THE 1988
INVESTOR'S COMP
TO THE

TOP 100

UK COMPANIES

THE 1988
INVESTOR'S COMPANION
TO THE

TOP 100

UK COMPANIES

Research by Shearson Lehman Hutton Securities

Graphs by Datastream

Financial Times Business Information

THE
INVESTOR'S
COMPANION

First published June 1988

© Adrian Munsey Limited and The Investor's
Companion Limited 1988

Material published in this book is copyright and
may not be reproduced in whole or in part for any
purpose nor used for any form of advertising or
promotion without the written permission of Adrian
Munsey Limited.

Whilst every effort has been made to ensure that the
information in this book is correct, no liability can
be accepted for any loss incurred in any way
whatsoever by any person relying solely on the
information contained herein. To the best of our
knowledge and belief, the facts stated are accurate as
known at the date of completion.

Packaged by Adrian Munsey Limited,
15 Dufour's Place, London W1V 1FE for The
Investor's Companion Limited and Financial
Times Business Information Limited

Published by Financial Times Business
Information Limited, 7th Floor, 50-64 Broadway,
London SW1H 0DB

ISBN 1 85334 012 X

For Shearson Lehman Hutton Securities

Research editor *Peter Jones*
Banks and property *Chris Davis, Paul Jarvis*
Breweries and leisure *Philip Shaw, Peter Jones*
City economics *Peter Warburton*
Diversified companies *Chris Alexander*
Electronics and telecommunications *Keith Hodgkinson*
Engineering and aerospace *Keith Hodgkinson, Christopher Will*
Financial analysis for the stock market *Peter Jones*
Food manufacturing *Tim Potter*
Food retailing *Peter Jones*
Health and household *Stewart Adkins, Ian Smith, Jo Walton*
Insurance *Shyam Mehta*
Mining *David Williamson, Rob Davies*
Miscellaneous companies *Peter Hitchens*
Motors *Christopher Will*
Oil and gas *Jeremy Hudson, Simon Trimble*
Property and building materials *Paul Jarvis, Paul Walton*
Publishing and packaging *Chris Alexander*
Statistics *Peter Hitchens*
Stores *Peter Jones, Michael Heery*
Technical analysis *Matthew Bounds*
Textiles *Ronnie Dunbar*
Traded options *Lesley Powell, Jonathan Glass*

For Adrian Munsey Limited

Editor *Adrian Munsey*
Associate editor *John Urling Clark*
Editorial co-ordinator *Philip Dampier*
Additional material by *John Sanderson*

Designed by Laurence Bradbury and Roy Williams
Graphs by Datastream
Typeset by MC Typeset, Chatham
Printed by Staples Printers Rochester Limited –
a member of the Martins Printing Group

CONTENTS

PREFACE

For many investors, it is hard to find out what companies do, and how well they do it.

The aim of this book is to try to make available to a wider audience the kind of information usually reserved by leading stockbrokers and merchant banks for their most important institutional clients.

UK companies have become increasingly diverse in nature. Familiar brands often have unfamiliar owners. Annual reports, by their nature, assume knowledge of the company and focus on the previous 12 months.

In each company profile we have tried to give an idea of how the company works, what it does, how its performance may be analysed and what the key figures and variables are.

The basis for the inclusion of a company in the book is its membership of the FT-SE 100 index – the joint index of the Stock Exchange and the *Financial Times*, based on the 100 largest UK quoted companies, measured by market capitalisation and calculated each minute that the stock market is trading. The constituents of the FT-SE 100 index are made up every three months. The 100 companies in this book are the constituents of the FT-SE 100 index as at 1 January 1988.

Companies move in and out of the index as their capitalisation rises and falls, or on a takeover. Four companies – constituents of the index when the writing of the text started in July 1987, but not any longer – are included in Appendix I as a guide to companies that have recently been or may again become index constituents. Britoil, a constituent of the index on 1 January 1988, was removed after the successful BP bid. Rowntree was the subject of a takeover bid when the book went to press.

The company profiles
These are based on research by Shearson Lehman Hutton Securities to a pro-forma specification. In all, 25 analysts worked on the book. Graphs provided by Datastream track the absolute share price of each company and the relative performance of the FT-A All-Share index, the widest measure of stock market performance.

The abbreviations used in the book are generally explained in the text. The following should be noted: ADR (American Depositary Receipt), ADS (American Depositary Share), CP (cumulative preference share), CUL (convertible unsecured loan stock) and ESC (Eurosterling convertible loan stock).

The names and addresses of leading company registrars form Appendix II. The details of other registrars are set out in the general information for each company.

In the share price history sections, the percentage figures used are calculated by dividing the company's share price by the FT-A All-Share index, expressed as a percentage. This is the basis for the calculation of all the Datastream graphs. The years in the five year financial information tables are financial years.

All information is generally up to date as at early May 1988. The market capitalisation figures were calculated on 1 January 1988 to facilitate annual comparisons and do not include convertible issues.

FT and FT-A categories are used throughout the book. The FT categories are those that form the basis of the prices pages of the *Financial Times*. FT-A categories are included to allow the calculation of relative sector performance through reference to the FT-A sector indices in the *Financial Times*.

Directors' holdings are based on the most up-to-date information available at the time of going to press – 9 May 1988.

THE INVESTOR'S COMPANION

INTRODUCTION TO FINANCIAL ANALYSIS FOR THE STOCK MARKET

Analysing a company listed on the stock market is a cross between an art and a science, combining a subjective feel for the market and the prospects for a business with a more rigorous analysis of the true value of the stock.

The key discipline employed to achieve this valuation is fundamental analysis. The historical statistics provided in this book have in some way underpinned the market prices and the dividend yields of the FT-SE 100 stocks.

THE MARKET

There is no sure way of relating a company's figures to the share price or dividends which a shareholder can expect to receive. Amazing leaps in the price of a share might accompany the belief that a company will generate more earnings or distribute more by way of dividend payments. Paradoxically, spectacular final year results may lead to a dip in the price of a share while extremely poor results may see the price rise. Why should this happen?

Professionals may comment that a good result was **in the price**, meaning that this performance was expected. If prospects for the following year are not so good, in the light of information disclosed with this year's results, the price will fall. The stock is judged to be **over-valued** in relation to its future capacity to generate earnings or its ability to increase the dividend paid. On the other hand, a price may have fallen so low as to appear cheap in terms of its valuation based on expectations of the following year's earnings. Buyers who have spotted this trend will increase the price.

For professional fund managers – the people looking after your pensions, insurance policies or savings – the actual price movement is only one measurement. Relative performance is usually how their success is measured, or, to put it simply, did their investment selection beat the average movement in the indices? If not, you may just as well have divided up the money and put equal amounts into each share represented in the indices.

The institutional investors, who dominate the market, have their own reasons for moving in and out of a stock. What proportion of a fund will this industry or this stock represent? What liabilities does the fund have to meet and when? Are there better opportunities in other markets or types of investment? Technical analysts consider the quantity of stock and the price at which it is available.

The art of financial analysis lies in knowing what weight to give fundamental analysis. The professionals have developed seemingly endless analyses of the limited financial disclosures which a company must make. But there is no easy way to get the numbers right. Timing and feeling are important. For the private investor, doing the numbers is part of the intellectual puzzle.

FINANCIAL INFORMATION

Companies are required by law, by accounting practice and by the Stock Exchange to provide basic financial information about their performance. But by the time it is published in their report and accounts, or in the interim statement, it is history. The company will disclose its **turnover**, that is sales made or income received during the year, and its **pre-tax profits**, that is the profit on sales after deducting various charges.

From this you can calculate the **profit margin** – turnover divided by profits. Is it up on last year? If so, management is doing well. Alternatively are other companies in the same industry achieving even better margins?

The year-on-year trend in results is important. If the cost of selling goods is going to be higher next year, or the price received in payment lower, then the profit margin may fall and pre-tax profits will not grow, and vice versa. Calculating costs and profit is not straightforward, and, in addition, variations in the way in which companies account may make comparison very difficult. How much credence can be attached to the bottom-line earnings numbers? This is the $64,000 question.

The **earnings per share** (**eps**) is the profit attributable to, or owned by, shareholders after all deductions such as tax – aside from those which are extraordinary and not expected to recur. The eps is expressed in pence per ordinary share.

The eps is crucial in valuing a company. When discussing a share the professional analyst will discuss its **multiple**, or **price/earnings ratio** (**PER**). How many times the reported earnings is a buyer prepared to pay to own a share? Anything from five times to 25 times is normal, depending on how fast the company's earnings are expected to grow, how consistent the company's performance is and whether it generates cash to invest for the future or has to go outside to raise additional funds. Not least is the speculative element. Is it likely that a company will receive a bid, and if so, at what price?

But which earnings should we consider? In fundamental analysis of a stock, the market is looking forward to the current year's performance, on which the company has already embarked, and towards the next year. Consequently our first assumption is to value future earnings.

There is a good correlation between the rise or fall in a share price and the earnings, and to some extent the dividends, which are ultimately reported. The share price anticipates earnings about six months to a year ahead. Nine months is a favourite gestation period.

This is not so surprising when you think about it. Professionals in the market are simultaneously acting on their own belief about the proper worth of a stock, and are collectively employing the same valuation techniques.

INCOME

So much for capital growth. Shareholders also receive payments of the dividend reported and, as this represents an interest payment, we can also talk about the **yield** of a stock – the dividend divided by the share price. To compare like with like, it is common to gross up the dividend to include an associated tax credit. The dividend is expressed in pence per ordinary share, net of income tax payment at the basic rate. The company effectively pays tax on your behalf. The dividend is a net dividend.

Yields, like multiple ratings, fluctuate throughout the year to reflect a changing price in the calculation. We give high and low figures for each company. But do not expect a high yield on equities. Over 6% to 7% is unusual. Often you would get a better return by putting your money on deposit in the bank or a building society. You would not experience capital growth on the sum invested, but nor would you run the risk of capital loss!

A company's ability to pay dividends is limited by the profits it can generate, less that proportion of earnings which are required to sustain and expand the business. To ascertain whether the present net dividend will be maintained, we calculate how many times the dividend is **covered**; the calculation is made by dividing the earnings per share by the net dividend. Above two times is usual, but closer to parity might suggest that the company is not really earning enough to justify next year's payout!

OTHER DEFINITIONS

Retained profits increase the value of a company. Since the only distribution the company can make is to the owners, collectively the shareholders, we can value what is left. Deducting all of a company's liabilities from its assets produces the **net assets**, representing the intrinsic worth of the company if it were to cease operation today. The **net asset value** is calculated by dividing the net assets attributable to shareholders by the number of ordinary shares, giving a valuation in pence.

Compare this valuation, the **break-up value**, against the market's valuation, the stock market middle price. Most FT-SE stocks trade at anything between two and ten times asset valuation. The market is prepared to pay more today in anticipation of a growth in earnings and dividends, as expressed by the PER multiple and the dividend yield, for the current and ensuing years. The art of analysis is to select a cheap stock today which will be awarded a premium rating in the not too distant future.

Other valuations exist. The **market capitalisation** is expressed as the stock market price multiplied by the number of ordinary shares. There is a more obscure calculation called the **present value** – the value today of future dividend payments.

This brief introduction, however, omits the basis on which accounts are prepared, and so ducks any criticism of the reality of reported financial statements. Analysis has improved but there is still room for a good deal of subjectivity in the preparation of company accounts and in interpreting them. If in doubt, ask your stockbroker to disentangle the numbers. It is one of the services by which he earns his commission!

The aim of this introduction is to explain the interaction of economic news with the market for ordinary UK securities. Before embarking on a detailed discussion of this interaction, it is helpful to consider the various types of data to which reference will be made.

ECONOMIC INFORMATION

Economic information falls into five broad categories. First, there is the regular continuous cycle of published economic indicators, which includes the monthly trade figures, money supply numbers and the retail price index. Major economic policy events such as Budget Day, the publication of the Autumn Statement and the Public Expenditure White Paper form a second category. Thirdly, there are surveys of company behaviour and intentions. The monthly and quarterly surveys carried out by the Confederation of British Industry (CBI) are probably the best examples. A fourth category comprises the regular reports of independent forecasting institutes. Of these, the London Business School, the National Institute for Economic and Social Research and the Organization for Economic Co-operation and Development are the best known. Finally, exchange rate and interest rate information form perhaps the most influential category of all.

The relationship between the price of ordinary shares, as represented by the FT-SE 100 index, and economic news can be extremely complex. To understand how the stock market is likely to react to a certain piece of news, it is necessary to answer three questions. Is the market worried that the domestic economy is growing too slowly or too quickly? On a consensus view, is the rate of inflation likely to fall or to rise in the coming months? Are international political and economic events of paramount or subordinate importance?

Taking the last question first, it is clear that a presidential election in the US, a debt default by a South American country, or an escalation of the war between Iran and Iraq could so preoccupy the stock market that domestic economic news would be ignored. There have been other occasions when the US has initiated a worldwide move towards lower or higher interest rates and the UK stock market has followed the Dow Jones index to the exclusion of almost everything else. Such episodes, though relatively uncommon, are important.

When international events are out of the limelight, the UK stock market will usually focus its attention on some aspect of the government's handling of the economy. As far as the market is concerned, the ideal situation is one in which the economy is growing vigorously, yet without strain on industrial capacity, inflation is low or declining, the exchange rate is constant and the balance of payments is in small surplus. In these circumstances interest rates would almost certainly decline, government tax revenues would be buoyant and government borrowing (the Public Sector Borrowing Requirement, PSBR) would be low. Stock prices would be liable to surge ahead.

During the months between the 1987 Budget and the General Election, the UK economy behaved almost exactly in this manner. However, this happy state of affairs is extremely rare. Immediately following the 1987 election, sterling's value slipped, poor monthly trade figures were announced and bank borrowing rose to a record level. From the tranquillity of the pre-election months, the equity market began to recognise the risk that the economy was growing too rapidly, or 'overheating'. In this environment, an increase in the annual rate of price or earnings inflation, a deficit on visible trade, faster than expected growth of bank lending or the money supply would all constitute 'bad news' and would be likely to send the FT-SE index lower. Even the announcement of faster growth of consumer spending or retail sales could depress the market.

At this point, the reader may think it paradoxical that the stock market could regard booming retail sales as a 'sell' signal. It is true that companies operating in the retail sector may later announce record sales turnover and record profits. However, the rapid growth of store company earnings may not match analysts' expectations in a situation where a sustained rise in stock prices has inflated the price/earnings ratio.

ECONOMIC SCENARIOS

The **ideal** scenario, where economic growth is high and inflation low or declining, and the **overheating** scenario, where national output is growing too quickly and inflation rising, are two of the four possible economic situations. The other two are described below.

Stagflation is the name given to the economic malaise of low, or even negative, output growth in combination with high or rising inflation. Here, any sign of economic recovery in the data for unemployment, industrial output, or a more optimistic CBI survey would tend to enhance share prices. Capacity constraints would be negligible. However, if expectations of rising output were accompanied by the prospect of higher producer and retail prices, then market reaction would be mixed. If inflation was so serious a problem that the market feared that higher interest rates or more burdensome taxation would ensue, then stock prices would be marked down.

Finally, a situation of low growth and low inflation is termed a **depression**. In the extreme case, the price level might fall, creating negative inflation. Whilst too much inflation is notoriously bad for the market, falling prices can be much worse. Imagine a company with a low rate of turnover of its stocks of finished goods.

Instead of recording stock appreciation in its accounts, it must record stock depreciation and therefore reduced historic cost profits. In such circumstances, cash would be an appreciating asset and one likely to outperform stocks and shares. Hence, a massive injection of public spending, financed by an increase in the money supply, would be wonderful news to the stock market in a depression.

GOVERNMENT POLICY

So far, the issue of government policy and its direct or indirect influence on economic events has only been touched upon. Since 1980, economic policy has operated in the context of the Medium Term Financial Strategy (MTFS).

The essence of the MTFS is a long term commitment to a reduction in the inflation rate, a reduction in the burden of direct taxation and a reduction in the size of the PSBR in relation to national income. The MTFS was originally formulated in terms of a PSBR target, a broad money target and a target for the standard rate of income tax of 25 pence in the pound. Within this policy framework it is natural for the stock market to attach great importance to the monthly PSBR and money supply figures. Income tax rates tend to be altered only at Budget time, which is usually in March, although there is no statutory restriction.

After a bad start, the MTFS was largely successful during the years 1982 to 1984. Since then, as broad money growth has strayed well outside its target range and so far without serious consequences, economic policy has become more pragmatic. In the early years of the MTFS, interest rates and sterling exchange rates were permitted to show a large degree of flexibility. For example, base lending rate was raised from 12% to 16% in 1981, and sterling appreciated by 15% in little more than a year during 1980.

More recently, the exchange rate has assumed a more prominent role, possibly foreshadowing entry into the exchange rate mechanism of the European Monetary System (EMS). Therefore, sterling's rate against the Deutsche Mark (DM) is watched very closely by the stock market.

Between February 1987 and February 1988, sterling traded in the comparatively narrow range of DM2.90 to DM3.00. During this period, foreign exchange market pressure for an appreciation of sterling was resisted repeatedly by the Bank of England. Over short periods, this resistance took the form of Bank purchases of foreign currency. When the pressure was sustained, UK interest rates were reduced. Thus, the behaviour of sterling within its range was important in its implications for the direction of interest rates. Lower interest rates would normally be a very positive factor for UK equities, and vice versa.

At the time of writing, May 1988, sterling has broken through the DM3.00 ceiling and UK exchange rate policy is far from clear. The unrestrained strength of sterling in the recent past has been viewed as 'bad news' by the stock market, on account of the high percentage of UK quoted companies' earnings which are derived in foreign currencies.

Despite the abandonment of a formal target for broad money M3 or M5 growth, the monthly money numbers remain important. The key items in these figures are the public sector contribution and the bank lending data. The public sector contribution to money growth gives clues about the state of the government's finances and whether it is likely to achieve its PSBR target. From an institutional point of view, it is also helpful in identifying the likely scale of future sales of gilt-edged securities and of privatisation issues. Both of these drain institutional cash resources. If projected asset sales are high, insurance companies and pension funds may be unwilling to absorb much of the new issue and stock prices, in general, may suffer.

OTHER INFLUENCES

Bank lending information is also of interest to the stock market. An unexpected surge in bank lending for house purchase by individuals or for inventory accumulation by companies may cause the market to worry that too much spending will result, leading to a worsening balance of payments and higher inflation.

Finally, a newly published report on the state of the economy by an influential research group can lead to a reaction in the stock market. If such a report sounds a note of caution, whereas its previous report had been optimistic, the FT-SE index may register a fall. Conversely, a bullish report from a conservative forecasting institute may lift the market, but such events are rare.

There is massive potential for the stock market to be influenced by economic news, but there can be no hard and fast rules. The determining factor in the relationship is the degree to which the market is worried about the state of the economy. Sometimes, a piece of economic news attracts no response in the equity market. At other times, the market may seize upon a highly volatile economic indicator, such as the monthly trade balance, and overreact wildly. The task of the city economist is to attempt to put the various items of news into perspective, to read the market in terms of its current concerns, and to save ecstatic proclamations for the rare occasions when they are justified.

TECHNICAL ANALYSIS

The use of fundamental arguments to draw conclusions over future price movement has enjoyed, and is likely to continue to enjoy, considerable success. However, at times where conflicting information is available, it is easy for the fundamental analyst's vision to become clouded. Furthermore, occasions frequently arise when widely unknown events, that have little or no bearing on the company's fundamental position, can have a dramatic, adverse effect on the price of its stock.

Examples could include: the liquidation by a fund manager of a substantial shareholding in a company that is enjoying considerable commercial success, in order to realise funds for use elsewhere; a predatory interest in an unsuccessful company; aggressive competition between market-makers; and the effects of large scale hedging and basket trading activities.

In a situation of increased divergence between bond and equity dividend yields, investment in equities clearly becomes more orientated towards capital gain rather than income growth and therefore more and more prone to the often violent forces of sentiment and rumour. It is at times such as this that the fundamentalist's task of assessing the impact of an event on a price, and the speed at which it becomes discounted, is difficult.

Under any circumstances, one of the underlying assumptions behind any decision to invest is that the price of investment instruments do not move in a completely random fashion. If this principle is accepted, then, by the same token, it must be accepted that there is some order to price movement. Through the study of price movement and volume alone, technical analysis seeks to identify that order. Whether the approach of a crowd psychologist is adopted or that of a mathematician, an objective analysis of recurring patterns should lead to the same conclusions.

The roots of technical analysis can be traced back to the turn of the century when, in a series of articles in the *Wall Street Journal*, Charles Dow summarised his theories and observations on the movement of stock prices and his now world famous stock averages. However, rather than ever intending to make detailed predictions, it is more likely that his efforts were directed towards constructing a barometric means of gauging long term commercial activity.

Empirically his observations categorised price movements into three basic components. The **primary trend** seldom lasts for less than a year. This would normally represent a move of at least 20%. Many now refer to these trends as bull and bear markets. The **intermediate trend** interrupts the progress of the primary trend. This generally lasts for about three months, and it commonly represents a retracement of one- to two-thirds of the previous move. Intermediate trends are made up of **minor trends**. These are minor fluctuations and rarely last for more than three weeks.

Simple as these observations may seem, they still serve anyone wishing to find a bearing in a market place that is frequently preoccupied with short term values.

Primary, secondary and minor trends

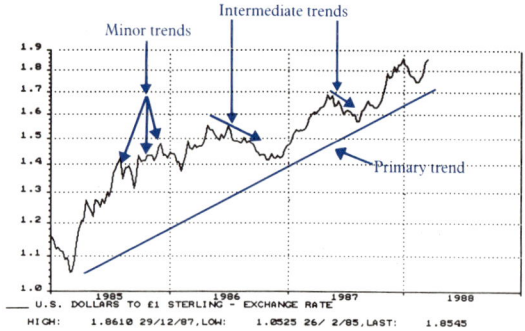

While these concepts are useful, it can easily be seen that through their application alone, it would not be until some time after the reversal of a primary trend that its occurrence would become apparent. Out of the need to establish effective signals for turning points and following the pioneering efforts of several professional traders and investors in the first half of the century, a series of tried and tested patterns became adopted by a growing number of technical analysts. Running the risk of over-simplification, they can be broadly outlined as follows.

TOPS AND BOTTOMS

A plethora of terms exists to describe these formations – head and shoulders, double and triple tops and bottoms, reverse head and shoulders or simply top and base formations.

Essentially these describe situations where at first a prevailing trend fails to carry the price into significantly higher or lower ground and then a gradual rounding reversal occurs. Their completion normally precedes a marked and prolonged reversal of the trend that it followed and can be said to be graphical representations of a waning tide of demand or supply. A good example of a head and shoulders top can be seen on Coloroll's price chart.

A head and shoulders formation

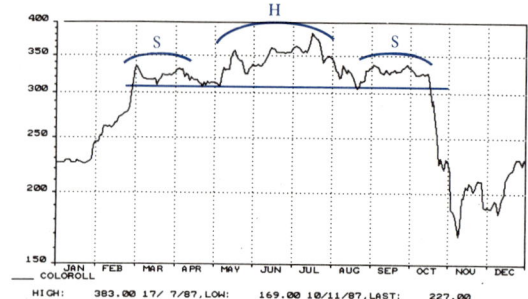

TRIANGLES

Frequently following a prolonged upward or downward move, price movement can be seen to become crowded into the boundaries of a triangle. These formations represent situations where a conflict between demand and supply exists and can be split into three categories.

Ascending triangles These patterns have an ascending lower boundary and a horizontal upper boundary. In these situations selling pressure remains constant while demand increases. A penetration of the upper boundary is normally followed by a prolonged upward move.

Albert Fisher (31 March 1986 to 21 March 1988) weekly high, low and close

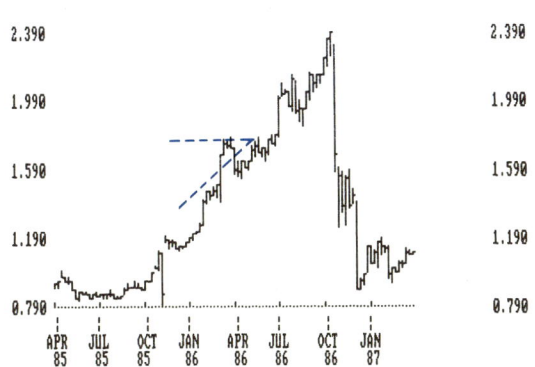

The chart of Albert Fisher shows an ascending triangle pattern between March and June of 1987.

Descending triangles These represent the reverse of the above situation. With a horizontal lower boundary and a descending upper boundary, selling pressure increases while demand remains constant. A penetration of the lower boundary normally precedes a prolonged downward move.

Ultramar's price chart shows a perfect example of a long term descending triangle pattern preceding the early 1986 sell-off.

A descending triangle formation

Symmetrical triangles As their name suggests, these have descending upper boundaries and ascending lower boundaries, and represent situations where the forces of demand and supply are increasing at the same rate. Where one force succeeds in overpowering the other, a significant move will commonly occur. Thus a penetration of the lower boundary would result in a prolonged downward move and vice versa.

A good example of a symmetrical triangle can be seen on the gold bullion price chart between January and May of 1986.

A symmetrical triangle

THE RECTANGLE

Extended periods of price movement between well defined horizontal upper and lower boundaries appear as rectangles on a price chart. Their occurrence indicates a period of equilibrium between supply and demand. Clearly, interested buyers must raise their bids to at least the lower limit of the developing trading range if they are to succeed in obtaining stock. Similarly sellers will not be able to sell at a price above the upper limit of the trading range. Thus when the price finally penetrates one of the boundaries, thereby signifying a drying up of supply if the break is on the upside or demand if on the downside, the price moves into an area where there is no opposing force and consequently makes a large move.

A good example of a breakout from a rectangle can be seen on Hoechst's chart between April and June 1987 where, following the development of a well defined trading range between DM2.85 and DM2.68, Hoechst broke above the upper boundary and accelerated away towards resistance at DM3.20.

Whether or not these explanations are treated with scepticism is unimportant. Their proven success alone justifies their use in any investment or trading strategy.

In conjunction with the patterns already mentioned, a wide range of mathematical tools – including Laplace and Fourier transforms, Markov chains, Bayes

A rectangle formation

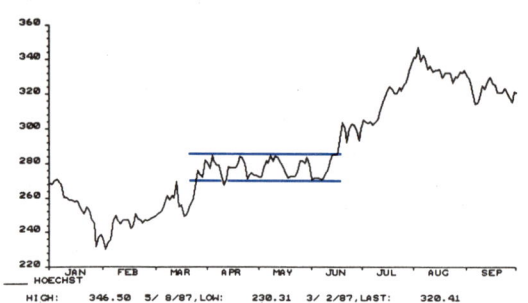

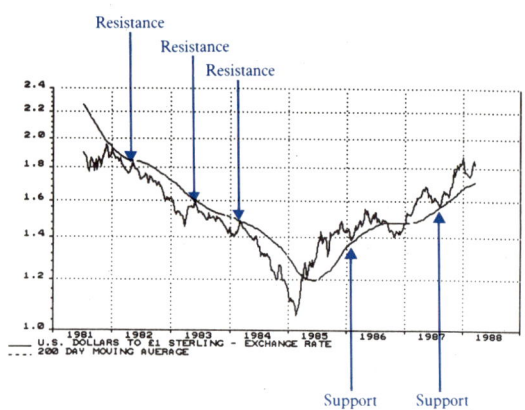

theorem, linear and curvilinear regression techniques and even quantum mechanics – have been adapted for trend evaluation in the financial markets over the years. The two most simple and widely used tools are the moving average and the momentum model.

THE MOVING AVERAGE

A moving average is simply the running average of a price over the last *n* days. It is calculated on a daily basis. When represented graphically it clearly shows the direction of the prevailing trend, while at the same time ironing out the sometimes confusing effect of day to day price ripples.

The widespread use of arithmetic moving averages in chart-dominated markets merits their inclusion in any technical study since many of the moves that they imply become self-fulfilling. Despite the fact that they lag the prevailing trend, their reaction time can be varied by altering the time of the average spans – a 30 day moving average reacts slower than a 10 day – and, as such, many possible combinations can be used to obtain a cross-section of long, medium and short term perspectives.

The principal uses of moving averages are to pinpoint support and resistance levels and highlight subtle changes in the price trend. In addition, the crossover effect that can arise from employing two or more moving averages can prove invaluable in locating chart pressure points.

These two types of study should be used to augment the technical picture, but their application should be tempered by the price chart itself since this is always the most important factor.

The sterling/US dollar chart shows the significance of the 200 day moving average not only in signalling a change in the trend but in acting as a support and resistance level.

THE MOMENTUM MODEL

Momentum models are widely used by technicians and although the different types of model vary, their one purpose is to determine the levels at which an instrument becomes overbought or oversold.

A typical example of a simple 10 day momentum model consists of the current price divided by the price 10 days before. The model will only be of any use if the running quotient has a well-established history (12 months for short term models and five years for longer term indicators) of fluctuating between well-defined limits of extension. When the 'momentum index' reaches such a limit, it clearly becomes improbable that it will extend much further in the same direction, thereby being a useful indicator of potential strength or weakness.

A balanced perspective of both long, medium and short term moves can be reached by looking at the 10, 20, 50 and 200 day momenta for any given instrument. Fisons' 10 day momentum chart shows how useful it has been in signalling the beginning and end of short term moves since the beginning of 1987.

Fisons and its ten day momentum below

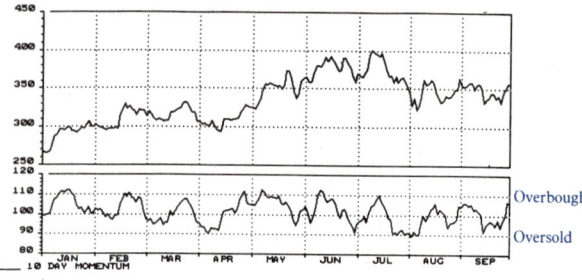

ADVANCE/DECLINE INDICATORS

An additional tool, which has been found very useful for gauging the breadth of bullish or bearish sentiment across a whole market, or a section of it, is the advance/decline indicator. Totalling the number of declines for a day and subtracting them from the total number of advances for the same day is useful in ironing out the distorting effect on an index of large moves being confined to a small number of stocks. A running total taken over a 10 or 20 day period is also useful in measuring extremes of bullish or bearish sentiment as the 10 day advance/decline indicator for the UK stock market shows. The running total fluctuates between fairly well defined upper and lower limits of extension. As with the momentum indicators, once a limit is achieved, further significant movement in the same direction becomes unlikely.

FT-A All-Share index and its ten day advance/decline line

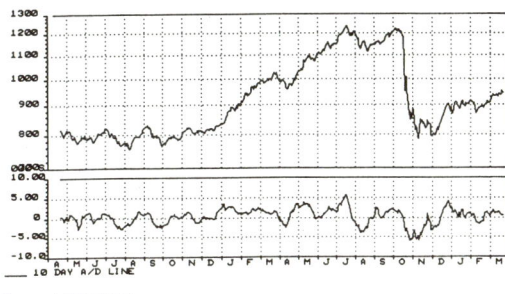

Source : Datastream

Contrary to popular belief, the use of technical analysis does not seek to undermine fundamentalist philosophy. Rather, one should be seen as complementing the other.

THE TRADED OPTIONS MARKET

Any visitor to the Stock Exchange gallery today will be struck by the emptiness of the once crowded floor. The majority of the dealers have retreated to their offices to trade 'off the screen' and there is only one remaining corner of the floor that is alive with activity. In this area multicoloured screens display banks of figures, and groups of dealers stand in small crowds around the podium and burst out shouting with apparently little provocation. It is here that the transactions of the London Traded Options Market are conducted.

In order to understand what is happening, an investor must take the time and trouble to understand why a traded options market came into existence, why it is the fastest-growing area of business in the International Stock Exchange and how it can be of use to the individual investor.

WHAT IS AN OPTION?

Most people understand what an option is – namely, an agreement between two parties that, in return for a sum of money, one party has the right, within a given time span, to require that the other party takes a certain course of action. It may be the sale of a house at a certain price, that orders for aircraft be given or a hundred and one different examples. If the giver of the option money has not taken up the rights conferred by the option within the allotted time, then the taker of the option money is released from his obligations and retains the option money. It is on this basis that traditional option trading has taken place in London since the end of the seventeenth century.

Translating this into stock exchange terms, the buyer of the option, who pays the option money (**premium**), acquires the right to purchase (**call**) or sell (**put**) shares in a specified company at a stated price (the **exercise price** or **striking price**) prior to the agreed **expiry date**.

This system had many disadvantages. Since there was a tied link between the giver of the option money and the receiver of the option money (the granter of the option), the option itself could not be sold to a third party. At all times, in order to establish a profit (or loss), the option had to revert to the underlying stock, with all the inherent expenses of doing so. As each option had to be negotiated individually, there could be no free market to determine the 'correct' price.

The **Traded Options Market** was introduced to deal with these shortcomings. A **Clearing Corporation** was formed to guarantee that the rights conferred by the options would be met. The options were allocated fixed expiry dates and specific striking prices were established. With these components in place the only remaining variables were the movement of the underlying stock and the passage of time.

To the uninitiated, much of the language used in the traded options market is mumbo-jumbo. It is therefore necessary to define carefully the basic terms used, and in their definition enable the investor to form an overview of the market itself. Many of the terms used originate from the traditional options market and their meaning is obvious.

Options come in two forms. The **call** option confers the right to buy shares at a certain price. The **put** option confers the right to sell shares at a certain price. Each option has a fixed date to mature – this is known as the **expiry date**. On equity options there is always a choice of three expiry dates, set three months apart. This is known as the **expiry cycle**. As one option month expires, a new option month with nine months' life is introduced. In the month of August, for example, a stock traded on the January, April, July and October cycle will have options available for October, January and April. As the October options expire, new options for July will be introduced. Other stocks will be allocated to the February, May, August and November cycle, while another batch will trade the March, June, September and December cycle.

The price at which the **holder** or buyer of the option may take up his right is known as the **exercise price** or **striking price**. The price or value of the option itself is known as the **option premium**. This can be divided into two elements – the **intrinsic value** and the **time value**. The intrinsic value is the 'real value element'; any excess is the 'time value'. An example should help clarify this.

ABC PLC has an **underlying price** of 101, i.e. it is quoted in the market at 100–102. Call options are available for October. A table quoting the prices may look as follows:

Exercise price	Premium	
90	15	11 points intrinsic (101–90), 4 points time value (15–11)
100	7	1 point intrinsic (101–100), 6 points time value (7–1)
110	3	No intrinsic value, 3 points time value

The 90 call option would be classified as an **in-the-money** option, the 100 call option an **at-the-money**, and the 110 call an **out-of-the-money**. However, for the put options with the same underlying price and strikes it is the 110 put option that is in-the-money, the 100 put is still at-the-money while the 90 put option is out-of-the-money. The table for the puts could look something like this:

Exercise price	Premium	
90	3	No intrinsic value, 3 points time value
100	6	No intrinsic value, 6 points time value
110	14	9 points intrinsic value (110–101), 5 points time value (14–9)

As the stock price moves up and down, and exceeds the striking prices quoted, new strikes are introduced to accommodate the stock price movement so that at all times there is at least one in-the-money and at least one out-of-the-money option available.

Each transaction in the options market is either dealt **to open** or dealt **to close**. Obviously, if there is no position in existence, the transaction is to open; if there is one in existence, it is to close. A position is closed by a transaction the opposite way to that which is open. A client, for example, has purchased five ABC Oct 100 calls; the instruction to close the position is to sell five ABC Oct 100 calls.

When giving instructions to the broker, a client must state if there are any limitations on the transaction. While a broker can give an accurate indication from the screen, the volatility of the market and speed of movement can mean that the price on the floor is different from that displayed. Instruction must be given as **at market** or **at best**, or **limited** at a certain price and whether the limit is **GD** (**good for the day**) or **GTC** (**good until cancelled**).

GD limits are automatically cancelled at the 3.40pm traded options market close. GTC are as stated – good until cancelled or the option series expires. Some clients are at first reluctant to issue a GTC order because they feel that if there is a sharp overnight move and they have left a GTC limit to sell at, say, 20 and the first price quoted is, say, 25 bid, the order will be completed at 20. This is not the case. The limit will be filled at the 25 level because, on opening, a GTC limit will be completed at the level indicated or at the first price quoted if it is to the client's advantage.

During trading, day limits will be filled as soon as possible. Use of the **public limit board** is especially beneficial to private clients because preference must be given to public limits before transactions in **the crowd** can be completed at the same price. The options market is based on an **open outcry** system and it is the **best bid** (the highest price at which someone is willing to buy) or the **cheapest offer** (the lowest price at which someone is willing to sell) that will get the business.

Traded options can be sold to open as well as sold to close. A holder of shares looking for a higher level at which to sell those shares should sell a call option. Either the shares will be called as a result of an **assignment** and delivered at the striking price, or the underlying share price will not be above the striking price at expiry and the shares will be retained plus the option premium.

Conversely a buyer of shares may wish to sell a put option as an attempt to acquire a holding below the current market price. When a client sells options to open, the client is known as the **writer**. When options are written, a **margin** to guarantee the position is required. For equity options the current rate is 20% of the underlying value plus or minus the amount the option is in-the-money or out-of-the-money. The table below illustrates the calculation.

ABC underlying price	101p
20% of underlying price	20.2p

Sold 90 call		Sold 90 put	
20%	= 20.2	20%	= 20.2
+ in the money	= 11.0	− out of the money	= 11.0
	31.2p		9.2p

Each contract is for 1,000 shares. The margin required on the call position is 31.2p × 1,000 = £312 per contract. The margin required on the put position is 9.2p × 1,000 = £92 per contract.

Margin may be provided in the form of cash, but this is a very inefficient way as no interest will be paid. More usually, cover in the form of **collateral** is lodged. This may be in any of the alpha stocks, any convertibles into these stocks, gilt-edged securities and Treasury Bills. The collateral lodged will be discounted to its market value. Your broker will be able to explain the technicalities of how to do this.

It is important to reassure writers that, while the stock will be transferred into a nominee name, there is no change of beneficial ownership and the transfer does not in any way affect the rights attached to the stock or the tax position of the holding.

Prior to opening an account, all clients, be they private or institutional, must sign a **Client Agreement Letter**. Accompanying this letter a broker will send out an appendix stipulating all **commission** charges, details of collateral and margin and terms of dealing.

Traded options are currently available on 59 UK stocks (including Vaal Reefs), two gilts, three French stocks, two currencies and on the FT-SE 100 index itself. New options are continually being introduced. It is possible that by the end of 1989 options will be quoted on all the FT-SE 100 index constituents.

This is a very condensed guide to the options market. The **Options Development Group** at the Stock Exchange will be more than happy to forward the introductory booklets and provide a list of brokers willing to accept new clients. They also run informative courses for beginners as well as more experienced investors.

The Traded Options Market is the only mechanism that enables an investor to manage his risk to a degree that is acceptable to him. This can range from total speculation to total protection. By taking the time and trouble to understand this market, an investor can enjoy high rewards for limited exposure. If an investor does decide that the options market is not for him, he should still be aware of its existence and the fact that its use by others will have an effect on individual shares and the market in general. 'Getting the market right' is not the prerogative of the professional investor. Using all the tools available can only help. Have fun!

THE TOP 100 UK COMPANIES

ALLIED-LYONS PLC

GENERAL INFORMATION

Head office	156 St John Street, London EC1P 1AR. Tel: 01-253 9911
Directors	Sir Derrick Holden-Brown CA (chairman), Sir Alex Alexander (deputy chairman), MCJ Jackaman (vice-chairman), RG Martin (chief executive), SH Alexander, CE Arnett – US, D Beatty, JJ Blanche CA, D Brown OBE, JA Giffen – Canada, MJ Griffiths, HC Hatch Jr – Canada, KR Jamieson, DG Jenkins, D Marshall, R Moss MIMechE, JB Silverman, WSF Wiley. *Non-exec:* SF Graham CBE DFC, Sir John Grenside FCA CBE, MR Lampard, Sir Philip Shelbourne
Advisers	SG Warburg & Co Ltd
Auditors	Peat Marwick McLintock
Registrars	RG Smith FCA, Allied-Lyons PLC, 156 St John Street, London EC1P 1AR. Tel: 01-253 9911
Brokers	Cazenove & Co
Solicitors	Ashurst Morris Crisp

GENERAL FINANCIAL INFORMATION

Market capitalisation	£2.578bn at 1 January 1988
Capital structure	
Issued ordinary shares (25p)	735m
Issued preference shares (£1)	4.6m CP 5.25%
	4.7m CP 3.85%
Warrants	None
Convertibles	£370m, fixed coupon of 29.7p per annum (convertible at 457p per share 1991–1994)
Traded options	Yes
ADRs	None
Shareholders over 5%	Bond Corporation Holdings Ltd 7%

FT CATEGORY

FT: Beers, wines and spirits
FT-A: Brewers and distillers

MAJOR ACTIVITIES

Allied-Lyons is the second largest UK brewer. It also has a substantial international wines and spirits business and considerable interests in the UK, European and US food business, in UK hotels, in soft drinks and in Dutch brewers.

The company has 14% of the UK beer market, with six breweries, 6,871 public houses and 950 Victoria Wine off-licences. Leading beer brands include Skol, Castlemaine XXXX and Swan lagers. Tetley bitter is the most important non-lager beer.

Wines and spirits brands include Harveys sherries, Teacher's Highland Cream, Lamb's Navy Rum, Cockburn's Port, and Gaymer's cider and Babycham. In November 1987 Allied-Lyons acquired the outstanding 49% of Hiram Walker–Gooderham & Worts, the Canadian international distilled spirits company, whose brands include Canadian Club, Ballantine's Scotch whisky, Courvoisier, Kahlúa and Tia Maria.

Products of its food division, J Lyons and Company, include Tetley teas, Lyons coffee and Lyons Maid ice cream. Lyons has substantial interests in the US, notably Baskin-Robbins ice cream, Tetley products and DCA cereal mixes.

The group's Embassy hotel chain has 43 units, of which three are in central London. Catering establishments and branded pub food outlets include Porterhouse Restaurants.

Allied has evoked criticism in the past due to the poor profits of its beer division. This culminated in the departure of senior executives. The wines and spirits business has been greatly enhanced by the acquisition of Hiram Walker and the food businesses have consistently done well, aided by small acquisitions from time to time. The outlook for profits growth over the next few years looks good.

FINANCIAL HISTORY

For the year ended 7 March 1987 group turnover increased by 4% to £3.6bn. Pre-tax profits rose 26.5% to £340.9m. Earnings per share, excluding property disposal profits, were up 28% to 33.8p. Dividends increased by 20% to 11.4p.

The beer division was the largest contributor, with sales of £1.058bn, and pretax profits of £157.5m. The wines and spirits division had sales of £870.5m and profits of £113.9m. The food division, including hotels, had turnover of £1.249bn and profits of £88.5m. Wines and spirits will assume even greater importance in 1987/88, with the full inclusion of Hiram Walker. £39.8m was written off below the line to cover the costs of closures, redundancies, and reorganisations within the food and beer businesses.

At the September 1987 interim, total turnover was up 25.4% on the comparable period in 1986/87 at £2.137bn, with pre-tax profits up 33.4% at £197.5m. Earnings per share were up 15.3% to 16.6p. The interim dividend was 11.5% to 4.35p per share. These figures include six months' profits of £57.6m from the group's subsidiary Hiram Walker, which at that time was 51% owned.

SHARE PRICE HISTORY

The share price soared in 1985 in anticipation of a bid from Elders IXL. The bid lapsed following its reference to the Monopolies and Mergers Commission and was not renewed following clearance by that body.

The shares performed well in the first half of 1987, both in absolute terms and relative to the Brewers and Distillers index. They fell sharply in the autumn crash, but relative to the market they were in the same position at the beginning of 1988 as at the beginning of 1987. In April 1988 bid speculation led to significant outperformance.

SENIOR MANAGEMENT

Sir Derrick Holden-Brown had been chairman and chief executive since 1982 until the roles were split in January 1988 in the new management structure created to take full account of the Hiram Walker acquisition. Sir Derrick remained chairman with a particular interest in long term strategy but Richard Martin took over as chief executive. Richard Martin remained as chairman of the beer division, Allied Breweries. Michael Jackaman was appointed vice-chairman of Allied-Lyons.

The boards of Allied Vintners and Hiram Walker were merged at the same time to create Hiram Walker-Allied Vintners with Michael Jackaman as chairman and chief executive. Sir Alex Alexander became deputy chairman of Allied-Lyons until his retirement at the AGM in July 1989. HC Hatch Jr remained as finance director, having previously been president and chief executive of Hiram Walker. Three new directors were appointed. In April 1988 six new directors were appointed to the board.

CAPITAL

In 1986 Allied-Lyons acquired 51% of Hiram Walker for an overall cost of £445m in cash. In January 1987 the company issued 14.27m shares as consideration for acquisition of the Drybrough Brewery from Grand Metropolitan. In July 1987 17.7m ordinary shares, 2.5% of the group's equity, were issued through an offering on the Toronto Stock Exchange to raise £80m. Allied disposed of Hiram Walker's shareholdings in Bacardi for £124m.

In November 1987 Allied acquired the remaining 49% of Hiram Walker. The total cost was £572m, of which £202m was in cash and the remaining £370m in convertible preferred stock, carrying a fixed coupon 29.7p per annum (representing a coupon of 6.5% at the conversion price of 457p), convertible into 80.9m ordinary shares in any of the years 1991 to 1994 inclusive, on the basis of one ordinary share for each convertible preference share.

If fully converted, GW Utilities' holdings would amount to 10% of Allied's issued equity capital. However, Allied has a standstill holding and voting agreement with GW Utilities and its 80% owner, Olympia and York Developments Ltd.

At 13 November 1987 the group, including all its subsidiaries, had a total indebtedness of £1.27bn and cash and other deposits of £75.8m. In December 1987 it increased its $500m multi-option facility to $755m, and extended the term to 31 March 1993. Gearing is estimated to be 65% after the acquisition of Hiram Walker, though this will fall in 1988/89.

GROUP REVIEW

Beer division A £70m capital expenditure programme is in progress at the Leeds, Warrington, Romford and Burton breweries in order to make Allied the lowest cost beer producer in the country by 1990. Cost reductions have been achieved, but this has meant writing off substantial sums in redundancy payments. This has been charged below the line rather than against current profits. The total debit, including items from the food division, in 1986/87 was £40m.

The company's beer trade is concentrated in the north and the south of the UK. Some of the west Midlands business was lost some years ago following a series of labour disputes which resulted in the closure of Ansell's Birmingham brewery.

The lager brands – Skol, Castlemaine XXXX and Löwenbrau – account for 51% of the division's sales. Löwenbrau sales are increasing at the rate of 50% per year. The licensing agreement with the Bond Corporation brings Swan Light and Swan Premium lagers to the range. In ales, Tetley Bitter is increasing its market share. Ansells and John Bull Bitter are both expanding sales.

In 1986/87 the group sold 190 pubs, but the purchase of the Scottish brewers Drybrough added 189 others to the Allied estate. The take-home trade is particularly strong.

The beer division includes Ind Coope's Muswells café bars, which should be ten strong by the end of 1987/88, the Vittle Inns, the New England Restaurant Group, the Victoria Wine chain of off-licences in the UK and the Haddows chain in Scotland.

Allied's soft drinks business is conducted through Britvic Corona, which was formed following Britannia Soft Drinks' acquisition of most of Beecham's soft drinks interests. PepsiCo took a 10% stake as part of the deal whereby the company became the UK distributor for PepsiCola and PepsiCo's other products. Allied owns 20%. Bass has 50% and operates the company.

Beer division turnover for 1986/87 was up 15.4% to £1.54bn. Pre-tax profits were up 33.1% to £157.5m. For the 28 weeks to 19 September 1987 pre-tax profits, excluding property disposals, were up 13.8% to £87.1m.

Hiram Walker-Allied Vintners The major development has been the acquisition of Hiram Walker and the integration of its business into the group. This began before the outright acquisition was completed in December 1987. Allied Vintners brands in North America have been transferred to Hiram Walker sales companies and reciprocal arrangements are being made in Europe.

For 1986/87 turnover was up 2.5% to £870.5m. Pre-tax profits were up 42% to £113.9m. Excluding Hiram Walker, profits were up 16%. At the September 1987 interim, pre-tax profits were £92.2m against £34.5m for the same period in 1986. The periods are not comparable because of the Hiram Walker acquisition. In the 28 weeks to 19 September 1987, Hiram Walker contributed profits of £57.6m, significantly ahead of its performance in the previous year. Without Hiram Walker, the division's interim profits were flat, up just 3% to £1.1m.

Prior to the acquisition of Hiram Walker, the division's largest single profit earner was the company's range of British wines, cider and perry, followed by spirits, fortified wines, sherry and port. There is a good export trade in many of these products. The international field is seen to hold real growth opportunities, hence the acquisition of Hiram Walker, which constituted an excellent brand fit with the group's existing products.

CHAIRMAN'S STATEMENT

'The group has successfully transformed itself over the years from being a United Kingdom based brewer into an international branded consumer products group operating in the food, drink and leisure sectors.

We are business builders. We aim to achieve above average returns for our shareholders by identifying and satisfying consumer needs – augmenting our existing brand portfolio by the introduction of new products and concepts to suit ever-changing consumer tastes.' *Sir Derrick Holden-Brown*

Allied's wine and spirits interests include: the Showerings and Whiteways cider, English wine and Babycham businesses; Harveys of Bristol; Teacher's whisky; Cockburn's Port; two Spanish sherry houses, Fernando A de Terry and Palomino y Vergara; a number of Dutch and Belgian wine and spirits companies, including Erven Warnink BV, the makers of the

							Price (p)		PER (x)		Yield (%)	
Year	Turnover (£m)	Pre-tax (£m)	Earnings (p)	Dividends net (p)	Dividend cover (x)	Net assets (p)	High	Low	High	Low	High	Low
1983	2,643.1	159.6	16.4	6.0	2.7	152	155	130	16.2	11.5	6.55	5.27
1984	2,850.5	194.9	21.2	6.8	3.1	186	179	138	15.1	10.2	6.71	5.00
1985	3,114.8	219.0	20.3	7.5	2.7	193	301	154	19.7	10.0	6.48	3.62
1986	3,301.8	269.5	26.4	9.5	2.8	273	363	253	19.0	13.1	4.77	3.47
1987	3,614.8	340.9	33.8	11.4	3.0	242	467	317	19.1	10.3	5.07	3.17

FIVE YEAR FINANCIAL INFORMATION

world-famous Advocaat; United Rum Merchants; and a 50.4% interest in the Irish soft drinks group Cantrell and Cochrane.

Allied has two joint ventures with Whitbread. European Cellars' aim is to build an international branded light wine business. The German Black Tower brand was acquired in 1986/87. Together with the existing Langenbach brand in Germany and Calvet in France, European Cellars is well positioned. It is also the largest wholesaler of wines and spirits in the UK. JR Phillips is the UK distributor of Courvoisier cognac, Grant's Standfast whisky and Glenfiddich.

Allied has spent considerable sums promoting its brands Monterez, Babycham and Copperhead (its new premium cider nationally available from 1988), and the relaunch of Rougemont Castle, its light British wine.

Food division This division has seen steady growth in sales and profits. It includes Allied's interests in food products, hotels, restaurants and catering.

UK food products include: the Lyons range of teas, coffees, cakes and biscuits; Lyons Maid ice cream; Lyons Seafoods, previously Flying Goose; the Applefords Cluster cereal bar; the Chic-O-Roll range of ethnic products; and Tetley teas. Many of these are sold internationally as well as in the UK.

European interests include Dutch cake and biscuit businesses, Panrico, the Spanish food mix and doughnut company, and Beckers, the makers of frozen meat-based snacks. US businesses include: DCA Food Industries, the cereal mixes company based in New York and now expanding rapidly internationally; Baskin-Robbins, the US ice cream maker, with joint ventures in Japan and South Korea; and Tetley Inc, launching new products throughout the US to complement its considerable tea and coffee business.

The group's chain of Embassy Hotels is undergoing a three year £31m investment programme. Amongst its objectives are increased conference capacity, and the upgrading of leisure facilities to include saunas, swimming pools and exercise equipment. Embassy Hotels has been modestly successful, but it does not seem to have achieved the same rate of growth achieved elsewhere in the industry.

The catering business wins many major contracts and caters for institutional events like the Wimbledon tennis tournament, Heathrow Terminal 4 and the whole of Gatwick airport. It also operates the Throgmorton Restaurant in the City, amongst others.

The food division includes Normand, the car distributor which is now the largest Mercedes dealer in the UK.

Food division turnover for 1986/87 was up 15% to £1.25bn. Pre-tax profits were up 18.8% to £88.5m. For the 28 weeks to 19 September 1987, pre-tax profits excluding property gains were up 14% to £41m.

Share price and relative to FT-A All-Share

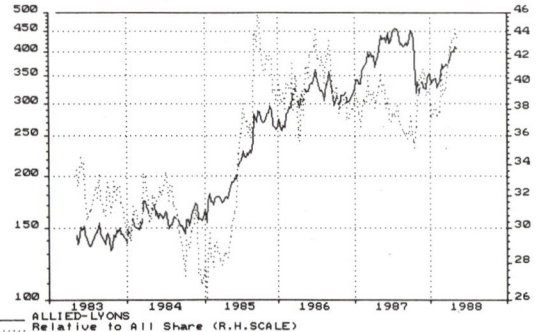

GEOGRAPHICAL REVIEW

Of the group's 1986/87 annual sales, 68% came from companies based in the UK, 5.6% from the Netherlands, 7.9% from the rest of Europe including the Irish Republic and 16% from North America. Export sales from the UK had a duty free value of £140m.

CORPORATE CALENDAR

Year end	first Saturday of March
Preliminary results	May
Report and accounts	June
AGM	early July
Final dividend paid	late July
Interim results	late November/early December
Interim dividend paid	late February/early March

DIRECTORS' HOLDINGS

	Beneficial interests	Share options
Sir Derrick Holden-Brown	50,000	58,941
Sir Alex Alexander	47,589	49,873
CE Arnett	—	8,865
D Beatty	5,962	32,208
JJ Blanche	38,129	49,268
D Brown	10,662	70,758
JA Giffen	—	8,865
ST Graham	3,500	—
Sir John Grenside	5,000	—
HC Hatch Jnr	3,500	46,000
MJ Howard	2,000	25,234
MCJ Jackaman	17,582	33,479
MR Lampard	1,500	—
RG Martin	30,000	37,687
D Marshall	11,000	28,415
R Moss	6,314	38,743
Sir Philip Shelbourne	1,000	—
JB Silverman	30,685	35,491
WSF Wiley	1,150	50,775

The above include any shares held by directors' families. The directors' remuneration in 1986/87 totalled £2.1m, including some pension provisions for past directors. The chairman and chief executive, who was the highest-paid director, received £293,225.

PRINCIPAL SUBSIDIARIES AND RELATED COMPANIES

Albrew Maltsters Ltd, Allied Breweries Nederland NV – Netherlands, Allied Breweries Overseas Trading Ltd, Allied Breweries Take Home Ltd, Allied Breweries Technology International Ltd, Allied Investments Ltd – Bermuda, Allied-Lyons Australia Pty Ltd – Australia, Allied-Lyons Canada Inc – Canada, Allied-Lyons Investments Ltd, Allied-Lyons Netherlands BV – Netherlands, Allied-Lyons North America Corp – US, Allied-Lyons Overseas Ltd, Allied Spirits & Wines Nederland BV – Netherlands, Alloa Brewery Company Ltd, Ansells Burslem Leisure Ltd, Ansells Cambrian Brewery Company Ltd, Ansells Ltd, Aylesbury Brewery Company Ltd, Baskin-Robbins Incorporated – US, Brierley Court Hop Farms Ltd, Brink BV – Netherlands, CG Hibbert Ltd, Callaway Vineyard & Winery – US, Calvet SA – France (50%), Cantrell & Cochrane Group Ltd – Irish Republic (50.4%), Chacalli De Decker & Co NV – Belgium, Chic-O-Roll Company Ltd, Cockburn Sithes & Cia Ltd, Coopers of Wessex Limited, Corby Distilleries Ltd – Canada (52.3%), Courvoisier SA – France, DCA Food Industries Inc – US, Donut Corporations of Málaga, Sevilla, Valencia and del Norte – Spain (50%), Embassy Hotels Ltd, Erven Warnink BV – Netherlands, European Cellars Ltd (50%), Fernando A de Terry SA – Spain, Frederick Wildman & Sons Ltd – US, Furgusons Ltd, George Ballantine & Son Ltd, George's Haverfordwest Ltd, Golden Oak Inns Ltd, Goldwell Ltd, Grants of St James's Ltd, HPC Inc – US, Hale-Trent Cakes Ltd, Halls Oxford & West Brewery Company Ltd, Harvey of Bristol Ltd, Hermann J Schmidt & Carl Schneemilch GmbH – West Germany, Hermann Kendermann GmbH Weinkellerei – West Germany (50%), Hiram Walker & Sons Inc – US, Hiram Walker & Sons Ltd – Canada, Hiram Walker Brands Ltd – Canada, Hiram Walker Europa SA – Spain (50%), Hiram Walker Inc – US, Hiram Walker International Ltd, Holt, Plant & Deakin Ltd, Hooimeijer BV – Netherlands, Ind Coope & Allsopp Ltd, Ind Coope (Isle of Man) Ltd, Ind Coope African Investments Ltd – Kenya, Ind Coope Burton Brewery Ltd, Ind Coope Ltd, Ind Coope Sales Ltd, Ind Coope-Benskins Ltd, Ind Coope-Friary Meux Ltd, Ind Coope–Taylor Walker Ltd, Ind Coope–

Romford Brewery Company Ltd, Industrie Riunite del Panforte di Siena SpA ('Sapori') – Italy, J Lyons & Company (Kenya) Ltd – Kenya, J Lyons Catering Ltd, J Lyons International Ltd, J Moreau et Fils SA – France, JR Phillips & Co Ltd (50%), John Harvey & Sons (España) Ltd, John Harvey & Sons Ltd, Joshua Tetley & Son Ltd, Kahlúa SA – Mexico, Langenbach & Co GmbH (50%) – West Germany, Lloyd & Trouncer Ltd, Looza SA – Belgium, Lyons Bakers Ltd, Lyons Brooke Bond (Pvt) Ltd – Zimbabwe (66.67%), Lyons Brooke Bond (Zambia) Ltd – Zambia (60%), Lyons Irish Holdings Plc – Irish Republic (75%), Lyons Maid Ltd (90%), Lyons Seafoods Ltd, Lyons Tetley France – France, Lyons Tetley Ltd, Maidstone Wine & Spirits Inc – US, Maker's Mark Distillery, Inc – US, Normand Ltd, Oldham Claudgen Ltd, Overseas Trading Corporation (1939) Ltd – Channel Islands, Palomino y Vergara SA – Spain, Panrico and Panificio Group – Spain (50%), Peter Walker Ltd, Showerings Group Ltd, Showerings Ltd, Skol International Ltd – Bermuda (95%), Sol-Tenco Ltd, Stansand Ltd, Steware & Sons of Dundee Ltd, Symbo Biscuits Ltd, Teacher (Distillers) Ltd, Tetley Inc – US, Tetley Walker Ltd, New England Restaurant Group Ltd, Victoria Wine Company Ltd, Tia Maria International Ltd, Tolchard & Son Ltd, Treliske Cellar Supplies Ltd, United Rum Merchants Ltd, Vine Products and Whiteways Ltd, Vittle Inns Ltd, Wm Teacher & Sons Brasil Ltd – Brazil (96.75%), Wm Teacher & Sons Ltd, Wrexham Lager Beer Company Ltd

BRAND NAMES

Advocaat, Ansells Bitter, Babycham, Ballantine's Scotch Whisky*, Baskin-Robbins, Benskin's Bitter, Bristol Cream, Burton Ale, Canadian Club*, Castlemaine XXXX, Celtic Vodka, Chic-O-Roll, Club Amontillado, Cluster, Cockburn's Special Reserve, Cointreau, Concorde, Country Manor, Courvoisier*, Drybrough, Embassy Gaymer's ciders, Gaymer's Old English, Glenfiddich, Golden Oak, Grand Marnier, Haddows, Harveys sherries, Hostess Kahlúa*, Ind Coope, Irish Mist, John Bull Bitter, Joshua Tetley, Lamb's Navy Rum, Lanson champagne, Limited Rum, Long Life, Löwenbrau, Lyons Maid, Lyons Quick Brew, Lyons cakes, Lyons coffee, Maryland Cookies, Muswells, New England Restaurants, Red Label, Ritz, Rougemont Castle, Showerings, Skol, Stolichnaya, Swan Light, Swan Premium, Tara Toffee Liqueur, Teacher's Highland Cream Scotch whisky, Tetley Bitter, Tetley Walker, Tia Maria*, VP, Whiteways, Victoria Wine Company, Vittle Inns

*Hiram Walker brands

CONTACTS AND FURTHER INFORMATION

Tony Pratt, Head of corporate affairs, Allied-Lyons PLC, 156 St John Street, London EC1P 1AR. Tel: 01-253 9911.

GENERAL INFORMATION

Head office	Brentwood House, 169 Kings Road, Brentwood, Essex CM14 4EF. Tel: 0277 228888
Directors	AM Sugar (chairman and managing director), K Ashcroft FCA FCMA, JL Dominguez – Spain, CJ Heald, MM Miller, JL Rice, Marion Vannier – France, RJ Watkins. *Non-exec* NF Shearman FCCA
Advisers	Kleinwort Benson Ltd
Auditors	Touche Ross & Co
Registrars	Lloyds Bank Registrar's Department
Brokers	James Capel & Co
Solicitors	Herbert Smith

GENERAL FINANCIAL INFORMATION

Market capitalisation	£628.5m at 1 January 1988
Capital structure	
Issued ordinary shares (5p)	556.2m
Issued preference shares	None
Warrants	None
Convertibles	None
Traded options	None
ADRs	None
Shareholders over 5%	AM Sugar 44.8%

FT CATEGORY

FT: Electricals
FT-A: Electronics

MAJOR ACTIVITIES

Amstrad is involved in the design, manufacture and distribution of consumer electronic products including audio equipment, video recorders, integrated TV and video recorder units, word processors, home computers, computer printers and most recently IBM-compatible personal computers.

Amstrad conceives its products, takes them through design, generally subcontracts their manufacture and then distributes them in the UK and abroad, increasingly through its own subsidiary distributors. The company covers all sectors of the personal computer market through its Amstrad and Sinclair brands from home entertainment to fully professional business computers.

Amstrad is susceptible to restrictive import quotas, the level of personal disposable incomes, inflation and exchange rate fluctuations.

Critics have said that the company is overdependent on the immediate success of any product it introduces. The company argues that this dependence is much diminished. As Amstrad has developed its product range, many of its earlier products have continued to sell well. Amstrad's results keep proving the critics wrong.

The expansion of its television and video recorder activities and a possible move into white goods will widen its product

CHAIRMAN'S STATEMENT

'The use of the word "consolidation" in my last annual report was, perhaps in hindsight, a wrong choice. It seems that some industrial analysts and journalists viewed the statement as a typical excuse given by company Chairmen when no growth potential exists. Clearly, the events of this latest six months demonstrate the seed planting plan coming together. The finalisation of both product design and market development, during the next six months will most definitely seal our expansion and growth for many years to come.' *Alan Sugar*

FIVE YEAR FINANCIAL INFORMATION

Year	Turnover (£m)	Pre-tax (£m)	Earnings (p)	Dividends net (p)	Dividend cover (x)	Net assets (p)	Price (p) High	Price (p) Low	PER (x) High	PER (x) Low	Yield (%) High	Yield (%) Low
1983	51.8	8.0	1.4	0.16	8.7	2.6	22.00	9.50	40.3	17.9	1.90	0.72
1984	84.9	9.1	1.2	0.19	6.3	6.0	24.00	13.20	26.4	13.9	1.47	0.71
1985	136.1	20.2	3.1	0.27	11.5	7.7	40.00	13.00	18.8	10.0	1.64	0.67
1986	304.2	75.3	9.5	0.35	27.1	16.1	150.00	36.00	36.5	13.1	0.75	0.21
1987	511.8	135.7	17.1	0.70	24.4	32.9	224.00	105.00	18.9	6.5	0.91	0.28

base further and make it less vulnerable to the sales failure of any one product. There are strong rumours of a video camera, more computer printers and even a cheap fax machine and photocopier, though the company denies interest in the latter two products.

Amstrad's audio and video products compete with those of Sony, Philips, Thomson, Toshiba and JVC. Its computer products compete with those of IBM, Atari, Zenith, Apricot and Acorn. Amstrad became personal computer market leaders within three months of introducing its PC-1512 to the UK market.

FINANCIAL HISTORY

Turnover for year ended June 1987 was £511.8m, 68% ahead of the previous period. It has increased almost tenfold over five years. Pre-tax profits were £135.7m for 1986/87, 80% ahead on the previous year and up fifteenfold over five years. Earnings per share increased from 9.54p to 17.13p. Dividends were increased for the seventh successive year to 0.97p, up 100% on the previous year's 0.49p.

The balance sheet was strong with net cash compared to shareholders' funds at around 52.5%. In 1986/87 cash of £35m was generated. Management performance ratios are high with pre-tax profit margin at 26.5% and asset turnover at 2.9 times.

The company produced excellent interim figures for the six months to 31 December 1987. Turnover at £351.06m was 28.8% up. Pre-tax profits at £90.1m were 26.5% up. Earnings per share of 11.58p were 24% ahead. The interim dividend doubled to 0.4p.

SHARE PRICE HISTORY

Since Amstrad's flotation in 1980 the company consistently outperformed the market until mid-1987. The October 1983 share split brought down the nominal value of shares from 25p to 5p. The rights issue of 1984 saw the share price deteriorate significantly due to the general lack of confidence in the personal computer market at that time. This was reversed following the successful introduction of the PCW-8256 when confidence was restored. In May 1986 there was a four for one scrip issue.

After their meteoric rise to 220p during the summer of 1987 the shares fell back sharply. They returned to 200p briefly but dropped dramatically before the general falls of the autumn. They then fell further still. They found a base at 110p before recovering sharply to the 160p level in mid-March 1988. The fine interim 1987/88 results were well received by the market and the shares then began to outperform again.

The period of active consolidation and related development the company sees ahead may improve its present rating, which is below the market average. Amstrad's acquisition of its distributors in practically all its major foreign markets has widened its capital base geographically, ensured the best possible marketing of its goods, and removed the middleman's profit margin.

SENIOR MANAGEMENT

Chairman and managing director Alan Sugar founded Amstrad Consumer Electronics in 1968 and floated the company in 1980. The initial attitude of the market was to suspect Alan Sugar as a whiz-kid intent on capitalising on the flotation who would prove unable to develop the company further. However, Alan Sugar has confounded his critics and shows no signs of reducing his efforts to keep Amstrad one of the UK's most successful enterprises.

Although the company is often portrayed as a one-man band, its speed of decision-making, its excellent marketing strategies and its record in product development could only have resulted from the work of a small, integrated and gifted team.

In 1987 Colin Heald, Marion Vannier and Jose Luis Dominguez joined the main board. Colin Heald has taken over some of the technical director's past responsibilities and arranges the procurement and manufacture of all the company's new and existing products. Marion Vannier, the chief executive of Amstrad's subsidiary in France, is involved in marketing and distribution developments there and in the Benelux countries. Jose Dominguez, founder of its distributor in Spain, now a wholly-owned subsidiary, continues his work there and will share the responsibilities for international marketing in other European territories and in South America.

Jim Rice continues as group operations director, Bob Watkins as technical director, Ken Ashcroft as group finance director and Malcolm Miller as sales and marketing director. Barry Young is managing director of Amstrad Distribution Ltd, and Ettore Accenti is managing director of Amstrad SpA, Italy. Stan Randall is managing director of Amstrad International Hong Kong, and Vernon Moore is the chief executive officer of Amstrad Inc, formerly Vidco, which he founded.

CAPITAL

Amstrad had not increased its capital base since the rights issue of 1984 until September 1987 when it acquired Vidco and Indescomp SA, its US and Spanish distributors. These deals involved the issue of a total of 16.4m new ordinary 5p shares, bringing the issued equity capital to £27.8m. Alan Sugar has a holding of 249.2m shares.

GROUP REVIEW

Amstrad's business philosophy is to identify a product for which there is a known demand, design it, arrange its manufacture at the lowest possible price, and then sell the maximum possible number. Its success has been achieved by emphasising the importance of the price of any new product and of the requirements it must meet. This emphasis is maintained from the product's initial conception throughout its design and manufacture to its eventual marketing programme.

Unlike many other electronics companies Amstrad does not sell its products on their technical superiority or innovative features. Instead it presents them as meeting, rather than surpassing, current state of the art standards at an unbeatable price.

The company divides its activities into two categories, business and leisure. Business consists of PC-compatible computers, word processors and printers. Leisure consists of home entertainment computers – the Sinclair and CPC ranges – video, and audio and television products.

For the year ended 30 June 1987 leisure accounted for 46% of sales at £234.4m while business accounted for 54% at £277.4m, compared with 62% at £188.9m and 38% at £115.2m for the previous twelve months.

Share price and relative to FT-A All-Share

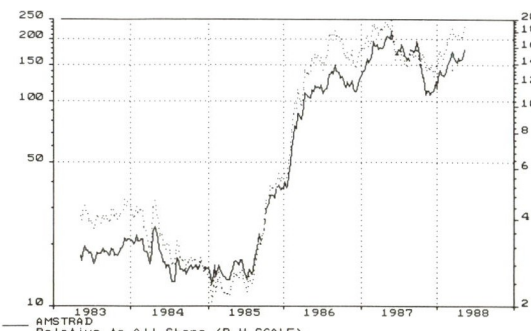

— AMSTRAD
...... Relative to All Share (R.H.SCALE)

Products Notable products of the Amstrad philosophy have been the PCW-8256 word processor and the IBM-compatible personal computer, the PC-1512. To meet demands for higher standards by some business users, these have been joined by the PCW-9512 word processor incorporating a letter quality daisy wheel printer, the PC-1640 personal computer, and the LQ-3500 dot matrix printer.

A major new product is Amstrad's range of portable computers, launched in November 1987. Amstrad's orders for them exceed by a factor of five the entire 1987 sales of all the other manufacturers put together.

The Spectrum Plus 3 with disc drive sells for £199 for the home computer market. The Amstrad combined television and video recorder unit continues to offer these two facilities at a far lower price than any two separate units. The company also makes a range of video products which it sells to retailers to market under their own brand names.

The most likely new product to be launched in the future is a video camera offering the same price competitiveness as all Amstrad's other products.

Manufacturing Manufacturing is generally contracted out to the most economic unit capable of satisfying the company's quality standards. These are usually fully independent of Amstrad. However, its Hong Kong subsidiary Amstrad Microtronics is now producing computer printers and will in the future make other products currently under development. In 1987 Amstrad also opened a joint venture factory in Shoeburyness with the Funai Electric Co Ltd of Japan.

Distribution In the UK Amstrad has established a distribution network involving major high street retailers like Boots, Rumbelows, Comet and, most importantly, Dixons. They have all succeeded in moving large numbers of Amstrad's products on their comparatively small margins. Now Amstrad is extending its network to small independent owners by tailoring its distribution service to meet their needs for low volume but frequent deliveries.

Abroad Amstrad has been most successful in France and Spain. The company has identified as the reason for this success its policy of only using exclusively Amstrad distributors. In its major markets it is setting up or acquiring its own fully owned subsidiaries. It has formed Amstrad SpA in Italy and acquired Vidco, its distributor in the US, and Indescomp SA, its Spanish distributor, and changed their names to Amstrad Inc and Amstrad SA respectively.

Amstrad International SA already exists in France. Amstrad International Hong Kong, aided by the Amstrad group's marketing division, continues to serve its smaller agents in Europe, the Middle East, the Far East and South America.

The latest distribution operation to be set up by Amstrad is in Germany, where the company is switching from Schneider and opening a wholly-owned subsidiary in Frankfurt. In 1988 the company has opened offices in Belgium and Australia, and will form a company in Holland.

GEOGRAPHICAL REVIEW

Amstrad has consistently pursued the objective of expanding the geographical scope of its operations. Geographical areas outside the UK account for 56.5% of total turnover. France, West Germany and Spain are the company's most important foreign markets. The build-up of a worldwide distribution of computer products has provided Amstrad with a massive customer base. It now plans to use this to market its future computer and non-computer products.

For the year ended June 1987 Amstrad's turnover in France, where it enjoys 41% of the computer market, was up 40% at £92.8m. In Germany it was up 70.4% at £63.9m. In Spain it was up 93.2% at £62.5m. In Australia it was up 40% at £11.2m. In Asia it was 77.3% up at £3.9m. Only in North America was it down, 20.3% lower at £13.7m.

CORPORATE CALENDAR

Year end	30 June
Preliminary results	October
Report and accounts	November
AGM	November
Final dividend paid	November
Interim results	February
Interim dividend paid	April

DIRECTORS' HOLDINGS

	Ordinary shares		Options
	(beneficial)	*(non-beneficial)*	
AM Sugar	249,218,750	—	—
JL Rice	57,050	—	1,176,000
NF Shearman	58,330	745,000	—
MM Miller	—	—	1,176,000
RJ Watkins	—	—	1,176,000
K Ashcroft	20,000	—	1,176,000

AM Sugar and NF Shearman jointly held a non-beneficial interest in an additional 350,000 shares.

In 1986/87 the total directors' remuneration was £391,000 of which the chairman, who was the highest-paid director, received £105,000.

ARGYLL GROUP PLC

PRINCIPAL SUBSIDIARIES AND RELATED COMPANIES

Amstrad Distribution Limited, Amstrad Espana SA – Spain, Amstrad GmbH – West Germany, Amstrad Inc – US, Amstrad International (Hong Kong) Limited, Amstrad International SA – France, Amstrad Microtronics (Mfg) Ltd – Hong Kong, Amstrad Pty Ltd – Australia, Amstrad SpA – Italy, Funai Amstrad Ltd (49%)

BRAND NAMES

Amstrad, Sinclair, Spectrum, CPC 464, PCW-8256, PCW-9512, PC-1512, PC-1640, LQ-3500

CONTACTS AND FURTHER INFORMATION

Nick Hewer, Michael Joyce Consultants, 19 Garrick Street, London WC2E 9BB. Tel: 01-836 6801.

GENERAL INFORMATION

Head office 8 Chesterfield Hill, London W1X 7RG. Tel: 01-493 0808
Registered office Argyll House, Millington Road, Hayes, Middlesex UB3 4AY. Tel: 01-493 0808
Directors JG Gulliver (chairman), MA Grant (chairman elect, chief executive), DTC Webster, CS Lawrie, TE Spratt CBE. *Non-exec* CGD Onslow MP, HM Plowden Roberts, CD Smith
Advisers Samuel Montagu & Co Ltd
Auditors Arthur Andersen & Co
Registrars Royal Bank of Scotland Registrar's Department
Brokers Panmure Gordon & Co Ltd, Rowe & Pitman Ltd
Solicitors Clifford Chance

GENERAL FINANCIAL INFORMATION

Market capitalisation £1.711bn at 1 January 1988
Capital structure
Issued ordinary shares (25p) 903.5m
Issued preference shares None
Warrants 4.69m, two ordinary shares for 60p each during October 1988
Convertibles £60m 4.5% ESC 2002 (338.983 shares per £1000 stock to 14 October 2002)
Traded options None
ADRs None
Shareholders over 5% None

FT CATEGORY

FT: Food, groceries, etc
FT-A: Food retailing

MAJOR ACTIVITIES

Within twelve months of its failure to acquire Distillers, Argyll completed the purchase of Safeway Stores from its US parent for £681m in February 1987 and embarked on disposing of its own interests in the drinks business and food manufacturing. Besides Safeway, Argyll's major retail chains are Presto and Lo-Cost discount stores.

The only interests the group now has outside food retailing are its major liquor store chains, Winterschladen and Liquor-Save, Mojo Cash and Carry and Snowking, the specialist frozen food distributors.

The acquisition of Safeway has transformed Argyll's prospects. Its market share has jumped from 5.5% to 10%, 3% behind J Sainsbury and Tesco, just 1% behind Dee who operate Gateway, and 3% ahead of Asda.

Safeway has a first class reputation for its products, particularly in the quality and range of the now important fresh produce area. This would have taken Argyll many years to build on its own. The group is taking advantage of this by converting 180 of the larger Presto stores to Safeway fascias. Argyll now looks clearly set to be one of the dominant forces in the UK food retailing industry in the 1990s and beyond.

As with all food retailers, food price inflation and the level of disposable income are crucial to Argyll. Food store shares are traditionally regarded as good defensive stocks as no one can survive long without their products.

FINANCIAL HISTORY

Total sales inclusive of VAT in 1986/87 were £2.1bn including £92m from Safeway for the four weeks ending 21 March 1987. This figure, which includes the food manufacturing and drinks businesses that have been sold off, was up 17% on 1985/86, and up 98% over five years. The sales growth reflects consistent organic growth through the existing businesses, as

FIVE YEAR FINANCIAL INFORMATION

Year	Turnover (£m)	Pre-tax (£m)	Earnings (p)	Dividends net (p)	Dividend cover (x)	Net assets (p)	Price (p) High	Price (p) Low	PER (x) High	PER (x) Low	Yield (%) High	Yield (%) Low
1983	1,310.5	25.9	6.1	—	—	22.5	73	68	16.5	15.4	4.69	4.37
1984	1,448.3	40.1	8.8	2.50	3.5	28.3	135	71	25.1	16.0	4.67	2.82
1985	1,677.0	53.6	10.1	3.13	3.2	30.2	172	126	29.3	18.8	3.21	2.32
1986	1,818.7	64.5	11.2	3.88	2.9	28.6	186	150	22.0	13.8	3.79	2.50
1987	2,025.0	79.6	12.5	4.55	2.7	20.8	247	159	22.5	10.1	3.82	2.51

well as the acquisition of Allied Suppliers in 1982/83.

Pre-tax profits were £80.6m (including £4.4m from Safeway for the four weeks ending 21 March 1987), 25% up on the previous year and over three times the figure achieved in 1982/83. Earnings per share increased by 8.5% from 22.4p to 24.3p in 1986/87 due to a higher tax charge and the partial dilution from the Safeway acquisition. The year's net dividend, however, was 16.8% ahead at 9.1p. The balance sheet showed gearing at 69% of shareholders' funds, but a one for eight rights issue declared with the figures raised £208m net of expenses and eliminated debt.

In recent years capital expenditure has only been modestly ahead of cash flow but this is likely to change with the substantial store expansion and conversion programme which lies ahead. The Argyll food division operating margin improved from 3.3% in 1985/86 to 3.9% in 1986/87. This compared with 4.8% achieved by Safeway. Similarly Presto's average weekly sales per square foot at £6.50 are well below Safeway's £10.10.

CHAIRMAN'S STATEMENT

'Our firm objective is to establish Argyll as an enduring quality retail group with our new Safeway division being developed as one of the most successful and respected food retailers of the 1990s.' James Gulliver

Safeway transformed the 1987/88 interim results. For the 28 weeks to 10 October 1987, the group's turnover for continuing businesses, including a full contribution from Safeway, was up 78% to £1.69bn. Operating profit was up 130% to £75.9m, an increase of 34%. Margins were up from 3.66% to 4.72%. Net profit, including the extraordinary credit of £23.4m arising from the sale of George Morton and the food manufacturing businesses, was £71.1m. Earnings per share, before exceptional items on a 35% tax basis, increased by 2% to 6.2p at 5.7p. Dividends were 17% up at 1.80p.

The group's decision to treat its Safeway 1990's modernisation programme as an exceptional rather than an extraordinary item was responsible for the decline in the group's earnings per share and will continue to do so until that programme is complete. Many groups would not have categorised these costs in this way and this reflects the group's conservative methods of accounting.

SHARE PRICE HISTORY

Adjusted for share issues, the Argyll share price has risen in absolute terms from around 75p in 1984 to 186p in February 1988. The all time high of 245p was reached prior to the 1986/87 results in mid-1987.

Relative to the FT-A All-Share index it rose from 17% in 1984 to 27% at the beginning of 1986. It subsequently underperformed the index substantially but since the autumn 1987 crash it has staged a considerable relative recovery, despite the group's decision to take the costs of its Safeway 1990's modernisation programme above the line.

The share price also recovered much of its autumn 1987 fall in absolute terms. In February 1988 it was 36p up from its autumn 1987 low at 186p and 21% of the FT-A All-Share index.

SENIOR MANAGEMENT

James Gulliver is chairman of the Argyll Group, having built up the business with two colleagues, Alistair Grant and David Webster, since 1977. Prior to this they were responsible for the development of Oriel Foods. Between 1965 and 1972, James Gulliver was chairman and chief executive officer of Fine Fare.

Alistair Grant, who originally joined James Gulliver at Fine Fare in 1968, is chief executive and will take over as chairman at the AGM in September 1988. David Webster, who joined Oriel Foods in 1973, is finance director. Charles Lawrie, another long-term associate of James Gulliver, is vice-chairman of Argyll Foods and is responsible for Presto and all the group business except Safeway. Terry Spratt, who has been in charge of Safeway UK since 1977 and joined the main board as vice chairman of Argyll Foods in April 1987, will continue to have operating and marketing responsibility for Safeway.

CAPITAL

Until the £620m issue of 194.1m shares for Safeway in February 1987, Argyll had been very sparing in its use of new equity. In 1982, 95m shares were issued in connection with the acquisition of Allied Suppliers, which gave Argyll its Presto and Lipton stores. In September 1984, 5.5m shares were issued as part consideration for the acquisition of Amos Hinton.

The Safeway acquisition was followed by a one for eight rights issue in July 1987 to raise £208m, and a one for one scrip issue in September 1987. £69m of convertible Eurobonds were issued in October 1987. Conversion would add 20.34m ordinary shares to the issued capital. Exercise of Argyll's warrants would add a further 9.38m. There are no declared stakes of 5% or more.

GROUP REVIEW

Food division At October 1987, Argyll's outlets outside the Safeway chain amounted to 860 stores, including 518 Presto stores, 201 Lo-Cost discount stores, 98 Cordon Bleu freezer food centres and 41 small Galbraith shops.

32 stores had 20,000 sq feet or more, and 127 had between 10,000 and 20,000 sq feet. The group's wholesale food outlets consisted of 25 Mojo Cash and Carry depots and eight

Snowking specialist frozen food distributors.

On acquisition, Safeway operated 142 stores with a total sales area of 2.2m sq ft. 86 were in Greater London and the south-east of England, 22 in central Scotland and 25 in the Midlands and north of England. These totals have subsequently increased to 165 and 2.7 sq ft with the opening of 15 new Safeway stores and eight more conversions.

From April 1988, 25 new Safeways will be opened every year and 60 Prestos converted to create a Safeway division of more than 350 stores. The group has confirmed that this programme will cost no more than £90m. Of this an estimated £45m is to be incurred in 1987/88, £20m in 1988/89 and the balance over the following two years.

In its last complete year before acquisition to September 1986, Safeway's turnover was up 23.2% to £1.04bn. Pre-tax profits were up 40% to £43.8m. Pre-tax margin was up from 3.7% to 4.2%.

Share price and relative to FT-A All-Share

Argyll's food division sales for the year to March 1987 were 7% up at £1.73bn. Operating profit was 27% up to £67.4m. Operating margins improved from 3.3% to 3.9%. The figures include a four week contribution from Safeway of £92m in turnover and £4.4m in operating profit, and a contribution to turnover of £19.3m and operating profits of £2.4m from the group's food manufacturing interests, Gold Crown Foods, the tea blenders and packers, and Paterson-Brontë and Turniss, the biscuit manufacturers. They were sold for an aggregate of £24m in July 1987.

The scale of the expansion brought about by the Safeway acquisition can be seen in the food division's 1987/88 interim results. In the 28 weeks to 10 October 1987, food division turnover, fully reflecting the Safeway acquisition, was up 60% to £1.7bn. Safeway, with sales 19% up at £678m, contributed 40%. By 1991 it is estimated that Safeway will contribute 80% of group turnover.

Safeway was also largely responsible for the rise in Argyll's pre-tax profits of 97% to £75.9m, and the 29% increase in operating margin from 3.5% to 4.5%. Turnover for Argyll's interests outside Safeway for the 28 weeks to 10 October 1987 was £1.02bn.

Drinks After the failure of the group to acquire Distillers, Argyll decided to pull out of the drinks business. It completed its disposal of Barton Brands in the US and Barton International for £26.7m before the 1987 year-end. Its disposal of George Martin to Seagram UK for £13.3m was not completed until 29 May 1987 and fell into the year to March 1988, giving rise to an extraordinary profit of £8.5m.

The group's only remaining drinks businesses, North West Vintners, Winterschladen and Liquorsave off-licences contrib-

uted £120.9m of the division's 1986/87 £304m turnover and £2.3m of its £13.4m operating profit. From 1987/88 they are to be included in Argyll's food division.

GEOGRAPHICAL REVIEW

Following the disposal of the overseas drinks businesses, the group's trading interests are now based purely in the UK, with the exception of a single store in Gibraltar.

Safeway is particularly strong in the south-east and in central Scotland. The Presto chain is completely national, but has a particularly strong presence in north-east England and central Scotland.

CORPORATE CALENDAR

Year end	4 April
Preliminary results	end June
Report and accounts	end July
AGM	September
Final dividend paid	October
Interim results	December
Interim dividend paid	January

DIRECTORS' HOLDINGS

	Ordinary shares	Options
JG Gulliver	7,641,000	350,000
MA Grant	1,387,386	490,000
CS Lawrie	40,000	300,000
CGD Onslow	7,996	—
HM Plowden Roberts	25,000	—
CD Smith	10,000	250,000
TE Spratt	—	150,000
DGC Webster	1,000,000	435,000

Total directors' salaries and fees for 1986/87 were £1.18m, with the chairman receiving the highest remuneration at £252,000.

PRINCIPAL SUBSIDIARIES AND RELATED COMPANIES

Argyll Foods Plc, Argyll Stores Ltd, Lo-Cost Discount Centres, Safeway Food Stores Ltd

BRAND NAMES

Presto, Safeway

CONTACTS AND FURTHER INFORMATION

Paul Heward, Argyll Group PLC, 8 Chesterfield Hill, London W1X 7RG. Tel: 01-493 0808.

ASDA GROUP PLC

GENERAL INFORMATION

Head office	ASDA House, Southbank, Great Wilson Street, Leeds LS11 5AD. Tel: 0532 435435
Directors	JN Hardman FCA (executive chairman), DM Gransby (deputy chairman), T Campbell, CS Carr, EW Lea FCA, GH Stow FIPM. *Non-exec* Sir Godfrey Messervy, KJ Morton FCA
Advisers	SG Warburg & Co Ltd
Auditors	Ernst & Whinney
Registrars	National Westminster Bank Registrar's Department
Brokers	Citicorp Scrimgeour Vickers Ltd, Cazenove & Co
Solicitors	No specified adviser

GENERAL FINANCIAL INFORMATION

Market capitalisation	£1.98bn at 1 January 1988
Capital structure	
Issued ordinary shares (25p)	1.15bn
Issued preference shares (£1)	1.9m 9.75% CPS
Warrants	None
Convertibles	£120m 4.75% ESC 2002 (conversion at 164p per ordinary share to 24 April 2002)
Traded options	None
ADRs	None
Shareholders over 5%	None

FT CATEGORY

FT: Food, groceries, etc
FT-A: Food retailing

MAJOR ACTIVITIES

The company underwent major change in 1987. Until the middle of 1987 ASDA–MFI retailed a wide range of food and household products through three store chains – ASDA Stores, Allied (often known as Allied Carpets) and MFI. It also manufactured and sold dairy and meat products through Associated Fresh Foods.

In August 1987 the dairy divisions of Associated Fresh Foods were disposed of. At the same time a management buyout of MFI was completed. The company had intended to dispose of Allied as well. In November 1987 the group announced that it had finally decided not to dispose of Allied but to concentrate on developing its full potential.

This has left Asda Group, renamed in February 1988, with two major businesses. ASDA Stores operates a chain of superstores and hypermarkets. Allied operates a chain of carpet, curtain and bedding centres. In addition, the residue of Associated Fresh Foods supplies packed meat and cooked provisions to retail outlets.

Despite the disposals Asda Group remains a group of major proportions whose annual turnover easily exceeds £2bn. The group had embarked on a programme of development and expansion of its ASDA Stores some time before the demergers. With several major new stores now open and the range of ASDA own-brand goods greatly extended, its management

forecast in September 1987 an annual percentage increase in ASDA Stores' sales well into double figures for 1987/88.

The group's disposals have certainly left it in a strong enough financial position to begin its announced programme of developing Allied and continuing to strengthen ASDA Stores. As it opens more stores in the south of England, ASDA's impact on its competitors – Tesco, J Sainsbury, Safeway and Gateway – could be considerable. At present Asda has 7% of the UK food retail market against 13% for Sainsbury and Tesco, 11% for Dee and 10% for Argyll.

As part of the MFI buyout the group took a 25% stake in Maxirace Ltd, the MFI management's vehicle for the acquisition of MFI and Hygena Kitchens (now renamed MFI Furniture Group Ltd).

FINANCIAL HISTORY

Turnover for the year to 2 May 1987 was £2.67bn, 6% up on the previous year. Pre-tax profits were £192m, up 15.4%. Earnings per share increased 11% from 10.1p to 11.4p. Net dividends for the year were 3.5p, up 12%. The combined pre-tax profits for 1986/87 of MFI and the disposed interests of Associated Fresh Foods (AFF) were £53.3m, 27.7% of the group's total for that year.

At 31 June 1987 group net debt of £165m was 32% of shareholders' funds, a level above the average gearing level for the sector as a whole. Cash flow was high at £147m but capital expenditure in the year amounted to £276m. Following the disposals of AFF and MFI the situation was transformed. Net cash on 16 November 1987 amounted to £290m and shareholders' funds were £860m.

Because of the disposals and the changed nature of the group, the 1987/88 interim results were of great significance. For the 28 weeks ended 14 November 1987, turnover was up 11.1% to £1.50bn. This included 28 weeks' contribution from MFI and 16 weeks' from AFF's disposed-of dairy division. £1.23bn was contributed by the group's continuing businesses, up 14.8%, and the balance by the discontinued businesses.

Pre-tax profits on ordinary activities were up 10% at £94.8m. More importantly, the continuing businesses were performing very strongly indeed. They contributed profits of £74.5m, up 29%. Earnings per share fully diluted were up 6.3% to 5.37p. Dividends per share were up 16.8% to 1.6p. The sales of MFI and AFF's dairy division produced an extraordinary profit of £284.6m.

SHARE PRICE HISTORY

From 1984 onwards the Asda share price traded in the 120p to 170p band, until it broke through to a high of 231p in the summer of 1987.

Compared to the market, Asda had been falling in relative terms from a high of 30% of the FT-A All-Share index in 1984

F I V E Y E A R F I N A N C I A L I N F O R M A T I O N												
Year	Turnover (£m)	Pre-tax (£m)	Earnings (p)	Dividends net (p)	Dividend cover (x)	Net assets (p)	Price (p) High	Low	PER (x) High	Low	Yield (%) High	Low
1983	1,519.1	77.4	5.74	1.87	3.1	28.9	128	88	29.8	22.0	2.61	2.05
1984	1,755.2	104.6	7.45	2.50	3.0	30.7	166	118	29.5	17.9	2.68	1.98
1985	2,259.1	158.2	7.81	2.75	2.8	30.7	166	130	28.4	15.6	3.02	2.18
1986	2,516.6	166.4	10.05	3.15	3.2	37.7	170	128	20.7	14.4	3.47	2.54
1987	2,667.1	192.0	11.21	3.50	3.2	42.0	220	142	20.1	14.2	3.24	2.18

to 15% in early 1987. However, it recovered to nearly 20% by December 1987, when it was trading at 172p.

The recovery partly reflects the traditional view of food stores as good defensive stocks in a recession. In addition the management's final decision regarding the group's future make-up has improved its rating.

SENIOR MANAGEMENT

John Hardman, group managing director, became executive chairman on 1 January 1988. David Gransby became deputy chairman. Derek Hunt gave up his post as group deputy chairman and chief executive to facilitate the demerger of MFI.

Edward Lea, group finance director, and Tony Campbell became joint managing directors of ASDA Stores on 1 January 1988. Tony Campbell joined the group board then. He was previously director of operations at ASDA Stores. Edward Lea is also on the board of MFI Furniture Group Ltd in which Asda has taken a 25% stake.

CAPITAL

In the early 1980s scrip issues were a regular occurrence, normally on a one for three basis. The last major share issue was in May 1985 when 338.2m ordinary shares were issued as part of the consideration paid for MFI Furniture Group. This represented 42% of the existing share capital at the time.

The group issued £100m of 9⅝% Bonds in May 1986. £120m of 4¾% convertible bonds were issued in March 1987. Conversion of those outstanding would result in the issue of a further 72.7m ordinary shares.

The group received total proceeds of £505m from the sale of MFI, and £80m from the dairy interests of AFF. £52m of the MFI proceeds was converted into a 25% equity stake in the new company, enlarged by the acquisition of Hygena, its major kitchens supplier.

GROUP REVIEW

ASDA Stores   ASDA Stores is one of the largest and best known multiple retailers in the UK. It serves an estimated two million customers a week, operating predominantly from superstores. Most have a sales area of more than 25,000 sq ft. ASDA Stores are achieving strong growth in profits.

In 1986/87 profits increased by 24% to £124.9m on turnover only 5% up at £2.02bn. Key trading ratios included weekly sales per square foot of £9.79. The trading margin was 6.19%, up from 5.33% in 1985/86, one of the highest in the sector. For the 28 weeks to 14 November 1987, sales rose 13.5% to £1.02bn. Operating profits were again sharply up 30.2% to £66.0m. The operating profit margin increased from 5.0% to 5.7%.

ASDA operates 120 stores with a total area of 8m sq ft and a sales area of 4.4m sq ft. It has had a far stronger presence in northern England but with around 20 sites planned for London and the home counties, a more satisfactory balance between north and south is beginning to emerge. Of the nine new stores opened in 1987/88, seven are in southern England, including the major development in Watford.

The current development and improvement of ASDA Stores has been based upon in-depth consumer research. It has ranged from architectural restyling to the provision of crèche facilities. The launch of ASDA brands has been very successful. A range of 2,500 quality own label brands has been

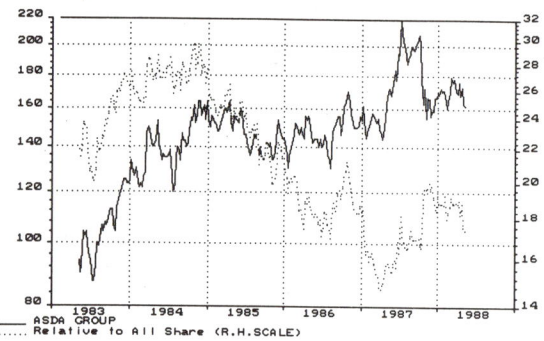

Share price and relative to FT-A All-Share

ASDA GROUP
Relative to All Share (R.H.SCALE)

launched to date.

In addition to the ASDA own-brand programme, development of fresh foods lines is taking place. Attention has also focussed on the development of the non-food business. A much improved, more refined product range has evolved including clothing and textiles, small electrical products, leisure goods, and DIY.

Allied   This division has 90 stores covering 1.7m sq ft. Since 1985 Allied has been transformed from a predominantly high street retailer of carpets to a more aggressive chain incorporating larger premises. Many of them are out-of-town and sell a much wider range of home furnishings, including carpets, curtains and textiles, beds and lounge suites.

Allied's sales and profits are growing well. In 1986/87 Allied's sales were up 28% to £118.7m and profits were up 30% to £9.6m. For the 28 weeks to 14 November 1987, sales rose by 38.7% to £79.5m. Operating profits were up 20% to £4.8m.

Associated Fresh Foods   The sale of the dairy division has radically reduced AFF's activities. The remaining business is mainly the supply of fresh meat and other fresh produce, and cooked pies and other pre-cooked provisions to ASDA's supermarkets. The division services ASDA's own-label products in this area. It also includes a smaller business which distributes products, manufactured by AFF and external suppliers, to supermarkets outside the group. These businesses made profits of £2.8m on a turnover of £80.4m for 1986/87. £79.2m of 1986/87 turnover represented intergroup sales.

Since the sale of the dairy division the rest of AFF's business has been consolidated in that of ASDA stores. For 1986/87 turnover of the discontinued business was £104.4m and operating profit was £9.6m. For the 16 weeks to 22 August

C H A I R M A N ' S   S T A T E M E N T

'The past six months have seen a radical change in the shape of the Group following the successful disposals of the dairy division of AFF and of MFI. The Group results, showing as they do an increase in both sales and profits before tax, do not reflect the significant growth of the core Asda superstore business which now contributes over 90% of Group profits.

The clear objective is for Asda to strengthen its position as the UK's leading superstore operator; I believe we have the management, the resources and the retailing formula to meet this objective and that the coming years will be ones of rewarding growth for the shareholders.' *John Hardman*

1987 when its sale was effected, its operating profit was £2.1m.

MFI Asda Group has a 25% stake in MFI Furniture Group Ltd which was formed on the completion of the management buyout. MFI is the market leader in the retailing of flat pack kitchen and bedroom furniture. It has 146 MFI stores in the UK and Eire, and five Priceless Kitchens stores in the US. Hygena, MFI's principal manufacturer, was also included in the management buyout. MFI is expected to go public in due course.

In 1986/87 MFI increased turnover by 11% to £420.5m, but profits were virtually the same at £46.5m. For the 28 weeks to 15 November 1987, turnover increased 5.4% to £233.9m but operating profit fell 24.9% to £17.8m.

GEOGRAPHICAL REVIEW

The entire business of the Asda Group and its wholly-owned subsidiaries is conducted in the UK. Its only exposure to the US is through its residual 25% holding in MFI which has five Priceless Kitchen stores there.

CORPORATE CALENDAR

Year end	30 April
Preliminary results	July
Report and accounts	August
AGM	September
Final dividend paid	October
Interim results	January
Interim dividend paid	April

DIRECTORS' HOLDINGS

	Ordinary shares		Options
	(beneficial)	(non-beneficial)	
JN Hardman	11,595	—	366,739
AE Gardiner	93,594	—	199,779
DM Gransby	5,225	—	204,342
EW Lea	147,651	—	323,821
Sir Godfrey Messervy	1,611	—	—
KJ Morton	10,000	—	—

Total directors' salaries and other fees for 1986/87 were £1.01m. Sir Noel Stockdale received £67,000 for his six months as chairman to 29 October 1986 and DL Donne received £38,000 for his six months in that office to 2 May 1987. The highest-paid director received £157,000.

PRINCIPAL SUBSIDIARIES AND RELATED COMPANIES

Allied Carpet Stores Ltd, ASDA Stores, Maxirace Ltd (25%)

BRAND NAMES

Allied, Asda, ASDA Stores

CONTACTS AND FURTHER INFORMATION

David Gransby, deputy chairman, Asda Group PLC, 21 Hertford St, London W1Y 7DA. Tel: 01-491 4019.

GENERAL INFORMATION

Head office	Weston Centre, Bowater House, 68 Knightsbridge, London SW1X 7LR. Tel: 01-589 6363
Directors	GH Weston (chairman), HW Bailey, PL Donovan, W Monaghan CBE, THM Shaw, WGG Weston
Advisers	Bank of Scotland, Lloyds Bank, National Girobank, National Westminster Bank
Auditors	Peat Marwick McLintock
Registrars	Lloyds Bank Registrar's Department
Brokers	Panmure Gordon & Co Ltd
Solicitors	No specified adviser

GENERAL FINANCIAL INFORMATION

Market capitalisation	£1.332bn at 1 January 1988
Capital structure	
Issued ordinary shares (5p)	446.0m
Issued preference shares (£1)	1m 4.2% CP
Warrants	None
Convertibles	None
Traded options	None
ADRs	One ordinary share per ADR
Shareholders over 5%	Wittington Investments (controlled by Weston family) 63%

FT CATEGORY

FT: Food, groceries, etc

FT-A: Food retailing

MAJOR ACTIVITIES

Associated British Foods (ABF) is one of the UK's leading milling and baking companies owning such well known brands as Sunblest, VitBe, Tip-Top and Allinson. It vies with Ranks Hovis McDougall for leadership in the bread market. This has led to very competitive conditions with margins constantly under pressure.

The group is also active in the biscuit market under the Burton and Ryvita names. The baking division owns a considerable retail presence through 1,300 outlets as well as 290 speciality hot bread shops.

Other food interests include: canning and preserves; Nelsons of Aintree; margarine and frozen products such as ice cream, gâteaux and pizzas; and Twinings, the famous speciality teas.

In the retail sector ABF owns two supermarket chains in Northern Ireland, Stewarts and Crazy Prices. In the Irish Republic, the Quinnsworth supermarket chain is owned along with Penneys, the textile retailer. Primark is a similar chain of textile shops owned in the UK.

ABF also has a 75% interest in the quoted George Weston Foods Group. This subsidiary is a major baker and miller in Australia and New Zealand. It produces cakes, pastry and biscuits.

The family-controlled ABF Group operates in basically mature industries where volume growth is limited and competition is great. Since 1983 there has been a considerable disposal programme that has left the group with a massive cash pile. £200m was raised from the sale of the Premier Group in 1984 and £557m from the sale of Fine Fare to Dee Corporation in 1986.

The lacklustre share price performance has not only reflected reduced returns from the UK gilts market, where a large portion of the cash is invested, but also the lack of any significant expansion strategy.

The management has been astute at selling businesses but has yet to display to the market its ability on the acquisition front. The 23.7% stake, costing £133m at 293p per share,

Year	Turnover (£m)	Pre-tax (£m)	Earnings (p)	Dividends net (p)	Dividend cover (x)	Net assets (p)	Price (p)		PER (x)		Yield (%)	
							High	Low	High	Low	High	Low
1983	3,366	146.5	29.9	4.27	4.9	174	167	129	12.4	9.4	4.73	3.57
1984	2,765	126.7	21.2	5.00	4.2	197	204	142	13.4	10.4	4.83	3.54
1985	2,931	132.3	19.8	5.40	3.7	211	270	194	15.4	12.0	3.76	2.88
1986	3.129	163.5	24.7	6.10	4.0	230	364	236	18.1	10.9	3.39	2.20
1987	2,201	190.5	30.3	7.30	4.2	330	414	288	15.0	9.9	3.59	2.41

FIVE YEAR FINANCIAL INFORMATION

acquired in S&W Berisford did, however, provide a pointer as to ABF's future plans.

The group launched a bid for Berisford in October 1987. Berisford owns British Sugar, which commands half the UK sugar market and is currently experiencing a marked revival in profits under new management. But, reflecting the stock market crash in mid-October, ABF allowed the bid to lapse even though it had gained more than 50% acceptances.

In the meantime ABF's profits should rise steadily, if unspectacularly, and the stock market will remain preoccupied with the management's acquisition plans.

FINANCIAL HISTORY

Group turnover was £2.202bn in 1986/87. Pre-tax profits at £190.5m were 17% up on those of the previous year. Earnings per share were 30.3p compared with 24.7p. The total dividend was up 20% at 7.3p, covered 4.2 times.

Shareholders' funds were £1.48bn, compared with £918m in 1985/86, boosted by the £371m profit on the disposal of Fine Fare. Pre-tax margins in 1986/87 were 8.6% against 8.0% on a reported basis, although at the trading level margins were 5.4% against 4.8% in 1985/86. Reflecting the sizeable liquid resources of £1bn, investment income totalled over £70m in 1986/87.

The past few years have been typified by large cash balances as ABF disposed of its South African subsidiary Premier Group in 1984 for £200m, and its UK retailing arm Fine Fare to Dee in 1986 for £557m.

Since 1982/83 profits have risen by 37% at the pre-tax stage, a rate of growth that does not compare favourably with its principal UK competitor, Ranks Hovis McDougall. Earnings per share have risen slightly faster than profits, however, and this largely reflects the absence of minority charges being eliminated on the Premier Group disposal. Dividend cover has remained at very high levels and stood at 4.2 times in 1986/87, down from 4.9 times in 1982/83.

At the 1987/88 interim to 26 September 1987, profits before tax increased by 15% to £82.7m on sales up by 6% to £1.068bn. Overseas sales were particularly strong since profits were up 24% at £19.3m on turnover up 8% at £372m. UK sales increased by 5% to £696m and trading profits by 13% to £34.1m.

SHARE PRICE HISTORY

Since 1984 ABF's share price has risen in relative terms against the market, although there have been some large swings. At the beginning of 1984 the share price rose strongly on news of the Premier Group disposal but then fell back subsequently in relative terms.

Throughout most of 1985 the share price began to show signs of more consistent gains against the market but disappointing returns from ABF's investment portfolio helped

cause a major correction in early 1986. However, confirmation of the Fine Fare disposal and better investment returns gave a considerable boost to the share price performance in mid-1986.

Overall, while the stockmarket has retained confidence in the management, the group's longer term strategy has perhaps been unclear, particularly given the large cash holdings. Since the October 1987 crash the shares have substantially outperformed because of the large cash pile and the defensive characteristics of the shares.

SENIOR MANAGEMENT

The chairman, Garry H Weston via Wittington Investments, controls 63% of ABF. The Weston family's businesses are centred in the UK food industry. The Weston family also controls Fortnum & Mason, the Piccadilly based retailer, and Weston Foods in Canada.

During the 1950s and 1960s Garry Weston's father was responsible for reshaping the structure of the UK milling and baking industry in a wide ranging acquisition programme, a strategy that the major competitors felt obliged to follow. Garry Weston continued the strategy and ABF's tough trading stance was allegedly responsible for Spillers' withdrawal from bread baking in the late 1970s. Thus the Westons have attracted the tag of being very competitive in the market place.

Patrick Donovan, who comes from a family that has a long history in flour milling, is in charge of the group's milling interests. Wallace Monaghan, who used to be in charge of Fine Fare, now heads the baking division. Galen Weston, Garry Weston's brother, also sits on the ABF board.

CAPITAL

At 31 December 1987 the issued share capital was 446m ordinary shares. This had been increased in December 1986 to that level upon the issue of 48.5m new shares to non-shareholders. The issue raised £148m in cash and was designed to reduce the Weston family control from 71% to 63% and avoid close company status which could have resulted in a considerably increased tax bill. The issue also increased the marketability of the shares.

GROUP REVIEW

Milling and baking Allied Bakeries own over 40 bakeries throughout the UK. Allied Mills operates 19 mills. Over the years, like most in the industry, ABF has found it very difficult to make reliable profits in the baking industry. Bread consumption has been in steady decline. More recently the trend towards brown and speciality breads has provided some offset.

Margins have remained very low given the strength of the

supermarkets and commodity nature of the product. Some respite to this pressure has traditionally been available from relatively good returns from flour milling, where, provided the quality of the domestic harvest is satisfactory, the millers can obtain useful economies of scale. ABF's market share in milling and baking is in the region of 30%.

Biscuits and crispbread   Burton's Biscuits has experienced a patchy history with profits and market share slipping in recent years. An extensive rationalisation programme has improved the cost base. A static and very competitive market, United Biscuits being the dominant and most efficient national supplier, has kept margins under pressure. The disposal of Fine Fare, a major customer, contributed to the difficulties experienced in 1986/87. Encouragingly in the crispbread market, Ryvita continues to trade very profitably. Ryvita enjoys brand leadership and is well represented in the export field, which represents 30% of sales.

Other foods   Anglia Canners is an own label canner of a range of vegetables that is relatively small in group terms. Nelsons of Aintree produces a range of preserves and marmalades. Its range of customers has been expanded to include not only retailers but also the catering industry and the food industry trade, which includes the ice cream and biscuit markets.

Share price and relative to FT-A All-Share

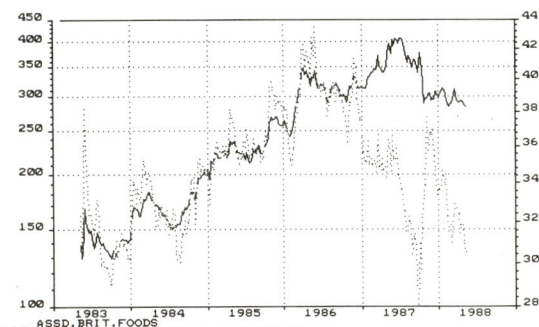

At Rowallan Creamery, retail margarines, fats, oils, and pastry and cake shortenings are produced, although its market share is very small. In frozen foods a range of pizzas, gâteaus and cheesecakes are produced under the Marietta brand. Considerable volume and profit growth has been achieved over the past year. Ice cream and ice lollies are produced for the retail trade, particularly in multi-pack form.

Twinings enjoys a very strong representation in the growing speciality tea market. This sector of an otherwise static tea market has been gaining increased supermarket shelf space in recent years with demand rising by 5% per annum. Twinings is the leader in this niche market and is also very well represented in overseas markets.

Yeasts and food ingredients   Mauri Products supplies baker's yeast while AB Ingredients produces bread improvers for the baking trade.

Retailing   The supermarket chains in Northern Ireland, Stewarts and Crazy Prices, operating in somewhat difficult conditions have reported satisfactory results. In the Irish Republic the Quinnsworth supermarket chain is undergoing some expansion. Penney's and Primark have both traded very well in recent years with Primark benefiting from new store openings.

Overseas activities   George Weston Foods operates 23

CHAIRMAN'S STATEMENT

'Shareholders will be aware of two major events in the past year [1986/87]. . . . We sold our interests in the Fine Fare companies . . . receiving in return cash and a major interest in The Dee Corporation Plc. Secondly . . . we issued for cash, 48.5m shares to raise approximately £150m. The immediate benefit of this move was twofold. Firstly, the company avoided the likelihood of a significant extra tax charge if it had retained "close" status, and secondly, by ceasing to be a "close" company, the marketability of our shares was enhanced. At the end of the year current asset investments exceeded £1,000m.' Garry Weston

bakeries, 17 flour mills, five biscuit factories and 23 other establishments throughout Australia and New Zealand. A major programme has concentrated on cost reduction in recent years.

George Weston Foods has endeavoured to maintain its competitive position, particularly in its largest bread market, New South Wales, where bread price controls have remained in force. Brand names in Australia include Tip-Top, Ryvita, Westons and Crackerbread. A range of bread and biscuits are marketed in New Zealand's North Island.

GEOGRAPHICAL REVIEW

In 1986/87 total group turnover was £2.202bn. Of this £721m or 33% derived from overseas activities. £256m, 12% of the total, came from Australia and New Zealand with the balance, £465m, mainly from Europe.

In terms of profit contributions the total overseas content was 20%, divided equally between Australia and New Zealand, and Europe.

CORPORATE CALENDAR

Year end	28 March
Preliminary results	May
Report and accounts	May
AGM	June
Final dividend paid	September
Interim results	November
Interim dividend paid	March

DIRECTORS' HOLDINGS

	Fully-paid ordinary shares		Options
	(beneficial)	(non-beneficial)	
GH Weston	341,230	998,775	—
WG Galen Weston	598,723	198,008	—
W Monaghan	7,700	—	100,000
PL Donovan	20,165	—	90,000
HW Bailey	33,055	550,000	75,000
THM Shaw	605	—	75,000

Total directors' remuneration in 1987 was £422,000, of which the chairman received £85,000.

PRINCIPAL SUBSIDIARIES AND RELATED COMPANIES

AB Exploration Ltd, AB Ingredients Ltd (95.7%), ABR Foods Ltd, H&R Ainscough, Allied Bakeries (NI) Ltd – Northern Ireland, Allied Foods Ltd, Allied Foods Ltd – New Zealand, Allied Grain Ltd, Allied-Love Adhesives Ltd (91.3%), Allied Mills Ltd, Alric Packing, Anglia Canners, Auckland Flour Mills Ltd – New Zealand (50%), Betabake, Bradford Bakeries, Brettsil Packaging Ltd, F Broomfield, Burton's Gold Medal Biscuits Ltd, Carrick's Caterers, Chancelot Mill Ltd, Chibnall's Bakeries, City Bakeries, E Cookson

BAA plc

& Sons, EJ Coombe, Coombe Bakery, Country Maid Bakeries, Cranfield Brothers Ltd, Crayford Mill, Crazy Prices, Crystal Drinks, CWII Ltd – Jersey, Dairy Tops, Deutscher Supermarkt Handels GmbH – West Germany (44%), Devonshire Ice Cream, S Edwards & Son, G Embrey, Fermentation Industries Pty Ltd – New Zealand (25%), Foods International SA – France, George Weston Foods Limited – Australia, Grosvenor Marketing Ltd – US, Harper Love Adhesives Corp – US (50%), Healings Flour Mills, Hickinbottoms Bakeries, Hunters the Bakers, James Neill Ltd, Joseph Sumner & Co, King's Mills, Koters (Liverpool) Ltd, Lax and Shaw Ltd, NB Love Industries Pty Ltd – Australia, Mardorf Peach & Co Ltd, Marietta Frozen Foods, Mauri Products Ltd (50%), Merrett's, Namosa Ltd, Nelsons of Aintree, HW Nevill (Sunblest), Parkers Bakeries, Parslows of Reading, Pendletons Ice Cream, Power Supermarkets Ltd – Irish Republic, Primark Ltd – Irish Republic, Primark Stores Ltd, Provincial Merchants Ltd, Rankin Flour Mills, Richard Sharrock & Sons, Rowallen Creamery, Seaforth Mill, Serpentine Securities Ltd, J&R Snodgrass, Speedibake, Stantons Bakeries, Stewarts Supermarkets Ltd, Sunblest Bakeries, The Ryvita Company Ltd, Thomas Sugden & Son, Tip Top Bakeries Holdings Pty Ltd – Australia, R Twining and Company Limited, R Twining & Co Ltd – US, RC Walmsley Limited, Watson's Food Holding Pty Ltd – Australia, Wesfeeds Pty Limited – Australia (50%), Weston Research Laboratories Limited, William King

BRAND NAMES

Allied Biscuits, Allinson, Baker's Oven, Burtons, Crackerbread, Crazy Prices, Harvest Bakery, Harvester, Marietta, Mighty White, Mix 'n' Bake, Nelsons of Aintree, Parisienne, Penneys, Primark, Quinnsworth, Ryvita, Stewarts, Sunblest, Tip Top, Twinings Tea, VitBe, Westons

CONTACTS AND FURTHER INFORMATION

PE Patchett, Group chief accountant, Associated British Foods plc, Weston Centre, 68 Knightsbridge, London SW1X 7LR. Tel: 01-589 6363.

GENERAL INFORMATION

Corporate office	130 Wilton Road, London SW1V 1LQ. Tel: 01-834 9449
Directors	Sir Norman Payne CBE FEng FCGI FICE FCIT (chairman), JJS Marshall (chief executive), G Bell CEng·MICE, N Ellis FCA, DMG King CEng FICE MIMechE, MP Maine MCIT. *Non-exec* JE Boyd CA (deputy chairman), MG Ashton FCA DL, DP Cassidy, JM Drinkwater QC, Sir Keith Stuart FCIT, Sidney Weighell
Advisers	J Henry Schroder Wagg & Co Ltd
Auditors	Touche Ross & Co
Registrars	Hill Samuel Registrars Ltd
Brokers	Hoare Govett Ltd
Solicitors	Herbert Smith

GENERAL FINANCIAL INFORMATION

Market capitalisation	£1.175bn at 1 January 1988
Capital structure	
Issued ordinary shares (25p)	500m
Issued preference shares	None
Warrants	None
Convertibles	None
Traded options	Yes
ADRs	None
Shareholders over 5%	None

FT CATEGORY

FT: Industrials
FT-A: Shipping and transport

MAJOR ACTIVITIES

BAA, formerly the British Airports Authority, was privatised in July 1987. The company's principal business is the ownership and operation of seven international airports in the UK. These are Heathrow, Gatwick and Stansted in the London area and Glasgow, Edinburgh, Aberdeen and Prestwick in Scotland. Of these, Heathrow and Gatwick are the two busiest international airports in the world.

The company's revenues were divided into two distinct categories for reporting purposes. Firstly there are the traffic revenues (1987: £212m) paid to BAA by airlines for the use of the airport's terminals, runways and other facilities. Secondly there are commercial revenues (1987: £227m) which derive from such activities as duty- and tax-free shopping, catering, car parking and hotel operations. Generally, these commercial activities are operated by outside companies on a concessionary basis. In future, in order to comply with the requirements of the regulator, the sources of income will be split into three categories – operational activities, divided into airport charges and other income, and other activities.

Traffic revenues are dominated by passenger charges (1987: £114m), which are payable by airlines on a fee per passenger basis. The level of this fee will vary according to the time of day and season – there are peak and off-peak rates at the London airports. Airlines are charged at a higher rate in peak periods for each passenger enplaned to an international flight than to a domestic flight. Airlines are also charged a landing and parking fee (1987: £78m), which vary according to the weight of the aircraft and there are various apron and other service charges (1987: £20m).

BAA does not have absolute freedom to raise these charges, except at their Scottish airports, where keen pricing can boost airport usage. Traffic tariff increases at the London airports are governed by a formula which limits annual tariff increases to a level 1% below inflation. Broadly this is expressed as the Retail

Price Index minus 1%. In 1992 the Monopolies and Mergers Commission is due to review this formula.

Most of BAA's commercial revenues derive from concessions (1987: £158m), although a proportion comes from the rental to airlines and others of land and property for such activities as cargo and baggage handling, hotels, offices and aircraft maintenance (1987: £69m). Services are provided to such tenants, providing additional revenues.

The concessionary income is provided by duty and tax-free shops, car parking, general retailing, catering, car rental and other services which include banks, hotel booking operations, and insurance agencies. BAA appoints concessionaires for the provision of services to passengers. These concessions are normally granted for a five year period, at the end of which the concession is re-bid on a percentage of revenues basis. Typically BAA provides the capital expenditure items – for instance, car park, restaurant and shop unit.

Post privatisation it is widely assumed that BAA will take advantage of its new freedom by seeking to maximise its commercial revenues in operating some of the activities itself as concessions expire, thus keeping a larger share of the revenues. In particular it is likely that BAA may start to build and operate its own hotels on airport land. This would mean that commercial revenues would become an even more significant part of total revenues. Even without these changes, commercial revenues have been growing faster than the regulated traffic revenues. In fiscal 1983 commercial revenues accounted for 46.7% of total turnover. By fiscal 1987 the proportion had reached 51.7%.

FINANCIAL HISTORY

BAA, like an airline, is dependent on growth in passenger traffic to stimulate profit growth. Also, like an airline, costs are largely fixed, leading to an exaggerated effect on profit of revenue enhancements. However, BAA's profit history is much steadier than any airline. This has two main reasons. Firstly BAA has very firm control on its costs, whereas airlines cannot easily control major expenses such as fuel costs and interest charges. Secondly, BAA is not overexposed to routes to particular destinations, such as the US, which may prove volatile. By its nature BAA serves a complete spread of destinations.

Since 1983 BAA has achieved, on a historic cost accounting basis, compound profit growth of 15% per annum, from £71m pre-tax in fiscal 1983 to £124m pre-tax in fiscal 1987. Profit growth of 10.5% was achieved in fiscal 1987 – albeit a low level – even though European airlines experienced severe profit downturns due to a shortfall in North Atlantic passengers.

Since 1983 BAA's total revenues have increased by 56.8% from £280m to £439m, 10.9% ahead of £396m in 1986. Traffic revenues contributed £212m (48.3%), concession income £158m (33.7%) and rents and services £69m (18%).

In the first half of fiscal 1988 strong traffic growth – 15.7% more passengers through the terminals – led to a 26% pre-tax profit increase from £108m to £136m. Turnover was 17.2% ahead at £307m against £262m in the previous period. The bulk of BAA's annual profit is earned in this half as it covers the busy months between April and September when revenues are therefore at their highest. Costs remain largely steady throughout the year.

SHARE PRICE HISTORY

BAA shares were offered for sale by the government in July 1987. 75% of the 500m shares were offered at a fixed price of 245p and 25% by tender at a cut-off price of 282p. In each case 145p was deferred until the second instalment on 19 May 1988.

The partly paid shares, 100p at the fixed price, opened at around 145p – close to the striking price for the tender offer – and reached 152p in October 1987 before falling to 87p in the market crash. The shares then consolidated for several months in the 95p to 105p range before climbing briefly again to over 120p in March 1988. BAA's perceived defensive qualities have permitted 25% outperformance of the market since the October crash.

SENIOR MANAGEMENT

Sir Norman Payne has been chairman since 1977, having joined BAA as director of engineering on its formation in 1965 after a career in airport and industrial consultancy. He handed the role of chief executive on to Jeremy Marshall shortly prior to privatisation.

Jeremy Marshall joined from Hanson, where he held positions as managing director of various subsidiary companies before becoming chief executive of Lindustries engineering division in 1979.

William Shaw was group financial director until his retirement in March 1988, when he was succeeded by Nigel Ellis, formerly group financial director of Hammerson.

CAPITAL

The Government sold all 500m ordinary 25p shares in July 1987, apart from sufficient shares to satisfy expected entitlements under a shareholder loyalty bonus scheme of one for ten held continuously until 31 July 1990.

There is a 'golden' share. No person is permitted by the Articles of Association of the company to be interested in shares carrying more than 15% of total voting rights.

GROUP REVIEW

London airports In fiscal 1987 the three London airports contributed £383m of revenue, 87.2% of the group total.

FIVE YEAR FINANCIAL INFORMATION

Year	Turnover (£m)	Pre-tax (£m)	Earnings (p)	Dividends net (p)	Dividend cover (x)	Net assets (p)	Price (p) High	Low	PER (x) High	Low	Yield (%) High	Low
1983	280	71	—	—	—	—	—	—	—	—	—	—
1984	316	84	—	—	—	—	—	—	—	—	—	—
1985	362	104	—	—	—	—	—	—	—	—	—	—
1986	396	122	—	—	—	—	—	—	—	—	—	—
1987	439	124	16.0	6.6	2.4	139	295	231	18.4	11.7	4.30	3.06

BAA owns and operates Heathrow, Gatwick and Stansted airports in the London area. It does not have a complete monopoly in the area since it owns neither Luton Airport nor the City Airport.

Heathrow is the world's busiest international airport in terms of international passengers, although certain US airports actually handle more passengers overall. Virtually all airline traffic handled is on scheduled flights. In the year to 31 March 1987, 31.7m passengers were handled.

Over 70 airlines operate from Heathrow to more than 200 destinations worldwide. British Airways is the principal user of the airport, accounting for 46% of the passengers using the airport in the year to 31 March 1987. Heathrow has two main runways and four airport terminals. Total revenue in fiscal 1987 was £269m, 8.9% ahead of 1986.

Gatwick became the second busiest international airport in the world during 1987, overtaking New York's JFK. In the year to 31 March 1987, 16.6m passengers were handled, of whom 58% were on charter flights and 42% on scheduled flights. British Caledonian Airways, now part of British Airways, Dan-Air and British Airways (including British Airtours – now renamed Caledonian Airways) each accounted for about 15% of passengers using the airport in the year to 31 March 1987. Gatwick has only one main runway and now has two terminals. In March 1988 the new North Terminal was opened, which should eventually allow 25m passengers each year to use the airport. Total revenue in fiscal 1987 was £110m, 14.6% ahead of 1986.

Share price and relative to FT-A All-Share

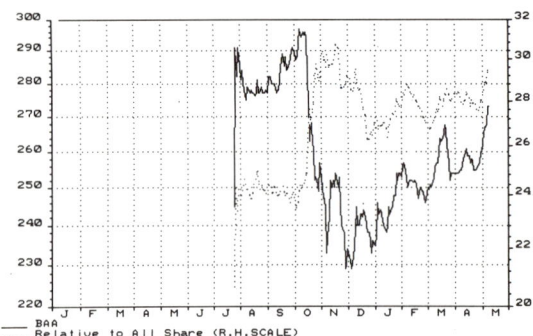

BAA
Relative to All Share (R.H.SCALE)

Stansted is being developed to become London's third airport. In the year to March 1987 there were only 0.56m passengers, of whom 75% were on charter flights. There is one runway and one airport terminal. Total revenue in fiscal 1987 was £4.7m, 20.5% ahead of 1986.

In June 1985, following a public enquiry, BAA was granted planning permission for the development of a new terminal at Stansted for the eventual accommodation of 15m passengers annually. This will be reached in stages. The terminal is scheduled to open in 1991 with initial potential for accommodating 8m passengers per annum. There is sufficient land available at Stansted for the construction of a second terminal, although this would require planning permission. A direct rail link is planned from the airport to Liverpool Street station in London.

Scottish airports   In 1987 the four Scottish airports contributed £55.3m of revenue, 12.8% of the group total.

Glasgow Airport is the fourth busiest in the United Kingdom, after Heathrow, Gatwick and Manchester Airport,

'The financial year 1986/87 was divided into two distinct halves. Passenger fears about terrorism and the fall in traffic following the Chernobyl incident cut passenger growth in the first half of the year but the second half saw a substantial recovery. Overall the rate of passenger traffic growth was 3.7% with a total of 55.3m passengers using BAA airports.

Taking account of the decline in traffic in several important markets in the first half of the year and the increase in operating costs and depreciation as Heathrow's Terminal 4 came into use in April 1986, the result for the year is satisfactory. . . .

The provision of new facilities and the redevelopment of existing facilities are key features of BAA's business. The first phase of the new North Terminal at Gatwick will open in March 1988 and work is on schedule with the terminal complex at Stansted and the redevelopment of Terminal 3 at Heathrow. Planning permission has now been granted for expansion at Glasgow Airport. The Company is continuing to evaluate opportunities for the further development of the business.' *Sir Norman Payne*

which is not owned by BAA. It has one main runway and one passenger terminal, which is to be expanded. In the year to 31 March 1987, 61% of the airport's passengers were carried on scheduled flights and 39% on charter flights. 38% of passengers were on flights to London. British Airways accounted for 41% of passengers. In the year a total of 3.1m passengers used the airport. Total revenue in fiscal 1987 was £26m, 23.8% ahead of 1986.

Edinburgh Airport was acquired by BAA in 1971, since when a new main runway and a new terminal complex have been built. Most passengers using the airport are on scheduled flights and in the year to 31 March 1987 70% of passengers using the airport flew on the London routes. In that year 1.7m passengers used the airport, of whom 53% were on British Airways flights. Total revenue in fiscal 1987 was £12.3m, 13.9% ahead of 1986.

Aberdeen Airport has one runway and two cross runways which are used for helicopter flights. The airport is a busy heliport because of North Sea oil exploration and production. In the year to 31 March 1987 one million passengers used the airport for fixed wing flights and 0.45m for helicopter flights. The reduction in oil exploration activity, exacerbated by the fall in oil prices in 1986, led to a 16% decline in passenger numbers in fiscal 1987. British Airways accounted for 55% of passengers on fixed wing aircraft in the year. Total revenue in fiscal 1987 was £10.6m, 3.8% down on 1986.

Prestwick Airport in Ayrshire, south of Glasgow, is, as a result of government policy, Scotland's long haul international airport but this policy is due for review in 1989. It has one main runway and one terminal building. The principal user of Prestwick is North West Airlines which operates on routes to the US. In the year to 31 March 1987 the airline accounted for 35% of the airport's 0.24m passengers. Total revenue in fiscal 1987 was £6.4m, 6.7% ahead on 1986.

GEOGRAPHICAL REVIEW

All of BAA's airports are in the UK and all revenue and operating profits are UK-based. The seven BAA airports accounted in 1987 for 73% of air passenger traffic and 85% of air cargo in the UK.

BAT INDUSTRIES p.l.c.

CORPORATE CALENDAR

Year end	31 March
Preliminary results	June
Report and accounts	July
AGM	July
Final dividend paid	August
Interim results	November
Interim dividend paid	January

DIRECTORS' HOLDINGS

	Fully-paid	Other (incl. options)
Sir Norman Payne	10,069	180,000
JJS Marshall	9,982	134,000
JE Boyd	2,000	—
HG Ashton	2,000	—
GD Bell	4,569	54,083
DP Cassidy	4,182	—
JM Drinkwater	4,182	—
NG Ellis	—	—
DMG King	3,287	85,083
MP Maine	287	70,083
Sir James Stuart	2,000	—
Sidney Weighell	4,082	—

Total directors' remuneration not available at April 1988.

PRINCIPAL SUBSIDIARIES AND RELATED COMPANIES

Aberdeen Airport Ltd, Airports UK Ltd, British Airport Services Ltd, Edinburgh Airport Ltd, Gatwick Airport Ltd, Glasgow Airport Ltd, Heathrow Airport Ltd, Prestwick Airport Ltd, Scottish Airports Ltd, Stansted Airport Ltd

BRAND NAMES

None

CONTACTS AND FURTHER INFORMATION

Caitriana Mackenzie-Williams, Investors Relations Manager, BAA plc, 130 Wilton Road, London SW1V 1LQ. Tel: 01-932 6653.

GENERAL INFORMATION

Head office	Windsor House, 50 Victoria Street, London SW1H 0NL. Tel: 01-222 7979
Directors	P Sheehy (chairman), BP Garraway (deputy chairman), GL Dennis (deputy chairman), B Bramley, EAA Bruell, MA Butt, JR Crosby, H Frigon, MS Lipworth, AC Long, DL Slobom, Sir Mark Weinberg, EJ Worlidge. *Non-exec* Sir Campbell Fraser, Sir Michael Palliser PC GCMG
Advisers	Lazard Brothers & Co Ltd
Auditors	Deloitte Haskins & Sells
Registrars	Lloyds Bank Registrar's Department
Brokers	de Zoete & Bevan Ltd, Cazenove & Co
Solicitors	Herbert Smith

GENERAL FINANCIAL INFORMATION

Market capitalisation	£6.554bn at 1 January 1988
Capital structure	
Issued ordinary shares (25p)	1.49bn
Issued preference shares	None
Warrants	None
Convertibles	None
Traded options	Yes
ADRs	One ADR per one ordinary share
Shareholders over 5%	None

FT CATEGORY

FT: Tobaccos
FT-A: Miscellaneous

MAJOR ACTIVITIES

BAT Industries is a major international tobacco company with a 20% market share. It has diversified successfully away from its core tobacco base to become a leading UK and US retailer, a leading speciality paper company, and a substantial UK financial services operator through Eagle Star and Allied Dunbar.

Despite a more than doubling of tobacco profits from £336m in 1980 to £722m in 1987, the percentage contribution from tobacco has declined from 72% to 50% during this period. 44% of profits accrue in North America with about 80% outside the UK. BAT is one of the UK's three largest non-utility companies. Its US operation would rank in the top 100 corporations there if independently quoted.

BAT has diversified away from tobacco more successfully and more quickly than any other international tobacco company. Yet BAT's rating has consistently stood at a discount to American rivals RJR Nabisco and Philip Morris.

BAT's immensely strong cash flows have enabled the company to fund its non-tobacco acquisitions with cash. BAT now includes the sixteenth largest US retailer, the third largest US tobacco company, the largest speciality paper company, and the second largest fund manager in the UK with £13.9bn under management. The $4.5bn tender offer announced for Farmers Group would take BAT into the top ten US insurance companies.

FINANCIAL HISTORY

Since 1982 pre-tax profits have increased from £856m to £1.39bn in 1986, compounding at 13% per annum. Profits marked time in 1987 at £1.394bn, using an exchange rate of $1.88 to £1 compared with $1.48 to £1 a year earlier. At a constant rate of exchange the growth rate would have exceeded 14%. From 1982 to 1986 earnings per share have risen on average by 14.5% per annum and the net dividend by 20% annually. In 1987 earnings per share rose by 1.4% and the

F I V E   Y E A R   F I N A N C I A L   I N F O R M A T I O N

Year	Turnover (£m)	Pre-tax (£m)	Earnings (p)	Dividends net (p)	Dividend cover (x)	Net assets (p)	Price (p) High	Low	PER (x) High	Low	Yield (%) High	Low
1983	13,839	979	37.57	8.25	4.6	236	185	131	8.3	5.2	7.50	4.45
1984	18,414	1,405	53.55	10.30	5.2	324	353	175	9.8	6.6	5.89	3.61
1985	17,051	1,166	45.72	12.10	3.8	281	385	255	10.6	5.2	6.16	3.31
1986	19,167	1,393	53.51	14.30	3.7	339	490	310	10.2	6.4	5.07	3.59
1987	17,208	1,394	52.78	16.90	3.1	270	707	395	13.4	7.2	5.31	2.90

dividend was increased by 18.2%.

Within BAT the profits mix has undergone a significant change through the £1.6bn acquisition of the financial services division, as the core retail activities have expanded organically, and as the contribution from speciality paper operations has grown from £75m to £209m.

The development of the financial services operation and the rapid growth of Argos and Wiggins Teape have given BAT a UK profits base that hitherto had been tiny. The dependence on both cigarette earnings and Third World earnings has been reduced significantly, in the latter instance to just 18%.

Strong cash generation, particularly from tobacco, has enabled BAT to reduce net gearing from 37½% in 1984 to 10% by the end of 1987. That BAT can contemplate a $4.5bn cash acquisition bears witness to the strength of the group's balance sheet and cash flow.

Shareholders' funds, adjusted for the appreciation of investments, grew from £2.991bn in 1982 to £3.946bn in 1987. Margins have increased by 36%, to reach a record 8.1% in 1987 on turnover 10% down at £17.208bn from £19.167bn in 1986.

The short term financial performance is influenced by currency movements, particularly the US dollar and the German mark against sterling. Sterling's extreme weakness in 1984 benefited BAT's profits considerably on translation but the distortion to stated profits that year accounted for almost all the subsequent shortfall in 1985 when sterling strengthened again.

At current exchange rates, for every one cent movement in the US dollar and dollar-related currencies relative to sterling, sterling-denominated profits are impacted by a swing of £7m to £8m. At constant exchange rates profits would have been £92m higher in 1987. This would have given an underlying profits growth rate of around 20% rather than the static position reported.

SHARE PRICE HISTORY

Tobacco stocks have sold at a significant discount to the market although tobacco earnings are highly visible and reliable. Relative to the FT-A All-Share index, BAT's status has improved from 30% in 1982 to 53% in early 1988. It peaked at 60% in 1984 after the Eagle Star acquisition. The price has improved from 125p in early 1983 to 420p in mid-April 1988.

Whilst the profits performance has been good and the broadening profits base has improved the perceived quality of earnings, the rating discount to the market is now almost as wide as before the move into financial services.

Adverse factors affecting sentiment include: the misconception that tobacco consumption worldwide is falling as fast as it is in the UK (where BAT has no tobacco representation); sterling movements; and the incidence and publicity of moves by the US anti-smoking lobby. There is also some correlation of BAT's share price movements to the price of RJR Nabisco and Philip Morris in the US.

SENIOR MANAGEMENT

Patrick Sheehey, the present chairman, succeeded Sir Peter Macadam in 1982, having spent his whole career with the company. There are two deputy chairmen, Gerald Dennis and Brian Garraway, the latter also being the senior of three finance directors.

The management structure is divided both by product and region. Areas with regional autonomy are threefold: the US under the BATUS Inc holding company, BATIG in Germany and Souza Cruz in Brazil. Until February 1988 no regional division was represented on the main board by any of its nationals, but this has now changed with two BATUS directors on the main board.

Barry Bramley succeeded Eric Bruell as chairman of BATCO, and heads the rest of the world tobacco operations; Michael Butt heads Eagle Star; Sir Mark Weinberg heads Allied Dunbar; John Worlidge heads Wiggins Teape; and Tom Long is chairman of BAT Stores Ltd.

CAPITAL

Because of the strongly cash positive nature of the tobacco industry, BAT has financed its expansion from its own resources without resorting to equity to finance acquisitions. Since 1984 net debt of £1.8bn had shrunk to £729m in 1986 and is expected to fall further to £440m by December 1987. Recent disposals of peripheral activities have raised over £1bn in two years.

The proposed $4.5bn acquisition of Farmers Group can be financed solely by cash, though putting net gearing up to 70%. The company is likely to partially finance the acquisition through a Euromarkets loan for $3.2bn led by JP Morgan, although Shearson Lehman are handling the $63 a share tender offer.

GROUP REVIEW

Tobacco BAT operates in 120 countries. In profit terms the most significant is the US. Brown & Williamson is the third largest tobacco company there with an 11% market share with brands like Kool, Richland, Barclay, Falcon, Capri, Raleigh, Viceroy and Belair. In 1987 Brown & Williamson achieved 19% higher profits in dollars, with export volume more than doubled by strong sales to Japan, China, Taiwan and the Middle East.

BAT's largest volume tobacco operation is in Brazil where the 75%-held Souza Cruz takes 81% of the market. Little profit is made from the Brazilian domestic market but a substantial profit is made by exporting good quality tobacco leaf for hard currency dollars. Venezuela with 84% market share, Germany with 25%, Canada with 50%, Malaysia, and the export-only UK are also important profit centres.

The key to profitability is efficient production with high capacity loadings. Price increases in the US are coming through early and often. The June 1987 price increase of $1.50 per 1,000 cigarettes on most brands, coupled with a December 1987 rise of $2.00 per 1,000 on mainline brands and $2.75 per 1,000 on generics, gives a US price increase of 12.5% in 1987. The cigarette industry allows significant pricing flexibility.

In 1987 tobacco trading profits were 5.5% down at £722m on turnover 16.8% down at £6.940bn.

Retailing In the US, the core businesses are Saks Fifth Avenue, an upmarket speciality fashion store with 46 outlets, and Marshall Field's, a top quality department store. Marshall Field's traded well in 1987 with a $1bn turnover for the first time, but Saks Fifth Avenue had reduced sales margins and profits fell. With Breuners' furniture retail operations on the west coast, Iveys and Thimbles, BATUS Retail is probably the 15th or 16th largest US retailer.

In the UK Argos is being built up rapidly. This operation has increased profits from £6.6m in 1982 to £47m in 1987. Argos has an aggressive store opening programme with a target of 550 stores compared with 208 at present.

In 1987 retailing trading profits were 3.8% down at £203m on turnover 17.1% down at £3.948bn.

Paper In the US and Europe, the BAT speciality paper interests, represented by Appleton and Wiggins Teape respectively, are the largest manufacturers of carbonless copying paper.

In the US, Appleton's share of the market has risen to a little over 50% in a market that has usually seen volume growth of over 10% per annum. In 1987, however, competitive pressure reduced volume growth, and profit was down 9%. Growth is geared to both the business forms market and the increasing substitution of carbonless copying paper for traditional carbon-in-bond. At present carbonless paper's penetration of the market represents only 40% of the potential. With major business forms printers such as the Moore Corporation scheduled to switch to 100% carbonless paper by the early 1990s, the long term outlook for Appleton is good.

In Europe, Wiggins Teape has about 33% of the market ahead of West German competition. Here carbonless paper takes a lower proportion of the market so the growth potential is greater. In Europe the company has rapidly growing interests in eucalyptus pulp mills in Portugal and Spain.

In 1987 pulp operations all did well. Profits rose again at Aracruz, which is spending $1bn to double capacity to 1m tons by 1993. Divisional trading profits in 1987 were 3.7% down at

£209m on turnover 3.6% down at £1.692bn.

Financial services Eagle Star is a leading composite assurance company. Allied Dunbar is the UK's largest unit-linked life assurance company.

Underwriting losses at Eagle Star are reducing sharply as the effect of improved premium rates, particularly on the household and motor accounts, comes through. With further rate increases, and a higher market share, a further big reduction in underwriting losses was achieved in 1987. The company takes a smoothed investment gain above the line each year which is neither taxable nor distributable. In 1987, following the stock market crash, such gains were severely reduced, with only £47m being brought into the group accounts against £149m in 1986.

Allied Dunbar is seeing a much improved flow of life premium business. In the longer term, Allied Dunbar should benefit from the new opportunities created in the life and pension fields after the 1987 and 1988 budgets. 1987 annual premiums were up 25% and pre-tax profits reached £71m.

Financial services trading profits in 1987 were 6% down at £265m on turnover 19.8% up at £3.809bn.

GEOGRAPHICAL REVIEW

In 1987 24% of revenues and 20% of trading profits were UK-based. The UK profits content has risen from under 5% in 1982 as the financial services operations have been acquired and as Argos has been developed.

North America, excluding associates, accounts for 44% of operating profits, Europe 16% and Latin America, principally Brazil and Venezuela, 10%. The Latin American and Third World content has fallen sharply since 1982.

CORPORATE CALENDAR

Year end	31 December
Preliminary results	March
Report and accounts	May
AGM	June
Final dividend paid	June
First quarter	May
Interim results	September
Interim dividend paid	November
Third quarter	November

DIRECTORS' HOLDINGS

	Ordinary shares (beneficial)	Options
BAT Industries plc		
EAA Bruell	51,176	104,945
GL Dennis	71,143	144,075
Sir Campbell Fraser	2,000	—
BP Garraway	35,984	129,975
Sir Jasper Hollom	10,125	—
MS Lipworth	—	101,161
AC Long	11,055	90,233
Sir Michael Palliser	3,074	—
P Sheehy	113,716	168,795
DL Slobom	7,155	64,003
Sir Mark Weinberg	104,210	—
EJ Worlidge	61,747	112,625
Allied Dunbar Assurance Plc		
MS Lipworth	1,402	15,000
Sir Mark Weinberg	—	15,000

Total directors' remuneration in 1986/87 amounted to £1.82m with the chairman receiving the highest at £223,918.

Share price and relative to FT-A All-Share

39

BET Public Limited Company

CHAIRMAN'S STATEMENT

'In terms of profit and cash flow the Group's tobacco interests still provide the vital underpinning for the continuing development of our business. It is essential that we safeguard them, by maintaining a strong and profitable presence with leading brands in many separate markets, and by further investing in marketing, production and research when appropriate.' *Patrick Sheehy*

PRINCIPAL SUBSIDIARIES AND RELATED COMPANIES

Allied Dunbar & Company Plc, Appleton Papers Inc – US, Argos Distributors Ltd, BAT Cigarettenfabriken GmbH – Germany, BAT Financial Services Ltd, BAT Industries, BAT Kenya Ltd (60%), BAT (UK and Export) Ltd, BATUS Inc – US, British-American Tobacco Co Ltd, Brown & Williamson Tobacco Corporation – US, CA Cigarrera Bigott Sucs – Venezuela (100%), Cia de Cigarros Souza Cruz – Brazil, Cia Souza Cruz Indústria e Comércio – Brazil (75%), Eagle Star Holdings Plc, Gresham Investment Trust Plc, Horten AG – Germany (51%), JB Ivey & Co – US, John Breuner Co – US, Marshall Field & Co – US, Nigerian Tobacco Co Ltd (59%), Nobleza-Piccardo SAICyF – Argentina (70%), Spicer-Cowan Ltd, The Jewellers Guild Ltd, The Wiggins Teape Group Ltd, Thimbles Specialty Stores Inc – US, VG Instruments Plc (69%)

ASSOCIATED COMPANIES

AMATIL Ltd – Australia (40%), Aracruz Celulose SA – Brazil, Imasco Ltd – Canada (40%), Scandinavisk Holding AS – Denmark (33%)

BRAND NAMES

Allied Dunbar, Appleton Papers – US, Argos, Barclay – US, Europe, Belair – US, Belmont, Plaza, Minster, Hollywood – Brazil, Belmont, Consul – Venezuela, Benson & Hedges – Germany, Capri – US, Coca Cola – Australia, Conqueror, Eagle Star, Falcon – US, HB – Germany, Idem, Jewellers Guild, Jockey Club – Argentina, John Player Special – Japan, Kim 25s – US, Kool – US, Lucky Strike – outside US, Prince Denmark – Germany, Raleigh – US, Richland – US, State Express 555, Viceroy – US

CONTACTS AND FURTHER INFORMATION

Christopher Meakin, BAT Industries p.l.c., Windsor House, 50 Victoria Street, London SW1H 0NL. Tel: 01-222 7979.

GENERAL INFORMATION

Head office	Stratton House, Piccadilly, London W1X 6AS. Tel: 01-629 8886
Directors	Nicholas Wills FCA (managing director), John Allan, William Boulton, Ronald Denny CEng FIERE, Tim Gold Blyth, John Griffiths FCA, Paul Rudder FCIT, Brian Thompson. *Non-exec* Sir Timothy Bevan (chairman), The Rt Hon Christopher Chataway, George Duncan FCA, Lord Mark Fitzalan Howard, The Rt Hon Norman Tebbit MP
Advisers	Baring Brothers & Co Ltd
Auditors	Deloitte Haskins & Sells
Registrars	Hill Samuel Registrars Ltd
Brokers	de Zoete & Bevan Ltd, Cazenove & Co
Solicitors	Linklaters & Paines, Waltons & Morse

GENERAL FINANCIAL INFORMATION

Market capitalisation	£1.512bn at 1 January 1988
Capital structure	
Issued ordinary shares (25p)	698.46m
Issued preference shares	None
Warrants	None
Convertibles	None
Traded options	None
ADSs	One ADS equals four ordinary shares
Shareholders over 5%	None

FT CATEGORY

FT: Industrials (miscel.)
FT-A: Conglomerates

MAJOR ACTIVITIES

BET is an international company which offers an integrated range of support services, primarily to industrial, commercial and public sector organisations. Until 1987/88 it reported under five headings – industrial services, construction, transport, electronics and leisure, and publishing.

In 1986/87, 34% of operating profit was derived from industrial services, 27% from construction, 18% from transport, 13% from electronics and leisure, and 8% from publishing. The company is being transformed from conglomerate to support services specialist.

Because of the international scope and diversity of the company, overall economic activity is the best indicator of the company's performance, with an emphasis on industrial activity and, to a lesser extent, the construction cycle.

FINANCIAL HISTORY

Since 1983, there has been a major strategy change. BET has sold businesses ranging from its North Sea oil interests to computers and the Rediffusion rental chain. It is moving away from leisure and towards industrial services, and is in the process of selling its flight simulation business and its radio systems division. In April 1988 BET announced that it was putting its publishing business, Argus Press, up for sale by auction through the investment bank Morgan Stanley. Turnover has increased by 77% since 1983.

Turnover in 1987 stood at £1.69bn, a 17.8% increase over 1986. However, it is pre-tax profits that have benefited most from the rationalisation of operations, including acquisitions, rising 26% over 1986 to £157.4m, more than doubling since 1983 from £85.9m.

Earnings per share rose by 15.8% over 1986, with a total increase of 46% since 1983 – 19.9p from 13.6p. Dividends increased 12.5% in 1987, and have risen 80% since 1983. There was a good improvement in margins to 10.8%, an increase of 48% over the 1983 figure of 7.3%. Gearing stood at 63% at 31 March 1987. The balance sheet should show a dramatic improvement at the 1988 year end, with the issue of ADRs valued at £69.7m in August 1987.

At the 1987 interim results to 30 September 1987, pre-tax profits were sharply up 56% at £92.1m, on turnover 38.2% up at £1.033bn. Despite issued shares being up 21% since the previous period, earnings per share were 29.8% up to 10p, from 7.7p.

SHARE PRICE HISTORY

The shares of BET have risen steadily from a low of 69p in 1982. In 1983 they broke the 100p barrier, rising to break the 200p barrier in 1986, and reaching 300p in 1987.

This growth in share price closely followed the performance of the FT-A All-Share index until early 1987 when there was moderate outperformance. With the October 1987 share crash, the shares fell to below 200p, before recovering by late April 1988 to the 230p level.

SENIOR MANAGEMENT

There have been a number of recent important changes in management. Sir Hugh Dundas retired as chairman to be succeeded by Sir Timothy Bevan. George Barter was replaced as financial director by John Griffiths. John Davies, who ran and then disposed of BET's leisure activities, retired in March 1988. In addition, Sir Peter Matthews has left the board and there are two new members: Brian Thompson, Initial's chairman and chief executive; and John Allan, chairman and chief executive of BET building services and BET security services. The Rt Hon Norman Tebbit has joined the board as a non-executive director. Nicholas Wills is managing director.

Other members of the management team are: William Boulton, chairman of BET Leisure Holdings and A-R Television; Tim Gold Blyth, chairman of Argus Press; Paul Rudder, chairman of United Transport; Reginald Parry, secretary; Neil Ryder, communication; and Rhoderick Warren, personnel and purchasing.

CAPITAL

The company has regularly issued equity for its acquisitions, which have been a major feature of its reorganisation. During 1984/85, 2.27m shares were issued to acquire Anglian Windows, the double glazing company, and 44.74m shares were issued as part consideration for Initial, the textile services group.

In 1986/87, 28.18m shares were issued as part consideration for HAT Group, the industrial contract painting and plant hire company; 4.86m shares were issued as part consideration for the acquisition of Brengreen Holdings, engaged in contract cleaning and waste disposal; and 7.24m shares were issued to

'Over the last five years, BET has made commendable progress in its goal of becoming the world's leading support service company.

We intend to continue down this route, with the benefit of the experience we have gained – in particular that of the desirability of emphasising profitable market share in our chosen service sectors.

As my predecessor indicated in his final statement as Chairman of BET, the company is in sound financial condition with the management resources in place to ensure an exceptionally bright future.' *Sir Timothy Bevan*

purchase Shorrock, which supplies electronic security services.

29.6m shares were issued in May 1987 to acquire Scott Greenham, the plant hire company. There were a series of smaller issues for a number of private companies bought in the UK and the US and a large number of small cash acquisitions.

There was a one for one scrip issue in April 1987. The repayment and the cancellation of the 4.2% cumulative participating preference shares, and the 5.6% non-cumulative preferred shares also took place in April 1987.

The £69m convertible Eurobond, issued in October 1986, was fully converted into equity in September 1987 by the company taking up its call option and issuing 21.8m ordinary shares to holders. In August and September 1987, £69.7m was raised by an ADR issue on the New York, Montreal and Toronto stock exchanges. Early in 1988 the company increased and upgraded its commercial paper programmes in the UK, the US and Europe.

There are no significant board holdings, nor any notification, as at 31 March 1988, of interest of more than 5% of the ordinary voting shares.

GROUP REVIEW

Industrial services The area consists of three divisions. They are UK textile rental and associated services, overseas textile rental and associated services, and cleaning and waste disposal. Operating profit in 1987 was up 19% from £50.0m to £59.3m on turnover 25.7% up at £436.0m, with the increase split evenly between acquisition and organic growth.

Initial, the UK textile rental business, provided more than one-third of turnover and almost two-thirds of operating profit while the overseas textile division provided more than 33% of turnover but only 20% of profit.

Parts of HAT, which was purchased for £109m, and Brengreen, acquired for £32m, were merged with Initial Service Cleaners Biffa Waste Services to form a new cleaning and waste division. Cleaning and waste disposal accounted for 25% of turnover and 15% of profit in 1987, but will benefit

Year	Turnover (£m)	Pre-tax (£m)	Earnings (p)	Dividends net (p)	Dividend cover (x)	Net assets (p)	Price (p) High	Price (p) Low	PER (x) High	PER (x) Low	Yield (%) High	Yield (%) Low
1983	1,002.3	70.1	13.6	5.0	2.7	125	139	83	16.8	10.5	7.04	4.36
1984	1,074.4	85.7	14.4	6.0	2.4	104	156	113	16.8	11.4	7.59	5.03
1985	1,064.0	92.8	13.8	7.0	2.0	97	195	140	15.4	11.6	7.07	5.36
1986	1,333.0	124.6	17.1	8.0	2.1	76	226	181	16.6	13.0	6.01	4.86
1987	1,576.4	157.4	19.9	9.0	2.2	64	310	198	18.6	10.9	6.23	3.98

FIVE YEAR FINANCIAL INFORMATION

Share price and relative to FT-A All-Share

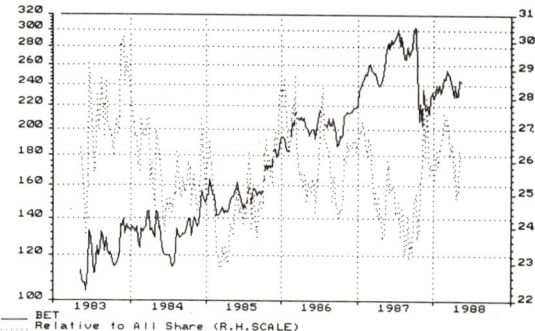

from improving margins as the new acquisitions are integrated and overhead is reduced.

At the 1987/88 interim, divisional operating profit was up 16% to £31.5m, with cleaning and waste disposal profit up 97%.

Construction The construction area consists of four divisions. They are plant services, joinery, home improvements and security services. Acquisition was a major factor in the 56% increase in 1987 operating profit, up from £30.8m to £48.4m on turnover 60.7% up at £504.1m.

The acquisition of Scott Greenham for £75m, as well as parts of HAT, were the largest contributors. Shorrock, the security company, was acquired for £33m. There were various smaller acquisitions in 1987.

Plant services produced nearly half the operating profit of the construction division in 1987. There were varying degrees of contribution from the acquisitions Four Seasons, MPS and Werner, trading as Saf-T-Green in the US. The largest profits came from the UK scaffolding and access companies, with hire, sale and contracting operations resuming their growth.

The joinery division saw the withdrawal from steel fabrication, and the closing of a joinery plant, resulting in a strong profit recovery. A new management team was also added.

The home improvements division saw an increase in operating profit of 13% due to the recovery of Anglian Windows and the purchase of Farouche Cuisine. Additional products are Roomsets and Metlex in the Hometrust company.

At the 1987/88 interim, construction operating profit was up 134% to £40m, with 44% of the increase coming from internal growth, and the remainder from acquisitions.

Transport United Transport International, BET's transport operating company, is active in freight and passenger transport, including tourism. Two-thirds of profits are derived from freight and one-third from passengers.

Operating profit in 1987 increased by 15% in local currencies, but by only 4% in sterling, to £32.5m on turnover 10.3% down at £359.4m. 57.8% of transport's profit comes from Africa, representing 7% of BET's net earnings. In 1983 Africa represented 36%.

At the 1987/88 interim, profits were up 1% to £15.6m, with freight increasing its weighting to 76%. Even after translation into sterling, freight's growth was 16%. It was the passenger area that suffered reduced profits, affected by the decline in the competitive position of the African bus companies and political and currency problems. The South African bus business has been divested.

Electronics and leisure The division consists of the world-leading flight simulator business, and various hotel, electrical,

leisure and entertainment interests.

BET announced in December 1987 that it was to sell all of the electronics and leisure businesses except those which provide audio-visual services for hotels, factories, ships etc. BET has agreed to sell Rediffusion Simulation to Hughes Aircraft Company for £151m and expected to complete the sale by the end of May 1988.

Operating profits were down slightly in 1987 from £23.2m to £22.9m, on turnover 10.0% down at £242.6m. At the 1987/88 interim, operating profit was 4% up from £9.8m to £10.2m.

Publishing The Argus Press publishes specialist business magazines, with two-thirds of operating profits derived from the US. In addition, several local UK newspapers are published.

In 1987, operating profit was up 18% to £14m on turnover 6.1% up at £143m, helped by a better US contribution, where tight cost controls, combined with the sale of *Atlanta* magazine, helped offset the weak dollar. At the 1987/88 interim, operating profit was 13% up to £7.6m. Local newspapers in the UK doubled their contribution to £1.8m, and consumer magazines' contribution was 44% up at £1.3m. The whole division is being divested.

GEOGRAPHICAL REVIEW

BET conducts the majority of its business in the UK, the US, Africa and to a lesser extent in Europe and the Pacific Basin. If operating profit is broken down by area, the UK in 1987 contributed 69%, North America 11.7%, Africa 10.3%, Europe 6.1% and other areas 2.9%.

CORPORATE CALENDAR

Year end	31 March
Preliminary results	June
Report and accounts	mid-July
AGM	end July
Final dividend paid	early August
Interim results	early November
Interim dividend paid	February

DIRECTORS' HOLDINGS

	Fully paid	Other (incl. options)
Sir Timothy Bevan	2,000	—
Nicholas Wills	529,994	75,872
John Allan	—	108,000
William Boulton	27,000	40,872
Rt Hon Christopher Chataway	20,000	—
Ronald Denny	—	165,872
George Duncan	1,000	—
Lord Mark Fitzalan Howard	3,332	—
Tim Gold Blyth	—	25,872
John Griffiths	5,000	130,138
Paul Rudder	20,000	33,872
Rt Hon Norman Tebbit	2,000	—
Brian Thompson	73,884	151,138

Total directors' salaries and other fees in 1987 were £1.10m, with the chairman receiving £76,695, and the highest-paid director £118,352.

PRINCIPAL SUBSIDIARIES AND RELATED COMPANIES

Argus Press PLC
Argus Books Ltd, Argus Business Publications Ltd, Argus Consumer Publications Ltd, Argus Health Publications Ltd, Argus Newspapers Ltd, Argus Press (International) Ltd, Argus Press Holding Inc – US, Argus Specialist Exhibitions Ltd, Argus Specialist Publications Ltd, Cardiff Publications Inc – US, Clareville Designs Ltd, Communications Channels Inc – US, Delta Mailing Services Inc – US, EW Communications Inc – US, FMJ International Publications Ltd, Farm Press Publications Inc – US,

Gemini Magazines Ltd, Guardian Communications Ltd, Hospital Publications Inc – US, International Business & Technical Magazines Ltd, International Symposia & Exhibitions Ltd, International Trade Publications Ltd, London & Essex Guardian Newspapers Ltd, London & West Surrey Newspapers Ltd, North London & Herts Newspapers Ltd, Polystyle Publications Ltd, Programme Publications Ltd, SM Magazine Distribution Ltd, SM Publications Ltd, Slimming Advisory Services Ltd, Slimming Magazine Clubs Ltd, Slimming Magazine Holdings Ltd, Surrey & South London Newspapers Ltd, The Reading Newspaper Company Ltd, The Reading Newspaper Printing Co Ltd, Trident Press Ltd, Windsor Newspaper Co Ltd

A–R Television PLC
Cosgrove Hall Productions Ltd, Euston Films Ltd, Thames Television International Ltd, Thames Television Ltd

BET Building Services Ltd
Anglian Windows Ltd, Aquatron (Showers) Ltd, Boulton & Paul (Building Services) Ltd, Boulton & Paul (Manufacturing) Ltd, Boulton & Paul (Sales) Ltd, Boulton & Paul (Scotland) Ltd, Boulton & Paul Plc, Farouche Cuisine Ltd, Hometrust Ltd, Metlex Industries Ltd

BET Leisure Holdings Ltd
Safety-At-Sea Films Ltd, Walport (Holdings) Ltd, Walport (Overseas) Ltd, Walport Aviation Programmes Ltd, Walport Ingram Ltd, Walport Ltd, Walport Telmar International Ltd

BET Plant Services PLC
ACL Ltd, Aberdeen Scaffolding Co Ltd, Access International Ltd, Arrow Security Systems Ltd, BET Security Services, Bijstede BV – Holland, Cheadle Plant Hire Ltd, Coventry Compressors Ltd, Deborah Insulation Ltd, Deborah Scaffolding Ltd, Eddison Plant Ltd, Four Seasons Roofing Group, Grayston Hire Services Ltd, Grayston Overseas Ltd, Grayston Scaffolding Ltd, Grayston White & Sparrow Ltd, HAT Engineering Ltd, HAT Interiors Ltd, HAT Merchanting Ltd, HAT Painters Ltd, HAT Painters Ltd (Northern Painting Div), Hireplant Ltd, Industrial Scaffolding Ltd, Laden Farmer Ltd, Leada Acrow Ltd, Martin Thomas Ltd (Aviation Equipment), Martin Thomas Ltd (Hi-Way and Sales Services), Metropolitan Alarm Systems Ltd, Plant Engineering Services Ltd, SG Aerial Platforms Ltd, Saf-T-Green Holdings Inc, Scott Greenham Plc, Shorrock Electronic Systems Inc, Shorrock Ltd, Shorrock Security Systems Ltd, Sparrows Industrial Services, Sparrows International Oilfield Services A/S, Sparrows Offshore Services, Spritebrand, Stephens & Carter Ltd, Stillasgruppen Norge A/S – Norway, Swing Stage Clima Inc – US, Taylor and Goodman, Zig Zag Scaffolds Ltd

Initial PLC
Ailsa Industrial Services Ltd, Apex Corporation, Biffa Waste Services Ltd, Descaling Contractors Ltd, Domestic/Contract Laundries (Advance), Domestic/Contract Services Ltd, Drinkmaster Ltd, Dudley Industries Ltd, Exclusive Cleansing Services Ltd, Exclusive Environmental Services Ltd, Harefield Contract Services, Hokatex BV – Holland, Hokatex GmbH – West Germany, Hotel Linen Services (Laundrycraft), IS Grob BV – Holland, Initial – Gaviota Group, Initial Automatic Services (Incorporation Colged & Skivvy), Initial Automatic Services Inc – US, Initial Contract Services, Initial Garment Manufacturing, Initial Holdings (Singapore) Private Ltd, Initial Holdings Inc – US, Initial Hospital Linen Services, Initial Property Maintenance, Initial Service Textiles, Initial Services (Australia) Pty Ltd, Initial Services (Ireland) Ltd, Initial Services (Malaysia) Sdn Bhd, Initial Textile Services, Initial Environmental Services Sdn Bhd, NV Friswit, Prathers Inc – US, Reckitt Cleaning Services SA Decroix, Spaldings Services Ltd, Strattwell Developments Ltd, United Service Company, Wastedrive (Manchester) Ltd, Wastedrive Ltd, White Cross Equipments Ltd, Worldwide Dryers

Rediffusion PLC
AMI Instruments Inc – US, Broadcast Relay Services (Hong Kong) Ltd, Jusan SA, RSI International Inc – US, Rediffusion (Hong Kong) Ltd, Rediffusion (Malaya) Holdings Sdn Bhd, Rediffusion (Malaya) Sdn Bhd, Rediffusion (Singapore) Private Ltd, Rediffusion (Trinidad) Ltd, Rediffusion (West Indies) Ltd, Rediffusion Belgium, Rediffusion Business Electronics Ltd, Rediffusion Business Electronics (M) Sdn Bhd, Rediffusion Channel Islands Ltd, Rediffusion Computer Graphics Incorporated, Rediffusion Electronic Systems Inc – US, Rediffusion Field Engineering, Rediffusion Films Ltd, Rediffusion International Music Ltd, Rediffusion Radio Holdings Ltd, Rediffusion Radio Systems Ltd, Rediffusion Services (Singapore) Private Ltd, Rediffusion Simulation (Canada) Inc, Rediffusion Simulation Incorporated – US, Rediffusion Simulation Ltd, Rediffusion Tulsa Incorporated, Rediffusion-Music, Reditune Thordson GmbH & Co, Startel Ltd, Trinidad Broadcasting Company Ltd

United Transport International PLC
AUT Pty Ltd – Australia, Block Hotels Management Ltd, Central Park Holdings (Private) Ltd, Containerlink BV, Containerlink Ltd, Copenhagen Transport Ltd, Coral Coach Express (Fiji) Ltd, Coriglade Ltd (trading as Buckingham Travel), DSI Transport Inc – US, East African Road Services Ltd, Econofreight United Transport Ltd, Erkatrans Internationale Spoedition, Express Motorways Africa (East) Ltd, IFF Europa BV, Indian River Transport Company, International Ferry Freight Ltd, Kenya Bus Services (Mombasa) Ltd, Kenya Bus Services Ltd, Kenya Hotels Ltd, Manchester Minibuses Ltd, Nairobi Travel Centre, Northern Territory Freight Service Pty Ltd, Nyali Beach Hotel Ltd, Passenger Transport Services Ltd, Seawheel GmbH, Seawheel Ireland Ltd, Seawheel Ltd, Seawheel NV, Seawheel Nederland BV, South Sea Island Cruises Ltd, The Birmingham & District Investment Trust Plc, The Electrical and Industrial Investment Plc, The National Electric Construction Plc, Tourism International (Bermuda) Ltd, Trans-Market Express Inc, Transport Management Services Ltd, Turtle Airways Ltd, UTH Hong Kong Ltd, United Air Charters (Private) Ltd, United CRT Bulk Haulage, United Distribution Systems Inc, United Tankers (Pty) Ltd, United Touring Company Ltd – Kenya, United Touring Company Ltd – Zimbabwe, United Touring Fiji Ltd, United Touring International Ltd, United Touring International Inc – US, United Touring International – Japan, United Transport (WA) Pty Ltd, United Transport Buses Ltd, United Transport Co Ltd, United Transport Contract Services Ltd, United Transport Line Ltd, United Transport Malawi Ltd, United Transport Oils Ltd, United Transport Overseas Services Ltd, United Transport Services Pty Ltd, United Transport Tankers Ltd, United Tyre Services (Private) Ltd, Unitrans Botswana (Pty) Ltd, Unitrans Bulk (Pty) Ltd, Unitrans Explosives (Pty) Ltd, Unitrans Lesotho (Pty) Ltd, Unitrans Lowveld (Pty) Ltd, Unitrans Ltd, Unitrans Natal (Pty) Ltd, Unitrans Reef (Pty) Ltd, Unitrans Sugar (Pty) Ltd, Unitrans Swaziland Ltd, Unitrans Zululand (Pty) Ltd, W Bos Transport-En Garagebedrijf BV – Holland, World Travel Bureau (Private) Ltd, Zimbabwe Omnibus Company Division, Zimbabwe United Freight Company Ltd, Zimbabwe United Passenger Company Ltd, Zimbabwe United Transport Holdings Ltd

BRAND NAMES

Anglian Windows, Argus Press Group, BET Plant Services, Biffa Waste Services, Boulton & Paul, Drinkmaster, Dudley Industries, Farouche, Hometrust, Initial, Initial Automatic Services, Initial Contract Services, Laundrycraft, Metlex, Metlex Aquatron, Rediffusion, Rediffusion Business Electronics, Shorrock, United Transport, Walport International, Worldwide Dryers

CONTACTS AND FURTHER INFORMATION

Neil Ryder, Head of corporate communication, BET Public Limited Company, Carlton House, Lower Regent Street, London W1X 6AS. Tel: 01-629 8886.

THE BOC GROUP plc

GENERAL INFORMATION

Head office	Chertsey Road, Windlesham, Surrey, GU20 6HJ. Tel: 0276-77222
Directors	RV Giordano (chairman), P Bosonnet (deputy chairman), D O'Connell Jnr (managing), JG Baldwin, DJ Craig. *Non-exec* R Malpas CBE, C Nevin, PJJ Rich, Sir Leslie Smith, D Taverne QC; C Tugendhat
Advisers	Lazard Brothers & Co Ltd
Auditors	Coopers & Lybrand
Registrars	Lloyds Bank Registrar's Department
Brokers	Cazenove & Co
Solicitors	No specified adviser

GENERAL FINANCIAL INFORMATION

Market capitalisation	£1.728bn at 1 January 1988
Capital structure	
Issued ordinary shares (25p)	454.6m
Issued preference shares (£1)	0.5m 4.55% CP
	1.0m 3.5% CP 2nd
	1.0m 2.8% CP 2nd
Warrants	None
Convertibles	None
Traded options	None
ADRs	One ADR equals one ordinary share
Shareholders over 5%	None

FT CATEGORY

FT: Industrials (miscel.)
FT-A: Chemicals

MAJOR ACTIVITIES

The BOC Group, formerly the British Oxygen Company, is a worldwide operation based on the production and supply of gases. It has diversified into health care and specialised products and services, largely developed from its core activities.

BOC's diversification into specialised pharmaceutical products and health care services has proved very successful, but its major investment in carbon products for the US steelmaking industry did not generate the expected return. Subject to the agreement of the US anti-trust agencies, it has been disposed of.

When the group first began to diversify, it did so by extending its product range and moving into activities by acquisition. Its current policy is to expand and develop its existing businesses through geographical expansion and market development.

BOC is seeking to expand by becoming number one or number two in activities, which because of the major capital and research expenditure involved, are unlikely to attract competitors.

FINANCIAL HISTORY

Since 1983 BOC's sales have risen 15.1%, but pre-tax profits have risen 85.9%, with margins rising from 8.3% to 13.4%. The rise in profitability reflects the increased efficiency of the group's operations, especially its gases business, and the disposal of many of its less successful operations.

The group's return to historical cost accounting will also tend to increase reported profitability. The recent growth in profits was achieved against a considerable adverse movement in the value of the dollar.

1987 turnover was modestly up 0.7% over 1986 at £1.959bn. Pre-tax profits were 23.3% up at £263.2m on 1986, excluding the 1986 exceptional £128m write-down of its $250m invest-ment in the US carbon business.

Earnings per share in 1987 at 36.32p were 22.2% ahead of those in 1986. Dividends were up 15.1% to 17.5p. Return on capital employed was 19.4%, up from 15.8%. Gearing was down to 28.1% from 32.4%. Capital expenditure was £221.1m.

For the first three months of the 1988 financial year ended 31 December 1987, turnover was down 6.2% to £464.8m. Pre-tax profits were up 7.6% to £63.6m. Earnings per share were up 12% to 8.93p.

SHARE PRICE HISTORY

BOC has outperformed the FT-A All-Share index since 1981, rising through 100p in 1980, 200p in 1982, fluctuating around 300p between 1984 and 1985, and reaching 559p at its peak in 1987.

The shares joined in the general share price fall in autumn 1987, but continued to fall to 380p by the end of 1987. This reflected fears of BOC's dependence on the US economy for 34.8% of its turnover and 35.6% of its operating profit.

These fears were not supported by the group's report for the first three months of its 1988 financial year.

SENIOR MANAGEMENT

Richard Giordano has been treated as something of a celebrity because of the large salary he draws from BOC. He was paid £782,300 in 1987. He became BOC's chief executive in 1979 after seeing through its absorption of Airco, of which he was president. Since 1985 he has combined the post of chairman with that of chief executive.

Paul Bosonnet, who became deputy chairman in 1985, has been involved with accounting, strategy and finance since joining BOC in 1957. Desmond O'Connell Jr is group managing director, with particular responsibility for gases and health care. David J Craig is managing director of engineering and technology.

CAPITAL

BOC has been sparing in the use of its equity capital. In October 1982, 17.5m ordinary shares were placed in connection with the acquisition of the group's interest in Osaka Sanso Kogyo. 29m shares were issued as part consideration for Glasrock Medical Services Corporation and its interest in Mountain Medical Equipment. A further 7.9m shares were issued as part consideration for three industrial gas businesses in South America.

Since then the only major issues have been of those of a total of 60.68m shares against the conversion of the £82m 9% convertible unsecured loan stock 2001/06. This was completely converted by July 1987.

There were no declarable stakes of 5% at the beginning of 1988.

GROUP REVIEW

BOC is engaged in the organic growth of its existing businesses and has disposed of lossmakers rather than developed by acquisition. Strong cashflow from the core gases business is helping to reduce debt. Gearing, and so interest charged, is reducing.

The prospects for growth in gases are good, particularly in areas where utilisation is below average like Japan and the Far East. Health care is capable of even faster growth and from a less substantial capital base. BOC believes it can double the

FIVE YEAR FINANCIAL INFORMATION

Year	Turnover (£m)	Pre-tax (£m)	Earnings (p)	Dividends net (p)	Dividend cover (x)	Net assets (p)	Price (p) High	Price (p) Low	PER (x) High	PER (x) Low	Yield (%) High	Yield (%) Low
1983	1,701.6	141.6	23.0	6.30	2.6	212	297	176	12.9	7.7	5.1	3.0
1984	2,103.0	176.4	26.5	7.70	3.1	258	307	228	11.6	8.6	4.8	3.6
1985	1,900.9	202.8	30.9	9.38	2.7	227	324	253	10.5	8.2	5.3	4.1
1986	1,944.6	213.4	29.7	10.79	2.2	208	382	283	13.9	9.5	5.4	4.0
1987	1,959.1	263.2	36.3	12.80	2.4	213	550	298	15.2	8.2	5.9	3.2

size of its health business in the next five years.

Gases and related products BOC's gas products cover both atmospheric and synthetic gases, including oxygen, nitrogen, argon, helium, hydrogen, xenon, krypton and neon. Applications are diverse, ranging from light bulbs to refrigeration. The diversity of its customers, new products created from new applications, and improved delivery methods distinguishes BOC from commodity gas suppliers.

In Europe, the demand for liquid nitrogen for refrigeration and food manufacturing, and for ultra-clean high purity gases for the electronics industry, outstrips the demand for more industrially-orientated gases like oxygen and acetylene, which are predominantly used in metal industries.

The UK is the second largest gases market in Europe. Substantial new capacity is being added in a number of locations. The division made progress in the electronic gases market in West Germany. Total European sales for 1987 were up by £11.9m to £302.6m, 21.4% of the division's total.

In the US, signs of revival in manufacturing industry helped sales volume and margins. The most important contributors are sales of argon for use in high precision engineering, carbon dioxide in food manufacturing and special gases for the electronics industry. The group is investing £82m in the US and Canada, with special emphasis on the recovery of high value argon. A number of new plants have been built. The aim is to spread delivery and reduce production costs. All of BOC's Latin American operations traded profitably in 1987.

Depressed by the fall of the dollar against the pound, the division's sales throughout the Americas were down £30.8m to £392.2m, 27.8% of the division's total.

Asia and the Far East are important growing points for the group. Increased demand is attending industrial growth in the region. Turnover is now greater than in either the Americas or Europe. In Japan BOC is adding low cost capacity through a major new plant in Osaka and selling technology direct to the end user. Equipment for a new merchant plant was shipped from BOC Cryoplants in the UK to Amagasaki. Japanese manufacturing businesses, particularly in electronics, began to show signs of recovery and this helped demand.

Joint ventures were signed with local partners in China, and in Turkey where BOC Cryoplants is building a liquid gas plant. The group is to install the most modern special gases purification and mixing equipment in Shanghai to serve China's growing electronics industry.

New markets are already profitable in Taiwan, Singapore, Hong Kong, Pakistan and India. Sales and profits showed particularly strong increases in Hong Kong, Malaysia and Singapore in 1987.

Sales in Asia and the Far East grew 2.4% to £573m in 1987, 40.5% of the division's total. It is here where the group sees the greatest opportunity for expansion of the gases business.

BOC's African interests did well, despite difficult conditions in South Africa and elsewhere in Africa. Though volatile, the region, starting from such a low base, offers excellent growth

prospects. Sales were 18.5% up in 1987 at £143.9m, 10.2% of the division's total.

Technology is crucial to develop new markets. The BOC Technical Centre in the US is emphasising work on: high value gases, like argon; improving cryogenic and non-cryogenic production processes, both in terms of cost and purity achieved; ultra-clean gases; the development of new process technology; gas cleaning systems for the semiconductor industry; argon recovery from ammonia; better use of carbon dioxide in paper pulping; and defence applications.

In 1987 gases and related products made up 60% of BOC's profits and turnover. Turnover was up slightly from £1.395bn to £1.412bn. Profits rose 11% to £197.4m.

Health care BOC has a portfolio of four related businesses in health care products and services. They are pharmaceuticals, concentrated on the Anaquest subsidiary; equipment and systems marketed under the Ohmeda name; intravenous disposable products, manufactured and marketed by the group's Viggo company; and home health care, centred around the Glasrock company. 63% of turnover comes from the Americas.

Anaquest is the major supplier of anaesthetics in the US. Anaquest's products include Forane, the most widely used anaesthetic in the US. Through Forane, BOC has moved away into the supply of special products for outpatient and paediatric departments.

Forane is building market share, paying off a significant marketing investment. Enlon is a second generic anaesthetic, a neuromuscular reversal agent, in which sales have grown markedly. Ethrane is a general anaesthetic widely used in US hospitals.

Ohmeda markets a range of medical equipment and systems. Its products cover anaesthesia, critical care, patient monitoring, medical engineering, and veterinary and dental treatment.

In February 1987 BOC took a 16.2% stake in Circon Corporation. Circon designs, manufactures and markets medical endoscope and video systems used mainly for diagnosis and surgery in urology, anthroscopy and other fields of

CHAIRMAN'S STATEMENT

'1987 was a very good year for The BOC Group . . . we achieved this excellent growth in profits and earnings per share in spite of another year of adverse currency movements, particularly the weakening US dollar, which reduced 1987 earnings through currency translation by £13.3m. . . . In any recession the diversity and defensive nature of the revenues of our gases business worldwide will serve us well. . . . Moreover the relative immunity of our substantial health care revenues from the effects of a recession will also prove to be a major asset.'
Richard Giordano

endoscopy. In June 1987 BOC took a controlling interest in Schmelter-Claas, one of West Germany's market leaders in visual displays and audio links.

Viggo makes intravenous therapy products, in which it is the European market leader. Viggo continued to grow in 1987.

Home health care is concentrated in the Glasrock subsidiary, acquired in 1982. Over 40 acquisitions have been made. More than 300 Glasrock branches in 41 states supply oxygen therapy for mainly elderly patients, and home medical equipment, ranging from pulse monitors to wheelchairs.

Glasrock made losses in 1987 because of reduced payments made by the US authorities to home health care providers. BOC is confident it will return to profit in 1988 with the restructuring and computerisation programme now in hand. It reported an improvement after three months of 1988.

The acquisition of Baxter Healthcare from Baxter Travenol for $59.5m should help sales and profits. BOC also operates a medical distribution network in Australia, CIG Medishield and a number of private hospitals in South Africa.

Spending on R&D is particularly important at Anaquest. Both Forane and Ethrane were developed internally. Three new compounds are under clinical trial.

Share price and relative to FT-A All-Share

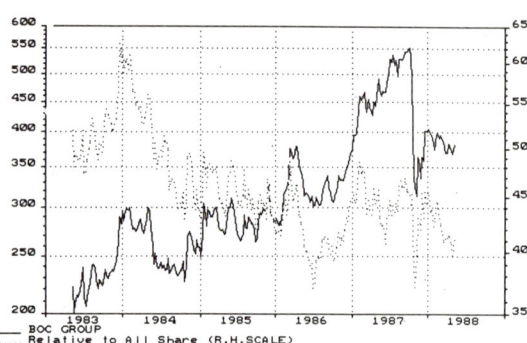

Health care is the second largest activity in BOC, accounting for 22% of turnover and 24% of operating profit. Currency influences held back both in 1987. Profits rise only marginally from £79.9m to £80.6m. Turnover fell from £516.8m to £513.3m.

Special products and services BOC combines other operations in a division in which unique technology, growth prospects and a relationship to the core businesses are combined.

There are two vacuum businesses, Edwards High Vacuum and Airco Solar Products. Edwards High Vacuum was spun off from the group's own process technology to sell vacuum pumps, coating systems and associated instruments to the electronics industry, and for freeze-drying pharmaceuticals. It now incorporates Airco Temescal's business of supplying the semiconductor industry with advanced vacuum metallising systems for the production of integrated circuits.

Airco Solar Products has about 85% of the world market in vacuum equipment and processes for architectural glass coatings. It has also sold Ford and General Motors the technology for a new generation of windscreen de-icing systems.

Transhield operates a highly profitable chilled warehousing and distribution system for Marks and Spencer food products. Euroshield is an undedicated cross-Channel and continental European distribution service. Thermit, the railway line welder, operates in the UK and South Africa.

The group's two carbide businesses are in Norway and the US. They produce calcium carbide for use in making acetylene, in desulphurising hot metal and as a feedstock for chemical derivatives. The group's US carbon business, now sold subject to the US authorities' approval, came into this division.

R&D in this division concentrates on the high vacuum technology business. Progress has been made in developing new processes for coating plastics and glass and in developing new vacuum systems.

In 1987 turnover rose from £361m to £423m. Profit more than trebled from £16.4m to £53.1m, in part because of the turnaround in the previously loss-making US carbon business. The division represents 18% of group turnover and 16% of group operating profit. Greater selectivity has led to the closure of 30 operations which did not meet group standards.

GEOGRAPHICAL REVIEW

BOC is spreading its activities geographically. Asia and the Far East represented 33% of sales and 20% of operating profit in 1987. The region offers the highest margins and the best potential for growth. This is because of a lower utilisation base and because the group is introducing operations where the development costs have been recouped elsewhere. This is reflected in the lower level of new capital investment of 13% of the group total.

Africa is highly profitable and represented 11.5% of sales and 10% of operating profit in 1987. New capital investment was 7.4% of the group total.

North and South America accounted for 39% of sales and 39% of operating profit in 1987, with over 40% of capital employed and over one-third of new investment. This exposes BOC to fluctuations in the dollar/sterling exchange rate. In 1987 this masked stronger underlying growth, but could prove positive in the future.

Europe, with over a quarter of sales and 29% of operating profit in 1987, is undergoing something of a revival. BOC is directing almost half of its capital spending to the region, much of it to the UK.

CORPORATE CALENDAR

Year end	30 September
Preliminary results	November
Report and accounts	December
AGM	January
Final dividend paid	April
Interim results	May
Interim dividend paid	October

DIRECTORS' HOLDINGS

	Ordinary shares		Options
	(beneficial)	(non-beneficial)	
JG Baldwin	13,069	—	296,922
P Bosonnet	8,522	—	211,755
DJ Craig	10,765	—	335,751
RV Giordano	68,614	—	400,000
R Malpas	22,483	—	—
C Nevin	541	—	—
D O'Connell Jr	6,983	—	390,714
P Rich	2,077	—	—
Sir Leslie Smith	13,250	—	—
D Taverne	24,331	—	—
C Tugendhat	1,072	—	—

Total directors' salaries and other fees for 1987 were £2.68m, of which the chairman, who was also the highest-paid director, received £782,300.

BPB INDUSTRIES PLC

PRINCIPAL SUBSIDIARIES AND RELATED COMPANIES

African Oxygen Ltd – South Africa (60%), Anaquest Inc – Puerto Rico (100%), Baxter Health Care Corp – US, Birlesik Oksjjen Sanayi AS – Turkey (50%), BOC Cryoplants Ltd, BOC Ltd, BOC Medishield SA – Spain (100%), BOC Transhield Ltd, Circon Corp Inc – US (16.2%), Datametrics Inc – US, Edwards High Vacuum Inc – US (100%), WA Flick & Co Holdings Pty Ltd – Australia (59%), Flick Termite & Pest Control Ltd – US (59%), Glasrock Home Health Care Inc – US (100%), Hong Kong Oxygen & Acetylene Co Ltd (50%), Indian Oxygen Ltd (40%), Lien Hwa Industrial Gases Co Ltd – Taiwan (50%), Osaka Sanso Kogyo KK – Japan, Schmelter-Claas GmbH – Germany (100%), Shanghai BOC Industrial Gases Co Ltd – People's Republic of China (50%), The BOC Group Inc – US, The Commonwealth Industrial Gases Ltd, US Viggo Inc – US (100%), Viggo AB – Sweden (100%)

BRAND NAMES

Anaquest, Airco, BOC, Enlon, Ethrane, Euroshield, Finapres, Forane, Glasrock Home Health Care, Lifepak 100, Ohmeda, Viggo, Stoneshield, Transhield

CONTACTS AND FURTHER INFORMATION

Luke Glass, The BOC Group plc, Chertsey Road, Windlesham, Surrey, GU20 6HJ. Tel: 0276-77222.

GENERAL INFORMATION

Head office	Langley Park House, Uxbridge Road, Slough SL3 6DU. Tel: 0753 73273
Directors	AG Turner CEng MIChemE (chairman and chief executive), A Brooks MIMM, CJ Bushell, A Creedon (vice-chairman), J-P Cuny – France, BJ Hogben FCA FCT, DR Reeves. *Non-exec* Sir Peter Carey GCB, RJ Day, D Fredjohn, GJ Hearne, JM Langham CE CEng FIMechE FIMarE, HB Pearson TD
Advisers	NM Rothschild & Sons Ltd
Auditors	Arthur Young
Registrars	Lloyds Bank Registrar's Department
Brokers	Cazenove & Co
Solicitors	Laces

GENERAL FINANCIAL INFORMATION

Market capitalisation	£1.042bn at 1 January 1988
Capital structure	
Issued ordinary shares (50p)	408m
Issued preference shares	None
Warrants	None
Convertibles	None
Traded options	None
ADRs	None
Shareholders over 5%	None

FT CATEGORY

FT: Building, timber, roads
FT-A: Building materials

MAJOR ACTIVITIES

BPB Industries is the largest manufacturer of plasterboard outside the US. It has dominated the UK market in plaster and plasterboard since ICI withdrew from the industry in the 1960s. It also manufactures a wide range of other building products and has related interests in bitumen, packaging and mining.

BPB is experiencing a steady increase in demand for its products from the growth in private housing and in commercial and industrial building. BPB's success has been underpinned by the doubling of the demand for plasterboard since 1977. But the plasterboard market is now attracting significant competition both in the UK and elsewhere. Given this, the principal challenges facing the group are to maintain its market share and increase productivity.

Substantial capital investment since 1982 in new plant and process development in the UK, France and Canada has increased the company's profitability by over a third since 1982. It is investing £750m in new manufacturing capacity and is opening a major plant on the Ruhr in West Germany, where it recently acquired important interests from the Intergips group.

Savings are expected from the use of a synthetic form of gypsum, the raw material in plaster and plasterboard filler. This is being made available from CEGB power stations which produce it as a by-product of the neutralisation of acidic flue gases.

Through its mining interests, BPB produces its own gypsum and its own factories manufacture the paper lining used in plasterboard. The vertical integration and the geographical spread of its operations should enable it to withstand the competition from Redland and the Australian group CSR as well as from any other producers emerging from continental Europe.

The group is dependent on the general level of activity in the private housing market. It is also affected by the level of activity in commercial and industrial building, and the growing repair and maintenance markets (now 40% of BPB's sales).

Buoyant domestic construction in particular regional areas like the south of England, France, northern Italy, the north-eastern seaboard of the US, and parts of Canada all contribute to strong growth in sales.

The sale of added-value products to the commercial market is more profitable than the domestic housing market, but it is not as dependable. Prices have held up in most areas of strong sales growth, but there is the risk that cheap imports in Europe and domestic competition in the US might keep prices flat in the future.

FINANCIAL HISTORY

BPB has expanded profitability since 1984 through expanding sales volumes. Turnover was £819.5m in 1987, up by over 20% on the year and by 64% over five years. Sales increased by 20% to £355.8m for the first half of 1988. Turnover in France and Italy will be boosted by BPB's continental acquisitions, namely: the Rigips group companies in West Germany, Austria, the Netherlands and Italy; VIC Italiana, Italgessi and Tomasetti in Italy; and Minera Fuente del Peral in Spain.

Pre-tax profits were £144.7m in 1987, up 40% on the period and 120% up over five years. Interim profits for the first half of 1988 increased by 31% to £90.9m. Profits were largely contributed by building materials in the UK, with fastest growth in France and Italy, and the highest margin in the Canadian operation.

Earnings per share grew more than 35% in 1986 and 1987, resuming an overall trend that had only been broken in 1985. This was despite increasing taxation affecting the French and Canadian operations. The balance sheet improved dramatically with net cash as opposed to debt generated in all areas, enabling the company to maintain plant and consider further acquisitions.

BPB is reducing risk by spreading its activities geographically and has not suffered from adverse exchange rate movements.

SHARE PRICE HISTORY

From 1982 to mid-1985 the shares underperformed the FT-A All-Share index by a considerable margin as the shares traded between 110p and 150p. In the summer of 1985 the shares took off, rising from 104p to 270p, before falling back to the 220p level.

The shares again outperformed from 225p in late 1986 to a summer 1987 high of 442.5p. Competition worries made the shares fall sharply to below 350p before the October 1987 crash took them to below 230p. The shares ended 1987 at 256p and were trading around the 280p level in mid-April 1988.

SENIOR MANAGEMENT

Chairman AG Turner, a chemical engineer, has been with the group since 1962, having worked his way up from the research and development department. He became a director in 1972, after management posts in the Gypsum company. He is president of the Eurogypsum industry organisation and a vice-president of the National Council of Building Materials.

A Creedon is group operating director and was appointed vice-chairman from February 1988. BJ Hogben is the finance and administration director. A Brooks is chairman of British Gypsum. CJ Bushell is chairman and managing director of

Davidsons. Non-executive directors include Sir Peter Carey, formerly permanent secretary at the Department of Trade and Industry, D Fredjohn, a member of Lloyd's of London, GJ Hearne, JM Langham, HB Pearson and RJ Day.

CAPITAL

BPB has issued share capital of 410m ordinary shares. Following an 11.8m share placing to raise £71m to finance the Rigips acquisition, a scrip issue doubled the capital in mid-1987. Other acquisitions have largely been made for cash. No director has a significant shareholding and there is no declarable shareholding of 5% or more.

GROUP REVIEW

Building materials This major division consists of gypsum products and other building materials. Worldwide building materials in 1987 produced operating profits 36.5% up at £118.8m on sales 30.5% up at £618.1m.
Gypsum products 75% of group sales and 82% of group operating profits depend on gypsum products. Key products include the traditional Carlite and Thistle plaster brands, glass reinforced Stucal plasterboard, Gyproc Veneer Finish plaster, short-setting Fast Fill joint cement and a large auditorium wall system capable of high quality sound insulation.

Gypsum is mined at East Leake, Robertsbridge, Newark, Kirkby Thore and Barrow-upon-Soar in the UK, and processed into plaster and plasterboard at several factories. Similar arrangements exist in Canada, France, Italy and Spain. Having recently extended the UK manufacturing plants, the company anticipates further spending in Europe.

Savings have been made by BPB in the calcination and plasterboard drying processes. Sufficient reserves of raw material are now assured. Processing the raw material is energy-intensive and therefore sensitive to energy prices.

The UK market has grown in recent years on the back of housebuilding and commercial construction in the south and south-east. The company offset the decline in public housebuilding through expansion of the repair and maintenance business.

BPB dominates the UK market with supplies of gypsum-based products. The East Leake works has now been fully commissioned after refurbishment, with a consequent improvement in margin. Lower energy prices have had a disproportionate impact on profitability. UK operating profits were 20% up at £62.8m on sales 9% up at £349.2m.

A continuing recession in the Eire construction industry has led to a cost reduction programme. Withdrawal of a government refurbishment scheme did not help sales. But cost savings improved the margin in 1987 and the subsidiary increased profitability. Eire profits in 1987 were 52% up at £4.1m on sales 10% up at £24m.

The group's principal French interest is its Placoplatre subsidiary, based near Paris. From here the group supplies the French market and exports to Italy. Margins on its operation have improved from 10.5% to 16.5% in 1987 due to lower energy costs, previous capital expenditure and firm long-run orders.

Despite a static construction industry overall, an increase in apartment building, a buoyant commercial sector around Paris, and increasing exports to Italy produced rapid growth in 1987.

French profits are being ploughed back into the operation to increase production capacity and, it is hoped, improve market share. New products are also being introduced. Government

FIVE YEAR FINANCIAL INFORMATION

Year	Turnover (£m)	Pre-tax (£m)	Earnings (p)	Dividends net (p)	Dividend cover (x)	Net assets (p)	Price (p) High	Low	PER (x) High	Low	Yield (%) High	Low
1983	465.9	65.4	11.2	3.0	3.74	63	149	116	20.1	13.2	3.68	2.64
1984	528.1	79.7	14.0	3.5	4.01	68	169	116	17.9	11.0	4.24	2.66
1985	564.3	78.6	12.5	3.8	3.25	76	189	106	15.6	9.4	5.16	3.06
1986	616.0	103.2	16.9	4.5	3.76	86	275	165	19.9	12.5	3.50	2.30
1987	750.5	144.7	23.1	6.2	3.70	101	437	215	18.9	6.3	4.46	1.58

spending on new housing projects is good news, but competition will increase from domestic suppliers.

The Italian market has been highly fragmented and under-capitalised. Hitherto BPB supplied it through its Placoplatre factory in Paris but in 1986 it acquired four small Italian companies. These have increased its presence and given it direct access to local manufacturing and reserves.

They should also make BPB proof against any substitution of imports with locally produced materials. In Italy as in all other European countries except the UK, gypsum products are still a small portion of the total building products market.

French and Italian operating profits were 117% up in 1987 at £27.4m on sales 39% up at £166.6m.

In 1987 BPB acquired a number of companies from the Intergips group in West Germany, Austria, the Benelux region and Italy, paying for the deal with a £71m share placing.

The Rigips deal brought BPB a 29% minority interest in the West German paperboard and plasterboard wrapping manufacturer Tecnokarton, adding significant additional capacity to that at the Aberdeen and Purfleet factories in the UK.

CHAIRMAN'S STATEMENT

'Sales of building materials in the UK continued to show steady growth over the year and profits improved as a result.... Progress in the UK was mirrored overseas, particularly in Canada and France where our activities achieved new records. ... The improved results derived from a combination of higher sales volumes and realisations, plus the effect of improved efficiencies resulting from the continuing capital programme to improve plants and processes.... We look forward to continued investment and growth in western European markets due to the penetration in the use of plasterboard systems, and while we may expect increasing competition in certain localities, recent acquisitions have opened up new markets.'
AG Turner

BPB is expanding other European interests. A Spanish investment brought access to major high grade gypsum reserves. The rest of Europe will be the major growth area in future.

Canadian Westroc Industries' relation to the US is similar to the French subsidiary's to Italy. It supplies a reasonable domestic market but also depends on export sales for real growth. Demand from the eastern seaboard housebuilding market is good, in particular from the widespread activity and improved price levels obtainable in the north-east US states. Now the Montreal plasterboard factory has been modernised and the Vancouver plant is still fairly new, Canada provides the highest margin in the group of over 22%. Profits of £17.5m were 23% up on sales 13.5% up at £78.3m.

The troubles and the economic recession in South Africa have led to a general reduction in profitability there.

Other building products 10% of building material sales are generated by a number of other minority activities. D Anderson & Son makes bitumen products such as roofing felt. The acquisition of a comparable business, Lanstar Coatings, capital spending on the existing factory, and good demand are generating better profits on flat sales.

Mountfield Roadstone is involved in asphalt coating but, because of increased competition, its profitability has suffered recently. Gyproc Insulation is extending its product line and is significantly profitable on the basis of value-added products. BPB also produces decorative finishing products like the Artex brand, of which a cold-water version has been launched, and Multiflek decorative mouldings.

Paper and packaging The Thames Group waste paper, board and paper case company, acquired in 1986, has now been fully integrated into the original plasterboard paper line company, Davidsons. Considerable capital expenditure has modernised Davidsons' three board mills in the production of plasterboard liner paper and in the recycling of waste paper. The Bischof + Klein (UK) related company has also upgraded its plant.

The Kartonfabriek company in Holland makes paperboard liner. In West Germany the Corovin operation produces spun-bonded non-woven materials.

The paper and packaging division, with profits 70% up at £23.6m on sales 41% up at £201.4m, produced 17.4% of the group's operating profits in 1987.

Wireline services BPB's wireline services division services North Sea oil companies. Greater exploration activity in the future will generate profits as oil industry activity is now starting to increase. Substantial progress has been made in the development of BPB's oilfield logging operation.

GEOGRAPHICAL REVIEW

BPB is now looking to expand sales geographically despite the significant challenge from Redland and the Australian group

Share price and relative to FT-A All-Share

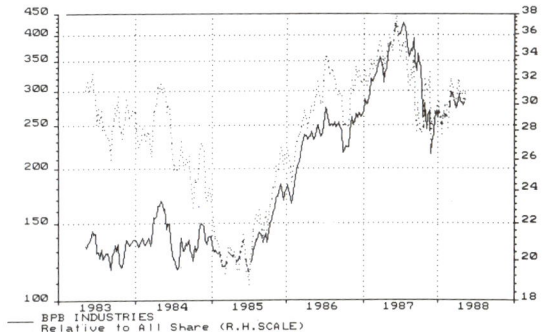

— BPB INDUSTRIES
...... Relative to All Share (R.H.SCALE)

CSR, among others, to loosen its monopoly position in the UK plasterboard market and challenge its dominant position in Europe.

Reliance on the UK construction market is falling. The UK produced less than 50% of BPB's profits for the first time in 1987. The group's geographical diversification has been aided by strong growth in continental Europe, in France, Italy, and most recently West Germany, and to a lesser extent from growth in its Canadian operation spreading into the US.

BPB has 90% of the UK and 50% of the European market for gypsum products.

CORPORATE CALENDAR

Year end	31 March
Preliminary results	late June
Report and accounts	July
AGM	July/August
Final dividend paid	August
Interim results	November
Interim dividend paid	January

DIRECTORS' HOLDINGS

	Fully-paid	Options
A Brooks	8,096	61,020
CJ Bushell	4,664	61,590
Sir Peter Carey	2,500	—
A Creedon	19,882	93,189
RJ Day	—	—
D Fredjohn	8,400	—
GJ Hearne	2,000	—
BJ Hogben	8,778	59,789
JM Langham	2,000	—
HB Pearson	16,564	—
DR Reeves	6,974	51,346
AG Turner	12,378	151,089

All interests are held beneficially. In the year ended 31 March 1987, the chairman's remuneration was £134,000. The company does not reveal the earnings of the board as a whole.

PRINCIPAL SUBSIDIARIES AND RELATED COMPANIES

Gypsum-based products
Börgardts-Sachsenstein GmbH – West Germany (20%), British Gypsum Ltd, Compañía Minera Fuente del Peral SA – Spain (50%), Gyproc AB – Sweden (25%), Gyproc Benelux NV – Belgium (44.9%), Gypsum Industries Ltd – South Africa (49.9%), Gypsum Industries Plc – Eire, Gypsum Industries (Private) Ltd – Zimbabwe, IECME SpA – Italy (60%), India Gypsum Ltd (40%), Irish Gypsum Ltd, Italgessi SpA – Italy, Les Plâtrières de Grozon SA – France (81.6%), Perlite SpA – Italy (49%), Perlit-Thermoputz-Ersen GmbH – West Germany (57.6%), Placoplatre Italiana SpA (98.5%), Placoplatre SA – France (98.5%), Placoplatre (Suisse) SA (99.5%), Rigips Austria GesmbH, Rigips Benelux BV, Rigips GmbH – West Germany, Rigips Italia Srl, Tomasetti Srl – Italy, VIC Italiana SpA – Italy, Westroc Industries Ltd – Canada

Other building materials
D Anderson & Son Ltd, Artex Ltd, Blue Hawk Ltd, Gyproc Insulation Ltd, Lanstar Coatings Ltd, Metrotect Ltd, Mountfield Roadstone Ltd, Moy Insulation Ltd – Eire, Plaschem, SOGECO SA – France (98.5%)

Paper and packaging
Alcoma BV – Netherlands (99.9%), Bischof + Klein (UK) Ltd (50%), Corovin GmbH – West Germany (99.9%), Davidsons Ltd, Kartonfabriek 'De Eendrach' NV (99.9%), Mutare Board and Paper Mills (Private) Ltd – Zimbabwe (40%), Tecnokarton GmbH – West Germany (29%)

Wireline services
Allegheny Nuclear Surveys Inc – US (56.6%), BPB Instruments (Australia) Pty Ltd, BPB Instruments (Canada) Ltd, BPB Instruments Inc – US, BPB Instruments Ltd, BPB Instruments Ltd und Co GmbH – West Germany

Holdings and services
Allied Manufacturing Industries (Private) Ltd – Zimbabwe, BPB Insurance Ltd, BPB Investments Ltd, BPB United Kingdom Ltd, Fulmar Insurance Company Ltd

BRAND NAMES
Anderson, Artex, Carlite, Fast Fill, Gyproc, Gyproc Veneer Finish, HT 125, HT 350, Kaleidoscope, Metrotect, Moy Insulation, Multiflek, Placoplatre, Stil Prim 100, Stucal, Thistle

CONTACTS AND FURTHER INFORMATION
RM Heard, Company Secretary, BPB Industries plc, Langley Park House, Uxbridge Road, Slough SL3 6DU. Tel: 0753 73273.

GENERAL INFORMATION

Head office	Silvertown House, Vincent Square, London SW1P 2PL. Tel: 01-834 3848
Directors	Sir Owen Green (chairman), JC Cahill (managing), RF Faircloth, P Fatharly, NC Ireland, AR Jackson, HW Laughland, Sir David Nicolson, BD Romeril, EE Sharp, JDM Smith, LJ Stammers, WDT Tapley, GJ Yardley
Advisers	Hill Samuel & Co Ltd, Morgan Grenfell & Co Ltd
Auditors	Ernst & Whinney
Registrars	Hill Samuel Registrars Limited
Brokers	Cazenove & Co
Solicitors	Norton Rose; Slaughter and May; Stoneham, Langton & Passmore

GENERAL FINANCIAL INFORMATION

Market capitalisation	£4.611bn at 1 January 1988
Capital structure	
Issued ordinary shares (25p)	421.96m
Issued preference shares	None
Warrants	None
Convertibles	£111.3m of 4.25% convertible subordinated bonds 1995 (convertible at 260p per share)
Traded options	Yes
ADRs	None
Shareholders over 5%	None

FT CATEGORY

FT: Industrials (miscel.)
FT-A: Other industrial materials

MAJOR ACTIVITIES

BTR is a broadly-based UK group, manufacturing industrial and consumer products. By becoming a well-balanced international holding company through many large and good-value acquisitions, BTR, once known as British Tyre and Rubber, has experienced over two decades of unbroken profits growth.

BTR has developed into a highly diverse company with no individual activity accounting for more than 5% of profits. Individual acquisitions include: Thomas Tilling, itself a diverse holding company; Dunlop, the tyre and rubber product makers; Nylex, the Australian plastics manufacturer; and early in 1987 Stewart Warner, the US engineering group.

BTR has bought undervalued and problem companies and dramatically improved their rate of return, tending, unlike Hanson, to concentrate on niche and higher technology operations with a high added-value component.

Before the major diversification of the mid-1970s, BTR made and distributed a variety of plastic and rubber engineering products such as conveyor belts for coal mines and reinforced hoses for fuel distribution. The acquisition and consolidation of Silentbloc, Huyck, Lindsay Wire, Serck, SW Industries and Worcester Controls widened the group's exposure to a vast number of markets such as gear speed reducers, liquid filters, dynamically balanced plug valves for the mining and oil industries, as well as to mid-tech industries such as papermakers, car manufacturers and shipbuilding.

Between 1983 and 1985 the acquisition of Thomas Tilling and Dunlop brought numerous consumer-related products into the portfolio, followed by disposals of less viable operations including Dunlop's tyre interests.

The 1983 acquisition of Thomas Tilling for over £600m was a British takeover record at the time, and signalled the advent of a period of major restructuring in British manufacturing industry. Its industrial core – the Newey and Eyre electrical equipment business, assorted building materials operations

and the Pretty Polly tights brand – were retained while Cornhill Insurance was sold in 1986 for £300m. The stake in Heinemann Books was swapped for one-third of Paul Hamlyn's fast growing Octopus Publishing, with the latter recently being purchased by Reed International.

Dunlop was a well-judged if unlikely takeover. BTR has begun to realise the value of subsidiary activities in industrial products and transport, and of the Dunlop and Slazenger consumer brands. The group acquired the complementary diversified US manufacturing company Stewart Warner for $220m in September 1987. BTR Nylex, BTR's 62%-owned Australian subsidiary, announced that it was completing its ambitious £600m acquisition of ACI International in late April 1988.

BTR comprises five divisions – construction, energy and electrical, industrial, transportation and consumer-related activities. Financial services were discontinued in 1986 with the disposal of Cornhill Insurance.

Consumer and industrial activities generate up to 25% of profits, followed by the three other divisions, each providing around 15% to 20% of profits. Half of the business is UK-based and about one-quarter arises in the US, while the growing European interests account for over 10% of sales and profits.

Key economic indicators affecting the group's performance include the level of disposable income in the UK, new car production and the level of capital investment and industrial demand. No single factor has an overriding impact.

FINANCIAL HISTORY

BTR has confounded its critics with the impressive and long-run growth in size, profitability and earnings. Since 1977 pre-tax profits and staff employed have increased over fifteen-fold. Since 1982, including the net effect of two major acquisitions, BTR's sales have advanced 472% from £725m in 1982 to £4.149bn in 1987. Pre-tax profits have kept in step, rising 451% from £107m in 1982 to stand at £590m in 1987.

In 1987 BTR failed to buy Pilkington, but has added the much smaller Stewart Warner which will significantly increase its US exposure. Having digested Tilling, Nylex and Dunlop, a 15% profit margin was achieved by the core industrial and transportation activities, which represent 50% to 60% of operating profits. Construction has also enjoyed a healthy margin improvement.

BTR has bought underperforming companies cheaply and realised their potential within a short period. Some critics, however, point to BTR's relatively small investment programme and a low research and development budget.

Shareholders have benefited from 274% and 340% growth respectively in earnings and dividends per share since 1982. Until 1987, BTR's regular advance of 30% to 40% in earnings per share and 40% to 50% in dividends per share was well above the market's average. Currency influences held growth back in 1987, although at constant exchange rates profits were up 28%.

SHARE PRICE HISTORY

Until early 1986, BTR has commanded a market premium because of excellent growth in earnings and profits and its possession of a strong management team. Since then the share price has remained somewhat lacklustre and now trades below the market for three reasons.

Much earnings growth has come from squeezing margins from twilight industries and how much more can be squeezed remains in doubt. Secondly, due to the large size of the company and lower growth potential of industrial interests, it would take increasingly larger acquisitions to maintain historical levels of growth – the company can only become so big. Thirdly, little emphasis appears to be put on research and development and long term planning. Future earnings potential remains uncertain.

The shares fell from their all-time high of 374p in September 1987 to a post-crash low of 228p in November, a fall of 39%. The shares then started to outperform the FT-A All-Share index and were trading around 270p in early March 1988.

SENIOR MANAGEMENT

BTR is well represented by its chairman and chief executive, Sir Owen Green. While credited for the development of BTR, this self-effacing and diplomatic man is not a household name. Having reached retirement age he remains as chairman but was succeeded as chief executive at the beginning of 1987 by John Cahill, previously head of BTR's US operations. Sir Owen's right hand man, finance director Norman Ireland, was succeeded in that post by Barry Romeril a few months later but the former remains on the board.

This changing of the guard was anxiously anticipated by the investment community, but the nervousness was muted given that the same executive directors remained in place after a management reorganisation.

CAPITAL

In line with the general aim of reducing interest charges, which were high following the acquisition of Dunlop, BTR redeemed the remaining £46.48m 5% dollar convertible subordinated bonds 1995 but not the ECU. Following a one for two scrip issue in May 1986 in which 550.4m shares were issued, BTR ended the financial year with 1.68bn ordinary shares in issue.

The major listing is still in London, but BTR is also traded on Swiss and West German exchanges. To coincide with a Tokyo listing in 1986 a further 3.2m shares were placed in Japan. BTR has a generous option policy for remunerating and rewarding successful executives.

GROUP REVIEW

BTR is known to be a lean, bureaucracy-averse group which follows the management philosophy and structure introduced by Sir Owen Green. He described the famous inverted saucer or a very flat pyramid as a means of decreasing the obstruction to communication within the group.

With over 300 operating companies, each of which has day-to-day autonomy in managing operations and in taking key strategic decisions, line management genuinely makes its own decisions on product development, manufacturing and marketing.

Central constraints placed on management are simple. Profit targets and financial ratios are imposed by the three regional offices, which operate like miniature banks in gauging the necessary period of return on an investment. Expenditure is seldom sanctioned if the payback period is beyond five years. The head office employs just over 20 people, a meagre one-quarter of one per cent of the group headcount, and the main Pimlico office is hardly palatial.

Construction Negligible growth of less than 1% in sales in 1987 was offset by much stronger margins, which rose to 12.8% from 8% in 1985 and 11.5% in 1986 and now approach the group average. A strong performances by Tilcon Inc was

not reflected when converted into sterling. UK construction had a good year and Pilkington Tiles was outstanding. In 1987 pre-tax profits were up 6.7% to £113m (£104m) on turnover 0.6% up at £883m (£878m).

The major operation is Tilcon, a provider of aggregates and associated products. There are numerous smaller companies in building services and products. The division is dependent on the public infrastructure plans of US and UK governments, which are being stepped up cautiously, and the general health of the private building market. Short-term trends can be affected by adverse weather conditions.

Tilcon has been increasing the volume of aggregates sold and consequently its margins. Sales, notably in road building and surfacing, have been strong in its home market within the north-eastern US. In late 1987, Tilcon bought Guyott, a Connecticut aggregates business as part of a $120m acquisition and development programme. Investments in new plant and equipment and continued acquisitions bode well for this division.

In the UK, adverse weather conditions disrupted sales in the first half of 1987 while prices reflected an extremely competitive market. New plants to process aggregates producing asphalt, concrete and mortar were commissioned. This is a highly capital-intensive business. Tilcon added to its reserve of Cheshire sands with the purchase of Cheshire Aggregates.

CHAIRMAN'S STATEMENT

'1987 celebrated the "coming of age" of our unbroken profit growth pattern. The twenty-first consecutive annual increase was achieved through resolute performances by many operations in differing business sectors in various world locations. They hold, however, to a common objective, the creation of wealth through the satisfaction of needs.' *Sir Owen Green*

The special products operation supplies foundry sand, industrial minerals and powders and products for the building industry. Sand, gravel and ready-mixed concrete are provided by the Hortons operation now integrated with Tilcon UK. Further mineral rights to extract marble and calcite were obtained in Spain, while in Ireland, SPD has entered a joint venture to develop a process for the high purification of quartz.

Graham Building Services, the builders' merchant, went through a difficult period from 1984 until it made a reasonable recovery in 1986 which continued in 1987. The business was restructured to move away from the new housing market towards repair and refurbishment. Until recently central government's reduced building programmes led to a reduced volume of business and prompted the integration of three regional trading companies into one. This process was completed by the end of 1986 and Graham returned to previous levels of profit.

Subsequently the upturn in infrastructure spending and a strong private housing market stimulated the business. Smaller acquisitions were made in 1986 such as Parkside Timber and the FJ Reeves timber outlets. In 1987, the timber importer and sawmiller J Baird was bought to serve this growth sector.

Specialist firms in the division include George Boyd, Beardmore and Goodman Croggan, and being sensitive to oil prices and agriculture, they have not performed particularly well. US Supply, the Texas and Midwest building and industrial materials distributor, had a difficult time for similar reasons and reduced its exposure in the worst affected states.

Pascon is a growing building services, plant hire and

F I V E Y E A R F I N A N C I A L I N F O R M A T I O N												
Year	Turnover (£m)	Pre-tax (£m)	Earnings (p)	Dividends net (p)	Dividend cover (x)	Net assets (p)	Price (p) High	Low	PER (x) High	Low	Yield (%) High	Low
1983	1,969.5	170.6	4.5	2.9	2.3	43.9	143	84	28.7	20.4	4.16	2.66
1984	3,486.7	284.2	12.2	4.3	2.2	53.2	205	138	31.6	19.1	3.23	2.38
1985	3,880.1	357.8	16.0	5.8	2.0	62.0	264	197	28.7	21.5	3.06	2.15
1986	4,019.2	489.8	21.2	8.3	1.9	74.1	330	241	28.7	18.2	3.63	2.29
1987	4,150.0	590.0	23.6	9.7	2.4	76.2	376	225	23.4	10.9	5.45	2.82

industrial maintenance activity which successfully integrated the Palmer Scaffolding, Selwood Hire and Plant Sales and Croker acquisitions during 1986. In Canada, Hamilton Kent supplies plastic gaskets for water and sewer pipes, and significant investment is being put into the operation. Another subsidiary, Pilkington Tile Holdings, which makes tiles, adhesive and grout, is trading particularly strongly.

Energy and electrical   Sales fell 4.4% in 1987, as competition intensified in the electricals sector and North Sea oil activity slackened. Improved margins in the higher technology companies offset the oil industry decline, leading to little net change in sales but a 9.3% rise in pre-tax profits to £82m (£75m) on turnover down £37m to £798m (£835m). Newey & Aire performed particularly strongly.

Newey & Eyre, one of the UK's leading electrical distributors with over 150 trading outlets, is increasing profits and overcame flat market conditions in 1987 by preparing staff and the business for anticipated growth. Wellco is maintaining its leading position in the DIY packaged electrical goods market. In the US, the Summers Group is an electrical distributor in the Midwest, west and southern sunbelt states where market conditions are difficult.

ADS-Anker is a European supplier of retail electronic point of sale equipment. The 44,000 units it shipped in 1986 included electronic cash registers, fund transfer terminals and cash handling systems for supermarkets, retail chains, restaurants and garages. Dunlop Enerka (Holland), Dunlop CCT (Belgium) and BTR Belting (UK) all supply coal mine belting. BTR Dunlop is expanding capacity in South Africa to serve the coal mining industry.

Charlton Leslie Offshore, which builds oil rigs, has suffered from the postponement of major projects due to oil industry recession and overcapacity. The offshore division was combined with the construction division under a single management to tackle a much reduced market, with initiatives in mechanical and electrical fitting and design services paying off, in particular with a £5m order from BP Chemicals.

Despite oil industry recession, Dunlop Oil & Marine is maintaining its position as the world's leading supplier of offshore marine hose. A new high pressure flexible pipe, Dunlop Armaline, is being produced for subsea oil and gas operations at a new Tyneside factory. A severe downturn in the US oil industry hit electrical group companies such as Valve Group and the Rochester Corporation, which supplies wire rope and wirelines.

Permali Gloucester manufactures densified wood, which is used to carry a liquified gas pipeline across the Western Australian desert and to support the flasks in which the UK Atomic Energy Authority transport spent fuel rods. BTR-Permali RP makes GRP antenna dishes for the emerging domestic satellite market. Facile Technologies in the US provides ENCODE identification tapes for cable television, advanced shielding composites for computer cables and magnetic storage media.

Industrial   Sales in 1987 rose 11.2% to £963m (£866m) and

pre-tax profits rose 6.5% to £149m (£138m). Margins declined slightly. This established division had seen major increases in 1986 demand with sales up almost 40% and a 2.5% margin improvement as many new activities contributed to higher profits.

Dunlop Hiflex, a relatively new company formed in 1985 from the hydraulic hose assembly operations of Dunlop and Hi-Flex International, has established 40 outlets and was a major, very profitable supplier of components for the Jaguar XI6 car. This is classic BTR treatment of an acquisition.

The industrial distribution companies are widespread throughout Europe, supplying a range of plastic, rubber and other finished parts. The cross trends in each market are complex, but in essence BTR is tackling slack and price competitive markets with the rationalisation of outlets, greater product diversity and more marketing by Farington and Dunlop Hydraulic Hose. Peter-BTR (Germany) now provides a range of products from conveyer belts to filter plates.

Dunlop Engineering installed the passenger conveyer units at Terminal 4 in London's Heathrow Airport, employing belts provided by Dunlop Enerka.

Weaker demand has hit the diverse UK businesses, especially in the rubber market. BTR Silvertown makes a wide range of products such as cutless bearings, line pipes, military overboots and submarine cradle pads. Leyland & Birmingham produces respirators, Dunlop Manchester makes flexible containers, Nuway makes entrance matting for industrial use and Dunlop Adhesives makes sealants, in particular for the double-glazing sector.

Other activities are the potentially world-beating Lonstroff-BTR (Switzerland), which makes elastometric components for the electronics industry. It has been voted IBM's best supplier in Europe for two years and has a reputation for zero defects. Serck Heat Transfer supplies cooler units to engine makers and won a major order from British Rail, despite flat market conditions. Gascoigne-Melotte makes milking equipment and, while sales were hit in 1986 by the adverse impact of milk quotas on UK farming, there is potential international expansion.

In South Africa, BTR merged its major interests with the Dunlop subsidiary in 1986, to form BTR Dunlop, a publicly quoted company of which 53% is held. In the US, Clarkson Industries is responsible for several engineering companies manufacturing a wide range of products.

In Australia, BTR Indeng services the hydraulics and construction markets. In Taiwan BTR Nylex's acquisition of major holdings in three quoted companies trebled its size. China General Plastics Corporation markets PVC resin and sheeting. Taita Chemical Company makes and markets styrenic polymers, including polystyrene, and Asia Polymer Corporation makes low density plastic materials. Nylex will help these companies bring their products to a wider market, including the BTR group.

Transportation   Integration of various Dunlop activities created this new and separate division in 1986. The division's

Share price and relative to FT-A All-Share

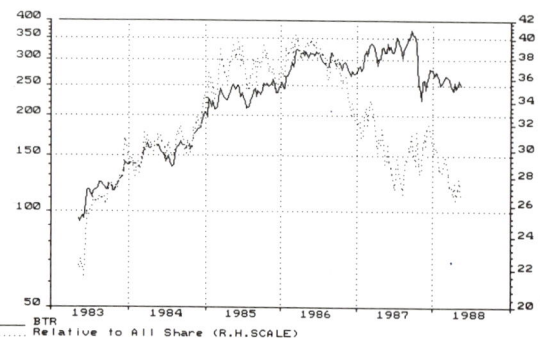

profit margin of 17.8% is higher than the group average. Margins increased 2.8% in 1987.

Pre-tax profits were 40% up at £126m (£90m) on sales 21.7% up at £706m (£580m). The increase in profits reflected increased volumes, new products and better productivity. In Europe in general, and the UK in particular, the automotive and aerospace areas were buoyant. Borg-Warner Australia was an important contributor.

BTR's various companies produce a vast number of component parts for the auto industry, predominantly in Europe. Dunlop Automotive supplies leading carmakers such as Ford, General Motors and Nissan with a range of rubber and industrial components. It is the sole maker of steel car wheels, but is moving away from heavy engineering into advanced hydraulic and electronic control systems.

Before the formation of Dunlop Automotive, Hertfordshire-BTR was the most important subsidiary with transport interests providing a range of car components, such as door seals and turbo-hoses. Metalastik Vibration Control Systems makes suspensions for the Jaguar XJ6, Rover 800 and for railcars on various rapid transit networks. Angus Fluid Seals is a major European source of hub seals for Ford and is opening up the West German market to imports. Peradin designs and manufacturers car suspension components for the XJ6, Rover 800, Mercedes 190/200/300 series and the 400 ES Volvo. Fatati BTR (Switzerland) provides car carpeting throughout Europe, and the UK subsidiary is adding to sales volume. BTR Kenno is the leading supplier of propylene-based moulded car carpets. Dunlopillo makes car seat foam mouldings, as used in the Ford Fiesta, Escort and Sierra, besides the XJ6.

In Australia BTR Nylex makes interior door panels and shelves, and in May 1987 acquired Borg Warner Australia. International Radiator Services supplies the radiator replacement market in the UK and the Middle East. In South Africa, Zambia and Zimbabwe, BTR Dunlop is in the replacement tyre market.

BTR is building up its aerospace interests with the supply of Dunlop Aviation equipment in aircraft built by British Aerospace and Fokker, in addition to smaller contracts for wheels, carbon brakes and brake control systems elsewhere. Dunlop Aircraft Tyres supplies the Advanced Harrier AV8B built by McDonnell Douglas. Dunlop Precision Rubbers supplies the market for airframe doors and window seals. Serck Aviation also supplies aircraft engine heat exchangers to SNECMA in France and Pratt & Whitney in the US.

National Tyre Service is a BTR subsidiary, a residual Dunlop interest retained after tyremaking was sold. Other interests include more basic materials like Silentbloc, which makes rail suspension blocks and aero engine suspensions and mountings; Cow Industrial Polymers; Permali Gloucester, composite materials technology; Russell Plastics Technology, supplying the US military; Dunlop Marine Safety; and Dunlop-Beaufort Air-Sea Equipment, makers of liferafts.

Consumer-related activities Sales fell 7% in 1987 to £799m (£860m) while pre-tax profits were marginally ahead at £151m (£150m). Currency effects masked some impressive gains at Dunlop Slazenger and the paper group. 1987 followed a difficult 1986, when BTR's sales were reduced by over a quarter and, despite a slightly improved margin of 15.5%, the profit contribution was reduced. The division consists of healthcare, paper and printing, sport and leisure and other activities.

The group has a number of generally unrelated healthcare interests. Through Interlab in the US, Nunc supplies specialised plastic products to other healthcare suppliers, such as the immunology devices used in making AIDS diagnostic kits. Bear Medical Systems makes ventilators for asthma sufferers. Cape Environmental Engineering provides complementary equipment. Penlon makes computer-controlled anaesthetic machines and Leyland Medical makes carbon fibre orthopaedic implants. Artificial limbs are made by JE Hangar, Vessa and Robert Kellie in the UK – with a move away from hand-crafted to machined limbs under way. Hosmer Dorrance markets limb products such as the UltraRoelite lower limb and myoelectric hands and Viennatone (Austria) makes hearing aids. Fidelity Hearing Instruments, acquired in 1986, will open up the US market for Viennatone.

The paper group is seeing significant new investment, updating manufacturing plant around the world with the ability to make the most sophisticated papermaking felts. Dunlop Graphic Products supplies printers' blankets. Roll covers and other manufacturing equipment in the papermaking process are also manufactured in Mexico and West Germany.

The sports and leisure interests were acquired with Dunlop. Dunlop Slazenger International makes a variety of equipment for tennis, squash, badminton and golf and also supplies both its own distinctive branded footwear and owns the UK agency for the West German Puma brand. Other activities include Pretty Polly tights which is seeing a period of innovation in industry design and growth in sales. Furniture and bedding is made in the UK by Rest Assured, Bridgecraft and Wm Lawrence. Dunlopillo provides a range of moulded latex products across Europe. Dunloplan provides pvc flooring.

Stewart Warner This US division is comparable to BTR in the manufacture of automotive equipment, heat exchangers and castors. It came close to merging with BTR in 1981, and there is obvious synergy between it and BTR's industrial and transport interests. The Chicago-based company had been losing money, but was probably bought at a discount to assets. The acquisition will allow BTR greater penetration of the US auto component market, which is currently low, and the lucrative new market for aerospace and defence.

GEOGRAPHICAL REVIEW

BTR derives almost half of its sales and profits from the manufacturing activities, which are predominantly in the UK, even though sales might ultimately be made abroad. The Pacific region is the fastest growing area, with sales up from 4% to 9% and profits from 5% to 10% in 1987. Australia is increasingly important. North and South America are BTR's second market, but various setbacks have depressed the proportion of sales and operating profits from 29% to 27% and

30% to 28%, respectively. Africa now makes up 4% of sales and 3% of profits.

CORPORATE CALENDAR

Year end	31 December
Preliminary results	March
Report and accounts	March
AGM	May
Final dividend paid	May
Interim results	September
Interim dividend paid	November

DIRECTORS' HOLDINGS

	Fully paid	Other (incl. options)
Sir Owen Green	1,000,000	161,696
JC Cahill	287,241	250,000
P Fatharly	—	—
NC Ireland	492,720	112,272
AR Jackson	45,000	152,500
HW Laughland	26,186	114,944
BD Romeril	—	100,000
Sir David Nicolson	2,037	
EE Sharp	3,000	125,000
LJ Stammers	192,500	118,210
WDT Tapley	600,000	7,272

Total directors' remuneration in 1987 was £1.347m, with the chairman receiving the highest remuneration of £225,000.

PRINCIPAL SUBSIDIARIES AND RELATED COMPANIES

Construction
Graham Building Services Ltd, Pascon Ltd, Pilkington's Tile Holdings Ltd, Tilcon Ltd, Tilcon Holdings Inc – US

Energy and electrical
ADS-Anker GmbH – West Germany, Charlton Leslie Engineering Ltd, Dunlop Oil & Marine, Facile Technologies Inc – US, Newey & Eyre Group Ltd, Permali, Summers Electric Co Inc – US, Worcester Controls Corp – US

Industrial
BTR Farington, BTR Silvertown, China Plastic Group – Taiwan (51%), Clarkson Industries Inc – US, DCE Group Ltd, Dunlop GRG, Dunlop Hiflex Ltd, Hansen Transmissions International NV – Belgium, Leyland & Birmingham Rubber, Lonstroff-BTR AG – Switzerland, Serck Heat Transfer, Vokes

Transportation
Borg Warner Australia, Dunlop Aviation, Dunlop Automotive, Dunlop Beaufort, Fatati-BTR SA – Switzerland, Dunlop Zimbabwe Ltd (70%), George Angus Ltd, Hertfordshire-BTR Ltd, International Radiator Services Ltd (70%), Metalastik Vibration Control Systems, National Tyre Services, Stewart-Warner

Consumer-related activities
A/S Nunc – Denmark, Bear Medical Systems Inc – US, Rest Assured Holdings Ltd, Dunlop GmbH – West Germany, Dunlopillo, Dunlop Slazenger International Ltd, Huyck Corp – US, JE Hanger, Pretty Polly, Sanshin Enterprises Ltd – Japan (70%), SW Industries Inc – US, Viennatone GmbH – Austria

Holding and related
BTR Dunlop Ltd – South Africa (53%), BTR Finance BV – Netherlands, BTR Inc – US, BTR Industries Ltd, BTR Nylex – Australia (62%), Dunlop Holdings Plc, Thomas Tilling Plc, Audco India Ltd – India (50%), Meggitt Holdings PLC (22%)

BRAND NAMES

Bridgecraft, Carlton, Cow Gum, Dunlop, Dunlopillo, Dunloplan, Fidelity, Maxfli MD, National Tyre Service, Pretty Polly, Puma, Rest Assured, Silentbloc, Slazenger, Starglide, Viennatone

CONTACTS AND FURTHER INFORMATION

DFP Sharrock, Company secretary, BTR plc, Silvertown House, Vincent Square, London SW1P 2PL. Tel: 01-834 3848.

GENERAL INFORMATION

Head office	54 Lombard Street, London EC3P 3AH. Tel: 01-626 1567
Directors	JG Quinton (chairman), PE Leslie (managing), Mrs M Baker, Sir Timothy Bevan, ARF Buxton, Lord Camoys, FR Dolling, FR Goodenough, Sir Martin Jacomb (deputy chairman), PE Leslie (deputy chairman), HT Norrington, BG Pearse, OH Rout, AJ de Nouaille Rudge, AG Tritton. Non-exec Dr DV Atterton CBE, IG Butler, DH Henderson, JR Henderson CVO OBE, Sir Christopher Laidlaw, HUA Lambert, Sir Nigel Mobbs, BG Pearse, Sir Richard Pease Bt, DR Pelly, The Rt Hon Lord Prior, OH Rout, Sir James Spooner, CH Tidbury, Sir Anthony Tuke, DV Weyer CBE
Advisers	Barclays de Zoete Wedd Ltd
Auditors	Price Waterhouse
Registrars	Barclays Bank Registration Department
Brokers	Cazenove & Co, de Zoete & Bevan Ltd
Solicitors	Durrant Piesse

GENERAL FINANCIAL INFORMATION

Market capitalisation	£3.329bn at 1 January 1988
Capital structure	
Issued ordinary shares (£1)	734.9m
Issued preference shares	None
Warrants	None
Convertibles	None
Traded options	Yes
ADRs	One ADR per four ordinary shares
Shareholders over 5%	None

FT CATEGORY

FT: Banks, HP and leasing
FT-A: Banks

MAJOR ACTIVITIES

Through Barclays Bank and various other subsidiary companies, the group provides a comprehensive range of banking, financial and related services in 3,000 UK branches, and internationally in over 1,200 offices in some 70 countries.

Barclays is a broadly-based banking group whose major activities include deposit banking and lending, credit cards and traveller's cheques, consumer finance, equipment leasing, investment banking, and other financial services for individual and corporate customers.

Domestic banking operations make the largest contribution to group profits, accounting for 52% in 1987. Other domestic businesses contributed 26% and overseas operations 22%.

The group is an innovator in banking and financial services in the UK having brought out the first personal credit card, Barclaycard. It also reintroduced Saturday openings, and recently launched the first debit card, Connect.

In April 1988 Barclays announced a £921m rights issue, the largest ever made by a UK bank, and the second largest UK issue ever. The bank announced that it wished to continue its rapid growth and that it would give Barclays the strongest equity to asset capital ratio in the clearing bank sector.

An integrated banking and financial services network has been developed on a global basis through the merger of the domestic and international operations. This is matched by the investment banking capability in Barclays de Zoete Wedd (BZW).

The contribution from BZW was at first minimal due to heavy start-up expenditure. BZW had made a good contribution of £25m to profits in the first half of 1987, but the heavy fall in equities in the autumn of 1987 caused losses in its market-making area. Since that time BZW has traded profitably.

In November 1986 the remaining 40% interest in Barclays

National Bank, a major South African bank, was sold.

FINANCIAL HISTORY

1987 pre-tax profits were down 62% to £339m after charging exceptional provisions of £713m in respect of problem loans to countries experiencing exceptional liquidity problems. Earnings per share were down 71% to 25.8p. Net dividends were up 10.7% to 23.5p. 1987 pre-tax profits before exceptional provisions were £1.052bn, 17.5% up on £895m in 1986.

UK domestic banking operations was the strongest divisional performer in 1987, experiencing profits growth of 31% to £548m after only a marginal improvement in 1986. BZW did well to restrict losses to £11m.

The dramatic £713m increase in Barclay's provisions means that it has provided for 35% of its total exposure of £2.026bn to developing countries and 12% of its £734m outgoings to developed countries, including South Africa.

The group has maintained consistent dividend growth, averaging 12.5% annually since 1983.

SHARE PRICE HISTORY

Adjusted for the 1985 deep discount rights issue, the share price rose by 80% in the three years to summer 1987. Compared with the market, the shares have underperformed by a substantial margin, falling from 75% of the FT-A All-Share index in early 1982 to 53% in early 1988. Factors responsible for this underperformance have included investor concern over sovereign debt exposure, adverse complications of the 1984 Budget, a large rights issue in 1985, disappointment with profits growth in 1986 and the debt provisions in 1987.

The shares fell with the market in the autumn 1987 crash before showing slight outperformance until the April 1988 rights issue announcement, when the shares fell sharply.

SENIOR MANAGEMENT

Chairman John Quinton (formerly a senior general manager), chairman of Barclays Bank UK and deputy chairman of Barclays, succeeded Sir Timothy Bevan as chairman of the group in May 1987. After the merger of the domestic and international banking operations, a new senior management structure was adopted in March 1987. It includes Derek Pelly as a deputy chairman and chairman of Barclays International, Peter Leslie as a deputy chairman and managing director, Sir Martin Jacomb as a deputy chairman and chairman of Barclays de Zoete Wedd, Andrew Buxton as vice-chairman and a deputy managing director, Brian Pearse as chief financial officer, Humphrey Norrington as executive director of overseas operations, Owen Rout as executive director of UK operations and Lord Camoys as chief executive of Barclays de Zoete Wedd.

CAPITAL

Recently the group has taken steps to strengthen its capital base and improve its capital adequacy ratios on the yardsticks used by the Bank of England. Total capital resources increased by 37% in 1985/86 compared with an 18% increase in consolidated assets. Equity capital increased by 48%. This reflected the £507m raised through the 1985 rights issue, and almost $2bn from updated capital notes, the bulk of which qualifies as primary capital for the purposes of Bank of England capital adequacy guidelines.

In May 1987, the group issued the equivalent of 41.5m shares through simultaneous offerings in the US and Japan. £110.4m was raised by the share issue in Japan and $198.9m through the ADR offering in the US.

In November 1987, the group issued £250m of Eurosterling bonds, and in December 1987 raised $400m in the US domestic market through its subsidiary Barclays North American Capital Corporation. Both will rank as capital under recent proposals for international convergence of capital measurement issued by the Bank for International Settlements.

Total assets increased 11% by £8.8bn in 1987, principally as a result of strong growth in UK lendings. Despite the effect of the exceptional provisions, capital resources increased by £454m in 1987 and stood at £6.8bn at the year-end. The bank's free capital ratio at the year end was 6.2% and equity as a percentage of total assets 4.8%, the lowest of the four major clearing banks.

In April 1988 Barclays announced a one for two rights issue at 250p to raise £921m. The issue was not underwritten. The effect of the capital raised would be to increase the free capital ratio to 7.4% and equity as a percentage of total assets to 5.9%. The averages for UK clearing banks are 6.6% and 5.5% respectively.

No director has a significant shareholding and there is no declarable shareholding of 5% or more in the group.

GROUP REVIEW

UK banking The large branch network in the UK continues to be the core of the group's domestic business as it allows Barclays to have a wide spectrum of customers and to monitor locally the quality of credit relationships. It also provides a stable base of deposits, a major factor in group profitability.

Priority has been given to developing a wide range of personal banking services, including mortgage lending and new premium or higher rate deposit accounts. The group has a mortgage book in excess of £5bn. A nationwide network of automated telling machine (ATMs) has been established. To

C H A I R M A N ' S   S T A T E M E N T

'Total assets rose by 11 per cent, to nearly £88 billion during 1987. Shareholders' funds increased by £398m, taking into account the share issues in New York and Tokyo and a revaluation of properties. The total capital resources of the Group increased by £454 million to stand at £6.8 billion at the year-end, but we believe they need further strengthening if we are to maintain our momentum of growth and are to take full advantage of the Group's considerable potential.

Our declared objective is to be a major international financial services group, recognised for the quality of our service to both corporate and retail customers. We will continue to build, as appropriate, on our domestic and international reputation and widespread representation, with particular emphasis on the major economies of Europe, the United States and the Far East.

. . .

In order both to fund the existing and expected growth in our business, and to support our declared objective, we require adequate capital resources and our need now is for additional equity capital. This rights issue is the largest call we have made on our shareholders, but we believe it is essential if our Group is to continue to grow and prosper in an increasingly competitive world.' *John Quinton*

F I V E   Y E A R   F I N A N C I A L   I N F O R M A T I O N

Year	Income[†] (£m)	Pre-tax (£m)	Earnings (p)	Dividends net (p)	Dividend cover (x)	Net assets (p)	Price (p) High	Low	PER (x) High	Low	Yield (%) High	Low
1983	3,190	557	53	15.1	3.5	546	337	243	9.3	5.7	8.10	5.86
1984	3,164	623	55	16.3	3.4	481	361	274	9.7	5.7	7.99	5.70
1985	3,508	840	70	18.6	3.8	473	477	332	8.3	5.5	7.04	5.05
1986	3,809	895	89	21.0	4.2	539	589	432	8.7	6.6	6.14	4.51
1987	4,259	339	26	23.3	1.1	560	655	425	17.1	5.5	7.09	4.39

[†]Unadjusted for subsequent accounting changes

meet the demands of the corporate sector, special professional teams have been set up to service the needs of large multinationals. There are also 325 Barclays Business Centres (centre-of-excellence branches) to serve medium-sized companies. UK domestic banking trading profits in 1987 were 31% up at £548m, contributing 52% of the group total before exceptional provisions.

Central retail services   This division includes Barclaycard, Gold Premier card, VISA Merchant Services, Masterloan and traveller's cheques. Barclaycard has over 8.5m cardholders in the UK. Cards can be used in outlets worldwide.

Traveller's cheque operations were enhanced in 1986 by the acquisition of the Chase Manhattan business. This acquisition and the effect of lower interest rates had a short-term adverse effect on profitability in 1986, but it left the group as the third largest issuer of traveller's cheques in the world.

Launch costs of Connect (a new debit card) and research and development expenditure held back profits growth in 1987 to 5% at £97m, 9.2% of the group total before exceptional provisions.

Mercantile Credit   Mercantile Credit is one of the largest writers of instalment credit and leasing business in the UK. The effect of changes arising out of the 1984 Finance Act has been to produce a lower level of tax-based leasing volume growth over the past two years. Mercantile Credit has benefited, however, from the continuing buoyancy of straight commercial leasing and the strength of personal sector credit demand.

Recent changes have included a new divisional operating structure for sharper focus on specific markets, and the acquisition of Motor Auctions Group, the third largest motor auction company in the UK. 1987 trading profits were fractionally down at £85m, 8% of the group total before exceptional provisions.

Barclays de Zoete Wedd   Barclays' commitment to the new capital and securities markets is principally through BZW, made up of Barclays Merchant Bank, the recently acquired stockbrokers de Zoete & Bevan, jobbers Wedd Durlacher Mordaunt, and Barclays Investment Management. The new entity began operations in June 1986.

BZW was reinforced by an increased capital base of £250m and advanced information, dealing and settlement systems. These include 600 dealing positions which are linked to BZW offices in all the major financial centres. BZW plays a leading role in the domestic and international equity and debt markets where it is one of the top three market-makers.

BZW also provides a full range of corporate financial services – capital raising, secondary offerings, flotations, acquisitions and mergers, and full treasury and security-related foreign exchange facilities. BZW has recently attracted some of Hill Samuel's corporate team and acquired a US clearing house.

In 1987 BZW lost £11m, a much better performance than

most of its competitors. It was profitable throughout 1987 except for the traumatic month of October.

Financial services   The financial services division incorporates the group's activities in retail financial services. It includes Barclays Bank Trust, Barclayshare, Broker Services Ltd, and the group's unit trust and insurance operations. Barclayshare is the retail stockbroking arm and was the first to launch a comprehensive Personal Equity Plan.

Broker Services Ltd provides settlement and other back office services to Stock Exchange trading members. The intention is to merge the unit trust and insurance operations with those of the trust company to provide a full range of personal financial products under the name Barclays Financial Services.

In 1987, profits increased by 22% to £56m, 5.3% of the group total before exceptional provisions. The division benefited from greater marketing through the branch network and the high levels of stock market trading experienced during most of the year.

International banking   Barclays has a strong international business, some handled from London. In London it is the leading provider of foreign exchange and treasury facilities. Profits have been under threat from the need to make provisions against sovereign debt. In the US, a new headquarters building was opened on Wall Street. The group's corporate activities are handled by the USA Banking Division. BarclaysAmericanCorporation handles the commercial markets.

In the rest of the world, profits are showing strong growth except in Italy and France. In France, Barclays is the leading private bank. Spain is a particularly successful operating country, as are Australia and Hong Kong. In Africa the group has deposits of £1bn.

In 1987, international banking trading profits, before exceptional provisions, increased 4.1% to £227m, 21.5% of the group total. Total provision for sovereign debt at the end of 1987 was £803m against outstandings of £2.760bn. Mexico has

Share price and relative to FT-A All-Share

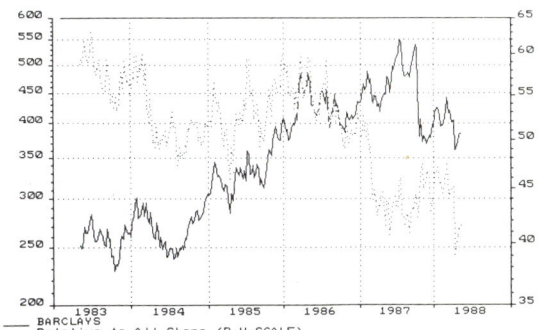

£580m outstanding, South Africa £533m, Brazil £359m and Argentina £338m. The group expects to get a tax credit on the write-offs. Sovereign debt is being reduced by the strengthening of sterling.

GEOGRAPHICAL REVIEW

At 31 December 1987, 61% of group assets were deployed in UK banking and financial service businesses. 10% were in UK-based foreign operations, including the greater part of cross-border lending and international treasury activities.

The group has a substantial presence in the US amounting to 13% of group assets. Through BarclaysAmericanCorporation the group has banking operations in 13 states and consumer and commercial finance activities in 35 states.

Barclays has a presence in 70 other countries throughout the world. Since the disposal of Barclays National Bank, none accounts for as much as 5% of total group assets and net income.

CORPORATE CALENDAR

Year end	31 December
Preliminary results	February
Report and accounts	March
AGM	April
Final dividend paid	April
Interim results	July
Interim dividend paid	October

DIRECTORS' HOLDINGS

	Ordinary shares		Options
	(beneficial)	(non-beneficial)	
JG Quinton	9,125	8,600	135,200
Dr DV Atterton	3,494	—	—
Sir Timothy Bevan	20,559	3,600	—
IG Butler	5,496	—	—
ARP Buxton	7,944	3,600	72,223
Lord Camoys	7,283	—	66,964
FR Dolling	8,179	—	—
FR Goodenough	13,609	290,022	—
DH Henderson	5,000	—	—
JR Henderson	7,000	—	—
Sir Martin Jacomb	1,488	3,600	96,438
Sir Christopher Laidlaw	1,680	—	—
HUA Lambert	13,100	5,501	—
PE Leslie	9,518	9,952	77,994
Sir Nigel Mobbs	4,472	4,896	—
HT Norrington	6,493	—	63,087
BG Pearse	1,122	—	69,910
Sir Richard Pease	11,949	454,404	—
DR Pelly	8,670	3,600	79,276
The Rt Hon Lord Prior	1,000	—	—
OH Rout	1,796	—	61,767
AJ de N Rudge	7,330	224	4,726
Sir James Spooner	1,000	—	—
CH Tidbury	4,176	978	—
AG Tritton	5,765	—	—
Sir Anthony Tuke	25,616	7,380	—
DV Weyer	4,474	—	—

Total directors' remuneration for 1987 was £2.50m with the chairman receiving £227,242 and the highest-paid director £222,819.

PRINCIPAL SUBSIDIARIES AND RELATED COMPANIES

BarclaysAmericanCorporation – US, Barclays Bank Australia Ltd – Australia, Barclays Bank Finance Co (Jersey) Ltd – Channel Islands, Barclays Bank of Botswana Ltd – Botswana (89.8%), Barclays Bank of California – US, Barclays Bank of Canada – Canada, Barclays Bank of Kenya Ltd (70.6%) – Kenya, Barclays Bank of New York NA – US (99.9%), Barclays Bank of Zambia Ltd, Barclays Bank of Zimbabwe Ltd – Zimbabwe, Barclays Bank Plc, Barclays Bank SA – France, Barclays Bank SA – Switzerland, Barclays Bank SAE – Spain (90.1%), Barclays Bank Trust Co Ltd, Barclays de Zoete Wedd Holdings Ltd, Barclays Finance Co (Guernsey) Ltd – Channel Islands, Barclays Financial Services Italia SpA – Italy, Barclays New Zealand Ltd – New Zealand (70.5%), Mercantile Credit Company Ltd, Investors in Industry Group Plc (18.8%), Republic Bank Ltd – Trinidad and Tobago (41.2%), Yorkshire Bank PLC (32%)

BRAND NAMES

Barclaycard, Barclays Unicorn Unit Trusts, Barclayloan, Barclayshare, Connect, Mercantile Credit

CONTACTS AND FURTHER INFORMATION

Christopher J Wheeler, Central Planning Department, Barclays PLC, 54 , Lombard Street, London EC3P 3AH. Tel: 01-626 1567 ext 3092.

GENERAL INFORMATION

Head office	30 Portland Place, London W1N 3DF. Tel: 01-637 5499
Directors	IMG Prosser (chairman and chief executive), OC Darby, DG Inns FCA, BD Langton CBE, AER Manners, AD Portno PhD, K Richards, JRD Swan, DA Urquhart. *Non-exec* Lord Bancroft GCB, GG Williams
Advisers	J Henry Schroder Wagg & Co Ltd
Auditors	Ernst & Whinney
Registrars	Hill Samuel Registrars, 6 Greencoat Place, London SW1P 1PL. Tel: 01-828 4321
Brokers	Cazenove & Co, Panmure Gordon & Co Ltd
Solicitors	Linklaters & Paines

GENERAL FINANCIAL INFORMATION

Market capitalisation	£2.760bn at 1 January 1988
Capital structure	
Issued ordinary shares (25p)	337m
Issued preference shares (£1)	3.4m 2.8% CPS
	3.2m 4.9% CPS
Warrants	None
Convertibles	None
Traded options	Yes
ADRs	None
Shareholders over 5%	Prudential Corporation 5%

FT CATEGORY

FT: Beers, wines and spirits
FT-A: Brewers and distillers

MAJOR ACTIVITIES

Bass is the largest UK brewery company. The main wines and spirits brand subsidiary is Hedges & Butler. The company's Crest Hotels are well established both in the UK and on the Continent.

Bass has recently acquired some of the US and all of the international interests of the Holiday Inn hotel business for $475m. These are additional to eight Holiday Inn hotels acquired in Europe in May 1987.

Bass has over 21% of the UK beer market, 13 breweries, 7,335 public houses and 646 Augustus Barnett off-licences. The company has a dominant market position in Scotland. The largest individual beer brand is Carling Black Label lager, followed by the Tennent's range of ales and lagers. It is by far the largest producer of traditional beer in the UK and has the biggest share of the take-home trade. It manages and has a 45% interest in Britvic Corona, the second largest soft drinks business in the UK.

In beers Bass is committed to the development of its own brands rather than the franchise of brand names and products from abroad. The most important wines and spirits brands are Mouton Cadet, Mateus Rosé, Bacardi, Dewar's, Otard Cognac, Bezique and White Satin. Other brands owned include Hirondelle table wines, Emva Cyprus sherry, Zamoyski vodka and the fine Bordeaux wines of the group's subsidiary Alexis Lichine.

In addition to the Holiday Inn hotels, there are 87 Crest Hotels, of which 37 are on the Continent, mainly in West Germany and the Netherlands. Other businesses include Horizon Holidays, 822 Coral betting shops, and 87 Coral social centres. Catering activities trade under the Toby name.

Bass competes with Ladbrokes and Grand Metropolitan in hotels and betting, with the other major quoted brewers (Allied-Lyons, Scottish & Newcastle and Whitbread) and with Courage, now owned by Elders IXL. Guinness competes with its beer, wines and spirits products.

FINANCIAL HISTORY

Profits in the year to 30 September 1987 increased by 17.6% over 1986 to £365.0m. All companies within the group had a good year. Property profits above the line were slightly down at £15.3m from £17.4m. There were extraordinary credits of £24.2m from surpluses generated on the sale of the stake in Yorkshire Television and the UK holiday centres, net of taxation of £12.7m. Earnings per share increased by 20.3% to 71.6p. Since 1983 earnings per share have doubled.

The business generates large amounts of cash. Gearing for four years until 1986 stood at an average of 17% and funds generated increased from £273m in 1983 to £575m in 1987. In spite of strategic investment amounting to £273m and expenditure of £331m on existing businesses, gearing at 30 September 1987 was still only 21.8%. Net asset value is 726p per share, including the effect of £830m surplus produced by its property revaluation in October 1986, up 105.1% over five years.

In 1987 Bass raised a total of £81.1m before tax from its sale of its Pontin Holiday centres in the UK, its 21% interest in Yorkshire Television and its 35.8% interest in the Castletown Brewery. In May 1987 Horizon Travel was acquired for less than 10% of the company's assets. This was followed up by the acquisition of the Wings, Blue Sky and OSL trade names in August. £90m was spent on the acquisition of eight English and European Holiday Inns. Its subsidiary Alex Lichine & Co spent £3m on the majority holding in Cognac Otard. Its related company Britannia Soft Drinks spent £120m on a major part of the Beechams soft drinks business and now trades as Britvic Corona.

Capital expenditure in 1987 totalled £573m, of which £300m was spent on new acquisitions. £100m was invested in retailing activities. Overall there was a £140m negative movement in liquid funds.

Since the October 1987 year end Bass has received £73.8m from the sale of 16 European Crest Hotels and subscribed for $100m of convertible debenture stock in Holiday Corporation Inc. The $475m consideration for the Holiday Inn acquisition was paid in March 1988.

Share price and relative to FT-A All-Share

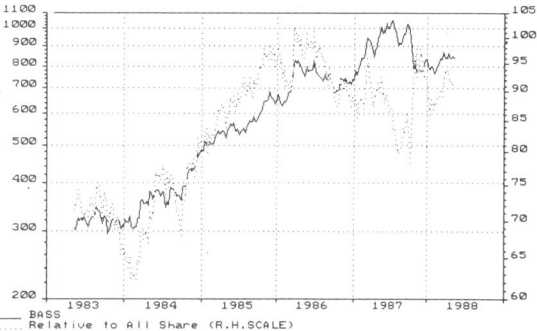

SHARE PRICE HISTORY

Since 1984 the Bass share price has risen from a base figure of around 350p to the mid-April 1988 price of around 840p after an all time high of 1050p in July 1987. This represents a good relative performance to the FT-A All-Share index and also to the FT-A Brewers and Distillers index.

In relative terms, the shares at the beginning of 1988, after

F I V E   Y E A R   F I N A N C I A L   I N F O R M A T I O N

Year	Turnover (£m)	Pre-tax (£m)	Earnings (p)	Dividends net (p)	Dividend cover (x)	Net assets (p)	Price (p) High	Price (p) Low	PER (x) High	PER (x) Low	Yield (%) High	Yield (%) Low
1983	1,988	175.0	34.9	11.36	3.1	354	347	287	17.9	11.7	5.36	4.27
1984	2,252	218.4	44.0	12.90	3.2	381	483	300	15.7	11.7	5.41	3.76
1985	2,410	255.1	50.4	14.70	3.4	419	689	473	16.8	12.8	3.90	2.76
1986	2,709	310.4	59.5	17.00	3.5	437	840	625	18.6	12.2	3.37	2.50
1987	3,213	365.0	71.6	19.50	3.7	726	1,052	759	18.6	10.8	3.48	2.28

falling back for most of 1987, were back at the peak levels achieved in 1985 and 1986. Bass has, for some time, been perceived as the quality stock of the sector.

SENIOR MANAGEMENT

Sir Derek Palmar, chairman since 1976, retired on 30 September 1987. He was succeeded as chairman and chief executive by Ian Prosser, previously managing director.

Other executive committee board members include OC Darby, AER Manners, K Richards and DA Urquhart. There are four other board members, including DG Inns, who is responsible for group finance. Each director is responsible for several subsidiary companies or group departments.

CAPITAL

Until recently, there had been little or no change in the equity capital of the company. In May 1987, however, 7.6m shares were issued to acquire the 74.4% of Horizon Travel not already held.

The $475m consideration for the Holiday Inns hotels deal is to be paid in cash and a promissory note to be redeemed over ten years. The convertible debentures Bass has bought in Holiday Corporation, if converted, would give a holding of 9.9%.

Directors' shareholdings and options in Bass are small. There are no large disclosable stakes apart from the 5% stake held by the Prudential. The group launched a £500m sterling commercial paper programme in December 1987.

GROUP REVIEW

The group is divided into two divisions – brewing, drinks and pub retailing, and leisure. The objective is to achieve a profits balance of 75% brewing and drinks and 25% leisure. Despite the growth in the leisure business, continued growth in the core divisions means that this position may not be reached in the immediate future.

Bass is arguably the most efficient of all the national brewing companies, which is reflected in a very good profits record. It has resisted the temptation to diversify or expand by too much acquisition, and the balance sheet gearing at 21.8% is low. Recently there has been a more aggressive acquisition policy. It is thought the group still wishes to extend its hotel interests. **Brewing, drinks and pub retailing** Despite having a relatively large number of breweries, Bass is one of the most efficient organisations in the industry. In order to achieve this maximum operating efficiency, it has manned down rather than closed breweries. As Britain's number one brewer, its pubs and free trade accounts extend throughout the country, but it is particularly strong, relative to the competition, in Scotland and the Midlands. Tennent's lager has 50% of the lager market in Scotland.

In Augustus Barnett, Bass has one of the most successful off-licence chains in the country. Branded catering in public houses incorporates the name of Toby grills, carving rooms and pantries. There are now 263 Toby outlets. Bass is increasing its market share in all areas. There will be considerable new investment over the next three to four years.

Hedges & Butler has many famous brand names in wines and spirits, including Bacardi, Hirondelle, Louis Kremer and Mateus Rosé. Alexis Lichine is Bass's Bordeaux wine subsidiary.

In addition to its portfolio of wines and spirits brands and agency lines, through Britannia Soft Drinks, Bass has a 45% interest in Britvic Corona, the second largest company in this field behind Coca Cola and Schweppes Beverages. Britvic Corona's interests arose from the merger of Canada Dry Rawlings and Britvic, the purchase in January 1987 of the major part of Beecham's soft drinks interests, and the UK distribution rights for the Pepsi and 7-Up brands. Bass's partners are PepsiCo, Whitbread and Allied-Lyons.

Bass also has a large and very profitable company in Barcrest, which manufactures and operates slot machines of the type found in public houses and arcades.

In 1987 the division made profits of £303.3m, 82% of the group's total, and 20% up on 1986. Beer volumes were up 1% to 2%, with lager increasing its share from 50% to 51.5%. **Leisure** The core business within this division is the Crest Hotel chain which is the fifth largest in the UK and has hotels in West Germany, Belgium, Italy, Spain, Austria and the Netherlands. Typically, they are three or four star business hotels. It is the company's policy to expand the hotel chain.

CHAIRMAN'S STATEMENT

'The major setback to world stock markets since 19 October 1987 has had its effect on the company's share price although, relative to most shares, the company's share price has held up well. The cause of the lack of confidence has been ascribed to a number of factors but notably to the American budget deficit. It has not, however, affected the underlying prospects for our businesses. We have confidence in the year ahead and look forward to further progress.' Ian Prosser

Bass initially purchased four UK Holiday Inns for £55m and four in Europe for a further £35m. Then it bought the whole of Holiday Inns outside North America for $475m. The Holiday Inns acquisition will greatly expand its hotel interests as well as taking them upmarket. Including the eight hotels already purchased, the deal gives Bass 185 hotels in all, made up of 114 franchises, 40 management contracts, 13 US hotels and nine joint venture projects. This amounts to 46,000 rooms though only 9 hotels are fully owned.

Initially the Holiday Inns' contribution will be negative.

The company anticipates a contribution of $28m before central overheads in a calendar year. Financing costs will be substantially more. Since the fully owned building element is low, Bass will be excluded from long term capital appreciation.

Bass has a considerable number of other leisure interests. They include Horizon Travel, which owns and operates 14 Mediterranean holiday sites, Horizon Holidays, Wings, Blue Sky and OSL. These companies operate in highly competitive markets subject to high levels of discounting and seasonal profit variation. Other leisure activities include 822 Coral Racing betting shops and 25 snooker halls.

Bass has an 85% stake in Delta Biotechnology, in which it is investing £20m over the next three years. The company develops serums for use in the treatment of shock and burns.

In 1987 the division made profits of £67.8m, 18% up on 1986. There was some contribution from the initial eight Holiday Inns acquired. Crest Hotels achieved substantial profit growth. Coral Social Clubs had a good year, but Coral Racing was unchanged.

GEOGRAPHICAL REVIEW

Overseas activities were small in total, contributing 6.4% of turnover in 1987. The Holiday Inns acquisition will increase this percentage in 1988.

CORPORATE CALENDAR

Year end	30 September
Preliminary results	December
Report and accounts	January
AGM	January
Final dividend paid	February
Interim results	May
Interim dividend paid	July

DIRECTORS' HOLDINGS

	Beneficial interests	Non-beneficial interests	Other (incl. options)
Lord Bancroft	250	—	—
OC Darby	1,369	72,500	38,527
DG Inns	760	—	21,615
BD Langton	858	—	22,372
AER Manners	1,478	—	35,537
Sir Derek Palmar	5,169	1,000	90,637
AD Portno	789	—	22,028
IMG Prosser	2,169	—	62,280
K Richards	2,169	—	35,372
JRDK Swan	1,589	—	22,270
DA Urquhart	1,602	—	37,930
GC Williams	1,000	—	—

Total directors' remuneration in 1987 was £1.34m, of which the retiring chairman received £71,940, and the highest-paid director £146,292.

PRINCIPAL SUBSIDIARIES AND RELATED COMPANIES

Holding companies Bass European Holdings – Netherlands, Bass Holdings Ltd, Bass Investments Plc, Bass Leisure Activities Ltd, Bass Leisure Group Ltd **Financial** Bass Continental Finance– Netherlands **Brewing, drinks and pub retailing** Augustus Barnett Ltd, Alexis Lichine et Cie SA – France (99.9%), Bass & Tennent Sales Ltd, Bass Brewing Ltd, Bass Ireland Ltd, Bass Maltings Ltd, Bass Mitchells & Butler Ltd, Bass North Ltd, Bass UK Ltd, Bass Wales & West Ltd, Britannia Soft Drinks Ltd (45%), Charrington and Company Ltd, Hedges & Butler Ltd, Taunton Cider Company Ltd (41%), Tennent Caledonian Breweries Ltd, Toby Restaurants Ltd **Export and overseas** Bass Export Ltd **Leisure** Bass Horizon Hotels Ltd, Bass Hotels & Holidays Ltd, Bass Leisure Ltd, Coral Racing Ltd, Coral Social Clubs Ltd **Other activities** Bass Computer Services Ltd, Bass Developments Ltd, Chandos Insurance Co Ltd (50.4%), Delta Biotechnology Ltd (85.0%), Horizon Travel, Standard Commercial Property Securities Ltd (51.0%), Trent Technology Ltd, White Shield Insurance Co Ltd – Gibraltar

BRAND NAMES

Alexis Lichine Wines, Allbright, Apple Splitz, Aveleda Vinho Verde, Bacardi, Barbican, Baron Philippe de Rothschild Wines, Bass, Bass Export, Bass Light, Bass Mild XXXX, Bass Special, Baton, Bezique, Boizel, Breaker, Brew XI, Britvic AM, Britvic, Bulls Blood, Caffrey's Ale, Canada Dry, Carling Black Label, Charger, Charrington, Corvo, Delas, Dewar's, DPA, Eisberg, El Coto Emva, Fernet Branca, Fowlers Wee Heavy, Grappa Bacchino, Hannocks PA, Hedges & Butler, Hemeling, Highgate Mild, Hirondelle, Jubilee, Lamot Pils, Les Routiers, Louis Kremer, M&B, Mateus Rosé, Jos Meyer, Alsace, Nodari Lambrusco, Mouton Cadet, Passion Splitz, Piper, Punt-e-Mes, R White, Shakers, Shandy Pilsner, Stones BB, Sweetheart, Tennent's, Tennent's Export, Tennent's Light Ale, The Antiquary, Tiffany, Toby, Toby Bitter, Umani Ronchi Verdiccio, Vallana Sopanna, Williams & Humbert's, Worthington, Zamoyski Pure Vodka

CONTACTS AND FURTHER INFORMATION

BJ Hanbury, Director of corporate affairs, Bass PLC, 30 Portland Place, London W1N 3DF. Tel: 01-637 5499.

BEECHAM GROUP p.l.c.

GENERAL INFORMATION

Head office Beecham House, Brentford, Middlesex, London TW8 9BD.
Tel: 01-560 5151
Directors RP Bauman (chairman), JW Robb (managing), HR Collum,
RM Gerber, JFB Hunter, Dr P Jackson, Dr KRL Mansford,
RE Newman, JD Pollard, RP Tatman. *Non-exec* DI Allport,
ARF Buxton, Sir Robert Clark, Sir John Kingman, J White
Advisers Kleinwort Benson Ltd, Hill Samuel & Co Ltd
Auditors Price Waterhouse
Registrars Hill Samuel Registrars
Brokers de Zoete & Bevan Ltd, County NatWest WoodMac
Solicitors Simmons & Simmons

GENERAL FINANCIAL INFORMATION

Market capitalisation	£3.325bn at 1 January 1988
Capital structure	
Issued ordinary shares (25p)	755.1m
Issued preference shares	None
Warrants	None
Convertibles	None
Traded options	Yes
ADRs	One ADR equals two ordinary shares
Shareholders over 5%	None

FT CATEGORY

FT: Industrials (miscel.)
FT-A: Health and household products

MAJOR ACTIVITIES

Popularly known for Beecham's Pills and Powders, the Beecham Group is now more involved in prescription medicines.

Beecham spent around £80m in 1986/87 on research and development of pharmaceuticals. The division accounted for around 51% of trading profit. In 1987/88 Beecham is increasing its expenditure on pharmaceutical research and development.

In 1986/87 the more widely-known over the counter (OTC) medicines business, with brands such as Setlers, Beecham's Powders and Night Nurse, accounted for around 13% of trading profit. The remainder of the business consists of toiletries, health drinks and cosmetics.

As Beecham operates worldwide, exchange rates and the economic status of some Third World countries influence Beecham's export business. However, economic indicators in the developed world have only a small bearing on Beecham's ability to sell its high-profile branded products.

The prescription medicine business is almost immune from broad economic influences since illness, like death and taxes, is inevitable. Strict comparisons in the UK are difficult. Beecham competes with Wellcome and Glaxo on prescription medicines, and Reckitt & Colman on OTC medicines and toiletries.

FINANCIAL HISTORY

Beecham has had a chequered financial history since 1982. In the difficult period between 1983 and 1986 earnings showed very little growth. This triggered significant management change and a major divestment programme. The understanding of what happened over this period is central to Beecham's perception in the stock market by investors.

The problems of Beecham were twofold. First, Beecham had a lack of new drug launches in the early 1980s, resulting in a slowdown of profits in an already mature drug division.

Second, earnings were diluted as a result of a rights issue in 1983 to make acquisitions in the consumer products area. Subsequently these acquisitions in areas such as home improvement and cosmetics did not perform, compounding the problems of the drug division.

Recognition of a number of managerial mistakes resulted in the resignation of the chairman Ronald Halstead in late 1985. This signalled the change in direction of the Beecham Group. As acting chairman Lord Keith of Castleacre initiated a strategy to refocus on core businesses in health and personal care.

This was continued and developed by the new chairman, Robert Bauman, and managing director, John Robb. In 1986/87, 13 businesses were divested, raising £236.8m, and a drive for productivity was initiated. As a result, earnings per share rose 17% in the year ending March 1987.

Since then DAP, Beecham's US-based retail and home-improvements business, has also been sold for $123m. Beecham now has a balance sheet with no debt. The businesses that remain are almost all in the categories of health and personal care.

In 1986/87, pre-tax profits were 15.3% up at £350.4m on turnover 4.9% up at £2.730bn. On continuing businesses, pre-tax profits were 22.1% up on turnover up 23%. Gearing was down to 4.3% from 33.3% in 1985/86 as a result of the disposals. Net assets per share were 167.5p, up 7.8%.

In the half year ended 30 September 1987, pre-tax profits rose 17.6% to £181.2m on turnover 11.4% down at £1.205bn because of further disposals. Trading profits of continuing businesses were up 8.1% after increased investment in advertising and in research and development. The balance sheet was ungeared and cash flow was running at an annual rate of between £125m and £150m.

SHARE PRICE HISTORY

As at mid-1987, Beecham had underperformed the FT-A All-Share index by 50% since the beginning of 1983, a reflection of its dismal financial record to date. This underperformance had been reduced to 44% in February 1988, as the market has come to appreciate the potential of new ethical drugs in development.

Since the October share crash, when Beecham shares fell from 590p to below 350p, the shares have strongly outperformed the market.

SENIOR MANAGEMENT

Chairman Robert Bauman, a US citizen, was recruited to Beecham from Textron. He is experienced in the marketing of fast-moving consumer goods, having spent much of his career with General Foods. John Robb is managing director, appointed in 1985 after 20 years with Beecham in consumer products management.

Finance director Hugh Collum was recruited from Cadbury-Schweppes in January 1987. The newest recruit to the Beecham board is Dr Peter Jackson, personnel director, appointed in June 1987. The current board team represents a new management group. Middle management is also being developed as part of Robert Bauman's emphasis on performance and incentives.

The other executive directors are: James Pollard, chairman of Beecham Pharmaceuticals; Dr Keith Mansford, chairman of Beecham Pharmaceuticals Research Division; John Hunter,

F I V E   Y E A R   F I N A N C I A L   I N F O R M A T I O N

Year	Turnover (£m)	Pre-tax (£m)	Earnings (p)	Dividends net (p)	Dividend cover (x)	Net assets (p)	Price (p)		PER (x)		Yield (%)	
							High	Low	High	Low	High	Low
1983	1,702.4	250.4	22.9	9.0	2.5	70	412	301	26.6	16.4	4.50	2.87
1984	1,944.0	279.6	22.8	10.2	2.2	100	390	286	18.6	14.2	5.09	3.91
1985	2,289.1	299.8	23.0	11.3	2.0	65	390	283	17.6	11.9	5.70	3.92
1986	2,602.7	303.8	23.2	12.0	1.9	85	442	320	19.1	13.5	5.04	3.79
1987	2,730.0	350.0	27.1	13.0	2.1	108	587	375	22.7	13.8	4.75	2.87

chairman of Beecham Products, Europe and International; Raoul Gerber, chairman Beecham Pharmaceuticals European Division; and RP Tatman, managing director, Beecham Pharmaceuticals.

CAPITAL

Following the unpopular rights issue in 1983 which raised £190m, Beecham has not needed to raise additional capital to make acquisitions.

Beecham disposed of 13 businesses for £236.8m in 1986/87. In August 1987 it sold DAP, its US-based retail and home improvement products business, to USG Industries for $123m.

It is possible that Beecham, with its ungeared balance sheet and strong cash flow, will bid for another company or division within it. Boots and the OTC divisions of a number of companies have been mentioned. There are no declared holdings over 5%

GROUP REVIEW

Prescription medicines   The division is dominated by anti-biotics, which account for around 70% of sales. Trading profits in 1986/87 were up 14.2% to £249.6m on turnover 10.1% up at £770.3m, somewhat reduced by price cuts in Japan, against the background of good progress elsewhere.

Sales of Augmentin, Beecham's broad spectrum oral anti-biotic, rose 81% to £115m in 1986/87. The recently launched Relifex for arthritis, and Eminase for the treatment of heart attacks and blood clots, are likely to add significant incremental sales over the next few years. New pharmaceuticals for depression, Paroxetine, and heart disease will be launched in the period to 1992. This will help lessen Beecham's dependence on antibiotics.

The division did particularly well in the US in 1987. At the 1987/88 interim, prescription medicines registered sales and profits growth of 8% and 15% respectively. Augmentin continued its strong performance with sales 50% up. Sales of Amoxil, the group's largest selling antibiotic, were steady. Timentin, the injectable antibiotic, showed good growth, with sales in the US up 58%. Eminase did well in Germany, and the company hopes to receive approval soon for sales in the US and UK. Relifex did well in the UK after its March 1987 launch, but disappointed in Germany.

Over the counter medicines   Major products include Tums antacid tablets, Oxy acne treatments, Sucrets and N'Ice throat lozenges, Vivarin energy products, Beecham cold and flu products, and Germolene antiseptic cream.

Tums, Beecham's Powders and Sucrets are receiving additional promotional support with encouraging sales results. Tums is doing particularly well because it is an effective treatment for calcium deficiency. Sucrets sales were up 50% in the US in 1986/87.

A full-year contribution of £8.5m after financing and other costs from Norcliff-Thayer, a US OTC medicine business acquired in 1985, pushed divisional profits by 61% in 1986/87 to £63.6m, on turnover 48% up at £229.1m.

In the first half of 1987/88, OTC medicines profits in the US were depressed due to increased advertising expenditure and the fall of the dollar, but sales were up. Oxy registered 14% sales growth, and Tums were up 17%. Second-half sales started well.

Toiletries, drinks and other consumer products   It is in this division that most changes have come about. 1986/87 saw the disposal of Beecham soft drinks (with brands like Corona and Quosh), Roberts Consolidated Industries (which produced home improvement products), Findlater Mackie Todd and the UK Coca-Cola franchise, among others. As a result of these disposals margins have improved, and the division is much more focused on health and personal care.

In 1986/87 the UK toiletries business had its best ever year. The three Beecham toothpaste brands, Macleans, Macleans Sensitive and Aquafresh, recorded a total sales increase of 23%. Silvikrin, Body Mist, Badedas and Brylcreem all did well.

European and US brands have performed well, although profits in the US were held back by the unsuccessful launch of a cold water detergent called Delicare. Expenditure on Delicare has now been curtailed and the future looks increasingly bright.

The UK food and drinks business lost its low margin operations when the soft drinks business was sold in January 1987. A substantial part of the business was reorganised under the new name of Beecham Bovril Brands. The speciality

CHAIRMAN'S STATEMENT

'Since arriving, I have been devoting considerable time to evaluating the company and working with its management to determine our objectives and strategies for the future.

Our aim is to enhance shareholders' value and the financial and business objectives described below are believed to be the best way to achieve this:

(1) earnings per share growth superior to comparable UK and US companies.

(2) return on equity of at least 20 per cent and return on operating assets of between 35 per cent and 40 per cent.

(3) positive cash flow generation from operations for reinvestment to build the company.

We are vigorously reviewing all aspects of our businesses against these objectives and are developing the programmes and actions to achieve them.' *Robert Bauman*

brands, most of them market leaders, include Lucozade, Ribena, Horlicks, Bovril, Marmite and Ambrosia.

In 1986/87, trading profits for continuing operations were 13.3% up at £128.8m. Progress in this division continued throughout 1987. Aquafresh and Massengill in the US, and Lucozade and Ribena in the UK, showed strong growth at the 1987/88 interim.

Cosmetics Following the rationalisation and disposal programme, the cosmetics and fragrances area reported the highest rate of profits growth at 32.4% to £41.7m in 1986/87. The strongest performance continues to be achieved by the Yardley and Lenthéric businesses based in the UK. Panache became the group's biggest selling fragrance.

In Europe the Astor, Lancaster and Jil Sander brands have performed well. In the US the launch of the Adidas range has more than made up for a small decline in sales of Jovan fragrances, which may be for sale.

GEOGRAPHICAL REVIEW

If research and development (R&D) expenditure is excluded, trading profits are split UK 35%, Europe 30%, the Americas 28% and the rest of the world 7%.

Sales at 26.8% of the total in the UK, including exports from the UK manufacturing base, tend to be higher margin than in other geographical regions, reflecting the dominant position of Beecham's marketing force in its domestic market. The sales mix contains a higher proportion of OTC medicines and toiletries than other markets for the same reasons. Most of Beecham's pharmaceutical R&D budget is spent in the UK.

Share price and relative to FT-A All-Share

Although Europe accounts for the largest contribution to sales with 40.1%, margins are below average. This is typical of a UK drug company operating in Europe, which is really a series of different markets, each requiring its own dedicated marketing and administrative infrastructure.

In the Americas, with 28.3% of sales, Beecham operates in Canada and Latin America, but the group's largest presence is in the US. Here it sells prescription and OTC medicines, toiletries and cosmetics. The US is the largest pharmaceutical market in the world. It is an important target for Beecham's further expansion.

Beecham operates in all Commonwealth markets as well as Japan, Nigeria, Pakistan and Singapore. The pharmaceuticals business has been difficult, particularly in Japan, because of government-imposed price cuts, and in Third World countries where lack of hard currency reduces their ability to pay.

CORPORATE CALENDAR

Year end	31 March
Preliminary results	June
Report and accounts	June
AGM	July
Final dividend paid	August
Interim results	November
Interim dividend paid	February

DIRECTORS' HOLDINGS

	Ordinary shares		Options
	(beneficial)	(non-beneficial)	
RP Bauman	5,000	—	664,170
JW Robb	5,092	—	200,000
DI Allport	440	—	—
ARF Buxton	500	—	—
Sir Robert Clark	2,420	—	—
HR Collum	3,650	1,750	158,000
RM Gerber	440	—	75,000
JFB Hunter	8,116	—	103,000
Sir John Kingman	400	—	—
KRL Mansford	8,343	—	103,000
JD Pollard	16,069	—	163,000
J White	500	—	—

Total directors' remuneration in 1987 was £2.68m, with the chairman, who was also the highest-paid director, receiving £368,883.

PRINCIPAL SUBSIDIARIES AND RELATED COMPANIES

Beecham AG – Switzerland, Beecham Animal Health, Beecham Australia Pty Ltd, Beecham Bovril Brands, Beecham Canada Inc, Beecham Cosmetics SA – Spain, Beecham de México SA de CV – Mexico, Beecham Département Vétérinaire SA – France, Beecham Farma BV – Netherlands, Beecham Farmacéutica SA de CV – Mexico, Beecham Hellas CISA – Greece, Beecham Home Improvement Products Inc – US, Beecham Inc – US, Beecham Italia SpA (51.0%), Beecham Laboratories – US, Beecham Laboratories Inc – Canada, Beecham Laboratories Ltd – Ireland, Beecham-Lamco A/S – Denmark, Beecham Ltd – Nigeria (40.0%), Beecham (New Zealand) Ltd, Beecham of Ireland Ltd, Beecham Pakistan (Private) Ltd (60.0%) – Pakistan, Beecham Pharmaceuticals, Beecham Pharmaceuticals Pte Ltd – Singapore, Beecham Pharmaceuticals Pty Ltd – South Africa, Beecham Pharma SA – Belgium, Beecham Portuguesa Produtos Farmacêuticos e Químicos Lda – Portugal, Beecham Products – US, Beecham Products BV – Netherlands, Beecham Products Far East Sdn Bhd – Malaysia, Beecham Products France SA, Beecham Products Overseas, Beecham Research International, Beecham SA – Belgium, Beecham South Africa Pty Ltd, Beecham Toiletries and Health Care, Beecham Venezuela SA, Beecham-Wülfing GmbH & Co KG – West Germany, Beecham Yakukin KK – Japan, Bond Street Cosmetics Ltd, Bovril Canada Inc, Bovril Ltd, Dr Lo Zambeletti SpA – Italy (99.0%), Fournex NV – Belgium, Horlicks Farms & Dairies Ltd, HMM Ltd – India (40.0%), Jil Sander Cosmetics GmbH – West Germany, Juvena Produits de Beauté AG – Switzerland, Laboratories Beecham-Sévigné SA – France, Laboratoires Néolait SA – France, Laboratorios Beecham SA – Spain, Lancaster SAM – Monaco, Lenthéric Morny Ltd, Lingner + Fischer GmbH – West Germany, Margaret Astor AG – West Germany, Monteil – France, Norcliff Thayer Inc – US, Perfumeria Parera SA – Spain, Societa Italo-Britannica L Manetti-H Roberts & C per Azioni – Italy (50.0%), Yardley & Co Ltd, Yardley of London Africa Pty Ltd, Yardley of London Colombiana SA – Colombia

BRAND NAMES

Ambrosia, Amoxil, Astor, Aquafresh, Augmentin, Badedas, Bactroban, Beecham's Powders, Body Mist, Bovril, Brylcreem, Chique, Clamoxyl, Clavamox, Complamin, Delicare, Eminase, Fluxarten, Germolene, Horlicks, Jil Sander, Jovan, Juvena, Lace, Lancaster, Lenthéric, Lucozade, Macleans, Macleans Sensitive, Marmite, Monteil, Neutro Robers, N'Ice, Norval, Odol, Oxy, Panache, Paroxetine, Parera, Pure Silk, Relifex, Ribena, Silvikrin, Sucrets, Synulox, Timentin, Tums, UHU, Vitabath, Vivarin, Vosene, White Satin, Williams Sport, Yardley, Yardley Black Label, Yardley Gold

CONTACTS AND FURTHER INFORMATION

Corporate communications department, Beecham Group p.l.c., Beecham House, Brentford, Middlesex, TW8 9BD. Tel: 01-560 5151.

BLUE CIRCLE INDUSTRIES PLC

GENERAL INFORMATION

Head office	Portland House, Stag Place, London SW1E 5BJ. Tel: 01-828 3456
Directors	Sir John Milne (chairman), D Poole (chief executive), J Bourdeaux – US, A Jackson OBE, J Loudon, J McColgan, D Simpson, M Spurr. *Non-exec* R Broadley, A Caldecott, D Hubbard, The Hon Geoffrey Wilson
Advisers	Baring Brothers & Co Ltd
Auditors	Pannell Kerr Forster
Registrars	National Westminster Bank Registrar's Department
Brokers	Hoare Govett Ltd
Solicitors	Slaughter and May

GENERAL FINANCIAL INFORMATION

Market capitalisation	£1.112bn at 1 January 1988
Capital structure	
Issued ordinary shares (£1)	258.81m.
Issued preference shares (£1)	0.30m 3.85% CP
Warrants	None
Convertibles	£60m 6.875% ESC 2002 (convertible at 232.558 per £1,000 bond)
	£75m 7.625% CUL 2010 (convertible at 25.974 per £100 stock)
Traded options	Yes
ADRs	None
Shareholders over 5%	None

FT CATEGORY

FT: Building, timber, roads
FT-A: Building materials

MAJOR ACTIVITIES

Blue Circle is the largest UK cement producer. It has diversified into other building materials such as bricks and ceramic products. New management has disposed of a number of overseas cement businesses in favour of acquisitions related to its core activities in the UK and the US.

Blue Circle derives most of its sales and profits from the supply of cement. Cement manufacture is a capital- and energy-intensive process. Because of the high bulk and low value nature of cement, distribution costs determine the localised nature of production.

The decline in demand in developed countries, and the general rise in production and energy costs since 1973, have forced modernisation and cost reductions in order to maintain profitability. The UK is still the most significant market. Blue Circle supplies around 7.8m tonnes annually to give it a market share of 55%, down from 60%.

Cement sales volumes have been stable for several years. The 53-year-old Common Price Marketing Agreement, which did not allow cement price competition, was disbanded in the UK in late 1986, after market assaults by subsidised Greek cement. Subsequently price levels have fallen.

Blue Circle has countered the downturn in UK demand by geographical development and diversification. In the 1960s and 1970s this was achieved by the organic growth of subsidiaries and associates in the Third World. Since 1982 there have been major acquisitions in the US. Less robust subsidiaries in Australia, New Zealand and Spain have been sold.

Through Armitage Shanks, Blue Circle is the leading supplier of bathroom fittings. Its sales and profits are making an increasing contribution to the group. Blue Circle has an increasing interest in the property development of its exhausted quarries and closed manufacturing plants. Property is generating a higher percentage of the group's sales and profits.

The group added to its US operations in July 1987 by the $35m acquisition of Raia, a New Jersey aggregates and ready-mixed concrete producer. Raia will not immediately boost UK profits, but has great potential when integrated with Blue Circle Atlantic and Williams Bros.

Blue Circle acquired the kitchen furniture businesses of Wrighton and Elizabeth Ann in November 1987, followed shortly after by the acquisition of Ockley Brick for £73m. In December 1987 Blue Circle failed in its bid for Birmid Qualcast by the narrowest of margins and retains a 44% stake.

FINANCIAL HISTORY

Turnover stood at £1.068bn in 1987, 2.6% down on the previous period, and 10.3% down over five years.

Increased capital expenditure in the UK between 1982 and 1987 has created 12 efficient cement plants which could still further improve profit margins.

In 1987 overseas interests in Australia, New Zealand and Spain were sold to reduce borrowings and provide the cash for new developments.

Pre-tax profits were £155m in 1987, 22% ahead on the year and 50.7% up over five years. Extraordinary profits of £71.2m were achieved. There was a £6.7m pension contributions holiday. Earnings per share increased 24.5% in 1987, continuing a recovery which started in 1985 after three years in decline. This upturn is partly due to a falling tax charge of under 20%, as a result of capital allowances and lower tax rates in some overseas countries, and partly due to substantial reductions in costs.

Dividend growth has improved with an increase of almost 10.5% from 21p to 23p in 1986, followed by a 30.4% increase to 15p in 1987, after growth of less than 5% since 1982.

The balance sheet is still improving, with gearing in 1987 falling from 42.2% to 15.6%, partly due to the foreign disposals and to the £60m convertible Eurobond issue in May 1987. There was a further £75m convertible preference share issue in December 1987.

Blue Circle is susceptible to exchange rate fluctuations because of its exposure to the dollar.

SHARE PRICE HISTORY

From the beginning of 1982 to 1985 the share price declined in both relative and absolute terms. The shares fell from around 280p to below 200p. In relative terms the fall was from 80% to 40% of the FT-A All-Share index.

From the second half of 1986 to mid-1987 Blue Circle stock doubled in price from 255p to 550p, acknowledging management's response to numerous problems. Compared to the market the price improved from 38% to 44% in relative terms.

In the October 1987 crash the shares fell from 516p to below 290p. A December 1987 dawn raid by a mystery buyer led to the shares shooting up to 480p, before consolidating around the 430p level in early March 1988.

SENIOR MANAGEMENT

Sir John Milne is chairman. Sir John was joint managing director until June 1987 and has been with the company for 39 years. David Poole is chief executive, having also been with the group for many years, during which time he was the architect of the group's entry into the US.

The managing team is relatively new, but collectively very experienced. John Bourdeaux is president of Blue Circle in the US, having joined from the acquisition of the Martin Marietta cement interests. James Loudon was recently appointed group finance director after handling similar tasks in the US subsidiary.

CAPITAL

In a one for one scrip issue Blue Circle capitalised its share premium account at the end of 1986. There are now 258.2m shares in issue. Businesses have largely been acquired for cash. There is potential dilution on the conversion of the preference share and Eurobond convertible issues.

No director has a significant shareholding and there is no declarable shareholding of 5% or more in the group. Towards the end of 1986 a subsidiary of The Adelaide Ship Company of Australia did build and declare a 10% stake, but this was subsequently disposed of via institutions.

GROUP REVIEW

Cement and allied products This division dominates the group's turnover and operating profit. The UK is the largest contributor followed closely by the US. Demand is governed almost entirely by the level of building activity. Another factor is the durability of construction goods, resulting in the postponement of projects in favour of more urgent priorities such as updating plant and machinery. There is also a shift away from new construction work towards repair and maintenance of existing building stock.

In common with other European countries, the British and Irish cement industries are highly concentrated as a result of the capital intensity of the business. Selling price is not a major determinant of demand. Cement plays a small part in overall construction costs, especially in relation to the cost of credit. Imports constrain domestic cement prices, which have risen little in the past five years, and actually fell in 1987.

Competition is also likely from substitutes with properties similar to cement, especially from fly ash. The profitability of the cement industry may improve if these substitutes can be distributed together with existing products. Blue Circle already participates in this market in the US.

Concentration within the ready-mixed concrete industry continues to increase, but price competition continues to be severe despite rumours of price-fixing agreements. Low margins are the rule.

Blue Circle will continue to replace obsolete and fuel-inefficient plant, albeit at a slower rate. No capacity expansion is planned now that supply and demand is in balance.

The steady prospects in home construction markets mean that most of the cement makers are continuing to focus on improved efficiency at home and on opportunities overseas, particularly in the US.

UK cement In 1987 operating profit at £45.6m was 58.3% ahead of 1986, buoyed by lower costs and increased efficiency. The group has been able to avoid price increases recently as it has negotiated lower fuel prices and also improved efficiency to increase margins. New integrated working systems, already in place at the Cauldon and Dunbar plants, are nearly complete in all 12 UK plants as part of a four year modernisation programme.

Blue Circle continues to market the Phoenix brand, an ordinary Portland cement and pulverised fuel ash mix. Besides cement, the group also produces London stock bricks in its Sittingbourne plant. The acquisition of Ockley Brick, a Surrey-based brickmaker, for £73m further expands capacity and improves reserves to 200 years. Blue Circle is strategically well placed to increase its share of the south-east market.

The company also markets a range of industrial minerals besides having patents on the Clariflow water filter process for sewage disposal works.

CHAIRMAN'S STATEMENT

'The cement industry worldwide has over the last few years been facing many problems, in particular that of excess capacity in many parts of the globe. One has seen in other industries such as steel, ship building, vehicle and textile manufacture, that in certain cases this over-capacity has brought about a very severe crisis which has necessitated government funds to find a solution to the industry's problems. This has not occurred on the same scale in the cement industry and owes a great deal to the correctness of investment decisions which have been taken in conjunction with rationalisation of the industry in many parts of the free world. This is a process which I have seen accelerating in the last two years and there are good reasons why the industry can look forward to more prosperous times in the future.' *John D Milne*

Home products In 1987 the division contributed 7.2% of the group's operating profit. Operating profit at £12.3m was 17.1% up on 1986.

Armitage Shanks has completed a five year investment programme to improve production and distribution of its well-known bathroom fittings. This autonomous subsidiary has over 30% of the UK market and has some overseas interests including a plant in the US.

Pressure is being put on margins from low quality Third World imports whilst some export markets are worsening. The Wrighton and Elizabeth Ann kitchen furnishing and fitting businesses were bought for £5m in late 1987 to offer new opportunities for growth in the home fittings market. Birmid Qualcast was identified as an ideal home products group for Blue Circle to acquire, but the bid narrowly failed.

Property In 1987 the division contributed 9.8% of the group's operating profit. Operating profit at £16.7m was 96% ahead of 1986.

Substantial landholdings are available to the group as old works are closed or quarries are exhausted. Several housing,

FIVE YEAR FINANCIAL INFORMATION

Year	Turnover (£m)	Pre-tax (£m)	Earnings (p)	Dividends net (p)	Dividend cover (x)	Net assets (p)	Price (p) High	Price (p) Low	PER (x) High	PER (x) Low	Yield (%) High	Yield (%) Low
1983	906.5	109.5	31.1	9.5	3.3	404	242	192	15.5	6.6	6.53	5.18
1984	870.3	113.2	31.0	10.0	3.1	427	248	179	11.8	8.8	7.58	5.48
1985	947.2	116.9	33.8	10.5	3.2	335	302	234	12.8	8.0	5.80	4.74
1986	1,098.0	127.0	38.4	11.5	3.3	335	358	263	13.1	8.5	5.53	3.99
1987	1,068.7	155.0	47.7	15.0	3.2	352	563	293	18.7	8.1	6.31	2.80

retail, light industrial and leisure sites are being developed, and will contribute to profits for some years.

Two current projects are the Sundon Springs shopping and leisure complex in Bedfordshire and the Blue Water Park in Kent, due to be completed in 1994 and 1991 respectively.

The group is developing an international ferry freight terminal on land at Dartford. Commercial sailings started in mid-1986. Its biggest housing project is the Chafford Hundred development at Grays in Essex.

US Blue Circle has built a considerable US base in the four years between 1983 and 1987. Recent acquisitions have shown its intention of becoming a major player in the US where demand in certain regions is growing rapidly though there is great pressure on margins. In 1987 operating profit fell substantially because of difficult trading conditions and dollar weakness.

Blue Circle Atlantic produces Portland cement at Ravenna on the Hudson River and serves the entire eastern seaboard by barge. Slag cement is produced from a smaller plant in Maryland. Atlantic Cement was acquired by Blue Circle from Newmont Mining in May 1985 for $145m.

Williams Bros is a more diverse building materials supplier, selling ready-mixed concrete from its Georgia base. It is expanding its retail chain of lumber stores. Williams Bros was the second major US acquisition by Blue Circle in 1985 at a cost of $90m.

The acquisition of Williams Bros amounts to vertical integration, providing outlets for Blue Circle's cement. Raia now offers a source of aggregates and ready-mixed cement in New Jersey.

Blue Circle believes that price levels will recover, improving US profitability in the second half of 1988. In 1987 US operations contributed £35.9m of operating profit, 27.3% down on 1986.

Mexico and South America Empresas Tolteca, the group's related company in Mexico, is the largest cement producer in the group outside the UK and the US. In 1986 it sold 4.3m tonnes of cement from its eight manufacturing plants. It also has substantial ready-mixed concrete operations. In Chile the group owns Cemento Melon, one of the two major cement producers. In 1987 these businesses contributed £30.4m of operating profit, 18.3% ahead of 1986.

Asia, Australasia and other interests Malayan Cement acts as a holding company for both Malaysia and Singapore. A sharp decline in profitability is being caused by the collapse of the cement market in Singapore due to an open market policy and a sharp fall in construction activity.

In February 1987 Blue Circle Southern Cement of Australia was sold for £117m. In May 1987 the majority interest in

Golden Bay Cement Company of New Zealand was sold for £23m.

In 1986 these operations contributed £26.1m of operating profit, though after disposals this was down to £8.4m in 1987.
Africa The group has interests in South Africa, Nigeria, Kenya and Zimbabwe.

The South African operation is now a 42%-owned associate after the acquisition for shares of D&H Materials. The acquisition has broadened the operating profile from cement manufacture into concrete and building materials with an important engineering operation retained in Hubert Davies to serve the mining sector.

Nigeria has seen demand for indigenous cement remain good but the lack of hard currency has cut imports of cement to a very low level.

The Zimbabwean and Kenyan operations have both been problematic in the recent past. This has centred around low levels of economic activity in their localities, a shortage of hard currency for spare parts and price controls. Kenya has also seen its export market in the Middle East become fiercely competitive as construction activity slowed and other exporters entered the market.

In 1987 these operations contributed £16.1m of operating profit, 25.8% up on 1986.

GEOGRAPHICAL REVIEW

In 1987 the UK accounted for 46.6% (30.6%) of operating profit, the US 21.1% (22.4%), Mexico 12.2% (11%), South America 6.9% (7.6%), Australasia 2% (12.8%) and the rest of the world 2.9% (4.6%).

CORPORATE CALENDAR

Year end	31 December
Preliminary results	March
Report and accounts	April
AGM	May
Final dividend paid	July
Interim results	August
Interim dividend paid	October

DIRECTORS' HOLDINGS

	Fully paid	Other (incl. options)
Sir John Milne	75,200	—
DAR Poole	10,318	87,668
JW Bourdeaux	2,000	—
R Broadley	2,000	25,000
JA Caldecott	2,400	—
RDC Hubbard	2,000	—
AJ Jackson OBE	32,050	20,088
JRH Loudon	1,364	63,000
JW McColgan	976	65,072
JK Shepherd	1,570	29,702
DA Simpson	7,400	1,796
AMM Spurr	12,720	18,884
Hon GH Wilson	2,000	—

Total directors' remuneration in 1986 was £1.022m, with the chairman, who was also the highest-paid director, receiving £124,403.

PRINCIPAL SUBSIDIARIES AND RELATED COMPANIES

Armitage Monobond Ltd, Armitage Shanks (Ireland) Ltd – Republic of Ireland, Armitage Shanks (South Africa) (Pty) Ltd – South Africa (58%), Armitage Shanks Group Ltd, Armitage Shanks Kilgore Inc – US, Armitage Shanks Ltd, Armitage Shanks Malaysia Sdn Berhad – Malaysia (55%), Armitage Shanks NC Inc – US, Ashaka Cement Company Ltd – Nigeria (32%), Associated International Cement Ltd, Associated Pan Malaysia Cement Sdn Berhad – Malaysia (29%), Bamburi Portland Cement Company Ltd – Kenya (37%), Beddington Commercial Motors Ltd, Blue Circle

Share price and relative to FT-A All-Share

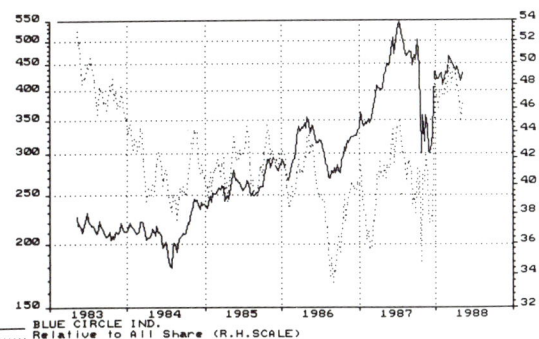

Atlantic Inc – US, Blue Circle Ltd – South Africa (42%), Blue Circle Property Holdings Ltd, BlueCem AG – Switzerland (50%), Cement Marketing Company (Singapore) Pte Ltd – Singapore (59%), Cemento Melon SA – Chile (97%), Circle Cement Ltd – Zimbabwe (62%), Damansara Developments Sdn Berhad – Malaysia (29%), Dartford International Ferry Terminal Ltd (50%), Davies Bros (Beebee) Ltd, Empresas Tolteca de Mexico SA – Mexico (49%), Johnson-Stewart-Johnson Mining Co Inc – US, Macnaughton Blair Ltd, Malayan Cement Sdn Berhad – Malaysia (59%), Marine Cement Ltd – Switzerland (50%), Metalair Ltd, PT Semen Andalas Indonesia – Indonesia (26%), Pan Malaysia Cement Works (Singapore) Pte Ltd – Singapore (29%), The West African Portland Cement Company Ltd – Nigeria (33%), Williams Bros Inc – US

BRAND NAMES

Armitage Shanks, Blue Circle, Elizabeth Ann, Phoenix, Wrighton

CONTACTS AND FURTHER INFORMATION

James Loudon, Blue Circle Industries PLC, Portland House, Stag Place, London SW1E 5BJ. Tel: 01-828 3456.

GENERAL INFORMATION

Head office	1 Thane Road West, Nottingham NG2 3AA. Tel: 0602-506111
Directors	RN Gunn (chairman), Sir James Blyth (chief executive), K Ackroyd FPS (managing), Dr EE Cliffe DPhil FIBiol FRSC (managing), PH Courtney FCA, AH Hawksworth TD ADC, GM Hourston FPS, TG Richardson, MF Ruddell, GR Solway, BHC Theobald. *Non-exec* AB Marshall (vice-chairman), The Rt Hon Sally Oppenheim-Barnes PC, IMG Prosser FCA, Sir Peter Reynolds CBE, DAG Sarre
Advisers	Morgan Grenfell & Co Ltd
Auditors	Peat Marwick McLintock
Registrars	National Westminster Bank Registrar's Department
Brokers	Rowe & Pitman Ltd
Solicitors	No specified adviser

GENERAL FINANCIAL INFORMATION

Market capitalisation	£2.164bn at 1 January 1988
Capital structure	
Issued ordinary shares (25p)	921m
Issued preference shares	None
Warrants	None
Convertibles	None
Traded options	Yes
ADRs	Two ordinary shares for each ADR
Shareholders over 5%	None

FT CATEGORY

FT: Industrials (miscel.)
FT-A: Stores

MAJOR ACTIVITIES

Most famous for its 1,000 high street stores, Boots operates through two principal divisions, retail and industrial. The retail division's principal activities are the sales of health and beauty products as well as a wide range of other merchandise. The industrial division is responsible for the research and development, manufacturing, and worldwide marketing of pharmaceuticals and consumer products. The business is based in the UK but enjoys wide overseas representation, especially in Europe and the US.

In 1986/87 profits divided 59% to 41% in favour of the retail division. In the first half of 1987/88 the industrial division's profits increased by 42.4%, whilst retail profits were up by just 0.7%. The balance, therefore, is moving in favour of the industrial division, now making 49% of group profits.

Key economic indicators affecting the business are personal disposable income, levels of consumer confidence, government and private healthcare spending, and foreign currency fluctuations.

On the retail side the main UK competitors are chemists and drugstores including Underwoods and Superdrug, and supermarkets. The main rivals of the industrial division include Beecham and Glaxo, and international pharmaceutical companies like Merck and Upjohn.

The group has the benefit of a very strong UK retail presence. The existing trading base has not yet been fully exploited in terms of sales and profits but recent evidence suggests a more determined management approach which holds promise for the future.

The industrial division's product portfolio had been dependent on ibuprofen which is maturing. However, the range of consumer products has been successfully expanded. In 1986 Boots acquired the Flint Division of Baxter Travenol of the US. This gave Boots its own US sales force and the successful product Synthroid for the treatment of thyroid deficiency. For the future the important heart drug Manoplax is on the horizon. If all goes well, this drug could transform the divisional profits in the 1990s.

FINANCIAL HISTORY

Group sales rose by 10% in 1986/87, to £2.35bn, to provide a five year increase of 58%. Over the period the industrial division has benefited from a decision to expand the consumer product interests in a period when the outlook for pharmaceutical business was less certain. The retail division has been subject to pressure on market share, given outside competitive activity, but the number of outlets has been rationalised to increase efficiency. Money thereby released has provided a valuable boost to cash flow and helped finance an upgrading of the remaining stores.

Since 1982 net margins have risen by 2%. An increased bias towards manufacturing has helped. There has also been a strong underlying improvement in profitability helped by increased levels of productivity. The group's pre-tax profits have more than doubled over the period.

Earnings per share rose by 4.8% in 1986/87 as the shares issued to finance the Flint acquisition were absorbed. Since 1982 a rise of 59% has been recorded. Dividends per share are showing a steady advance, with an increase of 12.7% in 1986/87, making up a five year rise of 88%. The balance sheet is ungeared, with net cash amounting to £88m as at March 1987. Capital expenditure of £100m per annum and rising is contained within cash flow, whilst working capital savings can be made given tighter stock controls.

The return on capital employed has been held at around 20%. A 1986 property revaluation showing a surplus of £326m has not been incorporated in the balance sheet, so that capital employed as shown is effectively understated.

The 1987/88 interims demonstrate the progress being achieved. There was a 15% increase in pre-tax profits to £120.1m, from £97.5m in the previous period. The industrial division's profits were up 42.4% with a strong contribution from Flint in the US. Because of overseas retail losses in Canada and France, the retail division increased its profits by only 0.7%. However, UK retail profits were up 10.7%. This was despite write-offs of £4.8m associated with development expenditure in the early trading and set-up of Childrens World.

SHARE PRICE HISTORY

In early 1988, the shares at 234p were selling 30% below their all-time peak of 336p. Compared with the stock market in total the performance since 1982 has been erratic, with the shares fluctuating between 40% and 25% of the FT-A All-Share index.

The decision to buy Flint produced a severe setback in the summer of 1986. Some temporary recovery was seen in early 1987 on the publication of encouraging news on the testing of the heart drug Manoplax. The shares, after severe underperformance because of poor earnings growth, are now off the bottom of their range at 28% of the index, reflecting the defensive qualities of the stock.

SENIOR MANAGEMENT

Robert Gunn had acted as vice-chairman and chief executive of the group from October 1983 until his appointment as chairman in October 1985. Sir James Blyth, previously managing director of Plessey, was appointed to the board in October 1987 and became chief executive immediately.

Dr Eric Cliffe is responsible for the industrial division, and Keith Ackroyd is managing director of the retail division. Peter Courtney is finance director, having been recruited from the Rank Organisation in February 1982. Non-executive directors include the Rt Hon Sally Oppenheim-Barnes, IMG Prosser, vice chairman and group managing director of Bass and Sir Peter Reynolds, chairman of Ranks Hovis MacDougall.

CAPITAL

The called-up share capital of the group at 30 September 1987 was 921m ordinary shares. 184.2m shares worth $555m were issued to acquire the Flint division of Baxter Travenol in the summer of 1986. This was felt to be expensive at the time. Clement Clarke, the opticians and ophthalmic manufacturer, was acquired for 4.8m shares and £7.2m cash. Edmund Wilkes and Curry & Paxton, retail optician chains, were subsequently acquired in 1987. There were no declared holdings over 5%.

GROUP REVIEW

UK retail A network of some 1,000 individual outlets, occupying 5m square feet of selling area, provides a dominant position within the UK chemists' goods market. The stores are one of the most frequently visited within the entire UK retail industry, particularly among female shoppers. The company enjoys an especially strong image and reputation.

Outside of a dispensing business, the product range includes medicines available without prescription, cosmetics and toiletries and, where space permits, photographic and electrical goods, records and tapes, household lines and kitchenware, health foods and appliances, and babywear. Boots has 25% of the UK toiletries market, 26% of healthcare and pharmacy, a third of the snapshot camera market, 35% of the women's make-up market and is a leading seller of portable televisions.

An increasing number of stores offer an optician's service which, together with the recently acquired Curry & Paxton, and Clement Clark and Boots Opticians – a separate chain of practices operating independently from the stores – gives the company the second largest share of the market.

F I V E Y E A R F I N A N C I A L I N F O R M A T I O N												
Year	Turnover (£m)	Pre-tax (£m)	Earnings (p)	Dividends net (p)	Dividend cover (x)	Net assets (p)	Price (p) High	Low	PER (x) High	Low	Yield (%) High	Low
1983	1,670.0	140.1	12.7	4.75	2.7	87.5	186	112	23.9	13.0	5.85	3.65
1984	1,832.8	165.1	14.4	5.50	2.6	94.3	213	143	22.6	13.8	5.99	3.55
1985	2,033.1	190.3	15.5	6.20	2.5	105.7	272	163	20.8	12.6	5.00	3.41
1986	2,126.1	210.4	18.6	7.10	2.6	113.4	286	210	21.9	12.9	4.76	3.25
1987	2,351.7	242.8	19.5	8.00	2.4	97.6	327	205	19.3	11.9	5.55	3.17

A number of initiatives have been undertaken to improve effectiveness. Management has been streamlined, stores have been refurbished, and improved layouts and methods of presentation have been introduced. Since 1984, 173 of the largest stores and 432 of the small stores have been refitted or had major initiatives introduced. Distribution systems have been tightened, electronic point of sale facilities developed, and marketing and merchandising policies strengthened, with own brands growing in importance. The number of shop within shop units is increasing. 37% of Boots The Chemists' sales are own brand products, and one-third are produced in Boots factories.

A recent diversification has begun into the childrens goods market through a specialist operation, Childrens World, operating through large superstores. Six units had been opened by December 1987 and a further three will be open by spring 1988. A total of 40 are planned to be opened within five years. The stores sell children's clothing, toys, furniture and hardware. They are designed to provide a convenient retail environment for shoppers with children.

UK retail sales for the year to 31 March 1987 were 9.4% up to £1.8bn. Trading profit, after £4.8m costs sustained in setting up Childrens World and restructuring Boots The Chemists, was up 11.4% to £124.8m. At the 1987/88 interim profits, excluding property and Childrens World, rose by 10.7%. Sales were up 11.5%, with real volume growth of 7.7%.

Share price and relative to FT-A All-Share

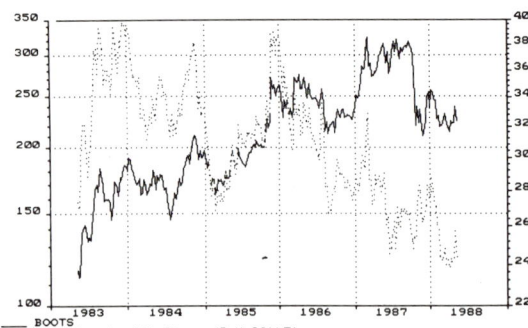

BOOTS
Relative to All Share (R.H.SCALE)

Overseas retail Chemists shops were operated in Canada until their sale in April 1988. The company has been represented there since 1977 with 180 stores trading as Boots Drugstores. A smaller operation is located in New Zealand with 14 shops trading as Boots The Chemist. Rapid expansion has occurred in France where 38 units are currently in operation under the name of Sephora, offering a range of cosmetic and beauty preparations.

Modest losses in 1986/87 deteriorated in the first half of 1987/88 to £4.3m due to poor trading in both France and Canada. The expansion of the French chain has been halted until conditions improve.

The retail division's worldwide sales for the year ended 31 March 1987 were up 9.4% to £2.01bn. Pre-tax profit was up 10.5% to £144.4m. For the six months to 30 September 1987, sales were 11.8% up to £1.00bn. Trading profit before the £5.8m surplus on property disposal was just £0.3m up at £43.0m, largely because of the overseas losses.

Industrial division The interests divide into drugs available on prescription and consumer products. The consumer products range from medicines available without prescription

CHAIRMAN'S STATEMENT

'Following the fall in world stock markets and the decline in the US dollar, the outlook is more uncertain than usual . . . following the major developments set in train last year the group is in a strong position to perform well in the changing economic circumstances.' *Robert Gunn*

to cosmetics and toiletries and other related chemists' goods products. Within the UK the most important prescription product is Brufen, an anti-rheumatic drug which is derived from the ibuprofen compound pioneered by the company and first marketed twenty-five years ago. Brufen is also available overseas under various names. Ibuprofen is now available as a painkiller without prescription in both the US and the UK under the names of Advil and Nurofen, and in other world markets. Other important brand names include Sweetex, Strepsils and Optrex and, following the acquisition of the business in 1986, Farley's.

Boots has a major presence in the US, where existing interests have been expanded following the acquisition of the Flint Division of Baxter Travenol, an established pharmaceutical company. Flint gives Boots a large sales force in the US as well as a highly successful main product in Synthroid. The contribution from Flint in the first half of 1987/88 at £18m was around 30% of the division's profits, with Synthroid's sales up 20% on increased margins.

There are important interests in West Germany, India and Pakistan, whilst a strong export business has been developed both to these and a wide range of other locations.

Increased investment has been made in research and development to find new products for the future. Particular interest surrounds the new heart drug, Manoplax, designed to combat cardiovascular difficulties and high blood pressure. If current tests prove successful this product is expected to generate significant additional sales for the company from the 1990s onwards. An important new anti-depressant, BTS 54 524, is also under test.

Turnover for the industrial division for the year ended 31 March 1987 was up 15.4% to £467.3m. Pre-tax profit was markedly up 26.9% to £84.5m. For the six months to 30 September 1987, turnover was up 15.5% to £262.8m. Pre-tax profit was up 42.3% to £57.8m, with a strong contribution from Flint.

GEOGRAPHICAL REVIEW

The Boots retail and industrial operations are based in the UK. In 1986/87 46% of industrial sales and 10% of retail sales were generated overseas.

The industrial division's overseas exposure has recently been increased by the acquisition of Flint group from Baxter Travenol in the US. Approximately 25% of the group profits are estimated to derive from overseas.

CORPORATE CALENDAR

Year end	31 March
Preliminary results	May
Report and accounts	June
AGM	July
Final dividend paid	July
Interim results	November
Interim dividend paid	January

BRITISH AEROSPACE PUBLIC LIMITED COMPANY

DIRECTORS' HOLDINGS

	Fully-paid ordinary shares	Options
K Ackroyd	18,104	120,211
EE Cliff	13,628	122,296
PH Courtney	11,794	105,879
RN Gunn	18,000	230,161
GM Hourston	12,730	94,396
AB Marshall	2,500	—
Rt Hon Sally Oppenheim-Barnes	2,149	—
IMG Prosser	1,000	—
Sir Peter Reynolds	1,500	—
TG Richardson	4,485	95,228
DAG Sarre	2,500	—
GR Solway	10,908	99,596
BHC Theobald	9,500	95,161

Total directors' remuneration for 1987 was £1.12m, of which the chairman, who was also the highest-paid director, received £163,000.

PRINCIPAL SUBSIDIARIES AND RELATED COMPANIES

Beauté, Hygiene et Soins SA – France, Boots-Celltech Diagnostics Inc – US (29.6%), Boots-Celltech Diagnostics Ltd (50.0%), Boots Co Pty Ltd – Australia, Boots Co SA – Belgium, Boots Co (Far East) Pte Ltd – Singapore, Boots Co BV – Holland, Boots Co Ltd – India (40.0%), Boots Co Ltd – Ireland, Boots Co Ltd – Kenya, Boots Co Ltd – Nigeria (40.0%), Boots Co Ltd – Pakistan (56.5%), Boots Co Inc – Philippines, Boots Co Pty Ltd – South Africa, Boots Co Ltd – Thailand, Boots Co Inc – US, Boots Drug Stores Holdings Ltd – Canada, Boots-Formenti SpA – Italy (55.0%), Boots International Ltd, Boots Laboratories Inc – US, Boots Opticians Ltd, Boots Pharmaceuticals Inc – US, Boots Puerto Rico Inc – US, Boots Pure Drug Co Ltd, Boots The Chemists Ltd, Boots The Chemists Ltd – New Zealand, Childrens World Ltd, Clement Clarke Holdings plc, Clement Clarke Inc – US, Clement Clarke International Ltd, Crookes Products Ltd, Farley Health Products Ltd, Flint Laboratories Inc – US, Hanwell Optical Co Ltd, John Weiss Ltd, Kanoldt Arzneimittel GmbH – West Germany (95.0%), Laboratoires Boots–Dacour SA – France (92.5%), Laboratorios Liade SA – Spain, Optrex Ltd, Optrex Sdn Bhd – Malaysia, OUR Boots Galenika – Yugoslavia (49.0%), Preservative Systems Ltd (50.0%), Technochemie GmbH Verfahrenstechnik – West Germany, Timothy Whites Plc, Whites Property Co Ltd

BRAND NAMES

Advil, Boots, Brufen, Childrens World, Complan, Country Born, Crookes, Esberiven, Eye Flyers, Farley's, Froben, Gluncodin, Hermesetas, Idom, Karvol, Manoplax, No 7, No 17, Nurofen, Optrex, Ostermilk, Plurivite, Prothiaden, 17, Reflex Spray, Rufen, SkinKindly, Strepsils, Sweetex, Syntaroid

CONTACTS AND FURTHER INFORMATION

Terry Steel, Director of public relations, The Boots Company PLC, 1 Thane Road West, Nottingham NG2 3AA. Tel: 0602-506111.

GENERAL INFORMATION

Head office	11 Strand, London WC2N 5JT. Tel: 01-930 1020
Directors	Professor Roland Smith (chairman), Sir Raymond Lygo KCB (chief executive), DE Bucknall, RH Evans CBE, DG Eustace FCA, BE Friend CBE, S Gillibrand, H Metcalfe OBE (deputy chief executive, operations), IR Yates (deputy chief executive, engineering). *Non-exec* Sir Kenneth Durham (deputy chairman), DO Gladwin CBE, HA Hitchcock DFC, Jack Wellings CBE, PW Wilkinson
Advisers	No specified adviser
Auditors	Peat Marwick McLintock
Registrars	Lloyds Bank Registrar's Dept
Brokers	Hoare Govett Ltd
Solicitors	Linklaters & Paines

GENERAL FINANCIAL INFORMATION

Market capitalisation	£820.9m at 1 January 1988
Capital structure	
Issued ordinary shares (50p)	250m
Issued preference shares	None
Warrants	None
Convertibles	None
Traded options	Yes
ADRs	None
Shareholders over 5%	None

FT CATEGORY

FT: Industrials (miscel.)
FT-A: Mechanical engineering

MAJOR ACTIVITIES

British Aerospace (BAe) is one of the world's major aerospace organisations. It is engaged individually or collaboratively with other aerospace companies in the design, development and manufacture of military and civil aircraft, guided missile systems, space equipment and electronic systems. Following the acquisition in 1987 of Royal Ordnance, it is also involved in the design, development and manufacture of munitions, guns, small arms and ordnance.

In 1987 military aircraft accounted for 45% of sales, guided weapons and electronics for 32%, civil aircraft 18% and space 4%. Group trading profits are largely earned half by military aircraft and half by guided weapons and electronics. Civil aircraft manufacturing is not yet profitable. Allowing for civil launch costs, which are then charged to trading profit, BAe's civil division has been losing money since 1982 at a rate equal to about a third of the total group pre-tax profit until 1987, when the group made an exceptional provision of £320m.

The group's military activities are primarily influenced by: British defence expenditure plans; those of its principal allies in Europe, Germany and Italy, with whom BAe has major collaborative ventures; and by competition for major defence contracts in non-European markets. Demand for civil aircraft is determined by the profitability of airlines, which in turn is influenced by fuel prices, traffic and economic activity, and by airframe life cycles and passenger traffic growth.

In March 1988 BAe agreed to purchase the UK government's shareholding in the Rover Group, subject to the approval of BAe's shareholders and the European Commission. The group believes that the combination of the engineering and commercial skills of an aerospace and car-manufacturing company will produce a synergistic combination.

BAe's principal aerospace competitors are the large international aerospace organisations, including Dassault and Aérospatiale of France, and Boeing, McDonnell-Douglas (with whom British Aerospace also collaborates) and General Dynamics of the US. In the UK, BAe faces limited competition from Short Brothers of Belfast, specifically in areas of light trainer aircraft and short-range ground-to-air missiles.

FINANCIAL HISTORY

In 1987 BAe announced a pre-tax loss of £159m on turnover 29.9% ahead at £4.075bn. The group made a £320m exceptional provision for anticipated currency and other losses on civil aircraft sales in the period 1988 to 1991. 1987 sales included Royal Ordnance, acquired during the year. Since 1982 sales have increased by 98%. The major increases have been in guided weapons and electronics, and in civil aircraft despite the lack of profitability.

Before exceptional items, pre-tax profits in 1987 were down 11.5% at £161m from £182m in 1986. Trading profit was static at £217m, the reduction in pre-tax profits largely being caused by the group moving from a net interest receivable position of £9m in 1986 to net interest payable of £18m in 1987. The failure of trading profit to match increased sales is largely due to conservative accounting of profits from military aircraft.

Weapons and electronic systems, helped by the contribution from Royal Ordnance, produced outstanding profits of £199m (£140m). Military aircraft were again to the fore with £155m (£146m), civil aircraft made a loss of £68m (−£8m) and space and communications activities a profit of £4m (£2m). The total order book at the 1987 year-end stood at £10.204bn (£8.600bn). Dividends in 1987 were raised to 18.7p, an increase of 7.5%.

In 1987 £210m of BAe's substantial cash resources were used to purchase Royal Ordnance. At the year-end, net liquid assets totalled £800m, the result of a large down payment on the order for 72 Tornadoes from Saudi Arabia, and the additional cash secured in 1985 from the primary share offer.

Pre-tax profit margins have risen from 4.2% in 1981 to 5.3% in 1987, the low ratio reflecting the large subcontract element of aerospace manufacture. Return on capital is somewhat below the UK industrial average, partly due to the large losses sustained on civil aviation activities, and partly due to its unusually large asset base which includes a significant number of UK airfields. Some asset disposals may be needed to

CHAIRMAN'S STATEMENT

'Despite the currency difficulties, we start 1988 in a strong trading position. In the past twelve months the Board has taken significant steps to broaden the base of the business by purchasing Royal Ordnance plc, a manufacturer of ammunition and weapon systems, for £190 million in cash, Steinheil Optronik GmbH, a specialist optics company in Germany, for £17 million and Ballast Nedam Groep NV, a large Dutch construction company with important interests in the Middle East, for $90 million, also for cash. We have established British Aerospace Enterprises Limited as a separate company to exploit related business and management activities which reflect developing technologies. We have invested in the fast growing systems and software industry through Systems Designers PLC. The order book of £10,204 million at the end of 1987 was a record.

Since the end of the year we have announced our discussions, and the subsequent conditional agreement reached, with HM Government for the proposed purchase of HM Government's shareholding in The Rover Group plc.' *Professor Roland Smith*

improve efficiency. By the end of 1989, the group expects 5,000 staff to leave, resulting in a saving of £65m in a full year.

SHARE PRICE HISTORY

In relation to the market, BAe has been a classic trading stock, the price having typically moved in a well defined band of between 50% and 75% of the FT-A All-Share index since flotation in early 1981. Short-term influences on the price have typically been announced or anticipated orders.

In 1987 optimism generated by orders gave way to fears of the adverse effect of the weak dollar on BAe's and Airbus Industrie's ability to compete with US manufacturers in the civil market. British Aerospace holds a 20% interest in Airbus Industrie.

Accordingly the share price slumped from a relative high of 65% of the All-Share index to a relative low of 28.5% at the end of 1987, the lowest it has ever been. The shares recovered sharply after consideration of the favourable effect of the likely acquisition of Rover Group.

SENIOR MANAGEMENT

Professor Roland Smith succeeded Sir Austin Pearce as chairman in August 1987. Sir Austin guided BAe through its stockmarket debut in 1981. Professor Smith is non-executive director of many industrial and financial companies. Sir Raymond Lygo, one of the UK's most respected industrialists, is chief executive.

Bernard Friend retires in May 1988 and will be succeeded as finance director by Dudley Eustace, who was recruited from British Alcan Aluminium. S Gillibrand and non-executive director PW Wilkinson joined the board in July 1987. RJ Parkhouse is divisional managing director of the new Dynamics Division.

CAPITAL

The total number of shares in issue is 250.1m. HM Government holds no shares in the company other than the special share. No other share issues have taken place. Acquisitions are being financed out of cash resources.

GROUP REVIEW

Civil aircraft 1987 sales were £753m against £762m in 1986. The principal constituents of BAe's civil aircraft range are: the BAe 146, an 80- to 112-passenger jet claimed to be the world's quietest jet airliner; its freight variant, the BAe 146-QT; the Jetstream 31, an 18- to 19-seater turboprop commuter airliner; and the BAe 125, a five- to ten-seater business jet. It is also developing the low noise, high economy ATP advanced turboprop.

BAe also manufactures the wings for the Airbus range – the A300, A310 and A320. This amounts to an average of 20% of the work involved in each aircraft. BAe is also involved in the development of the next generation of Airbuses – the A330 medium range model and the A340 long-haul, four-engined version.

In 1987 BAe delivered 56 Jetstreams, 23 146 regional airliners, 31 HS125s, 24 A300 and A310 wing sets, and 15 A320 wingsets. BAe received orders for 52 Jetstreams, 31 146s, and 27 125s. In 1987 Airbus Industrie received 114 orders for the family of Airbus airliners.

1987 also produced a commitment from TNT, the international transportation group, to purchase 72 146-QTs, BAe's

						Price (p)		PER (x)		Yield (%)	
Year	Turnover (£m)	Pre-tax (£m)	Earnings (p)	Dividends net (p)	Dividend cover (x)	Net assets (p)	High	Low	High	Low	High	Low
1983	2,300	82.3	41.1	9.10	4.5	459	241	171	13.0	10.9	7.06	4.77
1984	2,468	120.2	53.5	13.65	4.0	459	393	217	19.3	11.0	5.80	3.31
1985	2,648	150.5	56.4	15.80	3.6	474	481	295	15.0	8.5	6.61	3.94
1986	3,137	182.2	51.4	17.40	3.0	490	608	423	15.4	9.8	5.37	3.34
1987	3,096	(159.0)	(43.9)	18.70	—	470	688	280	16.7	6.2	8.76	3.36

(FIVE YEAR FINANCIAL INFORMATION)

total planned production of that model to 1992. Airbus Industrie has also received options and commitments for over 200 aircraft, including the A330 and A340 officially launched at the Paris Airshow in June 1987.

Despite these orders and the up to date product range, the division continues to make losses – £8m in 1986 and £68m in 1987. The division is not profitable when the pound moves above $1.50. Airbus accounted for £38m of the deficit. The reasons for this are: the enormous launch costs, still £42m in 1987; the development expenditure involved in civil aircraft production; the long development cycle from launch to revenues from first deliveries; and the weakness of the dollar which both favours the US competition and depresses the world market for BAe products.

The problems of a weak dollar are particularly acute for BAe because civil aircraft are priced in dollars worldwide, but BAe and its partners sustain most of their expenses in sterling or other European currencies.

Military aircraft In 1987 BAe delivered 56 Tornadoes and parts for a further 40, 10 Harriers, 40 fuselage sections for the AV8B and six Hawk trainers. These figures are in line with previous years, confirming the maturity of the Tornado programme which is turning down following the completion of production by its Italian partner to whom BAe supplies parts. The significance of the Saudi order for 72 Tornadoes is to stretch out production into the early 1990s, rather than higher annual production rates in the short term.

The AV8B programme, the US version of Harrier II, has come under pressure in the US, with a reduction of one-third of annual procurement for fiscal year 1988 compared with fiscal year 1986. However, the Indian government has contracted to purchase a third batch of Harriers and the Royal Saudi Air Force and the Swiss Military Department have placed orders for 30 and 20 Hawk aircraft respectively. BAe has continued its investment in its one-third share in the new European fighter aircraft launched in 1985. The Experimental Aircraft Programme has been adopted for Eurofighter development work.

1987 trading profit was 6.2% up at £155m on turnover 58.7% ahead at £1.854bn.

Guided weapons Fewer major orders were booked in 1987 compared with 1986, which included the British government's award of the development contract for the Rapier 2000, an advanced technology version of the successful short range air defence missile system. The development and initial production contract is worth £1bn.

In 1987 the biggest order received was for Royal Ordnance's 81mm mortar, worth $105m from the US Department of Defense.

In December 1987 BAe signed a partnership agreement to join 12 other companies under the leadership of General Electrics Electronic Systems Department to compete for the NATO Anti-Air Warfare System contract. The Naval Sea Systems Command of the US is expected to issue a request for a proposal in the immediate future.

In January 1988 BAe formed a new Dynamics Division from the combined resources of the Air Weapons, Army Weapons and the Naval and Electronic Systems Divisions. This division will have probably the widest range of missiles and defence-related products in Europe. Early in 1988, BAe received a £40m contract for the development of a lightweight Seawolf missile.

Turnover for the guided weapons division in 1987, including Royal Ordnance, was up £304m to £1.315bn and profits were up £59m to £199m on the same period in 1986.

Royal Ordnance In April 1987 BAe acquired Royal Ordnance (RO) for £190m cash and £1m worth of BAe ordinary shares. For the year ended 31 December 1986, RO reported pre-tax profits of £25m on sales of £460m. As part of the deal, the Ministry of Defence and BAe have entered into a new agreement for the supply of explosives and propellants to British forces.

Since Vickers acquired the tank factory, RO's business consists of the manufacture of ammunition, small arms, rocket motors and a range of fighting vehicles. Major rationalisation of RO is incomplete although covered by a £70m provision in the 1986 accounts. BAe's sales in 1987 included about £300m from Royal Ordnance.

Space and communications As well as being the prime contractor for Giotto, the satellite which intercepted Halley's Comet, BAe is responsible for 11 communications satellites. In 1987 BAe became the first company outside the US to win a satellite order from NATO. It is to supply it with two communications satellites worth over £100m.

The group supplied NASA with the roll-out solar arrays and the photon detector assembly for the Hubble Space Telescope in 1986, and has started design work on Space Platform, a free-flying, orbiting equipment-carrier to be operated in conjunction with NASA's planned permanently manned space station. Feasibility study work continued on the revolutionary Hotol spaceplane being developed with Rolls-Royce.

In 1987 space and communications made a profit of £4m on a reduced turnover of £175m, but this compares to a profit of

Share price and relative to FT-A All-Share

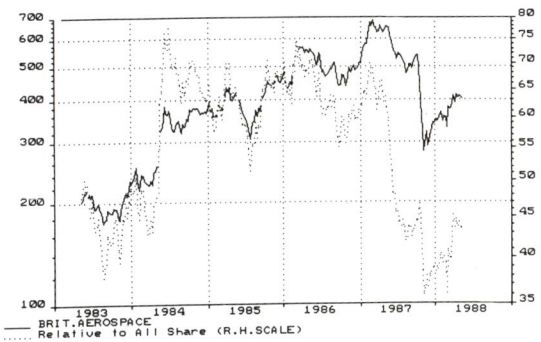

BRIT.AEROSPACE
Relative to All Share (R.H.SCALE)

£2m for the twelve months to 31 December 1986 on turnover of £196m.

British Aerospace Flying College In 1986 BAe established the British Aerospace Flying College Ltd as a wholly owned separate subsidiary. Related to this enterprise, in June 1987 BAe acquired a stake in Reflectone, the Florida-based flight simulator and training systems maker, and an option to bring its shareholding in the corporation to 51%.

Systems Designers PLC In 1986 BAe acquired a minority holding in Systems Designers to strengthen its involvement in the systems software market.

Research and development BAe spent a total of £405m on research and development. Much of this was borne by customers' contracts but the group spent £73m on private venture R&D in 1987, and has established the Sowerby Research Centre to develop the technology required for new products likely to be designed in the next five to 15 years. In 1987 the group spent £73m on company-funded development.

GEOGRAPHICAL REVIEW

In 1986 and 1987 exports accounted for around two-thirds of group sales, including Europe with 20% of total sales, the Middle East with 20%, the US and Canada with 17%, and the Far East with 5%.

The European figure includes mainly transfers of parts of aircraft to partners working on collaborative programmes, while the Middle East figure was boosted from just 7% of group sales in 1985 by the first delivery of equipment in the £5bn Saudi contract.

The US and Canada figure includes transfers of parts for the AV8B to McDonnell-Douglas, but mainly comprises sales of civil aircraft.

In general, exports to Europe and the US show relatively consistent patterns, due to the effects of long-term projects relevant to those areas, whereas the rest of the world fluctuates according to the timing and scale of aircraft and weapons deliveries.

CORPORATE CALENDAR

Year end	31 December
Preliminary results	March
Report and accounts	mid-April
AGM	May
Final dividend paid	June
Interim results	September
Interim dividend paid	November

DIRECTORS' HOLDINGS

	Ordinary shares (beneficial)	Options
Professor R Smith	500	—
Sir Austin Pearce	2,341	112,384
Sir Kenneth Durham	200	—
Sir Raymond Lygo	4,916	122,957
DE Bucknall	1,000	47,393
KM Bevins	875	—
RH Evans	333	56,574
BE Friend	3,500	70,895
S Gillibrand	—	54,386
DO Gladwin	—	—
JL Glasscock	591	49,761
CB Gough	937	—
HA Hitchcock	5,000	—
H Metcalfe	572	82,001
Sir Jack Wellings	1,250	—
PW Wilkinson	400	—
IR Yates	473	77,065

Total directors' remuneration in 1987 was £1,222,400, of which the chairman received £192,500 and the highest-paid director £210,500.

PRINCIPAL SUBSIDIARIES AND RELATED COMPANIES

Arab British Dynamics (30%), British Aerospace (Holdings) Inc – US, British Aerospace (Insurance Brokers) Ltd, British Aerospace (Insurance) Ltd, British Aerospace Australia Ltd, British Aerospace Flying College Ltd, British Scandinavian Aviation AB – Sweden, Euromissile Dynamics Group (33.3%), Panavia Aircraft GmbH – West Germany (42.5%), Reflectone Inc – US (41%), Royal Ordnance Plc, Steinhill-Lear Siegler AG, Satcom International (50%), Société Européene de Production de l'Avion ECAT SA – France (50%), Systems Designers PLC (29%)

BRAND NAMES

AALAAW, ASRAAM, ATP, AV8B, Active Sky Flash, Airbus, Alarm, BAe 125, BAe 146, Condor, EAP, EFA, Goshawk, Harrier, Harrier II, Hawk, Hawk 200, Hawk T45A, Inmarsat, Jetstream 31, Merlin, Rapier Darkfire, Rapier Laserfire, Sea Dart, Sea Eagle, Sea Harrier, Sea Skua, Sea Urchin, Seawolf, Sky Flash, Skynet, Swingfire, Tornado ADV, Tornado IDS, Towed Rapier, Tracked Rapier, Trigat, VEMS

CONTACTS AND FURTHER INFORMATION

Andrew Wrathall, Manager – City Relations, British Aerospace, 11 Strand, London WC2N 5JT. Tel: 01-930 1020.

BRITISH AIRWAYS Plc

GENERAL INFORMATION

Head office	Speedbird House, Heathrow Airport, Hounslow TW6 2JA. Tel: 01-759 5511
Directors	Lord King of Wartnaby (chairman), Sir Colin Marshall (chief executive), NGE Dunlop (chief financial officer). *Non-exec* RA Henderson (deputy chairman), BES Collins CBE, AM Davies, JW Jessop CBE, Sir Francis Kennedy CBE, HUA Lambert
Advisers	Lazard Brothers & Co Ltd
Auditors	Ernst & Whinney
Registrars	Lloyds Bank Registrar's Department
Brokers	Phillips & Drew Ltd, SG Warburg & Co Ltd
Solicitors	Linklaters & Paines

GENERAL FINANCIAL INFORMATION

Market capitalisation	£1.044bn at 1 January 1988
Capital structure	
Issued ordinary shares	720.2m
Issued preference shares	None
Warrants	None
Convertibles	None
Traded options	Yes
ADRs	10 ordinary shares per ADR
Shareholders over 5%	Mercury Asset Management 10.57%

FT CATEGORY

FT: Industrials (miscel.)
FT-A: Shipping and transport

MAJOR ACTIVITIES

British Airways (BA) is one of the world's principal airlines. Measured by the number of scheduled passengers carried, it ranks behind only the largest US domestic airlines and Japan Air Lines. It carries more scheduled passengers internationally than any other airline. The company was privatised in early 1987.

BA's principal activities are the operation of international and domestic scheduled and charter air services for the carriage of passengers and cargo. The bulk of this activity is scheduled passenger services, which accounts for approximately three-quarters of the group turnover. The cargo operation, which carries both freight and mail, is integrated with the passenger business since cargo is generally carried in the holds of aircraft flying scheduled passenger services.

The company's charter activities are principally operated by Caledonian Airways, formerly British Airtours, BA's wholly-owned subsidiary. The airline provides other services such as passenger and cargo handling, and aircraft and engine maintenance. In addition, the group's operations include certain non-airline activities, the largest of these being the sale of package holidays.

In December 1987 BA took control of British Caledonian, against a background of considerable business and political opposition.

FINANCIAL HISTORY

The airline industry is extremely profit-volatile, being sensitive to changes in passenger growth (which affect the crucial load factor) and to the oil price, because aviation fuel can constitute between 10% and 33% of an airline's operating costs. Many short-term costs are fixed and the job of management is to forecast accurately passenger growth and schedule flights accordingly. If passenger numbers fall significantly below expectations, the lack of variable costs will lead to an exaggerated impact on overall profitability.

In the year ended March 1987, BA made a pre-tax profit of £162m compared with the previous year's £195m. Turnover excluding discontinued activities was up 4.3% to £3.245bn. Earnings per share in 1986/87 were 20.5p, down from a theoretical pre-flotation 26.8p the previous year. A final dividend of 4.1p net was paid.

The downturn in profits was a consequence of the sharp fall in North Atlantic summer traffic in 1986, which stemmed from fears of terrorism in Europe and the Chernobyl explosion. Had aviation fuel prices not fallen, the downturn would have been significantly greater. The result interrupted a sequence of five years of profit improvement. As recently as 1982, the group was reporting losses in common with many other carriers.

BA's balance sheet was particularly strong for an airline at 31 March 1987. Net debt of £128m represented only 21% of shareholders' funds of £605m. This low gearing is largely the result of the availability to the industry of aircraft on an off-balance-sheet operating lease basis. The acquisition of British Caledonian will raise gearing to a level more typical of the international airline industry at around 80%.

Return on capital of 17.0% was achieved in 1987, compared with a more representative 21.6% in 1986. Higher returns achieved in earlier years reflected depleted shareholders' funds levels. During 1987, a total of over 20m passengers were carried and 41.4bn revenue passenger kilometres were recorded on scheduled services. The scheduled passenger load factor of 67.0% compared with a break-even factor of 62.0%.

For the nine months to 31 December 1987, pre-tax profits jumped to £267m compared with £178m in the previous period. Turnover was up 13.8% to £2.841bn. Earnings per share were 24.2p against 24.0p after a much increased tax charge. The number of scheduled passengers carried rose 14% to 15.2m, and scheduled revenue passenger kilometres improved to 36.6bn. The scheduled passenger load factor for the period was 6.2 points up at 73.1%.

SHARE PRICE HISTORY

British Airways' 720.2m shares were offered by the UK Government in February 1987 at a price of 125p, of which 65p was payable on application and the balance in August 1987. The partly paid shares opened near 120p and reached a peak of 178p amid pre-election euphoria in May 1987, equivalent to 238p fully paid.

After this peak the shares went into relative decline and fell sharply in the October share crash to below 120p fully paid. They subsequently recovered in both relative and absolute terms to trade in March 1988 in the range of 165p to 180p.

CHAIRMAN'S STATEMENT

'While British Airways holds an enviable place in the front rank of the world's airlines, we see a need for a much greater understanding in Britain of the scale and nature of the competition we face from United States, European and Far Eastern airlines.

If we are to maintain and increase our strength – and it is in the interest of the country and our customers, as well as of the Company that we should do so – then we *must* ensure that there are no externally imposed restrictions on our growth. We look to the future with confidence, provided we are allowed to operate in an environment of free and fair competition.' *Lord King*

SENIOR MANAGEMENT

Lord King of Wartnaby was appointed chairman of BA in 1981 and is considered responsible for ensuring privatisation by applying persistent pressure on the Government. He is also generally credited for the substantial turnaround in BA's fortunes.

Sir Colin Marshall was appointed chief executive in 1983 after a career spent largely with Avis and Hertz. Gordon Dunlop has been chief financial officer since 1982.

CAPITAL

In February 1987 the UK Government sold all 720.2m shares in the company. Some 18% of the share capital is owned by foreign nationals at February 1988.

BA bought British Caledonian in December 1987 for £250m in cash. British Caledonian was making substantial losses at the time of acquisition. BA believes that rationalisation of both operations will lead to substantial benefits.

BA has a 9.7% strategic stake in Hogg Robinson Travel, the second most important source of customers for BA after Thomas Cook.

GROUP REVIEW

Airline operations For BA to compete with the new breed of US mega-carriers, who are now eager to expand outside their deregulated homeland, it is essential that it is permitted to expand. Deregulation in Europe would remove some current capacity and pricing constraints, although progress towards a more liberalised environment is gradual.

Mergers and alliances within the European industry are now widely believed to be inevitable, in order to create strong airlines with wide route networks, which give protection against downturns in individual regions and provide passengers with a complete service from a single carrier.

In December 1987, BA won control of British Caledonian, the UK's second largest scheduled airline, for £250m. The reasons were to extend the route network, and particularly to compete in new markets like the southern states of the US and West Africa. At the same time BA announced a major worldwide marketing partnership with United Airlines, the second largest US domestic carrier.

An airline's route network is the basis of its business. The combined route network of BA and British Caledonian extends to some 165 destinations in 81 countries. The centre of the network is Heathrow Airport in London, which handles more international passengers and offers more international services than any other airport.

Most of the company's routes originate from Heathrow, but BA also operates a number of services out of London's Gatwick Airport, British Caledonian's hub, and certain regional cities in the UK. The group also operates services between West

Berlin and other West German cities. Its domestic UK services, the busiest of which are run primarily on a shuttle basis, are managed as an integral part of the company's European operations.

The fleet numbered 166 aircraft at 31 December 1987, with a further 36 on order. Of these, 16 are of the new extended-range Boeing 747-400 type, due for delivery from 1989. This order is being financed on an off-balance-sheet operating lease basis under a $2.3bn syndicated loan facility. The company's 19-strong Lockheed TriStar fleet is due for replacement, probably on an operating lease basis, in the 1990s. 11 Boeing 767s have been ordered for Super Shuttle and major European routes.

Route profitability varies widely, both over time and between the routes themselves. Apart from factors under BA's control such as the capacity offered, type of aircraft flown, and the standard of service provided, route profitability is subject to external influences such as economic and political conditions, the competitive and regulatory environment and exchange rate fluctuations. Airline tariffs and cost structures also vary from route to route with long-haul routes normally offering lower costs per available tonne kilometre than short-haul routes.

The routes to the Americas are the most significant in operating profit terms. New York is the most important US destination with two supersonic and three subsonic flights daily for most of the year. BA operates its own terminal at JFK Airport, New York.

Airline operations constitute 94.1% of BA's total turnover and produce all of the operating profit. Passenger and excess baggage traffic made up 79.4% of airline operations turnover, freight and mail 8.5%. All classes were slightly up in 1987.

BA's charter flight operation is run by Caledonian Airways, formerly British Airtours. From its base at London Gatwick, Caledonian Airways flies to holiday destinations principally within Europe. It provides transport to other tour operators as

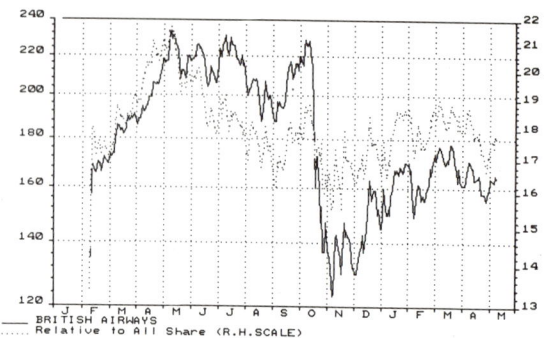

Share price and relative to FT-A All-Share

BRITISH AIRWAYS
Relative to All Share (R.H.SCALE)

F I V E Y E A R F I N A N C I A L I N F O R M A T I O N												
Year	Turnover (£m)	Pre-tax (£m)	Earnings (p)	Dividends net (p)	Dividend cover (x)	Net assets (p)	Price (p) High	Low	PER (x) High	Low	Yield (%) High	Low
1983	2,497	74	8.9	—	—	—	—	—	—	—	—	—
1984	2,514	185	25.4	—	—	17.8	—	—	—	—	—	—
1985	2,943	191	25.8	—	—	39.7	—	—	—	—	—	—
1986	3,149	195	26.8	—	—	66.6	—	—	—	—	—	—
1987	3,263	162	20.5	4.1	5.0	84.0	234	123	17.3	5.7	6.76	3.51

well as servicing its own package holidays. Group non-scheduled turnover in 1987 was down 6.6% to £141m, 4.6% of total airline operations turnover.

BA runs a substantial aircraft maintenance business and provides related services to other airlines. Turnover in 1987 was up 22% to £227m.

Inclusive tour holidays BA's two major package holiday interests are Redwing and Overseas Air Travel. Redwing was formed after a merger with Sunmed in September 1987 and includes the Sovereign, Enterprise, Flair and Martin Rooks brands. It is the fourth largest UK holiday operator. Overseas Air Travel operates the Poundstretcher and Dollarstretcher operations. BA's inclusive-tour holidays are loss-making. Pre-tax losses in 1987 were £9m.

Other BA's main business in this category is Travicom (Travel Automation Services), which promotes and provides automated multiple access booking services for the travel industry. The overall area of other activities is loss-making with a £1m pre-tax loss in 1987.

In May 1988, BA paid $113m for an 11.3% stake in Apollo, the computer reservations system of United Airlines. Together with its Galileo partners – Alitalia, KLM and Swissair – and the US airline US Air, BA is taking a 50% stake in Apollo as a step towards creating a global distribution system to make available airline, hotel and travel-related services electronically.

GEOGRAPHICAL REVIEW

In the year to 31 March 1987, Europe and the UK represented 44% of revenue and produced 32% of the airline's operating profit. The Americas generated 30% of revenue and 37% of operating profit. Australasia and the Middle and Far East accounted for 20% of total revenue and 19% of operating profit. The relatively more profitable African activities produced 6% of total revenue and 11% of operating profit.

CORPORATE CALENDAR

Year end	31 March
Preliminary results	May
Report and accounts	June
AGM	June
Final dividend paid	31 July
Interim results	November
Interim dividend paid	January

DIRECTORS' HOLDINGS

	Ordinary shares (beneficial)	Options
Lord King	30,000	—
RA Henderson	700	—
CM Marshall	25,436	224,719
NGE Dunlop	14,120	179,775
BES Collins	3,000	—
AM Davies	5,000	—
JW Jessop	3,500	—
Sir Francis Kennedy	500	—
HUA Lambert	1,000	—

Total directors' remuneration in 1987 was £364,627, of which the chairman received £52,740 and the highest-paid director received £112,288.

PRINCIPAL SUBSIDIARIES AND RELATED COMPANIES

Alta Holidays Ltd (51%), British Airways Associated Companies Ltd, British Airways Engine Overhaul Ltd, British Airways Holidays Ltd, British Airways Pension Administration Ltd, British Airways Tour Operations Ltd, British Caledonian plc, Caledonian Airways Ltd, Chartridge Centre Ltd, Martin Rooks & Co Ltd, Travel Automation Services Ltd

BRAND NAMES

British Airways, British Caledonian, Caledonian Airways, Club Europe, Club World, Concorde, Dollarstretcher, Enterprise, Poundstretcher, Sovereign, Speedbird, Super Shuttle

CONTACTS AND FURTHER INFORMATION

Graham Watts, British Airways Plc, Speedbird House, Heathrow Airport, Hounslow TW6 2JA. Tel: 01-759 5511.

BRITISH & COMMONWEALTH HOLDINGS PLC

GENERAL INFORMATION

Head office   Cayzer House, 2 & 4 St Mary Axe, London EC3A 8BP. Tel: 01-283 4343

Directors   JH Gunn (chairman), P Buckley (deputy chairman), PL Goldie (chief executive), RA Ashman (finance), C Brown, Miss MV Callaghan, CGR Cary-Elwes, RC Lacy, JFK Lee, P Myners. *Non-exec* Sir Peter Miles, Lord Cayzer (hon life president)

Advisers   Barclays de Zoete Wedd Ltd

Auditors   Deloitte Haskins & Sells

Registrars   Ravensbourne Registration Services Ltd

Brokers   Baring Brothers & Co Ltd, de Zoete & Bevan Ltd

Solicitors   Ashurst Morris Crisp, Slaughter and May

GENERAL FINANCIAL INFORMATION

Market capitalisation	£1.465bn at 1 January 1988
Capital structure	
Issued ordinary shares (10p)	324.03m
Issued preference capital (£1)	149.3m of 4.75% CP 1990–2002 (16.53 ordinary shares per £100 stock)
Warrants	None
Convertibles	£298m of 7.75% CULS 2000 (30 ordinary shares per £100 stock)
Traded options	Yes
ADRs	None
Shareholders over 5%	None

FT CATEGORY

FT: Finance, land, etc
FT-A: Other financial

MAJOR ACTIVITIES

British & Commonwealth (B&C) is a broadly diversified conglomerate which has recently been subject to a major change in corporate strategy and in management. B&C's traditions lie in the shipping industry, where it operated under the direction of the Cayzer family. Following the appointment of John Gunn as chief executive in 1986, B&C disposed of the last of its vessels.

B&C has been restructured as a major financial and commercial services group with nine core activities. Each will enjoy a high degree of operational autonomy but will be subject to strict financial controls laid down by group management.

Under the new structure, financial services comprise: moneybroking through Exco International (acquired in late 1986); forfaiting through a 40% holding in its recently floated associate London Forfaiting Company; investment management through Gartmore and Oppenheimer; professional financial services through Abaco; merchant banking through British & Commonwealth Merchant Bank; leasing through Woodchester Investments; and development capital through B&C Ventures.

The commercial and service companies, renamed Bricom, are divided into three areas of activity. These are: Bristow Helicopters and Air UK in transport and aviation services; Steel Brothers and JN Nicholls (Vimto) in the general commercial area; and Royale Resorts and B&C Leisure in the hotel and leisure sector.

FINANCIAL HISTORY

Pre-tax profits, earnings and dividends all more than doubled between 1981 and 1985. This was mainly due to a substantial increase in the contribution from the associated companies, especially Exco. However, in November 1985, a year before a bid was launched for the whole of Exco, a 21.6% shareholding was sold. A 19.8% interest in Overseas Containers was also sold in the same year.

These disposals were a major factor behind a 35% decline in group profits in 1986. At the operating level, however, there was a 23% increase due principally to the good performance of the financial service companies, especially Gartmore and Woodchester Investments. Against this, the transport operations suffered from a downturn in North Sea oil activity, profits on aircraft sales were lower than in previous years, and the result from the office equipment business reflected a difficult trading background.

In 1987 pre-tax profits were up 154% to £130.9m on turnover more than doubled at £919.7m. Because of the substantial amounts of goodwill arising on many of B&C's acquisitions (£750m at the 1987 year-end), the group decided to amortise the goodwill against the profit and loss account instead of against shareholders' funds (£450m of tangible assets at the 1987 year-end). In 1987, amortisation of goodwill reduced pre-tax profits by £14.6m. Profits will continue to be depressed over the next 25 years by this accounting treatment.

Earnings per share in 1987 increased by 22.3% after goodwill amortisation, but this rises to 52.7% if the amortisation is excluded.

Heavy losses in Kaines – the US commodity trader which is being closed – led to an extraordinary provision of £30.7m. $20m had been taken above the line in the first half against losses.

There were one-off disposal profits in B&C's development capital and investment activities arising from the realisation of B&C's historic investment portfolio.

In 1988 the disposals of Bricom and Mercantile House's wholesale broking interests are expected to produce £600m in cash.

SHARE PRICE HISTORY

Recent share price history divides into four main periods. Between mid-1982 and mid-1985 the shares moved strongly upwards from around 80p to around 370p. The share price relative to the FT-A All-Share index moved from 25% to 50%.

This rise was brought to an abrupt halt by a sharp profits downturn in 1985/86. The share price fell back to 230p within four months. Relative to the FT-A All-Share index it slumped to 30%.

The third period follows John Gunn's appointment as chief executive in October 1986 and the subsequent restructuring of the group. The shares rose from 250p to 330p in a month. By mid-1987 they had further improved to 530p.

In the fourth and most recent phase, the shares underperformed badly during the October 1987 stock market crash. By early 1988 they had recovered to 300p, but in relative terms stood at only 35% of the index.

SENIOR MANAGEMENT

John Gunn joined the group as chief executive in October 1986 and succeeded Lord Cayzer as chairman in June 1987. He was previously chairman of Exco International.

Chief executive Peter Goldie and finance director Rusty Ashman both held similar positions at Abaco Investments, the diversified financial services group which came under the B&C umbrella in February 1988. Bricom is managed by Julian Lee, Exco International by Richard Lacy, Gartmore by Paul Myners, B&C Merchant Bank by Bruce Ursell and Abaco by Cameron Brown.

FIVE YEAR FINANCIAL INFORMATION

Year	Turnover (£m)	Pre-tax (£m)	Earnings (p)	Dividends net (p)	Dividend cover (x)	Net assets (p)	Price (p) High	Price (p) Low	PER (x) High	PER (x) Low	Yield (%) High	Yield (%) Low
1983	350.3	58.5	17.0	3.5	4.9	140.0	198	118	23.7	15.4	3.35	2.19
1984	376.5	66.2	17.3	4.0	4.3	165.0	234	164	23.9	14.5	3.06	2.14
1985	402.4	76.8	19.0	5.0	3.8	235.0	338	227	30.2	13.9	2.47	1.69
1986	428.0	68.7	11.4	6.0	· 1.9	170.1	388	213	23.2	13.9	3.31	1.62
1987	919.7	145.5(a)	22.5(a)	8.0	2.8(a)	n/a	568	270	38.4	14.6	3.58	1.45

(a) before goodwill amortisation

Only Peter Buckley remains on the board as the representative of Caledonia Investments, following the reduction of its shareholding to 4.9%.

CAPITAL

A significant feature of the 1986 management changes was the declared commitment to issue B&C shares to finance acquisitions.

This policy was reflected in the issue of 105m shares against the acquisition of Exco International. A further 16m were issued against the acquisition of the minority shareholding in Steel Brothers, 60m ordinary shares and 149m preference shares against the acquisition of Mercantile House and 19m against the acquisition of Abaco Investments. In contrast, 90m shares were cancelled as a result of a reduction in the shareholding of Caledonia Investments.

More recently the group has entered the international debt markets as a means of raising additional capital. The clearest example of this is the issue of £100m 10.5% 2012 unsecured loan stock in December 1987.

No director has a significant shareholding, and that of Caledonia Investments has been reduced to a residual 4.9%.

GROUP REVIEW

Commercial and service activities   These have recently been integrated into Bricom, which has three main divisions.

The transport and air services division consists of Bristow Helicopters, Air UK, Airwork, ANC and IML, Walford Maritime, and Servisair.

Hotel and leisure activities consist of B&C Leisure, Royale Resorts, Hoteles Canarios, the Mount Nelson Hotel, Conference Holdings, and the Manor House Hotel in Castle Combe, Wiltshire.

Bricom's commercial businesses comprise: Neville & Gladstone, office equipment; Office International; Steel Brothers, engineering, construction and catering; Celltech, biotechnology products and services; and JN Nicholls (Vimto), the soft drinks manufacturer.

In February 1988, Julian Lee, Bricom's chief executive, put a management buy-out proposal to the B&C board. The bid is thought to be worth in excess of £350m. Divestment of Bricom has always been a possibility since John Gunn became chairman of B&C.

In 1987 Bricom made an operating profit of £30.5m, 17.9% of the group's total and 12.1% up on 1986.

Moneybroking   Exco International undertakes both deposit and currency broking activities. As part of a recent reorganisation, Exco's operations have been restructured mainly through the establishment of London Forfaiting as a separate subsidiary. This has enabled Exco to concentrate on the traditional core agency moneybroking business, as well as the non-agency

business of LM (Moneybrokers), Purcell Graham & Company, Eurobond broking, and Williams, Cooke, Lott and Kissack, gilt inter-dealer broking.

In April 1987 Exco acquired an 85% interest in RMJ Holdings, a leading US government securities dealer which is scheduled to open new offices in London and Tokyo.

In 1987 moneybroking made an operating profit of £44.7m, 26.2% of the group total. Comparisons with the previous period are not relevant as Exco was not part of the group.

Leasing   In August 1986 a 53% controlling interest in the Irish-based quoted leasing company Woodchester Investments was acquired.

Since then the acquisition of Hamilton Leasing has further strengthened Woodchester Investments' presence in the Irish sales and leasing market. The acquisition of Bowmaker Bank has expanded its consumer finance interests.

Woodchester took over the 25.5% shareholding in Moorgate Mercantile Holdings which was previously held by B&C. Woodchester successfully bid for the rest of Moorgate Mercantile in February 1988.

In 1987 leasing made an operating profit of £9.1m, 5.3% of the group's total and 264% up on 1986.

Forfaiting   London Forfaiting has grown rapidly over recent years and is now a leading participant both in its traditional area of non-recourse trade finance and in its securitised international lending operations. B&C's 85% interest, derived from Exco, was reduced to 40% in the successful public offer for sale of the company in February 1988.

In 1987, forfaiting made an operating profit of £16.5m, 9.7% of the group's total. Comparisons with the previous period are not relevant.

Investment management   Following the partial and incomplete break-up of Mercantile House and the subsequent retention of Oppenheimer, the US investment management business, B&C now possesses an Anglo-American fund management operation of undoubted pedigree.

Together with Gartmore, the enlarged division was esti-

Share price and relative to FT-A All-Share

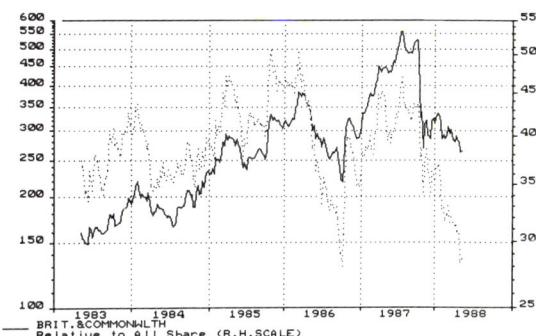

BRIT.&COMMONWEALTH
Relative to All Share (R.H.SCALE)

CHAIRMAN'S STATEMENT

'1987 represented a year of enormous change for B&C: the management of the Group, the sources of turnover and profits, and the shareholding structure have all changed almost beyond recognition. B&C is now emerging as a strong group that is capable of adapting to the fast changes that are taking place in financial services. . . .

In order to reflect more adequately the strength of the Group's balance sheet, we have decided to capitalise the goodwill arising on acquisitions of financial service subsidiaries. However, to comply with SSAP 22, we are amortising goodwill through our profit and loss account over 25 years. We do not believe that, in reality, there is any annual diminution in the value of these businesses.' *John Gunn*

mated to have approximately $9bn of funds under management at the end of 1987. This figure was reduced by just $1bn by the massive drop in share values which occurred soon after the Mercantile House takeover because of Oppenheimer's huge presence in the cash and deposit fund area.

UK pension fund assets under management more than doubled in 1986. Gartmore has been keen to expand its overseas presence, and is seeking permission to offer discretionary investment management services to Japanese institutions.

B&C sold the stockbroking arm of Mercantile House, Alexanders Laing & Cruickshank, to Crédit Lyonnais for approximately £90m in September 1987. It had intended to sell the wholesale broking division, MW Marshall and William Street Holdings, to Quadrex Holdings for £280m. In February 1988 Quadrex failed to complete the purchase. B&C is taking legal action at the same time as putting the wholesale broking division up for sale again.

In 1987 investment management made an operating profit of £14.9m, 8.7% of the group's total and 73.2% up on 1986. Part of the profits came from the realisation of B&C's historic investment portfolio and are not repeatable in the short term.

Professional financial services The group's wholly owned subsidiary, Abaco Investments, was acquired in February 1988. B&C previously held a 26% stake. The bid valued Abaco at £202m. Prior to acquisition by B&C, Abaco was expected to make pre-tax profits of around £12m in 1987. Abaco was accounted as an associate company in the 1987 results.

Abaco has grown rapidly since 1985 to become one of the largest professional financial services groups in the UK. Abaco's principal area of activity is residential estate agency, carried out through 125 branches located across southern England (all now consolidated under the Hamptons name), and commercial estate agency, including chartered surveying.

It also operates in the areas of national and international loss adjusting, bridging finance through Provincial Trust and mortgage consultancy services through John Charcol.

Banking The group's new merchant banking operations were launched in December 1987. The existing Cayzer and Banque de Rive banking subsidiaries, together with the 50.1% interest in stockbrokers Stock Beech acquired in 1986, were relaunched as British & Commonwealth Merchant Bank.

An injection of up to £100m capital has been made available, with £40m already contributed. An additional £50m is set aside for acquisitions. Initially, B&C Merchant Bank will concentrate on debt related deals, capital market transactions, corporate finance, private client management and trading in treasury-type instruments. There will be a particular emphasis on property and film financing.

In 1987 banking made an operating profit of £3.1m, 1.8% of the group's total.

Development capital B&C is expanding its development capital interests, in which it has a long history. B&C Ventures was established in October 1987 with a capital of £100m to carry out B&C's development capital activities and manage its existing portfolio.

In 1987 development capital made operating profits of £46m, 27% of the group total. Part of the gains arose from the disposal of B&C's historic investment portfolio and are not repeatable in the short term.

Property B&C intends to centralise its diverse property interests in a single division under central management with a view to enhancing capital values.

In 1987 the property division made an operating profit of £2.2m, 1.3% of the group's total. The fall of 50% was largely because of the disposal of B&C's interest in Country and New Town Properties.

GEOGRAPHICAL REVIEW

Such has been the changing structure of B&C that any geographical profit breakdown is of little significance to the group in its current form. Currently the majority of trading is UK-based and most of the 1987 profit was generated there.

The recent acquisition of Mercantile House and subsequent consolidation of Oppenheimer Fund Management will significantly increase the proportion of dollar denominated profits. However, these will remain low as a proportion of the group total.

CORPORATE CALENDAR

Year end	31 December
Preliminary results	April
Report and accounts	May
AGM	June
Final dividend paid	July
Interim results	October
Interim dividend paid	January

DIRECTORS' HOLDINGS

	Beneficial interests	Non-beneficial interests	Other (incl. options)
JH Gunn	53,000	13,500	665,000
PN Buckley	279,547	83,333	160,000
PL Goldie	—	—	638,000
CGR Cary-Elwes	40	—	122,000
The Hon CW Cayzer	6,500	—	—
HW Denman	1,100	—	145,000
NM Forster	1,100	—	150,000
DO Kinloch	—	—	178,000
RC Lacy	330,316	—	—
JFK Lee	—	—	638,000
P Myners	—	—	—
MG Wyatt	2,750	—	—

JH Gunn held £41,025 of B&C CULS as trustee, CGR Cary-Elwes held £122 of B&C CULS, RC Lacy held £1.11m of B&C CULS and MC Wyatt held £27,000 of B&C CULS.

Total directors' remuneration in 1987 was not disclosed. The chairman, who was the highest-paid director, received £988,847.

PRINCIPAL SUBSIDIARIES AND RELATED COMPANIES

Abaco Investments Plc, Air UK Ltd, Airwork Ltd, Astley & Pearce Ltd, Becorit Ltd, Bristow Helicopter Group Ltd, Bristow Helicopters Ltd, British & Commonwealth Merchant Bank Ltd, Celltech Ltd (36.0%), Christy Hunt Plc (18.5%), Continental Lime Inc – US, Exco Capital Markets Ltd, Exco International Plc, Gartmore Investment Management Ltd, Hoteles Canarios SA – Spain, International Resorts Ltd – Bermuda, JN Nichols (Vimto) Plc

BRITISH GAS plc

(34.8%), Kaines Corporation Ltd – Bermuda (23.5%), Kaines Holdings Ltd – Bermuda (49%), Leopold Joseph Holdings Plc (15.6%), London Forfaiting Company Plc (40%), Manor House Hotel (Castle Combe) Ltd, Meldrum Investment Trust Plc (75%), Moorgate Mercantile Holdings Plc, Mount Nelson Hotel Ltd, Neville & Gladstone Ltd – US (70%), Office International Ltd, Oppenheimer Fund Management Ltd, Premier Portfolio Ltd, Purcell Graham & Co Ltd, Servisair Ltd, Spinneys 1948 Ltd, Steel Brothers Holdings, Stock Beech & Co Ltd (50.1%), Williams, Cooke, Lott and Kissack Ltd, Woodchester Investments Plc (52.4%).

BRAND NAMES

Air UK, Bristow Helicopters, John Charcol, Gartmore, Hamptons, Oppenheimer

CONTACTS AND FURTHER INFORMATION

Sophie Bracher, Corporate communications, British & Commonwealth Holdings PLC, King's House, 36–37 King Street, London EC2V 8BE. Tel: 01-600 3000.

GENERAL INFORMATION

Head office	Rivermill House, 152 Grosvenor Road, London SW1V 3JL. Tel: 01-821 1444
Directors	Sir Denis Rooke CBE FRS FEng (chairman), R Evans CBE (chief executive), CW Brierley CBE, CE Donovan, J McHugh, WR Probert, A Sutcliffe. *Non-exec* RH Boissier, S Kalms, Sir Martin Jacomb, Sir Leslie Smith
Advisers	Kleinwort Benson Ltd
Auditors	Price Waterhouse
Registrars	National Westminster Bank Registrar's Department, PO Box 343, Caxton House, Redcliffe Mead Lane, Bristol BS99 7SQ. Tel: 0272-294188/306600
Brokers	Hoare Govett Ltd
Solicitors	No specified adviser

GENERAL FINANCIAL INFORMATION

Market capitalisation	£6.81bn fully paid equivalent at 1 January 1988
Capital structure	
Issued ordinary shares (25p)	4.15bn
Issued preference shares	HMG has one special rights redeemable preference £1 share
Warrants	None
Convertibles	None
Traded options	Yes
ADRs	One ADR per ten ordinary shares
Shareholders over 5%	None

FT CATEGORY

FT: Oil and gas
FT-A: Oil and gas

MAJOR ACTIVITIES

British Gas's primary activity is the purchasing, distribution and sale of natural gas. Allied to this is a gas appliance marketing operation and a customer services division.

British Gas was denationalised in December 1986. At the time the flotation was the largest UK equity offering ever, valuing British Gas at the offer price at £5.6bn.

British Gas supplies 99% of the natural gas used in the UK. It is the largest integrated gas business in the western world. Most gas sold does not originate from gas fields owned by British Gas, but from third parties. British Gas supplements these purchases by its own exploration and production activities.

British Gas has been cutting costs and improving efficiency for some years and this is likely to continue in the newly privatised structure. New growth will probably come from entrepreneurial activities in marketing and acquisitions in exploration, in addition to more modest growth in the core business.

In December 1987 British Gas signed an agreement to

CHAIRMAN'S STATEMENT

'With the benefits in the contract market from the stronger oil price and with domestic sales also doing particularly well, we have been able to increase our profitability. Apart from the difficulties in contract gas sales in the earlier part of the year, all aspects of our activities have performed well, making increased contributions to the group's profitability. Now that we are free from the constraints of public sector status we shall have the opportunity to move into new areas of activity.' *Sir Denis Rooke*

FIVE YEAR FINANCIAL INFORMATION

Year	Turnover (£m)	Pre-tax (£m)	Earnings (p)	Dividends net (p)	Dividend cover (x)	Net assets (p)	Price (p) High	Low	PER (x) High	Low	Yield (%) High	Low
1983	—	—	—	—	—	—	—	—	—	—	—	—
1984	6,395	909	—	—	—	395	—	—	—	—	—	—
1985	6,914	712	—	—	—	413	—	—	—	—	—	—
1986	7,687	782	—	—	—	452	151	135	10.8	9.7	6.78	6.08
1987	7,610	1,062	13.9	6.5	2.1	408	240	149	16.9	7.4	6.12	3.71

acquire a 51% interest in Bow Valley Industries Ltd, a Canadian independent oil and gas exploration and production company. Bow Valley has significant oil and gas interests in western Canada, in the Brae field in the North Sea, and in Indonesia.

There are no direct competitors in British Gas's principal business in the UK. It is sensitive to weather conditions and the prices of competing energy sources like oil and electricity. The closest comparison with another quoted utility company would be with British Telecom.

FINANCIAL HISTORY

Turnover in the year to March 1987 was 1% lower than the previous year, due mainly to lower sales in the contract gas market following intensive competition from cheap oil products. Nevertheless, as a result of large reductions in costs, pre-tax profits rose by 36% to £1.062bn in 1986/87. Operational efficiency gains and lower gas purchase costs were the main beneficial factors. Earnings per share rose 43% on a current cost accounting (CCA) basis, the company's preferred method of results presentation.

Comparisons with the previous year assume that the current structure of debt in the balance sheet, introduced by the government at the time of flotation, was in existence in 1986. Earlier comparisons are not meaningful, due to the control of the government over British Gas and its trading environment.

Capital gearing in 1986/87 fell to only 9% as British Gas repaid £750m of debt injected by the government on flotation. Cash generation was strong. Even after this debt repayment, payment of tax and capital expenditure, there was a £131m surplus at the 1986/87 year end.

Demand for gas in the first half of the financial year is only one-third of the annual total. On a pro-forma basis, in the first six months of 1987/88 the CCA earnings loss was reduced from £161m to £69m. This is equivalent on an historical cost basis to an improvement from a loss of £54m to a profit of £73m. Earnings per share were 1.8p compared with a loss of 1.3p. Cash and short term investments stood at £1.69bn but the end of September position is an annual peak.

SHARE PRICE HISTORY

British Gas shares have only been traded since December 1986. At their July 1987 partly-paid peak of 203p, they rose 6% faster than the total market. British Gas is in the oil and gas sector. Against the sector, they rose 8% slower. British Gas is perceived as a leading UK market stock and, as such, is less influenced by oil price considerations than other shares in the sector. This status could change as British Gas makes acquisitions in oil and gas exploration.

The shares have traded in a range of 12½% to 16% of the FT-A All-Share index. During the October 1987 crash they fell from 175p to 110p, before recovering at the year-end to around the 135p level. Regarded as a defensive stock, they outperformed the market by 15% on the way down.

SENIOR MANAGEMENT

Chairman Sir Denis Rooke has been described as one of the most accomplished engineers since Brunel. He has presided over the development and expansion of British Gas's high pressure mains system. He is a strong leader and his treatment of the investment community is blunt.

The day-to-day management of the business is the responsibility of chief executive Robert Evans, who has worked for British Gas for 31 years. Other executive members of the board include Chris Brierley, who is managing director, resources and new business, and has been with British Gas since 1970; Jim McHugh, who is managing director, production and supply, and joined the gas industry in 1946; Charles Donovan, who is managing director, personnel, and joined British Gas in 1966; Ron Probert, managing director, marketing, with 30 years' service; and Allan Sutcliffe, managing director, finance, who joined British Gas in 1970.

CAPITAL

As a public sector company, British Gas was used as a cash-generating vehicle by the Government. However, the cash remained within the assets of the company and the balance sheet remained very strong. When British Gas was floated, the Government took the opportunity to raise additional funds by injecting £2.5bn of debt into the balance sheet. This was also seen as clipping the wings of British Gas's potentially acquisitive ideas following privatisation, although the first tranche was repaid from internal cash flow.

A special share is held by the Government, which blocks any change in the Articles of Association that would remove the 15% limit on single shareholdings. This thereby prevents a takeover.

GROUP REVIEW

British Gas is a fully integrated gas supply business. It is involved in: the extraction and collection of gas; the distribution of gas across a nationwide transmission system; and the installation and servicing of the appliances that consume gas.

By far the largest and most profitable of its divisions is the gas supply operation. It is the heart of the business. The other divisions, which are largely support operations, include: installation and contracting; the marketing of appliances such as cookers, heaters and central heating; and consultancy work where British Gas sells its expertise in engineering and management to foreign countries. British Gas also has an exploration division which is seeking to add to its directly owned reserves of oil and gas.

Gas supply There are three types of gas customer. Domestic consumers are individual households in the UK. They account for approximately 60% of total gas sales. Next in importance are the industrial consumers. They account for a fluctuating proportion of gas sales, ranging from 20% to 30%. The third category is the commercial consumer, mainly shops, offices, hotels and schools. They account for a relatively steady 15% of total sales.

Charges are differentiated on the basis of the volume of supplies made. For those customers who take less than 25,000 therms per annum British Gas sets a tariff. For larger customers gas prices are individually negotiated. Tariff customers comprise individual households and about half of the commercial consumers. Industrial consumers, together with the remaining commercial consumers, make up the contract customers.

Share price and relative to FT-A All-Share

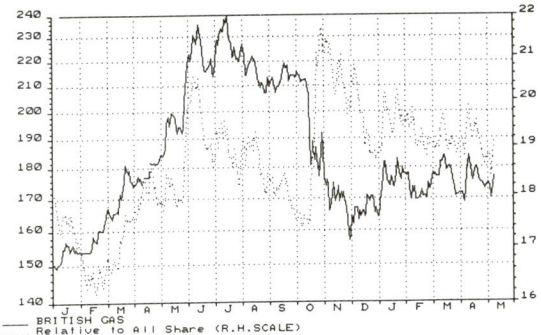

BRITISH GAS
Relative to All Share (R.H.SCALE)

Tariff sales have been relatively insensitive to the prices of competing energy sources. They continue to grow with the gradual extensions of the mains system to new households and with the conversion of other systems to gas.

Contract sales are sensitive primarily to the price of oil. In 1986/87 large numbers of industrial customers exercised their right to switch to cheaper fuel oil. Industrial sales fell 6% over the year. Tariff sales were up about 4% and reflected the very cold January conditions which occurred at a time of seasonal high consumption.

Price control exists in the tariff sector where British Gas is subject to a formula to limit the price. This is related to the costs British Gas bears in acquiring the gas it sells, and is a factor which assumes an element of continuing operational efficiency. In 1987/88 for example, the formula has actually caused a tariff cut to be introduced.

In the contract sector, competition between rival energy sources acts as a control on prices, especially in the interruptible contract sector where customers can switch off or be switched off.

Gas supply made operating profits in 1986/87 of £924m (+31.4%) on turnover of £6.967bn (−2%), 92.3% of the group total. For the seasonally weaker six months to 30 September 1987, gas supply turnover was down by £105m to £2.21bn (−4.5%), though this was entirely due to milder weather. On a CCA basis a loss of £133m improved to a loss of £22m.

Installation and contracting Essential service work tends to

be a highly seasonal activity. In order to counterbalance this, installation and contracting work has been developed. Although a long way behind gas supply in profit, this activity is the second highest profits contributor, with operating profits in 1986/87 of £28m (+154%) on turnover of £310m (+11.3%), 2.5% of the group total.

Servicing central heating has been a growth business in recent years. For the six months to 30 September 1987, installation and contracting turnover was up £11m to £149m (+8%). Operating profit was up £5m to £16m (+45.4%).

Appliance trading British Gas uses its network of almost 800 showrooms to sell a wide range of appliances as well as to collect customers' payments. Sales of central heating systems, space heaters, cookers and other appliances support wider gas use in the domestic market. It generated operating profits in 1986/87 of £19m (+58%) on turnover of £300m (+7.3%), 1.9% of the group total.

This aspect of British Gas operations could be interesting in future with its potential for other marketing and retailing activities. Turnover and profits in the first half of 1987/88 were very slightly down.

Exploration This division has been somewhat curtailed over recent years. In 1984 an extremely attractive and valuable interest in the onshore UK Wytch Farm field was disposed of under the direction of an Act of Parliament. Earlier in 1983 a selection of British Gas producing oil fields and exploration acreage in the North Sea was parcelled up and floated in the market as Enterprise Oil. British Gas received no compensation for either disposal.

The interests that remain today comprise equity shares in Leman and Indefatigable in the southern North Sea, and oil and gas fields under appraisal and development. The Morecambe gas field is in the second stage of development and is producing. Drilling is going on in the English Channel off Bournemouth and in Irish waters. British Gas is a partner in the drilling of 15 other wells, and consortia in which it is involved have been awarded two production licences under the tenth round of UK offshore licensing. A number of new UK onshore licences have also been obtained in Devon and Somerset, and Lancashire and Merseyside. The Welton oilfield, the second largest UK onshore field, opened in 1986.

About 15% of UK gas reserves are owned by British Gas but only a very small proportion of UK oil. Following the purchase of a major interest in Bow Valley of Canada in December 1987, this division is likely to be enlarged with further acquisitions.

Exploration subsidiaries in 1986/87 made profits of £23m, 2.3% of the group's total, on turnover of £189m, a turnaround from losses of £43m on turnover of £94m. For the six months to 30 September 1987, losses were reduced from £26m to £13m on turnover up from £34m to £51m (+50%).

GEOGRAPHICAL REVIEW

Apart from its consultancy service and its interests in Bow Valley Industries, British Gas has no substantial interests or business outside the UK.

CORPORATE CALENDAR

Year end	31 March
Preliminary results	June
Report and accounts	July
AGM	August
Final dividend paid	October
Interim results	November
Interim dividend paid	March

THE BRITISH PETROLEUM COMPANY p.l.c.

DIRECTORS' HOLDINGS

	Fully-paid ordinary shares	Options
Sir Denis Rooke	7,838	5,522
R Evans	7,519	5,522
CW Brierley	6,409	5,522
CE Donovan	6,813	5,522
J McHugh	6,643	5,522
WR Probert	6,026	5,522
A Sutcliffe	3,907	5,522
RH Boissier	1,800	—
Sir Martin Jacomb	2,400	—
Sir Leslie Smith	1,000	—

All interests are beneficial.

In 1987 the total directors' remuneration was £637,000, of which the chairman, who was also the highest-paid director, received £109,446.

PRINCIPAL SUBSIDIARIES AND RELATED COMPANIES

Bow Valley Industries Ltd – Canada (51% of equity but only 33% of voting rights), Gas Council (Exploration) Ltd, Hydrocarbons GB Ltd, Hydrocarbons Ireland Ltd

BRAND NAMES

British Gas

CONTACTS AND FURTHER INFORMATION

Ivan Whitting, British Gas plc, 326 High Holborn, London WC1V 7PT. Tel: 01-242 0789.

GENERAL INFORMATION

Head office	Britannic House, Moor Lane, London EC2Y 9BU. Tel: 01-920 8000
Directors	Sir Peter Walters (chairman), PG Cazalet (deputy chairman), BRR Butler OBE FEng, PJ Gillam, R Horton, R Malpas CBE FEng, DAG Simon. *Non-exec* Sir Lindsay Alexander, The Hon Sir John Baring CVO, Sir Campbell Fraser FRSE, Sir James Glover KCB MBE, CF Knight, Sir Robin Nicholson, Sir Alastair Pilkington FRS, LT Preston, P Sheehy
Advisers	No specified adviser
Auditors	Ernst & Whinney
Registrars	Registrar's Office, BP House, Third Avenue, Harlow, Essex CM19 5AG. Tel: 0279 447000
Brokers	No specified adviser
Solicitors	Linklaters & Paines

GENERAL FINANCIAL INFORMATION

Market capitalisation	£15.550bn at 1 January 1988
Capital structure	
Issued ordinary shares (25p)	5.952bn
Issued preference shares (£1)	7.0m 5.6% first CP
	5.0m 6.3% second CP
Warrants	21.48m, 12 ordinary shares or one ADS exercisable at $80
Convertibles	None
Traded options	Yes
ADSs	12 ordinary shares equals one ADS
Shareholders over 5%	Government of Kuwait Investment Office 21.8%

FT CATEGORY

FT: Oil and gas
FT-A: Oil and gas

MAJOR ACTIVITIES

BP is engaged in all aspects of the oil industry, from exploration, production and transportation to the refining and marketing of oil products. It also has major investments in minerals and other natural resources as well as other business areas such as nutrition.

BP is the largest industrial concern in the UK by revenue, the second largest in Europe and one of the largest in the world. Profits from sales of its oil and gas production, together with those from the refining and marketing of petroleum products, dominate other activities.

Though there is a partial compensation to earnings from refining and marketing when oil prices fall, reduced earnings from oil and gas production are greater in size and therefore BP benefits most from rising sterling oil prices.

After a period of rationalisation, BP is now in a growth phase, although cost-cutting is still occurring, with poorly performing assets being sold and savings being achieved in the refining area.

The strategic decision to acquire the minority interest in Standard Oil has opened the way for BP to make future US acquisitions without a conflict of interest, and fully benefit from Standard Oil's cash flow. The emphasis in the next five years will probably be on exploration and production. Among the world's major oil companies, BP will continue to be one of the most highly geared to a rising oil price.

BP acquired Britoil in February 1988 for just under £2.5bn, thereby gaining greatly enhanced oil and gas reserves, particularly in the North Sea where its own interests are declining. Britoil made pre-tax profits of £403.9m on turnover of £1.182bn in 1987.

FINANCIAL HISTORY

1987 was a better year than 1986, BP's poorest year since 1982 as a result of the oil price collapse. Turnover, not particularly meaningful as a measure for an integrated company like BP, was up 1.5% to £27.578bn.

Historical cost profits after tax rose 70.3% to £1.391bn. 1986 profits had been down 49% from £1.598bn to £817m, severely affected by stock losses of £962m from the falling oil price. 1987 historical cost profits were back to 1984 levels of £1.402bn. Replacement cost profits fell in 1987 from £1.779bn to £1.308bn. In 1986 replacement cost profits, which exclude stock holding gains and losses, benefited from the improvement in downstream margins resulting from the sharp fall in crude oil costs.

Upstream production and exploration operating profit virtually doubled to £1.998bn from £1.005bn, whilst refining and marketing profits, in a reversal of 1986, plunged 67.1% to £429m. Upstream profits were greatly helped by the reduced exploration write-off of £439m against £1.006bn in 1986.

Earnings per share in 1987 rose 67.1% to 24.9p. Dividends were increased 7.1% to 12.5p net. Capital gearing was only 32% at the end of 1987, though this increased to 40% after the Britoil takeover. Asset sales are likely in 1988 which will reduce gearing to the company's preferred 30% level.

SHARE PRICE HISTORY

From 1980 to early 1982, BP shares underperformed the FT-A All-Share index by 22%, falling from a relative of 50% to 27%. By mid-1984 they had recovered to a relative of 34%, before falling to just 24% in early 1986. Despite relative underperformance to the FT-A All-Share index, BP outperformed the oil sector by a substantial margin.

BP experienced a very strong share price rise in the 12 months to July 1987, moving from 190p to 400p, rising to a relative of 34%. In a little over a year, BP outperformed the UK equity market by 10%. This performance reflected not only the recovery in oil prices but the ongoing improvement in the image of BP in the minds of professional investors as rationalisation has improved efficiency.

The share issue by HM Government in October 1987 led to the most traumatic period in BP's share price history. The offer for sale was priced at 330p. BP shares were trading at around 360p. The first payment due on the part-paid shares was 120p. In the week after the October 19 share crash, BP's share price fell to 260p and subsequently to 240p. The part-paid shares opened at around 80p.

The issue was saved by HM Government putting a floor of 70p under the part-paid price and by the surprise intervention of the Government of Kuwait Investment Office, who quickly amassed a 21.8% stake from energetic and continuous buying of the part-paid shares. The underwriters to the issue made large losses.

In May 1988 Lord Young, the Trade and Industry secretary, ordered an investigation into the Kuwaiti stake by the Monopolies and Mergers Commission to decide whether it was against the public interest.

SENIOR MANAGEMENT

Since his appointment in 1981, chairman Sir Peter Walters has successfully overseen a major rationalisation period for the group. He has been a main board director since 1973. Peter Cazalet joined the board in 1981 and was appointed deputy chairman in 1986. Patrick Gillam is chairman of BP Coal, BP Minerals and BP Shipping. Robert Malpas is chairman of BP Chemicals and BP Ventures.

Now that Standard Oil is wholly owned by BP, Robert Horton, BP America's deputy chairman, has returned to the UK and is expected to compete with David Simon, managing director with responsibility for finance, to be the next chairman.

Britoil has its own board of directors, and the company remains based in Glasgow. John Saint, a BP employee, is chief executive. Three directors are retained from the pre-acquisition board.

CAPITAL

In March 1987 BP acquired the remaining minority interest in Standard Oil of the US for $71.50 per share and a warrant issue. If the warrants were exercised, BP's ordinary capital would be increased by 4.7%. The total consideration was approximately £4.700bn. There was a two for one scrip issue in April 1987.

In October 1987 HM Government sold its remaining 31.7% stake of 1.735bn shares at 330p per share to raise approximately £5.650bn. The company issued 458.6m new ordinary shares to raise approximately £1.450bn.

The 330p offer price is to be paid in three instalments – 120p on issue, 105p on 30 August 1988 and 105p on 27 April 1989. After a trying and troubled two week period both the Government and BP received their money, at the particular expense of the UK and US underwriters and 270,324 private investor applicants who applied for a total of 70.7m shares, 3.2% of the 2.194bn offered for sale.

In February 1988 BP successfully bid for Britoil at 500p per share in cash or one BP share plus 240p in cash. The bid valued Britoil at £2.520bn. BP successfully fought off a rival offer from Atlantic Richfield and persuaded the Government to waive its golden preference share and allow the takeover to go ahead.

GROUP REVIEW

Exploration and production BP and its subsidiary company Standard Oil are renowned in the oil industry for their ability to discover oil and gas. In recent years BP has hit the headlines in the North Sea, Alaska and China achieving great success in the North Sea and Alaska, but being disappointed in China. It has become known as the elephant hunter looking for the giant oil and gas fields that will sustain the long term reserve base. This approach contrasts with other leading companies which tend to seek a large spread of smaller prospects.

The group is the third largest holder amongst the major oil companies of proved reserves of oil and gas in the world. Its oil reserves are located primarily in Alaska and on the UK continental shelf, with further oil reserves mainly in Canada, Norway and onshore UK. Gas reserves are located primarily on the UK continental shelf, with further gas reserves in the US, Australia, New Zealand and Canada.

BP Exploration is responsible for the group's interests in oil and gas exploration, development and production – the upstream activities – and in processing and marketing natural gas.

During 1987 a substantial gas discovery was made in Papua New Guinea. Oil was discovered ten miles offshore from the existing UK Wytch Farm UK onshore field. In the Forties, Magnus and Ula fields in the North Sea and in Alaska, upward revisions of estimates have been made. At the same time 5.7

FIVE YEAR FINANCIAL INFORMATION

Year	Turnover (£m)	Pre-tax (£m)	Earnings (p)	Dividends net (p)	Dividend cover (x)	Net assets (p)	Price (p) High	Price (p) Low	PER (x) High	PER (x) Low	Yield (%) High	Yield (%) Low
1983	32,381	2,593	15.8	8.0	2.0	531	151	99	14.2	9.5	9.77	6.40
1984	37,933	3,455	25.6	10.0	2.6	636	180	131	12.9	7.6	8.46	6.35
1985	40,986	3,613	29.1	11.3	2.6	546	202	158	9.3	6.2	8.71	6.73
1986	27,171	958	14.8	12.0	1.2	549	242	173	18.6	6.1	9.34	6.59
1987	28,578	2,387	24.9	12.5	2.0	557	410	235	34.4	9.8	7.29	3.89

trillion cubic feet of Alaskan gas reserves were deleted due to uncertainty surrounding their commercial development. Oil represents around 75% and gas 25% of the group's proven reserves on an energy equivalent basis.

The group produces oil and gas in thirteen countries. The major sources of production are the Prudhoe Bay field in Alaska and the Forties and Magnus fields in the North Sea.

Crude oil production averaged 1.51m barrels per day (b/d) in 1987, compared with 1.43m b/d in 1986 and 1.40m b/d in 1982. Average gas production increased from 847m cubic feet per day (mcf/d) in 1986 to 909 mcf/d in 1987. UK oil production was down 4.1% to 464,000 b/d. Oil production represents about 90% of BP's output.

The acquisition of Britoil greatly enhances BP's production and reserves from the North Sea. Britoil's annual production in 1987 was 70m barrels of crude oil and 86.2bn cubic feet of gas. Britoil expected production of an average of 220,000 b/d for 1988 to 1993, rising to 290,000 b/d in 1994.

Before the Britoil acquisition the group expected to maintain its overall production at around current levels until 1992 with production from other developments replacing declining production from the Prudhoe Bay and Forties fields. The 1987 upward revision of recoverable reserves in the Forties field, in which BP has an 83.1% interest, was 319m barrels, equivalent to three years' output at current rates of production.

Replacement cost operating profit in 1987 was £1.998bn, 71.7% of the group's total. The 98.8% gain over 1986 reflected the improvement in crude oil prices and the reduction in exploration write-offs from £1.006bn to £439m. Turnover was 14.2% ahead at £6.970bn.

Refining and marketing BP Oil International is responsible for the supply, trading, refining and marketing of oil – the downstream activities – with the aim of providing wholesale and retail customers with crude oil, refined oil products and associated goods and services.

The group is one of the world's major traders of oil and refined products, dealing extensively in physical and futures markets. Downstream activities can, as a matter of policy, be operated independently of BP's own upstream production. The spot markets are used to reduce risk, seek cost effective supplies and take advantage of changes in margins of individual products.

BP Oil International has a network of refineries around the world which process oil produced from BP fields as well as purchased oil. Refined products such as gasoline, diesel and fuel oil are sold to industrial and domestic consumers through BP's retail outlets and a fleet of road tankers.

Having been a little slower than other major oil companies in improving the efficiency of marketing, BP has always been ahead in refining but is now on a par with most leading companies in marketing. Refining capacity has been reduced by around 20% since 1982 to take capacity utilisation up by around the same amount to approximately 80%. About half of refinery supplies come from BP's own production and half is

bought in. The group regularly sells on a significant amount to other refiners.

The group's products are sold principally under the BP brand. In the US a variety of trade names are used, including Sohio. A quarter of BP's products are represented by petrol sold through 23,000 service stations worldwide, 8,000 of which are located in the US and 10,000 in Europe.

Refined products other than petrol, the remaining three-quarters of the total, are marketed through other channels such as bulk delivery to the customer by road and rail. These products include diesel motor fuel, aviation and marine fuels, heating oils for domestic and industrial users and a wide range of automotive, industrial and marine lubrication oils and greases.

BP Shipping operates a fleet of tankers and a number of support vessels for offshore oil and gas exploration and production. It carries cargoes for third parties as well as for BP and offers services and systems to marine and onshore customers. Only one large tanker remains and the smaller bulk tanker fleet is trading profitably. BP also specialises in vessels which support offshore exploration activities and in floating production systems which enable low cost extraction of small oil accumulations.

Replacement cost operating profit was £429m in 1987, 15.4% of the group's total, and down 67.1% from 1986. Turnover was 0.2% down at £19.128bn. Unlike 1986, product prices failed to keep pace with rising crude oil prices, leading to depressed refining margins and lower retail margins, which had been exceptional in 1986.

Chemicals BP manufactures a range of chemicals based from petroleum feedstocks. From these it makes plastics, coatings and packaging materials and markets them world-wide.

Basic petrochemicals businesses have suffered from over-capacity problems, particularly in Europe. BP has therefore concentrated on developing technology to reduce production costs. This has led to a focusing on four strategic areas.

Share price and relative to FT-A All-Share

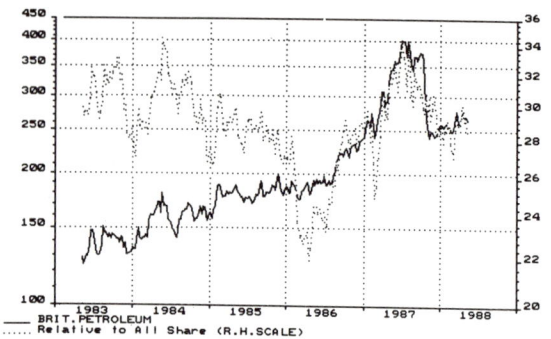

BRIT. PETROLEUM
Relative to All Share (R.H.SCALE)

Polyethylene is used in the packaging, housewares, building and construction industries. Acetyls are used in the paint, textile and adhesives industries. BP is the largest European producer of acetyls and number two in the world. Acrylonitrile is used in the synthetic fibres and rubber markets. BP licenses 90% of worldwide capacity and is the lowest cost producer. Speciality chemicals include oil and fuel additives, fire-proofing materials, coating materials for wire and cables, speciality plastics for applications such as insulation or brake linings, foamed materials for car interiors, and synthetic paper.

BP also produces and sells a range of household cleaning products. It supplies private label and unbranded lines for supermarkets across Europe. Rationalisation is expected to increase profitability. In 1987 a number of new speciality chemicals were added to BP's range. BP's presence in the advanced materials business was expanded greatly through the acquisition of HITCO, a leading US supplier of structural composites to the aerospace and defence industries.

CHAIRMAN'S STATEMENT

'1987 has been one of the most significant years in the company's history. In the second quarter, the remaining 45% of Standard Oil was acquired for approximately £4,700m. In October, in conjunction with the offer for sale by H.M. Government of its 31.5% interest in the company, BP raised approximately £1,450m by the issue of new ordinary shares. The combined offering took place during a period of extreme volatility in world stock markets....

Compared with recent years, crude oil prices remained relatively stable at around $18 per barrel, the level sought by OPEC, and were on average some $4 per barrel higher than in 1986. Downstream, the high refining margins experienced during most of 1986 were quickly eroded by product oversupply, abundant stockholdings and excess refinery capacity; in consequence the higher crude oil costs in 1987 were difficult to recover in the marketplace.' *Sir Peter Walters*

There was a general strengthening of petrochemicals markets in 1987 with a resulting improvement in sales and margins, but detergents incurred rationalisation expenses and US profits suffered on sterling translation. There was also additional depreciation and a write-off of goodwill on the acquisition of HITCO. Replacement cost operating profit at £218m, 7.8% of the group's total, was down 8.4% on turnover 12.3% up at £2.559bn.

Minerals BP mines principally for selected precious and base metals including gold, copper and uranium. In the US a major modernisation programme costing £250m is being carried out at Bingham Canyon in Utah, the world's deepest open-pit copper mine. BP, through its subsidiary QIT, is the world market leader in the supply of titanium dioxide feedstocks to the pigment industry.

The strengthening copper and gold prices, together with the build-up of production from Bingham Canyon and a benefit from asset trading, led to 1987 profits being 177.7% ahead at £125m on turnover 6.5% down at £446m.

Nutrition BP Nutrition is one of the world's largest millers of animal feed, supplements and special diets for the livestock industry; owns 112 feed mills in the US and Europe; processes meat and poultry in 18 plants in Europe; and is a major supplier of hybrid breeds of poultry, pigs and sheep from breeding farms in Europe and North America.

BP is investing heavily in this growing division, particularly in the US. Purina Mills, the largest animal feed supplier in the US, was purchased for £371m in October 1986, taking BP's total new investment in the nutrition division to £600m since 1982.

1987 operating profit was down 7.1% to £52m on turnover 35.2% up at £1.843bn. There were difficulties in the trading environment, especially in European poultry processing, and profits were hurt on translation into sterling.

Coal BP Coal's activities include the production and marketing of coal as well as the buying and selling of coal produced by third parties. Production is around 28m tonnes. BP has interests in mines in Australia, South Africa and the US. It is actively seeking opportunities for investment in low cost coal production in the US, Australia, Indonesia and Northern Ireland.

In 1987 the division turned a 1986 operating profit of £65m into a loss of £29m. Turnover was 15.0% down at £627m. The deterioration was caused by depressed coal prices, adverse exchange movements, additional depreciation and rationalisation.

Other businesses and corporate With £1.283bn of liquid resources at the end of 1987, BP's cash management is a substantial operation. Liquid resources totalled £2.529bn at the 1986 year-end, having been built up for the Standard Oil acquisition and to repay debt. For several years cash management and the provision of internal advice on project finance, debt structuring and currency management has been undertaken by an internal bank-like finance operation, called BP Finance International. It has established a first class reputation through its profitable currency and debt management.

BP Ventures identifies, develops and manages technology-based business opportunities which offer the potential to become part of the group's long term business portfolio. BP agreed to sell its Scicon computer software and systems subsidiary to Systems Designers for around £80m.

This group of businesses and central corporate costs produced an £8m loss in 1987 against an £85m loss in 1986.

GEOGRAPHICAL REVIEW

The acquisition of the remaining 45% minority holding in Standard Oil increased the significance of the US in the geographical constitution of BP's 1987 profits. The contribution of the UK and Europe was further reduced because the greater proportion of refining and marketing profits are derived from these areas and they fell severely in 1987.

In 1987 the US made up 52.7% of operating profit against 22.6% in 1986, the UK made 26.9% against 36.5%, Europe made 11.2% against 26.2% and the rest of the world made 9.3% against 13.7%.

CORPORATE CALENDAR

Year end	31 December
Preliminary results	early February
Report and accounts	end February
AGM	end April
Final dividend paid	May
First quarter result	May
Interim results	August
Interim dividend paid	November
Third quarter result	November

BRITISH TELECOMMUNICATIONS plc

DIRECTORS' HOLDINGS

	Fully paid	Other (incl. options)
Sir Lindsay Alexander	3,600	—
Lord Barber	3,771	—
Sir John Baring	13,000	—
BRR Butler	9,804	205,500
PG Cazalet	25,098	250,263
Sir Campbell Fraser	8,184	—
PJ Gillam	8,877	254,112
Sir James Glover	3,200	—
CF Knight	12,000	—
R Malpas	17,896	1,000
Sir Robin Nicholson	1,000	—
Sir Alastair Pilkington	2,565	—
DAG Simon	9,045	205,263
P Sheehy	7,014	—
Sir Peter Walters	32,326	384,000

Sir Alastair Pilkington also holds 12,000 non-beneficially as trustee.

Total directors' remuneration in 1987 was £1.705m, excluding pensions, of which the chairman, who was also the highest-paid director, received £347,212.

PRINCIPAL SUBSIDIARIES AND RELATED COMPANIES

Abu Dhabi Gas Liquefaction – Abu Dhabi (16%), Abu Dhabi Marine Areas (37%), Abu Dhabi Petroleum (24%), Alexander Duckham, BP (Oil Exploration) Company New Zealand – New Zealand, BP (Schweiz) – Switzerland, BP Africa, BP Alaska Exploration – US, BP Arabian Agencies, BP Australia – Australia, BP Austria – Austria, BP Canada – Canada (65%), BP Capital, BP Capital – Netherlands, BP Chemicals, BP Chemicals International, BP Chimie – France (87%), BP Coal, BP Developments Australia, BP España – Spain, BP Exploration – Scotland, BP France – France (79%), BP Gas International, BP Hong Kong Trading – Hong Kong, BP International, BP Ireland – Ireland, BP Japan Trading, BP Maatschappij Nederland – Netherlands, BP Malaysia – Malaysia (82%), BP Minerals International, BP Norge – Norway, BP America – US, BP Nutrition, BP of Greece, BP Oil, BP Oil International, BP Oil New Zealand – New Zealand, BP Olie-Kompagniet – Denmark, BP Petroleum Development, BP Petrolleri – Turkey, BP Pipelines – US, BP Portuguesa – Portugal, BP Shipping, BP Singapore – Singapore, BP Southern Africa – South Africa, BP Zimbabwe – Zimbabwe (50%), BPCA Finance – Australia, BPNV – Belgium (85%), Bristol Composite Materials, British Petroleum – Netherlands, Deutsche BP – Germany, Distugil – France (44%), Erdölchemie – Germany (50%), Europa Oil NZ – New Zealand, Noordzee Selection – Netherlands, Petroleum Refineries Unisel Gold Mines – South Africa (33%), Purina Mills – US, Raffinaderij Nederland Hendrix International – Netherlands, Robert McBride, Ruhrgas – Germany (25%), Shell and BP South Africa – South Africa (50%), Standard Oil – US, Svenska BP – Sweden

BRAND NAMES

BP

CONTACTS AND FURTHER INFORMATION

Peter Aslett, UK investor relations, The British Petroleum Company p.l.c., Britannic House, Moor Lane, London EC2Y 9BU. Tel: 01-920 8000. R Nash, US investor relations, BP America Inc, 200 Public Square, Cleveland, Ohio, 44114-2375. Tel: (216) 586-6077.

GENERAL INFORMATION

Head office	81 Newgate Street, London EC1A 7AJ. Tel: 01-356 5000
Directors	IDT Vallance (chairman), GDW Odgers (managing director), M Bett, AJ Booth, CAP Foxell CBE, JAC King, REG Back CBE, B Romeril. *Non-exec* JM Raisman CBE (deputy chairman), EA Ash CBE, PG Bosonnet, JF Goble, Sir David Scholey CBE, Rt Hon Norman Tebbit MP
Advisers	SG Warburg & Co Ltd
Auditors	Coopers & Lybrand
Registrars	Lloyds Bank Registrar's Department
Brokers	Cazenove & Co
Solicitor	JBK Rickford (in-house)

GENERAL FINANCIAL INFORMATION

Market capitalisation	£13.287bn at 1 January 1988
Capital structure	
Issued ordinary shares (25p)	6bn
Issued preference shares (£1)	250m 11.95% CP
	One special rights redeemable preference share issued to HM Government
Warrants	None
Convertibles	None
Traded options	Yes
ADRs	One ADR equals ten ordinary shares
Shareholders over 5%	HM Government 49.7%

FT CATEGORY

FT: Electricals
FT-A: Telephone networks

MAJOR ACTIVITIES

British Telecom (BT) is the major supplier of telecommunications for the UK, carrying both domestic and international traffic in voice telephony, data telecommunications, facsimile and telex. It also provides telecommunications equipment and directories.

BT has 4.4m business connections and 17.6m residential connections through 7,000 exchanges, 100,000 telex lines and 78,000 public payphones. It is one of the UK's largest employers with 234,400 employees and an annual turnover of £9.424bn.

An important part of BT's business is the renting of private circuits to businesses. There were over a million in use by the end of 1987. They are employed for inter-company voice and data communications and to provide group access to data information services. BT is introducing advanced fibre optic systems to service certain localities. The first of these was unveiled in the City of London in January 1988.

BT is solely responsible for the UK's ship-to-shore and emerging air-to-ground telephone service and the public call box network. BT's other value-added services include telephone news and consumer information services and a telephone-linked home security system. In partnership with Securicor, BT operates the Cellnet cellular radio-telephone network.

BT provides a wide range of business information services accessible via computer. Its Prestel network, originally intended as a mass market information service available to subscribers via their adapted television set, has developed primarily into a business network.

BT's principal foreign interests are its 51% holding in Mitel, a Canadian telecommunications equipment manufacturer, and the US arm of its newly consolidated Dialcom electronic mail and information service business.

BT is engaged in overseas consultancy and project work and the sale of communications equipment abroad. BT's foreign

F I V E   Y E A R   F I N A N C I A L   I N F O R M A T I O N

Year	Turnover (£m)	Pre-tax (£m)	Earnings (p)	Dividends net (p)	Dividend cover (x)	Net assets (p)	Price (p) High	Low	PER (x) High	Low	Yield (%) High	Low
1983	6,414	1,031	—	—	—	—	—	—	—	—	—	—
1984	6,876	990	—	—	—	—	186	130	15.7	11.0	7.14	5.01
1985	7,563	1,480	15.1	6.5	2.3	98.5	247	185	20.8	15.0	5.02	3.76
1986	8,387	1,833	17.1	7.5	2.3	118.2	278	178	17.9	10.1	5.93	3.55
1987	11,670	2,067	20.9	8.45	2.5	125.7	334	205	17.5	9.3	5.91	3.22

operations provide a very small proportion of its annual turnover and none of its profits.

The major influence of BT's business is general economic conditions which determine the rate of growth of telecommunications traffic. In addition, advancing technology provides new opportunities for adding to services and growth.

BT is beginning to meet competition for the first time. This is now emerging in all areas of activity. In equipment supply, BT competes with its suppliers – GEC, Plessey and STC – and others from overseas, such as Northern Telecom and Ericsson.

In basic telecommunications, Mercury has been licensed to compete in switched voice telephony. It started to offer a full UK service in mid-1987, with a growing list of international links. Mercury has also been given permission to compete in the payphone area. In cellular radio, BT and Cellnet face competition from Racal's Vodafone. There will be four suppliers of the new national radiopaging service, including Mercury and Racal. In computer data information services the competition includes Extel.

BT is a utility with the capability of showing very steady growth and continuing strong margins. The new technology now available in radio communications, satellite communications and fibre optics provide strong new growth markets. BT is endeavouring to become more competitive and also to broaden its geographical spread. Simply because of its sheer size this is of necessity a long term task.

FINANCIAL HISTORY

British Telecom's public flotation in November 1984 was at the time the largest ever in the UK. Since then the financial record has been one of steady progress, with sales rising at around 8% to 10% per annum in the core business of telecommunications. Call growth rates have also been steady at 6% to 8% for inland and 11% to 12% for intercontinental.

Due to its near monopoly position, BT is regulated by means of the terms of its operating licence, which is interpreted and implemented by the Office of Telecommunications, Oftel.

Apart from detailed requirements as to quality of service and on inter-connection with the operators, the most important aspect of the licence is the requirement not to raise the prices of a basket of main inland rentals and services by an amount greater than the rate of inflation less 3%. This remains in force until July 1989.

Despite this constraint BT has been able to achieve profits growth by improving its efficiency through introducing digital switching in the form mainly of System X, and also by implementing modern working methods for the workforce. Sales per BT employee rose from £28,100 in 1984 to £39,900 in 1987, and profits from £6,300 to £9,900. This improvement has also been achieved by reducing debt and interest charges and, at the level of earnings per share, by a falling tax charge.

Pre-tax profits in the year to 31 March 1987 rose 11.7% to £2.067bn on turnover 12.4% higher at £9.424bn. Earnings per share rose 20% to 20.9p in 1987 from 17.1p in 1986. Dividends were up 12.7% to 8.45p per share. Net assets were up 9% to £11.500bn.

At the 1988 interim, pre-tax profits were up 11.3% at £1.12bn on turnover up 7.4% at £4.95bn. Earnings per share at 11.5p increased by 13.1%. The interim dividend was up 11.9% to 3.35p. Recent complaints about quality of service have led to an increase in the workforce. Staff costs for the first half of 1988 increased by 6.3% but this is not expected to affect profitability.

BT's spending on fixed assets is high at £2.107bn in 1987, but even after paying tax and dividends it is largely capable of generating its requirements internally. The spending programme is heavy until 1990 as the initial modernisation of the network is undertaken. BT will always need to spend to maintain its high return on capital of 28%.

SHARE PRICE HISTORY

The shares were originally issued part-paid and with a voucher scheme to allow for reductions in domestic telephone bills. As an alternative to the voucher scheme a one for ten bonus share scheme was offered. Holders were able to take up these bonus shares in November 1987. The issue was highly successful and the shares more than doubled in the first six months after the offer for sale.

A relative peak was reached in the middle of 1985. This was followed by a period of underperformance due to political fears of a change of government, and to the growing realisation that achieving higher margins in telecommunications would take decades rather than years. The shares were very strong around the time of the 1987 election but once the Conservative government was re-elected performance was lacklustre.

After the autumn 1987 crash the shares started to outperform the market, rising from 22% to 27% of the FT-A All-Share index. In absolute terms they consolidated around the 240p level, well down from the June 1987 post-election high of 337p but only modestly down from the pre-crash level of 277p. In the long term the shares are generally expected to follow the economy and therefore the market.

SENIOR MANAGEMENT

The majority of management have grown up through the company. There are also new outsiders to provide a greater commercial impetus and in particular to improve financial records.

Iain Vallance, chief executive, took over as chairman in September 1987 after the unexpected resignation of Sir George Jefferson. Graeme Odgers became managing director and J Raisman became non-executive deputy chairman at the same time. In 1988 the company appointed a new group finance director, Barry Romeril. A group development director is to be appointed later in the year. The Rt Hon Norman Tebbit joined as a non-executive director in November 1987.

Mike Bett is the managing director of UK communications; Anthony Booth is the managing director of British Telecom International; John King is managing director of the overseas division; and John McMonigall is the managing director of the international products division.

CAPITAL

BT had 6bn ordinary shares in issue at 1 January 1988. The Government owns 49.7% and a special rights redeemable preference share. HM Government's remaining holding can be sold from 9 April 1989. ADRs for BT were listed in August 1987.

Of the £750m 11.95% redeemable cumulative preference shares originally issued to the Government, £250m were redeemed in March 1987 and a further £250m in December 1987. The Government also owns £2.592bn unsecured loan stock at rates of 12.25% to 12.75%, redeemable over the years to 2006, and a special rights preference share to ensure BT's independence.

In September 1986 the group made a $250m Eurobond issue, repayable in 1996. A dollar-sterling currency swap eliminates the foreign exchange exposure. A further $150m was issued in July 1987 and similarly hedged. BT's total indebtedness at 31 March 1987 was £2.4bn. Gearing was 27.5%.

GROUP REVIEW

During the 1987 financial year BT operations were re-organised into five trading divisions. They are UK communications, British Telecom International, overseas division, international products division and British Telecom Enterprises.

UK communications The division is responsible for running the basic domestic telephone network. Nearly 70% of BT's turnover comes from its traditional telephone business in the UK.

There has been much criticism of BT's monopoly position. The management is taking the problem seriously. The company is determined to react positively to public criticism.

The division's major task is the replacement of the old electromechanical telephone exchanges with the digital System X and AXE10. All the exchanges in BT's trunk network and some in rural areas have been replaced. London exchanges are currently being replaced by System X.

The division's other major development is the introduction of optical glass-fibre cables. In addition to increasing clarity of voice communication, optical fibre cables can carry computer data with far more versatility than wire telephone lines. They can also transmit television pictures. In January 1988 BT unveiled its £70m fibre optic business network, the Flexible Access System.

The other principal interests of the division are equipment sales, the payphone network, which is not profitable, the LinkLine services, directory enquiries and BT phone shops.

BT would like to charge for its directory enquiry service in line with most other national telephone networks. If Oftel's approval were forthcoming, this could form an important source of income in the future.

British Telecom International This division (BTI) is responsible for international communication by voice, telex and computer data. It includes the air, sea and offshore telephone services.

BTI's operations cover all international calls made by UK customers via the international operator or via the direct dialling network. This was extended to nine new countries in 1987, bringing the total available to 173. BTI has been successful in developing the UK as an important transit centre for other countries' telecommunications and as the international communications hub for many multinational corporations.

BTI is the major partner in the first transatlantic optical glass-fibre cable planned to open in 1988. The world's first commercial international undersea optical fibre cable between the UK and Belgium was opened by BT in October 1985.

BTI has considerable satellite expertise. Ship-to-shore and the emerging air travellers' telephone services are relayed via satellite. Business Television and other broadcasting and interactive services are offered.

Overseas division The division has been set up to sell BT's knowledge and experience to other countries. India, Africa and China are the major areas of this division's activities.

In India BT has begun a joint venture with Mahindra & Mahindra to modernise the Indian telephone service. In China BT entered into an agreement to develop telecommunications in Zhejiang Province until the year 2000. In Nigeria BT is designing and supervising the installation of the first optic fibre network to be installed in Africa. In Saudia Arabia BT is

Share price and relative to FT-A All-Share

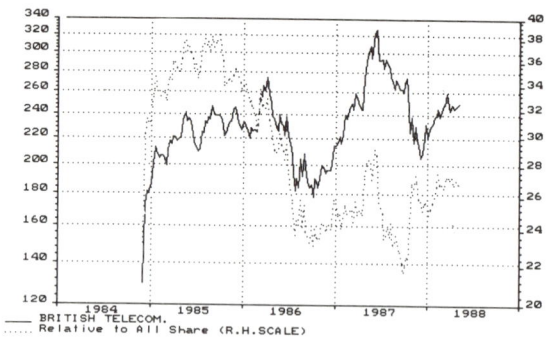

to manage, operate and maintain the Saudi telex, teletex and data networks until 1990 in a joint venture.

The division was strengthened in June 1987 with the acquisition of International Aeradio, the international airport ground service operator with interests in training and telecommunications services.

International products division The division designs, develops, manufactures and markets telecommunication and information technology products worldwide. It manages the group's two Canadian telecommunications companies Mitel Corporation and CTG. Mitel has been restructured and its manufacturing capacity cut back.

BT Datacomms supplies specialised computer equipment via its local agents in the Netherlands, Switzerland, Italy, Germany and Japan. In the US it has formed a joint marketing arm with Mitel.

The Teletrade unit exports public exchanges and transmission equipment from the UK worldwide. It is actively marketing its City Business and Key Business Systems in Australia, France, Germany, India, the Far East and North America.

British Telecom Enterprises This division includes the Cellnet cellular mobile radio-telephone service, jointly owned

C H A I R M A N ' S   S T A T E M E N T

'The board is committed to improving quality of service and to pressing ahead with telephone network modernisation.' *Iain Vallance*

with Securicor, and its 90% interest in the home security company, Telecom Security.

BT Enterprises also operates the group's electronic mail and other value-added data services. In January 1988 these operations, primarily based in the UK and the US, were consolidated into an enlarged Dialcom group, the US company acquired in 1986. In the UK this service, known as Telecom Gold, is the market leader.

Dialcom's other products include BT's business services, and Prestel, which publishes information on subjects ranging from tourism and trade to agriculture and financial data. Dialcom is in the process of setting up a telephone share-dealing service.

Engineering and procurement BT's research and development programme, mostly based at its Martlesham research laboratory in Suffolk, is carried out by this division.

In 1987 BT spent £144m on in-house research, £13m more than in 1986. It also spent a further £14m on the development of System X in conjunction with GEC.

In 1986 BT launched its joint venture with the DuPont company, BT & D Technologies, to manufacture and market worldwide a range of lasers and detectors. Such devices have been used to quadruple the capacity of glass-fibre optical trunk network cables.

BT is also carrying out research into artificial intelligence and how to extend the use of the limited radio spectrum available to the radio-telephone system.

GEOGRAPHICAL REVIEW

The UK accounted for 97% of the group's turnover in 1987. North American operations generated most of the remaining 3%.

CORPORATE CALENDAR

Year end	31 March
Preliminary results	June
Report and accounts	July
AGM	July
Final dividend paid	September
Interim results	November
Interim dividend paid	February

DIRECTORS' HOLDINGS

	Fully-paid ordinary shares	Options
IDT Vallance	5,413	124,190
GDW Odgers	5,000	236,363
REG Back	3,613	104,812
M Bett	5,213	124,190
AJ Booth	4,413	111,355
PG Bosonnet	1,600	—
CAP Foxell	2,013	69,929
JF Goble	2,580	
JAC King	3,033	119,402
JM Raisman	2,400	—
Sir David Scholey	7,500	—

Total directors' remuneration for 1987 was £1.27m, of which the chairman received £136,338 and the highest-paid director £153,661.

PRINCIPAL SUBSIDIARIES AND RELATED COMPANIES

Aberdeen Cable Services Ltd (30.0%), British Telecom Ltd, BT Consumer Electronics Ltd, BT & D Technologies Ltd (50.0%), CTG Inc – Canada, Coventry Cable Ltd (74.0%), Dialcom Inc – US, Fulcrum Communications Ltd, International Aeradio plc, Manx Telecom, Mitel Corporation – Canada (51.0%), Swindon Cable Ltd, Telecom Securicor Cellular Radio Ltd (60.0%), Westminster Cable Co Ltd (37.0%).

BRAND NAMES

British Telecom, Business Television, Cellnet, Freefone, LinkLine, Phonecard, Prestel, Qwertyphone, SatStream, Telecom Gold, Text-Direct, Tremolo, Tribune, Yellow Pages

CONTACTS AND FURTHER INFORMATION

Hugh Merrill, Investor relations manager, British Telecommunications plc, 81 Newgate Street, London EC1A 7AJ. Tel: 01-356 4909.

BUNZL PLC

GENERAL INFORMATION

Head office   Stoke House, Stoke Green, Stoke Poges, Slough SL2 4JN.
Tel: 0753 693693
Directors   EG Beaumont (chairman), J White (managing), KR
Anderson, FJ David, J Farago, BF Ford, PDM Gell, DC
Latimer, P Lorenzini – US, TCF Simpson, PD Whyman,
JJD Williamson. *Non-exec* FJ Briggs, B McGillivray
Advisers   SG Warburg & Co Ltd
Auditors   Peat Marwick McLintock
Registrars   Ravensbourne Registration Services Ltd
Brokers   Hoare Govett Ltd
Solicitors   Freshfields, Belmont Craymer

GENERAL FINANCIAL INFORMATION

Market capitalisation	£646.8m at 1 January 1988
Capital structure	
Issued ordinary shares (25p)	405.7m
Issued preference shares	None
Warrants	None
Convertibles	£26.1m 7% CULS 1995/97 (550.54 ordinary shares for £1,000 stock to 1 July 1997)
Traded options	None
ADRs	None
Shareholders over 5%	None

FT CATEGORY

FT: Paper, printing and advertising
FT-A: Packaging and paper

MAJOR ACTIVITIES

Bunzl has grown rapidly through acquisition since recognising in the early 1980s the weakness of its dependence the manufacture of cigarette filters and paper trading. It is now a substantial, diversified group with five divisions whose operations span the globe but are concentrated in the US, the UK and Australia.

Its distribution division sells paper and plastic disposable products, fine quality papers, coarse paper, foods, building materials and electrical systems and products. The merchanting division trades in pulp paper and board. The transportation division runs express parcel and other specialised transport services and manufactures trailers and specialist vehicle bodies. The Filtrona division manufactures electronic measuring instruments and plastic and paper-based packaging products as well as cigarette filters. The industrial division manufactures and converts specialised paper and plastic products.

Bunzl aims to expand organically and by acquisition in its core markets, by buying under-performing companies cheaply and seeking to improve their return with improved management and through inclusion in a larger group. Often, as in the case of several acquisitions in distribution, Bunzl buys a division from a company not primarily engaged in distribution and at the same time retains the custom of the ex-parent company.

The group's performance is influenced by several economic variables, not least the price of plastics and paper, and the value of the dollar. A rise in the price of plastics or paper provides the group with stock profits and higher margins. A fall in the value of the dollar has a depressing effect on the sterling value of its sales since so much of it, over 50% in 1986 and in 1987, is derived from the US.

Bunzl has no competitors across the full spectrum of its activities. Perhaps one of the problems with several of Bunzl's interests is that their function is already performed in-house by large organisations.

FINANCIAL HISTORY

External sales of the group in 1987 stood at £1.471bn. Compared with the 1981 level of £246m, this represented the exceptional compound growth rate of 29% per annum.

Trading profit has grown even more quickly. The 1987 figure of £85.7m compared with £8.1m in 1981, a compound growth rate of 40%. Over the same period the proportion of trading profit arising from the production of cigarette filters and associated products and paper trading fell from 81% to only 31%.

Although much of this expansion has been equity-funded, the 1987 earnings per share of 13.1p and net dividend of 5p still reflect a five year compound growth rate of over 25%. These figures are substantially in excess of those for the stock market as a whole. Despite this, 1987 pre-tax profits disappointed. Earnings per share in 1987 were up just 10% from 11.9p to 13.1p.

At the end of the 1987 financial year, the balance sheet was 24% geared with net borrowings of £62.7m against net cash and short term investments of around £46.5m in 1986. The group's 1987 trading margin of 5.8% looks low. Stripping out the naturally low margin but high volume business of paper trading gives a much healthier figure of 7.4%.

SHARE PRICE HISTORY

Having doubled in both 1983 and 1984, the Bunzl share price has since been a much less spectacular performer. Despite its excellent growth in earnings per share, the shares have considerably underperformed the FT-A All-Share index since the July 1986 peak of around 30% of the index.

Although the funds it raised have been well deployed, stock outstanding from the 1986 £197m rights issue still overhangs the market. The comparatively low growth rates of its continuing business support the belief that the group can only maintain its growth rate in earnings per share with a level of acquisitions that will automatically entail further equity issues.

Since the autumn 1987 crash, the share price has been additionally held back by worries about the future levels of the dollar and fears of a US recession. These are all the greater since over 50% of the group's sales are now made in the US and none of its interests there export.

SENIOR MANAGEMENT

James White succeeded Ernest Beaumont as chairman at the 1988 AGM in May and continued as chief executive. Patrick Whyman is chairman of the transportation division, James Williamson of the Filtrona division and Peter Gell of the industrial division. Brian Ford is managing director of the distribution and merchanting divisions. Terry Simpson is managing director of the Filtrona and industrial divisions. Other executive members of the board are group finance director Ken Anderson, group services director Donald Latimer and J Farago.

CAPITAL

Bunzl's rapid expansion by acquisition in the 1980s has been equity-funded with a host of small issues. Since 1984 there have been four major capital developments.

F I V E   Y E A R   F I N A N C I A L   I N F O R M A T I O N

Year	Turnover (£m)	Pre-tax (£m)	Earnings (p)	Dividends net (p)	Dividend cover (x)	Net assets (p)	Price (p) High	Price (p) Low	PER (x) High	PER (x) Low	Yield (%) High	Yield (%) Low
1983	540.6	17.3	5.2	1.7	3.1	38.1	62	34	17.3	11.8	5.27	3.43
1984	857.2	27.6	7.1	2.3	3.1	38.1	134	61	25.9	16.1	3.49	2.09
1985	787.6	42.7	9.5	3.2	3.0	44.8	176	134	30.9	17.0	2.89	1.99
1986	1,067.5	64.8	11.9	4.2	2.8	45.0	237	156	24.9	17.8	3.01	1.96
1987	1,471.6	85.7	13.1	5.0	2.6	66.0	278	139	25.0	10.9	4.48	2.07

The first was a one for four rights issue of 15.3m ordinary shares in January 1985. This was followed at the end of 1985 by the issue of 18.7m ordinary shares and £26.1m of loan stock to part-fund the purchase of United Parcels and Stewart Plastics.

In mid-1986 there was a two for one scrip issue and in September 1986 the group made a one for three rights issue. A further 12.9m shares were issued to fund the acquisition of Robert Moss, and to complete the funding of the United Parcels and Stewart Plastics acquisitions.

During the latter part of 1987 Bunzl acquired over a dozen companies for around £150m. It also disposed of its Flexpack film packaging subsidiary to Redfearn National Glass for £19.5m.

Full conversion of the convertibles issues would result in the issue of some 14.37m shares. There are no declarable holdings over 5%. The group agreed a £250m multi-option facility with the National Westminster Bank in December 1987.

GROUP REVIEW

Distribution In 1987 distribution was, by a considerable margin, the group's largest contributor to trading profit and turnover, with 35.6% of profits at £28.5m and 42.1% of sales at £636.8m. Turnover was up 57.5% on the previous year and profits were up by 29.5%. Both were depressed by the effect of a lower dollar on the sterling value of the group's US earnings and weaker plastics prices. However, plastics prices are strengthening in 1988.

In the US the division's principal interests are a network for the distribution of coarse paper and disposable plastic products like plastic cups, and a building materials distribution operation. In the UK it has a fine paper distribution network, and in Australia it distributes coarse paper and other products.

The US business, which began 1981, has virtually achieved its aim of forming a national network of coarse paper and disposable plastic product distribution with its acquisitions of Collins Foodservice for $34m in May 1987, and of Papercraft in January 1988 for $11.3m.

The division's building materials distribution operation was substantially increased by the purchase of the Hudson Group in December 1986 for £32.5m. Hudson, based in Chicago, is a leading US trader in timber panelling and distributes speciality building material to builders' merchants, home centres and industrial users. The group's aim is to build this operation into a national network. Bunzl is already one of the largest independent specialist building suppliers but in 1987 Hudson produced disappointing results.

Bunzl moved into US electrical distribution with the acquisition of EESCO in October 1987 for $64m. EESCO distributes electrical systems, wire, cabling, lighting and control systems from 33 locations in 16 states. It is the sixth largest distributor in the highly fragmented US electrical

market with 6,000 distributors. Bunzl will try to realise profitable growth from an otherwise low margin business, but one with a national turnover of $35bn per annum. EESCO had expected annual sales to February 1988 of $200m and pre-tax profits of $8m. The acquisition of EESCO brought the value of Bunzl US distribution turnover to more than $1bn.

In 1987 Bunzl strengthened its UK fine paper distribution operation by purchasing London distributor Thom & Cook for £14m in February 1987. Thom & Cook had annual sales of £25m and pre-tax profits of £2.6m. Bunzl also made the smaller acquisition of Brighton and Canterbury based Southern Paper and bought the minority interest in Donald Murray. Bunzl is a national distributor with 15 distribution locations.

In Australia the group is the strongest independent distributor of paper, plastic, janitorial, food service and other disposable products, covering the country's major population centres. A typical Bunzl move in 1987 was its acquisition and merging of three distributors in catering and other industries to provide a one-stop shopping and distribution centre in South Australia.

Merchanting The merchanting division, one of Bunzl's traditional areas, is not so much a paper merchant as a paper broker with a major international presence in both pulp and paper. It has centres in Europe, the US, and – through an associate – in Japan. The division acts as a principal.

More recently the division has entered the job-lot market in the US through the acquisitions of Grant Paper, GB Goldman and Paper Group in Chicago. These companies take seconds from the paper mills and market them as unbranded paper to the converting and printing industries.

Share price and relative to FT-A All-Share

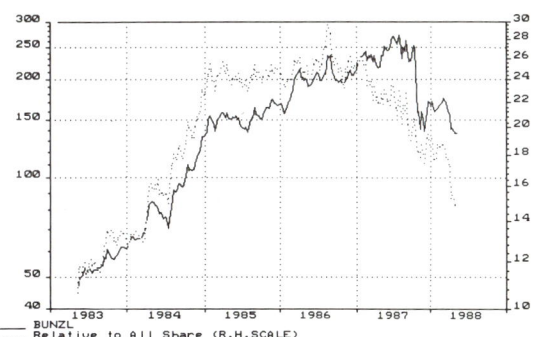

BUNZL
Relative to All Share (R.H.SCALE)

In Europe the acquisition of Wilhelm Seiler in December 1987 provides Bunzl with the number one paper merchant in the fragmented West Germany market. The smaller £1m acquisition of the Italian paper merchant Carteria Tenti gives Bunzl access to the southern Europe market.

In 1987 the merchanting division contributed 42.1% of sales and 11.8% of group trading profits. Turnover for the merchanting division was up £232.6m to £636.8m. Trading profit was up £1m to £9.5m.

Transportation The division was formed following the acquisition of United Parcels in November 1985. The three businesses it covers are parcel delivery, which contributes 75% of the division's profits, specialist transport and transport engineering. The group's delivery operations were reorganised in 1986.

The express parcels network of United Carriers, Atlas Express and Sovereign have been combined into a single network, providing services differentiated by the required speed of delivery. Multifreight, the 24-hour delivery service, uses a unique modular vehicle system for which the group claims considerable cost savings.

The specialist textile transport business consists of Scorpio, which works for companies who traditionally have operated their own in-house fleets, the textile carriers JM Young, and Hudson Shepherd, acquired in 1986. In 1987 several acquisitions were made which substantially strengthened this operation. Mann and Sons London (Holdings), an automotive shipping agent, was acquired in May 1987, followed by Robson's Distribution Services, which provides warehousing and distribution services, Thompson Jewitt International, an international freight forwarder with scheduled direct trailer services to 13 countries in Europe.

GROUP CHIEF EXECUTIVE'S STATEMENT

'During the year we continued our programme of strategic acquisitions to improve our market position in the core business areas.

We have recently implemented a new management structure to handle the growing scale of Bunzl's activities and to build upon existing management strength so that the Group is well placed to continue its planned future growth.

Despite the current weakness of the dollar, we have made an encouraging start to the current year.' *James White*

Transport engineering consists primarily of the York Transport engineering centres, the makers of the world famous York trailer and the Neville Charrold range of tipping bodies and gritters, and Glover Webb, the municipal security and special vehicle manufacturer whose customers include the Ministry of Defence.

The transportation division contributed 11.1% of group sales and 14.6% of group trading profits in 1987. Turnover was up £37.6m to £167.6m and trading profit was up £1.2m to £11.7m.

Filtrona This division, named after Bunzl's original cigarette filter business, produced 8.6% of group sales and 19.3% of trading profits in 1987. Through this division Bunzl has remained the world's leading independent cigarette filter manufacturer, consistently managing to avoid the terminal decline many outsiders had predicted and even expanding its sales overseas in Europe, Brazil, Australia and Asia.

This area, which has received minimal investment, has been an excellent cash provider for the rest of the group and a calling card for its worldwide electronic instrument business. This used to be a manufacturer of test stations for the multiple testing of cigarettes and filters, but now includes Microwave Systems Ltd, the largest independent calibration specialist in

the UK, and Sensonics, which supplies transducers to seismic and machine health monitoring systems.

In 1987 the group developed Filtrona's US base with the $13.2m Techmet acquisition. Techmet makes laser-based non-contact measuring devices which complement the Filtrona range of tape and gauging equipment.

The Filtrona plastics and packaging interests include: Rolex Paper, the UK tube-winder and its Australian associate Rolex Paper Pty; Filtrona Brasileira, a plastic bottle, tube, cap and stopper supplier to the Brazilian cosmetics industry; and a German plastic components supplier to the writing instrument business.

Turnover for the Filtrona division in 1987 was up £27m to £129.8m. Trading profit was up nearly £4m to £15.5m.

Industrial division This division contributed 8.5% of sales and 18.6% of trading profits in 1987. It has also been the focus of a considerable portion of the group's overall acquisition activity, though it disposed of Flexpack to Redfearn National Glass after having made several acquisitions in 1985 and 1986. The division is in four business sectors – speciality paper, consumer plastics, industrial plastics and graphic arts.

In speciality paper, the largest sector – Wycombe Marsh – produces a variety of medical papers. JR Crompton produces teabag tissue and sausage casings. Consumer plastics was established in 1985 with the acquisition of Stewart Plastics, and was expanded in 1986 by the purchase of North West Plastics, part of Robert Moss and Dialene. Products include a wide range of plastic housewares, and garden and patio products.

Industrial plastics started in 1986 with the acquisition of Robert Moss, which with Banbury Plastics produces a very wide range of plastic mouldings for UK industry. It also now includes Alliance Plastics, a major maker and supplier of plastic caps and plugs to the US automotive and general engineering industry.

In graphic arts the principal businesses are Coated Specialities and Channel Creasing Matrix, acquired in June 1987. These provide specialist products and services to the UK printing and packaging industries.

Turnover for the industrial division in 1987 was up £24.7m to £128.6m. Trading profit was up £3.6m to £14.9m.

GEOGRAPHICAL REVIEW

In 1987 50.8% of the group's sales were made in the US, 24.5% in the UK and 8.2% in Europe, with the rest of the world making up the balance. Much of the group's US turnover is in relatively low margin businesses and produced only 32.2% of the group's trading profit while the UK produced 52.5%.

1987 acquisitions have increased US sales rather more than UK sales. Fluctuations in the dollar-sterling exchange rate will have a crucial impact on whether the US makes a greater contribution to group profits in the future.

CORPORATE CALENDAR

Year end	31 December
Preliminary results	March
Report and accounts	April
AGM	May
Final dividend paid	July
Interim results	September
Interim dividend paid	November

DIRECTORS' HOLDINGS

	Fully-paid ordinary shares	Options
EG Beaumont	108,020	—
J White	55,000	423,951
KP Anderson	43,200	177,065
PDM Gell	47,000	111,939
FJ David	4,000	—
J Farago	6,887	207,830
FJ Briggs	10,000	—
B McGillivray	10,000	
JTD Williamson	8,000	115,953
DC Latimer	7,083	177,213
BP Ford	13,398	277,616
PD Whyman	16,665	256,909

Total directors' renumeration in 1987 was £1.8m, of which the chairman received £61,030 and the highest-paid director £354,226.

PRINCIPAL SUBSIDIARIES AND RELATED COMPANIES

Management
Bunzl Finance Ltd, Bunzl Group Services Ltd, Bunzl US Holdings Inc – US, Friendly House Property Investment Co Ltd

Distribution Division
Bunzl Australia Ltd, Bunzl Building Materials Service Inc – US, Bunzl Corporation – US, Bunzl Distribution USA Inc – US, Bunzl Fine Paper Ltd, EESCO Inc – US, Bunzl Foodservice Inc – US, Donald Murray (Paper) Ltd, The Hudson Group Inc – US

Merchanting Division
American Paper Sales Inc – US (75%), Atlantic Kraft Corporation – US, Bunzl Pulp & Paper Srl – Italy, Bunzl Pulp & Paper (Sales) GmbH – Austria, Bunzl Pulp & Paper Sales Inc – US, Bunzl Pulp & Paper Sales Ltd, Cartaria Tenti Spa – Italy (70%), Fay France Sarl, GB Goldman Paper Co – US, Grant Paper Co – US, Intercontinental Cellulose Sales Inc – US (51%), Intercontinental Cellulose Sales (UK) Ltd, The Paper Group Inc – US (60%), Raccolta Papierexport GmbH – Austria (63%), Wilhelm Seiler GmbH – West Germany

Transportation Division
Atlas Express Ltd, Bunzl Transportation Ltd, Glover Webb Ltd, Mann & Son London (Holdings) Ltd, Multifreight Ltd, Neville Charrold Ltd, Scorpio International Ltd, Thompson Jewitt International Ltd, United Carriers Ltd, United Parcels Properties Ltd, United Rentals Ltd, York Trailer Holdings Plc

Filtrona Division
Bunzl Industries Ltd – Australia, Bunzl Instrumentation Ltd, Cigarette Components Ltd, Filtrona Brasileira Indústria e Comércio Ltd – Brazil, Filtrona Española SA – Spain (75%), Filtrona Filter GmbH – West Germany, Filtrona Instruments & Automation Ltd, Filtrona International Ltd, Filtrona Ltd, Microwave Systems Ltd, Oesterreichische Zigarettenfilter GmbH – Austria (51%), Precision Engineering, Rolex Paper Co Ltd, Sensonics Ltd

Industrial Division
Alliance Plastics Inc – US, Banbury Plastics Ltd, Channel Creasing Matrix Ltd, Coated Specialities Ltd, Dialene Plc, Dupré Vermiculite Ltd, JR Crompton Plc, Microfine Minerals & Chemicals Ltd, Moss Plastic Parts Ltd, North West Plastics, Stag Plastics Ltd, Stewart Plastics Plc, Wycombe Marsh Paper Mills Ltd

Associated Companies
Bunzl Trading Ltd – Japan (50%), Filtrati SpA – Italy (49%), Securiseal Ltd – UK (50%)

BRAND NAMES

Bunzl, Dialene, Filtrona, Glover Webb, Microwave, Multifreight, Rolex Paper, Southern Paper, United Parcels

CONTACTS AND FURTHER INFORMATION

DC Latimer, Director of Group Services, Bunzl plc, Stoke House, Stoke Green, Stoke Poges, Slough SL2 4JN. Tel: 0753 693693.

GENERAL INFORMATION

Head office	214 Oxford Street, London W1N 9DF. Tel: 01-636 8040
Directors	Sir Ralph Halpern (chairman and chief executive), Laurence Cooklin (joint deputy managing director), David N Legg, Paul G Plant (joint deputy managing director), Gerald A Slater, W Michael Wood, Dr Robert C Woodman. *Non-exec* Richard T Harris, Mark Littman QC, Ladislas O Rice (deputy chairman)
Advisers	SG Warburg & Co Ltd
Auditors	Price Waterhouse
Registrars	National Westminster Bank Registrar's Department
Brokers	Capel-Cure Myers, Cazenove & Co, Citicorp Scrimgeour Vickers Ltd
Solicitors	Clifford Chance

GENERAL FINANCIAL INFORMATION

Market capitalisation	£1.234bn at 1 January 1988
Capital structure	
Issued ordinary shares	548.8m
Share options	11.4m
Issued preference shares	None
Warrants	26.7m, exercisable at 272p per share
Convertibles	£102m 8% CULS (357 shares per £1000 stock)
	£110m 4.75% Eurobond 2001 (317.46 shares per £1000 stock)
Traded options	No
ADRs	Yes
Shareholders over 5%	None

FT CATEGORY

FT: Drapery and stores
FT-A: Stores

MAJOR ACTIVITIES

The group operates through two core businesses. The first is composed of a number of specialist retail chains, catering primarily to the men's and women's clothing markets. The second is represented by the Debenhams department store business, which was acquired in August 1985 in a hard fought takeover battle. Group selling area amounts to over 8m sq ft.

A financial services division provides an integral contribution to the mainstream retail activities and is separately managed. This offers an interesting alternative activity, as does a newly-formed property sector.

The main economic indicators affecting the business are levels of personal disposable income, consumer confidence and movements in interest rates. Other factors include demographic changes within the UK population – traditionally the group has catered to younger age groups, although an older profile is now beginning to emerge – plus weather patterns, which can influence demand for clothing.

Principal competitors include Marks and Spencer, Next, Storehouse, Sears and the unquoted House of Fraser and John Lewis Partnership department stores. The financial services area has competition from the clearing banks.

The core specialist clothing chains are growing rapidly and command a strong industry presence. The task now in hand is to translate the same degree of authority to the newer Debenhams business. The programme is at an early stage (25% of stores had been updated at March 1988) but initial results have been encouraging. The potential for improving sales and profits is considerable. Phase II of the two year Debenhams development programme is under way, to take the total of new and updated square footage to 70% by autumn 1988.

FINANCIAL HISTORY

For the twelve months to 31 August 1987, group sales rose by 16% to £1.303bn on ongoing businesses. For the five years to 1986/87, sales growth amounted to 447%. During 1986/87 pre-tax profits rose by 14.5% to £183.4m, to complete a five year advance of 469%. The 1987 increase would have been 21.5% but for the sale and leaseback programme carried out during the year, undertaken as part of the balance sheet reconstruction, which resulted in increased rents during the year.

Since 1982, profit margins have widened by over five points as management has successfully strengthened the business. The increase would have been greater but for the acquisition of the less profitable Debenhams operation, which also involved a sharply increased group financing charge. Basic earnings per share in 1986/87 rose by 21.9%, to complete almost a 261% five year advance. Dividends were increased by 26%, 288% up since 1982. The return on capital employed for 1986/87 was an exceptionally high 35.1%.

As at August 1987 group borrowings amounted to £222.1m, to produce capital gearing of 43%, up 13% on 1985/86 because of the group's store development programme. The level of gearing had been more than halved during 1985/86 as the opportunity was taken to reduce borrowings through the sale of peripheral Debenhams activities. A heavy capital expenditure programme is being pursued.

At the 1987/88 interim, pre-tax profits increased by 18.8% to £109.5m, while profits from on-going businesses increased by 19.7%. Multiple retailing's margins improved, from 15.1% to 15.6%, to take trading profits up 22% to £72.7m on sales up 18.2% to £465.1m. Debenhams' margins declined from 15.9% to 14.8% as sales increased by 25.6% to £323.6m, but trading profits were still up 16.3% to £47.8m. The decline in margins reflected the decreased importance of concessionaire business, down to 34% from 50% when Burton took over Debenhams. Group turnover was up 16.8% to £795.6m. Earnings per share increased by 18.3% to 12.9p and dividends by 20% to 2.4p.

SHARE PRICE HISTORY

The all time high for the shares is just above the 350p level, reached in both 1986 and 1987. Relative to the stock market as a whole, the shares have been in decline from 1986. Some uncertainty over the Debenhams acquisition has emerged during 1987, though there has been outperformance since the October 1987 crash. The relative share price performance remains impressive, taking a longer five year view.

SENIOR MANAGEMENT

The present team was formed during the late 1970s and early 1980s and has successfully expanded the profits base from a previously depressed level and built the group into its present size. The chairman and chief executive is Sir Ralph Halpern. He succeeded as chairman in 1981, having been appointed joint managing director in January 1980, sole managing director in July 1980, and managing director and chief executive in November 1980.

Other executive main board directors include the two joint deputy group managing directors, Laurence Cooklin and Paul Plant, as well as Michael Wood (group finance director), David Legg (managing director, financial services), Gerald Slater (company secretary) and Dr Robert Woodman (systems and distribution). The president is Stanley H Burton.

CAPITAL

In August 1985, 91.4m new ordinary shares were issued to fund part of the Debenhams acquisition plus the smaller acquisition of the Colliers menswear chain. The new shares increased the equity base by 51.9%. Since August 1985 the number of ordinary shares in issue has grown by under 2% to 549m.

In January 1987 the group issued £110m of 4.75% convertible Eurobonds, continuing the restructuring of the balance sheet started by the sale and leasebacks of group property and stores undertaken in 1986. There are no individual shareholdings above 5%. A total of 9.5m options to subscribe for ordinary shares are outstanding, representing 1.7% of the existing ordinary share capital.

GROUP REVIEW

Multiple retailing The core clothing chains occupy 3.8m sq ft of high street selling area, plus another 0.5m sq ft within Debenhams. Selling area is growing by around 10% to 15% per annum. Considerable attention is devoted to maintaining an attractive and up to date in-store shopping environment through a regular programme of shop refits and refurbishments.

Allowing for 20% of the business which is estimated to be derived from concessionaires – covering such related fashion areas as shoes, jewellery and cosmetics – sales per square foot are high, at around £300 per annum, whilst margins are attractive.

Separate chains have been developed which are carefully targeted at individual customer groups, identified by age and lifestyle. In certain cases, other sub-sectors of demand are also catered to, where these can be accommodated alongside the mainstream ranges. The key businesses, which together form the single largest collection of specialist clothing chains in the UK, include Burton, Dorothy Perkins, Top Shop and Top Man, Principles and Champion Sport.

Sales of the core specialist clothing business increased by 19% in 1986/87, with results from the newer divisions, Principles, Principles for Men and Champion being particularly strong. New space accounted for 6% of the increase, while inflation was 3%, leaving volume growth at 9%. After adding back extra rents following the property sale and leaseback programme, trading margins are calculated to have risen from 15.5% to 16% in 1986/87, providing an underlying profits increase of 26.1% to £147m.

At the 1987/88 interim, trading profits were up 22% on sales up 18.2%.

Burton The name derives from the original menswear tailoring operation but bespoke suits now form only a part of total sales, whilst smart but casual clothing provides a core area

CHAIRMAN'S STATEMENT

'The British shopper, wishing to express individuality and a sense of style, continues to demand a wider and increasing specialised range of products and services.

The Burton Group has built its success on meeting the specialised needs of the largest and most profitable market sectors by developing a widespread but integrated portfolio of national large and small space retail chains.

The Burton Group intends to continue to pursue this strategy in order to become Britain's pre-eminent fashion retailer.' *Sir Ralph Halpern*

FIVE YEAR FINANCIAL INFORMATION

Year	Turnover (£m)	Pre-tax (£m)	Earnings (p)	Dividends net (p)	Dividend cover (x)	Net assets (p)	Price (p) High	Low	PER (x) High	Low	Yield (%) High	Low
1983	299.2	39.12	7.8	2.50	3.1	71	106	71	23.0	17.9	3.93	3.11
1984	415.9	56.41	10.1	3.25	3.1	74	211	106	28.9	16.5	3.64	2.08
1985	551.0	80.20	14.1	4.40	3.2	68	313	205	30.3	20.4	2.77	1.96
1986	1,228.8	148.70	17.1	5.70	3.0	80	352	242	27.7	15.2	3.11	1.80
1987	1,303.3	182.40	19.9	7.20	2.8	95	357	211	19.1	10.8	4.55	2.34

of demand. The age range is still broad with a core market in the 20 to 40 year age range, although ranges of childrenswear have also been added. At February 1988, there were 491 outlets.

Dorothy Perkins The business was acquired in 1979 and has subsequently been reshaped to offer reasonably priced but fashionable clothing within the 18 to 40 womenswear market. Separate departments include Expressions (aimed at more sophisticated customers), Mum's the Word (maternity wear), and Perks (for 9 to 14 year olds). At February 1988, there were 432 outlets.

Top Shop and Top Man Top Shop was launched in the mid-1960s, with Top Man following in the late 1970s. Both cater to the fashionable 15 to 25 year old market, covering womenswear and menswear respectively. Extensions to the core range in Top Shop include Top Notch (20 to 30 year olds), Streetwise (younger, trendier), and Top Girl (9 to 14 year olds). At February 1988, there were 296 outlets.

Top Man has Wild Boys (10 to 14 year olds), Portfolio (25 to 30 year olds, more classic styles), Physique (18 to 24 year olds, leisure and sportswear), and Collections (designer fashion). At February 1988, there were 223 outlets.

Champion Sport Champion Sport is the UK's second largest sportswear chain, operating the sports departments in Debenhams in solus sites and shop in shop. At February 1988, there were 91 outlets.

Principles for Women and Principles for Men Both businesses are relatively new and are aimed primarily at the 25 to 45 age groups, offering medium to higher priced clothing featuring stylish but classic looks. At February 1988, there were 273 outlets.

Evans The business is long established but has been refined in recent years to provide women requiring larger size garments, from size 14 upwards, with a choice of more fashionable merchandise. The main age range is 25 to 49. This business was first introduced in 1985 and caters to the fast-growing market for fashionable sports and leisurewear, for both men and women, covering the ages of 15 to 35 plus. At February 1988, there were 183 outlets.

New retail activities The most recent innovations include Alias, aimed at the fashionable 25 to 40 year old men's casualwear market, and Secrets, offering high quality lingerie. In each case, previously neglected but significant segments of the clothing market, worth £600m and £330m respectively, have been identified and targeted. Radius, started in November 1987, is being developed as an experimental business, with a range of men's formalwear and casualwear. At March 1988, there were 22 Alias outlets, 10 Secrets and six Radius.

Department stores The prestigious Harvey Nichols department store in Knightsbridge was inherited through the acquisition of Debenhams. The business has been retained and is being developed.

Most attention is focused on the mainstream department store business, where the group is represented on a nationwide

basis through 69 branches. Debenhams is the UK's second largest department store operator. About 40% of turnover was derived from concessions during 1986/87 but the contribution is deliberately being reduced in favour of higher margin own-bought merchandise which can offer greater coherence in terms of range and presentation.

Excluding concessions, an estimated 70% of sales derive from clothing with the balance consisting of household goods. The operation is being remodelled under the new management. Following a £16m investment, the new look Oxford Street flagship store was unveiled early in 1987 and the remainder of the chain is now undergoing a modernisation programme, which is due to be completed during the course of the next two to three years. Sales after modernisation were 40% up in the Oxford Street store. Preston is another new flagship store. There are important new stores in Hounslow, Colchester, Bolton and Southend. Phase II will be completed in autumn 1988, taking the new and updated square footage to around 70%.

Particular emphasis is being given to encourage customers to shop throughout the store, including the often unproductive basement and upper floors, as well as the more frequently inhabited ground and first floors. Product ranges are being strengthened and improved, to attract middle to upper income groups by offering more distinctive and higher quality merchandise. As a result of these initiatives, previous relatively modest sales and profits per sq ft are showing a significant improvement. New ranges of women's fashions are being introduced. In menswear and home furnishings there has been expansion of own-label merchandise.

Sales increased by 13.2% in 1986/87 despite disruption caused by modernisation. Volume growth was 8%, with inflation contributing 4% and the new store at Preston 1%. Trading profits increased from £70.4m to £74.4m, a modest 5%, whilst trading margins dropped 1% to 15.1%, as a result of higher rents caused by the sale and leaseback programme. Adjusting for this, trading profits increased by 14.8%, and margins by 1.3%.

Share price and relative to FT-A All-Share

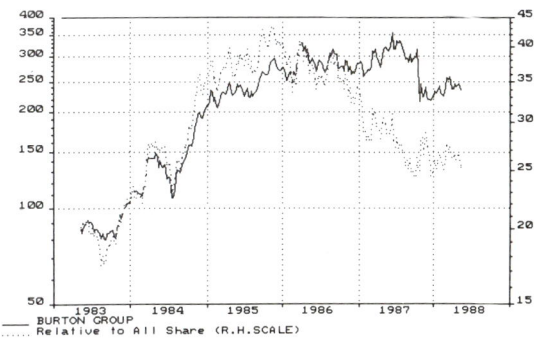

CABLE AND WIRELESS plc

At the 1987/88 interim, trading profits increased by 16.3% on sales up by 25.6%.

Financial services The division operates as an in-house credit card facility available to the group's retail businesses. A total of over 2.5m card holders have been recruited, with a particularly high penetration amongst 18 to 25 year olds. Other activities are also being introduced to capitalise on this customer base, covering house purchase, mortgages, personal loans, stockbroking, and investment and insurance facilities.

Property At 31 August 1987 the group managed a portfolio of 1,600 properties with a market value of £460.4m. The property division services the group's own shop development requirements and is also involved in schemes for other retailers. The operation has been strengthened by the recent acquisition of Pengap Estates. Activity is increasing, with a particularly important development due for completion at Dartford, Kent in spring 1989.

GEOGRAPHICAL REVIEW

No geographical analysis of sales and profits is available, but following the disposal of the French shoe retailing business, the company operates entirely in the UK.

CORPORATE CALENDAR

Year end	31 August
Preliminary results	November
Report and accounts	December
AGM	January
Final dividend paid	February
Interim results	March
Interim dividend paid	July

DIRECTORS' HOLDINGS

	Fully-paid ordinary shares	Options
Laurence Cooklin	16,582	1,850,552
Sir Ralph Halpern	74,738	2,775,796
RT Harris	18,500	—
M Littman	3,720	
PG Plant	16,582	1,848,016
LO Rice	102,000	
GA Slater	212,454	545,050
Non-beneficial	3,531,381	—
WM Wood	251,706	1,221,784
Dr RC Woodman	53,060	492,630

Total directors' remuneration in 1986/87 was £6.027m, of which the chairman, who was also the highest-paid director, received £1.359m.

PRINCIPAL SUBSIDIARIES AND RELATED COMPANIES

Burton BV – The Netherlands, Burton Capital BV – The Netherlands, Burton Group Financial Services (Holdings) Ltd, Burton Property Trust Ltd, Collier Holdings Ltd, Debenhams (Aruba) NV – The Netherlands Antilles, Debenhams Plc, Dorothy Perkins Ltd, Dorothy Perkins Retail Ltd, Evans Ltd, FPI Development Company Ltd, Freebody Properties Ltd, Harvey Nichols & Company Ltd, High Street Property Investments Ltd, John Collier Menswear Ltd, Pengap Estates Ltd, Peter Robinson Ltd, Welbeck Finance

BRAND NAMES

Alias, Burton, Champion, Debenhams, Dorothy Perkins, Evans, Harvey Nichols, In Store, John Collier, Principles, Principles for Men, Radius, Secrets, Top Man, Top Shop

CONTACTS AND FURTHER INFORMATION

Michael Mitchell, The Burton Group PLC, 214 Oxford Street, London W1N 9DF. Tel: 01-636 8040.

GENERAL INFORMATION

Head office	Mercury House, 110–124 Theobalds Road, London WC1X 8RX. Tel: 01-242 4433
Directors	Sir Eric Sharp CBE (chairman and chief executive), T Chellew, JH Crouch CBE, MG Gale, RJ Olsen, GMW Owen, BA Pemberton, JHM Solomon. *Non-exec* D Berriman, Sir Gordon Brunton, Sir Peter Carey GCB, AW Clements
Advisers	Kleinwort Benson Ltd
Auditors	Deloitte Haskins & Sells
Registrars	National Westminster Bank Registrar's Department
Brokers	Cazenove & Co
Solicitors	Speechly Bircham

GENERAL FINANCIAL INFORMATION

Market capitalisation	£3.376bn at 1 January 1988
Capital structure	
Issued ordinary shares (50p)	1.20bn
Issued preference shares (£1)	One special rights preference share of £1
Warrants	None
Convertibles	None
Traded options	Yes
ADRs	None
Shareholders over 5%	None

FT CATEGORY

FT: Electricals
FT-A: Telephone networks

MAJOR ACTIVITIES

Cable and Wireless (C&W) is one of the world's most progressive telecommunications carriers and facilities manager, providing business and domestic users with telecommunications services including telephone, telex, facsimile and data transmission.

It operates on a global basis as a provider of telecommunications services to sovereign governments in 46 different countries. Network operations, accounting for 86% of worldwide turnover, offer C&W higher margin value-added services from areas like teletext and electronic messaging.

Although C&W has an operating profit of 30% of turnover, there is an upper limit to growth. In the past C&W had total responsibility as a telecommunications carrier and facilities manager. Recently, government awareness of the potential profits and related benefits has meant that C&W has often had to take a joint venture approach.

The group is heavily exposed to exchange rate movements. Its international operations are usually dependent on currencies related to the dollar. Other factors affecting C&W include politics (for instance, Hong Kong's future after 1997) and its involvement in newly deregulated markets. These are completely different from C&W's normal type of operation.

The business operations of C&W involve it in long term investments capable of generating huge profits in the future. Major growth opportunities are being exploited by a heavy investment programme. This includes a 17% stake in International Digital Communications in Japan; Hong Kong Telecommunications; Mercury in the UK; and a joint venture with Nynex in the US.

C&W's aims to link its existing geographical bases with a global digital telecommunications network. Significant progress has already been made. All these factors indicate an acceleration in C&W's growth rate. In addition, C&W's influence on the market-place is likely to reduce prices. As a result, a significant increase is likely to occur in the uses made of telephone networks. In Hong Kong for instance, the facsimile market has exploded, with business growing at an

FIVE YEAR FINANCIAL INFORMATION

Year	Turnover (£m)	Pre-tax (£m)	Earnings (p)	Dividends net (p)	Dividend cover (x)	Net assets (p)	Price (p) High	Low	PER (x) High	Low	Yield (%) High	Low
1983	418.4	156.7	12.1	2.8	4.1	65	173	110	24.6	17.4	3.12	2.26
1984	673.1	190.1	12.6	3.2	3.8	65	224	138	25.0	17.4	3.38	2.11
1985	861.5	245.2	15.9	3.9	4.0	53	326	223	30.0	19.4	2.34	1.67
1986	907.0	295.0	19.4	4.8	4.0	69	368	277	24.6	17.8	2.42	1.85
1987	913.0	340.0	22.0	5.6	3.9	104	509	280	28.5	15.7	2.72	1.49

annual rate of 168%.

C&W is an established market leader. It is a totally international telecommunications company. Competitors include AT&T and British Telecom.

FINANCIAL HISTORY

Turnover was £913m at 31 March 1987, representing a marginal increase of 0.7%. Turnover for the five year period from 1982 increased 118%. Pre-tax profits were £340m against £295m in 1986, 15% ahead on the period, reduced by the weak dollar. Nevertheless, they had doubled since 1982. The Asia & Pacific operations provided 81% of trading profit.

Earnings per share increased by 14% from 19.3p to 22p. The dividend was increased by 17% to 5.5p. Spending on fixed assets increased to £355m as a result of the investment in Mercury and the further development of C&W's global digital highway. In the future C&W may need to commit as much as $2bn to capital investment.

The £330m rights issue in 1985 left interest income substantially higher at £46m, up from £14m. Management performance ratios were good. Asset turnover was 0.76 times and return on capital employed was 17.4%.

At the September 1987 interim, profits were 3.2% up at £165m after £14m had been lost from currency swings. The growth in earnings in the currencies in which C&W operates was 16%. Turnover was 6.6% ahead at £467m.

SHARE PRICE HISTORY

After the company's privatisation in 1981, the share price responded slowly. Following the market's realisation of the company's prospects, the share price increased steadily, though from mid-1983 to 1984 there was a period of instability as worries regarding the future of Hong Kong surfaced.

When these doubts were resolved, the price rose with only temporary setbacks to a high of 518p in September 1987. Share price fluctuation occurred as a result of exchange rate concerns, which in 1987 reduced profits by £34m.

CHAIRMAN'S STATEMENT

'Significant progress has been made towards the establishment of the Group's major corporate objective of a global telecommunications network connecting the primary economic and financial centres of the world. The significant investments which this strategy requires the Group to make are pivotal to securing future profitability and growth as the global regulatory environment for telecommunications continues to change and provide new opportunities for innovation. The Group is not alone in pursuing this vision of the future. Strategic allies in various locations around the globe will share in the cost of installing the new competitive facilities.' *Sir Eric Sharp*

In relative terms the shares peaked in 1985 at 46% of the FT-A All-Share index. They fell severely in the October 1987 share price collapse to 262p before recovering in early 1988 to the 350p level, 37% of the index.

SENIOR MANAGEMENT

Chairman and chief executive, Sir Eric Sharp is the company's architect. It is he who has been in the forefront of shaping global strategy. C&W's knowledge of the market-place, its contacts, diplomacy and general entrepreneurial character is in marked contrast to its old nationalised character and that of its rivals.

CAPITAL

Profits from ordinary activities and cash from the 1985 rights issue have helped C&W build up a cash reserve of £214m. This capital is to be used to finance the implementation of the global digital highway. The number of shares in issue is 1.02bn, with a special rights preference share of £1. There are no declared holdings over 5%.

GROUP REVIEW

Public telecommunications C&W's main area of activity is international and domestic telecommunications, including telephone, telex and telegram services, normally provided under agreements with licensing governments.

Ownership and operation of worldwide communications systems, amounts charged for maritime telecommunication services, and management fees had a turnover of £786.4m in 1987, an increase of 4.5% on the period, and 86% of the group's overall turnover.

Cable ships The group operates a fleet of seven vessels and two submersible vehicle systems for the laying, burial and maintenance of submarine cable systems. Income is generated from charters and from the use of the group's ships under agreement with other cable owners and manufacturers. Turnover for 1987 fell by 16% to £25.5m.

Contracts The group provides a telecommunications consultancy, operating both outside and within the UK. Turnover in 1987 was £51.0m against £84.6m in 1986.

Equipment and other activities This includes the group's involvement in the sales, leasing, rental and maintenance of terminals, communications systems and association activities. 1987 turnover increased 27% to £50m.

GEOGRAPHICAL REVIEW

Cable and Wireless is a legacy of the British Empire, involved in 46 countries around the world. It provides international telephone connections for 36 countries and internal networks for 18 countries. Due to C&W's complex nature, it requires a

Share price and relative to FT-A All-Share

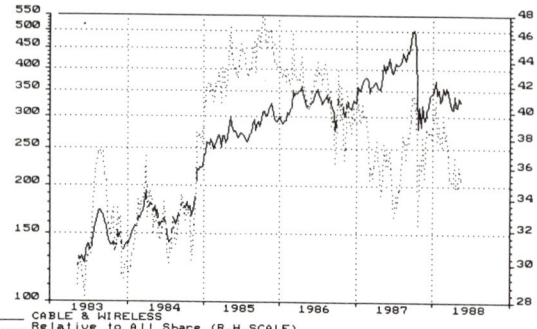

CABLE & WIRELESS
Relative to All Share (R.H.SCALE)

detailed geographical breakdown.

Asia & Pacific The Asia & Pacific region is the major source of revenue, accounting for £525m of turnover in 1987, an increase of 7% from £490m in 1986. Profits were up 18% to £234.7m from £198.5m. The strong growth in the area was helped by a 40% annual increase in the volume of traffic through the Hong Kong Telephone Company.

Cable and Wireless (Hong Kong) Limited and the Hong Kong Telephone Company Limited have been merged to create Hong Kong Telecommunications, which will provide major economies of scale in Hong Kong and opportunities in China in due course. C&W plans to reduce its stake by 5.5% through a local offer for sale, though this is subject to market conditions.

Future contributions to earnings will come from the company's 49% stake in a joint venture with Malaysia's state-owned telecommunications company. In addition C&W, through its 17% stake in the International Digital Communications consortium and leading partner C Itoh, has now received a category 1 licence, enhancing its future presence through direct operations in Japan.

Strong growth continued at the 1987/88 interim. Profits were up 21% at £127m on turnover 9.6% up at £273m.

Middle East, Indian Ocean & Africa Turnover in 1987 was £59.4m, a reduction of 25% from £79.9m on the period. Trading profit was 22.8% down at £26.7m.

C&W has a 40% equity stake in the Bahrain Telecommunications Company (Batelco). Developments have included a new cellular mobile automatic telephone system and alpha-numeric paging. Despite Bahrain's sustained growth, profits have been affected by the fall in the price of oil and the effect of the war between Iran and Iraq.

In the Seychelles C&W provides the island's national and international public telecommunications services. C&W is expanding in the Yemen Arab Republic where there are good prospects of revenue growing as a result of newly discovered oil resources. C&W is under contract to the UK Ministry of Defence to provide a major communications project for the Saudi Arabian National Guard, further emphasising the group's involvement in the region.

At the 1987/88 interim, trading profits were 43.7% down at £9m on turnover 30.3% down at £23m.

United Kingdom C&W's UK involvement is concentrated on Mercury Communications, formed to provide a public telephone network operator service in the newly deregulated UK market. Mercury's operating loss in 1987 was close to expectations. This was despite the increase in costs caused by rapid expansion in demand from the City, where Mercury has 10% of all lines.

C&W is also engaged in various turnkey projects and marine activities. UK turnover was £94m in 1987, compared to £114.1m for the previous period. Losses were £3.8m. Mercury was performing well at the 1987/88 interim, with turnover up 450% to £17m and losses unchanged at £10m.

Western Hemisphere C&W's business is mainly in the Caribbean, where in 1987 turnover decreased slightly due to tougher competition experienced in the US. This resulted in reduced margins for the US telephone business. 1987 sales fell to £223m from £235m. Profits were £32m against £33m. However, in the first half of 1987/88 profits were up 50% to £24m from £16m on turnover 4.4% up at £118m.

CORPORATE CALENDAR

Year end	31 March
Preliminary results	June
Report and accounts	July
AGM	July
Final dividend paid	October
Interim results	November
Interim dividend paid	March

DIRECTORS' HOLDINGS

	Ordinary shares (beneficial)	(non-beneficial)	Options
D Berriman	20,000	—	—
Sir Gordon Brunton	41,686	—	—
Sir Peter Carey	3,130	—	—
T Chellew	20,110	—	97,022
AW Clements	1,000	—	—
JH Crouch	3,468	—	254,902
MG Gale	2,278	—	132,674
RJ Olsen	14,594	—	107,300
GMW Owen	20,194	—	109,766
BA Pemberton	9,094	—	359,028
Sir Eric Sharp	75,212	—	335,742
HM Solomon	200	—	67,100

Total directors' remuneration in 1987 was £3.27m, of which the chairman, who was also the highest-paid director, received £258,654.

PRINCIPAL SUBSIDIARIES AND RELATED COMPANIES

Anderson Square Development Company Ltd – Cayman (30%), Bahrain Telecommunications Co Bsc – Bahrain (40%), Barbados External Telecommunications Ltd – Barbados (65%), Barbados Telephone Company Ltd – Barbados (65%), Cable & Wireless Communication Inc – US, Cable & Wireless (Far East) Ltd – Hong Kong, Cable & Wireless Management Services – US, Cable & Wireless Marine Ltd, Cable & Wireless NY Inc – US, Cable & Wireless North America Inc – US, Cable & Wireless West Indies Ltd – West Indies, Communication Services Ltd – Hong Kong, Companhia de Telecomunicações de Macau SARI – Macau (75%), Computasia Ltd – Hong Kong (97.5%), Eastern Telecommunications Philippines Inc – Philippines (40%), Electra Communications Corporation US (50%), Fiji International Telecommunication Ltd – Fiji (49%), Hong Kong Telecommunications Ltd – Hong Kong (79.5%), Huaying Nanhai Oil Telecommunications Ltd – Jamaica (39%), Mercury Communications (ECL) Ltd, Mercury Communications Ltd, Oceanic Wireless Network Inc – Philippines (40%), Shenda Telephone Company Ltd – China (49%), Sierra Leone External Telecommunications Ltd – Sierra Leone (49%), Solomon Islands International Telecommunications Ltd – Solomon Islands (51%), St Kitts & Nevis Telecommunication Ltd – St Kitts (80%), Trinidad & Tobago External Communications Co Ltd – Trinidad and Tobago (49%), Vanuatu International Telecommunications Co SARL – Vanuatu (50%)

BRAND NAMES

Cable and Wireless, Mercury

CONTACTS AND FURTHER INFORMATION

Ms Anna Cloke, Cable and Wireless plc, Mercury House, 110–124 Theobalds Road, London WC1X 8RX. Tel: 01-242 4433.

CADBURY SCHWEPPES p.l.c.

GENERAL INFORMATION

Head office   1–4 Connaught Place, London W2 2EX. Tel: 01-262 1212
Directors   Sir Adrian Cadbury (chairman), RA Henderson (deputy chairman), ND Cadbury (chief executive), NC Bain, HJM Blakeney, DR Williams, DP Nash, PH Reay CBE, JP Schadt. *Non-exec* Sir James Blyth, JG Day, RP Hornby, TO Hutchison, GH Waddell
Advisers   Kleinwort Benson Ltd
Auditors   Arthur Andersen & Co, Coopers & Lybrand
Registrars   Lloyds Bank Registrar's Department
Brokers   Hoare Govett Ltd
Solicitors   Slaughter and May

GENERAL FINANCIAL INFORMATION

Market capitalisation	£1.344bn at 1 January 1988
Capital structure	
Issued ordinary shares (25p)	593.84m
Issued preference shares (£1)	3.3m 3.5% CP
Warrants	None
Convertibles	$9.9 m 8% CUL 2000 (2,358 ordinary shares per $5,000 stock)
Traded options	Yes
ADRs	10 ordinary 25p shares for each ADR
Shareholders over 5%	General Cinema Corporation holds 17.7%

FT CATEGORY

FT: Food, groceries, etc
FT-A: Food manufacturing

MAJOR ACTIVITIES

Cadbury Schweppes is the largest British-owned confectionery and soft drinks company. Its brand names are internationally recognised. They enjoy leadership in the UK market, in several other European countries and in Australia.

In the UK soft drinks market, Schweppes' link with Coca-Cola at the beginning of 1987 brought together the two strongest brands in the market. The confectionery division is the market leader in the UK, followed by Rowntree and the privately owned US-based Mars Group.

In recent years, the management has deliberately focused attention on the group's two main business streams, confectionery and beverages. This has led to divestments, including the Typhoo tea brand and Jeyes household cleaners.

The group's products are sold in more than 110 countries around the world.

FINANCIAL HISTORY

The group's results showed a sharp recovery in 1986 and 1987 after an unexpected loss in North America in 1985. A new management team and considerably improved financial controls were installed in 1986 in the region. It is now destined for consistent growth and has been considerably expanded in the beverage sector.

Turnover in 1987 was up 10.4% to £2.031bn. Pre-tax profits jumped by 34.7% to £176.1m after a 40% rise in 1986 to £130.7m. Trading margins rose by 1.3% to 8.9% in 1987 after a rise of over 1.5% to 7.6% in 1986. They are now well above the record 7.7% of 1984. The return on operating assets climbed 2.5 points to 23.6%. In 1986 there had been a remarkable recovery to 21.1% from a decreased 1985 level of 14.6%.

Gearing rose to 24.6% in 1987 after falling in 1986 from 43% to 17%, while earnings per share rose by 33.4% to 19.05p.

SHARE PRICE HISTORY

The share price performance in the first half of 1987 was particularly exciting, reflecting improved financial results as well as the strategic stake taken by General Cinema Corporation, the US's largest bottler of Pepsi-Cola.

The General Cinema stake made Cadbury a potential takeover target, pushing the share price into new ground and to a 1987 high of 291p. However, against the market as a whole, the rally only partially recovered the ground lost during 1985, when the trading results were disappointing.

In 1984 the price relative had moved up quite sharply, after a relative decline in 1983, following a long bull run between 1980 and 1982. During the 1980s the share price performance has tended to move up and down in anticipation of changes in the group's rate of earnings growth.

The shares, along with rest of the market, fell sharply in October 1987 to a low of 185p. Since then there has been marked outperformance reflecting further General Cinema buying of the stock and the good 1987 results.

In the middle of March 1988 the shares stood at 259p, 28% of the FT-A All-Share index. Late in April, takeover speculation, prompted by the Nestlé bid for Rowntree and an ambiguous statement from General Cinema, led to the shares rising to 379p, before falling back to the 330p level in early May.

SENIOR MANAGEMENT

Sir Adrian Cadbury has served as chairman since 1974. A descendent of the founding Cadbury firm, Sir Adrian has considerable industrial experience and is also a director of the Bank of England and IBM United Kingdom Holdings. His younger brother, Dominic Cadbury, was appointed chief executive at the end of 1983. He joined the company in 1964, and became a member of the board in 1974.

NC Bain is the managing director of group confectionery operations. He joined the board in 1981 as strategic planning director. JP Schadt, managing director of the beverages stream, is also on the parent board. Mervyn Blakeney joined the company in 1959 and became a director in 1979. He has been responsible for the Schweppes businesses in Europe,

CHAIRMAN'S STATEMENT

'The strategy which led to the restructuring of the Group was based on concentration on the Group's core markets and on its leading brands in those markets. It involved selling those businesses which were outside the two main streams and putting the resources released behind those international brands and markets which had the best growth prospects. . . .

To carry the strategy forward an active acquisition policy was put in place, aimed at strengthening stream positions in leading markets. The outcome of that policy in 1987 was the acquisition of the Red Cheek and Mr and Mrs "T" drinks businesses in the United States and of the Woodroofe company in South Australia. We also acquired the Beatrice Company's confectionery interests in Australasia and agreed to purchase Chocolat Poulain in France. These companies were acquired because of their close fit with the strategies of their respective business streams. They also met the further test that Cadbury Schweppes could add value to their activities, as well as building on them for future growth.' *Adrian Cadbury*

F I V E   Y E A R   F I N A N C I A L   I N F O R M A T I O N

Year	Turnover (£m)	Pre-tax (£m)	Earnings (p)	Dividends net (p)	Dividend cover (x)	Net assets (p)	Price (p)		PER (x)		Yield (%)	
							High	Low	High	Low	High	Low
1983	1,703	106.9	13.6	5.4	2.5	89	131	97	14.6	11.5	7.36	5.13
1984	2,016	124.0	15.6	5.9	2.7	102	163	116	16.6	11.7	6.65	4.82
1985	1,874	93.3	9.3	5.9	1.6	90	176	131	17.9	11.2	6.43	4.46
1986	1,840	130.7	14.3	6.7	2.1	82	195	142	21.8	12.6	5.94	4.41
1987	2,031	176.1	19.0	8.0	2.4	83	289	183	24.8	11.9	5.05	3.21

Africa, Asia and Latin America. DR Williams, appointed to the board in 1986, is managing director of Coca-Cola & Schweppes Beverages.

David Nash joined the company and the board at the beginning of March 1987 as finance director. He was previously with ICI. P Reay joined the company in 1954, became personnel director in 1981 and joined the board in 1984. R Henderson is the group's non-executive deputy chairman. He is chairman of Kleinwort Benson Lonsdale, Cadbury's principal merchant bank adviser.

CAPITAL

During 1986, 35m shares were issued in connection with the acquisition of Canada Dry. There was an issue of 60m shares in ADR form in 1984. At March 1987, 11.4% of the issued equity was in this form, though after the autumn 1987 stock market crash this had fallen to 4.4%.

In March 1985 the group issued $80m of 8% convertible bonds 2000 in bearer form. The bonds may be converted into 2,358 ordinary shares for each $5,000 bond on or after 15 January 1986 and up to and including 8 December 2000. Upon full conversion of the outstanding balance the issued ordinary share capital will expand by 5%.

General Cinema Corporation increased its initial 8.2% stake to 17.7% in late 1987, after the crash. General Cinema issued an intriguing £110m Eurosterling convertible bond in 1987 with a 5% coupon, allowing conversion into Cadbury Schweppes ordinary shares, and including a put option.

GROUP REVIEW

Cadbury Schweppes is one of the UK's major branded food manufacturing companies, although for a long period of time the group failed to take advantage of its inherent brand strength, particularly during the 1970s.

Recently the management has adopted a more competitive approach to the business. There has been a greater concentration on the two main business areas, which led to acquisitions and disposals. There has been a much sharper market focus on products. This has necessitated the introduction of new management that has been more willing to adopt an aggressive stance in the marketplace.

The new competitive stance, however, has not gone unnoticed by possible predators. The 17.7% equity stake purchased by General Cinema signalled that Cadbury Schweppes was a possible international takeover target.

The current management has begun to reorganise assets along more profitable lines. Given the very strong brand names involved, this would mean that if a third party were to launch a bid, the independent minded Cadbury management would be able to justify a substantial premium over asset value.

Drinks Products are sold under world-famous brand names such as Schweppes, Canada Dry, Rose's, Sodastream and Sunkist. Cadbury Schweppes is the world's third largest soft drinks business.

The manufacturing base includes bottling plants in the UK, Australasia and Europe. In North America the group operates exclusively through a system of franchise bottlers, rather than its own bottling plants. The group also owns a 34% stake in Dr Pepper, one of the most famous drinks in the US, and which is particularly popular in the southern states. Dr Pepper recently merged with 7-Up in the US.

In the UK, the group led the most significant restructuring in the history of the beverages market by merging its Schweppes operations with Coca-Cola UK. The group retains a 51% stake with Coca-Cola holding the balance. In March 1988 the group announced a £50m investment to build the largest soft drinks plant in Europe at Wakefield, West Yorkshire.

In the US, the acquisition of Canada Dry gave the group a near 10% market share, although it remains a niche product company. In the UK, the expanded drinks operation is the market leader and distributes the two premier brands, Schweppes and Coca-Cola. The group also has a very strong position in Australia with a 22% market share.

The long term outlook for soft drink consumption is one of steady growth. Consumption per head in Europe trails that of the US by a very long way. Given its strong distribution network, Schweppes is well positioned to take advantage of most trends in a highly segmented market.

The drinks operation accounted for 56.8% of group sales in 1987 and 49.3% of trading profit. In 1987 trading profit was 34.3% up at £89.3m on sales 41.9% up at £1.154bn.

Confectionery The confectionery operation enjoys a very high profile around the world with the Cadbury brand name strong in the UK, South Africa and Australia. In North America, the group's main brands are sold under the Peter Paul banner, a company acquired in 1978, as well as the Cadbury brand name. Products are exported to over 100 countries.

Share price and relative to FT-A All-Share

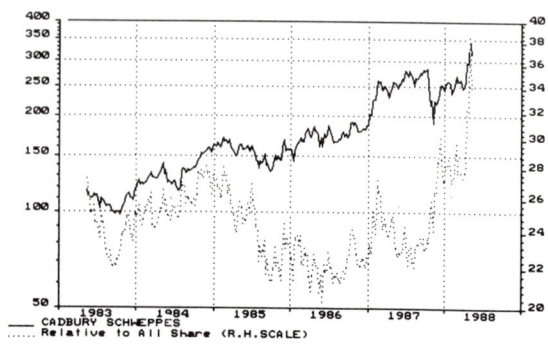

CADBURY SCHWEPPES
Relative to All Share (R.H.SCALE)

As well as having such established leading brands as Cadbury's Dairy Milk, Crunchie and Creme Eggs, the group has enjoyed success with new products, especially Wispa. This was launched three years ago and is now the fourth largest brand in the UK chocolate bar market.

In North America, poor management led to losses in 1985, but new management and a reappraisal of the business meant that 1986 and 1987 saw a sustained recovery. The group has made plans to generate sustainable growth, with greater support being given to the key brands such as Mounds, Almond Joy and York Peppermint Patties. Market share in the US is 8%, some way behind Hershey, with 31% and Mars with 42%. In the UK Cadbury is market leader with 28%, ahead of Rowntree with 25% and Mars with 23%. At the end of 1987, the group acquired Chocolat Poulain, the famous French confectionery company, for £94m in cash.

In 1987 confectionery represented 43.2% of group sales and 50.6% of trading profit. In 1987 trading profit was up 39.2% at £91.3m on sales 4.2% up at £877.0m.

GEOGRAPHICAL REVIEW

The group is international with approximately 53.0% of sales and 53.6% of profits being generated outside the UK. In 1987 Europe accounted for 16.0% of sales and 20.4% of trading profit, North America had 18.5% of sales and 10.6% of trading profit, up from only 4% in 1986. The rest of the world, mainly Australia and Africa, had 18.5% of sales and 22.7% of trading profit.

CORPORATE CALENDAR

Year end	31 December
Preliminary results	March
Report and accounts	April
AGM	May
Final dividend paid	May
Interim results	September
Interim dividend paid	November

DIRECTORS' HOLDINGS

	Ordinary shares		Options
	(beneficial)	(non-beneficial)	
Sir Adrian Cadbury	538,566	1,061,702	6,045
RA Henderson	15,000	—	—
ND Cadbury	400,025	3,700	138,189
NC Bain	46,025	—	74,959
HJM Blakeney	123,025	—	3,022
Sir James Blyth	2,000	—	—
RP Hornby	1,000	—	—
TO Hutchison	1,048	—	—
DP Nash	—	—	196,857
PH Reay	73,945	—	43,111
JP Schadt	3,000	—	221,000
DR Williams	25	—	222,502

Total directors' salaries and other fees for 1987 were £1.47m, with the chairman receiving £119,887, and the highest-paid director £184,358.

PRINCIPAL SUBSIDIARIES AND RELATED COMPANIES

Allied Foods Ltd – Ghana, Amalgamated Beverage Industries Pty Ltd – South Africa (19%), Beatrice Australia Ltd, Bromor Foods (Pty) Ltd – South Africa (53%), Cadbury Confectionery Malaysia SB, Cadbury Ireland plc, Cadbury Ltd, Cadbury Nigeria Ltd (40%), Cadbury Schweppes Australia Ltd (70%), Cadbury Schweppes (Canada) Inc, Cadbury Schweppes de España SA – Spain, Cadbury Schweppes GmbH – West Germany, Cadbury Schweppes Holdings Pty Ltd – South Africa, Cadbury Schweppes Holdings Inc – US, Cadbury Schweppes Holdings Ltd – Kenya, Cadbury Schweppes Hudson – New Zealand (70%), Cadbury Schweppes Kenya Ltd, Cadbury Schweppes Pty Ltd – Australia (70%), Cadbury Schweppes Research Ltd (51%), Cadbury Schweppes South Africa Ltd (53%), Cadbury Schweppes Zambia Ltd, Canada Dry Corp Holdings Inc – US, Canada Dry Ltd – Canada, Coca-Cola & Schweppes Beverages Ltd, Cottee's General Foods Ltd – Australia (70%), Crystal Candy Private Ltd – Zimbabwe (49%), Dr Pepper Co – US (34%), Greek Juice Processing and Canning Industry – Greece (24%), Hindustan Cocoa Products Ltd – India (40%), Kissan Products Ltd – India (33%), Mitchell's Fruit Farms Ltd – Pakistan (25%), Red Cheek Ltd – UK and US, Schweppes AG – Austria, Schweppes Central Africa Ltd – Zimbabwe (46%), Schweppes France SA, Schweppes SA – Spain (66%), Sodastream Deutschland GmbH – West Germany, Sodastream Ltd, Sunkist Soft Drinks Inc – US

Export and franchises
Cadbury International Ltd, Canada Dry Corporation Ltd – Irish Republic, Schweppes International Ltd

Finance and holding companies
Cadbury Schweppes Finance Ltd, Cadbury Schweppes Investments BV – Netherlands, Cadbury Schweppes Investments (Jersey) Ltd, Cadbury Schweppes Overseas Ltd, Cadbury Schweppes USA Inc

BRAND NAMES

Almond Joy, Almond Mound, Biarritz, Buttons, Cadbury's Dairy Milk, Canada Dry, Creme Egg, Crunchie, Double Decker, Dr Pepper, Flake, Go, Hepburn Spa, Malvern Water, Milk Tray, Motts, Muesli Munch, Rose's, Schweppes, Snacker, SodaMate, SodaStream, Solo, Sunkist, Top Deck, Tropical Spring, Twirl, Wispa, York Peppermint Patties

CONTACTS AND FURTHER INFORMATION

Chris Milburn, Cadbury Schweppes p.l.c., 1–4 Connaught Place, London W2 2EX. Tel: 01-262 1212.

COATS VIYELLA Plc

GENERAL INFORMATION

Registered office	Bank House, Charlotte Street, Manchester M1 4ET. Tel: 061-236 3272
Directors	Sir James Spooner (chairman), D Alliance CBE (deputy chairman and group chief executive), J McAdam (deputy chairman and deputy group chief executive), J Ashton, CM Bell, JL Hewitt, JM Houston, NCD Kuenssberg, AH Macdiarmid, W McEwan, JDF Miller, CB Rothera OBE, WJ Shelton, PM White. *Non-exec* HAS Djanogly CBE, WC Thomson
Advisers	NM Rothschild & Sons Ltd
Auditors	Spicer and Pegler
Registrars	Fenchurch Registrars Ltd, 8–16 Earl Street, London EC2A 2DY. Tel: 01-247 5644
Brokers	Cazenove & Co, de Zoete & Bevan Ltd
Solicitors	Nabarro Nathanson

GENERAL FINANCIAL INFORMATION

Market capitalisation	£1.374bn at 1 January 1988
Capital structure	
Issued ordinary shares (20p)	525.18m
Issued preference shares (£1)	3.1m 4.9% CP
Warrants	None
Convertibles	None
Traded options	None
ADRs	One ADR equals four ordinary shares
Shareholders over 5%	None

FT CATEGORY

FT: Drapery and stores
FT-A: Textiles

MAJOR ACTIVITIES

Coats Viyella is Europe's largest textile company. Formed in March 1986 by the merger of Vantona Viyella with the Scottish-based Coats Patons, the group has a large stable of household names such as Jaeger, Country Casuals, Byford, Dorma, Van Heusen, Viyella, Peter England, Lancaster Carpets, Royal Wilton and Patons.

The group's main activities centre on leisure and craft products, retail shops and fashionwear, home and industrial sewing products and precision engineering. It manufactures in over 30 locations around the world and sells its products in over 100 countries.

The group carries out the manufacture, processing and distribution of a wide range of garments, woven and knitted fabrics and carpets. Products range from shirts to bandage fabric, and lace to military uniform. The precision engineering division incorporates the non-textile interests of the group, principally small precision components in zinc alloys and plastic under the Dynacast name, and the development and distribution of a range of medical and rehabilitation products.

Coats Viyella is establishing itself as a major force in world textiles, with a product range that spans a wide spectrum backed by some of the foremost brand names, an essential ingredient for any manufacturer with international aspirations.

Changes in economic cycles have long been the scourge of the textile industry, but by increasing the breadth of operation, the group has softened the effect of localised trading downturns. Its economies of scale, production and technology offer a degree of protection against short-term, cut-throat competition or dumping by competitors.

Coats Viyella is emerging from a dull period with an aggressive plan to expand, to improve productivity, gain larger market share and wider distribution for existing products.

If the group can continue to gauge the prevailing moods and directions at the fashion end of the market and adapt its products on an international basis, it should continue to expand.

FINANCIAL HISTORY

Turnover for 1987 was 2.5% higher at £1.794bn. On a like for like basis turnover was up 7.0%. Pre-tax profits were 17.1% up at £212.8m. Earnings per share increased 22.9% to 29.0p as the group benefited from a lower tax charge in both the UK and overseas.

In 1987 the largest division was thread and handknittings which generated 34.4% of turnover, followed by garment manufacture and retailing with 26.2%, household textiles and carpets with 16.8%, yarns and fabrics with 16.1% and precision engineering with 6.5%.

Gearing fell to nothing from 2.3% in 1986. Net asset value is around 136p on the enlarged equity. Ordinary dividends increased from 7.25p to 8.7p (+20.0%) and were covered 3.3 times by earnings.

Coats Viyella has the authority to buy back 78.2m of its own shares, 14.9% of the total.

SHARE PRICE HISTORY

From 1984 to the 1987 market peak Coats Viyella shares quadrupled. The strong period of outperformance relative to the FT-A All-Share index was from mid-1984 to mid-1985, when the shares more than doubled. Until October 1987 the shares performed roughly in line with the market index.

The shares virtually halved in the autumn 1987 share crash, falling from 424p to a low of 217p. They were particularly hard hit, though since then they have recovered to the 250p level in mid-April 1988.

SENIOR MANAGEMENT

Sir James Spooner is non-executive chairman of the group. David Alliance is deputy chairman and group chief executive. Iranian-born, he arrived in Manchester 31 years ago and commenced building the group to its present size with the acquisition of Spirella.

J McAdam is deputy chairman and deputy group chief

FIVE YEAR FINANCIAL INFORMATION

Year	Turnover (£m)	Pre-tax (£m)	Earnings (p)	Dividends net (p)	Dividend cover (x)	Net assets (p)	Price (p) High	Price (p) Low	PER (x) High	PER (x) Low	Yield (%) High	Yield (%) Low
1983	307.3	15.5	12.8	3.8	2.6	90.7	84	51	19.3	8.2	11.10	6.76
1984	606.9	39.4	15.0	4.8	3.1	95.6	135	82	23.4	10.4	7.60	5.27
1985	674.9	160.1	18.0	6.0	2.5	109.7	230	134	20.8	12.6	5.31	3.57
1986	1,750.0	187.8	23.6	7.2	2.4	122.1	277	214	21.1	15.5	4.01	3.03
1987	1,794.0	212.8	29.0	8.7	2.4	143.0	420	216	22.5	9.5	4.88	2.51

executive. He joined the enlarged group from his position as chief executive of Coats Patons, having joined Coats from school over 40 years ago.

CAPITAL

Coats Viyella is the result of several mergers. The most significant in terms of shares issued were the 14.52m issued by Vantona for Carrington Viyella in 1983, the 58.7m issued by Vantona Viyella for Nottingham Manufacturing in 1985 and the 158.5m issued by Vantona Viyella for Coats Patons in 1986. There was a one for one scrip issue in June 1987.

David Alliance, with 2.28m shares, and HAS Djanogly, with 0.61m shares, have the two largest director's holdings, with total directors' holdings amounting to 6.04m, or 1.15% excluding non-beneficial holdings. There are no holders of 5% or more of the equity.

GROUP REVIEW

Vantona Viyella's merger with Coats Patons brought together Vantona's proven UK growth record and Coats Patons' established international presence. The full benefits will be felt in 1988 and beyond.

Capital investment has been maintained at a high level and a number of exceptional overseas opportunities have been identified. Strong organic growth is expected in home furnishings in Europe and North America, and in precision engineering through expansion of overseas facilities, characterised by the establishment of the Dynacast metal component factory in South Korea.

Price pressure and uncertain demand have historically limited growth. Margins rose from 9.4% in 1985 to 10.7% in 1986 and 11.9% in 1987. Cash flow is healthy. Of the £84m capital expenditure made in 1987, one-third went on thread and knitting, a further third on garment and retail, and the balance generally throughout the business.

Margins and profits improved in all major activities. The group is in a healthy liquid position, maintained despite high capital spending and investment in the latest technology. This should enable the group to continue gaining market share.

Thread and handknittings In 1987 the division represented 34.4% of the group's turnover and 48.2% of operating profit. Operating profit increased 14.3% to £103.6m on turnover 2.0% up at £617.4m. It consists of four areas – industrial sewing products, home sewing products, leisure and craft products and handknittings.

Industrial sewing products comprise sewing threads for industrial use, zip fasteners, inter-linings and a variety of related haberdashery and other products with strong market positions in most countries. The area is being successfully restructured. Significant growth is being experienced in the US. Stitchcraft, a Los Angeles distributor acquired in 1986, provided a base for further growth on the west coast.

Home sewing products cover a broad range of articles – home sewing threads, zippers and related products – marketed under a number of strong brands in countries around the world. New channels of distribution and cost effective international sourcing have been developed. Leisure and craft products include threads and yarns for embroidery, tapestry and crochet sold worldwide.

Handknittings are sold under the Patons, Jaeger, Red Heart, Schachenmayr and Cisne brands. The group has several design studios. Recently there has been a move back to a more classical look in handknittings.

The group sold its 54% interest in Bonds Coats Patons in Australia to Pacific Dunlop in 1987 and bought back 100% of the Bonds Coats Patons thread and handknitting division to produce a £35m net cash gain.

Garments – manufacturing and retail In 1987 the division represented 26.2% of the group's turnover and 16.7% of operating profit. Operating profit fell 7.9% to £36.0m on turnover 10.4% down at £469.9m. These figures are not directly comparable because of the sale of Bonds Coats Patons in Australia.

The division consists of a number of areas – menswear, knitwear, contract fashion clothing and hosiery, uniforms, and retailers Jaeger, Country Casuals, Viyella and Jean Muir – the haute couture business.

Menswear has been the subject of a major investment programme and additional production capacity became available in 1987. The group is the market leader in men's shirts with brands like Viyella, Van Heusen and Rocola. The cost of making these shirts has been halved since 1984.

In knitwear, the group is seeking to capitalise on the strength of brand names like Jaeger, Byford and Dalkeith to supplement its position as a supplier to major store groups.

In contract fashion clothing and hosiery there have been notable improvements in childrenswear, sportswear, and waterproof garments. The installation of advanced machinery has enabled quicker reaction to fashion changes and has helped exports.

Uniform sales have suffered from overcapacity and public sector spending constraints. A realignment of capacity is taking place.

In retailing Jaeger is well placed to expand internationally. The group is closing down Jaeger's wholesale business to protect the brand's upmarket appeal and has plans to increase the number of US outlets substantially. Jaeger's London flagship store in Regent Street was completely refurbished in 1987.

Country Casuals trades from 129 stores. Viyella is much smaller and concentrates on weekend spectator sportswear. Jean Muir is one of Britain's best known ladieswear designers. The business is being expanded in both the UK and North America.

Household textiles and carpets In 1987 the division represented 16.8% of the group's turnover and 12.1% of operating profit. Operating profit increased 32.0% to £26.0m on turnover 11.7% up at £270.2m.

The group is the leading UK supplier of bed-linen and duvets. Through Dorma it markets a total bedroom concept using a variety of co-ordinated fabrics. Dorma established a company in France in 1986 and the first Dorma Design House was opened in the UK in the same year.

The group is strong in towels and table-linen. In manufac-

C H A I R M A N ' S   S T A T E M E N T

'For the year as a whole, planned gross capital expenditure will be around £100m as the group continues to invest in new plant and technology in its businesses around the world. Already benefits from this are in evidence in the form of improved margins whilst better performances in certain hitherto difficult areas will further enhance profits.

The present and anticipated generation of a healthy positive cash flow will permit flexibility with regard to acquisitions in certain key areas both in the UK and abroad.' *Sir James Spooner*

turing the division provides fabric finishing and printing operations and a wide range of commission services.

In carpets, the Lancaster brand is marketed to the independent retail sector and CV Carpets concentrates on the larger multiple retailers. Donaghadee operates primarily in the wholesale sector and the emphasis of Carrington is in the contracts area.

Carpet production is being concentrated on two main sites. In 1987, the group took over the troubled Irish carpet maker Youghal Carpets, with its strong Wilton Royal brand name.

Yarns and fabrics In 1987 the division represented 16.1% of the group's turnover and 13.3% of operating profit. Operating profit increased 35.7% to £28.5m on turnover 19.4% up at £289.8m.

The group believes it can make textiles in the UK as cheaply as anywhere in the world. Yarn spinning is benefiting from increased capacity. The customer base has widened and imports are being checked. Fabric production is being concentrated into fewer sites, while workwear fabrics show continuing strong growth especially in exports.

Share price and relative to FT-A All-Share

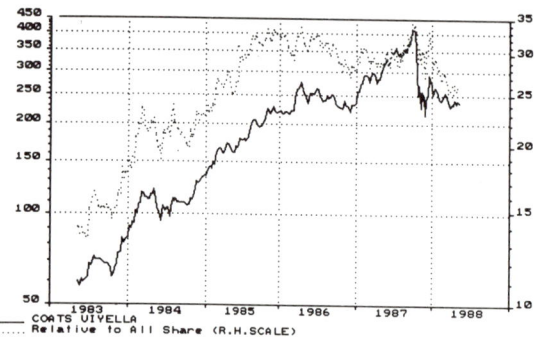

COATS VIYELLA
Relative to All Share (R.H.SCALE)

In December 1987, the group increased its minority holding in Consoltex Canada, the fabric and garments maker, to 80.8% at a cost of C$18m.

Precision engineering In 1987 the division represented 6.5% of the group's turnover and 9.7% of operating profit. Operating profit increased 9.4% to £20.9m on turnover 8.5% up at £116.0m.

The Dynacast components business is the major activity in the division. It has plants in Europe, North and South America and the Pacific region, serving a range of high technology industries. Dynacast makes small precision components in zinc alloys and plastics, which are key components in computer disc drive units and leading disc cameras.

The medical group manufactures products such as sterilised disposable surgical items, micro ophthalmic instrumentation and vascular grafts. Nottingham Group distributes educational and rehabilitation products.

GEOGRAPHICAL REVIEW

In 1987 the UK and its exports represented 57.6% of turnover and 44.1% of profits, Europe 14.5% of turnover and 9.0% of profits, North America 13.7% of turnover and 12.2% of profits, South America 7.3% of turnover and 26.6% of profits and Africa, Asia and Australasia 6.8% of turnover and 8.1% of profits.

CORPORATE CALENDAR

Year end	31 December
Preliminary results	March
Report and accounts	May
AGM	June
Final dividend paid	July
Interim results	September
Interim dividend paid	January

DIRECTORS' HOLDINGS

	Ordinary shares		Options
	(beneficial)	(non-beneficial)	
Sir James Spooner	29,700	—	—
D Alliance	4,557,980	132,466	—
J McAdam	15,336	—	143,440
J Ashton	33,332	—	78,000
CM Bell	21,000	—	153,983
HAS Djanogly	1,224,000	2,203,500	—
JL Hewitt	7,300	—	164,092
NCD Kuenssberg	5,370	—	116,410
AH Macdiarmid	6,998	—	96,092
W McEwan	5,000	—	164,092
JDF Miller	14,200	—	118,879
CB Rothera	96,090	—	81,440
WJ Shelton	12,092	—	121,942
WC Thomson	3,176	—	—
PM White	4,000	—	131,473

Total directors' remuneration including fees in 1986 was £1.45m, of which the chairman received £34,000 and the highest-paid director £104,000.

PRINCIPAL SUBSIDIARIES AND RELATED COMPANIES

Albert Hartley Ltd, British Van Heusen Co Ltd, Carrington Viyella Garments Ltd, Cia Anón Hilaturas de Fabra y Coats – Spain (65%), Cia de Linha Coats & Clarke Lda – Portugal, Cia Ind Hilos Cadena SA – Chile (66%), Coats & Clarke Inc – US, Coats de Venezuela SA (49%), Coats Patons (North America) Inc, Coats Patons plc, Consoltex Canada Inc (80.8%), Country Casuals Ltd, Cucirini Cantoni Coats SpA – Italy (67%), CV Home Furnishings Ltd, CV Woven Fabrics Ltd, D Byford & Co Ltd, Dalkeith Knitwear Ltd, Diana Cowpe Ltd, Donaghadee Carpets Ltd – Northern Ireland, Dynacast Deutschland GmbH – Germany (75%), Dynacast do Brasil Ltda, Dynacast International Ltd, Dynamold International SA, Ewart Liddell Ltd, Filature & Filtéries Réunies SA – Belgium (76%), Gelvenor Textiles (Proprietary) Ltd – South Africa (50%), Harlander Coats GmbH – Austria, Hilos Cadena SAC el – Argentina (90%), J Compton Sons & Webb Ltd, Jaeger Holdings Ltd, J&P Coats (Canada) Inc, J&P Coats Ltd, J&P Coats Pakistan (Pvt) Ltd (60%), J&P Coats (South Africa) (Proprietary) Ltd, J&P Coats (UK) Ltd, Lancaster Carpets Ltd, Linhas Corrente Ltda – Brazil, Madura Coats Ltd – India (40%), Mansfield Knitwear Ltd, Mansfield Leasing Ltd, Mez AG – Germany (97%), F Miller (Textiles) Ltd, Needle Industries Group Ltd, Nottingham Group Ltd, Nottingham Manufacturing Co plc, Pasolds Ltd, Patons & Baldwins Canada Inc, Patons & Baldwins Ltd, Priest (Lindley) Ltd, Santral Dikis Sanayii AS – Turkey (75%), Schachenmayr Mann & Cie GmbH – Germany, Stott & Smith Group Ltd, Thomas Burnley & Sons Ltd, Vantona Ltd, Vantona Viyella plc, VV Household Textiles Ltd, Wardle Fabrics Ltd, West Riding Worsted and Woollen Mills Ltd, William Hollis & Co Ltd

BRAND NAMES

Aero, Aertex, Allen Solly, Anchor, Aptan, Axicut, Beehive, Byford, Carrington, Chair, Chilprufe, Chortex, Clydella, Country Casuals, CV Carpets, Cyclone, Dalkeith, Diana Cowpe, Donaghadee, Dorma, Drima, Duet, Dynacast, Epic, Evvaprest, Jaeger, Jean Muir, Koban, Ladybird, Lancaster, Lance, Louis Phillipe, Mansfield Knitwear, Milwards, New-Tec, Nomeq, Nomotta, Panotex, Paragon, Patons, Penelope, Peter England, Red Heart, Royal Ascot, Royal Wilton, Sclipspun, Steriseal, Super Sheen, Trident, Van Heusen, Vantona, Vascutek, Viyella

CONTACTS AND FURTHER INFORMATION

Jay Webb, Coats Viyella Plc, Charlotte Street, Manchester M1 4ET. Tel: 061-236 3272.

COMMERCIAL UNION ASSURANCE COMPANY plc

GENERAL INFORMATION

Head office	St Helen's, 1 Undershaft, London EC3P 3DQ. Tel: 01-283 7500
Directors	AB Marshall (chairman), AL Brend, JGT Carter, LW Hammick, AB Wyand. *Non-exec* NH Baring (deputy chairman), JFG Emms (deputy chairman), RA Brooks, MH Fisher, RC Hampel, Sir Martin Jacomb, J Linborn, The Hon Sir Peter Ramsbotham GCMG GCVO
Advisers	Kleinwort Benson Ltd
Auditors	Coopers & Lybrand
Registrars	Lloyds Bank Registrar's Department
Brokers	Hoare Govett Ltd, Cazenove & Co
Solicitors	Linklaters & Paines

GENERAL FINANCIAL INFORMATION

Market capitalisation	£1.394bn at 1 January 1988
Capital structure	
Issued ordinary shares (25p)	415.0m
Issued preference shares (£1)	1.75m
Warrants	£7m, 243 shares per warrant, exercisable at 345p
Convertibles	None
Traded options	Yes
ADRs	None
Shareholders over 5%	None

FT CATEGORY

FT: Insurances
FT-A: Insurance (composite)

MAJOR ACTIVITIES

Commercial Union is a large diversified composite life and non-life insurance company operating in the UK, the US, Canada, the Netherlands, and in 80 other countries.

The group provides a wide range of financial products to members of the public in the UK and overseas. The products sold include: general branch policies like private and commercial motor car insurances; domestic contents and buildings insurances; policies covering public liability and accidents; life assurance; investment policies providing protection against accident or death; savings contracts; and retirement policies.

An important part of the group's activities relates to the acceptance of large commercial risks. It insures structure, contents and liability risks for aircraft and ships, and provides cover for commercial motor fleets and against industrial fire damage. It is active in the reinsurance market, providing insurance cover to insurance companies wishing to protect themselves from adverse developments on their own portfolio of accepted risks.

CHAIRMAN'S STATEMENT

'Our results . . . show a good improvement. . . . This recovery has been achieved in part through a general advance in the major markets in which we operate, but more particularly as a result of the decisions and actions taken to alter the composition of our business over the last few years. . . .

The outlook for the insurance industry is better than for many years and there should be greater stability in the markets in which we operate. Despite the worldwide economic uncertainties and increasing competition in our industry, the prospects for 1988 are generally good. The Group has been strengthened substantially by the actions taken in recent years and we look forward with confidence to further profitable development.' *AB Marshall*

Most of the group's business is derived from agents and independent brokers who receive commission as payment for the introduction of business to the group. Reliance on the broker market for the bulk of UK business means that sales volumes and profit margins depend greatly on the state of competition in the insurance industry. The group's fortunes also depend on exchange rates, because a large part of its business is conducted overseas, and on the stock market, because its huge asset base is invested primarily in gilts and equities.

The group's competitors include: the other quoted sector composite insurers General Accident, Guardian Royal Exchange, Royal Insurance and Sun Alliance; the large mutual insurers like Norwich Union; and the life companies, particularly Prudential Corporation, Standard Life and Legal & General. Commercial Union's entry into the house mortgage market faces a challenge from the building societies and banks, whilst its entry into unit trusts and PEPs is in competition with the unit trust management groups.

FINANCIAL HISTORY

Premium income in 1987 at £2.845bn was 30% higher than in 1982. Life assurance premium income more than doubled to £831m, and non-life premiums increased by one-tenth to £2.014bn.

The group has been contracting in the US since 1984. Non-life premium income there at about £600m is below the 1981 level, despite premium rate increases and inflationary trends in the intervening period. Elsewhere in the world the group is expanding, particularly in its life business.

The composite insurance companies have volatile earnings patterns. Consequently a breakdown of profits in any one year is little guide to the likely distribution in the next year. The industry has just recovered from a major downturn and may now be entering another, hopefully less severe, phase of increased competition.

Commercial Union's profit in 1987 of £170.1m has finally reached the levels seen at the peak of the last cycle in 1978 when it made £142.2m. The group's life profits of £90.6m in 1987 have been and continue to be a major source of stability.

Earnings per share amounted to 26.4p in 1987, compared with 20p in 1986 and losses of similar amounts in 1984 and 1985, the trough of the insurance cycle. Management's confidence in the future was reflected in a 23% increase in the dividend from 13.0p to 16.0p.

The autumn stock market fall was the main factor behind the fall in shareholders' funds, from £1.43bn at the end of 1986 to £1.14bn at the end of 1987. Nevertheless, the ratio of shareholders' funds to non-life premium income at 57% shows that the group is in a very healthy financial position. Losses in the October storms were reckoned to be about £15m.

SHARE PRICE HISTORY

Relative to the market, the company's shares trade between 30% and 40% of the FT-A All-Share index. Generally firm during 1983 and the first part of 1984, the shares fell back sharply from the middle of 1984 to the first part of 1985 as news gathered pace about asbestosis and other claims made against the group arising from a number of discontinued lines of business.

In common with other insurers, the price improved in the spring of 1986 as evidence of the healthier business climate for the insurance industry appeared. The relatively poor dividend

F I V E   Y E A R   F I N A N C I A L   I N F O R M A T I O N

Year	Turnover (£m)	Pre-tax (£m)	Earnings (p)	Dividends net (p)	Dividend cover (x)	Net assets (p)	Price (p) High	Low	PER (x) High	Low	Yield (%) High	Low
1983	2,285	9.3	(1.99)	11.8	—	254	191	125	—	—	13.49	8.83
1984	2,655	(72.8)	(21.44)	11.8	—	260	230	163	—	—	10.34	7.33
1985	2,306	0.2	(21.93)	11.8	—	281	259	175	—	—	9.55	6.45
1986	2,766	119.1	20.05	13.0	1.54	346	334	230	16.7	11.5	7.83	5.39
1987	2,845	170.1	26.37	16.0	1.65	273	454	267	17.2	10.1	8.08	4.75

news held the shares back for the remainder of 1986. The likelihood of increasing competition in the UK insurance industry was also a factor.

The shares fell from a high of 454p to 267p in the October 1987 crash. Optimism about dividend prospects helped the share price during the latter part of 1987. Outperformance of the index took the relative up towards 40% again. The share price was helped by the re-emergence of speculation about the possibility of the group being taken over.

SENIOR MANAGEMENT

The company's chairman is Alexander Marshall. Tony Brend, chief executive, is responsible for the day-to-day control of operations. The director in charge of investment and finance is AB Wyand. The group's financial management is also under the control of JH Webb, the group actuary. John Larke is in charge of the group's operations in the UK, Ken Duffy the US, Dr Guus Zoutendijk the Netherlands, Harry Greer Canada and Leslie Hammick the rest of the world.

Among the non-executive directors are N Baring of Barings; Sir Martin Jacomb, deputy chairman of Barclays Bank; and Sir Peter Ramsbotham, former British Ambassador to the US.

CAPITAL

At the end of 1987 there were 415m issued shares. No major changes have taken place in the last three years. The recent quotation on the Paris Bourse increased the number of shares by 3.5m.

The SFr 200m bond issue in June 1986 was accompanied by an issue of warrants which could result in up to 9.7m ordinary shares being issued. There is no declarable stake in the group but the Adelaide steamship company of Australia holds 4.7% of the issued shares.

GROUP REVIEW

United Kingdom The non-life division showed substantial growth in 1987 with premiums up 12% to £838m, following 23% growth in 1986. This reflected the effects of premium rate increases in 1985 and 1986, which were needed following the disappointing results in the years 1982 to 1985. The profit of £95.5m earned in 1987 was a big improvement on the 1985 and 1986 results of £34m and £65m respectively.

Marine and aviation and reinsurance premiums amounted to £219m in 1987. Of the remaining domestic premiums of £618m, motor insurances accounted for £172m and domestic and commercial property insurances for £220m.

The company has a very strong and profitable life division in the UK. It has been successful in expanding new business sales, through its various sales channels – advertising, direct selling and the network of contacts with insurance brokers. Life profits in 1987 amounted to £38m.

United States The group's business in the US is split evenly between personal and commercial insurances. Substantial premium rate increases, which continued up to the end of 1986 (particularly on the problem commercial lines insurances), resulted in a much reduced loss of £3.5m in 1987, compared with £23m in 1986 and £179m in 1985.

The group has been very selective in its acceptance of business since 1984. Premium volume has been reduced from £1.086bn in 1984 to £590m in 1987. Staff numbers have been reduced and the lists of agents who introduce business to the group have been pared. But the group's business in the US remains unprofitable in contrast to the good UK operations and successful Dutch life business.

Netherlands Commercial Union's business in the Netherlands is conducted through its subsidiary Delta Lloyd, which made profits of £42.5m in 1987 compared with £50.1m in 1986. The business is run on very conservative lines.

Life is the main business. The existing block of policies will ensure profits for years to come. New life business, which is sold primarily through intermediaries, is the main source of profits growth. Life business is very profitable.

The Dutch non-life market is fiercely competitive. The fire and motor accounts, which together account for over half the Dutch business, are particularly unprofitable at present. Delta Lloyd has paid out for many years more in expenses and claims than it receives in premiums. These losses are covered by the investment income generated by the non-life assets. A review of operations has recently been undertaken to improve profitability.

Rest of the world and Canada Commercial Union's other principal overseas divisions are in Canada, Belgium, France, Italy and Spain. The remaining interests are in the rest of Europe including Eire, the Far East, Australia and New Zealand, South America, the West Indies and Africa.

Apart from the US and the Netherlands, the operations in Canada are the largest of Commercial Union's overseas divisions. As in the US, non-life business, which predominates

Share price and relative to FT-A All-Share

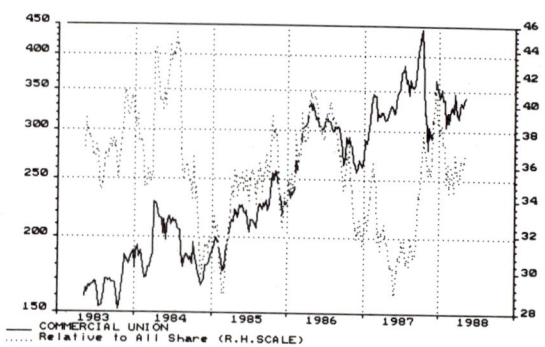

COMMERCIAL UNION
Relative to All Share (R.H.SCALE)

over life business in Canada, has emerged recently from a prolonged downturn. The property insurance portfolio is now profitable, although motor policies – which account for about a half of the total portfolio – continue to be unprofitable.

Pre-tax profits for Canada were £7.6m in 1987, compared to £6.5m in 1986. Operating pre-tax profit for the rest of the world was up £0.1m to £26.4m.

GEOGRAPHICAL REVIEW

The territorial distribution in 1987 of the group's non-life premium income is UK 31%, US 29%, Netherlands 12%, Canada 7%, Belgium 3%, France 1%, Italy 1%, Spain 1%, other areas 4%, marine and aviation worldwide 9% and reinsurance worldwide 2%.

Profits vary greatly from year to year for each territory, but life profits emerge primarily in the UK and the Netherlands.

CORPORATE CALENDAR

Year end	31 December
Preliminary results	March
Report and accounts	March
AGM	April
Final dividend paid	May
Interim results	August
Interim dividend paid	November

DIRECTORS' HOLDINGS

	Fully-paid ordinary shares	Options
NH Baring	7,000	—
AL Brend	3,725	794
RA Brooks	4,411	—
JGT Carter	2,667	—
JFG Emms	5,803	2,777
MH Fisher	1,000	—
LW Hammick	4,629	794
RC Hampel	200	—
Sir Martin Jacomb	12,105	—
J Linbourn	9,056	5,555
AB Marshall	4,267	—
The Hon Sir Peter Ramsbotham	1,526	—
AB Wyand	4,409	—

Total emoluments paid to the directors in 1987 amounted to £670,373, of which the chairman was paid £56,100 and the highest-paid director £139,972, exclusive of pension contributions.

PRINCIPAL SUBSIDIARIES AND RELATED COMPANIES

American Employers' Insurance Company – US, Ashton Tod McLaren (77.9%), British & European Reinsurance Company Limited (3%), CU Fire, Marine and General Insurance Company Ltd – Zimbabwe, Commercial Union Corporation – US, Commercial Union Life Insurance Company of America – US, CU Trading Corporation – US, Canada Accident and Fire Assurance Company – Canada, Commercial Union Asset Management Limited, Commercial Union Assurance Company of Canada, Commercial Union Capital Limited, Commercial Union Equipment Finance Limited (80%), Commercial Union Finance BV – Netherlands, Commercial Union Financial Services Limited, Commercial Union IARD – France, Commercial Union Leasing Corporation – US, Commercial Union Life Assurance Company Limited, Commercial Union Life Assurance Company of Canada, Commercial Union Pensions Management Ltd, Commercial Union Properties Ltd, Commercial Union Risk Management Ltd, Commercial Union Trust Managers Limited, Commercial Union Vida Seguros y Reaseguros SA – Spain, Commercial Union of America – US, Commercial Union of Canada Holdings Ltd, Delta Lloyd Levensverzekering NV – Netherlands, Delta Lloyd Schadeverzekering NV – Netherlands, Delta Lloyd Verzekeringsgroep NV (99.9%) – Netherlands, Edinburgh Assurance Company Ltd, Employers' Fire Insurance Company – US, Employers' Liability Assurance Corporation Ltd, Fleet Motor Management Group (51%), Indemnity Marine Assurance Corporation Ltd, L'Epargne de France SA (78.2%) – France, North British and Mercantile Insurance Company Ltd,

Northern Assurance Company Ltd, Northern Assurance Company of America – US, Ocean Accident and Guarantee Corporation Ltd, Ocean Marine Insurance Company Ltd, Plant Safety Ltd (50%), Stanstead & Sherbrooke Insurance Company – Canada, Travellers' Insurance Association Ltd

BRAND NAMES

The Dual Driver policy introduced in April 1986 is perhaps the best known of the company's products. Recent television campaigns 'Don't make a drama out of a crisis' and 'CU Life is for Living' have brought an increased awareness of Commercial Union to the public.

CONTACTS AND FURTHER INFORMATION

Jacky Naylor, Investor Relations Department, Commercial Union Assurance Company plc, Commercial Union House, 69 Park Lane, Croydon CR9 1BG. Tel: 01-283 7500.

CONSOLIDATED GOLD FIELDS PLC

GENERAL INFORMATION

Head office   31 Charles II Street, St James's Square, London SW1Y 4AG.
Tel: 01-930 6200

Directors   RIJ Agnew (chairman and group chief executive), The Rt
Hon the Lord Errol of Hale PC TD (president), ME Beckett,
PD Fells, AP Hichens, A Sykes, JHA Wood. *Non-exec* CMcC
Anderson, CNA Castleman, JN Clarke, PJ Elton MC, RAE
Herbert, J Ogilvie Thompson, GR Parker, RA Plumridge
DMS, JRAM Storar

Advisers   J Henry Schroder Wagg & Co Ltd, SG Warburg & Co Ltd
Auditors   Ernst & Whinney
Registrars   Lloyds Bank Registrar's Department
Brokers   Cazenove & Co
Solicitors   Freshfields

GENERAL FINANCIAL INFORMATION

Market capitalisation   £2.033bn at 1 January 1988
Capital structure
Issued ordinary shares (25p)   212m
Issued preference shares   None
Warrants   None
Convertibles   £110m 6.75% convertible subordinated
bonds 2002 (92.592 ordinary 25p shares
for every £1,000 stock)
Traded options   Yes
ADRs   Four ordinary shares per ADR
Shareholders over 5%   Mineral and Resources Corporation
28.75%, Gold Fields 7.6%

FT CATEGORY

FT: Mines – finance
FT-A: Mining finance

MAJOR ACTIVITIES

Consolidated Gold Fields (CGF) is the UK's largest gold mining group, with attributable gold production totalling approximately 1.7m ounces per annum. Through its wholly-owned subsidiary, ARC, formerly Amey Roadstone Corp, it is also a major producer of quarried stone products.

CGF is principally a large mining finance house with interests in the UK, North America, South Africa and Australia. Apart from its wholly owned North American gold subsidiary Gold Fields Mining Corporation (GFMC) and ARC, the group does not exercise direct managerial control over its interests.

CGF's major listed assets in order of value are: a 38% stake in Gold Fields of South Africa (GFSA), recently reduced from 48%; a 49% stake in Newmont Mining Corporation, the large US gold and energy group; a 49% stake in Renison Goldfields Consolidated (RGC), an Australian mining house; 70% of Mount Goldsworthy; 7% of Driefontein Consolidated; 15% of Deelkraal; and 12% of Kloof.

CGF also has a 12% direct interest in a new platinum mining development which is being brought to production by GFSA, and a 50% stake in Renown Energy. CGF has an active share dealing department located in London, which made over £50m in 1987.

ARC's UK activities are centred around quarrying operations and manufacturing heavy building materials. In the US, ARC America (ARCA) is the country's largest supplier of concrete drainage pipes. In March 1987 it moved into the US quarried stone business when it bought American Aggregates for $240m cash.

In 1987, 43% of operating profits were derived from gold mining operations, 8% from other minerals and energy, 25% from construction materials and 24% from share dealing and investment management. The most comparable listed com-panies are Anglo American in South Africa, RTZ in the UK and Western Mining in Australia. UK competitors in the building materials industry include Redland and Tarmac.

With more than 50% of total pre-tax profits attributable to gold mining operations, CGF's fortunes remain closely linked to the performance of the gold price. However, its mining operations are of exceptional quality. With breakeven costs of between $100 and $200 per ounce, leverage to the gold price is not high. Further, as a result of the company's substantial exploration budget, it has several new mining projects coming on stream over the next five years. These provide it with organic growth even if the gold price remains flat. The company has adopted a policy of reducing its dependence on South African earnings: in 1987 these constituted 17%, down from 33% in 1986.

The construction materials business has performed well. The group expects to increase its profits from this area by means of organic growth, especially of the value-added product business, and by acquisition. This business should provide the shares with some downside protection whenever bullion moves into bear markets.

FINANCIAL HISTORY

Turnover has been relatively flat since 1982, while pre-tax profits have risen 171% to £244m in 1987 from £97m in 1982. Earnings per share have risen from 39.0p in 1982 to 82.2p in 1987. The major portion of this rise occurred during the 1987 financial year.

Operating profits have been growing at an annual rate of 7.7% since 1982. This growth has come unevenly from gold mining operations and steadily and progressively from organic growth within the construction materials business owned by ARC. ARC's profits of £35.2m in 1982 rose to £83.6m in 1987.

The dividend was raised 3.0p to 27.5p in 1987. The 1987 balance sheet was geared at 42%, but recent disposals have strengthened it and ordinary shareholders' total funds are a long way from reflecting the true value of its important unlisted assets ARC and GFMC. Net debt stood at £504m at 30 June 1987 and return on capital was 26.4% and has averaged 16% over five years.

At the 1988 interim, CGF's pre-tax profits were sharply ahead, up 87% from £97.5m to £182.7m. Turnover was 11.3% up at £619.9m. Earnings per share rose by 58% to 58p. The dividend of 10p net represented a rise of 5.3%.

ARC's profits were 38% up at £57m from £41.3m with strong performances in the UK and the US, despite the weak dollar. The US operations contributed 40% of ARC's profits.

Share price and relative to FT-A All-Share

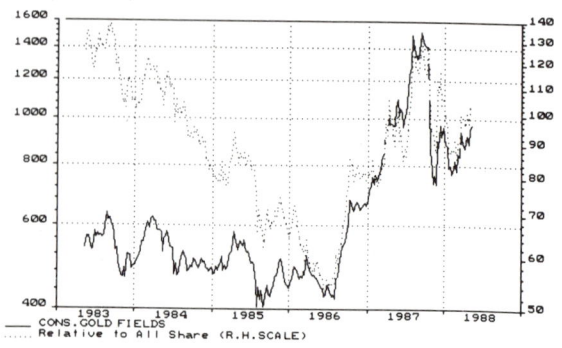

CONS.GOLD FIELDS
Relative to All Share (R.H.SCALE)

Year	Turnover (£m)	Pre-tax (£m)	Earnings (p)	Dividends net (p)	Dividend cover (x)	Net assets (p)	Price (p) High	Low	PER (x) High	Low	Yield (%) High	Low
1983	1,046	89.7	30.5	24.5	1.3	334	634	462	45.2	19.1	7.58	5.52
1984	1,200	105.0	38.2	24.5	1.6	361	627	464	26.1	16.3	7.54	5.58
1985	1,115	114.9	40.7	24.5	1.7	350	582	397	19.1	12.3	8.82	6.01
1986	1,200	110.9	35.1	24.5	1.4	258	699	414	19.9	12.3	8.45	4.94
1987	1,111.8	244.4	82.2	27.5	3.0	342	1515	670	22.4	6.9	5.40	2.53

Mining profits fell by 25% to £52.6m from £70.1m. Amongst several factors involved, the most important were: the reduction in the share of profit from Newmont Mining, down from £13m to £8.7m, arising from interest charges on the increased stake and the defence against the bid from Ivanhoe Partners; lower South African profits due to the reduction in the GFSA holding; and a small loss of £2.1m at the Goldsworthy iron ore operation in Western Australia brought about by adverse exchange movements.

Financial profits from dealing in mining shares were dramatically ahead at £101.5m from £8.1m. There was an £82m gain on the sale of the 10% beneficial interest in GFSA, which was taken above the line.

Net interest paid was £6.1m higher, despite the £266m net cost of increasing the stake in Newmont Mining by 23.6%. Much of the company's debt is dollar-denominated and benefited from the weak currency. Net gearing was 53% of shareholders' funds, though if the £765m unrealised appreciation of listed investments was taken into account this would fall to 32%.

SHARE PRICE HISTORY

Between 1984 and mid-1986 the share price traded between 580p and 400p, building up a massive bottom formation. A strengthening in the gold price and a positive upward rerating of global gold stocks sparked a strong rally from 420p in August 1986. A purchase of a 5% stake in the company through the market by American Barrick, and the subsequent bid speculation which amounted to nothing, pushed the shares to new highs of 700p. After a short period of consolidation, the realisation by the market that profits would probably double in 1987 pushed share prices from the 700p level to highs of £15. But the price subsequently fell back dramatically in the autumn 1987 crash and started 1988 around the 900p level.

SENIOR MANAGEMENT

Chairman and chief executive Rudolph Agnew, a through-the-ranks CGF man, was appointed chairman in 1983. Managing directors are Antony Hichens, who is chief financial officer, Michael Beckett, Alan Sykes, Humphrey Wood and Peter Fells. CMcC Anderson is managing director and chief executive officer of RGC. GR Parker is chairman and chief executive officer of Newmont Mining. RA Plumridge is chairman and chief executive officer of GFSA.

CAPITAL

CGF's issued share capital totals 212m shares. 23m new shares have been issued since 1984: in order to finance the purchase of Bath and Portland; on conversion of a convertible Euro-bond; as part of the scrip for their dividend scheme; and to

follow the Newmont rights issue.

The 23.6% increase in CGF's stake in Newmont Mining to 49.7% cost $1.55bn, financed from CGF's cash and loan resources. The 15.8m shares acquired, together with the existing stake, immediately received a $33 per share dividend, thereby reducing the acquisition cost significantly. CGF increased its stake to protect its interests in Newmont after the aggressive tender offer by Ivanhoe Partners.

Minorco owns 28.75% of the issued shares and GFSA and Driefontein jointly hold 7.6% of the company's stock.

GROUP REVIEW

Gold mining CGF's mining activities are essentially based around gold production. It is in this area, particularly in the US, where growth is expected to take place.

The Mesquite operation in California has started life successfully. Grades encountered so far have proved to be better than expected, and production reached 180,000 ounces in 1987. Mesquite is an open pit operation with a life of 15 to 20 years. Breakeven costs are $120 per ounce. Chimney Creek is a new open pit gold mine located in the recently discovered Nevada gold belt. This mine was brought to production in December 1987, on budget and three months ahead of schedule. It will produce 160,000 ounces per annum at full capacity. Its annual operating costs are low at around $120 per ounce. It is also expected to have a life of between 15 and 20 years. Both of these mines are totally owned by GFMC, and CGF may list this company separately in the near future and float off between 5% and 10% of it. If and when the listing takes place, CGF's asset value should be substantially increased.

Newmont Mining is also in the process of expanding its gold operations. Newmont's listed US subsidiary, Newmont Gold, is bringing on new capacity to push output to more than 900,000 ounces in 1988 and 1.6m ounces by 1991.

In South Africa, CGF's gold interests are held through direct holdings in three South African gold producers – Driefontein 7%, Kloof 12% and Deelkraal 15% – and through GFSA. GFSA acts as adviser to gold, base metal, and coal mines in southern Africa, and administers some of the richest and lowest cost mines in the world. Production from gold mines in the GFSA group was 123.2 tonnes in 1987. GFSA's attributable interest in gold production amounted to 1.3m ounces.

Driefontein and Kloof are South Africa's two lowest cost gold mines, recording production costs of $145 per ounce and $135 per ounce respectively in June 1987. Driefontein is the world's third largest gold producer with an output of 2.0m ounces per annum. Kloof's annual output is 50% of this, but the company is to double its ore treatment capacity over the next 15 years by opening up a new mining section, Leeudoorn.

Renison Goldfields Consolidated (RGC) has a 60% interest in the Pine Creek open-pit mine in the Northern Territory,

Australia. Production is running at 60,000 ounces of gold per annum. RGC also owns a small gold mine in Wau, Papua New Guinea. Its most exciting potential development is the 33% stake it owns in Porgera, Papua New Guinea. This is reported to be the largest undeveloped gold prospect in the world but it will take until the early 1990s to bring it into production at between 20 and 25 tons of gold a year.

Other mining RGC's major business other than gold mining is the extraction of mineral sands. Principal products are ilmenite, monazite, rutile and zircon. The company also has major tin operations in Tasmania. These are profitable despite the sharp fall in the price of tin that followed the collapse of the International Tin Council, because the ending of the official production quota system has allowed the mine to return to full production.

Newmont Mining has a 50% interest in Peabody Coal. This is the largest US coal producer, operating 39 mines in 11 states. 85% of the coal it produces is sold to electricity utilities under long term contracts. Its coal output totals 60m tonnes per annum. Newmont also produces 3,700 barrels of oil per day. Most of Newmont's copper interests were floated off in March 1987 by the issue to shareholders of scrip in Magma Copper Co. CGF received 21% of Magma, but has subsequently reduced its stake to below 20% so that it can treat it as a portfolio investment.

CHAIRMAN'S STATEMENT

'To those of you who have followed the strategic thrust of our policy closely in recent years, this sharp improvement in our results should come as no surprise. Despite the adverse economic conditions experienced by the mining industry as a whole, we have continued to invest heavily in the highest quality, lowest cost ore-bodies available to us. In my statement last year, I predicted that financial success would follow from the realisation of these plans. I am delighted to have been proved right so soon and believe the Group is set fair to build on the sound base now established.' *Rudolph Agnew*

CGF has a 12.7% direct interest in the Northam platinum venture in north western Transvaal. This is in addition to its indirect interest through GFSA which owns 78% of Northam. Development of the $270m venture is proceeding and production of platinum group metals is scheduled to commence in 1992.

Goldsworthy Mining, 70% owned by CGF, mines iron ore in Australia. The group is committing $80m to refurbish this operation's mine. In December 1987 CGF took a 50% stake in Kleinwort Benson Energy for £42m, now called Renown Energy, with the option of increasing its stake to 75% in three years.

Construction materials ARC is a major producer of heavy building materials. In the UK its primary products are crushed rock, sand and gravel, together with value-added products like coated stone, ready-mixed concrete, pre-mix mortar, concrete pipes, blocks, bricks and roofing tiles. The company also undertakes contracting work.

In the US, ARCA's principal business is Hydro Conduit, the country's largest supplier of concrete drainage pipes. In April 1987 ARCA bought American Aggregates for $240m. Its aggregate operations will complement ARC's existing business in the US.

ARC Properties holds an extensive property portfolio. Property development is an integral part of the group's business. When mineral reserves are exhausted from one of the group's sites, it becomes a candidate for development. Sometimes ARC Properties buys adjacent sites to maximise a development project's potential. Of particular potential is the property it owns around junction 13 of the M25 motorway.

GEOGRAPHICAL REVIEW

As a result of the company's policy over the last few years the reliance upon South Africa has been reduced and the profit contribution from North America increased. South Africa contributed 17% of profits in 1987 against 47% in 1983. A further reduction will occur in 1988. In terms of assets at market value the breakdown is South Africa 19%, US 46%, UK 29% and Australia 6%.

CORPORATE CALENDAR

Year end	30 June
Preliminary results	September
Report and accounts	October
AGM	November
Final dividend paid	December
Interim results	March
Interim dividend paid	May

DIRECTORS' HOLDINGS

	Fully-paid ordinary shares	Options
RIJ Agnew	5,138	154,515
CMcC Anderson	1,000	—
ME Beckett	1,100	75,309
JN Clarke	102	—
PJ Elton	2,569	—
PD Fells	100	45,742
RAE Herbert	100	—
AP Hichens	1,027	86,809
J Ogilvie Thompson	125	—
GR Parker	500	—
RA Plumridge	125	—
JRAM Storar	1,200	—
A Sykes	200	76,600
JHA Wood	192	76,042

All beneficial.

Total directors' salaries and other fees for 1987 were £706,000, with the chairman receiving the highest remuneration at £243,784.

PRINCIPAL SUBSIDIARIES AND RELATED COMPANIES

Gold mining
Black Mountain Mineral Development Co (Pty) Ltd – South Africa (26%), Deelkraal Gold Mining Co Ltd – South Africa (14%), Doornfontein Gold Mining Co Ltd – South Africa (16%), Driefontein Consolidated Ltd – South Africa (7%), EI du Pont de Nemours & Co – US (1%), Foote Mineral Co – US (41%), Gold Fields Coal Ltd – South Africa (34%), Gold Fields Mining Corp – US, Gold Fields of South Africa Ltd (38%), Goldsworthy Mining Ltd – Australia (70%), Kloof Gold Mining Co Ltd – South Africa (12%), Libanon Gold Mining Co Ltd – South Africa (16%), Magma Copper Co – US (26%), Newmont Gold Co – US (44.8%), Newmont Mining Corporation (49.7%), Newmont Oil Co – US (49.8%), O'okiep Copper Co Ltd – South Africa (28%), Palabora Mining Co Ltd – South Africa (8%), Peabody Holding Co Inc – US (24.9%), Pinto Valley Copper Corp – US (26%), Renison Goldfields Consolidated Ltd – Australia (49%), Southern Peru Copper Corp – Peru (3%), Telfer Gold Mine – Australia (18%)

Construction materials
ARC Ltd, ARC America Corporation – US

Finance
CGF Capital BV – Netherlands, Consolidated Gold Fields Finance Plc, Gold Fields Finance BV – Netherlands

Other investments
British-Borneo Petroleum Syndicate Plc (26%), Renown Energy (50%)

COOKSON GROUP plc

BRAND NAMES

ARC Concrete, ARC Marine, Hydro Conduit

CONTACTS AND FURTHER INFORMATION

Graham Williams, Consolidated Gold Fields PLC, 31 Charles II Street, St James's Square, London SW1Y 4AG. Tel: 01-930 6200.

GENERAL INFORMATION

Head office	Clements House, 14 Gresham Street, London EC2V 7AT. Tel: 01-606 4400
Directors	I Butler FCA (chairman), R Iley (managing), R Oster (managing), M Henderson (group chief executive), J Bickers, F Munro FCCA, Sir Peter Matthews AO, Sir Nigel Mobbs, M Sindzingre, B de Villeméjane
Advisers	Lazard Brothers & Co Ltd
Auditors	Peat Marwick McLintock
Registrars	Ravensbourne Registration Services Ltd
Brokers	Phillips & Drew Ltd
Solicitors	Linklaters & Paines

GENERAL FINANCIAL INFORMATION

Market capitalisation	£910.6m at 1 January 1988
Capital structure	
Issued ordinary shares (50p)	181.1m
Issued preference shares (£1)	1.3m 4.9% CP
	0.5m 4.9% preferred ordinary
Warrants	None
Convertibles	None
Traded options	None
ADRs	None
Shareholders over 5%	None

FT CATEGORY

FT: Industrials (miscel.)
FT-A: Other industrial materials

MAJOR ACTIVITIES

Cookson Group, formerly Lead Industries, is a manufacturer of a wide range of specialist industrial materials for use in industry. Principal activities include refining, fabricating non-ferrous and precious metals and the manufacture of chemicals, ceramics, refractories, plastics and printing products.

The group operates from three divisions – Cookson Metals and Chemicals, Cookson Ceramics and Plastics, and Cookson America. It holds a 50% interest with ICI in Tioxide, a producer of titanium dioxide, and a major contributor to profits.

The group serves industries in aeronautics, automobiles, building, ceramics, engineering, electronics, electronics, steel, glass, jewellery, medical and nuclear equipment, paint, paper, printing and textiles. Cookson is the world's largest consumer of tin.

FINANCIAL HISTORY

Between 1983 and 1987 Cookson's turnover increased by 117.4%. Pre-tax profits increased by 562.6%. Earnings per share were up 307.5%. Dividends were up 135%.

Sales in 1987 totalled £1.189bn, up 22.3% over £972.1m in 1986, despite negative currency movements, particularly the dollar. 1987 pre-tax profits of £143.8m showed a 52.2% increase over £94.5m in 1986. Margin on sales in 1987 was 13% compared with 12% in 1986 and 10.2% in 1985.

Net interest payable fell from £18.2m to £10.5m. Earnings per share improved to 54.2p in 1987 from 41.5p in 1986 and 36.3p in 1985, an increase of 30.6% and 18% respectively. After the rights issue in February 1987, net borrowings fell from 41% to around 16% of total funds employed.

FIVE YEAR FINANCIAL INFORMATION

Year	Turnover (£m)	Pre-tax (£m)	Earnings (p)	Dividends net (p)	Dividend cover (x)	Net assets (p)	Price (p) High	Price (p) Low	PER (x) High	PER (x) Low	Yield (%) High	Yield (%) Low
1983	574.0	21.7	13.3	5.10	2.6	206.4	118	58	30.3	8.1	11.40	5.63
1984	763.8	52.3	35.7	6.25	5.7	214.5	238	118	19.6	9.6	6.00	3.23
1985	867.3	67.6	36.3	7.75	4.7	179.4	385	230	17.4	8.7	3.35	2.33
1986	972.1	94.5	42.8	8.75	4.7	211.1	568	356	17.9	11.2	2.62	1.64
1987	1,188.8	143.8	54.2	12.00	4.5	n/a	830	405	20.4	8.1	3.38	1.44

SHARE PRICE HISTORY

Since late spring 1984, Cookson shares have shown good growth for a number of reasons. Analysts recognised the benefits derived from a rationalisation and cost reduction programme. There was a decreasing reliance on the UK market following acquisitions in the US. There was a move from cyclical commodity-type industrial materials to more specialised value-added products.

The share price responded, rising from a low of 118p in 1984 to a high of 831p in 1987. The major period of outperformance of the FT-A All-Share index was from mid-1984 to early 1986. The shares climbed from 125p in mid-1984 in a continuous bull run to 400p a year later. The shares fell back to 300p before rapidly climbing again to near 600p in early 1986.

The shares halved after the October 1987 share crash from 800p to 400p, before recovering to the 540p level in April 1988.

SENIOR MANAGEMENT

In April 1987 Cookson separated the roles of chairman and chief executive. Michael Henderson became chief executive in June 1987. Ian Butler remained as chairman. The company is embarking on management training to promote a more homogeneous management style among the different subsidiaries.

CAPITAL

In 1984 Cookson decided to have its first rights issue in the 54-year history of the company. Since that time there have been several other issues. The most recent was a one for four rights issue in January 1987 to raise £162.3m.

The company has kept acquisitions below £50m, concentrating on areas the company already knows about. In 1987 the company made a series of acquisitions. In May 1987 it purchased the remaining 50% of Vesuvius Crucible for a total

CHAIRMAN'S STATEMENT

'1988 has started well. Uncertainties which may have caused or resulted from the fall of many share prices last autumn have not materialised, although there is perhaps less confidence in the world about levels of economic activity in 1989. The UK must be encouraged by its economic performance, but both here and in the USA the adverse balance of trade needs correction. As always, economic uncertainties are a concern but the Group is well placed to take advantage of the opportunities and the planned continued growth of the Group is being maintained.'
Ian Butler

consideration of $105m. In August 1987 it agreed with the US company Plibrico to acquire all its plastic and castable refractory operations outside the US for $60m cash.

In September 1987 Cookson purchased Polyclad, the US producer of laminates for circuit boards, for $74m including a placing of 5.64m shares at 800p.

The company is proposing a one for one scrip issue at its AGM in May 1988.

GROUP REVIEW

Cookson metals and chemicals division This division, formed in 1987, brings together Cookson Materials and Cookson Fry.

The division is involved with metal smelting and refining, producing products such as lead, lead chemicals, shot and sheeting, copper foil and lithographic printing plates. Further activities include plastic stabilisers, plastic recycling and engineering plastics.

The past few years have been difficult due to low oil prices, which depress the price of virgin polymers. The division has seen rationalisation of its products and manufacturing processes. This should lead to higher margins and an increase in revenue, particularly if trading conditions in chemicals and stabilisers improve. Particular emphasis has been placed on improving the effectiveness of marketing and selling operations.

The old Cookson Fry area serves industry in general but has particular strengths in electronics, automotive, aviation, household appliances, printing and general engineering. The product range, which is based on non-ferrous metals, includes solders, fluxes, brazing alloys, printing metals, die-castings, bearings, bronze, aluminium and low-melting-point alloys.

All companies improved their performances in 1987. Operating profit was up 37% to £31m (£21.1m) after a rise of 61.1% in 1986.

Cookson ceramics and plastics division Organic and development growth prospects are good, due to the completion of the reorganisation started in 1985.

Antimony profits are well up. Margins have improved and contributed to a profit rise in ceramics. Potterycraft has also seen an increase of profitability from rationalisation. Zircon should benefit from major capital expenditure programmes in both the UK and Spain.

In 1987 the division saw a good increase in operating profit of 70% to £27.5m (£15.6m) after a rise of 46% in 1986. Half the rise came from Vesuvius, the ceramics maker fully acquired in June 1987. The European companies produced excellent results.

Cookson America division This division virtually mirrors the two preceding divisions. The only difference is that the manufacturing and marketing takes place in North America. There are 38 operating companies employing 4,000 people in 45 locations in the US, two in Canada and one through a related company in Mexico.

Acquisitions have continued to build a business dedicated to specialised industrial materials in high margin niche markets. The most recent acquisition was Neptco in April 1988, a US chemicals company manufacturing polymeric materials mainly for the insulated wire and cable industry. The initial consideration was $40m.

The group is the world's major consumer of tin. After the collapse of the International Tin Council, Cookson America formed Cookson Market Tin, a worldwide marketing organisation, to guarantee a reliable source of supply.

In 1986 and 1987 the division showed an increase in profit despite the continuing recession in the electronics market. Operating profit was up 21% to £23.0m in 1986 and rose 38.1% in 1987 to £29m. About £6m of the increase came from new acquisitions Polyclad and Vesuvius. The weak dollar reduced profits by £4m.

Share price and relative to FT-A All-Share

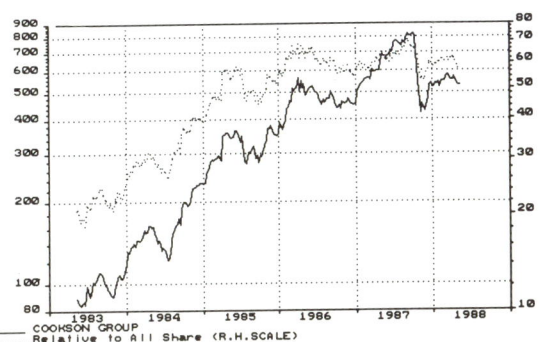

Vesuvius group Vesuvius was accounted as a related company in the first half of 1987, but after the acquisition of the remaining 50% in May 1987, its activities were accounted for in Cookson America and the Ceramics and Plastics division. Though not a division itself, Vesuvius group is a distinct entity within Cookson.

Vesuvius's most important products are ladle shrouds and crucibles, used in steel-making and metal foundries. Other products include slide gate refractories, slide gate mechanisms, fused silica rolls, casting runners and engineered ceramics.

Sales increased by 25% in 1987, all subsidiaries showing improvement, with significant increases in the Americas, Eastern Europe and the Far East. A new manufacturing plant is being commissioned in Spain. Acquisition of new strategic technologies and development of new processes is an important part of Vesuvius's activities.

Titanium dioxide The buoyant demand for titanium dioxide paint pigment continued throughout 1987 with all markets contributing to another record year for Tioxide.

This important division is 50% owned by the company and 50% by ICI. Tioxide contributed operating profit of £75m in 1987, up 31% and 52.2% of the group total.

Lower production costs, partly attributable to reduced energy prices, were assisted by increased output and greater sterling stability of new material costs. Reduced borrowings were reflected in lower interest charges. Tioxide will need to improve its anti-pollution measures over the next five years at a cost of around £50m.

Tioxide is increasing production capacity to meet a growth in world demand of 2.5% a year. This is being achieved by increasing efficiency at a number of existing plants and creating additional capacity of 100,000 tonnes by 1992 to make a total of 550,000 tonnes.

GEOGRAPHICAL REVIEW

Cookson has initiated a policy of diversifying markets away from a reliance on the UK, primarily through acquisition in the US.

In 1987 North America accounted for 38.9% of turnover with £462.8m, the UK 23.7% with £282.6m, Europe 25% with £298.4m and the rest of the world 12.2% with £145m. Despite the high turnover, less than 20% of Cookson's profits come from North America. These are offset by lower interest rate dollar borrowings.

CORPORATE CALENDAR

Year end	31 December
Preliminary results	April
Report and accounts	April
AGM	May
Final dividend paid	July
Interim results	September
Interim dividend paid	November

DIRECTORS' HOLDINGS

	Fully-paid	Other (incl. options)
IG Butler	135,978	107,208
MJG Henderson	39,012	138,210
JL Bickers	12,953	102,746
R Iley	83,750	89,187
Sir Peter Matthews	6,250	—
Sir Nigel Mobbs	—	—
FFC Munro	10,000	76,987
RM Oster	78,548	62,638
MJ Sindzingre	—	—
B de Villeméjane	—	—

Total directors' remuneration in 1987 was £1.12m, of which the chairman, who was also the highest-paid director, received £184,232.

PRINCIPAL SUBSIDIARIES AND RELATED COMPANIES

Cookson materials and chemicals division
Alpha Metals Ltd, Alpha Metals SARL – France, Alpha Metals SpA – Italy, Chemson GmbH – Germany (50%), Cookson (SA) (Pty) Ltd – South Africa, Cookson Industrial Materials Ltd, Eyre Smelting Ltd – India (74%), Frank Horsell Group Plc, Fry's Diecasting Ltd, Fry's Metals Ltd, The Mining Company of Ireland & Strachan Brothers Ltd – Ireland, Trent Alloys (Repton) Ltd, Wolverhampton Die Casting Ltd
Related companies
Alpha Grillo Lotsysteme GmbH – West Germany (50%), Chemson GmbH – West Germany (50%), Zimco Holdings (Pty) Ltd – South Africa (45%)

Cookson ceramics and plastics division
Almiberia SA – Spain (80%), Almitalia SpA – Italy (97%), Colorificio Ceramico Faenza SpA – Italy, Cookson Ceramics & Antimony Ltd, Lucas Cookson Syalon Ltd (50%), Vesuvius International Corporation, Vesuvius Crucible Co Ltd, Vesuvius Crucible Company Inc – US, Vesuvius Crucible GmbH – West Germany, Vesuvius Crucible NV – Belgium, Vesuvius SA – France

Cookson America division
Alpha Metals Inc – US (80%), Alpha Metals Ltd (Hong Kong) – Hong Kong, Anzon Inc – US, CB Edwards & Co Inc – US, Cookson Graphics Inc – US, Cookson Market Tin Inc – US, Electrovert Ltd – Canada, Federated-Fry Metals Inc – US (80%), Hammond Engineered Plastics Corp – US, Key-Tech Inc – US (80%), Monmouth Plastics Inc – US, AJ Oster Co – US, Stern Metals Inc – US, TAM Ceramics Inc – US, Texapol Inc – US (80%), Vesuvius Crucible Company – US (50%), Weiner Metals Inc – US (80%)

Vesuvius group
Vesuvius Crucible Company Inc – US, Vesuvius Crucible NV – Belgium, Vesuvius SA – France, Vesuvius Crucible GmbH – Germany, Vesuvius Crucible Company Ltd
Related company
Vesuvius Italia SpA – Italy (50%)

Titanium dioxide
Tioxide Group Plc (50%), Australian Titanium Products Pty Ltd – Australia, Tioxide Canada Inc – Canada, Tioxide España SA – Spain, Tioxide France SA – France, Tioxide Italia SpA – Italy, Tioxide UK Ltd

Holding and service companies
Cookson America Inc – US, Cookson (Europe) SA – Switzerland, Cookson Investments Ltd, Cookson Overseas Ltd, Mainsail Insurance Ltd – Bermuda

BRAND NAMES

None

CONTACTS AND FURTHER INFORMATION

Cookson Group plc, Clements House, 14 Gresham Street, London EC2V 7AT. Tel: 01-606 4400.

COURTAULDS plc

GENERAL INFORMATION

Head office	18 Hanover Square, London W1A 2BB. Tel: 01-629 9080
Directors	Sir Christopher Hogg (chairman and chief executive), RM Woodhouse (deputy chairman), GA Campbell, DJ Giachardi, S Huismans, RD Lapthorne, GE Morris, JA Nightingale, JM Taylor. *Non-exec* Sir Geoffrey Allen, EE Barr, Sir Colin Corness, G Maitland Smith
Advisers	Hill Samuel & Co Ltd
Auditors	Price Waterhouse
Registrars	Courtaulds plc, PO Box 67, Bocking Church Street, Braintree, Essex CM7 5NE. Tel: 0376 20444
Brokers	Cazenove & Co, Greenwell Montagu Securities
Solicitors	No specified adviser

GENERAL FINANCIAL INFORMATION

Market capitalisation	£1.272bn at 1 January 1988
Capital structure	
Issued ordinary shares (25p)	387.2m
Issued preference shares (£1)	0.8m 3.5% first CP
	4.0m 4.2% second CP
Warrants	None
Convertibles	None
Traded options	Yes
ADRs	One ordinary share equals one ADR
Shareholders over 5%	None

FT CATEGORY

FT: Textiles
FT-A: Textiles

MAJOR ACTIVITIES

Founded in 1816, Courtaulds is a textiles and industrial materials producer, moving over a long history from natural fibres and the first man-made fibres to produce a range of textiles, fibres, coatings, fine chemicals and advanced materials, packaging materials and wood pulp.

The major businesses are still in textiles and fibres with the more recent growth of operations in packaging, coatings, chemicals and materials. The group has been investing in high technology and higher margin growth areas, but its fortunes are to an extent still dependent on consumer demand for older materials like Courtelle, viscose, and acetate fibres and yarn for textiles.

The group has purposefully focused on six core business sectors – textiles, fibres, coatings, films and packaging, chemicals and materials, and wood pulp – on which to base long-term growth. In recognition of the proven rejuvenation within the group evident in the 1980s, a new corporate logo was introduced in 1987 to promote a more aggressive image.

Although the company has been investing in higher growth markets, it is still sensitive to changes in demand for textiles and fibres, particularly in the consumer area. The textiles division is vulnerable to dollar weakness.

Well-known Courtaulds brand names include Courtelle acrylic fibre, Amtico luxury flooring, Lyle & Scott knitwear, Gossard foundationwear and Aristoc tights.

FINANCIAL HISTORY

Over the past five years Courtaulds' sales have advanced slowly, by around 20% from £1.950bn in 1982/83 to £2.261bn in 1986/87. 1986/87 growth was in line with this trend, up 4%.

This apparently dull performance masks the rationalisation and growth which has taken place. The group is rarely acquisitive. Divested businesses, accounting for £500m of turnover since 1983, suggest that despite the published trend organic growth has gathered pace.

Margins on retained businesses doubled from 4.3% in 1982/83 to 8.9% in 1986/87. Consequently pre-tax profits have increased by almost 220% from £63.3m in 1982/83 to £201.1m in 1986/87.

The major changes took place in 1986/87, with pre-tax profits up by over 40% from £143.0m in 1985/86 to £201.1m in 1986/87. Margins rose from 6.6% to 8.9%. Courtaulds has become a more attractive company, in what was otherwise a badly under-performing textiles sector.

Earnings per share have seen the greatest advance, up almost 245% since 1982/83. Since 1984/85, earnings per share have risen by nearly 60%. In 1986/87 they were up 27.8% to 38 2p. Dividends have trebled since 1982/83, rising over 45% from 6.5p to 9.5p in 1986/87. The Courtaulds balance sheet is strong, with gearing at around 25%.

At the 1987/88 interim, turnover was up 5.7% to £1.159bn. Pre-tax profits were up 25% to £102.2m. Earnings per share before extraordinary items were up 26.7% to 19.7p. Net dividends per ordinary share were up 14.6% to 2.75p.

SHARE PRICE HISTORY

Since Courtaulds' dismal performance in the late 1970s and early 1980s, investors have remained cautious, although there has been greater enthusiasm for the shares as the financial picture has improved. This is partly due to fears that Courtaulds is still dependent on cyclical business such as clothing and textiles.

The share price has risen from a 1982 low of 48p to a 1987 high of 535p. In relative terms the shares have climbed from 18% of the FT-A All-Share index to 44% at the all-time 1987 high. The two periods of outperformance were 1983 and 1985/86.

The shares were hard hit in the autumn 1987 share crash, falling from 535p to below 300p. The shares have not fully recovered, standing at the 350p level at the end of April 1988.

SENIOR MANAGEMENT

Senior management at the Courtaulds group is relatively young, with a few senior executives in their thirties and forties. The chairman and chief executive, Sir Christopher Hogg, who has been with the company for 18 years, is largely credited with turning around and re-directing its fortunes in the 1980s. His deputy is Mike Woodhouse, another veteran with 26 years' experience, who was managing director and chairman of the International Paint operation for much of that time.

Allan Nightingale has managed the textiles division since its formation in 1985, but in the middle of 1987 he became divisional chairman. His successor as managing director is Martin Taylor, who joined the group in 1982 after working for the *Financial Times*.

Sipko Huismans joined the group from the Swaziland-based Usutu woodpulp company. He has been managing director of Courtaulds Fibres since 1982 and chairman of International Paint from 1987. Gordon Campbell joined Courtaulds Research in 1968, progressing through Courtaulds' acetate and fibres divisions to become managing director of Saiccor and chairman of Advanced Materials. Richard Lapthorne joined the group in 1983, becoming finance director in 1986.

David Giachardi has been in charge of research and development since 1982, becoming chairman of the chemicals operation in 1986. Non-executive directors include: Ed Barr, the head of the US Sun Chemical Corporation; Sir Colin Corness, chairman of Redland; Geoffrey Maitland Smith,

chairman and chief executive of Sears; and Sir Geoffrey Allen, head of research and engineering at Unilever PLC and a director of Unilever PLC and Unilever NV.

CAPITAL

Courtaulds has hardly changed its issued capital in recent years with 387.2m ordinary shares outstanding at the end of 1987.

The acquisition of Fothergill & Harvey in spring 1987 involved the relatively minor issue of 7.7m shares. The acquisitions of Martin Processing and Porter Paint Company in 1987 were for cash.

Options are outstanding on 12.5m shares. There are no declarable stakes over 5% held in the company.

GROUP REVIEW

The group has been transformed from a vertically integrated, over-extended textiles business making pre-tax profits in 1981 of £5m on sales of £1.7bn, to an efficiently run, highly profitable and diverse group, made up of some 40 reporting businesses making pre-tax profits in 1986/87 of over £200m on sales of £2.261bn.

Fibres Courtaulds is the world's leading supplier of acrylic fibre with factories in the UK, France and Spain. The fibres division, representing 21.0% of the group's sales and 28.9% of operating profit in 1986/87, is divided into three areas – Courtelle, viscose staple and acetate yarn.

Courtelle is Courtaulds' single most important business. The main uses for Courtelle include knitwear, handknitting, jersey, pile and fleece fabrics and domestic textiles. With strong demand for acrylic fibre continuing worldwide, the Courtelle plants enjoy high levels of capacity utilisation.

Viscose is used in non woven products for medical, hygienic, disposable and industrial applications, and cotton-type spun yarns for clothing and furnishings. A measure of the improvement in Courtaulds' position in viscose is that during 1986/87 good results were earned in a year when trading conditions were becoming much more difficult. The best results for many years were achieved in North America.

Courtaulds is a major producer of Dicel and Tricel acetate yarns. Its main uses are dress fabrics, linings and lingerie. Courtaulds owns 50% of Novaceta, the larger of the two Italian acetate yarn producers. Considerable steps were taken to reduce costs and improve quality standards, and this is helping profitability. Novaceta is performing well and leads the industry in southern Europe.

In the development of the new solvent spun cellulose fibre, tencel, a pilot plant came on stream in 1987. Good progress has been made on the next stage of production which will make commercial quantities available.

Turnover growth in fibres in 1986/87 was minimal, from £499m to £509m, but operating profit jumped over 50% to £61m. At the 1987/88 interim, turnover was down 10.6% to £226m. Operating profit was down 7.6% to £24m.

Wood pulp Courtaulds' wood pulp division, representing 4.8% of the group's sales and 14.2% of operating profit in 1986/87, consists of a two-thirds interest in the South African company Saiccor and a 50% interest in the Swaziland company the Usutu Pulp Company.

Saiccor produces dissolving pulp for the manufacture of viscose fibres, packaging films and cellulose-based chemicals. Saiccor's cost advantage stems primarily from its input of raw material. The fast-growing subtropical eucalyptus is recognised to be a most important element in the profitable

Share price and relative to FT-A All-Share

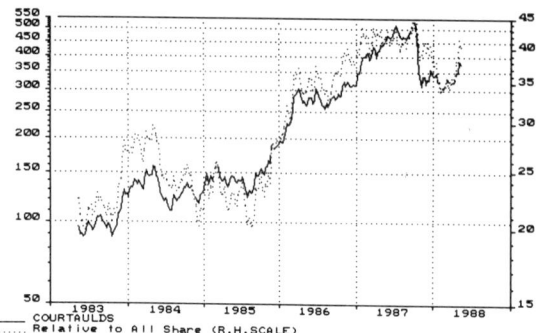

COURTAULDS
Relative to All Share (R.H.SCALE)

production of market pulp. 75% of Saiccor's timber comes from its own forests or from land on long term leases.

Usutu Pulp produces unbleached kraft pulp. Earnings from Usutu's unbleached kraft pulp, which have struggled for a long period in a depressed market have rebounded strongly as demand and prices improve. Usutu is self-sufficient in timber resources.

Over half of the combined sales of the two pulp businesses are to Far Eastern markets. A new pulp marketing organisation has been established with headquarters in Hong Kong.

1986/87 saw strong world demand for wood pulp as a whole. Sales were up 5.3% to £118m and operating profit was 114.3% up at £30m. Operating margins improved from 18% to 25%.

At the 1987/88 interim, turnover was down 5% to £57m. Operating profit was up 40% to £14m. Turnover was adversely affected by the loss in production caused by a flood in September 1987.

Chemicals and materials The division, representing 7.0% of the group's sales and 7.6% of operating profit in 1986/87, is concerned with engineered industrial intermediates and serve the needs of customers in the plastics, fibre, medical, defence, pharmaceutical and tobacco industries. It is divided into four areas – fine chemicals, advanced materials, acetate products and non-woven products.

Fine chemicals' main products are flame-retardant and sulphur-based chemicals, water-soluble polymers and aliphatic esters. In 1987 modernisation of the carboxymethyl cellulose facility and the manufacture of aroma chemicals began.

The advanced materials area comprises carbon fibre through Courtaulds Grafil, engineered fabrics, composite and sheet plastics and fabrications. The area also includes Fothergill & Harvey, acquired in spring 1987 and possessing a number of new business opportunities in the advanced materials field. Main uses are in the aerospace, defence, construction and sports goods industries.

Acetate products manufactures acetic anhydride, acetic flake, filter tow and acetate plastics. Main uses are in the chemical, fibre and tobacco industries.

The non woven products area consists of BFF. Main uses of its products are in the textile, medical and consumer industries. The group's recent major investment programme in this area produced a new heat bond facility and the most advanced spun lace production line in Europe due to come on stream in 1988.

1986/87 divisional turnover was up 12.5% to £168m. Operating profit was up 45.5% to £16m. At the 1987/88 interim, turnover was up 46% to £132m. Operating profit was up 33.5% to £8m.

Coatings The division represented 14.7% of the group's sales and 9.8% of operating profit in 1986/87. Through International Paint, Courtaulds is the world's leading supplier of marine coatings for ships, oil rigs and yachts. It is also a leading international supplier of other heavy duty protective coatings, metal packaging coatings and power and coil coatings.

International Paint has built up strong positions in certain international industrial product finishing markets. In metal packaging coatings, the company has a leading market position in Europe, Australasia, Brazil and South-east Asia.

Much of International Paint's development effort has been devoted to adapting the coatings and paints used on heavy shipping for use on small yachts and major metal structures like oil rigs. It has also developed a new coil coatings technology, Pruflex, which is beginning to be commercially marketed around the world.

In October 1987 Courtaulds purchased the leading US protective coating and architectural paint maker, Porter Paint Company, for $140m. The acquisition of Porter more than doubled the coatings division's interests in the US and diminishes the sector's dependence on the declining marine market. Porter specialises in protective coatings and architectural paints for the professional market.

Turnover saw a negligible increase to £357m from £355m in 1986/87. Operating profit dropped nearly 9% to £21m, from £23m. In the US, problems created by the low oil price in the major market of offshore oil platforms had a significant effect on performance. At the 1987/88 interim, turnover was up just £1m to £186m. Operating profit was up 7.7% to £14m.

Films and packaging The division, contributing 11.9% of the group's sales and 9.6% of operating profit in 1986/87, consists of four areas – Cellophane, OPP (oriented polypropylene) and other films, flexible packaging and Betts & Amtico. The businesses are being brought together in Courtaulds Films and Packaging. Apart from Cellophane, which accounted for about a third of turnover within the division, they are all growth businesses.

BCL is the world's largest producer of transparent cellulose packaging film with a total capacity of 50,000 tonnes from factories in the UK and Canada.

Shorko is a leading producer of coextruded OPP films for the growing US and European markets with factories in the UK and France. Other products include polyethylene stretch, shrink packaging, horticultural and building films. BCL has a 50% interest in an Australian OPP operation.

The flexible packaging area consists of 16 businesses in Europe, southern Africa and Australasia. Products include film printing, laminating, bag-making and bag-in-box liquid packaging.

CHAIRMAN'S STATEMENT

'Several times in its long corporate life Courtaulds has shown the capacity to rejuvenate itself. We believe it has done so again in the 1980s . . . the Company made one fortune out of fabrics in the 19th century and another from pioneering man-made fibres in the first half of the 20th. . . . The range of industries in which it is now engaged should contain enough opportunities over time to satisfy any reasonable growth aspirations. . . . We have been able over time to extend well beyond our textile and man-made fibre origins by building on the skills and market position these gave us. . . . We have deliberately avoided becoming a "conglomerate".' *Sir Christopher Hogg*

F I V E	Y E A R	F I N A N C I A L		I N F O R M A T I O N							
Year	Turnover (£m)	Pre-tax (£m)	Earnings (p)	Dividends' net (p)	Dividend cover (x)	Net assets (p)	Price (p) High	Low	PER (x) High	Low	Yield (%) High	Low
1983	1,905.5	63.3	11.1	3.10	3.6	126.3	130	70	15.8	10.3	5.87	3.79
1984	2,038.1	117.8	21.3	4.20	4.5	122.0	159	110	14.1	7.3	5.56	3.10
1985	2,151.9	128.2	23.9	5.00	4.8	136.8	194	122	10.4	7.2	5.85	3.90
1986	2,172.7	143.0	29.9	6.50	4.6	149.0	327	191	16.5	10.0	4.00	2.43
1987	2,261.9	201.1	38.2	9.50	4.0	168.8	535	306	18.7	8.8	4.28	2.11

Betts makes collapsible tubes for toothpaste, pharmaceuticals and other products; closures and other mouldings for food, toiletries, pharmaceuticals and carbonated beverages; and capsules for wines and spirits. These are the wrappers which cover corks and screwtops. Amtico makes luxury vinyl flooring for homes, stores, offices and hotels.

In August 1987 the group acquired for $99.2m Martin Processing, a performance films business based in southern Virginia in the US. Martin specialises in enhancing polyester film to reduce solar glare in vehicles and buildings and for reprographic equipment.

Turnover for 1986/87 was up slightly at £289m from £280m. However, operating profit doubled from £10m to £20m, indicating an operating margin up from 3.6% to 7%.

At the 1987/88 interim, turnover was up 5.1% to £167m. Operating profit was again sharply up, rising 66.7% to £15m. This was the result of a variety of factors including reduced costs and firmer prices and realisation of the benefits of extensive reinvestment.

Textiles This is the group's largest division, contributing 38.6% of the group's sales and 29.9% of operating profit. There are nine businesses grouped together as Courtaulds Textiles – spinning, finishers and converters, apparel fabrics, home furnishings, industrial fabrics, international fabrics, contract apparel, brands and retail and distribution.

Courtaulds Textiles is one of Europe's largest textile groupings. Group policy is to internationalise operations, improve the portfolio of businesses and move into market areas where speedy response times can give competitive advantage.

The spinning area produces a comprehensive range of yarns from both natural and man-made fibres, spun mainly on the cotton system but with some worsted yarns. Courtaulds factories in the UK manufacture about half of the total UK output of cotton-spun yarns. There are also factories in France. Applications include knitted fabrics and garments, home furnishings, surgical and industrial applications and fancy yarns.

The finishers and converters area consists of fabric printing, dyeing and finishing, and the converting of plain and printed fabrics for furnishings, bedding, fashion apparel and workwear.

Apparel fabrics is involved in the weaving of cotton-type, woollen and textured polyester yarns, and warp and weft knitting of fabrics for a wide range of apparel end-uses.

Home furnishings manufactures terry towels and towelling products, baby linens, bedlinen, curtains, upholstery fabric and fabrics for the automotive trim market. Brands include Christy, Sundour, Zorbit and Harringtons.

Industrial fabrics manufactures specialist fabrics for packaging, military and institutional end-uses.

International fabrics weaves and finishes linings and manufactures fancy narrow ribbons in France. It produces warp and weft knitting for apparel and automotive end-uses in New Zealand and South Africa. Penn International produces elastomeric knitting in North America and Europe. Hamilton Adams merchants linen fabrics in the US.

Contract Apparel is an own-brand manufacturer for large retail chains, mail order houses and department stores. Its UK market share is significant in lingerie and foundationwear, underwear, childrenswear and knitwear. A number of factories have been closed to concentrate on the most attractive market segments.

The brands businesses sell clothing which bears famous brand names to department stores, mail order and independent shops in both the UK and many overseas countries. Principal brands are Lyle & Scott knitwear, Jockey and Y-Front underwear, Wolsey knitwear and socks, Glenalva schoolwear, Gossard and Berlei foundationwear, Aristoc and Kayser hosiery and Slazenger, Dunlop and Carlton knitwear and sportswear in the UK. John Hampden Press, printers, are also owned.

Retail and distribution consists of the Contessa retail chain and McIlroy department and specialist stores. There is also a wholesale distribution operation.

In July 1987 Courtaulds strengthened its lace interests by buying 83.3% of the French company DLR Textiles and buying out the remaining minority state in Long Eaton Fabric, the UK lacemaker it already controlled.

In 1986/87 textile sales volumes achieved by Courtaulds' textile division was virtually unchanged in the UK and other developed economies. The fall in the value of the dollar made imports from dollar-based Far Eastern economies overwhelmingly attractive. In three years Courtaulds had to contend with the exchange rate moving from $1.10 to $1.75 to the pound.

Nevertheless in 1986/87 the division produced a 14.5% increase in overall operating profit to £63m from £55m, thanks to the division's increased efficiency. Sales were just 2.5% up at £935m.

At the 1987/88 interim, turnover for textiles was up 4.9% to £452m. Operating profit again rose strongly, up 16.7% to £28m. Strong contributions came from home furnishings and the new lace businesses.

Courtaulds Engineering In addition to serving the group, Courtaulds Engineering provides project management and engineering design services to a wide range of industries in the UK and overseas. It manufactures special purpose process machines, spinnerettes and plastics fabrications. Clients include Royal Ordnance Explosives, Kodak, McKechnie Metals and others in the food, fine chemicals and pharmaceutical industries.

GEOGRAPHICAL REVIEW

In 1986/87 UK home sales contributed 41.6% of the group's sales. Exports from the UK contributed a further 17.0%. The rest of Europe contributed 18.5%, North America 11.1%, Africa 5.3% and the rest of the world 6.4%.

THE DEE CORPORATION PLC

The UK contributed 54.5% of operating profit, the rest of Europe 21.8%, North America 2.4%, Africa a high margin 14.2% and the rest of the world 7.1%.

CORPORATE CALENDAR

Year end	31 March
Preliminary results	May
Report and accounts	June
AGM	July
Final dividend paid	August
Interim results	November
Interim dividend paid	January

DIRECTORS' HOLDINGS

	Fully-paid ordinary shares	Options
Sir Christopher Hogg	35,000	375,000
RM Woodhouse	3,508	200,000
EE Barr	2,666	—
GA Campbell	2,000	105,000
Sir Colin Corness	2,000	—
DJ Giachardi	2,000	105,000
S Huismans	2,500	180,000
RD Lapthorne	2,000	130,000
G Maitland Smith	2,000	—
GE Morris	2,266	200,000
JA Nightingale	4,666	135,000
Sir Peter Thornton	2,666	—

Total directors' remuneration in 1986/87 was £969,000, of which the chairman, who was also the highest-paid director, received £171,789.

PRINCIPAL SUBSIDIARIES AND RELATED COMPANIES

Ashton Brothers & Co (Holdings) Ltd, BCL Ltd, Bells Packaging Inc – US, Clutsom-Penn International Ltd, Courtaulds Apparel Fabrics Ltd, Courtaulds CPD Inc – US, Courtaulds Clothing Ltd, Courtaulds Distributors Ltd, Courtaulds Engineering Ltd, Courtaulds Fabrics (Holdings) Ltd, Courtaulds Fibres Exports Ltd, Courtaulds Fibres Ltd, Courtaulds Grafil Ltd (80%), Courtaulds Intimate Apparel Ltd, Courtaulds North America Inc – US, Courtaulds Retail Ltd, Courtaulds SA – France, Courtaulds Woollens Ltd, Envi BV – Netherlands, Fin Novaceta SpA – Italy, Fothergill & Harvey Plc (92%), George Brettle & Co Ltd, Hamilton Adams Imports Ltd – US, Hysol Grafil Inc – US (80%), International Paint plc, International Paint (Nederland) BV – Netherlands, International Paint (USA) Inc – US, International Paint Italia SpA – Italy, International Paint Kuwait ksc – Kuwait, International Paint de Portugal Lda – Portugal (96%), Long Eaton Fabric Co Ltd (51%), Macanie (London) Ltd, National Plastics Ltd, Neopak SA – Greece, New Zealand Fabrics Ltd – New Zealand, Penn Elastic Co Inc – US, Photoflex Printing & Packaging (Pty) Ltd – South Africa, Robert Usher & Co Ltd – Irish Republic, Saiccor (Proprietary) Ltd – South Africa (66.66%), Shorko Australia Pty Ltd – Australia, South African Fabrics (Pty) Ltd – South Africa, South African Gossard (Pty) Ltd – South Africa, Standfast Dyers & Printers Ltd, Taubmans Industries Ltd – Australia (56%), Taubmans International (NZ) Ltd – New Zealand (56%), Tricot France SA – France, Wrightcel (NZ) Ltd – New Zealand (75%), Wrightcel Ltd – Australia

BRAND NAMES

Amtico, Aristoc, Berlei, Carlton, Dunlop, Glenalva, Gossard, International Paint, Jockey, John Hampden, Kayser, Lyle & Scott, Slazenger, Wolsey, Y-Fronts

CONTACTS AND FURTHER INFORMATION

Donald Anderson, Courtaulds plc, 18 Hanover Square, London W1A 2BB. Tel: 01-629 9080.

GENERAL INFORMATION

Head office	Silbury Court, 418 Silbury Boulevard, Milton Keynes MK9 2NB. Tel: 0908 607171
Directors	DAG Monk (chairman & chief executive), AB Butler, KW Edwards, DM Fisher, JJF Francis, RK O'Keeffe, AS Perelman, P Stubbs, P Thistleton. *Non-exec* DG Coughlan, Mrs A Ferguson, RC Stapleton
Advisers	Lazard Brothers & Co Ltd, Morgan Grenfell & Co Ltd
Auditors	Grant Thornton
Registrars	National Westminster Bank Registrar's Department
Brokers	Rowe & Pitman Ltd, de Zoete & Bevan Ltd
Solicitors	Herbert Smith, Cannons

GENERAL FINANCIAL INFORMATION

Market capitalisation	£1.856bn at 1 January 1988
Capital structure	
Issued ordinary shares (5p)	883.8m
Issued preference shares	None
Warrants	None
Convertibles	5% convertible bonds 2002 (convertible into ordinary shares at 302.5p per ordinary share)
Traded options	Yes
ADRs	Yes
Shareholders over 5%	Associated British Foods 15.28%

FT CATEGORY

FT: Food, groceries, etc
FT-A: Food retailing

MAJOR ACTIVITIES

The Dee Corporation is a widely diversified retail and distribution group with interests in: food retailing, drugstores and cash and carry wholesaling in the UK; food retailing, cash and carry and wholesale distribution in Spain; and sporting goods retailing in the US.

UK food retailing is by far the largest activity accounting for 73% of sales and 79% of trading profits in the year to April 1987. Gateway is the major trading name and the division has nationwide representation trading from over 829 stores, which range up to 70,000 sq ft in size. The US sporting goods retailer, Herman's, acquired in April 1986, is the second largest contributor to profits. It trades from 200 stores. Dee also owns Linfood Cash and Carry, a major wholesaler to independent grocers.

Food price inflation and personal disposable income are key economic factors affecting performance, although in a static food market the strength of Gateway's competitive stance is the key variable. Sainsbury, Tesco, Asda and Argyll Group with Presto and Safeway are the major competitors.

Alec Monk and his team have made a dramatic impact on the group, which since 1982 has been transformed from a

CHAIRMAN'S STATEMENT

'The main businesses of the group have been totally reshaped in a very short period of time. These changes have enhanced the group's competitive position and improved the services offered to customers. Much work still needs to be done but the planned schedule is being maintained within budget.

Management foresaw that the major changes which have been undertaken would be disruptive and would impact earnings in the short term but this stage of the integration of Fine Fare has now substantially passed and the future is being tackled with vigour and confidence.' *Alec Monk*

minor food distributor into what is now a leading retailer in the UK, and which has the potential to be a major international trading company. The integration of Fine Fare with Gateway has been completed. The refurbishment of the Fine Fare stores and their conversion to Gateway fascias is going to plan and will be completed by April 1989. The management's track record to date indicates that problems will be resolved and the division built to a level where it can be a major competitive food retailing force for the 1990s.

FINANCIAL HISTORY

Total sales excluding VAT in 1986/87 at £4.839bn were 20.7% ahead of the previous year. Sales were 249% up over three years and 366% over five years. As well as good results from acquisitions, good organic growth was achieved through existing businesses. Pre-tax profits were £192.2m, 52% ahead on the period and compared to only £11.9m achieved five years ago. UK food retailing continues to dominate the group's profitability although the smaller businesses have also shown steady growth. Earnings per share increased by 10.6% to 17.7p, but on a restated basis they increased by 29.2% from 13.7p per share.

The year's net dividend was 11.1% ahead at 8.0p from 7.2p. The balance sheet remained strong with net debt only 11% of shareholders' funds. Trading margin in the supermarkets division is the key ratio and has progressed well from 3.5% to 4.5%.

At the November 1987 interim, Dee reported very disappointing pre-tax profits, down 19% at £63.6m from £78.2m on turnover 6% up at £2.62bn. Herman's made losses of £5.5m and group interest charges were up. There were heavy costs in absorbing Fine Fare into its Gateway chain. For the full year Dee is forecasting profits £7.2m down to £185m.

The poor results and uncertainty about future profits led to considerable dissatisfaction with Dee. The bid from Barker & Dobson was welcomed by many who felt ill-informed about Dee's progress and prospects. However recovery is expected for the full year from the depressed interim.

SHARE PRICE HISTORY

Over the past three years the Dee share price has risen from less than 100p to the 20% at the beginning of 1988. It has been as high as 300p in the period.

Compared to the market Dee has had mixed fortunes, rising in relative terms from 20% of the FT-A All-Share index in 1982 up to 40% at the end of 1985. It has steadily fallen since.

Dee fell with the market in October 1987 until the Barker & Dobson bid drove the price to 220p. The shares have fallen again as the bid has failed.

SENIOR MANAGEMENT

Alec Monk has been chairman and chief executive since 1981. He has been the architect and driving force behind the group's development, Keith Edwards is chairman of Gateway and has had 36 years experience in grocery retailing. Tony Butler is planning and business development director, having previously been finance director, a position now filled by Alan Perelman. Kevin O'Keeffe is business development director for the US, and is based in New York.

The executive board is completed by: Jeremy Francis, legal, property and administrative director; Peter Stubbs, special projects director; David Fisher, group marketing director; and

Share price and relative to FT-A All-Share

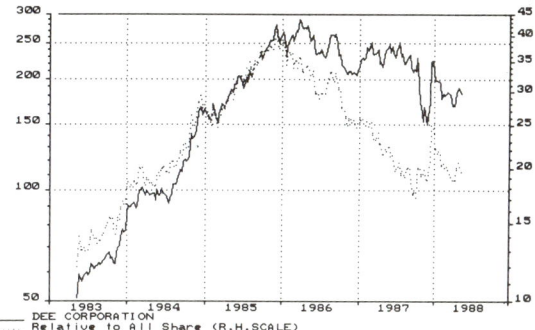

Peter Thistleton, managing director of Gateway.

Non-executive directors are: Professor RC Stapleton, formerly Professor of Finance at New York University and Manchester Business School and now fellow of Churchill College, Cambridge; Dermot Coughlan, chairman of Toronto-based Derlan Industries; and Mrs Anne Ferguson, publicity and marketing advisor to ICI.

CAPITAL

Dee Corporation has been an aggressive issuer of shares for its acquisitions. These have included 141.6m for International Stores in December 1984, 125m for Herman's Sporting Goods in April 1986 and 282.5m for Fine Fare in June 1986.

At 31 December 1987, 883.8m shares were in issue, a fourfold increase since Alec Monk became chairman. Associated British Foods holds 135m shares, 15.28% of the total issued, as part of the consideration for Fine Fare. Options for 32.5m shares are outstanding under the senior executive share option scheme and savings-related share option scheme.

The weakness of Dee's shares after the full prices paid for Fine Fare and Herman's leaves it open to a bid. In December 1987 Barker & Dobson offered £2bn in shares and cash.

GROUP REVIEW

Gateway Dee trades through 829 Gateway stores in the UK, with a total selling area of 8.6m sq ft, by far the largest in the industry. 419 Fine Fare stores covering 3.8m sq ft were acquired in June 1986 from Associated British Foods. Dee's policy is to convert all the Fine Fare stores, together with its existing Carrefour chain, into a single Gateway chain.

69 Gateway stores are superstores, with over 25,000 sq ft of selling area, and a strong emphasis on non-food sales. There have been closures of a large number of the smaller stores. At the same time Gateway continues to expand strongly, opening 1.23m sq ft in 1986/87, with 0.6m sq ft planned in 1987/88. Market share is 12%, placing Gateway third behind Tesco and J Sainsbury.

In 1986/87 Gateway made profits of £152.9m on turnover of £3.42bn. Like for like sales growth was 6.7% in the old Gateway stores, and only 1.8% in the former Fine Fare stores. Integrating Fine Fare with Gateway is expensive and takes a lot of time.

At the 1987/88 interim the problems came into sharper focus. Turnover was marginally up at £1.827bn, but profits

F I V E   Y E A R   F I N A N C I A L   I N F O R M A T I O N

Year	Turnover (£m)	Pre-tax (£m)	Earnings (p)	Dividends net (p)	Dividend cover (x)	Net assets (p)	Price (p) High	Low	PER (x) High	Low	Yield (%) High	Low
1983	910	15.4	4.8	3.2	1.5	27.1	86	48	28.1	18.4	8.53	5.67
1984	1,387	27.4	8.0	3.8	2.1	38.3	168	86	33.8	20.2	5.99	3.57
1985	2,434	56.4	12.0	5.8	2.1	60.6	285	150	43.3	22.9	4.39	2.91
1986	4,008	119.1	12.9	7.2	1.8	81.1	293	201	34.7	16.4	5.13	3.32
1987	4,838	187.1	17.2	8.0	2.2	76.5	257	150	20.8	10.7	7.31	3.98

were down from £70.8m to £68.6m. The trading margin was down to 3.76% and there were high levels of shrinkage at the former Fine Fare outlets. A recovery in both margins and profitability is expected in the second half. Dee is convinced that it will resolve the problems, but bidders Barker & Dobson believed they could do it better and possibly other predators think the same.

FA Wellworth Dee acquired its Northern Ireland subsidiary FA Wellworth in December 1983. It has doubled trading profits to £9.0m in 1986/87, despite adding only seven stores to the original 24. Profits were 10% up at the 1987/88 interim.

Cash and carry Linfood Cash and Carry trades through 100 depots serving a wide range of trade customers, including independent grocers, caterers, the licensed trade, and confectioners, tobacconists and newsagents. Although depot numbers have only grown slightly since Dee acquired the business, there has been a transformation in the division's fortunes.

Sales nearly doubled between 1981/82 and 1986/87 to reach £790.6m. The business has been restored to profitability, though at a low margin level, of £8.2m in 1986/87. This is a highly competitive, high volume, low margin sector. Linfood has a 15% market share, second only to the market leader, Nurdin & Peacock. Although future growth prospects are limited, reflected in the fall in profits at the 1987/88 interim, the division is capable of expanding by opening new units, acquisitions, and by sales and margin advances.

Medicare Dee purchased this drugstore chain in November 1986 by issuing 4.97m shares. It has already increased store numbers from the 49 acquired to 68 at the 1986/87. In 1987/88 numbers will be doubled by using redundant small supermarkets from the Gateway chain.

This is one of the fastest growing UK retail markets, although sales and profit contributions, at £12.3m and £0.2m respectively in 1986/87, are minimal. Medicare should make a growing contribution in future years. This is reflected in the 1987/88 interim when sales were £21.5m and profits £0.5m.

Herman's Sporting Goods Dee acquired the company, which sells ski-related and sporting goods in the US, in April 1986. Store numbers have been ambitiously built up from the 131 acquired to 200, taking the group away from its original base in the north-east of the US.

In 1986/87 the chain made profits of £25.4m on sales of £371m, and was growing strongly in a rapidly expanding market. At the 1987/88 interim this healthy trend reversed, with losses of £5.5m on sales of £170.2m. This was partly due to sterling translation and partly to increased advertising and overhead costs. Costs are escalating and there are worries about demand from high spending US consumers going into reverse. Only £8m is expected for the whole of 1987/88 on sales of £400m, although trading is always stronger in the second half.

Digsa Dee's Spanish operation achieved sales of £131m and profits of £3.3m in 1986/87, 28% up and 43% up respectively. Improvement continued at the 1987/88 interim.

Digsa has over 100 wholly-owned shops, 380 franchise shops and 10 cash and carrys based in north-east Spain and the Madrid area. The subsidiary has been built up by Dee's new management and is performing well.

GEOGRAPHICAL REVIEW

In 1986/87 89.7% of sales and 86% of trading profits were derived from the UK; 7.7% of sales and 12.4% of profits from the US; and 2.7% of sales and 1.6% of profits from Spain.

Dee had hoped that the US proportions would increase, but it remains to be seen how well Herman's Sporting Goods can recover from slackening demand, and the prospect of the dollar remaining weak for profits translation.

CORPORATE CALENDAR

Year end	26 April
Preliminary results	July
Report and accounts	August
AGM	September
Final dividend paid	October
Interim results	December
Interim dividend paid	February

DIRECTORS' HOLDINGS

	Fully-paid ordinary shares	Options
DAG Monk	50,000	3,665,745
AB Butler	8,501	1,433,245
DG Coughlan	50,000	—
KW Edwards	84,375	1,764,495
A Ferguson	2,000	—
DM Fisher	37,500	1,193,750
JJF Francis	25,911	1,538,245
RK O'Keeffe	31,000	1,232,500
AS Pepelman	—	800,000
DS Stapleton	10,000	—
P Stubbs	61,213	1,068,245
P Thistleton	51,502	1,176,995

All interests are beneficial. The total directors' remuneration, including fees, was £1.42m in 1986/87, of which the chairman, who was also the highest-paid director, received £181,494.

PRINCIPAL SUBSIDIARIES AND RELATED COMPANIES

Dee Realty Inc – US, Distribuciones Gimenez y Compañía SA – Spain, FA Wellworth and Company Ltd, Gateway Foodmarkets Ltd, Herman's Sporting Goods Inc – US, Linfood Cash & Carry Ltd, The Dee Corporation of America Inc – US, Medicare Ltd

BRAND NAMES

Compre Bien, Digsa, Fine Fare, Gateway, Herman's, Linfood Cash & Carry, Linfood Stock Exchange, Medicare, My Mums, Red Balloon Restaurant, Supermercados Compre Bien, Wellworths

CONTACTS AND FURTHER INFORMATION

Walter Raven Public Relations, 104–110 Goswell Road, London EC1V 7DH. Tel: 01-490 1552.

DIXONS GROUP plc

GENERAL INFORMATION

Head office	29 Farm Street, London W1X 7RD. Tel: 01-499 3494
Directors	S Kalms (chairman and chief executive), Egon von Greyerz (vice chairman), M Souhami (managing director), B Bennett. *Non-exec* H Lewis, P Oppenheimer
Advisers	Morgan Stanley, SG Warburg & Co Ltd
Auditors	Touche Ross & Co
Registrars	WH Stentiford & Co, Woodland House, Cellingwood Road, Essex CM8 2TS. Tel: 0376 515755
Brokers	Cazenove & Co
Solicitors	Titmuss Sainer & Webb

GENERAL FINANCIAL INFORMATION

Market capitalisation	£763m at 1 January 1988
Capital structure	
Issued ordinary shares (10p)	393.6m
Issued preference shares	£123.9m 5% convertible preference 2002 (26.67 shares per £100 stock)
Warrants	None
Convertibles	None
Traded options	Yes
ADRs	None
Shareholders over 5%	None

FT CATEGORY

FT: Drapery and stores
FT-A: Stores

MAJOR ACTIVITIES

Dixons' core activity is electrical retailing, where the company is the UK market leader through 309 Dixons and 567 Currys outlets.

The electrical retailing division accounted for 93% of group sales, and 79% of group profits in 1986/87. The electrical retailing division includes a related photo-processing operation, which also enjoys a dominant position within the market. The remaining contribution to profits was derived from financial services, which yielded 9%, and property, which provided 12%.

Financial services are closely linked to the retail businesses, providing customers with credit facilities and extended product warranties. A network of 41 service centres provides retail customers with a nationwide after sales service.

In 1987 the company gained control of Silo, a US speciality electrical retailer, and Tipton Centers, another US electrical chain, to provide an entry to the world's largest consumer market. Worldwide, the group controls over 3.5m square feet of selling space through 1,411 individual stores.

The group has taken full advantage of a buoyant climate for electrical consumer demand within the UK in recent years. It has established an exceptionally rapid pattern of growth, as well as a dominant share of the total market.

Above-average growth had been expected to continue until, in October 1987, the group was hit by a sudden downturn in demand. The company believed this was caused by the decline in world stock markets. An equally likely cause was the group being overstocked, and the public finding no new product to capture their imagination.

Key economic indicators include personal disposable incomes, consumer confidence and expenditure, credit demand, levels of interest rates and the standing of the US dollar against sterling. Major competitors include Comet, which is part of Woolworth, Rumbelows, owned by THORN-EMI, and Laskys, part of Granada. Competitors in the US include Circuit City and Federated.

FINANCIAL HISTORY

In 1986/87 sales rose by 17.8% to £1.11bn. Since 1982/83 an increase of 342% has been recorded. Pre-tax profits for 1986/87 rose by 31.4% to £102.6m, to complete a remarkable five year rise of 721%. Over this period margins have almost doubled.

The company has taken an increasing share of a buoyant market for electrical products by increasing sales through existing outlets and by rapid physical expansion. An especially important breakthrough was made in November 1984 when the company acquired the larger Currys business.

Following the introduction of new management and direction, Currys has been strengthened to take full advantage of the dominant position which the enlarged group enjoys within the industry. Extra shares were issued to fund the acquisition, but earnings per share have risen by 282% since 1982/83. This includes an increase of 38.3% during 1986/87. Over a five year period, dividends per share have risen by 325%, with a 33.3% rise in 1986/87.

At April 1987, £68.0m of euroconvertible bonds, and £55.9m of convertible unsecured loan stock, which have since been transferred into convertible preference shares, were outstanding. This was the result of the acquisition of Silo, which was bought for an effective consideration of $311m. Cash holdings amounted to £37.5m, and investments to £83.3m. A high rate of return on capital has been maintained, with 24% achieved in 1986/87.

At the 1987/88 interim for the 28 weeks to 14 November 1987, pre-tax profits increased by £9m to £49.5m, but £4.6m of this came from a first time contribution from Silo, and there were contributions totalling £17.5m from financial services and property. The key UK retailing pre-tax profits fell by 6% to £27.4m. Earnings per share increased by 6.8%, and the dividend by 8.3%. Profits for the full year are expected to be disappointing.

SHARE PRICE HISTORY

The acquisition of Currys in November 1984 marked the start of a major re-rating of Dixons in recognition of their position as the leading force within a rapidly expanding electrical goods market. The share price enjoyed a swift increase throughout

FIVE YEAR FINANCIAL INFORMATION

Year	Turnover (£m)	Pre-tax (£m)	Earnings (p)	Dividends net (p)	Dividend cover (x)	Net assets (p)	Price (p) High	Price (p) Low	PER (x) High	PER (x) Low	Yield (%) High	Yield (%) Low
1983	268.4	14.0	5.97	1.02	5.9	41.5	61	45	22.1	13.7	3.19	2.19
1984	350.8	20.5	7.41	1.25	5.9	45.3	140	53	30.7	13.2	3.25	1.49
1985	606.7	39.6	8.93	1.50	6.0	39.3	237	128	32.8	23.3	1.64	0.88
1986	943.4	78.1	14.10	3.00	4.7	47.0	419	213	47.8	23.6	1.39	0.62
1987	1,111.1	102.6	19.50	4.00	4.9	56.4	418	190	28.4	10.6	2.88	1.21

1985 to reach a peak of 400p in 1986.

The attempted bid for Woolworths in 1986 halted the upward trend, and the share price traded within a 300p to 425p range. Although reapproaching peak levels in absolute terms, the price fell sharply from a high of 45% to around 30% as a percentage of the FT-A All-Share index. The possibility of further acquisitions and some doubts over the continuing strength of the UK consumer economy combined to hold back the performance.

In late 1987, the shares experienced a precipitous and overwhelming decline, caused first by the October share crash, and then by the poor 1987/88 interim results. At the low after the interims, the shares fell to 178p, 25% of the index. In mid-April 1988, the shares had only recovered to 175p. There was no let-up in the decline relative to the index.

SENIOR MANAGEMENT

Stanley Kalms, who is chairman and chief executive, has been instrumental in building up the business from modest beginnings. The vice chairman is Egon von Greyerz, who was appointed in March 1986 from the position of group finance director. Also in March 1986 Mark Souhami was appointed group managing director, having been promoted from chief executive of the retail division. Other main board directors include Brian Bennett, who heads the property division, Henry Lewis and Peter Oppenheimer.

CAPITAL

As at November 1987 issued share capital amounted to 393.6m ordinary shares. Significant share issues have included 116.4m, after adjusting for subsequent capitalisation issues, for the Currys acquisition in 1984. In February 1986, there was a three for one scrip issue.

In July 1986 the bid for Woolworth of 15 ordinary shares and 22 4.3% convertible preference shares for every ten Woolworth shares failed. Cyclops Corporation, the US owner of Silo, was acquired in 1987 for cash and the issue of convertible preference shares. The net cost was $311m. Tipton, a US electrical retail chain, was acquired for $30.4m in cash in July 1987.

A proposed ADR share placing was cancelled on 7 October 1987, before the crash, because of depressed market conditions in the US speciality retail sector, though the listing went ahead.

Options are outstanding covering 16.3m ordinary shares under the group's share option scheme. There are no declared holdings over 5%. As at August 1986 Stanley Kalms beneficially held 1.3% of the issued share capital.

GROUP REVIEW

UK retail The division operates as Dixons and Currys within the electrical retail market. A market share around 15% is estimated to be twice as large as the nearest competitor. As at April 1987, 1.7m sq ft of selling area was in use. Dixons accounted for 0.6m sq ft and Currys 1.1m sq ft.

Dixons does most of its business in high street locations where it has a total of over 300 outlets. The average size of its premises is approximately 2,000 sq ft. A number of shops over 5,000 sq ft have been opened recently, but, at the same time, smaller stores are being introduced into smaller towns which had previously been neglected. These are now proving viable given the dominant local market share which can be realised. Floorspace is planned to rise by 13% in 1987/88.

The product range consists primarily of brown goods, including televisions, video recorders, hi-fi systems and personal computers, but approximately 20% of sales are derived from photographic goods. A strong own-brand presence has been established, which cleverly makes use of and promotes the Saisho name. Sales per square foot are amongst the highest within the retail industry, at over £700 in 1986/87. An exceptionally strong profits trend has been established, which was reversed for the first time at the 1987/88 interim.

Currys operates in the high street. It also has larger out of town stores originating from the business which initially traded as Bridgers. In addition to brown goods, a wide range of white goods is also offered. These are items such as refrigerators, deep-freezers, washing machines and dishwashers, as well as smaller domestic appliances. In the high street there are nearly 530 stores, which provide 886,000 sq ft of selling area. This gives an average store size of nearly 1,700 sq ft. Selling area is scheduled to rise by 9% in 1987/88, with new units at least twice the size of existing stores.

Since Currys joined the group a new management strategy has been adopted. Outdated stores have been closed and the money has been used to modernise the remaining outlets. In addition, more effective marketing and merchandising policies have been introduced. A strong own-brand presence has been built up through the Matsui and Carlton labels. Unproductive rental and hire-purchase activities have been discontinued. Following these changes, sales per square foot have more than doubled, and, with margins improving, profits have risen strongly.

The out of town operation is, as yet, in its infancy. However, it is now subject to rapid expansion in order to take advantage of expected market trends. The selling area is scheduled to grow by 250% in the two years to April 1988. Average selling area per store is approximately 7,000 sq ft, and shoppers have the advantage of extensive car-parking facilities.

CHAIRMAN'S STATEMENT

'The precipitous fall of World Stock Markets which started on 19 October had an immediate and significant effect on our UK retail business. Sales per square foot, which before this date had shown an increase, then declined against the previous year. This severely affected both the half year results and our important Christmas trading. Even in hindsight it would have been difficult to anticipate this market reversal and it was not possible to make the adjustments necessary to mitigate the volume decline.' *Stanley Kalms*

The future of the group's UK retailing interests is dependent upon a revival of demand. This is most likely to be brought about by a successful new product to take the place of video recorders and compact disc players, which have powered the growth of the last few years, or by a major event like the Olympics to revive interest in the older products. Satellite broadcasting is on the horizon and this could be a growth area. **Photo-processing** The business is now a part of the retail division. A network of seven laboratories, which includes the well-known names Truprint and SupaSnaps, provides customers with a fast and efficient film processing service.

The company operates mainly within the mail order market, where it has the largest share of all UK sales, and also through retail outlets. These include third party franchise arrangements under the name of Horizon. Orders are also taken through the group's own stores. In October 1986 a specialist

Share price and relative to FT-A All-Share

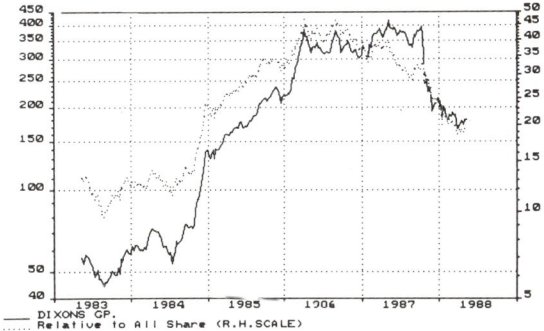

DIXONS GP.
..... Relative to All Share (R.H.SCALE)

photo-processing chain, trading as SupaSnaps, was acquired. This operation has some 340 outlets and is likely to be expanded under the new management.

Pre-tax profits in 1986/87 for the retail division, including photo-processing, were up 20.3% at £81.6m, on turnover 19.7% up at £1.04bn. At the 1987/88 interim to 14 November 1987, turnover was 17.1% up at £565.1m, but pre-tax profits were 5.8% down at £27.4m.

US retail   In April 1987 the group acquired the Silo and Busy Beaver businesses in the US through the takeover of Cyclops Corporation. Busy Beaver operates a handful of DIY outlets. The stores have an average selling area of approximately 30,000 sq ft, giving the chain a total selling area of nearly 500,000 sq ft.

More importantly, Silo, known as a 'power retailer', is the third largest speciality electrical retailer. Its share of the market is growing rapidly. Its position is expected to be further enhanced as group financial resources are used to expedite the opening of new stores. Additional management skills will be brought in to introduce more effective trading policies.

Since the acquisition of Silo the publicly quoted Tipton Centres has also been acquired. It has 24 outlets operating in and around St Louis, Missouri. At the 1987/88 interim, first-time pre-tax profits from the US acquisitions were £4.6m on turnover of £206.2m.

Financial services   Credit facilities provide an important marketing device for the Dixons and Currys chains. A decision has been taken to form the group's own credit card venture. Between 1988 and 1991 this will replace existing credit arrangements, which include a joint venture with Club 24, part of Next, within which Dixons Retail is the single most important customer. Dixons and Currys together already boast a total of more than one million accounts.

An insurance company was established in July 1986 to offer extended product warranties to cover sales through the retail division. Policies are being sold at the rate of almost one million per annum.

Pre-tax profits in 1986/87 were 142% up at £9.2m from £3.8m. At the 1987/88 interim, another excellent performance resulted in profits up 37% at £6.3m.

Property   Within the UK, activity is concentrated on shop developments, which account for 80% of funds invested. A particularly important scheme in Cardiff was completed at the end of 1987. Office developments make up the balance. The group is also represented overseas, in particular in Belgium, where both office and retail schemes are being implemented successfully.

In 1986/87, pre-tax profits were up 14.8% at £11.8m on turnover 4.3% up at £75m. At the 1987/88 interim, the property division reported pre-tax profits sharply up 64.7% at £11.2m on turnover 12.6% up at £49m.

GEOGRAPHICAL REVIEW

In recent years trading activity has been concentrated largely within the UK. However, surplus funds have been strategically invested overseas to provide a valuable additional source of income.

Following the acquisition of Silo, the overseas contribution to group profits in 1987/88 is estimated to approach 20% of the total, most of which is from the US.

CORPORATE CALENDAR

Year end	2 May
Preliminary results	September
Report and accounts	September
AGM	October
Final dividend paid	October
Interim results	January
Interim dividend paid	March

DIRECTORS' HOLDINGS

	Fully-paid ordinary shares		Options
	(beneficial)	(non-beneficial)	
S Kalms	5,155,284	40,000	612,000
Egon von Greyerz	224,780	—	507,960
M Souhami	381,500	18,500	491,640
B Bennett	103,520	8,000	358,020
H Lewis	16,000	—	73,440
P Oppenheimer	1,200	—	—

Total directors' remuneration was £1.6m, of which the chairman, who was also the highest-paid director, received £659,202.

PRINCIPAL SUBSIDIARIES AND RELATED COMPANIES

Astrominster Ltd, Busy Beaver Building Centers Inc – US, Clubfair Ltd, Colortrend (Holdings) Ltd, Currys Group Plc, Dixons Arizona Properties Ltd – US, Dixons Group (Capital) Plc, Dixons Group Distribution Ltd, Dixons Insurance Services Ltd, Dixons Investments Ltd, Gratispool International Holdings Ltd, Lea Park Developments Ltd, Martin Brent Developments Ltd, Silo Inc – US

Related companies
Bill Donald Investments Ltd, Dovelamb Ltd, Easdram Ltd, Jayhold Ltd, Timelark Ltd

BRAND NAMES

Blu-Chip, Busy Beaver, Currys, Currys Superstores, Dixons, Fotopost Express, Gratispool, Horizon, Logik, Mastercare, Matsui, Miranda, National Film Club, Saisho, Silo, SupaSnaps, Tipton, Truprint

CONTACTS AND FURTHER INFORMATION

Richard Kalms, Dixons Group plc, 29 Farm Street, London W1X 7RD. Tel: 01-499 3494.

ENGLISH CHINA CLAYS P.L.C.

GENERAL INFORMATION

Head office John Keay House, St Austell, Cornwall PL25 4DJ. Tel: 0726 74482
Directors Sir Alan Dalton (chairman), Dr SR Dennison (chief executive), RW Carlton-Porter (finance), DA Langford, GRW Lovering, TW Stobart, J Reeve. *Non-exec* DHL Hopkinson (deputy chairman), BG Allison, Lord Chilver, SJ Titcomb
Advisers J Henry Schroder Wagg & Co Ltd
Auditors Peat Marwick McLintock
Registrars National Westminster Bank Registrar's Department
Brokers de Zoete & Bevan Ltd
Solicitors Slaughter and May, Stephens & Scown, Sullivan & Cromwell – US

GENERAL FINANCIAL INFORMATION

Market capitalisation	£822.8m at 1 January 1988
Capital structure	
Issued ordinary shares (25p)	211.54m
Issued preference shares	None
Warrants	None
Convertibles	None
Traded options	None
ADRs	One ADR equals three ordinary shares
Shareholders over 5%	None

FT CATEGORY

FT: Industrials (miscel.)
FT-A: Other industrial materials

MAJOR ACTIVITIES

English China Clays (ECC) is the world's largest producer of china clay and supplies calcium carbonate and a range of other industrial minerals. The group is also engaged in quarrying activities, in the development and sale of residential housing in the UK and in the sale of specialised drilling fluids worldwide. UK sales represent half the group's turnover, European markets generate 33% and the rapidly expanding US market accounts for 8%.

ECC depends on industrial minerals for over half its sales and pre-tax profits. The paper industry is a major customer. The group also supplies the ceramics, paints, rubber, polymer and homecare industries. Sales to the building materials sector are increasing. Capital spending, funded from the group's strong cash flows, has paid for geographical diversification of the mineral activities, particularly in the US. It has also been used to gain market share.

The quarrying division extracts raw materials such as granite, limestone, sand and gravel, and also manufactures concrete products and tarmacadam for road construction. In volume terms, the company is the UK's fifth largest producer of aggregates and the leading producer of decorative concrete products.

ECC's construction division is one of the UK's top 20 housebuilders with sites throughout England, completing some 1,200 units per annum. The group has been in the housebuilding industry for over 40 years, and sells houses from starter homes through to executive residences. ECC also owns 29.9% of Bryant, a major Midlands-based housebuilder.

The falling oil price has depressed the profits of ECC's drilling fluids division, but it remains well placed to take advantage of any industry upturn.

Early in 1986, the group's leisure interests were sold to Rank. The funds from this and other disposals have been reinvested in the group to focus on those businesses generating the required margin.

The group remains intent on further expansion both by acquisition and joint venture, and by organic development of the core businesses. Group assets are largely medium and long-term in nature, especially mineral reserves and a land bank for housebuilding, and there is a constant programme to find replacements. Present and future profitability is affected by the rate and extent of capital spending, which in the past has represented about half of group profits.

ECC has aimed to develop a balanced portfolio of reserves. In the short term, improved earnings are easier to generate through acquisition. Sylacauga Calcium Products in Alabama, purchased for $25m at the end of 1986, is a significant addition to existing Georgia- and Texas-based mineral operations. The purchase of JL Shiely for $73m in January 1988 demonstrates further that the US is a key growth area.

ECC's chairman has taken issue with the Government over legislation related to planning permission for housebuilding and mineral extraction. He cites the Government's inability to define and to establish an efficient planning system which adequately takes account of local views without sinking the whole process into a ferment of inquiry and delay.

There is no significant domestic UK competition in the dominant china clay business, but ECC competes with a number of overseas producers. ECC is committed to overseas expansion in the US, Europe and, more recently, the Pacific.

FINANCIAL HISTORY

ECC's turnover has grown progressively since 1983, after adjusting for disposals of the small oil and gas interests and the sale of the leisure division in 1985/86. A steady margin of about 10% has maintained growth in pre-tax profits.

Turnover was £762.5m in 1987, 10.7% up on 1986, and 55.5% up since 1983. Management has set itself the task of boosting sales by increasing the added-value products in its minerals and aggregates division for specific market requirements. Quarrying is also rapidly increasing its contribution to the group.

Pre-tax profits in 1987 were £112.1m, 24% up on 1986 and 140% up since 1983. Earnings per share grew by 23% in 1987, compared with 10% in 1986. Since 1983, earnings per share have grown by 107%. Dividend growth has mirrored earnings growth.

ECC's balance sheet has improved dramatically. A rights issue in 1985, strong cash generation in 1986 and the ADR-issue proceeds in 1987 brought gearing down substantially.

CHAIRMAN'S STATEMENT

'Last year I reported to you that we had taken decisive steps to focus our skills and other resources on what we had identified as our key areas of expertise. We have continued with this strategy in the current year and the more concentrated drive is producing the benefits of those decisions. There is clearly more to do; each division has a major commitment to expansion for which funds have been voted and that investment will progressively strengthen the Group's already powerful stance in markets. Orderbooks are currently healthy, cash flow is strong and we look forward resolutely in the certain knowledge that we shall never be satisfied with our performance and that there is always room for improvement in everything we do.' *Sir Alan Dalton*

ENGLISH CHINA CLAYS P.L.C.

There is more to ECC than china clay

International Drilling Fluids

Supplying drilling muds, production chemicals and technical engineering services to the oil industry throughout the world.

ECC Construction

One of the top 20 UK housebuilders under its trading names of SNW and Bradley Homes.

ECC Quarries

Amongst the top five aggregate producers in the UK, supplying a wide range of materials and blacktop to the road, construction, house building and contracting industries.

ECC International

An industrial minerals group, mining, processing and marketing china clay (Kaolin) of which we are the world's largest producer, together with a range of other minerals which play a critical role in products used in every household in the land.

A careful study of the ECC Group's worldwide performance and growth of profitability reveals the wisdom of an investment in fundamental businesses serving stable markets.

In the year to 30th September 1987, Group sales reached £762M, profits before tax climbed to £112M and earnings per share rose 23% to 34.88p. and the final dividend is up 15% to 9.5p.

Our first priority is to seek always to provide first class products supported by first class service, backed by substantial reserves of minerals and other relevant assets and concentrated in the basic businesses we know well. We believe that this is a strategy that ensures high performance in good years, and perhaps, more importantly, provides flexibility and strength under difficult conditions.

The Company's shares are traded on the International Stock Exchange and the NASDAQ National Market System in the form of ADR's, under the symbol ECLAY.

For further information and a copy of our 1988 Interim Results and the Annual Report, write to, telex or fax our Chairman,
Sir Alan Dalton,
English China Clays P.L.C.,
John Keay House, St. Austell,
Cornwall PL25 4DJ, UK.
TELEX 45526 ECCSAU G.
FAX (0726) 623019.

FIVE YEAR FINANCIAL INFORMATION

Year	Turnover (£m)	Pre-tax (£m)	Earnings (p)	Dividends net (p)	Dividend cover (x)	Net assets (p)	Price (p) High	Price (p) Low	PER (x) High	PER (x) Low	Yield (%) High	Yield (%) Low
1983	490.2	46.7	16.85	8.75	1.97	206.4	220	161	13.6	10.7	7.10	5.37
1984	604.2	64.2	22.13	9.60	2.36	215.8	261	198	18.4	12.4	6.40	4.73
1985	713.9	74.6	25.97	11.60	2.24	219.4	303	216	13.6	9.7	7.08	4.68
1986	688.6	90.4	28.44	12.50	2.29	230.4	380	263	15.1	10.5	5.98	4.14
1987	762.5	112.1	34.88	14.50	2.32	236.2	578	308	17.9	9.8	5.72	3.14

SHARE PRICE HISTORY

Since 1983 the shares have been steady performers, rising from the 200p level to 579p at the peak of the 1987 bull market. Relative performance has been volatile, with strong outperformance in the first half of 1985, 1986 and 1987.

In the autumn 1987 crash they markedly underperformed, falling from 579p to 300p, a drop of 48.2%, substantially more than the market as a whole. Since then the shares have recovered well, standing at around 415p in late April 1988.

SENIOR MANAGEMENT

Sir Alan Dalton has been chairman since 1984, when Lord Aberconway retired. Other directors include: chief executive Dr SR Dennison; TW Stobart, managing director of ECC Quarries; J Reeve, managing director of ECC Construction; RW Carlton-Porter, finance director; GRW Lovering, managing director of ECC International; and company secretary DA Langford. Non-executive directors are deputy chairman DHL Hopkinson, Lord Chilver, BG Allison and SJ Titcomb.

CAPITAL

ECC had issued share capital of 211.54m ordinary shares at 30 September 1987. There have been two capital issues since 1983. In June 1985, 40.56m shares were issued in a one for four rights issue at 220p. In August 1987 an ADR issue of 8.63m shares at 510p raised £34.6m net.

Early in 1986, the group's leisure interests were sold to Rank for £37.5m. In November 1986 ECC made an unsuccessful share offer to buy Bryant Holdings, the West Midlands housebuilder. Although the offer was lost by just 2%, with 48% of the capital committed to ECC, the company now owns 29.9% of Bryant. No director has a significant shareholding, and there is no declarable shareholding of 5% or more.

Many of the company's acquisitions and disposals have been for cash. In 1987 the group spent a total of £85m on acquisitions, including the stake in Bryant Holdings. After the 1987 year-end, £43.3m in cash was spent in acquiring Microcal, an Italian calcium carbonate operation, and JL Shiely, a Minnesota-based aggregates company.

GROUP REVIEW

International division ECC International is the world's largest producer of china clay. It produces 90% of UK output, of which 80% is exported. Other products include calcium carbonate, ball clays, calcined clays and other minerals.

In 1987 divisional operating profit was 12.9% up at £69.3m, on turnover 12.8% up at £421.1m. The division contributed 58.1% of the group's total divisional operating profit and 55.2% of its turnover.

Applications for clay and its derivatives range from the high volume end of the paper market to bone china and ceramics. It is also used in the manufacture of thermoplastic and PVC audio, video and computer tapes. ECC's expanding range of industrial minerals are showing signs of growth. An example is calcium carbonate, used in paints, car fittings, and domestic and high performance electrical goods.

The group is maintaining its position in the bulk paper and specialist bone china clay sectors at the same time as developing new markets. The capacity increase in the Cornwall and Devon manufacturing sites – together with the building of slurry plants in Sweden, Finland and Belgium – will enable it to meet growing demand. A new high quality ceramic clay produced in Devon has been well received in Europe.

The international operation includes a profitable plant in Brazil, a majority share in a company in Portugal, two clay plants in Spain and one in France. There are also calcium carbonate plants in Sweden, Belgium, France, Italy and Japan.

The US operation includes Anglo-American Clays in Georgia, Southern Clay Products in Texas and calcium carbonate plants in Sylacauga, Alabama. US activities have been reorganised to develop a strong corporate image. The group is now selling into higher value markets with specialist products for paper, paint, homecare and personal care.

The paper industry is very profitable. Mineral pigments derived from clay production are important in making coated paper. The industry today is less cyclical, and demand for paper and board remains high. Additional capacity to meet demand is being added in the coating and filler grades.

A prepared body plant to produce ready mixed concrete material has been commissioned at Stoke-on-Trent. This has been well received. Demand for calcined clays is now very strong. The paint and polymer industries, particularly in Europe, are taking increased quantities of calcium carbonate and other calcined products.

The group is developing a profitable and expanding operation in the southern hemisphere. ECC Pacific is servicing the area from its Singapore base, with production operations in Japan and Australia. The recent acquisition of its New Zealand agent, Polychem, has added strength to this important geographical market.

The paper industry accounts for 75% of the division's turnover; the paint, rubber and plastics industries 13%; and the ceramics industry 11%. 76% of revenue is derived from Europe, 19% from the US, and 5% from the Pacific Rim.

Quarries division The division is one of the top five UK companies in the extraction of aggregates, producing 12m tonnes a year. Products include crushed and graded stone, industrial sand and natural gravel. 1.2m tonnes a year are further processed to produce coated stone used for road surfacing. The division is a market leader in decorative concrete products and building blocks, flagstones and kerbs.

In 1987 improved margins have pushed up profits to be

27.2% of the group's total divisional operating profit and turnover to be 31.8% of total group turnover. Operating profit increased 33% to £32.4m on sales 12.2% ahead at £242.3m. The UK-based business is enjoying a high demand for all its products.

The concrete business is extremely competitive. Thirteen static concrete block works located across the UK supplied over 70m concrete blocks during the year. The Bradstone and Countryside masonry brands of concrete are market leaders in sales to the DIY trade, but this business is subject to the vagaries of the British weather.

Associated Asphalt is the group's road surfacing business. It supplies tarmacadam for road construction. The company handled 40% of the surfacing of the M25 London orbital motorway, and has a number of major contracts in the south of England.

Share price and relative to FT-A All-Share

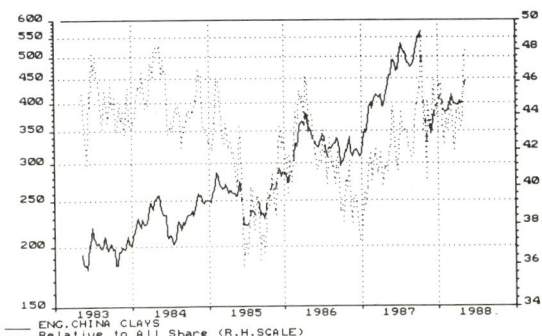

ECC's largest quarry is situated in Leicestershire. Over £10m is being spent on rebuilding the operation, which will enable it to produce 3m tonnes of granite per year. The quarry is rail linked. ECC is developing depots in the London area where further processing of the stone will take place.

The quarrying division in the UK now has a much better split of sales between the public and private sectors. Only a serious economic recession would badly damage volumes.

In a major US acquisition in January 1988, the group acquired JL Shiely for £41.7m. JL Shiely produces specification quality aggregates in Minneapolis, Denver and Colorado Springs.

Construction The division is one of the UK's top twenty housebuilders. Under the SNW Homes and Bradley Homes brand names, the division completed 1,144 domestic dwellings in 1987.

In 1987 the division represented 8.2% of group turnover and 13.7% of total divisional operating profit. Turnover rose 19% to £62.6m and profits more than doubled to £16.3m. The group's bid to control Bryant Holdings would have strengthened its geographic position. ECC has built up a large land bank in the south and south-west of England and is moving into the growth area of the construction of sheltered housing.

The division is concerned about high land prices which inflate new home costs. Despite seeking inner city sites for redevelopment, it believes that more green field sites must be released. A major example of this is ECC's participation in the Haydon Sector development north-west of Swindon. The group owns 200 acres, with planning permission pending, of the 1,500-acre site. This is one of the largest private enterprise town expansion schemes in Europe.

The division cannot help but perform well in 1988, benefiting from sharply rising house prices and being able to price according to buoyant market conditions. With input prices rising by some 7%, and house prices rising by 20% to 25% – the houses built on land bought at prices of three years ago – the company's concern about rising land prices inflating new house costs is not likely to affect profits in the short term. The company made a profit of £11,150 per house in 1987 compared with £6,800 per house in 1986.

The division's subsidiary activities, in particular its joinery business, have been rationalised to bring margins in line with the rest of the group.

International drilling fluids Mineral-based drilling fluids are used by all the major oil companies. The division has become an international market leader in the supply of high quality fluids to the oil and gas industry. Its major market is the North Sea, but West Africa and North America are growing in importance.

Demand from exploration activities has been disappointing. This has been partially offset by the introduction of ECC's Trudrill system into the Middle East and the North Sea. Major contracts for the system are pending in West and North Africa. ECC's Trudrill system allows higher rates of penetration and less down time.

The division's sales and profits have suffered as the falling oil price has curtailed international activity. Turnover dropped 22.1% from £46.9m in 1986 to £36.5m in 1987. Profits fell 62.9% from £3.5m to £1.3m. There is intense competition in all markets, though the division may benefit from the withdrawal of several competitors from the market.

GEOGRAPHICAL REVIEW

In 1987 the UK accounted for 49.5% of group turnover, Europe for 33.2%, North America for 8.6% and the rest of the world for 8.7%. It is estimated that profits in 1987 were derived equally from the UK and the rest of the world, taking into account that the major proportion of international division operating profit is not derived from the UK but from exports.

CORPORATE CALENDAR

Year end	30 September
Preliminary results	December
Report and accounts	January
AGM	February
Final dividend paid	April
Interim results	May
Interim dividend paid	September

DIRECTORS' HOLDINGS

	Fully-paid ordinary shares		Options
	(beneficial)	(non-beneficial)	
Sir Alan Dalton	10,423	—	—
DHL Hopkinson	3,000	—	—
Dr SR Dennison	7,510	—	—
Lord Chilver	3,003	—	—
TW Stobart	7,414	—	—
RW Carlton-Porter	2,704	—	2,382
BG Allison	3,683	—	—
DA Langford	1,133	—	2,251
SJ Titcomb	5,000	—	—
J Reeve	3,249	—	—
JMM Banham	625	—	—

Total directors' remuneration in 1987 was £526,000, of which the chairman, who was also the highest-paid director, received £110,275.

ENTERPRISE OIL plc

PRINCIPAL SUBSIDIARIES

AB CDM – Sweden, Anglo-American Clays Corporation – US, Associated Asphalt Company Ltd, Caosil SA – Spain, Compañia Española de Caolines SA – Spain (81.6%), ECC America Inc – US, ECC Ball Clays Ltd, ECC Calcium Carbonates Ltd, ECC Construction Ltd, ECC International (Sales) Ltd, ECC International AB – Sweden, ECC International Ltd, ECC International Oy – Finland, ECC International SA – Belgium, ECC International SA – France, ECC International SpA – Italy, ECC International Verkauf GmbH – West Germany (51%), ECC Japan Ltd – Japan, ECC Joinery Ltd, ECC Overseas Investments Ltd, ECC Pacific (Australia) Pty Ltd – Australia, ECC Pacific (NZ) Ltd – New Zealand, ECC Pacific Ltd, ECC Ports Ltd, ECC Quarries Ltd, ECCA Calcium Products Inc – US, English China Clays Finance NV – Netherlands, English Kaolin Holland BV – Netherlands, Fordamin Company (Sales) Ltd, George Garside (Sand) Ltd, Haul-Waste Ltd, Heavy Transport (ECC) Ltd, IDF International BV – Netherlands, Kaolin Australia Pty Ltd – Australia, Lime Distributors (ECC) Ltd, Polychem Marketing Ltd – New Zealand, Ronez Ltd, Société des Kaolins du Finistère SA – France (98.75%), Southern Clay Products Inc – US, Thomas Black Ltd, Western Excavating (ECC) Ltd, Western Express Haulage (ECC) Ltd, Whitfield Chemicals Ltd

RELATED COMPANIES

Bryant Group plc (29.9%), Watts Blake Bearne & Co P.L.C. (20.8%)

BRAND NAMES

Bradley Homes, Bradstore, Countryside, SNW Homes

CONTACTS AND FURTHER INFORMATION

Ivor Bowditch, Corporate and public relations manager, English China Clays P.L.C., John Keay House, St Austell, Cornwall PL25 4DJ. Tel: 0726 74482.

GENERAL INFORMATION

Head office 5 Strand, London WC2N 5HU. Tel: 01-930 1212
Directors WE Bell CBE (chairman), GJK Hearne (chief executive), JM Bowen OBE, EJ Harris, PE Wingston, JA Walmsley, JF Watt. *Non-exec* SE Churchfield OBE, JA Gardiner, TO Hutchison, IC MacLaurin, GM Ramsay, PG Rogerson, Sir Brian Shaw
Advisers J Henry Schroder Wagg & Co Ltd, SG Warburg & Co Ltd
Auditors Peat Marwick McLintock
Registrars Hill Samuel Registrars Ltd
Brokers Cazenove & Co, James Capel & Co
Solicitors Herbert Smith

GENERAL FINANCIAL INFORMATION

Market capitalisation	£739.2m at 1 January 1988
Capital structure	
Issued ordinary shares (25p)	287.64m
Issued preference shares (£1)	One special rights preference share held by the Secretary of State for Energy, redeemable on 31 December 1988
Warrants	None
Convertibles	None
Traded options	None
ADRs	None
Shareholders over 5%	ICI 25%, LASMO 25.3%, Norwich Union 8.11%

FT CATEGORY

FT: Oil and gas
FT-A: Oil and gas

MAJOR ACTIVITIES

Enterprise is the UK's leading independent exploration and production company. It was formed in May 1983 as part of HM Government's plans for reducing public sector involvement in the UK oil industry. In July 1984 Enterprise was floated on the stock market by way of an offer for sale. Today it is the largest producer of the UK independent explorers and derives almost all of its revenues from sales of oil and gas from the UK continental shelf.

Its financial performance is sensitive to the spot price of North Sea Brent crude, a benchmark for other grades, and to the sterling/dollar exchange rate. LASMO, a company with greater overseas interests but a smaller North Sea presence, is the company most resembling Enterprise.

FINANCIAL HISTORY

Turnover of £227.9m (£142.2m) in 1987 was 60.3% higher than in 1986, reflecting the contribution from the oil and gas assets acquired from ICI in early 1987. Sterling oil prices also assisted this improvement, averaging £11.06 a barrel in 1987 compared to £10.45 a barrel in 1986.

Pre-tax profits of £72.5m in 1987 rose very sharply from £2.9m in 1986, but fell well short of the 1985 figure of £111.1m when oil prices averaged £21.41 a barrel. Profits after tax were £50.7m in 1987, a result somewhat enhanced by tax credits. Earnings per share rose 63% to 17.6p but dividends for the year rose only 11.8% to 9.5p, reflecting the fact that they had been held when earnings fell sharply the previous year.

At the end of 1987 the balance sheet was exceptionally strong with no net debt and net cash of £130m. This achievement is remarkable, given that Enterprise has had to spend considerable sums on acquiring additional assets and on drilling since its flotation, and has been able to preserve the net cash position it started with in 1983.

Cash flow in 1987 was little altered from 1986 levels despite the ICI assets acquired. Funds generated from operations amounted to £93.7m and after capital expenditure and dividends there was a surplus of £8.1m.

SHARE PRICE HISTORY

Enterprise was floated at 185p and only broke above 200p conclusively in the spring of 1987. It rose strongly subsequently, reaching 350p before the October 1987 crash. The shares fell far more heavily in the crash than the market generally, losing 43%, but rapidly retraced this fall, rallying to 360p following BP's bid for Britoil. Notwithstanding this, only now have the shares recovered to the same level relative to the market as they were at flotation in 1984.

SENIOR MANAGEMENT

Chairman William Bell has held office since flotation. He presided over a period of major development decisions in the northern North Sea as a managing director of Shell UK from 1976 to 1980 before becoming a director of Shell International Petroleum Company.

Graham Hearne has been chief executive since flotation, having been chief executive of Tricentrol and managing director of Carless Capel. John Walmsley, former tax partner with Arthur Andersen, has been finance director since flotation and has been praised for his skilful treasury management.

Myles Bowen, a geologist with 30 years' experience with Shell, is exploration director, and Peter Kingston, a petroleum engineer of 18 years' experience, is technical director.

CAPITAL

Enterprise was floated with 212m shares in 1984. During 1985, 3.73m additional shares were issued to acquire Saxon Oil. Following this on 30 January 1987, 71.9 million new shares were issued to ICI to acquire its oil and gas interests.

There are three large shareholdings in Enterprise. LASMO holds 25.27%, ICI holds 25% and Norwich Union holds 8.11%. There is one special 'golden' share held by the Secretary of State for Energy, which conveys the ability to block a takeover. It expires on 31 December 1988.

GROUP REVIEW

Enterprise explores for oil and gas, plans the development and physical extraction of these resources, and then sells its share of production. It is a pure upstream company, concerned only with exploration and production, as opposed to the refining and marketing of petroleum products.

When Enterprise was offered for sale in 1984, it had an

CHAIRMAN'S STATEMENT

'Enterprise Oil had another active and successful year in 1987. The most encouraging feature of last year's performance is the clear evidence that the sharp fall in oil prices has not impaired our ability to develop the business in line with our original strategy. . . .

If we look ahead, against the expectation that oil prices will be on the rise in a few years' time, the group is well placed to benefit. Our production from the North Sea is set to double in the early 1990s, and with our financial strength and proven record of exploration success, we can look forward with confidence to the next phase of the group's development.'
William Bell

interest in five producing oilfields and exploration acreage in 25 UK offshore blocks. Its production in 1984 averaged 31,000 barrels of oil a day. In form, Enterprise was rather like a junior exploration company, in that it lacked a portfolio of good exploration prospects which would provide the fields of the future. Although its balance sheet had £69m of net cash and it had a strong cash flow from its producing assets, Enterprise needed to seek substantial additions to its exploration acreage.

In September 1985 Enterprise clinched the takeover of Saxon Oil for £138m. This deal gave Enterprise a substantial stake in the Miller field, one of the largest UK oilfields currently under development for production in the 1990s. It also contributed a wide addition to exploration acreage.

Enterprise was still not satisfied with its acreage position or its future prospects. During much of 1985 the company pursued a series of farm-in deals whereby it obtained a share of interesting exploration licences by contributing to costs or by swapping unwanted acreage. It made a number of smaller acquisitions too, such as Lennox Oil and Tanks Oil and Gas. Net acreage more than doubled during 1985.

During the oil price collapse of 1986, Enterprise contained its costs very effectively. The original budget for drilling on its now extensive acreage interests was trimmed substantially. Spending was 33% below 1985 levels at £28m but 34 exploration and appraisal wells were drilled in 1986, four more than in 1985.

1986 was a year of consolidation for Enterprise with further work on several future prospects confirming their commercial potential. Fields like Arbroath, Ness and North Ravenspurn all began to show potential to improve the long term production profile.

At the end of 1986 an opportunity to add reserves cheaply in the aftermath of the oil price decline presented itself. Enterprise merged its assets with the oil and gas assets of ICI. It proved to be an astute deal which, because of the cash in the ICI subsidiary acquired, made it particularly good value. Enterprise production almost doubled after the deal and by

F I V E Y E A R F I N A N C I A L I N F O R M A T I O N													
Year	Turnover (£m)	Pre-tax (£m)	Earnings (p)	Dividends net (p)	Dividend cover (x)	Net assets (x)	Price (p) High	Low	PER (x) High	Low	Yield (%) High	Low	
1983	—	—	—	—	—	—	—	—	—	—	—	—	
1984	267	63	29.5	8.0	3.7	76	210	175	9.1	7.9	5.71	4.98	
1985	266	63	25.9	8.5	3.5	100	207	152	9.2	6.1	7.52	4.93	
1986	142	23	14.1	8.5	1.7	85	178	99	11.4	3.7	12.09	6.73	
1987	228	51	17.6	9.5	1.9	93	344	180	45.4	11.7	6.58	3.38	

Share price and relative to FT-A All-Share

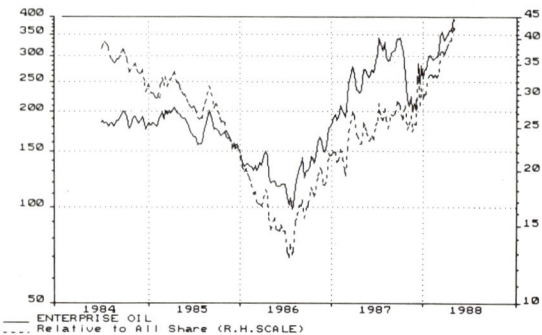

ENTERPRISE OIL
Relative to All Share (R.H.SCALE)

Far East and other Following the ICI deal, Enterprise acquired a potentially commercial oilfield in Indonesia, the Tiaka prospect in east Sulawesi. At present there is no production from Indonesia from any of its contract areas. In August 1987 Enterprise acquired a large tract of acreage offshore the Seychelles. There is no production currently.
North America Enterprise has more than 50 leases in Alberta, Canada. Production is not significant, and the leases are up for sale.

CORPORATE CALENDAR

Year end	31 December
Preliminary results	March
Report and accounts	April
AGM	May
Final dividend paid	May
Interim results	September
Interim dividend paid	November

DIRECTORS' HOLDINGS

	Ordinary shares	Options
WE Bell	40,000	180,822
JM Bowen	8,100	160,381
SE Churchfield	1,000	
JA Gardiner	5,800	
EJ Harris	6,754	154,979
GJ Hearne	13,500	287,207
TO Hutchison	—	
PE Kingston	—	178,727
IC MacLaurin	1,000	
GM Ramsay	15,000	
PG Rogerson	—	
Sir Brian Shaw	—	
JA Walmsley	10,000	182,571
JF Watt	—	129,031

Total directors' emoluments in 1987 excluding pension provisions amounted to £818,000, of which the chairman was paid £83,000 and the highest-paid director £135,000.

issuing shares to ICI it gave itself a degree of protection from the potential takeover threat from LASMO. ICI was issued with 25% of the new enlarged share capital of Enterprise and LASMO's holding was diluted from 29.9% to 22.5%.

Since that time, Enterprise has been sifting its numerous exploration assets and has made a series of disposals of peripheral interests in return for larger shares of specific licences.

This has improved efficiency and targeted certain areas which have the capacity to contribute significantly to the future of the company. North Sea block 22/11, 125 miles north-east of Aberdeen, is an example of a prospect for which Enterprise had high hopes. It swapped small interests in discoveries elsewhere for large percentages in this block, finally acquiring 100% ownership. When it was drilled in March 1988 it produced a significant oil flow and is almost certainly a commercial oilfield which could be producing in the mid-1990s. It was named the Nelson field by Enterprise and is its largest commercial discovery since its formation.

As at March 1988, the outlook for Enterprise is very promising. It has several fields under development and others which together could increase production from 58,300 barrels of oil a day in 1987 to over 100,000 barrels of oil a day in the mid-1990s. Its management is extremely highly regarded following a series of well received deals and the company has grown into a worthy successor to Britoil in the FT-SE 100 index.

PRINCIPAL SUBSIDIARIES AND RELATED COMPANIES

Enterprise (E&P) Ltd, Enterprise Oil Exploration Ltd, Enterprise Petroleum Ltd, Saxon Oil Ltd

BRAND NAMES

None

CONTACTS AND FURTHER INFORMATION

John Walmsley, Finance director, Enterprise Oil plc, 5 Strand, London WC2N 4HU. Tel: 01-930 1212.

GEOGRAPHICAL REVIEW

UK operations Enterprise has interests in seven producing oilfields. Together these account for about 2% of the UK's North Sea output. 99% of current production comes from the UK. At the beginning of 1988, Enterprise had an estimated 347m barrels of proven and probable oil and gas reserves. The Nelson discovery raises this to some 447m barrels, of which an estimated 95% lie in the UK. Enterprise has at least nine potential future fields in the UK either under development or under appraisal.

North-west Europe Having sold its Dutch gas production interest in P6 in December 1987, Enterprise now has no European production of oil or gas. Its exploration acreage lies onshore France, onshore Italy, onshore and offshore Denmark, offshore Ireland, and offshore Netherlands. Of all these areas, the best prospects for commercial future fields appear to lie in the Netherlands on blocks J/3 and J/6, where a potential gas field exists.

GENERAL INFORMATION

Head office	Fison House, Princes Street, Ipswich, Suffolk IP2 1QH. Tel: 0473-232525
Directors	JS Kerridge (chairman and chief executive), DR Peters, CA Scroggs, RD Thomas, GP Fothergill, JF Valentine. *Non-exec* EP Chappell CBE, Sir Alan Cottrell FRS, PVM Egan, Sir Philip Harris, Lord Plumb
Advisers	No specified adviser
Auditors	Price Waterhouse
Registrars	Barclays Bank Registration Department
Brokers	County NatWest WoodMac
Solicitors	Linklaters & Paines

GENERAL FINANCIAL INFORMATION

Market capitalisation	£1.219bn at 1 January 1988
Capital structure	
Issued ordinary shares (25p)	493.5m
Issued preference shares	None
Warrants	None
Convertibles	£33.7m of 5.25% convertible bonds 2001 (convertible at 322p per ordinary share at fixed rate of $1.4465 to the pound)
Traded options	None
ADRs	Four ordinary 25p shares for each ADR
Shareholders over 5%	None

FT CATEGORY

FT: Industrials (miscel.)
FT-A: Health and household products

MAJOR ACTIVITIES

In contrast with other drug companies, Fisons only concentrated its interests on drugs during the 1970s, diversifying away from its traditional base in fertilizers, agrochemicals and horticulture. This decision contributed to the dramatic turnaround in the group's performance, with compound earnings per share growth of 60% since 1981.

The pharmaceutical division is the largest in terms of profits, providing 64% of operating profit in 1987, whilst only contributing 37% of sales. The principal products are for the treatment of allergy-related problems. They include Intal for asthma, and Nasalcrom and Opticrom for nose and eye. Tilade, a further advance in the treatment of adult allergy and respiratory problems, was launched at the end of 1986. Fisons also owns the Sanatogen range of vitamins, and is a sizeable manufacturer of generic drugs in both this country and in Australia.

The scientific equipment division accounted for almost 54% of sales in 1987, but only 27% of profit. Fisons is one of the world's largest suppliers of laboratory equipment, supplying scientists in over 100 countries. Fisons operates national distribution businesses in the US, Australia and the UK. Recent acquisition activity has seen Fisons building up the more specialist side of the scientific division.

The horticulture business provides most of the easily recognisable brand names of Fisons, including the Gro-bag and other amateur garden products such as the Evergreen lawncare treatments, Levington composts and Fisons seeds. It is the largest of its kind in the UK although the smallest of Fison's divisions.

Fisons competes against a number of companies in various different markets. In pharmaceuticals Glaxo is the other British company involved in asthma therapy. Foreign competitors include Astra of Sweden and Sandoz of Switzerland.

The scientific equipment division operates in separate markets in the UK, the US, Europe and Australia. In the UK,

Fisons is dominant in the supply of educational equipment.

In the UK amateur horticulture market, Fisons is a market leader with competitors including ICI and Pan Britannica. In the US, the market for peat is more fragmented and the group's principal competitors are small family concerns.

FINANCIAL HISTORY

The disposal of the agrochemical and fertiliser activities in the early 1980s returned strength to the balance sheet and allowed the group to concentrate on international growth industries with a record of profitability for successful participants. Tight financial management and the availability of tax losses from the group's disposals have enabled the group to make the most of its return to growth.

Whilst sales have grown at a compound rate of 7% since 1982, pre-tax profits have grown at an average rate of 54%, and earnings per share at 60%. Market capitalisation has grown from around £40m in 1980 to £1.22bn at the beginning of 1988.

On the way Fisons has raised cash twice by way of rights issues to fund future expansion, and in 1987 proposed placing shares overseas to broaden the share base. However, the latter plan was dropped when some UK investors were concerned at the dilution of their shareholdings that such a placing would create. The group is in net neutral position with regard to cash and debt.

1987 pre-tax profits were £109.1m, up 28.2% on 1986, and 2,871% up on the 1980 figure of £3.8m. Earnings per share were 26.1% up at 17.4p. 1987 turnover was £760.3m, up 8.2% on 1986, and 67.6% up on 1980.

SHARE PRICE HISTORY

Since 1984 the shares, in common with other shares in the sector, have performed well, with growth in the share price of 60% from the end of 1985 to its July 1987 high of 407p.

During the October 1987 market crash, the shares fell from around the 400p level to a low of 216p. The price had recovered to the 255p level in April 1988.

The company in recent years has been consistently on a premium to the market, reflecting its earnings growth and strength of management. From 1984 to mid-1986 the shares significantly outperformed the market, but then turned gently downwards in relative terms.

SENIOR MANAGEMENT

The chairman and chief executive is John Kerridge. He joined Fisons in 1967, was appointed chief executive in 1980 and became chairman in 1984. RD Thomas has been finance director since 1977. DR Peters became director of planning and administration in 1981.

The three divisional chairmen are GP Fothergill, pharmaceutical division, JF Valentine, horticulture division and CA Scroggs, scientific equipment division.

CAPITAL

The capital structure has changed dramatically over the last five years as this rapidly growing group has asked shareholders to fund its expansion through rights issues and vendor placings.

The paid-up share capital grew from £37.3m in 1982 to £61.1m at the 1986 year end. Rights issues have raised

FIVE YEAR FINANCIAL INFORMATION

Year	Turnover (£m)	Pre-tax (£m)	Earnings (p)	Dividends net (p)	Dividend cover (x)	Net assets (p)	Price (p) High	Low	PER (x) High	Low	Yield (%) High	Low
1983	365	31.2	7.00	1.80	3.9	52	96	49	38.7	24.0	3.67	2.25
1984	553	48.3	9.40	2.16	4.3	46	144	82	32.1	19.9	3.15	1.94
1985	647	72.3	12.15	2.75	4.4	65	227	131	32.1	22.1	2.22	1.53
1986	703	85.1	13.70	3.20	4.3	68	323	205	36.9	25.6	1.69	1.20
1987	760	109.1	17.40	4.00	4.3	74	401	220	35.8	17.9	2.18	1.11

£125.4m along the way. There was a one for five rights issue in 1983, and a further one for five rights issue in March 1985. A one for one scrip issue in 1987 increased the issued share capital to £123m, represented by 493.5m ordinary shares at the 1987 year end.

GROUP REVIEW

Fisons pioneered a new type of therapy for asthma with the introduction of Intal some years ago. Unlike other asthma products, it gives no instant symptomatic relief but used prophylactically it helps prevent attacks occurring. A relatively expensive therapy, around £20 for a full month's course in an aerosol inhaler, the drug took a while to gain acceptance but is now widely used in this country. Overseas doctors have prescribed different sorts of drugs, but if the UK pattern is followed, there is still massive potential for increased sales.

Fisons have extended their respiratory range with Tilade, a drug targeted at adult respiratory problems including bronchitis. It is still too early to assess its long term potential as it has only been on the market since 1986.

The group has a good reputation for research and development, but following the failure of a drug in a late stage of clinical trials some years ago, the company is less forthcoming about future developments than some of the other companies in the sector.

A critical care heart failure drug, Dopacard, should be launched in 1988. Beyond that the group has potential interests in the cardiovascular, gastrointestinal, and anti-inflammatory areas.

Pharmaceutical division The division represents 37% of group sales and 64% of profits. In 1987 operating profit was 26.1% up at £62.8m on turnover 12.9% up at £281.9m.

The main focus of the division is on asthma and allergy drugs sold worldwide. They include Intal, Rynacrom and Opticrom, each a different formulation of the same basic chemical. In 1987 Intal, Opticrom and Nasalcrom increased sales by almost 60% in the US. Generic drugs, over the counter drugs and an assorted portfolio of ethical drugs make up the remainder of the business.

The group runs a small but successful research and development (R&D) programme in Loughborough with annual expenditure of £25m to £30m. The most recent product to emerge from R&D into the market place is Tilade, another anti-asthmatic agent, but believed by Fisons to be applicable to a much wider population of patients with respiratory disorders.

In the early 1980s the margin on sales in this division was in the low teens, reflecting the high fixed cost burden that Fisons had to carry with an inadequate revenue base. Now, however, Fisons has critical mass and the growth in revenues, particularly in the US, is making a significant impact on profits as the margins widen.

It is this feature of Fisons, its small earnings base relative to its international competitors, and its recent achievement of critical mass, that makes the company so interesting to investors. The impact of even a moderately successful drug on the small earnings base of Fisons could have a very big impact on earnings growth.

Tilade, recently launched in the UK and expected to be rolled-out worldwide over the next four to five years, could be such a drug with sales potential of $100m to $200m. New formulations of Tilade, making it applicable to treat hay fever and allergic conjunctivitis, are expected to follow. In addition, Dopacard, a drug for acute cardiac failure, could be on the first European market in 1988.

One feature of Fisons pharmaceutical business which distinguishes it from its many peers is that the marketing of its products does not require huge and costly sales forces. In the US, for example, Fisons markets Intal, the asthma drug, principally to specialists, of which there are few in number relative to ordinary physicians. This feature of Fisons and the therapeutic category in which it operates allows Fisons to compete successfully with companies many times its size.

Scientific equipment division The division, accounting for 54% of group sales and 27% of group operating profit, operates in three areas – laboratory supplies in the UK, biomedical supplies in the US, and advanced scientific instruments worldwide. Operating profit was 16.4% up in 1987 at £27.0m on sales 7.7% up at £410.0m.

The UK business, which is estimated to account for about 12% of divisional sales, is a supplier of traditional laboratory-ware, with Gallenkemp and Griffin & George perhaps the best-remembered names from chemistry lessons at school. 1987 was overall a difficult year.

In the US, Fisons runs the second largest distributor of

CHAIRMAN'S STATEMENT

'In 1987 Fisons achieved its seventh consecutive year of profit growth. Profits of £109.1m were 28% up on 1986, and there has been commensurate progress in the quality of our earnings per share and in the return on investment. As a management we place considerable importance upon the quality of our earnings, as well as their quantity, and it is particularly pleasing to be able to report sustained progress in this regard.

I have stated in previous reports the basis of our Group strategy, which remains sound, and is the essential cornerstone of the Group and its ability to maintain progress. But strategies, however sound they may be, are of no avail if they are not implemented operationally by skilled, competitively-orientated management. We place considerable emphasis upon this in Fisons, and by so doing feel that we put our assets to maximum profitable use.' *JS Kerridge*

Share price and relative to FT-A All-Share

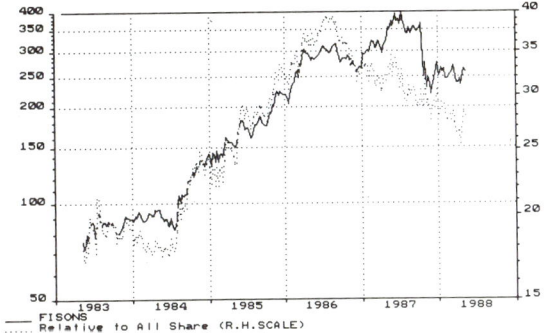

FISONS
Relative to All Share (R.H.SCALE)

leading products like Sanatogen multi-vitamins, Paracodol analgesic and Radian B. Through CP Pharmaceuticals Fisons also runs a very profitable generic drugs manufacturer.

US   The US is the largest of Fisons' markets, representing about 45% of sales and 35% of profit. The majority of sales come from CMS, the distributor of scientific equipment, but Fisons has a fast growing pharmaceutical operation and a sizeable commodity peat business here also.

Rest of the world   Europe represents about 17% of total sales and 37% of profit, mostly from pharmaceuticals. There are a small number of high technology scientific equipment manufacturers in Europe – in Germany and Italy in particular – but their contribution is small. Outside Europe, Fisons operates in Africa, Asia, Australasia and Latin America. Perhaps the business most worthy of note is the strong generics manufacturer Orbit Pharmaceuticals in Australia.

biomedical laboratory equipment and reagents, Curtin Matheson Scientific (CMS). CMS, acquired by Fisons in 1984, is operationally very efficient and has gained market share each year since then. It supplies everything from blood cell counters to pregnancy test kits to the target market of hospitals, pharmaceutical research labs and physicians' offices. It is growing at a steady 7–8% a year and continuously gaining market share.

CMS plans to increase its content of own-manufactured products and improve market penetration, thereby maintaining strong revenue growth and widening margins.

The instruments group manufactures and distributes high technology scientific instruments. Since 1985 Fisons has acquired a number of scientific equipment manufacturers. Carlo Erba Strumentazione, an Italian manufacturer of gas chromatographs was acquired in 1985. Applied Research Laboratories, a leading manufacturer of spectrometers, was acquired in 1986.

From gas spectroscopy to viscometry the demand for the instrument group's products is high. Fisons' criterion for acquisition is that the target company should operate in inherently attractive markets and have high market share. If Fisons' companies maintain their technological lead then the niche nature of the business will guarantee a continuing market leadership and hence good growth.

Horticulture division   This is the smallest division, contributing 9.0% of the group's sales and 8.7% of operating profit.

In the UK Fisons sells Gro-bags, Levington compost, garden chemicals and houseplant products. The division is very dependent on the weather. The quality of earnings is not as good as elsewhere in the group.

In North America Fisons owns large tracts of peat bogs and operates a commodity peat business selling peat to market gardeners. It also sells a small range of garden products through retailers in the US.

In 1987 operating profit was 7.5% up at £8.6m on turnover 5.3% down at £68.4m.

GEOGRAPHICAL REVIEW

UK   The UK is Fisons' second largest market, contributing about 20% of group sales and representing the largest base for manufacturing and exports. The UK is also the home of group pharmaceutical R&D and administrative headquarters.

Each division is represented in the UK but in addition the UK is the most significant market for Fisons' over-the-counter pharmaceutical range. The Consumer Health operation has

CORPORATE CALENDAR

Year end	31 December
Preliminary results	March
Report and accounts	April
AGM	May
Final dividend paid	July
Interim results	September
Interim dividend paid	January

DIRECTORS' HOLDINGS

	Fully-paid ordinary shares	Options
EP Chappell	10,654	—
Sir Alan Cottrell	4,434	—
PVM Egan	—	—
Sir Philip Harris	80,000	—
JS Kerridge	21,720	2,862
DR Peters	53,672	4,596
Lord Plumb	6,240	—
CA Scroggs	40,400	2,345
RD Thomas	111,900	2,345
JF Valentine	8,856	2,345

Total directors' remuneration for 1987 was £1.10m, of which the chairman, who was also the highest-paid director, received £253,181.

PRINCIPAL SUBSIDIARIES AND RELATED COMPANIES

Applied Research Laboratories Inc – US, Applied Research Laboratories SA – Switzerland, Arzneimittel GmbH – West Germany, Atlantic Chemical Corp Ltd – Bermuda, Carlo Erba Strumentazione SpA – Italy, Chemical Corp Ltd, Curtin Matheson Scientific Inc – US, Fisons AG – Switzerland, Fisons Arzneimittel GmbH – West Germany, Fisons A/S – Denmark, Fisons (Bangladesh) Ltd (51%), Fisons BV – Netherlands, Fisons Corp – US, Fisons Corp Ltd – Canada, Fisons Farmaceutici SpA – Italy, Fisons Pharmaceuticals (Pty) Ltd – South Africa, Fisons Pty Ltd – Australia, Fisons Western Corp – Canada, FSE Pty Ltd – Australia, Fujisawa-Fisons KK – Japan (50%), Gebrüder Haake GmbH – West Germany, Laboratoires Fison SA – France, Laboratoires SCAC-Fisons SA – France, Rallis India Ltd (29.9%), SCAC-Fisons SA – France

BRAND NAMES

Aggregate Plus, Dopacard, Evergreen, Fisons Lawncare, Flowerite, Gro-bag, Intal, Levington, Liquinure, Nasalcrom, Opticrom, Paracodol, Radian B, Rynacrom, Sanatogen, Tilade, Tomorite

CONTACTS AND FURTHER INFORMATION

C Fletcher-Smith, Fisons plc, Fison House, Princes Street, Ipswich, Suffolk IP1 1QH. Tel: 0473 232525.

GENERAL ACCIDENT ASSURANCE CORPORATION p.l.c.

GENERAL INFORMATION

Head office	Pitheavlis, Perth, Scotland PH2 0NH. Tel: 0738 21202
Directors	The Rt Hon The Earl of Airlie KT GCVO PC DL (chairman), BC Marshall CA (chief executive), AB Cleaver, JC Corcoran, JC Frangoulis FAII ACIS AIFA, IC Menzies CA, T Roberts FCII, WN Robertson FCII. *Non-exec* RW Adam CA (deputy chairman), L Bolton, Sir Nicholas Goodison, Sir Duncan McDonald CBE, Sir Norman Macfarlane, The Rt Hon The Earl of Mansfield DL, The Rt Hon Lord Moore of Wolvercote GCB GCVO CMG QSO PC, Sir David Nickson KBE DL, FR Noel-Paton
Advisers	J Henry Schroder Wagg & Co Ltd
Auditors	Peat Marwick McLintock
Registrars	Lloyds Bank Registrar's Department
Brokers	Hoare Govett Ltd
Solicitors	Slaughter and May

GENERAL FINANCIAL INFORMATION

Market capitalisation	£1.536bn at 1 January 1988
Capital structure	
Issued ordinary shares (25p)	191m
Issued preference shares (£1)	0.25m 3.85% CP
Warrants	None
Convertibles	None
Traded options	None
ADRs	None
Shareholders over 5%	None

FT CATEGORY

FT: Insurances
FT-A: Insurance (composite)

MAJOR ACTIVITIES

General Accident is the UK's fourth largest insurer by market capitalisation. It transacts all major classes of insurance business except industrial life.

General Accident is one of the largest UK motor insurers, and is also a substantial motor insurer in the US. It is active internationally in reinsurance, in domestic and commercial property insurance, and in marine and aviation. Life assurance contributes approximately 10% of its total premium income.

About two-thirds of General Accident's general business is overseas, including 35% from the US. The group's substantial US exposure means that the share price is vulnerable during periods of dollar weakness. The greater emphasis on the less volatile personal insurance business means that the shares can be better compared with the GRE and Sun Alliance than with Royal Insurance.

FINANCIAL HISTORY

Business volume has increased by 75% since 1982. Non-life competition limited the company's ability to increase premiums during the period 1981 to 1985. Consequently the group incurred very substantial underwriting losses in each of the years 1982 to 1986, though the trend is now improving.

Although these losses were more than offset by the investment income earned on the group's investments, profits during the period were very depressed. In 1986 and 1987 a substantial recovery took place. Underwriting losses were down 15% at £180.9m in 1986 and to £98.3m in 1987. Pre-tax profits at £127.3m in 1986 and £204.4m in 1987 provided a satisfactory return on shareholders' funds. Throughout this period dividends increased. The 1987 dividend was 25% higher than in 1986 and 106% higher than in 1982.

The group has a very cautious accounting policy and the free assets available to cover the effects of a prolonged downturn in the insurance industry or a stockmarket decline are the largest of all the UK quoted sector composite insurers. They stand at about 79% of non-life premium income.

SHARE PRICE HISTORY

The share price drifted in relation to the improvement seen in UK equities generally for most of 1984. 1985 saw an increased ability of insurance companies to increase premium rates. This was reflected in the group's 1986 results and the 40% rise in its share price, 20% up on the market as a whole.

Share price and relative to FT-A All-Share

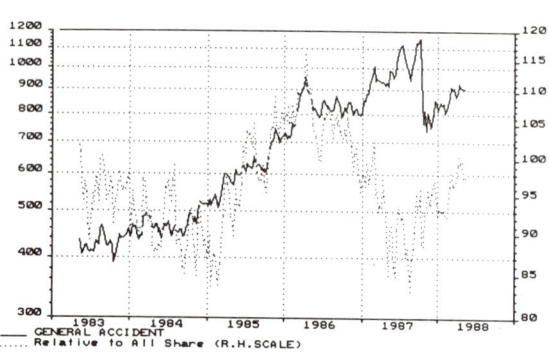

After the spring of 1986 it was generally believed that the upward trend in premium rates would not be sustained, even though they had not yet reached an historically high level of profitability. The shares underperformed until the autumn 1987 crash. Since then the fundamental strengths of the group have led its shares to outperform the market once again.

SENIOR MANAGEMENT

The chairman, the Rt Hon The Earl of Airlie succeeded GR Simpson in May 1987. The group's chief general manager is BC Marshall. JC Corcoran, JC Frangoulis, IC Menzies, T Roberts and WN Robertson are the other general managers.

CAPITAL

At the end of 1987 the company's issued share capital amounted to 190m ordinary 25p shares and 0.25m cumulative £1 preference shares. There have been only two major changes in the group's capital structure in the last few years.

In 1986 the group issued 16m shares, 14.3m relating to the acquisition of the Pilot Insurance Company of Canada, and the balance for the purchase of six chains of estate agents. In 1987 the group issued 6.3m shares in purchasing 22 more chains of estate agents. It also issued £1.6m of loan stock in the purchase of one of them.

Total shareholders' funds at the end of 1986 amounted to £2.011bn. The group had loans outstanding of £52.8m. Cash held at the end of 1986 totalled £25.6m. Following the market crash in October 1987, the group's net assets fell, but remained at a very healthy £1.708bn at the end of 1987.

FIVE YEAR FINANCIAL INFORMATION

Year	Turnover (£m)	Pre-tax (£m)	Earnings (p)	Dividends net (p)	Dividend cover (x)	Net assets (p)	Price (p) High	Low	PER (x) High	Low	Yield (%) High	Low
1983	1,538	65.6	37.0	19	1.90	677	476	354	12.9	9.6	7.67	5.70
1984	1,879	3.9	5.9	20	0.30	828	538	430	91.2	72.9	6.64	5.31
1985	1,896	26.5	20.5	22	0.90	940	753	508	36.7	24.8	6.13	4.14
1986	2,388	123.2	60.5	28	3.36	1,091	954	705	15.8	11.7	5.50	4.06
1987	2,383	204.4	86.2	35	2.46	896	1166	720	13.5	8.4	6.54	4.04

GROUP REVIEW

UK Motor insurance accounts for about 35% of total premium income, £820m in 1987. The number of car insurance claims has been increasing rapidly for a number of years with the result that, despite substantial premium increases, the loss for this account in 1986 increased. In 1987, however, the deficit fell substantially.

About 45% of premiums relate to property contents and buildings insurances. In recent years this class of business has been adversely affected by severe weather conditions. The cold weather in January 1987 resulted in an unusually large number of burst pipe claims, and the October 1987 hurricane took a substantial toll (£60m, of which £30m was met by the group's reinsurers). Premium rates in 1985 and 1986 were increased to take account of the increased occurrence of severe winters. Substantial improvements in profitability took place in 1987 despite the weather losses.

The group has a relatively small but expanding life business in the UK. The life fund has a strong balance sheet. In addition, the group acquired 27 chains of estate agencies in

CHIEF EXECUTIVE'S STATEMENT

'The general improvement in conditions reported last year has been maintained and, as more realistic underwriting attitudes have continued to prevail, yet further progress has been achieved. It is therefore ironic, albeit not unexpected, that an incipient downturn in underwriting experience is being postulated for some areas of activity in major markets.

As yet, evidence of any general move in that direction is limited, and it is to be hoped that the appalling experience of recent years will serve to deter those who may view current profitability as an irresistible invitation to relax the discipline on which has been based the progress now being achieved. Meanwhile, recent events in financial markets worldwide will have underlined, opportunely, the speciousness of the cash-flow underwriting philosophy.' *Buchan Marshall*

1987, bringing the total to 33, with 435 branches. These factors, together with an ability to provide a complete package of both life and non-life products to the agents and brokers who sell General Accident's policies, are likely to result in long-term growth in life profits. Life profits net of tax in 1987 amounted to £11.5m.

US and Canada The US provided £724m of total group non-life premium income in 1987, Canada a further £240m. The group's largest business is motor insurance. Of total underwriting losses of £37m in 1987 for these two territories, a substantial part related to the motor vehicle accident and liability accounts, both of which face strong competition and rising claims costs.

In 1986 General Accident acquired Pilot Insurance Company at a cost of about £103m. Pilot Insurance operates in Ontario and concentrates on personal rather than commercial insurances. It is well known as an efficiently run motor insurer in Canada.

As elsewhere in the world, General Accident has a strong balance sheet in North America so that underwriting losses are more than offset by investment income on the group's North American investments.

Rest of the world General Accident operates in a large number of countries around the world. In Europe it is represented in Ireland, France, Belgium, the Netherlands, West Germany, Denmark, Sweden, Greece, Italy, Malta, Cyprus, Gibraltar and Switzerland. It also has branches or subsidiaries in the Caribbean, South America, Australasia, and in the Near, Middle and Far East. In 1987 the group was making progress in virtually all these markets.

GEOGRAPHICAL REVIEW

The territorial distribution of the group's general business premium income in 1987 was UK 37.8%, US 33.4%, Canada 11.6%, Europe 6.9%, the rest of the world 10.8%. Life profits stem primarily from the UK.

CORPORATE CALENDAR

Year end	31 December
Preliminary results	March
Report and accounts	April
AGM	May
Final dividend paid	July
Interim results	September
Interim dividend paid	January

DIRECTORS' HOLDINGS

	Fully-paid ordinary shares	Options
RW Adam	1,000	—
The Earl of Airlie	1,000	—
L Bolton	400	—
JC Corcoran	1,000	25,347
JC Frangoulis	909	14,542
Sir Nicholas Goodison	1,200	—
Sir Duncan McDonald	1,000	—
Sir Norman Macfarlane	6,000	—
The Earl of Mansfield	2,500	—
Lord Moore	—	—
BC Marshall	1,766	27,871
IC Menzies	1,800	16,876
Sir David Nickson	5,000	—
The Hon FR Noel-Paton	—	—
T Roberts	1,677	18,540
WN Robertson	1,125	18,156

Total directors' remuneration in 1987 was £1,114,310, of which the chairman received £28,366, and the highest-paid director received £124,529.

PRINCIPAL SUBSIDIARIES AND RELATED COMPANIES

American Trust plc (15%), La Brabançonne SA Belge d'Assurances – Belgium (91.3%), Brighton, Worthing & District Property & Investment Corp Ltd, The Camden Fire Insurance Association – US (99.9%), Centrovincial Estates Plc (18%), Edinburgh Fund Managers plc (15%), General Accident Assurance Company Kenya Ltd (57%), The General Accident Assurance Company of Canada (99.8%), General Accident Financial Services Ltd, General Accident Insurance Company New Zealand Ltd, General Accident Insurance Company of America (99.9%), General Accident Insurance Company Puerto Rico Ltd – Puerto Rico (80%), General Accident Insurance Company South Africa Ltd (71%), General Accident Life Assurance Ltd, General Accident Linked Life Assurance Ltd, General Accident Reinsurance Co Ltd, Grampian Properties Ltd, The Guarantee Society Ltd, Intercontinental Life Insurance Company of Puerto Rico Ltd (66%), The Lancashire & Yorkshire Reversionary Interest Co Ltd, Lynton Property & Reversionary PLC (11%), McKay Securities PLC (24%), Multiple Credit Services Ltd, Oregon Automobile Insurance Co – US, Pennsylvania General Insurance Co – US (99.9%), Pilot Insurance Company – Canada, The Potomac Insurance Co of Illinois – US, The Road Transport General Insurance Co Ltd, Scottish Boiler & General Insurance Co Ltd, Scottish General Insurance Co Ltd, Scottish Insurance Corporation Ltd, Yorkshire-Corcovado Companhia de Seguros – Brazil (86.4%), The Yorkshire Insurance Co Ltd

ESTATE AGENCIES

Bancroft Groves Ltd, Banks and Silvers Ltd, Beales Property Services Ltd, Calvert Hunt and Barden Ltd, Clayton Booth & Partners Ltd, Cobbs Property Services Ltd, Collinson & Harvey South Ltd, Dee & Atkinson Ltd, Dudley Charlton Ltd, Edward Leslie Ltd, Flatt & Mead Ltd, Fox & Sons (Southern) Ltd, Fox & Sons (Western) Ltd, Fulljames and Still, Garton's Property Services Ltd, Gibbing and Mornborrow, Goodman and Mann Ltd, Hedley France Ltd, Hoddell Pritchard Ltd, JM Warwick & Co Ltd, JW Wood, Jackson & Jackson Estate Agents Ltd, Jacksons (Hereford) Ltd, Jacksons (Leominster) Ltd, Jacksons (Ludlow) Ltd, John H James Holdings plc, Lawson Larg & Co, Lawson Larg Ltd, Mawers Harrogate Ltd, Martlet Property Services Plc, Maureen Freeman Ltd, Naylor Hayward Ltd, RJ Harrison & Co Ltd, Saxtons Ltd, Scott James (Estate Agents) Ltd, Slater Dann Ltd, Stuart Wyse Ogilvie Estates Ltd, Thompson of Derby Ltd, Walker Barnet & Hill Ltd, Warwick Estates Ltd, Wateridge & Owen, Watsons (East Anglia) Ltd, Weller Hill Hubble, Worsfolds Property Services Ltd

BRAND NAMES

None

CONTACTS AND FURTHER INFORMATION

Jason Frangoulis, Director and general manager, General Accident Fire and Life Assurance Corporation p.l.c., Becket House, 87 Cheapside, London EC2V 6AY. Tel: 01-606 1030.

THE GENERAL ELECTRIC COMPANY plc

GENERAL INFORMATION

Head office	1 Stanhope Gate, London W1A 1EH. Tel: 01-493 8484
Directors	The Rt Hon Lord Prior (chairman), Lord Weinstock (managing), Sir Kenneth Bond (vice-chairman), RH Grierson (vice-chairman), MR Bates (deputy managing), DH Roberts CBE (joint deputy managing), RJ Davidson, M Lester, Dr IG MacBean, Hon Mrs S Morrison, JE Pateman CBE, D Powell, RG Reynolds, AJ Rogers, RJ Williams, S Weinstock. *Non-exec* Lord Catto, SZ de Ferranti, RH Grierson, Professor ET Hall, FR Johnson, Sir William Rees-Mogg, PA Weiller
Advisers	Hill Samuel & Co Ltd, Lazard Brothers & Co Ltd, Morgan Grenfell & Co Ltd, J Henry Schroder Wagg & Co Ltd, SG Warburg & Co Ltd
Auditors	Touche Ross & Co
Registrars	RS Taylor, GEC Registrars, Coppenhall, Stafford ST18 9BN. Tel: 0785-51446
Brokers	Cazenove & Co, de Zoete & Bevan Ltd, Warburg Securities
Solicitors	Freshfields, Jaques & Lewis

GENERAL FINANCIAL INFORMATION

Market capitalisation	£4.27bn at 1 January 1988
Share structures	
Issued ordinary shares (5p)	2.7bn
Issued preference shares	None
Warrants	None
Convertibles	None
Traded options	Yes
ADRs	One ADR per ordinary share
Shareholders over 5%	Prudential Corporation 7.1%

FT CATEGORY

FT: Electricals
FT-A: Electronics

MAJOR ACTIVITIES

The General Electric Company (GEC) is engaged in the manufacture of electronic systems, electrical equipment and power generation apparatus and systems. It is the largest electronic and electrical engineering group in the UK.

GEC has nine core activities, namely: electronic systems and components; telecommunications and business systems; automation and control; medical equipment; consumer products; power generation; electrical equipment; distribution and trading; and research and development (R&D). In 1987 the largest contribution to operating profits came from the electronic systems and components division with 38%.

GEC's major customers are the Ministry of Defence (MoD), which represents 17% of sales, and British Telecom, representing 8% of sales. Sensitive factors for the company are interest and exchange rates, inflation, and defence and public sector expenditure.

The company has recently demonstrated a more entrepreneurial approach, pursuing opportunities for merger, acquisition and joint venture. GEC attempted to take over Plessey but was blocked by the Monopolies Commission. GEC has since combined its worldwide telecommunications business with Plessey. £430m was spent on acquisition in the UK and the US in 1987.

Competition varies with each activity. The electronic systems and components division competes with British Aerospace, Plessey, Ferranti, Ericsson, Philips and Siemens. The telecommunications and business systems division competes with companies such as Plessey, STC, AT&T, Ericsson and Alcatel. Electrical equipment competitors include Matsushita, NEI, Siemens, CGEE Alsthom, Brown Boveri and Westinghouse, who also feature heavily in power generation and automation and control.

FIVE YEAR FINANCIAL INFORMATION

Year	Turnover (£m)	Pre-tax (£m)	Earnings (p)	Dividends net (p)	Dividend cover (x)	Net assets (p)	Price (p) High	Price (p) Low	PER (x) High	PER (x) Low	Yield (%) High	Yield (%) Low
1983	4,625	670	14.2	3.00	4.7	76.5	248	173	22.6	15.3	2.60	1.56
1984	4,800	671	14.2	3.45	4.1	81.5	236	162	20.0	14.1	2.80	2.09
1985	5,222	725	14.9	4.00	3.7	89.4	220	150	16.7	10.8	3.81	2.37
1986	5,253	701	16.0	4.30	3.7	97.9	222	160	15.9	10.4	3.79	2.61
1987	5,247	668	15.8	5.30	3.0	109.0	254	152	16.0	9.3	5.05	2.43

The consumer products division has recently been strengthened by the company's acquisition of Creda. Competitors for this activity include Electrolux of Sweden and Philips of the Netherlands.

FINANCIAL HISTORY

Turnover in 1986/87 was £5.25bn, 11% below the previous period and only 13% up over five years. Pre-tax profits were £668m in 1986/87 against £701m in 1985/86. Although this was a fall of 4.7%, earnings per share fell by only 1% due to a falling tax charge, from 16.0p to 15.8p. Dividends increased by 23% to 5.3p.

The major proportion of operating profit is derived from two divisions, electronic systems and components, including Marconi, and telecommunications and business systems. The remaining six divisions together contribute 43% of profits, therefore requiring a significant change in any one if the company's overall trading pattern is to be affected.

The balance sheet remains strong, with net cash compared to shareholders' funds at around 50% at 31 September 1987, down from the year end because of acquisitions. The cash reserve of £1.3bn generates the second largest source of pre-tax income. Over a number of years this large cash reserve has become the subject of criticism. It is often seen as evidence of an attitude of excessive caution and indecision on behalf of management, and the return is lower than can be earned on the capital in the business.

1986/87 was the fourth successive year of flat turnover and trading profit, accompanied by a decline over the period in pre-tax margins to 12.2% in 1986/87 compared with 14.0% in 1983/84. Asset turnover was 2.2 times and return on capital employed 18%.

At the 30 September 1987 interim, turnover was flat at £2.53bn. Pre-tax profits were £9m up at £284m. Profit attributable to shareholders, excluding extraordinary items, was 4.7% up at £178m. Earnings per share were up 4.7% to 6.7p. Dividends per share were up 20% to 1.8p.

SHARE PRICE HISTORY

Since reaching a peak in 1982, the shares have fallen more than 70% relative to the FT-A All-Share index. This is partly because of GEC's poor profit performance. It also expresses the opinion of observers who feel that the company has failed to innovate and expand.

Portfolio managers who have downgraded GEC from its prime position as a core holding for long term funds have also influenced the downtrend of the share price. The prospective P/E ratio is now below the market average, against the period in the early 1980s when GEC was rated at double the rest of the market.

SENIOR MANAGEMENT

The chairman of GEC is the Rt Hon Lord Prior. Senior management is headed by Lord Weinstock, managing director, who has been synonymous with the company for more than two decades. His style of management is decentralised with rigorous, centrally-administered financial control systems and devolved operating responsibility. MR Bates is deputy managing director. DH Roberts is joint deputy managing director with technical responsibility for the group. RH Grierson and Sir Kenneth Bond are vice-chairmen. Dr IG MacBean and Simon Weinstock, Lord Weinstock's son, joined the board in December 1987.

CAPITAL

There are 2.7bn shares in issue, of which the Prudential Corporation holds 7.1%. Significant directors' holdings include Lord Weinstock with 0.5%.

During 1984/85 the company started buying in its own shares for cancellation to help increase earnings per share. In the two years ended 31 March 1986, the company purchased 79.6m shares for £166.8m. The company has authority to buy a further 250m shares at up to 350p per share.

GROUP REVIEW

Electronic systems and components This division consists largely of Marconi and GEC Avionics in the UK, collectively the largest supplier of electronics equipment to the MoD, and represents about 30% of turnover. The product range includes avionics, command and control systems, instrumentation, radar, radio, ships built by Yarrow Shipbuilders and torpedoes. Major subsidiaries exist in Canada, the US and Italy.

The division showed a 4% decline in trading profits to £198m from £206m in 1986/87, due partly to the difficulties experienced in radar activities, and in particular the cancellation of the Nimrod project. For the six months' to 30 September 1987, turnover was up 1% to £930m. Trading profit was up 12.9% to £87m, but was virtually unchanged if the Nimrod costs are excluded.

Notable developments include a partnership with Rockwell International, which has won a major contract to develop a new anti-jamming radio for the US Navy worth over $450m. This could lead to production orders worth $3bn over ten years. In partnership with Alsthom of France the division won the contract for the instrumentation and control systems for the new Sizewell nuclear power station.

In July 1987 the group acquired Astronics and Development Sciences, the avionics subsidiaries of Lear Siegler for $205m. Astronics and Development Sciences had combined estimated sales of $124.8m and pre-tax profits of $15m for the year to 30 June 1987.

Share price and relative to FT-A All-Share

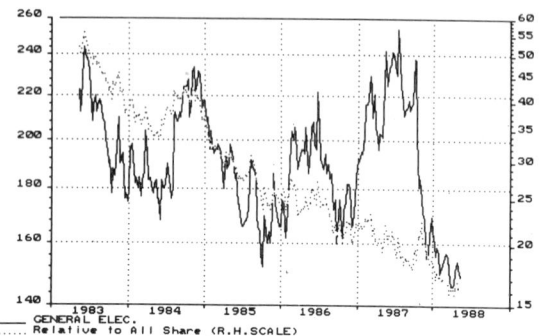

GENERAL ELEC.
Relative to All Share (R.H.SCALE)

Telecommunications and business systems All ot GEC's UK telecommunications business is now included in the joint venture with Plessey. In February 1988, GEC and Plessey formally announced the creation of a joint venture combining all their UK telecommunications interests. GEC and Plessey each hold a 50% share in GEC Plessey Telecommunications Holdings (GPT), which combines the two groups' interests in main switching, PABXs, transmission systems and telephone handsets.

Other divisional products include computers and software, and photocopiers. In June 1987 the group purchased Micro Scope, the videotext products specialist, for £18.8m. AB Dick, a US subsidiary, is involved in office automation products such as printers.

The division achieved a 12% increase in trading profits to £94m in 1986/87 from £84m in the previous year. This was a result of the increased sales of System X public telephone exchanges. At the 1987/88 interim, turnover and profits were slightly down.

Automation and control This division is responsible for the manufacture and installation of automation and mechanical handling systems for factories, airports, ships, coal mines, motor traffic management and other applications. It also supplies control equipment to manufacturers and retailers.

Familiar products are the Avery-Hardoll petrol pump and Satchwell central heating control units. The division is developing a unique contactless smart card. In June 1987 the group took a 30.6% shareholding in Berkel, the Dutch weighing machine manufacturer. In July 1987, the group extended its interests by acquiring Gilbarco, the world's leading supplier of petrol pumps, for $250m. Gilbarco had sales of $252.4m and pre-tax profits of $24.6m for 1986.

Turnover for the division increased by 3% to £457m in 1986/87 while profits declined 2% to £46m. Turnover for the six months to 30 September 1987 was up 10% to £230m. Trading profits were down 32% to £15m.

Medical equipment This division principally comprises Picker International, whose main products include X-ray equipment and magnetic image resonance scanners. In 1986/87 a new business was formed to develop sales to military customers. This gained orders for imaging systems from the German army and mobile X-ray systems from the US army. A planned joint venture with Philips proved abortive.

The division produced a larger contribution in 1986/87 than in recent years, generating profits of £26m against £22m, but this reversed at the 1987/88 interim when profits fell by 50% to £6m, hit by the declining dollar, a strike and production

problems.

Power generation The division manufactures turbine generators and gas turbines, in which the company is well positioned amongst competitors. It also produces diesel engines although it is not so strong in this area. The company is leading the British consortium for the Channel Tunnel high-speed train, which is to be built in conjunction with Alsthom of France. It also engaged in the development of a new family of aero engines with General Electric and other US companies.

Profits for the division fell to £50m from £58m in 1986/87, due to a strike and weak demand. For the six months to 30 September 1987, turnover was down 16.9% to £261m. Trading profit was down 4.3% to £22m.

Electrical equipment Products of this division include: switchgear and other electrical distribution equipment; generators for hydro-electric schemes; propulsion units for the Type 23 frigate; and cars for the Docklands Light Railway.

Although turnover was reduced in 1986/87 by £47m to £723m, profits increased 19% to £51m, following a period of rationalisation. Turnover for the six months to 30 September 1987 was up 3% to £349m, and trading profit was up 31.6% to £25m.

Consumer Products of the division include: Hotpoint, the manufacturer of the current best selling washing machine; Redring Electric, the space-heater maker; GEC-Xpelair, the extractor makers; and Osram-GEC the electric bulb makers. GEC (Radio and Television) and Cannon Industries, the oven maker, are both undergoing redevelopment. Turnover for 1986/87 was up 17% at £387m, profits up 3% at £35m.

In June 1987 the group acquired Creda Group from TI Group for £125m in cash. Creda made operating profits of £14m on a turnover of £142.4m in 1986. It had a very positive effect on the division's performance for the first half of 1987/88. Turnover at £249m was up 39.1%. Trading profit was up 50% to £24m.

C H A I R M A N ' S   S T A T E M E N T

'Despite the difficulties and setbacks which nowadays seem to be an integral part of industrial and commercial life, I remain confident that the Company's resources and skills will carry us forward to the realisation of our ambition for profitable expansion during the years ahead.' *The Rt Hon Lord Prior*

Distribution and trading The division is mainly involved in the overseas trading of group products. It supplies a wide variety of electrical switchgear, telecommunication and video conferencing systems, elevators, ventilation systems and other equipment to North America, Australasia, Africa, Bangladesh, Hong Kong and Singapore, as well as in the UK and the Irish Republic.

Turnover in 1986/87 was down 3.3% to £202m, and profits were down 7.7% from £13m to £12m. For the six months to 30 September 1987, turnover was down 3% to £101m and trading profit was unchanged at £6m.

Associated companies Turnover of this division comes from GEC's interests in the National Nuclear Corporation, Avery India, Cable Makers Australia, GEC South Africa and the General Electric Company of Malaysia.

Turnover for 1986/87 was up £1m to £308m, and profits were up £3m to £14m. For the six months to 31 September 1987, turnover was down 20% to £39m. Trading profit was up 20% to £7m.

In January 1988 GEC paid £12m for a 40% stake in Summit Group, the financial services and property arm of computer lessor Atlantic Computers. GEC's aims seem to be: to develop its financial services expertise; to make more active use of its cash mountain; and to join in Summit's joint venture with British Land and a Dutch property company in London's Docklands.

Research and development GEC commits substantial resources to research, to product development and to new design and manufacturing methods. GEC research explores new areas of science and engineering, as well as providing support to operating units and undertaking demonstration projects for new products and processes.

Areas where GEC research has proved pre-eminent include optical techniques, silicon integrated circuits, gallium arsenide, microwave sensor technology (used in satellite communication receivers and target homing systems), communication and radar techniques, and artificial intelligence.

GEOGRAPHICAL REVIEW

GEC is primarily engaged in the UK, which accounted for 53% of total turnover in 1986/87, worth £2.934bn. Europe took approximately 12%, worth £654m, the Americas took 16%, worth £914m, Australasia took 4%, worth £222m, Asia took 13%, worth £722m, and Africa took 3%, worth £185m. The recent acquisitions may slightly increase the US weighting though this will be offset by the dollar's weakness.

CORPORATE CALENDAR

Year end	31 March
Preliminary results	June
Report and accounts	July
AGM	September
Final dividend paid	October
Interim results	December
Interim dividend paid	March

DIRECTORS' HOLDINGS

	Fully-paid ordinary shares		Options
	(beneficial)	(non-beneficial)	
Sir Kenneth Bond	420,145	15,308,065	—
MR Bates	25,000	—	356,297
Lord Catto	440,000	—	—
RJ Davidson	10,000	10,000	256,297
SZ de Ferranti	19,200	—	—
RH Grierson	232,525	—	—
M Lester	110,000	15,995,735*†	254,228
IG Macbean	13,895	—	203,954
S Morrison	10,500	—	121,514
J Pateman	10,810	—	152,000
D Powell	145,000	—	203,897
The Rt Hon Lord Prior	30,000	—	150,000
Sir William Rees-Mogg	10,000	17,245	—
RJ Reynolds	10,000	—	200,000
DH Roberts	10,000	—	253,794
AJ Rogers	61,405	—	151,297
Lord Weinstock	8,801,470	1,000,000*	—
SA Weinstock	31,350,235*†	1,443,565	100,000
RJ Williams	10,000	—	250,000

*Of these holdings, 1,000,000 were held jointly by Lord Weinstock, SA Weinstock and M Lester.
† Of these holdings 6,500,000 were held jointly by SA Weinstock and M Lester.

Total directors' remuneration in 1987 amounted to £1.84m, with the chairman receiving £81,000, and the highest-paid director £221,000.

PRINCIPAL SUBSIDIARIES AND RELATED COMPANIES

Associated Electrical Industries Ltd, English Electric Co Ltd, GEC-Elliot Automation Ltd

Electronic systems and components
Astronics Inc –US, Cincinnati Electronics Corp – US, Circuit Technology Inc – US, Development Sciences Inc – US, EEV Canada Ltd – Canada, EEV Inc – US, English Electric Value Co Ltd, Esams Ltd, GEC Australia Ltd, GEC Avionics Inc – US, GEC Avionics Ltd, GEC Ceramics Ltd, GEC Sensors Ltd, Marconi Co Ltd, Marconi Command and Control Systems Ltd, Marconi Communication Systems Ltd, Marconi Defence Systems Ltd, Marconi Electronic Devices Ltd, Marconi Instruments Ltd, Marconi International Marine Co Ltd, Marconi Italiana SpA – Italy, Marconi Radar Systems Ltd, Marconi Space Systems Ltd, Marconi Underwater Systems Ltd, Salford Electrical Instruments Ltd, Yarrow Shipbuilders Ltd

Telecommunications and business systems
AB Dick Co – US, AEI Telecommunications Ltd – Canada, GEC Computers Ltd, GEC New Zealand Ltd, GEC Optical Fibres Ltd, GEC Reliance Ltd, GEC Software Ltd, GEC Telecommunications Ltd, Micro Scope Plc, Telephone Cables Ltd (74.5%)

Automation and control
Avery-Hardoll Ltd, English Electric Co – India (66.7%), GEC Australia Ltd, GEC Composants SA – France, GEC Electrical Projects Ltd, GEC Industrial Controls Ltd, GEC Marine & Industrial Gears Ltd, GEC Measurements Ltd, GEC Mechanical Handling Ltd, GEC Meters Ltd, GEC Traffic Automation Ltd, Gilbarco Inc – US, PM Services Ltd, W&T Avery Ltd

Medical equipment
Picker International Inc –US

Power generation
GEC Australia Ltd, GEC Diesels Inc – Canada, GEC Turbine Generators Ltd, Ruston Gas Turbine Inc – US, Ruston Gas Turbines Ltd

Electrical equipment
AG Hackney & Co Ltd, AEI Cables Ltd, English Electric Co Ltd – India (66.7%), Express Life Co Ltd, GEC Ltd – New Zealand, GEC Distribution Switchgear Ltd, GEC Engineering-Accrington Ltd, GEC Foundries Ltd, GEC Installation Equipment Ltd, GEC Large Machines Ltd, GEC Reinforced Plastics Ltd, GEC Small Machines Ltd, GEC Switchgear Ltd, GEC Traction Ltd, GEC Transformers Ltd, GEC Transmission and Distribution Projects Ltd, GEC Transportation Projects Ltd, LH Marthinusen Ltd – Zimbabwe, Micanite & Insulators Co Ltd, Rodco Ltd (60%), Vactite Ltd, Vacuum Interrupters Ltd, Vynckier NV – Belgium, Woods of Colchester Ltd

Consumer products
Cannon Industries Ltd, Creda Group, GEC Radio & Television, GEC-Xpelair Ltd, Hotpoint Ltd, OSRAM-GEC Ltd (51%), Redring Electric Ltd

Distribution and trading
English Electric Corporation – US, GEC Australia Ltd, GEC Canada Ltd, GEC New Zealand Ltd, GEC Zambia Ltd, GEC Zimbabwe Ltd, General Electric Co – Bangladesh, General Electric Co Hong Kong Ltd – Hong Kong, General Electric Co of Singapore Private Ltd, Walsall Conduits Ltd

Principal associated companies
Avery India Ltd (39.9%), Cable Makers – Australia (36.8%), GEC South Africa (Pty) Ltd – South Africa, General Electric Co – Malaysia (30%), National Nuclear Corp Ltd (30%)

BRAND NAMES

Ace, AEI, AN/AAR44, AN/ARC 205, Avery, Avery-Hardoll, BATES, Berkel, Cannon, Centrex, Checkmate, Creda, AB Dick, Dupletron, English Electric, EEV, Excel, Express Life, GEC, GEC Avionics, GEC Computers, GEC Reliance National One, GEM 80, GENOS, Gilbarco, Hotpoint, ICS3, In-Print, Ishida, Kelvin, Key Express, Lyric, Marconi, Marconiphone, Marksman, MASTER, Micro Profile, Micro Scope, Midata, MIDOS, M–O, Monarch, Moteurs Badouin, Napier Turbochargers, Oceanray, Osram, Paxman, Picker, Redring, Ruston, Rustronic, Salford, Satchwell, Scriptomatic, Secure Radio, Sentinel, Sting Ray, System X, Tornado, Tracker, TRC-180, Unicoil, Unipak, UXD5, Velenta, Videojet, Xpelair, Yarrow

CONTACTS AND FURTHER INFORMATION

Malcolm Bates, Deputy Managing Director, The General Electric Company plc, 1 Stanhope Gate, London W1A 1EH. Tel: 01-493 8484.

GLAXO HOLDINGS p.l.c.

GENERAL INFORMATION

Head office	Clarges House, 6–12 Clarges Street, London W1Y 8DH. Tel: 01-493 4060
Directors	Sir Paul Girolami (chairman), BD Taylor (chief executive), Dr M Fertonani, Dr E Mario, Dr H McCorquodale, CB Newcomb, JJ Ruvane Jnr, Dr RB Sykes. *Non-exec* Sir Ronald Arculus KCMG KCVO, Professor RG Dahrendorf KBE FBA, Sir Alistair Frame, JM Raisman CBE
Advisers	Lazard Brothers & Co Ltd
Auditors	Coopers & Lybrand
Registrars	National Westminster Bank Registrar's Department
Brokers	Shearson Lehman Hutton, Citicorp Scrimgeour Vickers Ltd
Solicitors	No specified adviser

GENERAL FINANCIAL INFORMATION

Market capitalisation	£7.270bn at 1 January 1988
Capital structure	
Issued ordinary shares (50p)	740m
Issued preference shares	None
Warrants	None
Convertibles	None
Traded options	Yes
ADRs	One ordinary share equals one ADR
Shareholders over 5%	BNY (Nominees) Ltd 10.04%

FT CATEGORY

FT: Industrials (miscel.)
FT-A: Health and household

MAJOR ACTIVITIES

Glaxo is the UK's largest pharmaceutical group, supplying around 11% of the prescription drugs dispensed in the UK, and manufacturing the world's single biggest selling drug, Zantac, for the treatment of peptic ulcers, with sales of over $1bn per annum.

Other major drugs include: Ventolin, for the relief of asthma; the new injectable antibiotic, Fortum; Zinacef, one of the most prescribed injectable antibiotics in Europe; Betnovate, used for many years for the treatment of eczema; and Trandate, a drug for the relief of high blood pressure.

Glaxo's activities are not confined to the UK, which now accounts for less than 20% of group sales, or continental Europe, which contributes 30% of group sales. The group is expanding fast in the large North American market, where sales have grown from virtually zero in 1983 to $1.09bn by June 1987, 38% of the group total.

In contrast to the other major UK drug companies such as Wellcome and Beecham, Glaxo has concentrated on ethical or prescription medicines, and has no over-the-counter medicine business. This partly explains why Glaxo has recorded one of the highest profit margins of any drug company in the world.

In common with most other drug manufacturers, Glaxo invests heavily in researching and developing new drugs.

Notable successes of past research include Zantac, formulated, tested and approved within only six years – a remarkable achievement – and more recently Ceftin, a reformulation of the highly successful Zinacef. Ceftin, launched in the US in 1987, is the first oral formation of a type of drug normally only given by injection, and as such represents a significant advance.

Glaxo is the fourth largest UK quoted company behind BP, British Telecom and Shell, and ahead of British Gas and ICI, with a market capitalisation of £7.27bn at the end of 1987.

Within the world pharmaceutical industry Glaxo is ranked fourth, with an estimated world market share of around 2.7%. Amongst its competitors are the European majors Ciba-Geigy, Hoechst and Sandoz, and the American companies Merck, Lilly, Smith Kline and Pfizer. Glaxo has the highest post tax profit margin, the highest five year historic growth rates and the greatest concentration in ethical medicines of any of its competitors.

FINANCIAL HISTORY

Glaxo's extraordinary success with Zantac and other drugs has been the major reason for the 22% average sales growth and 44% average pre-tax profits growth seen since 1983.

In the year to 30 June 1987, turnover increased by 27% to £1.730bn. Trading profits were 33% up at £665m, and pre-tax profits were 22% up at £746m. Investment income made up £51m of the total, reduced from 1986 because of the absence of extraordinary profits. Earnings per share were 23.8% up at 67.0p. Dividends totalled 19p, up 35.7% from 14p in 1986.

The consequences of this and previous years' success have led to the building up of substantial cash reserves, which reached over £700m by June 1987. These are providing the resources to step up the efforts in research and development, thereby ensuring the flow of new products. In 1987, £149m was spent on research and development, up 32%. Capital expenditure totalled £193m, a small decrease.

There was some disappointment in certain quarters with the 1987 results, and some analysts have argued that Glaxo's meteoric period of growth is over.

At the 1988 interim to 31 December 1987, group turnover was 6% up at £924m, against £873m in the previous period. Pre-tax profits were 6% up at £397m, against £376m in the previous period. Earnings per share were 12% up at 36.5p, against 32.6p. The interim dividend was increased by 40% to 7p from 5p.

Glaxo's results were affected by large adverse movements in exchange rates and increasing research and development expenditure. In constant currency terms trading profits would have been 16% up instead of the 4% reported. Research and development expenditure increased from £67m to £101m, a rise of 51%, reflecting Glaxo's commitment to future growth and its hopes of bringing several promising compounds to market in the next two or three years.

FIVE YEAR FINANCIAL INFORMATION

Year	Turnover (£m)	Pre-tax (£m)	Earnings (p)	Dividends net (p)	Dividend cover (x)	Net assets (p)	Price (p) High	Price (p) Low	PER (x) High	PER (x) Low	Yield (%) High	Yield (%) Low
1983	756.8	186.4	14.9	4.5	3.3	74.0	483	313	42.4	25.6	1.83	1.11
1984	891.6	256.0	22.9	6.5	3.5	91.8	550	350	39.0	22.6	1.99	1.47
1985	1,160.6	402.9	37.7	10.0	3.8	115.0	790	538	29.8	20.8	2.18	1.48
1986	1,407.0	612.0	54.1	14.0	3.9	147.0	1,115	757	30.4	16.9	2.20	1.34
1987	1,740.0	746.0	67.0	19.0	3.5	200.0	1,845	970	35.0	15.0	2.68	1.11

CHAIRMAN'S STATEMENT

'This year's figures, with their increases in sales and profits following six years of rapid and uninterrupted growth, confirm the continuing vitality of the Group's products, as well as indicating their potential for further growth. Looking only at the major categories, we see that ranitidine, our anti-ulcerant, which was first put on the market in 1981, showed an increase in sales of 37%; while in the respiratory area, salbutamol, introduced as far back as 1969, grew by 21%, and beclomethasone, first introduced in 1972, by 37%; our systemic antibiotics, as a class grew, by 25%, and even the sales of betamethasone, which has been on the market for twenty-five years, increased by 5%.' *Sir Paul Girolami*

SHARE PRICE HISTORY

Glaxo's share price between 1981 and June 1987 can only be described as meteoric. A tenfold increase in share price, adjusted for scrip issues, outstripped most other companies and followed the unparalleled success of Glaxo's drug Zantac.

Past success, however, breeds great expectations that can be difficult to deliver in a situation where current sales are so great that individual new products are unlikely to make as big an impact on Glaxo as they would on the performance of smaller companies.

For this reason, whilst the share price continued to rise, the valuation of the company measured as the price/earnings ratio started to fall relative to that of other companies from 1984.

The disappointment of investors with the 1987 results, combined with the October market crash, resulted in the share price falling from above £18 to below £10.

SENIOR MANAGEMENT

Sir Paul Girolami, the current chairman, has served as a director of Glaxo for nearly 20 years. He was elected chairman in 1985, succeeding Sir Austin Bide after having been the chief executive officer since 1981. Sir Paul Girolami can be credited with much of Glaxo's recent success and, despite handing over the reins of chief executive in 1986, is still closely involved with the day-to-day running of the group.

Bernard Taylor, chief executive since 1986, joined the main board in November 1984 after wide experience within the group below main board level. Bernard Taylor joined the group in 1964 as sales manager in New Zealand, and became marketing director in 1965. In 1967 he came to the UK as new products manager for Glaxo Laboratories, and in 1971 was appointed managing director of the Australian subsidiary, a position he held until 1984. He then returned to the UK as chairman and chief executive of the UK subsidiary Glaxo Pharmaceuticals, and was appointed to the main board.

Dr Richard Sykes, the director in charge of research and development, succeeded Dr David Jack in 1987. Dr Sykes joined Glaxo Research in 1972 as head of the antibiotic research unit, a position he held for five years before leaving to take up the appointment of assistant director, Department of Microbiology at the Squibb Institute for Medical Research. Dr Sykes rejoined Glaxo in September 1986 as deputy research director, before taking up his present position in January 1987.

Dr Ernest Mario, president of Glaxo Inc, was appointed to his present position in September 1986 and to the board of Glaxo Holdings from 1 April 1988, having previously been group vice-president of Squibb Corporation and president and chief executive officer of Squibb Medical Products.

Charles Newcomb FCA joined Glaxo as financial controller in 1978, a post he held until 1981, when for a brief spell he left the group to pursue other interests. On his return in 1983, Charles Newcomb was appointed to the main board where he holds responsibility for financial functions.

CAPITAL

The sharply cash-generative nature of Glaxo's business and lack of acquisitions has resulted in Glaxo building a very sound financial base for the future. Net cash of over £800m at December 1987 shows every sign of increasing further in future years.

The global nature of the drug industry has fostered global interest in the companies involved. Glaxo has recently responded to this by becoming listed on both the New York and Tokyo stock exchanges, in addition to London. This is bringing with it a greater disclosure of the activities of the group in line with US tradition.

In March 1988, Glaxo completed the sale of its animal healthcare business in the UK, Ireland, Italy and New Zealand to Pitman-Moore of the US. Separate negotiations were going on for the rest of the world.

GROUP REVIEW

Glaxo started life as a trading company, operating out of New Zealand in 1873, moving into dried milk for infants a few years later. It launched its first medical product, vitamin D, in the 1920s. Large scale production of penicillin in 1943 was followed by success in producing other vitamins and hormones. Rapid expansion in the 1960s and 1970s was accompanied by the launch of drugs such as Ventolin in 1969, Zinacef in 1978, and culminating in the first launch of Zantac in 1981.

Glaxo's major areas of interest are: anti-ulcerants; respiratory agents; systemic antibiotics; cardiovascular agents; dermatological agents; and other, including commodity antibiotics.

Anti-peptic ulcerants Zantac, Glaxo's most important anti-ulcerant, was the second drug to be launched into the H2 antagonist market after Smith Kline's Tagamet, and is the best-selling prescription medicine in the world.

Given that the market had already been opened up by Tagamet, the success of Zantac in overtaking Tagamet's lead was unexpected at the outset. The fact that it subsequently occurred has been put down to superior marketing, as the result of better dosage regimes – twice a day versus four times a day, and then later once a day versus twice a day – and a superior side-effect profile over Tagamet.

Anti-ulcerants contributed 47.9% of the group's turnover in 1987 of £1.73bn. Sales of £829m were up 37% on 1986.

Respiratory In the respiratory area, Ventolin, used in the treatment of bronchial asthma, is one of the world's top 20 ethical pharmaceutical products by sales. In 1987, Glaxo achieved impressive growth with its inhaled steroid-based asthma products – Becotide, Beclovent and Becloforte. Beconase, used for the treatment of hay fever, is producing strong growth in certain territories.

Respiratory agents contributed £362m of group turnover in 1987, 21% of the total, and up 26% on 1986.

Systemic antibiotics Fortum, an injectable cephalosporin, is Glaxo's most important systemic antibiotic compound. Fortum was extremely successful in Japan in 1987, the world's largest antibiotics market, and in the US, Italy, northern Europe and Spain.

In the oral cephalosporin category, Glaxo expects a strong performance from the recently launched oral antibiotic cefuroxime axetil – Zinnat in the UK and Ceftin in the US – with a launch in Japan in June 1988. Increased sales were achieved in 1987 of the earlier injectable Zinacef and oral Ceporex antibiotics.

Systemic antibiotics contributed £226m of the group's turnover in 1987, 13% of the total, and up 25% on 1986.

Cardiovascular Trandate, Glaxo's major cardiovascular product for the treatment of hypertension, is growing faster than the world market rate of growth, particularly in the US and France, enjoying a 10% market share in the latter country. Generally, however, the group is at present under-represented in the cardiovascular area. The US subsidiary has recently licensed in a number of cardiovascular compounds from other companies.

Cardiovascular agents contributed £46m of group turnover in 1987, 2.7% of the total, and up 28% on 1986.

Dermatological In the dermatological area, Glaxo is well-established and is the second largest company in the world topical steroids market. Significant advances are being made in the US.

Dermatological agents contributed £86m of group turnover in 1987, 5% of the total, and up 12% on 1986.

Other Commodity antibiotics are sold by the Sefton division of the group's UK manufacturer, Glaxochem Ltd. Penicillin is the major product. Sales were down 13.8% to £50m in 1987, 2.9% of total group turnover.

Share price and relative to FT-A All-Share

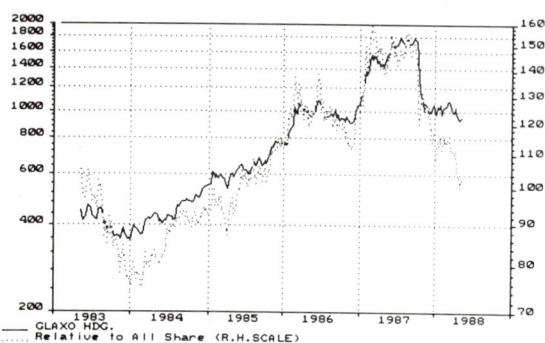

The group's fine chemicals business largely produces codeine phosphate. UK sales increased in 1987, though export sales fell, due to lower prices.

Glaxo's animal healthcare business was sold in March 1988. Its main product was Cepravin, a dry cow intra-mammary antibiotic. Animal healthcare contributed £30m of group turnover in 1987, 1.7% of the total, up 15.9% on 1986.

Research and development Glaxo's research commitment should produce a steady stream of new drugs, which are developed as quickly as possible by performing clinical trials in many major markets simultaneously. The group feels confident that it can identify winners early in development and that it will not be faced with large bills for multiple trials for a drug which ultimately does not reach the market.

Such prompt development of ideas, whilst undoubtedly carrying more risk, promises high rewards as early commercialisation of drugs maximises the use of patent protection, which usually guarantees eight to ten years free of competition. The group is involved in many areas with particularly interesting compounds in development for treatment of schizophrenia and migraine.

In April 1988, the group announced a major expansion of its worldwide research and development resources. £1bn will be invested over the next five years, including £500m in the UK. In all, Glaxo has 13 compounds in exploratory development and a further seven are now in full clinical studies for the treatment of major illnesses such as asthma, skin conditions, migraine and cardiovascular disorders. 4,000 people work in R&D, with the majority (2,800) in the UK.

GEOGRAPHICAL REVIEW

Out of total group turnover of £1.730bn in 1987, the UK contributed 13.2% with £228m, Europe 34.5% with £597m, North America 38.2% with £662m, Central and South America 2% with £34m, Africa and the Middle East 3.2% with £55m, South-east Asia and the Far East 6.2% with £108m and Australasia 2.7% with £46m. The company does not analyse the geographical distribution of profits.

UK Glaxo supplies 11% of the UK prescription medicine market with a large presence in both the general practitioner and hospital markets. The company continued to expand its production facilities.

As part of its policy on concentrating on core innovative activities, Farley Health Products were sold in March 1986. In October 1986 Evans Medical was sold for £27m as a management buyout. The animal healthcare businesses were in the process of disposal at the end of 1987.

In 1987 UK sales increased by 22% to £209m, a sharp increase after three years of 10% to 11% growth. Total exports from the UK in 1987 were £395m, up 2%.

Europe Products such as Zantac have achieved leading positions in many Continental markets, with Italy, Germany and France being of particular importance. In Italy Glaxo is in the top three of all drug companies. In addition to marketing drugs in Italy, Glaxo also operates major manufacturing and research facilities in Verona.

The French subsidiary is one of the fastest-growing drug companies in that country on the back of Zantac, Trandate, a cardiovascular drug, and Ventolin, which is now the leading product in the French asthma drug market. In 1987 European turnover increased by 19% to £597m.

North America Glaxo Inc was the seventh largest drug company based on prescription sales in the US in the year to June 1987, rising from eleventh position in 1986. 1987 US sales increased by 51% to $937m. Glaxo had 44% of the anti-peptic-ulcerant market. Zantac represented 70% of total sales in the US.

Glaxo is still expanding its infrastructure in the world's most profitable market place, with the number of employees rising by over 40% to 2,200 people. North American turnover increased by 41% to £662m in 1987.

Rest of the world In Japan, the world's second largest drug market, Glaxo operates through three associate companies. The launch of a locally produced anti-ulcer drug famotidine, brand name Pepcid, has impacted on sales of Zantac in Japan, although the fast growth in the market means that whilst market share may be falling, sales are little changed.

Elsewhere in Asia the group is expanding operations to develop markets with a new subsidiary recently introduced in Taiwan. Turnover for the rest of the world in 1987 was up 16.8% to £243m.

CORPORATE CALENDAR

Year end	30 June
Preliminary results	September
Report and accounts	October
AGM	December
Final dividend paid	January
Interim results	March
Interim dividend paid	June

DIRECTORS' HOLDINGS

	Fully-paid ordinary shares		Options
	(beneficial)	(non-beneficial)	
Sir Paul Girolami	15,076	9,600	84,000
BD Taylor	1,000	—	75,600
Sir Ronald Arculus	400	—	—
JV Burke	400	—	19,200
Professor RG Dahrendorf	400	—	—
DJR Farrant	400	—	48,000
Dr M Fertonani	500	—	84,000
Sir Alistair Frame	—	—	—
Dr H McCorquodale	400	—	25,300
CB Newcomb	2,000	—	34,200
JM Raisman	2,800	—	—
AH Raper	816	—	52,800
JJ Ruvane Jnr	600	—	49,867
Dr RB Sykes	1,500	—	20,000

Total directors' remuneration in 1987 was £3.05m, of which the chairman, who was also the highest-paid director, received £308,724.

PRINCIPAL SUBSIDIARIES AND RELATED COMPANIES

Adescha SA – Switzerland, Bonomelli SpA – Italy (50%), Cascan GmbH & Co KG – West Germany (50%), Duncan Farmaceutici SpA – Italy, Glaxo AEBE – Greece, Glaxo AG – Switzerland, Glaxo Animal Health Ltd, Glaxo A/S – Norway, Glaxo Australia Pty Ltd, Glaxo Bangladesh Ltd (70%), Glaxo BV – Netherlands, Glaxo Belgium SA, Glaxo Canada Inc, Glaxo Ceylon Ltd – Sri Lanka (78%), Glaxochem, Claxochem (Pte) Ltd – Singapore (98%), Glaxo de México SA de CV, Glaxo del Perú SA, Glaxo do Brasil SA, Glaxo East Africa Ltd – Kenya, Glaxo Export Ltd, Glaxo Far East (Pte) Ltd – Singapore, Glaxo Farmacéutica Chilena Ltda – Chile, Glaxo Farmacêutica Lda – Portugal, Glaxo Finance Bermuda Ltd, Glaxo Group Ltd, Glaxo GmbH – West Germany, Glaxo Group Research Ltd, Glaxo Inc – US, Glaxo Insurance (Bermuda) Ltd, Glaxo Korea Co Ltd (50%), Glaxo Laboratories (Pakistan) Ltd (70%), Glaxo Laegemidler A/S – Denmark, Glaxo Lakämedel AB – Sweden, Glaxo Ltd – Ireland, Glaxo (Pty) Ltd – South Africa, Glaxo (Thailand) Ltd (90%), Glaxo Malaysia Sdn Berhad, Glaxo New Zealand Ltd, Glaxo Nigeria Ltd (40%), Glaxo Operations UK Ltd, Glaxo Panamá SA, Glaxo Pharmaceuticals Ltd, Glaxo Pharmaceuticals Oy – Finland, Glaxo Pharmazeutika GesmbH – Austria, Glaxo Philippines Inc, Glaxo SA – Spain, Glaxo-Sankyo Co Ltd – Japan, Glaxo Singapore Pte Ltd, Glaxo SpA – Italy, Glaxo SUSTAS – Turkey (71%), Glaxo Taiwan Ltd (90%), Glaxo Uruguaya SA, Glaxovet SpA – Italy, Glaxo-Vidhyasom Ltd – Thailand (90%), Glindia Ltd – India (40%), Laboratoires Glaxo SA, Laboratorios Glaxo (Argentina) SACeI, Laboratorios Glaxo de Colombia SA, Laboratorios Glaxo de Venezuela CA, Marfarlan Smith Ltd, Milborrow & Co (Pty) Ltd – South Africa, Nippon Glaxo Ltd – Japan (50%), Shin Nihon Jitsugyo Co Ltd – Japan (50%)

BRAND NAMES

Aclovate, Azantac, Becloforte, Beclovent, Beconase, Becotide, Betnovate, Ceporex, Ceftin, Ceporin, Dermovate, Fortaz, Fortum, Glazidem, Modacin, Oracef, Raniplex, Rotadisk, Temovate, Trandate, Ventide, Ventolin, Volmax, Zantac, Zinacef, Zinnat

CONTACTS AND FURTHER INFORMATION

Mrs Miranda Evans, Glaxo Holdings p.l.c., 61 Curzon Street, London W1Y 7PA. Tel: 01-493 4060.

GENERAL INFORMATION

Head office	Electra House, Temple Place, Victoria Embankment, London WC2R 3HP. Tel: 01-836 7766
Directors	DW Hardy FCA FCIT (chairman), CH Black LLB (deputy chairman), JG West FCA (managing). *Non-exec* GJ Chandler, The Hon EDG Davies, AMM Grossart LLD CA, QM Morris FTII, MC Stoddart FCA, NKS Willis FCA, RN Young FCA
Advisers	Baring Brothers & Co Ltd
Auditors	Deloitte Haskins & Sells
Registrars	Lloyds Bank Registrar's Department
Brokers	Cazenove & Co
Solicitors	Linklaters & Paines

GENERAL FINANCIAL INFORMATION

Market capitalisation	£672.2m at 1 January 1988
Capital structure	
Issued ordinary shares (25p)	525.3m
Issued preference shares	None
Warrants	None
Convertibles	£4.54m 11.5% CULS 1990/95 (254 ordinary 25p shares for every £100 stock)
Traded options	None
ADRs	None
Shareholders over 5%	British Coal Board Pension Funds 28.4%

FT CATEGORY

FT: Investment trusts
FT-A: Investment trusts

MAJOR ACTIVITIES

Globe is the largest UK investment trust with gross assets of over £1.03bn at 1 January 1988. Globe adopts investment and dividend policies which aim to provide income growth sufficient to support dividend increases at least in line with any upward trend in the retail price index, and a growth in asset values better than that achieved by the FT-A All-Share Index. Not more than 40% of Globe's assets are concentrated into a small number of large significant investments, whether listed or unlisted.

Trusts quoted in the UK with assets of over £500m, and so in competition with Globe, include Alliance Trust, British Assets Trust, Edinburgh Investment Trust, Foreign & Colonial Investment Trust, Govett Strategic Trust, Scottish Investment Trust, Scottish Mortgage & Trust, TR Industrial & General Trust and Witan Investment Trust.

FINANCIAL HISTORY

Gross assets stood at £1.03bn at 31 December 1987, 5.3% down on those of the previous year but still 213% up over five years. Globe's assets were affected by the autumn 1987 market crash although the trust had been building up cash on deposit and fixed interest investments throughout the year. In the six months before the autumn crash to 30 September 1987, Globe's assets had been 21% ahead. All this gain and more was then lost.

Globe has kept a high weighting in the UK in order to maximise its dual objectives of growth in capital and income. Unquoted investments have been built up in both the UK and the US. 13.5% of the assets are now invested in unquoted stocks, and this will be expanded further.

In 1986/87 a switch of investment policy was undertaken. In March 1985 the trust had 65% invested in the UK, 24% in North America, 10% in the Far East, and 1% in other markets. By 31 December 1987 the trust had increased its UK assets to 77.4%, reduced North American exposure to 13.3%, kept

FIVE YEAR FINANCIAL INFORMATION

Year	Income (£m)	Pre-tax (£m)	Earnings (p)	Dividends net (p)	Dividend cover (x)	Net assets (p)	Price (p) High	Price (p) Low	PER (x) High	PER (x) Low	Yield (%) High	Yield (%) Low
1983	25.7	20.7	2.74	2.77	1.00	89.8	70	51	25.4	19.1	7.33	5.81
1984	27.3	23.4	3.02	3.00	1.03	113.7	84	66	30.0	21.9	6.49	4.92
1985	32.9	25.3	3.40	3.30	1.05	127.6	102	83	30.7	24.9	5.57	4.62
1986	36.4	29.9	3.67	3.67	1.07	163.0	129	97	35.9	27.8	4.97	3.92
1987	41.9	33.4	4.35	4.11	1.10	196.6	195	119	44.9	27.4	4.89	2.88

Japan at around 7%, and reduced its holdings to 2.2% in other markets like Australia.

Dividends were up from 3.7p to 4.1p in 1986/87. The interim dividend for 1987/88 showed a further 9.5% increase to 2.3p from 2.1p. Since 1982, dividends have increased by 56%.

Gearing was increased by 18% by the raising of a £100m debenture stock. Half the proceeds were invested in high yielding equities, which were mostly unquoted and many of them management buyouts. The other 50% was invested in the gilts market.

The net asset value total return for the year to December 1987 was 94.7% (−5.3%) – a slightly above-average performance for an investment trust.

SHARE PRICE HISTORY

Since 1983 the Globe share price has risen from 40p to the mid-April 1988 price of 136p, a rise of 240%. This outperformed the FT-A Investment Trust index, a very good performance for a large non-specialist trust.

The 1987 share price high was 196p. In the October 1987 crash the shares fell sharply to a low of 118½p, further relatively than the FT-A All-Share index. By December 1987 there had been a modest recovery in the share price to around 130p, although the relative underperformance reflected the investment trust sector's general underperformance.

Over the year to December 1987, Globe had outperformed the FT-A Investment Trust index by 5% due to its 10% unquoted shareholdings and its 18% cash and fixed interest weighting.

SENIOR MANAGEMENT

David Hardy was appointed chairman in 1983. He is also chairman of MGM Assurance, Swan National and Leisuretime International, as well as being deputy chairman of Agricultural Mortgage Corporation, and a director of other companies.

Colin Black is deputy chairman. He is also chairman of Scottish Widows Fund, a director of Electra Investment Trust, Clyde Petroleum and other companies.

James West is managing director. He is also a director of Candover Investments, Stanhope Securities and other companies.

CAPITAL

Called-up share capital at 31 December 1987 was 525.3m shares. The trust also has a £100m 10% Debenture Stock 2016, foreign currency loans of £96.78m, £4.45m 11.5% convertible unsecured loan stock 1990/95 and other long term borrowings of £679,000. The British Coal Board Pension Funds holds 28.4% of the ordinary shares.

GROUP REVIEW

The bulk of Globe's portfolio as at 1 January 1988 was invested in the UK, which represented 77.4%. 7.86% was invested in fixed interest securities.

The major holdings, as a percentage of the portfolio, were: Electra Investment Trust (7.6%), British Government securities (5.4%), Argyll Group (4.9%), British & Commonwealth Holdings (4.5%), Dee Corporation (3.9%), Hanson (3.6%), Reed International (2.8%), Caradon (2.4%), Maxwell Communication Corporation (2.1%) and Stanhope Properties (2%).

UK portfolio The UK market has ranked amongst the best performing of the world's major equity markets. Globe has benefited since Big Bang from the ability to trade shares in better size, contain commission charges and invest in companies that have benefited from deregulation of the stock market.

Globe holds 26.3% of Electra Investment Trust, which invests between 50% and 75% of its portfolio in unlisted investments both in the UK and USA. This holding helps to increase the spread of investments. Two of Globe's most profitable unlisted investments were Caradon, a management buyout, and Stanhope Properties, one of the most successful of the UK property developers, particularly with Rosehaugh in Broadgate, and in the London Docklands. Flotations of these two companies, Globe's largest unquoted investments, were made in the first and second quarters of 1987/88.

Recently, Globe has re-established a sizeable holding in BP, and added to its existing holdings in FKI Babcock and Burgess Group.

North American portfolio 13.3% of the total portfolio was invested in North America at the beginning of 1988. The largest holding at 0.4% of the portfolio is in Boise Cascade Corporation. Major changes to the portfolio have been made and exposure to North America, after a reduction in 1986/87,

CHAIRMAN'S STATEMENT

'In the nine months [to 31 December 1987] the fully diluted asset value fell from 192.02p on 31st March 1987 to 160.70p on 31st December 1987, a decline of 15.79 per cent. The F.T.-Actuaries All-Share Index declined by 12.98 per cent. Over the same period the New York Stock Exchange declined by 28.02 per cent., and Tokyo's by 5.31 per cent. after adjusting for currency changes. . . .

During the third quarter Globe was a core investor in the largest European buy-out ever, the purchase of MFI from Asda-MFI Group. As a result MFI is now our largest unquoted holding. . . .

A now much changed portfolio should perform well as more stable conditions return.' *David W Hardy*

was to have been increased on a very selective basis in 1987/88 before the general share crash. Recent strategy has been to build up holdings in basic industries. About half the portfolio is protected from a fall in the currency by dollar loans.

Far Eastern portfolio 10% of the portfolio was invested in Japan at the end of May 1987 but this was reduced to 7% as at 1 January 1988. The trust had been bullish of financial stocks in Japan and also overweight in pharmaceuticals and chemicals. The largest holding at 0.3% in the portfolio is Yamanouchi Pharmaceutical. The portfolio was restructured after the October 1987 crash to be reasonably defensive in nature. Half the portfolio is protected by yen loans.

The 3% of the portfolio that was invested in Hong Kong, Australia and other Far Eastern markets was liquidated after the severe falls in these markets in October and November 1987. Investment had been concentrated into a small number of holdings and a policy that had been successful was terminated.

Unquoted portfolio 13.5% of the portfolio is held directly in unquoted stocks with a further commitment through the trust's holding in Electra Investment Trust. There are large direct stakes in MFI, Hays Group, TIP-Europe, Berketex Holdings, Haden Group, Simplex, the *Daily Telegraph* and Parker Pen. £22.5m was invested in property. Globe has a major development project with P&O at Chelsea Harbour.

The unquoted portfolio of the trust is being developed. These investments generally take several years to produce a good return, since valuations tend to be conservative in the early years and achieving the capital return target depends on the realisation of the investment by disposal or flotation. After the October 1987 crash, Globe reduced the value of its unquoted holdings by 9%.

Fund management In addition to its trust investment activities, plans are under way for Globe to expand its management of pension funds and provide additional fund management services. The new share investment scheme for small investors, offering reduced commissions for regular savings or occasional investment of small sums, has been successful.

CORPORATE CALENDAR

Year end	31 March
Preliminary results	May
Report and accounts	June
AGM	June
Final dividend paid	July
Interim results	October
Interim dividend paid	January

DIRECTORS' HOLDINGS

	Ordinary shares		Options
	(beneficial)	*(non-beneficial)*	
DW Hardy	21,973	—	189,248
CH Black	17,517	—	189,248
JG West	6,133	—	178,571
GJ Chandler	30,000	90,000	—
The Hon EDG Davies	8,400	160,000	—
AMM Grossart	—	—	—
QM Morris	9,000	—	—
MC Stoddart	86,664	50,400	—
NKS Willis	—	4,200	—
RN Young	—	4,500	—

Total directors' remuneration in 1987 was £449,000, of which the chairman, who was also the highest-paid director, received £105,578.

PRINCIPAL SUBSIDIARIES AND RELATED COMPANIES

Aberdeen, Edinburgh and London Trust Ltd, Effold Properties Ltd, Electra House Ltd, Electra Investment Trust Plc (26.3%), Globe Finance Co Ltd, Globe Group Services Ltd, Globe International Ltd – Bermuda (71.7%), Globe Leasing Ltd, Globe Ltd – Finsbury Avenue, Globe Management Ltd, Rothesay Trust Ltd

BRAND NAMES

None

CONTACTS AND FURTHER INFORMATION

John Craze, Company Secretary, Globe Investment Trust P.L.C., Globe Management Ltd, Electra House, Temple Place, Victoria Embankment, London WC2R 3HP. Tel: 01-836 7766.

GEOGRAPHICAL REVIEW

Globe's portfolio at 1 January 1988 was invested 77.4% in the UK, 13.3%% in North America, 7.1% in Japan, and 2.2% in the Far East and other countries.

Share price and relative to FT-A All-Share

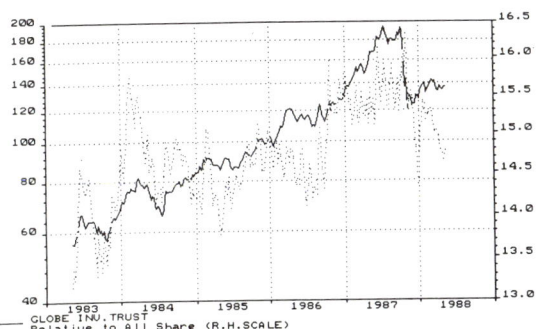

GLOBE INV.TRUST
Relative to All Share (R.H.SCALE)

GRANADA GROUP PLC

GENERAL INFORMATION

Head office	36 Golden Square, London W1R 4AH. Tel: 01-734 8080
President	Lord Bernstein LLD
Directors	A Bernstein (chairman), Sir Denis Forman (deputy chairman), D Lewis (managing), W Andrewes, D James FCIS, D Plowright, G Powell, D Quayle, A Quinn. *Non-exec* P Davis, M Littman QC, Q Morris
Advisers	SG Warburg & Co Ltd
Auditors	Peat Marwick McLintock
Registrars	Ravensbourne Registration Services Ltd
Brokers	Hoare Govett Ltd, SG Warburg & Co Ltd
Solicitors	Freshfields, Turner Kenneth Brown

GENERAL FINANCIAL INFORMATION

Market capitalisation	£860m at 1 January 1988
Capital structure	
Issued ordinary shares (25p)	278.18m
Issued preference shares (£1)	£123m 7.5% net convertible preference 2002 (convertible at 33.33 shares per £100 stock until 2002)
Warrants	None
Convertibles	None
Traded options	None
ADRs	None
Shareholders over 5%	None

FT CATEGORY

FT: Industrials (miscel.)
FT-A: Leisure

MAJOR ACTIVITIES

From its beginnings in cinema, broadcasting and TV rental, Granada Group has progressed to become a broadly-based leisure company. It is the only TV contractor to be part of a highly diversified group.

Granada's range of interests includes: TV contracting; TV and video retail and rental, both in the UK and abroad; specialist tour operators; bingo; cinemas; motorway service stations; budget hotels; multi-activity leisure centres; computer maintenance; and property.

Since 1985 Granada has been focusing on four main business areas. It has strengthened its position by both organic growth and acquisition. These acquisitions have included DPCE Holdings, Electronic Rentals, Laskys, NASA in France and WSL Holidays. Granada is also a leading member of the winning UK satellite TV consortium BSB.

In 1987 television retail and rental, primarily rental, accounted for 53% of pre-interest profits (two-thirds from the UK and one-third from overseas); broadcasting 17%; and the other varied leisure, consumer and services to business interests most of the balance.

A key characteristic of the TV rental business has been its ability to generate strong cash flow as the rental base matures. Black and white television was succeeded by colour television, whilst in the early to mid-1980s the video boom took off. Each phase of development was characterised by heavy capital investment as demand built up for the rental product, coupled with an inevitable increase in debt.

As the demand for a particular rental product reaches maturity, the annual capital expenditure declines sharply and the cash flow turns sharply positive, reflecting the very strong cash flow from the installed rental base.

In the past there has always been a prospective mass market rental product on the horizon to replace the current product. At present there is no obvious medium term mass market replacement for the VCR. Granada has entered a period of very strong cash generation. In this way Granada has been able to embark on a number of new ventures, some of which will require ongoing funding.

The acquisition of Electronic Rentals will enable Granada to save substantial costs out of the combined rental businesses which, in the medium term, should enhance the company's cash flow characteristics further.

The acquisition of DPCE Holdings in May 1988 makes Granada the largest independent computer servicing operator in the UK and doubles the size of its services to business division.

FINANCIAL HISTORY

Growth has been achieved organically and by acquisition. In recent years, the acquisition of Rediffusion's UK rental activities have made the biggest contributions to growth. The acquisition of the Electronic Rentals Group will now add significantly to group profits.

As the TV and video recorder rental base has matured, depreciation charges have fallen relative to divisional revenues, thus cash flow has been translated into pre-tax profits. Reflecting very buoyant TV advertising revenues, the broadcasting operation has increased profits dramatically.

The services to business division, including the independent computer maintenance operation, is doing well. Bingo and service stations have performed well whilst the substantial investment property portfolio has benefited from encouraging rent reviews.

As a result Granada's profits have broken out of the doldrums which it experienced in the 1980 to 1984 period, when pre-tax profits moved erratically in a £42.5m to £53.7m range with setbacks in 1982 and 1983.

Pre-tax profits expanded to £92.4m in 1986, helped by rationalisation benefits and the Rediffusion acquisition in no small way. In 1987 they were 20% ahead at £111.1m and could reach £155m in 1988.

Of the group's 1987 turnover of £1.02bn (+21.2%), UK TV rental and retail contributed £325.9m (+26.1%); overseas TV and rental £174.9m (+24.3%); TV broadcasting and programme production £222m (+12.4%); leisure and consumer services £214.5m (+33.8%); services to business £73.8m (+80.9%); and other activities £9m (−79.5%).

Of the group's 1987 pre-tax profits of £111.1m (+20.2%),

CHAIRMAN'S STATEMENT

'Last year, for the first time, Granada's turnover exceeded £1 billion and profits before tax exceeded £100 million. This achievement was a further major step forward after our substantial increase in profits in the previous year.

At £111.1 million, profit before tax was up by 20% after allowing £1.7 million for the Employee Share Scheme. Earnings per share increased by 20%, and the dividend was increased by 15%....

We have continued to adjust and improve the quality of Granada's portfolio of businesses, both through acquisition and disposal. These have been in line with our clearly defined strategy for encouraging the development of our four business areas. We aim to achieve a leading position in the markets we compete in and to ensure that sufficient resources are made available to allow businesses we acquire to grow into major contributors to Group profits within a reasonable period.' *Alex Bernstein*

FIVE YEAR FINANCIAL INFORMATION

Year	Turnover (£m)	Pre-tax (£m)	Earnings (p)	Dividends net (p)	Dividend cover (x)	Net assets (p)	Price (p) High	Low	PER (x) High	Low	Yield (%) High	Low
1983	521	43.4	12.5	5.8	1.1	105.3	212	144	17.9	12.5	5.42	3.56
1984	634	53.8	15.2	6.4	2.3	107.0	236	143	18.8	10.0	6.29	3.51
1985	767	64.4	12.6	7.1	1.8	105.6	230	146	17.9	11.3	6.49	4.12
1986	841	92.4	21.3	8.5	2.5	145.0	308	206	24.3	18.6	4.92	3.29
1987	1,020	111.1	25.5	9.8	2.6	152.5	374	238	17.7	9.6	5.17	3.12

UK TV rental and retail contributed £44.8m (+10.1%); overseas TV and rental £21m (+12.9%); TV broadcasting and programme production £20.8m (+15.5%); leisure and consumer services £25.1m (+36.4%); services to business £7.2m (+323.5%); and other activities £5.8m (−19.4%). Net interest was £11.9m (+12.3%) and the employee share scheme received £1.7m (+6.2%).

Earnings per share in 1987 were 25.5p (+19.7%) and dividends were 9.8p (+15%).

SHARE PRICE HISTORY

The underperformance of Granada's share price relative to the market had led to a substantial de-rating of the shares, with the price through most of 1987 barely above the level of Rank's bid of early 1986. The shares underperformed the market by 25% in the year to the summer of 1987 as the UK market hit new highs.

Since early 1982 Granada's price relative to the FT-A All-Share index has cascaded from 75% to 31% in early 1988. This is probably as much the result of the 50% increase in equity over the period as the influence of the ex-growth investor perception of the core business.

In the autumn 1987 share crash, Granada fell with the market, but has started to outperform subsequently, and has retraced some of 1987's underperformance whilst more recently moving in line with the stock market.

SENIOR MANAGEMENT

Chairman Alex Bernstein succeeded his uncle Lord Bernstein in 1979 whilst managing director Derek Lewis was recruited as finance director to replace Christopher Stanton in December 1984.

Much of the remaining senior operational management is long standing. Sir Denis Forman is deputy chairman, having headed the broadcasting interests; Bill Andrewes heads the consumer television interests; and David Plowright is chairman of the broadcasting interests.

David Quayle is chairman of the leisure and consumer services division. He was the founding Q in the B&Q chain.

CAPITAL

Reflecting improved profitability but also acquisition funding equity issues, net assets employed have risen from just £161m to £437.8m at the end of 1987. However, the pre-tax return on net assets has declined from 29.2% in 1982 to 25.4% in 1987 – a figure up from 20.3% in 1984. The share capital has increased by more than 50% in the period. Net debt stood at £92m at the 1987 year-end after £135.3m had been spent on acquisitions, leaving net gearing at 23%.

During 1987 Granada acquired WSL for £45m in cash and shares and the National Video Corp of the US for $27m in cash. It sold certain overseas TV rental interests to THORN EMI for £53m cash and passed on local debt of £11m. This move marked Granada's withdrawal from Denmark, France, Italy, Spain and Switzerland. Subsequently Granada has acquired the Electronic Rentals Group for £244.8m, financed by a mixture of cash and convertible preference shares. This has raised net gearing to around 60% but disposals of parts of Electronic Rentals are likely to reduce this figure in due course.

DPCE Holdings was acquired for £110m in May 1988 through a mixture of ordinary shares and convertible preference shares. There was a partial cash alternative.

In March 1986 Granada received a £740m bid from the Rank Organisation, which was subsequently blocked by the Independent Broadcasting Authority, backed by the courts. In January 1986 Granada had announced it was in merger talks with Ladbroke, which subsequently terminated. It may have been this latter move which precipitated the bid from the Rank Organisation.

GROUP REVIEW

UK TV rental and retail Granada is the second largest UK TV and video rental specialist company with over 40% of the market. Before the acquisition of Electronic Rentals it had 26% of the market, 610 branches and 1.75m subscribers. Electronic Rentals brings another 450 branches and 1.25m subscribers. Significant rationalisations will be achieved.

The acquisition of Laskys in November 1986 enhanced Granada's retail content with substantial long term scope to increase currently thin margins. Retail operations have been run in tandem with rental in 550 of Granada's branches since early 1986. Electronic Rentals' Visionhire chain also combines rental and retail.

The overall UK rental market is in steady decline, losing up to 5% of subscribers per annum. Only 20% of new TV and VCR demand is satisfied by rental. The rental industry has been forced into the retail market in order to achieve better use of staff and space and has undergone rationalisation as larger groups have sought through acquisitions to increase the density of subscribers in their outlets and spread costs over more customer contracts.

Granada has benefited in recent years from full integration and rationalisation of the Rediffusion acquisition and expects to do so in a similar way with Electronic Rentals' Visionhire chain.

Overseas TV rental and retail The overseas operations are concentrated in Germany, Canada, the US, France and Spain. Rental operations in other European markets have been either sold or wound down. Outside the UK there is a greater VCR content.

In 1987 overseas retail and rental accounted for just under a third of the divisional total of £65.8m operating profit. Five smaller businesses were sold to THORN EMI in 1987, reducing potential income in 1988.

In the US and Canada Granada is the market leader in renting televisions in the hospital market. In France the group's presence has been strengthened by the exercise of the option to take up 100% of the NASA chain. An entry has been made in the Spanish retail market with the acquisition of 76% of the Kapy chain.

Services to business With an expertise in video products maintenance, Granada, via acquisition, has become established as the UK market leader in the provision of independent computer maintenance services with over 2,000 contracts.

In May 1988, Granada acquired DPCE Holdings for £110m, thereby doubling the size of the division. Granada now has a quarter of the independent computer servicing market, which represents up to 15% of the overall UK market.

Through the acquisition of SMS Granada now has a foothold in France, Germany and Spain, where the third party maintenance market is significantly less well developed. Granada is particularly optimistic about the potential for this business.

Share price and relative to FT-A All-Share

Additionally, the services to business division supplies hardware or software to multi-site commercial users including the hotel industry and building societies.

Granada is aiming for divisional growth compounding at 30% per annum and believes the division is capable of producing over £10m of operating profit annually from the existing business base. In the current financial year DPCE is expected to add between £7m and £8m to divisional profits.

Television broadcasting and programme production Granada is the longest established independent TV broadcaster in the UK, running the Manchester-based north-west England contract. In advertising revenue share terms, it is currently the fourth largest of the major contractors and is starting to regain lost market share.

The TV broadcasting industry is unusual in that revenues and costs move independently. Overheads are governed by labour and programming costs, the latter tending to move erratically, reflecting major blockbuster programme production and purchase expenses.

Revenues are derived largely from advertising. These depend on the pressure of demand, principally from packaged goods companies, for advertising time. Factors influencing demand include new product launches, the state of competitors, corporate liquidity and the buoyancy of consumers' disposable incomes. In 1987 TV advertising revenues expanded by just over 12%. Overall revenues across the industry should increase by 8% to 10% in 1988.

Granada's secondary income source is the sale of programmes overseas. With a large back catalogue and a history of ambitious schedules – as well as soaps like *Coronation Street* – including *Brideshead Revisited*, *The Jewel in the Crown* and a substantial drama base, the company is well positioned to maximise sales.

Current uncertainties in the domestic industry, including the possibility that franchises may be auctioned when next renewed, have led Granada to begin to acquire a spread of interests in broadcasting. These now include part ownership ownership of Pipa Vidéo in France, and a stake in the satellite broadcasting consortium BSB. Granada's 3% stake in Canal Plus, the French subscription channel, was sold for £23m in May 1988, having been bought for £3m in 1986. Other investments are actively being sought.

Leisure and consumer services The division includes over 50 Granada bingo clubs, motorway services, 17 service stations and six budget price Granada Lodge hotels. More service areas and lodges are due to open in 1988.

Park Hall Leisure consists of multi-activity leisure sites with theme parks, including a mock Spanish village and Camelot theme park, a new hotel and a night club. Two further sites opened in 1987 – American Adventure in Ilkeston and the Pine Lake watersports and hotel complex in the Lake District.

The acquisition of WSL brought Granada into the travel industry. WSL's activities include school tours through Schools Abroad, Travelaway and Hourmont, group ski holidays, the high quality Magic of Italy holiday operation and Pilgrim-Air, the largest supplier of air transport between the UK and Italy.

WSL is continuing to achieve very substantial growth and can be expected to outperform Granada's longer established interests. WSL made a number of acquisitions during 1987 including Quest Adventure holidays, Villas Italia and the Neilson Leisure group. WSL is the largest supplier of ski holidays in the UK.

Other businesses Granada owns 67.75% of Barranquilla Investments, a London-based property investment company. Some of Barranquilla's properties have been sold, leaving it with a core of City of London properties. At these sites, the company is benefiting from a progressive series of rent reviews. At 3 October 1987, freehold properties were valued at £200m, of which investment properties probably accounted for close to a half.

GEOGRAPHICAL REVIEW

Granada is largely UK-based. In 1987 overseas revenue accounted for no more than 19% of the group total. The main contributors were North America with 6.5%, Germany 8.5% and France 2.5%.

Identified overseas profits amounted to 16.8% of the total, represented by TV and video rental with a small contribution from sales of television programmes.

CORPORATE CALENDAR

Year end	30 September
Preliminary results	December
Report and accounts	February
AGM	March
Final dividend paid	April
Interim results	July
Interim dividend paid	October

GRAND METROPOLITAN PLC

DIRECTORS' HOLDINGS

	Fully-paid ordinary shares		Options
	(beneficial)	(non-beneficial)	
W Andrewes	5,882	—	164,500
A Bernstein	1,559,395	1,910,503	207,000
Sir Denis Forman	164,798	—	220,500
P Davis	2,000	—	—
D James	15,229	2,913,022	101,500
DC Lewis	2,000	—	168,500
M Littman	3,081	—	—
Q Morris	2,500	—	—
D Plowright	11,110	—	148,500
D Quayle	2,000	—	—
A Quinn	4,994	—	103,000

Total directors' remuneration in 1987 was £1.07m, of which the chairman, who was also the highest-paid director, received £168,000.

PRINCIPAL SUBSIDIARIES AND RELATED COMPANIES

Barranquilla Investments Plc (67.75%), Computer Field Maintenance Ltd, Electronic Rentals Group Plc, Granada Canada Ltd, Granada Computer Services Ltd, Granada Leisure Ltd, Granada Motorway Services Ltd, Granada Overseas Holdings Ltd, Granada Properties Ltd, Granada TV Rental Ltd, Granada Television International Ltd, Granada Television Ltd, Hardman HiFi Centres Ltd, Mainstay Group PLC, National Video Corp – US, Novello and Company Ltd, Park Hall Leisure Plc, Servicepoint Ltd, Telerent Fernseh-Mietservice GmbH & Co KG – Germany, WSL Holdings Plc

BRAND NAMES

CFM, Finlandia, Granada, Kapy, Laskys, Mainstay, NASA, Novello, Park Hall, SMS, Sterisystems, Tashiko, Visionhire, WSL

CONTACTS AND FURTHER INFORMATION

J Tibbitts, Assistant secretary, Granada Group PLC, 36 Golden Square, London W1R 4AH. Tel: 01-734 8080.

GENERAL INFORMATION

Head office	11–12 Hanover Square, London W1A 1DP. Tel: 01-629 7488
Directors	AJG Sheppard FCMA FCIS (chairman and chief executive), IA Martin CA, GJ Bull, C Strowger FCA. *Non-exec* RV Giordano – US, Sir John Harvey-Jones MBE (deputy chairman), FJ Pizzitola
Advisers	SG Warburg & Co Ltd
Auditors	Peat Marwick McLintock
Registrars	Barclays Bank Registration Department
Brokers	Cazenove & Co, County NatWest WoodMac, Panmure Gordon & Co Ltd
Solicitors	Herbert Smith, Slaughter and May

GENERAL FINANCIAL INFORMATION

Market capitalisation	£3.849bn at 1 January 1988
Capital structure	
Issued ordinary shares (50p)	853.5m
Issued preference shares (£1)	1.2m at 3.225%
	3.3m at 4.375%
	7.7m at 5%
Warrants	None
Convertibles	£100m 6.25% subordinated convertible bonds 2002 (14.814 shares per £100 stock)
Traded options	Yes
ADRs	One ADR per ordinary share
Shareholders over 5%	None

FT CATEGORY

FT: Hotels and caterers
FT-A: Brewers and distillers

MAJOR ACTIVITIES

Grand Metropolitan is a broadly-based growing company operating principally in the UK and US. The group's major activities are reflected in its divisional structure of wines and spirits, brewing, UK consumer services, foods, hotels and US consumer products.

Among its interests in wines and spirits are International Distillers and Vintners (IDV), Heublein, and Almaden. Its brewers are Watney Mann & Truman. UK consumer services businesses include Mecca Bookmakers, Berni Inns and Chef & Brewer. Food companies include the Express Foods Group. Hotels include the Inter-Continental chain. US consumer products businesses include Pearle Eyecare, ALPO Petfoods and a number of Pepsi-Cola bottling plants.

Following the acquisition of Heublein in March 1987, the drinks activities account for approximately 50% of trading profit. IDV is the largest wines and spirits marketer in the world, with key brands like Smirnoff, J&B, Baileys, Gilbey's, and Le Piat d'Or. In the UK the group is a major brewer with brands like Holsten, Budweiser, Foster's, Carlsberg, Webster's and Ruddles.

Retailing interests include 3,800 Watney Mann & Truman tenancies, 1,800 managed outlets of the Berni and Host Group, Peter Dominic off-licences, 650 Mecca Bookmakers and 1,340 Pearle Eyecare centres in the US.

During 1986 the group was perceived as having lost its way, particularly with the disappointing performance of a number of its acquisitions in the US. However, confidence in the group recovered substantially with the completion of the $1.2bn Heublein acquisition, and the appointment of AJG Sheppard as chairman in July 1987.

The group is now one of the world's leading international drinks businesses comparable to Seagram. The bid for Martell, although unsuccessful, reflects the group's determination to improve its standing even further.

Grand Metropolitan competes with Ladbroke in betting and hotels. In drinks and brewing its competitors are Allied-Lyons, Bass, Guinness, Scottish & Newcastle and Whitbread, all of which have some interests in hotels as well.

FINANCIAL HISTORY

For the year ended 30 September 1987, total turnover increased 8% to £5.7bn. Pre-tax profits increased by 24% to £456.1m, with earnings per share up 21% to 38.9p. Dividends were up 17% to 12.0p.

Trading profits for all divisions were all well up. Wines and spirits increased by 51%, brewing 11%, UK consumer services 17%, foods 13%, hotels 23% and US consumer products 15%.

At the 1988 interim to 31 March 1988, pre-tax profits were up 38% to £232.2m on turnover 12% ahead at £2.884bn. All divisions performed strongly. The US earnings were affected by the weak dollar. Earnings per share increased by 31% to 18.8p and the interim dividend, at 5.5p, was raised by 22%.

SHARE PRICE HISTORY

Grand Metropolitan's share price has risen from 270p in 1984 to the 450p level in early 1988. The all-time high was in July 1987 when it reached 605p. The performance against the FT-A All-Share index has been erratic, ranging from 42% to 62%.

Underperformance in 1984/85 was caused by fears about Liggett's profits being hit by a cigarette price war in the US. Outperformance in 1986 was caused by takeover speculation. In 1987 underperformance was caused by dollar exposure worries.

The shares were hit hard in the autumn 1987 crash. This was overdone and the shares have started to outperform again.

SENIOR MANAGEMENT

AJG Sheppard succeeded Sir Stanley Grinstead as chairman in July 1987. Other executive board members are GJ Bull (wines and spirits), IA Martin (GrandMet US and Inter-Continental) and Clive Strowger (finance and foods).

CAPITAL

Changes in share capital in recent years have been largely limited to capitalisation issues. The last rights issue was in June 1982 and virtually all the company's acquisitions have been paid for in cash.

The group issued £100m of 6.25% subordinated convertible bonds in August 1987. In December 1987 the company arranged a $1bn multi-option facility, renewable annually for five years. Directors' shareholdings are small and there are no disclosable stakes.

GROUP REVIEW

Wines and spirits Following the 1987 acquisitions of Heublein and Saccone & Speed, IDV is the largest marketer of spirits in the world by volume with 1986 case sales estimated at 47.5m, compared with 42.8m cases for Seagram. The major brands include Smirnoff, J&B, Popov, Baileys, Gilbey's, Black Velvet, Malibu, Croft, Le Piat d'Or and Sambuca Romana.

IDV owns four Scotch whisky distilleries, and 12 other spirits distilleries worldwide. It has a 25% shareholding in Cinzano International SA. In the UK IDV's brand licences and agencies include Cointreau, Hennessy, Cinzano, Jack Daniels and Southern Comfort.

Heublein was acquired in March 1987 and has proved very successful. A 10% interest was acquired and a trading agreement signed with Martell in June 1987. This was followed by a bid for Martell in December 1987. The bid was not successful.

Turnover for the division in 1987 was £1.79bn, up 67%. Trading profit was £222.3m, up 51%. At the 1988 interim, trading profits were 51.4% up at £125.1m on turnover 63.2% ahead at £1.126bn.

CHAIRMAN'S STATEMENT

'Grand Metropolitan's businesses are robust against the immediate economic outlook, and commercially are well placed in all markets. Management morale is high. The new financial year has started well and the prospects for growth in earnings are encouraging. We remain confident and determined for the current year.' *AJG Sheppard*

Brewing and retailing Watney Mann & Truman has 12% of the UK beer market. The main brands include Foster's, Carlsberg, Holsten and Budweiser in lagers, and Webster's, Wilsons and Ruddles in ales. Sales volumes were up 4.5% in 1987, with lager accounting for 55% of beer volume.

Both the take-home and on-trade businesses performed well in 1987. Turnover was £613.8m, up 11%. Trading profit was £100.4m, also up 11%. At the 1988 interim, trading profits were 19.9% up at £60.2m on turnover 13.4% ahead at £575.9m.

UK consumer products and services In addition to the Berni & Host Group restaurants and public houses, UK consumer services operates 750 Mecca Bookmakers outlets, six London casinos, and 830 Peter Dominic, Bottoms Up and Roberts & Cooper off-licences in the UK. Licensed retailing showed strong growth in 1987.

Mecca Bookmakers profits were disappointing because of reduced margins, though its position has been enhanced by the

FIVE YEAR FINANCIAL INFORMATION

Year	Turnover (£m)	Pre-tax (£m)	Earnings (p)	Dividends net (p)	Dividend cover (x)	Net assets (p)	Price (p) High	Price (p) Low	PER (x) High	PER (x) Low	Yield (%) High	Yield (%) Low
1983	4,469	295.2	25.3	7.29	3.5	195	277	228	20.1	14.4	4.22	3.27
1984	5,075	334.3	29.4	8.36	3.5	216	327	244	18.8	12.8	4.34	3.18
1985	5,590	347.3	31.9	9.09	3.5	230	364	253	17.0	11.7	4.80	3.43
1986	5,291	386.1	32.1	10.2	3.1	238	484	332	19.5	14.1	3.91	2.75
1987	5,705	456.1	38.9	12.0	3.2	204	595	357	20.2	10.9	4.12	2.47

Share price and relative to FT-A All-Share

GRAND MET.
Relative to All Share (R.H.SCALE)

Satellite Information Services venture. The first overseas casino was acquired in Cannes, France.

Turnover for the division in 1987 was £1.05bn, up 10%. Trading profit was £79.1m, up 17%. At the 1988 interim, trading profits were 10.8% up on turnover 11.5% ahead at £271.8m.

Foods The foods division includes: the Express Dairy liquid milk processing and distribution business; Eden Vale chilled dairy products, including the Ski brand; and the Express Foods operation which manufactures and markets cheeses and butter. A number of acquisitions have been made recently.

Turnover for 1987 was £825.2m, up 10%. Trading profit was £44.1m, up 13% despite the continuing drop in the doorstep milk trade. At the 1988 interim, trading profits were 24.3% up at £24m on turnover 23.9% ahead at £460.7m.

Hotels This includes the 87-strong deluxe Inter-Continental chain and the 13 Forum first class hotels. There are six hotels in the UK, of which five are in London. Elsewhere the distribution is Europe 34, Middle East 13, North America 11, Latin America 11, Pacific/Asia 12 and Africa 10.

Inter-Continental was badly affected in 1986 by the sudden drop in US visitors to Europe following the Libyan air raid and the Chernobyl disaster. The first half of 1986/87 continued to be depressed. However, there was a 41% increase in trading profit for the Inter-Continental chain for the second half of 1987/88, and an 8% increase in occupancy overall for the whole year.

Turnover for the year as a whole was down £5m to £337.9m, but trading profit was up £7m to £37.4m (+23%). At the 1988 interim, trading profits were 72.8% ahead at £17.8m on turnover 2.3% ahead at £163.5m.

US consumer products and services The US businesses include ALPO Petfoods, the Atlantic Soft Drink Company, the Pepsi-Cola San Joaquin Bottling Company and Pearle Health Services, the 1,340-strong chain of eye care outlets. During 1987 ALPO Petfoods purchased the Blue Mountain and Jim Dandy pet food businesses. In April 1988 the Vision Express chain of 27 optical superstores was bought by Pearle Eyecare for $40m cash. In May 1988 the Eye + Tec chain was acquired for $32m.

The Liggett Group cigarette business was sold in October 1986. Quality Care was sold in July 1987. Diversified Products, the home fitness product business, was sold in September 1987. Children's World was sold in October 1987.

The division's turnover for 1987 was £635.5m, up 20%. Trading profit was £67.8m, up 15%. At the 1988 interim,

trading profits were 3% ahead at £24m on turnover 5.4% down at £285.9m. Dollar results were up by 24% and 13% respectively.

GEOGRAPHICAL REVIEW

Of group turnover in 1987 the UK contributes approximately 62%, North America 30.5%, continental Europe 4.5% and the rest of the world 3%. Of group profits the UK contributes 61%, North America 30.6%, continental Europe 5.6%, and the rest of the world 4%.

CORPORATE CALENDAR

Year end	30 September
Preliminary results	December
Report and accounts	January
AGM	March
Final dividend paid	April
Interim results	May
Interim dividend paid	October

DIRECTORS' HOLDINGS

	Beneficial interests	Non-beneficial interests	Other (incl. options)
AJG Sheppard	7,538	—	157,918
GJ Bull	11,500	—	114,520
IA Martin	—	—	107,920
JC Orr	11,000	—	153,062
WD Scott	5,500	—	110,000
C Strowger	—	—	107,370
RV Giordano	—	—	—
Sir John Harvey-Jones	—	—	—
FJ Pizzitola	13,200	—	—

Total directors' remuneration in 1986/87 was £1,873,734, of which the chairman received £176,504.

PRINCIPAL SUBSIDIARY COMPANIES

UK brewing Brewliners Ltd, G Ruddle & Co Plc, Holsten Distributors, Manns Northampton Brewery Co Ltd, Phoenix Brewery Co Ltd, Samuel Webster and Wilsons Ltd, The Norwich Brewery Co Ltd, Ushers Brewery Ltd, Watney Combe Reid & Truman Ltd, Watney Export Ltd, Watney Mann & Truman Brewers Ltd, Watney Mann National Sales Ltd

UK consumer services Clifton Inns Ltd, Grand Metropolitan Cardholders Ltd, London Clubs Ltd, Mecca Bookmakers Ltd, The Berni & Host Group Ltd

UK foods Aylesbury Foods Ltd, Eden Vale Ltd, Express Dairy (NI) Ltd – Northern Ireland, Express Dairy Co Ltd (Eire) – Eire, Express Dairy Ltd, Express Foods Group (International) Ltd, Express Foods Group Ltd, Express Foods Ltd

US consumer products ALPO Petfoods Inc – US, Atlantic Soft Drink Company Inc – US, Blue Mountain Pet Food Inc, Jim Dandy Inc, GrandMet USA Inc – US, Pearle Health Services Inc – US, Pepsi-Cola San Joaquin Bottling Company – US

Hotels Inter-Continental Hotels Corporation – US, Forum Hotels International Ltd

International wines and spirits Almaden Vineyards Inc – US, Carillon Importers Ltd, Croft & Ca Lda – Portugal, Croft Jerez SA (66.7%) – Spain, Gilbey Canada Inc – Canada, Gilbeys of Ireland Ltd – Eire, Heublein do Brasil Ltda – Brazil (70%), Heublein Inc – US, IDV (UK) Sales Ltd, International Distillers and Vintners Ltd, International Distillers and Vintners France SA – France, International Distillers and Vintners (UK) Ltd, International Distillers (Developments) Ltd, Justerini & Brooks Ltd, Peter Dominic Ltd, R & A Bailey & Co Ltd, Roberts and Cooper Ltd,

THE GREAT UNIVERSAL STORES P.L.C.

Saccone and Speed Ltd, Selviac Nederland BV – Holland, The Paddington Corporation – US, W & A Gilbey (SA) (Pty) Ltd (51%) – South Africa, W & A Gilbey Ltd, Wyvern International Ltd

Other   Grand Metropolitan Community Services Ltd, Grand Metropolitan Information Services Ltd, Holsten Distributors Ltd (51%)

PRINCIPAL RELATED COMPANIES

Apsley Hotels Ltd (50%), Cinzano International SA – Luxembourg (25%), Gávea Hotelaria e Turismo SA (Brazil 40%), Grands Hotels du Zaire SZARL – Zaire (50%), JE Mather & Sons Ltd (24.1%), Swift and Moore Pty Ltd – Australia (35%), The Bangkok Inter-Continental Hotels Co Ltd – Thailand (30.4%)

BRAND NAMES

Absolute Vodka, Alpo, Amaretto di Saronno, Aylesbury Foods, Baileys Original Irish Cream, Barnaby's Carvery, Berni, Black Velvet, Bombay Dry Gin, Budweiser, Carlsberg, Chef & Brewer, Cinzano, Clifton Inns, Croft Original, Dunhill Old Master, E, Eden Vale, Express Dairy, Express Foods, Forum Hotels International, Fosters, GMK, Gilbey's Gin, Grand Marnier, Hennessy, Holsten, Intercontinental Hotels, J&B, Le Piat d'Or, Malibu, Manns, Mecca Bookmakers, Norwich Brewery, Old Orleans Restaurant, Open House, Pastificio, Pearle Vision Centers, Pepsi-Cola, Phoenix, Ruddles, Sambuca Romana, Ski, Smirnoff, Truman, Ushers Brewery, Watney Combe Reid & Truman, Webster's Yorkshire Bitter

CONTACTS AND FURTHER INFORMATION

T Halford, Director of Public Affairs, Grand Metropolitan PLC, 11–12 Hanover Square, London W1A 1DP. Tel: 01-629 7488.

GENERAL INFORMATION

Head office	PO Box 1BZ, Universal House, 251–256 Tottenham Court Road, London W1A 1BZ. Tel: 01-636 4080
Directors	Sir Isaac Wolfson FRS (president), Lord Wolfson of Marylebone FBA (chairman), H Bowman (deputy chairman), AT Spittle FCA (deputy chairman), VJ Barnett, EM Barnes, JG Harris FCIB, ST Peacock, RHC Pugh LLB FCA. *Non-exec* Sir Philip Harris
Advisers	SG Warburg & Co Ltd, Whiteaway Laidlaw & Co Ltd
Auditors	Deloitte Haskins & Sells
Registrars	Hill Samuel Registrars Ltd
Brokers	Cazenove & Co
Solicitors	Linklaters & Paines, Paisner & Co

GENERAL FINANCIAL INFORMATION

Market capitalisation	£2.852bn at 1 January 1988
Capital structure	
Issued ordinary shares (25p)	5.4m ordinary voting shares
	245.1m non-voting 'A' shares
Issued preference shares (£1)	1.01m 4.9% CPS 'B'
	0.64m 3.15% CPS 'C'
Warrants	None
Convertibles	None
Traded options	None
ADRs	One ordinary share for each ADR
Shareholders over 5%	The Wolfson Foundation has 49.6% of the ordinary shares and 6.8% of the 'A', the Prudential Corporation has 9% of the ordinary

FT CATEGORY

FT: Drapery and stores
FT-A: Stores

MAJOR ACTIVITIES

The Great Universal Stores (GUS) is the leading UK mail order company, a high street retailer and also has a substantial financial services and property division.

The mail order and home shopping catalogue operation accounts for 62% of group sales and 51% of profits. Retail shops provide a further 20% of turnover and 15% of profits. The balance comes from property and financial services with 15% sales and 20% profits, and exports and manufacturing with 3% sales and 5% profits.

The UK represents the largest single market with 78% of group sales and 81% of post-tax profits, although a wide spread of business has been built up overseas. Since 1985/86 wholly-owned high street stores have declined in importance for GUS. However, a number of important outside shareholdings have been acquired, including a 23% stake in Harris Queensway, the leading UK home furnishings retailer.

Diverse interests and conservative accounting and management techniques have together resulted in a remarkably consistent, if at times unexciting, pattern of growth. It is interesting to note that a more aggressive management stance has emerged recently.

There has been a reorganisation in the area of high street shopping, and the group's inherent above average trading strengths seem to be receiving greater publicity and recognition than usual.

Key economic indicators are personal disposable incomes, consumer confidence, housing activity, fluctuations in interest rates and foreign currency movements. GUS's main competitors include the unquoted Littlewoods, Next, Empire, Marks and Spencer and Sears, as well as the UK clearing banks and other finance houses.

FIVE YEAR FINANCIAL INFORMATION

Year	Turnover (£m)	Pre-tax (£m)	Earnings (p)	Dividends net (p)	Dividend cover (x)	Net assets (p)	Price (p) High	Low	PER (x) High	Low	Yield (%) High	Low
1983	1,833	201	45.9	14	3.3	380.0	623	498	15.2	12.9	4.02	3.14
1984	2,033	227	53.1	16	3.4	464.0	707	488	15.3	10.7	4.62	3.03
1985	2,099	254	61.5	18	3.4	487.0	904	677	16.3	12.3	3.53	2.84
1986	2,270	298	72.6	21	3.5	646.0	1,150	726	19.0	12.0	3.69	2.33
1987	2,472.4	337.6	89.1	24.5	3.6	647.0	1,470	1010	19.2	11.3	3.36	2.05

FINANCIAL HISTORY

In 1986/87 turnover rose by 9% to £2.47bn, and profits by 15.9% to £345m. Since 1981/82 an increase of 49% has been recorded. Pre-tax profits have risen by 82% in the period. Margins continue to strengthen, with a 2.5% advance registered over five years, of which a nearly 1% rise was achieved in 1986/87.

Progress reflects a determined effort by management to improve profitability. In particular, previously unproductive high street retail interests have been sold off (but the freehold and longer leasehold properties were retained), and associate or other third party investments have been made, of which the most notable is the 23% interest acquired in Harris Queensway.

Earnings per share have risen by 115% over the last five years. An especially rapid increase of 21.9% to 92.0p, including property, was seen in 1986/87. Five year dividend growth has amounted to 88%. The figure for 1986/87 was 16.7%.

The balance sheet is exceptionally strong, with no borrowings. Net cash as at March 1987 amounted to almost £300m. There were outstanding trade debtors of £993.9m, of which £664.9m was payable within one year. A return on capital employed of under 20% reflects the mix of credit orientated business and a low-risk investment profile.

SHARE PRICE HISTORY

The shares are divided into ordinary and 'A' non-voting shares. The 'A' shares have shown steady progress in absolute terms but have failed to achieve any particular breakthrough as a percentage of the FT-A All-Share index. Since 1984 they have traded between 105% and 140%, and in late February 1988 stood at 119%.

Conversely, the ordinary shares have been performing well, and in late February 1988 represent 187% of the FT-A All-Share index, which is very nearly a five year high. Interest in a possible enfranchisement of the non-voting shares has grown.

Both groups of shares were initially affected by the October 1987 share crash, but the strong cash position of the group and defensive characteristics of the shares has led to strong relative outperformance.

SENIOR MANAGEMENT

Sir Isaac Wolfson, who is chiefly responsible for building the group towards its present dominant position, was appointed honorary life president in December 1986. At that time, his son Lord Wolfson of Marylebone became sole chairman, and Harold Bowman and A Trevor Spittle were both promoted from assistant managing director to deputy chairman. Other main board directors include EM Barnes, responsible for retailing and business information, and RHC Pugh, who is responsible for the catalogue and mail order division.

In October 1987 JG Harris was appointed managing director of financial services, ST Peacock is managing director of Burberrys and V Barnett joined the board with responsibility for the group's North American activities. Sir Philip Harris, the chairman of Harris Queensway, joined as a non-executive director in July 1986.

CAPITAL

The issued share capital as at March 1987 amounted to 250.5m ordinary and 'A' non-voting ordinary shares.

In April 1987, however, GUS offered shareholders in Pantherella a combination of shares and cash when it acquired the company. In total 82,257 'A' non-voting ordinary shares were issued. Andy Hampers was also bought for cash and shares in July 1987. In a total £3m consideration, 196,128 'A' non-voting shares were issued.

As at March 1987, the Wolfson Foundation held 49.9% of the ordinary shares and 6.8% of the non-voting 'A' shares. Between them, Sir Isaac and Lord Wolfson held 1.6% of the ordinary shares. The Prudential Corporation held 9% of the ordinary shares.

GROUP REVIEW

Home shopping and related activities Within the UK the group dominates the mail order market with a market share of over 40%. The nearest competitor, Littlewoods, has 25% of the market. The business derives principally from two separate subsidiary companies, GUS Catalogue Order and Kay and Co.

GUS Catalogue Order operates through warehouses and administrative centres situated throughout Greater Manchester and Lancashire. Kay and Co has its warehouse and distribution centres in Worcester and Leeds. Each of these two houses publishes a wide selection of catalogues, including Great

Share price and relative to FT-A All-Share

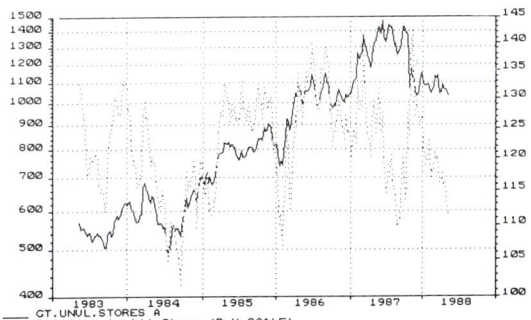

GT.UNUL.STORES 'A'
Relative to All Share (R.H.SCALE)

Universal, John England, Marshall Ward, John Myers, Choice, Kays and Kit. They offer a wide range of clothing and household goods.

The number of publications is increasing as more use is made of computerised databases to target the marketing effort towards individual groups of customers. The business remains heavily biased towards the traditional mail order market. It has a network of over three million agents who receive twice-yearly catalogues to generate orders. The company also handles deliveries and the return of unwanted merchandise. Sales are usually made on credit, with repayments extended over a 20 week or longer period.

A more recent departure has been the development of direct sales, which bypass the agency system. By making use of bank credit cards, the amount of paperwork and other administrative effort is reduced.

CHAIRMAN'S STATEMENT

'The Group's policy continued to be one of expansion and rationalisation in order to maximise stockholders' assets, earnings and dividends per stock unit.

To improve productivity we shall go on investing in modern systems and technology for warehouses, offices, and delivery services. We will seek to improve further our marketing and merchandising techniques and identify new areas of trade wherever these can produce, within a reasonable period, a suitable return to stockholders.

The continued strength of the Group can be seen in terms of the growth of earnings, dividends and assets per stock unit. In the last five years total earnings per stock unit have advanced from 42.63p to 91.99p. Dividends per stock unit have risen from 13p to 24.5p and stockholders' funds in the Consolidated Balance Sheet have increased from £781m to £1,846m. The distribution of the Group's assets is well-balanced between net current assets and property. The market value of our investments at 31st March 1987 was substantially in excess of book cost.' Lord Wolfson

Another aspect of the home shopping market which is being exploited by the company is the provision of hampers, containing an assortment of foods and other merchandise. The business has recently been expanded by acquisition. GUS Transport is also extending its activities. Its White Arrow nationwide delivery network is extending its services to external customers.

Other mail order businesses operate within Austria, The Netherlands, Sweden and Switzerland. However, it is the UK which provides the bulk of divisional sales and profits.

Retailing The division's direct retail interests have recently been reduced. In the UK, Paige, a ladies' clothing business, was acquired by Next. Times Furnishing, a substantial high street furniture retailing operation, and Home Charm, a chain of DIY shops, were sold to Harris Queensway in exchange for a 23% shareholding of the company. Freehold and long leasehold property rights have been retained for all of these businesses. Thoms Household Stores was also sold to Harris Queensway.

In Australia a furniture retailing chain has been sold in exchange for cash and a share stake in the acquiring company. These moves were intended to boost the group profit performance as a result of a productive exchange of assets and of gaining outside retail expertise. So far, however, the Harris Queensway holding has proved to be a disappointment.

The remaining directly-controlled shop retailing activities in the UK include Lennards. This chain operates through 300 outlets, but probably commands under 2% of the UK footwear market. It also includes the Burberrys and Scotch House operations. Both of these trade from selected locations and offer a range of high quality and premium priced rainwear, knitwear and other clothing lines.

The Burberrys retail business is also represented within the US, France, Belgium, Switzerland and West Germany. Burberrys is experiencing strong growth in royalty income through licensing its products, particularly in Japan. Successful furniture retailing operations are owned in Canada and South Africa.

Finance and property An expanding portfolio of freehold and long leasehold properties is used to generate rental income from outside the group. A number of developments are in hand or are about to commence.

Financial services are conducted through General Guarantee and Whiteaway Laidlaw, which operate through a network of over 45 branches spread throughout the UK. The business caters to private and corporate customers, and offers a range of hire purchase and other credit facilities as well as leasing finance. Whiteaway Laidlaw is also a bank, but most of its banking business is conducted on an inter-group basis.

A further source of revenue comes from CCN Systems which provides business information services. It uses the expertise gained from the group's own financing involvement to provide a service to outside businesses. A similar operation is established in the US.

Export and manufacturing The group manufactures beds and upholstery in the UK. The fastest growing and most important area of activity is provided by Burberrys, which sells into the UK market and overseas. It has already received five Queen's Awards for Exports. The products include rainwear, sportswear, knitwear and children's clothing. The recent acquisition of Pantherella has added men's hosiery to the range.

GEOGRAPHICAL REVIEW

In 1986/87, 80.9% of group profits after tax were generated within the UK. A further 8.4% came from Western Europe, 6.4% from North America and 2.5% from Africa. The remainder derived from the Far East and Australia. The overseas activities include mail order and retail.

CORPORATE CALENDAR

Year end	31 March
Preliminary results	July
Report and accounts	October
AGM	November
Final dividend paid	December
Interim results	December
Interim dividend paid	March

DIRECTORS' HOLDINGS

	Ordinary shares	'A' non-voting shares
EM Barnes	1,000	—
H Bowman	1,000	19,437
Sir Philip Harris	1,000	—
ST Peacock	2,500	12,500
RHC Pugh	1,000	—
AT Spittle	1,000	1,000
Lord Wolfson of Marylebone	43,447	353,872
VJ Barnett	10,437	361,570
JG Harris	1,000	—

Total directors' remuneration in 1986/87, including fees, was £0.6m, of which the chairman, who was also the highest-paid director, received £129,450.

GUARDIAN ROYAL EXCHANGE plc

PRINCIPAL SUBSIDIARIES AND RELATED COMPANIES

Andy Hampers Ltd, BH Ries Ltd, Burberrys – Belgium, Burberrys – France, Burberrys – Germany, Burberrys – Holland, Burberrys – Switzerland, Burberrys Ltd, Burberrys Ltd – US, Burberrys (Products) Ltd – US, CCN Systems Ltd, Family Hampers Ltd, GUS Canada Inc, GUS Catalogue Order Ltd, GUS Export Corporation Ltd, GUS Holdings Inc – US, GUS Merchandise Corporation Ltd, GUS Property Management Ltd, GUS Transport Ltd, General Guarantee Corporation Ltd, Great Universal Stores (Europe) AG – Switzerland, Great Universal Stores (South Africa) (Proprietary) Ltd, Halens Postorder AB – Sweden, JJ Silber Ltd, Kay and Co Ltd, Lennards Ltd, Lewis Stores Ltd – South Africa, Pantherella Plc, The Scotch House Ltd, Universal Bedding and Upholstery Ltd, Universal Versand GmbH – Austria, Vedia SA – Switzerland, Wehkamp BV – The Netherlands, Whiteaway Laidlaw & Co Ltd, Woodrow-Universal Ltd

BRAND NAMES

Burberrys, CCN Systems, Cherney, Choice, Family Album, Fashion Extra, General Guarantee, Great Universal, Halens, Hector Powe, John England, John Myers, John Noble, Kays, Kit, Legaré, Lennards, Lewis, Marshall Ward, Personal Selection, Royal Welsh Warehouse, Sanders Meubelstad, The Scotch House, Trafford, UBU, Universal, Wehkamp, White Arrow, Whiteaway Laidlaw, Woodhouse, Woodrow Universal

CONTACTS AND FURTHER INFORMATION

AT Spittle, Great Universal Stores P.L.C., 251–256 Tottenham Court Road, London W1A 1BZ. Tel: 01-636 4080.

GENERAL INFORMATION

Head office	Royal Exchange, London EC3V 3LS. Tel: 01-283 7101
Directors	JEH Collins MBE DSC (chairman), CEA Hambro (deputy chairman), PR Dugdale CBE (managing), SMF Harris FCII, SA Hopkins ACII, NE Shepherd. *Non-exec* Hon Edward Adeane CVO, Sir David H Burnett MBE TD, D Gordon, A McCorquodale, JM Menzies, Sir Peter Reynolds CBE, JJLG Sheffield
Advisers	Hambros Bank Ltd, Morgan Grenfell & Co Ltd
Auditors	Coopers & Lybrand
Registrars	Ravensbourne Registration Services
Brokers	Alexanders Laing & Cruickshank, Warburg Securities
Solicitors	Herbert Smith, Slaughter and May

GENERAL FINANCIAL INFORMATION

Market capitalisation	£1.327bn at 1 January 1988
Capital structure	
Issued ordinary shares (25p)	160m
Issued preference shares	None
Warrants	None
Convertibles	None
Traded options	None
ADRs	None
Shareholders over 5%	None

FT CATEGORY

FT: Insurances
FT-A: Insurance (composite)

MAJOR ACTIVITIES

Guardian Royal Exchange (GRE) provides a comprehensive service in all principal classes of insurance, primarily in the UK, but also in some 70 countries throughout the world. Its roots lie in the old Royal Exchange, one of the first insurance companies to be granted legal status by Royal Charter in 1720, and the Guardian Assurance Company, founded in 1821.

The group's main activities relate to the provision of personal – property, motor, life and pensions – and commercial – property, liability, motor, marine and aviation – insurances. The UK is the largest single territorial division, followed by Germany and the US.

Demand for GRE's products depends on its ability to quote a competitive price to the numerous insurance intermediaries who supply the group with proposals on behalf of the public. In turn, this ability depends on the GRE's ability to keep its expenses down, to limit the commission levels to intermediaries and to invest the assets under its management, about £8.5bn, profitably.

GRE's shares are often compared with those of the other four main quoted sector composite insurance companies in the UK: Commercial Union, General Accident, Royal Insurance and Sun Alliance. Commercial Union, General Accident and Royal Insurance have a substantially greater exposure to the US; consequently the direct comparison is often with Sun Alliance.

FINANCIAL HISTORY

Since 1982 the group has been expanding rapidly with non-life premiums rising by about 50% to £1.45bn in 1987, and life new business rising 125%.

GRE, and non-life insurance companies generally, experienced a difficult period between 1981 and 1985. The improving trend which began in 1986 continued into 1987. Group pre-tax profits in 1987 amounted to £165.0m, compared with £143.8m in 1986, having reached a low point of £3.5m in 1985.

F I V E   Y E A R   F I N A N C I A L   I N F O R M A T I O N

Year	Turnover (£m)	Pre-tax (£m)	Earnings (p)	Dividends net (p)	Dividend cover (x)	Net assets (p)	Price (p) High	Low	PER (x) High	Low	Yield (%) High	Low
1983	1,366	122.1	42.6	23.00	1.9	554	546	354	12.8	8.3	9.28	6.02
1984	1,652	92.2	34.5	26.00	1.3	625	693	508	20.1	14.7	7.31	5.36
1985	1,797	3.5	(8.7)	28.75	—	558	770	621	—	—	6.55	5.28
1986	2,145	143.8	63.6	34.00	1.9	720	954	720	15.0	11.3	6.52	4.92
1987	2,142	165.0	67.2	41.00	1.6	676	1135	751	16.9	11.2	7.35	4.86

During this period, life assurance profits have been a stabilising influence, amounting to £24.8m in 1987.

The net dividend was increased by 20.6% in 1987, to 41.0p per share, the increase reflecting the better trading prospects for the group. Earnings per share amounted to 67.2p, resulting in the dividend being covered 1.6 times.

The GRE has a very healthy balance sheet with a solvency ratio of about 75%. The solvency ratio is calculated by dividing shareholders' funds used in support of the non-life business, £101bn, by the premium volume of non-life business, £1.45bn. Barring a protracted downturn in the insurance industry or a major acquisition, GRE should have sufficient capital to finance the expansion of its business for years to come. The life funds are also in a very strong financial position.

SHARE PRICE HISTORY

GRE's share price has been relatively stable since 1984 compared with the other major quoted UK composite insurers. For much of 1986 and 1987 the price drifted down against UK equities, although it had increased by 25% in absolute terms at the summer 1987 peak.

A large part of its assets are invested in fixed interest securities and overseas assets, and consequently GRE does not participate fully in the rises and falls of the UK equity market. Relative to other equities, GRE's share price improved following the fall in world stock markets in October 1987.

SENIOR MANAGEMENT

JEH Collins is chairman of the group but retires at the end of May 1988. The board has selected Charles Hambro as his successor. Peter R Dugdale is managing director. Sidney A Hopkins is a director and general manager of UK operations and for the worldwide life operations. Michael F Harris, director and general manager, is responsible for the group's worldwide operations.

The group's investment and finance activities are controlled by Norman E Shepherd who is a director and general manager. The West German insurance companies, under the name Albingia, are run by Herbert Singer. Victor Yerrill is president of GRE of America Corp; Harold N Levick is managing director of the Australian subsidiary GRE Insurance Limited; and Norman Curtis is president of Guardian Insurance Company of Canada. The company secretary is JMR Evans.

CAPITAL

There are 160m issued ordinary shares. There have been no major changes to the issued capital since 1984 but the board is proposing to split the shares on a five for one basis after the AGM. Under the terms of the employee share option scheme,

there are options to subscribe for a total of 5.63m shares in the period up to 1996. Total shareholders' funds at 31st December 1987, excluding the value of the life operations, amounted to £1.1bn.

In addition, at the end of 1986 the group has loan capital and other loans outstanding amounting to £62.1m, made up of: 7% unsecured loan stock 1986/1991, £23.5m; 5.75% to 10.75% secured debenture stock of a subsidiary company repayable 1990/95, £4.8m; 8% unsecured US dollar bonds 1987, £0.8m; other secured loans, £6.8m; secured loans from bankers, £7.0m; and unsecured loans from bankers, £19.2m. These loans and the loan capital were more than matched by deposits, bank and cash balances which at the end of 1986 amounted to £281.2m.

GROUP REVIEW

In the UK, GRE accepts all the major types of insurances. Total non-life premium income in the UK amounted to £595.2m in 1987, out of a worldwide total of £1.45bn. As for other UK insurers, the personal lines insurances have been a problem area in recent years. The continuing rise in the frequency of motor car accidents has led to substantial premium rate increases. In 1987 the freeze in January, windstorms in March and storms in October all affected the household account. Claims payments for the October storms are likely to total £53m, although part of the cost has been met by reinsurance recoveries.

The increased occurrence of severe winter weather conditions in the last few years, and the increase in crime, has led to increase in premium rates for household contents and structures insurances, particularly in the inner city areas. The GRE writes a substantial amount of commercial insurance business and is particularly known for its marine and aviation division.

The group has a substantial life assurance division which, as for the rest of the group, depends primarily on independent intermediaries for new business sales. A strong balance sheet,

Share price and relative to FT-A All-Share

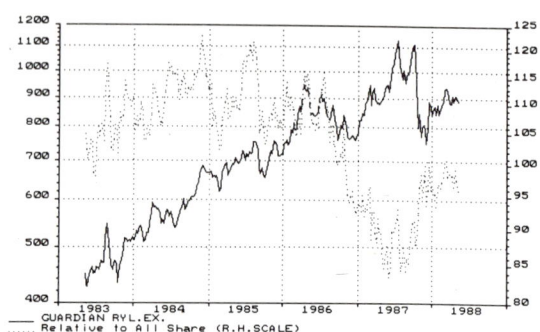

GUARDIAN RYL.EX.
Relative to All Share (R.H.SCALE)

competitive bonus rates, and good connections with a number of leading building societies led to buoyant sales in 1987.

GRE obtained £232m of premium income in Germany in 1987, trading under the Albingia group of companies. The German market is a difficult and highly regulated one, needing substantial economies of scale in order to operate profitably. The GRE runs a well established and sizeable branch network in Germany giving it an advantage over its UK competitors in that country.

CHAIRMAN'S STATEMENT

'For the last two years I have spoken of improving trends in our main areas of business and 1987 has been a year which, with major catastrophe claims arising from severe climatic conditions in North West Europe and South Africa, a tornado in Canada and an earthquake in New Zealand, has fully tested the depth of that improvement. In my judgement we have amply demonstrated the strength and quality of our book of business in producing improved profits in such a year. It is worth observing that for the first year since GRE was established we have been obliged to claim on the Group's catastrophe reinsurers, even though our policy has been to buy external protection at such a high level that we considered any claim to be a remote possibility that would involve a really major disaster. It is probable that the October windstorm will turn out to be such a disaster for the world insurance industry.' *JEH Collins*

1986 and 1987 saw a major improvement in profitability in both the US and Canada. Premiums received in 1987 in the US amounted to £155m, down from £160m in the previous year. Over the years GRE's operations in the US have been, and are likely to remain, extremely profitable. In Canada, premiums were down 13% to £113m, the result of exchange rate changes. Other territories in which the GRE has a major presence include Australia, Ireland, France, Holland, Portugal, South Africa, Zimbabwe and Brazil.

Despite the ups and downs of insurance markets, the GRE has increased its dividend by at least 10% in each of the last sixteen years since 1971. Its concentration of non-life activities in the UK and Germany provide an additional degree of stability to group profits, as do the substantial and increasing life profits emanating primarily from the UK.

GEOGRAPHICAL REVIEW

The territorial distribution in 1987 of the group's non-life premium income is UK 41%, US 8%, Canada 8%, Eire 4%, France 2%, Germany 16%, the Netherlands 1%, Australia 5%, South Africa 3%, other areas 4% and marine and aviation worldwide 8%. A distribution by profits is not shown because profits for non-life business vary greatly from year to year for each territory. Life profits primarily emerge in the UK.

CORPORATE CALENDAR

Year end	31 December
Preliminary results	March
Report and accounts	April
AGM	May
Final dividend paid	July
Interim results	September
Interim dividend paid	January

DIRECTORS' HOLDINGS

	Fully-paid ordinary shares		Options
	(beneficial)	(non-beneficial)	
JEH Collins	6,250	—	—
CEA Hambro	1,382	—	—
PR Dugdale	3,982	—	52,240
Hon Edward Adeane	1,000	—	—
Sir David H Burnett	831	—	—
D Gordon	5,230	—	—
SMF Harris	1,230	—	34,555
SA Hopkins	212	—	32,932
A McCorquodale	1,000	—	—
JM Menzies	2,000	—	—
Sir Peter Reynolds	1,000	—	—
JJLG Sheffield	3,000	—	—
NE Shepherd	16,679	—	35,677

Total directors' remuneration for 1987 was £614,445, of which the chairman received £27,500 and the highest-paid director £134,649.

PRINCIPAL SUBSIDIARIES AND RELATED COMPANIES

Insurance Companies

Albany Insurance Co – US, Albingia Lebensversicherungs-Aktiengesellschaft – Germany, Albingia Versicherungs-Aktiengesellschaft – Germany (86%), Amsterdam London Verzekering Maatschappij NV – Netherlands (99%), Atlas Assurance Co Ltd, Atlas Assurance Co of America, Caledonian Insurance Co, Globe American Casualty Co, GRE Insurance Ltd – Australia, GRE Linked Life Assurance Ltd, GRE Pensions Management Ltd, Guardian Assurance Plc, Guardian Insurance Co of Canada (99%), Guardian National Insurance Co Ltd – South Africa (51%), Guardian Royal Exchange Assurance IARD – France, Guardian Royal Exchange Assurance of New Zealand Ltd, Guardian Royal Exchange Assurance plc, Guardian Ruckversicherungs-Gesellschaft – Switzerland, Mid-American Fire & Casualty Co, North Pacific Insurance Co Ltd – Hong Kong, Royal Exchange Assurance, Royal Exchange Assurance of America Inc – US, Seguradora Brasileira Motor Union Americana SA – Brazil (99%), Talbot Bird & Co Inc – US, The Midwestern Indemnity Co – US, Tower Insurance Co Inc – US, Union Insurance Society of Canton Ltd – Hong Kong

Other companies

Aquis Securities Plc, British Field Products Ltd, Bruton Property Holdings Ltd (91%), Compass Securities Ltd (98%), GRE Corporation Ltd – New Zealand, GRE Financial Ltd – Canada, GRE Holdings Ltd – Australia, GRE of America Corp – US, GRE Personal Financial Management Ltd, Guardian Royal Exchange Unit Managers Ltd, Royal Exchange Trust Co Ltd, The Metropolitan Trust plc

BRAND NAMES

GRE, Polisy

CONTACTS AND FURTHER INFORMATION

Tony Williams, Guardian Royal Exchange plc, Royal Exchange, London EC3V 3LS. Tel: 01-283 7101.

GUINNESS PLC

GENERAL INFORMATION

Head office	39 Portman Square, London W1H 9HB. Tel: 01-486 0288
Registered office	Bodiam House, Twyford Abbey Road, London NW10 7ES. Tel: 01-965 7700
Directors	Sir Norman Macfarlane (chairman), AJ Tennant (group chief executive), Sir David Plastow (deputy chairman), BF Baldock, SC Dowling, FL Fitzpatrick. *Non-exec* FI Chapman, AA Greener, CE Guinness CVO, Hon JB Guinness, The Earl of Iveagh (president), MF Julien, IC MacLaurin
Advisers	No specified adviser
Auditors	Price Waterhouse
Registrars	Ian Brockie, Guinness PLC, 33 Ellesly Road, Edinburgh EH12 6JW. Tel: 031-225 3843
Irish Branch Registrars	Miss MJ Walsh, Guinness PLC, St James's Gate, Dublin 8. Tel: 0001-756701
Brokers	Cazenove & Co, James Capel & Co
Solicitors	Herbert Smith

GENERAL FINANCIAL INFORMATION

Market capitalisation	£2.397bn at 1 January 1988
Capital structure	
Issued ordinary shares (25p)	832m
Issued preference shares (£1)	300m 5.75% convertible redeemable preference 1990–1996 (28 ordinary shares per £100 stock)
Warrants	None
Convertibles	£74m 8.25% CULS 2001 (34.48 ordinary shares per £100 stock)
Traded options	Yes
ADRs	Five ordinary 25p shares per ADR
Shareholders over 5%	None

FT CATEGORY

FT: Beers, wines and spirits
FT-A: Brewers and distillers

MAJOR ACTIVITIES

At one time Guinness's primary business was that of brewing the renowned stout. Since the acquisition of Arthur Bell and Distillers this activity has been considerably overtaken in terms of scale and profits by distilled spirits. Guinness is now number one, ahead of International Distillers and Vintners and Seagram, in the world league of spirits marketers in terms of profitability.

Guinness stout, although highly visible, accounts for no more than 4% of the beer market in Great Britain. In the Republic of Ireland the company's beer products are dominant with a 75% market share. As a Scotch whisky producer Guinness had an impressive 36% share of world markets including 40% in the UK. The company's Gordon's Gin ranks number one in the UK and in the world.

The Martin Retail group of shops, mainly newsagents but including some chemists, has been sold. Other peripheral businesses have also been sold so that the company can concentrate on its beverage activities.

The scandal concerning the alleged illegal support operation for the share price during the bid for Distillers in 1986 received wide publicity. This is the subject of a Department of Trade and Industry (DTI) investigation which has yet to be published. Most of the key features surrounding the case now seem to be known.

Guinness appears to be recovering quickly from the effects of the publicity. The new chief executive, Anthony Tennant, is extremely experienced in the international drinks field. He established International Distillers and Vintners as a world leader during the 15 years that he was with Grand Metropolitan. Some of the key management staff at operating level recruited by Ernest Saunders remain in place and their undoubted skills in re-establishing the brands augur well for the future. Guinness stout itself is making good sales progress in the UK market, but the outlook worldwide is very patchy, with the important Irish market remaining depressed.

FINANCIAL HISTORY

Profits in 1985/86 are not comparable with those of the previous year due to the inclusion of Distillers, acquired in April 1986, and a change in the accounting year to a December year-end. However, on a pro-forma basis, earnings per share increased from 25.2p in the year to September 1985 to 28.6p in the year to December 1986 (+13.5%).

On a pro-forma basis, 1987 pre-tax profits were up 9% to £408m on turnover down 9% to £2.818bn. Earnings per share were up 8% to 30.9p and the net dividend for the year of 9.2p was up 13%. Gearing was down from 81% to 57%. Sales and profit were affected by exchange rate fluctuations and the strengthening pound.

During 1987 the group acquired Schenley Industries, its US distributor, for £320m and disposed of several non-core businesses for £400m. Positive cash flow is running at around £200m per annum.

In 1987 spirits contributed 48% of turnover and 76% of trading profit, brewing 31% and 17%, and general commercial and discontinued businesses the balance.

The group wrote off £125m in 1986 as a provision against various liabilities arising from the Distillers bid.

SHARE PRICE HISTORY

Once the darling of the stock market under the former chairman, Ernest Saunders, the shares fell sharply following the announcement on 5 December 1986 of a DTI investigation into the affairs of the company and Ernest Saunders' subsequent dismissal. More recently, confidence has returned with the appointment of a new chief executive and a new financial director. The shares fell with the market in the October 1987 crash but have been modestly outperforming since.

SENIOR MANAGEMENT

The present chairman, Sir Norman Macfarlane, was appointed on 1 January 1987, following the termination of Ernest Saunders' employment. Two new key appointments were made in March 1987 with Anthony Tennant as group chief executive from Grand Metropolitan, and Michael Julien,

Share price and relative to FT-A All-Share

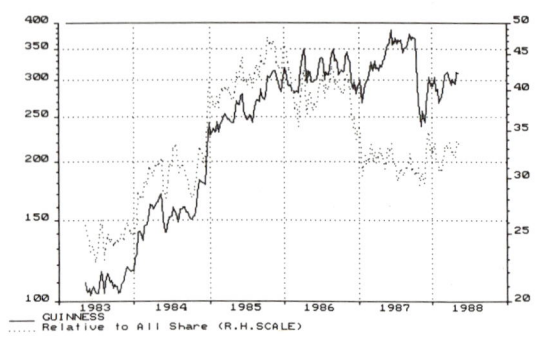

FIVE YEAR FINANCIAL INFORMATION

Year	Turnover (£m)	Pre-tax (£m)	Earnings (p)	Dividends net (p)	Dividend cover (x)	Net assets (p)	Price (p) High	Low	PER (x) High	Low	Yield (%) High	Low
1983	872.4	58.8	17.1	5.7	3.0	125	125	100	13.0	8.4	7.58	5.90
1984	923.4	70.4	20.9	6.4	3.3	124	243	116	19.6	8.6	6.53	3.48
1985	1,187.7	86.1	25.3	7.2	3.5	89	321	225	19.6	12.0	4.09	3.20
1986	3,101.0	376.0	28.6	8.2	3.5	72	353	276	16.1	10.3	4.07	2.90
1987	2,818.0	408.0	30.9	9.2	3.4	122	388	228	14.5	8.2	5.53	2.88

director of finance and administration, from Eurotunnel. In June 1988, Frank Fitzpatrick, formerly finance director of the BBC, takes over from Michael Julien.

CAPITAL

The number of ordinary shares has increased substantially as a result of acquisitions. At 1 October 1985 there were 298m shares. This was increased by the acquisitions of Arthur Bell & Sons and Distillers to 832m shares at 31 December 1987. As part consideration for the Distillers offer, 300m 5¾% convertible cumulative redeemable preference shares were issued during 1986.

GROUP REVIEW

Brewing Although the Guinness stout is sold in some 120 countries worldwide and is the product for which the company is best known, its importance in profit terms is steadily declining. The Republic of Ireland remains the largest single market and production centre. The St James's Gate brewery has seen considerable capital expenditure in recent years to bring it into the twentieth century. The Park Royal brewery in London services the home market and also produces Harp lager.

Other products, particularly Kaliber, have been launched. Kaliber is now the market leader in the UK of the non-alcoholic-beer market. Some success has been achieved in US with a range of imported beers. A production, distribution and marketing arrangement for Carlsberg in Ireland was recently announced. Other Guinness breweries were established many years ago in some of the old colonial territories. Their progress has been hit by economic and currency problems.

Brewing operating profit in 1987 was 5.7% down at £83m on turnover 4.7% down at £890m. Total beer volumes increased in the year.

Spirits Now operating under the title of United Distillers, this international business sells over 40m cases of distilled spirits annually, of which 26m are Scotch whisky. The most profitable markets in order of importance are: the US, Venezuela, Japan, UK, France and Italy.

Distillers was criticised in the past as being a production-orientated company. The objective of Guinness management is to increase the emphasis on consumer marketing. The board intends to take more control of distribution, and to work with the group's various distributors and associates around the world to further improve the company's competitive position. This is vital given the lack of growth for the distilled spirits industry in many world markets, particularly North America.

Achievements since the acquisition of Distillers in April 1986 include: the integration of bottling and blending under one management; integration of the brand companies; establishment of a worldwide sales and marketing group; closure of surplus bottling capacity; the merger of Distillers' home trade with that of Bell's; a distribution joint venture in the Far East with Moët-Hennessy; and the acquisition of several important overseas distributors including Schenley in the US, which gave the group control of the US distribution of its major brands – Dewar's and Gordon's. Guinness is now involved in the management of the distribution of 75% of the volume of its spirits sales against just 25% in 1986.

Spirits operating profit in 1987 was 10.5% up at £357m on turnover 1% down at £1.343bn.

Other Since the acquisition of Distillers, in excess of £500m has been realized from the disposal of peripheral businesses and investments. The principal disposals in 1987 were the Martin retail group, Richter Brothers in the US, Neighbourhood stores and the Drummond pharmacy group. There remain a number of small businesses including the health farm Champneys and the outstanding Gleneagles Hotel.

GEOGRAPHICAL REVIEW

In 1987 the UK accounted for 46% (48%) of group turnover, the Republic of Ireland 14% (13%), continental Europe 10% (9%), North America 15% (16%), Africa 4% (4%) and the rest

GROUP CHIEF EXECUTIVE'S STATEMENT

'On the spirits side, the year was highlighted by further moves designed to give the Group a more direct involvement in the sale and distribution of our premium brands in key international markets.

The acquisition of Schenley in the US was a major strategic move which brought us control over the distribution of Dewar's and Gordon's in the US as well as the ownership of such valuable brand properties as IW Harper, the number one bourbon in Japan, now the second largest and most rapidly growing bourbon market in the world.

We have negotiated joint venture agreements with Moët-Hennessy in the US, Japan and South East Asia. Added to our most recent agreement in France, we are now able to create a scale of operation better equipped to service our own brands in the world's most important markets.

In Japan we have acquired Caldbeck Dodwell from Inchcape. . . . Elsewhere in the Far East we are entering into a number of other joint ventures with the Caldbeck subsidiaries of Inchcape and its associates.

As a result of these agreements – and arrangements with Bacardi in Spain and West Germany, and Underberg in West Germany – over 75 per cent of our spirits volume is handled by distribution networks in which we have a direct involvement in the management. This compares with only 25 per cent a year ago.' *Anthony Tennant*

of the world 11% (10%).

In 1987 the UK accounted for 76% (75%) of operating profit, the Republic of Ireland 11% (11%), continental Europe 1% (1%), North America 7% (8%), Africa 1% (2%) and the rest of the world 4% (3%). With the acquisition of Schenley the US proportion is likely to increase in 1988.

CORPORATE CALENDAR

Year end	31 December
Preliminary results	March
Report and accounts	April
AGM	May
Final dividend paid	May
Interim results	September
Interim dividend paid	October

DIRECTORS' HOLDINGS

	Beneficial interests	Non-beneficial	Options
Earl of Iveagh	5,899,280	3,765,027	1,904
Sir Norman Macfarlane	50,000	—	—
BF Baldock	1,000	—	158,812
FI Chapman	2,000	—	—
SC Dowling	3,291	—	146,532
AA Greener	10,000	—	179,347
CE Guinness	20,808	—	5,677
Hon JB Guinness	1,509,252	122,253	—
MF Julien	—	—	177,330
IC McLaurin	1,000	—	—
Sir David Plastow	2,000	—	—
AJ Tennant	30,000	38,333	366,491

Duplications of shares included above amount to 866,560.

Total directors' renumeration in 1987 was £1.63m, of which the chairman received £197,773 and the highest-paid director £229,000.

PRINCIPAL SUBSIDIARIES AND RELATED COMPANIES

Arthur Bell & Sons Plc, Arthur Guinness Son & Co (Great Britain) Ltd, Arthur Guinness Son & Co (Dublin) Ltd – Eire, Caldbeck Dodwell – Japan, Guinness Cameroun SA – Cameroun, Guinness Malaysia Berhad – Malaysia, Guinness Nigeria Ltd (25.5%) – Nigeria, Guinness Superlatives Ltd, Irish Ale Breweries Ltd – Eire, James Buchanan & Co Ltd, John Begg Ltd, John Dewar & Sons Ltd, John Haig & Co Ltd, Peter Dawson Ltd, Scottish Grain Distillers Ltd, The Harp Lager Co Ltd (75%), United Glass Holdings Plc (50%)

BRAND NAMES

Bell's, Black & White, Booth's, Budweiser, Cardhu Malt, Carlsberg, Champneys, Cossack Vodka, Cranks, Dewar's, George Dickel Tennessee Whiskey, Funstenberg, Gleneagles Hotel, Gordon's, Guinness, Guinness Book of Records, Haig, Harp, IW Harper, Hine, Johnnie Walker, Kaliber, Kalua, Medicard, Old Fitzgerald, Pimm's, Rebel Yell, Tanqueray, Vat 69, White Horse

CONTACTS AND FURTHER INFORMATION

Simon Duffy, Director of group strategy and finance, Guinness PLC, 39 Portland Square, London W1H 9HB. Tel: 01-486 0288.

THE HAMMERSON PROPERTY INVESTMENT AND DEVELOPMENT CORPORATION plc

GENERAL INFORMATION

Head office	100 Park Lane, London W1Y 4AR. Tel: 01-629 9494
Directors	Sydney Mason FSVA (chairman and joint managing), JR Parry FRICS (joint managing), W Tindale FRICS, HR Vogt FRICS, EB Heyland MBA, RS Johnson FCIS, JMD Scott FRICS, JH Riddell LLB CA FCMA ATII. *Non-exec* RAC Mordant FCA, GD Gwilt FFA, AM Glick BS LLB JD, AS Bell FFA FPMI
Advisers	No specified adviser
Auditors	Touche Ross & Co
Registrars	Hill Samuel Registrars Ltd
Brokers	Henderson Crosthwaite Ltd, Hoare Govett Ltd
Solicitors	Herbert Smith

GENERAL FINANCIAL INFORMATION

Market capitalisation	£892.2m at 1 January 1988
Capital structure	
Issued ordinary shares (25p)	35.2m
	126.2m 'A' ordinary (limited voting)
	There is one vote per 5p of ordinary stock and one vote per 30p of 'A' ordinary limited voting stock
Issued preference shares	None
Warrants	None
Convertibles	None
Traded options	None
ADRs	None
Shareholders over 5%	Standard Life Assurance 20.3%, Australian Mutual Provident Society 7.3%

FT CATEGORY

FT: Property
FT-A: Property

MAJOR ACTIVITIES

Hammerson is the UK's third largest property investment company. Its major activities are the redevelopment and refurbishment of office and retail premises.

The group portfolio consists of an evenly balanced mixture of office and retail properties, valued at £1.62bn at the 1987 year end. The largest single property within the portfolio is the 1.5m sq ft Bow Valley Square, Calgary, Canada. The largest UK property in terms of area is the popular Brent Cross shopping centre, covering 800,000 sq ft of North London.

Together with Laing, the group is recognised as the country's leading overseas developer with an extensive and experienced foreign management team. This is reflected in the group's portfolio structure, 42% of which is based in the UK, 23% in Canada, 13% in Australia and 9% in continental Europe.

The group has also been successful at exploiting in recent years the local financial markets of the countries where it operates. The most recent example of this was a £220m multi-currency facility through a tender panel.

FINANCIAL HISTORY

Net reported assets per share stood at 650p at the 1987 year end. They were 8% higher than 1986 and 25% up since 1983. This is a key indicator for property companies. Assets represent an anticipated stream of earnings from future site development or rental income. Liquidation of a property company should in theory generate the net assets indicated.

1987 pre-tax profits for the group were 10% up at £54.3m (£49.3m), being held back by adverse currency movements. 58% of Hammerson's rental income is derived from outside the UK. Currency swings led to gross rental income being 10% lower than it would otherwise have been. Gross rental income at £124.8m was flat, affected by disposals as well as currency influences.

Property sales totalled £57.5m, with gross profits from property trading down 23% at £5.1m on 1986, a particularly good year. Earnings per share were 24% up at 23.34p (18.76p), benefiting from a low 18% tax charge. Dividends were up 9.5% to 11.5p net.

SHARE PRICE HISTORY

Hammerson's share price remained within a static trading range between 1984 and 1986 of 400p to 450p. The recent surge in UK property values, and the change in sentiment towards the property sector that went with it, enabled the share price to break well clear of its former levels to reach a peak above 700p in mid-1987.

Despite this substantial rise, the shares have underperformed the property sector by 20% over the period, mainly reflecting the group's heavy overseas exposure and the currency risks that go with it. Since the October 1987 share crash, the shares have recovered from below 400p to around 550p in spring 1988.

SENIOR MANAGEMENT

Sydney Mason is the chairman and joint managing director, together with JR Parry. JH Riddell is the finance director.

CAPITAL

Recent changes in Hammerson's share capital have occured as a result of some shareholders electing to take new shares in lieu of cash dividends and following the exercise of options by executive directors and senior staff members.

The group has also used shares to acquire minority interests in non-wholly owned subsidiaries. Declarable interests in the group's capital are held by the Standard Life Assurance Company (20.3%) and Australian Mutual Provident Society (7.3%).

GROUP REVIEW

United Kingdom Hammerson's UK investment and development activities have over recent years been concentrated mainly on the City office market. This was in response to Big Bang and the subsequent demand for substantial office complexes particularly from major overseas institutions. The

Share price and relative to FT-A All-Share

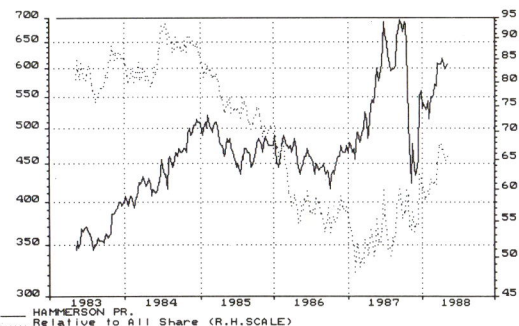

office portfolio now totals almost 2m sq ft of air conditioned floor space, a figure which is expanding rapidly.

During 1986 the group purchased the 70,000 sq ft freehold of Stone House EC2 for future refurbishment or redevelopment. A site was acquired at Tower Hill with planning permission for approximately 90,000 sq ft of offices for completion in mid-1988. Planning consents for the redevelopment of River Plate House, Finsbury Circus and Dominant House, Queen Victoria Street have been won to provide approximately 148,000 sq ft and 150,000 sq ft of offices respectively.

The UK retail properties have remained important constituents of the investment portfolio. The most significant of these is the Brent Cross shopping centre covering some 800,000 sq ft of floor space. Hammerson has recently been reviewing procedures for improving road access and building various extensions to the complex.

Canada The Canadian investment portfolio is focused on the Ontario office market. In contrast to the UK portfolio, attention has recently been concentrated on the group's retail interests. The group's main retail property in Canada is the 1.05m sq ft Square One shopping centre at Mississauga. This was reopened following a refurbishment and a 300,000 sq ft extension in August 1986. A further 300,000 sq ft extension is being developed. The centre had been virtually fully leased by the opening. This, coupled with excellent trading levels, has led the group to implement its plans to build a second phase. Phase two will start producing rental income in 1988.

Further recent events have included the finalisation of plans for the renovation and expansion of one of the Ontario office buildings to provide approximately 150,000 sq ft of new space, and the completion of the sale of the Mississauga industrial and residential land.

Australia and New Zealand The Australasian portfolio is a balanced mix of office and retail properties providing some

Year	Turnover (£m)	Pre-tax (£m)	Earnings (p)	Dividends net (p)	Dividend cover (x)	Net assets (p)	Price (p) High	Price (p) Low	PER (x) High	PER (x) Low	Yield (%) High	Yield (%) Low
1983	74.8	26.9	12.89	7.5	1.4	520	405	320	44.5	31.0	2.90	2.29
1984	109.9	33.4	14.31	8.5	1.4	602	520	392	42.0	31.2	2.73	2.20
1985	116.5	40.1	16.01	9.5	1.5	559	520	430	42.0	30.6	2.82	2.20
1986	127.8	49.3	18.76	10.5	1.6	601	495	410	34.5	24.7	3.26	2.45
1987	124.8	54.3	23.34	11.5	2.0	650	723	423	38.5	19.5	3.72	1.99

F I V E   Y E A R   F I N A N C I A L   I N F O R M A T I O N

C H A I R M A N ' S   S T A T E M E N T

'In the United Kingdom virtually all our properties are fully let and we are continuing our plans for upgrading and improving the various assets. . . . Although the generally unsatisfactory state of the local economy in Australia has not prevented us from continuing to achieve our goals of improving and extending our major assets the weakness of the Australian dollar and the exceptionally high cost of money have proved a significant deterrent to the evaluation and acquisition of new projects.' *Sydney Mason*

21% of group net rental income. This proportion would undoubtedly be higher but for the unfavourable currency translation effects caused by the persistent weakness of the Australian dollar over recent years as well as high financing costs. The company has recently acquired a listing on the Australian stock exchange.

The refurbishment programme being carried out on the company's Australian properties has continued during 1987 at Warringah Mall, Sydney, a 990,000 sq ft shopping centre, and at the 60,000 sq ft office building at 145 Eagle Street, Brisbane. In New Zealand the company has recently purchased a 19,000 sq ft freehold office building in Queen Street, Auckland.

US   The US company is relatively small as a proportion of the group, contributing approximately only 5% of net rental income. In the east, the company has been carrying out a rationalization programme which is now largely complete. The group is looking to expand modestly its interests in New York, Boston and Washington. The two Los Angeles buildings have benefited from the recent upturn in the Los Angeles office as a financial centre. The company's largest US property is the 635,000 sq ft Main Place office complex at Buffalo on the New York state border.

Continental Europe   The portfolio is made up of properties located in France, Germany and Holland. The most significant events recently have been the sale of a number of properties in Paris, acquired in the portfolio from the ICI pension fund, and the acquisition of two former department stores located in Essen and Bremen, West Germany. Between them, these two buildings should provide some 223,000 sq ft of new retail and office when redevelopment is complete in 1988.

GEOGRAPHICAL REVIEW

Hammerson's property investment portfolio is situated in five main areas of the world. They are the UK with 42% of the total, Canada with 23%, Australia 13%, US 13% and continental Europe 9%. Of these areas the UK contributes 42% to net rental income, Canada 29%, Australia 19%, the US 5% and continental Europe 5%.

CORPORATE CALENDAR

Year end	31 December
Preliminary results	April
Report and accounts	May
AGM	June
Final dividend paid	June
Interim results	October
Interim dividend paid	December

DIRECTORS' HOLDINGS

	Fully-paid ordinary shares		Options
	(beneficial)	(non-beneficial)	
S Mason	200,000	6,158,952	—
JR Parry	—	—	56,000
S Ferrada	18,705	—	—
RAC Mordant	10,400	6,158,952	—
W Tindale	—	—	80,000
NG Ellis	—	—	87,600
HR Vogt	—	—	77,000
EB Heyland	—	—	120,000
AM Glick	1,202	—	—

S Mason holds 6,158,952 ordinary shares and 315,866 'A' ordinary shares and RAC Mordant holds 6,158,952 ordinary shares and 256,290 'A' ordinary shares non-beneficially.

Total directors' remuneration in 1986/87 including fees was £752,000 of which the chairman, who was the highest-paid director, received £102,000.

PRINCIPAL SUBSIDIARIES AND RELATED COMPANIES

Casewick Properties Ltd (51%), DOB Estate Ltd (65.2%), Hammerson (Amethyst) Properties Ltd, Hammerson BV – Holland, Hammerson Europe, Hammerson GmbH – Germany, Hammerson Group Management Ltd, Hammerson Holdings (US) Inc, Hammerson (Newchat) Properties Ltd, Hammerson Property (NZ) Ltd, Hammerson Property Pty Ltd – Australia, Hammerson UK Properties Ltd, JV Holdings Ltd, Mascan Corporation – Canada, Orbisa Bassano SA – France, The Hammerson Property (West US) Corporation

BRAND NAMES

Not applicable

CONTACTS AND FURTHER INFORMATION

RS Johnson, Company Secretary, The Hammerson Property Investment and Development Corporation plc, 100 Park Lane, London W1Y 4AR. Tel: 01-629 9494.

HANSON PLC

GENERAL INFORMATION

UK head office	1 Grosvenor Place, London SW1X 7JH. Tel: 01-245 1245
US head office	410 Park Avenue, New York, NY10022. Tel: 212 759-8477
Directors: Hanson Plc	. Lord Hanson (chairman), DN Rosling (vice-chairman), AGL Alexander, HG Ashton DL, DC Bonham, ED Collins – US, A Hagdrup, BA Hellings, JH Pattisson, MG Taylor. *Non-exec* Sir Gordon Booth KCMG CVO, CGF Harding
Directors: Hanson Industries	Sir Gordon White KBE (chairman), DH Clarke (president), JG Raos (senior vice president), ED Collins (vice-president), GH Hempstead (vice-president). *Non-exec* R Reiss, CG Robinson
Advisers	NM Rothschild & Sons Ltd, J Henry Schroder Wagg & Co Ltd
Auditors	Ernst & Whinney
Registrars	Lloyds Bank Registrar's Department
Brokers	Hoare Govett Ltd, Parsons & Co Ltd
Solicitors	No specified adviser

GENERAL FINANCIAL INFORMATION

Market capitalisation	£4.59bn at 1 January 1988
Capital structure	
Issued ordinary shares (25p)	3.68bn, 4.61 m fully diluted
Issued preference shares (£1)	149.0m of 5.75% CP 2005 (74.08 ordinary shares per £100 stock)
Warrants	130m, exercisable at $18 for one ADR
Convertibles	£1058m of 10% CP 2007/12 (77.52 ordinary shares per £100 stock)
Traded options	Yes
ADRs	Five ordinary shares equal one ADR
Shareholders over 5%	None

FT CATEGORY

FT: Industrials (miscel.)
FT-A: Conglomerates

MAJOR ACTIVITIES

Hanson has developed over a twenty-four-year period to become one of the top five non-oil companies in the FT-SE 100 index, of which it accounts for 2%.

Hanson, which has developed rapidly on each side of the Atlantic, has acquired a portfolio of basic businesses, catering for everyday needs with a visible and predictable demand curve. These operations are not high-tech, nor fashion setters but relatively mature businesses that can achieve high returns and high cash flows by achieving high capacity loadings.

Typical Hanson subsidiaries are brand leaders or companies that have substantial market shares with well known brands. These include Ever Ready batteries, Players and WD & HO Wills tobacco products. Many of the companies acquired had been inefficient and under-managed. Much of Hanson's growth has come from instituting sound management and strict financial controls rather than expanding already mature markets.

In 1986 Hanson successfully took over Imperial Group in the UK and SCM in the US. Extremely successful disposals were made of constituent companies that Hanson did not wish to retain, including Courage the brewers. Cash from disposals has always formed part of the group's acquisition philosophy.

Major events in 1987 were the successful integration of Kaiser Cement and the purchase of Kidde, both in the US. Since purchasing Kaiser Cement, Hanson has already achieved more than the price it paid through three disposals.

There is speculation that Hanson would like to realise cash from its UK interests. Ross Young's frozen foods was sold to United Biscuits for £335m in March 1988. Other possibilities are Crabtree and Ever Ready.

FINANCIAL HISTORY

Hanson has well outstripped the UK and US growth averages but the underlying growth rate is now slowing. Between 1982 and 1987 Hanson has achieved a compound growth rate of pre-tax profits of over 51% per annum compared with UK and US market averages of 11% and 3.5% respectively. Earnings per share have grown 38% and dividends 30% per annum over the same period. These results have been achieved not in industries that are in any sense glamorous or high risk, or even participate in fast expanding markets, but by the efficient streamlined management of basic businesses.

Without acquisitions, Hanson's growth rate would have been much more pedestrian than with its history of a string of hitherto successful purchases. This is not to denigrate the underlying performance but to stress the management's success in identifying investment opportunities that can enhance the group's earnings growth.

Including the $1.7bn cash acquisition of Kidde, a US conglomerate, acquisitions have cost £3.1bn in the UK and $3.6bn in the US since 1981, whilst disposals have yielded £2.85bn. Businesses acquired for a net £1.5bn should yield £540m pre-tax this year.

The return on capital employed and the net return on equity has improved consistently, helped by the prudent practice of writing off goodwill.

Pre-tax profits in 1987 jumped 60% to £741m on turnover 55% up at £6.6bn. Earnings per share increased by 31% to 14p, while dividends went up 38% to 4.4p per share. But, adjusting totals for the full effect of acquisitions which contributed only partly to 1986's results, and the effects of a weaker dollar, the underlying growth at the operating level is estimated at some 12%.

The practice of buying UK businesses for equity and selling peripheral operations for cash meant that before the Kidde acquisition, Hanson was cash rich. After Kidde, it became a net 50% geared on a diminished shareholders' funds base, following the extinction of Kidde's £612m of goodwill. Hanson purchased Kidde for £930m, and took on with the acquisition a further £280m of debt. But, with the conversion of the 8% convertible loan stock in March 1988, the Ross Young's and other disposals and cash flow, Hanson is likely to be net cash positive by the middle of 1988.

SHARE PRICE HISTORY

The share price outperformed the FT-A All-Share index by 150% from the beginning of 1982 to the end of 1984, with the share price moving from 20p to 120p.

However, apart from a period in late 1986, the shares since then have been in relative decline to the index, moving from

C H A I R M A N ' S   S T A T E M E N T

'Firm British government policies over the last eight years have enabled UK companies to flourish in the healthy economic climate of lower inflation, lower taxation and encouragement of business enterprise. We rank seventh in the UK corporate order and, as Hanson increases in size, so do our opportunities for continued growth. The outlook for your company is excellent and we look forward to further challenges. Your directors are unanimous in their confidence in the company's future.' *Lord Hanson*

F I V E Y E A R F I N A N C I A L I N F O R M A T I O N												
Year	Turnover (£m)	Pre-tax (£m)	Earnings (p)	Dividends net (p)	Dividend cover (x)	Net assets (p)	Price (p) High	Low	PER (x) High	Low	Yield (%) High	Low
1983	1,484	91.1	5.5	1.2	4.6	25.2	67	43	20.7	16.2	3.87	2.60
1984	2,382	169.1	8.1	1.8	4.5	23.7	126	60	25.1	16.8	2.92	1.90
1985	2,675	252.8	11.0	2.4	4.6	39.5	131	101	23.1	15.8	3.33	2.00
1986	4,312	464.0	11.2	3.2	3.5	40.8	160	106	22.0	14.1	3.89	2.63
1987	6,682	741.0	15.2	4.4	3.5	48.4	193	113	17.5	8.7	5.02	2.51

20% of the index in early 1985 to below 16% in late February 1988, a 20% underperformance.

The factors responsible for this underperformance may include an overhang of shares and convertible stock issued to help fund acquisitions and stock from earlier rights issues.

In the October 1987 share crash, the shares fell from the 180p level to below 115p, before recovering to the 130p level in late April 1988.

SENIOR MANAGEMENT

The senior management structure is unusual in the sense that the UK and US operations function independently without main board representation for Sir Gordon White, who runs the US operation, on the UK board. There are two boards of directors, one for Hanson PLC and one for Hanson Industries in the US. Only one man, ED Collins, sits on both.

For Hanson PLC Lord Hanson is chairman, with D Rosling as vice-chairman. The executive directors include A Hagdrup, B Hellings, M Taylor, A Alexander, J Pattisson, D Bonham, E Collins and H Ashton. Non-executive directors include C Hardin and Sir Gordon Booth.

On the US side Sir Gordon White is the chairman with D Clarke as president. The executive directors include E Collins, J Raos and G Hempstead, while the non-executive directors are R Reiss and C Robinson.

CAPITAL

Hanson had 3.68bn ordinary shares in issue in March 1988. If all the convertible stocks and warrants were converted, the fully diluted share capital would be 4.735bn shares. The 8% convertible loan stock was fully converted into equity in March 1988.

US acquisitions have always been funded by cash, either from Hanson's own resources or by US bank borrowings. In the UK acquisitions have been for a mixture of convertible share issues and cash.

The most notable acquisitions since 1983 have been Ever Ready, Imperial Group, SCM, Kaiser Cement and Kidde. Hanson has raised £1.37bn from convertible preference shares and convertible bonds.

GROUP REVIEW

The major single event of 1987 was Hanson's acquisition of Kidde in November 1987 for £930m in cash, with accompanying debt of £280m.

The consituents of Kidde are: the old-established Kidde Fire Protection Company; Weber Aircraft, makers of aircraft interiors and seating; Grove Crane; Farberware, cookware products; a number of recreation companies; Jacuzzi; and lighting and office supply companies. It is thought that Hanson would like to sell the Weber Aircraft division of Kidde.

Hanson bought Kidde at the top of the market. However, Hanson's skills in achieving high disposal values from its assets should never be underestimated.

UK consumer The Imperial Tobacco cigarette subsidiary in the UK was the largest domestic cigarette company, with a production capacity of 30bn cigarettes a year, but has now slipped into second place. In 1987 Imperial Tobacco accounted for 19% of pre-tax profit.

Estimated market share has fallen from 41% to 35% since 1984. Substantial overhead reductions are being achieved, particularly on the marketing front, accompanied by substantial profit demands which have yet to materialise. Brands include the Players and WD & HO Wills portfolios.

Ever Ready is by volume the largest dry battery producer in the UK, with a 72% share in the zinc carbon and a rising 27% share in the alkaline manganese battery markets respectively. It has supplemented its product range by producing a complementary range of handlamps, bicycle lamps and torches.

The group's department store chain has 12 UK outlets, occupying 1.7m sq ft. Through Allders, Hanson is the largest operator of duty free stores at UK ports and airports. It also runs the *QE2* and *Canberra* cruise concessions and has expanded into Canada and the US.

Divisional trading profits in 1987 were up 112.5% to £3.4bn on turnover 120% up at £207m.

UK building products Hanson is the world's largest brick maker through London Brick and Butterley Brick. A buoyant market, efficiency gains, quality improvements and a recent price rise all contributed to a good 1987 performance. The division has, however, been constrained by a lack of capacity but will be helped in 1988 by a useful price increase. The other major company in the division is Crabtree Electrical Industries, makers of wiring accessories and circuit breakers.

Divisional trading profits in 1987 were up 17.7% at £73m on turnover up 3.8% at £246m.

UK industrial Hanson manufactures a wide range of engineered products including automotive parts, meters, fuel effect fires, rubber components and mobile accommodation units for the UK market.

Companies include Lindustries, makers of automotive heaters and air conditioning units; Smiths Meters, makers of gas meters and central heating control units; Robinson Willey, manufacturers of Magicoal gas fires; Barbour Campbell, makers of fine linen yarn; and Rollalong portable accommodation units.

Divisional trading profits in 1987 were 73.4% up at £85m on turnover 24.8% up at £387m.

UK food Imperial Foods, in its first full year as part of Hanson, achieved a strong profits advance, and an improved return on capital. Hanson sold its Ross Young's subsidiary to United Biscuits in March 1988 for £335m. Other operations include Lea & Perrins, HP sauces and baked beans, Elizabeth

Shaw chocolates and confectionery, and the Seven Seas range of fish oil and vitamin supplement health foods.

Divisional trading profits in 1987 were 90.9% up on turnover 131.5% up at £623m.

US consumer The Smith Corona typewriter unit takes over 50% of the US portable typewriter market. With a streamlined product range, including a new word processor, and production facilities, the company is recovering strongly helped by the disadvantages placed on Japanese exports by a strong yen. New products are expected.

Carisbrook produces a range of speciality textiles and where possible concentrates on the upper end of the market nationally or mid-price bracket where it has a substantial market share in a defined region.

In footwear, Endicott Johnson is an integrated manufacturer, wholesaler and retailer of hoes and boots in the mid-price bracket. Results have been disappointing and the company is for sale.

Divisional 1987 trading profits were 4.8% up on turnover 0.4% down at £528m.

US building products Through USI Lighting, Hanson is the third largest lighting company in the world. Recently the operation has suffered from soggy conditions in the commercial property market.

Building supplies manufactured include wooden doors, windows and mouldings, timber, concrete blocks and aluminium doors and windows. The division's performance is geared to the US housing market.

Share price and relative to FT-A All-Share

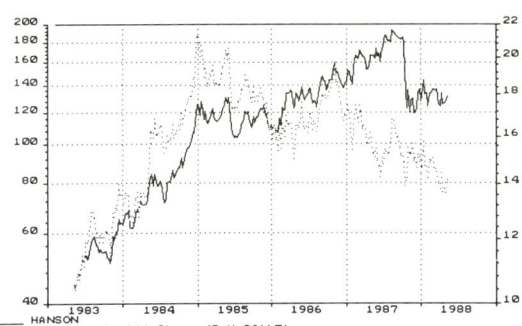

Building products benefited from nine months' inclusion of Kaiser Cement, California's largest cement producer. Profitability has been improved by cutting costs and increasing efficiency. It is thought to have contributed $20m to the period. Disposals have more than paid for the acquisition and still left Hanson with 50% of Kaiser's capacity.

Divisional trading profits in 1987 were 39.6% up on turnover 18.2% up at £500m.

US industrial SCM Chemicals is the world's third largest producer of titanium dioxide. Currently there is an industry capacity shortfall and the price is rising, although some industry observers see an oversupply by 1990. SCM is commissioning a new plant and converting the remaining plant to the more efficient chloride process. The immediate outlook is excellent.

Hanson's office furniture operation is the second largest US manufacturer under the Office Group America holding company. Though 1987 was a disappointing year, return on capital employed is estimated to exceed 60%.

Other products include oil industry related equipment and

moulded plastics. The outlook is mixed. Trading profits for the division in 1987 were 3.8% up at £81m on turnover 18.8% up at £620m.

US food Through its subsidiary Hygrade, Hanson is the second largest producer of hams, bacon and frankfurters in the US, selling under the Grillmaster and Ball Park brands. The Durkee subsidiary produces a wide range of frozen bakery products, coatings and vegetable oils. Improvements in service and food quality have resulted in increased sales and record profits at Ground Round's moderately priced, family-style restaurants.

Trading profits for the division increased 50% to £21m on turnover up 20.4% to £408m.

Financial income In 1987 financial income, including an estimated £60m of revenue gains, contributed £114m, 15.3% of trading profits. In the current environment such gains may not be repeatable. Hanson is likely to be nursing significant losses on its Midland Bank and Morgan Grenfell stakes.

GEOGRAPHICAL REVIEW

In 1986, 54% of operating profit arose in the UK, but the impact of the Imperial Group acquisition raised this to 65% in 1987. As Kidde should just cover the financing costs until such time as some disposal proceeds flow in, in a less fertile environment for disposals, this acquisition is unlikely to change the picture radically. The long term aim is for 50% of profits to occur on each side of the Atlantic.

CORPORATE CALENDAR

Year end	30 September
Preliminary results	December
Report and accounts	December
AGM	January
Final dividend paid	February
Quarterly figures	Feb, August
Interim results	May
Interim dividend paid	July

DIRECTORS' HOLDINGS

	Fully-paid ordinary shares		Options
	(beneficial)	(non-beneficial)	
Lord Hanson	12,349,618	—	1,605,797
DN Rosling	259,498	—	1,039,523
BA Hellings	586,273	12,982	1,778,748
A Hagdrup	500,000	—	542,998
MG Taylor	306,080	—	640,824
AGL Alexander	621,802	15,429	552,998
CGF Harding	47,333	—	220,373
JH Pattisson	190,500	15,000	428,500
DC Bonham	335,000	—	783,549
Sir Gordon Booth	188,280	—	356,143
ED Collins	173,805	—	553,628
HG Ashton	—	—	115,233

Total directors' remuneration in 1987 was £6m, of which the chairman received £1.26m.

PRINCIPAL SUBSIDIARIES AND RELATED COMPANIES

UK
Allders Ltd, British Ever Ready Ltd, Butterley Brick Ltd, Hanson Engineering Ltd, Imperial Foods Ltd, Imperial Tobacco Ltd, Lindustries Ltd, London Brick Company Ltd, SLD/Barbour Campbell

US
Allied Paper Products Inc, Carisbrook Industries Inc, Durkee Foods Corporation, Endicott Johnson Corporation, Ground Round Inc, Hanson Building Products, Hygrade Food Products Corporation, Kaiser Cement Corporation, Kidde Inc, Office Group America, SCM Chemicals Inc, SCM Chemicals Ltd – UK, Smith Corona Corporation, Smith-Corona Inc, USI Furniture, USI Lighting

HAWKER SIDDELEY GROUP PLC

BRAND NAMES

AS Tool, Allders, Ball Park frankfurters, Castella, Castella Classic, Durkee, Embassy, Ever Ready, Gold Block, Golden Virginia, Grill Master, Ground Rounds restaurants, HP Baked Beans, HP Sauce, Henri Wintermans, Hofels, Hygrade frankfurters, Jacuzzi, John Player's Specials, Lambert & Butler, Lambert & Butler 100's, Lea & Perrins, New Era, Panama, Player's No 6, Regal, Regal 100's, Ross, Seven Seas, Smith Corona typewriters, St Bruno, Superkings, Tom Thumb, WD & HO Wills, West Virginia hams

CONTACTS AND FURTHER INFORMATION

Martin Taylor, Hanson PLC, 1 Grosvenor Place, London SW1X 7JH. Tel: 01-589 7070.

GENERAL INFORMATION

Head office 18 St James's Square, London SW1Y 4LJ. Tel: 01-930 6177
Directors Sir Peter Baxendell CBE (chairman), BR Bensly (managing director and chief executive), Sir Lindsay Alexander, BM Bonfield, DG Bury FCA, Sir James Hamilton KCB MBE, Q Hazell CBE, M Parkinson, TWB Sallitt, RA Willford, Sir Rowland Wright CBE
Advisers SG Warburg & Co Ltd
Auditors Price Waterhouse
Registrars Lloyds Bank Registrar's Department
Brokers Cazenove & Co
Solicitors Simmons & Simmons

GENERAL FINANCIAL INFORMATION

Market capitalisation	£873.0m at 1 January 1988
Capital structure	
Issued ordinary shares (25p)	197.05m
Issued preference shares (£1)	6.0m 5.5% CP
Warrants	None
Convertibles	None
Traded options	None
ADRs	One ordinary share for each ADR
Shareholders over 5%	None

FT CATEGORY

FT: Engineering
FT-A: Electricals

MAJOR ACTIVITIES

Hawker Siddeley is a major UK-based international electrical and mechanical engineering group, which focuses on the manufacture and sale of electric motors, generators, electrical transmission equipment and systems, diesel engines, primary and secondary batteries, railway equipment and power systems, electric motors, drives and electrical transmission systems.

Latterly the group has built up a position in controls and instrumentation, and has also increased its involvement in aerospace overseas. Its UK aerospace interests were nationalised in 1977 to form part of British Aerospace. Its aeronautical history included making the Hurricane fighter and Lancaster bomber.

The principal markets for its main products are the transport, mining, industrial process and factory automation, defence, mineral extraction and electricity generating industries. Hawker is also active in providing basic infrastructure such as irrigation and water treatment for Third World government projects.

The group largely produces intermediate goods – products that are mainly incorporated into complete systems or manufactured goods supplied to end-users by other organisations.

The principal influences on its business are industrial investment, especially in power generation, transport and mining, and the growth of Third World economies, particularly members of the Organisation of Petroleum Exporting Countries (OPEC).

It has no single competitor across its entire product range. In the UK, the nearest are GEC's non-electronic interests and NEI, while the German company Klöckner-Humboldt-Deutz is a major international competitor.

FINANCIAL HISTORY

Turnover reached £1.743bn in the year to December 1987, up 8.4% on the 1986 figure, and has compounded at an annual rate of around 3% since 1982. US acquisitions continue to be a

FIVE YEAR FINANCIAL INFORMATION

Year	Turnover (£m)	Pre-tax (£m)	Earnings (p)	Dividends net (p)	Dividend cover (x)	Net assets (p)	Price (p) High	Price (p) Low	PER (x) High	PER (x) Low	Yield (%) High	Yield (%) Low
1983	1,457	137.5	43.0	11.0	3.9	393.9	406	270	16.0	8.8	5.19	3.27
1984	1,524	143.0	41.6	11.8	3.5	441.0	474	352	15.8	9.3	4.13	3.28
1985	1,592	160.3	48.8	14.5	3.4	414.0	461	361	13.2	8.2	4.67	3.52
1986	1,608	152.0	44.3	17.0	2.6	385.0	619	406	14.8	9.1	5.20	2.84
1987	1,743	163.2	48.5	18.5	2.6	400.0	630	385	14.0	8.5	6.23	3.70

positive influence.

Pre-tax profits in 1987 rose 7.3% to £163.2m, partly due to increased demand for diesel engines, a sector where profits more than halved in 1986.

Since 1982, pre-tax profit growth has averaged 6% a year. This included earnings setbacks in 1982 and 1986, with strong growth in between when profits rose by 11% a year. The main overall reason for the relatively limited growth was the diesel side of the business, where profits fell sharply, until recovering significantly in 1987.

Earnings per share in 1986 fell 10% to 44.3p while the dividend was increased from 14.5p to 17.0p net. In 1987, earnings per share increased by 9.5% to 48.5p while the dividend increased by 12.5% to 13.5p.

The balance sheet remains strong despite expenditure of £120m in 1986 on acquisitions, financed by cash. At the 1986 year-end, cash and short-term investments of £263m exceeded loans, overdrafts and debentures by £46m. £66m was spent on acquisitions in 1987, but there was a positive cash flow in the year, to leave cash net of long debt at £46m at the year end. Pre-tax margins of 9.4% in 1987 were almost 1% higher than in 1982.

SHARE PRICE HISTORY

Since 1982, the Hawker Siddeley share price has markedly underperformed the FT-A All-Share index, with its relative price falling from a peak of 108% to 56% in early May 1988.

The major influence on Hawker Siddeley has been the lacklustre earnings performance, which has been substantially less in growth terms than that of other UK quoted industrials. The 1987 profits, however, were well received and the shares started to outperform.

The shares fell from above 600p to below 400p in the October 1987 share crash, before recovering to 520p in early May 1988. The asset value at December 1987 was 400p.

Share price and relative to FT-A All-Share

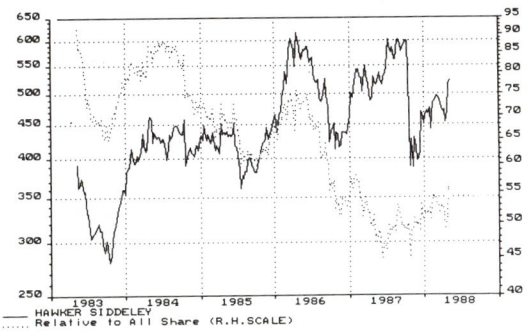

SENIOR MANAGEMENT

The current chairman is Sir Peter Baxendell who succeeded Sir Arnold Hall in the position. Sir Peter is also a director of Shell Transport & Trading, and Inchcape. R Bensly was appointed managing director in March 1984, having previously been responsible for the group's diesel engines business, and its major Australian interests. At the same time J Durber was promoted to deputy managing director. D Bury was appointed group finance director in March 1986, having been group chief accountant. The non-executive directors are Sir Lindsay Alexander, Sir James Hamilton, Q Hazell and Sir Rowland Wright.

CAPITAL

The total number of shares in issue is 197.05m, unchanged since 1982. This unusual state of affairs arises from the group's ability to generate cash and its preference to make cash acquisitions.

In 1986, the group purchased no less than thirteen companies for £120m, paying considerations of between $3.1m and $59.7m entirely in cash. In 1987, the group spent £66m on further acquisitions. There have also been a smaller number of disposals in the period.

There are no holdings above 5% and no significant directors' holdings.

GROUP REVIEW*

Major operations are grouped into electric motors and generators, electrical distribution and controls, electrical specialised equipment, diesel engineering, mechanical specialised equipment and other trading activities.

Electric motors and generators The division produces some 12m motors and generators each year. Applications are as varied as office machines and cement kiln drives for motors, while generators up to 150 megawatts are produced for all types of prime mover.

In small machines, Fasco Industries is continuing to expand. It is one of the largest companies in its sector in the US. Integration of Torin Engineered Blowers computer-related applications is extending the group's coverage in the US.

Brush Electrical Machines has been particularly successful in exporting large turbo alternators to General Electric in the US, and to Japanese and Middle East customers.

The division registered pre-tax profits of £26.6m in 1987, up 19.8% on 1986. Turnover was 5.4% up at £232m. Both small and large motor businesses are performing well, although the exposure of the former to the dollar is reducing profits on translation.

Electrical distribution and controls Products of this division range from the fuselink, a complete power complex with switchgear, transformers and cables, through to sensitive instrumentation, or sophisticated computer-controlled monitoring systems.

Daytronic Corporation, which specialises in measurement and control instrumentation, was bought for $22.5m. Electro Corporation, which makes motion, presence and position-sensing components, was acquired for $10m. This is a real growth area and profits will continue to advance strongly.

The US acquisitions are performing particularly well, and a big increase in orders is expected from the Middle East. Dollar weakness, however, could blunt the impact of these companies in sterling terms in 1988. Despite this, management has clearly identified this as a worthy area of expansion, capable of good future growth.

Pre-tax profit increased to £40.2m, up 18.2% from £34m, during 1987 as sound progress was made in the heavy business, with improved efficiency and good volumes. 1987 turnover rose 22% to £460m.

CHAIRMAN'S STATEMENT

'Our aim has been to restructure the Group towards a faster rate of growth and to do this not by further diversification, but by building on our existing strength in those areas of business where we see greatest growth potential. The acquisition policy has reflected this aim, and over the last two years we have spent nearly £200m on acquiring companies which have been based mainly in the light electrical areas, instruments and controls and aerospace.' *Sir Peter Baxendell*

Electrical specialised equipment The division is built around electro-chemical technology, electrical railway equipment and power conditioning products. The battery activities form a major sub-grouping, and places Hawker Siddeley as the largest manufacturer of batteries in Europe.

The battery business which represents a substantial part of the division's turnover, performed well during 1986 and 1987 with good progress in both rechargeable and primary businesses.

A 93.6% holding in Power Conversion was acquired in July 1986 for £60m. The company is a pioneer of lithium battery technology for which there is increasing demand from the defence sector.

An important feature of the rail equipment businesses has been the growth in rail traction orders, and a strong advance is expected in this area in 1988. Major subsidiaries include Westinghouse Signals (railway signalling systems and equipment and automatic train control equipment), Brush Traction (diesel electric locomotives, rail traction power equipment and control gear) and Dimetronic (a Spanish railway signalling and automation systems company).

Pre-tax profits amounted to £30.6m in 1987, up 9.7% on turnover up 15.1% at £335m.

Diesel engineering Hawker Siddeley diesel engines have applications ranging from British Rail's InterCity 125 High Speed Train to standby diesel generators for hospitals and computer installations.

As an immediate consequence of the 1986/87 oil price fall, OPEC demand for small diesels for agricultural pumping applications slumped. This forced the UK operation into loss as exports dwindled. Domestic UK and European sales were also affected, because many of Hawker Siddeley's customers addressed Middle East markets. In 1987, however, diesel engineering recovered strongly.

Onan Corporation, 37%-owned by Hawker Siddeley, returned to profit in 1986 and 1987 after heavy losses in 1985. Development and manufacture of the L range of diesels ceased, thereby stopping a significant drain of resources.

There are signs that the small diesel market has now bottomed out. Strong growth is being experienced in European sales. The introduction of a new engine range by Lister-Petter in 1988 will aid this sector.

This division experienced a sharp increase in pre-tax profits in 1987 to £13.7m, up 90.3% on turnover up 1.3% at £154m.

Mechanical specialised equipment The residue of Hawker Siddeley's aerospace interests sits alongside its mechanical railway equipment and mining equipment activities in this division. The group has significant interests in Australia and the Pacific Rim in higher added-value aerospace support services, component manufacture and marketing activities.

Weakness in the Canadian and Australian dollars has had a significant impact on this division's profitability, which has also been affected by the depressed Canadian rail freight market. The Trenton Works freight cars operation has had bad years, and an agreement to sell the company to Lavalin Trenton Works Inc was concluded in March 1988.

In other areas, agriculture has recovered somewhat, while mining staged an upturn following the miners' strike. Reduced demand from British Coal during 1987 was evident, however. Aerospace turnover is substantial, principally from Australia and Canada.

This division recorded a trading profit of £40.6m for 1987, down 6.9% on turnover down 2.1% at £504m.

Other trading activities The units in this sector comprise retail stores, thermoplastic sheeting, whisky distilling and timber products.

Invergordon Distillers, 65%-owned, continues to do well. In 1986 it acquired three new whiskies – The Original Mackinlay, the Isle of Jura and Glayva.

In 1987 profits rose 12.6% to £10.7m on turnover 9.4% up at £58m.

GEOGRAPHICAL REVIEW

The UK accounted for 34% of group sales in 1986, with about 33% of that supplied to UK customers for export in the form of complete products. The US represents 20% of sales, as a result of recent acquisitions, while Australia represents 13% of sales, following the acquisition of the Commonwealth Aircraft Corporation. Hawker Siddeley's exposure to the Far East and Europe, at 7% and 8% respectively, has shown the strongest growth.

Hawker Siddeley is experiencing strong growth outside the UK, with the US leading the way. European business is growing, and orders from OPEC are reviving. These trends can offset any possible weakness in the US. Hawker Siddeley's general niche orientation is in any event a strong defensive influence.

CORPORATE CALENDAR

Year end	31 December
Preliminary results	April
Report and accounts	May
AGM	June
Final dividend paid	July
Interim results	October
Interim dividend paid	December

DIRECTORS' HOLDINGS

	Fully-paid ordinary shares	Options
Sir Lindsay Alexander	1,000	—
Sir Peter Baxendell	5,000	—
BR Bensly	200	38,111
BM Bonfield	2,500	19,420
DG Bury	200	13,644
JM Durber	200	25,245
Sir James Hamilton	500	—
Q Hazell	2,000	—
M Parkinson	2,000	17,160
TWB Sallitt	200	20,473
RA Willford	200	18,798
Sir Rowland Wright	2,000	—

Total directors' remuneration for 1986 was £1.05m, of which the chairman received £50,671 and the highest-paid director £106,345.

PRINCIPAL SUBSIDIARIES AND RELATED COMPANIES

Electric motors and generators
Brook Control Gear Ltd, Brook Crompton Parkinson Motors Ltd, Brook Crompton Parkinson Pty Ltd – Australia, Brush Electrical Machines Ltd, Crompton Greaves Ltd – India (37.5%), Fasco Industries Inc – US, Hawker Siddeley Electric Africa Pty Ltd – South Africa, Kirkloskar Electric Co Ltd – India (20.3%), Torin Ltd

Electrical distribution and controls
A&M Instrument Inc – US, Aluminium Wire & Cable Co Ltd, Brush Fusegear Ltd, Brush Fuses Inc – US, Brush Switchgear Ltd, Brush Transformers Ltd, Cables and Plastics Ltd, Crompton Metermaster Inc – US, Crompton Parkinson Cables Ltd, Crompton Parkinson Instruments Ltd, Daytronic Corporation – US, Elmwood Sensors Inc – US, Elmwood Sensors Ltd, Fasco Controls Corp – US, Hawker Siddeley Dynamics Engineering Ltd, Hawker Siddeley Electric Africa Pty Ltd – South Africa, Hawker Siddeley Engineering Pty Ltd – Australia, Hawker Siddeley Power Transformers Ltd, Hawker Siddeley Switchgear Pty Ltd – Australia, Meters & Instruments Corporation – US, South Wales Electric Pvt Ltd – Zimbabwe, South Wales Switchgear Ltd, South Wales Transformers Division, Westinghouse Systems Ltd

Electrical specialised equipment
Brush Electrical Machines Ltd, Crompton Batteries Ltd, Crompton Lighting Ltd, Crompton Stud Welding Ltd, Crompton Vidor Ltd, Dimetronic SA – Spain (80.5%), KW Battery Co – US, Oldham-Crompton Batteries Ltd, Oldham France SA, Power Conversion Inc – US (93.6%), PowerTech Inc – US, Safetran Systems Corporation – US, Tungstone Batteries Ltd, Uniross Batteries Ltd (70%), Westcode Semiconductors Ltd, Westinghouse Brake & Signal Co – Australia (85%), Westinghouse Davenset Rectifiers Ltd, Westinghouse Signals Ltd

Diesel engineering
Hawker Siddeley Power Plant Ltd, Lister-Petter Ltd, Mirrlees Blackstone (Stamford) Ltd, Mirrlees Blackstone (Stockport) Ltd, Onan Corporation – US (37.1%)

Mechanical specialised equipment
Bunnings Ltd – Australia (25%), CGTX Inc – Canada (55%), Can-Car Division – Canada, Canadian Steel Foundries Division, Canadian Steel Wheel Division, Dosco Overseas Engineering Ltd, Gardiner & Sons & Co Ltd, HD Forgings Ltd, Hawker de Havilland Ltd – Australia (70%), Hawker Pacific Pty Ltd – Australia, Hawker Siddeley Brackett Ltd, Hawker Siddeley Water Engineering Ltd, Hollybank Engineering Co Ltd, Kockums CanCar Corp – US (80%), Lister Shearing Equipment Ltd, Noyes Bros Pty Ltd – Australia, Orenda Division – Canada, Petter Refrigeration Ltd, The Dosco Corp – US, Tree Farmer Equipment Company Inc – US, Westcode Inc – US, Westinghouse Brakes & Signal Co – Australia (85%), Westinghouse Brakes Ltd, Westinghouse Foundry Ltd

Other trading activities
Gardiner Sons & Co Ltd, Invergordon Distillers (Holdings) Plc (65%)

Related companies
Bunnings Ltd – Australia (25%), Crompton Greaves Ltd – India (37.5%), Kirloskar Electric Co Ltd – India (20.3%), Lister Blackstone de Colombia SA – Colombia (44.1%), Onan Corporation – US (37.1%), Salister Diesels Pty Ltd – South Africa (35%)

BRAND NAMES

Brush, Crompton, Crompton Parkinson, Daytronic, Gardiner Sons & Co, Glayva, Hawker, Hawker Siddeley, Isle of Jura, Oldham, The Original Mackinlay, Vidor, Westinghouse

CONTACTS AND FURTHER INFORMATION

Charles D Hewitt, Hawker Siddeley Group PLC, 18 St James's Square, London SW1Y 4LJ. Tel: 01-930 6177.

HILLSDOWN HOLDINGS plc

GENERAL INFORMATION

Head office	Hillsdown House, 32 Hampstead High Street, London NW3 1QD. Tel: 01-794 0677
Directors	H Solomon (chairman), JA Jackson FCA (deputy chairman), K O'Sullivan FCA, A Brice, BC Legg FCCA ATII, DA Newton. *Non-exec* DB Thompson
Advisers	Kleinwort Benson Ltd
Auditors	Jayson Arnold & Fowell, Peat Marwick McLintock
Registrars	Lloyds Bank Registrar's Department
Brokers	Hoare Govett Ltd, Warburg Securities Ltd
Solicitors	Herbert Smith

GENERAL FINANCIAL INFORMATION

Market capitalisation	£1.186bn at 1 January 1988
Capital structure	
Issued ordinary shares (10p)	411m
Issued preference shares (£1)	None
Warrants	None
Convertibles	£150m 4.5% ESC 2002 (convertible at 240.385 ordinary shares per £1,000 bond)
Traded options	None
ADRs	One ADR equals four ordinary shares
Shareholders over 5%	Government of Kuwait Investment Office 7.5%, DB Thompson and family 14.7%

FT CATEGORY

FT: Food, groceries, etc
FT-A: Food manufacturing

MAJOR ACTIVITIES

Hillsdown Holdings is one of the fastest growing companies in the UK with activities in many different sectors. It is primarily involved in food production and processing, but also has substantial interests in furniture, timber, stationery, property, travel and house building. The company was incorporated in 1975 and by 1987 had achieved an annual turnover of over £3bn and pre-tax profits of over £110m. It employs more than 40,000 workers.

Hillsdown seems to have an insatiable appetite for acquisitions and is not afraid of diversifying into completely new areas. Central to the group's success is its ability to identify and acquire sound and profitable businesses. It is also successful in turning round loss-making or marginally profitable operations by motivating middle management and by unlocking inherent potential within the business. Hillsdown regards the development of subsidiaries as fundamental to the future of the group.

A characteristic of the group has often been its periodic high level of gearing. However, it is both adept at financing its acquisitions and also generates strong cash flow. The stock market has been broadly pleased with the group's history as a public company since 1983. No doubt the group will continue to expand both organically and by acquisition.

FINANCIAL HISTORY

In 1987 group turnover rose 78% to £3.038bn and pre-tax profits more than doubled to £110.3m. Pre-tax margins registered a rise from 3.2% to 3.6%.

Earnings per share improved by 35% to 22.0p and dividends per share increased by 25% to 4.75p. Shareholders' funds increased by 8.9% to £383.3m. The group generates strong cash flow and in 1988 gearing is likely to reduce from the 1987 year end level of 100%.

£600m was spent in 1987 on new capital projects and the acquisition of more than 50 new businesses. £400m of this was provided from the company's own cash resources, the balance from an ordinary share and a convertible bond issue.

Since 1983 turnover has increased more than fourfold and pre-tax profits by over eightfold. Earnings per share have risen nearly threefold from 5.6p in 1983 to 22p in 1987. Dividends have increased by no less than 4,650% from 0.1p in 1983 to 4.75p in 1987.

SHARE PRICE HISTORY

Hillsdown was floated on the stock market in early 1985 via a tender offer. Its debut proved a major success with the striking price of the tender put at 40% above the minimum tender price. Since then, after an initial lull, the price has climbed rapidly to a peak of 358p, more than two and a half times higher than the adjusted price on the first day of dealings.

Hillsdown's policy of organic growth supplemented by continual acquisitions has led to a sharply rising profit trend resulting in a share that has gained a wide following. While the pace of growth has at times been quite hectic, Hillsdown's results have generally exceeded consensus forecasts. This has helped to maintain a high rating for the shares.

The share price fell from 358p to 214p during the autumn 1987 crash, but had recovered to 299p by the beginning of March 1988. In relative terms the shares were again outperforming after a neutral period from mid-1986.

SENIOR MANAGEMENT

David Thompson and Harry Solomon founded the group in 1975 and acted as joint chairmen until April 1987, when David Thompson stepped down to become a non-executive director. At this time, Mr Thompson and his wife sold 55.4m shares in Hillsdown, half their holding, to leave their stake at 14.7%.

John Jackson joined Hillsdown in 1976 as chief accountant. He became group finance director in 1977. Since January 1988 he has been deputy chairman. Tony Brice was appointed to the board in September 1986. He is chairman of Cartwright Brice, the stationery and paper merchanting business which became part of Hillsdown in 1981.

Barry Legg, company secretary since 1982, became a director in September 1986. David Newton was appointed to the board in September 1986, after becoming managing director of Buxted in 1984. Kevin O'Sullivan became Hillsdown's finance director on 1 January 1988.

CAPITAL

When Hillsdown was floated in February 1985, the issued share capital was 189m ordinary shares. At the end of 1986 the issued capital had risen to 391m. There was a one for three capitalisation issue in October 1986 at which time Hillsdown placed an additional 82.5m shares to raise £161m. Since then a further 23m shares have been issued to partially fund some of the more than 50 acquisitions undertaken by the group in 1987.

CHAIRMAN'S STATEMENT

'The continued internal development and growth of operating subsidiaries is fundamental to the future success of the Group's business. . . . The directors have continued to follow the acquisition strategy which has been a feature of the Group's development since it was founded in the mid seventies.' *Harry Solomon*

FIVE YEAR FINANCIAL INFORMATION

Year	Turnover (£m)	Pre-tax (£m)	Earnings (p)	Dividends net (p)	Dividend cover (x)	Net assets (p)	Price (p) High	Low	PER (x) High	Low	Yield (%) High	Low
1983	569.7	11.5	5.6	—	—	41	—	—	—	—	—	—
1984	983.2	18.9	8.3	2.62	3.2	49	—	—	—	—	—	—
1985	1,135.5	33.4	12.2	3.15	3.8	65	152	107	27.4	19.3	3.50	2.46
1986	1,702.6	54.9	16.3	3.80	4.3	90	241	135	32.2	21.8	2.76	1.87
1987	3,038.6	110.3	22.0	4.75	4.6	96	358	215	32.5	14.5	2.55	1.53

In August 1987 Hillsdown issued £150m 4.5% convertible Eurobonds to finance the £169m acquisition of Maple Leaf Mills. If the bonds were all converted, the resulting shares would represent 4% of the group's current issued capital.

The Hillsdown board holds approximately 20% of the equity. The largest individual holding is David Thompson's 14.7%. The Kuwaiti Investment Office holds 7.5%.

GROUP REVIEW

The group is organised into seven operating divisions. They are: food processing and distribution; fresh meat and bacon; furniture and timber distribution; poultry, eggs and animal feed; stationery and office equipment; property; and travel and specialist operations. The shape of these divisions can change quite significantly as acquisitions are made.

Over 40 companies were acquired in 1986 and 50 in 1987. The biggest was Maple Leaf Mills, acquired from Canadian Pacific in August 1987 for £169m. It takes Hillsdown into the Canadian flour milling and baking market, poultry and animal feed industries, as well as Canada's pet food, baking mixes and grain merchandising sectors. These activities are split between several divisions. Hillsdown quickly set about cutting head office overheads at Maple Leaf.

1987 saw dramatic growth of the group's fish interests through Hillsdown's part-owned subsidiary Canadian Clearwater Fine Foods and a near fourfold increase in furniture and timber distribution and property division profits.

In late 1987 the group made a number of disposals, including Nitrovit to J Bibby and the J Evershed shops to Circle K. Some of Maple Leaf Mills is expected to be sold off in 1988.

Poultry, eggs and animal feed The division processes over 75m chickens and 6m turkeys a year. It also produces over a billion eggs and over one million tonnes of animal feed annually.

Buxted is the largest UK poultry producer and is among the top three in the EEC. The business has its own farms, hatcheries, factories and mills. Customers include all the major retail store groups. Products are processed and packed either branded or with the customer's own label. A wide range of processed products are sold, from frozen whole birds to high added-value chicken products.

The Buxted Duckling Co subsidiary is the second largest UK duck processor. Church Farm Turkeys is the largest specialist producer of fresh catering turkeys in the UK. Twydale Turkeys, acquired in 1987, is a leader in the production of high quality turkey products. Other poultry companies include Harvest, a producer of both frozen and fresh chickens, and Hermanns Poultry, a leading supplier of fresh, oven-ready chickens.

Daylay Eggs is the largest integrated UK egg producer and distributor. The company owns 55 farms and six modern egg packing stations. It has three feed mills which fulfil 75% of its own feed requirement. Daylay eggs are to be found in most of the major high street multiples in England and Wales. In Scotland the eggs are marketed by Homestead Eggs, in which Daylay has a 50% shareholding.

Ross Breeders is the leading UK breeder and exporter of poultry breeding stock. Ross has successfully developed and marketed worldwide a range of breeds for both broiler meat and commercial egg production. Ross Poultry Breeders Inc is its US subsidiary. Ross Poultry Great Britain has six hatcheries and over 100 farms, either owned or under contract, which produce live poultry for use by large specialist producers and by small farmers.

Nutrikem and Peter Hand produce a wide range of vitamin and mineral supplements, medical feed additives and medications.

In 1987, turnover of the poultry, eggs, and animal feed division was up 40.2% at £452.9m, 14.9% of the group total. Operating profits were up 26.7% at £27.5m, 20.4% of the total.

Fresh meat and bacon This division includes FMC and North Devon Meat. FMC processes and distributes beef, lamb, and pork to both home and export markets. It has 40 plants located across the major UK livestock producing areas. FMC is the leader in its sector, but the industry operates on very small margins and suffers from considerable excess capacity. FMC also operates three fellmongeries and has interests in hide and skin markets in the west country.

North Devon Meat was originally established as a livestock producer's co-operative over 30 years ago. Some 3,000 producers sell their livestock direct to the company which has become a supplier to many of the country's most quality-conscious retail outlets.

The Harris Bacon Group is the largest UK bacon curer with 10% of the total bacon market. One million pigs are purchased annually under contracts which aim to encourage the production of top quality pigs. A wide range of bacon products is sold nationally under the Harris Crown Quality brand name. A range of sausages, pies and cooked meats is regionally available.

Farm Kitchen Foods processes pigs. Two-thirds of its output goes to the major multiple supermarkets, the remainder is sold under the Farm Kitchen label to butchers, grocers and catering establishments.

Hillsdown, through three subsidiaries, is the leading supplier of meat products to the catering industry. Ludlum, based in Sheffield, supplies beef to restaurants and hotels. Pyke, with ten factories offering a national distribution service, supplies high quality meat and poultry to major catering outlets. Meadow Farm is the country's fastest growing meat and poultry butcher and supplies both the catering and retail markets.

In 1987, divisional sales were up 22.4% at £630.4m, 20.7% of the group total. Operating profit was up 97.5% at £15.8m, representing 11.7% of group earnings.

Food processing and distribution   The division covers more than 20 different product and processing operations.

Principal activities include: fruit and vegetable canning and freezing; manufacture of canned and dry pet foods; speciality fish procurement and processing; meat import and export; manufacture of sugar confectionery and ice-cream; manufacture of pies, quiches, and sandwiches; a growing presence in the expanding chilled salads market; and the import, packing and distribution of fresh fruit and vegetables.

The trading activities – which include B Thompson, Swan Foods, Northam Food, AS Juniper, CR Barron, Towers and David T Boyd – have an international presence with operations in Canada, Hong Kong and Uruguay.

The rapidly developing Canadian-based Clearwater group of companies has fish procurement and processing operations in Canada, the US and the UK. In May 1987 Clearwater bought six Canadian fishing companies. In November 1987 it bought Pinneys, the UK's largest producer of smoked salmon and a big Marks and Spencer supplier. Hillsdown has a 57.1% interest in Clearwater, whose turnover totals C$400m and is rising dramatically.

Hillsdown's first major step in expanding its food interests was in 1981 with the purchase of Lockwoods Foods from the receiver, whose activities include fruit, vegetable and soft drink canning. It went on to add other canning companies, including Smedleys, John Morrell, Wilsons of Scotland, Mortons and Sterling Wygate.

In the sugar confectionery market, Hillsdown owns four ice-cream companies, including Classic Ices and Hortons Ice Cream, Blue Bird, notable for its toffee, and Needlers, renowned for its glacé fruit and barley sugar drops. Hillsdown also holds a 6% equity stake in Bassett Foods, famed for its liquorice all-sorts.

Other food processing companies include Henry Telfer, well known for its quality meat and bakery products, and AJ Mills, a leading importer of food products, specialising in canned meats, fruit, fish and dairy products, many of which are sold under the Emblem brand.

In the fresh produce area, Guy Morton and the Beeson Group are leading potato merchants in the traditional market. Poupart is one of the largest independent wholesalers of fruit, flowers and vegetables in the UK.

In 1987 the division's sales were up 90.4% at £1.046bn, 34.4% of the group total. There was a major contribution from the Maple Leaf Mills acquisition. Divisional operating profit was 82.5% up at £28.1m, 20.8% of the group total.

Furniture and timber distribution   Over 500,000 suites of furniture are produced and sold by the group every year, and it is now the country's largest furniture manufacturer.

The division includes Christie-Tyler and Walker & Homer.

Christie-Tyler is the UK's largest manufacturer of upholstered furniture, operating mainly in the middle and upper sectors of the market. Christie-Tyler acquired Sleepeezee and Simmons, the European bedding manufacturer, in April 1987. Walker & Homer operates in the lower and middle price market, and sells to the major high street retailers and to the large mail order catalogues.

Beresford and Hicks manufactures high quality reproduction Regency furniture. Wilkinsons Furniture produces a range of office and contract furniture.

The timber activities have undergone enormous change in 1986 and 1987. The acquisition of Mallinson-Denny, a timber distributor, and the quoted timber group May & Hassell enlarged the scale and scope of operations. Earlier in 1986, Hunter acquired a Scottish subsidiary, Christie & Vessey.

A formal reorganisation of Hillsdown's timber interests has taken place, with Hillsdown taking a 73.5% interest in the enlarged quoted Hunter group, which now owns all the group's timber and plywood subsidiaries.

In 1987, divisional sales were more than trebled to £669.8m, 22.0% of the group total. Operating profit more than quadrupled to £34.7m, 25.7% of the total.

Stationery and office equipment   The Cartwright Brice group of companies has two main businesses. Stationery and office equipment is distributed nationally through a network of 18 strategically located depots, operating under the HJ Chapman and Cartwright Brice names. Specialist printers' materials and equipment are supplied to the printing and graphics industry under the PS&E and TGS graphics names.

Sales in 1987 were up 11.4% at £59.7m, 2.0% of the group total. Operating profit was 5.8% up at £5.5m, 4.0% of the total.

Property   The division grew rapidly in 1986 and 1987. The most recent substantial acquisition was Fairview New Homes in July 1987, a well known and established builder of flats and houses, predominantly in north London and the Home Counties.

Rugby Securities has a development programme in hand worth more than £30m. Rugby's operations encompass larger commercial office and retail schemes as well as smaller developments.

Hillsdown itself has two substantial residential developments in Regents Park, London. Abco, the Gibraltar-based subsidiary of Hunter, is engaged in property development in Gibraltar, and plans are going ahead to expand into Spain.

The division's turnover in 1987 was up fourfold to £81.5m, 2.7% of the group total. Operating profit was also up fourfold to £19.9m, 14.8% of the total.

Travel and specialist operations   The principal companies in this division are: the IEL Travel group, specialising in business travel; Colloids, a manufacturer of specialist plastics and colour concentrates; Tredegars, a distributor of video films; and Hillgas, which distributes liquid petroleum gas both in bulk and in gas bottles.

In 1987 this division generated sales up 157.6% to £98.2m, 3.2% of the group total. Operating profit trebled to £6.0m, 4.4% of the total.

GEOGRAPHICAL REVIEW

In 1987, 85% of group sales were generated in the UK. North America, at just over 8%, was the main overseas contributor. However, the international contribution will rise appreciably following the acquisition of the Canadian-based Clearwater

Share price and relative to FT-A All-Share

group and Maple Leaf Mills. Their joint turnover is C$1bn a year, equivalent to 17% of the enlarged whole.

CORPORATE CALENDAR

Year end	31 December
Preliminary results	March
Report and accounts	March
AGM	April
Final dividend paid	July
Interim results	September
Interim dividend paid	December

DIRECTORS' HOLDINGS

	Fully-paid	Other (incl. options)
DB Thompson	60,508,828	—
H Solomon	9,531,470	448,000
A Brice	6,278,785	180,320
JA Jackson	645,007	444,000
BC Legg	611,301	332,000
DA Newton	160,042	292,000
KC O'Sullivan	5,838	76,667

Total directors' remuneration in 1987 was £1.2m, of which the chairman, who was also the highest-paid director, received £223,660.

PRINCIPAL SUBSIDIARIES AND RELATED COMPANIES

AC Morrell & Co Limited, AJ Mills & Co Ltd, AS Juniper & Co Ltd, Abco Holdings Ltd – Gibraltar, Action Furniture Ltd, B Thompson Ltd, Beeson Group Ltd, Beresford and Hicks Ltd, Blue Bird Confectionery Holdings Plc, Bransbys Ltd, Bridgend Timber Products Ltd, Buxted Poultry Ltd, C&T Harris (Calne) Ltd, CR Barron Ltd, CR Barron (Meats) Ltd, Cambria Mobel Ltd, Cartwright Brice & Co Ltd, Case Foods Inc – US, Charnwood Upholstery Ltd, Christie & Vesey Ltd, Christie-Tyler Plc, Church Farm Turkeys (Highleigh) Ltd, Classic Associates Ltd, Classic Ices Ltd, Clearwater Fine Foods Inc – Canada, Colloids Ltd, Compagnia Italiana Simmons Spa – Italy, Compagnie Continentale Simmons SA – France, Contour Mobel Ltd, Creative Upholstery Ltd, Culrose Foods Ltd, Danegoods (London) Ltd, David T Boyd Ltd, Daylay Eggs Ltd, Derwent Upholstery Ltd, Dom Holdings plc, Dovedale Fabrics Ltd, Duresta Upholstery Ltd, Eastern Quebec Seafoods Inc – Canada, Eastwood Thompson (Belvedere) Ltd, Eastwood Thompson (Nottingham) Ltd, Enigma Designs Ltd, FMC (Meat) Ltd, FMC Plc, Fairview New Homes Plc, Farm Kitchen Foods Ltd, Firstan Ltd, Formation Furniture Ltd, Formwood Limited, Forrest Hodgkinson Holdings Co Ltd, Fresh Country Foods Ltd, Guy Morton & Sons Ltd, HJ Chapman & Co Ltd, HLF Ltd, Hampstead Properties Ltd, Harvest Poultry Ltd, Henry Telfer Ltd, Henry W Peabody Grain Ltd, Hermanns Poultry Ltd, Hillgas Ltd, Hillsdown Distribution Ltd, Hillsdown Investment Trust Ltd, Hillsdown Insurance Services Ltd, Hillsdown International Ltd, Hillsdown Ltd, Hortons Ice Cream Company Ltd, Hunter Plc, Hunter Plywood (Bristol) Ltd, Hunter Plywood Ltd, IEL Travel Ltd, Inghams Nitrovit Ltd, J Evershed & Son Ltd, JB Eastwood Ltd, JT Stanton & Co Ltd, John Silver Holdings Ltd, King & Prince Seafood Corporation – US, Lewis Bros Ltd, Lifestyle Upholstery Ltd, Litera-Graphics Ltd, Ludlam's Catering Butchers Ltd, Malden Distribution Limited, Mallinson-Denny Limited, Maple Leaf Mills Limited, May & Hassell Plc, Meadow Farm Produce Plc, Miles Mitchell & Sons Ltd, Needlers Plc, Nitrovit Ltd, North Devon Meat Ltd, Northam Food Trading Inc, Nutrikem Ltd, Outline Upholstery Ltd, PS & E Ltd, Perimax Meat Co Ltd, Peter Fairfax Ltd, Peter Hand GB Limited, Pierce Fisheries Ltd – Canada, Pyke Holdings Plc, Pyke-Biggs Ltd, Quartgrade Ltd, REH Kennedy Ltd, Robert Wilson Holdings Ltd, Ross Breeders Ltd, Ross Poultry Breeders Inc – US, Ross Poultry Great Britain Ltd, Rowe Manchett & Till Ltd, Rugby Securities Ltd, Sleepeezee Limited, Smedley's Ltd, Spacehire (Goole) Ltd, Sterling Wygate Ltd, Swan Foods International Ltd, TGS Graphics Ltd, TJ Poupart Group Ltd, Tiverton Poultry Limited, Towers & Company Ltd, Tredegars Wholesale Video Leasing Centres Ltd, Tuskmark Ltd, Twydale Turkeys Limited, Vic Hallam Plc, Walker & Homer Group Plc, Walker & Homer Ltd, Wilkinsons Furniture Ltd, Wirral Foods Ltd, Wyvern Upholstery Ltd

BRAND NAMES

Action, Arkana, Barron, Blue Bird, Buxted Poultry, Cambria, Charnwood, Christie-Tyler, Church Farm Turkeys, Classic Ices, Clearwater, Contour, Creative, Culrose Foods, Daylay eggs, Duresta, Emblem, FMC meat, Farm Kitchen, Harris Crown Quality, Harvest Henry Telfer, Hortons Ice Cream, Inghams Nitrovit, John Morrell, Juniper, King & Prince, Lebus,

Lockwoods, Meadow Farm, Mortons, Needlers, North Devon Meat, Nutrikem, Perimax, Ross, Sleepeze, Smedley's, Solo, Sterling Foods, Stylrite, Swan, Three Castles, Tredegar's, Twydale, Vic Hallam, Washington, Wilson's of Scotland

CONTACTS AND FURTHER INFORMATION

John Jackson, Hillsdown Holdings plc, 32 Hampstead High Street, London NW3 1QD. Tel: 01-794 0677.

IMPERIAL CHEMICAL INDUSTRIES PLC

GENERAL INFORMATION

Head office	Imperial Chemical House, Millbank, London SW1P 3JF. Tel: 01-834 4444
Directors	DH Henderson (chairman), F Whiteley (deputy chairman), JDF Barnes CBE, AW Clements, RC Hampel, C Hampson, TO Hutchison, Sir Robin Ibbs, CH Reece. *Non-exec* Sir Alex Jarratt CB, WGLL Kiep, Sir Patrick Meaney, Sir Jeremy Morse KCMG, S Saba, The Rt Hon Lord Thomson of Monifieth KT, P Volcker – US, TH Wyman
Advisers	No specified adviser
Auditors	Peat Marwick McLintock
Registrar and transfer office	BP Mould, PO Box 251, Wexham Road, Slough SL2 5DP. Tel. 0753 31151
Brokers	Citicorp Scrimgeour Vickers Ltd, Hoare Govett Ltd, Panmure Gordon & Co Ltd, Rowe & Pitman Ltd
Group solicitor	VO White

GENERAL FINANCIAL INFORMATION

Market capitalisation	£7.314bn at 1 January 1988
Capital structure	
Issued ordinary shares (£1)	676m
Issued preference shares	None
Warrants	£62.7m, warrants to subscribe to 117 ordinary shares of £1 each, exercisable at 540p up to 1 June 1990
Convertibles	8.5% sterling convertible bonds 1989/99 (convertible at 800p per £1 share of ordinary stock); 9.75% convertible US dollar bonds 1990 (convertible into sterling bonds at $1.5773/£1); 6.75% Eurodollar bonds (convertible until 1997 into ordinary stock at 460p, with a fixed rate of exchange on conversion of US$1.7423=£1)
Traded options	Yes
ADRs	Four ordinary stock units for each ADR held
Shareholders over 5%	None

FT CATEGORY

FT: Chemicals, plastics
FT-A: Chemicals

MAJOR ACTIVITIES

ICI is one of the UK's largest industrial companies. The group's activities are reported under three industry segments – consumer and speciality products, industrial products and agriculture. Oil and gas interests (other than oil trading and refining) were merged into Enterprise Oil in exchange for 25% of Enterprise's enlarged share capital early in 1987.

Consumer and speciality products contributed 44.3% of ICI's overall trading profit in 1987; the segment has pharmaceuticals, paints and other effect chemicals as its major business. Industrial products contributed 45.9%. Agriculture made a significant recovery in 1987 and contributed 3.7% to the total.

ICI's profitability is linked into the prospects of so many industries in such a wide range of countries that its overall progress follows that of the general growth in world economies.

Much has been done, however, in recent years to restructure the group and focus on more value-added products so that ICI should not feel the effects of any slowdown in world growth or economic recession to the same extent as it did in the early 1980s.

Under Sir John Harvey-Jones, chairman until 31 March 1987, ICI was revitalised and started an agressive acquisition programme. Under his successor, Denys Henderson, the signs are that ICI will continue to exploit acquisition or divestment opportunities aggressively.

Key economic indicators affecting the group's performance include oil prices, the agricultural economy, and the general level of economic growth in industrial countries. Exchange rate movements, in particular those relating to the German mark, impact on profitability.

ICI is now well balanced with respect to the dollar; sales and purchases largely offset each other, so that currency movements have minimal impact on profits. Since ICI has more Deutschmark sales than purchases, changes in the sterling to Deutschmark rate have a more immediate impact on profit.

There are no similar companies in the UK. However, Bayer and Hoechst in Germany, and DuPont and Dow in the US, would be fair comparisons.

FINANCIAL HISTORY

Turnover stood at £11.123bn in 1987, 9.7% up on £10.136bn in 1986. Growth came from all three segments, with a particularly strong performance from industrial products. Sales volume rose by 11%, with 6% from organic growth and 5% the net effect of acquisitions. Pre-tax profits were sharply up 29.1% to £1.312bn.

1987 pre-tax profit was above the 1984 record of £1.034bn and over five times higher than in 1982, a particularly bad year.

Earnings per share were up 23.5% to 113.6p in 1987, nearly four times up on 1982. Dividends have shown a steady increase, rising from 36p to 41p in 1987. Stronger margins have helped to keep profits up in declining industrial sectors. The balance sheet remained strong with gearing at 26.9% even after the Stauffer acquisition. The major contribution to the improvement in margin arose in the industrial products segment, reflecting strong sales volumes, relatively low year-on-year inflation on input costs and strength in European currencies.

In 1987 ICI acquired Stauffer from Unilever, primarily for its agrochemicals business. This acquisition cost $1.7bn, pushing gearing up to 40%, but subsequent disposals of non-agrochemical parts of Stauffer have reduced this to under $0.8bn.

Group profit for the first quarter of 1988 was 7.2% ahead of the corresponding period in 1987 at £354m. Turnover at £2.937bn was 6.4% up. There was strong growth in the US and continental Europe, but level volume in the UK. The group stated that currency movements were having an impact on profits.

CHAIRMAN'S STATEMENT

'The Report for 1987 is one of record sales, record pre-tax profit and record earnings per share, with stockholders rewarded by a dividend increase from 36p to 41p per share – all of which adds up to a picture of a Group which is driving forward with every expectation of further progress to come, confident in the strength of a world class business. . . .

Thus, the keynotes of 1987 have been record financial results, day-to-day success in the market-place, continued expansion of research and development and a succession of initiatives to maintain the momentum of our main business strategies which will continue to be implemented with vigour and consistency.'
Denys Henderson

FIVE YEAR FINANCIAL INFORMATION

Year	Turnover (£m)	Pre-tax (£m)	Earnings (p)	Dividends net (p)	Dividend cover (x)	Net assets (p)	Price (p) High	Low	PER (x) High	Low	Yield (%) High	Low
1983	8,256	619	65	24	2.4	545	660	345	22.7	12.1	7.80	4.33
1984	9,909	1,034	98	30	3.0	617	746	526	15.4	8.0	6.88	4.41
1985	10,725	912	86	33	2.3	538	882	632	11.5	7.5	7.00	4.21
1986	10,136	1,093	83	36	2.3	558	1,116	727	15.2	9.3	5.99	4.30
1987	11,123	1,312	114	41	2.8	510	1,645	965	16.4	8.1	5.43	3.18

SHARE PRICE HISTORY

Shares in ICI have risen dramatically since 1982. This reflects ICI's effort to change its shape, including the restructuring and rationalisation of its cost base.

The first half of 1987 saw a rise in price to 1645p against a high of 882p in 1985 and a high of 1116p in 1986. Until recently ICI, called the bluest of blue chip stocks, was considered a good indicator of UK industry overall. Due to increasing exposure outside the UK economy this perception is changing.

The shares fell very sharply in the October 1987 crash to below 1000p and had hardly recovered by mid-April 1988.

SENIOR MANAGEMENT

The unorthodox Sir John Harvey-Jones retired as chairman to be replaced by Denys Henderson in April 1987. Alan Clements is financial director and Trevor Harrison is chief financial officer.

Principal executive officers of major business units are RI Lindsell, ICI Chemicals & Polymers Ltd; ATG Rogers, colours and fine chemicals; HM Scopes, paints; D Friend, pharmaceuticals; A Hayes, agrochemicals and seeds; HE Miller, advanced materials and electronics; JFH Park, films; BA Killner, polyurethanes; and BH Lochtenberg, speciality chemicals.

Paul Volcker, the distinguished American banker, became a non-executive director on 28 April 1988.

CAPITAL

Even though ICI used some borrowings to augment its strong cash flow so as to finance the 1986 US acquisition of Glidden Paints, gearing remained comfortable at below 30%. In a somewhat unconventional deal, ICI swapped its gas and oil assets for a 25% interest in the enlarged share capital of Enterprise Oil in a deal valued at £115m. Smaller acquisitions were made for cash generated by operations.

In June 1987 ICI agreed to buy Stauffer Chemicals from Unilever for $1.69bn (£1.06bn). This was financed by short term dollar borrowings and additional debt of $233m, pushing gearing up to around 40%. However, most of the non-agrochemical activities have been sold off for $1.1bn, reducing the net purchase cost to below $800m, and bringing gearing at the 1987 year end to 26.9%.

GROUP REVIEW

ICI is structured into several major business units and has a matrix structure in its organisation. Differentiated and high added-value speciality and effect products are marketed internationally on a worldwide basis. The main commodity chemicals businesses, most of which are part of the industrial products group, were combined in a new wholly-owned subsidiary, ICI Chemicals & Polymers Ltd, to get economies of scale. For reporting purposes ICI groups its businesses into three major industry segments.

Consumer and speciality products This comprises pharmaceuticals, paints and other effect products. The last category includes colours and fine chemicals, polyurethanes, speciality chemicals, advanced materials and films.

Pharmaceuticals make the largest contribution to the segment trading profit. In 1987 this totalled £306m and accounted for 53.3% of the segment's trading profit and 23.6% of ICI's overall trading profit. The bulk of ICI's pharmaceutical portfolio is made up by products for the treatment of heart-related problems.

Tenormin is the leading product for control of hypertension and angina. Inderal's use is being extended into non-cardiovascular uses. New evidence on another major product, Nolvadex, has shown that it can extend the life of some patients suffering from breast cancer, and this will continue to expand its use. Zestril, an ACE inhibitor, has been licensed from Merck, who in turn have licensed the diabetic product Statil from ICI.

ICI has become the leading world paint supplier after the acquisition of Glidden from Hanson in 1986 for $580m (£389m). Dulux is the leading UK brand. ICI's vehicle refinish paints business is the largest based outside the US. In 1987 the paints business provided 29.8% of the segment's turnover and 16.0% of profits with strong demand in Europe and from Glidden in the US.

Among the other effect products, polyester films and speciality chemicals in particular are growing strongly. Advanced polymers and composites show good potential but profits are being held back by high development costs. The colours and fine chemical business benefited from worldwide demand for stronger colours and for dyes and related products for the leather industry. Other effect products businesses are becoming increasingly important to the group as it tries to move away from some of the more cyclical businesses. In 1987 it provided 44.9% of the segment's turnover and 30.7% of trading profit.

Industrial products The segment comprises general chemicals, petrochemicals and plastics, synthetic fibres and industrial explosives.

ICI Chemicals and Polymers Group – comprising the group's main plastics and petrochemicals, general chemicals, fibres and fertilizer businesses – is basically a bulk commodity chemicals business. Its new management structure allows better utilisation of resources and closer co-ordination of business direction. The new group had a turnover of £4.2bn and a trading profit of £473m.

ICI's oil and gas business has seen a fundamental shake-up. In January 1987, ICI merged the majority of its oil and gas interests into Enterprise Oil, in exchange for a stake of 25% in the enlarged company valued at £115m. The group's oil activities retained, including oil trading, are now included in the industrial products segment results as part of the petrochemicals and plastics business.

In 1987 turnover for the industrial products segment was up slightly to £5.170bn. Trading profit, however, was up substantially by 29.9% to £595m, due to improved trading conditions and especially strong sales volume.

There were strong performances in 1987 in the UK, continental Europe and in Australia. General chemicals and petrochemicals and plastics experienced strong demand, helped by the stronger Deutschmark. Fibres' profits declined though added-value nylon products maintained their market share.

Agriculture During 1986, the difficult trading conditions experienced in 1985 became more pronounced. As a result, turnover and trading profit were down sharply. Turnover dropped 8% to £1.657bn, and trading profit plunged to £7m from £156m. The fertilizer business accounted for about 55% of segment turnover. In 1986 it saw a loss of £21m against a profit of £74m in 1985.

In 1987 the agriculture segment staged a strong recovery. Turnover was up 5.3% to £1.744bn and trading profit rose £41m to £48m. Agrochemicals and plant breeding, which now make up the bulk of the segment trading profit, saw this rise 85.7% to £52m. The majority of this business is in herbicides, fungicides and plant breeding.

The agrochemicals interests of the Stauffer Chemical Company group, acquired from Unilever in June 1987, is now part of the International Agrochemical business, producing particularly corn (maize) and rice herbicides.

GEOGRAPHICAL REVIEW

ICI's sales in 1987 are now healthily spread across the major markets of the world – with, in round terms, 25% in the UK, 25% in continental Europe, 27% in the Americas and 23% in other markets. Of this, UK exports accounted for £2.927bn.

ICI continues to support its successful UK businesses and to seek further growth in the US, continental Europe and the Asian Pacific countries; the last-named now account for 23% of the world chemicals market. Sales to customers in the Americas more than doubled to £3.048bn since 1982 and turnover rose 19%, notwithstanding adverse currency movements.

Australasia, Japan, the Far East and other countries, including India, accounted for the remainder of business, with turnover of £2.556bn in 1987.

Share price and relative to FT-A All-Share

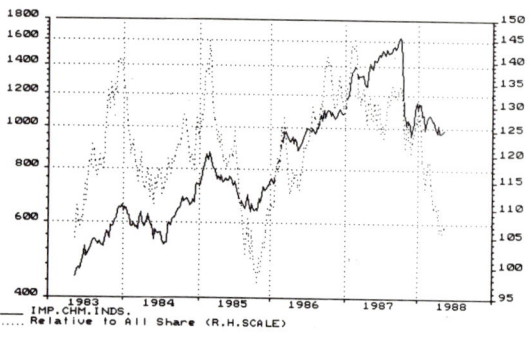

IMP.CHM.INDS.
Relative to All Share (R.H.SCALE)

CORPORATE CALENDAR

Year end	31 December
Preliminary results	February
Report and accounts	March
AGM	April
Final dividend paid	April
Interim results	July
Interim dividend paid	October

DIRECTORS' HOLDINGS

	ICI Ordinary Stock		Options
	(beneficial)	(non-beneficial)	
JDF Barnes	2,813	—	51,400
AW Clements	10,622	—	38,216
RC Hampel	3,508	—	61,566
C Hampson	560	—	—
DH Henderson	10,100	—	106,900
TO Hutchison	2,616	—	59,000
Sir Robin Ibbs	14,112	—	77,300
Sir Alex Jarratt	562	118	—
WGLL Kiep	500	—	—
Sir Patrick Meaney	1,325	—	—
Sir Jeremy Morse	1,819	—	—
CH Reece	6,785	—	69,100
S Saba	500	—	—
Lord Thomson	500	—	—
F Whiteley	9,065	—	—
TH Wyman	500	—	—

Total directors' remuneration was £2.41m in 1987, of which the chairman, who was also the highest-paid director, received £283,283.

PRINCIPAL SUBSIDIARIES AND RELATED COMPANIES

Principal subsidiaries
Chemical Company of Malaysia Berhad – Malaysia (52%), C-I-Linc – Canada (72%), Deutsche ICI GmbH – West Germany, Duperial SAIC – Argentina, ICI American Holdings Inc – US, ICI Australia Ltd – Australia (62%), ICI Brasil SA – Brazil, ICI (China) Ltd – Hong Kong and China, ICI Finance PLC, I.C.I. France SA – France, ICI Holland BV – Holland, ICI Japan Ltd – Japan, ICI New Zealand Ltd – New Zealand (75% by ICI Australia Ltd), ICI Pakistan Ltd – Pakistan (62%), ICI-Pharma Ltd – Japan (60%), ICI (South Africa) Ltd – South Africa, IEL Ltd – India (51%), Imperial Chemicals Insurance Ltd, Nobel's Explosive Company Ltd, Scottish Agricultural Industries PLC

Principal related companies
AECI Ltd – South Africa (38%), Enterprise Oil plc (25%), European Vinyls Corporation (Holdings) BV – Holland (50%), Tioxide Group PLC (50%)

TRADE MARKS

Anvil, Apatef, Aquabase, Asterite, Cefotan, Corwin, Diprivan, Dulux, Ecosyl, Fluon, Force, Fusilade, Glidden, Gramoxone, ICI, Impact, Inderal, Maranyl, Melinar, Melinex, Nolvadex, Perspex, Propafilm, Proxel, Sabrex, Stabar, Statil, Tactel, Tactesse, Tempro, Tenormin, Victrex, Zestril, Zoladex

CONTACTS AND FURTHER INFORMATION

N Taylor, Imperial Chemical Industries PLC, Imperial Chemical House, Millbank, London SW1P 3JF. Tel: 01-834 4444.

LADBROKE GROUP PLC

GENERAL INFORMATION

Head office	87 Wimpole Street, London W1M 7DB. Tel: 01-935 2853
Directors	C Stein (chairman and group managing director), CH Andrews FCIS, KG Edelman, PM George, JF Jarvis FHCIMA, MB Hirst FHCIMA, JF O'Mahony FCA. *Non-exec* Sir Kenneth Cork, JBH Jackson, The Rt Hon Greville Janner QC MP
Advisers	Charterhouse plc
Auditors	Ernst & Whinney
Registrars	Royal Bank of Scotland Registrar's Department
Brokers	Rowe & Pitman Ltd
Solicitors	Norton Rose

GENERAL FINANCIAL INFORMATION

Market capitalisation	£1.365bn at 1 January 1988
Capital structure	
Issued ordinary shares (10p)	422.8m
Issued preference shares	None
Warrants	None
Convertibles	None
Traded options	Yes
ADRs	None
Shareholders over 5%	None

FT CATEGORY

FT: Hotels and caterers
FT-A: Leisure

MAJOR ACTIVITIES

Ladbroke began 1987 as a diversified group with major interests in betting, hotels, retailing and property, and lesser interests in media and holiday camps. It ended 1987 as one of the world's leading hotel operators. This transformation was effected by the acquisition of the Hilton International hotel chain.

Before the Hilton acquisition, off-track betting contributed 41% of operating profits, hotels 23%, property 18%, and retailing including minor activities contributed 18%. In 1988 the four core business should contribute in the following proportions – hotels 43%, off-track betting 30%, do-it-yourself retailing 14% and property 13%.

During 1987 and 1988 Ladbroke has made strategic disposals to concentrate on its four core activities. Sales made before the Hilton acquisition were Laskys, the group's bingo halls, the 20% shareholding in Central Television, Senews, the Rodeway Inns franchise in the US and Olivers. Subsequent to the Hilton acquisition Ladbroke sold eight of its Scottish and two of its north of England hotels, its 79% holding in United Trade Press, its 17 UK holiday centres, the Astey's restaurant business in South Wales, Scottish snooker interests and Home & Law publications.

The principal component of Ladbroke's racing interests is its chain of UK off-track betting shops but it also operates in Belgium, Eire, the Netherlands and the US. Texas Homecare, the DIY chain acquired in April 1986, is the second largest in the UK market. Ladbroke's property interests include some important holdings in the US and Europe as well as in London and elsewhere in the UK. However, the dominant division currently is hotels, where Hilton operates 144 hotels with 45,000 rooms in 46 countries. The brand name of Hilton has been extended in April 1988 to a new category of hotels called Hilton National.

Key economic indicators affecting Ladbroke's sales are personal disposable income, tourist traffic and those affecting the property market. The group has a unique combination of activities and consequently faces different competitors in each of them. Bass, Grand Metropolitan, Trusthouse Forte and other major international groups compete with it in hotels. Major competitors in betting are Corals, owned by Bass, Mecca, owned by Grand Metropolitan, and William Hill, owned by Sears.

FINANCIAL HISTORY

Turnover stood at £2.135bn in 1987, 21% ahead of 1986, and 180.2% up since 1982. Diversification continues away from racing (85% of the group's activity in 1981) into other service industries (more than 60% in 1987), helped by strategic acquisitions. Organic growth is marked in property development and letting. Pre-tax profits were £160.2m in 1987, 58% ahead on 1986 and an advance of 325.5% since 1982.

Earnings per share increased by 26.5% in 1987 on 1986 from 23.2p to 29.4p. Dividends were up almost 20%, from 11.59p to 13.89p on significantly higher capital. The balance sheet showed gearing of around 48%, having been brought down by disposals towards the year-end from its 77% high point in 1986. In the core operations the performance ratios of the individual divisions continued to be amongst the best in their industries.

The acquisition of Hilton International and the rights issues will have a major bearing on the group's performance in 1988. Disposals of businesses and fixed assets raised net proceeds of £190m in 1987.

SHARE PRICE HISTORY

Over the three years to October 1987 the Ladbroke share price rose steadily in absolute terms from under 200p to a peak of 471p. Relative to the market the price fluctuated between 35% and 45% of the FT-A All-Share index.

The group has historically traded on a multiple of between 12 and 15 times future earnings, at or above the market average. Forecast growth of earnings per share in 1988 is expected to be in the 15% to 20% range.

The shares fell sharply in the October 1987 crash to below 280p, 36% of the index. They recovered by February 1988 to 360p, although they remained at the bottom of their trading range relative to the market, and rose to 420p ahead of the final figures, representing a strong period of outperformance overall since the crash.

SENIOR MANAGEMENT

Chairman and managing director, Cyril Stein, who guided Ladbroke to the Stock Market 20 years ago, still plays the major role in the group. On the acquisition of Hilton International John Jarvis relinquished his chairmanship of Texas Homecare to become chairman, president and chief executive officer of Hilton International.

Michael Hirst is deputy chief executive officer of Hilton International. Peter George is executive chairman of Ladbroke Racing and Berjis Daver is managing director. Keith Edelman is now executive chairman of Texas Homecare. Jerry O'Mahony is finance director and Christopher Andrews is an executive director and group company secretary.

Ernest Sheavills is managing director of Ladbroke Group Properties. Tony Grant was appointed president and chief executive officer of Ladbroke's US property division in July 1987.

FIVE YEAR FINANCIAL INFORMATION

Year	Turnover (£m)	Pre-tax (£m)	Earnings (p)	Dividends net (p)	Dividend cover (x)	Net assets (p)	Price (p) High	Low	PER (x) High	Low	Yield (%) High	Low
1983	847	41.8	17.8	8.80	2.0	116	236	158	23.8	15.3	6.72	4.93
1984	1,116	50.2	18.0	10.00	1.8	143	274	180	26.8	14.0	7.78	4.36
1985	1,343	75.1	21.2	11.25	1.9	266	336	239	24.7	15.2	5.93	4.50
1986	1,766	101.3	25.0	12.50	1.9	245	399	309	20.0	15.1	5.09	4.13
1987	2,135	160.2	29.3	13.89	2.1	293	471	275	20.2	10.2	6.50	3.69

CAPITAL

Ladbroke has regularly issued shares to finance its acquisition and expansion programme. The group issued 81m new ordinary shares in March 1987 to develop and expand its four core businesses and a further 70.4m in October 1987 as part of the arrangements to finance its acquisition of Hilton Hotels. Those issues raised approximately £294m and £256m respectively net of expenses.

The total indebtedness of the group prior to the October 1987 rights issue was £355.8m. Total indebtedness of Hilton International at acquisition was $116.7m. As at December 1987, the group's net borrowings stood at £602m. There is no declarable stake in the group of 5% or more.

GROUP REVIEW

Hotels and holidays The major event in 1987 for Ladbroke's hotel division was the acquisition of Hilton International in October for £645m. By April 1988, the Hilton chain, perhaps the most famous brand of hotels in the world, had 144 hotels with 45,000 rooms located in 46 countries. These include existing UK Ladbroke hotels, which have been re-branded as Hilton International or Hilton National hotels.

A further 13 Hilton International hotels are due to open in 1988 and 1989, all to be operated under management contracts. Their locations include Newark Airport in the US, Tokyo Bay, Ankara, Beijing, Vienna and Munich.

Ladbroke disposed of its Rodeway Inns franchise chain in the US for $20m in June 1987. It disposed of its 17 UK holiday centres and the Astey's catering business in South Wales for £50m cash and three million shares to Mecca in December 1987. Ladbroke retained its 50% interest in Los Zocos holiday complex on Lanzarote and the year-round villa resort in Eilat, Israel. This is being upgraded and will be operated by Hilton. The Eilat Ladbroke Hotel is being converted into a Hilton. In December 1987 Ladbroke sold its UK holiday centres and its Astey's catering business to Mecca Leisure for £55m. In February 1988 Ladbroke sold its Scottish snooker interests to Edenderry for £10.25m.

The turnover of the hotels division in 1987 was up £136m to £223m. Pre-tax profits were up £25.4m to £47.2m, including a record 11 weeks' trading contribution from Hilton. Hilton International had operating income for 1987 of $65m.

Racing Ladbroke's is the largest of the big four bookmaking chains in the UK and Eire and as at April 1988 traded from 1,766 outlets, up 106 from the end of 1986. In recent years the group has invested substantially in new technology both to improve management information and to enhance the enjoyment of the customers.

The Ladbroke Electronic Showboard, which is expected to be installed in 1,000 outlets by the end of 1988, offers 12 screens with datatext and enhanced coverage of sporting events. Live coverage by satellite of dog and horse races is provided by Satellite Information Services of which Ladbroke is a founder shareholder. Betting shop regulations are very gradually becoming liberalised and Ladbroke takes advantage of all new opportunities as they occur.

Outside the UK Ladbroke dominates the Belgian market where it operated 1,038 off-track betting units at the end of 1987 through Tiercé Ladbroke. Belgian betting is exclusively done through the totalisator system, and Ladbroke has gained the opportunity to use its Belgian experience to develop outlets in Holland where the group has an exclusive licence for 20 years. Other opportunities are likely to emerge in Europe over the next few years. Racing turnover is being boosted by the liberalisation of betting regulations.

In the US, Ladbroke owns Michigan's major racecourse at Detroit and took advantage in 1986 of the beginnings of more liberal legislation by enabling customers to bet on races transmitted live from other tracks. Off-track betting of the kind familiar in the UK is limited in the US and Ladbroke continues to be the prime mover to develop enabling legislation.

In mid-March 1988 it was learned that Ladbroke had won the sole franchise to develop off-track betting in Wyoming – a significant breakthrough – and although it will be a few years before the operation becomes a contributor to profits, the news does hold out hope of relatively early developments in other states.

Turnover in 1987 for all racing operations was up £132m to £1.32bn – 62% of the group's total. Profits were up £12.5m to £62m, 34.5% of the group's operating profits.

Property The US property portfolio is being expanded, through the London & Leeds subsidiary. It acquired two major freeholds in Washington DC for $67m at the end of 1986. Together with the existing Plaza West and Commonwealth Buildings they provide 560,000 sq ft of office space. More than half the 230,000 sq ft available at London & Leeds' site in Washington's golden triangle between 19th and M streets has been let. In New York the group has let the

Share price and relative to FT-A All-Share

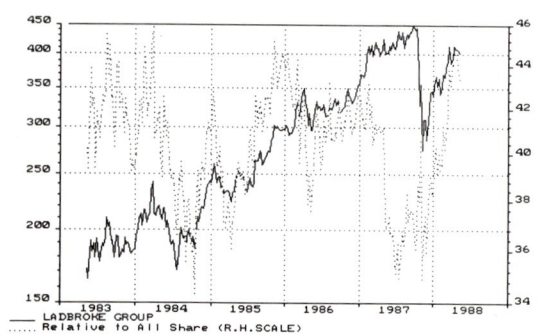

180

C H A I R M A N ' S   S T A T E M E N T

'While the acquisition in October of Hilton International was the highlight of the year and a great coup for us, the record results achieved in 1987 by all our major businesses reflect the underlying strength of the group. . . .

The acquisition of Hilton International has transformed our hotel business from a national operation to a world leader and it is now the largest division in the group. Since the acquisition, Hilton has opened six new hotels from California to Shanghai and we now operate 144 hotels with 45,000 bedrooms in 46 countries. The £13.8m profit earned by Hilton International since acquisition was an all time record for the company.' *Cyril Stein*

35-storey Manhattan Tower.

US tax changes benefit Ladbroke's partnership development ethic. Industrial warehousing developments are being sought in the area covering the Boston to Washington corridor. In total the group has two million sq ft of development already completed or under construction in the US. A further one million sq ft will be added by the end of 1988.

Residential and retail units on Wigmore Street in London were let in 1986 as part of the Debenham & Freebody redevelopment. Further homebuilding is in prospect after the acquisition of Gable House Properties in 1986, which operates in the nursing home market and also in medium price residential property in the south-east.

Ladbroke City and County Land has retail developments in progress in Cwmbran, Maidstone, Birmingham, Blackpool, Preston, Bristol and Winchester. The completion value of Ladbroke City and County Land's development programme amounted to £700m at the beginning of 1988.

Pre-tax profits in 1986 were up £3.4m to £21.4m, 16.4% of the group's operating profits. In 1987 profits rose 4% to £22.3m, after a year in which Ladbroke sought to add value to existing interests rather than dealing actively in the property market.

Retailing The acquisition in April 1986 of Texas Homecare, the second largest UK chain in the home improvements sector after Woolworth's subsidiary B&Q, created a fourth core business. To meet increased demand, which is growing with the buoyant housing market, Texas has been increasing its selling space at an annual rate of more than 20%, having at the end of 1987 a total of 5m sq ft, with 6m planned by the end of 1988. According to current plans, it will be trading from 192 stores by the end of 1988.

Turnover of Texas Homecare for 1987 was £351m. Pre-tax profits were £26m.

In 1987/88 the group disposed of virtually all its media interests. Only Cable Tel Communications, which is installing a cable TV network in the Ealing area, remains.

GEOGRAPHICAL REVIEW

The acquisition of Hilton International has given the group's hotel interests a much wider geographical profit exposure although surprisingly Hilton International's exposure to American visitors in 1987 was under 20%.

Betting profits are largely derived from the UK with the Belgian interests thought to contribute around £6m a year. Elsewhere the retail division is concentrated in the UK but an important element of the property division is US-based and a smaller element of property income is sourced in Europe.

CORPORATE CALENDAR

Year end	31 December
Preliminary results	March
Report and accounts	May
AGM	June
Final dividend paid	July
Interim results	August
Interim dividend paid	December

DIRECTORS' HOLDINGS

	Shares (beneficial)	Shares (non-beneficial)	Options
C Stein	2,667,603	—	51,116
Sir K Cork	50,700	2,870,230	—
CH Andrews	32,317	—	105,397
KG Edelman	—	—	64,185
PM George	84,660	—	182,029
MB Hirst	68,908	—	119,340
JF Jarvis	19,051	—	195,999
JF O'Mahony	2,658	—	101,686
JBH Jackson	9,098	—	—
G Janner	1,300	—	—

The aggregate annual salaries of the executive directors amounted to £1,225,000 in 1987. The chairman and chief executive, who was the highest-paid director, received £281,000.

PRINCIPAL SUBSIDIARIES AND RELATED COMPANIES

Gable House Estates Ltd (75%), Gable House Properties Plc, Gable Retirement Homes Ltd (85%), Ganton House Investments Ltd, Hampden Homecare Plc – Northern Ireland (29.9%), Hilton International Co – US, Ladbroke & Co Ltd, Ladbroke City & County Land Ltd (90%), Ladbroke Group Homes Ltd (75%), Ladbroke Group Properties Ltd, Ladbroke Hotels Ltd, Ladbroke Racing Corp – US, Ladbroke Racing Int BV – The Netherlands, Ladbroke Racing Ltd, London & Leeds Corp (72%) – US, London & Leeds Estates Ltd (87%), London & Leeds Investments (Belgium) SA (77.5%), Multicolor (Wallpapers) Ltd, Retail Parks Ltd, Satellite Information Services Ltd (27.75%), Texas Homecare Ltd, Tiercé Ladbroke SA – Belgium

BRAND NAMES

Hilton, Hilton National, Ladbroke, Texas Homecare

CONTACTS AND FURTHER INFORMATION

John Harounoff, Head of public affairs, Ladbroke Group PLC, 87 Wimpole Street, London W1M 7DB. Tel: 01-935 2853.

LAND SECURITIES PLC

GENERAL INFORMATION

Head office	Landsec House, 21 New Fetter Lane, London EC4P 4PY. Tel: 01-353 4222
Directors	PJ Hunt FRICS (chairman and managing director), IJ Henderson FRICS, W Mathieson FRICS, DM MacKeith CA, JM Moar FRICS. *Non-exec* J Hull (deputy chairman), RAW Caine FCA, HI Connick LLB
Advisers	J Henry Schroder Wagg & Co Ltd
Auditors	Price Waterhouse
Registrars	Lloyds Bank Registrar's Department
Brokers	Rowe & Pitman Ltd
Solicitors	Nabarro Nathanson

GENERAL FINANCIAL INFORMATION

Market capitalisation	£2.326bn at 1 January 1988
Capital structure	
Issued ordinary shares (£1)	503.4m
Issued preference shares	None
Warrants	None
Convertibles	£84m of 6.75% CULS 2002 (148.81 shares per £1000 stock)
Traded options	Yes
ADRs	None
Shareholders over 5%	Prudential Corporation 7.4%

FT CATEGORY

FT: Property
FT-A: Property

MAJOR ACTIVITIES

Land Securities is the UK's largest property investment and development company, concentrating on the redevelopment and, where appropriate, the refurbishment and re-letting of offices in the City, the West End and Victoria in London, and shops, retail warehouses, food superstores and industrial premises throughout the UK.

Land Securities is a broadly based property investment company, owning a substantial portfolio valued at over £3bn. The group's portfolio breaks down into four clearly defined areas. These are: office buildings mainly in London 56%, retail premises 38%, warehouses 4%, and industrial premises 2%. Almost all the group's properties are located in south-east England. The remainder is widely diversified throughout the UK. Some better-known buildings within the portfolio are the Hilton Hotel, the Home Office and New Scotland Yard.

The group has undertaken over recent years a number of major redevelopment and refurbishment programmes, principally within the central London office market. It has successfully re-let the resulting space. The group is currently concentrating upon the redevelopment of its own holdings and newly acquired office and retail schemes.

The retail side of the portfolio has gradually been expanded as a proportion of the whole over recent years. The company now has a retail presence in most major towns in the UK.

FINANCIAL HISTORY

Net assets per share stood at 488p in July 1987, up 16% from the 420p achieved in July 1986, and up 52% over the last five years. A combination of oversupply in the office markets and the low rental growth that went with it led to a particularly pedestrian period of asset value growth in the early 1980s.

Recent demand, however, including that from major overseas buyers, has led to an explosion in City office values since 1986. This is reflected in the impressive rate of net asset value (NAV) and rental growth in 1987, the latter rising by 15% to £189.6m in 1987. Recent financing programmes in the European bond markets have diluted the NAV figure, but the long term benefits of the group's development programme should more than offset this.

Earnings per share, whilst not being of much significance to a property investment company, have more than doubled over the past five years to 17.8p in July 1987. The net dividend for 1987 was 11p, representing an increase of more than 50% since 1984. The balance sheet remains in a healthy state with shareholders' funds standing at a record £2.45bn. Total debt remains low as a proportion of this figure. It stood at 29% in March 1987, though since then gearing has risen to 45%.

SHARE PRICE HISTORY

In the face of sluggish rental and asset value growth within the property sector over the past decade, the shares have been a traditional underperformer. Having historically traded on an approximate 20% discount to NAV, the shares had advanced by only 30% between 1982 and 1986. However, the 1987 property explosion that has led to dramatic rises in property values and rents in the south east especially has engendered a change in sentiment towards property shares. In 1987 Land Securities' price rose by some 40% and stood on a par to NAV.

SENIOR MANAGEMENT

After the death of The Lord Samuel of Wych Cross, Peter Hunt became the company's chairman and remained managing director. Donald Mackeith was appointed to the position of finance director in October 1987.

CAPITAL

The share capital of the company has remained unchanged since the capitalisation issue of 1983. Since then all financing requirements have been met through the issue of various bonds and debentures. The current ordinary capital of the company is 503.4m shares. The only major shareholding is that of the Prudential with 7.4%.

GROUP REVIEW

Office portfolio The major redevelopment and refurbishment programme the group is undertaking in central London continues apace with a further one million sq ft of City floorspace planned for development. Those sites earmarked for redevelopment are the Milton Court development in EC2, Salisbury Square House EC4, Ling House EC2, Leith House EC2, Moorgate Hall EC2, and Regis House EC4. The company has also recently acquired the leasehold interest in 158–170 Aldersgate Street EC1, where redevelopment will provide 190,000 sq ft of air conditioned offices.

In the West End planning permission has been won to redevelop the site of Grand Buildings and Standard House

CHAIRMAN'S STATEMENT

'Throughout our holdings active portfolio management continues and opportunities are being taken to buy in leases for redevelopment, refurbishment and reletting. Selected sales at satisfactory prices have been achieved. . . . A number of redevelopment schemes from within the portfolio are under consideration and we shall continue to seek acquisitions and future developments as and when appropriate.' *Peter J Hunt*

FIVE YEAR FINANCIAL INFORMATION

Year	Turnover (£m)	Pre-tax (£m)	Earnings (p)	Dividends net (p)	Dividend cover (x)	Net assets (p)	Price (p) High	Price (p) Low	PER (x) High	PER (x) Low	Yield (%) High	Yield (%) Low
1983	130.6	78.2	9.45	6.6	1.4	348	270	198	28.4	22.4	4.53	3.61
1984	137.7	84.0	10.15	7.3	1.4	377	318	250	32.5	26.3	4.07	3.32
1985	148.4	95.6	11.72	8.1	1.4	401	324	260	29.2	22.5	4.48	3.46
1986	171.5	113.0	15.79	9.8	1.6	420	349	279	25.4	19.8	4.54	3.64
1987	204.1	120.6	17.78	11.0	1.6	488	610	337	35.7	21.0	4.24	2.47

WC2 to provide approximately 164,000 sq ft of air conditioned offices plus banking and shopping areas. Work has commenced on the redevelopment of Ontario House SW1 which is due for completion at the end of 1988. Work at both Kingsgate House and Queen's House SW1 has been completed and lettings agreed for both. Planning application has been made for a redevelopment behind existing façades of 1–3 Sanctuary Buildings, together with 14 and 22 Great Smith Street SW1 to provide some 225,000 sq ft of air conditioned offices.

Shop portfolio The retail portfolio has become an increasingly important part of the whole over recent years. Under current plans this will be extended in 1987/88 when over 650,000 sq ft of new covered shopping centres is completed. In the south-east at Newbury, the Kennet Centre is to be further expanded following the recent expansion of Sainsbury's 53,000 sq ft store. In Canterbury the group has acquired the company controlling the Longmarket site, situated in a prime city centre position. Redevelopment is expected to commence in 1989. In the Midlands the 12 shop scheme in Walsall has recently been completed and virtually all units let. The group has also acquired a 185,900 sq ft covered shopping centre adjoining the completed units.

The northern retail developments are to undergo continued significant expansion. Two major shopping centre developments at Darlington and Hull, the former providing some 200,000 sq ft, the latter providing a similar amount of floor space sited over water in the town's docks area, are currently in progress. In Scotland, work has recently commenced on the Olympia Shopping and Leisure Centre at East Kilbride. This is due for completion in 1989. Work in Irvine New Town has been delayed due to further negotiations with the local Development Corporation. The relatively small presence of the group in Northern Ireland has recently been expanded by the acquisition of the 250,000 sq ft Ards Shopping Centre in Newtownards.

Retail warehousing Retail warehousing has become an attractive area for property investment and development over the past few years. Sites possessing access to major travel routes like the M25 are becoming in short supply. The group has built up since 1985 a considerable presence in this sector. It has recently acquired the freehold of the 300,000 sq ft Lakeside Retail Park situated at West Thurrock adjacent to the M25. Work has already commenced on the site in concert with Lakeside Trading Estate Limited. The opening is scheduled for Easter 1988. In all, the warehousing portfolio consists of two million sq ft constructed and let, and a further 1.8 million sq ft situated in 46 locations throughout the UK in various stages of development.

GEOGRAPHICAL REVIEW

The group portfolio is made up entirely of UK properties, the bulk of which are located in the South East and Central London. However, the group also owns a substantial amount of mainly retail properties in the South West, Midlands, north Scotland and Northern Ireland. The group has no overseas exposure.

CORPORATE CALENDAR

Year end	31 March
Preliminary results	May
Report and accounts	May
AGM	June
Final dividend paid	July
Interim results	November
Interim dividend paid	December

DIRECTORS' HOLDINGS

	Fully-paid ordinary shares (beneficial)	(non-beneficial)	Options
J Hull	407	323,721	—
PJ Hunt	18,362	323,721	142,879
RAW Caine	50,000	7,050	—
JM Moar	7,879	323,721	89,226
HI Connick	500	—	—
W Mathieson	3,893	—	78,636
IJ Henderson	3,833	3,175	79,226

Total directors' remuneration for 1986/87 was £238,000, of which the chairman received £65 and the highest-paid director £107,000.

PRINCIPAL SUBSIDIARIES AND RELATED COMPANIES

The City of London Real Property Company Limited, Land Securities Properties Limited, Ravenseft Industrial Estates Limited, Ravenseft Properties Limited, Ravenside Investments Limited

BRAND NAMES

None

CONTACTS AND FURTHER INFORMATION

LA Jones, Company Secretary, Land Securities PLC, Landsec House, 21 New Fetter Lane, London EC4P 4PY. Tel: 01-353 4222.

Share price and relative to FT-A All-Share

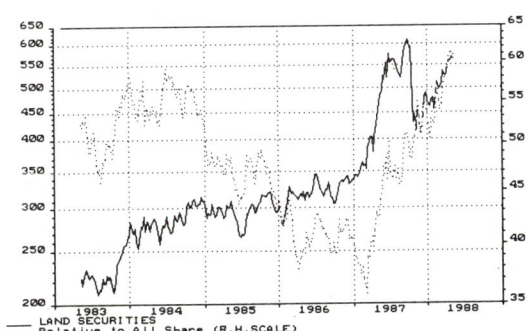

LEGAL & GENERAL GROUP Plc

GENERAL INFORMATION

Head office	Temple Court, 11 Queen Victoria Street, London EC4N 4TP. Tel: 01-248 9678
Directors	Professor Sir James Ball (chairman), KHM Dixon (vice chairman), TJ Palmer (chief executive), JK Elbourne, AJ Hobson, DJ Prosser, JM Skae. *Non-exec* RH Clutton, Sir John Egan, WJR Govett, JFC Hull, JS Kerridge, Sir Richard Lloyd Bt, The Hon TJ Manners
Advisers	No specified adviser
Auditors	Price Waterhouse
Registrars	Legal & General Group Plc, Registrar's Department, Temple Court, 11 Queen Victoria Street, London EC4N 4TP. Tel: 01-248 9678
Brokers	Citicorp Scrimgeour Vickers Ltd
Solicitors	No specified adviser

GENERAL FINANCIAL INFORMATION

Market capitalisation	£1.307bn at 1 January 1988
Capital structure	
Issued ordinary shares (25p)	470m
Issued preference shares	None
Warrants	None
Convertibles	None
Traded options	None
ADRs	None
Shareholders over 5%	None

FT CATEGORY

FT: Insurances
FT-A: Insurance (life)

MAJOR ACTIVITIES

Legal & General Group, capitalised at £1.307bn at the beginning of 1988, is a major UK insurance company with interests in all the principal classes of insurances. It has a special emphasis on life assurance and pensions business, and is a market leader in the provision of insurance, investment services and the management of company pension schemes.

About 70% of the group's long-term business is obtained in the UK. The balance is in Australia, the group's reinsurance subsidiary the Victory, the US, Europe, and the rest of the world. The long-term business is split between life assurance, investment business and pensions business.

Legal & General's general non-life insurance business is derived primarily in the UK. The bulk of the domestic insurance consists of household and commercial buildings and contents insurances, although premiums for the motor account are considerable. Most of the non-UK business is written in the Victory Reinsurance Group. Victory provides insurance cover to other insurance companies wishing to limit their exposure to particular risks or lines of insurance business which they have written.

Most of Legal & General's premium income is obtained from independent intermediaries. The group has strong connections with the building societies. However, an increasing proportion of its income is brought in by the group's expanding direct sales force, and also by direct marketing techniques like advertising and direct mail. The direct sales force is likely to number 2,300 by the end of 1988 compared with 2,000 in April 1988. It produces new premium income of some £30m per annum. Legal & General has been very successful in developing its estate agency network, with over 1,000 offices in 850 firms acquired at a cost of about £20m to date.

The quoted life companies, the composite insurers, and big mutual offices like Norwich Union and Standard Life, are the group's main competitors. The company's shares are most often compared with those of the Prudential but can also be compared with the other life companies, including Abbey Life, Pearl Group and Sun Life.

FINANCIAL HISTORY

Total premium income in 1987 amounted to over £1.53bn compared with £819m in 1982, up 88% over five years, with an expansion in most areas of activity.

Legal & General is a traditional with-profits office which means that profits earned from the with-profits life and pensions business accrue primarily to the policyholders. The shareholders benefit from transfers each year equal to about one-eighth of the value of the bonuses granted to policyholders. Profits from the unit-linked, investment and non-life insurance business accrue directly to the shareholders.

Bonus distributions tend to be fairly stable, although one-off bonuses in 1986 and 1987 contributed £28.3m and £10.9m, respectively, to the increase in shareholders' profits. The consistency of life profits helps to reduce the impact of volatile non-life earnings.

Total pre-tax profits in 1987 amounted to £79.2m compared with £101.8m for 1986. The fall is attributable to the cost of the October hurricane, £42m.

SHARE PRICE HISTORY

The share price fell early in 1984 on the expectation that the abolition of Life Assurance Premium tax relief in the 1984 Budget would lead to a decline in the sale of regular premium life assurance products. The possibility of government encouragement for private pensions provision led to an increase in the Legal & General share price early in 1985.

Since then the shares have fallen relative to UK equity markets generally on fears that consumer protection legislation would lead to increased competition and a reduction in the number of insurance intermediaries as a result of increased regulatory compliance costs.

More recently, the Social Security Act 1986 increased the attractiveness of private sector pensions and the share price has increased, reflecting the view that pensions sales will increase substantially. Life profits are fairly stable and because of this the share price outperformed equity markets during the October 1987 crash.

SENIOR MANAGEMENT

The group's chairman is Professor Sir James Ball and the group chief executive is Joe Palmer. The group's finances are controlled by Tony Hobson, general manager, finance. Managing director of the UK Life and Pensions division is John Elbourne. Brian Palmer runs the UK General Insurance division. Ted Tilly controls the International division. DJ Prosser is the newly appointed general manager of the Investment departments. WM Abbott is group chief actuary.

CAPITAL

Shareholders' funds used in support of the group's activities amounted to £281.4m at the end of 1986 and borrowings totalled £110.3m. The vast bulk of the borrowings are unsecured bank loans and overdrafts. At the end of 1987, total shareholders' funds totalled about £260m. There is no shareholder with an interest in excess of 5% of the issued share capital.

F I V E   Y E A R   F I N A N C I A L   I N F O R M A T I O N

Year	Turnover (£m)	Pre-tax (£m)	Earnings (p)	Dividends net (p)	Dividend cover (x)	Net assets (p)	Price (p) High	Price (p) Low	PER (x) High	PER (x) Low	Yield (%) High	Yield (%) Low
1983	989.8	55.6	9.40	6.17	1.52	47	176	108	18.7	11.5	8.16	5.01
1984	1,175.0	48.1	9.76	7.17	1.35	52	192	139	19.7	14.2	7.37	5.33
1985	1,160.5	31.5	7.86	8.17	0.96	51	258	182	32.8	23.2	6.35	4.48
1986	1,231.5	101.8	14.83	9.75	1.52	61	286	218	19.3	14.7	6.18	4.71
1987	1,536.7	79.2	11.0	11.50	0.96	56	395	220	35.9	20.0	7.03	3.92

GROUP REVIEW

Legal & General is one of the largest life offices in the UK. It has an extensive range of contacts with insurance intermediaries, including the building societies which should help the group to expand organically in the increasingly competitive insurance markets. Legal & General is a particularly active provider of pensions contracts and should benefit greatly from the government's encouragement to private sector pension provision.

Life assurance and pensions In the UK, the greater part of the group's life new business relates to the sale of endowment assurances which are used as security for the repayment of house mortgage loans. Legal & General is the market leader in the provision of these products. 1986 and 1987 were particularly buoyant years, although increasing competition resulted in some tailing off in growth during 1987. The changes made to capital transfer tax in the 1986 budget led to cessation of sales of Legal & General's Capital Preservation Plans. Despite this, single premium life policy sales rose by a quarter in 1986 and by over one third in 1987.

Legal & General maintains a strong position in the group pensions market but rising stock market values and also various legislative changes have reduced the level of contributions required by company pension schemes to support the benefits prospectively payable. Growth in this market was slow during 1986. The trend in 1987 was for a reduction in contributions.

The group also writes a substantial volume of individual pension business for the self-employed, for persons in non-pensionable employment who effect retirement annuity contracts to provide for their old age, and for directors of small companies who wish to have their own individual retirement schemes. Sales of these contracts increased by one third in 1987 and are likely to be given a further boost in 1988 when the 1986 Social Security Act takes effect and encourages the use of private provision for pensions.

Total pre-tax profit contributed by UK Life and Pensions in

1987 was £74.1m. This included £10.9m arising from the non-recurrent special bonuses granted to policyholders.

The group is committed to expanding its international operations. It is strong in Australia, where business is booming. In the US it owns Banner Life, where it is continuing to invest in the development of its agency network. As a result new business levels are accelerating. There are subsidiaries in France, the Netherlands and Zimbabwe.

Overseas life profits amounted to £12.8m in 1987, of which £5.1m stemmed from Australia, £5.4m from the group's US life subsidiary Banner Life and £2.2m from the Victory reinsurance subsidiary.

C H A I R M A N ' S   S T A T E M E N T

'The physical storm of October was accompanied by a financial storm, the longer term consequences of which are hard to predict. As far as profit is concerned the stock market crash had little effect on the 1987 results. In the long term the consequences for your company will depend more heavily on the effect of the financial shock on the economy as a whole. At the time of writing no overall consensus on this matter has emerged. I expect a slowdown in economic growth in 1988 compared with 1987, but this is largely due to the deterioration of the position *vis-à-vis* net exports rather than the fall in the stock market. There is no reason to believe that this will significantly damage the prospects for the development of personal pensions and house purchase related business, both of which are important to us.' *Sir James Ball*

Non-life insurance In the UK, Legal & General writes a substantial amount of non-life insurance. Premium volume in 1987 was £225.5m, mainly consisting of personal lines as distinct from the insurance of bigger commercial risks. A large part of this business is domestic buildings insurances obtained through the group's strong building society ties.

The property account underwriting result, the excess of premiums over claim payments and expenses, turned from a profit of £10.7m to a loss of £28.1m in 1987, reflecting the worst natural disaster in the UK for 200 years. Losses on the group's motor business and on the remaining business were much reduced so that, taken in conjunction with investment income, satisfactory returns were achieved.

The total underwriting loss of £30.6m was offset by investment income on the non-life assets of £20.8m, giving rise to a total general insurance pre-tax loss in the UK of £9.8m. There was a pre-tax profit on the group's international and reinsurance business of £5.4m. Overall, the non-life result in 1987 was adequate once account is taken of the UK weather losses.

Investment management The group has funds under management of over £12bn. Of this total, the main life and

Share price and relative to FT-A All-Share

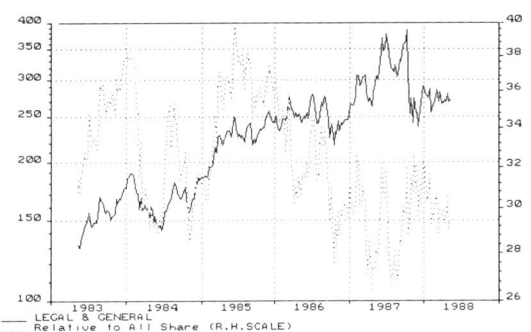

pensions insurance funds account for about £7bn. Assets under management for corporate pension scheme clients total about £3bn. About 25% of the total assets are invested in property, 40% in equities, and the balance mostly in fixed interest securities. The group needs to obtain good returns on its invested assets in order to compete effectively within the intermediary markets and so it has undertaken a substantial development of its investment management arm.

Other In December 1987 the group acquired a 41.5% interest in Parker's of Reading, a chain of estate agents in the M4 corridor. It also increased its stake in Connells Estate Agents to 14.6%. The group is also interested in acquiring investment intermediaries. Fairmount Trust was bought in 1986 as a first stage and is performing well, with profits of about £1m.

GEOGRAPHICAL REVIEW

Life assurance business constitutes the major part of the group's total business. The distribution of total life and pensions pre-tax profits of £77.3m (excluding the exceptional bonus payments) in 1987 was UK 83.4%, US 7.0%, Australia 6.6%, Europe 0.1% and Victory 2.8%.

The group's non-life insurance business provides a relatively small part of total profits. Of total premium income of £314.5m in 1987, £225.5m was written in the UK and £75.9m through the Victory subsidiary, which operates throughout the world.

CORPORATE CALENDAR

Year end	31 December
Preliminary results	March
Report and accounts	April
AGM	May
Final dividend paid	June
Interim results	September
Interim dividend paid	December

DIRECTORS' HOLDINGS

	Fully-paid ordinary shares		Options
	(beneficial)	(non-beneficial)	
Sir James Ball	33,000	—	—
RH Clutton	2,182	3,600	—
KHM Dixon	300	—	—
Sir John Egan	315	—	—
JK Elbourne	10,780	—	40,483
WJR Govett	720	—	—
AJ Hobson	—	—	34,800
JFC Hull	300	—	—
Sir Richard Lloyd	606	7,500	—
TJ Manners	606	2,190	—
Sir Jeremy Morse	39,480	9,000	—
TJ Palmer	76,906	—	70,500
JM Skae	25,803	—	82,162

Total directors' remuneration in 1987 was £747,140, of which the chairman received £43,100 and the highest-paid director £134,380.

PRINCIPAL SUBSIDIARIES AND RELATED COMPANIES

Aviation & General Insurance Co Ltd (12.0%), Banner Life Insurance Co – US, City and Urban Development Ltd (41.5%), Cogent (Holdings) Ltd, Connells Estate Agents Plc (14.6%), European Life (Channel Islands) Ltd – Channel Islands, Fairmount Trust Ltd, Guinea Insurance Co Ltd – Nigeria (20.0%), Heritage Insurance Co Ltd – Kenya (24.5%), Heritage Insurance Co of Zimbabwe (Private) Ltd (35.0%), Legal & General America Inc – US, Legal & General Assurance Holdings (Australia) Ltd, Legal & General Assurance of Zimbabwe (Private) Ltd, Legal and General Assurance (Pensions Management) Ltd, Legal and General Assurance Society Ltd, Legal & General Financial Services Ltd, Legal & General Holdings (France)

SA, Legal & General International Ltd, Legal & General (Investment Management) Ltd, Legal & General (Money Managers) Ltd, Legal & General Netherlands Holdings BV, Legal & General Property Fund Managers Ltd, Legal and General (Unit Assurance) Ltd, Legal and General (Unit Pensions) Ltd, Legal & General (Unit Trust Managers) Ltd, Pegasus Insurance Co Ltd – Greece (35.0%), Portsoken Reinsurances Ltd (45.0%), Victory Insurance Holdings Ltd

BRAND NAMES

Cashplan 2000, Treasury Chest 2000

CONTACTS AND FURTHER INFORMATION

J Neill FCIS, Group Secretary, Legal & General Group Plc, Temple Court, 11 Queen Victoria Street, London EC4N 4TP. Tel: 01-248 9678.

LLOYDS BANK Plc

GENERAL INFORMATION

Head office 71 Lombard Street, London EC3P 3BS. Tel: 01-626 1500
Directors Sir Jeremy Morse KCMG (chairman), Sir Lindsay Alexander (deputy chairman), Sir John Hedley Greenborough KBE LLD (deputy chairman), NW Jones CBE TD (deputy chairman), AJ Davis RD (vice chairman), Sir William Harding KCMG CVO, BI Pitman (chief executive), MHR Thompson (deputy chief executive), EJ Dawson, AL Kingshott. *Non-exec* Viscount Caldecote KBE DSC FEng, FW Crawley, G Duncan, Sir Robin Ibbs, Sir George Jefferson CBE FEng, GC Kent, Sir Peter Matthews AO, RJ Medlam, Sir Alec Merrison DL FRS, Lord Plumb DL, IMG Prosser, JM Raisman CBE LLD, The Hon Sir Peter Ramsbotham GCMG GCVO, CR Smith CBE, E Swainson CBE
Advisers Lloyds Merchant Bank Ltd
Auditors Price Waterhouse
Registrars Lloyds Bank Registrar's Department
Brokers Hoare Govett Ltd
Solicitors Linklaters & Paines; Murray, Beith & Murray

GENERAL FINANCIAL INFORMATION

Market capitalisation	£1.973bn at 1 January 1988
Capital structure	
Issued ordinary shares (£1)	808.82m
Issued preference shares	None
Warrants	None
Convertibles	None
Traded options	None
ADRs	None
Shareholders over 5%	None

FT CATEGORY

FT: Banks, HP and leasing
FT-A: Banks

MAJOR ACTIVITIES

Lloyds Bank and its subsidiary and associated companies provide a comprehensive range of domestic and international banking and financial services. Operations in the UK are conducted through over 2,600 branches and offices. International business is conducted through over 400 offices in 42 countries worldwide, as well as in the UK.

The principal business of the group in the UK is the transmission of payments, the acceptance of deposits, and the provision of a full range of lending facilities to companies and individuals. Other services provided by the group include export finance; equipment leasing; estate agency; registrar's services; and executor, trustee and insurance services.

Overseas, Lloyds Bank conducts a range of international and local banking business, including retail and corporate banking, money market and foreign exchange dealing, export and trade finance and correspondent banking.

Merchant banking activities are carried out by Lloyds Merchant Bank in capital markets, corporate finance, development capital, stockbroking and investment management services.

Lloyd's is one of the most exposed of the UK clearing banks to the risk of default on sovereign debt. In 1987 the group made exceptional provisions of £1.066bn for countries in payment difficulties.

FINANCIAL HISTORY

Group profits more than doubled between 1982 and 1986, mainly due to the strong performance of the domestic retail and corporate businesses whose profits increased by over 160% over the same period, whereas those of the international operations rose by only 35%. Returns from the domestic side were boosted by the combination of strong volume growth overall together with greatly increased lending to the personal sector. International returns were adversely affected by the incidence of higher debt provision, especially in 1984/85.

In 1987 Lloyds made its first ever pre-tax loss of £248m, against a pre-tax profit of £700m in 1986. Exceptional provisions of £1.066bn were made against total cross-border outstandings of £3.932bn. But for these provisions Lloyd's pre-tax profits were up 16.8% to £818m.

Underlying business growth in 1987 was strong, with total income for the year up by £272m to £2.720bn. Excluding the exceptional provisions, earnings per share were up 9% to 63p, putting the group on a PER of just over four. UK retail banking was outstanding with pre-tax profits up 32% to £562m from £427m. Dividends per share in 1987 were up 10% to 13.2p.

The trend of earnings in recent years has been distorted by fluctuations in the group's effective tax rate, principally brought about by the changes in the 1984 Finance Act impact on the group's leasing business. Since then the tax charge has benefited from a shift from general to specific debt provisions.

SHARE PRICE HISTORY

The shares have traditionally participated fully in the short term volatility of the sector and, because of above-average sovereign debt exposure, have proved sensitive to developments on that front. After falling sharply against the market in 1982 at the time of the Mexican debt crisis they subsequently outperformed the sector by a substantial margin and rose by 30% against the market in the three years to mid-1987. Factors contributing to this outperformance included the strong profits performance of the domestic banking operations, the maintenance of balance sheet ratios of above average strength, and a progressive dividend policy. However, the shares retraced part of that earlier outperformance in the latter half of 1987 when balance sheet ratios suffered an above average deterioration in the aftermath of mid-year exceptional debt provisions in excess of £1bn.

SENIOR MANAGEMENT

Sir Jeremy Morse has been chairman since 1977 and is supported by Sir Lindsay Alexander, Sir John Hedley Greenborough and NW Jones as deputy chairmen, and AJ Davis as vice-chairman. Senior management includes Brian Pitman, chief executive; Michael Thompson, deputy chief executive; John Dawson, director of UK retail banking; Len Kingshott, director of international banking; Bob Marshall, director of support services; Robert Medlam, director of corporate banking; Alan Moore, director of treasury and investment banking; David Horne, chief executive, merchant banking; and Leon Wilkinson, chief financial officer.

CAPITAL

Although the group is alone among the leading UK clearing banks in not having made a rights issue in the 1980s, it was able to maintain above average capital ratios on the yardsticks used by the Bank of England throughout the period to end-1987. This was as a result of retained earnings coupled with effective control of balance sheet growth. In addition, $1.85bn of undated loan capital, which qualifies as primary

FIVE YEAR FINANCIAL INFORMATION

Year	Income (£m)	Pre-tax (£m)	Earnings (p)	Dividends net (p)	Dividend cover (x)	Net assets (p)	Price (p) High	Low	PER (x) High	Low	Yield (%) High	Low
1983	1,820	419	35	7.0	5.0	277	143	98	8.3	4.0	8.33	6.08
1984	2,080	468	29	7.9	3.7	259	160	126	8.8	4.5	8.11	5.94
1985	2,230	561	41	9.3	4.4	289	228	154	6.7	5.1	7.25	5.23
1986	2,469	700	58	12.0	4.8	341	315	197	7.1	5.1	6.50	4.43
1987	2,764	(248)	(28)	13.2	—	296	427	220	—	—	7.74	3.85

capital for the purposes of Bank of England guidelines, was raised in 1985 and 1986.

As a result of the substantial increases in provisions and the payment of the 1987 dividend out of reserves, the primary capital ratio at the 1987 year-end stood at 7.9%, down from 8.9% at the 1986 year-end, but a recovery from the 7.2% ratio of June 1987, when most of the exceptional provisions were made.

Shareholders' funds fell by 8.5% to £2.393bn in 1987 and primary capital by 16.7% to £3.534bn.

There was a scrip issue of 268.9m ordinary shares in June 1987. No director has a significant shareholding and there is no declarable shareholding of 5% or more in the group.

GROUP REVIEW

General The group is committed to focusing on those activities where it has, or can obtain, a competitive advantage through selectivity, market segmentation and a concentration of resources. Recent years have witnessed, therefore, a series of acquisitions and disposals.

In 1984 the Royal Bank of Scotland's minority holding in Lloyds and Scottish, since renamed Lloyds Bowmaker Finance, was purchased. The investment banking business and certain parts of the commercial banking business of the German bank Schröder, Münchmeyer and Hengst were acquired in 1984. 90% of the Continental Bank of Canada was acquired, and in 1986 was merged into Lloyds Bank Canada.

Disposals have included the sale of a longstanding 16.5% shareholding in the Royal Bank of Scotland in 1985, as well as an additional 5% shareholding which had been acquired in 1983. Lloyds Bank California was sold off in 1986. Under the Lloyds Bank (Merger) Act 1985, the business of Lloyds Bank International was vested in Lloyds Bank Plc which, in the following year, made an unsuccessful bid for Standard Chartered.

UK retail banking UK retail banking services are provided by some 2,200 manned high street outlets; by supplementary networks of close on 200 unmanned service sites which provide cash withdrawal and other facilities 17 hours a day for seven days a week; and by nearly 2,000 Cashpoint machines. UK Retail Banking has consistently achieved strong growth in profits.

Priority in recent years has been given to developing a wider range of personal banking services. A noteworthy example is the innovative one-stop package for home buyers centred around the Black Horse Agencies, now one of the largest estate agency groups in the country. This is backed up by a large increase in mortgage lending.

Other examples include the launch of a high interest cheque account, the extension of Cashpoint facilities to deposit account customers, and the introduction of an asset management service. Other services provided cover a full range of investment management, insurance, executor and trus-

teeships. The acquisition of full control of Lloyds Bowmaker has resulted in the development of both new and existing specialist credit facilities, and a leading presence in the factoring market.

In 1987, UK retail banking increased its pre-tax profits by 32% to £562m (£427m), 68.7% of the group total before exceptional provisions.

International banking The international banking division is organised into six main regions – Latin America, Australasia, Europe, the Far East, the Middle East and Africa, and North America. Through its predecessors the group has been operating in Latin America for 125 years. An extensive branch network there gives it a strong presence in the retail and corporate banking markets. In Australasia, the group's principal investment is The National Bank of New Zealand, again with a strong retail base. This is reinforced by South Pacific Merchant Finance, which is engaged in merchant banking and the more recently established Lloyds Bank NZA in Australia.

In Europe, recent development has primarily focused on expanding from commercial banking business into personal investment, including discretionary portfolio management, and trust services. In North America, despite the sale of Lloyds Bank California, the group still has a substantial presence in the wholesale markets.

In 1987, pre-tax profits fell 15.8% to £117m, 14.3% of the group total before exceptional provisions. There were improved results in the Far East and Middle East, but a decline in the US.

Share price and relative to FT-A All-Share

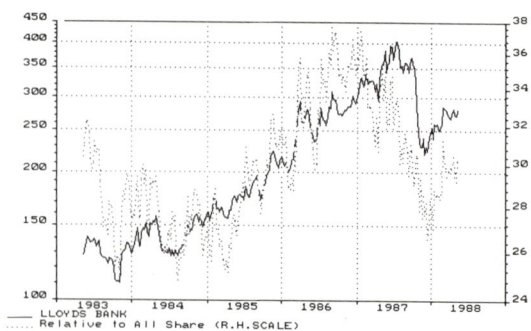

At the 1987 year-end total group cross-border outstandings were £3.932bn, against which the group had total provisions of £1.333bn (34%). The outstandings were Brazil £1.117bn, Mexico £763m, Argentina £405bn, rest of Latin America £968m and rest of the world £679m. The group is expecting a tax credit on the provisions. The total sovereign debt is being reduced by sterling strength because the outstandings are largely denominated in US dollars.

Corporate banking This division specialises in servicing the large corporate customer through facilities such as raising capital in the debt market, managing interest and exchange rate exposure through the swap markets, leasing and registration services. It also provides electronic information and fund transfer systems like Cashcall and Fundsflow, and an employee relocation system through the Black Horse Agency.

C H A I R M A N ' S   S T A T E M E N T

'1987 was a year of mixed fortunes for Lloyds Bank. Our retail businesses, principally in the UK, went from strength to strength. On the other hand, the margins on large corporate lending declined further; there were losses and cutbacks in the capital markets activities of Lloyds Merchant Bank; and worsening conditions in a number of developing countries led us to make very large exceptional provisions of £1,066 million at the half year.' *Sir Jeremy Morse*

1987 pre-tax profits increased by 13% to £80m, 9.8% of the group total before exceptional provisions.

Merchant banking The various merchant banking businesses of the group were brought together into Lloyds Merchant Bank in 1985. Its four major areas of activity are corporate finance, development capital, stockbroking and investment management.

In 1987 the division made a loss of £18m before tax against a profit of £70m in 1986, partly as a result of losses made in its discontinued activities in gilts and eurobonds.

Treasury A primary responsibility of the treasury division is in funding the group's deposits, which involves liquidity considerations and asset management techniques, and the control of exposure to interest rate movements. Dealing operations are carried out globally and in a broad range of financial markets, but especially the foreign exchange, commercial paper and money markets.

In 1987 pre-tax profits increased by 10% to £77m, 9.4% of the group total before exceptional provisions.

GEOGRAPHICAL REVIEW

Of total assets of £44.9bn at the end of 1987, 62% were employed in the UK, 11% in North America, 10% in Australasia and the Far East, 8% in Europe, 7% in Latin America and 2% in the Middle East and Africa.

Of the group's 1987 pre-tax profits of £818m before exceptional items, the UK contributed 85% (£693m), Europe, the Middle East and Africa 6% (£50m), North America 1% (£10m), Latin America −0.5% (−£4m) and Australasia and the Far East 8% (£69m).

CORPORATE CALENDAR

Year end	31 December
Preliminary results	February
Report and accounts	March
AGM	April
Final dividend paid	April
Interim results	July
Interim dividend paid	October

DIRECTORS' HOLDINGS

	Fully-paid ordinary shares	Options
Sir Lindsay Alexander	8,200	—
Viscount Caldecote	2,732	—
FW Crawley	24,935	9,084
AJ Davis	10,768	—
Sir John Hedley Greenborough	1,012	—
Sir Robin Ibbs	1,687	—
Sir George Jefferson	562	—
NW Jones	7,329	—
GC Kent	1,071	—
Sir Peter Matthews	10,253	—
Sir Alec Merrison	910	—
Sir Jeremy Morse	8,663	—
BI Pitman	55,541	216,954
Lord Plumb	1,059	—
JM Raisman	3,558	—
Sir Peter Ramsbotham	1,012	—
CR Smith	8,625	—
E Swainson	568	—
MHR Thompson	9,828	166,539

Total directors' remuneration in 1987 was £1.37m, of which the chairman received £145,056 and the highest-paid director £188,124.

PRINCIPAL SUBSIDIARIES AND RELATED COMPANIES

Alex Lawrie Factors Ltd, Banco Anglo Colombiano SA – Colombia (49%), Bankers' Automated Clearing Services Ltd (24%), Bank of London & Montreal Ltd – Honduras, Black Horse Agencies Ltd, Black Horse Life Assurance Company Ltd, Black Horse Relocation Services Ltd, General Finance Ltd – New Zealand, International Commodities Clearing House Holdings (22%), International Factors Ltd, Investors in Industry Group Plc (14%), Joint Credit Card Company Ltd (30%), LBI Bank & Trust Company (Cayman) Ltd, LBI Finance (Hong Kong) Ltd, Lloyds America Securities Corp – US, Lloyds Asia Ltd, Lloyds Bank (Belgium) SA, Lloyds Bank Canada, Lloyds Bank Export Finance Ltd, Lloyds Bank Finance (Isle of Man) Ltd, Lloyds Bank Finance Ltd – Jersey, Lloyds Bank Insurance Services Ltd, Lloyds Bank International Ltd – Bahamas, Lloyds Bank International Ltd – Guernsey, Lloyds Bank Ltd – France, Lloyds Bank NZA Ltd – Australia, Lloyds Bank Stockbrokers Ltd, Lloyds Bank Trust Co Ltd – Channel Islands, Lloyds Bank Unit Trust Managers Ltd, Lloyds Bowmaker Finance Ltd, Lloyds Development Capital Ltd, Lloyds International Corp – US, Lloyds International Ltd – Australia, Lloyds International Management SA – Switzerland, Lloyds International Merchant Bank (SEA) Ltd – Singapore, Lloyds Leasing España SA – Spain, Lloyds Leasing Ltd, Lloyds Merchant Bank Ltd, Lloyds Trust Co BV – Netherlands, Multiplic Banco de Investimento SA – Brazil (50%), Zealand Savings Bank Ltd, Schröder, Münchmeyer, Hengst & Co – West Germany, South Pacific Merchant Finance Ltd – New Zealand (70%), Travellers Cheque Associates Ltd (36%), Yorkshire Bank Plc (20%)

BRAND NAMES

Black Horse, Cashcall, Fundsflow, Lloyds Bank

CONTACTS AND FURTHER INFORMATION

John Robson, Press Office, Lloyds Bank Plc, 71 Lombard Street, London EC3P 3BS. Tel: 01-626 1500.

LONRHO Plc

GENERAL INFORMATION

Head office	Cheapside House, 138 Cheapside, London EC2V 6BL. Tel: 01-606 9898
Directors	The Rt Hon Sir Edward du Cann KBE (chairman), RW Rowland (managing and chief executive), RG Badger FCA, RF Dunlop, N Kruger – Zimbabwe, MJJR Leclézio – Mauritius, TJ Robinson FCA, PGB Spicer, PM Tarsh FCA, RE Whitten FCA, Sir Peter Youens CMG OBE
Advisers	No specified adviser
Auditors	Peat Marwick McLintock
Registrars	National Westminster Registrar's Department
Brokers	Capel-Cure Myers
Solicitors	No specified adviser

GENERAL FINANCIAL INFORMATION

Market capitalisation	£923.8m at 1 January 1988
Capital structure	
Issued ordinary shares (25p)	442.1m
Issued preference shares (£1)	None
Warrants	None
Convertibles	£39.6m 4.75% convertible guaranteed bond 2001 (convertible at 212p per share at fixed conversion rate of $1.4684 to £1) £60m 4.5% convertible guaranteed bond 2002 (convertible at 268p per share)
Traded options	Yes
ADRs	None
Shareholders over 5%	RW Rowland 15.2%, Mutual Shares Corporation, Mutual Beacon Fund, Mutual Qualified Income Fund, Nas Ltd and Heine Family Fund 6.9%

FT CATEGORY

FT: Overseas traders
FT-A: Overseas traders

MAJOR ACTIVITIES

Lonrho is a diversified international organisation controlling 800 companies in over 80 countries. Operations are predominantly based in the UK, central Africa and South Africa.

Lonrho's principal activities are centred around seven core areas – motor and equipment distribution; general trade; manufacturing; leisure, wine and spirits; mineral extraction and refining; financial services; and agriculture. In 1987 the largest contribution to pre-tax profits came from mineral extraction and refining (29.5%), leisure, wine and spirits (16%) and motor and equipment distribution (15.5%).

The group is becoming increasingly mining orientated. The group owns the third largest platinum mine in the world and produces significant quantities of gold, as well as copper, coal, oil, palladium and rhodium.

The motor distribution interests include the UK Volkswagen, Audi and SEAT distribution franchises and extensive franchises in Africa. Leisure activities include the Metropole and Princess hotel chains and Whyte & Mackay, the Scotch whisky distillers. Printing and publishing interests include the *Observer* newspaper, George Outram and Greenaway·Harrison, the security printers.

Agriculture operations include ranching and production of sugar and tea. The group has freight forwarding and warehousing interests and is involved in the engineering and manufacture of steel and glass products.

In February 1987 Lonrho bought the remaining 49% minority stake in Western Platinum and is in the process of expanding gold operations in Ghana, Zimbabwe and South Africa. Because of this the shares are expected to move more closely with the underlying gold and platinum price and volatility is therefore likely to increase. The company could be considered a hedge stock against inflation.

The thrust of the group's non-mining interests is now being focused upon increasing oil and gas business exposure and expanding opportunities in northern Europe.

Economic factors which affect the company's profitability are the level of world inflation, which partly determines precious metal prices, UK personal disposable income and international tourist traffic. Comparisons are difficult to make because of the group's wide-ranging interests, but in the mining sector RTZ in the UK and Anglo-American in South Africa are the listed companies which probably have most in common with Lonrho.

In April 1987 Lonrho finally succeeded in gaining a government inquiry into the £615m acquisition of House of Fraser by the Al-Fayed family. The Department of Trade is investigating the affairs of House of Fraser Holdings with particular reference to the circumstances surrounding the acquisition of shares in House of Fraser in 1985 and 1986. A Lonrho bid for House of Fraser was blocked by the Monopolies Commission in 1981. Lonrho then sold its stake in House of Fraser to the Al-Fayeds in 1984 who later launched an agreed bid for House of Fraser three days before Lonrho was given the go-ahead by the Monopolies Commission to bid itself.

This permission came too late for Lonrho, since the Al-Fayeds gained control of House of Fraser five days later, after a lightning share purchase.

FINANCIAL HISTORY

Since 1983 Lonrho's turnover and pre-tax profits have increased by 27% and 39% respectively. More significantly, earnings per share have increased by 135%. Steady growth has been led by the group's mining interests. The more recent improvement in group performance has been against the background of unfavourable exchange rate movements. Pre-tax margins have increased from 4.8% in 1983 to 6.6% in 1987.

Pre-tax profits in 1987 increased by 21.3% to £200.2m on turnover 13.7% ahead at £3.013bn. Earnings per share increased by 29.7% to 30.1p. Lonrho has always had high dividend payouts. In 1987 the dividend increased by 19.2% to 13p. Net asset value at the 1987 year end was 246p per share.

Lonrho's tax charge in 1987 was 41.4% at £83m, higher than the average for UK companies because of the higher tax charges incurred by overseas profits. The tax charge for South Africa, for instance, is 57.5%. There was an extraordinary profit of £43.6m, mainly due to the £71.1m profit on the sale of the Metropole Casino group. There was a £22.4m charge for losses and closure costs on the disposal of News UK.

Share price and relative to FT-A All-Share

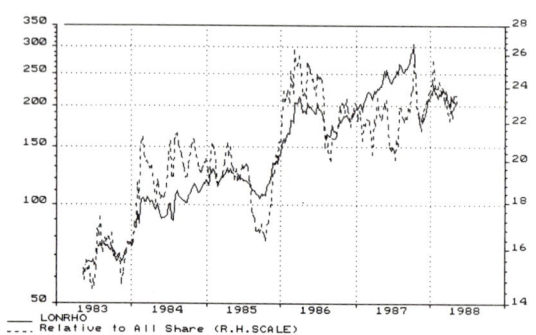

LONRHO
Relative to All Share (R.H.SCALE)

F I V E   Y E A R   F I N A N C I A L   I N F O R M A T I O N

Year	Turnover (£m)	Pre-tax (£m)	Earnings (p)	Dividends net (p)	Dividend cover (x)	Net assets (p)	Price (p) High	Price (p) Low	PER (x) High	PER (x) Low	Yield (%) High	Yield (%) Low
1983	2,356.5	113.2	12.8	7.5	1.7	164	89	68	27.6	8.0	15.68	11.90
1984	2,367.5	135.4	17.3	9.1	1.9	199	140	94	29.9	10.4	11.28	8.34
1985	2,586.2	158.3	21.2	9.9	2.1	199	165	123	12.9	6.8	11.03	8.21
1986	2,651.0	165.1	23.2	10.9	2.1	182	246	168	14.5	7.4	8.26	5.71
1987	3,013.9	200.2	30.1	13.0	2.3	246	362	202	14.9	6.7	8.82	4.92

During 1987 the company spent: $30m on a 50% interest in the Hondo Oil & Gas Company, a joint venture with Robert O Anderson, founder of Atlantic Richfield; £28.1m on the freehold of Cheapside House, the group's head office; $75m on the remaining 49% interest in Western Platinum; and DM48m for an 80% interest in Ruhrglas, the major German glass manufacturer.

Balancing this expenditure the company raised a net £158.4m from the sale of its casino interests, the freehold of 45 Park Lane and the disposal of News UK. Lonrho's Japanese listing and convertible issue raised £110.8m. Though gearing remained high, the balance sheet was strong, with total cash and unused facilities exceeding £1bn at the 1987 year end.

SHARE PRICE HISTORY

Lonrho's share price has risen strongly from a level of 120p in September 1985 to a high of 368p in October 1987. The initial price move was prompted by good results and strong bid rumours supported by US buying. The shares then attracted widespread support following what was seen as Lonrho's bargain acquisition of the remaining holding in its platinum producer, Western Platinum. It was pushed higher by firmer precious metal prices and the expectation of excellent results, reaching its high of 368p just before the autumn 1987 crash.

Apart from the major share price re-rating in late 1985 and early 1986, the shares have moved in line with the market. Relative to the FT-A All-Share index, Lonrho has traded in a range between 24% and 28% since mid-1986.

SENIOR MANAGEMENT

Managing director and chief executive is Roland 'Tiny' Rowland, whose entrepreneurial flair has built the company up from a relatively small concern to its present size.

Sir Edward du Cann is chairman. Alan Ball, who was deputy chairman and had been a director since 1951, died in October 1987. The company also lost Lord Duncan-Sandys, who had been both chairman and president of Lonrho, on his death in November 1987.

CAPITAL

At 22 April 1988 there were 442.1m ordinary shares in issue, following the one for six scrip issue of 63.1m new shares. Since 1982 there have been three scrip issues altogether, the other two in 1986 and 1987 increasing the share capital by 27.4m and 30.7m shares respectively.

Since 1982 35.9m shares have been issued against the conversion of convertible loan stock. In July 1987, 20m shares were issued on the group's listing in Tokyo at 280.4p per share. In August 1987 Lonrho Finance, a wholly-owned subsidiary, issued £60m of 4.5% convertible guaranteed bonds due 2002, convertible at 268p per share. Conversion of the outstanding loan stock would result in the issue of 35.1m new shares.

The group has the right to buy in 50.5m of its own shares. 'Tiny' Rowland has a 15.2% holding and the Mutual Share Corporation, Mutual Qualified Income Fund, Mutual Beacon Fund, Nas Ltd and the Heine Family Fund have 6.9%. There are no other declarable stakes over 5%.

GROUP REVIEW

Mining and refining In 1987 mining and refining represented 5% of group turnover and 29.5% of pre-tax profits.

Lonrho owns and operates the third largest platinum mine in the world – Western Platinum. The mine and refinery, which is located in the Brits region of South Africa, produced 258,000 ounces of platinum group metals in 1987. Output includes platinum, palladium and rhodium. Western Platinum is the lowest-cost producer in the industry.

Ore is mined by underground methods and a recently built base metal refinery located on site processes concentrated ore to a precious metal concentrate, which is further refined to platinum metals. Refined metal is sold on contract, the major client being car manufacturer Mitsubishi of Japan. Additional shafts are being sunk and construction has started on a third plant designed to mill and treat an additional million tonnes of ore per annum from the middle of 1989.

Other operations in South Africa are gold and coal mines held through listed subsidiary Duiker Exploration, in which Lonrho has a 67% beneficial interest. Duiker has a 36% interest in the new Erfdeel gold mine in the Orange Free State being brought into production by Anglo-American. Initial production began in 1987 and is planned to increase to 400,000 ounces of gold a year over the next few years. Coal sales reached record levels of 3.5m tonnes in 1987 but were affected by lower dollar prices and adverse exchange rates.

Total group gold production reached 442,000 ounces in 1987. Lonrho's major gold operations are located in Ghana, where the group holds 45% of Ashanti Goldfields, a producer of 300,000 ounces of gold a year. $160m is being invested in Ashanti and production is scheduled to increase by 50% over a five year period. Lonrho also has important gold interests in Zimbabwe, through a 49% interest in Corsyn Consolidated Mines, which operates a number of small gold and copper mines in Zimbabwe. Lonrho has entered into a joint venture with the government of Zimbabwe to promote the mining and marketing of amethysts.

In October 1986 Lonrho formed a partnership with Robert O Anderson, founder of Atlantic Richfield, by taking a 50% stake in Hondo Oil & Gas. With proven reserves of 43m barrels, Hondo was merged into the quoted Californian refiner Pauley Petroleum, to create one of the very few US integrated independent oil companies. The joint venture has an 80% stake in Pauley, which is listed on the American Stock Exchange.

In 1987 turnover was up 8% to £150.8m. Pre-tax profits were up 32.3% to £59.1m.

Leisure, wine and spirits In 1987, leisure, wine and spirits represented 11.2% of group turnover and 16% of pre-tax profits.

The group's hotel interests are made up of the Princess group of Bermuda, the Metropole Hotel group of the UK and the Mount Kenya Safari Club.

The Princess group operates hotels in the Bahamas, Mexico, Bermuda and most recently in Arizona. Two casinos are operated in the Bahamas. The Metropole group owns prestigious hotels in London, Brighton, Birmingham and Blackpool, with major conference facilities available in Birmingham and under development in London. In June 1987 Lonrho sold its UK casino interests and the freehold of 45 Park Lane to Brent Walker.

Louis Eschenauer is the group's wholly-owned Bordeaux vineyard owner and wine merchant, producing top quality classified wines. Whyte & Mackay is the second largest brand-owning company in the UK Scotch whisky market. Deluxe 21-year-old blend is a significant seller at the top end of the market in the Asian and Pacific regions. Lonrho has 23 breweries in Africa, 19 of which are in partnership with governments and municipalities.

Turnover in 1987 was 14.9% up at £339m. Pre-tax profits rose 77.3% to £32.1m.

Motor and equipment distribution In 1987 motor and equipment distribution represented 43.4% of group turnover and 15.5% of pre-tax profits.

The group's interests are predominantly based in the UK. Lonrho imports and distributes Volkswagen and Audi motor cars through VAG (UK), which is the largest importer of European cars into the UK. The agreement with Volkswagen expires in 1995 and in 1987 was renegotiated to allow Volkswagen a greater interest in the distribution of its products in the UK. Record sales of 120,000 units were achieved in 1987, with a major product launch of the new Audi 80 and 90 range.

Lonrho also distributes Volkswagen and MAN trucks and buses and in 1987 introduced the MAN F90, Truck of the Year. Through its subsidiary SEAT Concessionaires (UK), Lonrho is the sole distributor of SEAT motor cars in the UK, recording a 57.7% sales increase in 1987. Lonrho imports and distributes Deutz-Fahr tractors and agricultural machinery in the UK.

UK garage businesses include Dutton-Forshaw, retailers of Rover Group and Jaguar cars, Dovercourt Motor Company, VW and Audi retailers and Jack Barclay, retailers of Rolls-Royce and Bentley cars.

In Africa Lonrho is one of the largest motor vehicle distributors with agencies for Mercedes Benz, Toyota, Peugeot, Audi, Volkswagen, Mitsubishi, Massey Ferguson, General Motors, Rover Group and several other manufacturers.

In Kenya, Associated Vehicles produce 65% of all vehicles assembled and Massey Ferguson (distributed by the group) has a 41% market share. Power Equipment distributes tractors and other agricultural equipment in Zambia.

In 1987 turnover was 11.9% up at £1.307bn. Pre-tax profits were 39% up to £31m.

Financial services In 1987 financial services represented 3.8% of group turnover and 11.9% of pre-tax profits.

Among the group's UK financial services businesses are FE Wright (Lloyd's insurance brokers), Balfour Williamson (export confirmers) and two property companies. Wright Nacora is a joint venture to handle all the international insurance broking business of Lonrho and the group's freight forwarders Kuehne and Nagel. Overseas the group has major interests in investment and property-holding companies in Belgium, Zaïre, Nigeria, South Africa and Zimbabwe.

In 1987 turnover was down 22.1% to £115.3m. Pre-tax profits were 22.1% down at £23.9m.

Agriculture In 1987 agriculture represented 2.9% of group turnover and 7.0% of pre-tax profits.

Lonrho is Africa's largest food-producing company with ranching and crop cultivation interests spread over a million and a half acres, located in west, east, central and southern Africa. The size of the group's herd is 125,000 head. Group sugar production from its seven estates in Swaziland, Mauritius and Malawi amounted to half a million tonnes in 1987.

Maize and wheat are the group's principal crops in Kenya and Tanzania. In Malawi the group produces coffee, chillies, macadamia and cashew nuts and 5m kilos of tea. Tea is also grown in Tanzania. In Mozambique Lonrho, in partnership with the government, employs over 3,000 people growing vegetables for local markets and exporting cotton lint. The group's cattle are concentrated in Zambia and Zimbabwe, where the group also grows coffee and wattles for use as tanning extract and in the manufacture of adhesives. Through Hondo Oil & Gas, the group acquired ranches of over 600,000 acres in New Mexico and Texas.

CHIEF EXECUTIVE'S STATEMENT

'Your Company has had a highly successful year in all respects and this is reflected in the results I am able to present to you. Profit before tax has increased to a record £200.2m and earnings per share are up at 30.1 pence on an increased share capital.

The Group balance sheet is strong with shareholders' funds substantially up at £924m and cash balances at the year end of £313m. The book value of the Group's assets is considerably below their real worth, and this is one of the reasons for the Lonrho share price reaching record highs during the year. Your Company's businesses are at varying stages of maturity and there is real growth throughout the Group. Lonrho's unused banking facilities and strong cash position give us immediately available funds in excess of one thousand million pounds to support further expansion without recourse to share issues.'

'Tiny' Rowland

In 1987 turnover was 9.8% up at £86.4m. Pre-tax profits were 61.3% ahead at £14m.

General trade In 1987 general trade represented 16.9% of group turnover and 8.4% of pre-tax profits.

Bauman Hinde is the group's cotton merchanting company. The PJH Group is the leading UK distributor of kitchen and bathroom equipment and electrical appliances. Lonrho represents Beechcraft, Sikorsky and Boeing and other American aircraft manufacturers in a number of African countries. The Kuehne and Nagel group of companies, 50%-owned by Lonrho, is engaged in the ocean freight business throughout the world and has recently expanded into air freight.

Turnpan Zambia imports and distributes mining machinery and spare parts. African Commercial Holdings distributes electrical goods and batteries, bottles Coca-Cola and manufactures and distributes paint. The Teal Record Company distributes records and tapes in Zambia.

1987 turnover was 20.4% up at £510m. Pre-tax profits were

down 8.2% to £16.8m.

Manufacturing   In 1987 manufacturing represented 16.7% of group turnover and 11.6% of pre-tax profits.

Manufacturing includes Lonrho's businesses in textiles, engineering, printing and publishing. Lonrho Textiles manufactures and distributes polyester cotton products through Brentfords and Accord outlets. David Whitehead and Sons manufactures domestic textiles in Preston.

In Africa the group has various associate textile businesses. Consolidated Textiles, acquired by the group in partnership with ZANU (PF) in 1987, has 80% of the blanket market in Zimbabwe. Blantyre Netting in Malawi is extending its netting business. The group's new cotton ginnery in Zambia ginned 10,000 tonnes of seed in 1987.

Products of Lonrho's engineering businesses include precoated aluminium strip, car transporters, stainless steel sinks, Sheer Pride office furniture and filing cabinets and commercial refrigeration equipment. In April 1987, the group acquired Ruhrglas, the largest manufacturer of table glass in West Germany and the fourth largest supplier of container glass, with total production of over a billion individual pieces. In December 1987 the group began negotiations to acquire a 50% stake in the West German industrial conglomerate Krupp-Handel, which has sales of over a billion pounds a year.

The manufactured output of its Nigerian associate John Holt ranges from boats and motor cycles to cosmetics and confectionery. W Dahmer in Zimbabwe sells AVM trucks and buses.

In its printing and publishing area, Lonrho owns the *Observer* and George Outram, printers and publishers of the *Glasgow Herald* and *Evening Times*. The *Observer* has moved to splendid new offices, started regional contract printing in five centres and is still regularly winning more British Press Awards than any other title. George Outram is benefiting from a £22.5m development programme, equipping it with the latest colour presses and an inserting system. Harrison and Sons and Greenaway·Harrison print stamps, bonds, vouchers and other documents for the UK and overseas markets. In July 1987 Lonrho sold its 78% holding in News (UK), the publishers of *Today*, to News International, after rescuing it when it was in difficulties.

Turnover in 1987 was 23.9% up at £504.8m. Pre-tax profits were 5.4% up to £23.3m.

GEOGRAPHICAL REVIEW

In 1987 the UK accounted for 61% of group turnover, east, central and west Africa for 10.4%, southern Africa for 7.7%, the Americas for 4.4% and Europe and the rest of the world for 16.5%.

In 1987 the UK accounted for 34.3% of group pre-tax profits, east, central and west Africa for 29.3%, southern Africa for 20%, the Americas for 11.5% and Europe and the rest of the world for 4.9%.

CORPORATE CALENDAR

Year end	30 September
Preliminary results	end January
Report and accounts	February
AGM	mid March
Final dividend paid	6 April
Interim results	June
Interim dividend paid	1 October

DIRECTORS' HOLDINGS

	Ordinary shares	Options
Sir Edward du Cann	13,378	·346,557
AH Ball	—	—
RW Rowland	66,764,771	1,336,591
RG Badger	13,409	199,008
RF Dunlop	68,649	465,615
N Kruger	80,305	91,758
MJJR Leclézio	63,847	91,758
TJ Robinson	12,140	497,039
PGB Spicer	43,259	460,471
PM Tarsh	344,542	16,799
RE Whitten	10,587	507,598
Sir Peter Youens	4,742	164,780

Total directors' remuneration for 1987 was £2.12m, of which the chairman received £127,536 and the chief executive, who was the highest-paid director, £650,251.

PRINCIPAL SUBSIDIARIES AND RELATED COMPANIES

African Commercial Holdings Ltd – Zambia, Ashanti Goldfields Corporation (Ghana) Ltd – Ghana (45%), Balfour, Williamson & Co Ltd, Baumann, Hinde & Co Ltd, Charter Estates Ltd – Zimbabwe, Chibuku Products Ltd – Malawi (70%), Church & Bramhall (Stockholders) Ltd, Coated Strip Ltd, Cominière SA – Belgium (57%), Companhia Agro-Industrial Lonrho-Moçambique Limitada – Mozambique (50%), Consolidated Holdings Ltd – Kenya (52%), Consolidated Textiles (Zimbabwe) Ltd (50%), Construction Associates (Pvt) Ltd – Zimbabwe (60%), Corsyn Consolidated Mines Ltd – Zimbabwe, David Whitehead & Sons (Malawi) Ltd (51%), David Whitehead & Sons Ltd, David Whitehead Textiles Ltd – Zimbabwe, Delkins Ltd – Zambia (66%), Dovercourt Motor Co Ltd, Duiker Exploration Ltd – South Africa (67%), Dutton Forshaw Facilities Ltd (25%), Dutton Forshaw (Machinery) Ltd, Dwangwa Sugar Corporation Ltd – Malawi, East African Tanning Extract Co Ltd – Kenya, FE Wright Group Ltd, Fassnidge, Son & Norris Ltd, Firsteel Ltd, Firsteel Metal Products Ltd, George Outram & Company Ltd, Greenaway · Harrison Ltd, Harrison & Sons Ltd, Harrison Decorative Papers Ltd, Heinrich's Syndicate Ltd (90%) – Zambia, Holmes McDougall Ltd, Hondo Oil & Gas Company – US (50%), Independence Mining (Pvt) Ltd – Zimbabwe, JHI Ltd – Nigeria (48%), Jack Barclay Ltd, John Holt Agricultural Engineers Ltd – Nigeria, John Holt Group Ltd, John Holt Group Ltd – Nigeria (60%), John Holt Ltd – Nigeria (40%), Kalangwa Estates Ltd – Zambia, Kuehne & Nagel (UK) Ltd (50%), Kühne & Nagel (AG & Co) – West Germany (50%), Kühne & Nagel Holding Inc – US (50%), Lightfoot Refrigeration Co Ltd, London City & Westcliff Properties Ltd, London City and International Ltd, Lonrho Exports Ltd, Lonrho Finance Plc, Lonrho International – Netherlands, Lonrho (Malawi) Ltd – Malawi, Lonrho Motor Holdings Ltd – South Africa, Lonrho South Africa Ltd – South Africa, Lonrho Sugar Corporation Ltd – Swaziland, Lonrho Textiles Ltd, Lonrho Zambia Ltd – Zambia, Lonrho Zimbabwe Ltd – Zimbabwe, Louis Eschenauer SA – France, LSA Motors Ltd – South Africa, Lusolanda SARL – Angola, MAN-VW Truck and Bus Ltd (80%), Makandi Estates Ltd, Matermaco SA – Belgium (88%), Merville Ltd – Mauritius (53%), Metropole Hotels (Holdings) Ltd, Motor Mart Group Ltd – Kenya, Mount Kenya Safari Club Ltd – Kenya (75%), Mufindi Tea Co Ltd – Tanzania (75%), Mumbwa Cotton Ginnery Ltd – Zambia, NAFCO Investments Ltd – South Africa, National Breweries Ltd – Zambia (49%), Newell Dunford Ltd, Nicol & Andrew (London) Ltd, PJH Group Ltd, PS Mandrides & Co Ltd – Nigeria (38%), Page Bros (Norwich) Ltd, Pauley Petroleum Inc – US (40%), Pland Stainless Ltd, Power Equipment Ltd – Zambia (75%), Princess Properties International Ltd – Bermuda, Ruhrglas AG – West Germany (80%), Saville Tractors (Belfast) Ltd, Saville Tractors Ltd, Scottish & Universal Newspapers Ltd, Scottish and Universal Investments Ltd, SEAT Concessionaires (UK) Ltd, Sheer Pride Ltd, Southern Watch & Clock Supplies Ltd, Sportworks Ltd, Stainless Steel Products Ltd – Malta, Star Commercial – Zambia, Teal Record Co (Zambia) Ltd – Zambia, The Blantyre Netting Company Ltd – Malawi (63%), The Dovercourt Motor Co Ltd (25%), The Observer Ltd, The Wattle Company Ltd – Zimbabwe, Turnpan Zambia Ltd – Zambia, VAG Finance Ltd (49%), VAG (UK) Ltd, W Dahmer & Co (Pvt) Ltd – Zimbabwe (60%), Wankel International SA – Luxembourg (72%), Watveare Ltd, Western Machinery & Equipment Company Ltd, Western Platinum Ltd – South Africa (99%), Western Platinum Refinery Ltd – South Africa, Whyte & Mackay Distillers Ltd, Willoughby's Consolidated Plc – Zimbabwe (51%), Zambesi Coachworks Ltd – Zimbabwe, Zimoco Ltd – Zimbabwe

BRAND NAMES

Accord, Brentfords, Buchanan, Château Rausan-Ségla, Château Smith Haut-Lafite, Claymore, Crawford's, Crawford's Five Star, Dalmore, *Evening Times*, *Glasgow Herald*, Haig, Harrison Jamie Stuart, John Barr, Louis

Eschenauer, Metropole, *Observer*, Old Fettercairn, Old Mull, Princess, Rulglas, San Marco, The Real Mackenzie, Tomintoul-Glenlivet, Whyte & Mackay

CONTACTS AND FURTHER INFORMATION

MT Pearce, Company Secretary, Lonrho Plc, Cheapside House, 138 Cheapside, London EC2V 6BL. Tel: 01-606 9898.

MEPC plc

GENERAL INFORMATION

Head office	Brook House, 113 Park Lane, London W1Y 4AY. Tel: 01-491 5300
Directors	RW Adam CA (chairman), CJ Benson FRICS (vice-chairman and managing director), JA Beveridge FCA, RM Squire FRICS, JL Tuckey FRICS (deputy managing director), IR Watters FRICS. *Non-exec* Lord Boardman MC TD DL, Sir Patrick Meaney, The Hon Angus Ogilvy, Sir Adam Thomson CBE LLD
Advisers	Hill Samuel & Co Ltd, County NatWest Ltd, Morgan Grenfell & Co Ltd
Auditors	Peat Marwick McLintock
Registrars	Barclays Bank Registrar's Department
Brokers	Warburg Securities, County NatWest WoodMac, Cazenove & Co
Solicitors	Clifford Chance, Linklaters & Paines

GENERAL FINANCIAL INFORMATION

Market capitalisation	£1.558bn at 1 January 1988
Capital structure	
Issued ordinary shares	316.4m
Issued preference shares (£1)	2.5m 3.15% net CP
Warrants	None
Convertibles	£5m 6.5% CULS 1995/2000 (30.303 shares per £100 stock)
	£7.8m 8.25% convertible US dollar bonds 1996 (convertible at a fixed rate of $2.373/£1 at 41.841 shares per £100 stock)
	£4m 8.75% convertible Australian dollar bonds 1996 (convertible at a fixed rate of Australian $2.04/£1 at 40.485 shares per £100 stock)
Traded options	None
Shareholders over 5%	Co-operative Insurance Society Ltd 15.8%, HJ Hyams 6.8%

FT CATEGORY

FT: Property
FT-A: Property

MAJOR ACTIVITIES

MEPC is the UK's second largest property company, owning and developing commercial property on an international scale. The property investment portfolio consists principally of office and retail buildings. It also includes a smaller proportion of industrial and high-tech space.

MEPC's portfolio is valued at £2.44bn. 76% of this is located in the UK and 8% is under development. The portfolio is located in five broad centres in which the UK predominates. The other centres are Australia, the US, Germany and the rest of Europe. Among the better known of UK properties are Centre Point, comprising 170,000 sq ft of office space on New Oxford Street, Ninety Long Acre, Drapers Gardens and the Friary Shopping Centre in Guildford.

FINANCIAL HISTORY

Growth in net assets during the early to middle 1980s was stunted by depressed conditions in the London and provincial office markets. The annualised rate of increase of only 4% between 1983 and 1986 was in line with that of other UK property companies.

With the onset of Big Bang and all that this implied for City office values, the 1986/87 growth in net asset value accelerated sharply by over 20%, from 440p to 533p per share. Similarly, growth in net rental income, pre-tax profits and earnings per share in 1987 showed significant improvements over the annualised rates recorded earlier in the decade, rising by 25%,

FIVE YEAR FINANCIAL INFORMATION

Year	Turnover (£m)	Pre-tax (£m)	Earnings (p)	Dividends net (p)	Dividend cover (x)	Net assets (p)	Price (p) High	Low	PER (x) High	Low	Yield (%) High	Low
1983	101.8	40.4	11.5	8.0	1.4	380	281	188	24.5	18.5	5.51	3.98
1984	117.7	45.2	13.6	9.0	1.5	411	335	250	26.6	20.3	4.63	3.60
1985	119.3	51.6	15.6	10.5	1.5	415	320	257	23.5	17.8	5.28	4.00
1986	144.1	58.4	16.3	11.5	1.4	440	380	277	24.3	17.7	5.42	3.00
1987	172.7	80.2	19.2	13.0	1.5	533	583	339	33.3	20.8	4.78	2.76

37% and 18% respectively, compared with annualised rates for the three previous years of 10%, 11% and 10%.

1987 pre-tax profits increased 37% to £80.2m, compared with £58.4m for 1986. Profits after tax increased by 39%. Earnings per share rose less, by 18% from 16.3p to 19.2p, because of the equity issued to acquire Oldham Estates. Dividends were up 13% to 13.0p from 11.5p in 1986.

SHARE PRICE HISTORY

Along with property shares in general, those of MEPC underperformed the FT-A All-Share index badly during the mid-1980s as rental and asset value growth showed no signs of accelerating. However, with the recent boom in south-east property prices came a move sharply upwards to a high of 592p, a level where they exceeded net asset value.

The autumn 1987 market crash brought this back to a level nearer to net assets. But by the end of 1987 the shares were at 445p, still registering a 32% gain on the year, and had outperformed the All-Share index by 20%.

SENIOR MANAGEMENT

RW Adam is chairman and CJ Benson is vice-chairman and managing director. CJ Barwick and DEM Hall are joint managing directors of MEPC Developments. AW Pearson is managing director of Ortem Developments. IR Watters is managing director of Metestates; RL Frost is chairman and managing director of MEPC Australia; NAS Barr is managing director of MEPC Germany; RMD Greene is managing director of MEPC Ireland; and DS Gruber is president of MEPC American Properties.

CAPITAL

At 30 September 1987, there were 316.4m ordinary shares and 2.167m cumulative preference shares in issue. Oldham Estates was acquired in March 1987. 75% was paid for by the issue of new ordinary shares, and the remaining 25% by the issue of long-dated 10½% unsecured loan stock or cash.

The group has continued its policy of raising longer term fixed rate finance to lengthen the overall maturity of debt and

CHAIRMAN'S STATEMENT

'Our development programme expands in line with our growth in assets and now amounts to some £900m. . . . It is based largely on developing assets already existing in our portfolio and is therefore sufficiently flexible to meet changes in market demands . . . while events affect the rate of future growth, I remain confident that the demand for future developments of the high quality in which MEPC specialises, will continue.' *RW Adam*

to reduce sensitivity to interest rate fluctuations. The debt profile is such that approximately 80% is repayable in more than five years and 88% is at fixed rate. The total value of the group's loan capital at 30 September 1987 was £794.2m, of which £539.2m was in sterling.

The conversion of all £18.1m convertible loan stock outstanding at 30 September 1987 would result in the issue of 7.38m shares. Since then 561,048 ordinary shares have been issued on conversion of $3.18m of the 8.25% convertible US Dollar bonds 1996.

GROUP REVIEW

United Kingdom Having recently won a fierce and long battle to gain control of Harry Hyams' Oldham Estates, the UK's largest private property company, MEPC now owns a UK portfolio valued at almost £1.9bn, 76% of its total assets.

The success of the group's £516.4m bid for Oldham represents a significant boost to MEPC's UK asset base. The management hopes to expand further its value through a thorough refurbishment and redevelopment programme on some of the more outdated properties within Oldham's portfolio.

Approximately two-thirds of MEPC's UK portfolio is made up of office and retail properties located in south-east England. The dominant holdings are central London office buildings. The group has recently completed two new office developments: a 37,000 sq ft building at 1 Liverpool Street EC2 let to Yasuda Trust (Europe) Ltd, and a 40,000 sq ft office block at 20 Farringdon Street EC4, let to Peat Marwick McLintock.

The 55,000 sq ft office development at Throgmorton Avenue EC2 should be complete by the end of 1988, and is pre-let to Morgan Grenfell. Work has also begun on the office development at Alban Gate, London Wall EC2, formerly known as Lee House. This, at 360,000 sq ft, is the largest development being undertaken, and involves demolishing the out-dated Lee House and starting again.

Australia Conditions in the Australian property market have remained favourable and results in local currency terms have been excellent. This has been disguised by the continuing weakness of the Australian dollar. Nevertheless, MEPC Australia has continued successfully to identify and complete development opportunities, principally in Melbourne and Sydney.

During 1986/87 the subsidiary company completed a 57,000 sq ft office development at Help Street, Sydney, and let the building to a single tenant. It purchased the 120,000 sq ft Carousel Shopping Centre, Sydney with a view to further expansion.

Europe In Europe the group has been particularly interested in West Germany, and also in France, Ireland, Luxembourg and the Netherlands. More recently Sweden has become an area of activity through Oldham's interests there.

Activity in Germany has proceeded largely as planned, with

Share price and relative to FT-A All-Share

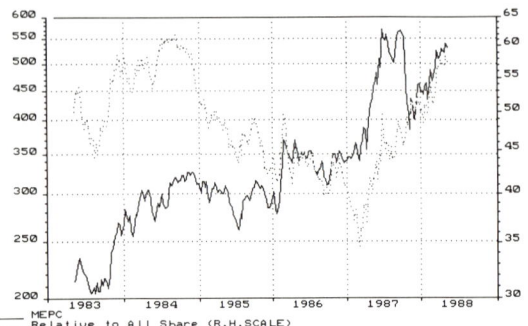

MEPC
Relative to All Share (R.H.SCALE)

PRINCIPAL SUBSIDIARIES AND RELATED COMPANIES

UK   English Property Corporation Plc, MEPC Developments Limited, Metestates Limited, The Oldham Estate Company Plc (99.8%)
Australia   Austore Property Trust (51.3%), MEPC Australia Limited
Europe   MEPC Germany GmbH, MEPC Ireland Limited, Metropolitan Estate and Property International NV – Netherlands
US   MEPC American Holdings Inc, MEPC American Properties Inc

BRAND NAMES

None

CONTACTS AND FURTHER INFORMATION

JPM Lee, MEPC plc, Brook House, 113 Park Lane, London W1Y 4AY. Tel: 01-491 5300.

the second phase of a 36,000 sq ft Stuttgart office development nearing completion and 70% pre-let, mainly to Nixdorf. Two sites have been acquired in Frankfurt. These are being prepared as potential office developments. In Ireland, a modest performance was as good as could have been expected during 1987, following the rationalisation program which disposed of industrial premises to leave a concentration on retail and office space.

United States   The US portfolio is reported to be performing satisfactorily, although a fair amount of space remains unlet due to a perceived national surplus, particularly in Denver and Dallas.

The Travelers Express Tower, a 235,000 sq ft office building in Minneapolis, is 75% let. The Colonnade development in Dallas remains 83% let, and the Marketplace at Denver is 60% occupied.

GEOGRAPHICAL REVIEW

At 30 September 1987 the geographical breakdown of gross rental income and other charges and assets were UK 70.1% and 76.3%, Australia 10.5% and 10.4%, Europe 9.0% and 7.3%, and the US 10.4% and 6.0%.

CORPORATE CALENDAR

Year end	30 September
Preliminary results	November
Report and accounts	December
AGM	January
Final dividend paid	January
Interim results	June
Interim dividend paid	July

DIRECTORS' HOLDINGS

	Fully-paid ordinary shares	Options
RW Adam	1,500	—
CJ Benson	357,947	182,600
JA Beveridge	5,315	122,500
Lord Boardman	600	—
Sir Patrick Meaney	—	—
The Hon Angus Ogilvy	1,200	—
RM Squire	13,118	130,600
Sir Adam Thomson	500	—
JL Tuckey	5,918	126,600

Total directors' remuneration in 1987 was £723,000 including fees. The chairman was paid £50,000, and the highest-paid director £152,530.

MARKS AND SPENCER p.l.c.

GENERAL INFORMATION

Head office	Michael House, 36–37 Baker Street, London W1A 1DN. Tel: 01-935 4422
Directors	The Lord Rayner (chairman), R Greenbury (chief executive), NL Colne, JA Lusher, JK Oates FCT, AS Orton, SJ Sacher, The Hon David Sieff, CV Silver, AKP Smith, PH Spriddell, DG Trangmar. *Non-exec* DV Atterton CBE, RAE Herbert, DG Lanigan, DR Susman, The Rt Hon Baroness Young
Advisers	No specified adviser
Auditors	Deloitte Haskins & Sells
Registrars	Ravensbourne Registration Services Ltd
Brokers	Cazenove & Co
Solicitors	Linklaters & Paines

GENERAL FINANCIAL INFORMATION

Market capitalisation	£4.838bn at 1 January 1988
Capital structure	
Issued ordinary shares (25p)	2.65bn
Issued preference shares (£1)	0.35m 7.0% CP
	1.0m 4.9% CP
Warrants	None
Convertibles	None
Traded options	Yes
ADRs	One ADR per one ordinary share
Shareholders over 5%	Prudential Corporation 6.4%

FT CATEGORY

FT: Drapery and stores
FT-A: Stores

MAJOR ACTIVITIES

The core business comprises UK multiple retailing. A total of 267 main stores and 17 smaller satellite branches were in operation as at March 1988, occupying 8.5m square feet of selling area, and offering a wide range of merchandise.

The Marks and Spencer retail chain has the largest single share of the UK retailing market. An estimated 96% or more of group profits derive from the UK retail division. Forming an integral part of UK retailing is a newly emerging financial services division, offering credit facilities to customers. Further contributions to group profits come from a growing export business, and from direct overseas retail representation in France, Belgium, Eire, Canada and, most recently, the US.

As the most profitable UK retailer the company is expected to build on its existing strengths within the home market, especially now its plans for a steady increase in selling area are being realised. In the medium term, its overseas operations could form a useful source of growth, especially given its decision to explore the US more fully.

CHAIRMAN'S STATEMENT

'We had a much improved second half in the U.K. with sales increased by 13.5% and Profits Before Tax 20.1% higher than last year. . . .

Since the year end we have acquired Brooks Brothers, a unique U.S. retailer, mainly of high quality mens clothing, which also has outlets in Japan. In addition we have secured from the Campeau Corporation certain preferential and exclusive rights for food and clothing retail sites in the United States and Canada. . . .

The major U.K. growth and investment plans will continue and the Marks and Spencer Group looks forward confidently to the future.' *The Lord Rayner*

In April 1988 Marks and Spencer successfully bid $750m for Brooks Brothers, the famous upmarket US shirtmakers and menswear chain.

The recently formed financial services division has good growth prospects. It is test-marketing personal loans available for general purposes, not restricted to making Marks and Spencer purchases, and is offering a legal protection scheme.

Key economic indicators influencing sales are consumer expenditure, personal disposable incomes, consumer confidence and interest rates. Principal UK competitors include: Burton, Next, Storehouse, Sears and GUS in clothing and household goods; J Sainsbury in food; and Burton and Next in financial services.

FINANCIAL HISTORY

In 1987/88 group sales rose by 8.5% to £4.6bn. Over five years the increase amounts to 82%. Pre-tax profits advanced by 16% in 1987/88 to £502m, making a five year rise of 110%. Since 1982/83, pre-tax margins have been fully maintained, helped by the 1986/87 improvement of 0.4% to 10.2% and the 1987/88 increase to 11%.

Within the UK retail division alone, margins are higher at an estimated 11.5%. The group return was held back by the less profitable overseas operations, and the initial development costs surrounding the financial services division. Earnings per share rose by 17.3% in 1987/88 to 12.2p, and by 137% over five years. The dividend increased by 13.3% and 100% respectively.

The group balance sheet at March 1988 was geared at just 3.1%. Shareholders' funds at £2.16bn have doubled over five years. After the Brooks Brothers acquisition, gearing will rise to 26%. The revaluation of UK properties at 31 March 1988 led to a £392.8m surplus, which was taken to reserves.

During 1986/87, a $150m Eurobond issue was completed. This received an AAA rating from both Moody's and Standard and Poor's, the first ever given by both agencies to a retail operation. In 1987/88 a further £150m was raised through a sterling Eurobond issue. Capital expenditure is accelerating, with £1.1bn earmarked for the four years to March 1990, but the group's cash flow is also rising strongly. In 1987/88 capital expenditure totalled £215m.

SHARE PRICE HISTORY

The shares reached an absolute peak of 280.5p in June 1987. But at 22% of the FT-A All-Share index this was lower than the relative highs of 30% in late 1982, and 28% in late 1985. The latter occurred when a number of stockbrokers were keenly recommending the shares on the grounds that a more aggressive management philosophy had emerged. Subsequent profits never quite matched their expectations.

The shares fell in the autumn 1987 crash to 160p. Although they subsequently recovered to 180p they returned to the 160p to 170p range on criticisms of the company's move into higher price merchandise.

SENIOR MANAGEMENT

Lord Rayner was appointed chairman in July 1984 on the retirement of Lord Sieff after 12 years in the position. Richard Greenbury was appointed chief executive in March 1988. He was previously group joint managing director. The group finance director, JK Oates, was recruited from outside the group in April 1984.

F I V E   Y E A R   F I N A N C I A L   I N F O R M A T I O N

Year	Turnover (£m)	Pre-tax (£m)	Earnings (p)	Dividends net (p)	Dividend cover (x)	Net assets (p)	Price (p) High	Price (p) Low	PER (x) High	PER (x) Low	Yield (%) High	Yield (%) Low
1983	2,517.4	239.3	5.15	2.55	2.0	43.3	113	96	27.1	22.3	3.81	2.97
1984	2,868.4	279.3	6.32	3.13	2.0	46.5	136	103	30.0	18.9	4.36	2.79
1985	3,208.1	304.1	6.90	3.40	2.0	50.2	192	115	27.8	20.1	3.95	2.66
1986	3,734.8	365.0	8.39	3.90	2.2	55.0	227	165	32.2	19.1	3.32	2.25
1987	4,220.8	425.3	10.24	4.50	2.3	59.5	277	159	27.3	15.1	4.01	2.23

CAPITAL

At 20 February 1988, a total of 2.65bn ordinary shares were in issue. No significant amounts of new equity capital have been issued in recent years. The Prudential Corporation holds 6.4% of the issued equity. There were no other declarable holdings over 5%.

GROUP REVIEW

UK retail   In 1987/88, clothing accounted for 48.3% of sales, homeware and footwear for 11.6% and food for 40.1%.

The company is the UK's largest clothing retailer, accounting for 16% of the total UK market. In certain areas, including lingerie and underwear, the company's market share is even higher, rising to 30% or more. In recent years, the company's already considerable presence in the market for ladieswear, childrenswear and basic menswear was extended to include men's suits, sports and leisurewear. Total sales of the company in clothing in the UK for 1987/88 increased 7.8% to £2.016bn.

The company is becoming an increasingly important retailer of footwear, with a UK market share increasing from 4.5% to around 5.0% in 1987/88. Homewares, gifts, household textiles and other furnishings have grown in importance. Sales of homewear and footwear for 1987/88 increased by 8.7% to £486.3m.

The share of the UK food market amounts to an estimated 5%, which represents a remarkably high penetration given that only a relatively narrow assortment of lines, numbering around 1,000, is available, compared with up to 7,000 within a conventional grocery store. Most activity is focused on fresh foods, plus ready-prepared meals and convenience foods. Non-food groceries are also stocked, plus a range of soft and alcoholic beverages. Sales of food for 1987/88 increased 12% to £1.671bn.

Traditionally, 90% of clothing products sold are sourced from the UK. Especially close links continue to be formed with all suppliers. This trend is being closely followed by an increasing number of rival UK retailers. The St Michael label is used exclusively to support the product range. The brand has achieved a very strong standing in its own right. As a result, an exceptionally high level of customer loyalty has been generated.

In 1987/88, estimated sales per square foot of close to £500 were recorded. This compares very favourably with the retail industry as a whole. An estimated net profit margin of 11.5% is impressive, given a high food content within the total product mix. Management's aim is to generate even higher returns in the future. Food sales were particularly strong in 1987/88.

The most recent innovation involves a move into the market for furniture, which is on offer within selected stores, and is accompanied by a home delivery service on request. To provide a more effective marketing approach, a direct selling operation is also being tested for large bulky items though this appears to be having mixed results.

By March 1988, 70% of the entire branch network had been modernised and upgraded. Improved systems of management information and control are being introduced. These will help to reinforce merchandising policies within the clothing and other fashion-orientated departments, which are designed to create greater customer interest by maintaining a regular flow of new product ideas during the course of any given season.

Closer attention is also being given to pricing policies to improve profitability. New selling area is being sought, either within the high street or in the newer out of town locations, such as the Gateshead Metro Centre. Selling area is growing by over 5% per annum.

In 1987/88, a total of 545,000 sq ft of new selling space was opened in the UK, with a new store in Telford and Cheshunt, and major extensions in Marble Arch, London, Edinburgh and Manchester. A new food-only store opened in Pinner.

The total combined turnover of the UK retail division in 1987/88 was up 9.6% to £4.173bn, excluding VAT. UK pre-tax profits were up 16.1% at £501.7m.

Share price and relative to FT-A All-Share

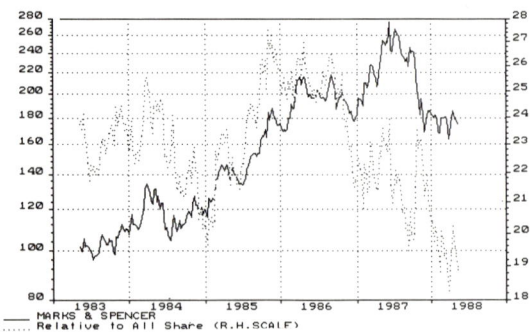

Adverse summer weather and a warm September produced a very disappointing sales performance in the first half of 1987/88. Clothing was worst hit. Excluding the effect of price inflation, clothing volume was flat. A move up-market also contributed to the disappointing performance. By February 1988, the group had recognised this, and was taking firm corrective action. Without the 6% extra space, turnover for the whole of the group would have been flat. Despite this, the group absorbed heavy development costs, and net margins increased from 8.8% to 9.5%.

The group confounded its critics by having an exceptionally strong second half in 1987/88. Sales increased by 13.1% and pre-tax profits by 20.1%.

Exports   For 1987/88 the group made export sales outside the group worth £46.5m. This was 3.3% up on 1986/87. The largest market for direct exports in 1987/88 was Europe, the second largest was the Far East.

Financial activities St Michael Financial Services offers credit facilities to the group's retail customers. A Marks and Spencer Chargecard was introduced nationally in 1985. This now includes Budget Account, acquired from Citibank Savings in June 1987. Previously no other credit instruments were accepted in-store. The card has grown rapidly in importance, with 2.2m in issue as at March 1988, accounting for 13% of UK retail sales during 1987/88, against 11% in 1986/87. The company reported that the credit operation achieved break-even in 1987/88.

The company is authorised as a licensed deposit-taker by the Bank of England, and is test-marketing personal loans which borrowers may use for any purpose. It is also marketing a legal protection scheme, Legal Line, offering 24-hours-a-day legal advice by telephone and insurance cover for legal expenses, excluding criminal defence costs, house conveyancing and divorce proceedings. Financial Services also includes the company's leasing and insurance activities.

Turnover for 1986/87 was up 25.4% to £45.9m. Two leasing companies were disposed of during the year for a profit of £6.2m. Pre-tax profits in 1987/88 were £4.2m against £4.8m for 1986/87.

Europe retail As at March 1988 the selling area totalled over 300,000 sq ft. France is the main area of activity. Most recently, a decision has been taken to concentrate on the Paris region, including a branch which was opened in the Velizy 2 shopping centre in autumn 1986. In November 1987 the company opened another major new store in Paris at Parly 2. With increased maturity an improving profits trend is now emerging.

Turnover for the company's business in Europe for 1987/88 increased by 13% in local currency. In sterling it was up by 10.3% to £131.7m. Pre-tax profits were up 41.3% to £18.8m in sterling.

North America retail Three separate chains are operating in Canada, trading as D'Allaird's (fashion clothing), Peoples (department stores) and Marks & Spencer (chain stores). As at March 1988, a total of 267 stores were open in Canada, with a total selling area of around 2.5m sq ft. In 1986/87 the company purchased the minority holding in Marks & Spencer Canada for £54m, following the relaxation of the Canadian government's rules controlling foreign investment. 1987/88 was a poor year for retailing in Canada, both for Marks & Spencer Canada and its competitors.

Most recently a decision has been taken to open four D'Allaird's stores in the US in New York State. If successful, more branches will be added. Moves to introduce the Marks and Spencer operation into the US are under active consideration, and a management team has been commissioned to consider suitable options. As a result of this initiative, Brooks Brothers, the famous US menswear chain, was acquired in April 1988 for $750m.

Profit and turnover declined in 1987/88, to £179.9m and £2.5m respectively. Sales per sq ft of D'Allaird's and Marks & Spencer are amongst the highest in the Canadian retail industry.

GEOGRAPHICAL REVIEW

Including the contribution from exports to third party customers, the UK accounted for 95.7% of group profits in 1987/88, with continental Europe 3.7% and Canada less than 1%.

CORPORATE CALENDAR

Year end	31 March
Preliminary results	May
Report and accounts	June
AGM	July
Final dividend paid	July
Interim results	October
Interim dividend paid	January

DIRECTORS' HOLDINGS

	Fully-paid ordinary shares		Options
	(beneficial)	*(non-beneficial)*	
Lord Rayner	87,555	—	315,692
R Greenbury	26,511	—	221,418
L Colne	15,582	—	269,351
JA Lusher	23,323	—	189,982
JK Oates	4,000	—	263,971
SJ Sacher	399,749	—	259,673
The Hon D Sieff	304,432	—	219,916
CV Silver	23,187	—	113,254
AKP Smith	—	—	—
PH Spriddell	28,665	—	170,243
DG Trangmar	14,719	—	179,390
DV Atterton	2,000	—	—
AE Frost	17,825	—	120,035
RAE Herbert	5,000	—	—
DR Susman	54,232	580,100	—
BJ Lynch	21,448	—	42,362
AS Orton	9,554	—	258,134

Total directors' remuneration in 1986/87 was £2.4m, of which the chairman, who was also the highest-paid director, received £287,234.

PRINCIPAL SUBSIDIARIES AND RELATED COMPANIES

Baker Street Leasing Ltd, Brooks Brothers – US, MS Insurance Ltd – Guernsey, Marks & Spencer Canada Inc, Marks and Spencer Finance (Nederland) BV, Marks and Spencer (France) SA, Marks and Spencer Holdings Canada Inc, Marks and Spencer Insurance Ltd, Marks and Spencer (Ireland) Ltd, Marks and Spencer (Nederland) BV, SA Marks and Spencer (Belgium) NV, St Michael Finance Ltd, St Michael Financial Services Ltd

BRAND NAMES

Brooks Brothers, Chargecard, D'Allaird's, Legal Line, Marks and Spencer, Peoples, Rez-de-Chaussée, St Michael

CONTACTS AND FURTHER INFORMATION

M Epstein Esq, company secretary, Marks and Spencer p.l.c., Michael House, Baker Street, London W1A 1DN. Tel: 01-935 4422.

MAXWELL COMMUNICATION CORPORATION plc

GENERAL INFORMATION

Head office	PO Box 283, 33 Holborn, London EC1N 2NE. Tel: 01-822 2345
Registered office	Headington Hill Hall, Oxford OX3 0BW. Tel: 0865 64881
Directors	R Maxwell MC (chairman and chief executive), R Baker FCA FCT (deputy managing director), J Holloran FCCA (executive vice chairman), JT Sullivan – US (executive vice chairman), I Maxwell, K Maxwell, R Mogg. *Non-exec* P Laister, The Rt Hon Lord Rippon of Hexham QC, The Rt Hon Lord Silkin of Dulwich PC QC (deputy chairman), R Woods
Advisers	Bankers Trust International
Auditors	Coopers & Lybrand
Registrars	Hill Samuel Registrars Ltd
Brokers	Alexanders Laing & Cruickshank
Solicitors	Freshfields, Lewis Silkin, Nicholson Graham & Jones

GENERAL FINANCIAL INFORMATION

Market capitalisation	£1.46bn at 1 January 1988
Capital structure	
Issued ordinary shares (25p)	608.28m
Issued preference shares	None
Warrants	None
Convertibles	None
Traded options	None
ADRs	None
Shareholders over 5%	Pergamon Foundation 51%

FT CATEGORY

FT: Newspapers, publishers
FT-A: Publishing and printing

MAJOR ACTIVITIES

Maxwell Communication Corporation (MCC) is effectively the publicly quoted printing and publishing vehicle of Robert Maxwell and his family, being 51%-owned by the Pergamon Foundation.

MCC is, by a considerable margin, the largest UK printer of magazines and catalogues, and, following recent substantial and dramatic acquisitions, has become the second largest printer in the US.

Through Pergamon Journals, Pergamon Books and Orbit Infoline, purchased from the parent company in 1986 and 1987, MCC is one of the world's principal publishers of scientific, technical and medical journals. It is also a substantial UK book publisher with imprints like Macdonald, Orbis and Futura.

Another link with the parent company is MCC's contract printing of the national newspaper titles of Mirror Group Newspapers. MCC is the market leader in virtually all other types of printing, and has a presence in packaging.

The group is rapidly developing its interests in the electronic dissemination of information.

The most important fluctuating economic background factor for the group is advertising expenditure, in both the UK and US, because of its subsequent impact on paginations. Elsewhere, particularly in its specialist publishing, demand is likely to be more stable.

In 1987 MCC was involved in a series of actual and rumoured takeover bids for: the major US book and journal publisher, Harcourt Brace Jovanovich; the Netherlands company, Elsevier; the security printer, De La Rue; the US company, Bell & Howell; and Extel, the information group. A rights issue raised £630m in June 1987.

Such is the pace of change set by Robert Maxwell, that it is

extremely difficult to forecast how rapidly MCC will grow. The group has undergone a remarkable transformation since its near bankruptcy prior to Robert Maxwell taking over.

Main competitors are RR Donnelly in US printing; St Ives in UK printing; and Elsevier, in which MCC has an 8.5% interest, in academic journal publishing.

FINANCIAL HISTORY

Since the arrival of Robert Maxwell in the early part of the 1980s there has been a major turnaround in the group's financial performance. There has been heavy capital investment of over £400m in new printing technology and much higher labour productivity.

Sales growth has until recently been slow. Turnover in 1980 of £213.7m compares with £265.1m in 1985. Since 1985 a number of rapid and sizeable acquisitions have resulted in substantial growth. In 1986 group turnover was £461.7m, a rise of 74.2% on 1985, up 139.8% since 1982. In 1987 group turnover rose 91.5% further to £884.1m.

At the pre-tax level, a 1980 loss of £11.3m compares with a profit of £25.5m in 1985, a huge 214.9% rise to £80.3m in 1986 and another substantial gain of 106.7% to £166m in 1987. Earnings per share moved from a loss of 29.3p in 1980 to 26.7p in 1987, up 15.1% on 1986, adjusted for the 1987 rights issue. The £630m raised from the June 1987 rights issue has left the group with net cash of £400m.

The period has also been marked by a restoration of the dividend payment. Adjusted for the rights issue this was 14p net in 1987, having been passed completely from 1980 to 1982.

The profile of the group has changed. In 1982, printing – largely of magazines, catalogues and packaging – dominated the group, accounting for 78% of sales. In 1987, printing – though still contributing 76% of group turnover and expanded in the interim by acquisition and the contract printing of newspapers – was much less significant in terms of pre-tax profits, making just 40% of the group total.

Publishing, renamed communications (including publishing) and particularly benefiting from the acquisition of Pergamon Journals, accounted for 31% of pre-tax profits – up from 21% in 1986 – and other activities, mainly property and treasury management, contributed 29%. Overseas sales have risen significantly since 1982, particularly following the recent US acquisitions.

MCC has stated its aim of achieving sales of over a billion pounds in 1988, and of becoming a global media concern with a turnover of between £3bn and £5bn by 1990, with half its profits, as opposed to the present 20%, coming from publishing, information systems and communications.

The core contract printing business is improving, greatly helped by acquisitions and investment. Further acquisitions are expected.

SHARE PRICE HISTORY

Although the original turnaround generated at MCC by Robert Maxwell lifted its shares from under 10% of the FT-A All-Share index to over 40% in the middle of 1984, the performance since then has been rather sluggish. The shares fell back to around 26% in mid-1987 as the market absorbed a £630m rights issue.

From mid-1984 to mid-1987 there were periods of strength in early 1986, following the acquisition of Pergamon Journals, which was perceived as having significantly improved the quality of earnings produced by the group, and in early 1987.

FIVE YEAR FINANCIAL INFORMATION

Year	Turnover (£m)	Pre-tax (£m)	Earnings (p)	Dividends net (p)	Dividend cover (x)	Net assets (p)	Price (p) High	Low	PER (x) High	Low	Yield (%) High	Low
1983	230.8	22.1	16.3	6	2.7	48.9	140	80	27.2	15.4	7.44	0.00
1984	266.5	37.9	29.6	11	2.7	82.4	214	133	29.7	15.6	9.52	3.78
1985	265.1	25.5	18.5	12	1.5	81.5	205	153	19.5	10.3	9.82	7.82
1986	461.7	80.3	23.2	12.9	1.8	59.1	302	186	33.7	13.7	8.53	5.60
1987	884.1	134.3	26.7	14	1.9	85	390	203	27.2	11.0	9.45	4.92

The 1987 bull market high was 395p, reached before the June rights issue at 265p per share.

The shares fell back to 197p with the general market collapse in autumn 1987, before recovering to the 240p level in March 1988.

SENIOR MANAGEMENT

Management has often been perceived as being dominated by Robert Maxwell, chairman and chief executive, and to some extent this may be fair. However, underneath his leadership, a team has steadily been built up.

Richard Baker has been deputy managing director since 1984, and in January 1987 John Holloran was recruited from McCorquodale, where he was chief executive. James Sullivan, vice-chairman in the US, joined in November 1986, having previously been president of the RR Donnelley magazine and book groups.

Two of Robert Maxwell's sons are executive directors. Ian Maxwell is responsible for group marketing. Kevin Maxwell is chief executive of Maxwell/Pergamon Publishing Corporation. The North American publishing management has been strengthened by the appointment of Donald Fruehling as president of Maxwell/Pergamon Publishing Corporation USA. Donald Fruehling reports to Kevin Maxwell and was formerly in charge of all McGraw-Hill publishing and broadcasting operations worldwide.

Reg Mogg is finance director. He assumed his post on the promotion of Richard Baker in 1984. Alan Roe is chief executive of the British Newspaper Printing Corporation.

The two non-executives are Peter Laister, formerly chairman and chief executive of THORN EMI and the Rt Hon Lord Rippon. The Rt Hon Lord Silkin acts as deputy chairman.

CAPITAL

Since spring 1985 MCC has used its capital and cash to fund considerable expansion without sacrificing the overall control of Pergamon Holdings.

First, it purchased Pergamon Journals in April 1986 from the holding company for £238m, satisfied by the issue of 107.5m ordinary shares. Then it bought Philip Hill Investment Trust in September 1986 for £331.3m, satisfied by the issue of 112.6m shares and £25.1m in cash, selling the underlying assets to provide liquidity.

In June 1987 the group announced a £630m two for three rights issue at 265p per share to help fund investment in its newspaper printing arm and provide resources for further acquisitions.

There are 608.28m shares in issue as at September 1987, with Pergamon Holdings owning 51%.

GROUP REVIEW

Printing The sector includes printing in both the UK and the US, as well as the group's packaging interests.

The UK printing side is split into four areas. The largest of these is publications, which consists of the group's magazine and catalogue operations. MCC is the clear market leader in the UK, with up to twice as much volume as its main competitor, St Ives. Catalogues printed by MCC include GUS, Littlewoods, Kays, Kauhof and Boots. Important magazine contracts include the *Radio Times*, *Punch*, *Woman's Own* and *Woman's Journal*.

The second area is security printing where MCC is the market leader in the production of cheques, credits and plastic cards. There is an increasing involvement in direct mail and the publication of reports and accounts. In August 1987 MCC bought Oyez Press, a leading city and financial printer, for £25m. In November 1987 MCC acquired a 14.9% interest in the security printer De La Rue.

The third area is book printing. Hazell, Watson & Viney is one of the UK's few major producers.

The fourth area is the group's pre-press operation, which provides full page make-up and computerised typesetting both within and outside the group. At BPCC Video Graphics the division has electronic design and animation facilities and provides a video-to-print transfer service.

MCC's packaging operations' main areas of interest are in cartons and labelling, with a presence also in the calendar market.

The group's printing interests in the US have been built up

CHAIRMAN'S STATEMENT

'Less than two years ago when our 1985 Annual Report and Accounts were published, I stated that our "strategic plan envisages our becoming an integrated global information and communications business by 1990 with sales in the £3,000–£5,000 million bracket per annum, with profit growth to match". Since the 1985 Annual Report and Accounts reported turnover of £265 million and pre-tax profit of £25.5 million, that statement startled media analysts and was greeted with some disbelief and scepticism.

I am now able to report that less than halfway through that period span Maxwell Communication Corporation plc has already achieved 1987 turnover of £884 million with pre-tax profits of £166 million. Indeed, had it not been for the fall in the United States Dollar in 1987 our turnover would have been approaching our first sterling billion turnover.

I am pleased to advise shareholders that we are therefore on course to achieve the objectives envisaged in our strategic plan.' *Robert Maxwell*

more recently by a series of acquisitions. The first deal was the purchase of The Webb Company of St Paul in October 1986 for $117.7m, followed by Providence Gravure of Rhode Island for $152.5m a month later and Diversified Printing Corporation, the printer and publisher of *Parade* magazine, in April 1987 for $134m. In early 1988 MCC bought Alco Gravure for $75.5m and successfully gained the $300m colour magazine printing contract for *USA Weekend*.

These deals have made MCC the second largest magazine and catalogue printer in the US. Among the titles printed by MCC are *Time*, *People*, *Sports Illustrated*, *TV Guide* and many others.

MCC has a number of other related US interests, including a 27% stake in Donohue, the Canadian newsprint producer, bought for £70m, and three satellite transmission services. AD/SAT transmits newspaper advertising in high resolution facsimile from New York simultaneously to newspapers nationwide. It serves 45% of the daily and 53% of the Sunday circulation of North America. Independent transmits data and pictures via satellite. Business News Wire beams disclosure and public relations items directly to newspapers and public relations agencies.

Share price and relative to FT-A All-Share

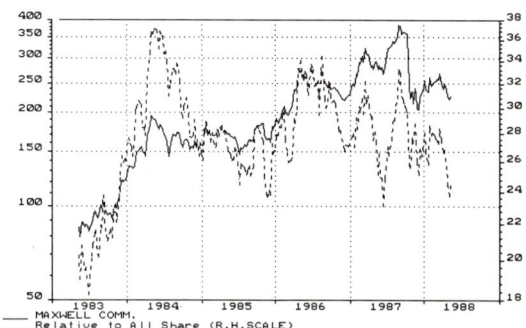

Contract printing of newspapers Operations mainly consist of printing carried out by MCC for its sister company, Mirror Group Newspapers (MGN). MGN is launching two colour magazines for the *Sunday Mirror* and *The People*.

Considerable development is planned with the provision of good quality colour web-offset presses in a regional network designed not only to perform a better job for MGN, but also to pick up contracts from the regional press. The group acquired Printec and QB early in 1987.

In 1987, MCC's total printing activities increased sales by 84.3% to £669.4m from £363.3m in 1986. Pre-tax profits in 1987 rose by 42.1% to £66.2m from £46.6m in 1986.

Communications (including publishing) Formerly the publishing division, the sector has been renamed to reflect MCC's increased interests in communications generally and electronic forms of publishing. The main areas fall into two categories – books and journals.

In book publishing MCC is a fairly sizeable UK publisher of illustrated books, adult fiction and children's books. Its best known imprints are Macdonald, Futura and Orbis.

Through the acquisition of Pergamon Journals in April 1986 for £238m, MCC became one of the world leaders in academic journal publishing. It produces around 375 titles in the scientific and technical areas. Some of this information is published through on-line databases by Pergamon Infoline.

Following the acquisition of a 70% stake in Nimbus Records for £24m in November 1987, information will also be available on compact disc.

The Maxwell Magazine Publishing Corporation is responsible for MCC's professional and trade publications. Its leading title is *Banking World*.

In 1987, after deciding not to proceed with acquisitions of Harcourt Brace Jovanovich and Elsevier, MCC made a number of important acquisitions to enlarge the publishing division.

In July 1987 it bought IPC Youth Group, which includes the UK book publishing licence for Walt Disney. In August 1987 the group acquired Headway Publications for £8m, and more importantly United Trade Press from Ladbroke in November 1987 for £34.8m.

In December 1987 MCC bought Pergamon Books, the parent company's UK- and US-based publisher of scientific, technical and medical works and defence books, and Pergamon Orbit Infoline, the parent company's US-based electronic publishing and information service, for £56m, with possible further payments up to a maximum of £100m. The group has identified this as an important area for expansion.

Other publishing developments include a plan to publish a Japanese business daily newspaper, the development of Comline News Service in Japan, a European daily newspaper based in Paris and new newspapers in Kenya, China, Canada and the UK.

In March 1988 MCC acquired Home and Law magazines from Ladbroke for £17m. Together with the group's existing Headway operation, MCC is one of the world's largest custom publishers, especially in the field of investor relations.

In 1987, MCC's communications (including publishing) activities increased sales by 88.9% to £184.4m from £97.6m in 1986. Pre-tax profits in 1987 rose by 210.7% to £52.2m from £16.8m in 1986. Pergamon Journals made an outstanding contribution.

Other It appears that the bulk of profits from this activity comes from the group's property activities and treasury operations, which invest sizeable sums of money on the back of the natural hedging opportunities which arise from the group's trade in a number of differing currencies.

In 1987, other activities sales increased to £30.3m from £0.8m in 1986. Pre-tax profits in 1987 rose by 181.6% to £47.6m from £16.9m in 1986.

Acquisitions From late 1986 onwards the group became very acquisitive and made a number of bids. Although Elsevier, De La Rue and Bell & Howell rebuffed MCC's approaches, the group acquired significant minority holdings in Extel, 27.13%; Donoghue, 27%; Elsevier, 8.5%; and De La Rue, 14.9%.

MCC withdrew from its bid for Harcourt Brace Jovanovich when it felt the price was too high. Following the June 1987 rights issue, the group had net cash of £400m, 36.4% of shareholders' funds, and is energetically continuing to make acquisitions.

GEOGRAPHICAL REVIEW

In 1987 the UK accounted for 52.8% (75.8%) of group turnover with £467.3m (£349.9m), continental Europe for 4.4% (6.4%) with £39.2m (£29.4m), North America for 39.1% (13%) with £345.8m (£59.8m), and the rest of the world 3.6% (5.6%) with £31.8m (£22.6m).

In 1987 the UK accounted for 69.6% (93.3%) of pre-tax profits with £115.6m (£74.9m), continental Europe for 1.7%

(1.8%) with £2.9m (£1.5m), North America for 28.5% (4.1%) with £47.4m (£3.3m) and the rest of the world 0.1% (0.8%) with £0.1m (£0.6m).

CORPORATE CALENDAR

Year end	31 December
Preliminary results	early April
Report and accounts	end April
AGM	mid-June
Final dividend paid	1 July
Interim results	end August
Interim dividend paid	early January

DIRECTORS' HOLDINGS

	Fully-paid ordinary shares	Options
I Maxwell	1,000	103,020
K Maxwell	2,863	150,000
R Maxwell	1,562,737	—
Rt Hon Lord Rippon	15,000	—
Rt Hon Lord Silkin of Dulwich	58,332	—
JT Sullivan	41,666	30,000

Total directors' remuneration in 1987 was £1.508m, of which the chairman, who was also the highest-paid director, received £250,000.

PRINCIPAL SUBSIDIARIES AND RELATED COMPANIES

Printing
AD Creative Ltd, Alco Gravure Inc – US, BPCC Colchester Web Offset Ltd, BPCC Direct Mail Ltd, BPCC Graphics Ltd, BPCC Northern Printers Ltd, BPCC Printing Corporation, BPCC Ultracard Ltd, BPCC Video Graphics, Carlisle Type-Setting Services Ltd, Carlisle Web Offset, Chromoworks Ltd, C&S Studios Ltd, Diversified Printing Corporation – US, Dorstel Press Ltd, E Hannibal & Co, Hazell Watson & Viney Ltd, Image Master Ltd (75%), Jas Broadlay Ltd, London Typesetting Centre Ltd, Nickeloid Computer Graphics Ltd, Numeric Arts Ltd, Odhams-Sun Printers Ltd, Oyez Press Ltd, Petty & Sons Ltd, Printec plc, Pulman Web Offset Ltd, Purnell & Sons Ltd, Purnell Book Production Ltd, Soman-Wherry Press Ltd, B Taylor & Co (Manchester) Ltd, Taylowe Ltd, Thomas Forman & Sons Ltd, T&T Gill Ltd, Waterlow Ltd, Waterlow Petty Business Forms Ltd, Waterlow & Sons (1984) Ltd, A Wheaton & Co Ltd, TM Woodhead Ltd

Contract printing of newspapers
BNPC Services Ltd, British Newspaper Printing Corp Plc, Donohue Inc – Canada (27%), Newsprint and Pulp Manufacturing

Communications (including publishing)
Aberdeen University Press, Angus Hudson Ltd, BPCC (Banking World) Ltd, British Magazine Publishing Corporation Ltd, Caxton & English Educational Programmes International Ltd, Cedibra Editora Brasileira Ltda – Brazil, Chess (Sutton Coldfield) Ltd, Delphin Verlag GmbH – West Germany (99%), Headway Publications Ltd, International Learning Systems (Japan) Ltd (65%), IPA Distribusjon A/S – Norway, IPA Produktion Forlag ApS – Denmark, KG Bertmarks Forlag AB – Sweden, Macdonald & Co (Publishers) Ltd, Macdonald Futura Australia Pty Ltd, Macdonald Middle East sarl – Lebanon (51%), Macdonald Publishers (NZ) Ltd – New Zealand, Orbis Book Publishing Corporation Ltd, Pergamon Books Distributers Ltd, Pergamon Books Inc – US, Pergamon Books Ltd, Pergamon BPCC Publishing Corp plc, Pergamon Brassey's Defence Publishers Ltd, Pergamon Journals Inc – US, Pergamon Journals Ltd, Pergamon Orbit Infoline Inc – US, Pergamon Orbit Infoline Ltd, Pergamon Press (Australia) Pty Ltd, Pergamon Press GmbH – Germany, Purnell Publishers Ltd, Regional Magazines Ltd, Standard Catalogue, Systems Publishing (Portugal) Editores Lda, United Trade Press Ltd, Verlag das persönliche Geburtstagsbuch GmbH – West Germany (66%), Webb Publishers Ltd, Webb Publishing Co – US

Printing communications
AD/SAT Inc – US, BPCC Holdings Inc – US, BPCC Printing Inc – US, Compucolor International – US, Independent Network Systems Inc – US (80.3%), Kable Printing Co – US, Maxwell Communication Corporation – US, Providence Gravure Inc – US, Standard Colorprint Corp – US, Texas Color Inc – US, Virginia Gravure Inc – US, Volkmuth Printers Inc – US, Webb Co – US, Webb/Midwest Printing Company – US

Service and holding companies
Birn Brothers Ltd, Bishopsgate Trust Plc, BPCC Corporate Management Services Inc – US, BPCC Financial Services Ltd, BPCC Group Services Ltd, BPCC Investments Inc – US, BPC do Brasil Comércio e Participações Ltda – Brazil, BPC Finance (Guarantees) Ltd, BPC Investments Ltd, BPC Sales Ltd, Camberry Ltd, Houses and Estates Ltd, KGBF Ltd, Legionstyle Ltd, Maxwell Communication Corporation (Australia) Pty Ltd, Paulton Holdings Ltd, Pergamon Realty Inc – US, Philip Hill Investment Trust Plc, Systems Publications BPC AB – Sweden, Thomson Printers Ltd

Joint ventures
Comline News Service (50%)

Other
Molecular Design Ltd, Maxwell Satellite Television

BRAND NAMES

Futura, Macdonald, Nimbus, Orbis, Pergamon, Purnell

CONTACTS AND FURTHER INFORMATION

Miss M Brannagan, Assistant secretary, Maxwell Communication Corporation plc, 10th Floor, 33 Holborn, London EC1N 2NE. Tel: 01-822 2345.

MIDLAND BANK plc

GENERAL INFORMATION

Head office Poultry, London EC2P 2BX. Tel: 01-260 8000
Directors Sir Kit McMahon (chairman and group chief executive), JA Brooks (deputy group chief executive), EW Brutsche, HP de Carmoy, BL Goldthorpe, HE Lockhart, IN Tegner. *Non-exec* KW Barker, Sir Kenneth Corfield, TJ Cunningham, IF Hay Davison, Sir Archibald Forster, Sir Trevor Holdsworth, Sir Alex Jarratt CB (deputy chairman), G Maitland Smith, Sir Patrick Meaney (deputy chairman), Ms D O'Cathain, Sir Michael Palliser (deputy chairman), Sir Eric Pountain DL, W Purves DSO
Advisers Samuel Montagu & Co Ltd, SG Warburg & Co Ltd
Auditors Ernst & Whinney
Registrars Ravensbourne Registration Services Ltd
Brokers Cazenove & Co
Solicitors Clifford Chance

GENERAL FINANCIAL INFORMATION

Market capitalisation £2.106bn at 1 January 1988
Capital structure
Issued ordinary shares (£1) 546.6m
Issued preference shares None
Warrants None
Convertibles None
Traded options Yes
ADRs None
Shareholders over 5% The Hong Kong and Shanghai Banking Corporation 14.9%, Hanson Trust 5.3%

FT CATEGORY

FT: Banks, HP and leasing
FT-A: Banks

MAJOR ACTIVITIES

Midland Bank and its subsidiaries provide a full range of banking, financial and related services. The UK banking sector has a network of over 2,000 branches, even after the recent sale of the Clydesdale and Northern banks and a recent reorganisation. This network is complemented by investment banking and global banking sectors.

With assets of £48bn, Midland is the third largest clearing bank in the UK. Services provided through its domestic and international branches and subsidiaries include deposit and lending facilities, funds transmissions, foreign exchange, money market facilities, Eurocurrency business, export finance, and cash and credit loans.

Financial services include instalment finance, leasing and factoring, insurance broking, investment management, and venture capital. Travel arrangements and traveller's cheques are offered worldwide through Thomas Cook, a wholly owned subsidiary of the bank and one of the largest travel companies and traveller's cheques issuers in the world.

The sale of Crocker National Corporation to Wells Fargo in 1986 greatly reduced Midland's exposure to the US. The group is still active there, principally through Midland Montagu Capital Markets, formed from its residual interests in Crocker, Midland's New York branch treasury and foreign exchange dealing operations and the activities of Samuel Montagu, New York.

Midland's UK activities have been at least averagely successful, but its expansion into foreign markets, adopted as a major corporate aim in the early 1980s, has proved very unhappy. In 1987 the group set aside provisions of £1.016bn against a total Third World lending exposure of £4.1bn.

Midland's capital base has recently been greatly strengthened by the sales of the Clydesdale and Northern banks, a £700m rights issue and a £383m investment by the Hong Kong & Shanghai Banking Corporation. The Hong Kong and Shanghai Banking Corporation thereby has a 14.9% stake in the group. A close working relationship and joint ventures are planned.

Midland's principal competitors in the UK are the major quoted clearing banks – Barclays, Lloyds, National Westminster, Royal Bank of Scotland and the TSB. Competition is also emerging from the major building societies.

FINANCIAL HISTORY

Midland Bank was the first to announce a UK banking loss this century in February 1988 when it reported 1987 losses of £505m. It was followed shortly afterwards by Lloyds and Standard Chartered. The loss was caused by an exceptional charge of £1.016bn for bad and doubtful debt provisions against loans to borrowers in countries with payment difficulties.

Midland's total exposure to these countries was £4.1bn, down from £5.1bn in 1986 due to the decline of the dollar. Midland now has provisions of £1.2bn against these debts, 29.3% of the exposure, or 34% if trade credits and other short term loans are excluded in line with US practice.

Of the £4.2bn outstanding from countries having actual or potential payment difficulties, Argentina owed £0.6bn, Brazil £1.2bn, Mexico £1.0bn, the rest of Latin America £0.7bn and the rest of the world £0.6bn. The provisions made by Midland against this debt are specific and therefore qualify for tax relief.

Before the exceptional provisions, Midland pre-tax profits increased in 1987 for the third year running. They were up £77m at £511m, 16.4% ahead of 1986. There was a major improvement in the group's balance sheet, with the ratio of equity to assets rising from 4.0% to 5.5%. The primary capital ratio was 7.5%, and the free capital ratio 8.3%. In 12 months Midland had changed from being one of the weakest UK banks to one of the strongest.

Before exceptional provisions, group profits increased by

FIVE YEAR FINANCIAL INFORMATION

Year	Turnover (£m)	Pre-tax (£m)	Earnings (p)	Dividends net (p)	Dividend cover (x)	Net assets (p)	Price (p) High	Price (p) Low	PER (x) High	PER (x) Low	Yield (%) High	Yield (%) Low
1983	2,357	135	45	18.9	2.4	613	337	209	9.4	4.4	11.62	7.85
1984	2,902	135	20	18.9	1.1	542	315	213	9.3	5.4	12.69	8.59
1985	2,855	351	39	18.9	2.1	594	341	240	16.6	8.3	11.31	7.94
1986	2,798	434	78	20.1	3.9	475	449	314	12.2	6.9	8.63	6.00
1987	2,726	−505	−145	20.1	—	500	562	320	—		8.60	4.90

128.8% between 1983 and 1987. They made a strong recovery from 1985 onwards as the situation stabilised within Crocker National, formerly the group's Californian subsidiary. UK banking profits showed a particularly impressive advance in 1986 and 1987, with higher loan volumes and healthy growth in fee and commission income.

Disappointingly, however, the cost to income ratio, traditionally high, increased from 72.5% in 1986 to 73% in 1987. Management has indicated that improvement of this ratio is a key priority but that the benefits of efficiency initiatives will take time to be reflected in an improved ratio since the changes required involve considerable investment in systems, training and product development.

CHAIRMAN'S STATEMENT

'The most dramatic developments for the group in 1987 were the reconstruction of our balance sheet, the improvement in the quality of our book and the increase in our capital ratios, taking us from a position of relative weakness to one of real capital strength: a very important attribute at a time when the economic outlook remains uncertain.

This strengthening of our financial position was brought about by the sale of the Clydesdale and Northern banks, the £700 million rights issue, the association we entered into with HongkongBank and, of course, the very large exceptional provisions we made against problem country debt. Granted the position we were in, and our current earning capacity, the unavoidable effect of this last measure was the £505 million loss we are showing in our accounts today.' *Sir Kit McMahon*

Investment banking profits, which had improved by more than 25% in 1986, fell sharply in 1987 due to a total loss of £46m in the institutional equities business, now closed.

International banking profits were much reduced in 1987 because of debt moratoria and lower interest margins, although other areas did well. There had been mixed results in 1986 with the European subsidiaries doing well, but continuing losses from Bracton, the subsidiary set up to work out the loan portfolio inherited from Crocker.

The trend of earnings in recent years has also been influenced by large fluctuations in the group's effective tax rate brought about by changes in the 1984 Finance Act, and by the incidence of unrelieved tax losses in the US. The dividend was left virtually unchanged throughout the period from 1982 to 1985, but was modestly increased in 1986. The total dividend in 1987 was maintained at 20.1p per share net.

SHARE PRICE HISTORY

Although the price has inevitably suffered from the traditional short term volatility of the bank sector, the dominant influences on performance in the 1980s have been the implications of the group's involvement with Crocker National, the above average exposure to problem sovereign debtors which the Crocker involvement brought in its train, and the effects of the tax changes announced in the 1984 Budget on Midland's leasing business.

Between mid-1983 and early 1985 the shares underperformed the market by nearly 50%. They enjoyed a partial recovery in 1986, reflecting the stabilisation of the Crocker National situation, the subsequent disposal of that investment,

and the strong improvement in domestic profitability. Bid speculation became a factor leading to modest outperformance in September 1987, particularly when Hanson announced a stake and Saatchi & Saatchi held abortive discussions with Midland.

The share price fell sharply in the autumn 1987 market falls, reaching a low of 308p before recovering to around 400p, partly on the news of the Hong Kong & Shanghai Banking Corporation (HongkongBank) stake.

SENIOR MANAGEMENT

Sir Kit McMahon, previously a deputy governor of the Bank of England, was appointed chief executive of the group in September 1986. He was appointed chairman in April 1987. The deputy chairmen are Sir Alex Jarratt, Sir Patrick Meaney and Sir Michael Palliser.

On completion of the deal with HongkongBank, Hongkong-Bank's chairman William Purves and KW Barber, its executive director resident in London, joined the Midland board. Sir Kit McMahon joined HongkongBank's board.

CAPITAL

Despite all the problems created by its involvement with Crocker National and an above-average exposure to problem sovereign debtors, Midland has taken a series of steps to maintain the adequacy of its capital ratios on the yardsticks used by the Bank of England.

Midland has had two rights issues in recent years, one in 1983 to raise £160m, and a much larger deeply discounted one in 1987. 232.93m new shares were issued on a one for one basis at 300p to raise £699m.

£383m was raised in 1987 through the issue of 80.6m new ordinary shares at 485p to HongkongBank. This not only had the effect of strengthening group capital ratios further, but also formed part of an agreement for a closer working relationship.

The group has raised a total of $1.550bn (£829m at end 1987) through undated loan capital which qualifies as primary capital for the purposes of Bank of England guidelines. Various disposals, including Crocker National and the Clydesdale and Northern banks, have also improved capital ratios by reducing balance sheet footings.

No director has a significant shareholding and the only declarable shareholdings of 5% or more in the group are those held by Hanson and HongkongBank.

GROUP REVIEW

In April 1987, the group announced a major reorganisation of its various operations which now fall within three clearly defined sectors – UK banking, investment banking (given the umbrella name Midland Montagu) and global banking.

UK banking This includes the retail and corporate banking businesses of the bank, together with the instalment finance, leasing, and factoring businesses of Forward Trust.

Priority in retail banking has been given to restructuring, redesigning and automating the branch network, and to developing new financial products and services. Specific examples of new financial products and services include extending the domestic residential mortgage portfolio and the introduction of a high interest cheque account. In 1987 Midland launched Vector and Credo, the first two of a new generation of sophisticated products.

In corporate banking, priority has been given to the development of specialist teams aimed at specific market sectors, notably agriculture, oil, aerospace, property and electronics.

In addition to mainstream banking activities, the group set up in 1987 a new Personal Financial Services division to bring together the various specialist subsidiaries – executor and trustee services, stockbroking, investment management and insurance broking. Within this area Midland has created its own life assurance company in partnership with Commercial Union.

In July 1987 Midland disposed of its wholly owned

Share price and relative to FT-A All-Share

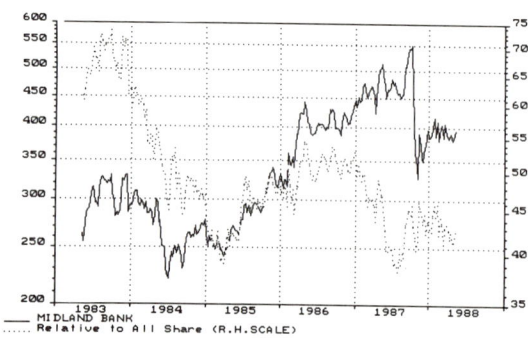

subsidiary banks, Clydesdale Bank, Northern Bank and Northern Bank (Ireland), to National Australia Bank for a total consideration of £420m, resulting in a profit of £60m.

In 1987, UK banking, excluding the Clydesdale and Northern banks, increased pre-tax profits by 35% from £294m to £396m. This included an increase in Forward Trust's pre-tax profits of 26.8%, up from £41m to £52m.

Investment banking The investment banking sector was formed in response to the increasing integration of financial markets, and to the changes in UK financial regulations governing the ownership of securities broking and market-making activities. All these activities are grouped under the Midland Montagu umbrella name.

This sector includes the group treasury, which conducts the UK wholesale banking business, and is a leading participant in the London foreign exchange and money markets. Operations in the fixed income securities markets have been consolidated into one business area, to incorporate commercial paper programmes and the trading and sales of international fixed income securities.

The group withdrew from equity market-making in March 1987 after minor trading losses. It was thereby spared the heavier losses other investment bankers sustained in the crash of October 1987. The remaining institutional sales business of Greenwell Montagu was closed in 1988 following substantial losses during 1987.

Overseas, moves to establish a global presence were recently boosted by the receipt of an integrated securities licence in Japan. Through the retention of Crocker National's capital market operations, the group maintains a presence in the US. Merchant banking business is carried out through subsidiaries in Australia, Switzerland, Norway, Sweden and Finland. The sector also has responsibility for the group's wholesale banking

activities in New York, Tokyo, Hong Kong and Australia.

Pre-tax profits of investment banking halved in 1987 from £83m to £41m. This largely reflected losses of £35m in the equities business and £11m provisions for the costs of withdrawing from that business in 1988. The other areas – treasury, gilt-edged dealing, corporate finance and venture capital – all did well.

Global banking The group's international commercial banking business is conducted through the UK offices of the global banking sector, the group's overseas branches and subsidiaries and its important correspondent banking operations. Two specialist units deal with private banking and international trade and export finance.

One of the group's long term objectives has been to diversify its operations beyond its traditional UK base. This it has done by expanding its overseas representation, principally through the establishment of, or investment in, wholly-owned or majority-held operations.

Geographically, the group has sought a direct presence in the principal financial centres, with priority given to the US, western Europe and the Pacific basin. The group also has branches in Athens, Bahrain, Hong Kong, Madrid, Manila, Milan, New York, Paris, Piraeus, Seoul, Singapore and Tokyo.

Under the recently concluded agreement with Hongkong-Bank, Midland will assume responsibility for operating or servicing most of HongkongBank's branches in Europe. HongkongBank will assume similar responsibility for certain of the Midland offices in the Far East.

HongkongBank will also acquire Midland Bank Canada, apart from its Thomas Cook division. Consolidation of other activities and the establishment of joint ventures will also be considered.

Pre-tax profits from global banking in 1987 fell from £54m to £13m. Debt moratoria, lower interest margins, and un-favourable conditions in continental Europe all overshadowed good performances in trade finance, corporate, correspondent, electronic and private banking, and CHAPS, where Midland has a 60% market share.

GEOGRAPHICAL REVIEW

Of the group's total assets at the 1987 year-end, 48% were classified as domestic and 28% were classified as UK-based international, a classification partly reflecting the allocation of internal management responsibility, but also reflecting the sizeable foreign currency operations conducted within the UK. A further 11% of total assets were located in Europe, 7% in the US, and 6% in the rest of the world.

The combination of exchange rate movements and the sale of Crocker Bank resulted in an 80% decline in the proportion of dollar denominated assets between 1984 and 1986. Sterling denominated assets increased by more than 30% over the same period.

CORPORATE CALENDAR

Year end	31 December
Preliminary results	March
Report and accounts	March
AGM	April
Final dividend paid	April
Interim results	July
Interim dividend paid	October

DIRECTORS' HOLDINGS

	Fully-paid ordinary shares	Options
Sir Kit McMahon	2,360	26,894
Sir Alex Jarratt	3,624	—
Sir Patrick Meaney	624	—
Sir Michael Palliser	600	—
KW Barker	1,500	—
JA Brooks	10,182	82,333
EW Brutsche	1,000	—
HP de Carmoy	200	2,685
Sir Kenneth Corfield	2,500	—
Sir John Cuckney	624	—
IF Hay Davison	600	—
Sir Archibald Forster	2,000	—
BL Goldthorpe	5,990	49,357
Sir Derrick Holden-Brown	4,000	—
Sir Trevor Holdsworth	624	—
G Maitland Smith	1,000	—
D O'Cathain	2,000	—
Sir Eric Pountain	3,000	—
W Purves	746	—
IN Tegner	1,158	46,258

Directors' remuneration in 1987 was £3.0m, of which the chairman received £176,510, and the highest-paid director £748,458.

PRINCIPAL SUBSIDIARIES AND RELATED COMPANIES

Forward Trust Ltd, Greenwell Montagu Gilt-Edged, Greenwell Montagu Securities, Greenwell Montagu Stockbrokers, Griffin Factors Ltd, Handelsfinanz Midland Bank – Switzerland (85%), Midland America Corporation, Midland Bank Canada, Midland Bank Group International Trade Services Ltd, Midland Bank Insurance Services Ltd, Midland Bank International Financial Services Ltd, Midland Bank SA – France (76%), Midland Bank (Singapore) Ltd, Midland Bank Trust Co Ltd, Midland Finance (HK) Ltd – Hong Kong, Midland International Australia Ltd, Midland International Financial Services BV – Netherlands, Midland Montagu Government Securities Inc – US, Midland Montagu (Holdings) Ltd, Midland Montagu Leasing Ltd, Midland Montagu Municipal Securities Inc – US, Midland Montagu Ventures Ltd, Samuel Montagu & Co Ltd, The Thomas Cook Group Ltd, Trinkaus & Burkhardt KGaA – West Germany (70%).

BRAND NAMES

Access, CarOwner Plus, Credo, Forward Trust, Griffin Factors, HomeOwner Plus, MasterCard, Midland, Thomas Cook, Vector

CONTACTS AND FURTHER INFORMATION

Keith Haslett, Investor and financing relations manager, Midland Bank plc, Poultry, London EC2A 2BX. Tel: 01-260 8000.

GENERAL INFORMATION

Head office	41 Lothbury, London EC2P 2BP. Tel: 01-726 1000
Directors	TP Frost (group chief executive), CF Green (deputy group chief executive), TA Green (deputy group chief executive), J Plastow. *Non-exec* The Rt Hon the Lord Boardman MC TD DL (chairman), Sir Edward Nixon CBE DL (deputy chairman), PW Wilkinson (deputy chairman), Sir Peter Walters (deputy chairman), The Rt Hon Viscount Boyne JP DL, The Hon Sir Richard Butler, Sir Alan Campbell GCMG, DM Child CBE MC DL, The Rt Hon the Earl of Crawford and Balcarres PC, Sir Hugh Guy Cubitt CBE JP DL, MR Harris, RAE Herbert JP DL, GF Jones, Sir Brian Kellett, JASL Leighton-Boyce, The Rt Hon the Lord MacLehose of Beoch KT GBE KCMG KVCO, CA McLintock, DB Money-Coutts, FJ O'Reilly, AR Pilkington, BStGA Reed, Sir Anthony Touche Bt, CS Tugendhat, Sir Leslie Young CBE DL, The Rt Hon Baroness Young PC
Advisers	County NatWest Limited
Auditors	Ernst & Whinney, Peat Marwick McLintock
Registrars	National Westminster Bank Registrar's Department
Brokers	Cazenove & Co, County NatWest WoodMac
Solicitors	Travers Smith Braithwaite, Wilde Sapte

GENERAL FINANCIAL INFORMATION

Market capitalisation	£4.436bn at 1 January 1988
Capital structure	
Issued ordinary shares (£1)	754.4m
Issued preference shares (£1)	14.0m at 4.9% CP
Warrants	16.8m, 325.5 ordinary shares per warrant exercisable at 459p to 31 July 1990
Convertibles	None
Traded options	None
ADRs	One ADR per three ordinary shares
Shareholders over 5%	None

FT CATEGORY

FT: Banks, HP and leasing
FT-A: Banks

MAJOR ACTIVITIES

Through the parent bank and various subsidiary companies, the group provides a comprehensive range of banking, financial and related services. It has over 3,200 banking branches in the UK, and its international representation extends to 36 countries.

The group is the most profitable banking concern in the UK. Its domestic business is principally retail and wholesale commercial banking. In the UK NatWest has developed its instalment credit and leasing business through Lombard North Central, its mortgage lending through National Westminster Home Loans and its Access credit card operations through the Joint Credit Card company.

Abroad NatWest is expanding its retail and commercial banking operations. The National Westminster Bank USA has 136 branches in the New York metropolitan area. In February 1988 the group completed the purchase of First Jersey National Corp, an American banking group with 114 branches in New Jersey, and since renamed National Westminster Bancorp NJ. In a joint venture with Banco NatWest March, the group has expanded in Spain.

GROUP CHIEF EXECUTIVE'S STATEMENT

'Our commitment to quality and the further investments we are making in our business at home and overseas will bring continued profitable progress. Our experience in 1988 is so far satisfactory and we take a confident view of prospects for the full year.' *TP Frost*

FIVE YEAR FINANCIAL INFORMATION

Year	Income (£m)	Pre-tax (£m)	Earnings (p)	Dividends net (p)	Dividend cover (x)	Net assets (p)	Price (p) High	Low	PER (x) High	Low	Yield (%) High	Low
1983	2,402	518	49	15.3	5.3	589	332	219	7.7	3.8	8.35	6.10
1984	2,863	671	56	16.2	3.5	465	379	270	8.4	5.0	8.07	5.57
1985	3,128	804	78	17.9	4.4	523	459	360	8.2	6.4	6.45	5.10
1986	3,721	1,011	94	20.5	4.6	617	593	428	11.9	5.0	5.96	4.31
1987	4,106	704	57	24.0	2.4	648	786	510	13.2	5.8	5.77	3.57

Investment banking is conducted through NatWest Investment Bank (NWIB). This was formed by bringing together Bisgood Bishop, Fielding Newson-Smith and County Bank. It is active in the world's principal capital markets in London, New York, Tokyo and Sydney. NWIB's purchase of Wood Mackenzie should strengthen its client list and research base still further.

FINANCIAL HISTORY

Group pre-tax profits more than doubled from £449m in 1982 to £1.01bn in 1986. This reflected continued improvement in domestic banking services.

In 1987 NatWest's pre-tax profits fell 30% to £704m. The group made a specific charge of £610m against problem country debt totalling £2.47bn. Excluding this provision, pre-tax profits on a comparable basis rose 14% to £1.266bn from £1.113bn in 1986.

There was an exceptionally strong performance from domestic banking, pre-tax profits rising 43% over 1986 to £1.001bn. Investment banking made a loss of £116m against a loss of £38m in 1986. Related banking services' pre-tax profits were up 24% to £158m. International banking made pre-tax losses of £339m against a profit of £223m in 1986, the result of the exceptional provision of £610m.

The group maintained its record of consistent dividend growth by raising the 1987 net dividend by 17% to 24.0p. From 1982 to 1986 dividends had increased by 10.75% annually. Earnings per share fell by 39% in 1987.

Despite the provisions made, shareholders' funds increased by 6% in 1987 to £4.883bn and net asset value by 5% to 648p per share.

The trend of net earnings in recent years has been distorted by large fluctuations in the effective tax rate of the group, principally since the 1984 Finance Act. The tax charge in 1985/86 benefited from lower provisions for bad and doubtful debts.

SHARE PRICE HISTORY

Adjusted for two deep discount rights issues between 1984 and 1987, the share price rose by 151% in the three years to mid-1987, reflecting one of the traditional characteristics of the sector – volatile short term price performance. Compared to the market, the shares underperformed by a substantial margin in 1984, under the combined impact of the tax changes announced in that year's Budget and the rights issue, and again in 1985 as a result of disappointment with first half profit trends.

Subsequently, relative share price performance has been more impressive, stemming partly from a sharp improvement in profitability, a wider recognition of the group's below average sovereign risk exposure and initial evidence of a more liberal dividend policy.

SENIOR MANAGEMENT

Lord Boardman has been non-executive chairman since 1983, when he succeeded Robin Leigh-Pemberton on his appointment as Governor of the Bank of England. 1987 witnessed a number of changes.

TP Frost has succeeded PW Wilkinson as group chief executive. Sir Peter Walters took over from The Earl of Harrowby as deputy chairman. The deputy group chief executives are CF Green and TA Green. The latter has assumed full executive responsibility for NatWest Investment Bank.

CAPITAL

A series of steps have been taken by NatWest to strengthen its capital position and improve its capital adequacy ratios on the yardsticks used by the Bank of England.

NatWest raised £236m through a deeply discounted rights issue in 1984. In the following two years there was a further increase in the capital base of 66%. Over the same period consolidated assets increased by 16.5%, whereas equity capital increased by 75%. This reflected the £711m net raised through a second deep discount rights issue in 1986, and £101m raised through a public offering of American depository shares in the US.

In addition, $2bn of undated loan capital, the bulk of which qualifies as primary capital for the purposes of Bank of England capital guidelines, has been raised since 1984. A further £100m of 9% Deposit Notes 1992 was issued in May 1987. 2.7m shares were issued in 1987 against the exercise of warrants. The exercise of the remaining warrants would result in the issue of 16.8m ordinary shares.

GROUP REVIEW

Domestic banking NatWest has the largest branch network in the United Kingdom. This extensive network gives it access to a wide customer base, allows it to monitor locally the quality of credit relationships, and provides a stable deposit base. This is a major factor in profitability, which is growing rapidly. Services provided through the bank's own domestic branches are supplemented by three banking subsidiaries: Ulster Bank, Coutts and Co, and Isle of Man Bank.

Priority in recent years has been given to developing a wider range of personal banking services, including: mortgage lending where National Westminster Home Loans now has a mortgage book in excess of £5bn; new premium or higher rate deposit accounts, including the Special Reserve Account; and a nationwide system of automated telling machines (ATMs). The group has traditionally been an important provider of banking services to larger multinational companies. To strengthen its presence in the medium-sized corporate market, NatWest is in the process of building up a network of some 90

Business Centres which will be completed in 1988.

The domestic banking division also participates in the Access credit card operation. The group had 3.4m Access accounts at the end of 1987. The card is accepted in more than 260,000 outlets in the UK and in more than 5.3m outlets world-wide through links with Mastercard and Eurocard.

International banking International banking is conducted through a number of specialist offices in the UK, through overseas branches and representative offices, located in virtually all the world's major financial centres, through International Westminster Bank, and through various overseas subsidiary and associated companies.

Following the purchase of First Jersey National Corp, now renamed National Westminster Bancorp NJ, the bank holding company, created along with National Westminster Bank USA, has assets approaching $17bn. Recent initiatives have included: acquiring NatWest March (49% owned); 84% of Banco de Asturias, a retail bank with 63 branches in northern Spain; the establishment of a representative office in Boston; and the creation of a branch in Gibraltar.

The group is a major participant in the foreign exchange markets through its London World Money Centre, one of the larger dealing rooms of its kind. The centre is directly linked to the group's other dealing rooms in financial centres across Europe, North America and Asia.

Related banking services The group offers a broad range of related banking services in the UK and internationally through the departments of the bank and through some subsidiaries and associates. Lombard North Central (LNC), with assets in excess of £5bn, is the major operation in this division. LNC is one of the largest instalment and leasing finance groups in the UK.

Other services include factoring, receivables financing, corporate security custody services, trustee and tax advisory services, transfer agent and registrar services, insurance broking, stockbroking, investment management and offshore personal banking services and computer services.

Investment banking services NatWest is active in the capital and securities markets through its subsidiary NWIB. With assets of close on £3bn, NWIB provides a full range of domestic and international merchant banking services, including corporate financial advice, securities broking, dealing, underwriting and investment management.

NWIB has gained a seat on the Tokyo Stock Exchange whilst in the US significant advances have been made. The government securities dealing subsidiary made substantial progress towards its aim of achieving primary dealer status in the US Treasury bond market. In Hong Kong the equities business continued to consolidate its position in the south-east Asian markets while in Australia the equities business captured over 10% market share.

In early 1988 NWIB bought stockbrokers Wood Mackenzie and merged the two market-making operations. £80m was injected into NWIB to cover development costs and trading losses after the October 1987 share crash.

GEOGRAPHICAL REVIEW

At the end of 1987 domestic offices accounted for 53% of the total group assets; international offices in the UK accounted for 20%; international offices in the US accounted for 13%; and international offices in the rest of the world accounted for 14%. The UK-based international offices include part of the assets of International Westminster Bank, which operates primarily in the Eurocurrency markets.

Domestic offices accounted for 149% of group net income.

UK-based international offices, which bore the brunt of the additional provisions on sovereign risk exposure, contributed a negative of 28%; US offices, reflecting the adverse effects of currency translation, a negative of 6%; and the rest of the world a negative of 2%.

Amounts outstanding at the 1987 year-end in Mexico, Brazil and other Central and South American countries were £508m, £471m and £810m respectively – £1.84bn in total. NatWest's total provisions for problem sovereign debt are £886m. This is 33% of its £2.47bn outstandings to the 33 countries in payment difficulties or rescheduling and is consistent with the maximum levels of provision suggested by the Bank of England matrix.

CORPORATE CALENDAR

Year end	31 December
Preliminary results	February
Report and accounts	March
AGM	April
Final dividend paid	April
Interim results	July
Interim dividend paid	August

DIRECTORS' HOLDINGS

Beneficial interests	Ordinary shares	Other	Options
Lord Boardman	5,000	—	—
Lord Harrowby	4,997	—	—
Sir Edwin Nixon	3,000	—	—
PW Wilkinson	3,841	—	1,083
Lord Boyne	17,640	11,400	—
Sir Richard Butler	2,616	—	—
Sir Alan Campbell	1,000	—	—
DM Child	4,640	4,607	—
Lord Crawford	2,700	—	—
Sir Hugh Cubitt	2,160	—	—
TP Frost	2,414	4,467	34,818
CF Green	5,916	4,577	33,832
TA Green	5,396	3,587	25,040
MR Harris	8,000	—	—
RAE Herbert	1,800	—	—
GF Jones	6,200	524	—
Sir Brian Kellett	3,000	—	—
JASL Leighton-Boyce	1,500	—	—
Lord MacLehose	3,000	—	—
CA McLintock	2,000	—	—
DB Money-Coutts	1,496	3,446	—
FJ O'Reilly	4,500	—	—
AR Pilkington	1,936	—	—
J Plastow	1,534	4,117	21,306
B St GA Reed	1,000	—	—
Sir Anthony Touche	1,000	2,500	—
CS Tugendhat	1,000	—	—
CN Villiers	1,922	4,401	17,205
Sir Peter Walters	1,500	—	—
Sir Leslie Young	4,000	—	—
Baroness Young	—	—	—

Total directors' remuneration in 1987 amounted to £2.26m, with the chairman receiving £154,987 and the highest-paid director £238,182.

PRINCIPAL SUBSIDIARIES AND RELATED COMPANIES

UK

The Agricultural Mortgage Corporation Plc (26.0%), BACS Ltd (22.4%), The Bankers' Clearing House Ltd (38.2%), Centre File Ltd, Coutts and Co, Credit Factoring International Ltd, International Westminster Bank Plc, Investors in Industry Group Plc (23.6%), The Joint Credit Card Co Ltd (30%), Lombard North Central Plc, National Westminster Home Loans Ltd, National Westminster Insurance Services Ltd, NatWest Investment Bank Ltd, Ulster Bank Ltd – NI, Yorkshire Bank plc (40%)

Overseas

Banco NatWest March SA – Spain (49.3%), CreditWest SpA – Italy (31%), Deutsche Westminster Bank AG – West Germany, F van Lanschot Bankiers NV – The Netherlands, HandelsBank NatWest – Switzerland, Isle of Man Bank Ltd – Isle of Man, National Westminster Bancorp NJ – US, National Westminster Bank Finance (CI) Ltd – Channel Islands, National

NEXT plc

Share price and relative to FT-A All-Share

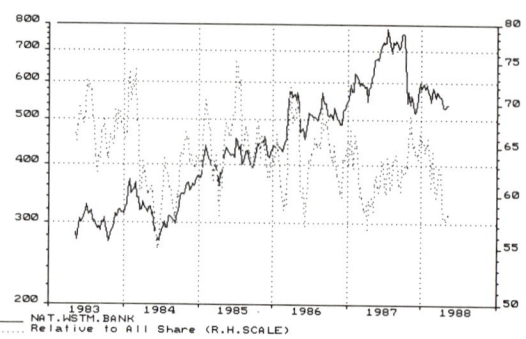

Westminster Bank of Canada – Canada, National Westminster Bank USA – US, National Westminster (Hong Kong) Ltd – Hong Kong, NatWest Australia Bank Ltd – Australia, NatWest International Trust Holdings Ltd – Bahamas

BRAND NAMES

Access, County NatWest WoodMac, Credit Zone, Eurocard, Gold Plus, Lombard Mastercard, NatWest

CONTACTS AND FURTHER INFORMATION

Warren Stokes, Senior Executive, Investor Relations, National Westminster Bank PLC, 41 Lothbury, London EC2P 2BP. Tel: 01-726 1103.

GENERAL INFORMATION

Head office	Desford Road, Enderby, Leicester LE9 5AT. Tel: 0533 866411
Directors	GW Davies (chairman and chief executive), David Jones (deputy chief executive), Mrs EK Davies, A Iversen, PF Lomas, TAO O'Malley, TJB Roberts, JH Whitmarsh. *Non-exec* R Marber, JT Rowlay, MC Stoddart
Advisers	Lazard Brothers & Co Ltd
Auditors	Arthur Young
Registrars	Lloyds Bank Registrar's Department
Brokers	Rowe & Pitman Ltd
Solicitors	Slaughter and May

GENERAL FINANCIAL INFORMATION

Market capitalisation	£1.046bn at 1 January 1988
Capital structure	
Issued ordinary shares (25p)	359.2m
Issued preference shares (£1)	0.1m 6% CP
	0.5m 7% CP
	0.489m 10% (50p) CP
Warrants	None
Convertibles	£100m 5.75% ESC 2003 (232.56 ordinary shares per £1000 stock)
	£48m 6.75% ESC 2002 (349.651 ordinary shares per £1000 stock)
Traded options	None
ADRs	None
Shareholders over 5%	None

FT CATEGORY

FT: Drapery and stores
FT-A: Stores

MAJOR ACTIVITIES

The company has grown out of the J Hepworth men's tailoring business. The core activities include retailing of men's and ladies' clothing and other consumer products, mail order, financial services and property. Next's major acquisitions have included Lord John, the Grattan mail order business and Combined English Stores.

The main economic factors influencing sales include consumer expenditure, levels of disposable income, consumer confidence and interest rates. Principal competitors include: Burton, Marks and Spencer, Sears and Storehouse in clothing; Freemans and GUS in mail order; and Burton, Marks and Spencer and the clearing banks in financial services.

CHAIRMAN'S STATEMENT

'A year which began with the harmonious blending of Next and Grattan blossomed into a period of major growth which included the acquisition of Combined English Stores Plc and Dillons. Each step that we have taken has been carefully and meticulously planned so that we could be confident of our ability to absorb any acquisition into the combined Group. That confidence has been rewarded in terms of the speed with which we have been able to implement our integration plans.' *George Davies*

The successful growth of the Next retail chains shows no sign of slowing down. Established product areas have proved capable of further extension whilst alternative ranges have successfully been introduced. The launch of the Next home shopping business in January 1988 provided an additional

Year	Turnover (£m)	Pre-tax (£m)	Earnings (p)	Dividends net (p)	Dividend cover (x)	Net assets (p)	Price (p) High	Price (p) Low	PER (x) High	PER (x) Low	Yield (%) High	Yield (%) Low
1983	98.6	8.56	4.6	1.83	2.5	85	74	36	39.3	20.5	5.34	3.52
1984	108.3	13.62	5.3	2.58	2.0	92	188	71	35.0	18.7	3.74	1.96
1985	146.0	20.06	8.7	3.75	2.3	103	244	156	37.5	24.8	2.58	1.66
1986	190.0	27.66	12.0	5.00	2.4	82	294	190	47.5	18.6	3.29	1.82
1987†	372.4	42.30	14.0	5.50	2.6	76	377	225	31.5	15.2	3.21	2.00
1988*	862.1	92.40	18.7	7.20	2.6	59	n/a	n/a	n/a	n/a	n/a	n/a

† Pro-forma to 31 July 1987
* Pro-forma to 31 January 1988

boost to the already highly successful Grattan operation. It fully utilises the management skills contained within Grattan, which are available to support the proposed new venture, whilst representing a valuable and increasing profit centre in its own right.

Club 24 and the property division provide further vehicles for development. Combined English Stores is being successfully integrated into the group. The group is developing its interests in the confectionery, tobacco, and newsagents area away from the high street, believing there is considerable growth potential. In April 1988 Next acquired the 175-strong Alfred Preedy newsagent chain.

FINANCIAL HISTORY

Next changed its year-end in 1985/86, making for a 17-month trading period to 31 January 1988. The company has therefore issued pro-forma 12-month figures for 1987 and 1988.

Pre-tax profits increased by 118% in the year to 31 January 1988, and earnings per share by 39% from 14.05p to 19.52p. Pre-tax profits amounted to £92.37m on turnover 131% ahead at £862.09m. At 31 January 1988, capital gearing was around 63%.

Innovative financing through low coupon convertible Eurobonds saves significantly on interest payments. A £400m acceptance facility was negotiated in 1986 to finance the development of the Club 24 financial business.

The scale of the group's development can be seen by comparison with the 1985/86 figures for the 12 months to 31 August 1986. Grattan was consolidated for one month only in 1986 and therefore contributed modestly to a 30.1% rise in group sales to £190.0m, and a 37.9% rise in pre-tax profits to £27.6m.

Over the five and a half years to 31 January 1988, an increase in group sales and pre-tax profits of 1,038% and 2,559% respectively was recorded. During the period, profit margins increased by a remarkable seven and a half points, as the previously poorly performing Hepworth business was converted into the highly successful Next retail format. Margins fell in 1987 by 1.7 points as the effect of some of the lower margin acquisitions was felt.

SHARE PRICE HISTORY

The all-time high of 360p was recorded in early 1987. In relative terms the shares rose from 10% of the FT-A All-Share index in 1982 to a peak of almost 40% in mid-1985. Since then, the shares have fallen back to under 30%, though there has been outperformance again in the second half of 1987.

Large share issues on the acquisition of Grattan and Combined English Stores have had to be absorbed. Mail order, which is now a significant contributor to group profits, tends to attract a rating below the stores sector average.

SENIOR MANAGEMENT

George Davies is chairman and group chief executive, taking over from Michael Stoddart as chairman in October 1987. Michael Stoddart remains a non-executive director.

George Davies was recruited in 1981 to head a new womenswear division, which was launched in 1982 under the name of Next. He was appointed to head the retail division in June 1983 and joined the main board soon after. He became joint managing director in July 1984 and was promoted to his present position at the end of 1984.

David Jones, who was formerly deputy chairman and managing director of Grattan, was appointed deputy chief executive of the enlarged group on its formation in July 1986. The other executive directors include Peter Lomas, group finance director, and John Whitmarsh, computer director – both ex-Grattan. Arnold Iversen, who is responsible for Club 24, and John Roberts, corporate development, are from the original Next operation.

CAPITAL

With the acquisition of Grattan in 1986, the group's ordinary share capital was increased by 89% to 254.6m ordinary shares. A £49m convertible Eurobond was issued in December 1986 with a 6.75% coupon.

To finance the June 1987 acquisition of Combined English Stores, a further 99.7m ordinary shares were issued, an increase in the share capital of 26.4%. 4.5m new ordinary shares were issued as part consideration for the acquisition of the outstanding 50% holding in the associate company, Paige. In April 1988 Next bid £21.4m for the 175-strong Alfred Preedy newsagent chain on the basis of 11 Next shares for every 12 Alfred Preedy shares.

Illustrating its financial shrewdness, Next issued a £100m convertible Eurobond in mid-1987 with a coupon of just 5.75%.

GROUP REVIEW

Retailing–high street The highly successful Next concept was launched in February 1982 as a ladieswear chain. Following this, a Next menswear chain was introduced in August 1984. A second ladieswear operation was started in August 1986, and a second menswear chain soon after. Other recent Next businesses to emerge include furniture and furnishings, shoes and accessories, and lingerie.

During this period the original Hepworth menswear business was run down and has now ceased to trade. Many stores were converted into use for Next. Coupled with the acquisition of space from outside the group and that of Combined English Stores, total selling area amounted to 2m sq ft as at September 1987. The average store size is under 2,000 sq ft but this includes locations where two or more of the separate Next businesses are operating under the same roof. The group's flagship is the large Next store in London's High Street Kensington.

In the largest outlets of 25,000 sq ft and over, a number of the businesses are combined together to provide a mini department store concept. The Next format has proved highly successful with margins of around 10% in 1986/87, in spite of paying pre-interest notional intergroup rents.

Within Next's target market of 25- to 45-year-olds seeking fashionable smart clothing, market share and penetration is significant. It was to prevent saturation that a second ladieswear chain was introduced. The two ladieswear chains are called Next Collection and Next Too. The two menswear chains are called Next for Men and Next for Gentlemen.

In September 1987 Next introduced its childrenswear chain, Next BG, which is trading well above expectations. Given the development of these additional businesses plus planned moves into still further product areas, a rapid store opening programme is being pursued.

Retail space has been increased by 0.7m sq ft as a result of the acquisition of Combined English Stores. The company operated different retail chains, including: Salisburys, handbags and leather goods; Zales, Collingwood and J Weir, jewellery; Allens, chemists; and in West Germany Biba, fashion clothing. A 100% interest was acquired in Paige, a UK ladies' clothing chain, which previously was only 50% owned by Combined English Stores. Other interests include a holiday company and wholesaling.

The business is being reorganised, with some of the trading names remaining and others rationalised absorbed within the Next mainstream activities. Collingwood, J Weir and Paige are being converted to the Next formula. Biba, Salisbury, Zales and Allens will continue to trade. The holiday company is being absorbed into the home shopping division.

Next has a credit operation operated at arm's length by the financial services division, Club 24. Credit sales give additional profit through the servicing of accounts, with income going direct to Club 24 under normal terms of business. The credit card operation does not merely fund Next's other operations. Next has expanding interests in financial services. It uses its extensive database of names and addresses to sell unit trusts,

provide credit reference to credit agencies, and create lists for direct marketing and mailing services.

A modern factory at Ashington near Newcastle sells to the group's own clothing stores. Other manufacturing investments have been made. These operations make a relatively modest contribution to group profits but provide an important captive source of supply and valuable vertical integration.

In the year to 31 January 1988, retailing-high street operating profit was 172% up at £49.87m (£18.36m), 49.9% of the group total.

Retailing–home shopping   Grattan is the UK's fourth largest mail order company. Each agent receives a Spring/Summer and Autumn/Winter catalogue which is supported by special promotional leaflets. Orders are received from the agents and delivered on an approval or return basis, with most payments extended over a 20-week period.

The product range divides between clothing and household goods. An increasing proportion of sales depend on alternative distribution methods which bypass the agency system, and effectively provide a cheaper and more cost-effective operation. In addition, computerised databases provide an opportunity to pinpoint individual customer groups and address them through special catalogues.

A further area of activity is direct response catalogues which are distributed under such names as Scotcade and Kaleidoscope to a selected mailing list. The business continues to be expanded, with agency numbers growing by 5% per annum and an increasing number of direct accounts opened.

In January 1988 a new mail order home shopping operation was launched under the name of Next Directory. Next Directory has 360 pages of fashion and accessories and is divided into 17 individual sections. Innovative photography and fabric swatches, as well as a sizing manual and tape measure, are just some of the new developments in the Directory. Through using courier services, Next Directory offers the revolutionary delivery time, for mail order, of 48 hours. The business combines the individual skills contained within the previously separate Next and Grattan companies, providing the opportunity for Next to tackle a larger proportion of the UK population than is available through the high street. Next Directory looks like being an outstanding success.

In the year to 31 January 1988, retailing-home shopping operating profit was 125% up at £34.38m (£15.29m), 34.4% of the group total.

Financial services   The business operates under the name of Club 24. Full ownership was acquired in September 1985. A total of over 1m accounts is now outstanding. Activity includes other retailers' credit card customers as well as the separate Next chains. The most important third party account is provided by Dixons, with whom a jointly-owned company has been established. The number of new accounts continues to rise.

In the year to 31 January 1988, financial services operating profit was 26% up at £8.28m (£6.59m), 8.3% of the group total.

Property   The division receives inter-group rents and undertakes property developments, both on behalf of the group's own retail businesses and externally.

In the year to 31 January 1988, property operating profit was 7% up at £7.46m (£6.97m), 7.4% of the group total.

GEOGRAPHICAL REVIEW

At present the group is almost entirely dependent on the UK, although manufacturing investments have been made overseas and the possibility of retail franchise agreements explored.

Share price and relative to FT-A All-Share

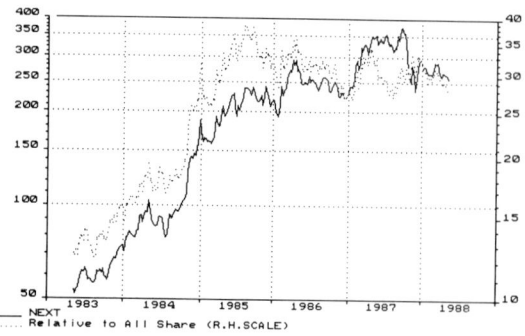

NEXT
Relative to All Share (R.H.SCALE)

PEARSON plc

CORPORATE CALENDAR

Year end	31 January
Preliminary results	March/April
Report and accounts	April/May
AGM	May
Final dividend paid	June
Interim results	September
Interim dividend paid	December

DIRECTORS' HOLDINGS

	Fully-paid ordinary shares		Options
	(beneficial)	(non-beneficial)	
GW Davies	87,859	659,143	1,029,240
DC Jones	483,430	—	721,167
EK Davies	75,162	—	319,513
PF Lomas	46,212	—	309,167
BS Marber	—	—	—
TA O'Malley	2,865	—	166,000
TJB Roberts	7,803	659,143	359,878
JT Rowlay	84,073	—	—
MC Stoddart	26,382	—	—
JH Whitmarsh	85,607	—	310,356

Total directors' remuneration in 1987 was not declared. The chairman received £205,596, and the highest-paid director £561,152.

PRINCIPAL SUBSIDIARIES AND RELATED COMPANIES

Alfred Preedy Plc, Allens Chemists Limited, Biba & Pariscop Duab, Club 24 Limited, Collingwood The County Jewellers Limited, Dillons Newsagents Limited, Eurocamp Travel Limited, Grattan plc, Kaleidoscope Limited, Next Properties Limited, Next Retail Limited, Paul James Knitwear Limited, Salisbury Handbags Limited, The Next Directory Limited, Van Dyke Limited, Zales Jewellers Limited

BRAND NAMES

Allens, Carefree Camping, Club 24, Dillons, Eurocamp, Grattan, Kaleidoscope, Look again, Manorgrove, Mercado, Next, Next BG, Next Collection, Next Directory, Next for Men, Next Originals, Next Too, Paul James Knitwear, Salisburys, Scotcade, Streets of London, Sunsites, You and Yours, Zales

CONTACTS AND FURTHER INFORMATION

P Bailey, company secretary, Next plc, Desford Road, Enderby, Leicester LE9 5AT. Tel: 0533 866411.

GENERAL INFORMATION

Head office	Millbank Tower, Millbank, London SW1P 4QZ. Tel: 01-828 9020
President	Viscount Cowdray
Directors	Viscount Blakenham (chairman and chief executive), F Barlow, MW Burrell, JAB Joll, DM Veit, AA Whitaker. *Non-exec* M David-Weill, J-C Haas, Sir Ian Fraser CBE MC, PG Gyllenhammar, JH Hale, Sir Simon Hornby, R Mark – US, D Stevenson CBE
Advisers	Baring Brothers & Co Ltd, Lazard Brothers & Co Ltd
Auditors	Deloitte Haskins & Sells
Registrars	Lloyds Bank Registrar's Department
Brokers	Cazenove & Co
Solicitors	Freshfields, Herbert Smith

GENERAL FINANCIAL INFORMATION

Market capitalisation	£1.461bn at 1 January 1988
Capital structure	
Issued ordinary shares (25p)	223m
Issued preference shares (£1)	501,000 3.5% CP
Warrants	None
Convertibles	None
Traded options	None
ADRs	None
Shareholders over 5%	The News Corporation Ltd 20.3%; companies associated with Lazard Frères et Cie, Paris 9.5%

FT CATEGORY

FT: Industrials (miscel.)
FT-A: Conglomerates

MAJOR ACTIVITIES

Pearson is a large diversified group with interests in information and entertainment, investment banking, fine china, and oil and oil services. Its most famous businesses are the *Financial Times*, Longman, Penguin Books, Madame Tussaud's, Royal Doulton and a 50% interest in Lazard Brothers.

Pearson is not dependent on any one area. In 1987, 60% of operating profits came from information and entertainment, 53% in 1986; 21% from investment banking, 21% in 1986; 10% from fine china, 13% in 1986; and 5% from oil and oil services, 5% in 1986.

Because of the group's breadth of interests, no particular narrow economic indicator is likely to have an overall impact, but several are important to specific areas. The oil price has an impact on the oil division, while consumer and advertising expenditure are important to many of the information activities. Levels of tourist activity in the UK are important to parts of the entertainment businesses and also to the fine china business.

The breadth of group interests also means that the competition is varied. Quoted competitors include United Newspapers and Associated Newspapers in newspapers, Collins in books, Waterford Glass in fine china, and the entire merchant banking sector.

FINANCIAL HISTORY

Earnings and dividends have shown good progress since 1982 when the group took its present shape, growing at annual compound rates of 23% and 22% respectively. Sales rose 32.5% from £718.5m in 1982 to £952.2m in 1987. The real benefit has come in trading margins, up from 10.7% in 1982 to 15.6% in 1987. At the pre-tax level the improvement was more marked with profits up 153.4% from £59.9m in 1982 to £151.8m in 1987.

Year	Turnover (£m)	Pre-tax (£m)	Earnings (p)	Dividends net (p)	Dividend cover (x)	Net assets (p)	Price (p) High	Low	PER (x) High	Low	Yield (%) High	Low
1983	730.4	77.4	22.6	7.0	3.22	179.1	205	135	12.9	7.9	5.97	4.34
1984	843.2	99.4	28.9	8.5	3.40	210.7	295	202	15.5	10.4	4.39	3.36
1985	970.1	109.3	30.0	10.0	3.00	198.1	428	287	15.4	10.6	4.67	3.00
1986	952.6	121.1	37.4	12.0	3.11	215.4	616	393	19.7	13.9	3.54	2.34
1987	952.2	151.8	46.7	15.0	3.11	266.5	1,012	525	25.4	13.3	3.36	1.76

Earnings per share went up 181.3% from 16.6p in 1982 to 46.7p in 1987. All the on-going core businesses, except oil services and fine china in 1986 and 1987, increased their profit contribution each year.

The balance sheet has also improved. Net interest changed from a debit of £17m in 1982 to a credit of £3m in 1987. Net borrowings of £124m in 1982 were transformed to net cash, though this will reverse again in 1988 due to the financing of Addison-Wesley and other acquisitions.

SHARE PRICE HISTORY

Pearson's improving financial performance resulted in a share price that rose from a 1982 peak of 145p to a 1987 peak of 1012p. Relative to the market the share price went from around 43% of the index's value at the start of 1984 to almost 85% at the 1987 high.

The shares were hit hard in the 1987 autumn crash. Pearson went down to the 500p level and 63% of the index, but in May 1988 the share price had recovered to the 675p level and 74% of the index. Bid speculation was the cause of the 1987 outperformance and will remain a factor in 1988.

SENIOR MANAGEMENT

President of the group is Viscount Cowdray, but it is Viscount Blakenham, who has been chief executive since 1978 and chairman since 1983, who has held the reins at Pearson. The other executive directors are: Frank Barlow, chief executive of the Financial Times and Westminster Press; David Veit, president of Pearson Inc; James Joll, group finance director; Mark Burrell; and Alan Whitaker.

There are many high calibre non-executive directors. They are: Michel David-Weill and Jean-Claude Haas, of Lazard Frères; John Hale, previously managing director of Pearson; Pehr Gyllenhammar, chairman of Volvo; Sir Simon Hornby, chairman of WH Smith; Reuben Mark, chairman and chief executive of Colgate-Palmolive; Sir Ian Fraser, deputy chairman of Vickers and TSB; and Dennis Stevenson CBE.

CAPITAL

Pearson has been conservative in the use of its shares. On a comparable basis the number in issue increased from 186m at the end of 1982 to 223m in May 1988. During 1985 there was a one for one scrip issue.

The group has attracted considerable takeover speculation. In September 1987 Rupert Murdoch of News International announced a 13.5% stake and increased it to over 20% in January 1988. Although he stated that a full bid was not intended, it became clear that he was interested in joint ventures and possibly the Financial Times itself. In addition

Michel David-Weill and associates have built up a holding of more than 20m shares.

In July 1987 the sale of Bracken House was completed for £143m in cash. This and the $37m received from the Cedar Fair stake led to the group having a substantial cash inflow.

In the second half of 1987 and early 1988, $80m was spent on purchasing the 35% stake in Camco that Pearson did not already own; C$11.5m was spent on acquiring 25% of the Canadian newspaper, the Financial Post; £20m cash was spent on the first payment on the Horseshoe Court development; £10m was committed to acquire Datasolve Information Online; and 7.37m and Fr 355m in cash and ordinary shares will be issued in two stages as part of the acquisition price of the French financial newspaper, Les Echos. The first stage of the Les Echos transaction was completed in May 1988.

In January 1988 the group arranged a £300m multiple option financing facility with a £250m standby committed. The group redeemed all the outstanding 5.75% 2001 convertible bonds not converted before 2 March 1988 on 10 March 1988. The US publisher Addison-Wesley was acquired for $283m cash in an agreed bid in February 1988.

GROUP REVIEW

Information and entertainment This is the largest of Pearson's four business divisions and contains a number of companies which are household names.

In newspapers Pearson owns the highly successful Financial Times (FT) and 50% of The Economist. Both papers are increasing circulation and the FT has been able to make cover price increases in 1985 and 1988, the previous one being in 1983. Pearson also owns the recently slimmed-down regional chain, Westminster Press, publishers of both paid-for and free newspapers throughout the UK.

The FT acquired Datasolve Information Online in October 1987 from THORN-EMI for £10m. This is an on-line information supplier and complements the FT's existing interests in FT Business Information, owners of the Investors Chronicle and electronic publishers. Datasolve has been renamed Profile Information.

The FT also acquired 25% of the Canadian business and financial news publisher, the Financial Post, in 1988 for C$11.5m. In January 1988 it signed a contract to acquire Les Echos SA, a French financial newspaper publisher, the first stage of the acquisition being completed in May 1988. Pearson is keen to develop an international network of financial newspapers. In May 1988 the group was in talks with Cinco Días, the Spanish financial daily.

In summer 1988 the production departments of the FT move to a new high-technology building in London's Docklands. In August 1987 the group purchased the Horseshoe Court development at Bankside, Southwark Bridge, from Regalian Properties for £74.4m, of which £20m was paid on exchange of contracts. This building will house the editorial and advertising staff of the *Financial Times* after they move from Bracken House.

Pearson's book publishing interests include Longman, the important professional and educational publisher, and Penguin.

In February 1988 Pearson greatly strengthened its international educational publishing interests by making an agreed bid of $283m for the US publisher Addison-Wesley. Addison-Wesley is the sixth largest college and ninth largest schools publisher in the US. The merged company, Addison-Wesley-Longman Group will have combined sales of £250m and will dominate both British and American English language teaching. It will also form a substantial force in scientific publishing. In 1987 Addison-Wesley made pre-tax profits of $15.4m on sales of $167.4m.

Other well-known names in the Longman group are Ladybird, Pitman and Churchill Livingstone, the UK's largest medical publisher.

Penguin has grown dramatically with the acquisition of several imprints from International Thomson in 1985 and the purchase of the New American Library (NAL) in December 1986. Penguin includes Puffin, Viking, Viking Kestrel, Hamish Hamilton, Michael Joseph, Sphere, Frederick Warne and Pelham, as well as NAL. NAL publishes mass-market paperbacks and hardbacks under its own imprint and that of EP Dutton, and Dutton and Dial books for children and young readers.

In entertainment Pearson owns Madame Tussaud's. This includes the famous waxworks, the London Planetarium and several other attractions, notably Warwick Castle, Wookey Hole and Chessington World of Adventures. A lease has been signed for part of the London Pavilion where a rock and roll music exhibition is planned to open in 1989.

CHAIRMAN'S STATEMENT

'Your company has had an exciting twelve months. Once again we have beaten our 20 per cent medium-term target in profits and earnings per share growth and have complemented organic development with important strategic acquisitions....

Put at its simplest, we believe that top quality products and services, marketed internationally by strongly motivated and highly skilled management teams, lead to strong market positions and superior business performance.' *Michael Blakenham*

In the US Pearson has an interest in the amusement parks of Cedar Fair, although its 33% stake was reduced to 8% following the public flotation of new partnership units in the business in May 1987.

The group has a 20.2% stake in Yorkshire Television and is one of the five founder partners of the British Satellite Broadcasting group, the satellite broadcasting franchise winner. This is expected to be launched in 1989 but is unlikely to produce profits for some years to come.

In 1987 divisional turnover was 17.9% up at £645m from £547.1m, with operating profit 27.2% ahead at £89.4m from £70.3m.

Newspapers and magazines increased operating profit by 16.3% to £40.6m (£34.9m) on turnover just 0.2% ahead at £255.4m (£255.0m) following some Westminster Press disposals. Book publishing operating profit, helped by a first time contribution from New American Library, was up 68.8% to

£39.5m (£23.4m) on turnover 33.7% ahead at £367.9m (£275.1m). Entertainment operating profit decreased by 22.5% to £9.3m (£12m) on turnover 27.6% ahead at £21.7m (£17m). The part disposal of Cedar Fair accounts for more than the whole profit decline in entertainment.

Investment banking Pearson's interests in investment banking are through its long-standing relationship with the Lazard Houses. After a reorganisation in 1984 Pearson owns 50% of Lazard Brothers, and has a 10% share of the profits of Lazard Frères, New York and Lazard Frères, Paris.

Following London's Big Bang, Lazard Brothers has taken an interesting approach by purchasing neither a jobber nor a broker but concentrating on areas of finance where its specialist advice and experience can be of use, but where it does not need to invest significant amounts of new capital. In 1987 profits attributable to Pearson were 7.4% up at £30.5m from £28.4m.

Share price and relative to FT-A All-Share

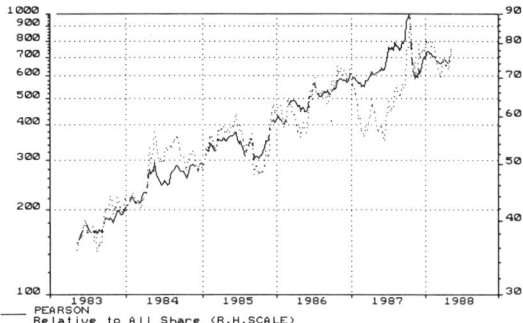

PEARSON
Relative to All Share (R.H.SCALE)

Fine china Pearson's fine china presence comes through its ownership of Royal Doulton and its associated major brands, Royal Crown Derby, Minton and Royal Albert. Much of the group's production is exported and marketed overseas with Canada, the US, Australia and Japan being the four largest markets. Steps are being taken to improve sales in continental Europe.

The level of tourism is an important factor in UK sales. The disappointing 1986 results were partly attributable to the fall in tourism which followed the bombing of Libya and the Chernobyl disaster.

In 1987 margins were hit by the weak dollar. Turnover was 3.1% up at £161.1m (£156.3m) but operating profit was 13.3% down at £14.3m (£16.5m).

Oil and oil services The bulk of the group's interests are held through its ownership of Camco, which had been separately quoted in the US. In July 1987 Pearson announced its intention to buy out the minority interest and this has now been concluded.

Camco produces a variety of equipment for the oil industry and performs a number of oil-related services. Pearson has direct interests in oil-bearing properties through Lignum Oil in the US and Whitehall Petroleum in the UK.

Pearson appears committed to the area in the longer term and has made a number of acquisitions at what is likely to be the bottom end of the cycle. These include Reed Tool in the US, a leading manufacturer of drilling bits with 1986 sales of $76m.

In 1987 operating profit was up 23.1% to £8m (£6.5m) on turnover 25.5% up at £137.9m (£109.9m). The increases were largely due to the acquisition of Reed Tool and the minority interest in Camco.

Other interests The group has a number of other interests. It is developing part of the West Thurrock estate in conjunction with Capital & Counties, and has received approval for a regional shopping centre. In May 1988 Pearson sold to Capital & Counties the freehold site of the shopping centre whilst retaining the remainder of its West Thurrock estate. Pearson owns 53.5% of Château Latour, the French wine producer.

1986 profits were sharply up at £5.5m from £0.7m. In 1987 operating profit rose 20% on turnover 32.3% ahead at £8.2m.

GEOGRAPHICAL REVIEW

Pearson's main presence is in the UK. In 1987 46% of sales and 57% of operating profits arose there. North America produced 38% of operating profits from 38% of sales, with the balance arising elsewhere.

CONTACTS AND FURTHER INFORMATION

P Emmerson, Company Secretary, Pearson plc, 17th Floor, Millbank Tower, Millbank, London SW1P 4QZ. Tel: 01-828 9020.

CORPORATE CALENDAR

Year end	31 December
Preliminary results	March
Report and accounts	April
AGM	May
Final dividend paid	May
Interim results	August
Interim dividend paid	November

DIRECTORS' INTERESTS

	Ordinary shares (beneficial)	(non-beneficial)	Options
Viscount Blakenham	57,609	99,520	116,217
F Barlow	23,318	—	43,027
MW Burrell	1,821,212	—	46,345
M David-Weill	20,852,300	—	54,084
Sir Ian Fraser	2,000	—	—
PG Gyllenhammar	—	—	—
J-C Haas	10,000	—	—
JH Hale	37,500	—	16,000
Sir Simon Hornby	2,000	—	—
JAB Joll	4,000	—	51,000
HD Stevenson	4,000	—	—
DM Veit	—	—	120,000
AA Whitaker	89,312	—	79,718

Total directors' remuneration in 1987 including fees was £1.78m, of which the chairman received £283,000.

PRINCIPAL SUBSIDIARIES AND RELATED COMPANIES

Camco Inc – US, Compressor Systems Inc – US (35.9%), Financial Times Group Ltd, Lazard Brothers & Co Ltd (50.0%), Lazard Frères & Co – US (9.8%), Lazard Frères et Compagnie and Maison Lazard et Compagnie – France (9.9%), Lazard Partners Ltd Partnership – US (50.0%), Lignum Oil Co – US, Longman Holdings Ltd, Longman Nigeria Ltd (40.0%), Madame Tussaud's Ltd, Pearson Inc – US, Royal Doulton Ltd, Société Civile du Vignoble de Château Latour – France (53.5%), The Economist Newspaper Ltd (50.0%), The Penguin Publishing Co Ltd, Westminster Press Ltd, West Thurrock Estate, Whitehall Petroleum Ltd, Yorkshire Television Holdings Plc (20.2%).

BRAND NAMES

BSB, Churchill Livingstone, Dial, Dutton, EP Dutton, *Financial Times*, Frederick Warne, Hamish Hamilton, Ladybird, Lazard Brothers, Longman, Madame Tussaud's, Michael Joseph, Minton, New American Library, Pelham, Penguin, Pitman, Puffin, Royal Albert, Royal Crown Derby, Royal Doulton, Sphere, *The Economist*, Viking, Viking Kestrel, Viking Penguin, Westminster Press

THE PENINSULAR AND ORIENTAL STEAM NAVIGATION COMPANY

GENERAL INFORMATION

Head office	79 Pall Mall, London SW1Y 5EJ. Tel: 01-930 4343
Directors	Sir Jeffrey Sterling CBE (chairman), BD McPhail (managing), AK Black, PJ Ford, TC Harris, AG Hatchett CBE, FW Lampl, HTHM Phelps, AM Robb, K St Johnston, P Thomas, PL Warner. *Non-exec* PG Cazalet, CEA Hambro, GC Hoyer Millar, O Marriott
Advisers	Hambros Bank Ltd, Barclays de Zoete Wedd Ltd
Auditors	Peat Marwick McLintock
Registrars	Royal Bank of Scotland Registrar's Department
Brokers	Panmure Gordon & Co Ltd, Rowe & Pitman Ltd
Solicitors	Freshfields

GENERAL FINANCIAL INFORMATION

Market capitalisation	£1.917bn at 1 January 1988
Capital structure	
Issued deferred stock (£1)	379.7m
Issued preference shares (£1)	3.34m at 5.5%
Concessionary preference shares (£1)	66.6m at 5.5%
Warrants	0.36m 1985/90, exercisable at 493p per ordinary share 26.59m 1988/92, exercisable at 750p per ordinary share
Convertibles	£58.0m 6.75% CULS 2006 (16.66 shares per £100 stock) £34.7m 6.3% CULS 1990 (29.41 shares per £100 stock) £75m 4.75% CULS 2002 (13.33 shares per £100 stock)
Traded options	Yes
ADRs	None
Shareholders over 5%	Prudential Corporation 5.8%

FT CATEGORY

FT: Shipping
FT-A: Shipping and transport

MAJOR ACTIVITIES

P&O is a diversified service group consisting of five core activities – passenger shipping, container and bulk shipping, transport services, property and development, and diversified service industries ranging from a catering operation to a security company.

Contribution to operating profit in 1987 was 17.4% from passenger shipping, 16% from container and bulk shipping, 21.4% from services, 33.2% from property and development and 16.8% from property investment. P&O is now the third biggest property company in the UK.

Because of the diversity of the company, a key economic indicator having an adverse impact on one company could prove beneficial for another. Factors include personal disposable income, fuel prices, and shipping rates in the areas of passenger, container and bulk shipping.

Interest rates and retail and commercial space demand are the determinants of profit and turnover in property development and investment.

FINANCIAL HISTORY

Turnover was £2.920bn in 1987, a 47.3% increase on 1986, and up 94.4% from 1983. Pre-tax profits increased 58% to £282.0m and were up 295% from 1983. Between 1986 and 1987 earnings per share increased 12.9% to 47.1p from 41.7p. Dividends showed a 15.8% increase to 22p from 19p. The balance sheet showed gearing at 46% in 1987 against 35% in 1986. This was reduced to 38.6% after the year-end through property disposals.

This earnings performance can be attributed to a policy change in 1983 which led to concentration on the group's core activities and a shedding of non-related companies. This was accompanied by a shift to a decentralised management style in which the divisional chairman is accountable directly to the board. Operating profit has shifted towards property and investment, away from shipping, and completely away from oil-related activities.

SHARE PRICE HISTORY

P&O has witnessed a steady rise in price share from a range of 101p to 158p in 1982 to a range of 425p to 776p in 1987, a major move of over 400%. In July 1987 P&O crossed the 750p barrier before falling in the autumn crash to 420p.

Relative to the FT-A All-Share index, the price rose from a range of 27% to 46% in 1982 to a range of 55% to 69% in 1987. The shares in April 1988 were trading around 600p, 65% of the index.

SENIOR MANAGEMENT

Sir Jeffrey Sterling, a dynamic entrepreneur who was largely responsible for the recovery of Town and City Properties after the property crash of 1973, and of his own Sterling Guarantee Trust services and property group, is responsible for the rationalisation of operations and turn-around at P&O. He has been serving as chairman since late 1983.

BD McPhail is managing director and AM Robb is finance director. The various key executive directors who also head divisions within the group are AK Black, HTHM Phelps, PJ Ford, TC Harris, FW Lampl, K St Johnston and PL Warner.

CAPITAL

P&O has generally used proceeds from the disposal of non-core subsidiaries as well as share issues to help finance acquisitions. In 1986/87 a number of major acquisitions were made.

In May 1986 the outstanding 52.6% of Overseas Containers Limited was bought for cash and the issue of £7.2m nominal of deferred stock. The acquisition of Stock Conversion in June 1986 required the issue of £69.7m nominal of deferred stock.

In January 1987 the acquisition of the ordinary and convertible share capital of European Ferries involved the issue of £48.9m nominal of deferred stock, £5.2m nominal of 6.3% convertible stock and £58.7m nominal of 6.75% convertible stock. Later in the year the European Ferries concessionary shares were exchanged for £66.6m nominal of P&O concessionary stock.

In April 1987, the directors declared an issue of ten 'Anniversary Warrants' for every £150 nominal of deferred stock, each such warrant giving the right to subscribe for £1 nominal of deferred stock at a price of 750p. In May 1987 the company issued £75m of 4.75% convertible bonds 2002.

P&O stock was listed on the Australian Stock Exchange on 22nd November 1987 and on the Tokyo Stock Exchange on 22nd December 1987.

GROUP REVIEW

Passenger shipping Activity is divided between North Sea Ferries, P&O Cruises, P&O European Ferries and P&O Ferries. P&O Cruises operates eight cruise liners, of which the

F I V E Y E A R F I N A N C I A L I N F O R M A T I O N												
Year	Turnover (£m)	Pre-tax (£m)	Earnings (p)	Dividends net (p)	Dividend cover (x)	Net assets (p)	Price (p) High	Low	PER (x) High	Low	Yield (%) High	Low
1983	1,502.2	71.4	28.2	12.5	2.3	318.2	254	106	22.2	6.6	13.23	5.54
1984	1,644.1	90.2	31.9	14.0	2.3	259.7	323	238	26.7	12.6	6.98	4.61
1985	1,629.3	125.6	34.9	16.0	2.2	274.9	448	303	20.4	13.4	5.88	4.70
1986	1,952.2	174.1	41.7	19.0	2.2	317.1	566	422	20.3	14.3	5.32	3.85
1987	2,920.0	274.7	47.1	22.0	2.1	386.0	773	440	20.5	12.2	6.38	3.37

Sea Princess and *Canberra* have recently been refurbished. In the US, integration of a cruise and rail service increased the range of tours offered. The US remains a competitive market.

P&O Ferries operates North Sea Ferries as a joint venture with the Royal Nedlloyd Group and Scottish services. The ferry operation expanded with the acquisition of European Ferries' Townsend Thoresen operation. 1987 was turned into tragedy by the loss of the *Herald of Free Enterprise* and many lives at Zeebrugge. Townsend Thoresen was renamed P&O European Ferries.

The area saw a 111.3% increase in operating profit in 1987 at £41.2m, up from £19.5m in 1986. P&O European Ferries had a difficult year with freight volumes maintained but passenger volumes slightly down. Both P&O Ferries and North Sea Ferries performed ahead of expectations against the background of the introduction of new ships. P&O Cruises performed well despite adverse exchange movements. *Royal Princess* did well in the US cruise market.

Housebuilding, construction and development The division, which includes Bovis and Town & City Properties (Development) Ltd, saw an increase in profits in 1987 of 116.9% to £108.9m from £50.2m in 1986, helped by buoyant conditions in construction markets in the US and the UK.

The purchase of Stock Conversion for £400m was partly financed by the divestment of Euston Centre Properties for £65.4m. This operation is now fully integrated with Town & City Properties.

Major Town & City Properties (Development) Ltd projects include: Chelsea Harbour with Globe Investment Trust; new shopping centres at Salisbury, Ashford, Thamesmead, Accrington and Braintree; and offices at Holborn Viaduct, Beaufort House (jointly with Stockley) and St Albans.

Bovis Construction completed the new Lloyd's headquarters and Queen Elizabeth II Conference Centre, as well as carrying out 55 separate projects for Marks and Spencer, the company's longest-established client. The Broadgate scheme, Chelsea Harbour and a major dealing facility for Salomon Brothers in Victoria were other major projects. Bovis Homes achieved record profits and turnover.

Container and bulk shipping The area changed significantly in 1986, with the purchase of the outstanding 52.6% of Overseas Containers Limited (OCL), valuing that company at £270m. OCL was renamed P&O Containers Ltd in 1987. Combined with the disposal of the interests in Panocean Storage and Transport, and Ocean Trading and Transport for £41.4m, the net effect was to internationalise the business.

Further consolidation was carried out by the disposal of the LPG shipping interest for £50m. Profitability was limited in 1986 by continued intense competition and over-capacity. Operating profit in 1987 was 17.2% up at £52.4m from £44.7m in 1986. Cargo volumes were particularly strong in the Europe-Far East trade. Results were affected by the weak US dollar but freight rate levels were maintained. The company has ordered a new ship and has reached an agreement with Sealand for economical capacity on the North Atlantic.

Investment property The acquisition of Stock Conversion had significant impact, doubling the value of the UK property portfolio which is predominantly in shopping and offices.

The division, through Town and Cities Properties Management Ltd, manages over 460 investment properties throughout the UK, including offices, shops and industrial premises. They house 3,600 individual tenants. The acquisition of Stock Conversion in 1986 brought an additional 115 properties and 1,100 tenants.

Arndale Shopping Centres Ltd owns or manages ten shopping centres situated throughout the UK. The largest are in Manchester, Luton and Wandsworth. A comprehensive range of services is provided, including letting and maintenance as well as marketing and promotion. The shopping centres total 4.8m sq ft.

Over 5m sq ft of space in Europe, North America and Australia have been developed by P&O Properties International Ltd, sometimes in conjunction with local partners. The major development activity is in the US where 3.5m sq ft of industrial buildings adjoining the centre of Boston are being updated progressively. The company also partially or wholly owns an additional 2.5m sq ft of office and industrial space in the US and in Europe.

CHAIRMAN'S STATEMENT

'Developments such as the Channel tunnel make change inevitable and we must, as responsible management, ensure that it is effectively implemented. In the face of unrelenting competition, in every Group company, commercial success and thereby the welfare of employees will only be achieved if we manage each and every business with total realism.

In all of this we must never lose sight of the human problems that arise and we must do our best to alleviate them.

1987 was a year of consolidation and development. We enter 1988 from a position of strength and I am confident of our ability to make further progress.

We secure our future by achieving sustained levels of profit on the capital we invest. This is the only way.' *Sir Jeffrey Sterling*

The division's international property interests expanded considerably with the acquisition of European Ferries' substantial US interests centred in Denver, Atlanta and Houston.

In 1987 investment property income at £55.1m provided 16.8% (22%) of P&O's total group operating profit and was up 20.8% on 1986 (£45.6m). The triennial valuation produced a surplus of £113m and there was a £29m profit on sales, taken as an extraordinary item.

Service industries The trade and conference group, which includes Earl's Court and Olympia, is the market leader. A

Share price and relative to FT-A All-Share

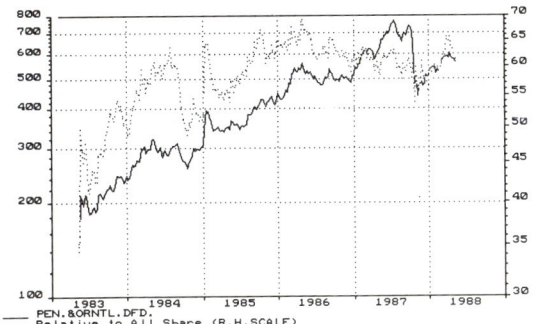

PEN.&ORNTL.DFD.
Relative to All Share (R.H.SCALE)

major extension to Earl's Court is under development. Sutcliffe Catering continues to grow successfully. The Felixstowe container port is expanding rapidly. Operating profit was 35.4% up at £70.0m from £51.7m in 1986.

P&O European Transport Services   The division consists of a group of sophisticated haulage companies, including Ferrymasters, Pandoro, Scott Packing & Warehousing, and P&O Roadways. Ferrymasters won the Queen's Award for Export Achievement in 1987.

GEOGRAPHICAL REVIEW

P&O is increasingly an international company in scope, with property interests in the UK, the US and Australia. In 1987, however, 61% of turnover continued to come from UK operations in spite of the international nature of the business. 12.2% of turnover is derived from continental Europe, 8.3% from Australasia and the Pacific, and 9.6% from the US and Canada.

CORPORATE CALENDAR

Year end	31 December
Preliminary results	March
Report and accounts	April
AGM	May
Final dividend paid	May
Interim results	September
Interim dividend paid	November

DIRECTORS' HOLDINGS

	Fully-paid ordinary shares (beneficial)	Options	Warrants
Sir Jeffrey Sterling	505,722	187,500	34,220
BD McPhail	209,041	137,500	14,194
AK Black	886	62,500	59
PG Cazalet	1,600	—	106
PJ Ford	130,871	75,000	8,732
CEA Hambro	—	—	—
TC Harris	31,438	62,500	2,102
AG Hatchett	18,744	75,000	1,251
GC Hoyer Millar	1,249		83
FW Lampl	11,841	70,000	788
O Marriott	18,181	—	1,309
HTHM Phelps	476	48,000	31
AM Robb	16,307	62,500	1,086
K St Johnston	675	65,500	45
P Thomas	6,565	47,408	437
PL Warner	1,429	79,794	265

Total directors' remuneration in 1987 was £1.70m, of which the chairman received £220,900.

PRINCIPAL SUBSIDIARIES AND RELATED COMPANIES

Service industries
Buck & Hickman Ltd, Earls Court & Olympia Ltd, Mackinnon Mackenzie & Company of Pakistan Ltd – Pakistan (70%), P&O Australia, P&O New Zealand, Sea Oil Homco Ltd, Sterling Guarantee Trust Plc, Sterling Guards Ltd, Sutcliffe Catering Group Ltd, Three Quays International Ltd

P&O European Transport Services
Butlers Warehousing & Distribution Ltd, Ferrymaster Ltd, Northern Ireland Trailers Scotland Ltd, P&O European Transport Services Ltd, P&O Roadtanks Ltd, P&O Roadways Ltd, Pandoro Ltd, Red Carnations Gum Ltd, Scott Packing & Warehousing Ltd

Passenger shipping
North Sea Ferries Ltd, P&O Cruises Ltd, P&O European Ferries Ltd, P&O Ferries Ltd, P&O Lines Ltd, Princess Cruises Inc – US, Swan Hellenic Ltd

Housebuilding, construction and development
Ashby & Horner Ltd, Bovis Construction Ltd, Bovis Homes Ltd, Bovis International Ltd, Town & City Properties (Development) Ltd, Wyseplant Ltd, Yeomans & Partners Ltd

Container and bulk shipping
P&O Containers Ltd, P&O Bulk Shipping Ltd

Investment property
Arndale Shopping Centres Ltd, P&O Properties Management Ltd, Town & City Properties Management Ltd

BRAND NAMES

Bovis, Ferrymasters, P&O, Townsend Thoresen

CONTACTS AND FURTHER INFORMATION

P Thomas, Director of Corporate Affairs, The Peninsular and Oriental Steam Navigation Company, 79 Pall Mall, London SW1Y 5EJ. Tel: 01-930 4343.

PILKINGTON plc

GENERAL INFORMATION

Head office   Prescot Road, St Helens, WA10 3TT. Tel: 0744 28882
Directors   Sir Alastair Pilkington (president), AR Pilkington (executive chairman), DE Cook (deputy chairman), PH Grunwell, GN Iley, Sir Robin Nicholson, G Nightingale. *Non-exec* Lord Croham, FR Hurn, H Kopper, JD Macomber, Sir Peter Thompson
Advisers   J Henry Schroder Wagg & Co Ltd
Auditors   Coopers & Lybrand
Registrars   National Westminster Bank Registrar's Department
Brokers   Cazenove & Co, Charterhouse Tilney, Rowe & Pitman Ltd
Solicitors   Slaughter and May

GENERAL FINANCIAL INFORMATION

Market capitalisation	£1.624bn at 1 January 1988
Capital structure	
Issued ordinary shares (50p)	734m
Issued preference shares	None
Warrants	10.6m, one ordinary share at 139.7p per share
Convertibles	None
Traded options	Yes
ADRs	None
Shareholders over 5%	None

FT CATEGORY

FT: Industrials (miscel.)
FT-A: Building materials

MAJOR ACTIVITIES

Pilkington is the world's largest glass producer with one-fifth of world glass output under its control. The group operates through 400 companies in 36 countries worldwide. Worldwide turnover is more than £2.1bn, about 77% of which is earned outside the UK. Pilkington successfully defended a bid by the conglomerate BTR at the start of 1987.

Pilkington makes a wide variety of basic glass products and derivatives such as common flat and safety glass. It has developing interests in glass and plastic ophthalmic products, electro-optical systems, and glass and mineral fibres. The group is also active in the glass merchanting, insulation contracting, defence, aviation and medical markets.

In the 1950s Pilkington developed the float glass manufacturing process, now the universal method of making high quality flat glass. The production revolution took place in the 1960s.

In the 1980s Pilkington experienced tough market conditions, including a price war in Europe, over-capacity and a strong pound. This forced Pilkington to seek major redundancies in its workforce. These cost £80m over a five year period.

The group attempted to soften the impact of this through a well managed voluntary redundancy programme. As a paternalistic employer it wished to lessen the impact on St Helens, which depends upon Pilkington as its major employer. Productivity gains accompanied the redundancy programme. Costs fell 30% between 1982 and 1984.

The BTR takeover bid spurred the group to make major changes. At the time of the bid Pilkington's future looked uncertain. But profits had in fact turned. Pilkington swapped a minority holding in Libbey-Owens-Ford (LOF) for the key acquisition of LOF's glass-making division. 1987 profits more than doubled. Shareholder and workforce faith in Antony Pilkington was well rewarded.

Strategic acquisitions in the US and West Germany have altered the balance of the business. In August 1987 Pilkington acquired Vision Care from Revlon for £361m. Vision Care has a significant market share in the world ophthalmic market. Through the LOF and Vision Care acquisitions, Pilkington has extended its geographical markets. Its intention is to increase the share of profits from advanced technology products to one-third by 1990.

Pilkington is a maturing business which is still undergoing the difficult transition from a single successful product. The next few years will test its ability to maintain a strong performance based on geographical diversification and improved productivity.

Pilkington believes that above average growth is possible from its core business, but if glass capacity increases or prices fall, it could again face the problems which failure to diversify from glass production represent.

FINANCIAL HISTORY

Between 1983 and 1986 Pilkington's sales increased by 29.2%. Operating profit increased by just 5.7%. Exceptional redundancy costs of between £10m and £21m per annum from 1983 reduced profits by 7% to 15%.

Growth returned to the glass business in 1987 as cost savings coincided with price increases. Turnover, including new acquisitions, was up by almost 60% on 1986 to £2.1bn. Pre-tax profits increased by 107.9% to £256m. Earnings per share were up by no less than 229.2% to 24.4p. This was partly due to a dramatic reduction in the tax charge from 50% to 31%, taking into account previous losses, and a lower UK tax charge.

Extraordinary costs of £32m in 1987 included £9.4m to defend the BTR bid. Dividends were 63% up in 1987 to 7.3p net. Licensing and technical income was 23% up at £32.1m. The LOF acquisition added sales of £450m and operating profit of £31m. Pilkington's balance sheet strengthened despite 24% higher capital expenditure of £213m, 10% of sales. Net gearing was 29.2% in 1987 and 28.6% in 1986, as higher cash flows allowed greater funding from the group's own resources.

At the 1987/88 interim stage, profits increased by 40% to £122.1m, on sales up 23% to £1.16bn. The overall growth in earnings per share was over 50% to 11p. The interim dividend was up only 8% to 2.35p.

SHARE PRICE HISTORY

Pilkington's share price has climbed out of the trough into which it was pitched by fears of a poor outlook. At the beginning of 1983 the shares had fallen to 50p. They recovered to around 75p by the end of the year and then fluctuated in a volatile manner around the 100p level until late 1985.

In 1986 the shares responded to recovery hopes and doubled in the year to over 200p. The BTR bid in 1987 lifted the price to 350p. The shares fell to 185p in the autumn 1987 share price crash before recovering to the 220p level in April 1988. In relative terms there was strong outperformance from late 1985 to the highs of mid-1987.

SENIOR MANAGEMENT

Antony Pilkington was appointed chairman in 1980, having been a director since 1973. Sir Alastair Pilkington is president. Derek Cook joined the board in 1984 and is responsible for flat and safety glass operations in Europe and the glass and mineral fibre businesses. He succeeded Denis Cail as deputy chairman on his retirement in August 1987. Peter Grunwell joined the board in 1985 and is responsible for finance and Pilkington's property companies.

Year	Turnover (£m)	Pre-tax (£m)	Earnings (p)	Dividends net (p)	Dividend cover (x)	Net assets (p)	Price (p)		PER (x)		Yield (%)	
							High	Low	High	Low	High	Low
1983	1,021.6	86	7.2	5.5	2.0	174	88	88	40.4	10.9	9.80	5.56
1984	1,214.4	110	8.0	3.8	2.1	178	114	114	21.4	10.9	6.99	4.27
1985	1,226.9	142	11.4	4.2	2.6	164	110	110	13.8	8.7	10.16	5.53
1986	1,321.1	123	7.4	4.5	1.6	119	221	221	31.6	11.8	9.84	4.68
1987	2,103.0	256	24.4	7.3	3.3	133	357	185	22.2	6.6	5.44	2.82

Geoffrey Iley joined the board in 1977 and is responsible for flat and safety glass outside Europe and North America. Sir Robin Nicholson became an executive director in 1986 and is responsible for the electro-optical, the ophthalmic division and for research and development (R&D). G Nightingale was appointed to the board during 1987, assuming responsibility for flat and safety glass, insulation and mineral fibres in Europe.

Non-executive directors include Lord Croham, an economist who is also a governor of the LSE, H Kopper, chairman of the Flachglas supervisory board and a banker with Deutsche Bank, Sir Peter Thompson and FR Hurn, who is also chief executive and managing director of Smiths Industries.

CAPITAL

After the 1984 rights issue, Pilkington was sparing in the use of its equity, probably because of its low share rating.

Pilkington made a major acquisition in April 1986 by exchanging its minority holding in LOF for 100% control of LOF's glass division, thereby adding a strong manufacturing presence in the US.

The remaining 50% holding in Argentina's leading safety glass-processor Santa Lucía Cristal was bought in July 1986, making it a wholly-owned subsidiary. The purchase of Swedlow in December 1986, a specialist in aircraft glazing, extended the group's existing Triplex Aircraft and Special Products operation.

During the 1987 financial year, there were eight other acquisitions and formations of small companies, two in the UK in micro-electronics and electro-optical materials, and six overseas in flat and safety glass. The group disposed of its shareholding in Tunnel Building Products and its investment in Rockware Group.

In August 1986 the company issued, in conjunction with £35m of 9.5% bonds, 10.64m warrants to subscribe for ordinary shares at 139p per share adjusted for the scrip issue. In July 1987 Pilkington's £1 ordinary shares were subdivided into two 50p shares followed immediately by a one for two scrip issue.

In August 1987 the company made a major share issue to acquire Vision Care, the Revlon subsidiary. Pilkington took advantage of its better share rating by paying for 70% of the £361m purchase price through a one for seven rights issue of 91.62m ordinary shares at 290p, to raise £255m. The balance of the consideration was in cash.

GROUP REVIEW

Flat and safety glass Pilkington is the world's leading manufacturer of flat and safety glass. The company divides its operations into three geographical areas – Europe, North America through Libbey-Owens-Ford, and the rest of the world. The division's 1987 sales were £1.681bn, with operating profit of £191.2m, 79.9% and 83.2% of the group's overall total respectively. Because of the LOF acquisition there is no 1986 comparison.

Flat glass is used in domestic, industrial, commercial and public buildings. In addition to clear glass, products include coated glasses, patterned glasses, wired and other resistant glasses, mirrors and tinted glasses. Safety glass products are supplied to automotive producers around the world. They are used in architectural glazing, in the home, as security glazing in shops and vehicles, and as windscreens and windows for all forms of transport. Technical developments are making the production of shaped and bent speciality glass much cheaper.

In Europe, Pilkington Glass, the Germany subsidiary Flachglas and the Scandinavian subsidiaries all contributed to a 26.4% increase in sales to £880.6m and a 324.7% increase in profits to £87.5m in 1987. Margins trebled to 10%.

Three large float glass lines were operating at a high level in the UK and the same was true of the West German operation. A new float line is being constructed in Finland by a related company. Better prices accounted for the improvement in margins, with a strong refurbishment market, a return to profit of the CIS Windows home improvement in the UK, and the substitution of higher value renovation products in the face of declining new residential housing demand in West Germany.

There has been improved demand for safety glass from multinational vehicle makers sited in Europe. More glass and higher value products, such as laminated solar glass and heated windscreens, are being specified.

Pilkington has a diverse Scandinavian operation, linked to the general automotive wholesale market, also manufacturing and distributing a wide range of non-auto safety glass throughout the region.

At the 1987/88 interim, European sales again moved up sharply, up 31.6% to £535.0m. Profits were 174.9% up at £59.1m., a remarkable performance reflecting impressive strength from West Germany and the UK.

In the US and Canada, Libbey-Owens-Ford made progress in 1987 improving low margins, largely as a result of lower energy costs, firm prices and good demand. Sales were £450.3m and profits £30.7m, with no comparable period in 1986. LOF's results are for four months as a related company and eleven months as a subsidiary.

LOF is rebalancing the customer base between bulk glass demand, which is slipping, and differentiated glass products. The market is generally flat, aside from an unexpected residential housing boom, which used up LOF's surplus capacity and allowed an improved market share with higher prices.

LOF has major contracts to supply windscreens for the Detroit motor industry. LOF's Ontario plant is developing its ElectriClear heated windshield for General Motors and is also a major retail supplier of replacement windscreens. LOF also operates a wholesale and retail glass supply business, concentrated on 58 centres in the western US.

LOF has a number of joint ventures in the automobile glass area with Nippon Sheet Glass Company of Japan (NSG). LOF's Mexican plant is being expanded in a joint venture with NSG to supply the bulk car windscreen and replacement market in North America. A Kentucky plant has also been built by the joint venture to be a principal supplier to Toyota in the US.

CHAIRMAN'S STATEMENT

'The most unwelcome event . . . was the hostile bid . . . by BTR. Our successful defence was firmly based on the conviction that BTR had nothing to offer . . . and on the knowledge that all the hard work which had been done over the past six years to reorganise, reshape and slim down the company was rapidly being translated into much improved returns to our shareholders. . . .

The acceleration of the Group's profitability, which we were anticipating and which was evident at the half-year stage, has continued to produce improving results throughout the world in the second half-year. The better geographical balance of the group following the full acquisition of the Libbey-Owens-Ford Co (LOF), gives confidence for the future. . . .

The Group's acquisition of the Vision Care businesses of Revlon Inc. is a major strategic move and one which achieves a world position in the vision care market. The acquisition is a major step towards the Group's objective of earning a third of the Group's profits outside the flat and safety glass markets. The Group's quality of earnings will also be enhanced by trading in this different market segment.' *Antony R Pilkington*

At the 1987/88 interim, US profits deteriorated sharply, affected by General Motors' loss of market share and the general softening of demand in the US new car market. Though sales were maintained, it may take time for the situation to improve.

Pilkington has major glass manufacturing operations in Australia, in a joint venture with ACI, South Africa and New Zealand. It supplies most of South America from Brazil and Argentina. Three new replacement float glass lines are planned in Argentina, Brazil and Australia. Contributions from these subsidiaries are often adversely affected by currency translation.

African production expanded despite difficult political and trading conditions. Pilkington's Chinese joint venture, capable of producing 350,000 tonnes of glass per annum, is now operational in Shanghai. An Indian float glass plant is planned to start production in 1989/90 as part of a joint venture.

Rest of the world sales in 1987 were 23.0% up at £350.9m and profits were 26.3% up at £73m. At the 1987/88 interim, sales were level at £175m and profits were 2.1% up at £38.1m.

Insulation glass and mineral fibres Fibres spun from molten glass and rock produce insulation materials for buildings and for plant. Other glass formulations produce fibres that can be used to reinforce Portland cement and rubber. Insulants for low temperature applications are produced from phenolic foams.

The benefits of restructuring brought this division back into profit in 1987. Sales were 8% up at £162.4m and operating profit was transformed from a loss of £0.8m to a profit of £23.8m.

Demand for energy saving insulation products and a more

buoyant building industry boosted demand. Glass fibre insulation is produced in Wales, Argentina and at St Helens, while rock fibre production has been transferred to Wales. Pilkington, through Kitsons, is the UK market leader in insulation contracting.

Pilkington Reinforcements activity was cut back in 1987 to concentrate on Cemfil fibres, which are used to reinforce Portland cement construction, and the supply of treated glass fibre cord.

At the 1987/88 interim, sales were down 24.3% to £63.3m but profits were 21.5% up to £7.9m.

Ophthalmic and special glass Pilkington make glass lens blanks, plastic and glass lenses for spectacles and sunglasses, contact lenses and spectacle frames. Trade with the leading Japanese camera makers was hit in 1987 by the strong yen, but the group is well placed in this market.

Acquisition of Vision Care, including the Barnes-Hind and Coburn ophthalmics operations, from Revlon, together with the existing Sola Syntex contact lens business, puts Pilkington in a dominant position in the industry. The Barnes-Hind soft contact lens and lens solution businesses complement Sola's hard lens operation, combining to make Pilkington world leader in the market. Coburn produces traditional spectacles and ophthalmic equipment. Sola is based in Australia.

1987 sales were up 52.3% and profits were 19.0% up at £10.0m. At the 1987/88 interim, sales were 26.6% up at £73.6m and profits were 80% up at £5.4m.

Electro-optical The three electro-optical business areas are defence, communications and medical. A fourth area of advanced materials has recently been launched.

Both the Barr & Stroud periscope and laser sights business and Pilkington PE, through overseas night vision orders, increased defence profits in 1987. UK procurement is now generally more competitive. Pilkington Electro-Optics opened in California to bid for US defence contracts.

Disposable fibre delivery systems are being developed for surgical lasers. Pilkington joined with BOC in the Living Technology joint venture to combine its technical and production expertise with BOC Healthcare's US marketing operations.

Share price and relative to FT-A All-Share

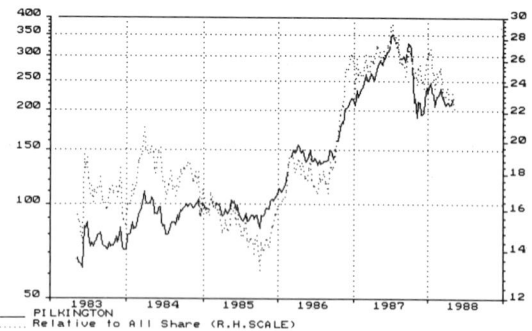

```
PILKINGTON
Relative to All Share (R.H.SCALE)
```

Defence sales were 20.4% up at £103.8m and profits were up 24.7% up at £9.6m. The new ventures made losses on low turnover. At the 1987/88 interim sales and profits were flat.

Aircraft and special products The division makes windshields, roof canopies and cockpit covers for a wide range of aircraft and other applications. The company places increasing importance on the area.

In December 1986 Pilkington acquired the US company Swedlow, makers of acrylic products for aircraft. Its contracts to supply the F111, F14, F15 and F18 aircraft complement the group's existing Triplex operation, which supplies the Westland Augusta EH101 helicopter, the British Aerospace ATP, the Airbus A320, the Jaguar fighter aircraft and much of the Boeing fleet of commercial airliners.

In 1987 sales, affected by the Swedlow acquisition, were 120% up at £21.4m. Profits increased by 7.1% to £1.5m. At the 1987/88 interim, sales were 392% up at £24.6m. Profits were 600% up at £2.1m.

Research and development Of the £65m – 25% of pre-tax profits – spent on R&D in 1987, one-third was externally funded. R&D expenditure increased to £34m in the first half of 1988.

Pilkington is acknowledged to be the world's leading glass technologist. A major area of expansion is in glass electronics. A major part of R&D work is concerned with adding value to existing products.

GEOGRAPHICAL REVIEW

In 1987, by market of sales, the UK contributed 23% (30%) of group sales with £481.3m (£392.9m), Europe (EEC) 24% (30%) with £506.8m (£399.1m), Europe (non-EEC) 7% (9%) with £149.2m (£119.1m), North America 27% (6%) with £560.3m (£79.8m), Australasia 7% (9.7%) with £152.4m (£127.8m), Africa 6% (9%) with £121.9m (£113.9m), South America 4% (4%) with £92m (£55.5m) and others 2% (2%) with £39.5m (£33m).

The company does not provide a full geographical breakdown of profit. UK companies contributed 27.7% (2.1%) of group trading profit in 1987, overseas companies 72.3% (97.9%). Within the flat and safety glass division, the largest, Europe contributed 45.7% (26.2%) of the division's trading profit in 1987, North America 16% (nil) and the rest of the world 38.2% (73.8%).

CORPORATE CALENDAR

Year end	31 March
Preliminary results	June
Report and accounts	July
AGM	July
Final dividend paid	August
Interim results	December
Interim dividend paid	February

DIRECTORS' HOLDINGS

	Fully-paid ordinary shares	Senior exec. share options	Savings-related options
AR Pilkington	1,469,757	465,741	—
GN Iley	16,488	268,575	7,917
Lord Croham	1,212	—	—
H Kooper	1,500	—	—
DE Cook	3,750	268,575	2,652
FR Hurn	2,007	—	—
Sir Peter Thompson	3,129	—	—
PH Grunwell	14,202	263,196	10,518
Sir Robin Nicholson	—	248,046	—
G Nightingale	522	127,854	2,199

Total directors' remuneration for 1987 amounted to £1.71m, of which the chairman, who was also the highest-paid director, received £177,137.

PRINCIPAL SUBSIDIARIES AND RELATED COMPANIES

UK
Andrewartha Ltd, Ashdowns Ltd, Barnes-Mind Ltd, Barr & Stroud Ltd, CIS Windows Ltd, Chance Brothers Ltd, Chance Pilkington Ltd, Elders Walker Millican (Holdings) Ltd, Kitsons Insulation Contractors Ltd, Kitsons Insulation Products Ltd, Mackenzie Glass (Exeter) Ltd, Micro Milling Limited, Pilkington Glass Ltd, Pilkington Industrial Estates Ltd, Pilkington Insulation Ltd, Pilkington Ophthalmic Products Ltd, Pilkington PE Ltd, Pilkington Properties Ltd, Pilkington Quarries Ltd, Pilkington Reinforcements Ltd, Rainford Venture Capital Ltd (67%), Triplex Holdings Ltd, Triplex Safety Glass Co Ltd

Overseas
Barnes Hind Inc – US, Barnes Hind SARL – France, Bauglas Grosshandel GmbH – Austria, Bauglasindustrie GmbH – West Germany, Cebrace – Companhia Brasileira de Cristal (42%) – Brazil, Cementos y Fibras SA – Spain, Cobum Optical Industries Inc – US, Concordia Vidros SA – Brazil, Cudo-Isolierglas GmbH – West Germany, Dahlbusch Verwaltungs AG (82%) – West Germany, EOM AG – Austria, Ernst Knock Glas & Spiegel Manufaktur KG (38%) – West Germany, FGP Ltd (40%) – India, FRG Thirty-one Corporation – US, FRG Twenty-seven Corporation – US, Flabeg GmbH – West Germany, Flachglas AG (77%) – West Germany, Flachglas International Beteiligungs BmgH – West Germany, Flachglas Vertriebs KG Meier & Sohn (38%) – West Germany, Floatex Glas AB – Sweden, Glas-Haller GmbH – West Germany, Glass South Africa (Pty) Ltd – South Africa, Glaszentrum Berlin Rafflenbeul & Loewe GmbH – West Germany, Glaszentrum Denzel GmbH – West Germany, Glaszentrum Eugen Frederich GmbH – West Germany, Glaszentrum GF Schweikert GmbH & Co KG – West Germany, Glaszentrum Ruhr Grosshandel GmbH – West Germany, Glaszentrum Stoermer GmbH – West Germany, Glaszentrum Weigand Otto Weigand & Sohn GmbH (38%) – West Germany, HW Ibsen GmbH (38%) – West Germany, Lamino OY – Finland, Libbey-Owens-Ford Co – US, New Zealand Window Glass Ltd (50%) – New Zealand, Nordlamex Safety Glass OY – Finland, Optics America Corporation – US, OyLahden Lasitehdas (44%) – Finland, PG Glass Holdings (Pty) Ltd – South Africa, PGN Ltd (40%) – Nigeria, Pilkington ACI Ltd – Australia, Pilkington ACI Operations Pty Ltd – Australia, Pilkington Brothers (New Zealand) Ltd – New Zealand, Pilkington Brothers South Africa Ltd – South Africa, Pilkington Flat Glass (Pty) Ltd – South Africa, Pilkington Floatglas AB – Sweden, Pilkington Glass (Jamaica) Ltd – Jamaica, Pilkington Glass (Zimbabwe) Pvt Ltd – Zimbabwe, Pilkington Holdings Inc – US, Pilkington International Holdings BV – Netherlands, Pilkington Sakerhetsglas AB – Sweden, Pilkington Shatterprufe Safety Glass (Pty) Ltd – South Africa, Providro Limitada – Brazil, Reflo AG – Switzerland, SOLA Corporation Ltd and wholly owned subsidiaries in Australia, Brazil, France, West Germany, Netherlands, Hong Kong, Italy, Japan, Malaysia, Singapore, Taiwan and Republic of Ireland, SOLA (US) Inc – US, Salanc Holdings (Pty) Ltd – South Africa, Santa Lucía Cristais Blindex Limitada – Brazil, Santa Lucía Cristal SACIF – Argentina, Shanghai Yaohna Pilkington Glass Co Ltd (12.5%) – China, Softint Inc – US, Swedlow Inc – US, Taiwan Glass Industry Corporation (7%) – Taiwan, Vidriería Argentina SA – Argentina, Vitro Plan SA (35%) – Mexico

BRAND NAMES

Barnes-Hind, CIS, Coburn, ElectriClear, Kappafloat, Libbey-Owens-Ford, Micropane, Pilkington, Shatterprufe, Sola

CONTACTS AND FURTHER INFORMATION

Group public relations, Pilkington plc, Prescot Road, St Helens WA10 3TT. Tel: 0744 692554.

THE PLESSEY COMPANY plc

GENERAL INFORMATION

Head office Vicarage Lane, Ilford, Essex IG1 4AQ. Tel: 01-478 3040
Directors Sir John Clark (chairman and chief executive), Lord Pennock (deputy chairman), WJ Sinsheimer (deputy chief executive), JC Bass, V Butler, D Dey, W Gosling, KB Huntbatch, AW Jones, AD Mayes, SR Walls. *Non-exec* Lord Brookes, Sir Alistair Frame, Sir Francis Sandilands, DAGR Simon, CR Thompson
Advisers First Boston Corporation, Lazard Brothers & Co Ltd
Auditors Deloitte Haskins & Sells
Registrars PAH Bull, The Plessey Company plc, Vicarage Lane, Ilford, Essex IG1 4AQ. Tel: 01-478 3040
Brokers Phillips & Drew Ltd, Warburg Securities
Solicitors Oppenheimers, Linklaters & Paines

GENERAL FINANCIAL INFORMATION

Market capitalisation £1.065bn at 1 January 1988
Capital structure
Issued ordinary shares (25p)   739.7m
Issued preference shares   None
Warrants   None
Convertibles   None
Traded options   Yes
ADRs   10 ordinary shares equal one ADR
Shareholders over 5%   Guardian Royal Exchange 11.583%

FT CATEGORY

FT: Electricals
FT-A: Electronics

MAJOR ACTIVITIES

Through the application of long-term strategies, Plessey manufactures technology-related products in areas such as telecommunications and defence. The group is involved in the design, development and manufacture of civil telecommunications, military communications, command and control networks, radar, sonar, electronic components, direct and satellite radio communications and traffic controls.

Half of the group's operating profit comes from telecommunications via a 50% shareholding in GEC Plessey Telecommunications Holdings, a further one-quarter from electronic systems and the balance from aerospace and electronic components. Major customers include the Ministry of Defence (MoD) and British Telecom (BT), which together are responsible for over half of total sales.

Sensitive factors for the company are UK defence policy and public sector expenditure, and BT's capital investment.

Competition varies with each activity. The telecommunications joint venture competes against LM Ericsson within the UK and with 11 other major telecommunications businesses worldwide, including AT&T, Siemens, Northern Telecom, NEC, Alcatel and Philips. Plessey has also entered into a joint venture with Racal to develop infrastructure and terminals for a new pan-European digital cellular system being introduced in the 1990s.

AT&T, Siemens, Northern Telecom, NEC Alcatel, Philips, Fujitsu and Italtel are competitors in the international field. Electronic systems competitors include Westinghouse, Siemens, Ferranti, GEC-Marconi and Racal. Competitors within the engineering and components activity include NEC, Fujitsu, Honeywell, Motorola and Gould.

FINANCIAL HISTORY

Turnover fell in 1987 by £31m to £1.430bn, a 2% decline against 1986, and only 28% up over five years. 1987 pre-tax profits were 8.2% ahead on 1986 at £184.2m, 25% up over five years. Although turnover was reduced, margins improved. Research and development spending rose 17% and £80m was spent on capital investment, but profits still increased.

Plessey's provision of quarterly figures highlighted the final three months of 1987. Turnover was down 10.9% at £404.8m and profits were down 11% at £51.7m. The fall was blamed on an exceptionally high delivery pattern in the fourth quarter of the previous year.

In 1987 telecommunications contributed half of the total operating profits, with electronic systems and equipment contributing 27.3%. Earnings per share grew 20% from 13.49p to 16.22p, mainly derived from a substantial increase in investment income of £15.8m against £5.9m. This was made possible by cash balances of £269m, £74m higher than in 1986, and a decrease in the effective rate of tax. A final dividend of 3.407p was made, bringing the total to 5.79p for the year, up 15%.

The balance sheet shows net cash to ordinary shareholders' funds at 45%, pre-tax margins of 11.6%, an asset turnover of 2.76 times, and return on capital employed of 32.5%.

For the 39 weeks to 1 January 1988, operating profit declined by 27.4% to £87.1m on turnover down by 13.7% to £884.2m. Pre-tax profits were down 20.5% at £105.3m. The company blamed the decline in profits on a bunching of telecommunications and defence orders. Pre-tax profits had declined for four successive quarters. However, the order book was 15% up on April 1987, standing at £1.551bn. The company expected a strong final quarter.

SHARE PRICE HISTORY

In 1987 the underperformance of Plessey's share price continued. This is a direct contrast to a period in the early 1980s when the share price was favoured by the market – due to improvements at board level, the implementation of more effective management and financial controls, as well as success in telecommunications (a glamour activity at the time).

In 1984, however, it became apparent that System X, the digital exchange, was unlikely to become an export success. Stromberg-Carlson (a manufacturer of public exchanges),

FIVE YEAR FINANCIAL INFORMATION

Year	Turnover (£m)	Pre-tax (£m)	Earnings (p)	Dividends net (p)	Dividend cover (x)	Net assets (p)	Price (p) High	Price (p) Low	PER (x) High	PER (x) Low	Yield (%) High	Yield (%) Low
1983	1,119.7	146.4	11.3	3.3	3.3	55.7	255	176	27.7	18.5	2.51	1.85
1984	1,252.4	176.1	15.3	3.8	3.5	68.1	249	188	21.9	15.5	2.89	1.98
1985	1,415.7	163.6	12.7	4.4	2.8	65.6	212	116	16.3	10.0	5.39	2.56
1986	1,461.1	170.2	13.5	5.0	2.7	71.7	246	162	19.9	10.5	4.38	2.70
1987	1,429.7	184.2	16.2	5.8	2.8	80.7	256	126	15.8	8.6	6.29	2.94

C H A I R M A N ' S   S T A T E M E N T

'We continue to maintain a high level of confidence in the Company's ability to achieve growth in the medium and longer term. This confidence has been strengthened by the events of the last quarter including the growing order book, opportunities presented by the joint venture with GEC in telecommunications, the acquisition of Ferranti's worldwide semiconductor business and Sippican in the US.

In addition, despite short term trading pressures, the Company has maintained its high level of investment in R&D which showed an increase of over 7% in the period. This commitment to maintaining the Company's technological excellence in our view is critical to future growth in sales and profits.' *Sir John Clark*

acquired in 1982, also proved difficult. These two factors had an adverse effect upon the share price at this time. Heavy losses in 1984/85 at Stromberg-Carlson were accompanied – as a result of the fall in oil prices – by a decline in military sales to the Middle East, weakening Plessey's share price relative to the market between 1982 and 1986.

The GEC bid helped the shares in 1986 and early 1987. The shares then went back into relative decline after the 1987 results and further downward revision of 1988 profit estimates. Early in 1988 bid rumours reappeared.

SENIOR MANAGEMENT

Britain's longest serving chief executive, Sir John Clark, with the reputation of being a strong leader, has been Plessey's chairman since 1970. Sir James Blyth resigned as managing director in October 1987.

GEC's abortive bid provided a catalyst for the management team to be strengthened, specifically by the promotion of Sir James Blyth to chief executive, signalling a change in corporate image with emphasis being placed upon a tougher and leaner profile.

There have been several appointments and resignations in 1987. Management is unlikely to be fully settled until the telecommunications deal with GEC is fully completed.

CAPITAL

The Guardian Royal Exchange and its subsidiary companies hold a total of 85,478,639 ordinary shares at August 1987, 10m less than at the year end. No other holding of 5% or more has been notified.

GROUP REVIEW

Plessey is a company which prides itself in technological achievement. Its research and technology programmes are strongly geared to meeting specific customer needs internationally.

Plessey's growth is usually organic, although more recently it has been achieved through collaborative agreements, with companies such as Westinghouse, GEC and Racal. Future attention is likely to be focused upon its role in international markets, accompanied by an expansion of its geographical base.

Telecommunications Plessey's largest business contributed £83.7m to operating profit in 1987 against £70.7m in 1986, 50.4% of the group total. It also provided the largest increase in operating profit of 18.4%.

The division is involved in the design, development and manufacture of public and private digital telecommunications exchanges, payphones, traffic controls and data communications. The public digital exchanges are System X and Stromberg's DCO system.

In October 1987 Plessey and GEC announced plans to merge their telecommunications activities, which was followed in March 1988 by the formation of GEC Telecommunications Holdings (GPT), in which Plessey holds 50% and which commenced trading on 1 April 1988.

GPT combines all of the UK telecommunications interests of GEC and Plessey, and Plessey's US subsidiary, Stromberg-Carlson. GPT now ranks ninth in world terms in the telecommunications industry overall, and eighth in world terms in main exchange equipment. In the UK, GPT is the dominant supplier of telecommunications equipment with an overall 50% share of the market, including over 80% of main exchanges, 50% of the PABX market and 60% of transmission.

The major product areas of GPT include digital switching, optical transmission equipment, multiplexes, private digital exchanges, telephone instruments, payphones, packet switches, microwave communications and telex switches.

With the UK market having declined in transmission systems and PABXs, and with System X facing competition from Ericsson's AXE10 switch for BT business, increased emphasis will have to be given to exporting.

Stromberg-Carlson made a £7m turnaround in 1987 and continued to strengthen its position in North America. Plessey hope that it will become a major supplier of small DCO exchanges to the Bell regional telephone companies following its success with a $100m order from Bell South in 1987.

The provision of traffic control systems and communications systems also continues to expand, accompanied by packet switching systems which are used extensively by BT, banks, the Inland Revenue, the Metropolitan Police and other commercial data networks.

For the nine months to 1 January 1988, sales were down 17% to £409.9m, with operating profit down 36.9% at £36.6m. The company said this was due to bunching and delays in orders.

Electronic systems Plessey's second largest activity contributed 27.4% to total operating profits in 1987. Operating profit was up 12.9% to £45.5m.

Major products and systems include facilities for gathering intelligence, effecting communications and implementing command and control in the support of military services.

Share price and relative to FT-A All-Share

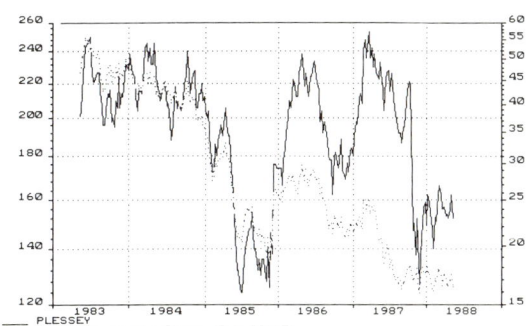

These products were all developed in the division's own research and development programmes, and represent about 40% of activity within the division.

Product specialism is battlefield communications systems, including Ptarmigan. Radar and sonar are the group's other main businesses. The company participates in a joint venture with Westinghouse to provide the radar for the RAF's AWACS early warning radar system. Offset work for other orders is likely to be received.

Recently Plessey has announced that it is to supply tactical radios to the Australian Army worth £160m. The company extended its interests through the purchase of Sippican in November 1987, which it is hoped will lead to more orders for the group as a whole from the Pentagon.

For the nine months to 1 January 1988, sales were 8.9% down at £313.7m, with profits 32% down at £22.6m. The company blamed the incidence of profit milestones on long term defence contracts.

Engineering and components This division is two businesses – aerospace and engineering, and microelectronics.

The operating profits of the aerospace and engineering business were almost halved in 1987 to £13m on turnover down 7.3% to £111.9m, due to lower civil aircraft spares sales and the costs of transferring the US dynamics side to new premises. In the nine months to 1 January 1988, turnover was down 6.9% to £78.2m, but profits were up 9.4% to £11.6m.

The microelectronics division concentrates on chip-based technology. The company believes the growth area is in ASIC semiconductors, which are custom-made and application-specific. Plessey has invested £50m in the world's most advanced six-inch CMOS wafer plant in Roborough, near Plymouth. Plessey is the fastest growing semiconductor manufacturer in Europe. The start-up costs involved in this new plant were the main reason for the fall in profits from £14.8m to £13.4m. In November 1987, Plessey bought Ferranti's semiconductor interests.

For the nine months to 1 January 1988, profits were 47% down at £3.5m on turnover 2.1% down at £95.7m. Slow sales in semiconductors and continuing start-up costs at Roborough held back profits severely.

GEOGRAPHICAL REVIEW

The international division, established in 1985, has steadily extended its sphere of influence in world markets, with new business penetration in many territories outside the UK, including Japan, China, Mexico and Sweden. The division liaises closely with the company's three core businesses, enhancing their international business prospects.

The UK is the group's main market with sales of £1.017bn, 71% of total turnover. North America has sales of £175m, representing 12.2%. Europe contributed £89.1m (6.2%), Africa £56.2m (3.9%), Australasia £41.2m (2.9%), Asia £42.1m (2.9%) and others £8.2m (0.6%).

CORPORATE CALENDAR

Year end	3 April
Preliminary results	May
Report and accounts	June
AGM	July
Final dividend paid	August
Interim results	February
Interim dividend paid	March

DIRECTORS' HOLDINGS

	Fully-paid ordinary shares	Options
Sir John Clark	1,008,950	—
Lord Pennock	3,000	
WJ Sinsheimer	59,958	23,100
JC Bass	37,939	88,900
Lord Brookes	18,000	
V Butler	4,100	64,000
Sir Alastair Frame	3,000	
W Gosling	2,000	19,100
AW Jones	2,000	46,300
AD Mayes	5,000	41,800
Sir Francis Sandilands	3,000	
DAGR Simon	2,000	—

Total directors' remuneration in 1987 was £2.02m, of which the chairman received £224,801, and the highest-paid director £237,347.

PRINCIPAL SUBSIDIARIES AND RELATED COMPANIES

Elettronica SpA – Italy (35%), Plessey Inc – US, Plessey (NZ) Ltd, Plessey Pacific Pty Ltd – Australia, Plessey South Africa Limited (74%), Plessey SpA – Italy, Plessey-UK Limited, Stromberg-Carlson Corporation – US, Telephone Manufacturers of South Africa (Pty) Ltd (50%)

BRAND NAMES

DCO Switch, Faxlok, IDX, ISDN, ISDT, ISDX, Ptarmigan, Raven, System X, System 4000, Voicelok

CONTACTS AND FURTHER INFORMATION

Norman Manners, The Plessey Company plc, Millbank Tower, 21–24 Millbank, London SW1P 4QP. Tel: 01-834 3855.

PRUDENTIAL CORPORATION plc

GENERAL INFORMATION

Head office	142 Holborn Bars, London EC1N 2NH. Tel: 01-405 9222
President	Sir Ronald Owen FIA
Directors	FB Corby FIA (group chief executive), RE Artus FSIA, DE Fellows FIA FPMI, JA Freeman FCA FCMA, MJ Lawrence FCA, B Medhurst FIA, MG Newmarch. *Non-exec* The Rt Hon Lord Hunt of Tanworth GCB (chairman), MD Abrahams, Mrs ME Baker, Sir John Butterfield OBE FRCP, The Rt Hon Lord Carr of Hadley PC, DS Craigen, The Hon Sir Victor Garland KBE, Sir Trevor Holdsworth, Sir Alex Jarratt CB (deputy chairman), PE Moody CBE FIA (deputy chairman), JAS Neave CBE JP DL, The Rt Hon JE Ramsden, The Rt Hon Lord Richardson of Duntisbourne KG MBE TD PC DL, Sir Ronald Dearing CB, FG Wood FIA ACII
Advisers	No specified adviser
Auditors	Deloitte Haskins & Sells
Registrars	Prudential Corporation plc, 142 Holborn Bars, London EC1N 2NH. Tel: 01-405 9222
Brokers	Rowe & Pitman Ltd
Solicitors	DF Roper, group legal adviser

GENERAL FINANCIAL INFORMATION

Market capitalisation	£3.005bn at 1 January 1988
Capital structure	
Issued ordinary shares (25p)	366m
Issued preference shares	None
Warrants	None
Convertibles	None
Traded options	Yes
ADRs	One ADR per ordinary share
Shareholders over 5%	None

FT CATEGORY

FT: Insurances
FT-A: Insurance (life)

MAJOR ACTIVITIES

On the basis of market capitalisation the Prudential is the largest insurance company in the UK. It provides a wide range of financial services including the sale of pensions, insurance, house purchase and investment products. The company also has sizeable interests in the US and Canada.

The Prudential has been a home service life office since 1854. Employed agents visit homes throughout the UK selling both life and non-life personal insurances. The group has for many years been diversifying and expanding. The bulk of the group's business in the UK is derived from the 11,000-strong sales force who write all types of personal insurance. This includes protection policies providing death and sickness cover, savings and mortgage-related policies and policies which allow saving for retirement.

Non-life policies sold include domestic contents and private motor insurances. In 1985 the group began selling unit trusts directly to the public. The Prudential has acquired and developed a chain of over 700 estate agents throughout England and Wales. These form part of the property services division which provides the public with a complete range of house purchase services.

In the UK, the Prudential is a market leader in the provision of pensions, acting both for individuals who save for their own retirement and for employers who have set up group schemes for their employees. The range of insurances accepted in the UK is completed by a service provided to cover the insurance needs of corporations. In addition the Prudential's reinsurance subsidiary, the Mercantile and General Reinsurance Company, provides cover to insurance companies throughout the world, protecting them against the risk of adverse developments on their own portfolios of accepted insurances.

The international division of the Prudential includes Canada, where the group writes personal insurances through its own agents and also obtains business via independent agents. In Europe the group has a subsidiary in Belgium, which transacts primarily general insurance business, and a subsidiary in the Netherlands. Other territories covered by the group include Australia, New Zealand, Italy (jointly with Benetton), the Far East and Africa.

In 1986 the Prudential acquired a medium-sized US life insurer, Jackson National Life Insurance Company. Jackson National was founded in 1961 by Tony Pasant who has remained chairman and chief executive since the acquisition. Prudential Insurance Company of the US is not connected with the Prudential Corporation in the UK. The Prudential has not hitherto transacted business in the US other than through its M&G Reinsurance subsidiary. In 1985 the Prudential acquired Insurance Corporation of Ireland, now renamed the Prudential Life of Ireland Ltd.

The remaining overseas insurance business consists of insurances accepted from foreign insurers as well as the insurances of ships and aircraft. The Group's new corporate identity was launched in September 1986, with the Prudence logo designed to project the organisation's new dynamism.

FINANCIAL HISTORY

Life and pensions new business premiums have increased by about 68% from 1981 to 1987. Single premium investment and unit trust business has been particularly buoyant during this period, as has the individual pensions business. Pre-tax profits have increased from £85.4m in 1982 to £206.0m in 1987. The bulk of this rise of 141% stems from organic growth in the life profits which have been boosted by buoyant stockmarket conditions. The 1987 result was buoyed by a return to reasonable profitability in non-life business following a small loss in 1986 and much bigger losses in 1984 and 1985.

Earnings per share have increased from 17.7p in 1982 to 41.7p in 1987, an average compound growth rate of just under 19% per annum. Dividends have also increased at a rapid rate, from 14.3p in 1982 to 34.0p in 1987, an average rate of increase of 19% per annum. The growth in dividend in 1987 amounted to 17%. At the end of 1987, total shareholders' funds amounted to £506m or 139p per share.

The Prudential announced in March 1988 that its results for 1987 and future years would be shown including a five year average of realised and unrealised capital gains. Pre-tax profits in 1987 allowing for this change amounted to £242.4m.

Share price and relative to FT-A All-Share

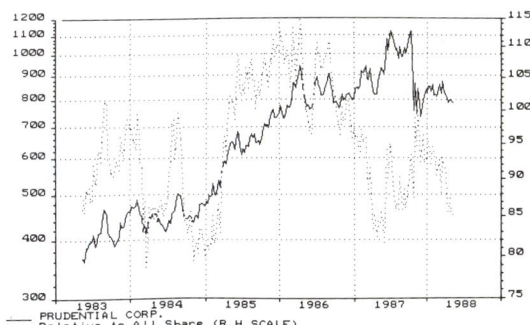

PRUDENTIAL CORP.
Relative to All Share (R.H.SCALE)

FIVE YEAR FINANCIAL INFORMATION

Year	Turnover (£m)	Pre-tax (£m)	Earnings (p)	Dividends net (p)	Dividend cover (x)	Net assets (p)	Price (p) High	Low	PER (x) High	Low	Yield (%) High	Low
1983	2,233	101.1	22.0	18.1	1.22	112	973	308	44.2	14.0	8.40	2.66
1984	2,600	78.0	14.40	21.4	0.67	124	511	412	35.5	28.6	7.42	5.98
1985	2,515	110.1	24.50	24.8	0.99	184	769	473	31.4	19.3	7.42	4.56
1986	3,226	178.1	34.50	29.0	1.19	160	942	721	27.3	20.9	5.56	4.26
1987	3,882	206.0	41.70	34.0	1.23	139	1,147	710	27.5	17.0	6.44	3.99

SHARE PRICE HISTORY

During the first few months of 1985 the Prudential's share price increased rapidly. This was due to expectations of a boom in pensions business, raised as a result of the government's consultative paper on pensions seeking to encourage private non-state provision for retirement. The drift in the share price during the latter part of 1986 was probably caused by a feeling that the Prudential was paying too much for its venture into the UK estate agency business and for Jackson National.

More recently there have been periods of boredom as well as periods during which the good long-term prospects for the group came to the fore. The group's 1987 high was 1147p. The share price tumbled dramatically during the autumn with the general fall in world stock markets. In the first quarter of 1988 the shares traded around the 850p level.

SENIOR MANAGEMENT

The non-executive chairman of the group is the Rt Hon Lord Hunt of Tanworth GCB, former Secretary to the Cabinet. Brian Corby, a leading figure within the actuarial profession, is chief executive. The chief actuary of Prudential Assurance is Derek Fellows, who also manages the UK Group Pensions Division.

Prudential Portfolio Managers, controlling the bulk of the group's investments, is chaired by Ron Artus, Chief Investment Manager at the Prudential, and is run by Mick Newmarch, chief executive and deputy chairman of the subsidiary. Ron Artus is also chairman of Prudential Property Services. The managing director for the UK individual division is Tony Freeman.

Brian Medhurst is managing director of the International Division. Michael Lawrence joined the board on 1 January 1988 as the finance director.

CAPITAL

The Prudential issued 60.258m shares in June 1986 in a rights issue which allowed shareholders to subscribe for one new share for each five already held at a cost of 600p. The rights issue raised £360m and was used in part to finance the acquisition of Jackson National Life and in part to pay for the acquisition of the estate agency branches. 823,000 shares were issued additionally in 1986 as part consideration for some of the estate agency chains.

In 1987 the group issued approximately 3.18m new ordinary shares, mostly in adding to the Prudential Property Services' chains of estate agencies. In May 1988, the shares were split in a five for one scrip issue.

At the end of 1987 the Prudential Corporation had bank loans, overdrafts and other borrowings amounting to about £350m. In 1987 it issued through Prudential Finance BV:

DM300m of 6% bonds due 1997; £150m of 9⅜% bonds due 2007; and SFr200m of 4.75% bonds due 1998. It also raised a further £250m in long term loans. In March 1988 the chairman said there was no present intention of making another rights issue.

GROUP REVIEW

UK individual division This division constitutes the core of the Prudential, with trading profits of £106.5m in 1987. Individual life policies and pensions as well as general insurances are obtained primarily from the Prudential's 9,000 agents, who are supported by 2,500 technical and managerial and other sales staff. Some general insurance business with a premium income in 1987 of £170m is obtained via insurance brokers. Life new business was buoyant, reflecting the boom in the house mortgage market and the extension of the Prudential Home Loans service to the whole of the UK.

Unit trust sales were also buoyant, because of excellent investment performance and the increase in the number of agents trained to sell them. Total single premium investments increased by 89% in 1987 to £474m. These developments, together with the new personal pensions legislation introduced in 1986, will result in sustained growth in life profits for the next few years. Sales of industrial branch and other long-term business remained static.

The AIDS virus may result in a large increase in the number of deaths in the UK in coming decades. Taking a reasonably pessimistic view, the Prudential has more than sufficient free reserves to meet the cost of the extra death claims likely to arise under its insurance policies.

General insurance business improved despite severe weather losses arising both in early 1987 and in the October hurricane. Premium rate increases effected during 1986 and 1987 and the partial withdrawal from the broker market should help to curtail losses on the motor account. The total contribution from general insurance business was £6.9m in 1987.

Prudential Property Services Prudential started its estate agency operation in 1985 and by the end of 1987 had built up a network of 622 residential outlets and 42 commercial and professional outlets at a cost of £174m. The target is to acquire or develop a national chain of 1,000 branches, with core firms located in twelve regions, and secondary firms developed to increase coverage within each region. At a cost of perhaps £200m the Prudential will own one of only about six truly national chains and have 6% of the UK market.

The network has not begun to contribute substantially to group profits but should do so in the future. Of major benefit to the Prudential in the long term is the possibility of selling Prudential insurance policies throughout the chain. In 1987 pre-tax profits amounted to £4.5m although profits of perhaps £20m are likely in 1988.

UK group pensions This division showed strong growth in 1986 and 1987, reflecting growth in the numbers of small

CHAIRMAN'S STATEMENT

'As well as being a time of very considerable change for companies in the financial services sector of the economy, the present is also one of considerable opportunity. The life insurance market in the United States is large, innovative and profitable and an acquisition there would also provide the opening for us to introduce other financial services. We expect Jackson National Life to make a significant contribution to our profits in the years ahead.... In the United Kingdom, we expect our estate agency business to provide a satisfactory return on investment from its main-stream operations, and in due course there will be an additional benefit from the sale of other Prudential products to new customers. This new and highly visible point of contact with the public will thus help to increase the future profitability of other parts of the Corporation.' *Lord Hunt*

pension schemes in the UK and the increasing level and numbers of transfer values payable when employees in a company scheme change jobs or become self-employed. Pre-tax profits amounted to £9.9m in 1987 and look set to increase in the coming years as the Government's legislation designed to encourage private sector pensions provision takes effect. They were held back in 1987 by various factors including the effects of the October stock market fall.

The Mercantile and General Reinsurance Company Trading profits at the M&G in 1987 amounted to £42.9m (£38.4m) and income on shareholders' funds to a further £27.1m (£28.4m). Life reassurance profits were held back – £21.9m compared with £24.5m in 1986 – because the company intends to have established reserves of about £110m by the end of 1988 to allow fully for a reasonably pessimistic view of AIDS claims costs. The non-life reassurance results were broadly satisfactory and significantly better than in 1986.

Investment management, unit trusts and PEPs A major part of the activities at the Prudential is concerned with the investment of policyholders' and other funds. At the end of 1987, the Prudential controlled investments of £29.8bn. The volume of funds under management continues to grow rapidly. 1987 pre-tax profits were £12.5m against £6.0m in 1986.

International division Rationalisation in a number of overseas territories took place during 1986. This included the withdrawal from the South African life market, the merger of the New Zealand interests with those of General Accident, and the merger of the Zimbabwean life branch with that of the Pearl Assurance.

In November Jackson National Life Insurance Company was acquired for about £400m. Jackson National is based in Michigan and has 600 staff helping to service 50,000 independent agents who place business with the company.

The rationalisation process bore fruit during 1987 with trading profits up from £23.2m to £42.6m, inclusive of a £14.6m (£0.6m) contribution from Jackson National.

GEOGRAPHICAL REVIEW

Life assurance business constitutes the major part of the group's total business. Total life pre-tax profits of £153.9m in 1987 were distributed as follows – UK 66.6%, USA 9.5%, Canada 1.9%, Australia and New Zealand 4.0%, M&G 14.2%, other countries 3.8%.

The territorial distribution of the group's non-life premium income in 1987, excluding the M&G, was UK 62%, Canada 16%, EEC 11%, marine and aviation worldwide 6%, other 19%. A distribution by profits is not given for non-life business because profits vary greatly from year to year for each territory.

CORPORATE CALENDAR

Year end	31 December
Preliminary results	March
Report and accounts	May
AGM	May
Final dividend paid	May
Interim results	September
Interim dividend paid	November

DIRECTORS' HOLDINGS

	Fully-paid ordinary shares	Options
Lord Hunt of Tanworth	2,650	—
MD Abrahams	2,400	—
RE Artus	2,000	62,956
Sir John Butterfield	2,400	—
Lord Carr of Hadley	2,400	—
FB Corby	1,400	99,229
DS Craigen	2,400	—
DE Fellows	2,400	36,477
JA Freeman	1,250	55,411
Sir Victor Garland	500	—
Sir Trevor Holdsworth	500	—
Sir Alex Jarratt	2,400	—
B Medhurst	2,400	54,511
PE Moody	2,400	—
JAS Neave	280,939	—
MG Newmarch	600	72,449
JE Ramsden	2,880	—
Lord Richardson of Duntisbourne	2,400	—
FG Wood	2,814	1,788

Total directors' remuneration in 1987 was £1,129,280, of which the chairman received £55,863 and the highest-paid director £197,279.

PRINCIPAL SUBSIDIARIES AND RELATED COMPANIES

Compagnie d'Assurance de l'Escaut SA – Belgium, Jackson National Life Insurance Company – US, The Mercantile and General Insurance Company plc, Prudential Corporation Canada – Canada, The Prudential Assurance Company Limited, Prudential Life of Ireland Limited (95%), Prudential Pensions Limited, Prudential Portfolio Managers Limited, Prudential Holborn Limited

BRAND NAMES

Holborn, Prudence, The Prudential, Prudential Property Services, Prudential Portfolio Managers

CONTACTS AND FURTHER INFORMATION

David Vevers, Group Public Affairs Manager, Prudential Corporation plc, 142 Holborn Bars, London EC1N 2NH. Tel: 01-405 9222.

THE RTZ CORPORATION PLC

GENERAL INFORMATION

Head office	6 St James's Square, London SW1Y 4LD. Tel: 01-930 2399
Directors	Sir Alistair Frame (chairman), JD Birkin TD (chief executive and deputy chairman), The Lord Clitheroe (deputy chief executive), AE Buxton, D Edwards, IC Strachan, RP Wilson. *Non-exec* M Littman QC, Sir David Orr MC, Sir Donald Tebbit GCMG, Sir Anthony Tuke, RS Walker MBE
Advisers	No specified adviser
Auditors	Coopers & Lybrand, Spicer & Oppenheim
Registrars	Central Registration Ltd, 1 Redcliffe Street, Bristol BS1 6NT. Tel: 0272 293296
Brokers	Hoare Govett Ltd, de Zoete & Bevan Ltd
Solicitors	No specified adviser

GENERAL FINANCIAL INFORMATION

Market capitalisation	£2.676bn at 1 January 1988
Capital structure	
Authorised share capital (10p)	£130.0m
Issued ordinary shares (10p)	£77.7m
Issued preference shares (£1)	£7.7m 3.325% 'A' cumulative £3.1m 3.5% 'B' cumulative
Warrants	32,999 warrants, exercisable into 10,394,685 shares of 10p
Convertibles	£170.1m 9.5% CULS 1995/2000 (51.44 shares per £100 stock)
Traded options	Yes
ADRs	Yes
Shareholders over 5%	None

FT CATEGORY

FT: Mines-miscellaneous
FT-A: Mining finance

MAJOR ACTIVITIES

Pre-eminent in mining, RTZ has evolved into a worldwide diversified natural resources company with substantial interests in related basic industries, including metal fabrication and building products, speciality minerals and chemicals. Together, these businesses constitute a major and highly competitive international asset base.

As well as its wholly-owned interests, RTZ has major listed assets. These are: CRA (49%), a large diversified Australian base, precious and ferrous metal mining producer; Rio Algom (53%), a Canadian copper, coal and uranium miner and speciality steel producer; Indal (61%), a holding and manufacturing company based in Canada; LASMO (29.7%), a UK oil and gas producer and explorer; and Palabora (39%), which mines and refines copper in South Africa.

Overall, RTZ has interests in 40 countries. Its subsidiary and related companies employ nearly 80,000 people, some 18,000 of whom work in the UK. RTZ is divided into two trading sectors – natural resources and related industry.

Comparable international natural resource companies are Anglo American in South Africa, Newmont (US), Noranda (Canada) and WMC and BHP (Australia).

FINANCIAL HISTORY

Turnover of £3.397bn in 1987 was up 35% over a five-year period but down nearly 3% on the record level of £3.502bn achieved in 1984, largely for reasons of currency changes.

Net attributable profit was £279.5m, compared with £244.8m in 1986. Around 63% of net earnings before corporate deductions came from the industrial businesses. The price of base metals (particularly copper and aluminium), as well as multiple currency relationships, are important factors that affect profitability.

Diversification into industrial interests has been taking place since the early 1970s when the Borax and Pillar businesses were acquired. Organic and acquisitive growth has been marked in RTZ's related industry sector, particularly within the speciality minerals and chemical businesses, RTZ Borax and RTZ Chemicals, and in the fabricated and engineered products business, RTZ Pillar, which supplies products for the building trade.

CHAIRMAN'S STATEMENT

'We intend to focus our energies on business areas where we have established competitive advantages and where we can identify scope for profitable development. With a strong balance sheet, a clear strategy and an excellent, highly motivated, management team, I see many opportunities for future profitable growth. We face the years to come with considerable confidence.' *Sir Alistair Frame*

Since 1981 the growth in RTZ's net earnings has averaged 14.5% per annum. Following the reduction in its stake in CRA from 52.3% to 49% during 1986, CRA's debt is no longer consolidated in RTZ's balance sheet. This has greatly improved RTZ's net debt position, which stood at £607m at 31 December 1987. The net debt to total equity ratio is a comfortable 24:76 or 31%.

SHARE PRICE HISTORY

From 1983 until March 1987 RTZ shares traded between 200p and 310p, significantly underperforming the UK equity market.

The shares reacted strongly to the recovery in metal and oil prices that began in the second quarter of 1987. They broke through the previous high of 310p in a sharp upward move to a new high of 580p before dropping in autumn 1987 to around 240p. During the first half of 1988 the shares traded around 370p.

RTZ's share price performance has historically often been linked to movements in the price of copper, though the company today is less orientated towards metal mining, particularly copper, than it has been in the past.

SENIOR MANAGEMENT

Sir Alistair Frame was appointed chairman in April 1985. He is a Scottish engineer. The chief executive is Derek Birkin,

Share price and relative to FT-A All-Share

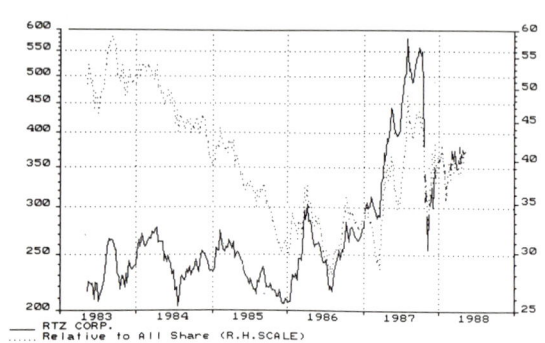

FIVE YEAR FINANCIAL INFORMATION

Year	Turnover (£m)	Net attributable profit (£m)	Earnings per share (p)	Dividends per share (p)	Dividend cover (x)	Net assets (p)	Price (p) High	Price (p) Low	PER (x) High	PER (x) Low	Yield (%) High	Yield (%) Low
1983	2,840	203	28.0	7.2	3.7	283	269	174	18.0	9.5	5.07	3.64
1984	3,502	247	31.9	8.0	4.1	282	284	203	12.5	9.1	5.07	3.42
1985	3,098	257	33.2	8.8	3.8	192	275	202	11.0	6.8	5.78	3.85
1986	3,344	245	31.6	9.4	3.4	208	307	204	10.3	6.8	5.80	3.81
1987	3,397	280	36.0	11.5	3.2	206	580	255	16.0	7.1	6.00	2.60

who joined RTZ from Tunnel Cement when that company was acquired by RTZ in 1982. Directors who are members of the chief executive's committee, which meets weekly to review strategy, are: Lord Clitheroe, deputy chief executive and chairman of RTZ Borax; Ian Strachan, finance director; Derek Edwards, industrial director and chairman of RTZ Pillar and RTZ Chemicals; Andrew Buxton, natural resources director; and Robert Wilson, who is planning and development director. Ian Strachan joined RTZ in October 1987 after 16 years with Exxon.

Management philosophy at RTZ is based on decentralised operations management coupled with financial control from the centre.

CAPITAL

Before the five for two share split in October 1987 the number of ordinary shares in issue had remained around 310m since 1984. The last large increase in the number of issued shares was in June 1983 when a one for six rights issue raised £192m in order to strengthen the equity base and finance acquisitions. The latter included a stake in Enterprise Oil, later exchanged for a 25.8% interest in LASMO, and several speciality chemicals businesses.

Approximately 86% of the RTZ equity is held in the UK with additional interests in France (4%), other Europe (4%) and the US (4.5%).

GROUP REVIEW

The steady profit performance of the RTZ group during the 1980s, a time of exceptionally depressed commodity prices, underlines the inherent managerial strength within the company. Many large mining groups, unlike RTZ, have cut dividends and been forced to resort to asset sales or plant closures to help reduce losses.

RTZ is divided into two trading sectors – natural resources and related industry. In 1987 the related industry sector was the main contributor to profits, with 63% of earnings before corporate deductions. Natural resources contributed 37%.

The related industry sector consists of a number of areas, each with several constituent companies. The speciality minerals and chemicals area is dominated by RTZ Borax (100%) and RTZ Chemicals (100%). The primary company in the fabricated and engineering products area is RTZ Pillar (100%). MK Electric, which was acquired in early 1988, will be incorporated into RTZ Pillar. In March 1988 RTZ sold its cement interests for £230m.

In the natural resources sector the main activity is the mining and smelting of aluminium, copper, gold, lead and zinc and the mining of iron ore. Through its holding in Rio Algom (53%), RTZ produces speciality steels and is involved in metals distribution. The holding in CRA (49%) is responsi-

ble for important areas of profit through copper and gold mining at Bougainville, aluminium refining and smelting at Comalco and iron ore at Hamersley Iron. Base metal prices in dollar terms have been recovering since mid-1987 and, should this trend continue, there is substantial scope for strong profit growth within the natural resources sector.

RTZ has coal, oil, gas and uranium interests. RTZ sold its 100% subsidiary RTZ Oil and Gas for £308m in April 1988. Its remaining oil and gas interest is a 29.7% holding in LASMO.

CRA (49%) RTZ's dependence upon CRA as a major source of earnings has gradually declined since the early 1970s. RTZ has developed its UK and US industrial interests and, as was always intended, has cut back its stake in CRA from 72.6% in 1979 to 49% to conform with the Australian government's policy of Australianising the ownership of Australian companies. In 1986 CRA made up 24% of RTZ earnings but by 1987 this had fallen to 19%.

CRA's most important operation in terms of profit contribution is Hamersley Iron. This produced around 39 million tonnes of iron ore in 1987. Hamersley's largest market is Japan. CRA also owns Kembla Coal and Coke and the Tarong coal mine and has a 50% effective interest in Blair Athol. Total output from these mines amounts to around 12 million tonnes per annum. CRA's copper and gold interests are held through its 53.6% interest in Bougainville Copper Limited. Aluminium exposure is through CRA's 67% stake in Comalco Limited, CRA also has a 57% holding in the Argyle diamond mine joint venture where full scale mining began at the end of 1986, the first full year of production. Argyle is the world's largest volume producer of industrial diamonds, producing some 30.3 million carats in 1987.

Rio Algom (53%) The company's four principal activities are: the underground mining of uranium; open pit mining of copper, molybdenum and metallurgical coal; the manufacture of stainless and speciality steels; and the marketing of these products. Rio Algom contributed 8.5% of RTZ's earnings in 1986 and 7.2% in 1987.

RTZ Borax (100%) This subsidiary has enjoyed strong profit growth since 1983. The company produces and sells borates to North America, Europe and other countries. Boron products are used by industry in the manufacture of detergents, glass, abrasives, as a flux in ceramic glazes and in many other applications. In May 1986 RTZ Borax acquired Ottawa Silica Company which has now been merged into its existing silica operation to form US Silica, now established as the largest US producer of high quality silica sand.

RTZ Borax provided 30% of the RTZ group's earnings in 1987, making it the leading contributor.

RTZ Chemicals (100%) Until the beginning of 1987 RTZ Chemicals was incorporated within RTZ Borax. Because of the growth of this business it is now reported separately. For 1987 its net attributable profit was £19.4m, up £6.5m on 1986. RTZ Chemicals is one of the largest UK-based speciality chemicals companies, with growing international interests, particularly in North America.

RTZ Pillar (100%)   Pillar reported net attributable earnings of £65.7m in 1987, against £63.7m in 1986. The company has important activities in the metal fabrication and building products field and is a substantial company in its own right with a turnover around £1.2bn in 1987.

RTZ Pillar owns 61.6% of Indal, a North American-based company which also supplies building products and manufactures auto parts, helicopter hauldown systems and glass products.

LASMO (29.7%)   LASMO is an oil and gas producer and explorer. Interests are located in the UK, US, Canada, Australasia and Indonesia.

Africa   RTZ's operations in Africa contributed 10% of net earnings in 1987. Its principal holdings in the region are 46.5% of Rössing Uranium which mines uranium oxide by opencast methods in Namibia and the Palabora open pit copper operation in South Africa, which is 38.9%-owned by RTZ.

Projects and other developments   The new Morro do Ouro gold mine in Brazil (RTZ 51%) came into production in December 1987. Total output is estimated at around 100,000oz per annum. The Neves Corvo copper project in Portugal is due to start production in 1989 with output expected at approximately 130,000 tonnes per annum. In Chile, there is the huge Escondida copper project (RTZ 30%) with reserves of around 675m tonnes. Via CRA, there are a number of gold prospects in Australia, Papua New Guinea and Indonesia as well as interesting uranium and rare earth finds.

On the industrial side, RTZ continues to make related acquisitions in the chemicals and construction components field where there is perceived synergy with existing activities (e.g. acquisition of MK Electric). Divestments such as RTZ Cement and RTZ Oil and Gas are undertaken where it is felt there are more attractive alternative prospects for growth or where it is concluded that a continuing presence would require a commitment of resources out of proportion to other group activities.

GEOGRAPHICAL REVIEW

The largest contribution to earnings is derived from North American businesses. The UK and Australasia are next in order of importance. The geographical analysis of 1987 earnings is North America 38%, UK 31%, Australasia 19%, other 12%.

CORPORATE CALENDAR

Year end	31 December
Preliminary results	April
Report and accounts	May
AGM	June
Final dividend paid	July
Interim results	September
Interim dividend paid	January

DIRECTORS' HOLDINGS

	Beneficial interests	Options
Sir Alistair Frame	2,437	253,737
JD Birkin	35,737	203,737
The Lord Clitheroe	12,200	114,410
AE Buxton	5,890	106,862
D Edwards	—	106,862
M Littman	23,435	—
Sir David Orr	5,195	—
IC Strachan	—	50,000
Sir Donald Tebbit	1,994	—
Sir Anthony Tuke	6,345	—
RS Walker	—	—
RP Wilson	—	96,652

Total directors' remuneration in 1987 was £1.9m. The highest-paid director in 1987 was the chairman, who received £205,219.

PRINCIPAL SUBSIDIARIES AND RELATED COMPANIES

Anglesey Aluminium Ltd (51%), CRA Ltd (49%) – Australia, Indal Ltd (61.6%) – Canada, London and Scottish Marine Oil PLC (29.7%), Palabora Mining Company Ltd (38.9%) – South Africa, RTZ Borax Ltd (100%), RTZ Chemicals Ltd (100%), RTZ Metals Ltd (100%), RTZ Pillar Ltd (100%), Rio Algom Ltd (53%) – Canada, Rio Tinto Zimbabwe Ltd (56.1%) – Zimbabwe, Rössing Uranium Ltd (46.5%) – Namibia

BRAND NAMES

Not applicable

CONTACTS AND FURTHER INFORMATION

Margaret Bull, Investor Relations Executive, The RTZ Corporation PLC, 6 St James's Square, London SW1Y 4LD. Tel: 01-930 2399.

RACAL ELECTRONICS PLC

GENERAL INFORMATION

Head office	Western Road, Bracknell, Berkshire RG12 1RG. Tel: 0344 481222
Directors	Sir Ernest Harrison OBE FCA Comp IEE (chairman and chief executive), DC Elsbury OBE (deputy chief exec), Sir Edward Ashmore GCB DSC, BJ Clarke, JE Coates, PG Crossland, JE Diggins MBE, GJ Lomer CBE, FIEE, DJ Peacock, MR Richardson FCMA, DA Webb, GA Whent
Advisers	Hill Samuel & Co Ltd
Auditors	Touche Ross & Co
Registrars	Hill Samuel Registrars Ltd
Brokers	Citicorp Scrimgeour Vickers Ltd
Solicitors	Stephenson Harwood

GENERAL FINANCIAL INFORMATION

Market capitalisation	£1.506bn at 1 January 1988
Capital structure	
Issued ordinary shares (25p)	626m
Issued preference shares	None
Warrants	None
Convertibles	£71.2m of 7% CULS 2009/2014 (one ordinary share for every 260p of stock, final redemption date 31 October 2014)
Traded options	Yes
ADRs	One ordinary share per ADR
Shareholders over 5%	Guardian Royal Exchange 7.7%, Millicom International Ltd 6.1%

FT CATEGORY

FT: Electricals
FT-A: Electronics

MAJOR ACTIVITIES

Racal is one of the UK's leading groups in professional electronics, fire and physical security, and telecommunications. Operations are conducted on a local, national and international basis. Racal's success has been rewarded by 36 Queen's Awards, 22 for export and 14 for technology.

Racal is engaged in six main areas of activity. These are security, data communications, radio communications, marine and energy electronics, defence radar and avionics, and telecommunications.

Margins in the security business, which contributed 31% of sales and 25% of operating profits in 1986/87, are low but improving. The data communications business provides high but volatile margins and yielded 35% of operating profits in 1986/87 on only 22% of sales.

Racal has just completed a programme of repositioning into security and telecommunications. This has led to static profits and high gearing since 1984 but has significantly altered group structure.

The outlook for 1988/89 is better with telecommunications likely to be the growth area in the future. International expansion seems set to be achieved through collaboration and joint venture. An example is the recent collaboration with Plessey in cellular electronics. This secures both a greater market share and wider geographical bases, strengthening Racal's competitive stance. In April 1988 Racal announced its intention to float its Vodafone subsidiary as an independent public company. Immediately afterwards, the company became the subject of bid rumours.

Factors liable to affect the group are interest and exchange rates. Due to historic customer dependence on oil revenue, Racal is sensitive to the effects of oil prices. The decline in world shipping has made an impact on results within the marine and energy division.

Competition in the security business comes from Securicor

and THORN EMI. Companies such as GEC, Plessey, STC, Cable and Wireless and British Telecom – as well as overseas-based companies like Siemens, AT&T, Ericsson, Northern Telecom and Alcatel – all compete in the areas of data communications, radio communications and telecommunications. Competition in the areas of defence radar and avionics comes from Ferranti, Westinghouse, GEC-Marconi and Plessey. Ferranti and Schlumberger are the main competitors in the specialist market of marine and energy electronics.

FINANCIAL HISTORY

The 1987 accounts showed, for the first time, the divisional breakdown. This highlighted sharply divergent performances within different areas, thus providing greater clarification and allowing a more detailed analysis to be made.

Turnover increased only marginally, by 1.9% to £1.29bn, up from £1.27bn in 1986. Pre-tax profits went up 11.1% to £100m, but this was still 24% down from the 1985 peak. Racal's original core activities were down overall, but diversification into security and telecommunications has provided stability, while the recent rationalisation has established a good platform for growth.

Earnings per share rose marginally to 11.27p from 10.7p, with a larger tax bill restricting any further increase. A final dividend of 2.495p per share net of tax made a total of 3.30p a share, an increase of 8.75%.

Total group borrowings stood at £237m. Deft equity ratio was reduced from 57% to 53% at the year end. It increased to 64% at the end of October 1987, though it should reduce again to 53% in March 1988. The need for substantial borrowing is due to the cost of establishing the telecommunications division. Future growth will reduce Racal's debt. Pre-tax margin was 7.8% against 15.5% in 1983. Net tangible asset turnover was 2.68 times and return on net tangible assets employed was 20.8%.

The 1987/88 interim showed that Racal's profits were recovering to what is likely to be around £132m for the full year, equal to the pretax record set in 1984/85. Telecommunications profits were well ahead of budget. Data communications were flat, with Racal–Vadic only breaking even. Security was growing slowly in difficult conditions. Marine and Energy recovered well, and other activities performed satisfactorily.

SHARE PRICE HISTORY

Apart from a flurry caused by the 1985/86 interim results, Racal's shares underperformed the market from the end of 1982 until late 1986. In absolute terms, the shares did not exceed the 300p level seen in late 1982 until the peak of the 1987 bull market in October 1987 when they topped out at 348p.

Loss of confidence in the company's performance was the cause. However, the prospects for telecommunications and security started a steady rise in Racal's relative share price performance from December 1986 onwards. The announcement of the flotation of Vodafone and bid rumours drove the share price sharply upwards in May 1988.

SENIOR MANAGEMENT

Racal operates an aggressive, market-orientated style of management. Senior management is headed by Sir Ernest Harrison, who is chairman and chief executive. DC Elsbury is

FIVE YEAR FINANCIAL INFORMATION

Year	Turnover (£m)	Pre-tax (£m)	Earnings (p)	Dividends net (p)	Dividend cover (x)	Net assets (p)	Price (p) High	Price (p) Low	PER (x) High	PER (x) Low	Yield (%) High	Yield (%) Low
1983	763.6	117.9	13.7	5.5	4.8	116.4	299	183	32.7	17.9	2.15	1.20
1984	815.6	119.2	14.8	2.9	4.4	68.5	284	190	24.7	17.5	2.20	1.40
1985	1,107.0	132.3	15.5	3.0	4.3	75.6	288	122	26.6	9.0	3.55	1.40
1986	1,266.3	90.2	10.7	3.0	2.7	75.7	226	148	21.9	11.8	2.89	1.90
1987	1,290.8	100.3	11.3	3.3	3.4	79.9	344	183	29.3	16.6	2.34	1.31

a dynamic and inspiring deputy chief executive.

JE Coates is financial director, and GJ Lomer is technical director. Other directors include BJ Clarke, PJ Crossland, JE Diggins, DJ Peacock, MR Richardson and GA Whent. The two non-executive directors are Sir Edward Ashmore and DA Webb.

CAPITAL

Racal has used its shares to diversify into security and telecommunications. In 1984/85, 35.58m shares were issued in part consideration of Chubb. In 1987, 52.16m shares were issued as part consideration of minority interests in Racal-Millicom, thereby giving Racal total control of the Racal-Vodafone network.

Directors' holdings account for only 0.31%. The Guardian Royal Exchange holds 7.73%, and Millicom International holds 6.08%.

GROUP REVIEW

Over the next few years Racal's profits mix is expected to change further, with the emphasis moving away from data communications and security, towards telecommunications, due to the rapid growth of the cellular market. Marine and energy may provide the opportunity for a potential management buyout.

Security This includes the protection of people, property and information from burglary and fire, and is the largest division within the Racal group. The acquisition of Chubb in 1984 provided an improved stability to counterbalance other more volatile divisions.

Maintenance of margins with an increase in turnover resulted in operating profits of £31m in 1987 on turnover of £395m. This was a strong performance which represented 31% of Racal's turnover and 25% of operating profits. The growth rate for locks and safes is calculated at 5% to 7% over the next two years. The growth rate of fire equipment is anticipated to reach 17%.

Racal is well positioned in the expanding area of data security, where growth rates are expected to double on an annual basis. With strong European revenues, growth of 18% in the area of alarm systems is expected. Racal-Transcom manufactures card authorisation electronic funds transfer point of sale (ETPOS) terminals. Notable US developments in 1986/87 included a car plant protection system and the provision of surveillance and monitoring systems for a new prison in New York.

Overall in recent years security has been the area for much of the group's diversification. An improved market share has been secured through further acquisitions and the effects of a 15% annual profit growth. In 1986/87 13 acquisitions were made, 11 of which involved alarm companies. Racal is one of the three market leaders, with a strong presence in 19 countries and manufacturing plants in 12. It has a wider product and geographical spread than any other security company.

Data communications Racal's products in this division range from simple modems for personal computers, multiplexers and local area networks, through to powerful packet switching systems, with network management to oversee the whole installation.

Racal is the world's largest data communications company, and is expert in the planning and implementation of corporate data networks. Consituent companies of the division include Racal-Milgo and Racal-Vadic in the US, and Racal-Milgo in the UK. Customers include the US Social Security Administration, American Airlines and the National Westminster Bank.

The data communications division remains the most substantial contributor to operating profits. These increased from £15m in 1986 to £44m in 1987. This dramatic rise was mainly due to a reduction in the basic costs of US operations, despite a dull market and the fall in the value of the dollar, and volume gains.

Radio communications Products include ranges of military hand-held, fixed and frequency-hopping radios, complete trunk communications systems, electronic warfare suites and communication security devices. Equipment is based on a modular design, allowing customers with restricted budgets progressively to acquire large complex systems.

Originally this division was the most successful area for Racal. However, tougher conditions in the UK market, the fall in oil prices, and the subsequent delays in Middle Eastern orders, caused sales to fall by 29% in 1987 from £184m to £131m. Operating profits dropped from £36.9m to £6.7m, resulting in the division's worst trading year in history. Racal has met this by introducing cost reductions including the loss of 750 jobs. The group is looking to a recovery in 1989, with prospects of diversification into paramilitary and civil applications.

Telecommunications This division is one of only two UK licencees for cellular radio telecommunications operations. Racal trades as Vodafone, in competition with Cellnet, owned by Securicor and British Telecom. Racal also supplies telecommunications equipment and services for extensive use in various applications, from one-man businesses to large

CHAIRMAN'S STATEMENT

'Our planned investment in the new business areas of Telecommunications and Security has continued and in 1988/89 operating profits for these two businesses will be well in excess of the £105m forecast last June. In addition, the rest of the Group will improve their contribution.

The Board remains confident of sustained growth.' *Sir Ernest Harrison*

corporations. There is also an expanding value-added network services company in operation, Racal-Vodata. It introduced radiopaging and Band Three Radio, a private mobile radio service, in 1987.

Cellular radio, which is one of the few growth markets in electronics, is expected to make exceptionally strong contributions. A start-up loss of £12.3m in 1986 turned into an operating profit of £10.2m in 1987. The costs of the cellular development mean that cash will not be generated until April 1988. Recent performance has encouraged the group to raise cellular profits forecasts for the next three years.

Share price and relative to FT-A All-Share

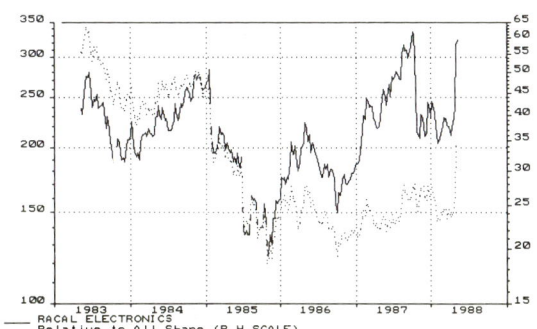

In 1987 Vodafone had 100,000 subscribers. Subscriber capacity can be substantially increased. This would be done by introducing 200 new frequencies and halving cell diameters in central London. Assuming that tariff policies remain similar to those of 1987, operating profits are expected to increase from £45m in 1987/88 to £75m in 1988/89, rising to over £100m plus in 1989/90. There remains, however, the possibility that Oftel may decide that the current high margins are not in the public interest.

The estimate for 1989/90 is equivalent to the pre-tax profits earned by the entire group in the year to March 1987. Forecasts suggest that telecommunications will probably eventually contribute 40% of Racal's operating profits rather than the 8% made in 1987.

After 1990 Racal will be in a very strong position to profit from increasing deregulation in the telecommunications market. Overall the outlook remains extremely positive. Future opportunities include Racal's participation in an agreement whereby 15 western European nations will introduce a digital pan-European cellular system in 1991. Racal has a joint venture with Plessey (Orbitel Mobile Communications) to develop infrastructure equipment and terminals.

In late April 1988 Racal announced its intention to float its telecommunications division as an independent public company.

Defence radar and avionics The division's major business activity is that of electronic warfare. Racal produces a family of electronic warfare products employing a common processor and man-machine interface, and high performance millimetre wave radars for use in low level air defence weapon systems.

The avionics sector provides flight management systems for civil, military, fixed- and rotary-wing applications. These control and display all aspects of navigation, flight performance, communications, monitoring and mission management.

Operating profits increased by 5.6% to £22.9m from £21.7m, although turnover was reduced from £131m to £127m due to reduced procurement by the Ministry of Defence,

squeezed margins and contract delays. Prospects continue to look attractive with orders worth £240m and significant AWACS work. Overall it has proved a steady business with high margins.

Marine and energy Products and services within the division range from radar, satellite equipment and bridge systems, to packages for ships' systems and offshore services.

This division was the only part of the group to incur a loss. The decline in the shipping and oil markets resulted in turnover falling from £132m to £110m, and an operating profit of £5m in 1986 was turned into a £5m loss in 1987. However, at the 1988 interim the division was back in profit.

These adverse results were accompanied by the problems of old technology. This led to restructuring and the implementation of cost reduction programmes to reduce capacity in line with demand.

Specialised business activities These include acoustics, health and safety equipment, micro-electronics, information systems, antennae, automated test and repair equipment, and instrumentation. The division contributed 14% of group sales in 1987. Operating profits were up 35.2% to £18.7m and turnover increased by 14.9% to £180.1m.

Research and development Racal funds its own R&D of products and systems. These are undertaken mainly by individual operating companies. R&D is aimed at identifying and investigating new technologies, and then applying them to commercial opportunities.

GEOGRAPHICAL REVIEW

Racal is one of the most international UK electronics manufacturers with over half its sales coming from overseas. It has many subsidiaries and related companies located throughout the world. It also exports products and services to over 50 countries.

In 1987, the UK provided 40% of total turnover, the Americas contributed 23%, continental Europe 17%, and Asia and Australia 15%. Africa accounted for 5%.

CORPORATE CALENDAR

Year end	31 March
Preliminary results	June
Report and accounts	July
AGM	August
Final dividend paid	August
Interim results	January
Interim dividend paid	March

DIRECTORS' HOLDINGS

	Beneficial ordinary shares	Options
Sir Ernest Harrison	1,642,856	348,431
DC Elsbury	25,810	511,098
Sir Edward Ashmore	8,080	—
BJ Clarke	3,030	171,378
JE Coates	9,930	203,575
PG Crossland	300	91,027
JE Diggins	1,754	176,607
GJ Lomer	17,530	186,409
DJ Peacock	—	139,433
MR Richardson	2,000	183,695
DA Webb	200,554	4,024
GA Whent	—	214,446

Total directors' remuneration in 1987 was £1.23m, of which the chairman received £188,291, and the highest-paid director £204,212.

THE RANK ORGANISATION

PRINCIPAL SUBSIDIARIES AND RELATED COMPANIES

Ablex Audio Video Ltd, Albert Marston & Company Ltd, Band Three (Holdings) Ltd (25%), British Communications Corporation Ltd, CE Marshall (Wolverhampton) Ltd, China Bohai Racal Positioning and Survey Company Ltd – People's Republic of China (50%), China Nanhai Racal Positioning and Survey Company Ltd – People's Republic of China (50%), Chubb & Son's Lock and Safe Company Ltd, Chubb Alarms Ltd, Chubb Australia Ltd – Australia, Chubb Electronics (Hong Kong) Ltd – Hong Kong (50%), Chubb Fire Security Ltd, Chubb Holding (Private) Ltd – Zimbabwe (69.1%), Chubb Holdings Ltd – South Africa (69.1%), Chubb Hong Kong Ltd – Hong Kong (50%), Chubb Ireland Ltd – Eire, Chubb Lips Nederland BV – Holland, Chubb Lips Systemen BV – Holland, Chubb Malaysia Sdn Bhd – Malaysia (30%), Chubb New Zealand Ltd – New Zealand, Chubb (NI) Ltd, Chubb Sécurité SA – France, Chubb Security Installations Ltd, Chubb Sicherheitstechnik Vertrieb GmbH – Federal Republic of Germany, Chubb Singapore Private Ltd – Singapore (70%), Chubb Wardens Ltd, Decca Contractors (SA) Pty Ltd – South Africa, Decca Electronics Ltd – Australia, Decca Survey Overseas Ltd, Fibre Form Ltd, Gispen and Staalmeubel BV – Holland, Hoermann Security Ltd – Eire, Hörmann Sicherheitstechnik GmbH – Federal Republic of Germany, Industrias Parsi SA – Spain, Internationale Navigatie Apparaten BV – Holland, Josiah Parkes & Sons Ltd, L&F Willenhall Ltd, Lips-Vago Elettronica SpA – Italy, Lips-Vago SpA – Italy, Orbitel Mobile Communications (Holdings) Ltd (50%), Pt Chubb-Lips Indonesia – Indonesia (76%), Racal Acoustics Ltd, Racal Airstream Inc – US, Racal Antennas Ltd, Racal Arbeitssicherheit GmbH – Federal Republic of Germany, Racal Automation Ltd, Racal Avionics Inc – US, Racal Avionics Ltd, Racal (Canada) Ltd – Canada, Racal Communication Inc – US, Racal Communications Ltd, Racal Defence Electronics (Radar) Ltd, Racal Defence Radar and Displays Ltd, Racal Electronics Pty Ltd – Australia, Racal Electronics (Singapore) Private Ltd – Singapore, Racal Elektronik System GmbH – Federal Republic of Germany, Racal Engineering Ltd, Racal Finance Ltd, Racal Group Services Ltd, Racal Information Technology Developments Ltd, Racal Leicester Ltd, Racal Management Services Ltd, Racal Marine Electronics Ltd, Racal Marine Inc – US, Racal Marine Ireland Ltd – Eire, Racal Marine Systems Ltd, Racal Microelectronic Systems Ltd, Racal Milgo SA NV – Belgium, Racal Norge A/S – Norway, Racal Panorama Ltd, Racal Properties Ltd, Racal Radar A/S – Denmark, Racal Radar Defence Systems Ltd, Racal Recorders Inc – US, Racal Recorders Ltd, Racal Research Ltd, Racal Safety Ltd, Racal Survey Inc – US, Racal Survey Ltd, Racal Survey (Malaysia) Sdn Bhd – Malaysia (70%), Racal Survey Norge A/S – Norway, Racal Survey (UK) Ltd, Racal Svenska AB – Sweden, Racal Tacticom Ltd, Racal Telecommunications Group Ltd, Racal Training Services Ltd, Racal-Cellular Ltd, Racal-Chubb Canada Ltd – Canada, Racal-Chubb Inc – US, Racal-Chubb Ltd, Racal-Chubb Security Systems Ltd, Racal-Comsec Ltd, Racal-Dana Instruments Inc – US, Racal-Dana Instruments Italia Srl – Italy (76%), Racal-Dana Instruments Ltd, Racal-Dana Instruments SA – France, Racal-Data Communications Inc – US, Racal-Decca Advanced Developments Ltd, Racal-Decca Canada Inc – Canada, Racal-Decca Electronics (Hong Kong) Ltd – Hong Kong, Racal-Decca Marine Navigation Ltd, Racal-Decca Navigator A/S – Denmark, Racal-Decca Service Ltd, Racal-Guardall (England) Ltd, Racal-Guardall Inc – US, Racal-Guardall SA – France, Racal-Guardall (Sales) Ltd, Racal-Guardall (Scotland) Ltd – Scotland, Racal-Guardall Srl – Italy, Racal-Guardata Ltd, Racal-MESL (France) SARL – France (99.5%), Racal-MESL Ltd – Scotland, Racal-Milcom Pty Ltd – Australia, Racal-Milgo GmbH – Federal Republic of Germany, Racal-Milgo Ltd, Racal-Mobilcal Ltd, Racal-Redac AB – Sweden, Racal-Redac BV – Holland, Racal-Redac Design System GmbH – Federal Republic of Germany, Racal-Redac Inc – US, Racal-Redac Italia Srl – Italy, Racal-Redac (Japan) Ltd – Japan, Racal-Redac Ltd, Racal-Redac Pty Ltd – Australia, Racal-Redac SA – France, Racal-Redac UK Ltd, Racal-Transcom Ltd, Racal-Vodac Ltd, Racal-Vodacom Ltd, Racal-Vodafone Ltd, Racal-Vodapage Ltd, Racal-Vodata Ltd, Sea Surveys Ltd – Eire, Security Industries SA-NV – Belgium, Societa Impianti Antincendio SpA – Italy, Société Lyonnaise de Protection Electronique SA – France (60%), Steelage Industries Ltd – India (40%), The Racal Corporation – US, Union Locks Ltd, Weyrad (Electronics) Ltd

BRAND NAMES

Apollo, Chubb, Cougarnet, Decca, Jaguar, Sabre, Sunrise, Tacnet, Vodafone, Vodapage

CONTACTS AND FURTHER INFORMATION

Ken Ward, Racal Corporate Communications Centre, The Racal Electronics Group, 21 Market Place, Wokingham, Berkshire RH11 1AJ. Tel: 0734 782158.

GENERAL INFORMATION

Head office	The Rank Organisation, 6 Connaught Place, London W2 2EZ. Tel: 01-629 7454
Directors	Sir Patrick Meaney (chairman), MB Gifford (managing director and chief executive), LH Bond, A Crichton-Miller, J Daly, Douglas M Yates, NV Turnbull FCA. *Non-exec* DV Atterton CBE, Sir Arthur Bryan, Sir Leslie Fletcher DSC, Sir Denis Mountain Bt, The Hon Angus Ogilvy, AW Stenham
Advisers	J Henry Schroder Wagg & Co Ltd
Auditors	Peat Marwick McLintock
Registrars	Hill Samuel Registrars Ltd
Brokers	Rowe & Pitman Ltd
Solicitors	Richards Butler

GENERAL FINANCIAL INFORMATION

Market capitalisation	£1.189bn at 1 January 1988
Capital structure	
Issued ordinary shares (25p)	215.5m
Issued preference shares (£1)	110m 6.25% CP
	£2.6m 8% second CP
Warrants	None
Convertibles	£20.2m 4.25% CUL 1993 ($14.523 of the loan convertible into one ordinary share)
Traded options	None
ADRs	None
Shareholders over 5%	Guardian Royal Exchange 5.7%

FT CATEGORY

FT: Industrials (miscel.)
FT-A: Conglomerates

MAJOR ACTIVITIES

The Rank Organisation is a diversified leisure-orientated company, with earnings split approximately equally between the Rank Xerox office equipment associate and the group managed and wholly owned leisure, entertainment and industrial interests.

The group is arguably best known for its film-related activities, which in 1987 accounted for 23.9% of sales and 16.3% of trading profit of the managed businesses. Rank has ambitious plans to launch a national pay-TV channel based on showing recently released feature films.

Branded leisure services, such as the Butlin's holiday centres, Haven Leisure centres and the Top Rank bingo chain, together with hotels and catering, accounted for 51.6% of group sales and 60% of trading profit of the managed businesses in 1987. Ladbroke social and bingo clubs and amusement centres were acquired in 1986, reinforcing Rank's position as one of the leading UK leisure companies.

Most of the remaining activities are in niche areas of metrology and vision-related equipment. Leisure property development is a sizeable activity in the US, and the acquisition in March 1988 of Ahnert Enterprises has significantly increased Rank's leisure industry presence in the US and this will increase significantly further if the proposed acquisition of Bell & Howell's videotape duplication business goes ahead.

Rank Xerox is effectively 34% owned by the Rank Organisation and 66% by Xerox Corporation, remitting a twice-covered dividend. Rank Xerox both manufactures and distributes a range of office equipment developed by itself and the Xerox Corporation. It is particularly well known for its photocopiers, for which 'xerox' is practically a generic term, and has the second largest sales and service organisation in the industry.

Despite speculation that Rank Xerox does not fit in the

F I V E   Y E A R   F I N A N C I A L   I N F O R M A T I O N

Year	Turnover (£m)	Pre-tax (£m)	Earnings (p)	Dividends net (p)	Dividend cover (x)	Net assets (p)	Price (p)		PER (x)		Yield (%)	
							High	Low	High	Low	High	Low
1983	742.9	69.3	14.3	10.0	1.4	230	196	102	20.0	5.5	14.84	5.83
1984	724.7	105.3	27.7	12.0	2.3	227	296	182	24.4	16.7	7.14	5.21
1985	.630.9	136.0	33.7	15.0	2.2	217	484	290	25.4	14.3	5.42	3.75
1986	718.1	164.1	45.4	18.0	2.5	271	589	424	19.9	13.7	4.75	3.64
1987	668.4	208.3	58.2	21.8	2.7	283	823	482	18.8	9.3	5.40	3.00

group, Rank had indicated that it is unlikely to sell this profitable associate. However, the budget changed the base date for capital gains computations, thus the disposal penalty may now be much reduced, making such a disposal a little less unlikely. In 1987 as a whole, Rank Xerox contributed £115.7m to group profits, 53% of the total.

FINANCIAL HISTORY

The most striking feature of Rank's development since 1982 has been a decline in sales of 10% but a 263% surge in trading profits. The trading margin on group managed activities has almost trebled in the period, from 5.1% to 15% by 1987. This was achieved largely by the disposal of unprofitable or low margin businesses, and a significant investment and acquisition programme costing £200m in 1986 and £129m in 1987.

At the end of 1987 net borrowings were £122.7m. In the last few years gearing has been reduced from almost 50% to under 20% as disposal proceeds have come in and higher cash flows have been generated. Since the year-end the acquisition of Ahnert Enterprises has pushed the gearing figure up to 35% to 40% on a pro-forma basis and perhaps a little higher in the first half of 1988 when cash tends to flow out of the group. Organic growth has been supplemented by acquisition.

Although Rank was able to buy the caravan parks of Haven Leisure, Ladbroke bingo and amusement centres and make a number of small acquisitions, it failed in early 1986 in a full bid for the complementary Granada leisure group due to IBA restrictions on the transfer of Granada shares.

Earnings per share have improved even more dramatically than pre-tax profits, rising at a 34% compound annual rate between the 1982 low point and 1986, as the tax provision fell from 54% to 40%, and growing again by 28% in 1987. Rank has pursued a progressive dividend policy throughout its recovery with payouts rising by 20% to 25% annually.

A £19.1m extraordinary item was charged against post-tax profit in 1986, mainly representing the costs of the abortive bid for Granada. In 1987 there was a £16.4m extraordinary credit chiefly due to surpluses derived from the sale of businesses.

Investment in the redevelopment of existing businesses began to pay off dramatically in 1984 and has improved further subsequently. In 1985 margins increased substantially with the doubling of operating profits from the holidays and recreation division. Of this, 60% resulted from the partial contribution made during the year by the Haven Leisure caravan parks and the Ladbroke social and bingo clubs, both now combined with Rank operations, and 40% from the growth of existing businesses.

The holidays and recreation division is the largest of the group's managed activities, representing just under one-third of sales and almost 44% of profits prior to consolidation of associates. The Wings package holiday subsidiary had re-

mained a persistent loss-maker, and was sold to Bass for £10m.

Paradoxically, investment in the hotels and catering division in 1986 failed to offset the impact of a dramatic increase in empty rooms in London hotels as American tourists stayed away from the UK in the wake of the Libyan air raid, the Chernobyl nuclear disaster and the weaker dollar. Empty rooms and lower customer spend meant that this division generated about 18% of sales and 15% of profit, but the 12% margin realised was well below the 15% to 20% which newly refurbished central London hotels are capable of achieving in a good year. In 1987 margins recovered to 14.2%.

Good steady growth was generated by the film and television services division with profits increasing substantially in the five years to 1987. Earnings can be affected by the general state of the market or by the quality of films available for exhibition. An excellent year for films, attendances and advertising resulted in a profits advance of 32.5% in this division in 1987. Many of the division's activities are in the more stable areas of servicing and are the largest of their kind in Europe. The film investment policy is designed to minimise risk in that film rights acquired are often pre-sold to reduce exposure. Rank has emerged as the major independent UK film distributor and has gained a substantial exposure to the fast growing home video market via its tape duplication and retail distribution interests.

Precision Industries contributed 14.2% of 1987 trading profits, down from 23.1% in 1986. It suffered from difficult conditions in the metrology and lighting markets in the US where 30% of the division's sales are derived. Rank Taylor Hobson in particular was affected by a fall in demand for capital equipment in the US car industry.

Leisure Developments, the division formed in 1987 to cover Rank's new leisure-related developments and operations, accounted for 8.9% of trading profits, with the Kingston Plantation resort in South Carolina contributing the majority of the figure. This percentage will rise in 1988 with the acquisition of Ahnert.

SHARE PRICE HISTORY

From a low of 100p in 1982, Rank's share price underwent a startling recovery, reaching a peak in mid-1987 of 826p. From 1984 to early 1986 the shares outperformed the FT-A All-Share index consistently. Thereafter they fell back slightly until the end of the year.

The share price outperformed the market in the first half of 1987 but fell away in the middle of the year as the stock market raced away. Rank then fell with the market in October 1987, losing around 250p from 740p to 490p, before recovering rapidly to outperform the market once again. The stock continues to be rated at an undeserved discount to the market and the leisure sector.

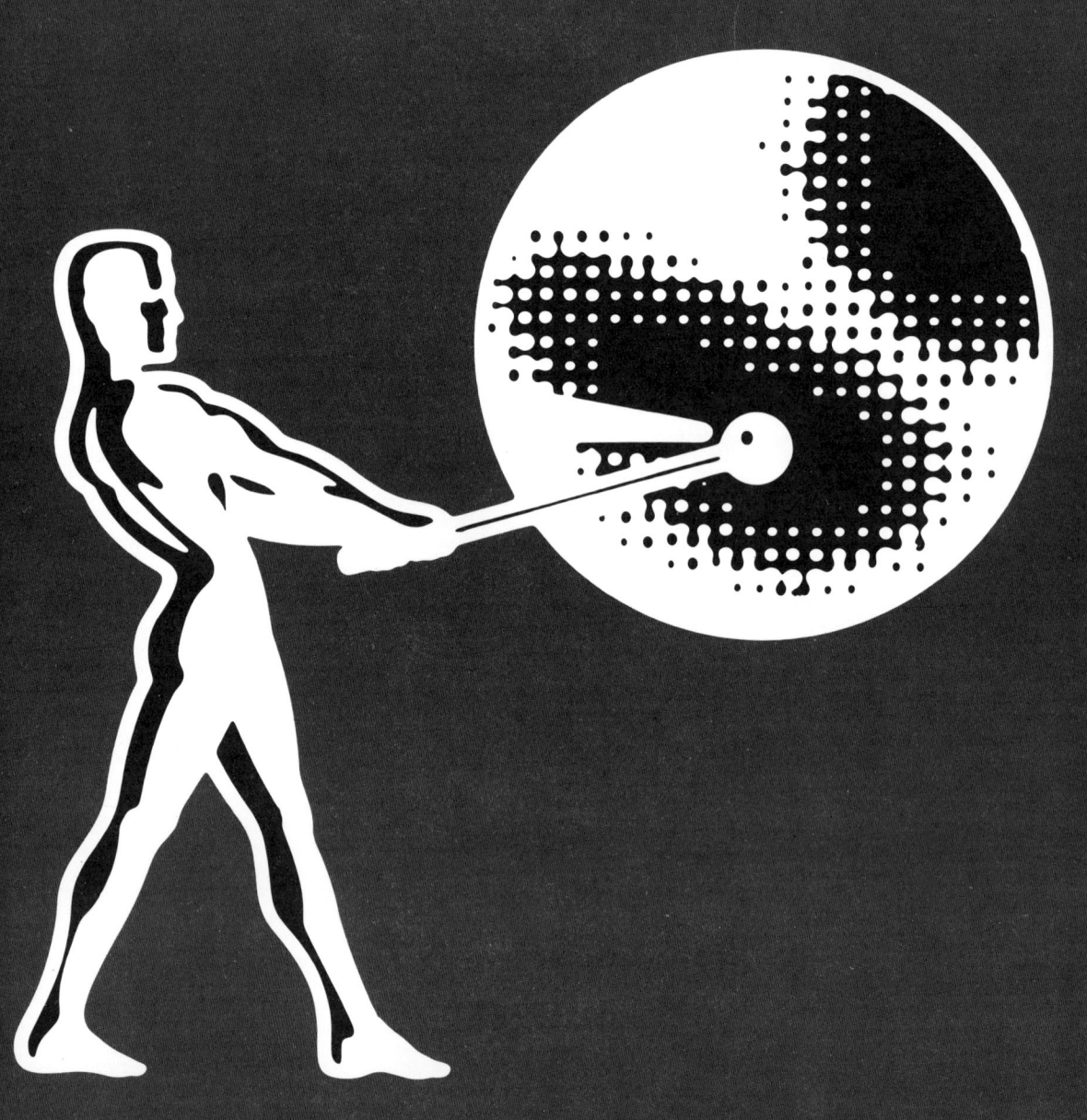

The Rank Organisation Plc   6 Connaught Place   London W2 2EZ   Tel: 01-629 7454

SENIOR MANAGEMENT

Sir Patrick Meaney, formerly chairman of Thomas Tilling, is the chairman and Michael Gifford, formerly finance director of Cadbury Schweppes, is the managing director and chief executive. Douglas Yates was the finance director until the middle of 1987, when Nigel Turnbull moved from a similar position at the oil company Tricentrol to take over. Douglas Yates is now responsible for a comprehensive strategy portfolio, including acquisitions, divestments and investment.

Other executive directors include Leslie H Bond, Angus Crichton-Miller and Jim Daly. Peter Blaxton and Stuart May are notable senior division executives. Non-executive directors include Sir Arthur Bryan, Dr David Atterton, Sir Leslie Fletcher, Sir Denis Mountain, Anthony Stenham and the Hon Angus Ogilvy.

CAPITAL

The group had 215.5m ordinary shares of 25p nominal value in issue, 12.5m of which were issued as part of the consideration to acquire Ladbroke's leisure interests, and approximately £12m preference shares (£2.5m 6.25% preference and the balance in 8% cumulative preference) at the beginning of 1987. It is planned to redeem these preference shares in the first half of 1988, enabling Rank significantly to increase its borrowing powers.

The group's holding in Rank Xerox is held through a number of subsidiary holding companies. The group holds 82% of A Kershaw & Sons, which in turn holds 43% of the preference and 40% of the ordinary capital of Rank Precision Industries (Holdings). This holding company in turn holds 50% of Rank Xerox Holdings.

There are £20.2m of borrowings in 4.25% Convertible Loan 1993. During 1986 0.2m were issued in exchange for loan stock and a further 2.4m shares may be converted. A further 3.35m shares are reserved for share option schemes.

In 1986 Rank sought shareholders' approval for the right to issue a proportion of unissued share capital for cash other than by a rights issue to all shareholders. Rank discloses one significant holding over 5%: Guardian Royal Exchange holds 12.3m shares, 5.7%.

GROUP REVIEW

Rank's directly managed business earnings advanced 22% in 1987, but this was bettered by the 43% advance in the contribution from Rank Xerox. Consequently, 54% of pre-tax profit was generated by the associates, largely Rank Xerox.

The holiday and hotel businesses are highly seasonal and the holiday operations are not consolidated into the first half results.

During both 1985 and 1986 the group disposed of and acquired £100m worth of businesses and this figure rose to £129m in 1987, refocusing on the growth segments in the leisure businesses and selling off less profitable manufacturing operations.

Rank Xerox Rank Xerox has the rights to manufacture and sell Xerox products outside the US, South America and Japan. It is best known for copier-duplicator products, which are either sold direct to customers or are placed on a rental agreement. Recently rental has given way to direct sales in most volume segments. These also form the basis of the 242 Xerox copy shop high street businesses in the office supplies division, which is also a major equipment distributor.

The latest 10 series of intelligent copiers launched in 1983 is extending the top end of the market, generating replacement business. Fast laser printers are selling well in the middle of the market, in particular for departmental publishing applications. Desk top copiers are also sold, but here Rank Xerox faces price competition from the Japanese, though this is less significant since the yen appreciated and EEC anti-dumping restrictions came into force.

Rank Xerox sources a number of low-end products from its Japanese associate Fuji-Xerox. More copier and office systems are now being sold and for the first time non-copier sales are outstripping copier sales. In Japan, Fuji-Xerox is currently doing very well.

C H A I R M A N ' S   S T A T E M E N T

'**Judicious investment is the key to profitable growth and £129m was spent on acquisitions and capital expenditure. Acquisitions were in areas where Rank could anticipate enriching profit by adding operations to existing businesses.**
. . .
Rank has clear objectives, capable management, strong resources and excellent opportunities to develop its activities at home and overseas. Despite repercussions from the substantial decline and frailty of stock market values with possible adverse influences on economic growth, we are confident that 1988 will be a further year of achievement and progress for your Company.' *Patrick Meaney*

A smaller but more rapidly growing market for integrated business systems – combining computers, work-stations, high quality printers, fax machines and other communications – is served by the systems business division. It provides the very successful Viewpoint desk top publishing systems.

Although Rank's stake in Rank Xerox leads to the group being perceived as having a heavy international exposure, it should be noted that the 1987 group results were scarcely affected by the major currency fluctuations of the period overall.

Film and TV services The health of the film or video industry is the major factor which affects the growth of companies in this division.

In 1987 Odeon cinema admissions were up by more than 10% and this was the third year of buoyancy in a row. *The Living Daylights* and *Crocodile Dundee* proved particularly attractive during the year, but the chain's success also reflects the group's efforts in refurbishment, stronger marketing and introducing a more flexible pricing policy.

Rank is involved with the production of films at Pinewood Studios outside London where the stagework for *Aliens* and the James Bond movie *The Living Daylights* was completed. The studio was badly hit from the second half of 1986 by a weak dollar and changes in UK tax law, deterring major Hollywood productions. Consequently, Pinewood slimmed down its workforce to a four-wall operation in May 1987, having previously been fully serviced, and has now returned to profitable operation.

Rank Video Services at Brentford is Europe's largest videotape duplication facility, with capacity to produce 8m tapes annually. As worldwide VCR ownership increases and tape usage rises, consumer demand for pre-recorded material should rise rapidly. The proposed $120m (£65m) acquisition of Bell & Howell's UK videotape duplication operation with its blue chip client base would increase growth prospects substantially.

Rank is the largest film processor in the UK and has recently opened a fourth processing laboratory in Glasgow. The company has gained substantial business from outside the UK.

Rank distributes films and owns a comprehensive film and video library. In addition the group announced in May 1987 a $100m revolving film fund which is available to independent producers in return for distribution rights. So far investment has been relatively modest. Rank Advertising has cornered the UK market, offering space in the Odeon and Cannon chains.

While advertising revenues are increasing, cinema profits are advancing more slowly, as further refurbishment costs temporarily reduce the profit margin. In time the benefits of a higher margin combined with healthy attendance levels at multi-screen sites ought to make the cinema operation more profitable. Profits on disposals of unwanted cinema sites contribute several million pounds annually.

At the same time combined cinema and leisure multiplex sites are planned. The first is being opened in Romford, outside London, and a second is due in Stoke-on-Trent. New screens are also being added in existing cinemas. The group's 50% share in the New Zealand Kerridge Odeon cinema chain was sold for £23.5m.

Holidays and recreation The benefits of a £45m investment in three important Butlin's holiday sites in winter 1986/87 are coming through as higher bookings at the upgraded sites. Rank benefits from premium pricing, having raised tariffs at the refurbished resorts by up to 20% in both 1987 and 1988. A further £35m will be invested during 1988.

Butlin's has been the star performer, with bookings up 10% in the face of an overall fall of 5% in the UK market. In 1986 this stemmed from gains at Minehead (Somerwest World) where redevelopment increased guest numbers by 36%. Bognor (Southcoast World) and Skegness (Funcoast World) have reopened. The Barry site was closed as it was uncommercial. The substantial uplift came, despite higher depreciation charges, by reducing establishment costs and raising prices for the better facilities offered.

Share price and relative to FT-A All-Share

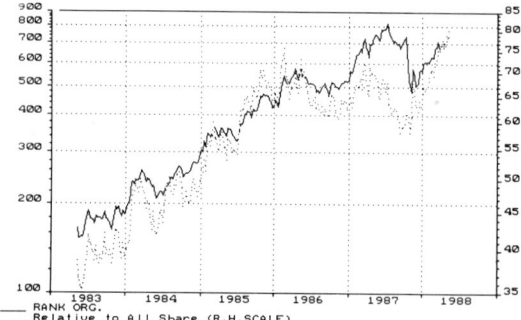

The group acquired Haven Leisure, an operator of caravan parks and some French boating, from English China Clays in 1986 for £37m, merging it with Rank operations. The UK had a mixed experience in 1987 but the French operations progressed ahead of expectations. Wings, the group's package tour operator with 5% of the UK market, was expected to make losses again in 1987 as a result of discounting as demand fell substantially short of expectations. Thus Rank's decision to sell to Bass falls into perspective. Cal Air International, the charter flight joint venture with British Caledonian, is

profitable and now operates three DC10 airliners.

Ladbroke's bingo and social club chain and 42 amusement centres acquired in 1986 are being integrated with the existing Top Rank operation, refurbished to the same standard, and contributed immediately to cash flow. The bingo 'National Game' was expected to bring in more customers, but this did not happen in a major way initially, although Rank has been successful in raising the per capita spend. Rank's acquisition of the Showboat Holdings' amusement centres in September 1987 has given it market leadership with over 100 inland centres, and additions are planned for 1988.

Hotels and catering Rank operates five four- and five-star hotels in central London, operates a number of motorway service stations and is developing a range of low-budget hotels and theme restaurants – including launching a Texan/Mexican chain in early 1988 called Texacana.

1986 saw a decline in hotel occupancy because of tourist fears about the risks of staying in London. Despite achieving improved room rates through increased prices after a major programme of capital refurbishment, the shortfall in guests hit profits. Hotel occupancy, despite unfavourable exchange rates, rose sharply in 1987.

The first half of 1987 showed a big profit bonus followed through for the full year and the company is well positioned to benefit from an increase in the number of tourists. The Royal Lancaster Hotel in London added a new restaurant in 1986 and this is seen as another way to generate revenue from existing sites. Rank also operates the Unicorn Hotel in Bristol, due for complete redevelopment in 1988, and manages the Hotel St Regis in Detroit. Rank formed Rank Hotels North America during 1987 to manage quality hotels, and has added three more management contracts, bringing its rooms under management to over 1,000.

Rank Motorway Services operates full service motorway service stations providing food, fuel and shops. A programme of modernisation is under way on a number of M4 and M6 sites. Major investments include the construction of a budget 60-room traveller's hotel on the M2 at Farthing Corner with more planned.

Rank is also planning to open more Texacana restaurants in 1988 and expects to have five in operation by the end of 1988. In aggregate these businesses are able to provide a relatively high margin to become cash-positive quickly, but are closely tied to the prevailing economic conditions in the UK.

Precision industries Rank controls a collection of UK- and US-based equipment manufacturers servicing highly profitable niche markets, the largest being Rank Taylor Hobson which manufactures metrology equipment and which is the world's leading supplier of surface geometry metrology equipment.

The industrial applications of metrology are now being exploited, linking precision metrology equipment to computer-controlled machine tools and robotics. A major portion of this company's output services the Japanese and US auto industries where demand has slackened recently. Other customers are mainly in the aerospace and electronics companies. Rank recently acquired Pneumo Precision in the US to enter the micro-surface generation equipment market to add to its micro-surface measuring capabilities.

Rank Cintel is the leading TV film scanner supplier to the world's TV and film industries. The Rank Cintel Mark III equipment is currently state of the art and has become an industrial standard in the Western world. Rank has recently demonstrated a high definition digital product.

Cintel also manufactures Slide File computer-based TV picture storage devices and has a marketing agreement with

Logica for large library systems. The Slide File product can be enhanced to include picture coloration and manipulative facilities. This is known as Art File. The company recently set up a joint venture company, Integrated Documatics, with Brown Root Vickers to manufacture and sell video micrographic systems.

Rank Electronic Tubes acquired the cathode ray tubes business of EMI in 1977 and Thorn Brimar in 1986. The company trades as Rank Brimar and is the largest cathode tube manufacturer in the UK. Rank Brimar manufactures specialist cathode ray tubes mainly for the military market and also manufactures associated equipment used in flight simulators and related products. The company's tubes are used in the F15, F16 and F18 aircraft, and most of the West's fighters.

Rank Pullin manufactures military sighting equipment for visual, infra-red and thermal imaging, and was sold in April 1988 for £22m to GEC.

GEOGRAPHICAL REVIEW

Rank is still predominantly a UK-based services business with a major worldwide associate, Rank Xerox. European and North American interests are growing but still represented only 14.1% of turnover in 1987, with the UK accounting for 84% and the rest of the world the balance.

North America clearly is being targeted as a major area for expansion in addition to the existing UK leisure interests, which should continue to repay capital investment well into the 1990s.

North America Strand Lighting is now the number one supplier of stage lighting in the US after Rank acquired its major competitor, Electro Controls of Salt Lake City in 1986. This boosted Strand's profits by 50%. Together with the subsequent acquisition of Quartz Color/Ianiro of Italy, the world's leading TV studio lighting equipment manufacturer, Rank is now a dominant provider of equipment and services to the film industry.

Rank Development, another US company, is responsible for the development of the Kingston Plantation hotel, residential and conference site at Lake Arrowhead, Myrtle Beach on the coast of South Carolina. The first phase of this luxury development started selling in 1986 with completion expected in 1988/89. The second phase is now beginning in what has been a very successful venture. Further similar ventures are likely.

Profits from North America could be approximately doubled in 1988 by the acquisition early in March for $180m (£102m) of Ahnert Enterprises, a leisure development company based in Bushkill, Pennsylvania, with substantial east-coast interests. The book value of the assets acquired was $154m and it was anticipated that property revaluation would reduce or even eliminate goodwill, on which basis Rank's gearing may have risen to 35% to 40%.

Ahnert's businesses include the operation of 14 private caravan resorts on the east coast of the US under the same Outdoor World. It owns 2,250 acres of land in the Pocono Mountains, 90 miles west of New York City, where it operates a wide variety of recreational facilities, sells plots of land and constructs and sells timeshare units. It also owns the franchises of the Yogi Bear Jellystone Park and Safari World resorts, under which 102 public caravan resorts operate.

In the year to April 1987 these businesses produced a pre-tax profit of $14m on turnover of $16m, and in addition to the price looking a good one for Rank, the acquisition appears to be a logical fit, since Rank has experience of this kind of business, has been seeking further US exposure and will bring financial muscle to develop Ahnert further.

Australia/Asia Recent closures and disposals have steadily diluted Rank's former long-standing operations in Australia and New Zealand and trading profits were £2.0m in 1987 against £3.1m in 1986.

CORPORATE CALENDAR

Year end	31 October
Preliminary results	January
Report and accounts	February
AGM	March
Final dividend paid	April
Interim results	July
Interim dividend paid	November

DIRECTORS' HOLDINGS

	Fully-paid ordinary shares	Options
DV Atterton	1,000	50,188
LH Bond	—	31,398
Sir Arthur Bryan	1,000	—
HA Crichton-Miller	—	60,000
J Daly	—	60,000
Sir Leslie Fletcher	1,000	2,418
MB Gifford	500	152,418
Sir Patrick Meaney	1,016	62,418
Sir Denis Mountain	8,465	
The Hon. Angus Ogilvy	2,679	2,418
NV Turnbull	2,500	39,940
DM Yates	50	62,418

Total directors' remuneration in 1987 was £752,000, of which the chairman received £79,000 and the highest-paid director £166,000.

PRINCIPAL SUBSIDIARIES AND RELATED COMPANIES

Film and television services
Pinewood Studios Limited, Rank Advertising Films Limited, Rank Audio Visual Limited, Rank Film Distributors Limited, Rank Film Laboratories Limited, Rank Theatres Limited, Rank Video Services Limited

Holidays and recreation
Ahnert Enterprises Inc – US, Butlin's Limited, Haven Leisure Limited, Rank Amusements Limited, Showboat Holdings Limited, Top Rank Limited, Wings Limited

Hotels and catering
Rank Hotels Limited, Rank Motorway Services Limited

Precision industries
Rank Precision Industries Inc – US, Rank Precision Industries Limited, Strand Lighting Inc – US, Strand Lighting Limited

Leisure developments
Rank Development Inc – US

Holding and other companies
A Kershaw & Sons Plc, Rank Holdings (UK) Limited, Rank Industries Australia Limited – Australia, Rank Overseas Holdings Limited, Rank Precision Industries (Holdings) Limited, Rank RX Holdings Limited

BRAND NAMES

Arital, Blue Line Cruisers, Butlin's, Cal Air International, Cintel, Gaumont, Haven Leisure, Odeon, Outdoor World – US, Pinewood, Rank Cintel, Rank Taylor Hobson, Rank Video, Rank Xerox, Royal Garden Hotel, Royal Lancaster Hotel, Safari World – US, Showboat, Strand, Texacana, Top Rank Clubs, Yogi Bear Jellystone Park – US

CONTACTS AND FURTHER INFORMATION

Rodney Rycroft, Public relations director, The Rank Organisation, 6 Connaught Pace, London W2 2EZ. Tel: 01-629 7454.

RANKS HOVIS MCDOUGALL PLC

GENERAL INFORMATION

Head office RHM Centre, Alma Road, Windsor, Berkshire SL4 3ST.
Tel: 0753 857123

Directors Joseph Rank FRCP (Hon) (president), Sir Peter Reynolds CBE (chairman), SG Metcalfe (managing and deputy chairman), TS Howden (assistant managing), P Coker FCA, RG Rogerson CA. *Non-exec* The Hon Patrick Best, JEH Collins MBE DSC, Dr J Edelman CBE, JH Gunn

Advisers Morgan Grenfell & Co Ltd

Auditors Hodgson Impey

Registrars Barclays Bank Registration Department

Brokers Cazenove & Co

Solicitors Richards Butler

GENERAL FINANCIAL INFORMATION

Market capitalisation	£1.194bn at 1 January 1988
Capital structure	
Issued ordinary shares (25p)	338.8m
Issued preference shares (£1)	2m 6% First CP
	2.2m 6% 'A' CP
	2.5m 6% 'B' CP
Warrants	None
Convertibles	59m 4¾% ESC 2003 (285.714 ordinary shares per £1000 bond)
Traded options	None
ADRs	None
Shareholders over 5%	Goodman Fielder Wattie Ltd 29.9%

FT CATEGORY

FT: Food, groceries, etc
FT-A: Food manufacturing

MAJOR ACTIVITIES

Ranks Hovis McDougall is the third largest UK food company. The group's products are on sale in every supermarket and food shop in Britain and in many countries abroad. It employs about 36,000 people in eleven countries. It has taken a little more than 100 years for RHM to grow from a young man working alone in a rented windmill to one of Europe's largest food processing companies.

The Company's foundations were laid in 1875 by Joseph Rank. In 1933, when the business was producing enough flour to provide one-seventh of the population of Great Britain with bread, Joseph Rank Ltd became a public company. Joseph Rank was a philanthropist on a large scale and set up several charity finances which still benefit educational establishments.

In 1957, Hovis and McDougall, two other British food groups, amalgamated to form Hovis-McDougall Ltd and five years later this company was acquired by Rank, to form Ranks Hovis McDougall. The range of packaged food brand leaders was extended in 1968 when RHM acquired Cerebos Ltd, and RHM Foods Ltd was subsequently created.

In 1987 RHM purchased Avana which increased the group's exposure to the growing value-added, chilled recipe dish market and in the branded preserves market with James Robertson & Son.

FINANCIAL HISTORY

Pre-tax profits in the year to September 1987 rose 28% to £116.1m, while attributable profits jumped 68% to £86.4m, reflecting a £12.7m extraordinary credit.

Profit margins continued to show a strong recovery from the very low levels five years ago. In 1987 they rose by 1% to 7.5%. Shareholders' funds fell in 1987 from £302.6m to £251.6m, reflecting the net effect of writing off goodwill arising on acquisitions, principally Avana. The last fiscal year also saw a further rise in the return on funds employed, up to 24.7% from the 1986 level of 20.1%. The 1982 rate of return was only 12%.

SHARE PRICE HISTORY

The most significant new development was the purchase by Goodman Fielder, the Australian food group, of a 14.9% stake in the group previously held by S&W Berisford. This purchase was made in August 1986 at a price of 259p, which at the time represented a 23% premium over the market price. In 1987, Goodman Fielder purchased further blocks of shares to bring its total holding up to 29.9%, the maximum holding permissible without triggering a full bid.

This change of ownership of a strategic minority stake has inevitably fuelled considerable takeover speculation. However, RHM has had to live with a significant minority holder of its equity since 1982 when British Sugar acquired a 14.9% stake. RHM responded by taking a 10.5% stake in British Sugar for strategic reasons. Subsequently RHM sold this stake to S&W Berisford and this had the effect of making British Sugar a subsidiary of Berisford's. Consequently, S&W Berisford inherited the British Sugar stake in RHM.

Throughout this period, RHM's shares have risen steadily in both absolute and relative terms as the management embarked upon major rationalisation and investment programmes, resulting in a substantial improvement in profitability. The shares quickly recovered after the October 1987 share crash, and have shown strong relative outperformance since mid-1987.

SENIOR MANAGEMENT

Joseph Rank became president of RHM in 1981, having previously been chairman from 1969. He began his RHM career in 1936 and became assistant managing director of the main operating company in 1952 when he joined the main board. Joseph Rank has considerable experience in the milling and baking industry and has twice been president of the Incorporated National Association of British & Irish Millers.

Sir Peter Reynolds CBE joined the group as assistant managing director in 1971, was appointed managing director the following year and in 1981 became chairman. He holds a number of appointments in the food industry and, following the award of the CBE in 1975, was created a knight in 1985. Sir Peter is a member of the Industrial Development Board for Northern Ireland.

SG Metcalfe joined the group in 1956 as a management trainee. From 1963 he held senior management appointments within the group before becoming responsible for the overseas division and in 1973 the cereals division. SG Metcalfe was appointed to the board in 1979, became deputy managing director in 1980 and managing director in the following year. He is a member of the executive committee of The Food and Drink Federation.

TS Howden joined the group in 1983, having spent much of the previous 15 years with the European operations of Reckitt & Colman. Following senior appointments in the cereals, grocery and bakeries divisions, he was appointed planning director of the group in 1985. In June 1987, TS Howden became managing director of Avana which had been acquired by RHM earlier in the year.

R Rogerson, a chartered accountant, joined the Cerebos group in 1957, and was appointed chief executive of RHM Foods Ltd in 1971 and of the general products division in 1975. He was appointed finance director in 1976.

FIVE YEAR FINANCIAL INFORMATION

Year	Turnover (£m)	Pre-tax (£m)	Earnings (p)	Dividends net (p)	Dividend cover (x)	Net assets (p)	Price (p) High	Price (p) Low	PER (x) High	PER (x) Low	Yield (%) High	Yield (%) Low
1983	1,634	44.1	10.9	4.0	2.7	90	78	52	11.0	8.3	10.70	7.25
1984	1,213	50.7	12.2	4.4	2.8	92	138	73	17.6	10.7	7.93	4.51
1985	1,314	70.8	15.5	5.3	2.9	97	186	123	16.3	10.7	5.06	3.53
1986	1,414	90.8	20.7	6.6	3.1	106	290	157	18.7	12.1	4.81	2.91
1987	1,544	116.1	24.0	8.5	2.8	86	368	242	19.3	10.6	4.11	2.66

Dr J Edelman joined the group in 1973 as head of research, having previously been Professor of Botany at Queen Elizabeth College, London. His research activities were mainly in the field of plant physiology and biochemistry. Dr Edelman, who has been a director since 1982, recently relinquished his role as director of research, and is now devoting more of his time to the development of myco-protein.

P Coker was appointed to the board in July 1987 to succeed T Howden as planning director. P Coker is also managing director of the general products division.

The Hon Patrick Best was appointed a non-executive director in 1984. JEH Collins has been a non-executive director of the group since 1965. He was chairman of Morgan Grenfell Holdings and is currently chairman of Guardian Royal Exchange Assurance. J Gunn was appointed a non-executive director in November 1987. He is chairman of British & Commonwealth Holdings.

CAPITAL

The equity base remained stable until May 1987, when the group acquired Avana via an issue of shares and cash. The number of shares increased from 284.2m in August 1986 to 338m.

There also exists £6.7m worth of preference shares which are issued in three different classes and which carry a coupon of 4.2% with a related tax credit. In November 1987 the company announced that it intended to issue a £59m convertible Eurobond issue with a view to saving interest costs of £2.5m per year.

By September 1987, options were outstanding on 9.2m shares, generally exercisable at various dates to 11 June 1997, at subscription prices ranging from 41p to 318p. Directors' holdings were 117,486 at 5 September 1987, and options held by directors totalled 1.198m.

GROUP REVIEW

RHM is a major UK food company with significant market shares in some important, if mature, grocery markets. During the 1970s it was long held as a disappointing concern, being badly placed in the milling and baking industry. However, the management has embarked on a bold investment strategy and has turned around the baking division into a considerably improved and efficient operation.

An acquisition and divestment programme, along with higher operating cash flow, strengthened the group's finances, so that in 1987 it was able to acquire Avana, a leader in value-added food products, even though the bid was strongly contested. Against this background, the management has had to live with a significant minority holder of the equity. The fact that this 29.9% holding is now held by the acquisitive Australian group Goodman Fielder has perhaps increased the

takeover speculation that surrounded RHM for the past few years. Whether any formal bid materialises remains to be seen. What is more certain is that the RHM management is determined to pursue its carefully devised strategy without feeling pressurised. So far the strategy has paid off, and with Avana now under its control the longer term outlook is considered very encouraging.

Bakery division British Bakeries operates 25 bakeries which supply about one-third of the wrapped loaves sold in Britain. These are sold under the Mothers Pride, Champion, Country Pride, Hovis, Windmill Bakery and Nimble brand names. An extensive range of morning goods is also sold under these labels. Mothers Pride is the nation's best known white sliced loaf. Wrapped bread sales, particularly those of wholemeal, are increasing through public awareness of bread as a healthy food, and a growing belief in the importance of fibre in the daily diet.

Hovis remains Britain's best known name in brown bread. It sells 25m stoneground wholemeal loaves a year. Under the Windmill banner, launched in 1981, RHM encouraged the resurgence in growth in brown and wholemeal bread, and is now the recognised leader and innovator in the brown bread market.

Share price and relative to FT-A All-Share

RANKS, HOVIS
Relative to All Share (R.H.SCALE)

While bread is a vast market, the commodity nature of the product has led to intense competition between the major bakery companies. Moreover, supermarkets have very often used bread as a loss-leader. In order to combat these pressures, RHM has been forced – along with the other majors in the industry – to implement a widespread reorganisation programme since 1982. In RHM's case this has encouraged a major turnround into profit and a substantial capital investment programme. The end result is that the group is now able to meet the shifting demands of the consumer and to face the increased strength of the supermarkets with greater confidence.

Cereals division Ranks Hovis makes and sells more flour than any other European miller, and supplies almost one-third of the UK flour market. Fifteen mills are strategically placed throughout the country. Many have undergone extensive remodelling and expansion as part of RHM's investment in its core businesses. A wide variety of flours is milled and the Hovis and Granary flours are exclusively milled. Much of the output goes to British Bakeries and free trade bakers for bread making. Some is packed by the grocery division and sold in supermarkets under the McDougalls and Be-Ro brand names, both market leaders in their field.

The division also includes RHM Ingredient Supplies, producers of rusks, crumb coatings and seasonings for commercial users and own-label breakfast cereals.

Also in the division is the Tenstar group of four companies. Tenstar Products are suppliers of starch syrups, glucose and gluten made from wheat flour for specialised purposes; Stadis is a joint venture with Distillers Company; Staper is a joint venture with Reed International.

The combined trading profits of the milling and baking divisions in 1987 were £45m, equivalent to 38% of the group total and up 27.1% on 1986. Turnover was £614.4m, up 1.4%.

Manor Foods division This division consists of: the group's packaged cake business Manor Bakeries, which produces the popular Mr Kipling and Cadbury's cakes; Heinzel, a frozen cake company; and a French bakery company, Sofrapain.

Mr Kipling cakes are baked at four English bakeries while Sofrapain, with 12 bakeries, is the largest baker of baguettes in France. The Mr Kipling range of cakes was launched in France in 1984 with good success. Heinzel (London & Vienna) Ltd was acquired in mid-1987.

The division has a good record of new product innovation while there is consistent investment in marketing. In 1987 trading profits at £16.9m represented 14.5% of the group total, up 11.1% on 1986. Turnover was £142.8m, up 9.5%.

Grocery division RHM Foods' brand names are familiar sights on supermarket shelves. They include such brands as Atora, Bisto, Be-Ro, Chesswood, Paxo, McDougalls flour and mixes, Saxa and Cerebos salt, One-Cal and Capri-Sun soft drinks. The Sharwood's range is the pre-eminent brand in the ethnic food category. Trading profits were £17.5m in 1987 and represented 15% of the group total, up 12.1% on 1986. Turnover was £182.4m, up 17.6%.

General products division This division includes bakery and catering supply companies, mushroom farms, a pulse packing factory, chocolate and bulk jam factories, coffee suppliers, fast food restaurants and a pasta company. Cheese making and processing factories were sold in mid-1987.

McDougalls Catering Foods supply schools, industrial outlets, institutions and hospitals with a complete range of mixes, soups, dried meats and vegetables together with a range of high quality chilled foods. They also process and supply Rombouts coffee filters and distribute the Old El Paso range of Mexican foods. Goldrei Foucard manufactures and distributes a wide range of bakery sundries to the baking industry.

Recent investment in the group's two mushroom companies, Chesswood Produce and Shepherds Grove Mushrooms, has applied the very latest technology to mushroom growing in Britain.

The chocolate company Stewart & Arnold Caxton continued its satisfactory development and again showed growth of bulk sales to biscuit, confectionery and ice-cream manufacturers.

RHM Retail operates more than 300 bakery shops, many with snack take-away and coffee-shop facilities, supplied by RHM's own specialist bakeries. A major refurbishment and conversion programme is under way with the new shops trading under the Three Cooks name. Pasta Foods is a brand leader and manufactures pasta products under the Record pasta label.

The division's 1987 profits were £12.4m, equivalent to 10.6% of the total, up 29.1% on 1986. Turnover was £239.7m, up 6.9%.

Avana There are ten main subsidiaries in Avana, many of which are being integrated with RHM's existing divisional structure. Avana Bakeries manufactures cakes and pastries for own-label customers while Avana Meat produces a range of own-label pies and savoury products. RF Brookes is Avana's principal chilled recipe dish company. Ledbury Preserves manufactures jams, preserves and De L'Ora fruit juice. At Lesme and OP Chocolate, chocolate couverture, wafer biscuits and chocolate novelties are produced. James Robertson produces a wide range of jams and marmalades under the Robertson's brand. Scotia Barry Foods packs dried fruits, and Viota is a major producer of own-label breakfast cereals. Peny SA in France is a vegetable canner.

The Avana division contributed £9.2m in four and a half months to 1987 trading profits, which represented 8% of total group earnings, on turnover of £80.3m.

Pacific region RHM's interests include food companies in

CHAIRMAN'S STATEMENT

'The Group's profit before taxation for the 53 weeks to 5th September 1987 rose by 28% to £116.1m compared with £90.8m for the previous year.... This further substantial increase in profits over 1986 was due to improvements in all aspects of the Group's business....

Packaged cake under the Mr Kipling brand produced record results and benefited from its accelerating programme of new product launches.... The Grocery division also achieved record profits....

Our milling and baking business improved its results substantially over the previous year. After many years of rationalisation and heavy capital investment, the bread bakeries achieved a full year of profitable trading....

The General Products divisions made record profits with good contributions coming from its mushrooms, industrial catering, pasta and food retailing operations....

Avana Group ... achieved results well above expectations and significantly ahead of the comparable period for last year.

The profits of our overseas operations were considerably improved despite the fact that the US pasta businesses were sold early in the financial year.... Cerebos Pacific Limited, despite difficult trading in the Far East, had a further record year with excellent contributions from Australia, New Zealand, and the growing restaurant business in Singapore.

Profits arising from disposals of surplus properties continued. The higher interest charges arose from funding part of the cost of acquiring Avana.

The directors recommend a final dividend of 5.84 pence per share ... which represents an increase of 30 per cent over last year's final dividend....

All shareholders are being sent with their copy of this Annual report my separate personal letter concerning Goodman Fielder's shareholding.... I shall be very pleased to hear from shareholders with their comments.

Although we are in the early stages of our new financial year, the profits to date are ahead of last year and I am confident that we shall have another record year.' *Sir Peter Reynolds*

Singapore, Malaysia, Thailand, Taiwan, Indonesia, Australia and New Zealand. Cerebos Pacific, quoted on the Singapore stock exchange and 70% owned by RHM, has 13 production units.

In 1987, Cerebos Pacific made a trading profit of £13.9m, equivalent to 12% of the group total, up 12.1% on 1986. Trading in Australia and New Zealand was strong, but in other parts of the Pacific Basin trading conditions remained difficult.

US RHM activities are focused on the production of apple juice, tomato sauce, peanut butter, pickles and preserves. There are 13 operating sites located mainly in the east and mid-east states of the country. Pilgrim Farms and Carriage House Foods were acquired in 1987.

In 1987 trading profits of £9.8m represented 8.4% of the group total, up 3.1% on 1986. Turnover was £184.1m, down 9%, though this was because of disposals. Continuing businesses increased sales by 20%, and underlying dollar profit growth was 15%.

GEOGRAPHICAL REVIEW

The largest single overseas market is the Pacific region where Cerebos Pacific is based. In 1987 it accounted for 12% of profits. The US operations contributed a further 8% bringing the total overseas content to 20%.

CORPORATE CALENDAR

Year end	5 September
Preliminary results	December
Report and accounts	December
AGM	January
Final dividend paid	January
Interim results	May
Interim dividend paid	July

DIRECTORS' HOLDINGS

	Fully-paid ordinary shares	Options
Joseph Rank	83,030	—
Sir Peter Reynolds	4,405	357,759
SG Metcalfe	500	220,405
The Hon Patrick Best	6,000	—
JEH Collins	12,500	—
Dr J Edelman	3,189	3,099
TS Howden	5,862	144,333
RG Rogerson	2,000	233,434
P Coker	—	239,179
Trustee holdings	976,453	—

In addition to the above, Sir Peter Reynolds, SG Metcalfe and TS Howden had beneficial interests in 9,000, 4,000 and 4,000 fully paid shares respectively of Singapore $0.50 each in Cerebos Pacific Limited.

Total directors' remuneration in 1986/87 is £781,000, of which the chairman received £101,000, and the highest-paid director £173,000.

PRINCIPAL SUBSIDIARIES AND RELATED COMPANIES

Avana Bakeries Ltd, Avana Meat Products Ltd, British Bakeries Ltd, Butterkup Foods Ltd, Cerebos (Australia) Ltd, Cerebos Gregg's Ltd – New Zealand, Cerebos Pacific Ltd – Singapore (70%), CGPA Peny SA – France, Ch. Goldrei Foucard & Son Ltd, Chesswood Produce Ltd, Heinzel (London & Vienna) Ltd, Hovis Ltd, Indian Summer Inc – US, JA Sharwood & Co Ltd, James Robertson & Sons Preserve Manufacturers, Ledbury Preserves (1928) Ltd, Lesme Ltd, Manor Bakeries Ltd, McDougalls Catering Foods Ltd, National Preserves Inc – US trading as Carriage House Foods, New Tech Snacks Inc – US, OP Chocolate Ltd, Pasta Foods Ltd, Pilgrim Farms Inc – US, RF Brookes Ltd, RGB Coffee Ltd, RH Clarke Ltd, RHM Computing Ltd, RHM Exports Ltd, RHM Foods (Ireland) Ltd, RHM Foods Ltd, RHM Ingredient Supplies Ltd, RHM Holdings (USA) Inc, RHM Ltd, RHM Research and Engineering Ltd, RHM Retail Ltd, Ranks Hovis Ltd, Scotia Barry Foods Ltd, Shepherds Grove Mushrooms Ltd,

Société Française de Panification et de Pâtisserie-Lyon SA – France, Stewart & Arnold Ltd, Supreme Salt Company Ltd, Tenstar Products Ltd, The Red Wing Company Inc – US, Theresa Friedman & Sons Inc – US, Tiffany Sharwood's Frozen Foods Ltd, Viota Foods Ltd, Western Foods Company Inc – US, William Brock & Son Ltd

BRAND NAMES

Atora, Be-Ro, Bisto, Capri-Sun, Cerebos, Champion, Chesswood, Country Pride, De L'Ora, Hovis, McDougalls, Mothers Pride, Mr Kipling, Nimble, Old El Paso, One-Cal, Paxo, RHM flour, Record pasta, Robertson's, Rombouts, Saxa, Sharwoods, Three Cooks, Viota, Windmill Bakery

CONTACTS AND FURTHER INFORMATION

GA Garnett, Company secretary, Ranks Hovis McDougall PLC, RHM Centre, Alma Road, Windsor, Berkshire SL4 3ST. Tel: 0753 857123.

RECKITT & COLMAN plc

GENERAL INFORMATION

Head office	One Burlington Lane, London W4 2RW. Tel: 01-994 6464
Directors	Sir Michael J Colman Bt (chairman), J St Lawrence (chief executive), IG Dobbie, RMM Foster, PC Knee, PJ Maydon, OT Parmenter, JJ West. *Non-exec* TJA Colman DCL, AJ Dalby, J-C Larréché, SM Peretz MBE FPS, MR Valentine, KH Walley FEng
Advisers	SG Warburg & Co Ltd
Auditors	Price Waterhouse
Registrars	National Westminster Bank Registrar's Department
Brokers	Cazenove & Co·
Solicitors	Slaughter and May

GENERAL FINANCIAL INFORMATION

Market capitalisation	£1.162bn at 1 January 1988
Capital structure	
Issued ordinary shares (25p)	148.3m
Issued preference shares (£1)	4.5m 4.5% CP
Warrants	None
Convertibles	None
Traded options	None
ADRs	None
Shareholders over 5%	None

FT CATEGORY

FT: Industrials (miscel.)
FT-A: Health and household products

MAJOR ACTIVITIES

Reckitt & Colman is a major international company with an annual turnover exceeding £1.3bn. It manufactures and markets a wide range of speciality food, household, wine, toiletry, pharmaceutical, and fine art and graphics products, including many popular and well-known brand names. It has manufacturing interests in 38 countries and markets its products throughout the world.

Over half the group's profits come from its household and toiletries division, 20% from the food and wine division, 17% from the pharmaceutical division, and the balance from its colours and fine art divisions. The group's industrial cleaning business was sold in late 1987.

There are no key economic variables that particularly affect the company. Historically it has proved to be relatively recession-proof in sales growth. However, because it is geared, the company is perhaps the most interest-rate-sensitive in the health and household sector.

Companies with which it is comparable include Beecham, which has a much larger pharmaceutical division, and Unilever, which is a much bigger company with a major consumer and toiletry business. Reckitt & Colman is relatively small in comparison to the majors in the branded consumer product market.

Growth by acquisition offers opportunities for production, marketing and administrative synergy. Reckitt has demonstrated its ability to respond to these opportunities through its acquisitions of Airwick, Durkee Famous Foods and Gold Seal.

FINANCIAL HISTORY

In 1987 pre-tax profits improved by £28.1m from £139.4m to £167.6m, an increase of 20.2%. This compares with an increase in pre-tax profits of 17.6% in 1986 over 1985. Turnover has shown steady increases, rising 12.3% to £1.492bn in 1987, and up 62.4% over 1982's turnover of £918.5m. This growth, however, can be attributed to acquisitions rather than organic growth, which is difficult to achieve

in the relatively static household and food markets.

In 1987 earnings per share showed growth for the seventh year in succession, increasing by 18% from 57.8p to 68.2p. This compared with growth in earnings per share of 19.9% in 1986 over 1985, and 121.4% over 1982's earnings of 30.8p. There was also a modest rise in pre-tax margins from 10.9% in 1986 to 11.2% in 1987. Dividends have shown a rise similar to earnings. They were up 17.3% in 1987 to 21.7p and up 103% over 1982.

SHARE PRICE HISTORY

Reckitt & Colman's shares trade on a price/earnings multiple in line with the average for industrial companies, much lower than the health and household average and conservative even for the foods sector.

The shares have enjoyed a steady rise since 1982, trading close to the FT-A All-Share index in relative terms. The price has increased from a trading range of 248p to 400p in 1982 to one of 668p to 1213p in 1987. Hard hit in the October 1987 share crash, the shares were trading in the 830p area in late April 1988.

SENIOR MANAGEMENT

John St Lawrence, who had been with Reckitt & Colman since 1953 and on the board since 1978, replaced John West as chief executive when he retired in May 1988. Sir Michael Colman is chairman and IG Dobbie is director of finance.

RMM Foster is group director for the UK and Europe. PC Knee is group director with responsibility for North America, PJ Maydon director for Latin America and Africa, OT Parmenter director for Australasia and Asia.

CAPITAL

In October 1984 Reckitt & Colman issued 24.7m shares in a one for five rights issue at 445p. In 1986 the group spent £175m on acquiring businesses and received £22.5m from disposals, a net expenditure of £152.5m. The businesses acquired were Durkee Famous Foods, Herb-Ox and Gold Seal. Consequently, net borrowings rose during the year by £106.9m from £41m to £148m. This was comfortably within the group's total financial capacity, leaving gearing at around 35% at the 1986 year-end.

In June 1987 the group purchased the Australasian manufacturing, marketing and distribution rights of various Beecham brands for £11.5m. In November 1987 Reckitt bought Kukident, the denture cleaning business, for £24m. A number of businesses were disposed of, including its Austra-

Share price and relative to FT-A All-Share

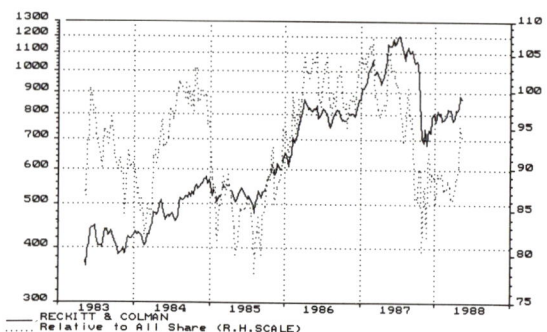

FIVE YEAR FINANCIAL INFORMATION

Year	Turnover (£m)	Pre-tax (£m)	Earnings (p)	Dividends net (p)	Dividend cover (x)	Net assets (p)	Price (p) High	Low	PER (x) High	Low	Yield (%) High	Low
1983	981.0	88.8	36.9	11.97	2.3	224	452	360	16.7	11.8	4.12	3.28
1984	1,124.0	106.4	41.9	14.14	2.2	277	578	403	17.0	12.5	3.94	3.31
1985	1,267.0	123.0	48.2	16.00	2.4	218	651	478	17.1	13.2	4.27	3.25
1986	1,329.0	139.5	57.8	18.50	2.5	185	900	608	22.0	15.0	3.48	2.53
1987	1,493	167.6	68.1	21.7	2.6	274	1,210	680	21.6	10.2	3.94	2.09

lian wine business, G Gramp, for £15.9m. Further acquisitions are expected in Germany, Italy and the US. Strong net cash flow reduced gearing at the 1987 year-end to just 11%.

In October 1987 the group realised £12.75m in cash from BET for its UK industrial cleaning operations and £9.3m in cash from the Swedish company Procordia for those in Denmark and Sweden. These formed the group's entire interests in this area.

GROUP REVIEW

Household and toiletry This is now Reckitt & Colman's largest division, contributing 46.2% of group sales and 50.8% of 1987 pre-tax profit in 1987. The acquisition of Airwick for £165m in 1985 and Gold Seal for £21m in 1986 have materially assisted the development of a strong global household product business.

In 1987 sales were up 6.3% to £689.6m and operating profits increased by 14.9% to £84.3m. An important reason for the profit increase was the better-than-expected results from the integration of Airwick.

Well-known products include Cherry Blossom and Meltonian shoe polishes, Robin laundry aids, Mr Sheen and Cleen-o-Pine, Mansion and Brasso polishes, Windolene, Steradent denture care, Supersoft shampoos and hairspray, and Nulon skin care. Australasian Beecham brands acquired in 1987 were Maclean's, Eno and Brylcreem. Kukident is a useful addition to Reckitt's existing Steradent brand in West Germany and should increase sales there by 50%.

In geographical terms, the US is a strong performer. The acquisition of Gold Seal towards the end of 1986 has made a significant addition to the portfolio of products there. Most of the markets in continental Europe are performing well. Latin America is subject to general volatility but is still achieving profits growth in local currency terms.

In the UK determined competition is encountered, but the business is holding its own and there is no shortage of innovative product and marketing ideas to be exploited in the future. The businesses in Australasia, the Far East and parts of Africa all performed satisfactorily in terms of local currency.

Food and wine In 1987 the division contributed 36.3% of group sales and 20.4% of pre-tax profit. Sales rose by 27.1% to £541.2m and pre-tax profits increased by 34.1% to £39.3m.

Well-known brands include Colman's mustards, condiments and cooking sauces and OK sauces. The Beecham brands recently licensed in Australasia include Bovril, Lucozade, Ribena and Horlicks.

Results for overseas businesses are being affected by adverse movements in exchange rates. An exception to this is Holland, where Conimex, the group's Indonesian food ingredients business is performing well. Significant events have been the disposal in the second half of 1985 of the US potato business and the acquisitions in 1986 of Durkee Famous Foods and Herb-Ox. The integration of Durkee with RT French has

proceeded well. This speciality US food business made rapid progress in 1987.

The UK is performing well. Work on the major site development project at Norwich was completed in 1987. The benefits of the modernisation will begin to be realised. The disposal of the Gale's honey and lemon curd business at the end of 1986 is enabling Colman's of Norwich to concentrate on its important soft drinks, baby food, savoury food and wine businesses. Colman's introduced a range of Home Style wet sauces in 1987 and disposed of its wine business in early 1988.

Pharmaceutical In 1987 the division accounted for 9.0% of sales and 15.7% of pre-tax profit. Total sales were up 8.4% to £134.3m. Pre-tax profits were up 9.2% to £26.1m. One-third of turnover is in the southern hemisphere.

Major specialist pharmaceutical product lines are analgesics and gastro-intestinal aids. Temgesic is a strong analgesic, which is performing well. Buprenex, the US equivalent of Temgesic, continues to make progress. Temgesic itself has yet to be launched in France, but is successful in Italy and Spain. Colven, a treatment for irritable bowel syndrome, introduced in the UK in 1985, is achieving its objectives. The division is developing some very promising new drugs for use in the treatment of ulcers and possibly other gastric conditions.

Over the counter products include Deep Fresh foam bath and gels, Dettol antiseptics, Valderma antiseptic soap and cream, and various proprietary medicines – Codis, Disprin, Disprol, Solmin, Gaviscon, LemSip, Senokot and Fybogel.

Fine art and graphics In 1987 the division accounted for 1.9% of the group's sales and 1.9% of pre-tax profit. Sales increased by 6% to £29m and pre-tax profit decreased by 8.6% to £3.1m.

Product lines include: Winsor & Newton paints, brushes

CHAIRMAN'S STATEMENT

'To ensure the further growth and prosperity of Reckitt & Colman, close attention will continue to be given to pursuing its corporate strategy of developing its core businesses by a carefully planned programme in the areas of:

  (i) innovation
  (ii) management skills
  (iii) acquisition

Strong emphasis is being placed on internal growth by innovation. Innovation means more than increased investment in research and development, although they are an extremely important part of it. The innovation workshop programme, which started in 1985, has extended to most parts of the business throughout the world and a climate has been created in which original thinking and fresh ideas are encouraged, with the ultimate objective of creating new markets, strengthening shares in existing markets and increasing operational efficiency by the introduction of new technologies and improved management techniques.' *Sir Michael Colman*

and canvases; Reeves art materials for children; and Dryad craft kits and books. There is a thriving export business to the US and a strong market position in the UK.

Colours In 1987 the division accounted for 2.9% of group sales and 6.9% of pre-tax profit. Sales increased by 13.7% to £43.4m and pre-tax profit by 29.2% to £11.49m.

The division's main activity is the production of pigments for paints and other industrial materials. Globo, the group's colours business in Brazil, is performing outstandingly. Exports, particularly to the US, are an increasingly important part of operations.

GEOGRAPHICAL REVIEW

Reckitt & Colman is a truly international company. In recent years, Reckitt & Colman has reduced its relative exposure in Australia, Asia and Africa through acquisition in the US.

In 1987 the UK accounted for 24.4% of turnover and 30.5% of pre-tax profits, including exports. Household products, toiletries, food and wine and pharmaceuticals were the major contributors.

Europe accounted for 21.4% of turnover and 11.6% of pre-tax profits, with household products and toiletries being the major contributors. North America contributed 27.8% of turnover and 17.6% of pre-tax profits, with food and household products and toiletries as the major items.

The remaining 26.4% of turnover and 40.3% of pre-tax profits from Australasia, Africa and Latin America is dominated by household products and toiletries, and, to a lesser extent, food. Australasia and Asia produced 16.6% of pre-tax profits on 12.3% of turnover.

CORPORATE CALENDAR

Year end	31 December
Preliminary results	April
Report and accounts	May
AGM	May
Final dividend paid	July
Interim results	September
Interim dividend paid	January

DIRECTORS' HOLDINGS

	Fully-paid ordinary shares	Options
Sir Michael J Colman	226,223	49,926
as trustee	69,852	
TJA Colman DCL	368,883	—
as trustee	104,558	—
IG Dobbie	283	9,512
RMM Foster	1,435	11,546
RC Knee	9,050	45,677
JC Larréché	1,000	—
PJ Maydon	2,484	50,649
T Parmenter	605	50,649
SM Peretz MBE FPS	2,160	—
JSt Lawrence	4,682	60,045
MR Valentine	500	—
KH Walley FEng	400	—
JJ West	4,880	72,025

Total directors' remuneration for 1986 was not disclosed. The chairman received £53,844 and the highest paid director £140,554.

PRINCIPAL SUBSIDIARIES AND RELATED COMPANIES

Airwick Industries Inc – US, Durkee Famous Foods Inc – UK, RT French Co – US, Reckitt & Colman – France, Reckitt & Colman Australia Ltd, Reckitt & Colman Ltd – Overseas Ltd, Reckitt & Colman Products Ltd, Reckitt & Colman South Africa (Pty) Ltd, Representações Reckitt & Colman Brazil Limitada

BRAND NAMES

Airwick, Bonjela, Brasso, Cardinal, Charbonnier, Cherry Blossom, Cleen-O-Pine, Codis, Colman's, Colven, Deep Fresh Play Tub, Dettol, Dettox, Disprin, Disprol, Dryad, Duraglit, Floret, Franz Reh, Fybogel, Gaviscon, Goldilocks, Gumption, Harpic, Haze, Junior Disprol, Junior Lemsip, Lemsip, Lloyd's Cream, Mansion, Meltonian, Moussec, Mr Sheen, Olasz Riesling, Oven Pad, Petits Domaines, Pripsen, Propert's, Reckitt's Blue, Reeves, Robin, Senokot, Silvo, Solmin, Sunny Jim, Temgesic, Timocort, Timodine, Timoped, Tokay, Transvasin, Valderma, Valpeda, Veuve du Vernay, Welsch Riesling, Wincarnis, Winsor & Newton, Wren's, Zebrite, Zip

CONTACTS AND FURTHER INFORMATION

David Clifford, Corporate public relations, Reckitt & Coleman Plc, One Burlington Lane, London W4 2RW. Tel. 01-994 6464.

REDLAND PLC

GENERAL INFORMATION

Head office	Redland House, Reigate, Surrey RH2 0SJ. Tel: 0737 242488
Directors	Sir Colin Corness (chairman), RS Napier (managing), T Walker MIMechE (managing), GMN Corbett, GTE Priestley, D Taylor DLC. *Non-exec* JE Bolton CBE DSC DL, Lord Ezra MBE LLD, Sir Christophor Laidlaw, JWM Wallace, J White CA
Advisers	Baring Brothers & Co Ltd, Morgan Grenfell & Co Ltd, Morgan Guaranty Trust Co New York, Morgan Stanley International, SG Warburg & Co Ltd
Auditors	Price Waterhouse
Registrars	Ravensbourne Registration Services Ltd
Brokers	Cazenove & Co
Solicitors	Slaughter and May

GENERAL FINANCIAL INFORMATION

Market capitalisation	£1.084bn at 1 January 1988
Capital structure	
Issued ordinary shares (25p)	269.7m
Issued preference shares (£1)	0.56m 5% CP
Warrants	£7.7m, 130.37 ordinary shares per warrant at 135p per share to 15 March 1991
Convertibles	£60m 7.25% ESC 2002 (18.52 shares per £100 of stock)
Traded options	None
ADRs	Five ordinary shares per ADR
Shareholders over 5%	None

FT CATEGORY

FT: Building, timber, roads
FT-A: Building materials

MAJOR ACTIVITIES

Redland is a UK-based multinational supplier of materials and services to the construction industry. Its principal products are concrete roof tiles, aggregates and clay bricks.

Other products include clay roof tiles and interlocking slates, readymix concrete and asphalt, plastic and metal roofing systems and ceramic wall and floor tiles. A recent addition to the group's range of products is plasterboard. In partnership with the Australian company CSR, Redland is making a challenge to BPB's domination of this market in the UK and Europe.

Redland is a major UK distributor of domestic and industrial fuels. Building materials account for approximately 80% of turnover and over 90% of operating profit.

The group operates in over 30 countries. More than half its assets are invested outside the UK. Most of the overseas businesses are joint ventures conducted in partnership with local shareholders and management. Most of the group's profits are derived from the UK, US, West Germany and Australia.

Redland's competitors vary according to activity and geographical region. Tarmac and RMC compete with its aggregates business. Tarmac competes with Redland in brick manufacture.

FINANCIAL HISTORY

Turnover for 1986/87, including that of related companies, was up just 0.7% to £1.300bn. Pre-tax profits were up 11.8% to £130.7m. Earnings per share were up 15.8% to 36p and annual net dividends up 23.9% to 13p.

Since 1982/83 Redland's turnover has increased modestly by 29%. During the same period pre-tax profits have increased by 106%. Earnings per share have risen by 111.8%.

The main reason for the rise in pre-tax profits has been the steady increase in the group's pre-tax margins, from 6.4% in 1982/83 to over 10% in 1986/87. An additional factor has been the group's reducing tax charge, because of declining UK tax rates and Redland's ability to offset previous US losses against the higher rates then current.

The 1986/87 results were depressed by the lower value of the dollar but in local terms the group's US businesses improved. Elsewhere progress was made in all the group's major regions except Australia, where poor results were exacerbated by a heavy fall in the Australian dollar.

The balance sheet is still improving with gearing rising around 25% to 30% in 1987. The net debt is increasing slightly as the group begins to use up cash on capital investment and acquisitions.

Acquisitions in 1986/87 totalled £296m. The most significant was the purchase of Genstar Stone Products in the US for £202m. Redland is good at managing its balance sheet, but because of the geographical spread of businesses it is susceptible to exchange rate fluctuations.

In December 1987 Redland agreed to sell its 50.1% holding in its Australian building materials subsidiary Monier for £125m to Equiticorp Tasman in return for buying out Monier's international roof tile interests for £116m.

At the 1987/88 interim, turnover including associates was up 31% to £760.9m. Pre-tax profits were 44% up to £51.1m. Earnings per share were up 17% to 18.9p. The UK divisions performed strongly, and though there were mixed performances in continental Europe and the US, the overall performance was good. 1987/88 pre-tax profits for the full year are expected to be around £165m.

SHARE PRICE HISTORY

Redland's share price doubled between 1985 and its all time high of 575p in summer 1987. Despite this, Redland has been underperforming the stock market in relative terms. During 1987 the shares were particularly supported by the expectation that the Conservative government would institute a programme of inner city reconstruction.

The shares fell 38.7% to 375p after the autumn 1987 share crash before recovering to the 430p level in early March 1988.

SENIOR MANAGEMENT

Sir Colin Corness, chairman since 1977, served as managing director during 1967–1982, and presently oversees the West German and US operations. He is also president of the National Council of Building Materials Producers and is founder of the Phoenix Initiative, a charity set up to fight inner city dereliction.

David Lyon stepped down as managing director in 1987 and made way for Robert Napier, previously finance director, and Tim Walker, previously responsible for roof tiles and bricks, to become joint managing directors responsible for international and UK operations respectively.

Gerald Corbett, formerly with Dixons, replaced Christopher May as finance director. The other executive directors are David Taylor, who is responsible for aggregates, and Eric Priestley, chief executive of British Fuels, who joined the board in April 1987.

CAPITAL

Redland had a total of 269.7m ordinary shares in issue at the beginning of 1988. Since 1983 the major changes in the

FIVE YEAR FINANCIAL INFORMATION

Year	Turnover (£m)	Pre-tax (£m)	Earnings (p)	Dividends net (p)	Dividend cover (x)	Net assets (p)	Price (p) High	Price (p) Low	PER (x) High	PER (x) Low	Yield (%) High	Yield (%) Low
1983	1,007.5	64.2	17.0	7.91	2.2	116.9	275	216	23.4	17.0	5.22	4.09
1984	1,184.2	100.6	24.1	9.30	2.6	125.3	309	215	22.7	11.5	6.17	3.83
1985	1,247.3	118.7	27.4	10.27	2.7	133.2	349	249	16.0	11.4	5.84	4.23
1986	1,291.6	124.7	31.1	11.30	2.8	133.0	471	334	21.1	13.5	4.54	3.22
1987	1,300.0	143.8	36.0	13.00	2.8	143.0	570	350	18.4	10.0	5.35	3.12

group's capital have been the issue of 4.5m shares in October 1984 as part consideration for acquisition of Thomas Wagg and Sons and the issue of 53.83m shares in November 1986 in a one for four rights issue at 350p per share to part finance the Genstar acquisition in the US.

In March 1987 the group issued £60m of 7.25% convertible bonds due 2002. They are convertible at 540p per share. There are warrants in issue which had been attached to 9.5% Guaranteed Bonds 1992.

GROUP REVIEW

Redland divides its UK businesses by activity while those overseas are divided by country or region.

UK aggregates Redland quarries rock, sand and gravel and processes them into graded aggregates for the construction industry. Aggregates form the basis of its road surfacing and smaller readymix concrete business and are the raw materials of some of its range of building products.

By industry standards Redland's reserves are not very large but they are particularly well placed to serve London and the south-east, the region with historically the greatest demand for aggregates. Most of Redland's reserves of sand and gravel are near London, for example at Tilbury or on the M1, A1 and A12 arterial roads.

Redland has further strengthened its position in the south-east by acquiring a major quarry at Budden Wood, Leicestershire. This contains some of the UK's granite reserves nearest to the London basin. There are no indigenous sources of crushed rock aggregates in the south-east. Budden Wood is a far cheaper source than dredging from the sea-bed.

Approximately one million tonnes of crushed stone are already transported to the south-east by rail every year. Redland sees this growing, as exhaustion of the south-east's reserves increases the price of local supplies.

Total crushed rock production from all Redland's quarries amounts to four million tonnes, equivalent to about 5% of the total UK aggregate market. The group owns at least 12 years' reserves of sand and gravel and at least 50 years' of granite at current rates of output.

Redland's readymix concrete interests are comparatively small but its 35 batching plants are strategically placed. A new one at Otterpool in Kent is within easy reach of the Channel Tunnel.

The group has upgraded its road surfacing operation, which played a major part in the construction of the M25, with the purchase of two drum mixers.

Operating profit for UK aggregates for 1986/87 was up 29.3% to £23.9m, 16.6% of the group's total.

UK roof tiles Redland Roof Tiles is the leading UK supplier of pitched roofing products and has the widest range available. These include traditional slate, concrete and modern tiling systems.

The group's 12 concrete roof plants in the UK command about 40% of the market. Demand for traditional plain tiles has kept its new plant at South Cerney, Gloucestershire, on three shifts per day. The group's CAD/CAM system, installed in 1984, has saved it considerable design lead time and tile machinery costs.

The Cambrian interlocking slate, launched in 1986, was recognised as a breakthrough in the application of state of the art technology to a traditional product and demand has been sufficient to bring a second production line into operation at the South Wales factory.

Other important additions to Redland's range of roofing tiles are the Rosemary range of plain and decorative clay tiles and the reconstituted slate tile manufactured at a new £3m factory in Wales. This utilises a process imported from Braas, Redland's West German company.

The UK tile market has attracted new entrants in recent times but none have made a significant inroad into Redland's market share. Tarmac has withdrawn its product after lack of success.

Operating profit for Redland's roof tile business for 1986/87 was up 9.3% to £11.8m, 8.2% of the group's total.

UK clay bricks Redland Bricks manufactures a wide range of bricks, including yellow London stock, blue facing Maunchwood Staffordshires and the new red North Down range.

The business used to be concentrated in the south-east of England, predominantly in Surrey, Sussex and Kent. The acquisition of the Rosemary Brick and Tile Company and Arden Brick have combined with the existing Stourbridge Brick and Birtley Brick activities to give Redland a strong Midlands base and almost 9% of the UK brick market.

The expansion of the Ashdown brickworks near Bexhill was completed in 1987. When the new plant at Wealden, near Horsham, and the expansion of the Chailey and Otterham plants are finished, Redland will have raised its annual capacity over a five year period by 50% to a total of 270m

CHAIRMAN'S STATEMENT

'Growth has been accompanied by a quite exceptional level of activity in extending the scope of our affairs by a combination of acquisition, new joint ventures and capital investment on a scale that surpasses that of any previous year in our history. We have also restructured our senior management in order to provide for the continued development ...

The improving economic climate in the United Kingdom has stimulated a rising trend over the last five years of construction work financed by private clients, particularly in the housing and commercial sectors; but, very welcome as this has been, it contrasts with gravely inadequate expenditure upon the renewal and maintenance of the public estate, which is indispensable to the well-being and international competitiveness of the country.' *Sir Colin Corness*

bricks a year.

The group has also committed itself to higher levels of sales, service and quality in the south-east. A newly formed house-building products division caters for the strong demand for more expensive housing developments using higher quality materials.

Operating profit for Redland Bricks for 1986/87 was up 37.7% to £14.6m, 10.2% of the group's total.

UK fuel distribution For many years Redland was a major UK distributor of coal and light and heavy fuel oil via its subsidiary, Cawoods. In December 1986 it agreed to merge its fuel distribution interests into the British Fuel Company, a joint venture between British Coal and AAH, but the deal required the approval of the European Commission in Brussels. This finally came through in July 1987. Now Redland has a 55% holding in British Fuels, the largest independent fuel distributor in the UK. A management buyout is under discussion.

Volumes are high in the fuel distribution business but profit margin at around 3% is relatively low. Operating profit for Redland's fuel business in 1986/87 was down 9.5% to £9.5m, 6.6% of the group's total.

UK plasterboard In September 1987 Redland formed Redland Plasterboard, a joint venture between Redland with 51% and Australian resources group CSR with 49%. CSR has annual sales of just over £1bn and accounts for just over half of the Australian plasterboard market, which is slightly smaller than the UK.

The joint venture is to invest £100m over the next few years in the UK and Europe and is building its first plant in southern England. During 1988 Redland will import rock gypsum from Spain and liner board from Sweden to make plasterboard in the UK.

To guarantee supplies, Redland acquired a controlling 44.9% interest in Norgips, the Norwegian plasterboard maker, in September 1987. CSR subsequently shared this interest, by buying 25% of Redland's stake.

This is Redland's first venture into plasterboard anywhere in the world. BPB Industries is estimated to currently hold about 96% of the UK market and 50% of the European one.

Continental Europe By far the group's largest activity in continental Europe is concrete tiles. Via two joint ventures, eight associate companies, two majority-owned subsidiaries and one fully-owned subsidiary, Redland is engaged in roof tiles in ten West European countries and in Hungary.

Redland's Italian majority-owned subsidiary, Wierer SpA, manufactures clay roof tiles and flat roofing products as well as concrete roof tiles. Its Spanish associate Industrias Transformadoras del Cemento Eternit SA makes concrete and clay roof tiles.

Redland's wholly-owned French subsidiary, SA Carrières de Pierre Bleue de Chooz-Givet, runs a sand- and gravel-winning to readymix concrete and road-surfacing operation.

Redland has major interests in West Germany through its majority-owned subsidiary Braas. In addition to concrete roof tiles Braas makes plastic products, mostly for the construction industry. Recently it has successfully introduced a rounded nose version of its best selling tile, the Frankfurter Pfanne in several European markets. It has also bought an Italian manufacturer of modified bitumen products and has established a joint venture to manufacture them in the US.

Redland Bouwprodukten is the largest producer of building materials in the Netherlands. Besides roof tiles its products include Mosa ceramic wall and floor tiles, clay bricks and Decostone kitchen sinks.

Operating profit for Redland's continental European businesses for 1986/87 was up 43.5% to £44.2m, 30.7% of the group's total.

US The group's principal activities in the US are its aggregates-winning to road-surfacing operations, roof sheeting and concrete roof tiles.

Via its joint venture with Koppers Company, Western-Mobile, its 87.5%-owned subsidiary Redland Worth and its wholly-owned subsidiary Genstar Stone Products, Redland is now one of the US's top ten producers of construction aggregates.

Share price and relative to FT-A All-Share

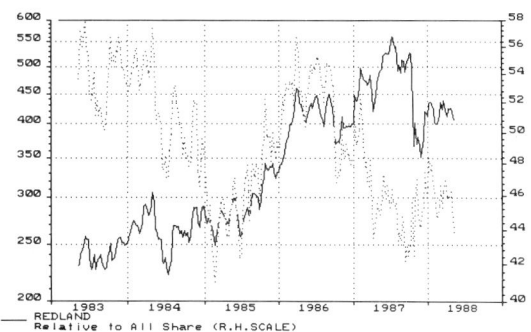

REDLAND
Relative to All Share (R.H.SCALE)

Western-Mobile, with three stone quarries and 19 sand gravel pits, covers Colorado, Kansas, Wyoming and New Mexico. Redland Worth, whose limestone quarry has an annual capacity of 15m tonnes per annum, is based in San Antonio, Texas. Genstar, with reserves of more than 1.5bn tonnes, is the most important producer of stone, sand and gravel in Maryland, which is among the US's fastest growing regions.

Redland disposed of its 78.2% of Gang Nail Systems in September 1987. Redland now owns 100% of Monier Roof Tile, based in Orange, California after its deal with Equiticorp Tasman.

Redland's interests in roof sheeting are through its 56.4%-owned New Jersey subsidiary, Barra Corporation of America, and its 28.2% of associate AGR Company, based in North Carolina.

Operating profit for Redland's US interests for 1986/87 was up 11.4% to £22.4m, 15.6% of the group's total.

Australia and the Far East Redland's leading businesses in these regions are the roof tile interests of Monier in Australia, acquired outright through its deal with Equiticorp Tasman in December 1987, and CI Holdings Berhad based in Malaysia and Singapore.

Monier Redland has a major share of the Australian market for concrete and clay roof tiles and also has smaller operations in New Zealand, Japan, Indonesia and Thailand. Its annual Australian sales are about A$150m.

CI Holdings Berhad has the local manufacturing and distribution rights of a range of branded building products including taps and sanitaryware. Its other products include concrete roof tiles, concrete paving, clay bricks and timber roof trusses. It supplies road-surfacing materials and carries out road-surfacing contracts.

Other overseas businesses are its associate South African concrete roof tile maker Coverland Roof Tiles, and its associated readymix concrete businesses in Bahrain, Kuwait, Oman and Qatar.

Operating profit for Redland's Australian and Far Eastern interests for 1986/87 were down 30.8% to £7.4m, 5.1% of the group's total, reflecting currency weakness and difficult trading conditions.

GEOGRAPHICAL REVIEW

In 1986/87 the UK accounted for 46% of the group's turnover with £600.2m, continental Europe for 27.6% with £357.9m, the US for 17.3% with £224.6m, Australia and the Far East for 7.8% with £101.5m and the rest of the world made up the balance with £15.8m.

The UK accounted for 48% of group operating profit in 1986/87 with £69.0m, continental Europe for 32.5% with £44.2m, the US for 15.6% with £22.4m, Australia and the Far East for 5.1% with £7.4m and the rest of the world made up the balance with £0.8m.

The UK had 25.2% of group net assets with £224.2m, continental Europe had 31% with £276m, the US had 39.0% with £346.4m, Australia and the Far East had 4.1% with £36.5m and the rest of the world made up the balance with £5.6m.

CORPORATE CALENDAR

Year end	26 March
Preliminary results	May
Report and accounts	August
AGM	September
Final dividend paid	October
Interim results	November
Interim dividend paid	January

DIRECTORS' HOLDINGS

	Ordinary shares	Options over ordinary shares
Sir Colin Corness	40,028	138,000
JE Bolton	625	—
Lord Ezra	2,500	—
Sir Christopher Laidlaw	2,500	—
JDR Lyon	6,853	110,959
RS Napier	1,000	127,618
D Taylor	17,713	101,903
T Walker	3,826	124,905
TWM Wallace	149,838	—
J White	625	—
GTE Priestley	400	94,833

Total remuneration received by the directors is not published but the chairman received a total of £131,375 in 1986/87.

PRINCIPAL SUBSIDIARIES AND RELATED COMPANIES

AGR Company – US (28.2%), B & C Danmark A/S – Denmark (18.8%), Barra Corporation of America Inc – US (56.4%), Braas & Co GmbH – West Germany (56.4%), Braas & Schwenk GmbH & Co – West Germany (39.5%), Bramac GmbH – Austria (28.2%), British Fuels Limited (55%), CI Holdings Berhad – Malaysia (30%), Cawoods of Northern Ireland (55%), Coverland Roof Tiles (Pty) Ltd – South Africa (33.3%), Delmon Ready Mixed Concrete and Products Co WLL – Bahrain (49%), Genstar Stone Products Company – US, Hartigan Readymix Ltd (50%), Industrias Transformadoras del Cemento Eternit SA – Spain (47%), Kuwaiti British Readymix Company – Kuwait (40%), Monier Redland Ltd – Australia (100%), Monier Roof Tile Inc – US, RBB NV – Belgium (50%), Readymix Abu Dhabi Ltd – UAE (40%), Ready Mixed Concrete (Eastern Counties) Ltd (50%), Readymix Gulf Ltd – UAE (40%), Readymix Muscat LLC and Premix LLC – Oman (40%), Readymix Qatar Ltd – Qatar (49%), Redland Aggregates Ltd, Redland Bouwprodukten BV – Netherlands, Redland Bricks Ltd, Redland Engineering Ltd, Redland Ibérica SA – Spain (47%), Redland of Northern Ireland Ltd, Redland Readymix Ltd, Redland Roof Tiles Ltd, Redland Technology Ltd, Redland Worth Corporation – US (87.5%), SA Carrières de Pierre Bleue de Chooz-Givet – France, Société Française Redland SA – France (42.7%), VÁÉV – Bramac Kft – Hungary (13.8%), Western-Mobile Inc – US (50%), Wierer SpA – Italy (56.4%), Zanda AB – Sweden (50%), Zanda A/S – Norway (24.5%)

BRAND NAMES

Bricks Ashdown, Castle, Funton, Haunchwood, Holbrook, Otterham, Pluckley, Southwater, Warnham, Wealdron
Roof tiles Cambrian, Cheslyn, Delta, Downland, Grovebury, Regent, Renown, Richmond, Rosemary, Stonewold

CONTACTS AND FURTHER INFORMATION

RGF Smith, Redland PLC, Redland House, Reigate, Surrey RH2 0SJ. Tel: 0737 242488.

REED INTERNATIONAL P.L.C.

GENERAL INFORMATION

Head office   Reed House, 6 Chesterfield Gardens, London W1A 1EJ. Tel: 01-499 4020
Directors   Sir Stanley Grinstead FCA (chairman), PJ Davis (chief executive), PH Burns, P Hamlyn, I Irvine, RG Segel – US, Sir Keith Skinner Bt, NJ Stapleton, JP Williams. *Non-exec* C Barker, LA Carpenter, Sir Derek Alun-Jones
Advisers   SG Warburg & Co Ltd
Auditors   Price Waterhouse
Registrars   Ravensbourne Registration Services Ltd
Brokers   Cazenove & Co
Solicitors   Allen & Overy

GENERAL FINANCIAL INFORMATION

Market capitalisation	£2.176bn at 1 January 1988
Capital structure	
Issued ordinary shares (25p)	542m
Issued preference shares (£1)	1.5m, 3.15% redeemable CP
	1.2m, 3.85% redeemable CP
	0.3m, 3.5% irredeemable CP
	1.1m, 4.9% irredeemable CP
Warrants	None
Convertibles	None
Traded options	None
ADRs	One ADR per ordinary share
Shareholders over 5%	None

FT CATEGORY

FT: Newspapers, publishers
FT-A: Publishing and printing

MAJOR ACTIVITIES

Following the disposal of a range of peripheral businesses, Reed is now clearly focused on two areas – publishing, and packaging and paper.

Operating profits in the year to March 1987 included a full contribution from the paint and DIY division since sold, and no contribution from Octopus Publishing purchased in August. In that year the various publishing operations contributed 51% of trading profit, with 38% coming from the packaging and paper operations.

With a sizeable portion of the group's earnings coming from North America, particularly the US, fluctuations in the dollar to sterling exchange rate can have an impact. Volatile commodity prices in certain paper and board products can also be important, although this is lessened by the integrated nature of the group's packaging and paper operations. The major economic influence on the publishing operations is advertising expenditure, in both the UK and the US, a variable widely held to move with consumer spending.

In UK publishing, EMAP and United Newspapers, although both are considerably smaller than Reed, would be the obvious quoted competitors. Both of these groups, as well

as Pearson, International Thomson and Associated Newspapers, own sizeable regional newspaper chains. Pearson is very strong in general book publishing.

Reed claims to be number one in US trade and technical magazines, and number one worldwide in creating and organising exhibitions.

On the packaging side, much of the activity is in corrugated board, where the main quoted competitors would be Bowater and David S Smith, who also compete in the paper manufacturing market.

FINANCIAL HISTORY

Turnover of £1.95bn in 1986/87 compared with £1.80bn four years earlier. But this apparently slow growth conceals the disposal of three entire divisions – Reed Building Products, Reed Decorative Products and Mirror Group Newspapers – which contributed £515m to sales in 1983. In Reed's continuing businesses there has been considerable development, and this is better shown by the increase in trading profit from £77.4m to £201m over the four years, up 160%.

This process of reshaping the group has continued since the end of the 1986/87 financial year, with the disposal of the Paint and DIY division to Williams Holdings for £260m, and the acquisition of Octopus Publishing for £540m. A crude adjustment suggests that these deals will leave the group with between 50% and 55% of sales and between 60% and 65% of trading profit in publishing, the balance being in packaging and paper.

During 1986/87 the group continued its impressive record. Earnings per share grew 34% to 26.6p, while the dividend was increased by 42% to 8.0p from 5.62p. However, during the year net borrowings rose by £110m to £188m, but this was largely due to the cost of several publishing acquisitions. Cash flow before disposals and acquisitions was positive by around £65m.

At the 1987/88 October interim, profits after tax were up 50% to £78.8m and pretax up 36.7% to £109.7m. Earnings per share were up 45%.

SHARE PRICE HISTORY

Since 1984, and despite the October 1987 share crash, Reed's share price has more than doubled relative to the FT-A All-Share index, while moving from around 110p to 400p in absolute terms, after adjusting for a scrip issue.

This outperformance has been reasonably consistent as the market has absorbed the benefits of the group's restructuring, but exceptionally good figures in October 1986 generated a particularly strong performance for the next two months. After the October 1987 share crash, the shares underperformed for three months before starting to move back up again in relative terms.

SENIOR MANAGEMENT

The senior executive team at Reed has changed significantly. Leslie Carpenter had been chairman since 1985, when he replaced Sir Alex Jarratt, but retired at the end of 1987. He remains on the board as a non-executive director. Towards the end of 1986 he had relinquished the post of chief executive to Peter Davis, formerly assistant managing director of J Sainsbury. At the same time Nigel Stapleton was appointed finance director, having previously been vice president, finance for Unilever US Inc.

The new chairman is Sir Stanley Grinstead, previously

C H A I R M A N ' S   S T A T E M E N T

'Last year, I referred to the long period of rationalisation and reconstruction which Reed International had undergone. As you will have seen from our recent press statements, this is a continuing process and we are now proceeding with further streamlining of our portfolio.

The outstanding results for this year should be seen against this background and should be recognised as reflecting the carefully thought through long term strategy for ensuring sustainable earnings growth.' *Leslie Carpenter*

F I V E   Y E A R   F I N A N C I A L   I N F O R M A T I O N

Year	Turnover (£m)	Pre-tax (£m)	Earnings (p)	Dividends net (p)	Dividend cover (x)	Net assets (p)	Price (p) High	Low	PER (x) High	Low	Yield (%) High	Low
1983	1,809	60.9	8.4	3.5	2.4	117	94	58	11.3	6.3	8.70	5.70
1984	2,043	96.4	14.4	4.1	3.5	126	136	94	13.8	8.3	5.83	4.53
1985	2,115	107.5	13.4	4.6	2.9	136	183	132	14.2	10.7	4.67	3.61
1986	1,931	137.4	19.9	5.6	3.6	132	308	164	19.6	10.5	4.20	2.85
1987	1,950	188.0	26.6	8.0	3.3	145	625	300	24.5	9.4	4.22	1.75

chairman of Grand Metropolitan, and a non-executive director of Reed since 1981. Paul Hamlyn and Ian Irvine joined Reed's board after the acquisition of Octopus Publishing in August 1987.

The board also contains the chief executives of the main business area. They are Sir Keith Skinner of UK publishing, Ron Segel of US publishing, and Peter Williams of European packaging and North American paper. Apart from Leslie Carpenter the other two non-executive directors are Colin Barker, chairman of the British Technology Group, and Sir Derek Alun-Jones, managing director of Ferranti.

CAPITAL

Until its £540m bid for Octopus when 64.4m shares were issued, Reed had proved reluctant to use its shares for acquisitions. The success of this deal meant that there are a total of 542m shares in issue, compared with 470m in 1982, adjusted for the one into four split of the summer of 1986.

Reed bought the US entertainment trade paper *Variety* for $50m in cash in October 1987 plus future performance-related payments not exceeding $35m. *Modern Bride*, the US magazine, was also acquired for $50m in cash in November 1987. Octopus acquired the general publishing interests of Associated Book Publishers in the UK, Australia and New Zealand for cash in December 1987.

At the end of 1987 there were no holdings of over 5%, though Rupert Murdoch had a stake of 2.5%. Although the directors' holdings were negligible, the board had almost 1.5m shares under option, with several times that available for other senior executives.

GROUP REVIEW

Reed Publishing UK   There are four separate sections. In 1987 the division made profits of £45.7m on turnover of £363m.

Reed Business Publishing, formerly known as Business Press International, produces 75 UK business journals, one-third of which are market leaders, and also has a number of successful directories. Well known titles include *Caterer & Hotelkeeper*, *Farmers Weekly*, *Computer Weekly*, *Flight International*, the *Kelly's* and *Kompass* directories, and the *Creative Handbook*.

The Butterworth Group comprises a wide range of professional publishing businesses, but is based around Butterworths itself, one of the world's leading legal publishers.

Reed Telepublishing includes the *World Airways Guide* and the ABC travel guides, and International Computaprint, a database management company. It is the fastest growing division of Reed Publishing UK. Its Telepublishing Services operation offers a variety of services ranging from keyboarding to online host databasing including optical disc technology.

Reed Regional Newspapers group has built up 104 titles from nothing in 1981, making it rank fourth in the UK in revenue terms. Its *Birmingham Daily News* is Europe's first morning free newspaper.

European Courtesy Magazines Group specialises in free distribution magazines with *London Portrait* as its flagship.

Reed Publishing US   There are three areas of which the largest is Cahners Magazines. In 1987 the division made profits of £42.1m on turnover of £291m.

Cahners comprises 52 titles, including 26 of the top 100 US specialist business magazines. These include *Interior Design*, *American Baby*, *Restaurants and Institutions* and *Plant Engineering*. It was considerably strengthened in October 1986 by Reed's $250m acquisition of the Technical Publishing Company titles from Dun & Bradstreet.

The second area covers Reed's exhibition activities, now all managed from the US. There is considerable synergy between promoting exhibitions and publishing business magazines, and partly on the back of its magazines Reed has become the clear world leader in exhibitions.

RR Bowker provides information for the book and library trades. Its *Books in Print* series and Ulrichs *Periodicals* were offered on compact disc for the first time in 1986/87 with very positive trade reaction. RR Bowker has been complemented by the purchase of a very similar German company, Saur.

Consumer publishing   The bulk of this division is made up by IPC Magazines, which has recently experienced a major turnaround in profitability because of rationalisation and improved performance of titles. The division made profits of £20.4m on turnover of £188m in 1987.

IPC Magazines' main strengths lie in the women's weekly market, where Reed owns *Woman*, *Woman's Own*, *Woman's Realm* and *Woman & Home*, and sells over 300m copies annually. Other well-known titles include *Country Life*, *New Scientist*, *Horse & Hound*, *Yachting Monthly* and *Ideal Home*. A new magazine *Essentials* was launched in late 1987 and has proved highly successful. Another part of the division is Carlton Magazines which produces four important titles for women including *Options* and *Woman's World*.

Octopus Publishing   Octopus Publishing was acquired for £540m in August 1987. It is one of the UK's largest general book publishers, and includes such well-known imprints as Secker & Warburg, Heinemann and Mitchell Beazley. It sold its 50% interest in Pan Books in September to Macmillan for £22m in cash after Macmillan exercised its pre-emption rights after Reed's acquisition of Octopus, but acquired Associated Book Publishers' general publishing interests in the UK, Australia and New Zealand in December.

Packaging   In the UK Reed is market leader in corrugated case manufacture and in the production of cartons for the food, drinks and tobacco industry. The group is also market leader in the Dutch corrugated market. In plastic packaging Reed owns both Reed Plastic Containers and the more recently acquired Smith's Containers. In 1987 the division made profits of £26.9m on turnover of £350m.

European paper   The European paper group covers not only paper and board manufacture in both the UK and the Netherlands, but also Reed Transport which handles 1.5m tonnes of freight each year. Profits of £21.5m were made on turnover of £183m.

In the UK Reed produces around 400,000 tonnes of paper per annum from its machines at seven mills, with a further 200,000 tonnes per annum produced in the Netherlands. Considerable effort has been expended in recent years to improve the energy efficiency of production and measures have been taken to use a consistently higher proportion of waste paper.

North American paper   By far the most significant part of this division is the mill in Quebec, which has been the subject of a major programme of investment and improvement. Following this programme the mill has operated at full capacity producing almost 400,000 tonnes per annum of newsprint and 50,000 tonnes per annum of other products. Reed also has a small associated chemicals and packaging business.

Share price and relative to FT-A All-Share

REED INTL.
Relative to All Share (R.H.SCALE)

Reed Trading   Following the closure of the unsuccessful Reed Carbonless Papers, this division has two main areas. The first is Spicer's, which manufactures stationery products and distributes a wide range of office supplies, not least through its increasingly successful catalogue.

The second area, J&J Maybank, is essentially complementary to the European Paper Business as its main supplier of waste paper. This forms the bulk of European Paper Business's raw materials. Recently Maybank has had a series of poor results, but this has been offset by low costs and higher profits from European Paper. In 1987 the division made profits of £8m on turnover of £173m.

In March 1987 Reed sold its Paint and DIY division, including Crown Paints and Polycell, for £250m net to Williams Holdings.

GEOGRAPHICAL REVIEW

Reed is mainly split between North America and the UK, with over 60% of sales coming from the UK even before taking account of the purchase of Octopus. Other operations are mainly the De Hoop paper and packaging companies in the Netherlands, with under 5% of sales arising elsewhere.

CORPORATE CALENDAR

Year end	31 March
Preliminary results	June
Report and accounts	June
AGM	July
Final dividend paid	August
Interim results	November
Interim dividend paid	January

DIRECTORS' HOLDINGS

	Fully-paid ordinary shares		Options
	(beneficial)	(non-beneficial)	
LA Carpenter	708	—	283,200
CF Sedcole	—	—	140,000
PJ Davis	8,000	—	200,000
Sir Derek Alun-Jones	1,000	—	—
C Barker	4,000	—	—
PH Burns	—	—	180,000
Sir Stanley Grinstead	2,000	7,000	—
RG Segel	—	—	180,000
Sir Keith Skinner	34,920	—	180,000
NJ Stapleton	58	—	140,000
JP Williams	—	—	180,000

Total directors' remuneration in 1986/87 including fees was £1.48m, of which the chairman, who was the highest-paid director, received £171,433.

PRINCIPAL SUBSIDIARIES AND RELATED COMPANIES

Butterworth & Co Ltd, IPC Magazines Ltd, King's Reach Investments Ltd, *RPH Ltd, Reed Business Publishing Ltd, Reed Inc – Canada, Reed Packaging Ltd, Reed Paper & Board (UK) Ltd, Reed Publishing (USA) Inc – US, Reed Services Inc – US, Reed Telepublishing Ltd, Spicers Ltd

Note: All are wholly-owned companies except for * where preference shares are held by outside interests.

BRAND NAMES

ABC Travel Guides, *Bankers' Almanac, Birmingham Daily News, Books in Print*, Butterworth, Carlton Magazines, *Caterer & Hotelkeeper, Catering Update, Commercial Motor, Community Care, Computer Weekly, Country Homes & Interiors, Country Life, Creative Handbook, Datamation, Design News, Doctor*, EDN, *Emergency Medicine, European Chemical News, Executive Travel, Farmers Weekly, Flight International, Futures*, Heinemann, *Horse & Hound*, IPC Magazines, *Ideal Home, Interior Design, Kelly's Business Directory, Kompass, London Portrait*, Mitchell Beazley, *Mizz, Motor Trader, Motor Transport, New Scientist, 19*, Octopus Publishing, *Options, Plant Engineering, Plastics World, Professional Builder, Restaurants and Institutions*, Secker & Warburg, Spicers, *Travel News, Woman, Woman & Home, Woman's Journal, Woman's Own, Woman's Realm, Woman's World, World Airways Guide*

CONTACTS AND FURTHER INFORMATION

Jan Shawe, Reed International P.L.C., Reed House, 6 Chesterfield Gardens, London W1A 1EJ. Tel: 01-499 4020.

REUTERS HOLDINGS PLC

GENERAL INFORMATION

Head office	85 Fleet Street, London EC4P 4AJ. Tel: 01-250 1122
Directors	Sir Christopher Hogg (chairman), G Renfrew (managing), ME Nelson (deputy managing), NL Judah. *Non-exec* DB Anderson, J Evans, PW Gibbings, PG Gyllenhammar, IR Maxwell MC, KR Murdoch, IG Park, Sir Richard Storey Bt, MV Suich, EJL Turnbull AO, WB Wriston. *Alternate* JA Burnett, DG Ure, A-FH Villeneuve
Advisers	SG Warburg & Co Ltd
Auditors	Price Waterhouse
Registrars	Bank of Scotland Registrar's Department
Brokers	Cazenove & Co, Hoare Govett Ltd
Solicitors	Linklaters & Paines

GENERAL FINANCIAL INFORMATION

Market capitalisation	£1.902bn at 1 January 1988
Capital structure	
Issued ordinary 'A' shares (10p)	100.1m
Issued ordinary 'B' shares (10p)	320.8m
Issued preference shares	None
Warrants	None
Convertibles	None
Traded options	None
ADRs	One ADR equals three 'B' shares
Shareholders over 5%	Abu Dhabi Investment Authority has 10.7% of the 'B' shares; Associated Newspapers 6.7% of the 'A' and 6.7% of the 'B'; Australian Associated Press Proprietary Ltd 13.9% of the 'A'; Pergamon Holding Foundation 5.9% of the 'A'; The News Corporation Ltd 9.5% of the 'A' and 3.2% of the 'B'; The Press Association Ltd 41.7% of the 'A'; United Newspapers 8.8% of the 'A'. There are four votes per 'A' ordinary share, and one vote per 'B' ordinary share.

FT CATEGORY

FT: Industrials (miscel.)
FT-A: Agencies

MAJOR ACTIVITIES

Reuters is the leading supplier of world news and information to the financial and business communities and news media of the globe. The vast bulk of revenues comes from the financial and business communities, an area which has grown exceptionally over the last dozen years. The number of Reuters-installed video terminals worldwide in December 1987 was 141,260, up an incredible 38,131 (+37%) from a year earlier.

Reuters' original opportunities arose out of the currency volatility following the collapse of the Bretton Woods agreement in 1974. Since then the combined trends of deregulation and globalisation of financial markets have created a huge demand for accurate and up-to-date information.

New developments at Reuters include the strengthening of the company's position in the international equities market through the introduction of its Equities 2000 product, the development of screen-based computer dealing, the introduction of Reuter Country Reports, and the development of satellite television news networks.

Over the shorter term the group's success is determined to an extent by business levels in the financial world, and the profitability of financial houses. Wider economic factors seem to have little impact and the group's policy of hedging parts of its foreign currency flows limits exposure to exchange rates. Competition to the group comes from a number of areas. Telerate is the best known and is separately quoted.

FINANCIAL HISTORY

A study of the group since 1983, including the last full year before the group was floated in 1984, reveals just how quickly Reuters has grown. With the aid of a number of relatively small acquisitions, turnover grew from £243m in 1983 to £866.9m in 1987, a compound rate of 37%. Pre-tax profits rose from £55.3m to £178.8m, a compound rate of 26.5%. Earnings per share rose from 8.5p to 26p, a compound rate of 25%.

The investment to fund this expansion has been substantial, with total spending on fixed assets of just over £410m in the five years. This has not in any way impaired the financial ratios. At December 1987 the group had net cash and investments, after deducting finance leases, of around £50m. Until the end of 1986 cash flow was heavily positive. In 1987, however, cash outlays on acquisitions and lower interest rates offset an increase in funds generated. Pre-tax return on capital employed in 1987 was 85%.

SHARE PRICE HISTORY

Reuters shares were floated in June 1984 at 196p, opening around 20p higher. In the ensuing three years they performed extremely well, roughly quadrupling, and significantly outperforming the FT-A All-Share index. The shares opened at 45% of the value of the index and at their peak stood at 72%.

The shares were amongst the most severely hit by the autumn 1987 stock market crash. They fell from 914p to a low of 385p. Analysts and investors felt that highly publicised cutbacks in the financial sector and Reuters dollar exposure would hit the company severely. A long period of outperformance of the FT-A All-Share index ended. There has been some recovery in the shares to the 500p level, 55% of the All-Share index, at the beginning of 1988.

SENIOR MANAGEMENT

The Reuters board is unusual in its structure. There are three executive directors – Glen Renfrew, chief executive officer; Nigel Judah, finance director; and Michael Nelson, deputy managing director. Because of its history as a trust there are twelve non-executive directors, of whom three are external representatives on the main board. These are headed by group chairman Sir Christopher Hogg (chairman of Courtaulds), Pehr Gyllenhammar (chairman of Volvo) and Walter Wriston (formerly chairman of Citicorp). In addition there is one alternate director to a non-executive director and two alternate directors to executive directors.

Among numerous other representatives are those of three of the major UK groups which formed part of the original ownership – Rupert Murdoch of News International, Robert Maxwell of Mirror Group and the nominee of Associated Newspapers. The newspaper representatives are elected by the various press associations.

CAPITAL

Reuters' share capital is split into 100m 'A' shares and 320.8m 'B' shares. Since its flotation the group has used its equity in small amounts and usually together with cash to purchase a number of companies. Most growth has been organic.

The largest recent acquisition was Instinet in 1986/87. In 1986 Reuters bought a 49% stake for £41.7m in cash and shares. The remaining 51% was acquired in 1987, financed by the issue of $52.3m worth of ADRs. In June 1987 the

FIVE YEAR FINANCIAL INFORMATION

Year	Turnover (£m)	Pre-tax (£m)	Earnings (p)	Dividends net (p)	Dividend cover (x)	Net assets (p)	Price (p) High	Price (p) Low	PER (x) High	PER (x) Low	Yield (%) High	Yield (%) Low
*1983	242.6	55.3	8.5	2.10	4.0	17.6	—	—	—	—	—	—
*1984	313.0	74.3	10.9	2.50	4.4	37.0	292	196	28.4	19.0	1.82	1.22
1985	434.1	93.6	13.2	3.25	4.1	44.4	399	270	37.7	18.8	1.98	1.06
1986	620.9	130.1	19.4	5.50	3.5	43.3	584	347	39.5	29.0	1.54	0.90
1987	866.9	178.8	26.0	7.3	3.6	n/a	913	389	40.1	15.0	2.57	0.83

*Figures for 1983 and 1984 are not restated to give retrospective effect of mergers or the acquisition of Rich Inc

Canadian company IP Sharp Associates was bought for £29m. In July 1987 a £100m sterling commercial paper programme was arranged and guaranteed by SG Warburg & Co.

The 'A' shares, which have four votes each, are held by the original newspaper owners of the group. Consequently a number of interests over 5% are declarable. Separately there is an independent Founders Share Company. The Articles of Association guarantee the independence of the group, precluding any takeover.

At the end of 1987 only Associated Newspapers still held over 5% of the 'B' shares, while the Abu Dhabi Investment Authority had built up a stake of just under 11%. Around 43% of the 'B' shares were held beneficially in the US at the most recent count.

GROUP REVIEW

Reuters' business can be viewed in a number of different ways – by product, by market served or by geographical area.

Markets The group identifies seven different areas which it serves. Media is now relatively small compared to the other six business and financial areas. These are money, commodities, energy, shipping, equities and bonds.

Of these, money is the largest, and covers foreign exchange dealing, the source of Reuters' explosive growth in financial markets. Commodities was also an early market served, though this has now been overtaken in scale by the supply of products to the securities houses who deal in the bond and equity markets. The shipping and energy markets are recent areas that have been targeted, and both are proving fruitful.

Products The key Reuters product is the provision of price information and news to business subscribers. Reuters obtains its information from exchanges and over-the-counter markets and from data contributed directly by individual traders and market-makers. Additionally it receives information from more than 1,000 of its own journalists worldwide. A series of acquisitions and technical advances in 1986 and 1987 have extended the range of Reuters' products and services globally.

In the bond and money markets, Reuters provides a Monitor Dealing Service through its screens and keyboards. In the equity and capital markets, Reuters' new Equities 2000 service is an important product providing real time coverage of the world's equity markets. Equities 2000 takes the company into the North American market for US equities quotations for the first time.

The recent Instinet acquisition provides the first international fully automated trading system for 8,000 equities and options. The principal difference between the Reuter Monitor Dealing Service and Instinet is that the Dealing Service supports conversational trading by telephone or telex, whilst Instinet is an automated order entry and execution system for large blocks of shares.

The Reuters product is either a screen and keyboard or the traditional telex, which is steadily going out of service. Reuters' commitment to advanced technology is reflected in the new Advanced Reuter Terminal, the TRIARCH digital switching technology, and the new Integrated Data Network. The acquisition of Rich Inc in 1985, a major supplier of dealing room systems to financial institutions, emphasises the group's commitment to providing the best and most sophisticated equipment. However, it is essentially what can be done with this equipment that constitutes the strength and range of Reuters' products.

Reuters also provides a news service to all the markets it serves, the quality of which is an important competitive point with which to sell the rest of its services.

There are 1,173 Reuters journalists, photographers and cameramen in 113 cities in 76 countries. The news services are distributed to newspapers, radio and television stations in 158 countries. Reuters is rapidly developing photographic and television news through its own photographers and through satellite feeds owned by its 88.75% subsidiary, Visnews.

GEOGRAPHICAL REVIEW

The most important geographical area for Reuters is Europe, where in 1987 it earned 56% of revenues. On the back of rapid deregulation and a relative lack of competition, revenues grew 48.4% to £495.9m.

Reuters' second most important area is Asia, Australia and New Zealand. This includes the Middle East, where the group has had historically a sizeable presence. Reuters hopes that the coming years will see a continued expansion of its business in Japan, where progress is steadily being made in terms of deregulation and the granting of access to foreign firms.

The group's North American presence is also that which faces the stiffest competition. The growth rate in revenue of 33% in 1987 in sterling terms was understated by the weakness of the Canadian and US dollars. The US is a mature financial

Share price and relative to FT-A All-Share

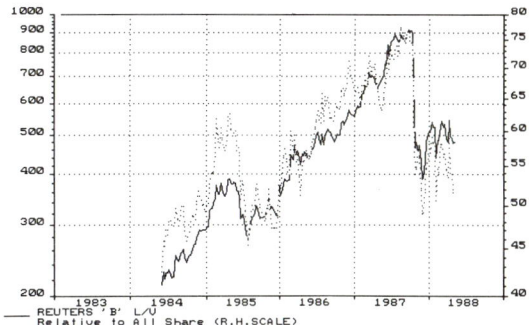

REUTERS 'B' L/U
Relative to All Share (R.H.SCALE)

ROLLS-ROYCE plc

CHAIRMAN'S STATEMENT

'The international market for Reuters integrated services is expanding constantly. Reuters leadership is based on its constantly developing communications network, the unmatched breadth of its databases and an unexcelled reputation for reliability and continuous innovation in the technology and marketing of information products. These standards ensure Reuters ability to deliver services of the highest quality.' *Sir Christopher Hogg*

market which is unlikely to experience the spectacular growth rates elsewhere in the world. Reuters is investing heavily to raise its profile and increase its presence.

Business elsewhere is concentrated in Latin America and Africa, and accounts for less than 5% of revenue. Despite the relative lack of political stability of some of the nations in these two continents, Reuters has still managed to produce growth, which ran at 8% in 1987.

CORPORATE CALENDAR

Year end	31 December
Preliminary results	February
Report and accounts	April
AGM	April
Final dividend paid	May
Interim results	July
Interim dividend paid	September

DIRECTORS' HOLDINGS

	'B' shares	
	(beneficial)	(non-beneficial)
DB Anderson	1,200	—
J Evans	350	—
PW Gibbings	4,500	—
Sir Christopher Hogg	14,700	6,000
NL Judah	287,650	188,250
KR Murdoch	12,186,459	110,850
ME Nelson	280,000	96,715
G Renfrew	1,149,378	—
Sir Richard Storey Bt	5,000	—
WB Wriston	3,000	1,200

KR Murdoch also owns 26,141,396 'A' shares.

The total emoluments paid to directors in 1987 were £1.01m, with the chairman receiving £30,000 and the highest-paid director receiving £334,000.

PRINCIPAL SUBSIDIARIES AND RELATED COMPANIES

AAP Reuters Communications Pty Ltd – Australia (43.9%), Comtelburo Ltd – France, IDR Inc – US, IP Sharp Associates Ltd – Canada, Instinet Corporation – US, LHW Wyatt Brothers Ltd, Reuter Nederland BV, Reuters Australia Pty Ltd, Reuters Hong Kong Limited, Reuters Information Services Inc – US, Reuters Japan Kabushiki Kaisha, Reuters Ltd (99.3%), Reuters Middle East Ltd – Bahrain, Reuters Singapore Pte Ltd, Reuters Svenska Aktiebolag – Sweden, Rich Inc – US, Visnews Ltd

BRAND NAMES

Equities 2000, Instinet, Reuter Monitor, TRIARCH

CONTACTS AND FURTHER INFORMATION

Michael Cooling, Reuters Holdings PLC, 85 Fleet Street, London EC4P 4AJ. Tel: 01-250 1122.

GENERAL INFORMATION

Head office	65 Buckingham Gate, London SW1E 6AT. Tel: 01-222 9020
Directors	Sir Francis Tombs (chairman), Sir Ralph Robins (managing director), Dr GR Higginson, JO Keir, SC Miller, J Ogilvie Keen, S Crichton Miller, JA Rigg, FT Salt CBE, JD Wragg. *Non-exec* Air Chief Marshal Sir Douglas C Lowe GCB DFC AFC, HG Mourgue, Sir Robin B Nicholson, Sir Philip Shelbourne
Advisers	NM Rothschild & Sons Ltd
Auditors	Coopers & Lybrand
Registrars	National Westminster Bank Registrar's Department
Brokers	Hoare Govett Ltd
Solicitors	Freshfields

GENERAL FINANCIAL INFORMATION

Market capitalisation	£953.7m at 1 January 1988
Capital structure	
Issued ordinary shares (20p)	801.47m
Issued preference shares (£1)	Special rights redeemable by Government
Warrants	None
Convertibles	None
Traded options	Yes
ADRs	None
Shareholders over 5%	None

FT CATEGORY

FT: Miscellaneous mechanical engineers
FT-A: Mechanical engineering

MAJOR ACTIVITIES

Rolls-Royce is one of the world's leading aero-engine makers with the ability to design, develop, manufacture and market civil and military turbofan and turbojet engines. Engines produced by Rolls-Royce are in service with 270 airlines, 700 executive jet operators and 110 armed forces. In addition, Rolls-Royce has supplied gas turbines to 175 industrial customers and 25 navies and is responsible for the design and supply of nuclear steam-raising plant for the Royal Navy's nuclear-powered submarine fleet.

In the civil aerospace market, Rolls-Royce has designed and developed in-house engines for the large turbofan market, which require 45,000 to 60,000 lb of thrust, the intermediate turbofan with 32,000 to 45,000 lb of thrust, and the small turbofan with 11,000 to 15,000 lb of thrust.

Through its 30% stake in IAE International Aero Engines, Rolls-Royce will enter the medium turbofan market in 1989, giving the group exposure to all civil turbofan markets. Medium engines produce 18,000 to 25,000 lb of thrust.

In the military market, Rolls-Royce is primarily dedicated to designing and developing engines for UK Ministry of Defence or European government funded combat aircraft programmes, such as the Tornado, Harrier and Hawk. Military aero-engine development is typically fully funded by the government procurement agencies.

Delivery prospects for Rolls-Royce civil aero-engines mainly depend on planned deliveries of new Boeing and Airbus aircraft. Two-thirds of Rolls-Royce civil aero-engine business is for engines on new aircraft. The other third is for spare parts. There is only limited business in re-engining any of the major types of commercial jets currently in service. However, because of its modular engine design, it can offer upgrade kits which bring the performance advantages of the latest generation of engines to existing units.

Engine production for the fixed-wing military aircraft programmes depend on the pace of aircraft shipments laid down by British Aerospace and its joint venture partners such

Year	Turnover (£m)	Pre-tax (£m)	Earnings (p)	Dividends net (p)	Dividend cover (x)	Net assets (p)	Price (p) High	Price (p) Low	PER (x) High	PER (x) Low	Yield (%) High	Yield (%) Low
1983	1,331	(115)	(19.2)	—	—	45.5	—	—	—	—	—	—
1984	1,409	26	3.0	—	—	48.8	—	—	—	—	—	—
1985	1,601	81	12.1	—	—	61.3	—	—	—	—	—	—
1986	1,802	120	18.9	—	—	79.8	—	—	—	—	—	—
1987	2,059	156	18.2	5.25	3.5	106.6	232	98	14.0	5.9	6.98	2.95

FIVE YEAR FINANCIAL INFORMATION

as Panavia and McDonnell Douglas in the US.

The world supply of large and medium-sized turbofans is dominated by Rolls-Royce in the UK and General Electric and Pratt & Whitney in the US. Several joint ventures are important, notably CFM International (a joint company between GE and SNECMA of France) and IAE International Aero Engines (a joint venture of Rolls-Royce, Pratt & Whitney, MTV of West Germany, Fiat and Japanese Aero Engines Corporation).

Rolls-Royce is the only quoted stock in the world whose principal activity is aero-engines.

FINANCIAL HISTORY

Turnover grew 14.3% to £2.059bn in 1987 and has compounded at 7% annually since 1982. This relatively low growth reflects a downturn in 1983 when turnover dropped 11% because of difficulties in the civil jet market. Pre-tax profit in 1987 rose 30% to £156m after jumping 48% in 1986 to £120m, continuing the recovery from losses of £115m in 1983. In the 1982 to 1986 period, Rolls-Royce reduced its workforce by 20%.

Earnings per share were up 6.5% to 20.1p in 1987 after rising 56% to 18.9p in 1986. The tax rate was 13% because of large tax losses brought forward. At 31 December 1987, the company had estimated tax losses of approximately £600m, which are available for relief against future trading profits.

Rolls-Royce has made significant improvements in its working capital ratios and cash controls in recent years. Pre-tax margins have recovered from nil in 1983 to 16.9% (15.1%) in 1987.

SHARE PRICE HISTORY

The shares were first dealt on 20 May 1987, and quickly moved to a substantial premium over the subscription price of 85p partly-paid (170p fully paid). The second instalment of 85p was paid on 23 September 1987. The fully-paid equivalent share price hit a peak of 242p immediately after the flotation and a low of 96p on 6 November 1987.

In addition to the October 1987 share crash, forced sales by foreign holders owning stock in excess of the 15% limit and the slump in the dollar have depressed the price severely. There has been a partial recovery in early 1988.

SENIOR MANAGEMENT

Chairman Sir Francis Tombs joined Rolls-Royce in 1982 and became chairman in 1985. He has held many senior positions in industry and is a director of NM Rothschild and Shell. Sir Ralph Robins became managing director in 1984 following a career spanning 31 years with Rolls-Royce. He was knighted in the 1988 New Year's Honours List. J Rigg was appointed director of finance in 1982. He has worked for Rolls-Royce for

34 years.

The non-executive directors are: Sir Arnold Hall, recently retired as chairman of Hawker Siddeley; Air Chief Marshal Sir Douglas Lowe; H Mourgue, also a vice-chairman of THORN-EMI; Sir Robin Nicholson, who became a chief scientific adviser to the Cabinet Office in 1983; and Sir Philip Shelbourne, formerly chairman of Britoil.

Sir Arnold Hall will retire at the AGM on 24 May 1988. Dr GR Higginson was appointed to the board on 1 April 1988.

CAPITAL

Total shares in issue following the May 1987 flotation totalled 801.5m. The UK Government retains a single special share, which it will exercise if it feels that ownership of the company is threatened. None of the directors had any interest in the shares of Rolls-Royce, but were permitted to apply for shares under the offer for sale, and participate in arrangements for employees and pensions.

GROUP REVIEW

Civil engine group In 1987 the division represented 46% of the group's turnover and 55.9% of operating profit. Operating profit increased 41.6% to £194m on turnover 25.9% up at £953m.

The group's principal civil engines are the RB211-524 series (which powers the Boeing 747 and Lockheed TriStar airliners), the 535 (which powers the Boeing 757) and the Tay (for the new Fokker 100 airliner and the new Gulfstream IV executive jet). Rolls-Royce has a 30% share in an international collaborative project to design and build the V2500 engine, due to enter service in the 150-seat Airbus A320 in 1989.

Deliveries of the RB211 are running at an annual rate of around 70. The rate of deliveries of aircraft types on which the RB211 is an option is 95. This option rate should increase to 250 by 1990 and could rise to 300 a year if Airbus selects the RB211-524L on the A330 aircraft.

The RB211-524D was certified in March 1988, with entry into service in 1989. It will produce 58,000 lb of thrust, will be the most economical power plant for the Boeing 747 and have the additional potential to power twins and trijets. The engine has Rolls-Royce's unique wide-chord fan and integrated exhaust nozzle. The company received the Queen's Award for Technological Achievement for work on the wide-chord fan in April 1987.

Rolls-Royce is proceeding with the certification of the RB211-524H on the Boeing 767 aircraft, 11 of which have been ordered by British Airways to replace part of its Tristar L1011 fleet. Other Tristar operators have been targeted by Rolls-Royce as customers for RB211-524H powered 767s.

The core of the larger RB211-22B engine was the basis for the 535 design, a 37,400 lb thrust power-plant. The 535E4 fuel-efficient engine is now approved for extended-range

Share price and relative to FT-A All-Share

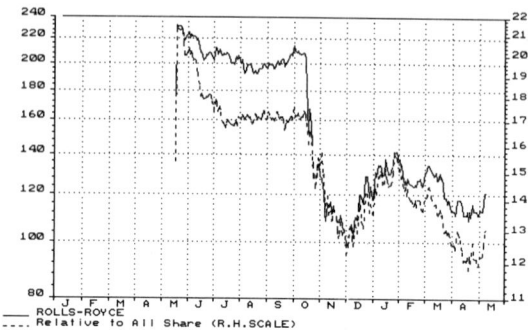

ROLLS-ROYCE
Relative to All Share (R.H.SCALE)

operations with the Boeing 757, the only power-plant currently approved for such operations with this twin-engined aircraft.

The fortunes of the 25,000 lb thrust V2500 engine are dependent upon the success of the Airbus airliners. Rolls-Royce's V2500 partners are Pratt & Whitney, Japanese Aero Engines Corporation, MTU of West Germany and Fiat Aviazione. Lufthansa opted for the competitor engine but the company remains optimistic.

At the smaller end of the market, Rolls-Royce has won orders for over 500 Tays. The Gulfstream IV business jet and Fokker 100 airliner, both powered by the Tay engine, have entered service. The Tay has also become the focus of a re-engining programme on the BAe One-Eleven regional jetliner, 160 of which are still in service.

Military engine group In 1987 the division represented 40% of the group's turnover and 38.3% of operating profit. Operating profit increased 12.7% to £133m on turnover 10.8% up at £820m. This area of the group has been relatively static for a number of years.

The division's main engine programmes are: the Pegasus for the Harrier and AV-8B; the Turbo-Union RB199 for the three-nation Tornado strike and air-defence aircraft; the Rolls-Royce Turbomeca Adour for the Hawk and Jaguar; the Viper for trainer and strike-aircraft; and the Gem, Gnome and RTM322 for helicopters. Rolls-Royce is also engaged in a collaborative programme aimed at supplying an advanced engine for the proposed new European Fighter Aircraft.

Rolls-Royce is virtually the sole supplier of aero-engines on aircraft operated by the UK armed forces. Accordingly the British Government is its most important military customer, with direct sales to MoD accounting for 31% of engine sales in the 1981 to 1986 period. Sales of the RB199 represented a further 35% of military engine deliveries. Sales to the US Department of Defense account for the largest element of the remaining 34%.

Deliveries of new engines, including parts to Rolls-Royce's European Turbo-Union partners, account for approximately half of total billings of the group's military aero-engine business. Repairs, overhauls and spares are of greater importance for military aero-engines than civil. This stems from the more rigorous nature of military engines of Rolls-Royce design still in service, but not in production.

The RB199 and Pegasus programmes offer the prospect of continuity of major engine production until the early 1990s, although it would be unrealistic to assume that annual delivery rates can increase above present levels. The gradual run-down of annual Tornado airframe production within Panavia,

following the completion of the Italian Air Force batch in 1986, probably means a corresponding reduction in the build rate of new engines by Turbo-Union. In addition, cuts in the procurement rate of the AV-8B in the US probably mean that the Harrier programme will not grow in terms of annual activity from recent levels, even though it includes the start of deliveries of GR5s to the Royal Air Force soon.

Industrial and marine In 1987 this division represented 7% of the group's turnover and 3.2% of operating profit. Operating profit increased 10% to £11m on turnover 11.1% down at £136m. Industrial and marine sales have increased only modestly since 1982, while profits – apart from an exceptionally strong 1985 – have been restrained.

The industrial and marine area produces gas turbines for power generation and for gas and oil pumping and has more than 175 industrial customers. It also provides gas turbine power for vessels of 25 of the world's navies including the Japanese Maritime Self Defence Force, for which the company is sole supplier of turbines.

Aero-engine-based gas turbine engines form a highly attractive means of providing electric or mechanical power with superior power-to-weight ratios than those achievable by more traditional gas turbines or diesel engines. Rolls-Royce industrial gas turbines are offered in the ten to 30 megawatt range, which is suitable for continuous power standby and load-following electric power applications and for mechanical drives associated with oil and gas exploration and production.

Over the past 20 years derivatives of aero-engines have been in naval applications. They are now the dominant power units for medium-size surface ships. An important future product development is likely to be the intercooled regenerative version of the highly successful Spey. Rolls-Royce has teamed with Allison, a General Motors subsidiary, and General Electric of the US to respond to a design contract placed by the US Navy, which if successful could form the basis of future naval propulsion.

Other activities In 1987 the division represented 7% of the group's turnover and 2.6% of operating profit. Operating profit increased 12.5% to £9m on turnover 1.3% down at £150m.

The repair and overhaul division works across Rolls-Royce's entire engine range. It is managed as a separate activity with sales split for reporting purposes between the civil engine group, the military engine group, and the industrial and marine division.

Rolls-Royce and Associates is responsible for the design and

C H A I R M A N ' S   S T A T E M E N T

'We enter 1988 with a sound balance sheet, with net cash funds of £137m, and with bank facilities of £250m (£150m committed) arranged in March 1987 in the form of a Multi-Option Facility. However, the US-based competition remains strong, aided by the weak dollar, and new business will only be won with excellent products backed up by impeccable customer service. I am confident we have both these attributes.

1987 was a year of particular significance since it saw the Company's successful return to the private sector after 16 years of public ownership....

The size of our order book, together with our wide range of engines and attractive market opportunities, gives confidence for continued progress in 1988 and a series of initiatives is under way to improve further the competitiveness of our products.' *Sir Francis Tombs*

supply of nuclear steam-raising plant for the Royal Navy's nuclear submarine fleet. The company also provides support for the Royal Navy in the maintenance and refuelling of operational nuclear-powered submarines. The company is bidding for work in support of civil nuclear power station programmes. These activities have shown a substantial expansion since 1983, due to the growth in nuclear reactor development work. Here, however, margins have been low and accordingly profits have not shown the same progress as turnover.

GEOGRAPHICAL REVIEW

Europe accounts for 27% of turnover, North America 48.4%, Asia 18.9%, Australasia 1.9%, Africa 1.4% and the rest of the world 2.5%. These percentages reflect a corporate policy of analysing engine sales by the country of domicile of the airframe manufacturer rather than by end-user. Thus the large US content reflects deliveries to Boeing of civil aero-engines and the Pegasus for the AV-8B programme, while Europe includes sales to Turbo-Union, the company responsible for the RB199 military engine.

CORPORATE CALENDAR

Year end	31 December
Preliminary results	March
Report and accounts	April
AGM	June
Final dividend paid	June
Interim results	September
Interim dividend paid	December

DIRECTORS' HOLDINGS

	Fully-paid ordinary shares	Options
	(beneficial)	
Sir Francis Tombs	21,811	146,300
Sir Arnold Hall	4,750	—
JO Keir	1,510	79,200
Sir Douglas Lowe	4,000	—
SC Miller	1,518	95,100
HG Mourgue	4,750	—
Sir Robin Nicholson	4,750	—
JA Rigg	6,045	136,500
Sir Ralph Robins	6,041	253,600
Sir Philip Shelbourne	4,750	—
JD Wragg	1,521	146,300

Total directors' remuneration in 1987 was £607,400, of which the chairman received £73,900 and the highest-paid director received £99,000.

PRINCIPAL SUBSIDIARY COMPANIES

Bristol Aerospace Limited – Canada, Deeside Titanium Limited (82%), Motores Rolls-Royce Limitada – Brazil, Rolls-Royce & Associates Limited (43%), Rolls-Royce (Canada) Limited – Canada, Rolls-Royce (China) Limited, Rolls-Royce (Far East) Limited, Rolls-Royce (France) Limited, Rolls-Royce Capital Inc – US, Rolls-Royce Credit Corporation – US, Rolls-Royce Holdings Inc – US, Rolls-Royce Inc – US, Rolls-Royce India Limited, Rolls-Royce Industrial Turbines (Saudia Arabia) Ltd – Saudi Arabia (51%), Rolls-Royce Industries Canada Inc – Canada, Rolls-Royce Leasing Limited, Rolls-Royce of Australia Pty Limited – Australia, Rolls-Royce Plant Leasing Limited

PRINCIPAL RELATED COMPANIES

Cooper Rolls Corporation (Canada) – Canada (50%), Cooper Rolls Inc – US (50%), Cooper Rolls Limited (50%), Eurojet Turbo GmbH – Germany (33%), GEC Rolls-Royce (Power Generation) Limited (50%), IAE International Aero Engines AG – Switzerland (30%), Rolls-Royce Turbomeca Limited (50%), Turbo-Union Limited (40%)

BRAND NAMES

Adour, Dart, 535, Gem, Gnome, Olympus, Pegasus, RB199, RB211-524, RTM322, Rolls-Royce, Spey, Tay, V2500, Viper

CONTACTS AND FURTHER INFORMATION

SJ Hollingsworth, Rolls-Royce plc, 65 Buckingham Gate, London SW1E 6AT. Tel: 01-222 9020.

ROTHMANS INTERNATIONAL p.l.c.

GENERAL INFORMATION

Head office	15 Hill Street, London W1X 7FB. Tel: 01-491 4366
Directors	Sir Robert Crichton-Brown (executive chairman), The Hon David CS Montagu (executive deputy chairman), VA Brink (chief executive), E De Jaegere, ME Thompson. *Non-exec* DSA Carroll (deputy chairman), JW Mayo, K Morgen, MJ Roux, N Senn, Baron Jacques de Staercke
Advisers	Samuel Montagu & Co Ltd, NM Rothschild & Sons Ltd
Auditors	Coopers & Lybrand
Registrars	Ravensbourne Registration Services Ltd
Brokers	Rowe & Pitman Ltd
Solicitors	Linklaters & Paines

GENERAL FINANCIAL INFORMATION

Market capitalisation	£1.195bn at 1 January 1988
Capital structure	
Issued ordinary shares (12½p)	315.3m ordinary and 'B' shares (18.4m ordinary with four votes per share; 269.6m 'B' shares with one vote per share)
Issued preference shares (£1)	0.3m 4.67% CP
Warrants	None
Convertibles	None
Traded options	None
ADRs	One ordinary share per ADR
Shareholders over 5%	Rothmans Tobacco (Holdings) Ltd 43%, Philip Morris 25%

FT CATEGORY

FT: Tobaccos
FT-A: Miscellaneous

MAJOR ACTIVITIES

Like many other large tobacco companies, Rothmans has attempted to diversify, but with limited success. At one stage, the substantial tobacco interests were just part of a group comprising: luxury goods, through Dunhill and Cartier; Chloé perfumes; beer in Canada and Ireland (Carling O'Keefe); oil and gas in Canada (Star); wineries in Canada (Jordan Valley); domestic appliances based in Germany (Rowenta Werke); and an assortment of minor diversifications by associates and former associates in New Zealand, Australia, Ireland, Malaysia and Singapore.

Such diversifications only proved moderately successful. Rothmans has subsequently undergone a programme of significant retrenchment. The most important disposal was that of Carling O'Keefe in Canada which, until 1985, had been a major success story, but which latterly had been wrongfooted in the beer market and suffered plummetting profits before being sold. Rothmans' principal diversifications are now limited to 51% of Dunhill Holdings (luxury goods), 47% of Cartier Monde (luxury goods), 51% of Montblanc (pens), and Chloé (fashion goods and perfumes) supplemented in April 1988 by the acquisition of a large stake in Piaget.

An exact analysis of sales and profits of Rothmans is almost impossible to derive – given the web of associates' holdings, the way results are presented and the fact that many associates are themselves diverse. Nonetheless, after adjusting the year to 31 March 1987 results for the disposals of Carling and Rowenta, it is estimated that some 58% of pre-interest operating profits came from tobacco and the bulk of the residue from luxury goods; at this pre-interest level, however, all the profits of the partly owned luxury goods subsidiaries and associates have been consolidated. On an equity account-ing basis, the tobacco content would rise to some 70% of operating profits. In 1988, as disposal cash has built up, a significant proportion of profits will be derived from interest receipts.

In 1987 it is estimated that over 75% of profits were outside the UK. The company's overall result has therefore been strongly influenced by the international value of sterling – particularly *vis-à-vis* the Canadian dollar, the Australian dollar, the German mark and the Middle Eastern currencies.

FINANCIAL HISTORY

Rothmans' financial performance has been mixed. 1984 pre-tax profits of £151m – struck after rationalisation costs of £24m – fell to £94m in 1986, when exceptional and rationalisa-tion costs amounted to £47m. By 1987 pre-tax profits had recovered to £195.5m after a further £15m rationalisation provision. Since 1982 the net dividend has risen 45%.

Equally since 1982, Rothmans has taken rationalisation costs of £140m above the line and emerged as a leaner and more efficient company. Increased cash flows from a more profitable operation, combined with disposal proceeds of Carling O'Keefe (£94m) and others, have transformed the balance sheet, which is now rich in cash. Cash and short term securities amounted to £483m at September 1987, against just £84m in March 1987. For perspective, as recently as 1985, total cash and near-cash of £191m compared with debt and convertibles totalling £289m.

In the six months to 31 September 1987, pre-tax profits doubled to £140m from £74m in the previous period, with a very significant rise in the contribution by the tobacco companies. Dunhill and the other luxury goods products raised profits by 50%. Rothmans moved from net interest payments to receipts in this latter period.

SHARE PRICE HISTORY

Between 1983 and 1986 Rothmans' share price performance was dull, trading between 115p and 175p. After reaching a short term high in December 1984, the price retreated to 120p in late 1985, and failed to return to the 1984 level until early 1987. During this period of falling profitability and mounting rationalisation costs, the share's price relative fell from 31% to the FT-A All-Share index to 17% – an underperformance of close to 45%.

1987 was the year of recovery in terms of profits, the share price and the market. In the space of eight months the shares moved from 175p in early 1987 to peak at 499p in October 1987 and the price-relative moved from 20% to 46%.

The shares fell back in the October 1987 crash to 335p. They have since recovered to over 420p and are back to their high relative to the market.

CHAIRMAN'S STATEMENT

'The Group's results for 1986/87 demonstrate that we are moving in the right direction after costly decisions to rationalise our various businesses in an unfavourable trading environment. Improving results are now coming through and as a result we have seen a substantial recovery in earnings and a stronger balance sheet with greatly improved liquidity. On that firmer base, the group is now much better equipped to move forward.... The encouraging progress made in the first half [1987/88] gives us further confidence in looking ahead. I can assure shareholders that we continue to strive for further progress in the group's performance.' *Sir Robert Crichton-Brown*

F I V E   Y E A R   F I N A N C I A L   I N F O R M A T I O N

Year	Turnover (£m)	Pre-tax (£m)	Earnings (p)	Dividends net (p)	Dividend cover (x)	Net assets (p)	Price (p) High	Low	PER (x) High	Low	Yield (%) High	Low
1983	1,831	130.5	23.9	5.3	4.5	307.4	129	102	4.5	2.9	7.72	5.04
1984	2,293	151.2	24.6	6.0	4.1	422.3	181	116	5.7	3.1	7.39	4.89
1985	2,719	121.9	14.2	6.4	2.2	459.5	200	115	6.3	4.5	7.95	4.43
1986	2,643	93.9	10.0	6.7	1.5	435.1	179	130	6.5	5.2	7.03	5.51
1987	2,736	195.5	28.6	7.7	3.7	510.6	499	178	12.9	5.9	5.54	2.14

SENIOR MANAGEMENT

The board of Rothmans International reflects the international spread of operations and effective control. Sir Robert Crichton-Brown, the executive chairman, succeeded Sir David Nicolson as chairman in 1985. David Montagu, who was appointed executive deputy chairman on 4 January 1988, will succeed Sir Robert Crichton-Brown as executive chairman on the latter's expected retirement at the end of 1989. Donal Carroll, the non-executive deputy chairman, is a long-standing board member. Vernon Brink, the chief executive, has served in this role since 1981. Malcolm Thompson, the finance director, has also served on the main board since 1978. Etienne De Jaegere is the other executive director on a board of 11, which includes Baron Jacques de Staercke and The Hon David Montagu.

CAPITAL

Rothmans' share capital is split into two classes of shares. There are 18.4m ordinary shares in issue, each share carrying four votes. At March 1987 there were additionally 248.8m 'B' shares issued, each carrying one vote. During 1987/88, the remaining junior and senior bonds were converted into 'B' shares, raising the 'B' share total to 296.9m shares.

The high-voting ordinary shares are almost all owned by Rothmans Tobacco (Holdings) Ltd, itself controlled by the Rupert Foundation SA, part of Rembrandt of South Africa. Additionally the Rupert Foundation owns 86m 'B' shares, giving it a total of 33% of the equity but 43% of the votes.

Since 1981, Philip Morris has had an interest in Rothmans, acquired from Rothmans Tobacco (Holdings). Currently, Philip Morris hold 107.4m 'B' shares, (36% of all the 'B' shares in issue) but 29% of the total equity and just 24.99% of the votes. The minority investing public accounts for 32% of the votes. It is understood that Philip Morris has undertaken to the European Commission to be a passive investor in the company.

The limited marketability of the stock and the presence of two large shareholders has traditionally detracted from the group's rating. In May 1988, Rembrandt announced that it intended to restructure its domestic and international quoted and unquoted holdings.

GROUP REVIEW

Rothmans has now slimmed down its operations into two principal categories – tobacco and luxury goods. The holding structure is complex, making it almost impossible to unravel the divisional contributions.

For the group as a whole, operating profits advanced from £115.9m in 1986 to £203.5m in 1987, before total interest charges of £7m. The operating profit advance in the first half of 1987/88 was to £128.7m from £78.3m (+64%), whilst following the sale of low-yielding assets and the conversion of the junior and senior bonds, interest payments were transformed into interest receipts of £11.3m. Pre-tax profits rose from £73.8m to £140.0m.

For the full 1987/88 year, pre-tax profits of £300m (£196m) are expected to be announced. In 1989 pre-tax profits should advance a further 15%, putting Rothmans on a comparable rating to Philip Morris and RJR Nabisco, but also on a significant premium to BAT.

Tobacco The important UK and German markets are served by wholly owned subsidiaries, but the significant Benelux and Canadian operations are 60% and 72% owned respectively, whilst Rothmans Canada actually holds just 60% of the tobacco operation, with Philip Morris holding the residual 40%. Elsewhere, Rothmans in Australia, Malaysia and Singapore is represented by 50%-held associates, whilst the Irish company, PJ Carroll and Company plc, is 39%-held.

The UK and German wholly-owned tobacco operations are now benefiting from the very substantial rationalisation that has taken place since 1982. Sadly in most markets Rothmans' market share has been shrinking – in the UK down to under 10% (against 14% in 1981) and to some 12% in Germany through Brinkmann, compared with 18% in the early 1980s. Rothmans, Dunhill and Peter Stuyvesant in the UK and Lord Extra, Lux and Peer in Germany have all declined. Operations in both these countries had been loss-making.

In Canada the amalgamation of Rothmans and Benson & Hedges (owned by Philip Morris) has bolstered market share to some 29% to 30%, but most mainstream brands have succumbed to the advance of Imasco (owned by BAT). The harshly competitive conditions in Canada in 1986 and part of 1987 depressed profits significantly, but margins are now being restored.

In Singapore, market share has dropped marginally to about 37%, but in Malaysia it has bounced to some 38% with the Dunhill brand performing very well. In Belgium and the

Share price and relative to FT-A All-Share

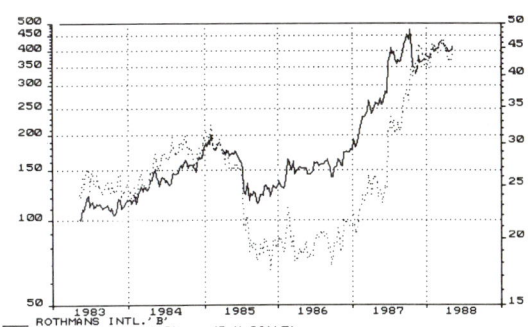

ROTHMANS INTL.' B'
Relative to All Share (R.H.SCALE)

Netherlands, Tabacofina's market share has held up well. In Australia, primarily with Winfield, Rothmans' market share is about 35% and is the market leader.

Between 1983 and 1987, profits from tobacco (consolidating 100% of associates' contributions) rose from £87.1m before interest to £205.9m, whilst in the first six months of 1987/88 tobacco profits almost doubled to £138.3m (£77.6m). Further advances are expected in 1988/89 as additional rationalisation gains come through.

Luxury goods Dunhill Holdings UK, a publicly quoted company, is 51% held by Rothmans International, which in turn holds Rothmans' stakes in Montblanc and Chloé. Cartier Monde is 47% held, directly by Rothmans.

Dunhill was originally a tobacco manufacturing and retail business which has transformed itself, both by organic growth and acquisition, into a broadly-based high quality branded goods business. Its range now includes clothing, watches, writing instruments, leather goods and fragrances. Cartier was brought to 47% ownership in 1984 with an exclusive jewellery business and with a wide range of luxury consumer goods. Both these businesses have an international flavour with premium priced products being sold in many markets, including America and Japan.

The luxury goods operations have moved from strength to strength – from £5.9m in 1983 to £68.8m (consolidating 100% of each operation) at the pre-interest level in 1987. Pre-interest profits added 50% to £31.3m in the first half of 1987/88.

GEOGRAPHICAL REVIEW

In 1987 only 5% of revenues arose in the UK – down from 7% in 1986. The profits content was probably marginally higher, with a possible contribution, including some profit on cigarette exports, of £30m – 15% of group profits. In 1987/88, reflecting the rationalisation gains in the UK tobacco business and good growth by Dunhill, the UK content of pre-tax profits could approach the estimated 19% achieved in the first half interim results.

35% of revenues arose in continental Europe in 1987, 28% in the Far East and Australasia, 12% in the Middle East – much of it represented by cigarette exports – and 20% in the Americas, principally Canada.

CORPORATE CALENDAR

Year end	31 March
Preliminary results	June
Report and accounts	July
AGM	July
Final dividend paid	October
Interim results	November
Interim dividend paid	January

DIRECTORS' HOLDINGS

	'B' ordinary shares	Options for 'B' ordinary shares
VA Brink	—	200,000
Sir Robert Crichton-Brown	—	300,000
E De Jaegere	—	83,000
JW Mayo	13,666	—
ME Thompson	—	100,000

E De Jaegere also holds 100 share in Tabacofina NV.

Total directors' remuneration in 1987 was £1.05m, of which the chairman, who was the highest-paid director, received £230,000.

PRINCIPAL SUBSIDIARIES AND RELATED COMPANIES

Carreras Group Limited – Jamaica (47%), Carreras of Cyprus Limited – Cyprus, Carroll Industries Plc – Republic of Ireland (39%), Cartier Monde SA – Luxembourg (47%), Chloé SA – France (51%), Dunhill Holdings Plc (51%), Martin Brinkmann AG – Germany, Montblanc-Simplo GmbH – Germany (51%), Rothmans (UK) Limited, Rothmans Holdings Limited – Australia (50%), Rothmans Industries Limited – Singapore (50%), Rothmans International Tobacco (UK) Ltd, Rothmans of Pall Mall (Malaysia) Berhad – Malaysia (50%), Rothmans, Benson & Hedges Inc – Canada (43%), Schimmelpenninck Sigarenfabrieken BV – Netherlands, Tabacofina NV – Belgium (60%), Turmac Tobacco Company BV – Netherlands

BRAND NAMES

Benson & Hedges – Canada, Carreras, Cartier, Chloé, Consulate – UK, Craven – Canada, Dunhill, Lane, Lord, Lux, Montblanc, Peer – Germany, Peter Stuyvesant, Piaget, Rothmans, Schimmelpennick

CONTACTS AND FURTHER INFORMATION

ME Thompson, Group finance director, Rothmans International p.l.c., 15 Hill Street, London W1X 7FB. Tel: 01-491 4366.

ROWNTREE plc

GENERAL INFORMATION

Head office	PO Box 202, York YO1 1XY. Tel: 0904 612261
Directors	KHM Dixon (chairman), D Cramb CBE (deputy chairman), DB Bowden, T Copley, J Guerin, RA Kaner, JL Mackinlay, NJ Nightingale, R Sugden. *Non-exec* DE Cook, Sir Michael Franklin KCB CMG, JAP Treasure, Sir Graham Wilkins
Advisers	J Henry Schroder Wagg & Co Ltd, County NatWest WoodMac
Auditors	Price Waterhouse
Registrars	Rowntree plc, PO Box 202, York YO1 1XY. Tel: 0904 612261
Brokers	Cazenove & Co
Solicitors	Slaughter and May

GENERAL FINANCIAL INFORMATION

Market capitalisation	£961.3m at 1 January 1988
Capital structure	
Issued ordinary shares (50p)	215m
Issued preference shares (£1)	1m 4.2% First CP, 0.8m 4.9% Second CP, 0.9m 5.25% Third CP
Warrants	8.86m, one ordinary share at 330p up to 1 October 1989
Convertibles	£69m, 4.5% convertible bonds 2002 (176.376 shares per £1,000 bond)
Traded options	None
ADRs	None
Shareholders over 5%	Suchard 29.9%; Nestlé 16%

FT CATEGORY

FT: Food, groceries etc
FT-A: Food manufacturing

MAJOR ACTIVITIES

Rowntree consists of over 30 companies making and selling confectionery, snack foods and grocery products throughout the world. It is one of the world's top three confectionery manufacturers and the UK's largest exporter of chocolate and sugar confectionery. It has a very long history and owns some of the world's best known confectionery brands. Its principal competitors, in a confectionery industry that is becoming increasingly international, are Cadbury, Nestlé, Suchard, Hershey in the US, and the privately-owned Mars group.

The Rowntree cocoa and chocolate business was founded in York in 1862. It became a public company in 1898 under the chairmanship of Joseph Rowntree, a leading Quaker and philanthropist. The firm's growth was sufficient to justify the formation of subsidiary companies in Australia, Canada, Ireland and South Africa.

In the 1930s the UK business established a number of confectionery brands that have since become leading international brands. They include Kit Kat, Aero and Black Magic. The merger with Mackintosh in 1969 gave Rowntree a number of additional toffee and chocolate products, including Quality Street.

In 1964 the group began to establish a continental European base. In 1981 the grocery products division was established in the UK. 1982 saw a move into snack foods, and in the following year the group acquired Tom's Foods, based in Georgia and a long established snack food company.

Further US expansion took place in 1983 with the acquisition of Laura Secord, a chain of speciality chocolate stores, and in 1985 with the purchase of the Original Cookie Company, a chain of hot cookie shops. In 1986 Sunmark, a sugar confectionery producer in the southern states of the US, and Hot Sam, 275 stores selling pretzels and hot dogs, were acquired. In 1988 Rowntree disposed of both its UK snack food operations and Tom's Foods in the US.

Rowntree dropped Mackintosh from its title in June 1987, reflecting the wider product base of the group and the increased international nature of its earnings.

As part of a reorganisation programme, Rowntree has rationalised its production facilities in the UK and Europe and has begun to benefit from some significant cost savings. This plan has also involved a move into specialist retailing that offers additional volume growth over the long term. This is a reflection of a management that is more market-orientated than previously, certainly less conservative, and much more aware of competition.

Given the continued moves to consolidate within the food industry on both sides of the Atlantic, it is almost inevitable that Rowntree will be deemed a takeover candidate from time to time. However, the management is showing very good signs of being astute custodians of a string of premier brand names to the benefit of employees, consumers and shareholders.

In April 1988 Rowntree became the subject of a bid of £2.1bn from Nestlé, the Swiss multi-national food company. Earlier in the month, Jacobs Suchard had made a dawn raid on Rowntree and built up a 15% stake. Nestlé then countered by making a full bid. Jacobs Suchard subsequently increased its stake to 29.9%. Though there was pressure on the Government to intervene to protect Rowntree's independence, it looked as if one or other of the bids would be successful.

The group headquarters are in York. The company employs some 33,000 people around the world.

FINANCIAL HISTORY

After very modest pre-tax profit increases from 1984 to 1986, Rowntree moved sharply ahead in 1987. On turnover 11% up at £1.427bn, pre-tax profits rose by 33% to £112.1m. Earnings per share were 17% up at 40.8p. The full year dividend was raised by 14% to 15.5p. There were strong profits performances from the UK and Europe.

Since 1983 pre-tax profits have risen 83.2% from £61.2m, while turnover has increased 50% from £951.9m. Margins have increased from 6.4% to 7.9%. Earnings per share are 36.5% up from 29.9p. Dividends have increased from 9.75p to 15.5p (+59%).

Rowntree's move into snack foods in both the UK and the US has been unsuccessful and contributed to the sluggish profits growth of the period 1984 to 1986. The 1987 results emphasise the wisdom of the group's decision to put these businesses up for sale. The UK snack foods company made trading profits of just £1.3m (£1.6m) and Tom's Foods in the US traded poorly with sterling profits falling 33% to £13m (£19.5m). Receipts from the two disposals are likely to cancel group debt of around £160m at the 1987 year-end.

SHARE PRICE HISTORY

Rowntree's share price has been influenced in the past few years by takeover speculation in 1984 and also by the relatively dull profits performance.

In 1984 the price rose from a low of 200p to a high of around 380p, a performance well ahead of the overall equity market. However, as the takeover speculation subsided with no evidence to justify what had been persistent rumour, the stock began to fall in the second half of 1985. It was during this time that profit expectations began to fall.

Between 1984 and 1986, pre-tax profits rose by a relatively pedestrian 13% as the group experienced some problems in Europe and only marginal growth in the US. This trend

						Price (p)		PER (x)		Yield (%)	
Year	Turnover (£m)	Pre-tax (£m)	Earnings (p)	Dividends net (p)	Dividend cover (x)	Net assets (p)	High	Low	High	Low	High	Low
1983	952	61.2	29.9	9.75	3.2	218	248	197	14.5	9.8	6.50	4.88
1984	1,156	74.5	34.8	11.00	3.3	244	388	213	18.8	10.5	6.02	3.68
1985	1,205	79.3	34.8	12.20	2.9	222	438	337	19.0	12.0	4.55	3.53
1986	1,290	84.0	35.0	13.60	2.6	207	530	370	18.9	11.9	4.76	3.24
1987	1,428	112.1	40.8	15.50	2.6	190	583	380	20.6	12.0	5.12	3.19

FIVE YEAR FINANCIAL INFORMATION

continued into 1986, culminating in the Sunmark US acquisition in August funded by a heavy and unexpected rights issue which raised £144m.

Between the first quarter and third quarter of 1986 Rowntree's share price fell from 530p to 380p. Although the share price reached new highs of about 580p in the summer of 1987, the performance was patchy when measured against the market.

The price fell to 379p during the 1987 autumn crash but had recovered to 460p in March 1988. Relative recovery may continue, given that at long last the profits outlook has improved.

In April 1988 Suchard made a dawn raid for Rowntree shares, bidding 630p a share for 15% of the company. Suchard wished to acquire a 25% stake, though it said that it would not make a full bid. The shares climbed above 730p. This was followed by a £2.1bn bid from Nestlé at 890p a share, leading to the shares rising above 900p.

SENIOR MANAGEMENT

The board consists of ten executive members with four directors for particular geographic regions, with the UK responsibilities split between confectionery and non-confectionery. There are four non-executive directors.

The group chairman is Kenneth Dixon, who was elected in 1981 on the retirement of Sir Donald Barron. He had previously been a deputy chairman and managing director of the UK confectionery division. He first became a director in 1970.

On the retirement of David Cramb in May 1988, Sir Graham Wilkins, a non-executive director and chairman of THORN EMI, became deputy chairman. Trevor Copley has been chairman of Wilson-Rowntree, Rowntree Hoadley and the export division since 1979.

Jean Guerin has been chairman of the group's European region since 1985. In 1988 Peter Blackburn was appointed chairman of the whole of Rowntree's UK and the Republic of Ireland region.

Lindsay Mackinlay is director, group human resources. Roy Sugden was appointed chairman of the North American region in 1988. David Bowden is group finance director. Nicholas Nightingale is company secretary and a group director.

CAPITAL

Rowntree has used its shares on a number of occasions since 1983, including having two rights issues. In 1981 £42m was raised by a rights issue. In 1986 a one for four rights issue raised £144m through the issue of 42.6m shares at 350p to fund the acquisition of Sunmark, a US sugar confectionery company.

· 17.5m shares were placed in 1983 to fund the £140m US acquisition of Tom's Foods. A £30m Eurobond was issued in 1984 with warrants attached granting rights to subscribe for 9.09m shares at 330p up to 1 October 1989. Full subscription would increase the issued share capital of 215m by 4%.

In February 1985, 8m ordinary shares were placed with institutions at 353.25p per share to part-finance the acquisition of the Original Cookie Company. In March 1987, £69m of convertible bonds were issued at a coupon of 4.5% and a conversion price of 567p per share, or 176.376 shares per £1,000 bond.

In January 1988 the company announced that it was seeking buyers for Tom's Foods in the US and Rowntree Snack Foods in the UK. The two disposals are expected to raise £180m. The first of these, Rowntree Snack Foods, was sold to Borden Inc for £34m in April 1988.

GROUP REVIEW

Rowntree is divided into four geographical regions – the UK and Republic of Ireland, North America, Europe, Australasia and rest of world.

The company's major export markets are Saudi Arabia, Kuwait, the lower Gulf, Hong Kong and Singapore. Repatriation of foreign workers from the Middle East led to lower export sales in 1986 and 1987.

UK and Republic of Ireland Along with Cadbury and Mars, Rowntree dominates the chocolate confectionery market. The market remains very competitive. In Kit Kat, Rowntree owns one of the most successful products in the confectionery market. It is the top selling item with sales at retail level worth over £150m in a market that in total was worth over £2.0bn in 1987.

Rowntree Sun-Pat is the grocery subsidiary, with particular strengths in table jelly, peanut butter, Pan Yan pickles and honey, trading under the Gale's and Judges brands.

The group purchased the Richoux restaurant business in October 1987 for £5.2m. Richoux sells quality continental chocolates and operates restaurants mostly in the London area.

Share price and relative to FT-A All-Share

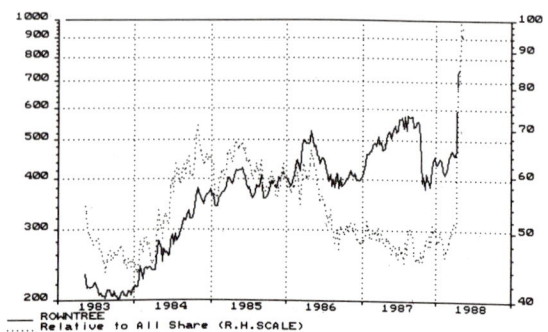

A further 10 restaurants were added to this business following the acquisition of Richards (Cakes) Ltd in April 1988.

In the Republic of Ireland a large range of products, including Kit Kat and Quality Street, is sold by a subsidiary company in Dublin.

The division employs 15,800 people spread around production facilities in seven cities and towns. In 1987 sales were up 5.7% to £566.4m (£536m), equivalent to 40% of the group total. Profits were 19.3% up at £61.7m (£51.7m).

North America Rowntree has both production and retailing interests in North America. It owns Laura Secord, which produces and retails chocolate products, and Sunmark, which produces and retails sugar confectionery. They were bought to further the group's move into speciality retailing. Other interests include the Original Cookie Company and Hot Sam, both of which bake and sell hot cookies, pretzels and hot dogs.

CHAIRMAN'S STATEMENT

'Rowntree plc exists to market branded products to consumers throughout the world at a profit for its shareholders.

We will concentrate on building strong positions in world confectionery markets by developing and buying high quality national and international brands.

We will continue to expand our smaller businesses: grocery products in the UK and specialist retailing of confectionery and related products worldwide.

We are committed to being responsible employers and good citizens in all communities in which we live.

We are open to change and new ideas.' *Kenneth Dixon*

Tom's Foods, a savoury snack business, was acquired in 1983. A strong cash generator but a disappointing profits performer, the company is based in the south, and has suffered from competition from Frit-O-Lay, a PepsiCo subsidiary. In 1987 Tom's Foods profits were 33% down in sterling terms and 26% down in dollars. In January 1988 Rowntree put Tom's Foods up for sale to concentrate on its sugar confectionery businesses. The sale was completed in April 1988 for $200m.

Rowntree does not manufacture Kit Kat and Rolo in America although they are produced and sold under licence by one of its competitors, Hershey. Royalty income is increasing substantially.

The group has embarked upon a programme of opening new retail outlets each year. The group's purchase of Gorant Candies, a small US chocolate business, has brought the total of shops operated by Rowntree in North America to 729. They are performing well.

In 1987 sales for North America were up 15.4% to £416.1m (£361m), equivalent to 29% of the group total. Profits were up 18.8% to £41m (£34.7m). Sunmark made an important contribution of £16.1m.

Europe Rowntree has production facilities in France, Germany and Holland. France leads European sales. The leading products – Lion, Polo mints and chocolate blocks – are all produced by the Noisiel factory. Quality Street, Lanvin assortments and Escargots are produced at Dijon. In August 1987 the group purchased the French retail group Sego-Martial, which controls 40 retail outlets located mostly near Paris, and has franchise agreements with over 60 shops throughout France.

The Hamburg factory in West Germany produces and sells

After Eight, Kit Kat, Polo, Smarties and Choco Crossies. In Holland, Nuts is the main product, made at Elst, near Arnhem. The group's products are also sold in Belgium, Spain, Sweden, Italy and most other European countries. Rowntree believes that it is well placed for the Single European Market commencing in 1992.

Sales in 1987 were 16% up at £300.4m (£260m), representing 21% of the group total. Profits more than doubled to £11m (£5.1m).

Australasia and rest of world This division covers Australia, South Africa and the export of product from the UK to the company's agents overseas. Rowntree Hoadley in Australia generated sales of £57.1m (£54.4m) in 1987. It has only recently begun to emerge from a period of extensive reorganisation. 1987 profits were 17.5% up at £4.7m (£4m). Production is now centred at Campbellfield, Melbourne.

With a market share of over 15%, the Australian operation is in a position to grow, even though the competition is intense, particularly from Cadbury, the clear market leader. To further the group's aims in retailing, a chain of 45 premium ice-cream parlours was purchased in 1986.

In South Africa, Wilson-Rowntree, established in 1925, is one of the leading confectionery companies with a 25% share. Major brands include Kit Kat, Smarties, Bar One and XXX mints. In 1987, rest of world turnover was £87.6m (£79.5m) and profits £11.7m (£10.4m).

GEOGRAPHICAL REVIEW

Over the past five years Rowntree has become much more international through an active acquisition programme that has centred mainly in North America. In 1987 trading profits from the UK accounted for 47% (49%) of the total, North America 31.5% (32%), Australasia 4% (4%), Europe 8.5% (5%), and the rest of the world 9% (10%).

With the disposal of Tom's Foods, the US share of profits will be reduced to 25%. The company's target in the medium term is 40%. The funds released from the disposal are likely to lead to acquisition in the US sugar confectionery business.

CORPORATE CALENDAR

Year end	31 December
Preliminary results	March
Report and accounts	April
AGM	April
Final dividend paid	July
Interim results	September
Interim dividend paid	January

DIRECTORS' HOLDINGS

	Fully-paid ordinary shares	Options
KHM Dixon	7,243	89,761
D Cramb	2,960	6,650
PH Blackburn	3,589	45,843
DB Bowden	2,961	53,203
T Copley	5,741	53,808
J Guerin	3,406	51,450
RA Kaner	7,811	47,437
JL Mackinlay	14,641	48,328
NJ Nightingale	2,020	46,239
R Sugden	9,289	50,993
JAP Treasure	500	—
Sir Graham Wilkins	1,250	—
DE Cook	500	—

Total directors' remuneration for the year to 2 January 1988 was £1.607m, of which the chairman received £138,000.

THE ROYAL BANK OF SCOTLAND GROUP plc

PRINCIPAL SUBSIDIARIES AND RELATED COMPANIES

Elect Chocolates Ltd, Gray, Dunn & Co Ltd – Scotland, Gorant Candies Inc – US, Holgates Honey Farm Ltd, Hot Sam Companies Inc – US, Judges Money, Laura Secord Inc – Canada, Multisnack Ltd, Nörgen-Vaaz Ice Cream Company Pty Ltd – Australia, Nuts Chocoladefabriek BV – Netherlands, Richoux Ltd, Rowntree DeMet's Inc – US, Rowntree Hoadley Ltd – Australia, Rowntree Ltd – Canada, Rowntree Mackintosh (Ingredients) Ltd, Rowntree Mackintosh BV – Netherlands, Rowntree Mackintosh Canada Ltd – Canada, Rowntree Mackintosh Confectionery Ltd, Rowntree Mackintosh Distribution Ltd, Rowntree Mackintosh European Export Ltd, Rowntree Mackintosh Export Ltd, Rowntree Mackintosh GmbH – West Germany, Rowntree Mackintosh Inc – US, Rowntree Mackintosh International BV – Netherlands, Rowntree Mackintosh International Finance BV – Netherlands, Rowntree Mackintosh International Ltd, Rowntree Mackintosh NV – Belgium, Rowntree Mackintosh SA – France, Rowntree Mackintosh SA – Spain, Rowntree Mackintosh SpA – Italy, Rowntree Mackintosh (Ireland) Plc – Ireland, SEG (Warehousing & Distribution) Ltd, Sooner Foods Ltd, Sunmark Inc – US, The Original Cookie Company Inc – US, Wilson-Rowntree (Pty) Ltd – South Africa

BRAND NAMES

Aero, After Eight, Big Cat, Black Magic, Blue Riband, Breakaway, Caramac, Coffee Crisp, Dairy Box, David, Fox's Glacier Mints & Fruits, Hot Sam's, Jellytots, Kit Kat, Laura Secord, Lion, Matchmakers, Menier, Mintola, Munchies, Nerds, Novo, Nuts, Polo, Quality Street, Rolo, Smarties, Sun-Pat, Sweetarts, Toffee Crisp, Turtles, Violet Crumble, Yorkie

CONTACTS AND FURTHER INFORMATION

Gavin Russell, Director of Public Relations, Rowntree plc, York YO1 1XY. Tel: 0904 53071.

GENERAL INFORMATION

Head office	42 St Andrew Square, Edinburgh EH2 2YE. Tel: 031-556 8555
Directors	Sir Michael Young-Herries OBE MC DL LLD DLitt (chairman), CM Winter (group chief executive), HE Farley (deputy group chief executive), MV Blank, HE Farley, RM Maiden, Dr GR Mathewson CBE. *Non-exec* PEG Balfour CBE, Sir Austin Pearce CBE PhD DSC (vice-chairman), The Rt Hon The Earl of Airlie KT GCVO PC DL, Sir Robin Duthie CBE LLD, IFH Grant JP DL, HLC Greig CVO CBE, AMM Grossart LLD, AM Hamilton CBE JP, JCR Inglis, JNC James FRICS, N Quick CBE DL LLD, CFE Shakerley, Sir Adam Thomson CBE LLD, The Rt Hon Lord Thomson of Monifieth KT PC LLD DLitt DSc FEIS
Advisers	Charterhouse Bank Ltd
Auditors	Deloitte Haskins & Sells
Registrars	The Royal Bank of Scotland Registrar's Department
Brokers	Alexanders Laing & Cruikshank, Bell Lawrie Ltd
Solicitors	Dundas & Wilson, Freshfields

GENERAL FINANCIAL INFORMATION

Market capitalisation	£1.051bn at 1 January 1988
Capital structure	
Issued ordinary shares (25p)	284.8m
Issued preference shares (£1)	None
Warrants	7.2m, one share at 443p per share till 3 November 1992
Convertibles	None
Traded options	None
ADRs	None
Shareholders over 5%	Kuwait Investment Office 14.44%

FT CATEGORY

FT: Banks, HP & leasing
FT-A: Banks

MAJOR ACTIVITIES

Through the Royal Bank of Scotland and subsidiary companies, the group provides a comprehensive range of banking, financial and related services. The group has an extensive branch network in Scotland and a rapidly expanding one in England and Wales.

The Royal Bank of Scotland and Williams and Glyn's Bank operated as two separate clearing banks prior to October 1985. The branch network of the former was mainly in Scotland and that of the latter primarily in the north of England. They now operate as one entity under the name of the Royal Bank of Scotland with a network of over 850 branches.

In 1985 the group acquired Charterhouse Bank, a member of the Accepting Houses Committee, and a provider of a full range of merchant banking services. Charterhouse had particular expertise in development capital operations.

Other divisions in the group include: the RoyScot Finance Group, which, with its subsidiaries is involved in leasing, factoring, hire purchase and instalment finance; the Royal Bank of Scotland Group Insurance Company Limited, which underwrites motor, home and credit insurance; and Royal Bank Group Services, which guides the technological development of the group and has responsibility for property, equipment and related resources. A long-standing involvement in Access and in Style Financial Services (in April 1988 the group increased its interest from 60% to 100%) are the bank's credit card interests.

The Royal Bank of Scotland Group's overseas representation includes branches and subsidiaries in the Channel Islands, the Isle of Man, Greece, Hong Kong, Singapore, France, Switzerland, Nassau and New York; an agency in San

FIVE YEAR FINANCIAL INFORMATION

Year	Turnover (£m)	Pre-tax (£m)	Earnings (p)	Dividends net (p)	Dividend cover (x)	Net assets (p)	Price (p) High	Price (p) Low	PER (x) High	PER (x) Low	Yield (%) High	Yield (%) Low
1983	406.5	95.5	33.7	7.1	4.7	351	215	109	11.0	5.6	8.50	4.70
1984	454.1	131.3	30.5	8.1	3.8	304	244	185	11.9	7.3	5.67	4.33
1985	556.5	166.3	35.7	9.6	3.7	311	294	216	11.9	7.6	5.37	4.00
1986	679.9	184.5	41.6	10.8	3.9	334	378	260	11.0	6.8	5.55	3.63
1987	821.6	197.2	45.0	12.7	3.5	369	440	280	11.2	4.7	5.80	3.55

Francisco; and representative offices in Sydney, Tokyo, Chicago, Houston, Los Angeles and São Paulo.

In April 1988 the group announced the purchase of Citizens Financial Group, the US retail and corporate bank based in Rhode Island, for $440m (£234m).

FINANCIAL HISTORY

Ignoring the incidence of an exceptional £77m provision in respect of the group's exposure to rescheduling countries in 1986/87, profits have almost trebled over the past four years.

Pre-tax profits for the year to 30 September 1987 before exceptional items were £274.2m, up 48.6%. After deducting exceptional items, profits were still up 6.9% at £197.2m. Part of this growth has reflected profits on the sale of premises resulting from the restructuring of the branch networks of the constituent banks, and part strong initial contributions from the Charterhouse Group on the back of higher levels of merchant banking activity

Profits within the banking business have essentially been a function of strong volume growth as the rate of return on average assets has remained relatively stable. Although problems with the group's exposure to the construction, oil and shipping industries dictated substantially higher debt provisions in 1985/86, domestic debt experience improved in 1986/87.

The trend of earnings in recent years has been distorted by fluctuations in the group's effective tax rate, principally brought about by the changes in the 1984 Finance Act. This has now converged on the standard rate of corporation tax, helped by a modest reallocation from general to specific provisions in 1985/86. In contrast to these fluctuations, the group has maintained a record of consistent dividend growth which over the past four years has averaged an annual 15.675%.

At the 1988 interim, pre-tax profits increased by 20.3% to £137.3m. Total assets exceeded £20bn for the first time and earnings per share were 16.6% ahead at 30.2p. The bad debt charge fell by £13.2m.

SHARE PRICE HISTORY

Share price performance over the past few years has been influenced by the continuing overhang of the abortive bids from Standard Chartered and the Hong Kong and Shanghai Banking Corporation in 1981. Although this has led to further bouts of takeover speculation, they have become less frequent. The shares underperformed the market by a substantial amount in the three years to mid-1987. Other factors which led to this underperformance were a lower perception of the quality of earnings that included larger contributions from the sale of properties and investments, and the delayed deteriora-

tion in group debt experience in 1985/86.

Since mid-1987, however, sentiment towards the shares has improved sharply. This can be attributed to the bank's limited exposure to troublesome Third World debt, and the increasingly visible benefits of the new group structure.

SENIOR MANAGEMENT

Sir Michael Young-Herries has been chairman since 1978. The present vice-chairmen are Peter Balfour, also chairman of Charterhouse plc and Sir Austin Pearce.

Charles Winter is group chief executive, and under the new management structure is supported by Rob Farley (deputy group chief executive), Bob Maiden (managing director, Royal Bank of Scotland plc), Victor Blank (chief executive, Charterhouse plc), Dr George Mathewson (director of strategic planning and development) and Kenneth Thompson (group finance director).

CAPITAL

The group has taken a series of steps to improve capital adequacy ratios on the yardsticks used by the Bank of England, and to maintain above-average ratios for the industry. The greater part of the cost of acquiring the Charterhouse Group was met by the proceeds of a £115m rights issue in 1985. In addition $300m was raised through the issue of undated floating rate notes which qualify as primary capital for the purpose of Bank of England capital guidelines.

No director has a significant shareholding but the Kuwait Investment Office has a declarable shareholding of 14.44%. A long standing shareholding by Lloyds Bank was disposed of in late 1985.

GROUP REVIEW

Domestic banking Since merging the two clearing banks, priority has been given to promoting the Royal Bank of Scotland name, particularly in England and Wales. This has involved the opening of new branches which in 1986/87 included locations in Ealing, Uxbridge, Burton-upon-Trent, Rugby and Burnley. Work has been commenced on branches in Milton Keynes and Loughborough. A major administrative centre has been inaugurated at The Angel, Islington.

Among new services specifically geared to the personal customer has been the high interest Gold Deposit Account. This complements the older Premium Account to which refinements have been made. The commitment to mortgage lending has been strengthened through a co-operative venture with John G McGregor Homes and closer links with estate agents and life assurance companies. A reciprocal automatic teller machine (ATM) agreement has been set up with Barclays, Lloyds and the Bank of Scotland, which provides customers with card dispenser facilities through 4,000 outlets.

For corporate customers, recent initiatives include a cash management service through a worldwide communications facility provided by National Data Corporation, and an integrated treasury and foreign exchange operation based in London backed by satellite operations in Glasgow and Manchester. A new pensions service has also been introduced, in conjunction with the Wyatt Company, to cater for small and medium-sized companies.

Whilst the bank emphasises its commitment to stimulating the growth of smaller businesses, there is a higher incidence of bad debt with medium-sized and smaller businesses. Over 60% of individual specific provisions are for amounts under £25,000.

Investment banking Acquisition of the Charterhouse Group in 1985 substantially increased the group's investment banking capability. This focuses on four major areas – merchant banking, development capital, investment management and securities.

In merchant banking, Charterhouse Bank has emerged as a major contender in corporate finance as a result of the larger customer base which it now enjoys through the group. It also provides a full range of commercial banking and treasury services. Development capital operations, including management buyouts and business expansion schemes, have long been recognised as one of Charterhouse's areas of expertise. Activities have been greatly strengthened in Scotland.

Investment management Tilney, the Liverpool-based stockbrokers, was acquired in 1986 and has enhanced the group's securities distribution and research capability, as well as giving it a more substantial private client customer base. Charterhouse's fund management has been merged into that of the Royal Bank of Scotland, and now has some £2bn under management. The new company, Capital House Investment Management Limited, forms the fifth operational division of the group.

C H A I R M A N ' S   S T A T E M E N T

'A continuing strong operating performance is the result of two main factors. Firstly and most importantly, we are now seeing tangible benefits from the merger, in 1985, of the group's two former clearing banks. This has enabled us to release substantial capital resources of over £100m by the disposal of surplus properties in the City of London for use in the profitable development and expansion of our business.... Secondly, our new group structure, which was introduced in October 1986, has allowed us to deploy our resources more effectively.' *Sir Michael Young-Herries*

Specialist finance RoyScot Finance is the newest of the group's operating divisions. It was established to bring together various specialist financing activities, some of which previously fell within the responsibilities of the clearing bank. As part of this restructuring, Charterhouse Japhet Credit has been merged into what is now RoyScot Trust to consolidate the group's hire purchase and instalment finance operations.

RoyScot Factors has simultaneously been set up as a new company to provide debt factoring services to companies.

These services were previously available through the group's link with Lloyds and Scottish, in which a 39% interest was sold to Lloyds Bank in September 1984.

Insurance Royal Bank of Scotland Group Insurance, the group's move into insurance underwriting, began with car insurance. Unique amongst UK banks, its Direct Line policies, based on the use of advanced technology, are sold either by telephone or coupon response. Because Direct Line

Share price and relative to FT-A All-Share

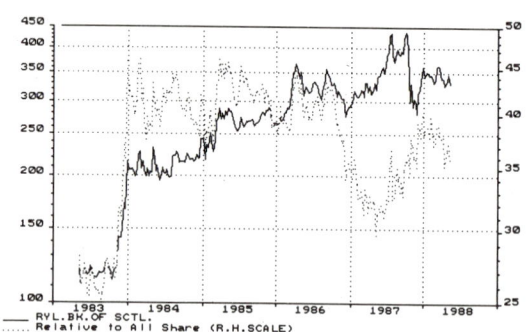

does not have to pay commissions, it is able to offer competitive rates which can be adjusted at short notice. Company policy is to concentrate business on the upper end of the market. The initial success of the operation may be gauged from a renewal rate of nearly 90%. The same Direct Line principles have since been applied to house insurance, the response to which is no less encouraging.

GEOGRAPHICAL REVIEW

The group does not publish a detailed breakdown of its geographical spread of assets and profits which would in any event be of little significance. However, as at 30 September 1987, international assets/liabilities accounted for close on 30% of total balance footings. They showed an 18½% increase over the previous twelve months, notwithstanding the effects of a lower dollar.

This was a result of a deliberate decision to allow the foreign currency book to expand again, partly in response to demand generated from the domestic side of the bank, and partly from investment management groups seeking to minimise the effects of wide swings in exchange rates. Group exposure to rescheduling countries in 1987 has been quantified at no more than £325.3m on which it has now established 32% specific provisions of £102m.

CORPORATE CALENDAR

Year end	30 September
Preliminary results	early December
Report and accounts	mid-December
AGM	mid-January
Final dividend paid	late January
Interim results	early May
Interim dividend paid	early July

ROYAL INSURANCE HOLDINGS plc

DIRECTORS' HOLDINGS

	Fully-paid ordinary shares	Options
The Rt Hon The Earl of Airlie	1,250	—
PEG Balfour	1,250	—
MV Blank	11,577	65,000
Sir Robin Duthie	2,500	—
HE Farley	9,809	68,525
IFH Grant	1,250	—
HLC Greig	1,250	—
AM Hamilton	5,000	—
JCR Inglis	2,500	—
RM Maiden	7,793	69,003
Sir Austin Pearce	1,250	—
N Quick	1,250	—
K Thompson	1,000	—
Sir Adam Thomson	1,000	—
The Rt Hon Lord Thomson of Monifieth	1,250	—
CM Winter	9,515	70,000
Sir Michael Young-Herries	6,250	90,000

Total directors' remuneration in 1986/87 was £1.1m, of which the chairman was paid £85,204 and the highest-paid director was paid £327,132.

PRINCIPAL SUBSIDIARIES AND RELATED COMPANIES

Owned by the company:
Capital House Investment Management Ltd, Charterhouse plc, Royal Bank Group Services Ltd, Royal Bank of Scotland Group Insurance Company Ltd, RoyScot Finance Group Ltd, The Royal Bank of Scotland plc

Owned by The Royal Bank of Scotland Plc:
Associated Merchant Bank Pte Ltd – Singapore (64%), RBS Trade Services Ltd, Royal Bank Insurance Services Ltd – Scotland, Royscot International Finance BV – The Netherlands, The Royal Bank of Scotland AG – Switzerland, The Royal Bank of Scotland (Guernsey) Ltd – Guernsey, The Royal Bank of Scotland (IOM) Ltd – Isle of Man, The Royal Bank of Scotland (Jersey) Ltd – Jersey, Williams & Glyn's (Nederland) BV – The Netherlands

Owned by Charterhouse plc:
Charterhouse Bank Ltd; Charterhouse Development Capital Ltd, Charterhouse Securities Ltd

Owned by Charterhouse Bank Ltd:
Charterhouse Bank and Trust International Ltd – Bahamas, Charterhouse (Suisse) SA – Switzerland

Owned by Charterhouse Development Capital Ltd:
Charterhouse Business Expansion Fund Management Ltd, Charterhouse SA – France

Owned by Charterhouse Securities Ltd:
Charterhouse Tilney

Owned by RoyScot Finance Group plc:
Royal Bank Leasing Ltd, RoyScot Factors Ltd, Royscot Financial Services Ltd, RoyScot Trust plc, RoyScot Vehicle Contracts Ltd

Owned by RoyScot Financial Services Ltd:
Style Financial Services Ltd – Scotland

Owned by Royal Bank of Scotland Group Insurance Company Ltd:
RBSG Bureau Services Ltd

Associated companies:
Charterhouse Development Capital Fund Ltd (47.6%), International Commodities Clearing House Holdings (11.1%), Investors in Industry Group plc (7.6%), The Scottish Agricultural Securities Corporation p.l.c. (33.3%), Travellers Cheque Associates Ltd (10%), Yorkshire Bank PLC (8%)

BRAND NAMES

Direct Line, Gold Deposit Account, Royline

CONTACTS AND FURTHER INFORMATION

Alwyn James, Chief Press Officer, The Royal Bank of Scotland Group plc, 42 St Andrew Square, Edinburgh EH2 2YE. Tel: 031-556 8555.

GENERAL INFORMATION

Head office	1 Cornhill, London EC3V 3QR. Tel: 01-283 4300
Directors	AA Horsford (chief executive), GR Kellett, EL Palmer, IL Rushton. *Non-exec* Sir John Cuckney (chairman), Sir John Nott KCB PC (deputy chairman), Sir Anthony Tuke (deputy chairman), Sir Derek Alun-Jones, KM Bevins CBE TD, RD Broadley, Sir John Milne, Sir Edwin Nixon CBE DL, Sir Max Williams
Advisers	Baring Brothers & Co Ltd, Lazard Brothers Co Ltd
Auditors	Deloitte Haskins & Sells
Registrars	Lloyds Bank Registrar's Department
Brokers	Hoare Govett Ltd
Solicitors	Linklaters & Paines

GENERAL FINANCIAL INFORMATION

Market capitalisation	£1.875bn at 1 January 1988
Capital structure	
Issued ordinary shares (25p)	474.4m
Issued preference shares	None
Warrants	None
Convertibles	None
Traded options	None
ADRs	None
Shareholders over 5%	Adelaide Steamship, Australia, has 6.05%

FT CATEGORY

FT: Insurances
FT-A: Insurance (composite)

MAJOR ACTIVITIES

Royal Insurance is one of the largest composite insurance companies in the UK. It transacts all types of life and non-life insurances, is active in pensions and related financial services and has recently started acquiring chains of estate agents.

Royal Insurance consists of six principal operating companies, 130 subsidiaries and 35 related companies. It has 500 offices in over 80 countries and employs more than 22,000 staff. The US and the UK are its leading markets.

The greater part of Royal's business is non-life insurance, providing cover for individuals and corporations against fire, accident and theft, and other contingencies that could result in loss or damage to property and liability claims.

As with any non-life insurer, profits vary considerably from year to year. A better guide to the distribution of business is premium income. Of the total life and non-life premium income of £4.0bn in 1987, about £1.4bn is derived from the US. Here, in contrast with, for example, General Accident, greater emphasis is placed on the insurance of small to medium-sized commercial risks rather than personal, motor and property, insurances.

Royal Insurance is strong in commercial insurances in the UK, though it still insures two million private homes, making it the second largest UK domestic property insurer. Total non-life premium income in the UK amounted to £1.060bn in 1987.

Royal Life Holdings is one of the top five life companies in the UK. Its life operation was given a major boost in September 1985 when Royal acquired Lloyd's Life, now called Royal Heritage Life. Royal's good links with many building societies help to promote its life business, as do its ties with about 700 estate agents.

Royal Reinsurance, the reinsurance arm, is based in London and accounts for about 4% of the group's total premium income. It accepts business from insurance companies and intermediaries and operates throughout the world.

Apart from its base in the UK and operation in the US,

Year	Turnover (£m)	Pre-tax (£m)	Earnings (p)	Dividends net (p)	Dividend cover (x)	Net assets (p)	Price (p) High	Price (p) Low	PER (x) High	PER (x) Low	Yield (%) High	Yield (%) Low
1983	2,179	98.4	17.0	11.40	1.5	348	226	171	13.3	10.1	9.52	7.21
1984	2,591	11.2	(1.2)	11.87	—	385	277	193	—	—	8.79	6.12
1985	3,147	41.4	6.1	12.87	0.5	401	398	258	65.2	42.3	7.06	4.58
1986	3,795	304.8	52.7	15.50	3.4	518	476	381	9.0	7.2	5.63	4.50
1987	4,033	274.0	37.8	19.25	2.0	422	598	335	15.8	8.9	7.75	4.34

Table title: FIVE YEAR FINANCIAL INFORMATION

Royal has a major presence in Canada and the Netherlands, and also in Australia where it is the leading insurance company. In the UK, Royal's principal competitors include the other quoted insurers, Commercial Union, General Accident, Guardian Royal Exchange and Sun Alliance.

Prospects for pre-tax profits for 1988 and 1989 appear good despite the volatile nature of the insurance business. Royal Insurance has ample resources to maintain and increase its dividends. In the context of its stated ability to pay dividends increasing by 15% per annum or more for the next three years, and the increase of over 20% in 1986 and 24% in 1987, the medium and long-term outlook is encouraging.

FINANCIAL HISTORY

Since 1983, non-life insurance premium income has nearly doubled to £3.2bn in 1987. Life assurance premium income in 1987 amounted to £823m, of which £386m arose from premiums payable under long-term regular premium contracts, and £437m from new single premium contracts. Unit trust sales totalled £377m.

Pre-tax profits in 1987 of £274m were below the 1986 level of £304.8m, primarily because of severe weather losses in the UK in January and October. Total weather losses in 1987 amounted to £190m compared with £57m in 1986. Profits in 1985 amounted to only £41.4m and the turnaround reflects the volatile pattern of non-life earnings, which depend not only on factors which are at least partially under management control, such as premium rates, commission payments and expenses, but also on natural factors, such as the severity of the winter weather and the numbers of hurricanes in the US.

The total 1987 profits of £274m are the sum of the underwriting balance (−£155.1m), investment income on the funds set aside to meet future claim payments and on the shareholders' funds (£361.9m), life profits (£36.8m) and the profits earned by associated companies (£30.4m). The cost of the 1987 dividend at £91.4m is substantially covered by after-tax profits of £179.2m.

A useful measure of the group's financial strength is the solvency ratio, which was 57% at the end of February 1988. This is calculated by dividing the shareholders' funds, excluding the value of the life operations (£1.830bn or 385p per share), by the non-life premium income (£3.210bn). The life operations are stated in the accounts to be worth on a conservative basis an additional £850m, or 179p per share.

SHARE PRICE HISTORY

The low point for the recession in the insurance industry was reached in 1984. News of the ability of companies to increase premium rates without the risk of a significant loss of business to their competitors helped the share price throughout 1985 and the first part of 1986.

Subsequently the prospect of increased competition in the US has driven the Royal share price down. Like all quoted companies, Royal's shares fell sharply in October 1987.

SENIOR MANAGEMENT

The group's non-executive chairman is Sir John Cuckney. The deputy chairmen are Sir John Nott and Sir Anthony Tuke. The group chief executive is Alan Horsford.

Day-to-day management of the group's affairs is in the hands of GR Kellett and IL Rushton, group general managers; RK Hollis and D Malcolm, deputy group general managers; DM Heather, group controller; and C Evans, group personnel manager. The company secretary is JP Barber.

In charge of the principal operating subsidiaries are GW Ansbro – US, PF Duerden – UK, RA Elms – Canada, WR Rowland – International, PJ Sherman – Reinsurance and WJ Scanlan – Life and related finance services.

CAPITAL

There were 474.4m ordinary shares in issue after the one for one scrip issue on 1 June 1987. There have been no other major changes to the share capital of the company in the last three years, other than the one for four scrip issue in 1984. An ADR facility is expected in 1988 in New York. In 1987 there were a number of sterling and dollar commercial paper programmes.

Under existing employee share option schemes, a maximum of 2.5m further shares were outstanding at 31 December 1986 to be subscribed in the years up to 1993. The company issued 1.1m shares in acquiring the Oyston Estate Agency Ltd in April 1987. The group had total borrowings of £303.8m at the end of 1986.

GROUP REVIEW

In early 1988, shareholders' approval was given for the creation of a non-insurance holding company, Royal Insurance Holdings plc, in order to ensure that the company's development would not be limited by legislation limiting an insurance company to insurance activities.

US This is the group's largest territory. The premium rate increases seen in the 30 months prior to the end of 1986 has had a major impact on profits in the US. The greatly reduced underwriting loss combined with the substantial and increasing investment income resulted in a pre-tax profit of £141.7m in 1986, compared with a loss of £22.7m in 1985.

Profits in 1987 at £152.7m were satisfactory and prospects for 1988 look encouraging although price competition has returned to the US non-life market.

UK As in the US, premium rates for non-life insurances have been increasing. The pre-tax profit increased from

£44.3m to £93.6m in 1986. In 1987 profits totalled £3.3m. As with other insurers, profits were adversely affected by the severe weather conditions in the early part of 1986 and in the first and fourth quarters of 1987. The October 1987 hurricane alone resulted in 150,000 claims and cost Royal about £105m.

The life operation, Royal Life Holdings, is of major importance to the group in the UK, providing a stable but increasing flow of profits. It has grown rapidly in recent years, especially after the acquisition of Lloyd's Life in 1985, now renamed Royal Heritage Life.

Share price and relative to FT-A All-Share

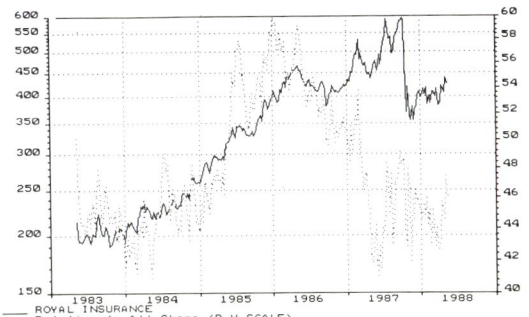

A number of estate agent chains are being injected into the life operation. They include Oyston's in the north-west, William H Brown in the east, and Fox and Sons in the south. Total UK life profits in 1987 amounted to £36.8m, up from £28.4m in the previous year.

Canada The Canadian market tends to follow that of the US. The group achieved a pre-tax profit of £36.0m in 1987 compared with £18.6m in 1986. Premium income in Canada amounted to £284.7m. Royal is the largest company in the Canadian market and is increasingly able to achieve the economics of scale necessary for long-term profitability. The freeze in Ontario auto premium rates is beginning to adversely affect results but the overall outlook remains healthy.

International The principal operating territories are the Netherlands, the rest of Europe and Australia. The pre-tax profit of £7.2m in the Netherlands in 1987 included investment income for the year of £12.3m. International profits for 1987 were up from £5.6m to £20.3m on total premiums written of £392.6m.

Apart from its interest in the Netherlands, the group is placing an increasing emphasis on development in western Europe. A major group stake is its holding of 20% of the insurance group Aachener und Münchener Beteiligungs. This German company conducted a major capital raising in the first half of 1987 in order to acquire 50% of the BFG German banking group.

Royal Insurance is consolidating its operations in Australia, reflecting the difficult local insurance environment. Total premium income in 1987 amounted to £68.3m, down from £101.7m and the group achieved a very satisfactory profit of £12.4m compared with a loss of £3.2m in 1986.

GEOGRAPHICAL REVIEW

The territorial distribution of the group's non-life premium income in 1987 was UK 33%, US 42%, Canada 9%, Netherlands 4%, Australia 2%, other areas 5%, marine and aviation worldwide 2%, reinsurance worldwide 3%.

A distribution by profits is not shown because profits vary greatly from year to year for each territory. Life profits primarily emerge in the UK.

CORPORATE CALENDAR

Year end	31 December
Preliminary results	February
Report and accounts	March
AGM	April
Final dividend paid	May
Interim results	August
Interim dividend paid	November

DIRECTORS' HOLDINGS

	Fully-paid ordinary shares		Options
	(beneficial)	(non-beneficial)	
Sir John Cuckney	4,062	—	—
Sir John Nott	1,000	—	—
Sir Anthony Tuke	10,000	—	—
Sir Derek Alun-Jones	1,250	—	—
KM Bevins	9,052	—	—
RD Broadley	1,250	—	—
AA Horsford	7,329	—	158,042
GR Kellett	4,241	—	79,674
Sir John Milne	4,374	—	—
Sir Edward Nixon	3,124	—	—
EL Palmer	1,000	—	—
IL Rushton	5,065	—	76,256
Sir Max Williams	1,000	—	—

Total directors' remuneration was £725,481, of which the chairman received £50,000 and the highest-paid director received £203,952.

PRINCIPAL SUBSIDIARIES AND RELATED COMPANIES

Aachener und Münchener Beteiligungs AC – West Germany (20%), Companhia Internacional de Seguros – Brazil (20%), Law Union and Rock Insurance Co of Nigeria Ltd, Mutual & Federal Investments Ltd – South Africa (49%), Oyston Estate Agency Ltd, Rodrick Holding BV – Netherlands, Roins Holdings Ltd – Canada, Royal Australian Holdings Ltd, Royal Group Inc – US, Royal Insurance Finance NV – Netherlands, Royal Insurance (Int) Ltd, Royal Insurance (UK) Ltd, Royal Life Holdings Ltd, Royal Reinsurance Co Ltd (80%)

BRAND NAMES

Car Shield 30, Car Shield 50, Home Shield

CONTACTS AND FURTHER INFORMATION

Roy Randall, Head of Corporate Relations, Royal Insurance Holdings plc, 1 Cornhill, London EC3V 3QR. Tel: 01-283 4300.

C H A I R M A N ' S   S T A T E M E N T

'I had hoped to be able to report to you that the recent improvement in the profits of the company had continued in 1987. Indeed, this has proved to be the case for five of our six operating companies, but the quite exceptional weather losses in the UK during the year and, in particular, the October storm has led to a lower pre-tax profit for the year of £274m.' *Sir John Cuckney*

STC PLC

GENERAL INFORMATION

Head office	10 Maltravers Street, London WC2R 3HA. Tel: 01-836 8055
Directors	Lord Keith of Castleacre (chairman), AS Walsh CBE (chief executive), PL Bonfield, Sir Raymond Brown OBE, WK Gardener, RA Gardner, NW Horne. *Non-exec* EB Fitzgerald – US, HRH Prince Michael of Kent, The Hon David Montagu, Sir David Nicholson, A Park, Lord Rawlinson of Ewell QC, JW Robb
Advisers	Morgan Grenfell & Co Ltd
Auditors	Deloitte Haskins & Sells
Registrars	National Westminster Bank Registrar's Department
Brokers	Cazenove & Co
Solicitors	Slaughter and May

GENERAL FINANCIAL INFORMATION

Market capitalisation	£1.267bn at 1 January 1988
Capital structure	
Issued ordinary shares (25p)	553.3m
Issued preference shares (£1)	None
Warrants	None
Convertibles	None
Traded options	Yes
ADRs	Yes
Shareholders over 5%	Northern Telecom 27.5%

FT CATEGORY

FT: Electricals
FT-A: Electronics

MAJOR ACTIVITIES

STC is primarily involved in the manufacture of communication and information systems. It is also involved in defence systems and component manufacturing and distribution operations. These activities are supported by extensive research and development.

ICL – the UK's largest computer manufacturer and acquired by the group in 1984 – accounted in 1987 for nearly all STC's information systems business and 63.4% of total group turnover. ICL manufactures a range of computer systems, from corporate mainframes to departmental and personal systems and provides related products and services.

The principal activity of the rest of the group is the supply of land-based telecommunications and submarine transmission systems and related equipment for system providers and users. The group has an impressive 50% share of the world market for submarine cables.

STC also manufactures and distributes advanced electronic components. It has recently expanded its electrical distribution business. Its defence systems division is now quite small.

Following severe financial and business problems in 1985, Lord Keith took over as chairman and instituted an intensive rationalisation programme. Its essential elements were cost reduction, debt control and concentration upon core businesses in computers and telecommunications. There were asset disposals outside these areas where necessary. The result was a dramatic recovery in the group's financial situation within twelve months, accompanied by signs of a bright future.

The group's long-term prospects are dependent upon its ability to expand its markets overseas, broaden its product range and develop new products. The group's research and development programme will become ever more vital as its existing products inevitably date and competition becomes more intensive.

The acquisition by Northern Telecom of STC shares previously held by ITT has been followed up by STC's purchase of Northern Telecom's UK telecommunications business and its European data systems operation. Closer collaboration is expected to be a feature of STC's development.

In computing, ICL competes with many companies including IBM. In telecommunications it competes with GEC, LM Ericsson, AT&T, Northern Telecom, Italtel and Fujitsu. In submarine systems, competition comes from the US, Japan and France. In defence its competitors include Ferranti, Westinghouse, Racal, GEC, Marconi and Siemens. Its components and distribution operations face competition from many smaller companies in the UK and Europe.

FINANCIAL HISTORY

1983 to 1984 saw turnover almost double on a pro-forma basis following the merger with ICL. However, since 1984 turnover has increased by only 9% and 1985 saw major losses.

1986 saw the remarkable turnaround in STC's financial position. Although turnover for the period was reduced by 3.2% to £1.933bn, due to the disposal of certain businesses, pre-tax profits rose to £134.2m, against a loss in 1985 of £11.4m. Earnings per share reached 15.9p compared with the 2.5p per share loss in 1985. A total of 4.5p per share was paid in dividends as against none in 1985.

The group's balance sheet was transformed. Divestment proceeds and substantially lower working capital requirements helped STC eliminate net borrowings of £211m, leaving a net cash balance of £37m. The combination of profit recovery and cash generation strengthened the balance sheet and restored shareholders' reserves to earlier levels. Pre-tax margins were 6.9%, asset turnover was three and a half times, and return on capital was 28.2%.

In 1987 turnover was up 6.9% to £2.066bn. Turnover in ongoing businesses was up nearly 10% to £2.049bn. Pre-tax profits were up 40.1% to £188.0m. Margins were up from 6.9% to 9.1%. Earnings per share were up 41.5% to 22.5p.

Improved profits, the continued emphasis on asset management and proceeds of £44m from disposals led to a build-up in cash balances to £196m in 1987 compared with £37m in 1986. The sale of the tantalum capacitors operation for £30m gave rise to an extraordinary profit of £11.5m. An exceptional charge of £6.1m was the result of further rationalisation costs.

SHARE PRICE HISTORY

In 1985 the share price dropped below 200p in February, and to less than 80p in October. The rights issue of 91m shares at 190p in March and general disenchantment with the electronic sector were responsible. During this period STC was badly affected by a downturn in demand for its electronic components, technical problems in its telecommunications operations and bottlenecks within its submarine cable businesses.

The shares turned round in late 1985 and quadrupled in eighteen months to the 1987 high of 331p. The share price rose particularly sharply in early 1987, reflecting a recovery in confidence, and reached a peak of 331p. They fell back to 160p in the autumn 1987 crash, before recovering to open 1988 at 229p.

SENIOR MANAGEMENT

Lord Keith of Castleacre has been chairman since the boardroom coup in 1985, when he took charge of the business. A Walsh was appointed chief executive soon afterwards. He had previously been with GEC.

Year	Turnover (£m)	Pre-tax (£m)	Earnings (p)	Dividends net (p)	Dividend cover (x)	Net assets (p)	Price (p)		PER (x)		Yield (%)	
							High	Low	High	Low	High	Low
1983	920.6	92.2	20.6	7.5	2.7	80.5	324	191	33.1	20.4	4.46	2.60
1984	1,966.7	140.8	18.9	9.0	2.1	87.8	370	257	26.9	17.1	4.98	2.90
1985	1,997.2	(11.4)	(2.2)	—	—	85.9	289	74	—	—	—	—
1986	1,993.4	134.2	15.9	4.5	3.5	99.3	177	100	11.1	6.3	8.38	4.73
1987	2,067.0	188.0	22.5	7.0	3.2	116.6	329	175	35.1	11.1	3.87	2.06

FIVE YEAR FINANCIAL INFORMATION

In 1987 A Park retired as deputy chief executive but remains on the board as a non-executive director. With the sale of ITT's stake in the company to Northern Telecom, JJ Chluski, DP Weadock and MC Woodward left the board, and EB Fitzgerald and Sir David Nicholson joined as non-executive directors.

CAPITAL

130.1m ordinary shares were issued to acquire ICL in 1984. In March 1985 there was a deeply unpopular one for five rights issue of 91.01m ordinary shares at 190p. In February 1987 7.2m ordinary shares were issued to acquire Whitworth Electric (Holdings) and Newey and Eyre Distributors Ltd.

Northern Telecom bought ITT's 24% shareholding and now owns 27.5% of the ordinary capital in October 1987. There are considerable points of contact between STC and Northern Telecom.

Two commercial paper programmes were arranged in December 1987, one of $150m and one of £100m.

GROUP REVIEW

In the recovery programme implemented in 1985/86, the group's operations were divided into five major activities.

Information systems ICL's strategy is to select target industries and produce specialist solutions for them based on its comprehensive range of systems and services.

The Series 39 VME mainframe computer and DRS range provide higher profit margins than their predecessors, though they will come under increasing pressure from US suppliers benefiting from the weak dollar. The next generation DRS and Series 39 VME are starting production. The number of customers using VME increased by 30% in 1987. Sales of ICL's software have continued to grow.

ICL has become the market leader in sections of the UK public services market, including health systems. It has also strengthened its position in local government. In retailing it has become the UK market leader. Overall UK sales were up by 16% in 1987.

In 1986 ICL's international growth was only 4% and in 1987 just 2%, largely because of exchange rate movements, but it believes that the introduction of open systems standards in Europe, which it has strongly supported, will enable it to take a greater share of the European market. ICL became the first European member of the US Corporation for Open Systems and implemented the emerging world standard Manufacturing Applications Protocol (MAP) in its manufacturing plants in 1986. ICL has won a significant share of the French market and has set up a manufacturing business centre in Dusseldorf, West Germany.

ICL Network Systems was formed from the ICL and STC networking departments. It is the UK market leader in electronic data and has set up joint ventures with Geisco and

Cable and Wireless to improve sales overseas.

ICL's research effort includes its participation as prime controller in the UK Alvey FLAGSHIP project at Imperial College, London, and the joint venture with Queen's University, Belfast, to develop advanced office systems applications.

Operating profit for 1987 was up 52% to £109.9m on turnover 63% up at £1.299bn. Since 1985 ICL turnover has grown nearly 40%, operating profit has grown over 170% and return on capital has more than doubled to 41%. The division contributed positive cash flow of £166m in the period.

Communication systems The division is divided into land-based telecommunications and submarine cable systems. Activities have been increasingly focused on optical transmission products and systems.

Telecommunications supplies capital equipment like exchanges and subscriber items like telexes and handsets. Continuing business from TXE4 public exchange equipment was declining as exchanges were replaced with System X and System Y but enhancements to the TXE4 exchanges are likely to support strong growth in 1988. STC is putting emphasis on transmission systems providing more sophisticated connections to end users.

STC has particular expertise in optical systems and the major part of growth in 1987 has come from this area. It has halved manufacturing costs for fibre optics and concentrates on single mode acrylic fibre. STC is taking 60% of British Telecom's orders in this area. PDMX, a unique programmable digital multiplexer for private exchanges in offices and factories, is achieving strong sales.

Because of its PDMX product and fibre optic expertise, STC was awarded a major part of the City of London fibre optic network, known as FAST. It also received British Telecom's initial award for ISDN equipment. It is installing optical lines for both British Telecom and Mercury.

STC is seeking to widen the geographical market for its land-based telecommunications systems and products. It has set up a new export marketing unit to handle all overseas sales

Share price and relative to FT-A All-Share

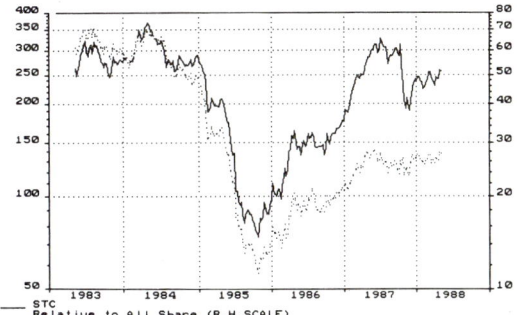

STC
Relative to All Share (R.H.SCALE)

of national telecommunication products outside the UK and the US. This has secured some orders in major markets including India and China. Its collaboration with Fujitsu has been extended to cover aspects of transmission and microwave radio equipment.

In submarine systems STC won 85% of the submarine projects open to international tender in 1986, including the 7,000 kilometre PTAT-1 optical link between the US and the UK valued at $350m. Activity in 1987 and 1988 is concentrated on the build-up towards the installation of the two transatlantic cables, TAT 8 and PTAT-1.

CHAIRMAN'S STATEMENT

'The momentum of business has continued strongly throughout 1987 and has resulted in record levels of turnover, profit and cash. At the end of the year, despite uncertain economic conditions worldwide and the additional turbulence caused by unsettled financial markets, demand is continuing to grow.

Turnover increased by 7 per cent to £2,067 million compared with £1,933 million in 1986. Excluding the discontinued businesses, the underlying growth was 10 per cent. The level of international business was almost unchanged after accounting for the adverse effects of exchange rate movements which reduced turnover by £10 million.' *Lord Keith of Castleacre*,

Turnover for submarine systems continued to fall for the first six months of 1987 but turned round sharply in the second half. Existing orders will lift sales in 1988 as many of them are completed. STC is confident that the market for optical systems pioneered by them will outstrip that for analogue systems.

In 1987 turnover rose 8.5% to £377.6m and operating profit rose 29.6% to £72.7m, a substantially greater rise than in 1986.

Defence systems This division provides sophisticated defence electronics and communication systems. The company saw the Ministry of Defence's decision to delegate responsibilities for project management to its contractors as a major opportunity for its defence systems division, but its performance has proved disappointing.

STC has supplied information systems for several major military command systems including the Royal Navy's, the fibre optic system for the Type 2400 submarine and the optical receiver for the ground station transmitter of the Scandinavian Space Agency. Its Trident towed array has completed its trials.

The division has won insufficient orders for these products or its laser technology to compensate for the end of the Ptarmigan contract. There were exceptional charges to cover rationalisation of the division's activities in 1986 and the first half of 1987.

The business has now stabilised at a lower level, supported by recent orders for the Boxer and Uniter projects and command and control systems. Turnover for 1987 was down 21.3% to £63.8m and operating profit was down 33.0% to £6.3m.

Components and electronic distribution STC manufactures and distributes electronic components. It has sustained manufacturing semiconductors in difficult market conditions. Despite price erosion and excess capacity in certain markets, trading margins improved in 1986 through cost reduction and control techniques improving competitiveness but fell away again in 1987.

Tantalum capacitors were disposed of in the second half of 1987 and the company is now concentrating on the manufacture of those components necessary to support the systems businesses.

STC Distributors, the electrical distribution business, services the electrical contractor and industrial markets. The acquisition of three smaller distributors, Whitworth Electric (Holdings), BTR's Newey & Eyre subsidiary, and Unitel from Brammer were designed to improve the business's competitiveness and increase its geographical coverage of the UK.

Earlier disposals and rationalisation programmes provided a radical turnaround in this division in 1986. Operating profit was up thirteenfold to £20m, before exceptional costs of £5.6m on turnover slightly higher at £287.1m. In 1987 turnover was up 15.8% to £308.6m but operating profit was down 1.0% to £20.2m because of poor results in components manufacturing.

Research and development The majority of research and development (R&D) is funded from STC's own resources. Its investment for 1986 totalled £161.3m, 8.5% of total group turnover, an increase of £7.8m despite rationalisation throughout the group during the year. In 1987 it rose to £176m, 8.5% of group turnover. Each company in STC is responsible for its own funding of R&D. A small resource exists for research work of common interest.

GEOGRAPHICAL REVIEW

In 1986 over 70% of total turnover was accounted for by the UK. Continental Europe accounted for 13%, while America, Asia and Australasia, Africa and the Middle East accounted for the remainder. The overseas business is concentrated in ICL and submarine systems.

CORPORATE CALENDAR

Year end	31 December
Preliminary results	March
Report and accounts	April
AGM	April/May
Final dividend paid	May
Interim results	August
Interim dividend paid	October

DIRECTORS' HOLDINGS

	Ordinary shares	Options
Lord Keith	9,000	—
AS Walsh	12,340	1,000,000
A Park	12,630	381,000
PL Bonfield	—	367,000
Sir Raymond Brown	700,000	—
WK Gardener	12,500	60,000
RA Gardner	10,000	300,000
NW Horne	5,000	205,000
HRH Prince Michael of Kent	11,400	—
Hon David Montagu	51,798	—
Lord Rawlinson	1,000	—

Total directors' remuneration in 1987 was £1.615m, with the highest-paid director receiving £276,000 and the chairman £71,000.

PRINCIPAL SUBSIDIARIES AND RELATED COMPANIES

CADCentre Ltd (50%), ICL Australia Pty Ltd – Australia, ICL Data AB – Sweden, ICL Deutschland International Computers GmbH – West Germany, ICL France International Computers – France, ICL Inc – US, ICL Nederland BV – The Netherlands, ICL UK Ltd, International Computers Indian Manufacture Ltd – India (40%), International Computers Ltd, International Computers South Africa Proprietary Ltd (46.5%), Newey and Eyre Distributors Ltd, Standard Telephones (Rentals) Ltd, STC Distributors Ltd, STC International Computer Ltd, STC International Marine Ltd, STC Investments Ltd, STC Marine Services (Benelux) Ltd, STC Northern Ireland Ltd, STC Properties Ltd, STC Technology Ltd, Unitel Ltd, Whitworth Electric Holdings plc

J SAINSBURY plc

BRAND NAMES

DRS, ICL, Oilcon Ballast Monitor, PDMX, Series 39, SCARAB, STC, TXE4, Viscount

CONTACTS AND FURTHER INFORMATION

Gareth Lewis, STC PLC, 10 Maltravers Street, London WC2R 3HA. Tel: 01-836 8055.

GENERAL INFORMATION

Head office	Stamford House, Stamford Street, London SE1 9LL. Tel: 01-921 6000
Directors	Sir John Sainsbury (chairman and chief executive), Sir Roy Griffiths (deputy chairman and managing director), DJ Sainsbury (deputy chairman), JHG Barnes (joint managing director), DA Quarmby (designate joint managing director), RT Vyner (assistant managing), RA Clark, I Coull, DE Henson, GC Hoyer Millar, RA Ingham, C Roberts, KC Worrall. *Non-exec* Mrs DC Eccles, The Rt Hon Lord Prior, Sir James Spooner
Advisers	SG Warburg & Co Ltd
Auditors	Clark Whitehill
Registrars	National Westminster Bank Registrar's Department
Brokers	Rowe & Pitman Ltd
Solicitors	Oppenheimers

GENERAL FINANCIAL INFORMATION

Market capitalisation	£3.229bn at 1 January 1988
Capital structure	
Issued ordinary shares (25p)	1.47bn
Issued preference shares	None
Warrants	None
Convertibles	None
Traded options	Yes
ADRs	One ordinary 25p share equals one ADR
Shareholders over 5%	DJ Sainsbury 22%, JS Portrait 10%, HON & V Trustee 10%, Vanheimer Trustee 9%, Sir John Sainsbury 7%

FT CATEGORY

FT: Food, groceries, etc
FT-A: Food retailing

MAJOR ACTIVITIES

The principal activity of the group is retail food sales. Other activities through subsidiaries and associates include the operation of home improvement and garden centres, hypermarkets, and pork and bacon production.

Through the Sainsbury's supermarket chain the group sells food, drink, toiletries and kitchen-related housewares. The Homebase subsidiary, in which the group has a 75% stake, is involved in garden centres and the retailing of DIY products. SavaCentre, a joint venture with Storehouse, retails the Sainsbury food and drink range together with a wide range of textiles and other non-food items from out-of-town hypermarkets at the lowest possible prices.

Haverhill Meat Products, in which Sainsbury's has a 50% stake, produces bacon and a wide range of pork products. Shaw's Supermarkets, which the group purchased outright in July 1987, retails food, drink and related products in the US.

With total food volume showing at best only modest growth, the key economic indicators affecting sales from the supermarket division are food price inflation and to a lesser extent

CHAIRMAN'S STATEMENT

'The steady rise in market share reflects our sustained supermarket opening programme, which has been at 15–17 new stores a year for the past seven years. . . . The five trading companies in which Sainsbury's has interests varying from 28.5% to 75%, now have sales amounting to over £1bn and profit amounting to £48m. They are all successful businesses with good prospects, and I expect them to contribute to an increasing proportion of Group profit in the future.' *Sir John Sainsbury*

F I V E Y E A R F I N A N C I A L I N F O R M A T I O N												
Year	Turnover (£m)	Pre-tax (£m)	Earnings (p)	Dividends net (p)	Dividend cover (x)	Net assets (p)	Price (p) High	Low	PER (x) High	Low	Yield (%) High	Low
1983	2,383.7	107.9	5.95	1.47	4.1	30.2	117	89	31.2	25.7	2.12	1.78
1984	2,574.8	127.3	6.32	1.89	3.4	34.0	154	114	33.2	26.0	2.19	1.64
1985	2,998.7	153.8	7.68	2.25	3.4	39.9	195	143	32.8	24.5	2.14	1.62
1986	3,414.7	186.8	8.84	2.75	3.2	46.6	212	172	29.3	21.0	2.25	1.62
1987	3,857.1	237.8	10.76	3.50	3.1	54.8	301	209	29.7	16.2	2.44	1.40
1988	4,791.5	297.6	13.10	4.20	3.1	62.0	249	217	19.3	16.0	2.50	2.02

personal disposable income. Competition is from other quoted multiple retailers, in particular Tesco, ASDA, Argyll with Safeway, and Dee with Gateway.

Sainsbury's looks set to remain the UK's pre-eminent food retailer. The supermarket division's share of national sales in food and drink shops increased from 10.2% to 10.7% in fiscal 1988. Productivity was up 4%. Its performance ratios are very difficult for others to match and its lead is maintained by the significant advantages it is building through the application of modern technology. Homebase and Shaw's look promising additional growth points for the future.

FINANCIAL HISTORY

Sales, including VAT, for the year to 19 March 1988 were £5.009bn, 23.9% above the previous year, and 116.3% up over five years. These include Homebase sales and Shaw's as a wholly-owned subsidiary for seven months.

Pre-tax profits on ordinary activities were £308.4m after profit sharing in 1988, an above average rise of 24.9% on 1987, and up 206% over five years. Earnings per share increased by 21.6% from 11.16p to 13.57p. Net 1988 dividends were 4.2p, up 20% on 1987.

Profit sharing by employees is a feature of Sainsbury's generous attitudes to staff relations. In 1988 no less than £23.9m, 7.2% of pre-tax profits, was paid out to Sainsbury's own staff. This may account in part for the very low turnover of staff the company experiences.

Group net debt at 19 March 1988 was 36% of shareholders' funds, a level above the average gearing level for the sector as a whole, but nonetheless still a manageable level.

Key trading ratios for fiscal 1988 included weekly sales per square foot of £16.30, up 5.7%; sales per employee of around £95,000, profit per employee of around £6,000; and a pre-interest margin of 6.62%, up 0.4 of a point.

SHARE PRICE HISTORY

Since 1984 Sainsbury's share price has risen steadily in absolute terms from around 125p to a high of 300p. Relative to the market it has fallen slightly, trading between 23% and 28% of the FT-A All-Share index.

At 300p per share, or 26% of a 1,150 point index, Sainsbury's had outperformed over the year to mid-1987. After the autumn 1987 crash, the price fell to 205p and had managed only a small recovery to 217p, nearly 25% of the FT-A All-Share index, by the beginning of 1988. By mid-May 1988 the shares were standing at around 220p.

SENIOR MANAGEMENT

Sir John Sainsbury has been chairman and chief executive since 1969. Lord Sainsbury of Drury Lane and Sir Robert Sainsbury, the senior members of the Sainsbury family, are joint presidents. Sir Roy Griffiths is deputy chairman and managing director until the 1988 AGM in June. DJ Sainsbury was appointed deputy chairman and finance director on 1 January 1988.

JH Barnes was appointed joint managing director on 1 January 1988 and took over Sir John Sainsbury's executive responsibility for retail operations, buying and marketing. DA Quarmby becomes joint managing director when Sir Roy Griffiths retires as an executive director and becomes a non-executive director in June 1988.

RT Vyner is assistant managing director, buying and marketing. C Roberts is head of meat, pork products and bakery buying. RA Ingham is head of dairy produce and off-licence buying. DE Henson is financial controller. KC Worrall is head of grocery and non-foods buying.

I Coull, who became an executive director on 1 January 1988, takes over as director in charge of development from GC Hoyer Millar at the 1988 AGM but GC Hoyer Millar will remain a non-executive director and chairman of Homebase. There are 30 departmental directors who are not on the main board.

CAPITAL

Apart from the annual issue of shares against options and those issued under the profit-sharing scheme, Sainsbury's has traditionally had a very conservative policy towards the issue of new shares that might dilute shareholders' interests.

However, the company's offer to take over Shaw's Supermarkets, its US associate, was financed by the issue of approximately 57m ordinary shares. There was a one for one scrip issue in June 1987. Such issues have been a feature of the group over the years.

Beneficial owners of shareholdings above 5% are DJ Sainsbury 22%, JS Portrait 10%, HON & V Trustee 10%, Vanheimer Trustee 9% and Sir John Sainsbury 7%.

GROUP REVIEW

Sainsbury's supermarkets Sainsbury's is one of the leading food retailers in the UK, accounting for 10.7% of national sales in food and drink outlets in 1988. By March 1988, Sainsbury's had 279 supermarkets with an average size of 18,500 sq ft, serving a total of 6.5m customers each week.

For many years the average size of Sainsbury's supermarkets has been increasing. Of the 279 trading, 126 have sales areas of more than 20,000 sq ft. With new stores averaging 30,650 sq ft, this number is steadily growing. In March 1988 the total sales floor area of all Sainsbury's stores of 5.46m sq ft was more than double the figure of ten years earlier.

In 1987/88 the company opened 16 new supermarkets, increasing the chain's sales area by 9.6%. 18 supermarkets are planned to open in 1988/89 and 20 in 1989/90.

The group has over 4,000 food and drink lines under its own

label, supplied by more than 700 manufacturers. The Sainsbury label accounts for over half the company's trade and offers exceptional value alongside branded products sold at highly competitive prices.

The full range of proprietary and own-label lines sold in traditional food and household departments has increased by about 20% since 1983 while the number of stores large enough to stock that full range has reached 135. Sainsbury's is the largest butcher and largest retailer of wine, fresh fruit and vegetables in the UK.

SavaCentre Sainsbury's and BhS, part of the Storehouse group, jointly own SavaCentre, a hypermarket company operating six stores with an average sales area of 72,000 sq ft and each generating average weekly sales of £925,000. Two more are under construction.

SavaCentre sells the full Sainsbury's food and drink range. It has been shown to be the retailing chain offering the lowest food prices in the country. SavaCentre also sells the extensive range of BhS textiles and other non-food items and is experimenting with the inclusion of the Habitat and Mothercare ranges. Trading profits in 1988 were up 18.5% to more than £20m.

Share price and relative to FT-A All-Share

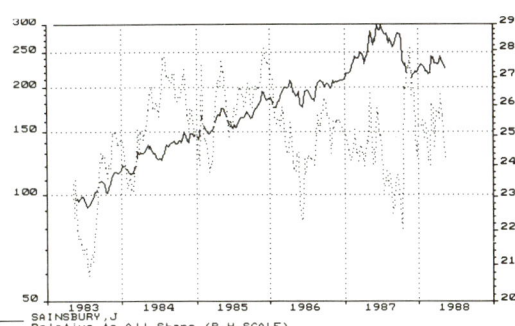

Homebase By March 1988 Homebase, Sainsbury's DIY subsidiary, had 38 home improvement and garden centres. It is planning to open at least 20 units by 1990. Sales in 1988 totalled £137m and trading profit was up 40.5% to £4.3m. An average Homebase comprises about 35,000 sq ft of covered sales area with an outside area of 17,500 sq ft for nursery plants and building materials. A minimum of 200 car park spaces is provided.

Homebase is following the Sainsbury's tradition of developing a growing number of its own-label products. The Base Price campaign, which consists of a selected range at long-term low prices, offers the customer exceptional value for money. The company's joint partner in Homebase is GB-Inno-BM, one of the leading DIY retailers in continental Europe.

Shaw's Supermarkets Shaw's Supermarkets, now 100%-owned, is a successful US food retailer, operating 47 supermarkets in New Hampshire, Maine and Massachusetts. Sales for the 60 weeks to 27 February 1988 were $1.419bn and trading profits were $37.7m. Five new stores were opened in 1986, two replacements and three in new marketing areas, adding 136,000 sq ft to total sales area. Eight new stores were completed in 1987, adding 15% to net sales area.

Shaw's became a 100% subsidiary of Sainsbury's on 24 July 1987. Of the £15.5m profit contributed to the group in fiscal 1988, £3.2m was as an associate and £12.3m as a subsidiary.

Haverhill Meat Products Haverhill, and its Palethorpes

subsidiary, is owned jointly by Sainsbury's and Canada Packers of Toronto. From its East Anglian and Shropshire factories it produces Tendersweet bacon and a wide range of pork products, mainly for Sainsbury's.

GEOGRAPHICAL REVIEW

Shaw's annual pre-tax profits of $37.7m for the 60 weeks to 27 February 1988 would represent approximately 6% of the group's total. Shaw's is the group's only interest outside the UK.

CORPORATE CALENDAR

Year end	last Saturday in March
Preliminary results	May
Report and accounts	June
AGM	July
Final dividend paid	July
Interim results	November
Interim dividend paid	January

DIRECTORS' HOLDINGS

	Fully-paid ordinary shares		Options
	(beneficial)	(non-beneficial)	
Sir John Sainsbury	23,745,338	1,050,000	—
Sir Roy Griffiths	49,007	64,587	107,893
DJ Sainsbury	168,608,608	251,528	105,220
GC Hoyer Millar	223,158	—	55,164
JHG Barnes	102,174	—	69,886
RT Vyner	15,729	—	90,696
C Roberts	61,163	—	115,165
RA Ingham	51,905	—	70,070
RA Clark	71,032	—	56,562
DE Henson	54,652	—	95,161
DA Quarmby	975	—	57,276
KC Worrall	49,540	—	89,848
Sir James Spooner	2,400	—	—
The Rt Hon Lord Prior	1,000	—	—
Mrs DC Eccles	1,000	—	—

Total directors' remuneration in 1986/87 is not disclosed by the company, but the chairman was paid £125,000, and the highest-paid director £190,000.

PRINCIPAL SUBSIDIARIES AND RELATED COMPANIES

Breckland Farms Ltd (50%), The Cheyne Investments Inc – US, The Cheyne Investments Ltd, Haverhill Meat Products Ltd (50%), Homebase Ltd (75%), Kings Reach Investments Ltd (28.76%), J Sainsbury (Farms) Ltd, J Sainsbury (Finance) BV – The Netherlands, J Sainsbury (Properties) Ltd, SavaCentre Ltd (50%), Shaw's Supermarkets Inc – US, The Sainsbury Charitable Fund

BRAND NAMES

Haverhill Meat Products, Homebase, J Sainsbury, SavaCentre, Tendersweet

CONTACTS AND FURTHER INFORMATION

Ewan Davidson, Treasurer, J Sainsbury plc, Stamford House, Stamford Street, London SE1 9LL. Tel: 01-921 6000.

SCOTTISH & NEWCASTLE BREWERIES plc

GENERAL INFORMATION

Head office   Abbey Brewery, Holyrood Road, Edinburgh EH8 8YS. Tel: 031-556 2591

Directors   Sir David Nickson KBE DL (chairman), AM Rankin CBE (chief executive), CJ Chalmers FCA, HD Page Croft, JHW Fairweather, Dr BC Kilkenny, AM Mowat, GB Reed, R Summers. *Non-exec* NM Shaw, JM Thompson

Advisers   Morgan Grenfell & Co Ltd, Noble Grossart Ltd

Auditors   Arthur Young

Registrars   Bank of Scotland Registrar's Department

Brokers   Bell Lawrie Ltd, Rowe & Pitman Ltd

Solicitors   Linklaters & Paines

GENERAL FINANCIAL INFORMATION

Market capitalisation	£786.7m at 1 January 1988
Capital structure	
Issued ordinary shares (20p)	362m
Issued preference shares (£1)	3.9m 3.85% CP, 7m 7.75% CP
Warrants	None
Convertibles	£67.7m 7% convertible preference shares (ten shares per £22 of stock 1989/99)
Traded options	None
ADRs	None
Shareholders over 5%	None

FT CATEGORY

FT: Beers, wines and spirits
FT-A: Brewers and distillers

MAJOR ACTIVITIES

Scottish & Newcastle (S&N) is one of the UK's top six brewers and one of Scotland's top ten companies. The present company was formed in 1960 by a merger between Scottish Brewers and the Newcastle Breweries and has its head office in Edinburgh. Scottish Brewers were themselves the result of a merger between William Younger and William McEwan.

S&N has 2,270 managed and tenanted public houses, concentrated in Scotland, northern England, north Wales and the Midlands. Through William Younger it has 70 tied outlets in southern England. In October 1987 S&N took control of Matthew Brown, increasing the number of its tied outlets by 270. All are in Lancashire and the Midlands. The acquisition of Matthew Brown brought the number of S&N's breweries to seven.

The group owes much of its success to the sale of its products in off-licences and supermarkets, the result of effective management and marketing of such brand names as McEwan's Export, Harp, Beck's, Newcastle Brown and Kestrel. This has been further strengthened by the Matthew Brown acquisition.

The group's off-licence business is conducted on a national basis and is successful throughout the UK. The group is outstandingly successful in supplying free public houses – those not tied to any particular brewer. 80% of S&N's beer business is carried out in the free trade area and it supplies more beer to the take-home trade than any other brewer.

S&N's other principal activity is its Thistle Hotel operation, the fourth largest hotel chain in the UK and present in most major UK cities. The group's wines and spirits wholesaling interests have been recently consolidated and do not make a significant contribution to profits.

Before buying Home Brewery in 1986 and Matthew Brown in 1987, the group considered buying Courage from Hanson but rejected doing so on the grounds of price. S&N competes with Grand Metropolitan, Whitbread, Courage and Bass. The group is often rumoured to be the target for a take-over.

FINANCIAL HISTORY

Since 1983 S&N's turnover has increased every year, achieving a 29% rise overall. Pre-tax profits over the period have advanced by 119.7%. Operating margins have risen from 8.1% in 1983 to 12.5% in 1987. Earnings per share rose by 94.7% in the period and dividends by 70.3%.

In the year to 3 May 1987, turnover was up 7% to £827.5m (£773.6m). Pre-tax profits were up 20.2% to £90.3m (£75.1m). Earnings per share were up 8.9% to 18.3p (16.8p) and dividends per share were up 13.4% to 7.95p (7.01p).

In October 1987 S&N acquired the regional brewer Matthew Brown for a mixture of cash and shares. S&N already owned 29.7% of Matthew Brown's share capital. In its last year of independence, Matthew Brown made a pre-tax profit of £10.13m on turnover of £56.63m.

At the 1988 interim to 1 November 1987, S&N's turnover was up 9% to £429.3m and pre-tax profits were up by 27.9% to £57.3m. Earnings per share were up 12.9% to 11.4p and the interim dividend rose 12.0% to 2.7p. Off-licence sales and improved profits from Thistle Hotels were the major factors in this upturn.

SHARE PRICE HISTORY

Since 1983 S&N's share price has moved from an annual range of 72.5p to 101.5p in 1983 to 189p to 268p in 1987. There has been a modest outperformance of the FT-A All-Share index in the period.

The shares fell in common with the market during the autumn 1987 crash but recovered strongly afterwards, outperforming the FT-A All-Share index by a considerable margin.

In early 1988 the price was driven up to a high of 293p on speculation that Australian brewers Elders would make a bid. As this possibility receded, they slipped back and were trading in the 260p region at the end of March 1988.

SENIOR MANAGEMENT

S&N's chairman, Sir David Nickson, is currently president of the Confederation of British Industry. He was knighted in June 1986 and is a member of the National Economic

CHIEF EXECUTIVE'S STATEMENT

'Turning now to the broader issue of the national beer market, we can see a continuation of the demand pattern of recent years. Though consumer spending has been positive generally, there has been little indication of any resurgence in demand for beer ahead of the other normal social-spend priorities.... Nevertheless, it could be argued that for beer generally the fall in per capita consumption may have levelled off, giving rise to some degree of optimism for the future.

Within this overall picture, beer products purchased for consumption off the premises continue to grow in volume and variety, the former by some 12 per cent in the year. By comparison on-trade sales showed a decline of about 1 per cent nationally.

These figures embrace an overall lager growth of 6 per cent and a consequent ale decline of 3 per cent, though there was growth in both categories in the take-home sector. Premium lagers demonstrated the strongest upward trend with growth of 20 per cent, reflecting confidence in quality and the relative weight of advertising investment.' *AM Rankin*

FIVE YEAR FINANCIAL INFORMATION

Year	Turnover (£m)	Pre-tax (£m)	Earnings (p)	Dividends net (p)	Dividend cover (x)	Net assets (p)	Price (p) High	Price (p) Low	PER (x) High	PER (x) Low	Yield (%) High	Yield (%) Low
1983	641.8	41.1	9.4	4.7	2.0	116	100	75	16.0	11.8	8.28	6.44
1984	692.5	55.2	13.5	5.4	2.5	123	135	102	15.3	11.1	7.24	5.46
1985	707.2	65.2	15.3	6.1	2.5	128	193	128	14.6	11.0	6.58	4.68
1986	773.6	75.1	16.8	7.0	2.4	163	234	165	17.2	11.6	6.06	4.27
1987	827.5	90.3	18.3	8.0	2.3	172	263	200	16.5	10.2	5.29	3.79

Development Council and the Scottish Economic Council. S&N's chief executive is Alick Rankin, who is also vice-chairman of the Brewers' Society. Group finance director is CJ Chalmers.

Dr BC Kilkenny is chairman of Thistle Hotels and Waverley Vintners. AM Mowat is chairman of Home Brewery and the take home sales company, Scottish & Newcastle Breweries (Sales). GB Reed is chairman of Newcastle Breweries and McEwan-Younger. R Summers is chairman and managing director of Scottish & Newcastle Beer Production Ltd, Moray Firth Maltings and Canongate Technology. HD Page Croft is chairman of Scottish Brewers and William Younger.

CAPITAL

There were 362m ordinary shares in issue at the end of March 1988. 48m were placed at 243p in late 1987 in the course of the acquisition of Matthew Brown, which was completed in January 1988.

Prior to the Matthew Brown acquisition, there had been two major changes in the group's capital since 1983. In 1984/85 11.06m ordinary shares were issued as part consideration for the acquisition of Moray Firth Maltings. In September 1986, 15.37m ordinary shares and 67.65m 7% convertible £1 cumulative preference shares were issued as part consideration for the acquisition of Home Brewery. Conversion of the convertible preference shares would result in the issue of some 30.75m new shares. This would represent 7.8% of the enlarged group.

There are no stakes above 5% in the group. However, Norwich Union own 4.79% and IEP Securities 4.84% of the enlarged share capital after the acquisition of Matthew Brown.

GROUP REVIEW

Beer In 1987 the beer division contributed 80.9% of the group turnover and 85.6% of operating profit.

Among S&N's best-known brands are Younger's Tartan Bitter, Kestrel Lager, McEwan's Export and Newcastle Brown Ale. The Matthew Brown acquisition added Theakston and Theakston's Old Peculiar. The group also has the national distribution franchise for the premium Beck's Bier and a bottling contract for Harp Lager.

S&N has four breweries and operates from seven divisions, to which have been added two breweries from the Matthew Brown acquisition.

Scottish & Newcastle Beer Production is responsible for the group's breweries in Edinburgh, Newcastle, Manchester, Nottingham, Blackburn and Masham, together with related production, packaging and primary distribution facilities. Scottish and Newcastle Breweries (Sales) is responsible for the sale of packaged beers to the retail and wholesale take-home trade.

In recent years the group's sales in public houses have declined, partly reflecting a run of bad summers but also a shift in drinking habits. Those in off-licences have grown substantially. The success of the group's off-licence sales strategy is reflected in the fact that one in every five purchases made in off-licences was of an S&N product.

The other five divisions are regional operating companies responsible for the retailing, wholesaling and distribution of beer products together with the operation of managed and tenanted public houses and restaurants in their respective areas.

Scottish Brewers has around 520 licensed premises in Scotland. The Newcastle Breweries has around 600 in north-east England. McEwan-Younger has about 200 in north-west England, Yorkshire and north Wales. Home Brewery, which was acquired in 1986 and into which the Midlands operation of William Younger was merged, has about 450 in the Midlands. William Younger has some 70 in southern England and Wales.

The acquisition of Matthew Brown added around 400 licensed premises to the group's tied estate and three breweries. These are concentrated in the Midlands and Lancashire. The breweries are comparatively small.

Within the beer division the group includes the Chandlers

Share price and relative to FT-A All-Share

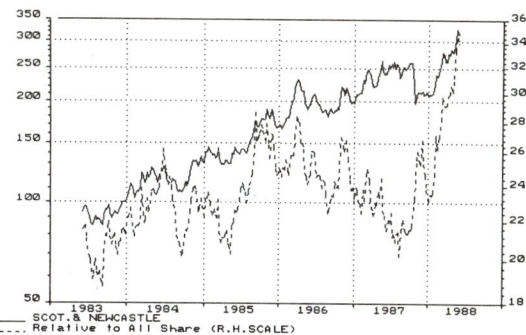

Restaurants chain and Moray Firth Maltings. Chandlers is a recently introduced catering concept at the upper end of the public house restaurant market. Moray Firth Maltings, alone among malting companies owned by brewers, supplies distillers both in the UK and internationally. It is one of the UK's largest traders in barley.

In 1987 turnover for the beer division, including beer wholesaling, public houses, tenancies and malting, was up 12.6% to £669.2m. Operating profit was up 15.4% to £83.3m.

Thistle Hotels In 1987 Thistle Hotels contributed 10.8% of the group turnover and 14.3% of operating profit.

Thistle Hotels is the fourth largest hotel group in the UK and the second largest in London. It operates 30 hotels, with eight four-star hotels in central London, including the Tower, the Royal Westminster, the Selfridge, the Royal Horseguards and the Royal Trafalgar. In 1987 Thistle Hotels received a Queen's Award to Industry for Export Achievement.

Thistle is developing several country house style hotels, the first of which – the Cannizaro House Hotel in Wimbledon – opened in 1987. The group is committed to expanding overseas, particularly in continental Europe.

In fiscal 1987 refurbishment of many of the division's hotels took place. The Donington Thistle Hotel was opened at East Midlands Airport, outside Nottingham. This is the group's first management contract.

In 1987 turnover was up 5.3% to £89.6m. Operating profit was up 5% to £14.7m. In common with other hotel groups, the division suffered from a shortfall of North American visitors in summer 1986, but this was not repeated in 1987 and the division produced exceptional results.

Wines & spirits In 1987 the division, including all exports, contributed 8.3% of the group turnover and 0.4% of operating profit.

Waverley Vintners is the group's wines and spirits wholesaling operation. In recent years the group has withdrawn from Scotch whisky production, built up its Scottish base and slimmed down Waverley's presence in England.

The division is now concentrating on becoming an effective supplier of wines and spirits to the group's tied and free retail accounts and in developing sales of the group's beers overseas. In 1987 turnover was down 27% to £68.5m. Operating profit was £0.4m against a loss of £0.5m in 1986.

GEOGRAPHICAL REVIEW

Of the group's 1987 turnover, the UK accounted for 98.5%, the US and Canada for 0.4%, Europe for 0.6% and the rest of the world for 0.5%.

CORPORATE CALENDAR

Year end	3 May
Preliminary results	July
Report and accounts	August
AGM	August
Final dividend paid	September
Interim results	December
Interim dividend paid	February

DIRECTORS' HOLDINGS

	Ordinary shares	Options
CJ Chalmers	10,998	106,289
HD Page Croft	918,285	91,749
JHW Fairweather	29,761	98,680
BC Kilkenny	17,486	103,571
AM Mowat	38,710	95,443
Sir David Nickson	5,000	—
AM Rankin	25,053	176,846
GB Reed	43,351	104,237
NM Shaw	1,000	—
R Summers	5,240	93,072
JM Thomson	1,000	—

GB Reed also holds 13,750 shares non-beneficially.

Total directors' remuneration for 1987 amounted to £626,000. The chairman received £33,355 and the highest-paid director £112,087.

PRINCIPAL SUBSIDIARIES AND RELATED COMPANIES

Canongate Technology Ltd, Coronation Inns Ltd (75%), Home Brewery Plc, Matthew Brown Plc, McEwan-Younger Ltd, Moray Firth Maltings Plc, Scottish & Newcastle Beer Production Ltd, Scottish & Newcastle Breweries (Sales) Ltd, Scottish and Newcastle Breweries (Services) Ltd, The Newcastle Breweries Ltd, Thistle Hotels Ltd, Waverley Vintners Ltd, William Younger and Company Ltd

BRAND NAMES

Beck's Bier, Castaway, Chandlers, Five-Star Bitter, Harp, Home Bitter, Home Mild, Hunter Bitter, Kestrel Super Strength Lager, Little John Special Strong Ale, Lion, McEwan's 60/–, McEwan's 70/–, McEwan's 80/–, McEwan's Best Scotch, McEwan's Export, McEwan's, McEwan's Lager, Newcastle Brown Ale, Newcastle Exhibition, Robin Hood, Ropiteau Frères, Shilling, Theakston's Old Peculiar, Younger's IPA, Younger's Kestrel, Younger's Scotch Bitter, Younger's Tartan, Younger's Traditional No 3 Scotch Ale

CONTACTS AND FURTHER INFORMATION

MJ Pearey, Company secretary, Scottish & Newcastle Breweries plc, Abbey Brewery, Holyrood Road, Edinburgh EH8 8YS. Tel: 031-556 2591.

SEARS PLC

GENERAL INFORMATION

Head office	40 Duke Street, London W1A 2HP. Tel: 01-408 1180
Directors	G Maitland Smith (chairman), JM Pickard (chief executive), L Sainer (president), HS Perlin, DJR Ward. *Non-exec* DC Macdonald, The Rt Hon Norman Tebbit CH MP, D O'Cathain OBE
Advisers	Kleinwort Benson Ltd
Auditors	Price Waterhouse
Registrars	Hill Samuel Registrars Ltd
Brokers	Cazenove & Co, Kleinwort Grieveson Securities Ltd
Solicitors	Titmuss Sainer & Webb

GENERAL FINANCIAL INFORMATION

Market capitalisation	£1.925bn at 1 January 1988
Capital structure	
Issued ordinary shares (25p)	1.5bn
Issued preference shares (£1)	2.0m 4.9% CP 'A'
	0.5m 8.75% CPS
	0.3m 5.25% CPS
Warrants	None
Convertibles	None
Traded options	Yes
ADRs	One ordinary share per ADR
Shareholders over 5%	House of Fraser 9.97%

FT CATEGORY

FT: Drapery and stores
FT-A: Stores

MAJOR ACTIVITIES

Sears is one of the UK's largest retailers, operating through 5,800 outlets a range of businesses which include footwear, department stores, home shopping, ladies' fashion, menswear, sportswear and jewellery. Footwear is the most important activity, accounting for 40% of group profits in 1986/87, including a small US contribution. Other retail activities contributed a further 33%. The balance of group profits was derived from licensed betting, 11%, and housebuilding and property development, 11%. A motor vehicles division, which has since been sold, provided 5%.

In December 1987 Sears successfully bid for Freemans, Britain's third largest mail order business, with a market share of 14%. Sears believes that there is a near perfect fit between the two businesses. The combination of Sears' brands and Freemans' distribution expertise will allow Sears to exploit the forecast growth in home shopping.

Alternative trading strategies have been developed in the footwear division to segment the market both by price and lifestyle. At the same time more resources are being directed towards ladies' fashions and menswear. Progress is encouraging. The past management record suggests that unproductive activities will be discontinued. The steady improvement in margins recorded in recent years should be maintained.

CHAIRMAN'S STATEMENT

'Certain group activities have been discontinued which no longer fit in with our new trading strategies and perceived way forward. A new corporate plan has been introduced on the footwear side recognising the need for consumer-led, strategic business units addressing clearly defined market segments.... There is undoubtedly a revolution going on in the high street and our biggest job is to manage change. One of the great strengths of Sears is its high street property base, enabling considerable flexibility in a growing specialist market place.'
Geoffrey Maitland Smith

In May 1988 the group announced that it was selling its Lewis's department stores and withdrawing from shoe retailing in the US.

Key economic indicators influencing the business include personal disposable incomes, consumer expenditure, consumer confidence and interest rates. Other external factors include government legislation, particularly that concerning the betting industry.

The group's main retail competitors include Burton, GUS, Marks and Spencer, Next, Storehouse, the unquoted John Lewis Partnership and House of Fraser. Mecca, Ladbroke and Coral compete in the betting industry, while Barratt, Trafalgar House, Beazer, Wimpey and Costain are competitors in the housebuilding market.

FINANCIAL HISTORY

For the year to 31 January 1988 turnover stood at £2.359bn, representing a 4.9% decrease over the previous period and a 28.3% increase over five years. The decline in turnover in 1987/88 was the result of the sale of Lewis's and the US shoe stores. Pre-tax profits were £245.7m, including non-trading items. This showed a 12% increase over the previous year, and a 51.8% improvement over a five year period. Pre-tax margins recorded a 1.6% increase in 1987/88. Since 1983 there has been a rise of nearly three and a half points, to give pre-tax margins of 10.4%.

Sears has disposed of its unproductive businesses and improved its remaining activities. The return on capital employed in 1987/88 was around 20%. This reflects a heavy investment in freehold and long leasehold retail premises. The 1987/88 property revaluation showed an increase of £395m over book amounts. In 1987/88, other income jumped £25.2m to £39.6m and accounted for most of the increase in pre-tax profits.

In 1987/88 earnings per share rose by 16% to 10.9p, to provide a five year advance of 49.3%. Dividends per share have been increased by 15% over one year, and by 140% since 1982.

Net debt at 31 January 1988 was £417m, representing 46% of shareholders' funds.

SHARE PRICE HISTORY

The shares' all-time peak was 190p in the summer of 1987. Since 1982 the shares have fluctuated between 13% and 18% off the FT-A All-Share index. In mid-May 1988 they stood at 13%. Recent profit trends have not matched the most optimistic stock market expectations, but any disappointments have been offset by speculative bid interest.

The Perth-based Bell Group and its associated company, JN Taylor, acquired an 8.2% stake in 1987. After the crash the share price fell to 110p. Robert Holmes a'Court subsequently placed the 127.9m share stake with the Al-Fayed brothers' House of Fraser, which, together with an existing holding, took its interest up to 10%.

SENIOR MANAGEMENT

Geoffrey Maitland Smith is chairman of the group. He was appointed to the board in August 1971 and became chief executive in 1978 and chairman in May 1985. He had worked with Sir Charles Clore, who built the group up as one of the UK's first conglomerates in the 1960s and 1970s.

Michael Pickard joined the board as deputy chief executive on 1 September 1986 and succeeded Geoffrey Maitland Smith

| F I V E   Y E A R   F I N A N C I A L   I N F O R M A T I O N | | | | | | | | | | | | |
Year	Turnover (£m)	Pre-tax (£m)	Earnings (p)	Dividends net (p)	Dividend cover (x)	Net assets (p)	Price (p) High	Low	PER (x) High	Low	Yield (%) High	Low
1983	1,590.5	112.3	4.93	1.87	2.6	52.7	86	57	21.1	15.7	4.26	3.33
1984	1,839.0	156.2	6.98	2.50	2.8	57.5	98	68	20.7	11.7	5.29	3.08
1985	2,019.4	169.8	7.87	3.00	2.6	63.7	121	79	17.5	12.9	5.26	3.66
1986	2,277.9	179.5	7.95	3.40	2.3	64.4	147	104	21.3	14.6	4.40	3.01
1987	2,480.3	211.7	9.09	4.00	2.3	67.6	186	118	21.4	12.4	5.05	2.95

as chief executive in February 1988. Before joining Sears he was chairman of Imperial Brewing & Leisure, holding responsibility for all Imperial's retail activities. Until 1984 he was chairman of Grattan and also founded the Happy Eater restaurant chain.

CAPITAL

The group generates a cash flow of over £100m a year. In April 1985, 130m ordinary shares were issued to acquire Foster Brothers, a clothing retailer. In July 1986, 9.53m shares were issued for the acquisition of Milletts Leisure, a sports and leisure goods retailer.

Horne Brothers, the speciality menswear retailers, was acquired for £34m in August 1987, of which £29.5m was paid in cash. By far the most important recent acquisition was Freemans in January 1988. It cost the group approximately £475m in cash and loan notes.

In 1986/87 there were a number of disposals of the group's peripheral interests. The most significant was the sale of the group's motor interests, Sears Motor Group, to Lex Service, which released cash of £86m. The surplus arising on the transaction was £25.5m. The engineering interests were also sold off for a loss of £14m.

As at 31 January 1987, employee options to subscribe for 25.8m ordinary shares, 1.7% of the issued share capital, were outstanding. The life president, Leonard Sainer, owned, either beneficially or non-beneficially, 7.8m ordinary shares, 0.5% of the total. The House of Fraser holds 10%.

GROUP REVIEW

Footwear retailing The main business is in the UK, where the company accounts for nearly 25% of the total market and therefore dominates the industry. A branch network covers 2,500 outlets, including both shops and concessions.

The operation has been reorganised into four separate areas of demand. These are: Dolcis, fashion shoes for younger buyers; Saxone and Manfield, high quality shoes for the higher spending and older age groups; Freeman Hardy Willis and Trueform, providing family footwear within the lower to mid-price ranges; and Curtess and Shoe City, mass market budget priced shoes.

The older shops are being modernised, and outdated stores are being replaced with large new stores. The aim is to strengthen the sales and profits performance in the face of increased competition in the footwear market from clothing and chain store retailers.

In May 1988 the group announced that it was selling its 600 US footwear shops to their management for approximately $50m. Sears will show a £34m extraordinary loss on the sale. The business has experienced difficult trading conditions and recent results have proved disappointing. They were only likely to break even in 1987/88. The 200 self-service outlets of Butler Shoe Corporation were closed down in 1986/87. The

company is also established in Holland with 200 branches.

In 1987/88 footwear retailing made profits of £106.2m, an increase of 23.2% on the previous year, with sales up 7.3% at £696.5m.

Department stores In May 1988 the group announced that its 10 Lewis's stores are to be sold to their management for £70m. Lewis's trades in important city centres such as Leeds, Manchester and Glasgow and other locations outside London.

Selfridges in Oxford Street, London, is extremely profitable and occupies a massive ten acres of floor-space. Tourist spending is important but the business enjoys a strong presence within the local market. It produces high levels of sales and profits per square foot and has recently been fully air-conditioned.

Clothing, sports and leisurewear A number of separate chains have been built up or acquired. In ladies' fashion clothing, Miss Selfridge and Wallis continue to expand and now trade from 211 outlets in total.

With the acquisition of Foster Brothers in 1985 Sears moved into the menswear market. With over 500 outlets it has the second highest number of specialist menswear stores in the UK. The business is growing rapidly in size. New operations are being launched, aimed at particular segments of the menswear market. Most recently, the Hornes and Zy chain of menswear stores was acquired.

The Foster's acquisition also brought in Adams, a childrenswear retailer, which now has over 125 outlets. Another part of the package was Millets which offers leisure and related merchandise. In 1986/87 business was expanded to 176 outlets.

A separate sports and leisure business has been developed by the group under the name of Olympus. There are 116 outlets now operating in the UK under the names Olympus, Supasports and Sportsave.

Jewellery retailing The business is concentrated on the high quality end of the market, under the prestigious Garrard and Mappin and Webb names. In 1986/87 the group launched In Time, a chain of lower priced watch retailers. The group also has a 25% interest in Aspreys.

Share price and relative to FT-A All-Share

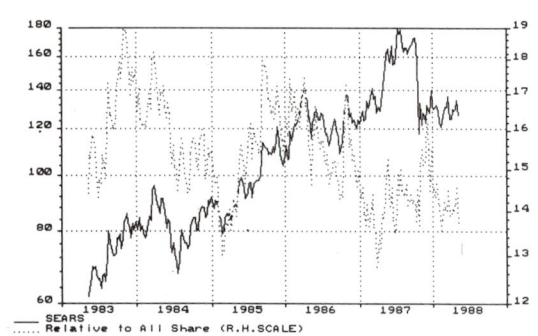

SEARS
...... Relative to All Share (R.H.SCALE)

In 1987/88 profits for the combined area of stores, fashion and speciality retailing totalled £80.9m, an increase of 14.3% on turnover up 15.9% on the previous year at £678.7m.

Freemans Freemans operates a catalogue mail order business selling primarily through agents in the UK. In addition to the main catalogue, Freemans publishes smaller specialist catalogues intended to appeal to distinct segments of the market. The Freemans group also sells fashion merchandise through its own retail stores and owns Warehouse, a womenswear retail chain.

In the year to 31 January 1987, Freemans reported pre-tax profits of £32.4m on turnover of £405.4m. However, 1987/88 was proving flat before the Sears acquisition. In the 28 weeks to 15 August 1987, Freemans reported pre-tax profits of £15.2m, up just £0.1m on the previous period. In 1987/88, Sears took in £6.8m of turnover and £0.5m of trading profit from the date of acquisition of 22 January 1988.

Despite paying a 93% premium over the pre-bid share price, Freemans is likely to be an outstanding acquisition for Sears. After Next's apparently successful entry into 'home shopping', the new name for mail order, Sears has followed quickly. Even before the Freemans bid, Sears had already developed focused mail order catalogues, called specialogues, for Wallis, Olympus and Miss Selfridge.

Miss Selfridge, Hornes, Fosters, Adams, Olympus, Millets, Wallis and Dolcis are an immensely strong brand portfolio. Sears has excellent prospects in its linking of high street retailing and home shopping.

Licensed betting The company operates as William Hill, and owns one of the largest betting office chains in the UK, second in size only to Ladbroke. The number of outlets rose from 845 to 870 in 1986/87. The introduction of live television coverage of horse and greyhound racing has provided an important boost. A new information service has been developed under the name of Hillsport to provide a further marketing edge.

In March 1986 a business in Belgium was acquired. The number of outlets there has already been increased from 345 to over 400.

1986/87 was an outstanding year, with profits up 41.8% to £24.1m. In 1987/88 the pace proved impossible to maintain, and profits were down 27.4% to £17.5m on turnover up 8.9% to £651.1m.

Housebuilding and property Full advantage is being taken of a buoyant UK housing market, with 1,100 homes completed in 1987/88 compared with 950 in the previous year and 800 in 1985/86. Activity is greater in the more prosperous southern half of the country. Major office and retail developments are under way both in the UK and overseas.

In 1987/88 profits were up 23.8% to £28.8m on turnover 37.1% ahead at £86.1m.

GEOGRAPHICAL REVIEW

In 1986/87, 86% of group sales and 91% of trading profits accrued in the UK. The US contributed 4% of trading profits. The balance came primarily from continental Europe.

CORPORATE CALENDAR

Year end	end January
Preliminary results	May
Report and accounts	June
AGM	June
Final dividend paid	July
Interim results	October
Interim dividend paid	December

DIRECTORS' HOLDINGS

	Fully-paid ordinary shares		Options
	(beneficial)	*(non-beneficial)*	
L Sainer	1,029,087	6,819,722	—
G Maitland Smith	73,750	—	540,995
JM Pickard	202,700	—	300,000
DJR Ward	81,000	—	263,852
DC Macdonald	4,500	—	—
HS Perlin	10,000	—	315,995

Total directors' remuneration was £1.02m, of which the chairman, who was also the highest-paid director, received £164,398.

PRINCIPAL SUBSIDIARIES AND RELATED COMPANIES

Footwear retailing
British Shoe Corporation Holdings Plc, British Shoe Corporation Ltd, Butler, Butler Shoe Corporation – US, Curtess, Dolcis, Freeman Hardy Willis, Hoogenbosch Beheer BV – Netherlands, Invito, Manfield, Saxone, Shoe City, Tip Toe, Trueform

Stores, fashion and speciality retailing
Adams, Asprey (25%), Dormie, Foster Brothers Clothing Plc, Fosters, Garrard, Garrard & Co, Horne Brothers Clothing Plc, Hornes, Jargon, Lewis's Investment Trust Ltd, Lewis's Ltd, Mallett (25%), Mappin & Webb, Mappin & Webb Ltd, Millets, Milletts Leisure Shops Plc, Miss Erika Inc – US, Miss Selfridge, Miss Selfridge Ltd, Olympus, Olympus Sport International Ltd, Selfridges Ltd, Sportsave, Supasports, Wallis, Wallis Fashion Group Ltd

Mail order
Freemans PLC

Licensed betting
La Générale Hippique Tierce SA – Belgium, Tierce Franco-Belge SA – Belgium, William Hill Organisation Plc

Housebuilding and property investment
Galliford Developments BV – Netherlands, Galliford Sears Estates Ltd, Leisure International Nederland BV, Sears Property Investments Ltd

BRAND NAMES

Adams, Bertie, Curtess, Dolcis, Dormie, Esquires, Fosters, Freeman Hardy Willis, Freemans, Galliford Sears, Garrard, In-Time, Invito, Jargon, Lewis, Manfield, Mappin & Webb, Millets, Miss Erika, Miss Selfridge, Olympus, Saxone, Selfridges, Shoe City, Sportsave, Supasports, Tip-Toe, Trueform, Wallis, William Hill, Your-price, Zy

CONTACTS AND FURTHER INFORMATION

SF Murray, Sears PLC, 40 Duke Street, London W1A 2HP. Tel: 01-408 1180.

SEDGWICK GROUP plc

GENERAL INFORMATION

Head office   Sedgwick House, The Sedgwick Centre, London E1 8DX.
                  Tel: 01-377 3456
Directors   CM Mosselmans (chairman), JD Rowlands (group chief
                  executive), JN Duncan (vice-chairman), RM Page – US
                  (vice-chairman), JM Payne (vice-chairman), JC Crane – US,
                  RRF Crofts, JS Gilbert, A Platt, S Riley, WH Sheridan, SA
                  Stewart Jr – US, JJH Swinglehurst, WR White-Cooper.
                  Non-exec AV Alexander CBE, HR Collum, Lord Fanshawe
                  KCMG, JR Harvey – US, FC Herringer – US, RN Hambro,
                  FJ Lutolf, PL Moussa, MJ de R Richardson
Advisers   NM Rothschild & Sons Ltd
Auditors   Coopers & Lybrand
Registrars   Lloyds Bank Registrar's Department
Brokers   Hoare Govett Ltd
Solicitors   No specified adviser

GENERAL FINANCIAL INFORMATION

Market capitalisation   £918m at 1 January 1988
Capital structure
Issued ordinary shares (10p)   347.2m ordinary. 79.9m 'A' ordinary.
                                   There is one vote for every four 'A' shares
Issued preference shares (£1)   None
Warrants   None
Convertibles   None
Traded options   None
ADRs   One ADR equals five ordinary shares
Shareholders over 5%   Transamerica Corporation holds 39% of
                                   the group's issued capital, including all
                                   the 'A' shares, but only 29% of its voting
                                   rights

FT CATEGORY

FT: Insurances
FT-A: Insurance brokers

MAJOR ACTIVITIES

Sedgwick Group is one of the leading insurance brokerage groups in the world and the largest in Europe. It is the only European international broker with a major presence in North America. Sedgwick has more than 300 offices in over 60 countries.

The group has always been well represented abroad with interests in Europe – particularly the Netherlands and Scandinavia – the Middle and Far East, and Australia.

C H A I R M A N ' S   S T A T E M E N T

'The group's operations in 1987 were dominated by two adverse factors, each familiar but rarely experienced simultaneously. Softening insurance markets and a weakening US dollar produced a situation of unusual severity for the business. These frustrated the prospects for profits growth which would otherwise have stemmed naturally from the successful establishment of the group in all significant insurance markets, including North America. Rates in the North American insurance market have fallen dramatically. Furthermore, premium rates in the United Kingdom and Europe, in certain classes, have moved in a downward direction. In addition, the dollar has continued to weaken and the price of oil has made only a partial recovery. The fall in exchange rates has produced a severe reduction in the net contribution from US dollar denominated business. All these factors have directly affected the group's revenue.' *CM Mosselmans*

Sedgwick's US acquisitions have transformed the group. It now derives a major part of its revenues from North America. The US interests have captured a greater share of the world's insurance market for the group but their profitability has not proved consistent.

The primary business of the group is to act as an intermediary between clients and insurers. It provides insurance, reinsurance and related risk management consultancy services to clients throughout the world.

In common with other brokers Sedgwick is susceptible to loss of client accounts and the loss of key employees as well as any downturn in premium rates. With about 70% of its activity dollar-related, it is also especially vulnerable to any weakening in the dollar in view of the substantial proportion of its costs denominated in sterling.

Sedgwick competes with big US brokers like Alexander & Alexander and Marsh McLennan, as well as the smaller UK companies. In the UK its shares are usually compared with those of other quoted insurance brokers, including CE Heath and Willis Faber.

FINANCIAL HISTORY

During the period 1982 to 1986, group turnover more than doubled and pre-tax profits rose by 50%. The reduction in corporation tax resulted in earnings increasing more quickly than profits. Earnings per share increased from 12.9p to 21.9p and the dividend rose from 7.0p to 12.0p.

Pre-tax profits in 1987, however, were 25% down to £101m. Sedgwick's US interests held profits back, as did the fall in the US dollar. The US contribution was down from £55.2m to £33.6m (−39.1%). Premium rate cuts and competitive conditions in many insurance markets led to reduced profit levels in most regions, except the Pacific.

Turnover in 1987 rose by £10m to £650.9 (+1.6%), the increase reflecting the acquisition of Crump, Armistead and Owen in 1986. Earnings per share declined from 21.9p to 16.1p (−26.5%), but the dividend was held at 12.0p. At the 1987 year-end the net assets of the group amounted to £161m or 38p per share. The group was strenuously cutting costs but the steps taken will take time to have effect.

SHARE PRICE HISTORY

Since 1982 the share price has risen from a low of 144p to a high of 345p in 1987. In the autumn 1987 crash the shares fell back to 168p before recovering to 215p in mid-April 1988. The group's share price is vulnerable to any fall in the value of the dollar and to any tendency for premium rates in the UK or US to fall.

SENIOR MANAGEMENT

The group chairman is Carel Mosselmans. David Rowland, formerly deputy chairman of Willis Faber, became chief executive in March 1988. Carel Mosselmans retires in April 1989.

Vice-chairman J Niven Duncan is chairman and chief executive of the main UK subsidiary, Sedgwick Limited. The other two vice-chairmen, RM Page and JM Payne, are chairman and chief executive of Fred S James & Co and EW Payne Companies respectively. The group finance director is Jack C Crane.

F I V E   Y E A R   F I N A N C I A L   I N F O R M A T I O N

Year	Turnover (£m)	Pre-tax (£m)	Earnings (p)	Dividends net (p)	Dividend cover (x)	Net assets (p)	Price (p) High	Low	PER (x) High	Low	Yield (%) High	Low
1983	366.9	98.6	18.3	8.0	2.3	43	251	179	13.7	9.8	6.38	4.55
1984	456.0	96.3	18.9	10.0	1.9	66	341	207	18.0	11.0	6.90	4.19
1985	581.0	124.3	21.5	11.0	2.0	56	405	331	18.8	15.4	4.75	3.88
1986	640.4	135.5	21.9	12.0	1.8	42	413	300	18.9	13.7	5.53	4.02
1987	650.9	101.1	16.1	12.0	1.3	38	350	165	21.7	10.2	9.79	4.61

CAPITAL

The group's business is financed by shareholders' net assets amounting at the end of 1987 to £161m, as well as bank loans, overdrafts and other borrowings which amount in total to £145m.

In the merger with the Fred S James Group in August 1985 the group issued 73.7m ordinary shares and 68.5m 'A' ordinary shares. All of the latter are held by Transamerica Corporation. In September 1986 the group made a rights issue with one new share being subscribed for each six shares previously held.

The number of ordinary shares in issue at the 1987 year-end was 347.2m. There were also 79.9m 'A' ordinary shares. In May and June 1987, 427,054 ordinary shares were issued in connection with the acquisition of BSi Inc by Sedgwick Tomenson Inc, a wholly owned subsidiary of the group. In December 1987, the group announced the signing of a $200m commercial paper programme and a $175m medium term loan facility.

GROUP REVIEW

Sedgwick trades through four principal divisions. They are Sedgwick Limited, James Group, EW Payne Companies Limited and Sedgwick Lloyd's Underwriting Agents Limited.
Sedgwick Limited This is principally a UK-based company providing retail and wholesale insurance services to a wide variety of clients. Areas it covers include aviation; marine; offshore oil and gas exploration and production; the construction, power and nuclear industries; employee benefits; and risk management to companies, professions and individuals.

In 1987 profits from the marine and aviation group were lower in the face of the continued contraction of the maritime industry and stiffer competition. Great emphasis was placed on efforts to reduce costs and safeguard long term profitability.

The special risks group covers the construction industry, including the Channel Tunnel Project (in which Sedgwick is the sole UK broker), and oil and gas exploration and production.

The group's retail operations had mixed results in 1987. In the UK its employee benefits company did well. The Dutch operation also progressed but combining the group's offices in France proved difficult and expensive.

In Australia and the Far East, Sedgwick Limited did well in 1987, especially in Australia where the group is the largest construction broker and a leader in oil and gas insurance.
James Group Also known as the Fred S James Co Inc, the James Group, acquired by Sedgwick in 1985, is primarily a US-based company. Its stated aim is to become North America's premier risk services company. Among the areas it covers are the Californian wine and US pharmaceutical industries and the provision of employee benefits consulting services.

In 1986 the Group strengthened its US standing by acquiring the Crump, Armistead and Owen companies. The acquisitions gave it access to the one-off risk reinsurance broking market and increased the depth and efficiency of its support services. They also widened its geographical spread especially in the southern states and the important Dallas area. The three companies were successfully integrated into the group during 1987.

1987 saw a continued reduction in premium rates, particularly for US property risks, and profits came under severe pressure. Nevertheless new business volume hit new records.

The Canadian subsidiary Sedgwick Tomenson did well in 1986 and increased its volume of business in 1987. In March 1987 it acquired BSi Inc, a private company engaged in actuarial, employee and executive benefits, and consulting and administration. BSi Inc had annual revenues of $4.4m in 1986 and profits of $1.1m.
EW Payne Companies Limited This is a UK-based international group of reinsurance brokers and is the UK's largest reinsurance broker. Its US subsidiary, Sullivan Payne Co, formed by the merger of John F Sullivan Co and EW Payne Inc, is the second largest reinsurance intermediary in North America. It also has subsidiaries in Australia, Greece and Sweden. In 1987 profits were suffering from significantly reduced earnings from Sullivan Payne, exacerbated by staff departures.

Share price and relative to FT-A All-Share

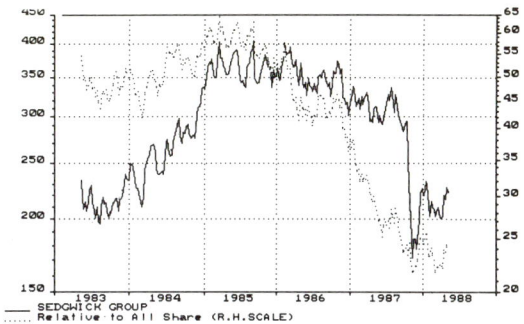

SEDGWICK GROUP
Relative to All Share (R.H.SCALE)

Sedgwick Lloyd's Underwriting Agents Limited The agency was formed after the divestment of Sedgwick Group's managing agency interests at Lloyd's. It now looks after the affairs of a substantial group of Lloyd's members, writing approximately 6% of all business underwritten at Lloyd's in 1986. Profits were well up at £5.6m compared with £4.2m in 1986.
Rivers Group Limited The Rivers Group monitors the Sedgwick Group's non-Lloyd's underwriting interests in the UK, Belgium, Bermuda, the Netherlands and Italy. Principal areas covered by the group included marine, property and the European motor business. It sold its 50% stake in Lloyd

THE "SHELL" TRANSPORT AND TRADING COMPANY, p.l.c.

Européen and its 100% holding in British Continental Office – Wigham Poland Belgium SA (BCO) for approximately £15m in cash to Group AXA-Belgium in June 1987. The Rivers Group's UK interests are concentrated in the River Thames Insurance Company, which has a capital base of £25m and is 51%-owned by Transamerica.

GEOGRAPHICAL REVIEW

Total profits in 1987 amounted to £101.1m, with the UK contributing 48%, the US 33.2%, Canada and Latin America 8.5%, continental Europe 2.8%, the Middle East and Africa 2.5% and the Pacific 5%.

Profits vary with the insurance cycle. Turnover, a less volatile indicator of business size, was split 35% in the UK, 6% in continental Europe, 49% in the US, 6% in Canada and Latin America and 4% in the Pacific. The group's exposure to the dollar is well over 50% because many non-US contracts are also denominated in dollars.

CORPORATE CALENDAR

Year end	31 December
Preliminary results	February
Report and accounts	March
AGM	April
Final dividend paid	April
Interim results	August
Interim dividend paid	October

DIRECTORS' HOLDINGS

	Ordinary shares (beneficial)	Options
CM Mosselmans	37,916	176,031
JN Duncan	24,498	176,031
RM Page	2,000	130,000
JM Payne	10,183	135,151
AV Alexander	63,100	—
HR Collum	3,000	—
JC Crane	5,000	100,000
RRF Crofts	4,550	100,000
Lord Fanshawe	5,330	
JS Gilbert	1,166	130,041
A Platt	3,943	117,777
S Riley	1,741	117,690
WH Sheridan	21,863	104,491
SA Stewart Jr	2,000	30,800
JJH Swinglehurst	37,844	135,151
WRP White Cooper	500	—

Total directors' remuneration in 1987 was £3.456m, of which the chairman received £310,000, and the highest-paid director £307,000.

PRINCIPAL SUBSIDIARIES AND RELATED COMPANIES

Sedgwick Aviation Ltd, Sedgwick UK (London), Sedgwick Personal Financial Management Ltd, Price Forbes Ltd, Sedgwick Ltd, Sedgwick Associated Risks Ltd, Sedgwick International Ltd, Sedgwick Employee Benefits Consultants Ltd, Fred S James & Co Inc – US, The Crump Companies Inc – US, EW Payne Ltd, Sedgwick Tomenson Inc – Canada, Sedgwick Chartered Hong Kong Ltd (50%), Sullivan Payne Co – US

BRAND NAMES

None

CONTACTS AND FURTHER INFORMATION

George Hilton, company secretary, Sedgwick Group plc, Sedgwick House, The Sedgwick Centre, London E1 8DX. Tel: 01-377 3456.

GENERAL INFORMATION

Head office	Shell Centre, London SE1 7NA. Tel: 01-934 1234
Directors	Peter Holmes MC (chairman), JS Jennings (managing), David Welham (managing), Sir Peter Baxendell CBE, Sir Robert Clark, The Rt Hon The Earl of Cromer KG GCMG MBE PC, The Rt Hon Edmund Dell PC, Robert Hart, Sir David Orr MC, The Rt Hon Sir Michael Palliser GCMG, W Thompson
Advisers	No specified adviser
Auditors	Ernst & Whinney
Registrars	Lloyds Bank Registrar's Department
Brokers	Rowe & Pitman Ltd
Solicitors	Slaughter and May

GENERAL FINANCIAL INFORMATION

Market capitalisation	£11.143bn at 1 January 1988
Capital structure	
Issued ordinary shares (25p)	1.105bn
Issued preference shares (£1)	2m first 7% CP, 10m second 7% CP
Warrants	None
Convertibles	None
Traded options	Yes
ADRs	Four ordinary shares per ADR
Shareholders over 5%	None

FT CATEGORY

FT: Oil and gas
FT-A: Oil and gas

MAJOR ACTIVITIES

Shell Transport and Trading is a 40% shareholder in the Royal Dutch/Shell group, the world's largest integrated oil company in terms of revenues, oil and gas production and reserves. The group explores for and produces oil and gas, refines and markets oil products, and is a major international chemical manufacturer.

The group explores for and produces oil and gas in 46 countries spanning six continents. Production of oil and gas has risen considerably compared to 1983. The group has been successful in finding new reserves over the same period.

The Royal Dutch/Shell group market oil products in more countries than any other oil company. Refining and marketing have been subject to considerable rationalisation and investment to maintain the group's pre-eminent position.

The group has 30 refineries operating in 15 countries and a share in 53 refineries in 34 countries. Twelve of these refineries are in North America. Refineries are being upgraded to produce greater quantities of light products. This process may increase the refineries' efficiency further beyond that of their competitors.

Under the distinctive Shell symbol, the group is renowned as a marketer of oil products with a programme of continued investment in selected market areas. The group has been able to increase total product sales in all but one year since 1983 during a period when demand for oil products was declining. The group experienced a setback in January 1988 when, as a precaution, the spark aider additive was withdrawn from leaded grades of Formula Shell premium petrol brands after technical problems.

The group's chemicals interests are rapidly expanding. Their contribution increased substantially in 1987 and currently represent more than a quarter of group business net income. The chemicals business is one of the world's seven largest chemicals companies.

The Royal Dutch/Shell group has developed considerable activities in coal and minerals. These are not as yet major sources of group revenue.

F I V E   Y E A R   F I N A N C I A L   I N F O R M A T I O N

Year	Sale proceeds* (£m)	Pre-tax* (£m)	Earnings (p)	Dividends net (p)	Dividend cover (x)	Net assets (p)	Price (p) High	Low	PER (x) High	Low	Yield (%) High	Low
1983	53,308	2,754	96.0	26.2	3.7	711	640	404	8.4	5.5	7.46	4.87
1984	63,542	3,648	127.5	33.0	3.9	926	705	545	7.6	4.7	6.87	4.92
1985	73,102	3,032	101.5	35.0	2.9	852	791	626	6.2	4.9	7.67	5.02
1986	55,547	2,540	82.0	43.0	1.9	906	985	660	11.4	5.9	7.27	5.15
1987	59,811	2,883	94.8	48.0	2.0	756	1515	930	19.1	10.5	6.78	3.89

* These figures refer to Royal Dutch/Shell, the remainder to Shell Transport.

FINANCIAL HISTORY

Post-tax profits of £2.883bn in 1987 for the Royal Dutch/Shell group showed a 13.5% increase on 1986 and a 21% fall from the 1984 peak.

Exploration and production earnings recovered partially, as oil prices rose from the low levels of 1986, to £1.796bn, up 20.2% from £1.494bn in 1986. Earnings benefited from the reduction of exploration write-offs from £931m in 1986 to £549m in 1987, enhancing earnings by £382m.

This was offset, in a reversal of 1986, by a £319m reduction in refining and marketing profitability. Total refining and marketing profits in 1987 were £674m, down 32.1% from the 1986 figure of £993m.

Chemical earnings were sharply up, benefiting from improved utilisation of capacity, firmer product prices and a £125m disposal profit on the sale of the group's holding in the Akzo consumer products business. Record profits of £764m were achieved, up 65.4% from £462m.

There was a net outflow of cash as working capital needs increased, due mainly to the effects of oil price changes. Cash and short term securities were £5.1bn at the end of 1987, as against £6.4bn at the end of 1986.

Since 1983 Shell has paid consistent increases in the dividend at above the average rate of UK inflation. The 1987 net figure of 48.0p was 11.6% up on 1986.

The rising dividend has been supported by a large dividend cover. 1987 earnings per share were 16.1% up at 95.2p. Net assets were 756p per share, 16.5% down on the 1986 figure of 906p.

SHARE PRICE HISTORY

From the beginning of 1986 to mid-1987, the Shell Transport share price rose from the 660p level to a high of 1515p. Oil price fears held the share price back in 1984 and 1985. However, investors gained confidence in the quality of earnings as refining and marketing profits recovered and the oil price rose. An above-market-average yield helped the share price to outperform the market.

Before the autumn 1987 share price collapse, however, the share price had retreated to the 1400p level. In the crash the shares fell to a low of 930p, before recovering to the early April 1988 level of 1080p.

The share price has always reflected investors' confidence in Shell's policy of consistent dividend growth at above the rate of inflation. The financial strength of the group, as the largest oil company, has given the shares a premium rating in the sector.

SENIOR MANAGEMENT

The Royal Dutch/Shell group is run by a presidium of six managing directors, three from Royal Dutch and two from Shell Transport. Shell Transport has a full board of directors made up of its chairman, two managing directors and a group of eight distinguished non-executive directors.

The chairman, Peter Holmes was appointed from 1 July 1985, having been a managing director since July 1982. David Welham was appointed a managing director from July 1986, and John Jennings was appointed from 1 July 1987. All three have worked for the Royal Dutch/Shell group for most of their business careers.

CAPITAL

Shell Transport and Trading has no operations of its own. Virtually the whole of its income derives from its 40% interest in the companies known collectively as the Royal Dutch/Shell group of companies. The other 60% is owned by Royal Dutch Petroleum Company, a Netherlands company.

Shell has issued capital of £276.21m, divided into 1.105bn ordinary 25p shares. There are two small issues of preference shares. ADRs are traded on the New York Stock Exchange.

None of the directors have a significant holding and there are no interests above 5%.

GROUP REVIEW

Oil and gas exploration and production The group has been successful in increasing reserves by 29% for oil and 10% for gas since 1979 at a time when oil and gas production was rising. This outstanding achievement is due to the group's expertise in increasing oil reserves in mature fields using enhanced oil recovery techniques. It is also due to the group's worldwide exploration activities, which are continuously locating commercial reserves throughout the world.

The acquisition of a 50% interest in the one billion barrel Caño Limón Field, Colombia, shows Shell's willingness to purchase oil reserves where it believes prices are reasonable. More investment in the heavy oil fields of California indicates Shell's belief that its expertise in enhanced oil recovery techniques can add value to known mature production.

In 1987 earnings were up 20.2% to £1.796bn, 62.3% of the group's total. The exploration write-off was reduced from £931m to £549m, accounting for the increase in earnings. 1987 production at 1.77m barrels per day was marginally down on 1986 levels. Natural gas sales volumes of 6.538m cubic feet per day were 5% up.

Manufacturing, marine and marketing The group is the world leader in refining and marketing oil products. In 1987 it sold 4.9m barrels of oil products a day and has 30 refineries operating in 14 countries and a share in 53 refineries in 34 countries. 1987 production was 11% up on 1986.

The continued growth in marketing facilities in 1987 has been reflected in the increased use of group refineries. Royal Dutch/Shell has one of the highest capacity utilisations of any major oil company.

The Royal Dutch/Shell group was foremost in the introduction of upgrading capacity at refineries to improve conversion efficiencies. This position has been eroded since 1982 as competitors raced to catch up. The implementation by the group of new techniques and processes at its various refineries currently in progress may again allow the group to leap ahead of its competitors.

Increases in US motor gasoline sales by four times the industry average made Shell the largest US gasoline retailer in 1986 and 1987. This drive for increased market share and lower oil prices helped the group to show profits of £993m in 1986, an increase of 59% over the previous year.

The rise in oil prices lowered earnings in 1987. Earnings were £674m, 23.4% of the group's total, and down 32.1% from the exceptional 1986 figures. Margins throughout the world were reduced. Intense competitive pressures more than offset the positive effects of increased sales volumes.

Unleaded fuels have been introduced in the UK and the continuing upgrading of retail outlets shows Shell's determination to remain the market leader in automotive products. The withdrawal of the spark aider additive in Formula Shell leaded gasoline in the UK and the Netherlands, after problems were discovered in some cars, is a disappointment given the success that the launch of this new product has had in both the leaded

Share price and relative to FT-A All-Share

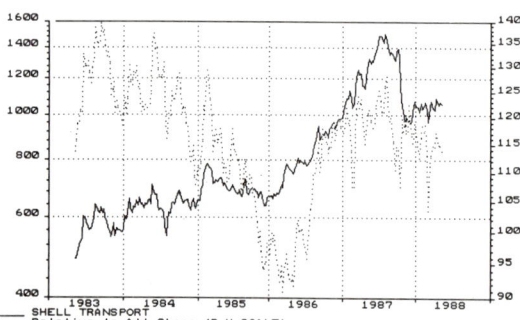

and unleaded gasoline market. But the Formula Shell brand gasolines continue to be marketed successfully in 31 countries.

The group has always maintained a strong presence in the marine tankerage of oil and products. The collapse of the tanker market in the late 1970s, as demand for Middle East crudes declined, forced the group to reduce its fleet of tankers from some 30mdt to 10.5mdt by the end of 1987.

Chemicals Sales from the group's chemicals business rank it among the world's seven largest chemicals companies. In 1987 chemicals accounted for 26.5% of the group's net earnings, a substantial increase on 1986's 18.2% contribution.

The 65.4% increase in chemical earnings to a record £764m in 1987 came after a 125% rise in 1986. This strong performance reflected a rise in sales volumes in petrochemicals, particularly styrene, lower olefins and aromatics, and from lower unit production costs, which benefited from very high plant loadings. Agricultural and speciality chemicals volumes were maintained and Royal Dutch/Shell was able to operate petrochemical sites at near capacity rates.

In 1986 the group disposed of its US agrochemical business to Du Pont, ending a long period of association with agrochemicals in the US. There was a disposal profit of £85m. This disposal reflects the competitive nature only of the US market, and the group have announced their intention to

CHAIRMAN'S STATEMENT

'Oil prices today are still well below the peak levels of the early 1980s. This decline has benefited the consumer in the short term, but has caused some problems in oil-producing countries.

Exploration and production activity by the industry was sharply cut back as prices dropped, and it is quite clear that this has had an impact on the rate of discovery and development of new reserves. There has been some resurgence of activity as prices have recovered, and a stable oil price at a level which will encourage the development of new oil reserves is, in the long term, as important for consumers as it is for producers. It should be noted also that the oil reserves of non-OPEC producers are gradually diminishing and that OPEC has about three-quarters of the world's proven oil reserves. More than 80% of these are located in Saudi Arabia, Kuwait, the United Arab Emirates, Iraq and Iran.' *PF Holmes*

expand their European and Far Eastern agrochemical interests. In 1987 the group sold its Akzo consumer products business for a gain of £125m.

Base chemical production is very vulnerable to oil prices and dollar exchange rates, though in 1987 there were margin gains reflecting buoyant demand in many countries. Shell continues to move further into higher value speciality chemicals as well as differentiated petrochemical products in order to provide for profitable growth and greater resilience to cyclical fluctuations.

Metals Aluminium production accounts for the largest part of the group's metal interest. This benefited from a steady rise in prices in 1987. Prices may soften in 1988 but earnings will continue to benefit from previous rationalisation programmes.

In 1987 the division made profits of £15m, against losses of £44m in 1986 and £156m in 1985. This represented 0.5% of the group's total. Whilst there was a non-recurring credit contribution, metals benefited from the sharp recovery in prices for most non-ferrous metals.

Coal Despite rationalisation creating lower operating costs, there is overcapacity in the world market with the prospect of further new producers operating in Colombia and China.

In 1987 there was a continued decline in already depressed coal prices. The division made losses of £26m, against a profit of £18m in 1986.

GEOGRAPHICAL REVIEW

The Royal Dutch/Shell group is spread globally with total assets being split fairly evenly between the eastern and western hemispheres. The US represents the bulk of assets in the western hemisphere and Europe dominates the eastern, but the rest of the eastern hemisphere is important too with 16% of group assets.

On a net proceeds basis, however, Europe accounts for nearly 50% of the total with the US yielding approximately 25%.

CORPORATE CALENDAR

Year end	31 December
Preliminary results	March
Report and accounts	April
AGM	May
Final dividend paid	May
Interim results	August
Interim dividend paid	November

DIRECTORS' HOLDINGS

	Fully-paid ordinary shares	Options
PF Holmes	1,000	140,745
JS Jennings	—	36,000
DR Welham	1,500	93,771
Sir Peter Baxendell	15,000	137,000
Sir Robert Clark	1,000	—
The Earl of Cromer	3,000	—
Edmund Dell	800	—
RM Hart	4,000	—
Sir David Orr	1,200	—
Sir Michael Palliser	2,500	—
WC Thomson	2,000	75,200

Total directors' remuneration in 1987 was £792,644, with the chairman, who was also the highest-paid director, receiving £265,430.

PRINCIPAL SUBSIDIARIES AND RELATED COMPANIES

Abu Dhabi Company for Onshore Oil Operations – United Arab Emirates (9.5%), Abu Dhabi Gas Industries – United Arab Emirates (15%), Abu Dhabi Petroleum Co – United Arab Emirates (23.75%), Aekyung and Shell – South Korea (50%), Africaine Shell Chimie – West and Equatorial Africa, Africaine de Raffinage – West and Equatorial Africa (12%), Akzo Consumenten Produkten – Netherlands (49%), Al Jomaih & Shell Lubricating Oil – Saudi Arabia (49%), Anadolu Tasfiyehanesi – Turkey (27%), Arab Solar Industries – Jordan (50%), Aughinish Alumina – Republic of Ireland (35%), Austen and Butta – Australia (45%), Bangladesh Shell – Bangladesh, Belgian Shell – Belgium, Billiton – Netherlands, Billiton Aluminium Ireland – Republic of Ireland, Billiton Australia Gold – Australia (30%), Billiton Española – Spain, Billiton Maatschappij Suriname – South America, Billiton Metals Canada – Canada, Billiton Metals and Ores Deutschland – West Germany, Billiton Portuguesa – Portugal, Billiton UK, BioShell – Canada, Braconnot – France, Brigitta/Elwerath – West Germany (50%), Brunei Coldgas – Brunei Darussalam (25%), Brunei LNG – Brunei Darussalam (25%), Brunei Shell Marketing – Brunei Darussalam (50%), Brunei Shell Petroleum – Brunei Darussalam (50%), Brunei Shell Tankers – Brunei Darussalam (50%), Burkina et Shell – West and Equatorial Africa (49%), Burshane (Pakistan) – Pakistan (31.5%), Butagaz – France (98%), Butagaz-Tunisie – Africa, Callide – Australia (30%), Capricorn Coal Developments – Australia (26%), Cerro Matoso – South America (47%), Colas East Africa – East Africa, Colas Products, Compañía Shell de Colombia – South America, Dansk Shell – Denmark, Deutsche Shell – West Germany, Distrigaz – Belgium (16.66%), Drayton – Australia (39%), Dukhan Service – Qatar (23.75%), Ecuatoriana de Lubricantes – South America (70%), Erdöl-Raffinerie Deurag-Nerag – West Germany (50%), First Philippine Industrial – Philippines (40%), Guatemalteca Shell – Central America, Iransen et Shell – West and Equatorial Africa (50%), Irish Shell – Republic of Ireland, Jambi Shell – Indonesia, Kent Heating – New Zealand, Kenya Petroleum Refineries – East Africa (12.75%), Kenya Shell – East Africa (50%), Kukdong Shell Petroleum – South Korea (50%), Malaysia LNG – Malaysia (17.5%), Maui Development – New Zealand (18.75%), Mitsubishi Yuka – Japan (26%), National Oil and Chemical Marketing – West and Equatorial Africa (40%), National Organic Chemical Industries – India (33.33%), Nederlandse Aardolie Mij – Netherlands, Nederlandse Gasunie – Netherlands (25%), New Zealand Refining – New Zealand (17%), Nickerson Seeds, Nickerson Zwaan – Netherlands, Norske Shell – Norway, North West Shelf Development – Australia (50%), Oliufelagid Skeljungur – Iceland (24%), Pakistan Burmah Shell – Pakistan (24.5%), Pakistan Refinery – Pakistan (15%), Pecten Cameroon – West and Equatorial Africa (80%), Pecten Malaysia – Malaysia, Pecten Syria – Syria, Peninsular Aviation Services – Saudi Arabia (25%), Petroleum Development Oman – Oman (34%), Petrolífera Española Shell – Spain, Petromali-Shell – West and Equatorial Africa (50%), Petromin Shell Refinery – Saudi Arabia (50%), Philippine Petroleum – Philippines (55%), Pilipinas Shell – Philippines (50%), Port Sudan Refinery – East Africa (50%), Private Oil Holdings Oman – Oman (85%), Qatar Shell Service – Qatar, Química Dominicana – Caribbean, Química Nicaragüense – Central America, Raffinerie de Cressier – Switzerland, Raffinerie des Antilles – Caribbean (24%), Refinería Dominicana – Caribbean (50%), Refinería Petrolera Acajutla – Central America (35%), Renewable Energy Systems – Netherlands, Réunionnaise de Produits Pétroliers – East Africa (50%), Rheinische Olefinwerke – West Germany (50%), Röhol-Aufsuchungs Gesellschaft – Austria (50%), Rotterdam-Rijn Pijpleiding – Netherlands (40%), Ruhrgas – West Germany (15%), Sabah Shell – Malaysia, Sarawak Shell – Malaysia, Saudi Arabian Markets & Shell Lubricants – Saudi Arabia (50%), Saudi Petrochemical – Saudi Arabia (50%), Shell (Hellas) – Greece, Shell (Pacific Islands) – Pacific Islands, Shell (Puerto Rico) – Caribbean, Shell (WI) – Caribbean, Shell Switzerland, Shell Antilles and Guianas – Caribbean, Shell Argentina de Petróleo – South America, Shell Australia – Australia, Shell Austria – Austria, Shell Aviation Guinée – West and Equatorial Africa, Shell BP and Todd – New Zealand (37.5%), Shell Bahamas – Caribbean, Shell Belize – Central America, Shell Bermuda – Caribbean, Shell Brasil – South America, Shell Cabo Verde – West and Equatorial Africa, Shell Cameroun – West and Equatorial Africa, Shell Canada – Canada (79%), Shell Centrafricaine – West and Equatorial Africa, Shell Chemical (Malawi) – Central and Southern Africa, Shell Chemical (Philippines) – Philippines (40%), Shell Chemical Eastern Africa – East Africa, Shell Chemicals (Hellas) – Greece, Shell Chemicals (Zambia) – Central and Southern Africa, Shell Chemicals Ireland – Republic of Ireland, Shell Chemicals Jamaica – Caribbean, Shell Chemicals UK, Shell Chemicals and Services (East Caribbean) – Caribbean, Shell Chile – South America, Shell Chimie – France, Shell China – China, Shell Co of the Islands – East Africa, Shell Coal China – China, Shell Colombia – South America, Shell Côte d'Ivoire – West and Equatorial Africa (50%), Shell Cyprus Trading – Cyprus, Shell Developments Zimbabwe – Central and Southern Africa, Shell Distribution – Philippines, Shell Djibouti – East Africa, Shell Eastern Petroleum – Singapore, Shell El Salvador – Central America, Shell Ethiopia – East Africa, Shell Exploradora y Productora de Colombia – South America, Shell Exploradora y Productora del Perú – South America, Shell Exploration (China) – China, Shell Exploration – East Africa, Shell Fiji – Pacific Islands, Shell Française – France (98%), Shell Gabon – West and Equatorial Africa (75%), Shell Gas (Philippines) – Philippines, Shell Ghana – West and Equatorial Africa (60%), Shell Gibraltar – Gibraltar, Shell Honduras – Central America, Shell Hong Kong – Hong Kong, Shell Italia – Italy, Shell Ivoirienne – West and Equatorial Africa, Shell Kosan – Japan, Shell Littoral Zairois – West and Equatorial Africa, Shell Luxembourgeoise – Luxembourg, Shell Malaysia Trading – Malaysia, Shell Marketing Borneo – Malaysia, Shell Markets/Trading (Middle East) – United Arab Emirates, Shell México – Central America, Shell Nederland Chemie – Netherlands, Shell Nederland Raffinaderij – Netherlands, Shell Nederland Verkoop – Netherlands, Shell Nepal – Nepal, Shell New Zealand – New Zealand, Shell Nicaragua – Central America, Shell Niger – West and Equatorial Africa, Shell Oil Botswana – Central and Southern Africa, Shell Oil Company – US, Shell Oil Lesotho – Central and Southern Africa, Shell Oil South West Africa – Central and Southern Africa, Shell Oil Swaziland – Central and Southern Africa, Shell Olie-og Gasudvinding Danmark – Denmark, Shell Pacific Developments – Taiwan, Shell Pacific Enterprises – South Korea, Shell Pacifique – Pacific Islands, Shell Papua New Guinea – Pacific Islands, Shell Paraguay – South America, Shell Petroleum Development Libya – Africa, Shell Petroleum Development Nigeria – West and Equatorial Africa, Shell Petroleum Development Somalia – East Africa, Shell Petroleum Development Tanzania – East Africa, Shell Petroleum Development PNG – Pacific Islands, Shell Portuguesa – Portugal, Shell Prospecting – Africa, Shell Química de El Salvador – Central America, Shell Química de Guatemala – Central America, Shell Química de Venezuela – South America, Shell Recherche – France (99%), Shell Refining (FOM) – Malaysia (75%), Shell Research, Shell Research – Belgium, Shell Research – Netherlands, Shell Sierra Leone – West and Equatorial Africa (60%), Shell Singapore – Singapore, Shell South Africa – Central and Southern Africa, Shell Spanje – Spain, Shell Sudan – East Africa, Shell Suriname Verkoop – South America, Shell Tankers (UK), Shell Tankers – Netherlands, Shell Tchad – West and Equatorial Africa, Shell Tchadienne – West and Equatorial Africa, Shell Thailand – Thailand, Shell Thailand Manufacturing – Thailand, Shell Tunisie – Africa, Shell Tunisienne – Africa, Shell Turkey – Turkey, Shell UK, Shell Uganda – East Africa (50%), Shell Uruguay – South America, Shell West Africa – West and Equatorial Africa, Shell Winning – Africa, Shell Zimbabwe – Central and Southern Africa (50%), Shell and BP South African Refineries – South Africa, Shell del Perú – South America, Shell des Antilles et de la Guyane Françaises – Caribbean, Shell du Laos – Laos, Shell du Maroc – Africa (50%), Showa Shell Sekiyu – Japan (50%), Showa Shell Sempaku – Japan (50%), Sierra Leone Petroleum Refining – West and Equatorial Africa (18%), Sunda Shell – Indonesia, Svenska Shell – Sweden, Swedegas – Sweden (15%), Syria Shell Petroleum Development – Syria, Tarakan Shell – Indonesia, Thai Oil – Thailand (15%), Thai Shell Exploration and Production – Thailand, Thaisarco – Thailand, Thyssengas – West Germany (25%), Tiram Kimia – Malaysia (49%), Togo et Shell – West and Equatorial Africa (50%), Turkse Shell – Turkey, Wavin – Netherlands (57%), Woodside Petroleum – Australia (40%), Worsley Alumina – Australia (30%), Yuka Shell Epoxy – Japan (63%), Zaire-Shell – West and Equatorial Africa (60%), oy Shell – Finland

BRAND NAMES

Shell

CONTACTS AND FURTHER INFORMATION

Group public affairs, The "Shell" Transport and Trading Company, p.l.c., Shell Centre, London SE1 7NA. Tel: 01-934 1234.

SMITH & NEPHEW plc

GENERAL INFORMATION

Head office 2 Temple Place, Victoria Embankment, London WC2R 3BP. Tel: 01-836 7922
Directors KR Kemp (chairman), E Kinder (chief executive and deputy chairman), AR Fryer, MJ Kiely, JL Rennocks, JH Robinson, TF Winter. *Non-exec* MAF Macpherson
Advisers No specified adviser
Auditors Ernst & Whinney
Registrars Lloyds Bank Registrar's Department
Brokers Kleinwort Grieveson Securities Ltd
Solicitors Ashurst Morris Crisp

GENERAL FINANCIAL INFORMATION

Market capitalisation	£1.245bn at 1 January 1988
Capital structure	
Issued ordinary shares (10p)	961m
Issued preference shares (£1)	0.45m, 3.85% CP
Warrants	None
Convertibles	$26m of 5½% $ Convertible Bonds 2000 (convertible into ordinary shares at 109p, at fixed exchange rate of $1.4202 to £1) £90m of 4% ESC 2000 (645.998 shares per £1000 stock, put option at 133.5p per ordinary share)
Traded options	None
ADRs	None
Shareholders over 5%	None

FT CATEGORY

FT: Industrials (miscel.)
FT-A: Health and household products

MAJOR ACTIVITIES

Smith & Nephew (S&N) is a health care group, oriented towards wound healing and orthopaedics. The company is noted for its strong management team and is comprised of five core groups – patient care, medical and other supplies, consumer, medical and other textiles, and plastics.

Patient care accounted for 56% of operating profit in 1987, while 12% came from medical supplies, 20% from consumer, 8% from medical and other textiles and 4% from plastics.

Key factors affecting the company are growth in medical demand, spending in the western world and new technology development. To a lesser extent the group is also vulnerable to changing weather in the UK, which affects the sales of toiletries, particularly sun preparations.

FINANCIAL HISTORY

Turnover was up 14% in 1987 at £546m, and has increased consistently through acquisition and organic growth. US turnover at £173.1m surpassed UK turnover at £159.3m for the first time in 1986 and in 1987 represented 35% of the group total. Pre-tax profits were up 24% at £110m in 1987, from £82.2m in 1986.

Operating profit continues to be substantially derived from the patient care division, whose activities have contributed over 50% of profits for some years. Total operating profits are up over 130% since 1983.

Earnings per share have also shown good growth. In 1987, earnings per share stood at 8.2p, a 15% increase over 1986's 7.1p, and up over 110% from 1983 levels.

Efficient handling of debt resulted in very low interest charges in 1985, 1986 and 1987. Tax was also low in 1986 and 1987, in part due to beneficial tax treatment from the Richards acquisition.

For the 12 weeks ended 26 March 1988, pre-tax profits were 11.9% up at £24.5m on turnover 5.8% ahead at £135.3m. Earnings per share were 11.1% up at 1.8p. Sales were reduced by £11.7m through the effect of movements of exchange rates.

SHARE PRICE HISTORY

The share price has also experienced solid growth. Adjusted for various share issues it has risen by an average of 37% a year from 26p at the start of 1982 to 135p at the end of December 1987. Recent years have seen consistent buy or hold recommendations due to underlying real growth of 10% to 12%, and excellent financial management.

The shares fell sharply in the share crash of October 1987. From their all-time high of 196p they fell 39.2% to 119p, though in relative terms they stayed near the top of their trading range. The group has historically sold at around a 50% premium above the FT-A All-Share index.

SENIOR MANAGEMENT

KR Kemp is chairman of S&N. E Kinder is chief executive and deputy chairman. JL Rennocks is in charge of group finance, and acts as company secretary. A Suggett is chief of group research.

AR Fryer, who joined the board in March 1987, shares responsibility for the UK with JH Robinson. In the US, J Blair is president of Richards Medical, and L Fern is president of Smith & Nephew Inc, formerly Affiliated Hospital Products. TF Winter has a co-ordinating role for North America. MJ Kiely heads up the Australasian business, while PJ Neethling is responsible for southern Africa. K Tatteshall is responsible for UK pharmaceuticals.

CAPITAL

In January 1986, S&N raised $60m (£42m) by the issue of 5.5% convertible bonds. S&N issued additional equity through a vendor placing in October 1986. The £127m proceeds went towards the purchase of Richards Medical in the US for $284m. There was a one for one scrip issue on 15 May 1986.

Additional capital was provided by the sale of Smith and Nephew Anchor, the group's US plastics and tapes business, for $55m in March 1987. Alberto Fernández, a leading Spanish manufacturer of latex surgeon's gloves, examination gloves and condoms was bought in March 1987 for £2.3m.

In April 1987, the company raised £90m through a convertible Eurobond issue with a 4% coupon. The bond contained a put option for investors, to yield 8.5% to put at par.

The company expects that the whole borrowing of the two convertible bonds will eventually be eliminated by conversion into equity. By mid-1987, $34m of the $60m 5.5% bond had been converted.

In September 1987, S&N bought two US companies, Donjoy and Sigma, for $32m. Donjoy manufactures and distributes orthopaedic knee braces used in sports medicine. Sigma manufactures and distributes peristaltic infusion pumps for patient care.

GROUP REVIEW

Patient care This is the largest division, which accounts for over half of turnover and operating profit. It is responsible for manufacturing wound-healing products, orthopaedic and

FIVE YEAR FINANCIAL INFORMATION

Year	Turnover (£m)	Pre-tax (£m)	Earnings (p)	Dividends net (p)	Dividend cover (x)	Net assets (p)	Price (p) High	Price (p) Low	PER (x) High	PER (x) Low	Yield (%) High	Yield (%) Low
1983	314.0	44.6	3.9	1.57	2.5	18.6	64	44	25.8	16.7	3.78	3.00
1984	374.1	55.5	4.9	1.89	2.6	21.1	94	60	30.0	17.6	3.23	2.52
1985	423.0	70.6	5.9	2.32	2.5	23.3	110	82	28.2	19.2	3.34	2.92
1986	480.0	88.0	7.1	2.70	2.6	22.0	133	94	26.3	19.3	3.09	2.37
1987	547.0	109.6	8.2	3.40	2.4	25.0	196	124	28.9	16.4	3.72	2.00

arthroscopy products and generic pharmaceuticals. Its well-known brand names include Opsite, and Dynacast and Minims.

This division, created in 1987 for reporting purposes, has been greatly expanded by a series of acquisitions, the most significant of which was Richards Medical Company, bought in October 1986 for $283.9m (£210m). Richards is a manufacturer of arthroscopy equipment and artificial joint replacement parts such as hips and knees. Employing 1,500 people it is one of the largest companies in the US dedicated to serving the orthopaedic market with surgical implants, equipment and instruments.

A fast-growing portion of this division is pharmaceuticals. Solopak, a company acquired in 1985 as part of Affiliated Hospital Products, specialises in injectable generic pharmaceuticals and has shown 30% per annum growth since then.

Manufacturing capacity at Solopak is to be doubled in 1988 and represents a commitment to an emerging niche pharmaceuticals business.

In 1987 the division increased profits by 51% to £57.6m on turnover up 52% to £277.8m.

Medical supplies and equipment This division, like patient care, was created in 1987 out of the old medical and healthcare division for reporting purposes. It is responsible for the manufacture of latex gloves, orthopaedic rehabilitation products and various items of surgical and medical equipment.

The most significant part of the business is latex gloves, a large portion of which was acquired as part of Affiliated Hospital Products in 1985. Glove capacity was increased 40% by the end of 1987 and a further five plants are coming on stream in 1988.

Sigma, a medical pump manufacturer, was acquired in 1987. 1987 profits were up 39% to £12.1m on turnover up 24% to £90.3m.

Consumer This division represents the amalgamation of the old toiletries and personal hygiene divisions with Tender Touch cotton wool and Elastoplast included. It is the classic cash cow with high margins and low capital investment. Many of the toiletry brands have their origin in Beiersdorf, a German company, which had many of its Commonwealth assets appropriated after the second world war. Smith & Nephew now works closely with Beiersdorf to protect and enhance the worldwide brand image of Nivea, which includes many skincare and toiletry products. The launch of Nivea hair care products early in 1987 was received well and budgeted market shares were attained. A further development of the Nivea name is planned. Other toiletry brands include Atrixo hand care products, Limara body spray and Labello lip care.

Personal hygiene products, manufactured in Birmingham, include a full range of tampons and sanitary towels. Branded products such as Dr White's and Lil-lets have maintained market position and reasonable growth has come from private label business for multiple retailers.

This division, accounting for 20% of operating profits at £20.2m, improved 8% in 1987 on turnover up 5% to £115.1m.

Medical and other textiles The division produces cotton yarn, woven fabrics, and bulk surgical cloth for the medical industry.

S&N is the largest UK producer of denim, the raw material used to manufacture jeans, which accounts for a third of the division's turnover. 1987 saw a deterioration in margin as a consequence of rising cotton prices, slackening demand and destocking by competitors. However, subject to the vagaries of fashion, underlying demand for denim continues to be strong, and the group has provided more added value to the product beyond the standard indigo dyed cloth.

Profits in 1987 were 4% up at £8.4m on turnover 12% up at £54.7m.

Plastics Products include adhesive tapes for ostomy products; polymeric nets for use as coverstocks, cheesenets, interlining, filters and medical products; custom moulded engineering components and containers; and yarns and fabrics for carpeting, industrial and leisure applications.

No longer considered a core part of S&N's business, the low margin Smith & Nephew Anchor was sold in early 1987 for $55m. Were it not for a disappointing performance from the Toronto plastics business, margins at this division would have improved. Growth should continue as the company reaps the reward of recent investment in the Australian subsidiary and the Toronto situation is rectified one way or another.

1987 profits were 2% down to £4.5m, on turnover up 2% on continuing business to £33.6m.

GEOGRAPHICAL REVIEW

The majority of S&N's business is derived from operations in the US and the UK. Although turnover is greater in the US, a greater percentage of operating profit is contributed by UK

Share price and relative to FT-A All-Share

C H A I R M A N ' S   S T A T E M E N T

'The stock market crash in October 1987 and subsequent financial volatility has added more hazard to the business of international planning and forecasting. The effect of wide fluctuations in currency rates on exports, raw material prices and translation of profits into sterling is nearly impossible to predict but trading conditions in local currencies will continue to show satisfactory progress in 1988.

Taking everything into account I am confident that your company will report a satisfactory earnings per share increase in 1988.' *Kenneth Kemp*

operations. The company's operations in Europe are expanding. Japan is also seen as a much larger potential market long term than current activity suggests.

The 1987 geographical breakdown of turnover is US 33.7%, UK 29.4%, Europe 19.5%, Australasia and Asia 9.3% and Africa and the Middle East 8.2%.

The 1987 geographical breakdown of trading profit is UK 34.6%, US 33.3%, Europe 18.3%, Australasia and Asia 7.3% and Africa and the Middle East 6.5%.

CORPORATE CALENDAR

Year end	31 December
Preliminary results	March
Report and accounts	April
AGM	May
Final dividend paid	July
Interim results	August
Interim dividend paid	January

DIRECTORS' HOLDINGS

	Fully-paid ordinary shares		Options
	(beneficial)	*(non-beneficial)*	
KR Kemp	548,929	20,708	726,078
E Kinder	253,874	40,000	931,650
AR Fryer	82,719	—	147,147
MJ Kiely	2,200	—	275,057
MAF Macpherson	10,000	—	—
JL Rennocks	160,000	—	239,893
JH Robinson	128,704	—	303,245
TF Winter	215,042	—	435,624

Directors' salaries and other fees in 1987 were £579,000, with the chairman receiving £33,000. The highest-paid director received £127,000.

PRINCIPAL SUBSIDIARIES AND RELATED COMPANIES

B Braun-Smith & Nephew GmbH – West Germany (50%), British Tissues Limited (50%), Clothing Industries (Mfg) Company Limited – Malta (30%), Dyonics Inc – US, Eurociencia CA – Venezuela (49%), Federal Industries Sdn Berhad – Malaysia, JL Morison Son & Jones (India) Limited (28%), Jack Chia–Smith & Nephew Limited – Thailand (49%), Laboratoires Fisch–Smith & Nephew SA – France, Osteo Ag – Switzerland, Osteo GmbH – West Germany, PT Central Sari Medical Supplies – Indonesia (50%), Productos Higiénicos Panamericanos SA de CV – Mexico (40%), Richards International Inc – US, Richards Manufacturing Gmbh – West Germany, Richards Medical Company – US, Richards Medical Company Australia Pty Limited – Australia, Richards Scandinavia AB – Sweden, Richards Scandinavia AS – Norway, Smith & Nephew Anchor Inc – US, Smith & Nephew (Australia) Pty Limited, Smith & Nephew (Belgium) SA, Smith & Nephew (Bermuda) Limited, Smith & Nephew Consumer Products Limited, Smith & Nephew Europe BV – Netherlands, Smith & Nephew (Far East) Limited, Smith & Nephew Finance Limited, Smith & Nephew Ibérica SA – Spain, Smith & Nephew Inc – US, Smith & Nephew Inc – Canada, Smith & Nephew Limited – South Africa, Smith & Nephew (Malaysia) Sdn Berhad, Smith & Nephew Medical Limited, Smith & Nephew Nederland BV, Smith & Nephew Orbel SpA – Italy (50%), Smith & Nephew Pakistan (Private) Limited (51%), Smith & Nephew Pharmaceuticals Limited, Smith &

Nephew Rolyan Inc – US, Smith & Nephew Scandinavia A/S – Denmark, Smith & Nephew (Singapore) Pte Limited, Smith & Nephew Southalls (Ireland) Limited, Smith & Nephew Textiles Limited, Smith & Nephew (New Zealand) Limited

Principal other investments
MMS Quirúrgica SA – Spain (50%), Sanortho SA – France (50%), Société Française de Fournitures Chirurgicales SA – France (50%)

BRAND NAMES

Atrixo, Cicagraf, Dande-pants, Dande-liners, Dixcel, Dr White's, Dry-Care, Dynacast XR, Elastoplast, Flamazine, Flexobande, Glauline, Hypal 2, Jelonet, Labello, Lil-lets, Limara, Melolin, Nivea, Opsite, Ozo, Primapore, Propax, Richards, Rogier, Southalls, Tender Touch, Vulco

CONTACTS AND FURTHER INFORMATION

John L Rennocks, Investor Relations, Smith & Nephew plc, 2 Temple Place, Victoria Embankment, London WC2R 3BP. Tel: 01-836 7922.

STANDARD CHARTERED PLC

GENERAL INFORMATION

Head office   38 Bishopsgate, London EC2N 4DE. Tel: 01-280 7500
Directors   Sir Peter Alfred Graham OBE DSc (chairman), Sir Yue-Kong Pao CBE LLD JP (group deputy chairman), MRH Holmes à Court (group deputy chairman), Sir Leslie Fletcher DSC FCA (deputy chairman), WCL Brown (managing), AD Orsich, RJB Stein MA FCA FCT. *Non-exec* RAM Baillie, J Louden, Sir Derek Mitchell, JB Page, Lord Pennock, PH Robinson, PKC Woo, AL Newman, S Yue-Kuo Pan
Advisers   J Henry Schroder Wagg & Co Ltd, Standard Chartered Merchant Bank Ltd
Auditors   Peat Marwick McLintock, Deloitte Haskins & Sells
Registrars   National Westminster Bank Registrar's Department
Brokers   Cazenove & Co
Solicitors   Slaughter and May

GENERAL FINANCIAL INFORMATION

Market capitalisation	£724.1m at 1 January 1988
Capital structure	
Issued ordinary shares (£1)	155.7m
Issued preference shares	None
Warrants	£1.4m, exercisable at 875p
Convertibles	None
Traded options	None
ADRs	None
Shareholders over 5%	Bell Group International Ltd 14.9%, Sir YK Pao 14.9%, Tan Sri Khoo Teck Puat 7.2%

FT CATEGORY

FT: Banks, HP & leasing
FT-A: Banks

MAJOR ACTIVITIES

The Standard Chartered group provides a full range of banking and related financial services in more than 50 countries around the world through one of the largest branch networks of its kind and associate companies.

The group possesses a number of characteristics which give it a unique presence in global banking markets. It has a coordinated network of more than 20 national banks and a direct presence in all five continents. There is a traditional emphasis on the financing of international trade. Initiatives have been taken in recent years to provide a wider range of international banking services and to enhance capital markets capability. Another feature is the extent to which the deposit base is retail in origin and therefore not dependent upon the wholesale or Eurocurrency markets.

On the group's own yardsticks, 50% of total deposits are currently derived directly from its own customer base. Lloyds Bank made a contested and unsuccessful bid for Standard Chartered in 1986.

FINANCIAL HISTORY

Group profits remained substantially unchanged in the five years to 1986. This was partly the result of adverse exchange rate movements which constrained sterling-denominated balance sheet growth. A deterioration in debt experience, particularly in the Asia Pacific region, was another significant factor in profits performance.

In 1987 the group made a pre-tax loss of £274m, after exceptional items of £441m, against a profit of £254m in 1986. At the trading profit level profits were down 8.1% to £362m from £394m. The charge for bad and doubtful debts increased from £184m in 1986 to £234m in 1987, to give a profit before exceptional items of £168m against £254m in 1986.

The decision to make an exceptional provision of £441m was occasioned by the group's total sovereign debt exposure of £2.468bn. At the beginning of 1987 the group had provisions of just £99m for this debt. By the 1987 year-end the provision had been increased by £519m to £618m, with £560m (32%) set against 28 developing countries' exposure of £1.729bn, and £58m (8%) set against four developed countries' exposure, including South Africa, of £739m.

Despite the heavy losses suffered in 1987 the group maintained its dividend at 35p. Shareholders' funds fell from £1.295bn to £717m.

SHARE PRICE HISTORY

Between early 1981 and early 1986 the shares underperformed the market by 60%. Factors contributing to this were the failure of the group's bid for the Royal Bank of Scotland after its referral to the Monopolies Commission at the start of 1981, and profits performance in subsequent years. Nevertheless the share price virtually doubled in the early part of 1986 before and during the bid by Lloyds Bank. Although that bid failed, resulting in a further period of share price underperformance, management recognises that if the group is to remain independent profitability now needs to be increased to justify a share price previously driven up on speculative grounds.

The shares halved during the autumn 1987 share crash. At the low of under 400p the shares were yielding well over 11%. They subsequently recovered. In April 1988 they were trading around the 450p level.

SENIOR MANAGEMENT

Sir Peter Graham, previously group managing director and senior deputy chairman, succeeded Lord Barber as chairman in May 1987. He is supported by Sir Yue-Kong Pao and Mr Holmes à Court as joint group deputy chairmen. Sir Leslie Fletcher is deputy chairman. Sir Peter retires later in 1988 and will be succeeded as executive chairman by Rodney Galpin.

A recent management reorganisation has emphasised the role of the executive committee as the key management body of the group. It is chaired by Bill Brown (managing director), and includes Richard Stein (executive director, finance systems and administration), Alan Orsich (executive director, interna-

CHAIRMAN'S STATEMENT

'Our strategy is to concentrate on Standard Chartered's distinctive network of international offices and the businesses based on them, and to provide diversified financial services as an international banking group. We see our best growth prospects in the Asia Pacific Region and the United Kingdom, supported by the capability to provide superior banking services in Third World countries – particularly in the economies of the Middle East, South Asia and Tropical Africa. Standard Chartered's presence in the European Community and its long established international banking presence in North America, which is managed from New York, add to its ability to service corporations operating around the world.

The disposal of the Union Bank does not impinge adversely on the Group's core businesses, but releases resources to support our main activities. Measures already taken to enhance productivity, to strengthen management, and to improve the control of credit should impact favourably on profitability this year and beyond.' *Sir Peter Graham*

FIVE YEAR FINANCIAL INFORMATION

Year	Turnover (£m)	Pre-tax (£m)	Earnings (p)	Dividends net (p)	Dividend cover (x)	Net assets (p)	Price (p) High	Price (p) Low	PER (x) High	PER (x) Low	Yield (%) High	Yield (%) Low
1983	1,238	268	77	28.0	2.8	817	504	350	7.5	5.2	9.82	7.13
1984	1,138	240	64	28.5	2.2	850	577	442	8.4	6.6	9.05	6.76
1985	1,062	268	85	30.5	2.8	797	534	422	8.4	5.1	9.99	7.49
1986	1,197	254	97	35.0	3.3	832	877	422	11.0	6.0	9.99	4.97
1987	1,221	(274)	(221.3)	35.0	—	460	840	405	—	—	11.84	5.71

tional banking, bullion and investment management), Peter McSloy (senior general manager, Asia Pacific region), Patrick MacDougall (chief executive, SCMB), Ian Paterson (senior general manager, UK banking) and Alan Wren (senior general manager, Africa, Middle East, South Asia and Europe).

In March 1988, as part of further far-reaching management reorganisation, Michael McWilliam agreed to resign as group managing director. RD Galpin, presently executive director of the Bank of England in charge of banking supervision, is to join the board as executive chairman designate as soon as he can be released from the Bank of England.

CAPITAL

The group has taken a series of steps in recent years to strengthen its capital position and to improve its capital adequacy ratios on the yardsticks used by the Bank of England. It raised £100m through a rights issue in 1983. Subsequently $1.1bn and £300m of undated loan capital was raised. The bulk of this qualifies as primary capital for the purposes of Bank of England capital guidelines.

The deconsolidation of Stanbic, once it became an associate bank, also improved capital ratios by reducing balance sheet aggregates. Ratios weakened again as a result of the £441m of special provisions on sovereign debt made in 1987.

The disposals of Union Bank and United Bank of Arizona, however, will improve capital ratios by realising approximately £550m, and the group has indicated that a rights issue is likely in 1988.

Three directors together hold 37% of the issued share capital. Robert Holmes à Court holds 14.9%, as does Sir YK Pao and his family interests. Tan Sri Khoo Teck Puat holds 7.2%.

GROUP REVIEW

United Kingdom The group has given priority to establishing a stronger presence in the UK market in recent years. The international banking division in London now provides a full range of wholesale banking services which includes trading in all major and many minor currencies. These services are supplemented by the Mocatta companies, leading participants in the bullion markets. A 20-branch network, located across the country, specialises in corporate banking business in general, and in the financing of overseas trade in particular.

The wholly owned Chartered Trust, a finance company, operates through 70 offices and is now also responsible for the group's UK Visa card business. Standard Chartered Merchant Bank has an expertise in project and international corporate finance. Scimitar Asset Management specialises in the provision of investment management services to overseas customers and high net worth expatriates. Chartered Trust and Savings is the group's domestic direct personal lending division.

Europe The group is represented through 21 offices across

11 countries in continental Europe. The majority are now committed to developing a niche banking business. Although this continues to include such traditional operations as the financing of international trade, greater emphasis has recently been placed on developing a new range of domestic treasury and capital market operations aimed at meeting the needs of a sophisticated client base. This has been reflected in the recent restructuring of the Italian operation, through the creation of Standard Bank Finanziaria SpA, and in the formation of a new capital markets subsidiary in France, Banque Française Standard Chartered SA.

North America The group's principal interest in the US was the wholly-owned Union Bank which, with total assets of close on $10bn, is the 27th largest bank in the country. In February 1988 the group signed a letter of intent with California First Bank, a 77%-owned subsidiary of Bank of Tokyo, to sell Union Bank for $750m.

In January 1988 Standard Chartered decided to sell United Bank of Arizona, subject to the necessary consents, to Citicorp for between $200m and $210m.

When Union Bank and United Bank of Arizona are sold, the group's representation will comprise branches in Chicago, New York and San Francisco; the Standard Bank of Canada; and Mocatta Metals Corporation.

Middle East and South Asia The group is represented in the Gulf through 19 offices in Bahrain, Oman, Qatar and the United Arab Emirates. All have a long-established presence there.

There are 40 branches in the Indian subcontinent in India, Bangladesh, Pakistan and Sri Lanka. The most important operation is in India, which now incorporates a merchant banking division and a minority interest in a Madras-based leasing company.

A branch was opened in 1986 in Istanbul. Its business is geared to multinational and first-tier Turkish companies.

Asia Pacific The group has an unusually strong franchise throughout the Asia Pacific region. It comprises more than 250 banking and financial service offices in 13 countries.

Share price and relative to FT-A All-Share

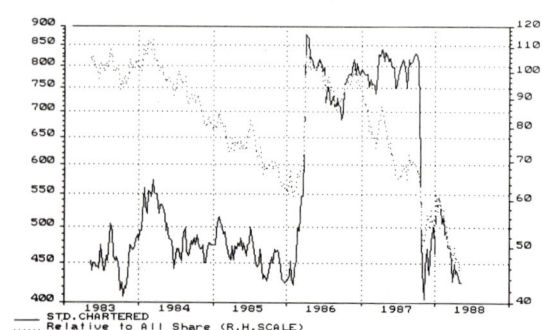

— STD. CHARTERED
..... Relative to All Share (R.H.SCALE)

The most important centre is Hong Kong, where Standard Chartered is one of the two note-issuing banks. It has a 116-branch network there, enjoying a strong involvement with the middle market Chinese business community, and possesses a substantial retail customer base.

In Singapore, the group has 26 offices with over a quarter of a million account holders, making it one of the leading banks in the country. In Malaysia, there are 44 offices with over three-quarters of a million account holders.

Other countries where the group is represented include Japan and Australia, where its operations have been integrated into a 69% interest in the publicly listed Standard Chartered Bank Australia. There are also branches in Indonesia, Taiwan, South Korea, the Philippines, Brunei and Thailand. In China there are currently three full branches and three representative offices.

Tropical Africa The group has a strong and long-established market position in tropical Africa, comprising more than 500 branches in 14 countries. It is the leading national bank in 12 of these countries. The group has a considerable presence in Kenya, Uganda, Zambia, Zimbabwe, Nigeria and Ghana. In 1986 representation was reinforced by the acquisition of a 66% interest in the renamed Standard Chartered Bank Cameroon SA, thereby re-establishing a significant presence in French-speaking Africa.

GEOGRAPHICAL REVIEW

The UK accounted for 38% of total group assets at the end of 1987, the Asia Pacific region for 26.3%, North America for 23.6%, continental Europe for 5.8%, the Middle East and South Asia for 3% and Africa for 3.1%. Before exceptional items and central financing costs, the UK accounted for 35.7% of group profits, North America for 28.1%, tropical Africa for 8.9%, Asia Pacific for 27.1%, the Middle East and South Asia for 3.7% and Europe for −3.6%.

CORPORATE CALENDAR

Year end	31 December
Preliminary results	March
Report and accounts	April
AGM	May
Final dividend paid	May
Interim results	August
Interim dividend paid	October

DIRECTORS' HOLDINGS

	Ordinary shares	Options
Sir Peter Graham	4,544	—
Sir Yue-Kong Pao	7,750,500	—
MRH Holmes à Court	23,329,052	—
Sir Leslie Fletcher	1,292	—
MD McWilliam	5,527	1,741
WCL Brown	1,500	35,000
AD Orsich	2,963	35,000
RJB Stein	500	35,000
RAM Baillie	2,260	36,741
JF Harrigan	500	—
Lord Inchcape	13,513	—
J Louden	500	—
DR Mitchell	1,292	—
Sir Derek Mitchell	900	—
AL Newman	500	—
JB Page	600	—
The Lord Pennock	600	—
Sir Idwal Pugh	1,424	—
PH Robinson	1,000	—
PKC Woo	7,750,500	—

Total directors' remuneration in 1987 was £1.1m, of which the chairman is paid £120,942, and the highest-paid director £192,396.

PRINCIPAL SUBSIDIARIES AND RELATED COMPANIES

Commercial banking
Standard Chartered Bank, Standard Chartered Bank Africa Plc, Standard Chartered Bank Australia Ltd, Standard Chartered Bank (Austria) AG, Standard Chartered Bank Botswana Ltd, Standard Chartered Bank Cameroon SA, Standard Chartered Bank (CI) Ltd – Channel Islands, Standard Chartered Bank Gambia Ltd, Standard Chartered Bank Ghana Ltd, Standard Chartered Bank Ireland Ltd, Standard Chartered Bank Isle of Man Ltd, Standard Chartered Bank Kenya Ltd, Standard Chartered Bank of Canada, Standard Chartered Bank Sierra Leone Ltd, Standard Chartered Bank Swaziland Ltd, Standard Chartered Bank Uganda Ltd, Standard Chartered Bank Zambia Ltd, Standard Chartered Bank Zimbabwe Ltd, Union Bank – US, United Bank of Arizona – US

Merchant banking
Banque Française Standard Chartered SA – France, Standard Chartered Acceptances Ltd – Kenya, Standard Chartered Asia Ltd – Hong Kong, Standard Chartered Australia Ltd, Standard Chartered Finanziaria SpA – Italy, Standard Chartered Merchant Bank Asia Ltd – Singapore, Standard Chartered Merchant Bank Ltd, Standard Chartered Merchant Bank Zimbabwe Ltd

Instalment finance and leasing
CEC Finance Ltd – Hong Kong, Chartered Trust Plc, Credit Corporation (Brunei) Berhad – Negara Brunei Darussalam, Credit Corporation (Singapore) Ltd, PT Standard Chartered Leasing – Indonesia, Standard Chartered Export Finance Ltd, Standard Chartered Finance Ltd – Australia, Standard Chartered Finance Ltd – Hong Kong, Standard Chartered Finance Ltd – Singapore, Standard Chartered Finance Uganda Ltd, Standard Chartered Finance Zimbabwe Ltd, Standard Chartered Leasing Co Ltd

BRAND NAMES

None

CONTACTS AND FURTHER INFORMATION

William Manser, Manager, Information Department, Standard Chartered PLC, 38 Bishopsgate, London EC2N 4DE. Tel: 01-280 7472.

STOREHOUSE PLC

GENERAL INFORMATION

Head office   The Heal's Building, 196 Tottenham Court Road, London
W1P 9LD. Tel: 01-631 0101
Directors   Sir Terence Conran, T Goddard, K Jones, F Lister, J Power,
J Stephenson. *Non-exec* Sir Maurice Hodgson, I Peacock
Advisers   Kleinwort Benson Ltd, Morgan Grenfell & Co Ltd
Auditors   Arthur Andersen & Co
Registrars   Barclays Bank Registration Department
Brokers   Rowe & Pitman Ltd, Citicorp Scrimgeour Vickers Ltd
Solicitors   Clifford Chance, Slaughter and May

GENERAL FINANCIAL INFORMATION

Market capitalisation	£1.033bn at 1 January 1988
Capital structure	
Issued ordinary shares (10p)	404.3m
Issued preference shares	None
Warrants	None
Convertibles	£24m of 9% CUMS 1992 (66 ordinary 10p shares for every £100 stock)
	£69m of 4.5% Eurosterling convertible subordinated bonds 2001 (1445.085 ordinary shares per £1000 stock)
Traded options	None
ADRs	None
Shareholders over 5%	Sir Terence Conran 7.2%

FT CATEGORY

FT: Drapery and stores
FT-A: Stores

MAJOR ACTIVITIES

The group is one of the largest UK retailers and also controls significant overseas interests in the US and continental Europe. Group selling area at March 1987 totalled 6.9m sq ft.

Storehouse prides itself on its design-led approach to retailing. The Conran Design Group provides the design resources for product development, store design and marketing needs across the group.

Principal businesses include Habitat, which in 1986/87 provided 11% of group retail profit; Mothercare, 26%; and BhS, 53%. The group also owns Richards, which contributed

CHAIRMAN'S STATEMENT

'The first year in the life of Storehouse has been one of great success. A new identity has been created and, using the combined strength of resources and management, the future growth and success of our existing businesses and the creation of new ventures will be secured. The year has been one of great activity across the whole group. This included the creation of the new BhS brand and corporate identity, new warehousing and distribution systems for Mothercare, the launch of an in-house credit card, the UK launch of Habitat's out of town operation, the completion of Richards revitalisation, the launch of the Anonymous fashion chain, the issue of a £69m convertible Eurobond and the continuing expansion of our overseas businesses and franchise operations. The portfolio of dynamic retail business will continue to be developed. A policy of expansion through organic growth, joint ventures and international franchise agreements will continue to be pursued and the group plans to strengthen further its international interests.' *Sir Terence Conran*

3% of profits; a 50% interest in SavaCentre; and a 20% interest in Fnac, a French retailer selling books, records and a range of related leisure merchandise.

In 1986/87 group sales divided into childrenswear 23%, housewares 20%, womenswear 19%, furniture 9%, toys and infant hardware 9%, menswear 7%, footwear and accessories 6%, in-store restaurants 4% and food 3%.

The group is in a period of transition. The original Habitat interests are showing a generally steady advance but Mothercare has been disrupted through changes in distribution and storage methods, and the upgrading of BhS is not yet complete. The potential for significant future profit improvement is substantial for both Mothercare and BhS. Outside the mainstream interests, both Richards and SavaCentre appear capable of providing increasingly valuable support.

The key economic factors affecting business include personal disposable incomes, consumer expenditure, consumer confidence and fluctuating currency movements. Demographic changes and fluctuating birth rates provide additional outside influences. Major competitors include Laura Ashley, Marks & Spencer, Next and Boots.

FINANCIAL HISTORY

The Storehouse group was formed in January 1986 following the merger of Habitat Mothercare with British Home Stores, now renamed BhS. Habitat Mothercare itself was formed as a result of the acquisition of Mothercare by Habitat in January 1982.

Between 1982 and 1987 profits before tax rose by 80%, from £75.2m to £129.3m. The margin on sales rose slowly in the period from 9.3% to 11.5%. Earnings per share information is not available throughout the period because the group is relatively newly formed and previous accounting dates have in some cases been changed. No formal profits or earnings record is therefore available.

For the year to March 1987, group sales rose by 5.9% to £1.12bn and pre-tax profits by 11.4% to £129.2m; this includes property. Net margins rose from 10.9% to 11.5%, helped by the elimination of loss-making food departments within BhS. Basic earnings per share rose by 2.8% to 22.2p, and ordinary dividends amounted to 8.6p net covering the first full 12 months in which the enlarged group was operating.

The results for the year to 1988 are expected to be disappointing, reflecting the distribution problems of Mothercare and slow Christmas sales.

As at March 1987 capital gearing amounted to 22%. Cash holdings of £52.9m were offset by bank loans of £14.9m, commercial paper £37.3m, and other long term loans £11.2m. The commercial paper programme was negotiated in October 1986 with agreed facilities of up to £150m including a US dollar option. The convertible Eurobond was arranged on an especially low 4.25% coupon. Multi-currency bank facilities of £200m are also available.

Since the year end the group has subscribed for 50% of Storecard Limited, which operates an in-store credit card business. The return on capital employed in 1986/87 was 21.4%. The asset base was understated since a number of properties had not recently been revalued.

At the 1987/88 interim, profits were disappointing, showing a fall of 3%. BhS had slow growth in sales, and Mothercare was held back by continuing distribution problems. However, margins at BhS improved and Habitat was trading well. The balance sheet remained strong, with borrowings virtually unchanged.

FIVE YEAR FINANCIAL INFORMATION

Year	Turnover (£m)	Pre-tax (£m)	Earnings (p)	Dividends net (p)	Dividend cover (x)	Net assets (p)	Price (p) High	Price (p) Low	PER (x) High	PER (x) Low	Yield (%) High	Yield (%) Low
1983	—	—	—	—	—	—	—	—	—	—	—	—
1984	—	—	—	—	—	—	—	—	—	—	—	—
1985	—	—	—	—	—	—	—	—	—	—	—	—
1986	1,057.8	116.1	19.0	7.7	2.4	101	360	260	20.1	14.2	4.33	3.01
1987	1,120.6	123.1	20.2	8.6	2.4	113	411	224	20.7	11.3	5.26	2.87

SHARE PRICE HISTORY

Since the formation of the enlarged Storehouse Group the shares have performed poorly, falling from a peak 45% of the FT-A All-Share index in early 1986 to only 25% in March 1988. Speculative activity provided a boost between August and September 1987 when the shares reached highs of just over 420p, selling at over 30% of the All-Share index. The shares were hit hard in the autumn crash and fell below 220p before modestly recovering in early 1988.

SENIOR MANAGEMENT

Sir Terence Conran founded the original Habitat business. Sir Terence remains chairman, but when the group was under threat from Mountleigh in the autumn of 1987, he announced that he would seek an external candidate for managing director. Major managerial changes were made. At the same time Denis Cassidy, chief executive of BhS and the then deputy chairman, resigned. It was widely believed this was because he felt snubbed in his ambition to be overall chief executive. With him went Colin Williams, the assistant managing director of BhS.

Geoff Davy moved over from being chief executive of Habitat UK to become chief executive of BhS. Francis Lister rose from assistant managing director to chairman of BhS. This was in addition to his executive role at Storehouse of world-wide franchises, product sourcing and development. Jim Power, formerly of BhS, is group finance and planning director. Geoff Davy was also appointed to the Storehouse board.

Other board members include Terry Goddard, property and pensions director, and John Stephenson, group design and marketing director. Kevyn Jones, chairman and chief executive of Habitat and Mothercare, will devote his full time to the Mothercare group as chairman and chief executive.

Non-executive directors include Sir Maurice Hodgson, a previous chairman of ICI, Dunlop and BhS, and Ian Peacock, previously finance director of Habitat Mothercare.

With effect from June 1988, Michael Julien, previously with Guinness, has been appointed group chief executive and chairman designate.

CAPITAL

As at March 1987 a total of 404.3m ordinary shares were in issue. On full conversion, the outstanding loan stocks and bonds would add 32m shares to the equity base or 8%. Sir Terence Conran owns 29.3m shares, representing 7.2% of the existing capital.

In August 1987 property group Mountleigh made a bid of 420p per share for Storehouse, only to withdraw it a month later. Immediately afterwards the small company Benlox also bid, but achieved only 0.8% acceptances for its plan to demerge the group.

Non-beneficial holdings by directors held under various trustee schemes total 5.0m ordinary shares, 1.2% of the total. Other than Sir Terence Conran's, there were no other holdings in excess of 5.0%.

GROUP REVIEW

Habitat As at March 1988 a total of 102 stores were trading, with 60 in the UK, 27 in France and Belgium and 15 in the US. Habitat is trading strongly, particularly in the US and France. Selling area amounted to just under 1.8m sq ft.

A range of furniture, home furnishings and household goods is offered. Initially there was a bias towards first time homemakers, but the product range has now successfully been developed to attract older age groups and to retain the loyalty of existing customers.

Encouraged by the experience in France, a network of out of town superstores is now being opened in the UK, and these are doing well. The first began trading at High Wycombe in April 1987. A total of five were planned by the end of 1987, with as many as 30 to be operational in the future. These outlets offer an extended range of merchandise, with a particular emphasis on furniture and an immediate delivery service. With extra space a more effective method of presentation and display can be employed.

The acquisition of Heal's has provided Storehouse with the opportunity to cater to the more expensive ends of the market, and to offer a more sophisticated selection of merchandise in the UK. Overseas, significant scope remains for additional physical expansion.

In 1986/87 divisional sales and profits increased by 14.2% and 9.8% respectively. A margin of 6.9% was achieved. At the 1987/88 interim, sales were up 11% and profits 26%.

Mothercare As at September 1987, 508 branches were trading with 238 in the UK, 231 in the US, and 36 in Europe. Selling area amounted to 1.5m sq ft. Within the UK, Mothercare is the leading specialist retailer catering for children up to age 10 and mothers-to-be.

A range of additional services is expected to be introduced within a number of stores. These should help sharpen the company's marketing edge. Extra space to house these services, which include crèches and changing and feeding facilities for babies, is being released as a result of moving to a new central distribution system, so that less storage space is required in-store. A new format, Mothercare+ is being tried.

There has been disruption during the changeover causing 1986/87 profits to fall by 9.1% following a 6.4% increase in sales. Profits fell again at the 1987/88 interim. In spite of this setback, and with the European and US operations as yet producing only a modest contribution, a divisional net margin of 11.4% provided a continuing high return. Mothercare will continue to expand in the UK and will develop in selected markets within continental Europe, especially West Germany.

The US is poised for an especially rapid programme to open new stores and, free from distribution problems, is showing strong gains in sales and profits.

BhS A number of franchises are being developed overseas but the operation is essentially geared towards the UK, where 129 stores are in operation with a total selling area of 3.4m sq ft.

Share price and relative to FT-A All-Share

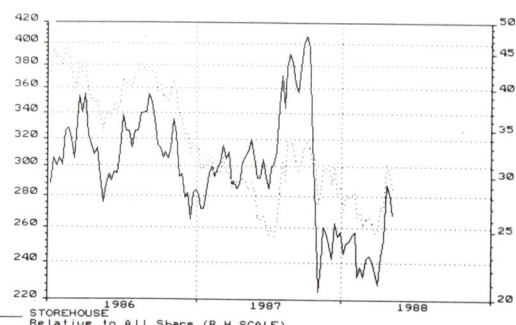

After food departments were discontinued in 1986, BhS has concentrated primarily on clothing, which contributes 60% of sales, footwear, lighting, gifts and other household items. Most stores also have catering facilities, with restaurants accounting for approximately 7% of sales.

Following the merger with Habitat Mothercare, a store modernisation programme has been accelerated. In September 1986, the 'Exclamations' campaign was launched, to provide a more interesting and eye-catching environment in the stores. The opportunity has also been taken to introduce stronger product ranges, using the Conran Design Group's merchandise development and buying skills to improve quality, value for money and presentation.

To broadcast the BhS message more widely, advertising and other promotional activity is increasing. The aim is to generate increased profits by improving sales per square foot. In 1986/87 these were estimated to have been under half those recorded by a major rival, Marks and Spencer.

In this period sales rose by 7.6%, discounting previous contributions from the discontinued food business. However, profits rose by 18.2% after the closure of the food departments. An effective net margin of 13.2% compares well with Marks and Spencer. In the first half of 1987/88 sales growth at 7% was slow despite increased operating efficiency.

Richards As at September 1987 the chain had 161 outlets and 327,000 sq ft of selling area. The business has been totally reorganised since it was acquired in 1983. A new management team has been responsible for closing poorly-located stores and for upgrading the remainder through a comprehensive modernisation programme. New product ranges have been introduced. Management information systems and distribution have also been improved.

The benefits became obvious in 1986/87 when sales rose by 41.2%. Pre-tax profits amounted to £5.6m compared with a loss in the previous year. A renewed period of expansion is now planned, and will provide a chain of over 200 stores. At the 1987/88 interim, sales and profits continued to show excellent progress.

SavaCentre This organisation is jointly owned with J Sainsbury, one of the UK's leading food retailers. It was an inheritance arising from the Habitat Mothercare merger with BhS. The SavaCentre range is divided between food, hard goods and toiletries. As at March 1987 six stores were in operation, with a total selling area of 365,000 sq ft. The business has proved successful. Sales have risen by 4% in 1986/87 and profits by 35%, to provide a net margin of 5.9%. This is very satisfactory given the high food content within the product mix and the chain's relative immaturity. A further four sites have been earmarked for new stores, subject, in certain cases, to receiving planning permission.

GEOGRAPHICAL REVIEW

In 1986/87, 85% of group sales, excluding discontinued business, and 95% of retail profits, not allowing for associate contributions, accrued in the UK. The remainder was derived from continental Europe, with 8% of sales and 3% of profits, and the US with 7% of sales and 2% of profits.

CORPORATE CALENDAR

Year end	31 March
Preliminary results	June
Report and accounts	June
AGM	July
Final dividend paid	August
Interim results	November
Interim dividend paid	February

DIRECTORS' HOLDINGS

	Non-beneficial	Fully-paid ordinary shares	Options
Sir Terence Conran	—	29,337,445	107,474
D Cassidy	—	6,935	153,036
T Goddard	—	44,362	121,494
Sir Maurice Hodgson	—	1,721	
K Jones	—	54,094	138,478
F Lister	—	11,330	107,028
I Peacock	272,009	338,592	
J Power	—	4,324	123,994
J Stephenson	—	225,934	106,464
C Williams	—	7,048	103,158

Total directors' remuneration including fees was £1.01m, of which the chairman received £99,517 and the highest-paid director £121,830.

PRINCIPAL SUBSIDIARIES AND RELATED COMPANIES

Belgian Designs SA – Belgium, BhS (Dublin) Ltd – Republic of Ireland, British Home Stores, British Home Stores (Jersey) Ltd – Jersey, Conran Design Group Ltd, Conran Mothercare US Inc – US, Conran Octopus Ltd (50%), The Conran Shop Ltd, The Conran Stores Inc – US, Habitat Designs Ltd, Habitat France SA – France, The Habitat Group Ltd, Habitat Holland BV – Netherlands, Habitat Mothercare Plc, Heal & Son Ltd, Mothercare AG – Switzerland, Mothercare BV – Netherlands, Mothercare GmbH – Austria, Mothercare GmbH – West Germany, The Mothercare Group Ltd, Mothercare SA – Belgium, Mothercare UK Ltd, Mothercare Stores Inc – US, Richard Shops Holdings Ltd (95%), Storehouse Finance Overseas Ltd – Cayman Islands, Storehouse Finance Plc, TCR Properties Ltd

BRAND NAMES

Anonymous, Barton, BhS, Café, Conran, The Conran Shop, Conran Design Group, Conran, Fnac, Habitat, Heal's, Mothercare, Quad, Richards, SavaCentre, Storecard

CONTACTS AND FURTHER INFORMATION

Jim Power, Group finance and planning director, Storehouse PLC, The Heal's Building, 196 Tottenham Court Road, London W1P 9LD. Tel: 01-631 0101.

SUN ALLIANCE AND LONDON INSURANCE plc

GENERAL INFORMATION

Head office	1 Bartholomew Lane, London EC2N 2AB. Tel: 01-588 2345
Directors	HUA Lambert (chairman), Sir Derrick Holden-Brown (deputy chairman), The Earl of Crawford and Balcarres PC (vice chairman), KG Addison OBE, ARC Arbuthnot, PH Bartrum, RK Bishop, G Bowler, Sir Alan Dalton CBE, JNC James, H Keswick, The Lord Kindersley, Sir Peter Matthews AO, DB Money-Coutts, RAG Neville VRD, WG Niven, P Quaile, Leopold de Rothschild CBE, JD Russell-Taylor, RJ Taylor, K Wilkinson, BA Wright
Advisers	Hambros Bank Ltd, Kleinwort Benson Ltd, NM Rothschild & Sons Ltd
Auditors	Deloitte Haskins & Sells
Registrars	Lloyds Bank Registrar's Department
Brokers	Cazenove & Co, Rowe & Pitman Ltd
Solicitors	Ashurst Morris Crisp; Berrymans; Collyer-Bristow; Lawrance Messer & Co; Maples Teesdale; Sacker & Partners

GENERAL FINANCIAL INFORMATION

Market capitalisation	£1.682bn at 1 January 1988
Capital structure	
Issued ordinary shares (25p)	197.24m
Issued preference shares	None
Warrants	None
Convertibles	None
Traded options	None
ADRs	None
Shareholders over 5%	Chubb Corporation 6%

FT CATEGORY

FT: Insurances
FT-A: Insurance (composite)

MAJOR ACTIVITIES

Sun Alliance is one of the biggest, as well as perhaps the oldest, providers of life and non-life insurances in the UK. It has a particularly high quality non-life operation. The life and non-life divisions both possess healthy balance sheets. The prospect for dividend increases in the next few years are excellent.

Sun Alliance derives over 60% of its business from the UK, a higher proportion than the other quoted composite insurers. The main other areas of operation are Europe (13% of total premium income), the US, Canada and Australia.

In the UK, the group writes all the major classes of insurance business, both personal lines – domestic household buildings and contents policies, and motor insurance, and commercial lines – industrial property, motor fleets, liability, and accident risks. It is the biggest property and motor insurer in the UK.

Following the purchase of Phoenix Assurance in August 1984, the group acquired a specialist reinsurance division. The volatility of results and the competitive state of the reinsurance market have led to a phased withdrawal from this field of activity. In future, a substantial part of new business sales are likely to emerge from intermediaries who have decided not to register under the terms of the Financial Services Act, but who have elected to become appointed representatives of the Sun Alliance.

Sun Alliance also writes a substantial volume of marine and aviation business, insuring hull, cargo and passenger risks.

The group's life assurance and pensions business is expanding strongly. In common with the rest of the group's business, most new sales are obtained from insurance intermediaries. However, over a quarter of new premiums are now derived from the group's own sales force, from direct mail shots and from advertising.

General Accident and the Guardian Royal Exchange are the most directly comparable quoted companies, but the company's shares may also be considered in relation to the other composite insurers.

The group is likely to benefit in the future from increasing links with the Chubb Corporation, who hold a 5% stake in the group. Sun Alliance holds a reciprocal 10% stake in Chubb and the group's US business is largely represented by a share of 14% in Chubb's insurance business.

FINANCIAL HISTORY

Total premium income in 1987 was £2.75bn, of which £1.99bn related to non-life insurance and £765m to life insurance and pensions. The group accounts for over 11% of the UK non-life market and about 2.5% of the life market.

The group did well in 1987, with the underwriting loss, the excess of claims payments and expenses over premiums, increased by only £30m to £107.7m, despite extreme weather claims in the UK, which increased from £39m in 1986 to £199m in 1987. Life profits were up 10% to £30m. Investment income increased by 8% to £249.2m.

1987 pre-tax profits were down marginally to £171.5m from £180.4m, but still compared favourably with £37.7m in 1985. The dividend was increased by 32% to 31p, following the 34% increase in the previous year. 1987 results were of course depressed by the effects of the severe weather losses in the first quarter and the October hurricane.

Sun Alliance's solvency ratio – shareholders' funds, assessed at market values, divided by non-life premium income – at the end of March 1988 was 89%. For a general insurance company, shareholders' funds are required in order to ensure that payments to policyholders can be met even if there are a succession of poor results or a fall in the market value of the invested assets. A solvency ratio of above 70% is a good indicator of a very strong balance sheet.

Sun Alliance's above-average solvency ratio should ensure that the group will be able to continue its policy of providing above-average growth in dividends per share for at least the next few years.

Sun Alliance has been growing organically and steadily for many years. The acquisition of Phoenix Assurance in 1984 almost doubled the scale of operations. However, Sun Alliance's pre-tax profits have been erratic. They were sharply down in 1984 and 1985 when underwriting losses increased substantially from £67.4m in 1983 to £198.7m in 1984 and £183.4m in 1985.

CHAIRMAN'S STATEMENT

'While we were in the hectic aftermath of the Great Storm, a hurricane of another kind fell upon the world's stockmarkets. Countless people have attempted to analyse this phenomenon, and I will confine myself to three comments. Firstly, market indices at the end of the year were but little changed from January levels. Secondly, the fall, if more precipitate, was less alarming than the menacing events of 1974–75 against the background of rising and seemingly unstoppable inflation, and, thirdly, and most importantly, the turbulence of the autumn of 1987 demonstrated the comfort to be derived by policyholders and shareholders alike from reliance upon an insurance company whose balance sheet is both strong and liquid. Despite the hurricanes, thanks to the quality of our investment management our solvency margin was still 85% at the end of the year.' *HUA Lambert*

FIVE YEAR FINANCIAL INFORMATION

Year	Turnover (£m)	Pre-tax (£m)	Earnings (p)	Dividends net (p)	Dividend cover (x)	Net assets (p)	Price (p) High	Price (p) Low	PER (x) High	PER (x) Low	Yield (%) High	Yield (%) Low
1983	1,179	73.4	23.3	14.0	1.67	563	363	223	15.6	9.6	8.97	5.51
1984	2,112	47.6	20.8	15.5	1.34	644	440	336	21.2	16.2	6.59	5.03
1985	2,236	37.7	14.0	17.5	0.80	668	571	401	40.8	28.6	4.34	
1986	2,699	180.4	64.2	23.5	2.73	837	769	520	12.0	8.1	6.25	4.22
1987	2,754.9	171.5	61.3	31.0	1.98	858	1215	645	19.8	10.5	6.46	3.43

SHARE PRICE HISTORY

The share price was on a rising trend relative to UK equities generally during 1985 and the first few months of 1986. Investors gained increasing confidence that the prospects for the UK economy were improving and that insurance premium rates were rapidly recovering from the depths seen in 1984.

In relative terms, the shares then drifted downwards to the end of 1986. Investors began to discount the possibility of a downturn in the insurance cycle commencing in 1988. Notwithstanding the weather losses in the first and fourth quarters of 1987 and the October 1987 share crash, the bullish prospects for the insurance market were increasingly recognised in the share price during 1987.

SENIOR MANAGEMENT

The chairman of the group is HUA Lambert. The chief general manager is Roger Neville, who succeeded Geoffrey Bowler in June 1987.

The management team includes deputy chief general manager Peter Quaile, and general managers PH Bartrum, William Niven, RJ Taylor, K Wilkinson and BA Wright. The company secretary is H Silver.

CAPITAL

Total shareholders' funds in December 1986 were £1.690bn. In addition the group made use of loans and borrowings totalling £89.7m to support its non-life activities. These were made up of £18.8m of 10.25% unsecured loan notes 1985/87, £68.1m of bank loans and overdrafts, and £2.8m of loans secured on properties.

At the end of 1987, shareholders' funds amounted to £1.693bn, equal to the 1986 level, despite the effects of the fall in world stock markets in October 1987 and of the rise in sterling against other currencies on the value of the group's overseas investments.

The issued share capital at the end of 1987 was 197.2m shares, a level which has not changed significantly for some years. Under the Sun Alliance savings-related share option scheme, there are options outstanding to subscribe for a total of 2.35m shares in the years up to 1993.

The agreed merger with Phoenix Assurance in 1984 represented the major milestone for the group. The acquisition has resulted in substantial cost savings for the enlarged group, with worldwide integration of the two operations resulting in reduced overheads and a wider spread of business.

GROUP REVIEW

United Kingdom Expansion in the UK is continuing, with an increase of non-life premium income in 1987 of 15% to £1.1bn.

This was the result of both premium rate increases and expansion in the underlying portfolio of accepted risks. The group, in common with most other insurance concerns, has incurred substantial underwriting losses since 1982, but achieved a major improvement in 1986. Losses fell from £71.0m to £16.1m. The October 1987 hurricane losses of £128m, together with the severe cold spell and gales earlier in the year costing £71m, combined to increase the underwriting loss in 1987 to £109.8m.

The motor accounts improved further in 1987 and the group is continuing to expand its share of the UK market. The domestic buildings account is set to benefit from an increase in the basic premium rate from 18p to 20p per £100 of sum insured from 1 June 1988. The underlying level of profitability, excluding abnormal weather losses, is good. The group has close ties with a number of building societies, including the Halifax and Abbey National.

Premium rates in the commercial lines market have been firm for several years and this too has benefited Sun Alliance, which is the premier commercial property writer in the UK.

Life and pensions profits have increased steadily during the last decade. Liabilities to policyholders are more than adequately covered by policyholders' assets, leaving the group with a long-term ability to compete effectively for new life and pensions business. 1987 saw a continuing trend of increasing sales, especially of house mortgage endowment assurances, pensions business, and savings- and investment-linked products.

Europe About 13% of the group's total business originates in Europe. Non-life underwriting losses were reduced in 1987 and results were satisfactory. The Dutch insurance market is a difficult one for all the UK insurers but the group achieved a significant improvement there in 1987. A small profit was made in France. Losses in the other territories (including Belgium, Denmark, Germany, Italy, Portugal and Spain) were more than offset by investment income on the non-life reserves and shareholders' capital employed. Total premium income in

Share price and relative to FT-A All-Share

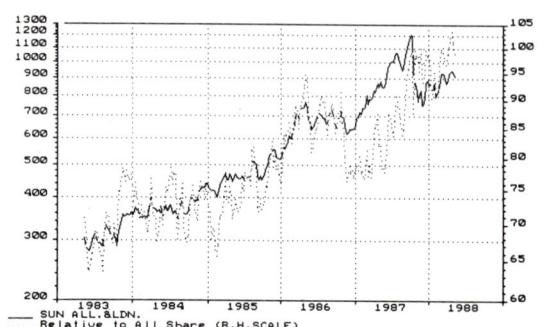

SUN ALL.&LDN.
Relative to All Share (R.H.SCALE)

1987 was £264.6m and the underwriting result was a loss of £16.9m compared with a £27.3m loss in 1986.

North America The group's US business derives primarily from its 10% holding in and links with the Chubb Corporation. Chubb Corporation is a large and exceptionally well regarded and profitable US insurer. Sun Alliance's results in the US benefit from overhead and other economies of scale.

Nearly 17% of the group's total non-life business is derived from the US and Canada. In both territories premium rate increases in the latter part of 1984, in 1985 and in 1986 have resulted in a big improvements in underwriting results.

Both the US and Canada achieved an underwriting profit in 1987, although premium income in sterling terms declined as a result of the fall in the value of the dollar. Premiums attributable to the US amounted to £216m in 1987 and £104.7m was written in Canada. The prospects in 1988 remain good, although the exceptional profitability in 1986 and 1987 are unlikely to be maintained.

Rest of the world The Sun Alliance has operations in Australia and New Zealand, the Far East, South Africa and the Caribbean. These territories account for 9% of the total non-life business.

Australia is a particularly difficult market, with competitive pressures preventing companies from setting adequate premium rates. Nevertheless, the group achieved a respectable result in 1987 – an underwriting loss of only just over £5m on premiums of £52m.

Business in the other geographical areas continues to produce satisfactory results with prospects generally remaining favourable. Total premium income in 1987 in the rest of the world, excluding Australia, amounted to £124.4m and an underwriting profit of £3.1m was produced.

Marine and aviation Marine and aviation business provides about 8% of the group's total non-life premium income.

The aviation account is particularly volatile, depending on the number of airliner losses and passenger or other deaths in any year. The marine insurance account is more stable but depends rather more on the state of competitive pressure to ensure an adequate level of premiums.

Trading results during 1985, 1986 and 1987 have been very favourable to Sun Alliance, although recently substantial competition and price-cutting has become a feature of the market.

GEOGRAPHICAL REVIEW

The distribution of the group's non-life insurance business premium income in 1987 was UK and Eire 57%, US 11%, Canada 5%, Denmark 4%, France 1%, Germany 2%, the Netherlands 3%, Australia 3%, South Africa 2%, the rest of the world 4%, marine and aviation 7% and reinsurance 1%.

Profits for non-life insurance business vary greatly from year to year and consequently their distribution is not shown. Life profits are 85% derived from the UK. 13% arise in the rest of Europe.

CORPORATE CALENDAR

Year end	31 December
Preliminary results	April
Report and accounts	April
AGM	May
Final dividend paid	July
Interim results	September
Interim dividend paid	January

DIRECTORS' HOLDINGS

	Fully-paid ordinary shares	Options
KG Addison	1,400	—
ARC Arbuthnot	3,440	..
PH Bartrum	400	1,992
RK Bishop	1,250	—
G Bowler	4,000	1,097
The Earl of Crawford and Balcarres	800	—
Sir Alan Dalton	600	—
Sir Derrick Holden-Brown	4,000	—
JNC James	532	—
H Keswick	5,200	—
Lord Kindersley	400	—
HUA Lambert	532	—
Sir Peter Matthews	4,800	—
DB Money-Coutts	1,000	—
RAG Neville	400	2,370
WG Niven	532	1,992
P Quaile	800	1,992
J Martin Ritchie	9,400	—
Leopold de Rothschild	6,000	—
JD Russell-Taylor	2,110	—
RJ Taylor	500	1,992
K Wilkinson	1,000	1,791
BA Wright	500	2,200

ARC Arbuthnot and RAG Neville hold 3,000 and 200 shares respectively non-beneficially.

Total directors' remuneration in 1987 was £1,025,959, of which the chairman received £28,750 and the highest-paid director £115,088.

PRINCIPAL SUBSIDIARIES AND RELATED COMPANIES

A/S Forsikringsselskabet Codan – Denmark (64.8%), A/S Forsikringsselskabet Codan Liv – Denmark (64.8%), Acrecrest Ltd, Alliance Assurance Co Ltd, Bradford Insurance Co Ltd, Comptoir Commercial du Caoutchouc (France) SA – France (99.1%), Ebor Phoenix Assurance Co Ltd, Fjerde Soforsikringsselskab A/S – Denmark, Guildhall Insurance Co Ltd, Hollandsche Verzekering Societeit van 1808 NV – the Netherlands, Liverpool Marine and General Insurance Co Ltd, London Guarantee & Accident Co of New York, London Guarantee & Reinsurance Co Ltd, London Seguradora SA – Brazil, National Vulcan Engineering Insurance Group Ltd, Phoenix Assurance Co of Canada, Phoenix Assurance Co of New York, Phoenix Assurance of South Africa Ltd (79.7%), Phoenix Assurance Plc, Phoenix Latino SA – Spain (81.4%), Phoenix Prudential Assurance of Zimbabwe Ltd (56.7%), Phoenix of East Africa Assurance Co Ltd – Kenya (61.6%), Property Growth Assurance Co Ltd, Protea Assurance Co Ltd – South Africa (79.7%), Securitas Bremer Allgemeine Versicherungs AG – Germany (98.1%), Securitas-Gilde Lebensversicherung AG – Germany (99.1%), Séza SA – France, Sun Alliance Australia Ltd, Sun Alliance Fund Management Ltd, Sun Alliance Holdings Ltd – Australia, Sun Alliance Insurance (Malaysia) Sdn Bhd (60%), Sun Alliance Insurance (Singapore) Ltd, Sun Alliance Insurance Company – Canada, Sun Alliance Insurance Co of Puerto Rico Inc (97.1%), Sun Alliance Insurance Ltd – New Zealand, Sun Alliance International Life Assurance Co Ltd – Channel Islands (Guernsey), Sun Alliance Life Assurance Ltd – Australia, Sun Alliance Linked Life Insurance Ltd, Sun Alliance Pensions Life & Investment Services Ltd, Sun Alliance Pensions Ltd, Sun Alliance Phoenix SA – Belgium, Sun Alliance and London Assurance Co Ltd, Sun Insurance Co of New York, Sun Insurance Office Ltd, The Acadia Life Insurance Company – Canada, The Century Insurance Co Ltd, The Century Insurance Co of Canada – Canada (99.9%), The London Assurance, The Pennine Insurance Co Ltd, The Provident Life Assurance Co Ltd – New Zealand, The Sea Insurance Co Ltd, Victoria-Gilde Krankenversicherung AG – Germany (50.1%), Yonge Wellington Property Ltd – Canada

BRAND NAMES

Sun Alliance

CONTACTS AND FURTHER INFORMATION

WG Niven, Sun Alliance and London Insurance plc, 1 Bartholomew Lane, London EC2N 2AB. Tel: 01-588 2345.

TSB GROUP plc

GENERAL INFORMATION

Head office	25 Milk Street, London EC2V 8LU. Tel: 01-606 7070
Reg office	16 Hope Street, Charlotte Square, Edinburgh EH2 4DD.
Directors	Sir John Read (chairman), Sir Ian Fraser CBE MC (deputy chairman), DM Backhouse, NR Barkes TD, L Bolton, Lord Bruce-Gardyne, Sir Robert Carr DSC, M Chalcraft, P Charlton OBE (managing director), GB Corser, DJ Davies, RT Ellis OBE DL, Sir Nicholas Goodison, JD Hamilton CBE, JPR Holt, RR Jeune OBE, JHF MacPherson CBE, DCM McCrickard, AD Martineau, KA Millichap, DC Nootham, PC Paisley, LW Priestley TD, Lady Prior JP, JS Rainey, NJ Robson, DM Stevens, Sir Paul Studholme Bt DL, DB Thorn (deputy managing director), E Wilson
Advisers	Lazard Brothers & Co Ltd
Auditors	Peat Marwick McLintock
Registrars	Lloyds Bank Registrar's Department
Brokers	Rowe & Pitman Ltd
Solicitors	Theodore Goddard, W & J Burness

GENERAL FINANCIAL INFORMATION

Market capitalisation	£1.68bn at 1 January 1988
Capital structure	
Issued ordinary shares (25p)	1.5bn
Issued preference shares	None
Warrants	None
Convertibles	None
Traded options	Yes
ADRs	None
Shareholders over 5%	None

FT CATEGORY

FT: Banks, HP and leasing
FT-A: Banks

MAJOR ACTIVITIES

The group conducts a major personal banking business through a 1,600 branch network in the UK, Channel Islands and the Isle of Man, and a developing commercial banking business. It additionally provides a broad range of related banking and financial services to both personal and corporate customers.

The group provides a wide range of banking services, through four companies – England and Wales, Scotland, Northern Ireland and TSB Channel Islands – to around seven million customers holding nearly 14m accounts. Although its branch network is nationwide, concentration is heaviest outside the south of England.

The principal non-banking services traditionally provided by the group are insurance and unit trusts, which cover a full range of investment, offshore fund, insurance and pension products. Since it was launched in 1968, TSB Life has been particularly successful in the single and regular premium unit-linked markets. TSB Trustcard was launched in 1978 as a member of the worldwide VISA network and the transfer to in-house processing was completed in 1986.

The move into finance house services was achieved through the acquisition of the United Dominions Trust Group in 1981, which at the same time gave the TSB Group a presence in the vehicle rental and leasing and distribution market via Swan National.

In July 1987, the Target financial services group was acquired. Target markets personal investment, pensions and other financial products. In November 1987, the group acquired Hill Samuel, the diversified merchant bank. Hill Samuel's principal activities are merchant banking, investment management services, insurance broking, employee benefits and shipping services.

Following these two significant acquisitions, TSB Group has some £12bn of funds under management and a further £6bn of funds under advice.

FINANCIAL HISTORY

The results of TSB's banking business have traditionally been influenced by the deployment of the greater part of its assets in gilt-edged and short term instruments and hence by its above-average sensitivity to interest rate movements. More recently, however, this sensitivity has been reduced by the build-up of the lending portfolio and a progressive shortening of the maturity of the money market related assets.

Profits have simultaneously been affected by development expenditure on additional data processing capability and the repositioning and upgrading of the branch network. Aggregate profits from the non-banking services on the other hand have shown both strong and consistent growth, largely reflecting the performance of the life and general insurance businesses.

The purchase of Hill Samuel for £777m and Target Life for £227m has used up much of the £1.27bn raised by the 1986 flotation. Though many regard TSB as having paid a full price for both acquisitions, particularly so in the case of Hill Samuel, the two acquisitions are likely to fill out and extend the group's product range and customer base very effectively.

Pre-tax profits for 1987, a 49 week period, were £275.5m against £205.6m in 1986. Profit from business operations on a pro-forma basis, which exclude income on capital held for investment, rose to £224.5m, an annualised increase of 19%. Earnings per share rose from 14.0p to 14.9p, an increase of 6.4%. There were particularly strong performances from financial services. In banking, profits were held back by a shift in the lending mix, the allocation of higher group overheads, and increased development expenditure. For the long term, there was impressive volume growth.

SHARE PRICE HISTORY

The shares enjoyed a spectacular stock market debut in late 1986 but by mid-1987 still stood below the level established in initial dealings, implying substantial underperformance against the market over the intervening period. They have nevertheless sustained a premium rating against other banks, partly by virtue of the unusual strength of the group's capital ratios and partly by virtue of negligible exposure to troublesome sovereign debtors.

Since the October 1987 crash the shares reacted from an absolute low of 95p to around the 100p level in mid-April 1988.

CHAIRMAN'S STATEMENT

'As Chairman I welcome this opportunity of reporting to shareholders on the sustained growth and achievement of the Group in the first full year of operation since TSB's successful flotation in September 1986. . . . Although banking continues to be the prime source of profits, the group's transition from a bank to a financial services group is apparent from the continued growth in non-banking profits. In 1986/87 non-banking profits contributed 36% of total profits from business operations, compared with 32% in the previous year and 28% in 1985. . . . By combining TSB activities with those of Hill Samuel, the TSB group has now become one of the most comprehensive financial service groups in the United Kingdom, with abundant potential for growth.' *Sir John Read*

FIVE YEAR FINANCIAL INFORMATION

Year	Income (£m)	Pre-tax (£m)	Earnings (p)	Dividends net (p)	Dividend cover (x)	Net assets (p)	Price (p) High	Low	PER (x) High	Low	Yield (%) High	Low
1983	559.6	99.4	—	—	—	—	—	—	—	—	—	—
1984	609.2	143.8	—	—	—	—	—	—	—	—	—	—
1985	689.7	169.3	—	—	—	—	—	—	—	—	—	—
1986	826.7	205.6	14.0	4.3	3.3	143	136	100	10.3	7.6	6.00	4.43
1987	965.1	275.5	14.9	4.7	3.2	151	154	100	20.1	9.1	5.84	3.79

SENIOR MANAGEMENT

The board of the group comprises the chairman, a deputy chairman, nine executive directors and other directors, of whom twelve were members or associate members of the previous central board with regional connections. Regional boards also operate in England and Wales to maintain the group's local involvement.

Sir Nicholas Goodison, chairman of the International Stock Exchange, was appointed a non-executive director from 1 April 1988, and becomes chairman on 1 January 1989.

CAPITAL

The authorised share capital of the group was increased to 2.021bn shares in September 1986, immediately prior to the offer for sale of 1.5bn shares at 100p, of which 50p was payable in that same month, and 50p in September 1987.

No director has a significant shareholding. The company's memorandum and articles of association restrict the maximum proportion of ordinary shares in which any one person may be interested to 5% until September 1991, and to 15% thereafter.

GROUP REVIEW

Banking Until 1976 the TSBs were severely limited in the services they could offer and the manner in which they could invest their customers' deposits. Since that time virtually all these restrictions have been removed, and the branches now offer a comprehensive range of banking services. These include cheque and deposit account facilities for personal customers similar to the products offered by other clearing banks and a range of other products, many of which are directed at specific market segments. These include premium deposit accounts, term deposits, monthly income bonds and contractual savings schemes.

The banks' personal lending business is principally in the form of mortgages and unsecured fixed rate personal loans. Other products include overdrafts, secured loans, bridging finance, probate and home improvement loans. TSB has installed more than 1,900 autotellers, available to both Speedbank and Trustcard holders. The link-up agreement with Midland and NatWest will substantially increase this number on its completion in 1988. As part of TSB's ambitious development plans, 200 branches were completely refurbished in 1987.

The group has progressively developed a range of corporate banking services, notably deposit accounts carrying market-related rates of interest, a high interest deposit discount, Marketlink, and Speedsend, an instant money transmission service.

Lending facilities are primarily geared to the requirements of small and medium-sized companies but large corporate lending, launched in 1981, now covers nearly half the 100 largest listed UK companies. This is complemented by a full foreign exchange business. The group has issued Trustcards within the VISA system since 1978.

In 1987 banking profits increased to £142.7m, 64% of total profits, and an annualised increase of 13.4%. Advances to customers increased by 18% to £4.2bn with especially strong growth in mortgage lending. Deposits grew significantly to £12.1bn with a substantial increase in cheque account balances. Despite the growth it was not necessary to increase the provision for bad or doubtful debts. The group has minimal exposure to Third World debt.

The corporate sector showed promising growth and will be greatly enhanced by Hill Samuel. A contribution in a full year of £60m pre-tax is projected for 1988.

Insurance and unit trusts TSB Trust Company, which includes TSB Life and TSB Unit Trusts, achieved striking growth in 1986 and 1987. 1987 profits were £41.7m, up £6.6m, representing 13% of the group's total pre-tax operating profits.

TSB Trust Company had close on 580,000 policies on file in 1986. At the 1987 year-end, the net assets of the life and pensions business was over £2.5bn. In 1987 new single premium business was up by 66%. Its marketing is primarily aimed at the group's customer base through a direct sales force operating in conjunction with TSB branches. The recently acquired Target Group operates primarily through intermediaries.

TSB Life funds have a large investment in TSB unit trusts, which cover a broad range of both general and specialist trusts. TSB is the seventh largest unit trust management business in the country. Direct sales of unit trusts grew by 79% to £90m. Other TSB Life products are a flexible pension plan and general insurance, particularly home contents, motor, travel, and loan repayment insurance against accident, sickness and unemployment. Premium income on general insurance business was up 38% to £76m in 1987.

Credit card operations TSB Trustcard currently has 2.8m

Share price and relative to FT-A All-Share

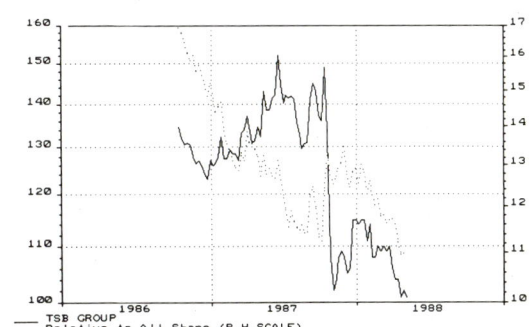

cards in issue, giving it a 12% share of the bank-issued credit card market in the UK. Trustcard is accepted in around 0.25m outlets in the UK, and through the VISA network, in 5m outlets worldwide. Transaction turnover in 1987 exceeded £1bn, 20% up on 1986. Recent initiatives include the launch of Trustcard Motoring Club, Trustcard Travel Club and Trustcard Shopping Hotline. 1987 annualised profits were 10% up at £11.6m, 5% of the group's total.

Finance house services UDT was reorganised in 1984 and the group now operates through five divisions: UDT Sales Finance, a point of sale division which specialises in fixed rate lending to customers for the purchase of cars, commercial vehicles and caravans; UDT Consumer Finance, a personal loan division which includes unsecured loans marketed through home improvement suppliers and direct advertising and mailings, and secured loans, principally mortgages through Mortgage Express; UDT Corporate Loans, specialising in loans for residential property development, purchases of plant and equipment and mortgages on commercial and industrial property; UDT Commercial Finance, offering confidential and full recourse recoveries financing; and UDT Bank, which is the largest independent finance house in Eire, offering a wide range of personal and commercial financial products.

1987 was an outstanding year. Profits were up by no less than 109% to £19.9m. There were reduced charges for bad debts. Mortgage Express, which markets mortgages through intermediaries, was started in late 1986. It has quickly built up its portfolio to £500m in the first year of operation.

Vehicle rental, leasing and distribution Through a network of nearly 100 branches, Swan National provides short term vehicle rental services to both personal and corporate customers. It increased its fleet by a third in 1987 to cover 9,400 cars and 700 vans and is a member of InterRent, an international association of car hire companies. Profits in 1987 were up 18% to £8.6m, 4% of the group's total. The division has been expanded in 1988 through the purchase of the Target Motor Company and Graham Motor Group.

Estate agencies TSB Scotland acquired Slater Hogg and Howison, a leading Scottish estate agency with 26 offices, in 1986. More recently, the group has begun the initial development of a network within England and Wales. At the beginning of 1988 the total number of offices was 81.

Future divisional structure In a management reorganisation announced in late April 1988, TSB is segmenting its activities into three areas – retail banking, corporate banking, and insurance and investment services. This will bring together and consolidate the activities of TSB and its recent acquisitions, Hill Samuel and Target.

GEOGRAPHICAL REVIEW

The group is represented outside the UK in the US, continental Europe, the Channel Islands and the Isle of Man, although its lending overseas is minimal.

CORPORATE CALENDAR

Year end	20 November
Preliminary results	January
Report and accounts	February
AGM	March
Final dividend paid	March
Interim results	June
Interim dividend paid	October

DIRECTORS' HOLDINGS

	Fully-paid ordinary shares	Options
Sir John Read	3,000	—
DM Backhouse	5,000	—
NR Barkes	11,500	—
L Bolton	5,300	—
Lord Bruce-Gardyne	3,400	—
M Chalcraft	500	—
P Charlton	6,150	142,857
GB Corser	51,700	50,000
RT Ellis	2,200	—
Sir Ian Fraser	10,000	—
JD Hamilton	2,500	—
JPR Holt	5,000	—
RR Jeune	2,000	—
JHF Macpherson	4,200	—
AD Martineau	6,000	—
DC McCrickard	4,650	100,000
KA Millichap	6,000	—
PC Paisley	4,000	—
LW Priestley	5,150	114,285
Lady Prior	2,500	—
JS Rainey	5,600	—
NJ Robson	5,000	—
DM Stevens	6,450	100,000
DB Thorn	5,150	114,285
E Wilson	5,150	85,714

Total directors' remuneration for 49 weeks in 1987 was £1.247m including fees and pension contributions. The chairman, who is the highest-paid director, received £116,593.

PRINCIPAL SUBSIDIARIES AND RELATED COMPANIES

Hill Samuel Group Plc, TSB England & Wales plc, TSB Scotland plc, TSB Northern Ireland plc, TSB Channel Islands Limited, Target Group PLC, TSB Commercial Holdings Limited, TSB Investment Management Limited, TSB Trustcard Limited, TSB Trust Company Limited

BRAND NAMES

Marketlink, Mortgage Express, Speedbank, Speedsend, Swan National, Trustcard, TSB, TSB Homecentre, TSB Life, TSB Unit Trusts, United Dominion Trust

CONTACTS AND FURTHER INFORMATION

Michael Fitzgerald, TSB Group plc Press Office, 25 Milk Street, London EC2V 8LU. Tel: 01-606 7070.

TARMAC PLC

GENERAL INFORMATION

Head office	Hilton Hall, Essington, Wolverhampton WV11 2BQ. Tel: 0902 307407
Directors	Sir Eric Pountain DL (chairman), BW Baker (managing), DT Carr (managing), TH Mason, J Mawdsley, IGS McPherson, A Osborne, SF Pickstock, NI Simms. *Non-exec* Sir Campbell Adamson, Lord Balfour of Burleigh, The Duchess of Devonshire, Sir Nicolas Henderson GCMG, AP Bamford
Advisers	No specified adviser
Auditors	Peat Marwick McLintock
Registrars	National Westminster Bank Registrar's Department
Brokers	Cazenove & Co, Rowe & Pitman Ltd
Solicitors	No specified adviser

GENERAL FINANCIAL INFORMATION

Market capitalisation	£1.597bn at 1 January 1988
Capital structure	
Issued ordinary shares (50p)	711m
Issued preference shares (£1)	0.2m 5.5% CP
Warrants	None
Convertibles	None
Traded options	None
ADRs	None
Shareholders over 5%	None

FT CATEGORY

FT: Building, timber, roads
FT-A: Building materials

MAJOR ACTIVITIES

Tarmac is the UK's largest construction and building materials group, having greatly extended its activities from its original road construction and resurfacing business.

Tarmac is now also engaged in: other areas of civil engineering; quarrying; the supply of bulk construction materials; the manufacture of building and other industrial products; housebuilding; and commercial and industrial property development.

The group remains predominantly UK-based but in 1987 it substantially increased its US operations with the acquisition of a 60% controlling interest in the Virginia and Carolinas businesses of Lone Star Industries. Since this acquisition Tarmac's US operations account for about 12% of its total turnover and its UK operations for about 80% against about 83% before.

The activities of the group's quarry products division include winning stone, gravel and sand, dredging aggregates from the sea-bed and making blacktop road-surfacing material and ready-mix concrete.

The group's clay brick, finished concrete products and monumental masonry businesses form the building materials division.

The group's US interests, including Tarmac–LoneStar, have been consolidated into Tarmac America. They include substantial ready-mix concrete, concrete products and cement-making operations. Reserves of aggregates total 1.5bn tonnes. Annual turnover is $500m.

Recently the group's housebuilding division, led by its McLean subsidiary, has achieved spectacular growth. In 1987 it overtook George Wimpey as the UK's leading housebuilder. After quarry products it is the group's largest source of sales, accounting for about one quarter of its total turnover, just ahead of the construction division.

Besides the construction division's road-building activities, it is involved in the complete range of construction types and contract size. Current civil engineering includes the Channel Tunnel and the Greater Cairo waste-water project.

The industrial products division refines bitumen and other building chemicals. Among its products are roof waterproofing membranes, mastic asphalt, curtain walling and industrial doors and shutters.

The properties division's major recent projects include the Heron Quays development in the London docklands.

Traditionally the level of much of the group's activities has been determined by the level of government spending on the nation's infrastructure. This dependence has been greatly reduced by its successful housebuilding operation and the broadening of its range of building products.

An important factor in Tarmac's future could be the increased role the UK Government and some local authorities are giving private sector contractors in urban redevelopment and major infrastructural projects. According to this, contractors share in the financing and ownership of these ventures and in the financial rewards flowing from the completed developments. Actual and possible examples include tolled tunnels, bridges and motorways, privatised council housing estates and contractor-owned or even contractor-operated urban railways.

The Tarmac-LoneStar acquisitions have increased the group's exposure to the unfavourable movement of the dollar. Like all contractors Tarmac is vulnerable to prolonged bouts of inclement weather. This is less of a factor in its US markets than in the UK.

Tarmac's principal competitors in many of its activities include Beazer, Costain, John Laing, Sir Robert McAlpine, George Wimpey and Taylor Woodrow. ARC (Consolidated Gold Fields) is a competitor in quarry products, building products and road building.

FINANCIAL HISTORY

The development of housebuilding, diverse building products and the American business should maintain above average growth rates.

Turnover was £2.2bn in 1987, a rise of 27% on 1986, well above the 10% rise in 1986 and somewhat above the good growth in 1984 and 1985. Since 1982 sales have doubled. The growth in profits has been more stable, up 56% in 1987 to £265.4m, following a rise of 26% to £170.5m in 1986 and up 286% since 1982.

Regular profit increases of 20% to 25% have been possible as Tarmac improved its margin from around 6.5% in 1982 to almost 10% in 1986 and 13.2% in 1987. Earnings growth was flat during the difficult 1984/85 period but grew by 27% to 35.7p in 1986 and by 32% to 23.5p in 1987.

A major shift in strategy is taking Tarmac away from lower

CHAIRMAN'S STATEMENT

'I am delighted to report such an outstanding result for 1987, which was once again a record year. Our great underlying strength is our ability to extract organic growth from all parts of the group. The managements, and indeed all employees of our seven strong divisions, did a wonderful job.

Excellent order books, wide-ranging investment in assets and management and unusually good weather have combined to launch 1988 in confident style. The group is well equipped to seize the opportunities of continuing strong construction markets and 1988 should be another year of considerable progress.' *Sir Eric Pountain*

F I V E   Y E A R   F I N A N C I A L   I N F O R M A T I O N

Year	Turnover (£m)	Pre-tax (£m)	Earnings (p)	Dividends net (p)	Dividend cover (x)	Net assets (p)	Price (p) High	Low	PER (x) High	Low	Yield (%) High	Low
1983	1,160.5	89.6	24.3	6.80	3.6	190	116	98	22.8	15.3	4.03	2.94
1984	1,321.2	109.6	25.8	8.00	3.2	244	132	102	19.9	12.0	4.79	3.08
1985	1,570.6	135.2	28.2	9.40	3.0	138	203	114	17.3	11.9	4.41	2.89
1986	1,735.0	171.0	17.8	11.09	3.2	108	258	173	22.0	14.7	3.75	2.27
1987	2,200.9	265.4	23.5	7.25	3.2	99	342	191	20.4	10.8	4.53	2.22

margin businesses such as quarry products and towards the higher margin finished market, be they building products or new homes.

SHARE PRICE HISTORY

Tarmac's share price rose from the 100p level in 1984 to a 1987 all-time high of 350p. In relative terms the strongest performance was in the first half of 1985. Since then it has marginally declined relative to the FT-A All-Share index.

The shares fell 43% in the autumn 1987 share price crash to below 200p. Subsequently they had recovered to 250p in late April 1988.

SENIOR MANAGEMENT

Sir Eric Pountain is chairman of Tarmac. Cecil Parkinson, who had been a board member since 1984, resigned as deputy chairman on his appointment as Minister for Energy in June 1987. Donald Carr and Bryan Baker are joint group managing directors.

Jack Mawdsley succeeded Donald Carr as chief executive of the quarry products division and joined the main board in January 1987. Terence Mason, who has been with the group for 20 years, joined the main board as group finance director in 1986. Neville Simms and Ian McPherson joined the main board in March 1988. AP Bamford was appointed to the board in January 1988 as a non-executive director.

Samuel Pickstock is chief executive of the housing division. Neville Simms is chief executive of the construction division. Tony Collins is chief executive of the properties division. Ian McPherson is chief executive of the industrial products division.

CAPITAL

Tarmac's issued ordinary capital amounted to 711m shares at the end of 1987. Tarmac has used its equity very sparingly. There were one for one scrip issues in June 1985 and May 1987.

The only major issue of shares has been to finance two stages of the Lone Star Industries acquisition. In October 1984, 14.3m shares were issued as part consideration for certain operations of Lone Star Industries. In January 1987 the group issued 40.3m shares in January to finance the acquisition of its 60% controlling interest in Lone Star's Virginia and Carolinas businesses. These were mostly taken up by existing Tarmac shareholders. Tarmac has an option to buy the remaining 40% of Lone Star in 1989.

There were small issues of shares in 1987 in part consideration of Feb International, Hawkins Tiles and Severn Valley Brick Company. In November 1987 SG Warburg arranged a $250m Euro-Commercial paper programme.

GROUP REVIEW

Quarry products division Since the group's reorganisation in January 1987 the division has continued its traditional quarrying and road surfacing in the UK and its ready-mix concrete and waste businesses. It also contains its residual interests in South Africa. Building materials and Tarmac America became autonomous divisions. In 1987 the division accounted for 19% of the group's turnover and 25.3% of its operating profit.

Tarmac has major UK resources of stone, sand and gravel from which it supplies the building and construction industry with crushed and graded aggregates. The majority of the group's reserves, which are primarily located in the north of England, are of rock and sand. Gravel accounts for only about 10% of sales. Despite its geographical distribution Tarmac is meeting with some success in its aim of developing sales in the more prosperous southern regions. It now commands about 17% of the total UK market for the supply of aggregates.

The group has about 30% of the UK market for blacktop, the name given to the compound generally used for surfacing roads.

Tarmac's ready-mix concrete business holds around 10% of the UK market. Like RMC is has a network of ready-mix plants and operates a fleet of mixer trucks which deliver concrete in liquid form. Much of its ready-mix output is also used in road construction.

Tarmac's waste disposal business accumulates the filling required to restore its exhausted sand and gravel sites into agricultural, forestry and recreational land. The group's remaining businesses in South Africa consists of quarrying and blacktop.

Turnover in 1987 was up 9.3% to £418.3m. Operating profit was 14.3% ahead at £72.1m. These figures include what is now the building materials and Tarmac America divisions.

Building materials division The division encompasses the group's brick, block concrete and natural products operations.

In recent years the group has been developing its building materials business in its own right and as an additional source of added value for its aggregates business. In 1985 it had no involvement in the concrete block market but now commands a 10% share in the UK. Its policy has been to achieve organic growth by developing its long-standing businesses and also to extend its operations through acquisition.

Tarmac made two significant purchases in 1987 – Hawkins Tiles and the Severn Valley Brick Company. The group's main brick-making operation is the Westbrick clay facing brick business. Severn Valley's annual output of 40m bricks has increased Tarmac's total brick production to about 200m bricks per annum. Its acquisition marks Tarmac's entry into the simulated hand made brick market and has significantly extended the geographical base of its brick and tile operations.

Westbrick's plants are located in Devon and Hawkins Tiles in Staffordshire. Severn Valley's Bristol location has easy access to London and the western home counties.

In 1987, turnover rose 24.3% to £102.2m, 4.6% of the group total. Operating profit rose 56.7% to £16.3m, 5.7% of the group total.

Tarmac America Tarmac's operations, with the newly acquired 60% of Tarmac-LoneStar and the Massey Sand and Rock company, extend across the states of Florida, Texas, California, Arizona, Virginia and North and South Carolina.

Total aggregate reserves of 1.5bn tonnes have an annual capacity of 20m tonnes and are distributed among 30 locations. Added-value activities comprise 82 ready-mix concrete plant locations with over 850 mixer trucks, 25 concrete block plants, three concrete pipe plants and a cement plant with an annual capacity of over one million tonnes.

The south and south-eastern US construction market is generally buoyant. The climate in most regions there allows constant activity throughout the year. In Texas, however, continuing economic difficulties deferred recovery. Infrastructure and housing expenditure levels are higher than in the UK.

In 1987, turnover rose 63.4% to £258m, 11.7% of the group total. Operating profit rose 113.2% to £46.9m, 16.4% of the group total.

Construction division In 1987 the division accounted for 24.2% of the group's turnover and 6.7% of operating profit. It has three main operating units – Tarmac Construction International, Tarmac Construction Regions and Tarmac Plant – and operated in 1987 from 650 sites.

Tarmac Construction International, from headquarters in Wolverhampton, executes major building and civil engineering projects in the UK and overseas. Tarmac's current traditional government-sponsored engineering projects include motorway construction for the Department of Transport, and work for the Welsh Office and the Property Services Agency. Tarmac was a founding member of the revived Channel Tunnel consortium and is now a prominent member of the construction team.

Perhaps inspired by the successful launch of the Channel Tunnel, Tarmac is increasingly adopting a principal's position in major developments whereby it acts both as constructor and part-owner of the project. An example of a project which it is co-promoting on this basis is the Mersey Barrage, an imaginative scheme to harness the tidal range in the Mersey estuary to generate electricity. The group is also promoting a major £150m service station on the M25 which is to include a rail link to Heathrow airport, a shopping centre and a large marina on the nearby Grand Union canal.

The Greater Cairo waste-water tunnel is Tarmac's most important overseas contract currently in hand.

Tarmac Construction Regions is planning a wide range of major mixed housing and commercial developments, some involving its properties and housing divisions.

Tarmac has set up an enlarged contract housing grouping to serve the market for building and modernising public sector housing. This is a member of a consortium set up to refurbish the now abandoned 1,000 acre Bradley Stone council housing estate outside Bristol, in a private development valued at £250m. The entrepreneurial approach taken by Tarmac and several other leading contractors has been given a considerable boost by the Government's plans for inner city local authorities to dispose of many of their derelict or underused assets for redevelopment by private enterprise.

Tarmac Plant supplies construction plant to other parts of the group in competition with outside suppliers.

Turnover for the construction division in 1987 was up 29.3% to £532.8m. Operating profit was up 52.4% to £19.2m.

Housing division In 1987 the division accounted for 25.3%

of the group's turnover and 36% of operating profit.

Tarmac has rapidly emerged as the major private housebuilder, with new developments in the Midlands and significant interests throughout the UK. The group replaced George Wimpey in 1987 as the UK's leading housebuilder. The annual total of new homes completed by the group has grown from 7,128 in 1984 to 11,236 in 1987. The latter figure represented a rise of 1,000 over 1986, at an average price of £48,000 – below the national average.

The division's output is slanted towards the more profitable second time buyers' section of the housing market and derives about 30% of its profit from sales in the south-east. The housing division is seen by Tarmac as a major UK growth area.

Turnover for 1987 was up 31.3% to £558m. Operating profit was up 66.9% to £102.8m, after a rise of 77.5% in 1986 to £61.6m.

Properties division This is by far the group's smallest division, accounting for 1.8% of turnover in 1987 and 2.3% of operating profit. Much of its activity is in the erection of retail outlets. Projects under way include those at Harrow and Lewes.

Share price and relative to FT-A All-Share

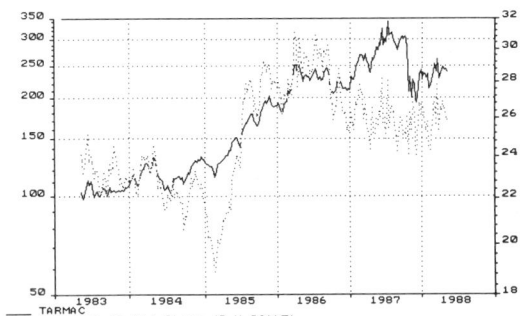

TARMAC
Relative to All Share (R.H.SCALE)

The Heron Quays development in the London docklands enterprise zone is one of its more important commercial developments. Another docklands project is a £1bn co-venture to redevelop the Royal Albert Dock. The division is also active in the high-tech industrial premises and warehouse market in the M3/M4 corridor.

Turnover for the properties division in 1987 was down 68.4% to £35.7m. Operating profit was up 50% to £6.6m.

Industrial products division In 1987 the division accounted for 13.4% of the group's turnover and 8.9% of operating profit.

Industrial products manufactures and installs a wide range of products mainly for industrial and commercial buildings in both the public and private sectors. These include roof waterproofing membranes, mastic asphalt, polyurethane insulation, metal decking and cladding, curtain walling, and industrial doors and shutters. This division also manages the group's bitumen-refining operation and manufactures building chemicals.

An important component of the division is the Permanite roofing-felt operation. Permanite was in a very poor position only five years ago. It is now a solid business with the most modern plant for making torch-applied bitumen membranes.

Other components of Tarmac's roofing-felt business are Villas Roofing Systems in the US and Briggs Amasco, the UK's leading roofing and cladding contractor. Briggs Amasco is also active in curtain walling and marine decking. Other interests include the French curtain-walling business Tectonic, Fyrespan and Bolton Brady – an industrial and commercial door and shutter business.

The extensive range of the division's branded roofing, roof-fixing and waterproofing products is led by BP Aquaseal, Permanite and Hydroflex. This was considerably broadened by the purchase of Feb International in February 1987.

Much of the division's bitumen-refining interests are being redeveloped via a joint venture with Shell. The group's principal bitumen business is Philmac, now completely bought out from Phillips Petroleum.

Turnover for the industrial products division in 1987 was up 16.4% to £295.9m. Operating profit was up 20.9% to £25.4m.

GEOGRAPHICAL REVIEW

In 1987 the UK accounted for 80% of group turnover, the US for 12%, with the balance made up by Europe and the rest of the world. The group does not disclose the geographical breakdown of operating profit.

CORPORATE CALENDAR

Year end	31 December
Preliminary results	April
Report and accounts	May
AGM	June
Final dividend paid	July
Interim results	September
Interim dividend paid	November

DIRECTORS' HOLDINGS

	Fully-paid	Share options
Sir Eric Pountain	886,224	204,524
Sir Campbell Adamson	3,160	—
BW Baker	110,224	234,524
Lord Balfour of Burleigh	10,838	—
AP Bamford	140,000	—
DT Carr	13,286	250,748
The Duchess of Devonshire	13,558	—
Sir Nicholas Henderson	4,258	—
TH Mason	30,224	49,600
J Mawdsley	50,224	49,600
A Osborne	339,480	114,600
SF Pickstock	120,000	109,600
NI Simms	2,500	140,892

In 1987 the directors' remuneration was not disclosed. The chairman, who was also the highest-paid director, received £213,000.

PRINCIPAL SUBSIDIARIES AND RELATED COMPANIES

Quarry products division
Arnold Waste Disposal Ltd (50%), Berwyn Granite Quarries Ltd (49%), Bryco Concrete Ltd, C&H Quickmix Limited, Econowaste Ltd, Marcon (London) Limited, Mineral Properties and Investments Ltd, North Tyne Roadstone Ltd (50%), Scunthorpe Slag Ltd (60%), Tarmac Quarry Products Ltd, Tarmac Roadstone Ltd, Tarmac Roadstone (Scotland) Ltd, Tarmac Topmix Ltd, Tarmac South Africa (Pty) Ltd – South Africa, Teesside Slag Ltd (50%), Tendley Quarries Ltd, United Marine Aggregates Ltd

Building materials
Bryco Concrete Ltd, Ferro Concrete Ltd, Francis Concrete Ltd, Hawkins Tile (Cannock) Ltd, Natural Stone Products Ltd, Severn Valley Brick (Avonmouth), Tarmac Building Materials Ltd, Tarmac Structural Concrete Ltd, Tarmac Topblock Ltd, Westbrick Ltd

Tarmac America
Amcon Products Inc, Chisman Company Inc (60%), Ellis Transportation, Massey Sand and Rock Company, Old Virginia Brick Company, Tarmac Florida Inc, Tarmac Roadstone Inc, Tarmac Texas Inc, Tarmac LoneStar Inc (60%)

Construction division
Go Plant Ltd, Hannen & Cubitts (Civil Engineering) Ltd, Kinnear Moodie (1973) Ltd, McWall Estates (50%), Pasco Engineering Ltd (97%), Saudi Tarmac Company Limited – Saudi Arabia (44%), Schal International Ltd (51%), Tarmac Construction (London) Ltd, Tarmac Construction Ltd, Tarmac Construction Plant Ltd, Tarmac International Ltd, Tarmac National Construction Ltd, Tarmac Overseas Ltd, Tarmac Regional Construction Ltd

Housing division
Groveside Homes Ltd, John McLean & Sons Ltd, McLean Homes East Anglia Ltd, McLean Homes Midlands Ltd, McLean Homes North East Ltd, McLean Homes North London Ltd, McLean Homes North West & Cheshire Ltd, McLean Homes Northern Ltd, McLean Homes Scotland Ltd – Scotland, McLean Homes South East Ltd, McLean Homes South West Ltd, McLean Homes Southern Ltd, McLean Homes Yorkshire Ltd, Midland & General Developments Ltd, Rivermead Homes Ltd, Tarmac Homes Bristol & West Ltd, Tarmac Homes Essex Ltd, Tarmac Homes Midlands Ltd, Tarmac Homes South Midlands Ltd, Tarmac Homes Yorkshire Ltd, Thameswey Homes Ltd, Thomas Lowe Homes Ltd, Thomas Lowe Joinery Ltd

Properties division
Clayform Retail Properties Ltd (50%), Farmcote Developments (Southern) Ltd, Farmcote Developments Ltd, Heron Quays Management Ltd, John McLean and Associates Ltd, McLean Investments Ltd, Newnham Court Commerce Centre Ltd (66%), Schofield Centre Ltd (50%), Tarmac Brookglade Properties Ltd, Tarmac Burford Properties Ltd, Tarmac Chepstow Developments Ltd (50%), Tarmac Developments Ltd, Tarmac Properties Home Counties Ltd, Tarmac Properties Investments Ltd, Tarmac Properties Ltd, Tarmac Properties Midlands Ltd, Tarmac Properties Securities Ltd, Tarmac Properties South East Ltd, Tarmac Properties Southern Ltd, Tarmac Provincial Properties Ltd, West Mercian Property Company Ltd, White Lion Walk Ltd (50%)

Industrial products division
Aquaseal Ltd, Bolton Brady Ltd, Briggs Amasco Ltd, British Hydroflex Ltd, Compagnie de Matériaux et de Services SA – France, Coolag Purlboard Ltd, Durastic Ltd, Feb International, Fyrespan Ltd, Irish Roofing Felts Ltd – Republic of Ireland, Markfield (Insurance Brokers) Ltd, Neuchâtel Asphalte SA – Switzerland, Permanite Asphalt Ltd, Permanite Inc – US, Permanite Ltd, Philmac Oils Ltd, Société de Pavage et des Asphaltes de Paris SA – France, Tarec International BV – Netherlands (50%), Tarec International SA – France (80%), TBP Industries Ltd, Tarmac Building Products Ltd, Tarmac Industrial Holdings Ltd, Tarmac Oil Products Ltd, Tarmac Roofing Systems Inc – US, Tectronic Ltd, Thomas Witter & Company Ltd, William Briggs & Sons Ltd – Scotland

Joint ventures
Anglo Egyptian Cairo Wastewater Consortium – Egypt (20%), Majes Consortium (22%) – Peru, Schal Associates – US, Thames Barrier (32%), Translink JV (20%)

BRAND NAMES

Aquaseal, Aquatex, British Hydroflex, Duraflex, Feb, Febflor, Feblex, Feblon, Febmix, Febond, Febseal, Febsilicon, Febspeed, Febstik, Febtile, Febtite, Febtone, Febwood, Permanite, Permanite Aquatex, Permaband

CONTACTS AND FURTHER INFORMATION

KA Jackson, Head of Press and Public affairs, Tarmac PLC, Hilton Hall, Essington, Wolverhampton WV11 2BQ. Tel: 0902 307407.

TESCO PLC

GENERAL INFORMATION

Head office	Tesco House, Delamare Road, Cheshunt, Hertfordshire EN8 9SL. Tel: 0992-32222
Directors	IC MacLaurin (chairman), VW Benjamin (deputy chairman), AD Malpas (managing), M Darnell, J Gildersleeve, FRN Krejsa FRICS, DE Reid CA, DC Tuffin. *Non-exec* Miss D O'Cathain OBE, JA Gardiner, JMF Padovan LLB BCL FCA, Sir Leslie Porter (president)
Advisers	County NatWest Ltd
Auditors	Price Waterhouse
Registrars	Lloyds Bank Registrar's Department
Brokers	Phillips & Drew Ltd
Solicitors	Berwin Leighton

GENERAL FINANCIAL INFORMATION

Market capitalisation	£2.252bn at 1 January 1988
Capital structure	
Issued ordinary shares (25p)	1.46bn
Issued preference shares	None
Warrants	None
Convertibles	£43m 9% CUL 2002/07 (243.30 ordinary shares per £100 stock to 30 August 2002) £115m 4% ES 2002 (190.84 shares per £1,000 stock to 12 February 2002)
Traded options	Yes
ADRs	None
Shareholders over 5%	None

FT CATEGORY

FT: Food, groceries, etc
FT-A: Food retailing

MAJOR ACTIVITIES

The principal activity of Tesco and its subsidiaries is multiple food retailing within the United Kingdom. Tesco sells food, drink, housewares, garden products, toiletries, textiles, clothes and petrol. In recent years the company has streamlined its operations substantially and determinedly. Today it has almost half the number of stores it had ten years ago yet its sales area has actually risen by over 35%.

Of primary importance has been the concentration on the development of superstores, those with sales areas of 25,000 square feet and above, which now account for over 60% of the company's sales.

With total food volume showing at best only modest growth, the key economic indicators affecting sales are food price inflation and to a lesser extent personal disposable income. Competition is from other quoted multiple retailers, in particular J Sainsbury, ASDA, and Argyll with Safeway.

Following disposal of its peripheral activities and its successful acquisition of Hillards, Tesco has clearly established itself as the UK's main superstore operator and the contender with J Sainsbury for the position of leading food retailer. It is now in a position to reinforce its identity and consumer franchise and looks set for several years' solid growth in market share and profits.

Looking further ahead to the 1990s, Tesco may well seek to diversify either into another form of UK retailing or overseas food retailing.

FINANCIAL HISTORY

Sales excluding VAT in fiscal 1988 at £4.12bn increased 14.6% on 1987 and 81% over five years. Pre-tax profits, excluding property, were £224m in 1988, 34.5% ahead on 1987 and 219% up over five years, well above the stock market average.

Diluted earnings per share, adjusted for the July 1987 two for one scrip issue, increased 17.8% from 8.2p to 9.6p. Net dividends were 17.3% up at 2.85p. The balance sheet is strong with year-end debt, including the convertible loan stock, of about £260m, giving a gearing level of 29%. Cash flow was high at about £180m, but capital expenditure was higher still at £407m.

Key trading ratios for 1988 included weekly sales per square foot up 7.8% to £11, sales per employee up 5.4% to £82,037, profit per employee up 24% to £4,808, and pre-interest margin up 26.8% to 5.2%.

Net margin continued to improve from 5% to 5.9%. All this was achieved on a sales increase of 15%, a volume gain after inflation of 12%, of which existing stores contributed 4%.

SHARE PRICE HISTORY

Since 1984 the Tesco share price has risen from around 50p to 158p. Compared to the market and despite the autumn 1987 crash, Tesco has also been rising in relative terms, moving from around 12% to 17% of the FT-A All-Share index.

The successful acquisition of Hillards and the potential gains from converting these stores to Tesco fascias may partly explain this optimism, given the increased potential for higher margins and profits growth. The high for the shares in July 1987 was 209p. They began 1988 at 158p.

SENIOR MANAGEMENT

Ian MacLaurin has been with the company for 28 years. He was appointed to the board in 1970 and became the first non-family chairman in 1985. David Malpas is managing director and has been a board member since 1979.

Recent board appointments have been David Reid (finance) and John Gildersleeve (personnel, buying and marketing). The executive board is completed by JW Benjamin, deputy chairman; M Darnell, distribution; FRN Krejsa, property and estates; HF Pennell, buying and marketing; and DC Tuffin, retail.

Non-executive directors are Sir Leslie Porter, president and former chairman; Miss D O'Cathain, managing director of the Milk Marketing Board; John Gardiner, chairman and chief executive of the Laird group; and JMF Padovan.

CAPITAL

Tesco broke with tradition in April 1987 when it made a hostile bid for the Yorkshire-based retailer Hillards, expanding its share capital to finance the acquisition. 42.4m Tesco shares were issued, representing 9.1% of the enlarged share capital. The previous major share issue was the one for five rights issue of 67.8m shares in May 1985.

£112m was raised in March 1987 through the convertible Eurobond issue. A two for one scrip issue was completed in

CHAIRMAN'S STATEMENT

'The benefits of the previous two years, which were essentially periods of rationalisation, have begun to emerge to reinforce the profit potential of our company. While sustaining a large and increasing investment programme in new stores, distribution and technology we have been able to maintain a very strong balance sheet.' *Ian MacLaurin*

FIVE YEAR FINANCIAL INFORMATION

Year	Turnover (£m)	Pre-tax (£m)	Earnings (p)	Dividends net (p)	Dividend cover (x)	Net assets (p)	Price (p) High	Low	PER (x) High	Low	Yield (%) High	Low
1983	2,276.6	53.5	3.96	1.17	3.4	31.3	58	36	23.2	16.0	4.05	2.81
1984	2,594.5	67.4	3.83	1.37	2.8	32.6	78	51	23.4	15.9	3.78	2.60
1985	3,000.4	81.3	4.54	1.62	2.8	36.8	100	73	23.6	18.5	2.91	2.33
1986	3,355.3	122.9	5.84	1.93	3.0	47.7	140	89	25.5	17.1	2.77	1.95
1987	3,593.0	166.5	8.17	2.43	3.4	54.2	206	131	23.5	14.1	2.54	1.62

July 1987. At 31 December 1987, 1.47bn ordinary shares were in issue. Conversion of the outstanding 9% CULS would result in 39.7m shares being issued and of the 4% ES 2002 convertible bonds a further 21.9m.

There are no declared holdings over 5% and the most significant director's holding is that of Sir Leslie Porter with 0.8%.

GROUP REVIEW

Tesco is one of Britain's largest and best known multiple retailers with superstores and supermarkets in England, Scotland and Wales. The group withdrew from retailing in Eire when it sold its small Tesco Stores Ireland operation in May 1986.

At February 1988, Tesco operated 379 stores taking in a total sales area of 8.2m sq ft, an average area per store of 21,700 sq ft. Of these, 136 stores, covering 65% of total selling area, were 25,000 sq ft or greater, while 111 stores, covering 8% of selling area, were under 10,000 sq ft.

The acquisition of Hillards added 40 stores to Tesco's portfolio. By August 1987 all had been converted to the Tesco fascia. New Tesco stores added in 1987 included Truro, New Malden and Doncaster, and a major extension was completed at Basingstoke. A further 14 stores were completed by December 1987, together with three new extensions totalling in all 657,000 sq ft. 16 new sites and three extensions are committed for 1988, amounting to 572,000 sq ft.

The main thrust of Tesco's development programme has concentrated on its superstore strategy in which the company has sought to build single-storey units with all services at ground level. New sites would ideally be around eight acres providing stores of 40,000 to 65,000 sq ft of sales area.

Tesco also seeks smaller stores of around 20,000 sq ft net sales area which concentrate on selling food and drink products only. A significant aspect of Tesco's development policy is its link-up with Marks and Spencer where both shops will trade together on new sites. The first scheme has begun trading very successfully in Hertfordshire.

The superstores stock up to 18,000 product lines, while supermarkets carry a product range consistent with their size and location. All stores carry fresh fruit and vegetables and have meat departments. One in three stores has an in-store bakery.

Delicatessen can be found in two-thirds of the supermarkets and in all the superstores. Fresh fish ranges are now available in 39 stores. Of the 308 licensed Tesco stores offering a wide range of wines, spirits and beers, 250 offer a self-service facility allowing customers to browse and select their purchase at leisure.

Conventional dry groceries, such as canned and packaged provisions, occupy half of the space allocated to food. A large proportion, around 40%, of Tesco's grocery sales are own-label products.

Tesco's recent policy towards own-label branding has aimed at creating and maintaining customer loyalty from quality products. The largest Tesco superstores carry a range of over 2,000 own-label products covering 90% of fresh foods, 90% of wines and 50% of spirits and beers.

GEOGRAPHICAL REVIEW

The acquisition of Hillards gave Tesco 12 superstores and 29 stores between 10,000 and 25,000 sq ft. Of these, six superstores and 11 others are in Yorkshire, an area in which Tesco was severely under-represented, thus filling a useful gap in its geographical coverage.

CORPORATE CALENDAR

Year end	last Saturday in February
Preliminary results	mid-April
Report and accounts	late-April
AGM	mid-May
Final dividend paid	early July
Interim results	late September
Interim dividend paid	November

Share price and relative to FT-A All-Share

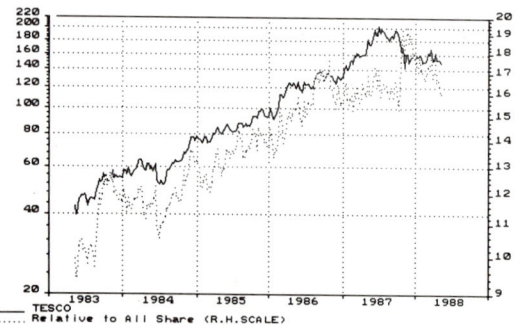

DIRECTORS' HOLDINGS

	Ordinary shares (beneficial)	(non-beneficial)	Convertible loan stock	Options
IC MacLaurin	136,863	90,000	750	406,161
VW Benjamin	75,000	—	—	89,121
AD Malpas	53,015	—	—	240,216
M Darnell	44,375	—	—	122,586
J Gildersleeve	27,000	—	—	152,805
FRN Krejsa	65,346	—	—	365,973
D O'Cathain	3,005	—	—	—
JMF Padovan	3,600	—	—	—
JA Gardiner	—	—	—	—
Sir Leslie Porter	8,542,453	10,174,341	91,104	5,562
DE Reid	—	—	—	339,974
DC Tuffin	44,052	—	—	130,437

Sir Leslie Porter held in addition £85,320 of the convertible unsecured loan stock non-beneficially.

Total emoluments of the directors in 1988 were £1.48m, of which the chairman, who was the highest-paid director, received £196,951.

PRINCIPAL SUBSIDIARIES AND RELATED COMPANIES

Tesco Stores Ltd, operated and registered in England and Tesco Insurance Ltd, operated and registered in Guernsey, are the only subsidiary companies which principally affect the amount of the profit or assets of the group. The issued share capitals of Tesco Stores Ltd and Tesco Insurance Ltd consist of £1 ordinary shares, wholly owned by Tesco PLC.

BRAND NAMES

Tesco

CONTACTS AND FURTHER INFORMATION

Lucinda Davies, Tesco PLC, City & Commercial Communications, Bell Court House, 11 Blomfield Street, London EC2M 7AY. Tel: 01-588 6050.

GENERAL INFORMATION

Head office	THORN EMI House, 4 Tenterden Street, Hanover Square, London W1R 9AH. Tel: 01-836 2444
Directors	Sir Graham Wilkins (chairman), C Southgate (chief executive), J Maxmin PhD, T Mayer CBE, Bhaskar Menon, R Nellist FCA. *Non-exec* M Angus, Sir William Barlow, D Barnes CBE, Sir Ian Trethowan
Advisers	No specified adviser
Auditors	Ernst & Whinney
Registrars	National Westminster Bank Registrar's Department
Brokers	Rowe & Pitman Ltd
Solicitors	Rowe and Maw

GENERAL FINANCIAL INFORMATION

Market capitalisation	£1.456bn at 1 January 1988
Capital structure	
Issued ordinary shares (25p)	217.6m
Issued preference shares (£1)	0.5m 3.5% CP
Warrants	12.96m, one ordinary share at 555p
Convertibles	£63.5m 7.0% second CP 1992/99 (four preference shares for 1.002 ordinary shares)
Traded options	Yes
ADRs	One ordinary share per every ADR
Shareholders over 5%	Prudential Corporation 5.2%

FT CATEGORY

FT: Electricals
FT-A: Leisure

MAJOR ACTIVITIES

THORN EMI is the leading television and video recorder rental group in the world. It also has a range of other consumer activities including lighting, music, small kitchen appliances, and retail outlets for brown goods, white goods and music. There are also activities in technology (principally defence electronics), security and software. The balance of THORN EMI's operations is made up by: INMOS, the UK transputer company originally funded by the Government; Thorn Ericsson Telecommunications; and THORN EMI Flow Measurement. There are extensive overseas operations.

After a period of severe problems and an extensive restructuring programme, including cost reduction and sell-offs of many activities, THORN EMI is now focused in four divisional headings.

Rental and retail is the largest, with just over a third of sales and just under three-quarters of operating profits in the year to March 1987. The technology and entertainment divisions each contribute a quarter of sales and around 15% of profits. The consumer and commercial division is smaller and provides the remainder of sales and profits. Roughly two-thirds of sales and profits are generated in the UK, while the rest splits half to Europe and half elsewhere.

In UK rental and retail, THORN EMI operates four major rental brands – Radio Rentals, DER, Focus and MultiBroadcast; the Rumbelows retail chain, to which Vallances in Yorkshire has recently been added; and the expanding HMV record shops.

There is a parallel operation called Fona in Denmark, and rental activities in 18 other countries around the world. The recent acquisitions of Rent-A-Center in the US and Granada rental operations in Denmark, France, Italy, Switzerland and Spain have further strengthened the rental and retail division of the company. THORN EMI is the leading world distributor of brown goods.

In entertainment the main activity is the music business

							Price (p)		PER (x)		Yield (%)	
F I V E Y E A R F I N A N C I A L I N F O R M A T I O N												
Year	Turnover (£m)	Pre-tax (£m)	Earnings (p)	Dividends net (p)	Dividend cover (x)	Net assets (p)	High	Low	High	Low	High	Low
1983	2,716	122.0	35.4	15.8	2.2	347	476	373	24.9	15.6	5.00	3.44
1984	2,821	156.8	47.8	17.5	2.7	365	643	411	23.8	9.4	6.65	3.34
1985	3,204	108.3	29.9	17.5	1.7	307	687	376	17.0	8.9	8.14	5.17
1986	3,316	104.7	26.5	17.5	1.5	271	484	307	22.4	11.1	6.63	4.77
1987	3,185	159.5	43.9	18.5	2.4	291	803	440	25.1	11.2	5.76	3.05

where THORN EMI operates major record labels such as Capitol and EMI/Manhattan. THORN EMI also makes compact discs with pressing capacity in the UK, the US and in Japan jointly with Toshiba and is a leading music publisher. The other contributor to this division is the associate investment of 28.75% in Thames Television.

Technology includes: THORN Security, in fire and burglar alarms; Software Sciences and Datasolve in software; defence activities in fuzes, thermal imaging, radar and some transport engineering products; a joint venture with Ericsson, Thorn Ericsson, in telecommunications; and the INMOS semiconductor activity with its emerging transputer 'computer on a chip'.

Consumer and commercial includes lighting and Kenwood small domestic appliances. THORN Lighting is UK market leader alongside GEC's Osram and Philips and also makes significant overseas sales. The recent acquisition of Jarnkonst, in Sweden, has confirmed THORN's position as the world's leading lighting fittings manufacturer outside the US and Japan.

Since 1985, THORN EMI has sold off a number of activities, including most recently its loss-making Ferguson television manufacturing activity to Thomson of France and its major domestic appliance activities to Electrolux. THORN EMI has also sold its film-making operation, part of its holding in Thames Television, THORN EMI Heating and several smaller operations.

Overall 60 businesses were sold for £364m, reducing the assets employed by £390m and employees by 18,500. The businesses were making a net annual loss of around £20m. The sale of group headquarters realised a major profit of £22m. A profit was also made on selling part of its Thames Television stake when it went public. The net result of the restructuring was a small capital profit.

The group is a major factor in most of its markets, competing with Granada in television rental, and a wide range of companies in retail. In defence technology, THORN EMI competes with GEC, Racal, Plessey and STC. In software, competitors include CAP, Logica, Systems Designers and Hoskyns. In music, competitors include Phonogram, Warner, CBS and other major US companies as well as independents. In food processing, THORN EMI meets Philips, Moulinex and Braun.

The principal influences on profitability are consumer spending, along with general economic conditions and interest rates. In addition, and particularly since the recent major deal to buy the US rental operation Rent-a-Center, exchange rates are becoming important.

FINANCIAL HISTORY

Thorn Electrical Industries acquired EMI in 1979/80 and, after some initial reasonable progress in sorting out EMI's problems, hoped to move forward. However, a series of

problems in a number of businesses, together with the acquisition of INMOS, led to a profits fall from a peak of almost £190m in 1983/84 to £154m in 1985/86. The earnings were equally problematic since shares were issued to buy INMOS, falling over the same two years from 47.8p to 26.5p.

Subsequently major management changes were led by non-executive directors in 1985. Since then there has been a major restructuring of the group. Profits rose from £104.7m in 1985/86 to £159.5m in 1986/87 with around £215m in view to March 1988 and perhaps £265m in the following year.

The 1986/87 recovery allowed the first dividend increase for three years, with earnings cover over two times compared to one a half times at its lowest. Margins are still low at 5% pre-tax but are better than at their lowest, when they were 3.2%. The sales of assets allowed debt to be reduced, so interest costs are falling. The return on capital recovered to 26% in 1986/87 from its low of 14.9% in 1984/85.

At the 1987/88 interim, pre-tax profits were 46.3% up on turnover 5.0% down at £1.421bn. All divisions performed well, with a strong turnaround in the music and consumer and commercial divisions. Earnings per share were 41.2% up at 13.7p.

In May 1988 THORN EMI announced the successful completion of a £450m multiple option facility.

SHARE PRICE HISTORY

The share price followed the downward slide of the company and then recovered strongly in 1987 as the benefits of the rationalisation became evident. The price rose by 77% from its low in the period leading to the results for 1986/87.

THORN EMI placed 53m shares at 695p for cash to acquire Rent-A-Center in August 1987. The shares were then hit by the general market collapse in autumn 1987 and shareholders virtually ignored their pre-emption rights to acquire the placed shares. The shares have performed strongly since, trading around 635p in early May 1988.

SENIOR MANAGEMENT

The chairman, Sir Graham Wilkins, led the rationalisation programme, but has now handed over the role of chief executive to Colin Southgate. The other executive directors are: Jim Maxmin, home electronics; Tom Mayer, technology; Bhaskar Menon, music; and Bob Nellist, finance. The non-executive directors are Michael Angus, Sir William Barlow, David Barnes and Sir Ian Trethowan.

CAPITAL

THORN had 219.5m ordinary shares in issue but the purchase of Rent-A-Center required a further 53.5m shares to be issued to make a total of 273m. Gearing fell from 58% in 1985/86 to 38% by the end of 1986/87 and has continued to fall. At the

1987/88 interim stage, gearing was between 15% and 20% of shareholders' funds.

There is £63.5m convertible preference stock in issue, but the effect of conversion on earnings is virtually nil for ordinary shareholders after saving the preference dividend payment. There are in addition 12.96m warrants outstanding each giving the right to subscribe for one ordinary share at 555p up to January 1992. The dilution effect of these is also minimal.

The Prudential Corporation held 5.2% of the shares prior to the Rent-A-Center issue. There are no other declared substantial holdings.

GROUP REVIEW

The restructuring of the group by the current management team has been one of the more remarkable industrial events of the mid-1980s.

Although the group reports under four divisional headings, it really contains six core areas. They are rental and retail, groupable as home electronics; music; lighting; security; defence electronics; and software.

Of the six cores, two (home electronics and music) now operate on a global scale, two others (lighting and security) are capable of global scale and the remaining two (defence and software) are international.

Broadly the group's restructuring, while greatly enhancing its financial strength, has put the management in a position to exploit all the opportunities of its main business areas by investment for organic growth or by acquisition, and the next few years are likely to see a high level of corporate activity by THORN EMI. The planned reduction of the group's share premium account and creation of a reserve against which the goodwill arising on acquisitions can be written off, has advertised to shareholders that they should expect a number of strategic acquisitions.

Rental and retail The restructuring of the group has left rental and retail the largest business area, likely to account for over 60% of profits in the year to March 1988.

The television rental market overall has been shrinking for some years in the UK, but THORN EMI has been able to gain market share by careful marketing, improvement of the service element of the rental deal and continuous upgrading of its machine base. Many commentators continue to believe that further declines in the rental subscriber base are likely, but THORN EMI's researches indicate that this is not necessarily

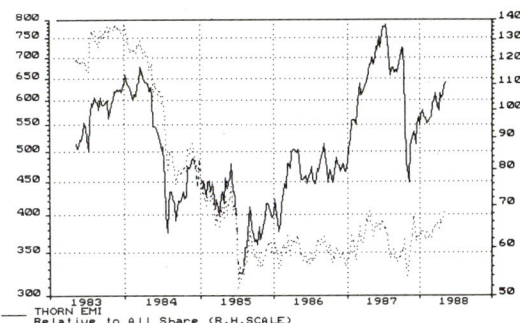

Share price and relative to FT-A All-Share

THORN EMI
Relative to All Share (R.H.SCALE)

so, and the acquisition of Rent-a-Center in the US has brought a new dimension to the group's outlook in this area.

THORN EMI's UK rental operations are segmented with four increasingly targeted brands. The fast growing Rent-a-Center chain in the US is broadly undifferentiated, while on the Continent, national qualities have different characteristics, with in Sweden, for example, rental having a premium cachet.

In retail the current THORN EMI management has repositioned Rumbelows, moving its rental activities out and concentrating on sales with newly designed outlets to capitalise on a niche market for brown and white goods retail. Similar attention has been given to the HMV store chain as more outlets are opened across the country. HMV is beginning to respond strongly to significant investment.

Lighting and Kenwood Lighting requires continuous investment in modernisation in highly competitive and cyclical market conditions. Despite this THORN EMI's strong market position is being maintained. THORN EMI has the world's fourth largest lighting business and is seeking to strengthen its position by integration of service and fittings capabilities and by acquisitions. Following the £15.9m November 1987 acquisition of the Swedish manufacturer Jarnkonst, THORN EMI bid for the quoted French group Holophare in April 1988 and announced a fittings manufacturing joint venture in Malaysia in May 1988.

A similar pattern is also true for Kenwood, THORN EMI's international small kitchen appliances business. 80% of turnover and 75% of profits are derived from outside the UK. It remains to be seen how far the existing product range permits international expansion.

Music Slippage in past years has meant that major investment in new artists has been needed since 1985. This is now beginning to achieve improved results. THORN EMI's focus is on the American market, which accounts for over 40% of sales worldwide and where its market stance has been underweight. The group is a leading world music publisher.

Technology Technology has generally been difficult, particularly due to reductions in the growth of defence expenditure and the very severe downturn in semiconductor markets. Restructuring and new products are enabling the defence order book to rebuild slowly and export prospects have improved.

INMOS remains a significant problem since acceptance of the transputer has been slow, but basic profitability is now within reach and the success of CLUT (colour look-up table) has significantly enhanced the prospects. The facilities, however, require continuous investment and THORN EMI is

---

C H A I R M A N ' S   S T A T E M E N T

'The contrast between your Company's fortunes now, and when I was invited to become Chairman and Chief Executive, in July 1985, substantiates the programme of actions initiated and demonstrates the energy with which they have been pursued by our management team.

Whilst certain problems have still to be resolved and operating efficiency must be increased further, the sustained improvement achieved to date provides a much better base for the future.

By concentrating on improving returns on capital employed, and on sharpening the efficiency of our financial management and utilisation of our assets, we have achieved a reduction in gearing over the last two years, while maintaining satisfactory levels of investment in the mainstream businesses.' *Sir Graham Wilkins*

---

actively seeking a partner to share this business, although since the Rent-A-Center acquisition this is perhaps a less urgent priority. The sale of the US manufacturing plant in Colorado Springs to Cray Research was announced in April 1988.

THORN EMI's restructuring is now said by its management to be substantially complete, and with divestments having reduced both gearing and future funding requirements the group is set to see steady progress with above average growth prospects.

The Rent-A-Center acquisition adds a growth dimension with around $50m of profits in a full year and a 35% annual growth rate, so better than average progress across an international consumer grouping now looks possible.

GEOGRAPHICAL REVIEW

Television rental is carried on throughout Europe and elsewhere and profitability has been rising steadily in recent years. The Fona retail activity in Denmark was, however, severely impacted by government credit restrictions. Music is very much an international business, with the bulk of revenues in the US. Security is active in the Far East and Europe, and defence electronics has an important manufacturing presence in California. The software business is increasingly international in scope.

Overall, THORN EMI aims to increase the international part of the business from the current one-third to over half and the Rent-A-Center acquisition comes a long way towards achieving this.

Europe takes around three-quarters of the business and the Americas have around 15%. Australasia has 5%, as does the combination of Asia and Africa.

CORPORATE CALENDAR

Year end	31 March
Preliminary results	July
Report and accounts	August
AGM	September
Final dividend paid	October
Interim results	December
Interim dividend paid	March

DIRECTORS' HOLDINGS

	Fully-paid ordinary shares	Options
Sir Graham Wilkins	9,935	177,500
CG Southgate	32,401	140,541+
Sir William Barlow	1,233	—
JDF Barnes	500	—
Sir Trevor Holdsworth	1,241	—
HJ Maxmin	106	110,041+
T Mayer	—	63,223+
RHH Nellist	—	82,000
IH Owen	444	91,473+
Sir John Read	1,946	—
Sir Ian Trethowan	400	—

+Includes ordinary shares under the Savings Related Share Option Scheme.

Total directors' remuneration in 1986/87 was £1.07m, of which the chairman received £172,500 and the highest-paid director £185,444.

PRINCIPAL SUBSIDIARIES AND RELATED COMPANIES

Capitol Industries – EMI Inc – US, EMI Records Ltd, INMOS International plc (99.9%), Kenwood Ltd, Thames Television PLC (28.75%), THORN EMI (Australia) Ltd (75.0%), THORN EMI Electronics Ltd, THORN EMI Home Electronics (UK) Ltd, THORN EMI Technology Group, Thorn Ericsson Telecommunications (Holdings) Ltd (51%), THORN Lighting Ltd, Toshiba-EMI Ltd – Japan (50%)

BRAND NAMES

Capitol, DER, Datasolve, EMI, EMI/Manhattan, Fona, Focus, HMV, Kenwood, Mazda, Modulight, Multibroadcast, Radio Rentals, Rumbelows, Software Sciences, Thorn

CONTACTS AND FURTHER INFORMATION

Sharon J Curley, THORN EMI plc, 4 Tenterden Street, Hanover Square, London W1A 2AY. Tel: 01-836 2444.

TRAFALGAR HOUSE PUBLIC LIMITED COMPANY

GENERAL INFORMATION

Head office	1 Berkeley Street, London W1A 1BY. Tel: 01-499 9020
Directors	Sir Nigel Broackes (chairman), EW Parker (group chief executive), DM Calverley, JWS Fletcher, I Fowler, AG Gormly, VA Grundy, AG Kennedy OBE, DStJ McDermott, JR Williamson. *Non-exec* GHB Carter, AW Clements, GE Knight CBE, WB Slater CBE VRD, The Marquess of Tavistock
Advisers	Kleinwort Benson Ltd
Auditors	Touche Ross & Co
Registrars	Ravensbourne Registration Services Ltd
Brokers	Shearson Lehman Hutton, Cazenove & Co
Solicitors	Ashurst Morris Crisp

GENERAL FINANCIAL INFORMATION

Market capitalisation	£1.51bn at 1 January 1988
Capital structure	
Issued ordinary shares (20p)	488.5m
Issued preference shares (£1)	1.5m 5.075% CP
	24.9m 3.5% CP
Warrants	None
Convertibles	None
Traded options	Yes
ADRs	One ADR equals five ordinary shares
Shareholders over 5%	None

FT CATEGORY

FT: Industrials (miscel.)
FT-A: Conglomerates

MAJOR ACTIVITIES

Trafalgar House has grown from its original property core to become a diversified company with substantial interests in property development and housebuilding, construction and engineering, cargo and passenger shipping and hotels. It also includes a number of small oil and gas exploration companies in the UK and US. The group has expanded on a basis of synergistic acquisitions.

Following a period of emphasis outside property, Trafalgar House is now concentrating more on its original core. It acquired Broseley Estates, a Midlands-based housebuilder, in December 1986 and Comben Homes in 1984 and a number of substantial commercial development sites that will impact on profits in 1988 and beyond. The successful bid for Chase Property Holdings brought the company significant London development projects.

The housebuilding operation, Ideal Homes, is the fourth largest in the UK and the largest single source of profits. It accounted for 28% of the group's total in 1987. The property division, which includes both the housebuilding and property investment activities, forms the largest part of Trafalgar House and provides 54% of the group's profit. This is followed by construction at 27%, shipping and hotels at 15% and oil and gas at 3%.

FINANCIAL HISTORY

Group profits before tax rose by 148% to £163.2m between 1982 and 1987. The 12.0% gain in 1987 on 1986 was achieved despite the inclusion of unusually high profits of £25.6m on the sale of investments being taken above the line in the 1986 figures. This increase in property profits continued to offset a decline from £30.5m in 1985 to £5.6m in 1987 in the oil and gas division contribution.

Trafalgar's oil interests have generally been accepted as having been disappointing. The build-up of the division at the top of the market for £250m preceded profits tumbling from £31.4m in 1985 to just £5.6m in 1987. In 1986 there was a £56m oil-related write-down.

In 1987 there were total provisions of £50.6m, including a provision for putting Scott Lithgow on to a care and maintenance basis, and the cost of remanning arrangements for the *QE2* and other passenger ships.

Earnings per share rose from 20.4p to 34.7p between 1982 and 1985, and subsequently contracted to a fully diluted 31.6p in 1987 but will be usefully up in 1988.

Historically the dividend has increased at an annual rate of 15%, but in the context of a lower inflation rate and the company's recent financial performance, 10% looks a more realistic medium term target.

At the 1988 interim for the six months to 31 March 1988, pre-tax profits increased by 57.7% to £85.3m on turnover 17.6% ahead at £1.207bn. Earnings per share increased by 24.5% before extraordinary items, reflecting the large share placing in summer 1987. There were particularly strong performances from the property and investment and shipping, aviation and hotels divisions.

SHARE PRICE HISTORY

Until late 1985 Trafalgar House's share price had shown substantial gains, rising from a 1982 low of 90p to 405p in late 1985, outperforming the market over this period. However, the collapse in the oil price and the realisation of the impact of this on Trafalgar House's newly constructed oil division, plus the implications of this on the hitherto important offshore construction operations, led to a thorough derating of the shares.

On static earnings the share price subsequently fell to 245p in 1986, falling back in relative terms to a pre-1982 position. Subsequently the appreciation of the potential for profits growth in the housebuilding and property operations, in the construction division with its vastly expanded order book, coupled with the benefits to the shipping business of more efficient capacity, led to a useful recovery in the share price back to late 1985 levels.

During the first half of 1987 there was a period of significant relative out-performance when the shares rose from 245p to 441p at the peak. The share price then suffered a set-back after the one for five share placing and then fell with the rest of the market in the October 1987 crash. The shares have performed well after Black Monday, recovering from a low of 257p to 325p in mid-April 1988.

SENIOR MANAGEMENT

Chairman Sir Nigel Broackes founded the business in 1956 and retains a significant shareholding. More recently he has relinquished posts outside Trafalgar House and is one of the main strategists in the company. Eric Parker, the group chief executive, has had a long career with the company, moving upwards from the role of finance director.

The current finance director, Dermot McDermott, joined Trafalgar House from Esso in 1987 and has a corporate strategy background. David Calverley (who succeeded Geoffrey Carter), property, and Vincent Grundy, construction, are long established. John Williamson, oil, was brought in to run the division in 1982 from BP. Alan Kennedy, shipping and hotels, joined the board in 1986 from Thomas Cook.

John Fletcher is another director with board experience in construction and engineering. He has been with the group for

							Price (p)		PER (x)		Yield (%)	
Year	Turnover (£m)	Pre-tax (£m)	Earnings (p)	Dividends net (p)	Dividend cover (x)	Net assets (p)	High	Low	High	Low	High	Low
1983	1,344	79.0	24.4	8.5	2.9	105.9	216	147	14.9	11.6	7.32	5.52
1984	1,614	113.2	30.6	10.0	3.1	121.1	332	196	18.4	12.3	6.68	4.23
1985	1,912	142.5	34.7	11.5	3.0	159.1	397	325	19.1	15.2	5.04	3.70
1986	2,071	145.8	32.7	13.2	2.4	119.8	349	250	15.9	10.1	7.44	4.71
1987	2,369	163.2	31.6	14.5	2.2	155.0	435	268	25.5	11.7	6.90	4.25

FIVE YEAR FINANCIAL INFORMATION

many years. He is presently responsible for business development and marketing. The appointment of Allan Gormly, following the John Brown acquisition in 1986, has strengthened the construction team. Ian Fowler is the company secretary. All executive directors are also members of the Chief Executive's Committee.

CAPITAL

Trafalgar's high level of capital spending in the last three years, particularly on the *QE2* in 1986/87, and the build-up of the property development portfolio, led to a significantly higher level of debt and higher gearing. Since 1983 net debt rocketed from £61.5m to £264m in 1986, and rose further to £437m in July 1987. During this period net gearing jumped from 23½% to over 70%.

A rights issue raised £170m in 1985, whilst equity valued at £110m was raised in 1987 to finance the acquisitions of Broseley Estates and Ellerman Lines. In summer 1987, the group raised £306m through a placing. This was intended to finance the purchase of Pension Fund Property Unit Trust. When this proved abortive, the issue had the immediate effect of increasing shareholders' funds to £700m, reducing net debt to £130m, and net gearing to 14%. Debt was subsequently eliminated by the year-end as a result of major property sales.

Increasingly Trafalgar House should become more strongly cash-positive as cash generation improves, for example from the *QE2* modernisation programme and the progressive sale of property in the course of development. The net asset value at the 1987 year-end was 155p.

The £198m acquisition of Chase Property Holdings is to be financed with cash. Net gearing will grow to 35%, but is expected to be reduced significantly as mature investment properties are sold. Trafalgar's balance sheet is enviably strong.

GROUP REVIEW

Property and investment The housebuilding operations are booming in the current very buoyant market conditions. Trafalgar House, following the acquisition of Broseley, is the UK's fourth largest, and probably the most profitable, of the major housebuilders. In 1987 Trafalgar built 5,500 houses, and has a 17,000-plot land bank. The company is active in seeking substantial sites in the major development areas. The company is involved with three or four green-field sites as country towns.

Ideal Homes is almost certainly the UK's most profitable housebuilder. Bringing the margins of Broseley Estates, acquired in December 1986, up to Ideal's as its operation trades up, will mean this important division should outperform the UK sector average in the medium term. About 5,500 houses should be completed in 1988.

Trafalgar has a reinvigorated interest in property develop-

ment with a number of important M25 corridor sites in the course of development. It also has a growing start-up operation in the tristate area of the north-east US. The recent $20m acquisition of Capital Homes, which operates in the Washington DC area, has helped to restore the group's small existing housebuilding operation in the north-east US and expanded its US housebuilding interests. The total developed value of the group's projects in the US exceeds $350m.

In the south-east of the UK a number of office sites are under development in the City and West End, including those of St Mary Axe Developments, bought in partnership with ARC Properties from Inchcape for £22m cash in October 1987. Elsewhere there is strong retail content in a business park, office and leisure portfolio mix.

Significant profitable property disposals have been made recently and more are expected in 1988 and beyond. Chase Property Holdings has enhanced the development portfolio substantially and contributes a useful number of modest City and West End medium term projects, thus improving profits visibility.

Turnover for the property and investment division for 1987 was up £183.0m to £534.9m. Profit was up £29.5m to £105.9m. At the 1988 interim, divisional pre-tax profits were 47.2% up at £50.5m, reflecting a continuing buoyant performance from commercial and residential property.

Construction and engineering The offshore business is faltering but there are prospects for a revival in 1989. Scott Lithgow, the subject of a massive 1987 provision, is to be put on a care and maintenance basis. Trafalgar House issued a writ against British Shipbuilders in April 1988, claiming damages of £186m for costs incurred after the acquisition of the business. John Brown, however, is prospering with a large number of contracts in hand. John Brown is also well placed to tap the potentially lucrative market for flue gas desulphurisation in the UK and the construction of proposed privatised power stations. In April 1988 John Brown set up the first joint Soviet–British engineering company and has the contract to modernise and expand two large polyethylene plants in the USSR.

The level of construction activity in the south-east is booming. An increase in the number of government funded infrastructure projects, particularly motorway and road building, has led to a substantially increased long term work load and should cause some firming of margins medium term – UK construction industry order books were up 22% in the last quarter of 1987.

Out-of-town retail store construction is very buoyant. The commercial steel operations are experiencing a massive surge in demand as the method of office building has switched to the fast-track principle. Cleveland Bridge & Engineering recently won the contract for the structural steel frame for the principal tower at the Canary Wharf project in London's Docklands. Margins have firmed considerably.

The Dartford Bridge contract, with its unique financing

package, is a major long term gain for the company. Work is expected to begin in late summer 1988. Gammon Construction of Hong Kong, owned jointly with Jardine Matheson, has recently been awarded a £145m franchise to build, own and operate a major new road tunnel between the New Territories in Hong Kong and the Kowloon peninsula. Overall it is believed that the order book has expanded from £900m in 1986 to £1.4bn in early 1988.

Cementation – SAUR Water Services, a Trafalgar House/ Bouyges SA joint venture, has been formed to develop the worldwide demand for water treatment and sewerage plants by providing turnkey packages, incorporating design, construction, finance and operational management services. The joint venture owns 22.6% of the voting stock of the Rickmansworth Water Company and 15.29% of North Surrey Water.

Turnover for the construction and engineering division for 1987 was up £48.0m to £1.35bn. Profits were up £8.7m to £52.9m. At the 1988 interim, divisional pre-tax profits were ¬ 4% up at £20.3m, with a further improvement in John ⌐ own's performance compensating for the timing delay before the enlarged construction order book flows through to profits.

Shipping, aviation and hotels Re-engining the *QE2* and the Associated Container Transportation (Australia) fleet had a negative effect in 1987 as expected. But they promise very significant efficiency gains in 1988 and beyond. The *QE2* upgrade cost over £100m and meant that the ship was out of commission during the first half of fiscal 1987, but the payback period from upgraded accommodation, more suites, and a more fuel-efficient engines that can cross the Atlantic faster, could be as short as four or five years.

Fuel efficiency gains will be made on the Australian service and its performance will be particularly helped by rising freight rates. Trafalgar House is a partner in both this service and the Atlantic Container Line. The Atlantic Container Line container ships have been stretched. The resulting efficiency gains, some industry capacity rationalisation, and the prospect of a rise in freight rates following a period of heavy discounting, combine to make the medium term prospects more encouraging.

The 1987 financial year carried all the costs and strains of the capital investment programme but few of the compensa-

CHAIRMAN'S STATEMENT

'The recent stock market collapse took everyone by surprise and it is still too early to comment on which, if any, of our activities will suffer from the resultant loss of confidence. The worldwide nature of the event gave us all a shock which is not to be under-estimated.

Within Trafalgar House we can only redouble our efforts and continue to be as flexible as possible in our responses. We are well placed to handle a pessimistic scenario, and even better placed to improve our position during a recession of lesser gravity or duration – in either event we continue to plan for the medium and long term future.

Inevitably this year will be harder than could have been foreseen two months ago but so far the only weakness we have observed is in cruise bookings – and in our case passenger shipping starts the year from a low base.

Nearly all prospective dollar revenues are covered on the forward exchange market, and whilst we share the almost universal apprehension of turbulent conditions in the year ahead we enter it with confidence.' *Sir Nigel Broackes*

tory gains. 1988 will show the full benefit of this programme and of the first full year contribution from Ellerman Lines, which was acquired for £24m. This should increase as the benefits of integration with the Cunard fleet come through.

Cunard runs seven cruise liners aimed towards the top luxury end of the market. Whilst 1986 was hit by problems damaging sentiment and bookings, and 1987's *QE2* refit prevented it from maximising profits, the company had looked forward with confidence to achieving its full potential in 1988. However, the depressed stock market and weak dollar has impacted, though to a limited extent, on bookings. However, this is expected to be temporary and the *QE2* has two Japanese charters in 1989 and 1990. HeavyLift Cargo Airlines traded reasonably in 1987.

Share price and relative to FT-A All-Share

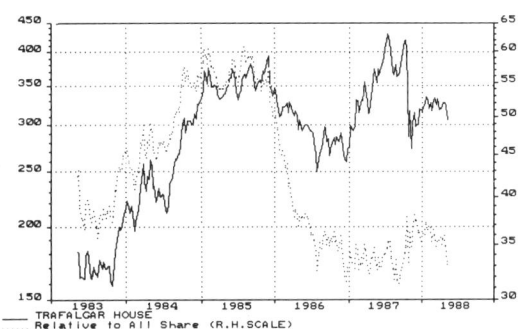

TRAFALGAR HOUSE
Relative to All Share (R.H.SCALE)

The group's hotels include the Ritz and Stafford in London, and one each in Barbados and St Lucia. They are showing a better performance. Trafalgar House is expected to increase its exposure to the luxury US hotel market by the acquisition of further hotel management contracts, adding to the Watergate in Washington and the Bellevue-Stratford in Philadelphia.

Turnover for the shipping, aviation and hotels division for 1987 was up £73m to £456.3m. Profits fell £8.4m to £30.1m. At the 1988 interim, divisional pre-tax profits were 92.6% up at £18.3m. Profits were helped by the return of the *QE2* to service and the acquisition of Ellerman Lines. Cruise ship and hotel booking levels have been affected by the weak dollar and stock market downturn, though the division's revenues are largely protected by hedging.

Oil and gas Trafalgar House's oil and gas interests were assembled in 1983 and were based on the acquisition of Candecca and a stake in the Forties field. The timing of the diversification was not successful, coinciding with both a fall in the oil price and weakness in the dollar, which in the second half of 1986 reduced the division to losses and resulted in a £57m asset write-down.

Profits peaked at £31.4m in 1984 and after £3.8m in 1986 recovered to only £5.6m in 1987. Following the sale of the group's two subsidiaries Candecca Resources and Cambrian Exploration to BP for £21m, the on-shore interests have been reduced to 28 licences. Half Trafalgar House's interest in Humbly Grove was included in the disposal, leaving Trafalgar House with a 12½% interest. Trafalgar House now holds 1.45% of Forties and stakes in 17 other North Sea licence blocks, including the Ravenspurn gas field, where a £534m natural gas drilling project has recently been approved.

In the US, Trafalgar House has interests in a large number of small oil and gas producing prospects. These include gas condensate interests in the Brit Ranch properties in the Texas Panhandle, a 50% stake in the Bear Head gas condensate field in Louisiana and the Spraberry oil field in west Texas, where the group is interested in over 500 wells. Spraberry accounts for an estimated 70% of the group's proven US reserves. Overall total US production is probably 12m cubic feet of gas and 1,500 barrels of oil per day.

The write-down of assets was made when the oil price was $14 to $15 a barrel. Subsequently a brief recovery to $20 a barrel enabled the division to achieve a return to profitability, aided by lower depreciation provisions. The value of the division is now higher than at the time of the write-down. Divisional production for 1987 totalled 2.4m barrels of oil and 4.6bn cubic feet of gas.

Although the prospects for the division may well have passed their worst, Trafalgar House is not expected to wish to expand in oil and gas. Turnover for the oil and gas division for 1987 was down £6.3m to £30m. The profit of £5.6m was a £1.8m improvement on 1986. At the 1988 interim, divisional pre-tax profits were 62.5% up at £3.9m. Both the UK and US operations improved and there are signs of a better future outlook.

GEOGRAPHICAL REVIEW

In 1987, 58.8% of revenues arose within the UK, 15.3% in Europe, the Middle East and Africa, 17.2% in the Americas, and 8.7% in India, the Far East and Australasia. Although no profit analysis is available it is believed that the UK profits bias is significantly greater, boosted recently by the acquisition of Broseley, Chase and Ellerman, and a generally reinvigorated property activity.

CORPORATE CALENDAR

Year end	September
Preliminary results	December
Report and accounts	December
AGM	January
Final dividend paid	February
Interim results	June
Interim dividend paid	July

DIRECTORS' HOLDINGS

	Fully paid	Share options
Sir Nigel Broackes	34,934,83	165,068
EW Parker	2,921	505,364
GHB Carter	5,051	81,910
WB Slater	24,409	68,279
The Marquess of Tavistock	15,000	—
VA Grundy	4,495	91,527
AW Clements	1,440	—
GE Knight	3,200	—
DM Calverley	911	101,204
JWS Fletcher	2,674	101,204
I Fowler	16,638	101,204
JR Williamson	1,500	101,204
AG Kennedy	—	75,000
AG Gormly	138	50,000
DStJ McDermott	—	75,000

Sir Nigel Broackes also held 66,601 ordinary shares non-beneficially.

Total directors' remuneration was £1.2m, of which the chairman received £160,000, and the group chief executive, who was the highest-paid director, received £236,000.

PRINCIPAL SUBSIDIARIES AND RELATED COMPANIES

United Kingdom
ABS Computers (Allied Business Systems Limited), Agent Plant Group Limited, Anderson Firmin & Collins Limited, Cementation Construction Limited, Cementation Frankipile Limited, Cementation Mining Limited, Cementation Piling and Foundations Limited, Cementation – SAUR Water Services Limited (50%), Cementation Research Limited, Chase Property Holdings plc, Cityline Catering Limited, CJB Developments Limited, Clark & Fenn Limited, Cleveland Bridge & Engineering Company Limited, Collin Wilson Insurance Brokers (London) Limited, Cunard Arabian Middle East Line, Cunard Crusader World Travel Limited, Cunard Ellerman Limited, Cunard Ellerman Shipping Services Limited, Cunard Hotels Limited, Cunard Line Limited, Dartford River Crossing Limited, Dowsett Construction Limited, Ellerman Lines PLC, G Jackson & Sons Limited, HE Moss & Co Limited, HeavyLift Cargo Airlines Limited (66.7%), Ideal Homes Anglia Limited, Ideal Homes East London Limited, Ideal Homes Holdings p.l.c., Ideal Homes London Limited, Ideal Homes Midlands Limited, Ideal Homes North East Limited, Ideal Homes Northern Limited, Ideal Homes North West Limited, Ideal Homes Scotland Limited, Ideal Homes Solent Limited, Ideal Homes Southern Limited, Ideal Homes South West Limited, Ideal Homes Thames Limited, Ideal Homes Wales Limited, Ideal Homes Western Limited, John Brown Automation Limited, John Brown Engineering Limited, John Brown Engineers & Construction Limited, John Brown Plastics Machinery Limited, John Brown PLC, Markham & Co Limited, Rashleigh Phipps Electrical Limited, RDL Contracting Limited, Redpath Dorman Long Limited, Redpath Engineering Services Limited, Redpath Offshore, RGC Offshore PLC, Richard Lees Limited, Samuel Elliott & Sons Limited, Scott Lithgow Limited, The Cunard Steam-Ship Company p.l.c., The Ritz Hotel (London) Limited, The Stafford Hotel Limited, Thermo Acoustic Products Limited, TH Engineering Services Limited, Trafalgar Brookmount Limited (80%), Trafalgar House Building and Civil Engineering Holdings Limited, Trafalgar House Business Parks Limited, Trafalgar House Construction Holdings Limited, Trafalgar House Developments Limited, Trafalgar House Offshore and Structural Limited, Trafalgar House Oil & Gas Limited, Trafalgar House Property Limited, Trafalgar House Residential Limited, Trollope & Colls (City) Limited, Trollope & Colls Construction Limited, Trollope & Colls Joinery Limited, Trollope & Colls Management Limited, Willett Limited

Overseas operating companies
ASETCO Limited (50%) – USSR, Capital Homes Inc – US, Cementation International Limited, Cementation (Middle East) Limited, Cemindia Company Limited (51%), Cleveland Bridge & Engineering Middle East (Pty) Limited (32.5%), Crozet Oil and Gas Limited (66.6%), Cunard Hotels and Resorts Inc – US, Cunard Resorts Limited, Dorman Long Overseas Limited, Federal Construction Co, Gammon Construction Limited (50%) – Hong Kong, John Brown Engineers & Constructors Inc – US, John Brown Engineers & Constructors BV – Netherlands, Lawrence-Allison & Associates West Inc – US, The Cementation Company (Africa) Limited (48.9%), The Cementation Company of America Inc – US, The Cementation Company (Zimbabwe) Limited, Trafalgar House Construction Management Inc – US, Trafalgar House Oil and Gas Inc – US, Trafalgar House Real Estate Inc – US, Trafalgar House Residential Inc – US, Trafalgar House Residential (Europe) Limited, Western Polymer Division, John Brown Plastics Machinery Inc – US, Zeetech Engineering BV – Netherlands

BRAND NAMES

Cementation, Cunard, Dowsett, Ideal Homes, *QE2*, Redpath Dorman Long, Ritz, Trollope & Colls, Willett

CONTACTS AND FURTHER INFORMATION

Ian Fowler, Company Secretary, Trafalgar House Public Limited Company, 1 Berkeley Street, London W1A 1BY. Tel: 01-499 9020.

TRUSTHOUSE FORTE PLC

GENERAL INFORMATION

Head office	166 High Holborn, London WC1V 6TT. Tel: 01-836 7744
President	Lord Thorneycroft
Directors	Lord Forte (chairman), Sir Charles Hardie CBE FCA (deputy chairman), The Hon Rocco Forte FCA (chief executive), GB Chiandetti (deputy chief executive), Dennis Hearn FCA (deputy chief executive), BF Combemale, Garry Hawkes, IAH Johnston, DA Main CA, The Hon Mrs O Polizzi, GFL Proctor LLB. *Non-exec* DD Durban CBE FCIS, E Hartwell CBE (vice chairman), Sir David McNee QPM
Council of trustees	The Hon Hugh Astor JP (chairman), The Rt Hon Lord Boyd-Carpenter DL, The Rt Hon The Earl of Gainsborough JP, The Rt Hon Lord Peyton, The Rt Hon The Earl St Aldwyn GBE TD DL, The Rt Hon The Earl of Westmorland KCVO, Sir Paul Wright KCMG OBE
Advisers	No specified adviser
Auditors	Price Waterhouse
Registrars	National Westminster Bank Registrar's Department
Brokers	Phillips & Drew Ltd
Solicitors	Linklaters & Paines, Paisner & Co

GENERAL FINANCIAL INFORMATION

Market capitalisation	£1.714bn at 1 January 1988
Capital structure	
Issued ordinary shares (25p)	782.5m
Trust shares (25p)*	780,000
Issued preference shares	None
Warrants	41.2m (exercise price 226p to 11 March 1992)
Convertibles	None
Traded options	Yes
ADRs	None
Shareholders over 5%	Lord Forte 6.5% (including non-beneficial interests)

On a poll of the company's members the trust shares are entitled to the same number of votes as the holders of all the other shares.

FT CATEGORY

FT: Hotels and caterers
FT-A: Leisure

MAJOR ACTIVITIES

Trusthouse Forte (THF) is primarily a hotel company. The substantial majority of its profits are earned in the UK. THF also has a group of rapidly expanding catering businesses which operate for the most part in the UK and include contract catering, motorway service areas, the Little Chef and Happy Eater chains and Harvester Inns.

Trusthouse Forte has over 800 hotels worldwide, with 240 in the UK, 33 elsewhere in Europe and 21 in North America. Amongst THF's flagship hotels are the Grosvenor House in London, the Plaza Athénée in New York, the George V in Paris and the Ritz in Madrid.

In North America the group owns the 475-strong Travelodge chain, ranging from motels to full service city centre hotels. In December 1987 the group purchased Skylight Inns, a chain of 13 modern economy hotels located in major US cities with a total of 1,500 rooms for £26m in cash.

In the UK Trusthouse Forte is by far the largest hotel operator, being some three times larger than any of its nearest rivals. As most of the properties are owned freehold or long leasehold, the company has good asset backing. THF owns 69% of the equity of the Savoy Group but this represents only 42.3% of the voting rights.

In 1986/87 the group's hotel business outside North America recovered significantly, and the group's expectations that its catering businesses would contribute a greater proportion of the group's trading profits have been fulfilled.

After clearance by the Monopolies and Mergers Commission, THF completed the acquisition in March 1987 of the Anchor Hotel and Imperial Inn hotel chains, and the Happy Eater and Welcome Break roadside restaurant businesses from Hanson for £190m in cash. This acquisition and its joint venture with Kentucky Fried Chicken International increased its catering interests substantially.

THF's catering interests now consist of Gardner Merchant contract catering, the Café Royal, 24 motorway service areas, 385 Little Chef and Happy Eater roadside restaurants, 90 Pier House Inns, a collection of steak houses, café bars and restaurants, and a 50% share in 330 Kentucky Fried Chicken outlets.

THF owns Harvester Inns, presently in the course of rapid expansion following a recent deal with Courage. As a further extension of its interests, THF made an agreed bid for Kennedy Brookes in March 1988, thereby acquiring 1,800 hotel rooms and a number of upmarket restaurants.

FINANCIAL HISTORY

After a disappointing profits performance in 1986 in the aftermath of the Libyan air raid and the Chernobyl disaster, the group enjoyed greatly improved results for the year ended 31 October 1987. Sales grew by 20% to £1.778bn. Pre-tax profits were up by 33% to £180m. Earnings per share were up by 31% to 16.3p. Dividends were up 18% to 7.1p. Net assets per share were up 43% to 202p. Gearing was reduced from 47% to 28%. A property revaluation produced a surplus of £484m and brought the total value of fixed assets to over £2.1bn.

Over the past four years pre-tax profit has grown by an annual average of 26.3%, with the proportion earned by the group's catering operations increasing from 20% to 32%.

SHARE PRICE HISTORY

Since 1984, THF's share price has broadly matched the FT-A All-Share index, although progress has been far from steady. During 1986, disappointing interim results and the shortage of

---

GROUP CHIEF EXECUTIVE'S STATEMENT

'The record profit of £180m before tax in 1987 continues the excellent growth of the last five years and is treble the figure of five years ago. This result was particularly encouraging, not only because of the very healthy improvement of 33 per cent over last year, but also because so many different parts of the Group contributed to that improvement.

We have continued to expand our operations by developing our core businesses and introducing new brands, whilst at the same time improving the products and operating margins in our existing operations....

We have continued to invest heavily with a £192 million programme of capital expenditure in the year ended October 1987. This policy will continue with a forecast spend of £210m (£150m in the UK) which will continue to underpin the Company's longer term profit growth....

... the work we have done over the past few years in expanding our operational base and in the development of our people will ensure strong growth in profitability for the Group in the coming years.' *Rocco Forte*

F I V E Y E A R F I N A N C I A L I N F O R M A T I O N												
Year	Turnover (£m)	Pre-tax (£m)	Earnings (p)	Dividends net (p)	Dividend cover (x)	Net assets (p)	Price (p) High	Low	PER (x) High	Low	Yield (%) High	Low
1983	1,012.0	82.1	7.9	4.1	1.9	81	98	76	31.6	21.6	6.53	5.10
1984	1,148.6	105.2	9.4	4.7	2.0	104	146	93	32.1	20.7	5.89	2.46
1985	1,244.5	129.6	11.1	5.4	2.1	117	162	119	32.2	17.8	5.86	3.79
1986	1,476.5	136.0	12.4	6.0	2.1	141	208	140	24.6	15.6	5.54	3.74
1987	1,778.0	180.0	16.3	7.1	2.3	202	290	178	25.8	13.5	4.77	2.93

tourists from North America, led to a substantial underperformance.

The share price fell with the FT-A All-Share index in the autumn of 1987. Subsequently its recovery to around 230p in mid-March 1988 was an outperformance of the index. Despite the problems posed by its share structure in any takeover of THF, there have been persistent bid rumours.

SENIOR MANAGEMENT

The chairman, Lord Forte, was the driving force behind the development of the company following its formation in 1970 through the merger of the Trusthouse hotel group with his own company Forte Holdings.

Lord Forte's son, The Hon Rocco Forte, took over as chief executive in 1983. Tito Chiandetti and Dennis Hearn became deputy chief executives at the same time. Tito Chiandetti heads up the group's food and catering services while Dennis Hearn is managing director of Trusthouse Forte Hotels.

Of the other executive board members, Garry Hawkes is managing director of Gardner Merchant, Ian Johnston is chairman of Trusthouse Forte Supplies, Donald Main is group finance director, The Hon Mrs Olga Polizzi is director of building and design and George Proctor is director of group commercial, legal and property services. Bernard Combemale is chairman and chief executive officer of Trusthouse Forte Inc, the US subsidiary.

Lord Thorneycroft is president.

CAPITAL

Since its narrow escape from a takeover attempt by Allied Breweries, now Allied-Lyons, in the early 1970s, Trusthouse Forte has issued relatively little new capital other than through a one for five rights issue in 1976, a one for four rights issue in 1981 and through capitalisation issues. There are 782m ordinary shares in issue.

Warrants to buy a further 41m ordinary shares at an exercise price of 226p were issued in February 1987 attached to an £85m issue of sterling Eurobonds with a coupon of 11.25% at 119%, giving net proceeds of approximately £99m.

The share structure of the company is unusual in that in addition to the ordinary shares there are 780,000 trust shares, which are controlled by a council of trustees, and which on a poll are entitled to the same number of votes as the holders of all the other shares. The existence of the trust shares is therefore a significant obstacle to any potential predator.

The chairman of the trustees is The Rt Hon Hugh Astor. The other trustees are The Rt Hon Lord Boyd-Carpenter, The Rt Hon The Earl of Gainsborough, The Rt Hon Lord Peyton, The Rt Hon The Earl St Aldwyn, The Rt Hon The Earl of Westmorland and Sir Paul Wright.

GROUP REVIEW

Hotels In the year to 31 October 1987 hotels in London recovered from the sudden unexpected downturn in North American visitors during 1986. The provincial UK hotel market continued to do well. In common with other major UK operators Trusthouse Forte's main source of profit growth in the UK hotel business has been a programme of hotel upgrading and refurbishment with subsequent tariff increases. Several new buildings are being added to the Post House chain each year.

THF has 17 hotels with 7,100 rooms in London and 195 UK provincial hotels with 14,200 rooms. With London tariffs significantly higher than provincial tariffs, the contribution of the much larger London hotels is clearly substantial.

In 1986/87 THF increased trading profits from its UK hotels by 27% to £110m, excluding its share of Savoy Hotel profits (which it does not consolidate). After strong efforts to broaden its market, North American tourists account for only 25% of THF's London business compared with 45% in pre-Libyan bombing and Chernobyl days. The group believes that this lower level should protect THF adequately from any reduction in North American tourists which might follow any further fall in the dollar. The share of Savoy Hotel profits contributed £9m.

THF's stake in Savoy Hotel is one of the longer standing odd sagas in the City at the moment. Although THF owns over 69% of the Savoy shares, Savoy's 'A' and 'B' capital structure – and in particular the tightness with which its 'B' shares are held – deny THF control of the group. In the period in which THF has been sitting on Savoy's shoulder, Savoy's profits have leaped ahead perhaps almost to the point where the management is now beginning to depend on the market's vicissitudes for significant further growth in profits. But acquisitions for paper would upset the balance of control and so are ruled out, in spite of THF's majority ownership.

The impasse may be resolved by moves THF is now making in the courts to question the legitimacy of issue of a part of Savoy's capital. But if these moves were to fail, it is difficult to foresee a solution, at least in Lord Forte's lifetime.

In the US, the major city centre hotels have performed satisfactorily, but the performance of the TraveLodge chain has continued to be somewhat disappointing, and has not yet responded to a radical management reorganisation. Trading profits for the group's US hotels for 1986/87 were up 9% to £9m.

New visa requirements restricted US tourism to France and this helped hold back the performance of the group's hotels in Europe. Trading profits for THF's hotels in Europe and elsewhere outside the UK and North America were up 10% to £16m.

Kennedy Brookes brings to THF on the hotel side the five-star Londonderry Hotel on Park Lane, adding usefully to

THF's existing Mayfair status (it already owns the Grosvenor House). It also brings the 172-room Onslow Hotel in Kensington, a four-star freehold, as opposed to the 103-year leasehold on the Londonderry. After the acquisition, THF's London portfolio amounts to over 7,500 rooms. In addition, Kennedy Brookes' hotels bring the 107-room Howard Hotel in Manhattan, and about 20 UK provincial hotels of a broad range of types. The majority of the portfolio had been purchased in 1987 by Kennedy Brookes as it sought to diversify from its traditional restaurant base.

Share price and relative to FT-A All-Share

TRUSTHOUSE FORTE
Relative to All Share (R.H.SCALE)

Catering The catering businesses, based for the most part in the UK, are seen by the company as the strongest area of profits growth in the near future. Not only do they present good opportunities for development, but their improvement requires very much less capital than the hotels.

The acquisition of the former Imperial businesses from Hanson has significantly strengthened THF's presence in the public catering and motorway service area market. This has gone up to 24 units. Its nearest competitor Granada has 16 units. In the branded roadside restaurant market, where the Happy Eater and Little Chef restaurant businesses of 385 outlets are the only operators of any size, THF is the dominant operator.

The 90 Pier House Inns, which were also part of the Hanson deal, consisted of 49 steak houses and 31 other restaurants and café bars. This division now plans over 100 outlets branded as the Harvester chain and Dome café bars and will expand very substantially following a recent deal with Courage to take over the running of a number of pubs. The trading profits of the catering businesses acquired from Hanson doubled to £24.5m in 1986/87, their first year under THF management.

THF has begun to capitalise on the Little Chef name and its hotel expertise by developing the Little Chef Lodge chain which may be 50-strong by the end of 1988. The chain offers single accommodation for £19.50 a night and is filling a gap which constant upgrading of existing chains and the development of the road network have opened up. Unchanged since 1985, the rates now offer reasonable value.

The Gardner Merchant contract catering business is projected to achieve very significant growth in the near future, as opportunities to build on the 3,500 existing contracts in hospitals, schools, and various self-operated factory or office staff restaurants are developed. Over 1,000 of the current contracts are operated overseas, and because of the nature of the business, expansion will require virtually no capital.

Contract catering also includes the airport services division of THF which continues to have a fine record of operation and

expansion in an extremely competitive market. This division also includes airport retailing operations where THF has been successful with some very high turnover specialities such as Shirt Factor and Drug Store.

For 1986/87, trading profits for the group's catering sector as a whole were up by a stunning 57% to £63.4m. The public catering businesses were up no less than 86%. Those for contract catering were up 24% to £23m.

The Kennedy Brookes catering interests bought include the Wheeler's chain, Mario & Franco's restaurants in London, Crusts and a clutch of individual London restaurants (including Locket's, Genevieve, the Braganza and L'Opera Terrasse). Finally, Kennedy Brookes adds the 50%-owned London Pavilion, a development site in London's Docklands, a fishmonger, a very successful wine merchants and an outside catering business.

Miscellaneous activities These include: food wholesaler Puritan Maid; Stangard, a commercial kitchen manufacturer; Giusti, a specialist manufacturer of pressure vessels; Lillywhites, the department stores; and Grosvenor Theatrical Products, the music and entertainment service for hotels and catering establishments within and outside the group. They made combined trading profits of £4m in 1986/87, the same as in 1985/86.

GEOGRAPHICAL REVIEW

In 1986/87 4.5% of the group's trading profits came from North America, and 8.1% from continental Europe and elsewhere outside the UK and North America. 87.4% came from the UK. The exposure to North America is in fact significantly higher due to the percentage of American visitors in group hotels, in particular in London.

CORPORATE CALENDAR

Year end	31 October
Preliminary results	January
Report and accounts	February
AGM	March
Final dividend paid	April
Interim results	June
Interim dividend paid	October

DIRECTORS' HOLDINGS

	Beneficial interests	Other* interests	Options
Lord Forte	13,094,406	37,729,208	160,806
The Hon Rocco Forte	29,958,590	3,258,988	389,191
GB Chiandetti	247,000	—	63,209
DD Durban	223,624	—	85,437
E Hartwell	3,559,902	26,821,116	—
JG Hawkes	126,328	—	79,082
D Hearn	371,582	9,000	109,203
IAH Johnston	119,000	—	88,759
DA Main	121,600	—	115,366
Sir David McNee	1,000	—	
The Hon Mrs O Polizzi	24,498,285	900,000	158,011
GFL Proctor	166,658	26,930,802	58,516

*Certain of these holdings include the same shares more than once in relation to trusts created by directors of which other directors are trustees, and also in respect of joint interests.

In 1986/87 the emoluments, excluding pension contributions, of the chairman were £230,222, and the highest-paid director received £234,577.

UNILEVER

PRINCIPAL SUBSIDIARIES AND RELATED COMPANIES

Airport Catering Services Ltd, Anchor Hotels Ltd, Forte & Company Ltd, Forte Holdings Ltd, Gardner Merchant Ltd, Grosvenor Theatrical Productions Ltd, Happy Eater Ltd, Kelvin Catering Ltd, Kentucky Fried Chicken (GB) Ltd (50%), Leased Hotels Ltd (50%), Les Grands Hotels Associés SA – France, Lillywhites Limited, Little Chef Ltd, Motorway Services Ltd (86%), Puritan Maid Limited, Quaglino's Plc (98%), Ring & Brymer Ltd (98%), The Savoy Hotel Plc (69%), THF International Management Ltd – Bermuda, THF Oil Ltd, TraveLodge International Inc – US, Trusthouse Forte Airport Services Ltd, Trusthouse Forte Bermuda Ltd – Bermuda, Trusthouse Forte Catering Ltd, Trusthouse Forte Group Finance NV – Netherlands, Trusthouse Forte Hotels Inc – US, Trusthouse Forte International Ltd, Trusthouse Forte Ireland Ltd – Irish Republic, Trusthouse Forte Service Areas Ltd, Trusthouse Forte (UK) Ltd, Welcome Break Ltd

Trusthouse Forte has 69% of the equity of Savoy Hotel Plc but only 42% of the voting rights.

BRAND NAMES

Anchor Hotels, Dome Cafés, Falstaff Bars & Grills, Gardner Merchant, Happy Eater, Harvester Inns and Steak Houses, Imperial Inns, Lillywhites, Little Chef, Motor Chef, Motorway Service Areas, Pier House Inns, Post House, Puritan Maid, Ring & Brymer, Roadside Catering Division, Skylight Inns, Travelodge, Trusthouse Forte Hotels, Viscount Hotels, Welcome Break Motorway Service Areas

CONTACTS AND FURTHER INFORMATION

John Robbins, Head of press and public relations, Trusthouse Forte PLC, 166 High Holborn, London WC1V 6TT. Tel: 01-836 7744.

GENERAL INFORMATION

Head office	Unilever House, PO Box 68, Blackfriars, London EC4P 4BQ. Tel: 01-822 5252
Registered office	Unilever PLC, Port Sunlight, Wirral, Merseyside L62 4ZA. Tel: 051-644 8211
Directors	MR Angus (chairman), FA Maljers (vice-chairman), Sir Geoffrey Allen, RW Archer, M Dowdall, PVM Egan, JP Erbé, MG Heron, JA Houtzager, H Meij, J Peelen, MS Perry, GKG Stevens, M Tabaksblat, T Thomas, EJ Verloop. *Non-exec* BW Biesheuvel, T Browaldh, Fletcher L Byrom, Sir Robert Haslam, A Herrhausen, The Rt Hon the Lord Hunt of Tanworth, D Spethmann, EP Wellenstein. *Hon non-exec* The Rt Hon the Viscount Leverhulme
Advisers	No specified adviser
Auditors	Coopers & Lybrand
Registrars	Unilever PLC, Port Sunlight, Wirral, Merseyside L62 4ZA. Tel: 051-644 8211
Brokers	Rowe & Pitman Ltd
Solicitors	Slaughter and May

GENERAL FINANCIAL INFORMATION

Market capitalisation	£8.587bn at 1 January 1988
Capital structure	
Issued ordinary shares (5p)	1.855bn, made up of 160.41m Unilever NV Fl4 shares and 790.75m Unilever PLC 5p shares. One Unilever PLC share equals 3/20ths of a Unilever NV share.
Issued preference shares (£1)	0.2m 5% First CP
	3.5m 7% First CP
	1.2m 8% Second CP
	0.2m 20% Third CP
Warrants	None
Convertibles	None
Traded options	Yes
ADRs	One ADR per five ordinary shares
Shareholders over 5%	Prudential Corporation 5.5%, Leverhulme Trust 6%

FT CATEGORY

FT: Industrials (miscel.)
FT-A: Food manufacturing

MAJOR ACTIVITIES

The Unilever group of companies is one of the world's largest businesses, employing 300,000 people and providing a wide range of products and services in 75 countries.

The larger part of Unilever's business is in branded and packaged consumer goods like washing powders, margarines, personal products and a wide range of frozen and other food and drinks. Unilever's other activities include speciality chemicals, agribusiness operations including plantations and animal feeds, and medical products. In addition, there are merchandising and service operations conducted in tropical Africa and the Arabian Gulf.

Unilever has recently expanded its US exposure through the acquisition of Chesebrough-Pond's. This move has strengthened the group in an important region where previously it has been under-represented.

In recent years the management has concentrated on its core businesses and this has involved in the period 1984 to 1987 disposal of over 80 businesses and the acquisition of 70 companies. The effect has been positive in terms of profitability and productivity.

Unilever NV, Rotterdam and Unilever PLC, London operate as nearly as is practicable as a single entity, have identical boards of directors and are linked by a series of agreements of which the principal is the Equalisation Agreement. This agreement equalises the dividends payable on the ordinary capital of NV and PLC. As a consequence the

FIVE YEAR FINANCIAL INFORMATION

Year	Turnover (£m)	Pre-tax (£m)	Earnings (p)	Dividends net (p)	Dividend cover (x)	Net assets (p)	Price (p) High	Price (p) Low	PER (x) High	PER (x) Low	Yield (%) High	Yield (%) Low
1983	13,386	769	20.6	6.2	3.3	170	179	139	9.6	6.7	5.93	4.62
1984	16,172	925	26.9	7.1	3.8	184	219	167	9.8	8.0	5.28	4.10
1985	16,693	953	27.6	7.7	3.6	182	276	202	10.4	7.0	5.02	3.69
1986	17,140	1,143	35.5	10.0	3.5	162	443	264	14.0	9.0	3.85	2.68
1987	16,550	1,327	40.5	11.8	3.4	189	718	465	17.7	10.4	4.48	2.91

combined affairs of NV and PLC are more important to shareholders than those of the two separate parent companies.

Unilever competes internationally with other very large companies like Proctor & Gamble, Colgate and Nestlé.

FINANCIAL HISTORY

In 1987 Unilever sales decreased 3% to £16.550bn (£17.140bn), while pre-tax profits rose 16% to £1.327bn (£1.143bn). Gross volume growth was 9%, of which 5% was attributable to acquisitions and disposals. Significantly, operating margins increased 1.7% from 6.6% to 8.3% in 1987, after a 1% rise in 1986. Earnings per share improved by 14% to 40.5p, while the dividend increased by 15% to 11.8p.

At constant exchange rates the figures would have been substantially better, with sales up 6%, pre-tax profits 27% and earnings per share 24%. In dollar terms earnings per share increased by 44%. Gearing at the year-end was 26%, down from 43.4% in 1986 and 31% at the end of 1985.

Operating profit in 1987 in North America more than doubled. In Europe there was a gain of 19% and promising results in Japan. Return on shareholders' funds was 20%.

Since 1983 turnover has increased by 23.6%, pre-tax profits by 78.5% and earnings per share by 97.1%. Dividends have increased by 92.2%.

SHARE PRICE HISTORY

The two years prior to July 1987 saw a dramatic rise in the share price of Unilever. From September 1985 the price jumped by three and a half times from 200p to a high of 719p. Investors were keen to buy the stock during this period in response to the group's reorganisation, its programme of selective investment and acquisition, and its capital investment in continuing operations. Investor sentiment was given a further boost in July 1987 when the shares were split on a five to one basis.

In the autumn of 1987 Unilever shares fell back with the market, sinking to 415p at their low before recovering to 460p at the year end.

SENIOR MANAGEMENT

Mike Angus has been chairman of Unilever PLC and vice-chairman of Unilever NV since 1986. He joined Unilever in the UK. In 1980 he moved to the US where he took control of Lever Brothers Company. Floris Maljers has been the current chairman of Unilever NV and vice-chairman of Unilever PLC since 1984. Floris Maljers joined Unilever in 1958 and was appointed chairman of Van den Berghs and Jurgens in 1969.

Unilever has a plural chief executive known as the Special Committee which is responsible for the long term objectives and strategies of the business as a whole. In addition to Mike Angus and Floris Maljers who joined in 1984 and 1982 respectively, its third member is J Erbé who is vice-chairman of Unilever NV as well as a senior director of Unilever PLC. In May 1988 GKG Stevens will retire from the board and CM Jemmett and Dr JIW Anderson will join it.

CAPITAL

Unilever shares are listed in London, Amsterdam, New York and other stock exchanges in continental Europe. On the New York Stock Exchange, Unilever NV is quoted in Fl4 stock while Unilever PLC is quoted in ADR form.

One of the largest single shareholders is the Leverhulme Trust. It owns about 6% of the ordinary capital and applies its income for charitable purposes. The issued capital has remained constant since the 1930s apart from the five for one split in June 1987.

GROUP REVIEW

Edible fats and dairy products Unilever is the world's largest producer of margarine with manufacturing units in every major country in which it operates. Many of Unilever's margarine and low fat spread brands – for instance, Flora, Becel, Rama, Blue Band, Planta, Fruit d'Or and Country Crock – are household names in their respective countries.

In many of its margarine markets Unilever sells ranges of cooking fats and oils for household, artisan and industrial consumption. In 1986 the group became market leader in the US margarine market and extended its position in 1987.

In 1987 turnover fell 13% to £3.235bn, but operating profit rose 9.8% to £280m, 20.4% of the group total.

Frozen foods and ice cream In response to the world wide growing demand for convenience foods in the home and catering trade, Unilever has quick-frozen food operations in most major countries. In continental Europe, these are marketed mainly under the Iglo brand, and in the UK as Bird's Eye. The major lines are vegetables, fish and meat products. Recently ready meals, snacks, pizzas and desserts have become increasingly popular.

Unilever markets a wide range of ice cream products internationally. Calippo, a new product, has been well received in continental Europe and Cornetto did well in more than 20 countries.

In 1987 profits for frozen food improved, especially in the UK, where the restructuring of Bird's Eye is now paying off, and in West Germany. Ice cream continued to be very profitable worldwide. Divisional turnover in 1987 was static, but operating profit improved by 15.3% to £124m, 10.4% of the group total.

Other food and drinks The division covers a wide range of products including tea, coffee, meat products, instant soups, canned foods, soft drinks, sauces, mayonnaise and salad dressings. Major brands include Brooke Bond and Lipton teas, John West canned salmon, Unox, Wall's, Mattesons and Fray Bentos meats, Oxo cubes, Calvé mayonnaise and dressings, and instant soups like Batchelors Cup-a-soup. In the US, Lipton also markets a variety of rice and pasta-based side dishes. 1986 saw the merging of Mattesons and Wall's in the UK and Unilever acquired the Spanish branded meat product market leader Ravilla. In 1987 Brooke Bond and Batchelors were merged.

In 1987 turnover rose 5% to £2.851bn, while operating profit rose 21.6% to £281m, 20.4% of the group total.

Detergents The Unilever detergents business started over 100 years ago when William Lever opened his first factory in the UK. It is now the largest manufacturer of detergents in the world, selling over 4m tonnes per annum in over 75 countries. Several brands launched many years ago, including Sunlight, Vim, Persil and Lifebuoy, are still important today.

Important modern products include: fabric softeners like Comfort and the teddy bear brand; liquid abrasive cleaners like Jif and Cif; detergent bars for use in countries where manual washing still prevails; Lux beauty soap, the largest-selling beauty soap in the world; Dove skin care soap; laundry powders like Surf and Omo; and liquid laundry detergents like Wisk. As a result of substantial investments made in 1986 Lever Brothers experienced a dramatic turnaround in the US in 1987 and greatly enhanced divisional profits.

Unilever also has an important industrial detergents business which operates in 25 countries manufacturing and marketing a range of cleaning and hygiene systems for use in factories, hospitals, laundries, hotels and kitchens.

In 1987 turnover fell 4.7% to £3.593bn, but operating profit rose 41.5% to £269m, 19.6% of the group total.

Personal products Unilever's personal products division encompasses a wide range of products concerned with health and beauty care for all age groups, including hair preparations, toothpastes, deodorants, skin creams, perfumes and cosmetics. Among its famous brand names are Signal, Pepsodent, Mentadent and Close-Up toothpastes; Clinic, Timotei and Sunsilk hair products; Rexon deodorant, Impulse body spray, Denim fragrance and Pears soap. These products make Unilever one of the world's most important manufacturers of personal care products, with major market shares in all main markets.

The Chesebrough-Pond's acquisition has added substantial sales and profits to the division. Chesebrough-Pond's brands include Pond's creams, Q-tips, Vaseline and the Cutex range of cosmetics. The group is now one of the two largest personal product makers in the world.

1987 turnover was 43.9% up at £1.510bn. Operating profit increased 124.2% to £139m, 10.1% of the group total.

Speciality chemicals Unilever has global presence in the speciality chemicals through four international groups, each world leaders in their field.

National Starch and Chemical Corporation manufactures speciality starches, adhesives and synthetic resins in the US. Its starches are used in papermaking textiles and foods, its adhesives in packaging, micro-electronics and construction, and its synthetic resins in cosmetics and paper coating.

Unichema International supplies a wide range of oleo-chemical products from its several locations in Europe, the US and the Pacific basin. PPF – based in Europe, North and South America and South-east Asia – produces fragrances and flavours for use in the food and perfume industries. Crosfield Chemicals, based in the Netherlands and the UK, primarily makes petroleum cracking catalysts and silicates.

In 1987 Naarden International, acquired in 1986, was merged with PPF to create Quest International, now a major worldwide supplier of fragrances, flavours and food ingredients.

In 1987 turnover was 1% up at £1.312bn. Operating profit rose 20.4% to £165m, 12% of the group total.

Agribusiness Unilever's interests in agribusiness consist of plantation companies, seed breeding and tissue culture, animal feeds and fish farming.

Originally Unilever's extensive palm plantations were intended to ensure a continuous supply of palm oil for its margarine and soap products. In 1986 the price of palm oil fell dramatically and cut back profits with no improvement in 1987. Partly as a consequence of this, Unilever has started palm oil production in Colombia where demand outstrips internal supply.

Despite a fall in the tea price, Unilever's tea estates in India and Kenya did well. Major factors in their success are the introduction of new technology, and the cloning of tea plants.

Share price and relative to FT-A All-Share

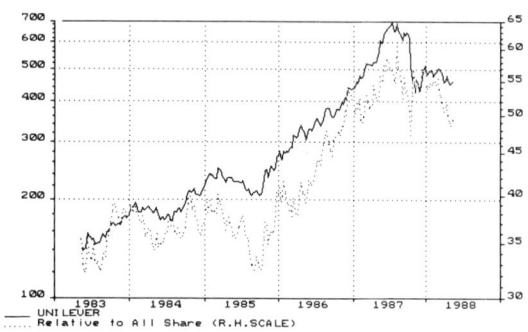

The animal feeds business originated in the utilisation of the by-products of the seed crushing process which produced oil for the manufacture of soap and margarine. These are processed into cattle-cake. Fish-farming is a new area for Unilever although it has been developing the appropriate technology for a number of years. The group's acquisition of the Plant Breeding Institute and National Seed Development Organisation will make a considerable impact.

1987 results were adversely affected by European milk quotas and the costs of restructuring an innovation. The division nevertheless remained profitable. Turnover was 17.9% down to £519m, but operating profit was 11.4% up at £39m, 2.8% of the group total.

Other operations Unilever is also involved in a number of other business areas. Amongst the most important are medical products. Developments in immunology, a specialist area for Unilever research scientists, have led to the establishment of Unipath, a new medical products business in the UK.

Turnover from other operations in 1987 was down 22.6% to £1.446bn, while operating profit fell 36.1% to £57m, 4.2% of the group total.

UAC International UAC International is primarily a distributor of specialised consumer and industrial products and of capital goods to tropical Africa and the Middle East. The principal product areas include African textiles, beers, foods, personal products, electrical and diesel equipment and materials, construction, earth-moving and agricultural equipment, and commercial and passenger vehicles.

CHAIRMAN'S STATEMENT

'The company is now well placed for further profitable growth and is better equipped to face the competitive challenge. We shall continue to concentrate our resources on those businesses in which we have the necessary skills to compete effectively.' *MR Angus, FA Maljers*

To an increasing extent, these products are manufactured or assembled using local raw materials, skills and labour, thus stimulating the economy of the area and reducing the need for imports.

Packaging Throughout the world Unilever spends several hundred million pounds each year on packaging its products. In some European countries it also produces packaging and packaging materials for sale to other Unilever companies and to third parties.

Fish and restaurants The Nordsee company, based in Germany, is involved in fish processing and runs a chain of restaurants.

Research and development During 1987 the group spent £329m on research, against £305m in 1986. This research effort is devoted entirely to benefiting the group. Some research is carried out on a generic scientific basis, not aimed at specific benefits for specific products.

GEOGRAPHICAL REVIEW

Of the group's global turnover for 1986 of £17.14bn, Europe took £10.47bn (61%), North America £3.01bn (17.6%) and the rest of the world £3.66bn (21.4%). Of the total operating profit of £1.12bn, Europe earned £632m (56.4%), North America £114m (10.2%) and the rest of the world £376m (33.4%).

Of the group's global turnover of £16.55bn in 1987, Europe accounted for £10.35bn (−2.7%), North America £3.08bn (+2.2%) and the rest of the world £3.12bn (−10.5%). Of the total operating profit of £1.37bn (+22.1%), Europe earned £789m (+19.2%), North America £239m (+109.6%) and the rest of the world £345m (−0.9%).

CORPORATE CALENDAR

Year end	31 December
Preliminary results	March
Report and accounts	April
AGM	May
Final dividend paid	May
Interim results	August
Interim dividend paid	December

DIRECTORS' HOLDINGS

	Fully-paid ordinary shares		Options
	(beneficial)	*(non-beneficial)*	
MR Angus	500	8,781,642	41,445
RW Archer	577	—	29,017
PVM Egan	3,000	—	29,017
GKG Stevens	300	—	722
FA Maljers	—	—	722
RW Archer	—	—	29,017
M Dowdall	—	—	24,650
JP Erbe	—	—	32,370
MG Heron	—	—	19,183
JA Houtzager	—	—	722
H Meij	—	—	722
MS Perry	—	—	23,524
M Tabaksblat	—	—	722
T Thomas	—	—	29,017
EJ Verloop	—	—	722

These figures do not reflect the share split of July 1987.

Sir Kenneth Durham, now retired, received remuneration of £68,767 for the period of 1986 he spent as chairman. Mr MR Angus received £85,640 for the period of 1986 he spent as chairman and an additional £56,888 for his other services.

PRINCIPAL SUBSIDIARIES AND RELATED COMPANIES

The letters NV or PLC after the name of each country indicate whether in the country concerned the shares in the companies listed are held directly or indirectly by NV or PLC.

Principal group companies
4P Drukkerij Reclame BV – The Netherlands NV, 4P Emballages France SA – France NV (99%), 4P Folie Forchheim GmbH – Germany NV, 4P Nicolaus Kempten GmbH – Germany NV, 4P Rube Göttingen GmbH – Germany NV, 4P Vrpackungen Ronsberg GmbH – Germany NV, A Sutter AG – Switzerland NV, A&W Food Services of Canada Ltd – Canada PLC, AB Sunlight – Sweden NV, Agra SA – Spain NV, Algemeen Vrachtkantoor BV – The Netherlands NV, Anderson Clayton & Co SA – Mexico NV (60%), Anderson Clayton SA Indústria e Comércio – Brazil NV (93%), Astra-Calvé SA – France NV (99%), 'Astra' Fett-und Oelwerke AG – Switzerland NV, BOCM Silcock Ltd, Batchelors Foods Ltd, Bird's Eye Wall's Ltd, Blohorn SA – Côte d'Ivoire PLC (80%), Brasseries du Logone SA – Tchad PLC, Brooke Bond Group Ltd, Brooke Bond Kenya Ltd – Kenya PLC (88%), Brooke Bond Oxo Ltd, Burgess Feeds Ltd, Bushells Pty Ltd – Australia PLC, CFCI SA – Côte d'Ivoire PLC (99%), CNF SA – France PLC (99%), CWA Holdings Ltd, Calvé-De Betuwe BV – The Netherlands NV, Compagnie des Glaces et Surgelés Alimentaires SA – France NV (99%), Compagnie des Margarines, Compañía Colombiana de Grasa 'Cogra-Lever' SA – Colombia NV, Croklaan BV – The Netherlands NV, Crosfield Chemie BV – The Netherlands NV, Deutsche Unilever GmbH – Germany NV, East Africa Industries Ltd – Kenya PLC (54%), 'Elais' Oleaginous Products AE – Greece NV (50%), 'Elbe' Transport GmbH – Germany NV, Elida Cosmetic AG – Switzerland NV, Elida Gibbs Ltd, Elida-Gibbs GmbH – Germany NV, Exportslachterij Udema BV – The Netherlands NV, Ford & Slater Group Ltd, Formosa United Industrial Corporation Ltd – Taiwan NV, Française d'Alimentation et de Boissons SA – France NV (99%), Française de Soins et Parfums SA – France NV (99%), Frigo SA – Spain NV (99%), Gailey & Roberts (Uganda) Ltd – Uganda PLC, Gailey & Roberts Ltd – Kenya PLC, Gibbs AB – Sweden NV, Glace-Bolaget AB – Sweden NV (90%), H Leverton Ltd, HB Ice Cream Ltd – Ireland PLC, Hartog NV – Belgium NV, Hatton et Cookson SA – Gabon PLC, Hindustan Lever Ltd – India PLC, Iglo Indústrias de Gelados Lda (74%), Iglo-Ola BV – The Netherlands NV, Iglo-Ola NV – Belgium NV, Indústrias Gessy Lever Ltda – Brazil NV (99%), Indústrias Lever Portuguesa Lda – Portugal NV (60%), Industrias Revilla SA – Spain NV (90%), John West Foods Ltd, Joseph Crosfield & Sons Ltd, KB Davies & Co (Zambia) Ltd – Zambia PLC, Koninklihke Maatschappij De Betuwe BV – The Netherlands NV, Langnese-Iglo GmbH – Germany NV, Lawry's Foods Inc – US NV 75% PLC 25%, Lever GmbH – Germany NV, Lever BV – The Netherlands NV, Lever Brothers (Ceylon) Ltd – Sri Lanka PLC, Lever Brothers (Ireland) Ltd – Ireland PLC, Lever Brothers (Malawi) Ltd – Malawi PLC, Lever Brothers (Malaysia) Sdn Bhd – Malaysia PLC (70%), Lever Brothers (Private) Ltd – Zimbabwe PLC, Lever Brothers (Thailand) Ltd – Thailand NV, Lever Brothers Bangladesh Ltd – Bangladesh PLC (61%), Lever Brothers Company – US NV 75% PLC 25%, Lever Brothers Ltd, Lever Brothers Ltd – Canada PLC, Lever Brothers Pakistan Ltd – Pakistan PLC (66%), Lever Brothers Singapore Sdn Bhd – Singapore PLC, Lever Brothers West Indies Ltd – Trinidad PLC (50%), Lever Chile SA – Chile NV/PLC, Lever España SA – Spain NV, Lever Hellas AEBE – Greece NV, Lever Industrial BV – The Netherlands NV, Lever Industrial Ltd, Lever NV – Belgium NV, Lever Oy – Finland NV, Lever SA – France NV (99%), Lever SA – Venezuela NV, Lever Sodel SpA – Italy NV, Lever Solomons Ltd – Solomon Islands PLC (60%), Lever y Asociados sacif – Argentina NV (99%), Leverinduis AB – Sweden NV, Lipton Export Ltd, Lipton Tea Company Ltd, Loders & Nucoline Ltd, Lucas Aardenburg BV – The Netherlands NV, Margarinbolaget AB – Sweden NV (55%), Marine Harvest Ltd, Mattesons Wall's Ltd, Mavibel International NV – Netherlands Antilles NV, Meina Holding AG – Switzerland NV, Meistermarken-Werke GmbH, Spezialfabrik für Back-un Grossküchenbedarf – Germany NV, Naarden International NV – The Netherlands NV (99%), Nabisco Brands – Canada PLC, National Starch and Chemical Corporation – US NV 75% PLC 25%, Nederlandse Unilever Bedrijven BV – The Netherlands NV (99%), Niger France SA – France PLC (99%), Niger-Afrique SA – Niger PLC (99%), Nippon Lever BV – Japan NV (incorporated in the Netherlands), 'Nordsee' Deutsche Hochseefischerei GmbH – Germany NV, Nordsee GesmbH – Austria NV, Nordsee GesmbH – Austria NV, Novia Lismedelsindustrier AB – Sweden NV, Osterreichische Unilever GesmbH – Austria NV, Oxoid Ltd, PBI/NSDO, PPO International Ltd, PT Unilever Indonesia – Indonesia PLC, Paasivaara Oy – Finland NV, Pamol (Nigeria) Ltd – Nigeria PLC (60%), Pamol Plantations Sdn Bhd – Malaysia PLC, Paul and Vincent Ltd – Ireland PLC, Philippine Refining Company Inc – Philippines NV, Pierre Robert AB – Sweden NV, Plantations Lever au Zaïre

UNITED BISCUITS (HOLDINGS) PLC

sarl – Zaïre NV, Plantations Pamol du Cameroun Ltd – Cameroun PLC, RW King SA – Cameroun PLC (99%), Sagit SpA – Italy NV, Sais AG – Switzerland NV, Savons et Cosmétiques au Zaïre sarl – Zaïre NV, Schafft Fleischwerke GmbH – Germany NV, Sedec sarl – Zaïre PLC, Shedd's Food Products Inc – US NV 75% PLC 25%, Sterling Industrial Ltd, Sudy y Cía – Uruguay NV, Sunlight AG – Switzerland NV, Svenska Unilever Forvaltnings AB – Sweden NV, Thames Board Ltd, The Wall's Meat Company Ltd, Thomas J Lipton Inc – Canada PLC, Thomas J Lipton Inc – US NV 75% PLC 25%, UAC International Ltd, UAC Ltd, UAC of Ghana Ltd – Ghana PLC, UAC of Sierra Leone Ltd – Sierra Leone PLC (87%), UAC of Tanzania Ltd – Tanzania PLC, UML Ltd, UVG Nederland BV – The Netherlands NV, Uni-Dan A/S – Denmark NV, UniMills BV – The Netherlands NV, Unichema Chemicals Ltd, Unichema Chemie BV – The Netherlands NV, 'Unichema' Chemie GmbH – Germany NV, Unifrost GesmbH – Austria NV, Unil-It SpA – Italy NV, Unilever (Schweiz) AG – Switzerland NV, Unilever Australia Ltd – Australia PLC, Unilever Becumij NV – Netherlands Antilles NV, Unilever Canada Ltd – Canada PLC, Unilever Capital Corporation – US NV 75% PLC 25%, Unilever España SA – Spain NV, Unilever Export BV – The Netherlands NV, Unilever Export France SA – France NV (99%), Unilever Export Ltd, Unilever Financieringsmaatschappij BV – The Netherlands NV, Unilever New Zealand Ltd – New Zealand PLC, Unilever South Africa (Pty) Ltd – South Africa PLC, Unilever UK Holdings Ltd, Unilever United States Inc – US NV 75% PLC 25%, Unilever-Is Ticaret ve Sanayi Türk Ltd Sirketi – Turkey NV (65%), Union Deutsche Lebensmittelwerke GmbH – Germany NV, Union NV – Belgium NV, United Agricultural Merchants Ltd, Uniwax SA – Côte d'Ivoire NV (67%), Valpon SpA – Italy NV, Van den Bergh en Jurgens BV – The Netherlands NV, Van den Berghs and Jurgens Ltd, Vinamul Ltd, W&C McDonnell Ltd – Ireland PLC, West Marton (AFF) Ltd, Zeepfabriek de Fenix BV – The Netherlands NV

Principal related companies
Associated companies
Aekyung Industrial Company Ltd – Korea NV (50%), Binzagr-Lever Ltd – Saudi Arabia PLC (40%), FIMA – Fábrica Imperial de Margarina Lda – Portugal NV (40%), Fritz Homann Lebensmittelwerke GmbH & Co KG – Germany NV (50%), Industrias Unisola SA – El Salvador NV (50%), Lever Brothers Nigeria Ltd – Nigeria PLC (40%), Margarinefabrikken Alfa-Solo A/S – Denmark NV (50%), Nigerian Breweries Ltd – Nigeria PLC (14%), UAC of Nigeria Ltd – Nigeria PLC (40%)

Trade investments
Gamma Holding NV – The Netherlands NV (37%)

Principal Chesebrough-Pond's companies
Subsidiary companies
3C Industriale SpA – Italy NV (95%), CP France Ltd – France NV (95%) (Incorporated in the United States of America), Chesebrough-Pond's (Canada) Inc – Canada NV (95%), Chesebrough-Pond's (Genève) SA – Switzerland NV (95%), Chesebrough-Pond's (Japan) Ltd – Japan NV (95%) (Incorporated in the US), Chesebrough-Pond's CA – Venezuela NV (95%), Chesebrough-Pond's Inc – US NV, Chesebrough-Pond's International Ltd – Australia NV (95%), Chesebrough-Pond's Ltd (95%), Pond's Argentina SAIC – Argentina NV (95%), Pond's Española SA – Spain NV (95%), Pond's GmbH – Germany NV (90%), Pond's de México SA de CV – Mexico NV (95%), Prince Matchabelli Inc – US NV, Ragu Foods Inc – US NV, Spectrum Group Inc – US NV

BRAND NAMES

Axis, Batchelors, Bird's Eye, Brooke Bond, Calvé, Clearblue, Comfort, Cookeen, Cutex, Delight!, Denim, Domestos, Du darfst, Fa Fa, Fiorela, Flora, Frigo, Frish, Fun Fruits, Jif, John West, Light and Lean, Lipton, LWC, Lynx, Mattesons, Mentadent, OXO, Pears Soap, Persil, PG Tips, Ponds, Prince Matchabelli, Q-tips, Ragu, Rayco, Revilla, Signal Plus, Signal Toothpaste, Snuggle, St Floriguy, Stork, Sunsilk, Surf, Swift, Timotei, Trust, Vaseline, Vaseline Intensive Care, Vim, Wall's, Wisk

CONTACTS AND FURTHER INFORMATION

Ian Barnard, Investor Relations Manager, Unilever PLC, Unilever House, Blackfriars, London EC4P 4BQ. Tel: 01-822 5252.

GENERAL INFORMATION

Head office	Grant House, PO Box 40, Syon Lane, Isleworth, Middlesex TW7 5NN. Tel: 01-560 3131
Registered office	United Biscuits (Holdings) Plc, 12 Hope Street, Edinburgh EH2 4DD
Directors	Sir Hector Laing (chairman), RC Clarke (chief executive), J Byth CA, TM Garvin, FW Knight, DRJ Stewart. *Non-exec* CA Fraser CVO (vice-chairman), EL Bondy Jnr – US, Sir James Cleminson MC, WP Gunn, MA Heller FCA, The Rt Hon Sir Michael Palliser GCMG, Lord Plumb MEP DL, The Rt Hon Lord Prior
Advisers	No specified adviser
Auditors	Deloitte Haskins & Sells, Arthur Young
Registrars	Royal Bank of Scotland Registrar's Department
Brokers	County NatWest WoodMac, Warburg Securities
Solicitors	W & J Burness

GENERAL FINANCIAL INFORMATION

Market capitalisation	£1.076bn at 1 January 1988
Capital structure	
Issued ordinary shares (25p)	412.6m
Issued preference shares (£1)	£110m 5.75% CP 2003 (convertible at 308p)
Warrants	10.6m, one ordinary share at 149p until 31 March 1989
	20.3m, one ordinary share at 247p until 25 June 1991
Convertibles	None
Traded options	None
ADRs	None
Shareholders over 5%	None

FT CATEGORY

FT: Food, groceries, etc
FT-A: Food manufacturing

MAJOR ACTIVITIES

United Biscuits (UB) is the leading UK biscuit company and the second largest biscuit manufacturer in the world. Through its acquisitions in the late 1960s and organic growth it also became the leading national supplier of snack foods. In addition the group has built up a major restaurant and fast food business, purchasing the Wimpy operation in the late 1970s and later the Pizzaland chain.

Part of the philosophy of the group's expansion has been to develop its overseas operations. The most important development was the acquisition of Keebler in 1974, the second largest biscuit manufacturer in the United States. Other US acquisitions have included those of Specialty Brands (which produces spices, seasonings and salad dressings) in 1979, and Early California Industries in 1985, both of which are being sold because of the lack of growth opportunities in their respective markets.

In the UK, UB moved into the chocolate confectionery market with the purchase of Terry's of York in 1982. UB also has a sizeable presence in the UK retail and catering frozen food markets.

The group made a bold attempt to merge with Imperial Group in a reverse takeover in 1986 but was eventually the loser to Hanson's successful bid.

In March 1988 UB bought Ross Young's from Hanson for £335m, thereby acquiring Imperial's frozen food business, the original reason for UB's bid for Imperial. Through the purchase UB becomes greatly strengthened with coverage of all the important frozen food sectors in the UK.

Despite continuing uncertainties about UB's North American businesses, it is clear that the company has a strong

F I V E   Y E A R   F I N A N C I A L   I N F O R M A T I O N

Year	Turnover (£m)	Pre-tax (£m)	Earnings (p)	Dividends net (p)	Dividend cover (x)	Net assets (p)	Price (p) High	Low	PER (x) High	Low	Yield (%) High	Low
1983	1,425	83.3	18.3	7.0	2.6	82	158	125	15.9	10.2	6.98	5.11
1984	1,743	87.2	19.1	7.5	2.5	94	193	132	14.9	10.5	6.99	5.05
1985	1,907	102.2	19.1	8.0	2.4	111	279	164	19.2	10.7	6.53	3.92
1986	1,932	125.2	20.3	9.5	2.1	111	267	217	17.0	12.4	6.17	4.42
1987	1,955	147.0	23.9	11.0	2.2	118	350	217	17.9	11.1	6.31	3.72

management team that is determined to improve upon its rather disappointing earnings per share record. In addition, UB has positioned itself in the UK grocery market to command a great deal of shelf space with brands that the leading multiples cannot afford to do without.

FINANCIAL HISTORY

UB sets itself corporate objectives which include a range of financial targets. The most important is return on average capital employed. This has been targeted at 25%, with a minimum of 20%. In 1987 the group's return on capital employed rose from 22% to 23%, 2% short of the group's target, on turnover up 1.1% from £1.932bn to £1.954bn.

A steady improvement in net profit margins is another of the group's objectives. In 1987 pre-tax profits rose 17% to £147m. Margins rose from 6.5% to 7.5%.

The objective for earnings per share is that they will grow more in line with the growth in pre-tax profits. In recent years the investment in developing businesses has reduced the earnings per share growth to below that of pre-tax profits. Earnings per share rose by 18% to 23.9p in 1987.

The dividend policy is to try to ensure that returns to shareholders grow in line with pre-tax profits. The 1987 dividend increase of 16% was in line with this.

The target for capital expenditure is that it should be not less than 4% of sales annually. In 1987 capital expenditure was 7.4% of sales, 3.4% up on the group policy, and demonstrating the significant investment for the future by the group.

Shareholders' funds in 1987 rose from £453m to £490.5m. Reflecting the improvement in cash flow, net debt fell by £30m to £65m, to represent a gearing ratio of only 13%, the lowest it has been for several years. The balance sheet benefited from the 1985 rights issue which raised £98m in cash.

The acquisition of Ross Young's will involve the writing-off of £130.5m of goodwill and an increase in group gearing. Shareholders' funds will fall to £386.2m after taking in a surplus of £48.6m on the sale of Specialty Brands.

SHARE PRICE HISTORY

The highlight since 1984 was a very large jump in the share price at the end of 1985, when Imperial Group announced merger terms with UB. The price rose by around 100p to nearly 300p at one stage, and remained high even though the deal foundered.

However, in relative terms the share price subsequently fell against the market as investors took the opportunity to reduce their commitment to a share which had disappointed the market in previous years. Bid speculation reappears from time to time.

The price fell to 220p during the 1987 autumn crash but recovered to the 260p level at the beginning of 1988, having outperformed the FT-A All-Share index in December 1987.

The disposal of UB's Specialty Brands and Early California businesses in the US may be a beneficial factor. By mid-April 1988 the shares were trading in a range between 245p and 270p.

SENIOR MANAGEMENT

The board of directors consists of fourteen directors, eight of whom are non-executive, an unusually high proportion compared with most other large companies.

Sir Hector Laing has been chairman since 1972. He has been a director since 1953 and has over 40 years' experience in the UK biscuit industry. Sir Hector is a director of the Bank of England and Exxon in the US, and was voted businessman of the year in 1979.

Sir Hector's experience and leadership has been the force behind UB's international expansion. He believes that it is particularly important for UK companies to become large at home and overseas in order to compete effectively with the much bigger US food companies.

Robert Clarke was appointed group chief executive in 1986 when the divisional structure of the group was reorganised. He has been with UB since 1971. James Blyth has been the group finance director since 1977. He is also responsible for the five companies that make up the small businesses division. He joined UB in 1965.

Tom Garvin joined the main board in 1983. He became chief executive of Keebler in 1978 and under the 1986 group reorganisation he became responsible for UB's North American manufacturing operations. Frank Knight joined the main board in 1986. He is responsible for the manufacturing activities in the UK and Europe. Frank Knight also heads the UB Foods Europe board. This consists of the managing directors responsible for the various manufacturing divisions and associated services.

DRJ Stewart joined UB as company secretary in 1972 and was appointed to the board in 1986.

CAPITAL

There are 416m ordinary shares in issue. The 1985 rights issue increased the equity base by 20% when 63.98m shares were issued to raise £98m. A further 21.5m shares were later issued to fund acquisitions.

In 1984 the group issued 17.5m warrants to subscribe on an adjusted basis for 17.5m ordinary shares at 149p until 31 March 1989, and followed this in 1986 by issuing 20.3m warrants to subscribe for 20.3m ordinary shares at 247p until 25 June 1991. Subscription of the outstanding 1989 and 1991 warrants would result in an increase in equity of 4.7%.

The acquisition of Ross Young's is being financed partly by the £90m sale proceeds of Specialty Brands and partly by a £160m 5.75% convertible preference issue with an ingenious rolling put option feature. The cash element is £139m.

GROUP REVIEW

United Biscuits is a major international food group, involved in a wide range of food products, as well as being the second largest biscuit manufacturer in the world. In the UK it is the leader in the biscuits and snacks markets and is well respected for its confectionery products, frozen foods, restaurants and fast foods retailing.

Internationally UB has built significant businesses in the US and continental Europe. It has established a sound base for further growth. Worldwide the group employs nearly 40,000 people.

The new divisional structure divides the group into four – UB Foods Europe, UB Restaurants, UB Foods US and Other.

UB Foods Europe The division consists of UB Brands, KP Foods, UB Frozen Foods, UB Distribution Services and UB Continental Businesses. In 1987 the division contributed 51% of group turnover and 64.8% of trading profits. 1987 divisional turnover was £993.6m, up 0.4% from £989m in 1986. Profits were up 23.4% at £107.6m from £87.2m in 1986.

UB Brands UB Brands is the UK's largest biscuit maker with around 48% of the branded sector and 41% of the own label sector. This represents over one-third of the total UK biscuit market. It also owns Terry's of York, famous for its chocolate assortments.

Share price and relative to FT-A All-Share

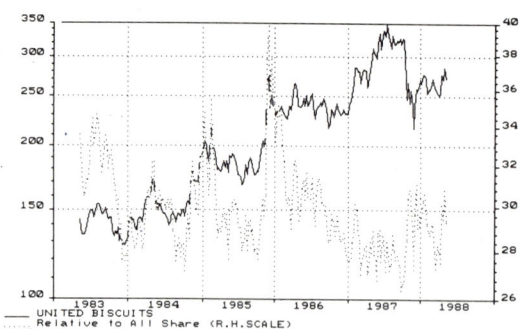

— UNITED BISCUITS
...... Relative to All Share (R.H.SCALE)

Well known brand names include McVitie's, Crawfords and Carr's. Almost half of all branded biscuits consumed in the UK are produced at UB's four main factories at Manchester, Carlisle, Tollcross in Glasgow and Harlesden in London.

This market strength has been built up by continuing heavy investment, the focusing on core brands like McVitie's Digestive, Chocolate Homewheat, Rich Tea and Penguin, and by introducing successful new products like Hob-nobs, 54321 and Natural Choice.

Sales in 1987 were virtually unchanged at £439.1m (£440.2m), while profits were 20.7% up at £58.2m from £48.2m in 1986.

KP Foods The KP Foods area is responsible for snack foods and is one of the largest and most profitable companies in this market in the UK. KP is the leading single brand, with a share approaching 23% of the total snack foods market.

The KP brand embraces nuts, crisps and savoury snacks with products like Hula Hoops, Skips and Space Raiders, and confectionery like Choc Dips and Toffee Dips. There is a substantial own label division which supplies a full range of snack foods to the leading high street multiple retailers.

KP Foods sales in 1987 were 10.5% up at £325.3m, while

'One of the major criticisms levelled at British industry in recent years has been that unit labour costs have risen faster than those of our international competitors making British products less competitive. This has not been the case in our company. Indeed, in the last few years in the greater part of our UK business average earnings of employees have risen at least 1% more than the cost of living each year, while at the same time our unit labour costs have declined so that they are now, in our UK biscuit business for example, lower than they were in 1980.'
Sir Hector Laing

profits were 23.9% up at £325.3m.

UB Frozen Foods UB Frozen Foods is a producer of high added value frozen and chilled foods for the UK retail and catering markets. In the retail market the major product groups are pizza, pasta, cakes and gâteaux, and desserts which are marketed under the McVitie's brand name.

In the catering market the Alveston Kitchens brand enjoys a good reputation with a range of starters, main courses, desserts and bar meals for the restaurant and pub catering segments.

The acquisition of Ross Young's in March 1988 makes UB number two in the UK frozen food market. Ross is the fastest-growing brand and Young's is the leading brand in high added value speciality fish products.

Sales in 1987 were 7.8% up at £108.7m, while profits were 43.2% up at £5.3m.

UB Continental Businesses European operations include Westimex, one of the Continent's largest crisp manufacturers, supplying crisps and snacks to the Dutch, French and Belgian markets under the Croky brand. Brand share is in excess of 33% in these countries.

Productos Ortiz, based in Spain, is being developed as a high quality biscuit company to add to UB's existing product range. The acquisition of a 30% shareholding in Industria Contezioni, the leading Italian crisp and snack manufacturer, should develop UB's European interests further.

In 1987 European operations' sales were 11.1% up at £77.6m, while profits were 19.5% up at £5.5m.

UB Restaurants This division consists of Wimpy International and Pizzaland. In 1987 the division contributed 6.8% of group turnover and 5.6% of trading profits. 1987 sales were 11.4% up at £134.2m, while profits fell 8.2% to £8.9m. This reflected the costs of reorganising and increasing investment in the Pizzaland chain.

Wimpy has 120 counter service and 268 table service units in the UK. Pizzaland was redefined in the first half of 1987 and consists of 167 company-owned Pizzaland restaurants and 73 Perfect Pizza franchised units. Non-pizza-based restaurants were transferred to an independent operation within the Other division.

UB Foods US used to consist of Keebler and Specialty Brands, the two UB food-processing operations in America. Specialty Brands was sold in January 1988. In 1987 divisional turnover was down 1.3% to £767.4m, 39.2% of the group's. Trading profit was 1.3% up at £44.4m, 28.1% of the group's.

Keebler is the second largest manufacturer of branded biscuits in America, behind Nabisco. It employs over 8,000 people and its products are made in six geographically dispersed plants. More recently the product range has been widened to include salty snack products.

Keebler has enjoyed consistent growth in dollar terms under UB ownership, although between 1984 and 1986 it met with increased competition in the cookie sector which adversely affected margins. The subsequent withdrawal of Procter & Gamble from the market has eased the margin pressure, although it is still pursuing a lawsuit against Keebler as well as Nabisco and PepsiCo for alleged patent infringement in the production of certain cookies.

Keebler's 1987 sales were flat at £679.8m, as were profits at £33.4m. In dollar terms trading profits were 18% up and margins 1% ahead.

Other The division consists of Shaffer Clarke in the US and Small Businesses in the UK. 1987 sales were 4.7% up at £113.8m, 5.8% of the group's total. Trading profits were 15.5% ahead at £5.2m, 3.3% of the group's total.

Shaffer Clarke is a US importer and distributor of speciality and other foods including meat and confectionery.

UK Small Businesses comprise Crawfords, a Scottish retailer; Capital, a Scottish frozen food retail chain with 57 outlets; Sayers, a Liverpool bakery with 130 retail outlets in Greater Merseyside and north Wales; Campbells, the Leith-based fresh meat supplier to the catering trade; Cochrane's Vehicle Holdings, a Ford main dealer; and the non-pizza restaurants extracted from the Pizzaland chain.

GEOGRAPHICAL REVIEW

In 1987 the UK and Ireland contributed 55% of group sales with £1.076bn, the US 40.4% with £789.2m, and Europe 4.4% with £86.9m. The UK and Ireland contributed 67.9% of trading profits with £107.1m, the US 28.5% with £45m, and Europe 3.4% with £5.4m.

CORPORATE CALENDAR

Year end	31 December
Preliminary results	March
Report and accounts	April
AGM	May
Final dividend paid	July
Interim results	September
Interim dividend paid	January

DIRECTORS' HOLDINGS

	Shares (beneficial)	(non-beneficial)	Options
Sir Hector Laing	1,722,590	1,634,484	70,232
RC Clarke	12,000	—	236,557
J Blyth	20,704	—	152,861
TM Garvin	2,000	—	40,816
FW Knight	2,000	—	278,105
DRJ Stewart	10,000	—	99,663
EL Bondy Jnr	3,273	—	—
Sir James Cleminson	2,200	413	—
CA Fraser	18,024	1,790,872	—
WP Gunn	103,994	—	68,270
MA Heller	1,106,392	1,024,254	—
Rt Hon Sir Michael Palliser	3,000	—	—
Lord Plumb	3,120	—	—
Rt Hon Lord Prior	31,243	—	—

Total directors' remuneration in 1987 was £2.11m, of which the chairman received £162,000 and the highest-paid director £224,000.

PRINCIPAL SUBSIDIARIES AND RELATED COMPANIES

Cochranes Vehicle Holdings Ltd (51%), Keebler Company – US, NV Westimex (Belgium) SA, Productos Ortiz SA – Spain, Shaffer Clarke & Co Inc – US, UB Finance BV – Netherlands, UB Investments Plc, United Biscuits (UK) Ltd

BRAND NAMES

Alveston Kitchens, Campbells, Carr's, Cochranes, Crawfords, KP Crisps, KP Foods, KP Nuts, Keebler, Mackays, Macfarlane Lang, Mackies, Mooco, McVitie's, Mr Vilies, Natural Choice, Pan Ortiz, Penguin, Pizzaland, Sayers, Simmers, Terry's of York, Wimpy

CONTACTS AND FURTHER INFORMATION

Alastair Clark, Group Financial Controller, United Biscuits (Holdings) PLC, Grant House, PO Box 40, Syon Lane, Isleworth, Middlesex TW7 5NN. Tel: 01-560 3131.

WELLCOME plc

GENERAL INFORMATION

Head office	The Wellcome Building, PO Box 129, 183 Euston Road, London NW1 2BP. Tel: 01-387 4477
Directors	AJ Shepperd (chairman), MR Brookman FCA, WM Castell, H Copestick CA, RC Devereux, D Godfrey, TE Haigler Jnr, PTG Hobbs, Dr TM Jones, C Matons LLB, Dr HJ Schaeffer. *Non-exec* Sir Michael Butler GCMG, AW Clausen LLB, Dr AT James CBE FRS, JF Lever QC, Sir Alastair Pilkington FRS
Advisers	Baring Brothers & Co Ltd, SG Warburg & Co Ltd
Auditors	Touche Ross & Co
Registrars	Ravensbourne Registration Services Ltd
Brokers	Cazenove & Co, Rowe & Pitman Ltd
Solicitors	Slaughter and May

GENERAL FINANCIAL INFORMATION

Market capitalisation	£3.102bn at 1 January 1988
Capital structure	
Issued ordinary shares (25p)	842.8m
Issued preference shares	None
Warrants	None
Convertibles	None
Traded options	Yes
ADRs	One ordinary share equals one ADR
Shareholders over 5%	The Wellcome Trust holds 74.9%

FT CATEGORY

FT: Industrials (miscel.)
FT-A: Health and household products

MAJOR ACTIVITIES

Wellcome is the second largest pharmaceutical company in the UK by market capitalisation. It transferred from private to public ownership through a listing on the London stock exchange in February 1986, when just over 25% of the company's issued share capital was made available to the public. The outstanding 75% was retained by the Wellcome Trust.

Wellcome is a major international research-based pharmaceutical group, with interests in both the human and animal healthcare markets. Human healthcare products include some over-the-counter lines. Research and development and production facilities are located in the UK and the US.

In 1987 the largest proportions of human healthcare sales came from anti-infective, antiviral and antibacterial agents 36%, cough and cold preparations 13%, anti-gout agents 8% and cardiovascular agents 8%. Total sales were £958m.

Antiviral sales are set to increase dramatically following the launch in 1987 of Retrovir, the only currently available agent for the treatment of AIDS. The over-the-counter business, which the company intends to expand, is led by cough and cold preparations.

The animal healthcare business is conducted through Coopers Animal Health, which Wellcome owns jointly with ICI. The company was formed in October 1984 by merger of the international animal health businesses of both companies, and had sales of £192m in 1987. This subsidiary is adjusting to the worldwide problems facing the agricultural sector, but turned a small loss in 1986 into a profit in 1987.

Wellcome's profitability is highly dependent on exchange rates, since only 11% of sales were in the UK in 1987.

FINANCIAL HISTORY

Turnover in 1987 was up 13% on the 1986 level at £1.132bn, despite continuing weakness of the US dollar. There has been a 68% increase in turnover since 1983, when the US dollar average exchange rate was similar to that in 1987.

Pre-tax profits at £169.1m were up 35% on the 1986 level, mainly due to margin improvements associated with the rapidly growing sales of Zovirax (used in the treatment of herpes) as it is introduced into new markets. Since 1983, pre-tax profits have increased by 174%.

Research and development expenditure in 1987 was up 7.5% at £142.4m. Earnings per share were sharply up 43.6% at 11.2p from 7.8p. Total 1987 dividends were 2.81p per share net. Return on shareholders' funds was 16.8%.

At the 1988 interim, turnover was 5.5% ahead at £588m, while pre-tax profits increased by 16.7% to £94.8m. Both turnover and profits were reduced by adverse currency movements. Earnings per share increased by 16.4% to 6.4p. Zovirax sales were particularly strong, and Retrovir made a contribution of £40m.

SHARE PRICE HISTORY

Following the flotation in February 1986 at 120p, Wellcome's share price has been driven largely by earnings expectations for its AIDS drug Retrovir, launched in the first half of 1987. The price doubled in the first two months of 1987 as attention focused on this agent. Much of the buying has been by US investors.

A high of 569p was reached in September 1987, though subsequently fell back to 280p on fears of competition for Retrovir and the general crash in share values. At 454p in late February 1988, the price has recovered well from its oversold position but further progress may be impeded by considerable overhead resistance.

SENIOR MANAGEMENT

Alfred Shepperd has been chairman and chief executive since 1977. He was first appointed to the board of the Wellcome Foundation in 1972 as finance director. The current group finance director is Martin Brookman. Harold Copestick is in

CHAIRMAN'S STATEMENT

'The process of bringing RETROVIR to the market entailed enormous efforts by the group's R&D and Production staff in collaboration with the medical and ancillary professions and government agencies around the world.

The indications for which RETROVIR has been approved are presently limited to the treatment of serious manifestations of human immunodeficiency virus ("HIV"), such as certain defined types of AIDS and AIDS related complex ("ARC"). However, studies aimed at extending its present indications are in hand.

AIDS was first described as a disease in 1981 and the causative virus was not isolated until 1983. The history of the disease is thus extremely short compared to man's experience of other diseases. . . .

Our work to date has given great encouragement for the future development of this drug, and we believe that we are making an important therapeutic contribution to the relief of this disease.

However, from a commercial point of view, our antiviral, RETROVIR, has made no contribution to the profit of the group this year.' *AJ Shepperd*

FIVE YEAR FINANCIAL INFORMATION

Year	Turnover (£m)	Pre-tax (£m)	Earnings (p)	Dividends net (p)	Dividend cover (x)	Net assets (p)	Price (p) High	Price (p) Low	PER (x) High	PER (x) Low	Yield (%) High	Yield (%) Low
1983	674.4	61.7	4.7	—	—	45.9	—	—	—	—	—	—
1984	806.4	89.0	5.9	—	—	52.5	—	—	—	—	—	—
1985	1,003.6	121.7	8.6	—	—	54.8	—	—	—	—	—	—
1986	1,005.4	125.3	7.8	2.08	3.7	60.9	235	120	31.2	16.0	2.48	1.2
1987	1,132.4	169.0	11.2	2.77	4.0	66.3	570	235	63.1	25.3	1.25	0.51

charge of group corporate planning. Dr TM Jones is in charge of research, development and medical in the UK. Dr HJ Schaeffer is vice-president in charge of research, development and medical in the US.

Non-executive directors are: Sir Alastair Pilkington, formerly chairman of Pilkingtons; Sir Michael Butler, retired diplomat; JF Lever QC; Dr AT James, formerly head of Unilever's biosciences division; and AW Clausen, formerly president of the World Bank.

CAPITAL

The issued share capital stands at 842.8m ordinary shares, with just over 25% in public ownership. The remainder is retained by the Wellcome Trust. No director has a significant holding, and there are no declared holdings over 5%.

It is anticipated that the Wellcome Trust will offer a further tranche of up to 25% of the issued share capital to the market by 1991.

GROUP REVIEW

In the short term, major interest is focused on the company's AIDS drug Retrovir. The share price reflects the high expectations for this agent. Interesting products in clinical trials will add incremental sales from 1990. The company also has a strong position in the techniques of biotechnology. Wellcome intends to expand its over-the-counter interests.

Human healthcare Sales of Wellcome's human healthcare products contributed £958m to the group's turnover in 1987, 84.6% of the overall total. The company is involved in a number of areas.

Anti-infective agents, which contributed 36% of human healthcare sales in 1987, include antiviral, systemic antibacterial and topical agents. The company has a leading position in antiviral therapy.

Zovirax, which contributed 16.7% of total human healthcare turnover with sales of £160m in 1987, is used in the treatment of herpes. This product's sales have continued to grow in all countries and are increasing at approximately 50% per annum. Authorisation for its use in shingles in a growing number of countries will provide further growth. At the 1988 interim, sales had advanced to £94m, 46% up at 1988 exchange rates over the previous period.

Another antiviral agent, Retrovir, is the company's most exciting and best publicised product. During 1987 Retrovir was granted a product licence for the treatment of AIDS in more than 25 countries, and is set to make a major contribution to sales. By May 1988 it had become available in 40 countries and sales at the 1988 interim had reached £40m, compared with £16m in the second half of 1987.

Amongst systemic antibacterials, the company's main product is Septrin, which accounts for 10% of sales. Topical anti-infective agents for skin, eye and ear infections also contributed 10%.

Retrovir and Zovirax, along with Tracrium, a muscle relaxant which contributed 3.8% of human healthcare sales, are the company's main agents still covered by patents in major markets. Patents on most of the other products have now expired, although Wellcome has maintained its sales volume in many product areas because of strong brand image and reputation.

The anti-gout preparation, Zyloric, is the most widely-prescribed agent for the condition. It contributed approximately 8% of healthcare sales. The company also markets cardiovascular agents, which contributed about 8% to sales, mainly Lanoxin for heart failure, and also analgesic agents, Calpol and Empirin.

Wellcome has a strong position in the techniques of biotechnology at both a research and production level through its subsidiary Wellcome Biotechnology. The company's human interferon, Wellferon, has resulted from this work, and other agents, including human tPA for heart attacks, are in the pipeline. Wellcome has recently established a joint venture company, WelGen Engineering, with Genetics Institute to manufacture biotechnology-based products.

Wellcome Biotechnology produces a number of vaccines against bacterial infections (cholera, tetanus, typhoid and whooping cough) and viral infections (German measles, yellow fever and polio). These agents account for only 1% of human healthcare sales, mainly to the DHSS.

Wellcome diagnostics systems include tests for streptococcal infections, thrombosis, and recently introduced tests for AIDS, hepatitis B and staphylococcal and meningitis infections. These kits contribute about 2% to sales.

Share price and relative to FT-A All-Share

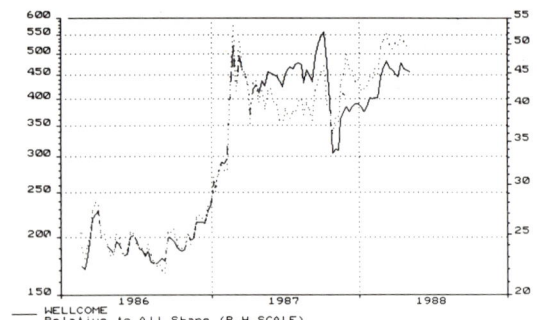

The group has a large presence in the cough and cold market. Actifed and Sudafed are market leaders in the over-the-counter market in the US, the largest geographic market for these products.

Wellcome also markets non-pharmaceuticals, largely insecticides and pesticides, whose major markets are in Australia and the Middle East respectively, and the Calmic range of hygiene products.

Research and development To ensure its position in international pharmaceutical markets in the future, Wellcome spends 12.5% of sales on human healthcare research and development (R&D), £142.4m in 1987, double the amount spent in 1982. The proportion was maintained at the 1988 interim, when Wellcome spent £74.8m on R&D.

The company has R&D centres with 1,200 staff in the US, and 1,800 in the UK. Coincident with its move to listed public company status, Wellcome is undergoing a reorganisation of its research interests.

Major areas of expenditure include infectious diseases, 35% of the R&D budget, including further work on AIDS and other antiviral agents; cardiovascular 18%, including agents for heart attack, cardiac arrhythmias, heart failure and high blood pressure; central nervous system 10%, including antiepileptic and antidepressant agents; cancer 11%; and inflammatory diseases 15%, including agents for rheumatoid arthritis and asthma.

Animal healthcare Coopers Animal Health, in which Wellcome holds a 51% stake and ICI 49%, now conducts all of the company's animal healthcare business. Turnover amounted to £192m in 1987. This resulted in a pretax profit of £5.3m, compared with a loss of £9.7m in 1986.

The animal healthcare market has been static over the past few years largely due to the depressed state of the world's major agricultural markets. A year of restructuring and investment in the UK and overseas has put Coopers Animal Health into profit for the first time since its foundation in 1984. Capital expenditure in 1987 was £9.3m.

Wellcome's products include animal pharmaceuticals (antiinfectives and vaccines), fertility regulators, feed additives and farm disinfectants. Coopers expects great things from its new product, tetronasin, a ruminant performance enhancer.

GEOGRAPHICAL REVIEW

Like other major participants in the field of research, development and marketing of pharmaceuticals, Wellcome is an internationally-oriented company, with its major R&D and production facilities in the UK and the US, and with worldwide geographic markets.

42% of 1987 sales were in North America, 17% in continental Europe, 10% in the UK, and 31% in other countries including exports from the UK.

In 1987 US sales increased by 14% in dollar terms, in a country that represents 30% of the free-world market. Continental European sales were up 20%, while in Japan, sales in local currency terms rose by 40%. Japan is Wellcome's third biggest market after the US and the UK, and forms 20% of the free-world pharmaceutical market.

CORPORATE CALENDAR

Year end	30 August
Preliminary results	November
Report and accounts	December
AGM	January
Final dividend paid	January
Interim results	May
Interim dividend paid	June

DIRECTORS' HOLDINGS

	Fully-paid ordinary shares	Options
AJ Shepperd	8,499	125,174
MR Brookman	8,449	67,204
Sir Michael Butler	—	
WM Castell	599	46,633
AW Clausen	7,000	—
H Copestick	6,933	60,424
RC Devereux	5,166	79,884
D Godfrey	4,166	78,799
TE Haigler Jnr	8,471	118,264
PTG Hobbs	4,166	58,236
Dr AT James	3,000	
Dr TM Jones	3,166	56,180
JF Lever	8,333	
C Matons	8,499	73,899
Sir Alastair Pilkington	7,000	—
Dr HJ Schaeffer	1,183	62,543

Total directors' remuneration in 1987 was £1.75m, of which the chairman, who was also the highest-paid director, received £236,000.

PRINCIPAL SUBSIDIARIES AND RELATED COMPANIES

Agribusiness Marketers Inc – US (51%), Biocontrol Ltd – Australia (49%), Burroughs Wellcome & Co (Hong Kong) Ltd – Hong Kong, Burroughs Wellcome Co – US, Burroughs Wellcome (Far East) Ltd – Hong Kong, Burroughs Wellcome Inc – Canada, Burroughs Wellcome (India) Ltd – 40%, Burroughs Wellcome International Ltd, Burroughs Wellcome de México SA de CV – Mexico, Calmic AG – Switzerland, Calmic GmbH – Germany (51%), Calmic Ltd, Cooper-Zeltia, SA – Spain (50%), Coopers Agropharm Inc – Canada (51%), Coopers Animal Health (Holdings) Ltd (51%), Coopers Animal Health Ireland Ltd (51%) – Republic of Ireland, Coopers Animal Health Ltd (51%), Deutsche Wellcome GmbH – Germany, Fairfield American Corporation – US, Gayoso Wellcome SA – Spain, Laboratoires Wellcome SA – France (51%), NV Coopers Agrovet SA – Belgium (51%), NV Wellcome SA – Belgium, Nippon Calmic KK – Japan (50%), Nippon Wellcome KK – Japan (55%), PT Burroughs Wellcome Indonesia – Indonesia (80%), Welgen Manufacturing Inc – US (50%), Wellcome AG – Switzerland, Wellcome Arabian Gulf Ltd – United Arab Emirates, Wellcome Argentina Ltd (51%), Wellcome Australia Ltd – Australia, Wellcome Austria Pharma GmbH – Austria, Wellcome Biotechnology Ltd, Wellcome Diagnostics Japan Co Ltd, Wellcome Diagnostics Ltd, Wellcome Foundation Ltd, Wellcome Italia SpA – Italy, Wellcome Kenya Ltd – Kenya, Wellcome Malaysia Snd Bhd – Malaysia, Wellcome New Zealand Ltd – New Zealand, Wellcome Nigeria Ltd – Nigeria (60%), Wellcome Pakistan Ltd – Pakistan (70%), Wellcome Plc, Wellcome (Private) Ltd – Zimbabwe, Wellcome (Singapore) Private Ltd – Singapore, Wellcome Southern Africa Ltd – South Africa

BRAND NAMES

Actifed, Alcopar, Calpol, Cortisporin, Empirin, Imuran, Lanoxin, Neosporin, Retrovir, Septrin, Staphaurex, Sudafed, Tracrium, Wellbutrin, Wellcogen, Wellcozyme, Wellferon, Zovirax, Zyloric

CONTACTS AND FURTHER INFORMATION

Dr Martin Sherwood, Wellcome plc, 183 Euston Road, London NW1 2BP. Tel: 01-387 4477.

GENERAL INFORMATION

Head office	Brewery, Chiswell Street, London EC1Y 4SD. Tel: 01-606 4455
Directors	SC Whitbread (chairman), PJ Jarvis (group managing director), BW King (deputy managing director), MC Findlay (vice-chairman), JD Pritchard-Barrett, LJ Ross, TC Thwaites. *Non-exec* MR Angus, NO Burrough CBE, JA Caldecott, Sir Ronald Dearing, AH Heineken, G van Schaik, CH Tidbury
Advisers	Kleinwort Benson Ltd
Auditors	Ernst & Whinney
Registrars	Barclays Bank Registrar's Department
Brokers	James Capel & Co
Solicitors	Field Fisher & Martineau

GENERAL FINANCIAL INFORMATION

Market capitalisation	£1.236bn at 1 January 1988
Capital structure	
Issued ordinary shares (25p)	412.11m 'A' limited voting shares
	16.60m 'B' ordinary shares
Issued preference shares (£1)	0.6m 3.15% first CPS
	0.4m 3.15% second CPS
	2.1m 3.85% third CPS
	3.7m 4.2% third CPS
	3.0m 4.9% third CPS
Warrants	None
Convertibles	None
Traded options	None
ADRs	None
Shareholders over 5%	Whitbread Investment Company Plc has 5.2% of the 'A' limited voting shares. Of the 'B' ordinary shares, Whitbread Investment Co Plc has 56.2%, HC Whitbread 11%, ECA Martineau 7.1% and FOAG Bennett 6.2%. There is one vote for every four 'A' limited voting ordinary shares but five' votes for each 'B' ordinary share.

FT CATEGORY

FT: Beers, wines and spirits
FT-A: Brewers and distillers

MAJOR ACTIVITIES

With 4,700 tenanted and 1,600 managed public houses and 910 off-licences, Whitbread is the UK's third largest brewer and the market leader in the take-home trade.

Like all major brewers Whitbread has followed a policy of geographical and business diversification. It has substantial interests in UK restaurant chains through 206 Beefeater Restaurants and 152 Pizza Huts; in wine wholesaling through European Cellars in partnership with Allied-Lyons; and in soft drinks through Britvic Corona in partnership with Bass, Allied-Lyons and PepsiCo.

CHAIRMAN'S STATEMENT

'The strength of the company is increasingly in its diversity. Though brewing and the sale of beer will always be the very important core of our business as it has been for nearly 250 years, other drinks and other forms of retailing will play an ever more vital part. I have no doubt that we have within the company the necessary skills and expertise to ensure that the company will flourish through the next period of development. The new investments we are making in the business are considerable and the prospects for growth are extremely encouraging.' *Sam Whitbread*

The company's acquisition of James Burrough, famous for Beefeater gin, reflects its determination to strengthen its international spirits division, especially in North America where real success has eluded the group despite substantial investment in the local wines, spirit-making and marketing industries.

The recent acquisition of the 75-strong Canadian restaurant chain branded The Keg and the joint venture of Whitbread Inc with Benedictine to market its liqueurs further reflect Whitbread's desire to increase its North American presence.

Whitbread's interests in the UK hotel industry, which amount to 44 establishments, are insubstantial when compared to the hotel interests of other major brewers. Whitbread's interests outside the UK and the US are small.

Whitbread's major competitors are Courage, Bass, Scottish & Newcastle, Allied-Lyons and Grand Metropolitan.

FINANCIAL HISTORY

Since 1983 Whitbread's turnover and pre-tax profits have more than doubled to £1.689bn and £187.2m respectively in the year to 28 February 1988. 1988 pre-tax profits were 17.8% up on 1987.

Dividends, which have also nearly doubled since 1983, were up 18.5% on 1987 at 10.55p. Earnings per share were up 10.2% in 1988, and had more than doubled since 1983.

SHARE PRICE HISTORY

Whitbread's share price rose steadily to a peak of 385p in July 1987. During most of 1985 and 1986 it underperformed the beers, wines and spirits index because of the stock market's disenchantment with the company's North American acquisitions.

The price fell substantially in the autumn 1987 crash with the general market correction. Since then it has partially recovered and traded in the 250–312p range. The stock market has traditionally regarded brewers as good defensive stocks on the basis that people drink perhaps even more in a depression.

SENIOR MANAGEMENT

The present chairman, Sam Whitbread, took over from Charles Tidbury in 1985. Peter Jarvis is managing director. In autumn 1987 Bernard King was made deputy managing director, responsible for the breweries, UK beer sales, the tenanted premises, central services and personnel. This was to allow Peter Jarvis to concentrate more on the overall strategy of the group and the developing aspects of its business. Timothy Thwaites, managing director of Whitbread Retail Division, also joined the main board in 1987.

Also in 1987 Freddie Heineken, Sir Ronald Dearing (former Post Office chairman) and Norman Burrough CBE (formerly of James Burrough) became non-executives.

The executive committee which co-ordinates the management of the group's various activities includes JW Andersen (North America), WG Blake (Services), and AH Fraser (Inns), in addition to the executive members of the main board.

CAPITAL

There are cross holdings between Whitbread and Co Plc and the Whitbread Investment Co Plc (WIC), another quoted company. Whitbread owns 49.89% of WIC and WIC has 29% of the voting control of Whitbread. Consequently Whitbread is

FIVE YEAR FINANCIAL INFORMATION

Year	Turnover (£m)	Pre-tax (£m)	Earnings (p)	Dividends net (p)	Dividend cover (x)	Net assets (p)	Price (p) High	Low	PER (x) High	Low	Yield (%) High	Low
1983	1,002	81.0	14.1	5.4	2.6	215.1	161	127	14.8	9.8	6.30	4.48
1984	1,186	95.1	19.3	6.3	3.1	224.2	219	128	13.8	9.5	6.25	4.21
1985	1,444	110.1	21.4	7.0	3.1	264.2	278	185	15.2	10.0	4.98	3.50
1986	1,533	136.8	24.9	7.8	3.2	280.3	316	228	16.1	11.1	4.63	3.26
1987	1,553	158.9	26.6	8.9	3.0	292.6	380	253	16.9	9.8	4.98	2.96

effectively controlled by members of the Whitbread family through their holdings in WIC and Whitbread and Co Plc.

The Whitbread 'B' shares account for 3.51% of the total equity, but 47% of the total votes of the company since only one vote is attached to every four 'A' shares but five votes to each 'B' share. ECA Martineau, FOAG Bennett and HC Whitbread are former senior members of the Whitbread board.

Approximately 32.4m new 'A' limited voting ordinary shares have been issued in 1987/88, the vast majority in connection with the acquisition of James Burrough. Overall total equity capital has increased very modestly over the last few years and all increases have been confined to 'A' limited voting ordinary shares.

GROUP REVIEW

Beer, brewing and wholesaling Since 1977 Whitbread has invested substantially in the reorganisation and modernisation of its breweries and its distribution of beers, wines and spirits to public houses, off-licences and supermarkets. The benefits of this programme are coming through in increased profits. For the year to 28 February 1988, profits were up 8.7% to £100.4m. Turnover was up 3.5% to £644.5m. Progress was being maintained at the interim stage.

Whitbread has a good mix of beer brands with Whitbread Best Bitter outperforming the total ale sector. Whitbread Trophy and its regional brands, Flowers in the south and Chesters in the north, are also doing well. It has also introduced a new low alcohol bitter, White Label, to meet growing consumer demand for less intoxicating drinks. Whitbread is proud of its considerable success with Heineken and Stella Artois lagers, which now account for 51% of the group's beer sales.

Retailing Whitbread's 1,600 managed public houses recorded higher than expected turnover and profits for the year to 28 February 1988. The group's programme of development continued, much of it devoted to the tavern, community pub, venue and Brewer's Fayre concepts with a further £60m invested in the year. More flexible licensing laws should improve the performance of public houses still further.

Whitbread's 206 Beefeater restaurants, 40 Roast Inns, two TGI Friday's restaurants and 152 Pizza Huts, co-owned with PepsiCo, all had good years in 1987/88. 40 new Pizza Huts were opened in the UK and an agreement with PepsiCo and GB Inno was reached to develop the Pizza Hut concept in France.

Whitbread has nine Pizza Huts in Belgium and five Quick hamburger restaurants in the UK. These are franchised from the successful continental chain. The newly acquired Canadian chain, The Keg, has 75 steak and seafood establishments. In December 1987 Whitbread purchased 16 restaurants in West Germany for DM2.5m, which it plans to turn into further outlets of its Beefeater chain.

The 850 Thresher off-licences recorded higher profits in 1987/88 after disappointing in 1986/87. The five Country Club Hotels enjoyed profit growth above expectations and that of the 24 Whitbread Coaching Inns was said to be encouraging. Seven more Coaching Inn conversions are being carried out and two more Country Club Hotels are being developed.

Whitbread entered into a partnership with JPM Holdings, the leading UK manufacturers of amusement-with-prizes machines, otherwise known as one-armed bandits, to increase the already considerable profits the group makes from this type of retailing. It sold its discothèque business, Aureon Entertainments, to Pleasurama in return for £22.8m and a contract to supply Aureon premises with beer in the future.

Overall retailing profits for the year to 28 February 1988 were up 19.7% to £83.1m and turnover was up 17.4% to £859.6m.

Wines, spirits and soft drinks This division of Whitbread has undergone major changes in the last few years. The group's European wine interests, Langenbach and Calvet, and the UK wines and spirits wholesaling arm, Stowells of Chelsea, were merged with the Allied-Lyons subsidiary Grants of St James's to form European Cellars. This joint company now has over 15% of the UK market.

Whitbread now owns 22.5% of Britvic Corona. This is the combine formed from Canada Dry Rawlings, into which Whitbread had previously merged its soft drink interests, Britvic and the Beecham soft drinks company. Britvic Corona has a long term contract for the distribution of Pepsi-Cola in the UK and PepsiCo has become a major shareholder in the business. Britvic Corona performed well in 1987/88.

Long John International is the group's whisky distilling business. Its brands include Long John and Black Bottle blended whiskies and Laphroaig and Tormore Glenlivet single malts. Overall profits for 1987 improved and exports reached their highest level since 1979, even though one million fewer cases were sold to the US.

The company sets great store on the benefits of merging the

Share price and relative to FT-A All-Share

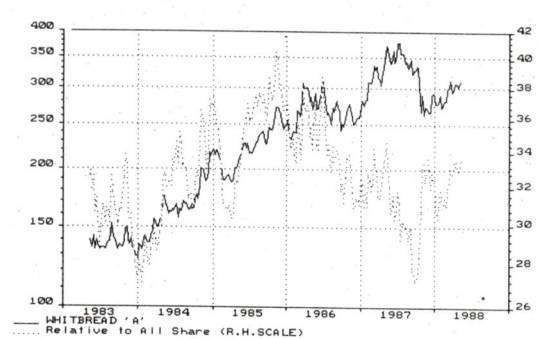

WHITBREAD 'A'
Relative to All Share (R.H.SCALE)

newly acquired James Burrough with Long John International. It is convinced that Beefeater gin, the market leader in premium gin throughout much of the world, will strengthen the sales of its whiskies.

Whitbread North America's principal businesses are the Buckingham Wile Company, Fleischmann Distilling Company and the Julius Wile and Sons label. Buckingham Wile markets Cutty Sark whisky and premium imported wines like Bollinger champagne. Fleischmann distils and markets gin, Scoresby Rare Scotch and Denaka Imported Vodka from Denmark. The group has decided to sell Fleischmann in order to concentrate on imported premium spirit brands and premium imported and domestic wines.

Julius Wile and Sons is the brand name of the wine produced by Whitbread's new joint venture with several Napa Valley wineries in California.

Overall profits and turnover of the wines, spirits and soft drinks division in the year to 28 February 1988 were up 19.6% to £31.7m and static at £333m respectively. Both turnover and profit benefited from a part-year contribution from James Burrough, but were adversely affected by the falling dollar.

GEOGRAPHICAL REVIEW

In the year to 28 February 1988, the UK accounted for 83% of turnover, the US for 12.9%, Europe outside the UK for 3%, and the rest of the world 1.1%. The company does not release a geographical analysis of profit.

CORPORATE CALENDAR

Year end	28 February
Preliminary results	May
Report and accounts	June
AGM	July
Final dividend paid	July
Interim results	November
Interim dividend paid	January

DIRECTORS' HOLDINGS

	'A' limited voting ordinary shares		Options for
	(beneficial)	(non-beneficial)	'A' shares
JA Caldecott	3,500	—	—
MC Findlay	8,442	29,500	65,368
PJ Jarvis	7,000	—	136,968
BW King	3,435	—	75,293
JD Pritchard-Barrett	3,600	—	57,694
LJ Ross	7,500	—	—
CH Tidbury	17,717	614,075	—
SC Whitbread	1,164,378	13,965	152,000

	'B' ordinary shares	
	(beneficial)	(non-beneficial)
MC Findlay	—	180,000
CH Tidbury	45,171	983,550
SC Whitbread	1,375,560	920,942

In the above table 1,715,750 shares have been shown against the names of more than one director.

Total directors' remuneration amounted to £846,000 in 1986/87, of which the chairman received £101,391, and the highest-paid director £120,692.

PRINCIPAL SUBSIDIARIES AND RELATED COMPANIES

All Brand Importers Inc – US (49%), WH Brakspear and Sons Plc (27%), Benedictine Whitbread Enterprises Inc – US (50%), Britvic Corona Ltd (22.5%), The Buckingham Wile Company – US, Country Club Hotels Ltd, European Cellars (Holdings) Ltd (50%), Fleischmann Distilling Company – US, JPM Holdings Ltd, Keg Restaurants Ltd – Canada, Long John

International Ltd, PCM Ltd, JR Phillips & Co Ltd, Pizza Hut (UK) Ltd, Whitbread Belgium – Belgium, Whitbread Investment Company Plc, Whitbread North America Inc – US, William Grant and Sons (UK Sales) Ltd, James Burrough Plc

BRAND NAMES

Beers Heineken, Stella Artois, Trophy, Whitbread Best Bitter, Whitbread Pale Ale, Gold Label, Kactenberg Diat Pils, Flowers, Chesters, White Label, Moosehead
Spirits Tormore Glenlivet, Long John, Black Bottle, Laphroaig, Beefeater, Fleischmanns*, Fleischmanns Preferred*, Canadian Ltd*, Denaka Imported Vodka*, Scoresby Rare Scotch*, Cutty Sark*
*US only
Retailing Coaching Inns, Whitbread Inns, Country Club Hotels, Pizza Hut, Roast Inns, Quick, Beefeater, TGI Friday's, Brewers Fayre, Threshers
All Brand Importers Inc Moosehead, Dos Equis, Clausthaler, Pilsner Urquell, Mackeson
Britvic Corona Britvic, Pepsi, Corona, 7-Up, Canada Dry, Quosh, Tango, Barbican, R Whites, Idris, Top Deck, Shandy Bass
European Cellars Black Tower, Calvet Reserve, Langenbach Crown of Crowns, Grants of St James's, Stowells of Chelsea, Don Cortez, Corrida, Piemontello, Romanoff Vodka
JR Phillips & Co Cognac Courvoisier, Champagne Lanson, William Grant's Whisky, Glenfiddich Pure Malt Whisky
Benedictine Whitbread Enterprises Inc B & B, Benedictine

CONTACTS AND FURTHER INFORMATION

Malcolm Burr Esq, Whitbread and Company, PLC, Brewery, Chiswell Street, London EC1Y 4SD. Tel: 01-606 4455.

WOOLWORTH HOLDINGS PLC

GENERAL INFORMATION

Head office North West House, 119 Marylebone Road, London NW1 5PX. Tel: 01-724 7749
Directors Sir Kenneth Durham (chairman), G Mulcahy (chief executive), A Norman, VJ Steel, N Whittaker, RS Goldstein. *Non-exec* M Hollinberry, Lady Howe, A Hurst-Brown, Sir Nigel Mobbs
Advisers No specified adviser
Auditors Deloitte Haskins & Sells
Registrars Regis Registrars, Balfour House, 390–398 High Road, Ilford, Essex IG1 1NQ. Tel. 01-478 8241
Brokers Rowe & Pitman Ltd
Solicitors Clifford Chance

GENERAL FINANCIAL INFORMATION

Market capitalisation £1.093bn at 1 January 1988
Capital structure
Issued ordinary shares (25p) 427.8m
Issued preference shares None
Warrants None
Convertibles £146.3m 8.5% CUL 2000 (44.94 shares per £100 stock)
Traded options Yes
ADRs One ADR per five ordinary shares
Shareholders over 5% Prudential Corporation has 7.6%

FT CATEGORY

FT: Drapery and stores
FT-A: Stores

MAJOR ACTIVITIES

Woolworth Holdings is a multiple retailer and property company with a range of retail interests. The group in its present form dates back to September 1982, when the Paternoster consortium bought out the 52.6% holding in FW Woolworth owned by its US parent, and then brought a new public company to the stock market. New management has been recruited, new trading policies adopted and a whole series of other retail operations acquired.

The Woolworths high street chain remains a key operation, although it now represents less than 50% of the group's sales and selling space. The group has successfully diversified out of town through the acquisition of the B&Q chain of DIY superstores and Comet, the electrical retailer.

In B&Q, the group possesses a first class operation, which is also the subject of a rapid expansion programme. The mainstream Woolworth operation and the newer Comet business are in the process of being reorganised and strengthened. The initial results are encouraging, although further work remains to be completed.

More recently Woolworth has acquired Superdrug, the smaller Tip Top and Share Drug chains of drugstores, the Charlie Browns car parts business, and added to its interests in electrical retailing by purchasing the Ultimate chain from Harris Queensway.

In 1983 Woolworth Holdings made its property interests into a separate division within the group. It has the third largest portfolio of retail property in the UK, with freehold or long leasehold retail outlets worth more than £800m. Most of the property division's income comes from the rents it charges the group's retail businesses, though it is increasingly involved with development.

A total of just over 17m square feet of selling area in 1,800 outlets was in operation in February 1988, to provide the UK's largest retail grouping in terms of square footage. In 1987/88 operating profit divided between Woolworth with 23.6% of the total, Superdrug with 6.8%, B&Q with 31.6%, Comet with 10.5% and property 28.5%.

Key economic factors affecting the group's business are personal disposable incomes, consumer expenditure, interest rates and housing activity. Principal competitors include the unquoted Littlewoods, Marks and Spencer, WH Smith, Boots and Storehouse in the high street; Ladbrokes, Ward White, WH Smith and J Sainsbury in DIY; and Dixons, Granada Group and THORN EMI in electrical retailing.

FINANCIAL HISTORY

Between 1982/83 and 1987/88, group sales rose by 93.9% to £2.172bn, and pre-tax profits increased twenty-eight fold from £6.1m to £177m. Group profit margins in the five years have advanced by nearly six points to 8.1%, with the Woolworth division largely responsible for this improvement.

Since 1982/83 earnings per share, before exceptional items, have increased fifteenfold, including a 24.9% increase in 1986/87 to 23.6p and a 43.6% increase in 1987/88 to 33.9p. The dividend has increased from 1.7p in 1982/83 to 9p in 1987/88.

In 1987/88 group turnover was up 18.8% on 1986/87 to £2.172bn. Pre-tax profits were up a dramatic 53.5% to £177m. This included a surplus on disposals of land and buildings of £6.4m and an exceptional item of £29.8m. Excluding the exceptional item, pre-tax profits were up 27.7% to £147.2m. Earnings per share were up 11% excluding exceptional items. Dividends were up 12.5% to 9p per share.

At 31 January 1988 the balance sheet contained cash of £61.5m but this was more than offset by borrowings totalling £462.6m. The balance sheet was reshaped during 1986/87 with the launch of a £150m commercial paper programme and a syndicated £150m multiple option facility. In 1987/88 the group total made exceptional profits of £29.8m, primarily due to property sale and leasebacks.

SHARE PRICE HISTORY

Following the restructuring of the company in 1982, the shares were refloated and commanded an initial price of around 40p. At the beginning of 1988 they stood at 277p which is 40% below their absolute peak of 461p. Since 1982 the shares have traded between 10% and 50% of the FT-A All-Share index. At the end of 1987 they stood at 33%.

The announcement in April 1986 of the bid by Dixons boosted the share price significantly. When the bid failed, the shares' relative performance weakened until recognition was given to the rapidly improving profit trend.

More recently the shares have again fallen back, reflecting both speculation over a possible bid for the rival Storehouse business, and pessimism about the earnings outlook. They initially outperformed the market after the October 1987 stock market crash, but then fell back before recovering somewhat after the 1987/88 results.

SENIOR MANAGEMENT

Sir Kenneth Durham was appointed chairman in March 1986, having joined the board in 1985. He served as chairman of Unilever until early 1986.

Geoffrey Mulcahy, the chief executive of Woolworth Holdings and chairman of Woolworths, was appointed chief executive in March 1986. He joined Woolworth Holdings at the beginning of 1983 as group finance director, and was

F I V E   Y E A R   F I N A N C I A L   I N F O R M A T I O N

Year	Turnover (£m)	Pre-tax (£m)	Earnings (p)	Dividends net (p)	Dividend cover (x)	Net assets (p)	Price (p) High	Price (p) Low	PER (x) High	PER (x) Low	Yield (%) High	Yield (%) Low
1983	1,124	42.6	9.8	2.0	4.9	194	86	41	100.8	11.5	5.10	0.00
1984	1,269	62.8	15.0	3.9	3.8	161	148	85	133.2	19.0	2.82	1.89
1985	1,661	89.3	16.8	5.0	3.4	162	303	139	28.4	19.5	2.96	1.96
1986	1,757	110.4	21.1	8.0	2.6	183	453	218	73.3	18.8	3.82	1.58
1987	2,172	140.8	23.9	9.0	2.7	175	458	238	26.7	11.6	4.89	2.39

appointed group managing director in August 1984.

Archie Norman joined as finance director in September 1986. He was formerly a partner of McKinsey & Co. Nigel Whittaker, corporate affairs director of Woolworth Holdings, was a member of the team that put together the initial bid for FW Woolworth. He is also chairman of B&Q and Charlie Browns.

In November 1987 Malcolm Parkinson, chief executive of Woolworth Retail since July 1986, resigned from the board. In June 1987 Ronald and Peter Goldstein, the joint chairmen and managing directors of Superdrug, became a director and alternate director of the Woolworth Holdings board respectively.

In March 1988, Vic Steel was appointed chairman of Woolworths and became a director of Woolworth Holdings in April. He joined the company from Guinness, where he was managing director of Guinness Beverage Group.

CAPITAL

Equity has been issued regularly to finance the development of the company. 13.37m 50p ordinary shares were issued as part consideration for the old FW Woolworth business. 12.5m 50p ordinary shares were issued as part consideration for Comet in May 1984. There was a one for one scrip issue in June 1985.

The group paid £19.5m in cash and loan notes for Charlie Browns in March 1987. 30.15m 50p ordinary shares were issued in consideration for Superdrug in April 1987. There was a subdivision of each 50p ordinary share into two 25p ordinary shares in June 1987.

In November 1987 Woolworth bought Ultimate very advantageously for £6.3m cash. The takeover of Tip Top Drugstores, agreed in January 1988, cost approximately £13m, in a combination of cash, loan notes and a further tranche of the 8.5% convertible unsecured loan 2000 stock. Woolworth's takeover of Share Drug, agreed in February 1988, is costing approximately £32m in a similar combination.

In January 1988 there were 427.8m shares in issue. Full conversion of the unsecured loan stock in issue before the Tip Top and Share Drug acquisitions would result in the issue of some 65.8m ordinary shares. This would represent 12.1% of the enlarged issued ordinary capital.

The Prudential's 7.6% holding was the only declared stake in January 1988.

GROUP REVIEW

The developing strategy for the group is to create three groupings – the high street group, consisting of Woolworth, drug stores and the experimental Kidstore and Volume One operations; the out of town businesses, consisting of B&Q, Comet and Charlie Browns; and the property group.

Woolworths In 1987 selling area totalled 6.9m sq ft. Activity is concentrated on the high street. New trading policies have been introduced under the Focus strategy which, whilst retaining much of the original mixed retailing approach, has made a significant reduction in the number of lines carried. A new second phase of the Focus strategy is currently in progress.

The business is being concentrated on five key product areas. These are: cosmetics and fashion accessories; entertainment – records and videocassettes; gifts and sweets; home, garden and kitchen; and children's toys and clothing.

Alongside the merchandise changes, new fixtures and fittings are being installed. By the end of 1987, over 4.0m sq ft had been upgraded to provide improved methods of presentation and display. The aim is to increase market share within the selected product ranges, beyond those in which Woolworth has traditionally enjoyed a strong or dominant position.

These moves have been taken a stage forward with the experimental Kidstore operation, which is designed to cater to the buying needs of babies to 13-year-olds, from clothes through to entertainment. In addition, some of the Woolworth store sites are being divided to accommodate new branches of Superdrug, the expanding discount toiletry acquired in April 1987.

The new trading strategies have already been reflected in profits, more than doubling since 1983/84. But a 1987/88 margin of around 8% still offers scope for further improvement. Trading profit of £10 per square foot is substantially less

CHIEF EXECUTIVE'S STATEMENT

'In the high street group, which includes Woolworths, Superdrug including Tip Top, Kidstore and Volume One, space will be configured in the second phase of the Focus strategy to accelerate the productivity improvements at Woolworths and the expansion of Superdrug to become the U.K.'s leading drugstore retailer. Stores which have already been divided into Woolworths and Superdrug are showing increases of sales per foot in Woolworths of up to 20 per cent.

In the out of town businesses, which include B&Q DIY, Comet, Charlie Browns Autocentres and B&Q Homecentres, the priority will be to consolidate B&Q's outright DIY leadership and establish Comet as the "first choice" electrical retailer.

In the property group, the aim is to unlock the value of the £800m property portfolio by redeveloping high street sites and realising some of the assets to finance specialist retail expansion....

Our strategy and objectives for 1988 are clear. Quite simply, we are going to take competitive action to grow market share and strengthen our brands; put even more emphasis on streamlining supply chains and overheads; accelerate our space productivity and property development programme; and ensure that we are developing our businesses for profit growth into the 1990s.' *Geoffrey Mulcahy*

than that achieved by its competitors.

1987/88 operating profit was 16.5% ahead at £45.1m from £38.7m in 1986/87.

B&Q In 1987 selling area totalled 6.8m sq ft. The next largest competitor within the DIY superstore field occupied far less. This industry dominance is reflected in B&Q's strong profits performance. In the four years to January 1987, its pre-tax profits have quadrupled. In 1986/87 pre-rental margins amounted to a high 9.5%. Record profits were achieved in the first half of 1987/88.

Average store sizes are around 30,000 sq ft. New stores average 40,000 sq ft. A wide product range of over 20,000 individual lines is carried. New management information systems are being introduced to increase efficiency and customer convenience still further. At least 60% of stores had fully computerised electronic point of sale and inventory control (EPOS) by the end of 1987.

B&Q's marketing effort is especially directed towards the key 25- to 35-years-old age bracket, the mainstream DIY customer group. Its rapid expansion continues, with 28 new stores and 10 relocated stores completed in 1987/88.

In 1987/88 operating profit was 32.3% ahead at £60.2m against £45.5m in 1986.

Comet In 1987 selling area, before the acquisition of Ultimate, totalled 764,000 sq ft of which 633,000 sq ft was in out of town locations, with the balance accounted for by smaller high street branches. The business is described as the UK's leading out of town electrical retailer.

The company estimates that out of town stores will increase their share of the total sales of electrical goods to 20% by 1990. This compares with under 5% in the early 1980s. In anticipation of this growth, Comet is increasing its out of town sales area, strengthening its product range and devising more sophisticated marketing strategies.

In the two years to mid-1987 the group increased its sales space by 28%. A total of 27 new or relocated stores opened in 1987/88, including the chain's two-hundredth branch at Barking in Essex. In the first half of 1987/88, Comet introduced more leading and expensive brands into its product offer, and launched its own Proline brand of a wide range of white and brown goods. Its new concept, new look store at Watford, which opened in November 1987, is the first of a new generation of Comet stores.

In November 1987 the group acquired Ultimate, the electrical retailing division of Harris Queensway. In pre-acquisition 1986/87, Ultimate made losses of £5.6m on turnover of £106.7m.

Ultimate's 94 outlets include self-standing high street and out of town sites, as well as concessions within Queensway and Debenham stores. They will be integrated within the Comet chain. The combined businesses have the second largest share of the UK electrical goods market. Ultimate increased selling area by 422,000 sq ft.

In 1987/88 operating profit was 15.5% ahead at £20.1m from £17.4m in 1986/87.

Superdrug Superdrug is the UK number one chain of drugstores. This concept was developed by the Goldstein brothers from a single shop in Putney to a chain of 260 outlets when Woolworth bought the business in the spring of 1987. The operation consists of selling toiletries and small household products cheaply in huge volumes. According to independent retail consultants, sales per square foot are currently £280 a year.

Since its acquisition Superdrug has already been considerably expanded. In March 1988 it had 339 stores operating from a total of 954,000 sq ft of retail space. Many of the new branches are located in store splits of larger Woolworth retail units. In two of its branches Superdrug is developing the group's new retailing concept for books, Volume One.

The group is building up its drug stores interests. It withdrew from bidding for Underwoods, but in January 1988 Woolworth made an agreed bid worth approximately £13m for Tip Top Drugstores, the third largest specialist drugstore chain in the UK, and the leading chain in the north of England. It trades from 110 outlets with a total sales area of 270,000 sq ft. In pre-acquisition 1986/87, Tip Top made pre-tax profits of £0.43m on turnover of £34.7m.

In February 1988 the group made an agreed bid of £32m for Share Drug Stores, the second largest specialist drugstore chain in the UK, with 145 stores trading from 340,557 sq ft. Many of its stores are located in parts of southern England where Superdrug is not represented. In the year to 24 August 1987, Share Drug made pre-tax profits of £2.2m on turnover of £50.1m.

In 1987/88 operating profit of Superdrug was £13m in a nine month period, 25% ahead of the £10.4m pre-tax profit made in the year to March 1986, its last year of independence.

Share price and relative to FT-A All-Share

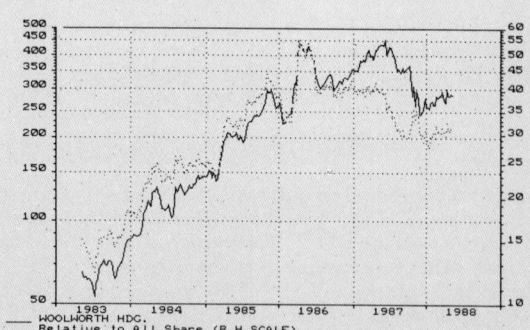

Charlie Browns Car Part Centres for £19.5m in cash and loan notes. The Charlie Browns management forecast pre-tax profits of not less than £1.35m for 1986/87.

Since its acquisition of Charlie Browns the group has been integrating its car spare centres at B&Q stores into the Charlie Browns business. The group sees Charlie Browns as a major candidate for expansion and the source of considerable profits in the future.

Woolworth Properties In addition to being the group's retail businesses landlord, Woolworth Properties runs a considerable property development operation and is to play a crucial role in the shaping of the group's future.

First, Woolworth Properties is carrying out a number of city centre developments with Shearwater Property Holdings, a subsidiary of Rosehaugh. Woolworth's joint ventures with Shearwater include the development of the older, massive Woolworth high street stores. For example, the Southampton Woolworths is being developed into a shopping mall.

Although the group's high street businesses, Woolworth Retail and Superdrug, will occupy some of the development space in most cases, many retail units will be sold off at a profit.

Second, by disposing of some of its portfolio investments, Woolworth Properties is to finance the group's expansion into further areas of specialised retailing.

Third, Woolworth Properties is planning, in conjunction with other retailers, to develop new out of town centres, where the group is convinced the major future growth in retailing will occur. At present five retail parks are under development. The group seeks to locate further branches of its predominantly out of town businesses – B&Q, Comet and Charlie Browns – in these developments. By the end of 1988, 1m sq ft of the group's high street property will be developed or under development. In May 1988, Woolworth Properties was re-named Chartwell Land PLC.

Income from property for 1987/88 was 6.1% up to £52.4m, including a surplus on disposals of £6.4m and development profits of £6.9m. The value of the group's properties, including acquisitions, was up 8.8% to £820m.

GEOGRAPHICAL REVIEW

Apart from a tiny and financially insignificant subsidiary in Barbados, the entire business of the group is in the UK.

CORPORATE CALENDAR

Year end	31 January
Preliminary results	March
Report and accounts	May
AGM	June
Final dividend paid	July
Interim results	September
Interim dividend paid	November

DIRECTORS' HOLDINGS

	Ordinary shares		Options
	(beneficial)	(non-beneficial)	
Sir Kenneth Durham	—	—	92,266
GJ Mulcahy	130,476	—	429,205
PD Goldstein	8,576,500	2,179,060	—
RS Goldstein	6,800,000	2,295,000	—
MJ Hollinberry	830,528	475,636	—
Lady Howe	200	—	—
AD Hurst-Brown	20,000	—	—
Sir Nigel Mobbs	—	—	—
AJ Norman	1,620	—	143,149
DWM Pretty	8,652	—	195,246
N Whittaker	40,316	—	217,911

Total directors' remuneration was £1.656m in 1987/88, of which the chairman received £68,000, and the highest-paid director £460,000.

PRINCIPAL SUBSIDIARIES AND RELATED COMPANIES

B&Q plc, Charlie Browns Autocentres Plc, Chartwell Land PLC, Comet Group Plc, Record Merchandisers Ltd, Share Drug Stores Plc, Superdrug Plc, Tip Top Drugstores Plc, Woolworths plc

BRAND NAMES

B&Q, Charlie Browns, Comet, Coverplus, Homecentres, Kidstore, Ladybird, Proline, Share Drug, Superdrug, Tip Top, Ultimate, Woolworth

CONTACTS AND FURTHER INFORMATION

Nigel Whittaker, Corporate affairs director, Woolworth Holdings PLC, North West House, 119 Marylebone Road, London NW1 5PX. Tel: 01-724 7749.

APPENDIX I

ADDITIONAL COMPANIES

JAGUAR
RMC GROUP
SAATCHI & SAATCHI COMPANY
UNIGATE

JAGUAR plc

GENERAL INFORMATION

Head office	Browns Lane, Allesley, Coventry CV5 9DR. Tel: 0203 402121
Directors	Sir John Egan FIC (chairman and chief executive), M Beasley C Eng MIProdE, J Edwards FCMA, WT Edwards CEng FIProdE MIMechE, G Whitehead CBE. *Non-exec* E Bond FCA FCT, Sir Austin Pearce CBE PhD
Advisers	Morgan Grenfell & Co Ltd, First Boston Corporation
Auditors	Coopers & Lybrand
Registrars	Barclays Bank Registration Department
Brokers	Cazenove & Co
Solicitors	Clifford Chance

GENERAL FINANCIAL INFORMATION

Market capitalisation	£567.7m at 1 January 1988
Capital structure	
Issued ordinary shares (25p)	181.3m
Issued preference shares	None
Warrants	None
Convertibles	None
Traded options	Yes
ADRs	One ADR per ordinary share
Shareholders over 5%	None

The Secretary of State for Trade holds one Special Rights Redeemable share of £1

FT CATEGORY

FT: Motors, aircraft trades
FT-A: Motors

MAJOR ACTIVITIES

The Jaguar Group designs, develops, manufactures and sells luxury cars under the marque names of Jaguar and Daimler. Since privatisation in August 1984 it has become Britain's leading dollar earner.

Jaguar manufactures and sells four ranges of cars. These are the new XJ6 saloon, the XJ-S sports car, the XJ12 variant of the old Series III saloon and the Daimler limousine. Saloons and sports cars accounted for all but 176 of the 48,020 units produced in 1987. The Series III was replaced by the new XJ6 in 1987, but limited numbers are produced in V12 form until the new model has been adapted to accommodate a 12-cylinder engine.

Although Jaguar's cheapest model, the XJ6 2.9 at £18,400, is priced lower than the up-market offerings of some of the volume manufacturers, for instance the Rover Sterling, most of its cars sell for over £20,000, a price which restricts Jaguar's market to the top wage earners.

The financially secure position of most of its customers renders the company less susceptible to economic downturn than its lower margin, high volume counterparts. After the autumn 1987 stock market crash, Jaguar sales held up well, although there has been a slowdown in demand in north-eastern states in the US.

In 1986, 81% of cars were exported, the US accounting for 66% of turnover and an estimated 70% of profits. In 1987, with the launch of the new XJ6, sales to the UK and West Germany increased significantly, reflecting pent-up demand for the new model which was launched in Europe at the end of 1986. US sales in 1987 were limited by the switch to the new model and supply problems, so that the US accounted for only 55% of turnover.

Jaguar's fortunes are clearly tied to the fluctuations of the sterling dollar exchange rate. A shrewd policy of currency hedging has helped to reduce its vulnerability to sudden dollar weakness. For long term security the company is concentrat-ing on higher productivity, increased production volumes and greater emphasis on other markets in Europe and the Far East.

Although volume manufacturers do produce luxury models, Jaguar's competitors are those whose image, if not their entire model range, is founded exclusively on high added-value luxury products. Not surprisingly the company's main rivals are based in the world's leading luxury car markets, the US and West Germany.

The former is dominated by Cadillac and Lincoln, wholly owned subsidiaries of General Motors and Ford respectively. Jaguar's West German rivals are BMW, especially the 6 and 7 series, Daimler-Benz with the S class, and Porsche. All three companies are quoted on the Frankfurt Stock Exchange.

FINANCIAL HISTORY

Jaguar's trebling of car sales since 1981 is reflected in its financial performance over the same period. In 1986, sales of £830.4m were 11.2% higher than 1985, and up 325% over five years. From a loss of £31.7m at its nadir, the company's pre-tax performance recovered to £120.8m in 1986. Zero earnings growth in 1986 was attributable to new model launch costs, which also restrained growth and hurt profits in 1987.

1987 was a year of continued growth in production and sales for Jaguar. Turnover was 20.7% up at £1.002bn. Pre-tax profits, however, fell 19.7% to £97m. The company blamed further significant weakening of the US dollar against sterling, a £15.3m increase in depreciation charges, a £15.2m increase in research and development and inefficiencies associated with the phasing-out of six-cylinder Series III production and the gradual build-up of new XJ6 saloon volumes.

Earnings per share fell 26.7% to 33.8p in 1987. Dividends increased by 10.5% to 10.5p. Shareholders' funds at the 1987 year-end were up 13.2% to £265m and the net asset value per share was 178p.

The company hedges its dollar earnings. In 1987 the rate achieved was $1.44 against an average spot rate of $1.64. Jaguar is completely hedged for 1988 and 50% hedged for 1989.

Profits are expected to recover in 1988 and 1989. Demand remains good and the company is experiencing considerable sales growth in the UK and continental European markets.

After several years of cash generation, 1987 marked the start of a more absorptive phase, although the robust balance sheet remains ungeared.

SHARE PRICE HISTORY

Jaguar shares have traded between 165p, their original offer for sale price, and 632p, a level reached early in 1987. In relation to the market, the price has ranged from 31% to 71% of the FT-A All-Share index.

CHAIRMAN'S STATEMENT

'Jaguar recorded further significant growth in 1987. Progress continued during a period of change, not just within the company, but also in terms of the economic environment in which it operates. This constituted a challenge which we have set out to use to the company's long-term advantage.

Demand for our products has remained buoyant and all our research indicates that the world luxury car market will grow in the future, thus enhancing the prospects for Jaguar in 1988 and thereafter.' *Sir John Egan*

Year	Turnover (£m)	Pre-tax (£m)	Earnings (p)	Dividends net (p)	Dividend cover (x)	Net assets (p)	Price (p) High	Low	PER (x) High	Low	Yield (%) High	Low
1983	472.6	50.0	27.5	—	—	36.5	—	—	—	—	—	—
1984	634.1	91.5	31.7	4.8	6.7	60.2	255	165	13.6	8.8	6.71	4.34
1985	746.5	121.3	48.5	8.6	5.6	92.9	362	241	19.3	6.9	4.59	3.06
1986	830.4	120.8	46.1	9.5	4.8	129.0	578	335	13.8	8.5	3.30	2.10
1987	1,002.1	97.0	33.8	10.5	3.2	146.1	628	266	16.5	7.5	5.10	2.00

FIVE YEAR FINANCIAL INFORMATION

Before the autumn 1987 share crash, Jaguar had outperformed the index by 41.7% since privatisation. Since the crash, the shares slumped to 31% of the index because of fears of world recession and the effect on profitability of a weaker dollar.

On a P/E basis, the shares have tended to trade at a 20% discount to the prospective market multiple, reflecting the market's wariness of what is generally regarded as a one product manufacturing company.

SENIOR MANAGEMENT

Sir John Egan, chief executive since 1982, was appointed chairman in 1986. He is credited with transforming Jaguar from the loss-making semi-autonomous British Leyland subsidiary of the early 1980s to the independent highly profitable concern of today. A public figure in his own right, his enthusiastic extrovert approach has enabled him to sell his company's image – a vital prelude to selling any exclusive product, not least a new model in the world's luxury car market.

CAPITAL

When Jaguar was privatised in 1984, the entire ordinary share capital of 180m shares was issued. Approximately 99% or 177.8m of these were made available to the market. The remaining 2.12m were allocated to the Jaguar employee share scheme.

Since November 1985, ordinary shares have been traded in the US on the NASDAQ system in the form of American Depository Receipts (ADRs). This is important in investment terms. At the beginning of 1988, 31.1% of Jaguar shares were held by US investors in ADR form.

Under the terms of the original offer for sale, the government, anxious to prevent Jaguar falling into foreign hands, imposed a limit on individual shareholders of 15% of the issued share capital. This condition will lapse on 31 December 1990, when the company redeems the Special Rights Redeemable or golden £1 share. Until then the golden share, which gives its holder the sole right to alter the 15% rule, can only be held by the government. Once the special share has been redeemed, Jaguar will become a legitimate takeover target, and the company will almost certainly be the focus of widespread bid speculation as the redemption approaches.

There were no individual holdings of over 5% at 16 April 1988.

GROUP REVIEW

The years 1986 and 1987 will probably be seen as a watershed in Jaguar's much publicised turnaround. An important hurdle was overcome with the development and launch of a new model. Until then the recovery had hinged on a design that had remained more or less unchanged for over 15 years.

By sustaining the momentum required to develop a new model from scratch, Jaguar has shown it has the financial and technological wherewithal to compete with its main rivals in the luxury sector. Moreover it has demonstrated that it can adapt its product to meet the demands of specific markets, even if this entails short term financial sacrifice.

A prime example of this is the fuel efficiency of the new XJ6, which enables it to be free of the US gas-guzzler tax of $850 per car paid by its predecessor. The new model is both easier and cheaper to produce than its predecessor, the Series III. Ease of production, combined with a range of on-line electronic fault-finding systems, should make high warranty costs a thing of the past, and further enhance the company's growing reputation for reliability.

1987 sales For the fourth successive year Jaguar achieved record sales. 46,643 cars were sold in 1987, up 14% on the 1986 total of 40,971. Production was 48,020 units.

UK sales were up 46% to 11,102 cars, the highest sales for 10 years. US sales were down to 22,919, from 24,464, because of supply constraints. In December 1987, Jaguar sold 2,848 cars, the second highest monthly US total, suggesting that fears about the effect of the stock market crash on Jaguar's US sales have probably been overdone. The XJ-S, with no delivery problems, had sales up 10% at 5,380 units. Canadian sales were 31% up at 2,660 cars.

Total European sales were up 51% to 6,550 cars. French sales doubled to 1,026 cars, Italy was up 131% to 610, Spain up 71% to 405, and the Netherlands and Belgium were up 62% and 58% respectively. In West Germany, Jaguar sales were up 16% to 2,156 units from 1,900.

The company is making the establishment of its presence in Europe's largest luxury market a priority, and has recruited a new managing director for its import company, Lars-Roger Schmidt, ironically a former sales director of Porsche. Jaguar decided not to market the new XJ6 aggressively in West Germany in the first half of 1987 because of extreme competition between the new BMW 7 series and Mercedes' established S class.

In Japan, Jaguar's new marketing and distribution company, Jaguar Japan KK, in partnership with the Seibu group, commenced trading in April 1987, and sold over 500 cars in the year. It has set medium term sales targets of 3,000 cars per annum for the early 1990s.

Model policy Jaguar is currently developing an out and out sports car codenamed XJ41, but more colloquially described as the F-Type, a spiritual successor of the legendary E-Type. When launched in the early 1990s, the new sports car will compete with cars like the Porsche 911 and 928.

For the foreseeable future, the new XJ6 will be the mainstay of Jaguar's sales. Its enthusiastic reception in Europe towards the end of 1986 and in 1987 has helped pave the way for success in the US, where the XJ6 was launched in the first week of May 1987. Several thousand new models were ordered unseen by US customers, and there is currently a waiting list outside the north-eastern states.

Production, productivity and capacity   Although productivity has almost trebled since 1980, current levels of four cars per man per annum fall far short of those achieved by Jaguar's German competitors. Such a comparison is not entirely fair, as Mercedes and BMW do not focus exclusively on luxury cars and can arguably be classed as volume producers. Nevertheless, Jaguar hopes to have reached six cars per man by 1990 by investing substantially in further automation and recruiting more specialist engineers.

At the 1987 year-end the workforce totalled 12,800, bringing recruitment to 2,800 in two years. Production and sales are expected to increase faster than payroll expenses. At 19% of total sales, Jaguar's payroll costs are low by industry standards.

By the end of the decade, the company hopes to be producing over 60,000 cars per year. Capacity could reach 80,000 cars in the mid-1990s, by which time it is hoped the double shift system will have been fully integrated, and industrial relations further improved. Following the strike in October and November 1986, a two year settlement was agreed, making Jaguar workers the best paid in the British Motor Industry. Nevertheless, relations between management and workforce are far from straightforward, negotiations being complicated by the need to satisfy eleven unions.

Distribution   The first contact that most potential customers have with any car company is the distribution network. As a result of an intensive dealership rationalisation programme, radical changes have taken place in the last six years.

Share price and relative to FT-A All-Share

The main theme has been the need to re-establish the sort of exclusive image which tended to be diluted when Jaguars were displayed in the same showroom as cars manufactured by its former parent company, Rover Group. Where possible, Jaguar dealers have been disentangled from multi-franchise operations and given their own identity. In the UK, Jaguar has 115 outlets, of which 78 are specialist Jaguar retailers.

Once established, such outlets are highly valued and jealously guarded, as evidenced by T Cowie's recent attempt to take over Appleyard, the Harrogate-based franchise holder. The above measures are merely the outward signs of the revolution in marketing strategy that has played as important a part in Jaguar's recovery as improved product quality.

Motorsport   Another important measure the company has taken to rehabilitate Jaguar's image is its commitment to motor

racing. In 1987 it won both the drivers' and manufacturers' titles in the World Sportscar Championship. This was the first time any British company had won it since 1959, and the first time Porsche have been beaten for over a decade. This success on the track has obviously been of tremendous psychological importance, giving the company widespread publicity in Europe, and providing research and development experience for the XJ41.

This success apparently drove Porsche to withdraw from the championship halfway through the series. It is believed that the decision was inspired by fears that its US image and performance were coming under considerable pressure. According to industry forecasts, Jaguar could well equal Porsche's US car sales for the first time ever in 1987. In the process, Porsche's US sales are forecast to fall by nearly 17%.

After-sales policy   The new approach is characterised by a more personal approach to the customer. The aim is that customer care should not stop at the point of sale, and that both buying and owning a Jaguar or Daimler should be a pleasant experience. Although new cars should be trouble-free, teething faults do occur. Annoyance and inconvenience are kept to a minimum if problems are rectified efficiently, politely and with the minimum of discomfort.

A good indicator of Jaguar's improved standards of customer care has been the favourable response of US owners. In a recent customer satisfaction survey conducted by the JD Power Organization, Jaguar's dealer ratings in the US were second only to Mercedes, and their service advisers were rated the highest in the industry for helpfulness, courtesy and understanding. The link between higher sales and profits and friendly personal service is self-evident. Since 1980, Jaguar's US sales have increased eightfold.

GEOGRAPHICAL REVIEW

In 1987, the US accounted for 55.4% of the company's turnover with £555.1m, the UK for 21.7% with £217.4m, Europe (excluding the UK) for 10.7% with £107.1m, Canada for 6% with £60.1m, and the rest of the world for 6.2% with £62.4m.

As the new XJ6 was introduced, sales increased in the UK and Germany, and the proportion of turnover in the US decreased. This distribution of turnover is perhaps untypical as US sales in 1987 were held back by the changeover to the new XJ6 early in the year, and by supply problems late in the year. However, US revenue still represented over half the company's 1987 record turnover, which exceeded £1bn for the first time.

Jaguar production, split between three plants, takes place entirely in the UK. Car bodies are made at Castle Bromwich, Birmingham. Engines and transmissions come from the plant at Radford, Coventry. The cars are assembled at Jaguar's headquarters – Browns Lane, Coventry.

CORPORATE CALENDAR

Year end	31 December
Preliminary results	March
Report and accounts	April
AGM	April
Final dividend paid	May
Interim results	August
Interim dividend paid	November

RMC GROUP p.l.c.

DIRECTORS' HOLDINGS

	Fully-paid ordinary shares	Options
Sir John Egan	12,150	302,112
M Beasley	3,000	146,329
E Bond	1,000	—
J Edwards	1,000	119,155
K Edwards	3,000	100,899
Sir Austin Pearce	—	—
G Whitehead	10,000	191,232

Total directors' remuneration for 1987 was £820,069, with the chairman, who was also the highest-paid director, receiving £210,335.

PRINCIPAL SUBSIDIARIES AND RELATED COMPANIES

Jaguar Canada Inc – Canada, Jaguar Cars Exports Ltd, Jaguar Cars Finance Ltd (20%), Jaguar Cars Inc – US, Jaguar Cars Ltd UK, Jaguar Deutschland GmbH – West Germany (35%), Jaguar International Finance Ltd – Cayman Islands, Jaguar Japan KK – Japan (40%)

MARQUE/MODEL NAMES

Jaguar, Daimler, XJ6, XJ-S, XJ12

CONTACTS AND FURTHER INFORMATION

Arnold Bolton, Manager, public affairs, Jaguar plc, Browns Lane, Allesley, Coventry CV5 9DR. Tel: 0203 402121.

GENERAL INFORMATION

Head office	RMC House, High Street, Feltham, Middlesex TW13 4HA. Tel: 01-890 1313
Directors	J Camden (chairman), PJ Owen (managing director), BBJ Baumgarten, DW Jenkins, A Jessup, GS Tyler, PL Young. *Non-exec* JW Gauntlett (deputy chairman), Sir Leslie Fletcher DSC, Sir Neil Macfarlane MP, JCS Mott
Advisers	J Henry Schroder Wagg & Co Ltd
Auditors	Coopers & Lybrand, Kidsons
Registrars	National Westminster Bank Registrar's Department
Brokers	Cazenove & Co, Hoare Govett Ltd
Solicitors	Linklaters & Paines

GENERAL FINANCIAL INFORMATION

Market capitalisation	£813m at 1 January 1988
Capital structure	
Issued ordinary shares (25p)	190.36m
Issued preference shares	None
Warrants	None
Convertibles	None
Traded options	None
ADRs	None
Shareholders over 5%	None

FT CATEGORY

FT: Building, timber, roads
FT-A: Building materials

MAJOR ACTIVITIES

RMC is a major supplier of ready mixed concrete, road stone and other materials to the construction industry in the UK and nine other countries. It has related interests in concrete products, aggregates, road surfacing, builders' merchants, DIY stores, waste disposal, burglar alarms and an amusement and watersports centre.

RMC pioneered the supply of concrete in ready mixed form and introduced it to the UK in the 1930s. The service RMC offered represented a major advance on existing construction practices because until then contractors met their own needs for concrete on site. For several decades RMC's business consisted of processing the necessary raw materials into ready mixed concrete and supplying it. In 1968, the group purchased a sand and gravel producer and since then has maintained substantial reserves of aggregates through an ongoing programme of acquisition. It now holds reserves in ten countries.

Outside the UK the group's major markets for its concrete aggregate, roadstone and other construction materials business are West Germany, Austria, Belgium, France, Israel, the Republic of Ireland and the US. In early 1988 it considerably increased its US interests by forming a joint venture in northern California with the major US cement maker, Lone Star Industries.

RMC's supply of ready mixed concrete, roadstone and aggregates now accounts for roughly two-thirds of its turnover. About a sixth is accounted for by its cement, lime and concrete productions operation. The balance is contributed by its builders' merchants, the Great Mills DIY store chain, its waste disposal and burglar alarm businesses and the Thorpe Park water sports and amusement centre, developed from an exhausted gravel pit.

RMC is susceptible to the general level of activity in the construction business but its geographical spread protects it from a downturn in any particular area. The vertical nature of its concrete operations in most markets also protects it against currency fluctuations. It is generally never buying materials in one currency and selling them in another. The group is

FIVE YEAR FINANCIAL INFORMATION

Year	Turnover (£m)	Pre-tax (£m)	Earnings (p)	Dividends net (p)	Dividend cover (x)	Net assets (p)	Price (p) High	Price (p) Low	PER (x) High	PER (x) Low	Yield (%) High	Yield (%) Low
1983	1,048.5	71.6	19.7	6.00	3.3	226.1	204	166	19.6	14.8	4.40	3.33
1984	1,174.9	81.3	22.5	6.50	3.5	268.9	233	165	18.4	8.7	5.19	3.36
1985	1,363.8	79.7	22.6	7.00	3.2	305.5	254	172	12.7	8.5	5.37	3.71
1986	1,633.5	108.5	30.5	8.75	3.5	365.5	344	221	16.2	11.0	4.27	2.87
1987	1,790.0	150.7	42.1	11.00	3.8	n/a	575	340	18.3	9.8	3.56	2.08

vulnerable in its extraction and delivery operations to increases in the costs of energy.

A recent history of overcapacity in most major markets has ensured that the key to the group's profitability is the efficiency and economy of its delivery and extraction operations. Its joint venture with Lone Star marks a major expansion of its overseas business.

FINANCIAL HISTORY

Group turnover for 1987 was £1.788bn. This was up 9.5% on 1986 and 70.6% on 1983. Pre-tax profits were up 38.9% to £150.7m. Earnings per share were up 38% to 42.1p. Annual dividends per share were up 25.7% to 11p.

In 1987 the group spent £169.3m on maintaining and expanding its UK and overseas businesses. At the year end, net borrowings represented just 13.2% of shareholders' funds against 10.1% in 1986 and 24.8% at the end of 1985.

The 1987 advance in turnover and profit reflected progress in sales and efficiency in all RMC's major markets.

After a number of small acquisitions in 1987, RMC entered into a 50/50 joint venture with Lone Star Industries, named RMC LONESTAR, in January 1988, subscribing $55m in cash to acquire this interest in the ready mixed concrete, aggregates, cement and builders' merchants business of Lone Star in northern California.

SHARE PRICE HISTORY

In absolute terms RMC's price virtually trebled between the middle of 1985 and the 1987 bull market high. The shares rose from 200p to a high of 575p. In relative terms the shares consistently outperformed the FT-A All-Share index.

The shares fell to the 375p level after the autumn 1987 share crash but recovered to the 480p level in April 1988.

SENIOR MANAGEMENT

The chairman of RMC is J Camden. PJ Owen is managing director. PL Young is in charge of general industries divisions in the UK, activities in Ireland, France and Spain, and corporate planning. DW Jenkins is the finance director and has been group finance controller since 1977.

Other directors include: BBJ Baumgarten, responsible for West Germany, Austria and Belgium; A Jessup, Far East and Australia; and GS Tyler, responsible for waste disposal, leisure and marketing. Non-executive directors include JCS Mott, who was formerly chairman of French Kier Holdings.

CAPITAL

There was a one for one scrip issue in June 1987, increasing the group's share capital to 190.36m. Apart from modest issues for acquisitions there have been no major issues of shares in recent years. At the beginning of 1987 no director had a significant shareholding and there were no declarable stakes over 5%.

GROUP REVIEW

Ready mixed concrete and aggregates Principal operations are ready mixed concrete, the winning of aggregates from land based reserves, dredging from the sea-bed, the supply of aggregates to the construction industry and the manufacture and supply of coated stone for use in road construction.

A major factor in RMC's ability to compete is the geographical distribution of its manufacturing plants and the maintenance of the level of its aggregate reserves. RMC has some 926 plants worldwide, approximately 3,400 truck mixers, 228 aggregate reserves and the largest fleet of specialised aggregate dredgers in Europe.

In the UK RMC owns 147 aggregate plants. These feed the group's network of 374 ready mixed concrete plants and supply its own roadstone factories as well as other companies. Although the group's plant base is well spread throughout the UK it is slanted towards the Midlands and the south of England where historical growth rates in demand have been most attractive. Supplies of aggregates in the south-east are augmented by aggregates won from the sea-bed. These are shipped along the coast as well as being brought inland by rail.

In the United Kingdom, the level of activity in the construction industry in 1987 rose significantly compared with previous years. This was reflected in increased sales of all RMC's principal products, where the combination of increased demand and cost control resulted in markedly increased profits.

The group's coated roadstone business is far smaller than its ready mixed concrete and aggregate operations. Recent expansion should enable it to take a major share if any upturn in road building materialises.

The group's West German interests manufacture ready mixed concrete and produce aggregates. RMC is a major market participant. Its ready mixed concrete operation has 63 batching plants.

RMC has important interests in a number of other European countries. It is particularly strong in France, where it recently acquired Rhône Agrégats Gravidrome, and in Israel, Austria and Spain.

In Israel RMC owns 35 ready mixed concrete plants and one aggregates plant. In the recent past Israel has been a remarkable source of profits and in 1987 increased demand from the private housing sector and general rationalisation led to improved profits.

In Spain the group's ready mixed concrete and aggregates plants experienced buoyant conditions in 1986 and 1987, and recorded increases in turnover and profit accordingly. Seven new ready mixed concrete plants and two new quarries were added in 1987.

CHAIRMAN'S STATEMENT

'We shall continue the development of the Group by the strategy which has served us well over many years. We will search for businesses where acquisitions at appropriate prices will complement or extend our existing operations and we will ensure improvement in the efficiency of those operations. Following this policy in 1987, we invested some £169.3 million in the maintenance and expansion of our operations, including £29.8 million on the last day of the year in our partnership in RMC LONESTAR. This was mainly financed from our strong cash flow and at 31st December 1987 net Group borrowings represented 13.2% of shareholders' funds.

This year [1988] has started well, assisted by an exceptionally mild winter throughout Europe. While the worldwide financial markets have been unsettled since October 1987, this does not appear to have had a material effect on economic activity in the countries in which we operate. In these circumstances I anticipate another good year in 1988.' *John Camden*

In the US the group's main interests prior to its RMC LONESTAR joint venture were its concrete businesses in North and South Carolina, Georgia and Florida. The RMC LONESTAR joint venture has added significantly to RMC's interests. RMC LONESTAR owns 33 ready mixed concrete plants with an annual output of approximately 2m cubic metres, two coated stone plants, with an annual production of 200,000 tonnes, and nine aggregate quarries with reserves of over 200m tonnes. It should double the group's US sales, though in 1987 US profits were slightly lower due to competitive pricing in certain markets.

Turnover for RMC's ready mixed concrete and aggregates business in 1987 was up 7.3% to £1.165bn. Operating profit was up 44.4% to £106.6m.

Cement, lime and concrete products With the growth of the group's core businesses in ready mixed concrete and aggregates has come the steady development of associated activities in the manufacture of cement, lime and concrete products.

In the UK RMC Industrial Minerals produces lime for a broad range of markets from high quality deposits at Buxton in Derbyshire. For many years RMC has been promoting the use of lime in mortar through its subsidiary RMC Mortars in the UK as well as in France, Germany and the Republic of Ireland. It now operates one of the largest networks of specialist mortar plants in the UK producing the branded product Readyspread.

The sector's other principal activity in the UK is the manufacture of both dense and aerated concrete products. The production of the latter is based on the technique of aerating concrete prior to casting it. After completion of new manufacturing plant, RMC will become the fourth largest supplier of concrete blocks in the UK. The group's aerated concrete products are marketed under the Durox Supabloc brand name and its dense concrete products as Readyblock. 1987 saw RMC benefiting from very strong levels of demand.

In West Germany the group manufactures Portland cement at its works in Beckum. This supplies the group's own requirements in the north Rhine area, limestone to the construction and iron and steel industries and to agriculture. The group's other principal activity in West Germany is the supply of lime and cement mortar. West Germany is the group's most important overseas operating area in terms of capital commitment. Profits were maintained in 1987 in a difficult market.

The Benelux countries form another important region for RMC's concrete products operations. In 1987, RMC's Dutch subsidiary, RWK Nederland, experienced increased sales and a major upturn in profits as a result of higher levels of activity in the Dutch construction industry. These advances were helped by the contribution from the group's aerated concrete factory at Bareht near Antwerp, purchased at the end of 1986.

In the US the production of concrete and paving blocks, pre-stressed units and concrete pipes accounts for a large part of the group's operations. A new pre-stress plant in Atlanta, Georgia, came on stream at the beginning of 1987. Further concrete pipe making capacity is being erected in eastern Florida. 1987 was a good year overall for RMC's US operations.

The RMC LONESTAR joint venture added a 20-year operating clause on a north Californian cement plant with an annual output of 775,000 tonnes, and two cement loading terminals to the group's US interests.

Turnover for RMC's cement, lime and concrete products business for 1987 was up 8.1% to £283.5m. Operating profit was up 4.8% to £28.2m.

Merchanting, DIY, waste disposal, security, leisure and others Hall & Co has over 50 locations and is the largest builders' merchants chain in southern England. The group also owns builders' merchants in Northern Ireland and Scotland, to give a total of 91 depots after the acquisition of 12 depots in the Midlands and north of England. Via its RMC LONESTAR joint venture it has acquired builders' merchants interests in the US.

The group's DIY interests consist of the Great Mills superstore chain. Another 70 outlets are due to be opened in 1988 after the opening of 11 new stores in 1987, to give a total of 64. The new stores are larger and increased total selling area by 25% to over 1.75m sq ft.

Hales Containers is a major UK operator of waste container services, having built on its experience in the removal of bulk materials from inaccessible sites. Hales is strong in the industrial, building and civil engineering sectors. The group's Wasteater industrial waste disposal vehicles have been introduced to many parts of the UK. Wheelie units cater for the smaller volume sector of the market.

Lander Alarms form the group's interests in security and is currently being restructured and consolidated. Lander's central security stations provide continuous automatic surveillance and communicate alarm calls to the appropriate authorities.

The group's leisure interests consists of the Thorpe Park water skiing and amusement centre situated some thirty miles

Share price and relative to FT-A All-Share

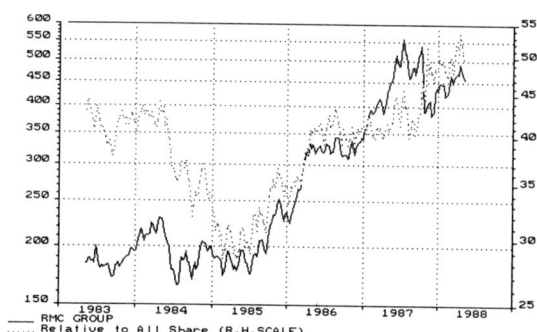

west of London. Annual attendances exceed one million but, though they fluctuate with the weather, profitability was maintained in 1987 despite disappointing weather.

The group's other interests include: the insurance brokers and services group C Rowbotham & Sons; the marketing of construction plant, agricultural machinery and fork lift trucks; the manufacture of insulating materials; and the installation through agents of loft and cavity wall insulation. In 1987 RMC began the development of a 250 acre site near Heathrow Airport in partnership with Rutland Hall.

Turnover for RMC's merchanting, DIY, waste disposal, security, leisure and other businesses for 1987 was up 19% to £339.3m. Operating profit was up 40.4% to £20.5m.

GEOGRAPHICAL REVIEW

Of the group's total turnover in 1987, the UK with £787.8m accounted for 44% (41%), West Germany with £474.3m accounted for 26.5% (29.1%) and other countries with £526.6m accounted for 29.4% (29.9%).

Of the group's operating profit in 1987, the UK with £85.8m accounted for 55.2% (53.5%), West Germany with £26.4m accounted for 17% (17.2%) and other countries with £43.1m accounted for 27.7% (29.3%).

CORPORATE CALENDAR

Year end	31 December
Preliminary results	April
Report and accounts	May
AGM	June
Final dividend paid	June
Interim results	November
Interim dividend paid	December

DIRECTORS' HOLDINGS

	Ordinary shares	Options
J Camden	78,096	104,566
JW Gauntlett	614	
P J Owen	106,000	104,566
BBJ Baumgarten	—	—
Sir Leslie Fletcher	2,500	—
DW Jenkins	5,000	104,699
A Jessup	18,108	103,333
JCS Mott	3,000	
GS Tyler	70,918	105,432
PL Young	20,776	102,401

Total directors' remuneration in 1987 amounted to £1.15m, of which the chairman, who was also the highest-paid director, received £139,972.

PRINCIPAL SUBSIDIARIES AND RELATED COMPANIES

Sand, gravel and readymix division
Atlas Aggregates Limited, Butterley Aggregates Limited, East Coast Aggregates Limited, Hall Aggregates (Eastern Counties) Limited, Hall Aggregates (South Coast) Limited, Hall Aggregates (South East) Limited, Hall Aggregates (Thames Valley) Limited, Northern Aggregates Limited, Quickmix Concrete Company Limited, Readicrete Limited, Ready Mixed Concrete (Eastern Counties) Limited (50%), Ready Mixed Concrete (East Midlands) Limited, Ready Mixed Concrete (Lincolnshire) Limited, Ready Mixed Concrete (London) Limited, Ready Mixed Concrete (Northern) Limited, Ready Mixed Concrete (North West) Limited, Ready Mixed Concrete (Scotland) Limited, Ready Mixed Concrete (South Coast) Limited, Ready Mixed Concrete (South East) Limited, Ready Mixed Concrete (South West) Limited (51%), Ready Mixed Concrete (Thames Valley) Limited, Ready Mixed Concrete (Transite) Limited, Ready Mixed Concrete (Wales) Limited, Ready Mixed Concrete (Western) Limited, Ready Mixed Concrete (West Midlands) Limited, Ready Mixed Concrete (Yorkshire) Limited, Scottish Aggregates Limited, South Coast Shipping Company Limited, St Albans Sand & Gravel Company Limited, Western Aggregates Limited

Roadstone products division
Lincs Surfacing Contractors Limited, McLaren & Company (Belford) Limited, Mid-Norfolk Concrete Company Limited, North West Aggregates Limited, Peakstone Bricks Limited, Peakstone Limited, RMC Concrete Products Limited, RMC Industrial Minerals Limited, RMC Mortars Limited, RMC Roadstone Limited, RMC Surfacing Limited, Roadstone Surfacing Limited, Springett Coated Stone Limited, Western Roadstone Limited, Wotton Concrete Products Limited, Wotton Roadstone Limited

Management and services
Hall Aggregates Limited, Ready Mixed Concrete (United Kingdom) Limited, RMC Engineering & Transport Limited, RMC Technical Services Limited, Rombus Finance Limited, Rombus Materials Limited, Testing Services Limited

General industries division
Aerated Concrete Limited, Great Mills (East) Ltd, Great Mills (North) Ltd, Great Mills (Retail) Ltd, Great Mills (South) Ltd, Lander Alarms Limited, Lander Alarms (North) Limited, Lander Alarms (Scotland) Limited, Lander Alarms (South) Limited, Readymix Drypack Limited, RMC Explorations Limited, RMC Panel Products Limited

Trading and environmental division
Hales Containers Limited, Hall & Co Limited, Hall & Co (Western) Limited, Hall Roofing Limited, Leisure Sport Limited, Olcope Limited, Rombus Insurance Brokers Ltd

Ready mixed concrete and aggregates
Allied Readymix Inc – US, Alsterbeton GmbH & Co KG – West Germany, Béton de France SA – France, Durox Gasbeton BV, Vuren – Netherlands, Ewell Industries Inc – US, Hans Baltus GmbH & Co – West Germany, Krehling Industries Inc – US, Le Béton Rationnel Contrôlé SA – France, Lieferbeton Ges mbH – Austria, Metromont Materials Corporation (75%) – US, NV Readymix-Belgium SA – Belgium, Piedmont Concrete Company – US, RMC Catherwood Limited (70%), RMC France SA – France, RMC Industries Corporation – US, RMC LONESTAR (50%) – US, RWK France SA – France, RWK Nederland NV, Vuren – Netherlands, Readymix AG für Beteiligungen (63.6%) – West Germany, Readymix Asland SA (50%) – Spain, Readymix Hüttenzement GmbH – West Germany (75%), Readymix Industries (Israel) Limited (67.5%) – Israel, Readymix Kies GmbH – West Germany, Readymix Plc (76.9%) – Republic of Ireland, Readymix Sand und Kies Ges mbH – Austria, Readymix Transportbeton GmbH – West Germany, Readymix (West Indies) Limited, Readymix Zementwerke GmbH & Co KG – West Germany (98.3%), Rheinisch-Westfälische Kalkwerke AG (99.4%) – West Germany, Sablières et Entreprises Morillon Corvol SA – France, Seyd & Heinrichs Transportkontor GmbH & Co KG, Berlin – West Germany, Singleary Block Inc – US, Singleary Concrete Products Inc – US, Transportbeton Schleswig-Holstein GmbH & Co KG, Kiel (75%) – West Germany, Union Beton Niedersachsen GmbH & Co KG (50%) – West Germany

Central services and finance
RMC Finance Ltd, RMC Group Services Ltd

BRAND NAMES

Durox, Great Mills, Hales, Lander, Readyblock, Readymix, Readyspread, RMC, Supabloc, Wasteater, Wheelie

CONTACTS AND FURTHER INFORMATION

AH Taylor, Deputy group secretary, RMC Group p.l.c., RMC House, High Street, Feltham, Middlesex TW13 4HA. Tel: 01-890 1313.

SAATCHI & SAATCHI COMPANY PLC

GENERAL INFORMATION

Head office 15 Lower Regent Street, London SW1Y 4LR. Tel: 01-930 2161
President JK Gill
Directors M Saatchi (chairman), JT Sinclair (deputy chairman), AK Woods (deputy chairman), SJ Mellor, VE Millar – US, DB Newlands, DS Perring, C Saatchi. *Non-exec* V Treves
Advisers County NatWest Ltd, SG Warburg & Co Ltd
Auditors Peat Marwick McLintock
Registrars National Westminster Bank Registrar's Department
Brokers Phillips & Drew Ltd
Solicitors Macfarlanes

GENERAL FINANCIAL INFORMATION

Market capitalisation	£701.1m at 1 January 1988
Capital structure	
Issued ordinary shares (10p)	156.01m
Issued preference shares (£1)	99.47m 6.3% CP (convertible at 18.713 ordinary shares per £100 stock)
Warrants	None
Convertibles	£7.5m 5% CUL 2015 (convertible at 24.65 ordinary shares per £100 stock)
Traded options	None
ADRs	Three ordinary shares per ADR
Shareholders over 5%	None

FT CATEGORY

FT: Paper, print, advertising
FT-A: Agencies

MAJOR ACTIVITIES

Having grown extremely rapidly, both organically and by acquisition in recent years, Saatchi & Saatchi is now the world's largest group of advertising agencies. The group has also begun to move into consulting services to provide market research, human resource consultancy, executive search and selection, litigation support, logistics and operations and a number of other supports to business. This fits in with the group's stated desire to provide business services in general, and not just advertising.

The key economic indicator for Saatchi is still advertising volume worldwide, but this has often been held to be related particularly to corporate profitability. As emphasis switches to providing a broad range of business services, this latter indicator may become more important. The company has argued that advertising volumes are rising in absolute terms and point to increased expenditure in times of recession.

In the UK stock market there are a number of other quoted advertising agencies including Boase Massimi Pollitt, WCRS Group and Lowe Howard-Spink and Bell. But following its purchase of JWT Group, the closest profile is now that of WPP, run by Martin Sorrell, ex-finance director of Saatchi & Saatchi.

FINANCIAL HISTORY

Fuelled partly by acquisition but also by organic growth, Saatchi's performance in recent years in financial terms has been exceptional. From September 1981 to September 1987, turnover rose from £102m to £3.954bn, a compound rate of 84%, while pre-tax profit has risen from £3.6m to £124.1m, a compound rate of 81%. In the same period earnings per share grew at a compound rate of 38%, to reach 45.9p, while dividends had a compound growth rate of 41% to reach 15.7p.

In the financial year to September 1987, 16.5% of revenue came from consulting, with 13.4% of profit from the same source. The balance came from communications, essentially advertising.

The balance sheet remained extremely strong with net cash of around £180m at 30 September 1987. Having said that, there has been frequent comment about the limited asset backing of the company, but realistically the business is not a great user of tied-up capital anyway.

The rate of growth in the group's profitability will be reduced from the historically high levels if the dollar remains weak. With 54.2% of operating profit coming from the US, local currency growth, estimated to be around 18% in 1988, will be reduced on translation into sterling.

SHARE PRICE HISTORY

Until early 1986 Saatchi & Saatchi's share price consistently outperformed the market, reflecting the exceptional earnings growth of the group. But since the announcement of a £400m rights issue in April 1986, the story has been quite different. Because investors have not fully understood the logic behind Saatchi's drive for size, the shares were comprehensively derated at a time when the market was going in the opposite direction.

In relative terms the shares lost approaching 35% of their value between mid-1986 and mid-1987. The shares were then hard hit by the October 1987 worldwide stock market falls. Coming after the unpopular flirtation with Midland Bank, investors sold the shares down to 327p, putting them at the time on a prospective P/E of around seven.

Subsequently the shares have made up some lost ground relative to the market, but have still underperformed by some 31% since April 1987. Fears about the dollar exposure have kept the rating of the company low, although advertising is more recession-proof than is commonly believed. In May 1988 the shares fell below 400p – the 1988 low.

SENIOR MANAGEMENT

The company was built up by the Saatchi brothers, Maurice and Charles, with Maurice Saatchi still retaining the overall chairmanship.

There are three crucial day-to-day executive posts which have recently been filled. David Newlands was recruited from Touche Ross to replace Martin Sorrell as group finance director. Victor Millar, formerly of Arthur Andersen's management consulting arm, was brought in to head up Saatchi's consultancy division and also now heads up the communication division.

Of the other board members Kenneth Gill is president, having formerly been chairman, and David Perring is secretary. Other board members are Simon Mellor, Andrew Woods and new members Jeremy Sinclair and Vanni Treves, non-executive, from Macfarlanes, the group's solicitors.

CAPITAL

The Saatchi share capital is split into two classes. At 30 September 1987 there were 156m ordinary shares and 99m convertible preference shares in issue. The preference shares were issued in April 1985.

The major recent developments have been the seven for eight rights issue in April 1986, followed by a one for three scrip issue in early 1987 and a euro-equity issue of almost ten million shares in March 1987.

FIVE YEAR FINANCIAL INFORMATION

Year	Turnover (£m)	Pre-tax (£m)	Earnings (p)	Dividends net (p)	Dividend cover (x)	Net assets (p)	Price (p) High	Price (p) Low	PER (x) High	PER (x) Low	Yield (%) High	Yield (%) Low
1983	603.2	11.2	13.2	4.4	3.0	75.5	280	207	32.2	24.0	2.35	1.61
1984	855.4	18.3	19.9	6.3	3.1	164.9	464	265	34.2	22.2	2.31	1.62
1985	1,307.4	40.4	31.6	9.8	3.2	204.8	571	417	25.3	17.1	2.78	1.83
1986	2,087.0	70.0	38.2	11.8	3.3	(7.8)	697	427	22.2	10.7	3.97	2.01
1987	3,954.2	124.1	45.9	14.5	3.2	(38.0)	698	325	20.2	8.6	5.49	2.40

There are no declared stakes of over 5%, although the directors, particularly the two Saatchis, hold sizeable amounts, and also have share options.

GROUP REVIEW

Communications division The acquisition of Ted Bates in autumn 1986 left Saatchi the clear world number one advertising agency but although substantial business was won following the merger, equally substantial business was lost, on the face of it because of conflict worries by clients. Clearly had this problem been allowed to escalate, it could have made the group's aim of having a 10% world market share quite difficult to achieve. Saatchi's response has been to form two separate worldwide agencies to cover the core of their communications division.

CHAIRMAN'S STATEMENT

'Over the last 17 years, the Company has devoted its energy and resources to building a worldwide position in the business of providing "knowhow". It has done this by assembling a wide range of knowhow skills – originally in advertising, marketing and communications; and more recently in management consulting, litigation services and information technology. Why has our company made this commitment?

In recent years there has been a profound shift in companies' investment strategies. The growth in investments has been in "brain" rather than "brawn".

In the UK between 1980 and 1987 advertising expenditure grew by 126%, twice as fast as officially recorded tangible or "real" investment.

In the same period management consulting fees grew by 443%.

In fact over the last ten years the share of total investment by companies accounted for by their investment in knowhow has doubled.

As one British financial journal put it: "One might even suggest that companies have entered a new evolutionary phase in which growing smarter (accumulating knowledge) is acquiring a higher priority than growing stronger (accumulating assets)."' *Maurice Saatchi*

The first of what the group calls its two global advertising agencies was created by a combination of the established Saatchi & Saatchi Compton agency and Dancer Fitzgerald Sample, to form Saatchi & Saatchi Advertising Worldwide. Saatchi's problem previously had perhaps been that although it was enormously powerful outside the US, its US billings of $1.4 billion may not quite have been sizeable enough to give it full credibility. The addition of $900m of billings from DFS has largely solved this.

The second agency has come from merging the Ted Bates and Backer & Spielvogel agencies to form Backer Spielvogel Bates Worldwide. The logic here was that although Ted Bates' New York presence was rather larger than that of Saatchi & Saatchi Compton, it did not have a matching creative reputation. Although relatively small, Backer & Spielvogel was well thought of in this respect and is expected to bring substantial benefits.

The two new global agencies are doing well, picking up some new business and continuing to win significant numbers of creative awards, although the loss of the RJR Nabisco accounts is a big blow. The last reported *Advertising Age* figures show Saatchi & Saatchi Worldwide having worldwide billings of $4.1bn and Backer Spielvogel Bates Worldwide having $3.7bn. Major clients include Procter & Gamble, Mars and Philip Morris.

The remainder of the group's interests are organised in what could be described as a series of loose federations – one for US advertising, one for other US communications services and one for Europe. It is perhaps in these areas that Saatchi also hopes to exploit its concept of power of scale, not doing it more cheaply, but actually doing it better. By co-ordinating media buying, media planning and research, among other things, the group feels it will be able to offer its agencies significant benefits to pass on to clients.

As an extension of its general reorganisation and concentration of its activities, Saatchi merged most of its worldwide public relations interests into Rowland Worldwide in October 1987.

Consulting division Saatchi now also has a presence in the apparently attractive consulting market, which it entered in 1984 through the purchase of the Hay Group. The current profile of activity contains the following broad areas.

Recruiting services are provided by MSL International, Moxon Dolphin & Kerby and Saatchi & Saatchi Recruitment. Market research is covered by Yankelovich Clancy Shulman.

Share price and relative to FT-A All-Share

Gamma International, based in France, gives consultancy in certain areas of information systems, a segment which has considerable scope for expansion.

The Hay Group provides a range of services under the broad banner of human resource consulting. In September 1987 Saatchi extended its consulting interests by buying Peterson, a US partnership providing consultancy on litigation, commercial disputes, and regulatory matters and contracts.

Saatchi & Saatchi's aim is to hold a 10% share in the consulting market worldwide, which in 1987 was estimated at around $120bn, with annual growth of around 20%. To achieve this will require acquisitions as well as organic growth. Victor Millar, recruited from Arthur Andersen, was credited there with building up an information consulting business with annual revenues of around $850m.

GEOGRAPHICAL REVIEW

55.5% of revenue and 54.0% of operating profit are derived from the US, 16.0% of revenue and 15.8% of operating profit from the UK and 28.5% of turnover and 30% of operating profit from the rest of the world. The group has hedged some of its dollar revenue forward in 1988.

CORPORATE CALENDAR

Year end	30 September
Preliminary results	early December
Report and accounts	late January
AGM	early March
Final dividend paid	early April
Interim results	end May
Interim dividend paid	end September

DIRECTORS' HOLDINGS

	Beneficial (ordinary)	Beneficial (preference)	Other (inc. options)
JK Gill	133,353	67	1,264
SJ Mellor	8,318	2,670	63,977
VE Millar – US	133,333	—	669,360
DB Newlands	4,445	—	186,770
DS Perring	26,666	—	83,631
C Saatchi, M Saatchi	4,349,538	4,726,744	213,529
AK Woods	11,862	6,000	228,953

JK Gill, DB Newlands and DS Perring held 216,345 ordinary shares and 39,410 preference shares jointly and non-beneficially.

Total directors' remuneration in 1987 was £3.98m, of which the chairman received £500,000, and the highest-paid director £500,000.

PRINCIPAL SUBSIDIARIES AND RELATED COMPANIES

AC&R/DHB & Bess Advertising Inc – US, Ace Compton Advertising Inc – Philippines (59%), Allick/Bates BV – Netherlands (90%), Backer Spielvogel Bates Worldwide Inc – US, Badillo/Compton Inc – Puerto Rico, Bates Gruppen SA – Norway (80%), Bates International Development Company SA – Luxembourg, Campbell Mithun Inc – US, Chow Lang & Partners SA – Switzerland, Clancy Shulman & Associates Inc – US, Cleveland Consulting Associates Inc – US, Cochrane Chase, Coerten SA – Belgium, Computer Marketing Services Inc – US, Conill Advertising Inc – US, Contur Werbeagentur GmbH – Germany (75%), Delvico Bates SA – Spain (60%), Dorland Advertising Ltd, D&H Dansmann GmbH – Germany, Dr Puttner & Ted Bates Worldwide Werbegesellschaft mbH – Austria (75%), Dupuy Saatchi & Saatchi Compton SA – France (53%), Fairfax Inc – US, Finnad Bates OY – Finland (90%), Gamma International SA – France, Gamma International Srl – Italy, Geindre Marketing Services SARL – France, George Patterson Pty Ltd – Australia (80%), Granard Rowland Communications Ltd, Grandfield Rork Collins Financial Ltd, Grupo Hay Asociados SA de CV – Mexico, Hall Advertising Ltd, Harrison Cowley (Holdings) Plc, Hay Argentina SA – Argentina, Hay Associates Australia Pty Ltd – Australia, Hay Associates New Zealand Ltd – New Zealand, Hay Consulting Group Ltd – Belgium, Hay Consulting Group Ltd – Italy, Hay Consulting Group Ltd – Netherlands, Hay Consulting Group Ltd – Switzerland, Hay do Brazil Consultores Ltda – Brazil (70%), Hay France SA – France, Hay Group Hellas Ltd – Greece (85%), Hay Group Inc – US, Hay Huggins Co Inc – US, Hay Iberica SA – Portugal (82%), Hay Ibérica SA – Spain (82%), Hay Italiana Spa – Italy, Hay Management Consultants GmbH – Germany, Hay Management Consultants Hong Kong Ltd – Hong Kong, Hay Management Consultants Ltd, Hay Management Consultants Ltd – Canada (61%), Hay Management Consultants (Malaysia) Sdn Bhd – Malaysia, Hay Management Consultants (Singapore) Pte Ltd – Singapore, Hay-MSL Ireland Ltd – Eire, Hay y Asociados Consultores de Direccion SA – Venezuela (96%), Huggins Financial Services Inc – US, Hunter Advertising Ltd – Eire, ICM International Ltd, ISSO Spa – Italy, Kingsway Public Relations Ltd, Klemtner Advertising Inc – US, KMP Humphreys Bull & Barker Ltd, Kobs & Brady Advertising Inc – US, Litigation Sciences Inc – US, Marlboro Marketing Inc – US, McBer & Company Inc – US, McCaffrey and McCall Inc – US, Moxon Dolphin & Kerby Ltd, MSL International Consultants Ltd – US, MSL International (UK) Ltd, O'Kennedy-Brindley Ltd – Eire, RCP Saatchi & Saatchi Compton SA – Spain, Rumrill-Hoyt Inc – US, Saatchi & Saatchi Compton Advertising Pte Ltd – Singapore (90%), Saatchi & Saatchi Compton BV – Netherlands, Saatchi & Saatchi Compton GmbH – Germany, Saatchi & Saatchi Compton Hayhurst Ltd – Canada, Saatchi & Saatchi Compton Ltd, Saatchi & Saatchi Compton (NZ) Ltd – New Zealand, Saatchi & Saatchi Compton Spa – Italy, Saatchi & Saatchi Compton (Sydney) Pty Ltd – Australia (69%), Saatchi & Saatchi Compton (Victoria) Pty Ltd – Australia, Saatchi & Saatchi Compton SA – Spain, Saatchi & Saatchi DFS/Compton Inc – US, Saatchi & Saatchi Wong Lam Ltd – China, Saatchi & Saatchi Wong Lam Ltd – Hong Kong, Scholz & Friends GmbH – Germany (51%), Siegel & Gale Inc – US, Team Reklame & Direct Marketing Adviesburo BV – Netherlands, Ted Bates AB – Sweden, Ted Bates Advertising and Managing Consulting SA – Greece, Ted Bates Advertising Inc – Canada, Ted Bates A/S – Denmark, Ted Bates España SA – Spain (60%), Ted Bates Holding Ltd, Ted Bates Inc – Italy, Ted Bates Ltd – Hong Kong, Ted Bates Ltd – Singapore, Ted Bates Ltd – Thailand, Ted Bates (Malaysia) Sdn Bhd – Malaysia, Ted Bates SA – Belgium, Ted Bates SA – France, Ted Bates Werbeagentur GmbH – Germany, The Kleid Co Inc – US, The Rowland Company Inc – US, William Esty Inc – US, Wolff & Partner GmbH – Germany (51%), Yankelovich, Skelly & White Inc – US

BRAND NAMES

None

CONTACTS AND FURTHER INFORMATION

Tim Jackson, Saatchi & Saatchi Company PLC, 15 Lower Regent Street, London SW1Y 4LR. Tel: 01-930 2161.

UNIGATE PLC

GENERAL INFORMATION

Head office	Unigate House, Western Avenue, London W9 0SH. Tel: 01-992 3400
Directors	J Clement (chairman and chief executive), DM Bullough, AR Dare, MD Eastaff, J Worby, RD Yeomans. *Non-exec* Sir Alex Alexander, IS Barter, WCJ Gates, Sir Brian Kellett, EH Sharp
Advisers	No specified adviser
Auditors	Peat Marwick McLintock
Registrars	Lloyds Bank Registrar's Department
Brokers	Cazenove & Co
Solicitors	Linklaters & Paines

GENERAL FINANCIAL INFORMATION

Market capitalisation	£645m at 1 January 1988
Capital structure	
Issued ordinary shares (25p)	228.1m
Issued preference shares (£1)	1.7m at 4.2%
	0.2m at 3.15%
Warrants	None
Convertibles	None
Traded options	None
ADRs	None
Shareholders over 5%	None

FT CATEGORY

FT: Food, groceries, etc
FT-A: Food manufacturing

MAJOR ACTIVITIES

Unigate is a leading UK company, specialising in food, transport and exhibition services, and operating from six divisions.

Unigate Dairies is one of the leading milk and dairy products companies in the UK, selling milk through a doorstep delivery system. St Ivel manufactures a range of dairy and other fresh products like yoghurt, low fat spreads, cheeses and fresh salad products. It has been very much to the fore in marketing food products under the health food banner. Unigate Poultry has also expanded in the poultry meat industry.

Through the Wincanton division the group is engaged in vehicle sales and service, vehicle contract hire, distribution and transport services. Giltspur is engaged in the exhibition industry, offering a full range of exhibition services, including furniture and floorcovering hire, and the design and construction of custom exhibits and displays; it also markets a range of modular display equipment. Unigate International is engaged in the restaurant business and cheese production in the US.

Since 1983 Unigate has become a much more profitable group, with margins more than doubling. The group has also expanded its non-liquid milk operations through a high level of capital expenditure and a planned acquisition programme. Although the base liquid milk operations offer little growth opportunities, they are a great source of cash flow. The St Ivel division has successfully exploited the growth available in the area of healthier type foods while the growth of the Wincanton business confirms the strength of the group's non-food activities.

During 1987 the management has continued its policy of strategic acquisition and disposal. It acquired the Middlesex-based dairy firm HA Job Ltd; Thornhill's Country Produce Ltd, a supplier of fresh and frozen chicken; United Exhibition Services Ltd and International Exhibition Services Ltd from Reed Plc; and PandaVan Hire (Exeter) Ltd. It has disposed of the Giltspur and Wincanton engineering and electrical service businesses.

So far these latest moves have not had a major positive impact on profits. Interim figures for the six months to November 1987 revealed a slight rise in turnover but a £1.7m fall in operating profits to £45.7m. This was at least partly due to the bad summer weather which caused a fall in demand for many of the group's food products.

FINANCIAL HISTORY

In the year to March 1987, turnover rose by 3% to £1.970bn. Pre-tax profit rose for the first time to above £100m. At £104.7m it was 26% above the previous year, while earnings per share registered an improvement of 24% to 30.6p. The dividend was increased by 19% to 11.5p. Operating margins rose to 5.5%, up from 4.8%, while the return on trading capital employed jumped from 23.5% to 28.3%.

Shareholders' funds totalled £335m at 30 March 1987. The level of net debt fell by just under £5m to £70m, implying a modest gearing ratio of 18%.

For the six months ended 3 October 1987, turnover was up £128.9m to £1.08bn. Pre-tax profits were down £6.8m to £40.3m. Profits attributable to shareholders after taxation and extraordinary items were down £2.1m to £29.7m.

SHARE PRICE HISTORY

Unigate has experienced a significant re-rating since 1985 with the share price rising from 150p to 440p at the high in mid-1987. This movement represented relative strength of over 60% during the period and can be attributed to Unigate's much improved rate of profitability.

The management has sharpened the group's image to investors over the past few years through an effective and consistent investor relations campaign. This has encouraged a greater understanding of its activities. At the same time the group has carried out an effective capital investment programme, which along with a carefully planned acquisition and divestment programme has raised the level of underlying profitability.

However, the reduced profits expected for the year to March 1988, caused in part by the impact of poor summer weather on demand for certain of the group's products, caused the share price from July 1987 to enter a period of consolidation at lower levels before falling with the rest of the market in October. It began 1988 at 283p.

SENIOR MANAGEMENT

John Clement, chairman and chief executive, has been with the group since 1949, and joined the board in 1973. He was appointed chief executive in 1976 and chairman and chief executive in 1977.

CHAIRMAN'S STATEMENT

'Your group's continued success and its ability to stay ahead of the competition has been achieved through the speed and skill with which each of the divisions has developed in new and expanding business areas and through an increasing number of well-considered acquisitions in the UK and the US. I have every confidence that this well established pattern of expansion by organic growth and acquisition will continue in the future.'
John Clement

FIVE YEAR FINANCIAL INFORMATION

Year	Turnover (£m)	Pre-tax (£m)	Earnings (p)	Dividends net (p)	Dividend cover (x)	Net assets (p)	Price (p) High	Price (p) Low	PER (x) High	PER (x) Low	Yield (%) High	Yield (%) Low
1983	1,662	43.7	14.1	6.8	2.1	136	117	91	12.2	8.4	10.20	8.29
1984	1,766	57.1	18.5	7.5	2.5	132	159	114	10.9	8.3	9.00	6.74
1985	1,932	63.6	18.3	8.2	2.2	140	238	142	14.2	9.5	7.80	5.09
1986	1,920	82.8	24.6	9.7	2.5	151	325	220	15.6	11.5	5.62	4.15
1987	1,970	104.7	30.6	11.5	2.7	149	442	257	16.2	8.8	6.37	3.45

David Bullough joined Unigate as managing director of Unigate Meat in 1981 and was appointed Special Projects director in 1985. He became chairman of Unigate Poultry in 1986.

Andrew Dare joined the group in 1971 in the international division. In 1979 he became managing director of St Ivel, and in 1983 marketing director of Unigate's cheese interests in Ireland. He was appointed to the board in 1987.

Maurice Eastaff joined Home County Dairies in 1947 and held various positions in the dairy business in the group before becoming managing director of Unigate Dairies in 1987.

David Yeomans joined Wincanton Transport in 1971 and was appointed managing director of the subsidiary in 1978. He was appointed to the board in 1984. John Worby joined the Wincanton Group in 1978 and, prior to his appointment as group finance director in 1987, had been group treasurer and had held posts as finance director of the dairy and Wincanton businesses.

CAPITAL

Since 1984 the only increase in the equity base has been through the exercise of options and the 4.75m shares issued in 1986/87 as part consideration for Oldacre Holdings. At 1 January 1988, the number of ordinary shares in issue was 225.1m, just 3% more than 1984.

GROUP REVIEW

The small head office staff of Unigate, based in West London, is concerned mainly with the development of the business and the implementation of strategy. The activities of the group are managed through six divisions.

Over the past five years Unigate has gone through a period of heavy capital investment designed to improve returns from the core businesses and to broaden the range of the group's products and services. The processed food divisions have also expanded through considerable new product development particularly at St Ivel. The restaurant interests in America have been expanded by acquisition. The non-food operations have been expanded further into car auctions and distribution.

St Ivel With a turnover of £416m in 1987 and pre-tax profits of £15.7m, 15% of the group total, this company produces, markets and distributes dairy and chilled products to the grocery and catering trade. It has a total of ten factories and during the peak period of milk production, more than one million litres are used daily for manufacture.

The main products under the St Ivel label are St Ivel Gold, a unique low fat spread made from milk protein and vegetable oils, the Shape range of low fat dairy products, the Real range of additive free and no added sugar products, Prize Italiano whipped yogurt, yogurts, cream, cheese, cottage cheese, salads, and St Ivel Five Pints and chilled pizzas.

Many major chain stores also sell products manufactured by

St Ivel under their own labels. Unigate Chilled Distribution also operates chilled distribution facilities for other companies as well as dedicated depots for several leading supermarket groups.

Hassy sells onions, celery, potatoes, carrots and special vegetables, such as mange-tout, to the major supermarkets. A subsidiary, Beddington Fruit Company, supplies a range of fruit conserves to food manufacturers and the retail trades.

Unigate Poultry Unigate Poultry, together with Malton Bacon Factory, form Unigate's meat interests. The division has recently been formed to create a framework for the company's planned expansion of its poultry interests. In 1987 sales were £127m and pre-tax profits were £8.4m, equivalent to 8% of the group total. The division is destined for significant expansion since in May 1987 the group announced a £55m project to build a completely new and wholly integrated chicken rearing and processing facility in South Humberside.

At present the group owns JP Wood of Shropshire, a major supplier of chicken and turkeys; Turners' Turkeys, a Lincolnshire-based turkey company; and Oldacre, a supplier of animal feedstuffs. Oldacre also supplies the in-house turkey and chicken rearing activities. In May 1987 the group acquired Thornhill Country Produce, which specialises in both fresh and frozen chicken and chicken-related products.

The Malton Bacon Factory supplies prime quality bacon and pork products to the retail trade.

Unigate Dairies Unigate Dairies is the country's biggest dairy company with 23 production and 260 distribution depots sited across the country. Market share in the liquid milk industry is around 30%. More than 6,000 managed and franchised rounds deliver over 46m pints of milk weekly to doorstep customers, shops and offices, restaurants and canteens, hotels and commercial premises.

Alongside the full range of fresh and long life, high and low fat milks with enhanced calcium content, there is a comprehensive selection of other foods and dairy produce delivered

Share price and relative to FT-A All-Share

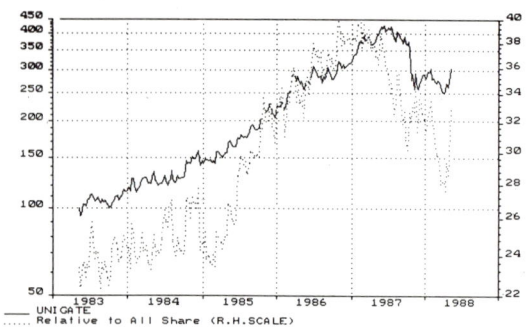

daily. Since 1983, some £50m has been invested in improving existing dairies and building new ones. For example, a new £12m non-returnable-container dairy in London has recently come on stream, meeting specific customer needs and setting new improved standards of service.

Through this type of investment Unigate Dairies has been able to improve profitability and compensate for the lack of volume growth in the liquid milk market. In 1987 sales were £585m and pre-tax profits £34.4m, equivalent to 33% of the group total. The acquisition of HA Job Ltd has expanded Unigate's dairy business further.

Wincanton Group Wincanton Group is Unigate's largest investment outside the dairy and foods businesses. It operates in three business areas: vehicle sales and service, vehicle contract hire, and distribution and transport services. In 1987 sales totalled £325m and pre-tax profits £11.4m, equivalent to 11% of the group amount. Wincanton's contract hire fleet exceeds 13,000 vehicles and continues to grow. Wincanton Distribution Services and Bullen's provide a wide range of distribution services and fleet and warehouse management. The vehicle sales and service activities include over 30 franchise vehicle outlets under the Arlington Motors banner and the six-location National Car Auctions.

Giltspur Giltspur was acquired by Unigate in 1981. It is an exhibition services and display equipment group with operations in the UK, Europe and the US. In 1987 sales were £145m and pre-tax profits £8.7m, equivalent to 8% of the group total.

Giltspur's exhibition services were recently expanded by the acquisition of IES and VES from Reed International. Marler Haley markets modular exhibition units and pedestrian guidance systems.

Unigate International Unigate International comprises the group's food interests in the US. 1987 sales were £218m and pre-tax profits were £11.3m, which represented 11% of the group total.

Unigate Restaurants with its headquarters in Dallas, Texas, consists of four restaurant and fast food chains operating over 180 units in the southern states of Texas, Colorado, Oklahoma and Arkansas. These are known as Casa Bonita (which serves Mexican food), Taco Bueno (fast-food and take-away Mexican food), Black-eyed Pea and Dixie House (southern country style full service sit-down restaurants) and Crystal (pizza and pasta dishes).

Unigate has amalgamated its two cheese companies in the US, Frigo Cheeses and Gardenia Foods. Frigo's Italian cheeses are sold nationwide across the US.

GEOGRAPHICAL REVIEW

The majority of Unigate's business is UK-based, although in recent years there has been an increase in the US content, largely through the acquisition of the restaurant chains. In 1987 86% of operating profits came from domestic operations, 13% from North America, and other countries made up the balance of 12%.

CORPORATE CALENDAR

Year end	31 March
Preliminary results	June
Report and accounts	July
AGM	July
Final dividend paid	October
Interim results	November
Interim dividend paid	April

DIRECTORS' HOLDINGS

	Fully-paid ordinary shares	Options
J Clement	184,000	64,022
Sir Alex Alexander	2,000	—
IS Barter	10,250	123,022
DM Bullough	52,370	31,500
AR Dare	32,000	27,022
WCJ Gates	21,150	—
Sir Brian Kellett	2,000	—
EH Sharp	164,327	—
JC Worby	11,000	23,500
RD Yeomans	20,000	35,545

Total directors' remuneration in 1986/87 was £593,000. The chairman, who was the highest-paid director, received £122,000.

PRINCIPAL SUBSIDIARIES AND RELATED COMPANIES

Arlington Motor Holdings Plc, The Beddington Fruit Co Ltd, Bullens Ltd, Casa Bonita Inc – US, Fermanagh Creameries Ltd, Frigo Cheese Corporation – US, Gardenia Foods Co Inc – US, Giltspur Ltd, Giltspur Expo Industries, Giltspur Inc – US, Hassy Ltd, Marler Haley Expo Systems Ltd, Malton Bacon Factory Ltd, WJ Oldacre Ltd, Nutricia – Netherlands (28%), Prufrock Restaurants Inc – US, St Ivel Ltd, Turners' Turkeys Ltd, Unigate (UK) Ltd, Unigate Dairies Ltd, Wexford Creamery Ltd – Eire (93%), Wincanton Distribution Services Ltd, Wincanton Contracts Ltd, Wincanton Vehicle Rentals Ltd, JP Wood of Shropshire Ltd

BRAND NAMES

Arlington Motors, Black-eyed Pea, Bullen's, Calcia, Casa Bonita, Colchester Car Auctions, Dixie House, Five Pints, Frigo Cheese, Gardenia, Giltspur, Gold, National Car Auctions, Prize, Real, St Ivel, Santa Fe Express, Shape, Taco Bueno, Turners' Turkeys, Unigate, Unigate Chilled Distribution, Wincanton

CONTACTS AND FURTHER INFORMATION

John Worby, Group Financial Director, Unigate PLC, Unigate House, Western Avenue, London W3 0SH. Tel: 01-992 3400.

APPENDIX II

COMPANY REGISTRARS

BARCLAYS BANK
REGISTRATION DEPARTMENT

PO BOX 34
OCTAGON HOUSE
GADBROOK PARK
NORTHWICH
CHESHIRE CW9 7RD
TEL: 0606 40440

HILL SAMUEL
REGISTRARS LTD

6 GREENCOAT PLACE
LONDON SW1P 1PL
TEL: 01-828 4321

LLOYD'S BANK
REGISTRAR'S DEPARTMENT

THE CAUSEWAY
GORING-BY-SEA
WORTHING
WEST SUSSEX BN12 6DA
TEL: 0903 502541

NATIONAL WESTMINSTER BANK
REGISTRAR'S DEPARTMENT

PO BOX 82
CAXTON HOUSE
REDCLIFFE WAY
BRISTOL BS99 7NH
TEL: 0272 306600

RAVENSBOURNE
REGISTRATION SERVICES LTD

BOURNE HOUSE
34 BECKENHAM ROAD
BECKENHAM
KENT BR3 4TU
TEL: 01-650 4866

ROYAL BANK OF SCOTLAND
REGISTRAR'S DEPARTMENT

PO BOX 27
34 FETTES ROW
EDINBURGH EH3 6UT
TEL: 031-442 4111